Alternative Educational Delivery Systems: Enhancing Instructional Options for All Students

Edited by

Janet L. Graden Joseph E. Zins Michael J. Curtis
University of Cincinnati

National Association of School Psychologists
Washington, DC

First Printing, 1988

Published by the National Association of School Psychologists
808 17th Street, NW #200
Washington, DC 20006

ISBN 0-932955-09-6

Printed in the United States of America

Acknowledgments

We gratefully acknowledge the assistance and expertise of several individuals in helping with this book: Lawrence Moran (copyediting); Judy Fulwider (typesetting); and Betty VanWagener, Natalee Braun, Rita Poth, Bruce Wess, and Karen Carey (proofreading). We also are indebted to Fran Floyd, our secretary, for her always capable assistance with all phases of this project, to Charlene Ponti for sharing her ideas on many facets of the book, and to our colleagues Dave Barnett and Ed Lentz. Elizabeth Berlage, Steven Coolahan, and Alicia Lateer helped with numerous tasks essential to completion of the book. Thanks also are extended to Cathy Telzrow, Chair of the Publications Committee, for technical assistance in producing the book.

We express our deepest gratitude to chapter authors, who dedicated their time and expertise to the project. Their contributions to this book are immeasurable. Also, we appreciate the contributions of the chapter reviewers, who provided practical suggestions in the revision process. Without both of these groups of professionals, the project could not have been completed.

From NASP Publications Policy Handbook

The content of this document reflects the ideas and positions of the authors. The responsibility lies solely with the authors and does not necessarily reflect the position or ideas of the National Association of School Psychologists.

List of Contributors

Bob Algozzine
Professor
University of Florida
Department of Special Education
G315 Norman Hall
Gainesville, FL 32611

Jack I. Bardon
Excellence Foundation Professor
University of North Carolina at Greensboro
School of Education
Greensboro, NC 27412-5001

David W. Barnett
Associate Professor
University of Cincinnati
516 Teachers College
University of Cincinnati
Cincinnati, OH 45221-0002

Wesley Becker
Associate Dean
University of Oregon
College of Education
University of Oregon
Eugene, OR 97403

Randy Elliot Bennett
Senior Research Scientist
Educational Testing Service
Princeton, NJ 08541

David C. Berliner
Professor
Curriculum and Instruction and
    Educational Psychology
College of Education
Arizona State University
Tempe, AZ 85207

Douglas Carnine
Associate Professor
University of Oregon
College of Education
University of Oregon
Eugene, OR 97403

Ann Casey
Assistant Professor
Iowa State University
Psychology Department
Ames, IA 50011

Sandra L. Christenson
Research Associate
Instructional Alternatives Project
University of Minnesota
350 Elliot Hall
75 East River Road
Minneapolis, MN 55455

Carolyn T. Cobb
Coordinator, School Psychology Section
North Carolina Department of
    Public Instruction
116 W. Edenton Street
Raleigh, NC 27603-1712

Jane Close Conoley
Associate Professor
University of Nebraska-Lincoln
135 Bancroft Hall
Lincoln, NE 68588-0348

Robert K. Conyne
Professor and Head School Psychology and
    Counseling
University of Cincinnati
527C Teachers College
Cincinnati, OH 45221-0002

Michael J. Curtis
Professor and Coordinator of School
    Psychology
University of Cincinnati
526 Teachers College
Cincinnati, OH 45221-0002

Donald D. Deshler
Director
University of Kansas Institute
    for Research on Learning Disabilities
223 Carruth-O'Leary
Lawrence, KS 66045

Douglas Fuchs
Associate Professor
George Peabody College
Vanderbilt University
Department of Special Education
Nashville, TN 37203

Lynn S. Fuchs
Assistant Professor
George Peabody College
Vanderbilt University
Department of Special Education
Nashville, TN 37203

Michael F. Giangreco
Special Education Coordinator
Cayuga-Onondaga Board of Cooperative
    Educational Services
234 South Street
Auburn, NY 13021

Janet L. Graden
Assistant Professor
University of Cincinnati
516 Teachers College
Cincinnati, OH 45221-0002

Alex Granzin
School Psychologist
Springfield School District
525 Mill Street
Springfield, OR

Mary Katherine Hawryluk
School Psychologist
South Brunswick Schools
Special Services Department
1 Executive Drive
Monmouth Junction, NJ 08852

Candice A. Hughes
Doctoral Candidate
Fordham University
New York, NY

Irwin A. Hyman
Professor
Temple University
College of Education
School Psychology Program
262 Ritter Annex
Philadelphia, PA 19122

Robert J. Illback
Director of Student Services
Fort Knox Community Schools
Fort Knox, KY 40121

Howard M. Knoff
Director and Associate Professor
School Psychology
University of South Florida
FAO 268
Department of Psychological and
    Social Foundations
Tampa, FL 33620

Louis J. Kruger
Assistant Professor
Department of Education
Lincoln Filene Center
Tufts University
Medford, MA 02155

Deborah K. Kundert
Assistant Professor
State University of New York at Albany
232 Education
1400 Washington Avenue
Albany, NY 12222

Naomi Lennox
Adjunct Professor
Temple University
College of Education
School Psychology Program
262 Ritter Annex
Philadelphia, PA 19122

Francis E. Lentz, Jr.
Assistant Professor
University of Cincinnati
526 Teachers College
Cincinnati, OH 45221-0002

Deanne Magnusson
Coordinator — K-6 School Based
    Resource Program
Department of Special Education
Minneapolis Public Schools
254 Upton Avenue, S.
Minneapolis, MN 55405

Douglas Marston
School Psychologist
Department of Special Education
Minneapolis Public Schoolls
254 Upton Avenue, S.
Minneapolis, MN 55405

Caven S. Mcloughlin
Associate Professor
Kent State University
412 White Hall
Kent State University
Kent, OH 44242

Luanna H. Meyer
Professor
Syracuse University
Division of Special Education and
    Rehabilitation
805 S. Crouse Avenue
Syracuse, NY 13244

Joel Meyers
Professor
State University of New York at Albany
School Psychology Program
ED 224
Albany, NY 12222

Kathleen D. Paget
Associate Professor
University of South Carolina
Department of Psychology
Columbia, SC 29208

Daniel J. Reschly
Professor and Director of
    School Psychology
Iowa State University
Psychology Department
Iowa State University
Ames, IA 50011

Maynard C. Reynolds
Professor
University of Minnesota
214 Burton Hall
178 Pillsbury Dr., SE
Minneapolis, MN 55455

Jean B. Schumaker
Coordinator of Research
University of Kansas Institute for Research
    in Learning Disabilities
223 Carruth-O'Leary
Lawrence, KS 66045

Lisa Levine Schwartz
Doctoral Candidate
Temple University
Philadelphia, PA 19122

Russell J. Skiba
Assistant Professor
Indiana University
Institute for Child Study
Bloomington, IN 47405

Diane L. Smallwood
School Psychologist
South Brunswick Schools
Special Services Department
1 Executive Drive
Monmouth Junction, NJ 08852

Susan Stainback
Professor
College of Education
University of Northern Iowa
Cedar Falls, IA 50614

William Stainback
Professor
College of Education
University of Northern Iowa
Cedar Falls, IA 50614

Mary Henning-Stout
Assistant Professor
Austin College
Sherman, TX 75090

Gerald Tindal
Assistant Professor
University of Oregon
Division of Teacher Education
275 Teacher College
College of Education
Eugene, OR 97403-1215

Stacey Vedder-Dubocq
School Psychologist
Hamilton County Office of Education
11083 Hamilton Avenue
Cincinnati, OH 45239

Margaret C. Wang
Professor and Director
Temple University Center for Research
   in Human Development & Education
13th St. & Cecil B. Moore Avenue
Ritter Annex, 9th Floor
Philadelphia, PA 19122

James E. Ysseldyke
Professor
University of Minnesota
350 Elliott Hall
75 East River Road
Minneapolis, MN 55455

Joseph E. Zins
Professor
University of Cincinnati
516 Teachers College
Cincinnati, OH 45221-0002

List of Reviewers

George Batsche
Assistant Director
Hammitt School
The Baby Fold
Normal, IL

Paul Bell
School Psychologist
Lexington, KY

John Berrens
School Psychologist
Hamilton County Office of Education
Cincinnati, OH

Natalee Braun
School Psychologist
Hamilton County Office of Education
Cincinnati, OH

Karen Carey
School Psychologist
Kenton County School District
Independence, KY

Sandra Christenson
Research Associate
University of Minnesota
Minneapolis, MN

Barbara Coolahan
Supervisor of School Psychologists Services
Hillsboro Special Education Regional
    Resource Center
Hillsboro, OH

W. David Driscoll
Psychologist
Rochester, NY

Margaret Dawson
School Psychologist
Exeter School District
Fremont, NH

Don Fleming
School Psychologist
Chesterfield County Schools
Chesterfield, VA

Evelyn Fleming
Attorney
Crews & Hancock
Richmond, VA

Martha Farrell Erickson
Coordinator for Project STEEP (Steps
    Toward Effective Enjoyable Parenting)
University of Minnesota
Minneapolis, MN

Janette Cahill Flower
School Psychologist
Kenton County School District
Independence, KY

Michael C. Forcade
Supervisor of School Psychologists
Hamilton County Office of Education
Cincinnati, OH

William G. Knauf
School Psychologist
Kenton County School District
Independence, KY

Francis E. Lentz, Jr.
Assistant Professor
University of Cincinnati
Cincinnati, OH

Beth Lowman
School Psychology Consultant
Programs for the Handicapped
South Carolina Department of Education
Columbia, SC

Marcia L. McEvoy
Prevention Specialist
Allegan County Community Mental
    Health Services
Allegan, MI

John J. Murphy
School Psychologist
Covington Independent Schools
Covington, KY

Jack Naglieri
Associate Professor
The Ohio State University
Columbus, OH

Daivd W. Peterson
Administrative Assistant
LaGrange Area Department of Special
  Education
LaGrange, IL

Charlene R. Ponti
School Psychologist
Hamilton County Office of Education
Cincinnati, OH

Margaret Potter
Assistant Professor
Moorehead State University
Moorehead, MN

Ronald Reeve
Associate Professor
University of Virginia
Charlottesville, VA

Jacqueline Schakel
School Psychologist
Anchorage, AK

Linda Stevens
Publications and Training Consultant
Pennsylvania Resources and Information
  Center for Special Education
King of Prussia, PA

Karen Stine
School Psychologist
Hamilton County Office of Education
Cincinnati, OH

Stacey Vedder-Dubocq
School Psychologist
Hamilton County Office of Education
Cincinnati, OH

Barbara Wehmann
School Psychologist
Hamilton County Office of Education
Cincinnati, OH

Bruce P. Wess
School Psychologist
Kenton County School District
Independence, KY

Preface

In April of 1985, the Delegate Assembly of the National Association of School Psychologists (NASP) adopted a position regarding the need to develop alternatives to current service delivery systems for students currently in special education as well as for all students needing supportive services. This position statement (reprinted following this Preface) represented an important step for NASP as an organization in taking a strong position on a controversial issue. Adoption of the position statement also demonstrated NASP's commitment not only to question some of the problems in current practices, but more importantly, to work toward solutions and improved practices.

To support these proposed changes, many measures have been taken by the organization since the adoption of this position: NASP has included the advocacy of alternative services as one of the long-range goals guiding the association, the Association has lobbied for appropriate changes in federal and state policies, and the Alternative Services Task Force of NASP has been active in pursuing goals relative to alternative services. NASP's goal of advocating for alternative services is demonstrated throughout all activities of the association including selection of convention topics and research awards, as well as the publication of this book to provide information on alternative services to NASP members and others.

The Publications Committee of NASP conducted a national search, in the spring of 1986, for editors of this book. We consider ourselves very fortunate to have been selected to develop this volume for NASP. We have assembled as authors some of the leading professionals who are at the forefront of efforts to develop, implement, and evaluate alternative services.

The book is organized into three major parts corresponding to (a) the need for alternatives, (b) information on possible alternative frameworks, and (c) means of facilitating the change process to implement alternative service delivery systems. Part I, which includes the chapters addressing the need for alternative delivery systems, provides the context and background for the changes proposed in later chapters. Descriptions of specific alternative services programs are included in Part II. It is subdivided into sections covering alternative practices in referral, assessment, and intervention, as well as alternative organizational frameworks for providing broad-based services at the school or district level. It also provides coverage of special topics relative to alternative services for individuals with severe disabilities, infants and toddlers, and preschoolers. Part III contains chapters about the change process — how to facilitate change at the state, district, and building level, how to evaluate the effectiveness of alternative programs, and how to deal with legal and ethical issues connected with alternative services. Finally, there are two closing chapters that integrate the major issues in alternative services and provide implications for those wishing to implement such services.

In providing readers with information on why alternative services should be implemented, how they can be implemented, and how to facilitate change toward the adoption of alternative services, we hope that this volume makes an impact on professional practices and the provision of improved services to children, families, and schools. We stand strongly behind NASP's commitment to alternative services delivery and hope that our efforts with this book provide an impetus to question practices that need to be questioned, and to work toward improving educational services for all students.

Position Statement: Advocacy for Appropriate Educational Services for All Children

PL 94-142 (The Education of All Handicapped Children Act) has achieved major goals in serving handicapped children, many of whom had been previously excluded from appropriate educational programs. Since its enactment in 1975, all handicapped children have been guaranteed a free and appropriate education, the right to due process, and individualization of program according to need. We strongly support the continuation of legislation which has mandated these guarantees.

We also recognize that serious problems have been encountered as school districts strive to meet these mandates and that quality education is still an elusive goal. Some of these problems reflect difficulties within special education; others appear to be special education issues but have their origins in the regular education system.

One major set of problems involves reverse sides of the issue of access to appropriate education: (1) On the one hand, access to special education must be assured for all significantly handicapped children who need and can benefit from it. (2) Conversely, children are being inappropriately diagnosed as handicapped and placed in special education because of: (a) a lack of regular education options designed to meet the needs of children with diverse learning styles, (b) a lack of understanding, at times, of diverse cultural and linguistic backgrounds, and (c) inadequate measurement technologies which focus on labels for placement rather than providing information for program development.

It is not a benign action to label as "handicapped" children who are low achievers but are not, in fact, handicapped, even when this is done in order to provide them with services unavailable in general education. School personnel often resort to labeling because it seems the only way to obtain needed services for children. This is an unfortunate result of categorical models which attach funding to classifications. Other problems originating in the classification system include:

- Labels that are often irrelevant to instructional needs.

- Categories, based on deficit labels, that are rather arbitrarily defined, particularly for mildly handicapped and low achieving students, but which come to be accepted as "real" and may prevent more meaningful understanding of the child's psychoeducational needs. The intent of this statement is not necessarily to endorse mixing children with different moderate to severe handicaps in a single special education classroom.

- Reduced expectations for children who are placed in special needs programs.

- Assessment processes aimed at determining eligibility which often deflects limited resources from the determination of functional educational needs and the development of effective psychoeducational programs.

- A decreased willingness on the part of regular education, at times bordering on abdication of responsibility to modify curricula and programs in order to better meet the diverse needs of all children.

As increasing numbers of children are classified as handicapped and removed from regular classrooms for special instruction, there has been a dramatic reduction in the range of abilities among children who remain within the general education system. Concurrently, as national standards for excellence are being raised, the number of children at risk for school failure is growing dramatically. Without provisions to prepare students for higher expectations through effective instructional programs, many of these children may also be identified as handicapped and placed in special education. This climate, in which children are tested and labeled as failures or as handicapped in increasing numbers, creates an urgent need for reexamination and change in the system which provides access to services.

In view of these problems, and based upon the commitment to see that all children receive effective and appropriate education irrespective of race, cultural background, linguistic background, socioeconomic status, or educational need, we believe:

- All children can learn. Schools have a responsibility to teach them, and school personnel and parents should work together to assure every child a free and appropriate education in a positive social environment.

- Instructional options, based on the individual psychoeducational needs of each child, must be maximized within the general education system. Necessary support services should be provided within general education, eliminating the need to classify children as handicapped in order to receive these services.

- Psychoeducational needs of children should be determined through a multi-dimensional, non-biased assessment process. This must evaluate the match between the learner and his or her educational environment, assessing the compatibility of curriculum and system as they interact with the child, rather than relying on the deficit based model which places the blame for failure within the child. Referral to the assessment and placement process must always relate directly to services designed to meet psychoeducational needs.

- In addition to maintaining current protection for handicapped children, protections and safeguards must be developed to assure the rights of children who are at risk for school failure and require services while remaining in general education without classification as handicapped.

We propose a new national initiative to meet the educational needs of all children:

We propose the development and piloting of alternatives to the current categorical system. This requires reevaluation of funding mechanisms, and advocacy for policy and funding waivers needed for the piloting of alternative service delivery models. It also requires the development of increased support systems and extensive retraining of all school personnel to enable them to work effectively with a broad range of children with special needs within the regular education system.

This initiative will encourage greater independence for children by enabling them to function within the broadest possible environment, and independence for school personnel by providing them with training and support so they can help a wide range of children.

The types and extent of change we are suggesting should be made cautiously. Targeted funds intended for children with moderate and severe handicapping conditions must be protected. Similarly, resources for children who are not handicapped, but who experience learning difficulties, must be protected even though these children are served within general education. We need to assure that no child is put at risk for loss of services while the change process is occuring.

Our task is to reduce the rigidities of the current system without taking away the protections offered by PL 94-142. All experimentation and research must take place within a framework of maximum protection for children. It is highly likely that this may require the development of temporary parallel systems — the traditional system of classification and placement under PL 94-142, and a system of experimental programs, primarily within general education — until satisfactory models can be developed which meet the requirements of accountability, due process, and protection of students' and parents' rights, and provide funding for students in need of services. In addition, while these recommended modifications might reduce the risk of misclassification due to cultural or linguistic differences, we caution that these issues must continue to be monitored and discussed during the transition period and beyond.

Because of the complexity of these issues, the generation of effective solutions will require a national effort of interested persons and organizations which we hope to generate through this task force. We will actively work toward the collaboration of a wide variety of individuals and organizations, joining together to develop a strong base of knowledge, research, and experience in order to establish new frameworks and conceptualizations on which to base decisions, design feasible service delivery options, advocate for policy and funding changes needed to implement these alternatives, and coordinate efforts and share information for positive change. We invite you to join with us.

Table of Contents

Part I: Need for Alternative Educational Delivery Systems
1

Part II: Alternative Frameworks for Educational Delivery Systems
33

Section 1: Alternatives in Referral Practices

Part III: Facilitating the Development and Operation of Alternative Service Delivery Systems
455

Part IV: Reactions and Conclusions
553

Part I:

Need for Alternative Educational Delivery Systems

The Need for Alternatives in Educational Services

Janet L. Graden
Joseph E. Zins, and
Michael J. Curtis
University of Cincinnati
Carolyn T. Cobb
North Carolina Department of Public Instruction

In its first decade, PL 94-142 assured inclusion. Now it is time to get on with the unfinished work of assuring to all students a quality education which can only be achieved in an integrated and unified school system. (Gartner & Lipsky, 1987, p. 471)

Throughout special education there is growing recognition that despite the gains accomplished over the last decade, there are significant problems with the way that these educational services are structured and provided to students. In fact, it is increasingly acknowledged that some of the problems with services (e.g., overidentification of handicapped students, lack of clear differentiation of categorical groups, segregated pullout programs) are a direct result of existing provisions and regulations intended to provide appropriate services to students with handicaps. Consequently, national leaders and national associations involved with special and general education are calling for major philosophical and structural changes in the way that services are provided to students currently labeled as handicapped, and to students experiencing learning and adjustment problems in school.

These problems with services are the result of well-intentioned practices of both general and special education systems. Current special education practices largely reflect the results of years of advocacy efforts to provide a free and appropriate education for the thousands of previously unserved and underserved students with disabilities. Following the implementation of PL 94-142, over 650,000 previously unserved students have been brought into public education (Gartner & Lipsky, 1987). Other gains derived from special education legislation include an increased emphasis on the individualization of instruction for students with learning problems, expanded participation of parents in the special education process, and improved services for handicapped students (Will, 1986). However, along with these gains came "unintended effects [making it difficult] for educators to teach . . . and children to learn" (Will, 1986, p. 4). These unintended results occurred, according to Copeland (1983), because with increased rights came money, and the money was linked to identifying students as handicapped. Essentially, current funding structures encourage a process of "bounty hunting" in order to find and label students as handicapped, sometimes mistakenly, in order that they may receive needed educational support services.

Changes in general education, including increasingly higher standards and exclusionary practices, also have contributed to current practices in special education. Throughout the history of education in the United States, there has been a tendency to exclude or isolate students experiencing problems from other students (Reynolds & Lakin, 1987). It is only through this combination of factors — general education's almost exclusive focus on the mainstream and special education's emphasis on categorical programs to serve "special" groups — that the current problems have come into existence. As Gartner and Lipsky (1987) have suggested, special and general educators have "made a deal" in which general education rejects students with problems and special education accepts them. In fact, for many years following the implementation of PL 94-142, special education explicitly encouraged the referral of students who were suspected of being handicapped. Many of these referred students were subsequently placed in special education (Algozzine, Ysseldyke, & Christenson, 1983). Thus, general education teachers have been reinforced for referring students to special education (Zins, Curtis, Graden, & Ponti, 1988).

Because both systems have contributed to the problems reflected in current practices, change efforts also must involve both systems. In fact, major restructuring to integrate general and special education may be necessary. Major structural changes in the educational system are being called for by a number of prominent educational leaders (e.g., Reynolds, Wang, & Walberg, 1987), and are reflected in landmark position papers adopted by national associations representing the educational and social needs of students (e.g., National Association of School Psychologists, 1985). Over the past few years, several reports and position papers have added momentum to the current trend toward changing the service delivery system. To understand the historical context for the changes being advocated, it is necessary to review several of these landmark events.

BACKGROUND TO THE CALLS FOR CHANGE

Major Reports and Positions Calling for Change

The National Academy of Sciences panel and report. Late in the 1970s, a national panel of experts was assembled to address the problem of minority overrepresentation in classes for the educably mentally retarded (EMR). The report of this panel, edited by Heller, Holtzman, and Messick (1982), emphasized that minority overrepresentation itself was a problem, but broader and more fundamental problems also existed in the way that services were provided to students with handicaps. The report called into question practices in referral, assessment, placement decision making, and special education programming, and made a number of recommendations that are similar to many of the reforms still being advocated. One of the panel's conclusions remains especially pertinent today. "It is the responsibility of the placement team that labels and places a child in a special program to demonstrate that any differential label used is related to a distinctive prescription for educational practices that lead to improved outcomes" (Heller et al., 1982, p. 94). This responsibility of demonstrating distinctive prescriptions for different categories and improved outcomes as a result of categorical programs still has not been met. Despite years of effort, researchers have not been able to demonstrate that differential labels lead to distinctive prescriptions and improved outcomes for students (Reynolds et al., 1987). In other words, students do not clearly benefit from categorical special education services.

The NASP/NCAS position statement. In 1985, as a result of extensive collaboration and background work, the National Association of School Psychologists (NASP) and the National Coalition of Advocates for Students (NCAS) adopted a position statement entitled "Advocacy for Appropriate Educational Services for All Children" (NASP/NCAS, 1985). Citing problems associated with current services, including unreliable and arbitrary categorical definitions, placement practices that have only limited relevance for instruction, reduced expectancies for students who are labeled, the abdication of responsibility by general education for many students with learning problems, and the growing numbers of students characterized as at risk, the position statement called for the development and piloting of alternatives to current categorical systems. This position statement has been a major stimulus for many current efforts to promote change. (It is reprinted in the front of this volume.)

"Rights Without Labels." A document entitled "Rights Without Labels" (NCAS, 1987) was developed and endorsed by the National Coalition of Advocates for Students, the National Association of School Psychologists, and the National Association of Social Workers, as a follow-up statement to the advocacy position statement. This document has been a stimulus for ongoing discussion and debate regarding change. Its purpose was to reaffirm the rights afforded by PL 94-142 and to identify recommended practices in alternative programs. "Rights Without Labels" reiterated the call for the development of programs that did not require students who have special needs to be labeled or removed from general education. The document specifically recommended such changes as prereferral interventions that are intended to benefit all children and to preserve the right not to be evaluated unless it is warranted; alternative evaluation measures (e.g., curriculum-based assessment) that reliably assess performance relative to instructional planning; and the transfer of some special education resources to the general education setting.

This document includes guidelines to assure that "rights without labels" are implemented appropriately to serve the best interests of children. Because of its practical utility in highlighting important variables discussed through this volume, a copy of the document is included in Appendix A.

The Regular Education Initiative. A significant landmark in the advocacy of alternative services is the report issued by the Office of Special Education and Rehabilitative Services (OSERS), United States Department of Education, entitled "Educating Students With Learning Problems: A Shared Responsibility" (Will, 1986). This document provides the groundwork for OSERS's Regular Education Initiative (REI). It is notable that this report comes from within special education, and yet it is candidly critical of some of the existing problems with special education and is courageous in calling for efforts to address these problems. According to Will (Assistant Secretary for Special Education and Rehabilitative Services), some of the current problems, or obstacles, within current services are (a) a fragmented approach to services delivery that focuses on categorical labels, (b) a dual system of segregated services (special education and general education), (c) the stigmatization of students labeled as handicapped, and (d) placement decisions as a battleground between schools with specific eligibility criteria for placement and parents desiring services for their children. In elaborating on these obstacles, Will discussed how organization by categorical services results in (a) misclassification of students (so that they can receive needed services), (b) monetary incentives to place students, and (c) limited general education options for students who are found to be ineligible for categorical services. The dual system also is seen as contributing to minimal communication and coordination between general and special education programs and personnel and diminished general education responsibility for students with special needs.

Changes are called for within general and special education that build upon the "intrinsic strengths" of both systems (Will, 1986, p. 10). Included in the proposed solutions are increasing support systems for teachers in general education, empowering principals to control programs at the building level, implementing effective educational approaches in general education, and piloting and experimenting with alternative approaches.

These reports and positions demonstrate the momentum that is building behind the exploration of alternatives to the way that special education services currently are provided. At the same time, there is debate and discussion regarding the pervasiveness of the problems cited in these reports and the suggested alternatives for resolving them.

Responses to the Calls for Change

Critics of the Regular Education Initiative and related efforts at implementing changes in services delivery have responded to some of the issues raised in the documents and have expressed concern regarding the changes being advocated. Expressing some of these concerns, the Council for Exceptional Children (CEC), the National Education Association (NEA), and the American Association of School Administrators (AASA) adopted a position statement (CEC, 1987) relative to the REI. The statement begins by noting a concern about "trends and events which we believe to be regressive" and further states that "exceptional students [are] one group . . . in terms of what they need to learn and how they can best learn" and that "special educators are the educational professionals qualified to provide specifically designed instruction to exceptional children." These statements appear to be in opposition to the previously cited positions and documents, whose central theme and assumptions are the need to diminish emphasis on categorical programs and integrate special and general education into a unified system.

The Teacher Education Division (TED) of CEC has responded specifically to the Regular Education Initiative (TED, 1986). While supporting some aspects of the initiative (e.g., improved instruction for "special-needs students," increased achievement in general education, and an emphasis on developing effective programs), their response took issue with other aspects of the report. Among their stated concerns are that special education services are cast in a negative light by proponents of change and that the initiative fails to recognize the improvements made in services to "special-needs learners." The Executive Committee of TED formed "The National Inquiry Into the Future of Education for Students With Special Needs" and formulated 250 questions to be addressed in this national inquiry regarding the Regular Education Initiative.

Interestingly, the Regular Education Initiative has been criticized both for going too far in questioning the education of mildly handicapped students in separate environments (e.g., Hallahan, Kauffman, Lloyd, & McKinney, 1988) and for not going far enough by leaving severely handicapped students out of the initiative (Gartner & Lipsky, 1987). Gartner and Lipsky (1987), as well as others (see Giangreco & Meyer, this volume), believe that students with severe handicaps should also be integrated into general education (e.g., should not be placed in separate schools but should be placed in schools with same-age peers, and should be integrated as appropriate for many activities). It is important to note that integration does not mean "dumping" students with severe disabilities into general education without supportive services (Gartner & Lipsky, 1987).

There are other concerns raised regarding the Regular Education Initiative. Among them are that general education is not equipped to deal with students with special needs and to provide increased instructional options (Kauffman, Gerber, & Semmel, 1988; Keogh, 1988), that there is a need for policy analysis of the implications of proposed alternatives (McKinney & Hocutt, 1988), and that proposed changes do not have adequate empirical support to warrant full-scale adoption (Hallahan, Keller, McKinney, Lloyd, & Bryan, 1988; Keogh, 1988; Lloyd, Crowley, Kohler, & Strain, 1988).

Additional Calls for Restructuring Education

One of the key arguments that opponents of the Regular Education Initiative pose is that general education has not joined in the parade of support for greater integration of mildly handicapped students into regular education classes. To the contrary, general educators appear to be increasingly aware of the large numbers of children who are not succeeding in our schools as they are currently structured. There are numerous initiatives proposed to meet the needs of the many "at-risk students" in our schools, — students who are not completing school or who are completing it without achieving the educational and personal skills that should be expected.

It was noted earlier that the National Education Association and the American Association of School Administrators have joined the Council for Exceptional Children in stating support for teaching "exceptional children" (a) as a group and (b) by specially trained teachers. However, both of these general education groups are also part of the Forum of Educational Organization Leaders (FEOL), a coalition of eleven national education groups that has issued a position statement entitled "Meeting the Needs of Children and Youth At Risk of School Failure" (FEOL, 1987).

Over the last 2 years, the Council of Chief State School Officers (CCSSO), which comprises state directors and superintendents of public instruction, has made as a priority restructuring schools to better meet the needs of increasing numbers of at-risk students. In their policy statement, "Assuring School Success for Students at Risk" (CCSSO, 1987), they noted (a) that we must make a commitment of will to a national goal of high school graduation for virtually all students, (b) that each person, with rare exceptions of severe disabilities, has the ability to obtain a high school diploma, and (c) that the way students are taught should vary but all students should have a challenging and common curriculum.

The Education Commission of the States also has targeted at-risk youth in a national initiative (Palaich, 1988). In presenting some of the next steps to promote new directions in services to at-risk students, the Commission noted policy areas including the restructuring of schools. Palaich (1988) concluded that "the question is whether social institutions and governmental agencies can reorient their traditional ways of delivering services to meet the challenges these young people represent" (p. 23).

These examples illustrate the involvement of education associations concerned with all students in the need to restructure educational and supportive service delivery systems. These statements recognize that new programs cannot be added to existing services, but rather that major changes are needed in the way we educate all students.

PROBLEMS WITH CURRENT SERVICES

Despite the debate on the philosophical underpinnings of change efforts and the ways in which change is being advocated, there is considerable empirical evidence documenting the significant problems with current service delivery approaches. An overview of these documented problems provides a conceptual and empirical basis supporting the need to develop alternative approaches.

Contemporary Problems in Education

Increasing numbers of students are being served in special education, especially in programs for the mildly handicapped. Approximately 80-90% of the students in special education are served in categories for the mildly handicapped — the most unreliable and scientifically controversial categories (Reynolds et al., 1987). In addition, there is a problem with minority overrepresentation in the categories serving students as mildly handicapped (Chinn & Hughes, 1987). Chinn and Hughes cite figures showing that black students continue to be overrepresented in classes for the educably mentally retarded, trainably mentally retarded, and severely emotionally disturbed. Black students are assigned to these categories at twice the rate expected on the basis of the proportion of black students in the school population (Chinn & Hughes, 1987).

The number of students in the general education population who are experiencing learning and adjustment problems also is increasing. Major concerns have recently emerged regarding students in "at risk" groups. The Children's Defense Fund, in reviewing a broad range of data sources, provides the following information (Children's Defense Fund, 1988). Each year, 700,000 students (approximately 25%) aged 14 years and older drop out of school. One of every five children (approximately 13 million) lives in poverty, one of every four preschoolers. Almost 500,000 are affected by malnutrition. In 1986, an estimated 2.2 million children were reported abused or neglected; about 40% of them were preschoolers. More children are living in single-parent homes and are surviving low birth weights. Each year, one U.S. teen-aged girl in 10 becomes pregnant. Only half of the teens who become parents before age 18 graduate from high school by their mid-twenties. All of these conditions increase the risk factor for certain educational and social/emotional problems. Palaich (1988) also cites the additional problems that substance abuse poses in putting students at risk.

This trend of growing numbers of students in need of different kinds of instruction and schooling is coupled with reform movements in general education that are leading to increasingly higher educational standards (e.g., National Commission on Excellence in Education, 1983). There are two problems with higher general education standards: General education has narrowed the definition of "normal," and students with handicaps and other educational needs have been ignored in national reform reports (Gartner & Lipsky, 1987; Lilly, 1987; Lipsky & Gartner, 1987; Shepard, 1987).

These two issues — higher standards in general education and increasing numbers of students "at risk" and needing alternatives — bring the problems of a dual system of general and special education to the forefront. With greatly increasing numbers of students who need supportive services and alternative instruction, it is clear that special education cannot and should not deal with all the needs that will be placed upon it to serve these students. It is equally clear that general education must develop options to provide appropriate services and programs for the vast numbers of students considered to be at risk (Reynolds & Lakin, 1987). In public hearings and a subsequent report, Howe and Edelman (1985) emphasized the need to restructure schools and create a wider range of general education options so that students' needs can be met without labeling. These goals may be accomplished best by developing a unified school system designed to meet the needs of all students (Gartner & Lipsky, 1987; Lilly, 1986; and Stainback & Stainback, 1984, this volume).

Challenging the Assumptions Inherent in the Dual System

Lipsky and Gartner (1987), strong proponents of a unified system of educational services for all students, offer persuasive arguments that challenge the assumptions underlying the dual system of special and general education. They assert that there are "fundamental flaws in the very conceptualization of general and special education" (p. 69). Stainback and Stainback (1984, this volume) have raised some of the same concerns about the flawed assumptions inherent in the dual system (e.g., that there are two distinct student populations — special and regular). Challenging the current assumptions, these authors have provided an alternative set of assumptions underlying a proposed unified system: That handicapped and "normal" children are more alike than different; that more attention is to be paid to individual differences than group differences; that even severely handicapped individuals are able to learn in most environments; and that the principles of effective schooling, including high expectations for achievement, must be applied to all students (Lipsky & Gartner, 1987; Stainback & Stainback, 1984, this volume).

Empirically Demonstrated Problems with Current Practices

In addition to the conceptual problems with the current dual system, there are problems from a practical perspective. A generic issue is that time and money spent on determining who is "special" and who is not could be better used to provide services to all who need it, regardless of any presumed handicap. Furthermore, considerable empirical evidence, as well as years of practical experience, demonstrates that changes are needed in the process of referral, assessment, and categorical placement.

Problems with referral, assessment, and placement practices. The special education referral-assessment-placement process is costly, complex, and of questionable validity and utility for instructional programming (Lilly, 1986). Referral often is subjective and idiosyncratic, and because high proportions of the students referred are subsequently placed in special education, teachers often learn to expect that referral automatically leads to placement (Galagan, 1985; Ysseldyke et al., 1983).

The assessment process, when primarily directed toward determining eligibility for categorical services, is of little practical utility for planning instructional interventions for students (Galagan, 1985; Reschly, in press). Many of the currently used tests also are of questionable technical adequacy with respect to the appropriateness of the norms, the reliability of scores (and of the subsequent decisions derived from scores), and the validity of the tests to make the placement decisions (Reschly, in press).

After 5 years of research on the referral, assessment, and placement process for labeling students as learning disabled, Ysseldyke and colleagues concluded that the placement process is unreliable and that there is no empirically defensible way to classify students as learning disabled (Ysseldyke et al., 1983). This same conclusion regarding the lack of reliability in categorical placements has been reached for the other mildly handicapping conditions (Reschly, in press; Reynolds & Lakin, 1987; Ysseldyke, 1987). As evidence of the unreliability of categorical placement practices, it has been demonstrated that categorical placement rates differ markedly between districts and states (Morsink, Thomas, & Smith-Davis, 1987; Ysseldyke, 1987).

Problems with categorical differentiation. It makes little sense to serve students according to categorical labels if the labels cannot be reliably differentiated and if there are no distinct educational prescriptions that result from the labels. The evidence in this regard shows that categories for the mildly handicapped are "scientifically questionable" (Reynolds et al., 1987, p. 392) and "nonquantifiable conditions" (Edgar & Hayden, 1984-1985, p. 531). There are no reliable and meaningful categorical differences in teaching methods for the mildly handicapped categories (Morsink et al., 1987) and no categorical differences in the effectiveness of programs for different groups of mildly handicapped students taught by teachers with various categorical certifications (Marston, 1987). Overall, similar practices appear to be effective for students in EMR, LD, or compensatory education (i.e., Chapter 1) programs (Heller et al., 1982).

Effectiveness of special education. All of the critiques regarding placement of students into categorical programs would be less important if there were clear evidence supporting special education's effectiveness in improving outcomes for students who receive these services. Although there are methodological problems associated with attempts to prove the overall effectiveness of special education (Epps & Tindal, 1987), the results of several studies, including a meta-analysis of 50 separate special education effectiveness studies, have failed to demonstrate the efficacy of special education (Carlberg & Kavale, 1980; Glass, 1983; Madden & Slavin, 1983). However, the failure to statistically prove the positive (that special education is effective) does *not* prove the negative (that special education is ineffective). In other words, although special education overall has not been shown to have positive effects, there may be benefits from specific programs or fo specific students that have not been uncovered by research. The question remains, however, as to whether these presumed benefits (e.g., effective teaching practices) can be derived only in categor ical programs.

Conclusions regarding current practices. The evidence that there is a clear need to develop alternatives to current special educational practices is overwhelming, but this should not be seen as an indictment of special education. The existence of regulations to provide categorical special education services to students reflects well-intentioned efforts and the best knowledge that was available at the time the regulations were developed. Now, however, is the time to consider the accumulated evidence from over the last decade and to apply it toward the improvement of educational practices. As summarized by Lilly (1986),

> Special education for students labeled "mildly handicapped," as currently conceptualized and implemented, overidentifies students, results in inefficiency in service delivery, and operates counter to mainstreaming principles. Supportive services are needed which are based in regular education, aimed at students who are low achievers and/or disruptive in school, do not require complex diagnostic testing and labeling of students as handicapped, and minimize "pull-out" of students from normal classroom activities. A single coordinated system of service delivery is preferable to the array of special programs currently offered in the schools. (p. 10)

DIRECTIONS FOR
ALTERNATIVE SERVICES

The remainder of this volume contains several chapters discussing in detail some suggested alternatives for providing effective services to all students with specific needs for supportive services. Some of these chapters describe alternatives that differ fundamentally from current categorical services (e.g., Stainback & Stainback; Wang, Reynolds, & Levine-Schwartz). However, since most

states continue to fund services categorically (West & Brown, 1987), the majority of the chapters describe alternatives that can be applied within the constraints of current service delivery systems. Alternative referral practices are described as a way to implement classroom interventions to avoid unnecessary evaluations for special education eligibility and to provide more supportive services in general education (Fuchs & Fuchs; Lennox, Hyman, & Hughes). These building-based support systems (described in more detail in Zins et al., 1988) are advocated by Will (1986) and "Rights Without Labels" (NCAS, 1986). According to a newsletter distributed by the Office of Special Education (1987), such building-based efforts are already being implemented to a large extent in many states.

In response to the numerous previously cited problems with current assessment practices, alternative assessment practices are described that include curriculum based assessment (Marston & Magnusson; Tindal) and instructionally relevant assessment (Ysseldyke & Christenson). These assessment alternatives are useful for instructional purposes; additionally, according to a legal expert, curriculum-based measures can constitute an evaluation under the Education for the Handicapped Act (Galagan, 1985).

There are numerous intervention strategies that have been proven to be effective for children with learning and behavioral problems, regardless of whether any designation as handicapped has been made, and regardless of categorical assignment if handicapped status has been designated. As stated by Algozzine and Maheady (1985), "Gains demonstrated by effective instruction are not bound to the setting in which the teaching occurred or the label assigned to the student who received it" (p. 488). Among the effective intervention strategies that are described in a number of chapters are behavioral interventions (Casey, Skiba, & Algozzine), social skills interventions (Knoff); reading interventions (Lentz), peer tutoring and cooperative learning (Hawryluk & Smallwood), direct instruction (Carnine, Becker, & Granzin), and principles of effective instruction compiled from the extensive research on effective teaching (Berliner).

In working towards change in practices, the process of implementing change is crucial. Strategies for implementing planned and lasting change are described by Illback, by Henning-Stout and Conoley (district-level change), and by Kruger (building-level change). Evaluation of the effectiveness of alternative practices is essential (Bennett), as is the consideration of legal and ethical issues (Reschly).

CONCLUSIONS

It is clear from existing research and years of experience that many current practices in special and general education must change. Although there is considerable evidence supporting this need for alternatives, the extent to which they actually occur is dependent on the concerted efforts of educational professionals in their classrooms, schools, districts, state departments, and professional associations, and in efforts to improve federal and state regulations. Fundamental changes in services that have been recommended (National School Psychology Inservice Training Network, 1984; Reynolds et al., 1987) now are seen to be on the horizon (Lilly, 1986; Reschly, in press). It is time to recognize the problems that exist and to work to improve practices so that the best educational services can be provided to *all* students, regardless of assumptions about whether they are handicapped. As concluded in the NASP/NCAS position statement,

> All children can learn. Schools have a responsibility to teach them, and . . . to assure every child a free and appropriate education in a positive social environment . . . necessary support services should be provided within general education, eliminating the need to classify children as handicapped in order to receive these services. . . . We propose a new national initiative to meet the educational needs of all children.

REFERENCES

Algozzine, B., & Maheady, L. (1985). When all else fails, teach! *Exceptional Children, 52,* 487-488.

Algozzine, B., Ysseldyke, J. E., & Christenson, S. (1983). An analysis of the incidence of special class placement: the masses are burgeoning. *Journal of Special Education, 17,* 141-147.

Carlberg, C., & Kavale, K. (1980). The efficacy of special versus regular class placement for exceptional children: A meta-analysis. *Journal of Special Education, 14,* 295-309.

Children's Defense Fund. (1988). *A call for action to make our nation safe for children: A briefing book on the status of American children in 1988.* Washington, DC: Author.

Chinn, P. C., & Hughes, S. (1987). Representation of minority students in special education classes. *Remedial and Special Education, 8*(4), 41-46.

Copeland, W. C., (1983). Strategies for special education in the 1980s: A conference epilogue. *Policy Studies Review, 2,* 243-260.

Council of Chief State School Officers. (1987, November). *Assuring School Success for Students At Risk: A Council Policy Statement.* Washington, DC: Author.

Council for Exceptional Children, National Education Association, and American Association of School Administrators. (1987). *The relationship between special education and general education.* Reston, VA: Council for Exceptional Children.

Edgar, E., & Hayden, A. H. (1984-1985). Who are the children special education should serve and how many children are there? *Journal of Special Education, 18,* 523-539.

Epps, S., & Tindal, G. (1987). The effectiveness of differential programming in serving mildly handicapped students: Placement options and instructional programming. In M. C. Wang, M. C. Reynolds, and H. J. Walberg (Eds.), *The handbook of special education: Research and practice* (Vol. 3, pp. 213-248). Oxford: Pergamon.

Forum of Educational Organizational Leaders. (1987). *Meeting the needs of children and youth at risk of school failure.* Position statement adopted by the Forum of Educational Organization Leaders.

Galagan, J. E. (1985). Psychoeducational testing: Turn out the lights, the party's over. *Exceptional Children, 52,* 288-299.

Gartner, A., & Lipsky, D. K. (1987). Beyond special education: Toward a quality system for all students. *Harvard Educational Review, 57,* 367-395.

Glass, G. V. (1983). Effectiveness of special education. *Policy Studies Review, 2,* 65-78.

Hallahan, D. P., Kauffman, J. M., Lloyd, J. W., & McKinney, J. D. (1988). Introduction to the series: Questions about the regular education initiative. *Journal of Learning Disabilities, 21*, 3-5.

Hallahan, D. P., Keller, C. E., McKinney, J. D., Lloyd, J. W., Bryan, T. (1988). Examining the research base of the regular education initiative: Efficacy studies and the adaptive learning environments model. *Journal of Learning Disabilities, 21*, 29-35, 55.

Heller, K., Holtzman, W., & Messick, S. (Eds.). (1982). *Placing children in special education: A strategy for equity.* Washington, DC: National Academy Press.

Howe, H., & Edelman, M. W. (1985). *Barriers to excellence: Our children at risk.* Boston: National Coalition of Advocates for Students.

Kauffman, J. M., Gerber, M. M., & Semmel, M. I. (1988). Arguable assumptions underlying the regular education initiative. *Journal of Learning Disabilities, 21*, 6-11.

Keogh, B. K. (1988). Improving services for problem learners: Rethinking and restructuring. *Journal of Learning Disabilities, 21*, 19-22.

Lilly, M. S. (1986, March). The relationship between general and special education: A new face on an old issue. *Counterpoint*, p. 10.

Lilly, M. S. (1987). Lack of focus on special education in literature on educational reform. *Exceptional Children, 53*, 325-326.

Lipsky, D. K., & Gartner, A. (1987). Capable of achievement and worthy of respect: Education for handicapped students as if they were full-fledged human beings. *Exceptional Children, 54*, 69-74.

Lloyd, J. W., Crowley, E. P., Kohler, F. W., & Strain, P. S. (1988). Redefining the applied research agenda: Cooperative learning, prereferral, teacher consultation, and peer-mediated interventions. *Journal of Learning Disabilities, 21*, 43-52.

Madden, N., & Slavin, R. (1983). Mainstreaming students with mild handicaps: Academic and social outcomes. *Review of Educational Research, 53*, 519-659.

Marston, D. (1987). Does categorical teacher certification benefit the mildly handicapped child? *Exceptional Children, 53*, 423-431.

McKinney, J. D., & Hocutt, A. M. (1988). The need for policy analysis in evaluating the regular education initiative. *Journal of Learning Disabilities, 21*, 12-18.

Morsink, C. V., Thomas, C. C., & Smith-Davis, J. (1987). Noncategorical special education programs: Processes and outcomes. In M. C. Wang, M. C. Reynolds, and H. J. Walberg (Eds.), *The handbook of special education: Research and practice* (Vol. 3, pp. 287-311). Oxford: Pergamon.

National Association of School Psychologists/ National Coalition of Advocates for Students. (1985). *Advocacy for appropriate educational services for all children.* Washington, DC: Author.

National Coalition of Advocates for Students. (1987). *Rights Without Labels.* Washington, DC: Author.

National Commission on Excellence in Education. (1983). *A nation at risk: The imperative for educational reform.* Washington, DC: Author.

National School Psychology Inservice Training Network. (1984). *School psychology: A blueprint for training and practice.* Minneapolis, MN: Author.

Office of Special Education and Rehabilitative Services, U. S. Department of Education. (1987). State roll call. *OSERS News in Print, 1*(3), 4-6.

Palaich, B. (1988, March 16). Youth at risk — Raising public awareness. *Education Week.*

Reschly, D. (in press). Special education reform: School psychology revolution. *School Psychology Review.*

Reynolds, M. C., & Lakin, K. C. (1987). Noncategorical special education for mildly handicapped students: A system for the future. In M. C. Wang, M. C. Reynolds, and H. J. Walberg (Eds.), *The handbook of special education: Research and practice* (Vol. 3, pp. 331-356). Oxford: Pergamon.

Reynolds, M. C., Wang, M. C., & Walberg, H. J. (1987). The necessary restructuring of special and regular education. *Exceptional Children, 53*, 391-398.

Shepard, L. A. (1987). The new push for excellence: Widening the schism between regular and special education. *Exceptional Children, 53*, 327-329.

Stainback, W., & Stainback, S. (1984). A rationale for the merger of special and regular education. *Exceptional Children, 51*, 102-111.

Teacher Education Division Council for Exceptional Children. (1986). A statement by the Teacher Education Division, Council for Exceptional Children on the Regular Education Initiative. Reston, VA: Author.

West, J. F., & Brown, P. A. (1987). State departments of education policies on consultation in special education: The state of the states. *Remedial and Special Education, 8*(3), 45-51.

Will, M. (1986). Educating students with learning problems: A shared responsibility. Washington, DC: United States Department of Education.

Ysseldyke, J. E. (1987). Classification of handicapped students. In M. C. Wang, M. C. Reynolds, and H.

J. Walberg (Eds.), *The handbook of special education: Research and practice* (Vol. 3, pp. 213-243). Oxford: Pergamon.

Ysseldyke, J. E., Thurlow, M., Graden, J., Wesson, C., Algozzine, B., & Deno, S. (1983). Generalizations from five years of research on assessment and decision making: Findings of the Minnesota Institute. *Exceptional Education Quarterly, 4,* 75-93.

Zins, J. E., Curtis, M. J., Graden, J. L., & Ponti, C. R. (1988). *Helping students succeed in the regular classroom.* San Francisco: Jossey-Bass.

APPENDIX A
Guidelines for Assuring Rights without Labels in Regular/Special Education Programs

Checklist

I. ASSURANCES: Any proposed alternative non-categorical program or system shall:

  A. Ensure that the fundamental rights afforded handicapped students and their parents under PL 94-142 are maintained and safeguarded. These include, but are not limited to:

  (1) Standards for fair and unbiased identification and evaluation of children who would qualify as "handicapped" in a categorical system.*   (1) _____

  (2) Individualized Education Programs (IEPs) for all students who would otherwise qualify under a categorical system.   (2) _____

  (3) Specialized instruction and related services for students who would otherwise qualify under a categorical system.   (3) _____

  (4) Least Restrictive Environment (LRE) standards in determining educational placement.   (4) _____

  (5) Appointment of surrogate parents when appropriate.   (5) _____

  (6) Non-discriminatory discipline procedures.   (6) _____

  (7) All timeline standards governing the above practices and procedures.   (7) _____

  (8) Parental rights in the identification, evaluation, IEPs and placement of students who would otherwise qualify under a categorical system.   (8) _____

  (9) Due Process rights for parents and students who wish to pursue concerns/complaints regarding educational evaluations, programs, and placements.   (9) _____

  (10) Local advisory boards to assist LEAs in planning for the provision of appropriate educational services.   (10) _____

  B. Provide parents of handicapped students with an alternative to selecting a traditional categorical approach to classification.   B. _____

  C. Provide full disclosure of the non-categorical system to parents including an explanation of resources, services, and rights that wil be afforded students in this system.   C. _____

II. GENERAL QUALITY OF ALTERNATIVE PROGRAM: Any proposed non-categorical program or system shall:

  A. Employ pre-referral screening/intervention measures and utilize evaluation procedures that include curriculum based assessments.   A. _____

  B. Employ methodology known to be associated with effective teaching/learning (for example, provide students with orderly and productive environments, ample learning/teaching time, systematic and objective feedback on performance, well-sequenced curricula, etc.).   B. _____

  C. Focus attention on basic skills as priority areas for instruction (for example, language, self-dependence, reasonable social behavior, mathematics, health and safety, etc.).   C. _____

  D. Provide procedures to identify and respond to the individual needs of all students, and in particular, those who may need modifications in their school programs.   D. _____

  E. Provide for special education aids, services, and resources to be delivered in regular education settings.   E. _____

III. ASSESSMENT OF OUTCOMES: Any proposed non-categorical program shall:

  A. Have an objective methodology for assessing the educational progress of students in major curriculum domains (including academic, social, motivational, and attitudinal variables) and for comparing such progress with results in traditional programs.   A. _____

  B. Contain and utilize a cost-benefit analysis to compare costs with traditional programs.   B. _____

IV. TEACHING STAFF AND FACILITIES: Any proposed non-categorical program shall:

A. Include instruction and services by teachers and staff who are qualified in accordance with current state certification standards.

A. _____

B. Include a delivery system that provides continuing staff development responsive to the training needs of the teaching staff and administrative personnel who will be implementing the requirements of the non-categorical program.

B. _____

C. Include appropriate instructional materials and other resources.

C. _____

---

*To provide these assurances, it is assumed that as part of the experimental procedures, it would be common to conduct a dual classification system, whereby, for example, a student who might be classified as "learning disabled" in a traditional system would actually be so identified. Although the student's record would reflect the traditional classification, the student would be considered in need of "supplemental services" (i.e., regular and special education services) for purposes of his/her participation in the non-categorical program. Only by such a dual system could assurance concerning "rights" be offered and safeguarded. Over the long term, the traditional classification system might be modified if all stake-holders are satisfied about the new procedures.

Reprinted with permission, Advocacy Center for the Elderly and Disabled, New Orleans, LA.

2

Changes Needed to Strengthen Regular Education

Susan Stainback
University of Northern Iowa
William Stainback
University of Northern Iowa

Reynolds and Birch (1982) have pointed out that "the whole history of education for exceptional students can be told in terms of one steady trend that can be described as progressive inclusion" (p. 27). Great strides in this movement have been made relatively recently (Biklen, 1985; Forest, 1986, 1987a; Gartner & Lipsky, 1987; Graden, Casey, & Bonstrom, 1985; Madden & Slavin, 1983; Stainback & Stainback, 1985a; Wang & Birch, 1984b). It has been reflected in the past several decades by the emergence of concepts such as deinstitutionalization, normalization, integration, mainstreaming, zero rejection, delabeling, and merger.

We now appear to be at a point in history in which we are no longer satisfied with just discussing the mainstreaming or integration of some students into regular education. Rather we have begun to analyze how we might go about integrating or merging special and regular education personnel, programs, and resources to design a unified, comprehensive regular education system capable of meeting the unique needs of all students in the mainstream of regular education (Forest, 1987a; Gartner & Lipsky, 1987; Lipsky & Gartner, 1987; Stainback & Stainback, 1984, 1985b; Stainback & Stainback, in press, a). Historical reviews of education have indicated that the trend is in the direction of integrating or merging special and regular education (see Gartner and Lipsky, 1987).

It is the contention of the authors that the historical trends of the past several decades will continue and we will eventually break down the barriers between special and regular education. There are a number of changes occurring at the present time that will propel us toward further eliminating the special and regular education dichotomy. For example, in the not too distant past, nearly everyone agreed that mainstreaming meant the integration of students labeled mildly handicapped into the mainstream of regular education. Thus, our task was to strengthen regular education to meet these students' needs. However, this is changing. The situation is becoming much more complex. A growing number of researchers, parents, and educators are beginning to advocate that *all* students be integrated into the mainstream of regular education, including those who have traditionally been labeled severely and profoundly handicapped (e.g., Forest, 1987a; Ruttiman & Forest, 1986; Jacobs, 1986; Gartner & Lipsky, 1987; Stainback & Stainback, 1987; Strully, 1986). They essentially believe that it is now time to stop developing criteria for who does or does not belong in the mainstream and instead turn the spotlight toward increasing the capabilities of the regular school environment, the mainstream, to meet the unique needs of *all* students.

As this movement intensifies and progresses, it will be *essential to remain* cognizant that regular education is not at the present time structured or equipped to successfully meet the unique needs of all students. To gear up, present-day special and regular educators will need to join together as one group with the purpose of organizing a strong and comprehensive regular system of education that can meet the needs of all students. This is the only way, in the authors' opinion, to eventually begin to meet the unique needs of all students in the mainstream of regular education, including those students now in regular education whose needs are not being met as well as those students we currently label as gifted, mildly handicapped, or severely and profoundly handicapped.

The purpose in this chapter is to outline and discuss some changes needed if a strong, comprehensive regular service system of education capable of meeting all students needs is to be developed. Before addressing the changes needed, however, a few key assumptions underlying the changes suggested are briefly outlined.

ASSUMPTIONS

Assumption #1

All children deserve a free and appropriate education. Currently, as stated in Public Law 94-142, it is accepted that all students with disabilities or handicaps deserve a free and appropriate education that meets their unique needs. As a result, individualized education plans and accountability procedures have been developed to assure that this occurs. However, to assume that an appropriate education geared to the individual needs of a student should be provided and protected only for one category of students such as those labeled handicapped or "special" is educationally discriminatory. *Every* student, regardless of any label or categorical assignment, is unique and worthy of individual consideration in regard to her or his educational needs.

Assumption #2

The education and related services any student receives should be based on his or her specific interests, needs, and capabilities. Currently, the category to which students belong (e.g. "special" needs versus "regular" needs) influences the education they receive. This is a poor instructional practice. For instructional purposes, it is more effective to view students as individuals. Once we begin looking at students as individuals, the data available concerning their instructional needs is far more specific and precise than a special or regular label or any other categorical label, making such labels virtually useless for educational purposes (Lilly, 1979). The problems involved in basing educational programs and related services on a categorical affiliation such as special or regular, or handicapped or nonhandicapped, are similar to those inherent in basing the education students receive on whether they are black or white, or male or female. When students or anyone else are approached according to a categorical affiliation, they are denied the individual consideration they deserve. As noted by Reynolds and Balow (1972): "In all of society there is a rising revulsion against simplistic categorizations of human beings" (p. 357).

Assumption #3

All students should have their needs met as a regular or normal practice in the public schools. At present, some students (approximately 10–12% of the student population) are provided educational and related services that meet their unique needs through "special" accommodations and practices (Ysseldyke & Algozzine, 1984). This is inequitable. There should be nothing special or charity-like about meeting the educational needs of *any* child in the public schools. That is, some students should not be viewed as special, charity cases *given* "special," individualized educational programs and services because of their needy or "special" condition. All students should receive an education geared to their capabilities and needs as a regular, normal, and expected practice. Equality suffers when the education of some students is viewed as special, different, and charity-like while the education of others is viewed as regular, normal, and expected. As noted by Biklen (1985): "Until accommodation for the disabled is seen as regular, normal and expected, it will be seen instead as special. As long as it is special, it will be, by definition, unequal" (p. 176).

It should be noted that what is being discussed here as inequitable is the *viewing* of some students' education as "special." This is not to imply that all the expertise, curriculum, and procedures currently considered under the auspices of "special" education (e.g., individualization of instruction, community-referenced daily life instruction, braille) are inappropriate or not needed.

Assumption #4

All students should be educated in the same basic system of education. There is little or no reason for some students to receive their education or related services from a special system of education and others receive theirs from a regular system. Maintaining a dual system of education establishes artificial barriers among educators. This results in the division of school personnel, students, and programs along handicapped/nonhandicapped lines in the public schools, which works against viewing all students as individuals and integral natural members of the same "regular" student body (Stainback & Stainback, 1984, 1985b).

CHANGES NEEDED TO STRENGTHEN REGULAR EDUCATION

The changes suggested in this section are based on the assumptions outlined above. There are a number of changes needed to strengthen regular education. They range across the gamut from grouping practices employed in the public schools to personnel preparation approaches. The following include several changes considered by the authors to be critical to the potential ability of regular

education to meet the individual needs of all students.

Each change must be recognized as only one part of a holistic effort. While the implementation of individual changes can assist in the development of a system to address unique needs, individual changes in isolation cannot be expected to strengthen regular education enough to meet the needs of all students.

Staff and Personnel Changes

Attitudes. It will be necessary to first change the attitudes of many educators (Forest, 1987b). Without an attitude change, there will be little motivation or commitment to strengthening regular education in any significant or comprehensive way. One critical attitude that requires change involves what should be done when regular education is considered not strong enough to meet the needs of some students. The prevalent current attitude is that if some students' needs cannot be met in regular education (primarily those labeled "truly" or severely/profoundly handicapped), a different or special education option is needed for them. If regular education is to be strengthened to meet the needs of *all* students, a different attitude will be necessary. An attitude or approach must be adopted that recognizes the need to modify, expand, or adjust regular education so that it is capable of addressing the unique educational requirements of all students. As long as a separationist or segregationist model is used that assigns some students to special education when regular education does not meet their needs, progress will be impeded rather than facilitated toward the goal of strengthening regular education to meet the needs of all students (Strully, 1986).

Support Staff. The availability of a strong support staff is critical to strengthening the ability of regular education to meet the unique needs of all students. It also is essential to the strengthening of regular education that support staff work directly with teachers and students in mainstream settings on specific problems.

The emphasis needs to be on instructional assessment and program planning in the mainstream as opposed to classification and eligibility for "special" placement outside regular education. Thus, one change that appears to be needed is the shift of some current support staff toward engaging in the development and implementation of more curriculum-based and instructionally focused assessment and educational planning procedures designed for use in mainstream setting. For example, consultants or resource teachers in areas such as instruction of the learning-disabled, behaviorally disordered, severely and profoundly handicapped, gifted, mentally retarded, deaf, or blind need focus away from specialization in categories of exceptional students and toward more functional, curriculum-based and instructionally related areas of expertise such as curriculum adaptations, behavior management, community-referenced daily living instruction, braille, creativity and problem solving, mobility or alternative communication skills. That is, we need to move away from having support staff who portray their expertise as being in categories of exceptional students or "special" education and have them develop and more clearly communicate their contribution to assessment and program planning in a curricular or instructional expertise area(s). This would bring support staff currently in special education into a position more parallel with support staff such as consultants and resource personnel in reading, speech, physical therapy, school psychology, science, and math. In addition, support staff in areas such as school psychology need to maintain an instructionally relevant focus to assist regular education. This would involve concentrating to a greater extent on ecologically and curriculum-based assessment and intervention procedures designed to meet the unique needs of individual students while moving away from traditional normative performance and expectations in assessment and intervention planning (Yssel-dyke & Christenson, 1986).

We also need to change the way many support staff currently operate in the public schools in order to strengthen regular education. Traditionally, specialized support staff such as school psychologists, physical therapists, occupational therapists, speech correctionists, resource teachers, and reading, learning, and behavior experts have concentrated their time in direct-service activities (Sternat, Nietupski, Messina, Lyon, & Brown, 1977). In general, support staff have taken the student(s) needing assistance to an isolated section of the classroom or school building to engage in intensive one-to-one or small-group activities. The resource room where students with learning and/or behavior difficulties are frequently taken for specialized assistance is a common example. Such traditional practices have done little to strengthen regular education.

Instead of the isolated services model described above, the use of an integrated support staff services model is needed to strengthen regular education. Such a model is designed to work in mainstreamed settings. In the integrated model, support staff work with the student(s) to assess needs and facilitate progress in mainstreamed settings in which the student is integrated. In this way regular education is strengthened in that the support staff provide a model for and teach not only the individual student but also the student's teacher(s), peers, and friends. As a result, there is an increase in the number of people who can provide cues and assistance to the student. An important ancillary benefit is that teachers and peers learn skills they can use with other students and friends they meet at other times who need the kind of assistance being provided.

Another support staff change that has the potential to strengthen regular education in meeting the unique needs of all students is a shift away from having some support staff (e.g. resource teachers/consultants) concentrate almost exclusively on providing services for individual students or small groups of "special" students. Instead, they need to expand their focus to assist the classroom teacher in adapting classroom procedures and activities to be responsive to the individual interests, needs, and capabilities of all class members. Recognizing that all students, including those traditionally labeled as "special needs students," can benefit when a classroom is organized to be responsive to individual differences could go a long way toward having support staff become more involved in strengthening regular education. Various consulting and prereferral intervention models could be employed to help bring about this change (Graden, Casey, & Bonstrom, 1985; Graden, Casey, & Christenson, 1985; Lilly & Givens-Ogle, 1981). Detailed information about consulting and prereferral intervention models can be found in the next three chapters in this book.

Personnel preparation. In order to strengthen regular education to meet the needs of all students, modifications are needed in current personnel preparation and certification practices. The critical impact of personnel preparation on the functioning of the elementary and secondary schools has been clearly pointed out by Sarason (1982), who noted that

> School personnel are graduates of our colleges and universities. It is there that they learn there are at least two types of human beings and if you choose to work with one of them you render yourself *legally* and conceptually incompetent to work with the others. . . . What we see in our public schools is a mirror image of what exists in colleges and universities. (p. 258)

A major change needed in personnel preparation is that regular education accept the personnel and instructional programming traditionally labeled "special" into college and university regular education departments, divisions, and programs. By doing so, universities can set a model for integration and comprehensive programming within regular education for the public schools as well as strengthen regular education personnel preparation.

Within an integrated preparation program for regular education personnel the bodies of knowledge and skills related to basic philosophies and processes of teaching and learning could be offered within a common core for all educators. Specializations focusing on each educator's interests and abilities in instructional content areas such as science, history, reading, math, individualized and adaptive learning approaches, behavior management, community-referenced daily life instruction, braille, or mobility could be offered as options for specialization to prospective and practicing educators to provide training, certification, and job assignment in all areas of expertise needed in the schools to meet all students' instructional needs. This type of reorganization would not only serve to de-emphasize the current categorical approach to personnel preparation and assignment, but also would provide an organizational structure in which students in the public schools would be provided more precise access to available personnel resources in respect to the particular instructional areas in which they need educational programming. For example, students who require programming in sign language or other alternative communication methods could be assigned within regular education to a teacher, consultant, or other resource personnel with specialized training in the area. Similarly, if community-referenced daily life instruction were needed, a student could be assigned to an experience in which the instructor or consultant had expertise in teaching community-referenced daily life instruction. Thus, personnel assignment in the public schools could be based on the instructional needs of students rather than by other grouping arrangements (e.g., special or regular) that are often not directly relevant to student learning needs.

Finally, it should become possible in an integrated, comprehensive regular education personnel preparation model to capitalize upon and integrate the diverse expertise among all faculty for the provision of a stronger preparation program for all educators. That is, with the diverse expertise available among the variety of faculty in a unified regular education personnel preparation program, the incorporation and sharing of the strengths available could lead to the development of a stronger core program for educators of all students, at the same time allowing for specialization in specific instructional areas. The reader interested in more detailed information about the reorganization of personnel preparation is referred to Stainback and Stainback (in press, b).

Organizational Changes

School structure. Several changes also are needed in the basic structure of regular education. One obvious change is the reincorporation of personnel, services, and resources currently labeled as special back into the regular education system. Special education was conceived as a means to accommodate the needs of students who were considered "different" or "special." However, through research and experience, there has been a gradual recognition that *every* student is "different" and "special" (Lipsky & Gartner, 1987). Thus such aspects of education as have been developed to deal with differences among students need to be reincorporated as an integral, natural part of regular education.

Another structural change needed is a break from the traditional lockstep, graded organizational structure that presently operates in the public schools (Stainback, Stainback, Courtnage, & Jaben, 1985). In this organizational scheme chronological age is the predominate criterion by which students are assigned to instructional groups. That is, at roughly 6 years a student is placed in grade 1; at 7 years in grade 2, and so on. This organizational structure is based on the following assumptions:

1. All students of the same chronological age are ready to be taught the same objectives.
2. All students require the same amount of time (i.e., an academic year) to master the predesignated objectives.
3. All students can master the predesignated objectives for the grade level across all curricular areas during the same year.

However, both experience and research

refute each of these assumptions (Fenstermacher, 1983). Furthermore, when the assumptions are considered collectively, only a narrow band of students could in all likelihood meet these criteria.

Because of the assumptions upon which it is based, the lockstep graded system impedes rather than facilitates the individualization of educational programming. Contrary to the assumptions underlying the graded system, students are unique, exhibiting a wide diversity of learning needs. "To attempt to encompass these enormous differences within the educational expectations and specifications of a grade, borders on futility if not irresponsibility" (Goodlad, 1970, p. 25).

Rather than continue in this mode, it is the contention of the authors that the school system itself should be modified so that it is based on assumptions that more accurately reflect the learning characteristics of students. The assumptions underlying the structure of regular education should be congruent with our strongest hypotheses regarding student needs based on findings from research and experience. At present we appear to need an educational structure based on the following assumptions:

1. Students vary from one another in regard to the age at which they are ready to learn specified objectives.
2. Students vary from one another in regard to the rate at which they learn given objectives.
3. Students vary within themselves in regard to how fast they progress through the objectives in different curricular areas.

During the past several decades, educational structures have been proposed that are more closely aligned with the assumptions noted above. Included are organizational structures such as "nongraded" (Goodlad, 1984) and "individually guided education" (Nussel, Inglis, & Wiersme, 1976) that attempt to accommodate wide diversity in learning characteristics among students as a regular or standard practice. Generally, in these more flexible systems modifications of the present graded system such as the following have been recommended: (a) nongraded grouping arrangements, (b) variable pacing and time requirements for learning, and (c) evaluation and programming based on individual students' characteristics and achievement levels (criterion-referenced) rather than group averages (norm-referenced). The adoption of a more flexible regular education structure would allow educators the opportunity to more readily employ more individualized and adaptive instructional procedures found to be successful in meeting students' diverse needs (Goodlad, 1984; Madden & Slavin, 1983; Moran, 1983; Wang, 1982). There are a growing number of people now in regular education who are advocating such a change (Goodlad & Anderson, in press). More representatives of school psychology and special education need to join them in their efforts.

Curriculum. Offering a much broader and more comprehensive curriculum than is currently available will be imperative if the unique needs of all students are to be addressed. In addition to traditional subject areas, the curriculum in regular education needs to include experiences in community-referenced daily life instruction and in competitive and supported employment, as well as sign language, braille, speech reading, self-control training, and the development of creativity and analytical thinking skills (Stainback & Stainback, 1987). In this way, students who require these curricular areas could gain access to them within regular education, rather than having to be assigned to "special" education to receive programming appropriate to their instructional needs.

The expertise among school personnel needed to expand the curricular base in regular education is already available in schools. It is precisely the curricular expertise currently available in what now constitutes "special" education. Professionals currently in special education could be brought into regular education, could become regular educators, and offer the curricular content of areas such as community-referenced daily life instruction, mobility training, braille, and the like

to students who need it as an integral part of the mainstream of regular education rather than as a "special" accommodation. As a result, no students would have to be classified as special and assigned to a special system of education with special personnel in special classrooms in order to receive instructional programs and services that meet their unique needs.

Instructional practices. At the present time, regular education tends to be dominated by instructional practices designed to teach to the "average" student, as opposed to a wide range of students with diverse backgrounds and characteristics. This will need to be changed if regular education is to be strengthened to meet the needs of *all* students. An increasing amount of research evidence in regular education, special education, and school psychology indicates ways of modifying mainstream instructional practices to make them more conducive to the social and academic needs of students with diverse backgrounds and characteristics (Goodlad, 1984; Gottlieb & Leyser, 1981; Guralnick, 1981; Johnson & Johnson, 1981; Madden & Slavin, 1983; Slavin, Leavey, & Madden, 1984; Strain, 1982; Wang, 1980, 1981, 1983; Wang & Birch, 1984a, 1984b). The following practices are some examples of what has been found to be useful in meeting diverse student needs within the mainstream of regular education. Although not widely implemented at this time, these practices have been accepted and successfully implemented by many classroom teachers throughout the United States.

One practice, commonly referred to as "individualized programming," is critical to strengthening regular education's potential for meeting the diverse instructional needs of students (Fenstermacher & Goodlad, 1983). Individualized programming is designed to accommodate specific educational characteristics and needs on a per-student basis. Instructional objectives, pacing, and materials are criterion-based — that is, they are selected according to their appropriateness to the individual student — rather than norm-referenced, or selected in accordance with the expected average for the student's peer group. Individualized programming practices can provide a means of allowing for each student's unique instructional needs, interests, and capabilities. (It should be noted that the emphasis here is on approaching students as individuals and planning educational programs according to their specific characteristics and needs. The emphasis is not on the value of individual or one-to-one teaching. In fact, research during the past decade (D'Zambo & Raiser, 1986) has indicated that students often learn more efficiently and effectively through group instruction.

Another practice that can be utilized in regular education to address diverse student needs is cooperative goal structuring, which involves group activities in which members are assigned a common goal and are encouraged to work together to reach it (Johnson & Johnson, 1981). Cooperative learning can be used as a method of bringing students of various achievement and intellectual levels together in a positive way, at the same time allowing each student to work at his or her own individual level and pace (Slaven, Madden, & Leavey, 1984). Positive interaction and enhanced academic achievement among students of varying backgrounds and characteristics is achieved since, if the group's goal is to be reached, all students must coordinate their skills to achieve the goal. Chapter 18 contains more information about cooperative learning programs.

Adaptive learning environments also have been found to be effective in providing appropriate instructional programming for students with diverse characteristics in the mainstream of regular education. Adaptive learning environments often include individualized and cooperative learning components. Wang & Birch (1984b) described an adaptive learning environment as containing

12 critical design dimensions which in combination, support (a) identification of learning problems through a diagnostic prescriptive monitoring system integrally related to the program's instructional component; (b) delabeling of mainstreamed "special" students and description of learning needs in instructional rather than categorical terms; (c) individually designed educational plans that accommodate each student's learning strengths and needs; and (d) teaching of self-management skills that enable students to take increased responsibility for their learning. (p. 33)

More information about adaptive learning environments can be found in Chapter 10. Through environmental arrangements of this type, the potential strength of regular education to meet the unique learning needs of all students could be substantially enhanced.

Grouping students for instruction. While the selection of any grouping arrangement should be based on the goal(s) to be achieved, the type of activity included, and the characteristics of the students, generally homogeneous grouping has been vastly overutilized in the current educational system. Homogeneous grouping of students, emphasizing categorization and "tracking," has had a dominant influence in education. This has been particularly true of tracking of students into "special" education. As a result, the potential for major learning benefits that can be derived from well-organized heterogeneous group composition has not been capitalized upon in regular education. Thus, regular education could be strengthened through recognition of the benefits of heterogeneous grouping arrangements and how they can be organized in easy and practical ways in the schools to benefit all students (Dawson, 1987; Oakes, 1985; Slavin, 1987).

Heterogeneous grouping, in which students are at various intellectual and achievement levels, allows for shared responsibility among students and for skill guidance and modeling in which peers learn from and help each other. Heterogeneous grouping can also offset the potential stereotyping and/or stigmatization that often results when students are frequently associated with a particular ability, disability, or achievement group and can promote better understanding of individual differences and similarities among all students.

However, if the potential benefits such as those noted above are to be realized, heterogeneous grouping arrangements must be organized in a way that allows for all students to function as contributing members of the group while fostering their needed individualized learning objectives. In addition, every student must be given the opportunity to be challenged and to be successful within the group structure if learning and positive peer interactions and attitudes are to be realized. The reader is referred to D'Zambo and Raiser (1986) for specific and practical examples of how heterogeneous group activities can be organized to meet each student's unique learning characteristics and goals. Also, the work of Johnson and Johnson (1981) and Slavin, Madden, and Leavey (1984) on cooperative goal structuring, discussed earlier in this chapter, should be of benefit in regard to the best ways of organizing heterogeneous groups.

Thus, regular education needs to move toward the inclusion of more heterogeneous grouping practices. This is not intended to imply that all educational activities should necessarily focus on heterogeneous grouping. There are times when students may need to work on an individual basis or be grouped according to their particular needs for specific instructional purposes. For example, not all students need systematic instruction in functional community-referenced daily life instruction in natural community settings. Similarly, some students may not be able to profit from advanced calculus or physics classes. But when such specific and hopefully age-appropriate groupings are made, they are based on the instructional needs of students rather than categorical labels (Stainback & Stainback, 1984). It is also critical that such grouping be kept flexible to avoid the development of a tracking system and to allow students to move in and out and across the groupings as their individual needs and interests dictate.

Student Related Changes

Eligibility for instructional and related services. Another way regular education could be strengthened would be for all educators to join together to reduce the current emphasis on basing eligibility for educational and related services on a category affiliation as opposed to the specific interests, needs, and capabilities of each student. At the present time, an elaborate procedure for classifying students is used to determine who is eligible for a variety of educational and related services. Classification and labeling is an unproductive activity that drains resources that could be used to strengthen regular education.

At the present time, eligibility for services such as occupational therapy, community-referenced daily life instruction, social interaction skills training, and creative thinking; access to instructional materials such as large print, talking, or braille books; and adapted seating or communication devices are generally determined on the basis of the category to which a student is assigned. However, these categories often do not reflect the specific educational needs and interests of students in relation to such services (Gardner, 1977). For example, some students categorized as visually handicapped may not need large-print books; others who are not labeled visually impaired and thus are ineligible for large-print books could benefit from their use. Similarly, not all students labeled behaviorally disordered may need self-control training, whereas some students not so labeled may need such training but not be eligible. Such categorization actually interferes with providing some students with the services they require and at the same time drains resources that could be better used to meet all students needs in regular education. Eligibility determinations for educational and related services, as pointed out by Gardner (1977) and Meyen (1978), should depend on the relationship of each student's abilities, interests, and needs to available instructional options and services, rather than on the student's inclusion in a categorical group.

Eligibility criteria serve only to determine whether some people are entitled to assistance and others are not. However, in education, all students are (or should be) entitled to assistance if they need it (Moran, 1983). The only criterion should be that their assessment profiles indicate that they need assistance. For instance, students who need assistance because of a letter reversal problem, a self-control problem, or a mobility problem should receive the best assistance available regardless of whether the criteria for inclusion in a categorical group are met. Any other handling is blatant discrimination against some students.

In short, current classification and labeling practices are unfair to students, inefficient, and ineffective in getting needed services to students, and they drain resources in the form of money, personnel, and time that could be used to make regular education more flexible, adaptive, and accommodating to the unique needs, interests, and capabilities of all students.

Assessment. Curriculum-based assessment, that is, evaluating each student's ability on skills related to the curriculum, has begun to receive increased attention and acceptance as "a way of matching student ability to instruction" (Tucker, 1985, p. 201). Similarly, instructional assessments, designed to evaluate the nature of a student's instructional environment, have been found to be a valuable asset in individualizing instructional programming to meet a student's specific needs (Ysseldyke & Christenson, 1986). Thus, curriculum-based assessment paired with instructional assessment procedures can provide regular education with the means of determining appropriate instructional programming for the individual student. For more information about what is meant by curriculum-based and instructional assessment procedures see chapters 7 and 8. Such procedures are well suited for use in individualized and adaptive instructional programs and they will likely play a central role in helping regular education to respond more precisely to diverse student needs.

Curriculum-based and instructional assessment procedures can also provide direction for accomplishing other needed changes in regular education. One practice requiring change is the method used to provide students recognition for educational achievement. In most instances, educational recognition is accorded those students who excel in performance in relation to their classmates or other students. That is, most educational recognition is based on "norm-referenced assessments," such as scoring highest on tests or writing the best poem. It is based on competition and comparison with a peer group. In a system that includes students with varying skills, abilities, and interests use of such student recognition is often demoralizing, inappropriate, and inherently unfair. Because of the diversity in students' academic characteristics each student possesses a different set of resources to put into the competition. This underlying inequity in resources can make competition with peers for recognition futile for some students, regardless of the effort expended, whereas other students require minimal effort to earn recognition. As a consequence, the norm-referenced educational recognition procedures commonly used in schools today can result in lack of motivation and even negative attitudes toward learning and achievement in many students. Assessment for positive attention and recognition should be focused on competing against one's own achievements rather than the achievements or performance of others. Assessment for recognition and attention in education should be criterion-based: Students should be encouraged to excel beyond their present highest achievements.

Also requiring change are the current assessment strategies used for reporting progress or achievement data to such groups as parents, educational agencies, and prospective employers. Most often such reporting has taken the form of a letter rating (i.e., A, B, C, D, F or S, U) determined by teachers on the basis of a norm-referenced comparison with class peers or with local, state, or national expected averages. In either case, from this information a clear understanding of what skills an individual has achieved is often not possible, because such factors as the grading approach of the teacher and the norms on which the grades were based can vary greatly from one state, school, or class to another or even from student to student. An alternative curriculum-based achievement reporting system could reduce this nebulousness in the meaning of grades. Using a curriculum-based reporting system, educators could provide a printout for every student listing briefly and concisely the highest level of skills mastered. Gains made from semester to semester and year to year could be easily discerned for each student. Similarly, prospective employers or educational agencies could determine whether a particular student has achieved the skills required to do a certain job, fill a specific position, or enter into a given course, program, or school and, if not, readily determine what skills are missing. Such reporting could be more clear and consistent across students and more useful in evaluating a student's skills and achievements. Such curriculum-based reporting could enable regular education to meet the instructional needs of all students by focusing on and communicating the specific educational skills gained by a student without requiring all students to be evaluated according to the performance of some group average or expectation.

In short, if regular education is to accommodate a wide diversity of students, it will be important to modify how students are evaluated and how grades are reported. If we adhere to a norm-referenced approach to setting standards and evaluating progress, there always will be some students for which the standards are too high and some for which the standards are too low. Inevitably, failure will result for some students and others will not be challenged, and there will be calls to establish "special" programs for these students. The wide adoption in regular education of criterion, curriculum-based, and ecological assessment procedures for instructional planning, monitoring, grading, and reporting of progress — coupled with individualized, cooperative, and adaptive instructional

programs — could help reduce considerably the need for "special" programs.

Students as active learners. In order for regular education to meet the needs of all students, educational personnel will need to assume a greater role as organizers of learning within instructional settings rather than attempt to function as a continuous source of direct input and supervision for students as passive receivers of information (Dorman, 1981; Duckworth, 1964; Goodlad, 1983; Jones & Jones, 1986). With greater diversity among students in regular education, educators will need to promote a greater degree of independent functioning on the part of students. That is, while it is essential for teachers to devote time to closely directed instruction, it also is important to systematically foster self-motivation and independent learning. Otherwise, it will be difficult to maintain a classroom organizational structure that keeps a heterogeneous group of students busy and on task throughout the day.

Student training in self-management, problem solving, and decision making can facilitate more active participation on the part of students as learners. This can help students become more independent and goal-directed both in school and in daily life outside of school. Students also can learn to share with each other and teach each other through various buddy systems and tutoring programs. As a result, students are provided the opportunity to learn about the interdependent nature of a humane society, in which individuals share with and assist one another and accept responsibility for the achievement of goals by others as well as themselves.

Advocacy and Service Model Changes

Advocacy. In order to prepare regular education to meet the needs of all students, the current policy of advocating for various special categories of students will require change. Lobbying for special categories of students (e.g., the gifted, handicapped, mentally retarded, blind, learning-disabled) to receive special school programs and services prompts a separation of these students from their peers. It also weakens potential advocacy in behalf of program flexibility in regular education to meet all students' needs.

Rather than advocating in behalf of categories of students for special school programs, advocacy efforts could focus on having the schools hire, as needed, support personnel such as physical therapists, school psychologists, speech and language specialists, and/or behavior management specialists. We also could support more instruction in areas such as basic community-referenced daily life instruction and vocational and competitive employment skills, as well as more instruction in sign language, braille, speech reading, self-control training, or the like. In addition, advocacy could be focused on increasing resources to enable schools to offer more flexible, individualized, and adaptive educational programs to meet the needs of all children, including those unserved or illserved in the past (or present).

More specifically, if it is documented that there is a deficiency of research, personnel preparation, or other resources in an area traditionally covered by special education (e.g., sign language and speech reading), it may well be necessary to lobby to have monies allocated for the particular deficient area(s), as is done when such a lack is identified in math or science. Rather than seeking "child-in-category" funding, advocates could lobby state and federal legislators to earmark funds to facilitate research, training, and the accumulation of resources in the deficient instructional area(s).

By doing this, it would no longer be necessary to call for "special" programs accessible only to certain categories of students as the sole means to ensure that a wide range of educational programs will be available to meet students' diverse needs. The alternative line of advocacy is important since advocating by categories of students ultimately leads to the division of school personnel, students, and programs into special and regular programs, which works against viewing all students as individuals and integral members of the same "regular" student body.

Finally, there is a need for all educators to pool their efforts and act in a supportive rather than competitive relationship. Currently, there are numerous advocacy organizations that lobby for a vast range of special interests: the behaviorally disordered, retarded, deaf, autistic, psychotic, blind, learning-disabled, schizophrenic, visually impaired, economically disadvantaged, socially maladjusted, linguistically disabled, brain-damaged, severely handicapped, gifted, emotionally disturbed, physically handicapped, neurologically impaired, and reading disabled. Recently, there has been a call for another advocacy group to be formed to work in behalf of the so-called "normal" students, since this "special" group has received so little attention in recent years (Powell, 1985). Unfortunately, as noted by Moran (1983), when advocacy groups are split, all lose in the long run. It also ultimately results in a fragmented and disjointed educational system. If all advocates in education joined together and coordinated their efforts, the potential force of such a large and powerful group could greatly increase the amount of funds allocated to broadening the scope of regular education, and permit the mainstreaming of all students.

Service model. If regular education is to meet the needs of all students as a matter of standard practice, a change in the basic model used to guide the services provided to students with disabilities will be needed. At the present time, students with disabilities are supplied educational services and programs that meet their needs on the basis of a *welfare* model. As an altruistic gesture society is willing to provide special, charity-like assistance to some students because of their needy, special, or "truly" handicapping condition. Thus, special education programs, at present, are analogous to the food stamp program and housing assistance for welfare clients in that some students must adequately demonstrate their needy or handicapping condition to receive educational programs appropriate to their needs.

Maintaining a welfare model in the

public schools is inappropriate and wasteful of educational resources. There simply are *no* students whose unique educational needs should not be met in the public schools *as a regular and standard practice.* Thus, there is no defensible rationale for special qualifications for those with disabilities nor for special education programs.

Equality suffers when the education of some students is viewed as special and different, as a charity operation. "Until accommodation for the disabled is seen as regular, normal, and expected, it will be seen instead as special. As long as it is special, it will be, by definition, unequal" (Biklen, 1985, p. 176). When we break away from the welfare model and recognize that an appropriate education is an inherent right for all students (disabled or not), we will be in a position to refocus our resources toward strengthening regular education to meet the specific needs of all students instead of investing our resources on trying to determine who is "truly" handicapped and deserving of special programs.

CONCLUSIONS

While many of the changes suggested in this chapter (e.g., curriculum-based assessment, adaptive learning programs) have been gaining increased attention and support, there still remains much to be done to enable regular education to meet the particular needs of all students. To help expedite future change, direct lines of communication among education groups — particularly special and regular educators — should be developed to enable educators to work together to foster change. One possible way to open lines of communication would be to reexamine the splitting of major educational organizations such as the Council for Exceptional Children and the National Education Association that occurred several decades ago. A reintegration of educators into a united group could potentially lead to focusing a wide range of talents and resources toward the study and incorporation of needed modifica-

tions into the current regular education system.

There are a number of constraints that will impede change from occurring as quickly as many of us would like to see it occur. Some people believe that the major constraint is that there is not enough scientific research that is beyond criticism to support the education of all students in regular education (see Kauffman, 1987, for example). We disagree, however. Among others, Forest (1987a) and Strully (1986), have clearly shown that we already know, and have known for a long time, all we need to know to educate all children in the mainstream of regular education. The major constraint, in our opinion, is a matter of attitude. As noted by Lipsky and Gartner (1987), "the establishment of a separate system of education for the disabled is an outgrowth of attitudes toward disabled people" (p. 72). Continued progress toward educating all students in the mainstream of regular education will require that attitudes of educators and the general public change through education and daily contact with people labeled handicapped or disabled. We are optimistic. Historical trends indicate that increasing numbers of people are in fact adopting an attitude that people with disabilities should be accepted into the mainstream of school and community life. People with disabilities are beginning to demand it (Hahn, 1987). As a result, we are beginning to "turn from the effort to perfect a separate special education system to the struggle of changing the educational system to make it both one and special for all students" (Lipsky & Gartner, 1987).

At the present time, it simply does not appear to be enough to continue with piecemeal, isolated efforts to help students and teachers function within the current regular education structure. The objectives inherent in the mainstreaming movement may never be fully realized until educators become willing to pool their various areas of expertise and resources to develop a strong, flexible regular education structure that accommodates individual differences. It has become increasingly apparent during recent years that, while it may be worthwhile, it is insufficient to only provide in-service or preservice information to regular educators and/or resource and consultative assistance in the public schools to facilitate needed changes. It appears it will be necessary for special educators to make a concerted effort to fully *integrate themselves* into the educational mainstream if substantive movement toward the development of a strong comprehensive system of regular education designed to meet all students' needs is to be realized. Unless fundamental changes occur in regular education, there is little likelihood that students being returned to the mainstream will be any more successful than they were before the advent of special education.

REFERENCES

Biklen, D. (1985). *Achieving the complete school.* New York: Columbia University Press.

Dawson, M. (1987). Beyond ability grouping: A review of the effectiveness of ability grouping and its alternatives. *School Psychology Review, 16,* 348-369.

Dorman, G. (1981). *Middle grades assessment program.* Chapel Hill, NC: Center for Early Adolescence.

Duckworth, E. (1964). Piaget rediscovered. In R. E. Ripple and V. N. Rockcastle (Eds.), *Piaget rediscovered: A report of the conference on cognitive skills and curriculum development.* Ithaca, NY: Cornell University, School of Education.

D'Zambo, M., & Raiser, L. (1986). A strategy for individualizing directed group instruction. *Teaching Exceptional Children, 18,* 190-196.

Fenstermacher, G. (1983). Introduction. In G. Fenstermacher and J. Goodlad (Eds.), *Individual differences and the common curriculum* (pp. 1-8). Chicago: University of Chicago Press.

Fenstermacher, G., & Goodlad, J. (Eds.). (1983). *Individual differences and the common curriculum.* Chicago: University of Chicago Press.

Forest, M. (1986). Just one of the kids. *Entourage, 1,* 20-23.

Forest, M. (1987a). Keys to integration: Common sense ideas and hard work. *Entourage, 2,* 16-20.

Forest, M. (1987b). Start with the right attitude. *Entourage, 2,* 11-13.

Gardner, W. (1977). *Learning and behavior characteristics of exceptional children and youth.* Boston: Allyn & Bacon.

Gartner, A., & Lipsky, D. (1987). Beyond special education. *Harvard Educational Review, 57,* 367-395.

Goodlad, J. (1970). The nongraded school. *National Elementary School Principal, 50,* 24-29.

Goodlad, J. (1983). A study of schooling: Some findings and hypotheses. *Phi Delta Kappan, 64,* 465-470.

Goodlad, J. (1984). *A place called school: Prospects for the future.* New York: McGraw-Hill.

Goodlad, J. & Anderson, R. (in press). *The nongraded school.* New York: Columbia University Press.

Gottlieb, J., & Leyser, Y. (1981). Facilitating the social mainstreaming of retarded children. *Exceptional Education Quarterly, 1,* 57-69.

Graden, J., Casey, A., & Bonstrom, O. (1985). Implementing a prereferral intervention system: Part II. The data. *Exceptional Children, 51,* 487-496.

Graden, J., Casey, A., & Christensen, S. (1985). Implementing a prereferral intervention system: Part 1. The model. *Exceptional Children Quarterly, 1,* 71-91.

Guralnick, M. (1981). Programmatic factors affecting child-child social interactions in mainstreamed preschool programs. *Exceptional Education Quarterly, 1,* 71-91.

Hahn, H. (1987). Civil rights for disabled Americans: The foundation of a political agenda. In A. Gartner and T. Joe (Eds.), *Images of the disabled, disabling images* (pp. 181-204). New York: Praeger.

Jacobs, J. (1986). *Educating students with severe handicaps in the regular program, all day, everyday.* Paper presented to the 1986 Annual Conference of The Association for Persons With Severe Handicaps, San Francisco.

Johnson, R., & Johnson, D. (1981). Building friendships between handicapped and nonhandicapped students: Effects of cooperative and individualistic instruction. *American Educational Research Journal, 18,* 415-424.

Jones, V., & Jones, L. (1986). *Comprehensive classroom management.* Newton, MA: Allyn & Bacon.

Kauffman, J. (1987). Research in special education: A commentary. *RASE, 8,* 57-62.

Lilly, S. (1979). *Children with exceptional needs.* New York: Holt, Rinehart and Winston.

Lilly, S., & Givens-Ogle, L. (1981). Teacher consultation: Present, past and future. *Behavioral Disorders, 6*, 73-77.

Lipsky, D., & Gartner, A. (1987). Capable of achievement and worthy of respect: Education of handicapped students as if they were full-fledged human beings. *Exceptional Children, 54*, 69-74.

Madden, N., & Slavin, R. (1983). Mainstreaming students with mild handicaps: Academic and social outcomes. *Review of Educational Research, 53*, 519-659.

Meyen, E. (1978). An introductory prospective. In E. Meyen (Ed.), *Exceptional children and youth,* (pp. 2-84). Denver: Love.

Moran, M. (1983). Inventing a future for special education: A cautionary tale. *Journal for Special Educators, 19*, 28-36.

Nussel, E., Inglis, J., & Wiersme, W. (1976). *The teacher and individually guided education.* Reading, MA: Addison-Wesley.

Oakes, J. (1985). *Keep track: How schools structure inequality.* New Haven, CT: Yale University Press.

Powell, A. (1985). Being unspecial in the shopping mall high school. *Phi Delta Kappan, 67*, 255-261.

Reynolds, M., & Balow, B. (1972). Categories and variables in special education. *Exceptional Children, 38*, 357-366.

Reynolds, M., & Birch, J. (1982). *Teaching exceptional children in all America's schools* (2nd ed.). Reston, VA: Council for Exceptional Children.

Ruttiman, A., & Forest, M. (1986). With a little help from my friends: The integration facilitator at work. *Entourage, 1*, 24-33.

Sarason, S. (1982). *The culture of the school and the problem of change.* Boston: Allyn & Bacon.

Slavin, R. (1987). Grouping for instruction in the elementary school. *Educational Psychologist, 22*, 109-127.

Slavin, R., Leavey, & Madden, N. (1984). Combining cooperative learning and individualized instruction. *Elementary School Journal, 84*, 410-422.

Slavin, R., Madden, N., & Leavey, M. (1984). Effects of cooperative learning and individualized instruction on mainstreamed students. *Exceptional Children, 50* 434-443.

Stainback, S., & Stainback, W. (Eds.) (1985a). *Integration of students with severe handicaps in regular schools.* Reston, VA: Council for Exceptional Children.

Stainback, S., & Stainback, W. (1985b). The merger of special and regular education: Can it be done? *Exceptional Children, 51*, 517-521.

Stainback, S., & Stainback, W. (in press, a). Classroom organization for diversity among students. In D. Biklen, D. Ferguson, & A. Ford (Eds.), *Disability and society.* Chicago: National Society for the Study of Education.

Stainback, S., & Stainback, W. (in press, b). Facilitating merger through personnel preparation. *Teacher Education and Special Education.*

Stainback, W., & Stainback, S. (1984). A rationale for the merger of special and regular education. *Exceptional Children, 51*, 102-111.

Stainback, W., & Stainback, S. (1987). Educating all students in regular education. *TASH Newsletter, 13*(4), pp. 1, 7.

Stainback, W., Stainback, S., Courtnage, L., & Jaben, T. (1985). Facilitating mainstreaming by modifying the mainstream. *Exceptional Children, 52*, 142-144.

Sternat, J., Nietupski, J., Messina, R., Lyon, S., & Brown, L. (1977). Occupational and physical therapy services for severely handicapped students: Towards a naturalized public school service delivery model. In E. Sontag, J. Smith, & N. Certo (Eds.), *Educational programming for the severely and profoundly handicapped.* (pp. 250-263). Reston, VA: Council for Exceptional Children.

Strain, P. (Ed.). (1982). *Social development of exceptional children.* Rockville, MD: Aspen Systems.

Strully, J. (1986). *Our children and the regular education classroom: Or why settle for anything less than the best?* Paper presented to the 1986 Annual Conference of The Association for Persons With Severe Handicaps, San Francisco.

Tucker, J. (1985). Curriculum-based assessment: An introduction. *Exceptional Children, 52*, 199-204.

Wang, M. (1980). Adaptive instruction: Building on diversity. *Theory Into Practice, 19*, 122-127.

Wang, M. (1981). Mainstreaming exceptional children: Some instructional design considerations. *Elementary School Journal, 81*, 194-221.

Wang, M. (1982). *Effective mainstreaming is possible–provided that . . .* Pittsburgh, PA: Learning Research and Developmental Center, University of Pittsburgh.

Wang, M. (1983). *Provision of adaptive instruction: Implementation and effects.* Pittsburgh, PA: University of Pittsburgh, Learning Research and Development Center.

Wang, M., & Birch, J. (1984a). Effective special education in regular class. *Exceptional Children, 50*, 391-399.

Wang, M., & Birch, J. (1984b). Comparison of a full-time mainstreaming program and a resource room approach. *Exceptional Children, 51*, 33-40.

Ysseldyke, J., & Algozzine, B. (1984). *Introduction to special education.* Boston: Houghton Mifflin.

Ysseldyke, J., & Christenson, S. (1986). *The instructional environment scale.* Austin, TX: PRO-ED.

Part II:

Alternative Frameworks for Educational Delivery Systems

3

Consultation: A Foundation for Alternative Services in the Schools[1]

Michael J. Curtis
University of Cincinnati
Joel Meyers
State University of New York at Albany

INTRODUCTION

The chapters in this monograph examine an array of alternative mechanisms and strategies for the delivery of special services in the schools. What is clear throughout these chapters is that the effective delivery of services is dependent on the collaborative efforts of parents, educational personnel and community-based professionals.

Consultation represents the foundation on which alternative services delivery systems are based. It is the problem solving process through which students' needs are clarified and appropriate strategies for intervention are developed and implemented (Zins, Curtis, Graden, & Ponti, 1988).

BACKGROUND

Two decades have passed since "consultation" was introduced as a major professional function for school-based special services personnel. Those twenty years have witnessed notable progress in this area of service delivery.

School-based consultation originated in the 1960s based on dissatisfaction with the medical model which seemed to permeate traditional psychology. Consultation emerged as part of what Hobbs (1964) called "mental health's third revolution" referring to the general revolt throughout professional psychology against failures of the "mental illness" orientation of the field.

The 1970s brought a growing consensus that consultation should occupy a more dominant place in the delivery of services (Bardon & Bennett, 1974; Meacham & Peckham, 1978). Similar preferences of teachers, superintendents and other school personnel have been well established (see Gutkin & Curtis, 1982 for an extensive review of related studies), as have those of parents and students (Raffaniello, Curtis, Heintzelman, Shannon, Van Wagener, Vesper, Taylor, & Blennerhassett, 1980).

However, the merits of a consultative approach do not rest solely on the "preferences" of special services providers and the consumers of their services. There is a substantial body of empirical support for the effectiveness of consultative methods. Extensive reviews of the research literature which have been conducted by Medway (1979), Medway and Updyke (1985), Mannino and Shore (1975) and Fullan, Miles and Taylor (1980) regarding the efficacy of consultation support this conclusion.

Research also has examined the "preventive" value of consultative techniques with encouraging results. Consultation has been found to positively affect conditions and outcomes for children in a variety of ways such as: improved professional skills for teachers (Gutkin, 1980; Zins, 1981); teacher attitudes regarding the "seriousness" of children's problems (Gutkin, Singer & Brown, 1980); improved teacher information and understanding of children's problems (Curtis & Watson, 1980); generalization of consultation benefits to other children in the same classroom (Jason & Ferone, 1978; Meyers, 1975); reductions in referral rates (Ritter, 1978); improved long-term academic performance (Jackson, Cleveland, & Merenda, 1975); and reduction of varying behavioral difficulties (Spivack, Platt, & Shure, 1976).

In view of the above information, it is only logical to assume that consultation would currently occupy a position of primary emphasis in school-based services delivery systems. Yet, despite twenty years of advocacy and mounting empirical support, there is a gap between the justified prominence of consultation and the reality that it continues to lack a place of priority in professional practice.

One reason for this inconsistency relates to the lack of a common understanding of consultation. This problem is caused by the overuse of the almost meaningless generic term "consultation." Consultation has been used to refer to practically every interaction between two professionals. However, as Curtis and Zins (1981) note, "consultation is beginning to achieve a level of sophistication whereby there is a fair degree of agreement and understanding regarding what is implied by the term when it is identified with a specific model" (p. xiv). Those with a background in consultation are very likely to understand what assumptions, objectives, and behaviors are associated with a particular model.

But the fact is, most special services personnel do *not* have a strong background in consultation. "The primary obstacle to the effective integration of consultation into special services rests in the failure of training institutions to address this area" (Curtis, 1983, p. 9).

For example, surveys of school psychology training programs have found that a minority of the respondent institutions include an emphasis on consultation (Bardon & Wenger, 1974, 1976). In a recent survey (Meyers, Wurtz, & Flan-

agan, 1981), only 40% of the responding programs offered a course focused solely on training in consultation. There also is an absence of consultation offerings through continuing professional development programs which compounds the problem for practitioners who have never received formalized preparation in this area. There is a pressing need for systematic and intensive training which includes an integrated practice component.

BASIC CONSIDERATIONS

The three major models for school-based consultation are the behavioral, mental health and organizational. Comprehensive discussions of each model are presented by Bergan (1977), Caplan (1970) and Schmuck and Runkel (1985), respectively. Although the three approaches differ in terms of their theoretical bases, they reflect numerous areas of commonality. This chapter offers a model for consultation which integrates those elements that are common to the other models within a systems framework.

A Systems Model of Consultation

Throughout this chapter, consultation will be defined as: *a collaborative problem solving process in which two or more persons (consultant(s) and consultee(s)) engage in efforts to benefit one or more other persons (client(s)) for whom they bear some level of responsibility, within a context of reciprocal interactions.*

This definition reflects nine major assumptions regarding effective consultation which are described below:

Assumption 1:
Participants in Consultation

Consultant and consultee. For ease in clarification of roles, we tend to describe the participants in a consultative relationship in terms of distinct identities. The *consultant* is generally the person who provides assistance to the consultee (the caregiver) regarding a work-related concern. Typically, we think of the special services professional as a consultant to a classroom teacher regarding a child for whom the teacher is responsible. However, other school personnel such as a principal or another special services provider also could be the consultee.

It is important to recognize that *a unique feature of the above definition is the potential for consultant and consultee to shift roles.* While the consultant (e.g., school psychologist) generally tries to help the consultee (e.g., teacher), there are times in the relationship when the teacher possesses the expertise needed to help the school psychologist. This is important because it emphasizes that *both* participants in the consultation relationship share power and influence in a process that truly is characterized as a reciprocal interaction.

Client. The client is the ultimate beneficiary of consultation. In a classroom situation, a student is typically the client. An entire class could be clients if consultation is focused on improving the professional performance of the teacher. Students would also be the clients in organizational consultation since the purpose would be to improve the educational environment for the benefit of students.

Assumption 2:
Collaborative Relationship

One of the most fundamental principles underlying this definition is that a genuinely collaborative professional relationship among those engaged in the problem solving process is essential for success. Unlike the medical model which assumes that the expertise for solving any given problem rests primarily within the consultant, this model assumes that *both* the consultant and the consultee have knowledge and/or skills necessary for problem resolution. The success of this relationship is dependent on the following characteristics.

Coordinate status. The relationship of those involved is non-hierarchical. The consultant does not operate from a position of authority, diagnosing the

problem and then either carrying out the remediation directly or prescribing the program to be implemented by others. Rather, the consultant and consultee both contribute to the development of problem solving strategies.

Consultee involvement in consultation. It is essential that the consultee(s) is actively involved in the consultation process by helping to assess and diagnose the problem, as well as by contributing to the intervention plans. Through active involvement, the consultee develops a sense of "ownership" of the plan. In most cases, it is likely that the consultee will bear primary responsibility for implementation of the plan. Failure to establish ownership may result in the likelihood that the strategy will not be carried out as intended. Besides, it often is the consultee who has the best sense of what is possible within the context of the school and classroom. By contributing ideas, the consultee helps to ensure that appropriate recommendations are developed.

Consultee's right to accept or reject strategies. The consultee must feel free to accept or reject any of the consultant's ideas. The consultant does not have the authority to impose a plan on the consultee. Moreover, it would be counterproductive to do so. If forced to implement a plan, the consultee is likely to carry it out in a manner which will ensure its failure, if it is implemented at all. If the consultee does not believe in an idea, there is little likelihood that it will work (Curtis & Anderson, 1976a). If the consultant genuinely believes that the consultee is a coordinate member in the consultation process, ideas generated by the consultee deserve equal consideration with those of the consultant. Even in those cases where the consultant does not favor the suggestions of the consultee, the consultee's plan should be tried as long as it does not appear to have detrimental implications for the client. The primary goal is to find some way to help the client, rather than to "win" a struggle over whose plan will be used.

Consultation is voluntary. Although

not always the case, consultation should be initiated by the consultee. When this occurs, it suggests that the consultee (a) recognizes that a problem exists, and (b) may be motivated to do something about it (Curtis & Anderson, 1976a). Unfortunately, there are many instances in schools where consultation is neither initiated by the consultee nor voluntary. Such situations are less likely to be effective than those in which the consultee is voluntarily involved.

Confidentiality. It is essential that information shared remain within the consultative relationship. The central issue here is one of trust. The likelihood of honest and open communication is diminished when the consultee believes that sensitive information may be available to others outside the relationship. Obviously, there is some information which of necessity must be shared with others (e.g., parents, administrators, or other specialists). However, under these circumstances, the consultant and the consultee should discuss ahead of time what information will be shared.

The "need to know" principle can be a helpful guide as to what information should be shared. In other words, only information that others need to know should be passed on. For example, both the principal and parents need to know about the behavioral program to be implemented for a given child. However, the teacher's feelings of inadequacy or anger regarding actions of the principal should not be a topic for outside discussion. This concept of confidentiality is intended to reflect upon the importance of an honest and open relationship. It does not relate to the legal status of confidential communication which is determined by the laws of each state.

Assumption 3:
The Need for Confrontation

Confrontation is an important component of the consultation process since this technique can be necessary to push the consultee toward action. However, the term "confrontation" has a negative connotation to some people. Confrontation, as used here, is a professional process which is not destructive *and* which is devoid of hostility. In fact, confrontation must be implemented in a manner which avoids a win-lose struggle and which preserves the consultee's right to accept or reject the consultant's ideas.

Two distinct approaches to confrontation have been discussed in the literature and both can be useful. The first, *Indirect Confrontation*, was described first by Gerald Caplan (1970). He suggested that indirect techniques were advantageous because they do not break down defenses. An example of this approach is to discuss the consultee's problem (e.g., difficulty dealing with rebellious pupils) as if it were a problem of the client (e.g., "Be careful how you deal with Johnny because *he* has difficulty dealing with authority figures.") See Meyers, Parsons and Martin (1979) for a more detailed discussion of indirect confrontation.

While indirect approaches are sometimes the only way to help the consultee without stimulating resistance, this method can be so subtle that the message is not received by the consultee. Under these circumstances, it may be necessary to use the second major approach, *Direct Confrontation*. However, this must also be done in a way that minimizes consultee resistance. To do this, it must be based on a strong relationship between consultant and consultee. Direct confrontation is a purposeful process in which contradictions, conflicts within the consultee or other problems are clarified and discussed openly. Direct confrontation must be communicated in a tentative manner, leaving the consultee with the clear option to reject what is offered. For example, when trying to initiate a discussion of a new teacher's conflict about being the authority figure the consultant might say, "Let's spend a few minutes thinking about what you just said. Do you think it implies that one important issue may have to do with your own ambivalence about being an authority figure to the students?" By opening a direct discussion of such a problem it becomes more likely that the consultee will be able to plan alternative interventions. A more detailed discussion of the variety of conflicts that may be the focus of direct confrontation during consultation is presented in Meyers, Parsons and Martin (1979).

Assumption 4:
Indirect Service

Consultation differs from direct service models such as counseling in that the consultant works primarily with another caregiver, rather than directly with the client. Typically, it is the caregiver (consultee) who works directly with the client. In other words, consultation is an indirect approach to service delivery which involves a triadic relationship. The consultant works with the consultee who, in turn, works directly with the client.

There can be situations in which a school psychologist would consult with a consultee *and* would engage in some form of direct service during the same period of time. One example occurs when a psychologist provides counseling services to a child and uses information obtained during counseling as a basis for consulting with the youngster's teacher. Such situations represent a combination of both direct and indirect services, with consultation being the indirect service.

Assumption 5:
Responsibility for Client

Historically, consultation models have emphasized that it is the caregiver/consultee who is responsible for the client. While the consultee may retain *primary* responsibility, it is important to note that the school psychologist must also assume some level of responsibility for the client. Participation on multidisciplinary teams and demands for accountability in service delivery require that the consultant share in responsibility for outcome.

Assumption 6:
Work-Related Focus

The focus of consultation is always on work-related concerns. This principle has two primary implications: (a) Consultation is differentiated from therapy based on this principle. While therapy focuses on personal concerns, the consultant is consistent in directing conversations towards work-related issues. When therapy is sought by the consultee, the consultant should make a referral to outside sources. This can be an important factor in defining the consultant's role clearly for the system. (b) The second implication is that while the consultant maintains a warm productive relationship with the consultee and uses procedures like empathy, the focus is not primarily on the consultee's feelings. Consultation is a problem solving process which involves two colleagues. Although attention would be paid to work-related feelings when they are relevant, the primary focus is on solving the problem at hand.

Assumption 7:
Goals of Consultation

This consultation model, like every other, has two goals. The first is explicit within the definitions, i.e., to resolve the referral problem. The second is to improve the consultee's understanding of and ability to respond effectively to similar problems in the future.

Assumption 8:
Systems Theory

A critical emphasis that is *not* reflected clearly in most other models is the basis in *systems theory* as illustrated by the inclusion of *reciprocal interaction* as one major concept. Operationally, this refers to the tendency for a change in any part of a system to affect other parts of the system. This concept moves away from the medical model view that the child "contains" problems and instead suggests that the child is part of a system. It is no longer sufficient to postulate that psychological disturbances are internal to the client. Attempts to resolve child-related problems in schools must be based on a sophisticated awareness of effects that the school and classroom environment have on the child, as well as of the child's effects on the environment.

The application of systems theory to consultation is valuable in two ways. First, it helps the consultant understand the consultative process itself as affected by numerous interactive variables (e.g., consultant characteristics, consultee characteristics, school climate, district philosophy) (Gallessich, 1973). Second, it offers a framework for examining child-related concerns and for developing strategies for addressing those concerns within the context of the child as *one* component in an environmental setting (system). Any problem reflects the interaction of numerous variables associated with the setting. An understanding of those variables is essential in developing meaningful interventions.

Assumption 9: Affective/Cognitive Components to Consultation

Consultation can be viewed as having two primary components (i.e., affective and cognitive).

Affective component. This refers to those aspects of the consultative interaction which address the interpersonal relationship between the consultant and consultee. This component would relate to core elements such as coordinate status between consultant and consultee, involvement of the consultee in the process, the consultee's right to accept or reject consultant suggestions, the voluntary nature of consultation and the confidential nature of the interaction. It reflects *how the consultant views the consultee.*

Cognitive component. This refers to those aspects of the interaction which reflect the consultant's theoretical base for problem solving. It reflects *how the consultant views the problem.* For example, the approach to the problem might indicate either a behavioral orientation (Bergan, 1977) or a mental health orientation (Caplan, 1970). The steps or stages for problem solving are included in the cognitive component and the same general pattern is consistent across different theoretical orientations.

Whether the consultant uses behavioral, psychodynamic, or cognitive-behavioral theory, the steps to problem solving follow a sequence which includes problem clarification, strategy generation, planning for implementation, and planning for evaluation.

Consultant skills. In order to fulfill the requisites of both the affective and cognitive components, the consultant needs four areas of expertise. The first relates to the interpersonal process and reflects both knowledge and skills pertaining to effective communication and the establishment of positive relationships. Good reflective listening skills as well as the use of Rogers' core conditions (i.e., empathy, genuineness, and non-possessive warmth) are needed for effective consultation and have been discussed by Gutkin and Curtis (1982) as the "technology of communication." It also is important to recognize that particular communication skills may have to be implemented in different ways depending on the socio-cultural context. For example, the way in which the consultant uses a skill like empathy may vary dramatically depending on whether the consultee is a teacher in a suburban upper middle class school district or an aide in a head start program located in an urban ghetto. Consultant awareness of socio-cultural differences in interpersonal style is essential (for example, see Kochman, 1981).

The second area of expertise relates to a strong foundation in the area of professional content specific to the consultant. In the case of the school psychologist, that would be a strong foundation in the understanding of human behavior. The view of human behavior adopted by the consultant will dictate the theoretical basis for problem analysis. Third, is expertise in problem solving accompanied by the ability to facilitate the problem solving process.

The fourth area of expertise is knowledge of systems theory. The systems model of consultation allows for the incorporation of other consultation models (e.g., behavioral, mental health, organizational) within a systems framework. The definition integrates those elements that are common to other models pertaining to relationship, goals, focus and being indirect in nature. It requires expertise in generic problem solving. Yet, it allows for differing theoretical orientations to human behavior. It establishes a context of reciprocal interaction within which problems are to be analyzed and resolved. This last element requires that consultants be skilled in systems analysis.

IMPLEMENTATION

Consultation and Direct Services

Since the earliest offerings, there has been a tendency in the literature to present consultation as an indirect service delivery system which is independent, if not dichotomous from direct service delivery systems. You either do consultation or you do other things. The message almost becomes one of being a consultant, rather than a school psychologist, counselor, or other special services professional (Curtis, 1983).

Essentially what has occurred is a confusion between the *role* of the consultant and the *function* of consultation. In reality, relatively few special services personnel are able to secure roles as consultants, i.e., their sole function is consultation. On the other hand, many have been successful in establishing consultation as an integral part of a comprehensive service delivery system (Curtis, 1983). "When direct service is applied appropriately, it invariably involves consultative aspects; thus to exclude direct service from consultation would be artificial" (Meyers et al., 1979, p. 89). In other words, consultation is most appropriately viewed as a set of skills that are complementary to and a part of direct services.

Entry into the System

Schools should not be viewed as isolated entities, but as systems which are influenced by the larger environment within which they exist, as well as by the various internal components of which they are composed. External factors such as legislation and community norms can affect the types of services expected. Internally, factors such as staff characteristics, morale and educational philosophy can influence receptivity to the use of mental health resources. For example, competition and anxiety among teachers may reduce their interest in collaborative efforts for improving classroom processes (Schmuck & Schmuck, 1979). It is essential that the practitioner maintain a systems perspective in understanding the numerous organizational variables that can influence consultation. Gallessich (1973) provides a helpful discussion of this topic.

Gaining sanction. Implementation of consultation involves acceptance by relevant administrators, as well as by the caregivers themselves (Meyers et al., 1979). Entry is an important on-going process, and should not be conceptualized as a single event (Curtis & Zins, 1981). Acceptance should be secured at the highest level possible in order to gain support and reduce resistance. Many of the following issues should be clarified during negotiations (Zins & Curtis, 1984; Meyers et al., 1979).

1. *Clearly define the consultation role.* Topics such as the functional meaning of consultation, how it fits in and confidentiality should be discussed. Short- and long-term goals should be established.

2. *Involve all relevant administrators.* Avoid identification of consultation as one person's "pet project." Access to all levels of the organization is needed.

3. *Present the rationale for consultation.* What are the benefits to the system? Emphasize efficiency and effectiveness of service delivery, mental health promotion, early identification of problems and skills development in consultees.

4. *Provide accountability data.* Agree to provide both formative and summative evaluation data after a specified period of time. Zins (1981) describes an effective program using this technique.

5. *Establish formal and informal contractual agreements.* Once an under-

standing has been achieved, an agreement or "contract" should be established which specifies all areas of agreement (this does not necessarily refer to a formal written document).

6. *Make provisions for review/renegotiation.* Arrange for an evaluation of the effort after a specified period of time.

7. *Develop formal job descriptions.* Once agreed upon, the entire range of services to be provided should be clarified in writing.

8. *Maintain open lines of communication.* As with many other processes, fine tuning or even significant adjustments might be necessary as time goes by. Problems should be dealt with promptly.

After negotiating with the administration, acceptance must be secured from the teachers and other school personnel who might serve as consultees. One effective method for doing this is the use of an "entry presentation" at a faculty meeting (even when it is not initial entry, but the introduction of a new professional function). In essence, the approach to the presentation should reflect the assumptions and philosophy underlying the consultation model. It is essential that a "collegial" atmosphere be established. A "down-to-earth" explanation of consultation should be provided in very functional terms and all jargon avoided (Zins & Curtis, 1984). Issues should be covered such as what consultation is, appropriate concerns to be addressed, the consultant-consultee relationship, initiation, responsibility, confidentiality, and the benefits of consultation (Curtis & Anderson, 1976a; Gutkin & Curtis, 1982). It is important to recognize that this presentation will help to establish a climate conducive to implementing consultation. Nevertheless, a realistic understanding of what consultation *can* be will depend largely on the behavior of the consultant during the early stages of entry. Also, these same issues are brought up informally with individual teachers at the beginning stages of a particular consultation relationship.

Changing role expectations. "Role expectations essentially are determined by history, title and behavior" (Curtis & Zins, 1986). *History* refers to the expectations that have been established by the behaviors of those who previously have fulfilled the same role. *Title* infers that regardless of previous direct experiences, certain expectations are instilled by the title of the individual, e.g., "school psychologist." Most importantly, the *actual behaviors* of the individual school psychologist eventually will become the dominant influence in determining role expectations. It is common to find that a school psychologist's role is determined more by what others *expect* than it is by what they *desire.* Chandy (1973) has demonstrated that a brief in-service program can influence the frequency and manner in which consultants are used. It is essential that special services personnel ensure that potential consumers and persons in influential positions have an accurate understanding of what such professionals *can* do before deciding what it is that they *will* do (Curtis & Zins, 1986). The entry presentation described above is one way of contributing to that understanding. However, misconceptions regarding the consultant's role will continue to arise and must be dealt with on an individual basis through discussions as well as through the modeling of appropriate behavior by the consultant. Some consultants have found it effective to repeat the entry presentation when role confusion persists. It is important to remember that change will be gradual, although some special services personnel have achieved remarkable differences within the first year of concentrated effort.

Value dilemmas. Special services personnel frequently confront value dilemmas in their efforts to provide services to children and their families. Those same types of conflict will persist in efforts to provide consultation. The consultant can use skills in systems analysis to assess the various contextual elements that result in value dilemmas. The values of the organization are as significant as are those of the individual consultee. A prerequisite to considering the values of other components in the system, however, is that the consultant be fully aware of personal values. Undoubtedly, each of us must make personal decisions regarding those activities, goals and objectives that we are willing to support or even condone, and we are best able to make those decisions based on an awareness of the values of components of the system, as well as our own personal values.

Accountability — assessing impact. When an activity is new or represents a distinct change, it often is necessary to demonstrate the value of that activity to those in a decision-making position. In view of the widespread misuse of the term "consultation," the scarcity of appropriately conducted consultation in most settings, and the fact that it represents a significant change in the role expectations for most special services providers, consultation requires program evaluation to demonstrate its efficacy. Such evaluations are conducted all too infrequently. Nevertheless, there is a variety of practical approaches to evaluation. Fairchild, Zins and Grimes (1983) have developed a multi-media program on accountability which includes a filmstrip, manual and book of accountability instruments. Also, Zins (1981) presents a case study which illustrates the use of data-based evaluation in the integration of consultation into school psychological services.

Downplay the intended change. It is important to recognize that consultation represents a dramatic shift in service delivery. Many people automatically resist change regardless of its potential positive effects. Therefore, it may be easier to gain acceptance for consultation by portraying it as an approach which is *similar to* rather than different from existing approaches. By minimizing the change involved, people may be more accepting at first. Then, as they become accustomed to the approach and see its benefits firsthand, they may be more receptive to expansion of the consultant role.

THE CONSULTATION PROCESS

The consultation process can be conceptualized in stages which include: (a) entry, (b) problem clarification and (c) problem solution. Entry was discussed in the preceding section.

Problem Clarification

The purpose of this stage is to define the problem as specifically and as comprehensively as possible. It must be emphasized that the intent here is to understand the problem within an environmental context in terms of reciprocal interactions. How does each component of the environment interact to contribute to the problem? In order to move on to the stage of problem solution, we first must consider the influence of the teacher, other children, classroom structure, curriculum, school norms, parents, home environment and child (in the case of a child-related problem). It is essential that both the consultant and the consultee develop a thorough understanding of all aspects of the problem and the various factors contributing to it. Bergan and Tombari (1976) found problem identification to be the primary determinant of consultation outcomes. In other words, they found that when the consultant and teacher agreed that the problem had been identified correctly, "problem solution almost invariably resulted" (p. 12).

Early in the problem clarification process, the consultant attempts to determine the level of the system at which consultative intervention would be most effective. That is, the consultant must determine whether to provide consultation directed toward: (a) the child; (b) the teacher and the classroom; or (c) the school as an organization. Although child-related problems could be dealt with through consultation at the individual child level, a significant number of such problems are addressed most effectively by focusing on the teacher or the organization. In other words, there are some situations where factors associated with the teacher, the classroom, or the school organization contribute significantly to the problems of individual children. For example, at an organizational level, very low morale among the teaching staff is likely to contribute to an increase in the incidence of student behavior problems. Improving morale in these situations is often followed by a decrease in behavior problems.

Since it is desirable to function at a preventive level, the consultant should attempt to intervene at the level where it is possible to benefit the maximum number of children. If problems are caused in large part at the organizational level and consultative efforts are directed at the child level, the consultant essentially is using a bandaid approach and failing to address the *cause* of the problems. The same is true when problems are caused by the teacher. It is most efficient to focus consultation on the teacher rather than on individual students when the skills of the teacher are causing student problems.

The priority for intervention would be from highest to lowest in terms of preventive influence. Accordingly, the consultant would first choose to work at the organizational level, then the teacher level, and finally at the child level. Of course, in cases where organizational or teacher-centered factors were not of primary importance, the focus of consultation would be on the individual child.

Regardless of the level of intervention, problem clarification uses information collected through data generating strategies and/or interviewing techniques.

Data generating strategies. Consultation involves the use of information from a variety of sources other than consultative interactions. Among the data sources are assessment procedures, clinical interviews, observational systems, educational records, and medical records. Additional data sources which may be more pertinent to organizational consultation include surveys, questionnaires, personnel records, organizational correspondence, meeting minutes, and so forth.

Interviewing techniques. Interviewing forms the basis for what most people see as consultation. It is that process of verbal interaction between the consultant and the consultee(s). First, it must be emphasized that all of the principles outlined earlier such as the characteristics of a collaborative relationship, work-related focus, dual goals, and systems emphasis form the foundation to the interactive process and serve as guidelines for the consultant's behavior.

Essentially, the consultant uses the skills of listening, asking questions and integrating information and ideas. Listening means interest in and attentiveness to what the consultee has to say. Questioning has been found to be the consultant behavior most highly correlated with overall effectiveness (Curtis & Anderson, 1976b). It tends to influence every other skill such as the abilities to establish a climate of trust, elicit information, and involve the consultee throughout the process.

The consultant should try to minimize the use of closed questions where the consultee can provide a "yes" or "no" response. Such questions, in essence, require the consultant to develop a mental checklist of possible information regarding the problem and to then request the consultee to indicate whether or not each possible piece of information is accurate. This method places most of the burden for information generation on the consultant who has to think of every conceivable possibility. It also limits the involvement of the consultee and thereby interferes with the collaborative relationship. In contrast, more open-ended questions require that the consultee provide a greater amount of information. Questions of this type tend to be more oriented toward stimulating the consultee to think about the problem under discussion. They also tend to facilitate the collaborative relationship by keeping the consultee actively involved in the process throughout. For example, instead of asking about a list of possible situations that might "set off" temper tantrums in a particular boy (Does he get upset when . . . ?), the consultant might ask, "What kinds of things cause him to lose his temper?" Also, effective consultants tend to ask proportionately more questions and make fewer statements of fact or opinion. It is important to note however, that the process is collaborative and involves the active involvement of *all* participants. It would be inappropriate for the consultant to hold back ideas and become non-directive. What is important is that ideas are shared in a way that allows the consultee to accept or reject them.

A critical consulting skill is the ability to integrate information and ideas. Quite often, it is necessary to consider information regarding a client from a variety of sources (assessment and observational data, teacher perceptions). The amount of information is expanded even further in a systems model since the influence of several additional variables must be considered. It is essential that the consultant be able to integrate all of the information in a way that is meaningful to the problem at hand.

Two related skills that facilitate integration of material by both the consultant and consultee are clarification and summarization. Clarification is a technique in which the consultant presents his/her perception of what the consultee just said. This lets the consultee know that the consultant understands the consultee's experience and it helps the consultant ensure that he or she understands correctly what the consultee has just said. While clarification reflects one specific statement of the consultee, summarization is used to integrate a variety of information that has been presented by the consultee. The goal is to help develop a conceptual bond for diverse information that has been discussed. Neither clarification nor summarization is designed to bring premature closure to the discussion. Instead, the purpose is to facilitate continued exploration of the topic.

The problem presented initially by the consultee may not be the problem that eventually is dealt with. Information generated during problem clarification should confirm the "agenda" which is often more complicated than the initial referral, even when the referral remains a partial focus of consultation. It cannot be stated too strongly that the problem must be clarified *thoroughly* before the process moves to the problem solution stage. When this does not occur, consultation frequently fails. Furthermore, there are cases

in which thorough problem clarification may be enough of an "intervention" to enable the consultee to resolve the problem without further assistance from the consultant (Curtis & Anderson, 1976a).

Problem Solution

Once the problem has been clarified thoroughly, the process moves to the problem solution stage. Since problem clarification will have been completed from a systems perspective, attempts at problem solution should reflect a similar approach.

As noted earlier, numerous articles have been published regarding the problem solving process and different steps have been suggested (Parnes, Noller & Biondi, 1977). Yet, as noted by D'Zurilla and Goldfried (1971), "there has been a remarkable degree of agreement among theorists and investigators working in different areas as to the general kinds of operations involved in *effective* problem solving . . ." (p. 111).

A representative list of the stages follows.

1. *Thoroughly clarify the problem.* Problem clarification, consistently identified as the first general stage has already been discussed.

2. *Specify objectives.* It is important that *specific* objectives be identified in an effort to reduce anxiety and to prevent the consultee from being immobilized regarding the problem. This step is particularly significant since global and vaguely defined problems inhibit problem resolution. The consultant should help the consultee identify objectives which are specific and realistic, and for which there is a reasonable probability of success.

3. *Explore resources available.* Although this might include information and materials available, as well as the assistance of other persons, professionals and parents, the consultee should not be overlooked as a resource. There may be a tendency to look too quickly for "outside" assistance.

4. *Evaluate and choose among alterna-*

tives. Developing alternative strategies allows the consultee to compare and contrast the different approaches in deciding which one is most likely to prove effective in resolving the problem at hand. In reality, a systems approach might require that several strategies be implemented in an effort to respond to the various environmental forces that contribute to the problem. Each strategy should be carefully examined. The consultant should strive to ensure that the strategy is selected based on its potential effectiveness. Other reasons should not be used (e.g., convenience, politics, etc.) unless the available options are equal in their potential efficacy. Since the consultee is the person who will carry out the plan, it is essential that the consultee is actively involved in this process. Therefore, the consultee should select the intervention strategy to be used.

5. *Clarify implementation procedures.* This step is particularly important. *Who* will carry out *what* action and by *when* must be clarified and agreed upon. A plan with tremendous potential will probably be of no value if it is not implemented as planned. Detail and responsibility are critical issues and they must be detailed if success is to be ensured.

6. *Implement the chosen strategy.* It is not safe to assume that the agreed upon plan will be implemented as planned. This does not necessarily infer that the consultee does not have the ability, or willfully chooses not to fulfill the agreement. There are many unanticipated legitimate obstacles that arise. These potential problems require systematic follow-up on the part of the consultant. In essence, this step reinforces the idea that consultation is an on-going process and not a one-time encounter.

7. *Evaluate the plan and recycle if necessary.* Planned evaluation of the intervention's effectiveness is essential. It is naive to think about problem solving in terms of finding *the* solution. There are few "guaranteed" solutions to problems involving human behavior, especially within a constantly changing environmental context. Therefore, it is essential that the consultant and consultee monitor

effectiveness once an intervention is implemented. Sometimes it will be necessary to revise the intervention. However, lack of success of the intervention also may occur because of a problem during the entry or problem clarification stages. For example, a problem with the entry stage can easily result in a consultee participating in consultation when all that was expected was that the consultant remove the problem with no involvement from the consultee. Similarly, an error in problem clarification could have resulted in interventions directed at an individual child, when what was really needed was a focus on the teacher or the entire school organization. Under these circumstances, the consultant would use the evaluation data as a basis for cycling back to an earlier stage of the consultation process.

SUMMARY

Consultation does not represent a panacea for the effective delivery of school-based special services. However, there is a substantial body of evidence indicating that consultation can contribute significantly to efforts to meet the school-related needs of children and their families. However, one major problem which continues to hamper the field in this regard is inadequate emphasis on the specific skills necessary for successful consultation. This chapter has outlined some of the important skills that are needed. A more detailed discussion of consultation skills can be found in Parsons and Meyers (1984).

In order for special services personnel to be able to provide these needed services, adequate training must be made available. First, it is essential that training programs provide quality formalized training in consultation. Second, pre-service and in-service teachers should receive training in the skills necessary to work effectively as consultees (Meyers, 1982). To enable special services professionals to meaningfully respond to the needs and demands that they face in the schools, training programs will have to take these steps. Furthermore, those professionals will have to be determined to integrate consultation into the services delivery system.

REFERENCES

Bardon, J. I., & Bennett, V. D. (1974). *School psychology*. Englewood Cliffs, NJ: Prentice-Hall.

Bardon, J. I., & Wenger, R. D. (1974). Institutions offering graduate training in school psychology: 1973-1974. *Journal of School Psychology, 12*, 70-83.

Bardon, J. I., & Wenger, R. D. (1976). School psychology training trends in the early 1970s. *Professional Psychology, 7*, 31-37.

Bergan, J. R. (1977). *Behavioral consultation*. Columbus, OH: Charles E. Merrill.

Bergan, J. R., & Tombari, M. L. (1976). Consultant skill and efficiency and the implementation and outcomes of consultation. *Journal of School Psychology, 14*, 3-14.

Caplan, G. (1970). *The theory and practice of mental health consultation*. New York: Basic Books.

Chandy, J. M. (1973). *The effects of an inservice orientation on teacher perception and use of the mental health consultant*. Unpublished doctoral dissertation, University of Texas at Austin.

Curtis, M. (1983). School psychology and consultation. *Communiqué, IX*, (7), 9.

Curtis, M. J., & Anderson, T. (1976a). *Consulting in educational settings: A collaborative approach* (slide/tape). Cincinnati: Faculty Resource Center, University of Cincinnati.

Curtis, M. J., & Anderson, T. (1976b). *The relationship of behavioral variables to consultant effectiveness*. Paper presented at the annual meeting of the National Association of School Psychologists, Kansas City.

Curtis, M. J., & Watson, K. (1980). Changes in consultee problem clarification skills following consultation. *Journal of School Psychology, 18*, 210-221.

Curtis, M. J., & Zins, J. E. (Eds.) (1981). *The theory and practice of school consultation*. Springfield, IL: Charles C Thomas.

Curtis, M. J., & Zins, J. E. (1986). The organization and structuring of psychological services within educational settings. In S. N. Elliott & J. C. Witt (Eds.), *The delivery of psychological services in schools: Concepts, processes, and issues*. Hillsdale, NJ: Lawrence Erlbaum.

D'Zurilla, T. J., & Goldfried, M. R. (1971). Problem solving and behavior modification. *Journal of Abnormal and Social Psychology, 78*, 107-126.

Fairchild, T. N., Zins, J. E., & Grimes, J. (1983). *Improving school psychology through accountability* (filmstrip). Washington, DC: National Association of School Psychologists.

Fullan, M., Miles, M. B., & Taylor, G. (1980). Organization development in schools: The state of the art. *Review of Educational Research, 50*, 121-183.

Gallessich, J. (1973). Training the school psychologist for consultation. *Journal of School Psychology, 11*, 57-65.

Gutkin, T. B. (1980). Teacher perceptions of consultation services provided by school psychologists. *Professional Psychology, 11*, 637-642

Gutkin, T. B., & Curtis, M. J. (1982). School-based consultation: Theory and techniques. In C. R. Reynolds & T. B. Gutkin (Eds.), *The handbook of school psychology*. New York: John Wiley.

Gutkin, T. B., Singer, J. H., & Brown, R. (1980). Teacher reactions to school based consultation services: A multivariate analysis. *Journal of School Psychology, 18*, 126-134.

Hobbs, N. (1964). Mental health's third revolution. *American Journal of Orthopsychiatry, 34*, 822-833.

Jackson, R. M., Cleveland, J. C., & Merenda, P. F. (1975). The longitudinal effects of early identification and counseling of underachievers. *Journal of School Psychology, 13*, 119-128.

Jason, L. A., & Ferone, L. (1978). Behavioral versus process consultation interventions in school settings. *American Journal of Community Psychology, 6*, 531-543.

Kochman, T. (1981). *Black and white styles in conflict*. Chicago: University of Chicago Press.

Mannino, F. V., & Shore, M. F. (1975). Effective change through consultation. In F. V. Mannino, B. W. MacLennan, & M. F. Shore (Eds.), *The practice of mental health consultation*. New York: Gardner Press.

Meacham, M. L., & Peckham, P. D. (1978). School psychologists at three-quarters century: Congruence between training, practice, preferred role and competence. *Journal of School Psychology, 16*, 195-206.

Medway, F. J. (1979). How effective is school consultation: A review of recent research. *Journal of School Psychology, 17*, 275-282.

Medway, F. J., & Updyke, J. F. (1985). Meta-analysis of consultation outcome studies. *American Journal of Community Psychology, 13*, 489-505.

Meyers, J. (1975). Consultee-centered consultation with a teacher as a technique in behavior management. *American Journal of Community Psychology, 3,* 111-121.

Meyers, J. (1982). *Consultation skills: How teachers can maximize help from specialists in schools.* Published by National Support Systems Project, University of Minnesota, M. R. Reynolds, Editor.

Meyers, J., Parsons, R. D., & Martin, R. (1979). *Mental health consultation in the schools.* San Francisco: Jossey-Bass.

Meyers, J., Wurtz, R., & Flanagan, D. (1981). A national survey investigating consultation training occurring in school psychology programs. *Psychology in the Schools, 18,* 297-302.

Parnes, S. J., Noller, R. B., & Biondi, A. M. (1977). *Guide to creative action.* New York: Scribners.

Parsons, R. D., & Meyers, J. (1984). *Developing consultation skills: A guide to training, development and assessment for human services professionals.* San Francisco: Jossey-Bass.

Raffaniello, E. M., Curtis, M. J., Heintzelman, G., Shannon, P., Van Wagener, E., Taylor, C., Vesper, J., & Blennerhassett, L. (1980). *School psychologists' roles: Parent and student perceptions.* Paper presented at the meeting of the National Association of School Psychologists, Washington, DC.

Ritter, D. (1978). Effects of a school consultation program upon referral patterns of teachers. *Psychology in the Schools, 15,* 239-243.

Schmuck, R. A., & Runkel, P. J. (1985). *The handbook of organization development in schools* (3rd ed.). Palo Alto, CA: Mayfield Publishing.

Schmuck, R. A., & Schmuck, P. A. (1979). *Group processes in the classroom* (3rd ed.). Dubuque, Iowa: Wm. C. Brown.

Spivack, G., Platt, J. J., & Shure, M. B. (1976). *The problem-solving approach to adjustment.* San Francisco: Jossey-Bass.

Zins, J. E. (1981). Using data-based evaluation in developing school consultation services. In M. J. Curtis & J. E. Zins (Eds.), *The theory and practice of school consultation.* Springfield, IL: Charles C Thomas.

Zins, J. E., & Curtis, M. J. (1984). Building consultation into the educational service delivery system. In C. A. Maher, R. J. Illback, & J. E. Zins (Eds.), *Organizational psychology in the schools: A handbook for professionals.* Springfield, IL: Charles C Thomas.

Zins, J. E., Curtis, M. J., Graden, J. L., & Ponti, C. R. (1988). *Helping students succeed in the regular classroom: A guide for developing intervention assistance programs.* San Francisco: Jossey-Bass.

FOOTNOTE

[1]This chapter is an adaptation of "Best Practices in School-Based Consultation: Guidelines for Effective Practice" by M. Curtis and J. Meyers, in *Best Practices in School Psychology* (1985), A. Thomas and J. Grimes (Eds.), published by the National Association of School Psychologists.

4

Mainstream Assistance Teams to Accommodate Difficult-To-Teach Students in General Education

Douglas Fuchs and Lynn S. Fuchs
George Peabody College of Vanderbilt University

Since passage of Public Law 94-142, there has been a sharp increase in special education enrollment. This increase partly reflects attempts to ensure that handicapped children receive an appropriate education. Nevertheless, there is growing suspicion that (a) too many students are being identified as handicapped and (b) this overidentification or misidentification exemplifies general education's failure to accommodate the heterogeneous nature of its mainstream population. In other words, many observers view general education as depending more and more on special education to deal with its difficult-to-teach pupils, thereby becoming increasingly exclusive in terms of the students judged appropriate for mainstream education.

Two basic strategies are emerging that aim to strengthen general education's capacity to deal more effectively with student diversity. The first is development of large-scale, full-time mainstreaming programs that attempt to reintegrate handicapped students into general education (see, for example, Johnson & Johnson, 1986; Slavin, Leavey, & Madden, 1984; Wang, Gennari, & Waxman, 1985). The second approach is prereferral intervention, which targets additional help for nonhandicapped difficult-to-teach pupils, thereby reducing or eliminating the need for referral to special education. We currently are involved in a three-year program of research, funded by the Office of Special Education in the U.S. Department of Education, to develop, implement, and validate a prereferral intervention model entitled Mainstream Assistance Teams (MATs).

The primary purpose of this chapter is to describe the MAT, including a detailed report on how it has worked during our first year. Specifically, we first present a rationale for prereferral assessment and intervention. Second, we discuss the social, political, and bureaucratic dimensions of the particular setting for which the MAT was developed. Next, we delineate the major dimensions of the MAT such as our use of Behavioral Consultation and written scripts* to assure fidelity of the consultation process. Fourth, we outline the implementation process, including a description of how we involved schools, consultants, general educators, and students and how we evaluated the effectiveness of the project. Finally, we present a summary of our evaluative data on the MATs and discuss the implications of these data for implementing similar assistance programs and conducting research on prereferral intervention in the schools.

During Year 1 we have generated information that should help guide school-based consultants currently engaged in, or contemplating future involvement with, prereferral intervention. However, we also uncovered many questions. We intend to present both resolved and unanswered questions, given the currently incomplete database, to avoid an oversimplified conceptualization of a process that many practitioners and researchers understand is complex and challenging. By sharing our questions about prereferral intervention, as well as presenting what we believe we *do* know, we hope to encourage practitioners and researchers to continue to explore how best to implement prereferral intervention and, more generally, school consultation.

RATIONALE FOR AN ALTERNATIVE APPROACH

Increasing Numbers of Mildly Handicapped Students

Since the U. S. Department of Education's first child count in 1976-1977, the number of students enrolled in special education has grown each year, with an increase of 17% from 1976-1977 to 1985-1986 (Singer & Butler, 1987). Dramatic increases in identification of mildly and moderately handicapped pupils account for much of the reported growth (Annual Report to Congress, U. S. Department of Education, 1984). It is probable that, at least to some degree, this results from legal, legislative, and professional initiatives directed toward assuring handicapped youth a free and appropriate public education. However, there is growing suspicion, both within the federal government (Annual Report to Congress, U. S. Department of Education, 1984) and among professionals (see, for example, Gerber & Semmel, 1984), that too many children are identified as handicapped. There are numerous and obvious reasons for the undesirability of incorrect identification. It causes unnecessary separation and stigmatization of children (Jones, 1972; Reynolds & Balow, 1972), disruption and fragmentation of school programs (Will, 1986), and additional costs to school districts (Wang, Reynolds, & Walberg, 1985).

These and other negative effects of misidentification argue for an attempt to understand the reasons for observed increases in the population identified as mildly and moderately handicapped. There are at least two important explanations. First, classroom teachers are referring increasingly large numbers of children for special education evaluation

(Ysseldyke & Thurlow, 1983; Ysseldyke, Thurlow, Graden, Wesson, Algozzine, & Deno, 1983). Second, comparatively few handicapped students are returned to the mainstream (e.g., Anderson-Inman, 1987; Weatherly & Lipsky, 1977; Ysseldyke & Thurlow, 1984). While each explanation appears essential to understand why special education enrollments are expanding, our project and this chapter focus on the phenomenon of increasing teacher referrals.

Frequency of teacher referrals. It has been estimated that, since 1977, the average number of referrals initiated each year by classroom teachers has nearly doubled, from 2.2 to 4.0 (Ysseldyke & Thurlow, 1983). Furthermore, evidence indicates that teachers' referrals are crucial to the ultimate identification of pupils as handicapped. Algozzine and Ysseldyke (1981) reported that over a three-year period 92% of referred students were evaluated and 73% of evaluated students were placed in special education. Similarly, Foster, Ysseldyke, Casey, and Thurlow (1984) found that 72% of students referred were placed in special education and that most were placed in the special education category for which they had been referred. Additionally, Ysseldyke, Algozzine, Regan, and McGue (1981) reported that, when faced with psychometric profiles indicating normal performance, "expert" diagnosticians labeled over 50% of the students with normal profiles as eligible for special education and cited teachers' referral reasons as justification for their referral decision.

Arbitrariness and precipitousness of teacher referrals. Despite the apparent confidence that diagnosticians and special educators place in classroom teachers' referrals, empirical evidence indicates that teacher referrals often are arbitrary, if not biased (Lietz & Gregory, 1978; Tobias, Cole, Zibrin, & Bodlakova, 1982; Tucker, 1980; Ysseldyke & Thurlow, 1984). Investigations have found that minority pupils, boys, and siblings of children identified as learning-disabled are overrepresented when referrals are initiated by teachers rather than based on objective measurement (Marston, Mirkin, & Deno, 1984). Additionally, contrary to reasons typically cited on referral forms, general educators frequently refer students primarily because of disturbing behaviors (Algozzine, 1977), which (a) tend to be defined idiosyncratically (Gerber & Semmel, 1984) and (b) often represent situation-specific problems rather than enduring student characteristics (Rubin & Balow, 1971).

In addition to findings that teachers' referrals often are arbitrary, if not biased, evidence suggests that teachers frequently make referrals in a precipitous, rather than a deliberate, manner. It seems that classroom teachers typically make few, if any, substantial programmatic changes prior to initiating referral (Ysseldyke, Christenson, Pianta, & Algozzine, 1983; Ysseldyke & Thurlow, 1980). The frequently observed result is that a high percentage of teacher referrals fails to meet local eligibility criteria (Marston et al., 1984; Shepard, Smith, & Vojir, 1983). Findings of arbitrariness and precipitousness in referral-related decision making suggest that many classroom teachers do not attempt, or do not know how to accommodate difficult-to-teach students. This is corroborated by a related research literature demonstrating that teachers provide instruction to low-achieving students that is qualitatively and quantitatively inferior to that made available to high-achieving pupils (Allington, 1980; Mosenthal, 1984).

Prereferral Assessment and Intervention

Analysis of the often arbitrary and precipitous nature of the process of referral to special education placement highlights the importance of modifying conventional practices in educational assessment to permit prereferral assessment and intervention in general education classrooms. Such activity aims to enhance general educators' capacity to instruct and manage difficult-to-teach pupils, thereby reducing the number of students referred for formal assessment and possible placement in special programs.

Traditional educational assessment. According to Salvia and Ysseldyke (1985), the traditional purposes of educational assessment are to specify and verify students' problems and formulate decisions about referral, classification, instructional planning, and program modification. The referral and classification phases constitute an identification process in which pupils' performance on nomothetic aptitude and/or achievement measures typically are compared to identify "outliers" who warrant placement in special programs. Contrastingly, the instructional planning and program modification phases together represent a process whereby assessment is relatively idiopathic and related to the content and methods of instruction.

Prereferral assessment. The concept of prereferral assessment requires that we reconceptualize the nature of educational assessment in at least two important ways. First, the concept of prereferral assessment explicitly has to do with activity that is preliminary or preparatory to teacher referral, which formalizes the decision whether to refer. Second, and in contrast to activity conventionally associated with referral and classification phases of assessment, prereferral assessment represents an opportunity to collect data helpful to the development of classroom interventions. Toward this end, information frequently is necessary about (a) the social and instructional characteristics of the classroom and (b) students' social behavior and/or academic performance in curricula used in the classroom. In addition to its potential contribution to the creation of classroom interventions, prereferral assessment signals effort to "fine tune" or validate these interventions. Thus, prereferral assessment typically is conceptualized as intervention-oriented, thereby necessitating the collection of data that are ecologically sensitive and curriculum-based. Moreover, such data may be used formatively to fashion classroom modifications that permit general educators to accommodate greater student diversity. Useful strategies for prereferral assessment include Curriculum Based Measurement (see Tindal, this volume, and Marston & Magnusson, this volume) and assessing the learning environment (see Ysseldyke & Christenson, this volume).

Prereferral intervention. There are at least five characteristics of the prereferral intervention model, a couple of which already have been discussed. First, it is consonant with the *least restrictive* doctrine set forth in PL 94–142, requiring educators to attempt to accommodate difficult-to-teach students' instructional and social needs in the most "normal" setting possible. Second, and related to the preceding point, prereferral intervention is meant to be *preventive*. According to Graden, Casey, and Christenson (1985), it focuses on (a) avoiding inappropriate referral and placement of students in special programs and (b) obviating future students' problems by enhancing general educators' capacity to intervene effectively with diverse groups of children.

Third, although some general educators may choose to develop and implement prereferral interventions independently, such activity typically is "brokered" by one or more special service personnel, such as school psychologists and special educators, acting as consultants. Usually working indirectly with targeted pupils through collaborative consultation with the classroom teacher, these consultants often employ a *problem-solving* approach borrowed from behavioral consultation (BC) to design, implement, and evaluate interventions (Curtis, Zins, & Graden, 1987). Fourth, prereferral intervention represents *immediate* assistance to pupil and teacher, since support is provided at the point at which the teacher contemplates referral. Finally, the typical prereferral intervention model encourages use of an *ecological* perspective that identifies teacher, physical setting, and instructional variables as well as the characteristics of the individual student as possible causes of learning difficulties. In other words, rather than assume the source of student problems resides within

the child, the prereferral intervention model challenges educators to investigate a larger context for the source(s) of and solution(s) to pupil difficulties.

As indicated by Curtis, Zins, and Graden (1987), there are many ways to implement a prereferral intervention program. Two general alternative approaches are for special service personnel to assist classroom teachers by working alone or as a part of a team. Cantrell and Cantrell (1976), Graden, Casey, and Bonstrom (1985), and Ritter (1978) have described programs in which support personnel consult independently; in contrast, Chalfant, Pysh, and Moultrie (1979) and Maher (cited in Curtis, Zins, & Graden, 1987) have mobilized teams of various professionals to deliver prereferral intervention.

MATs. In designing an approach to prereferral intervention, we attempted to make the MAT project a state-of-the-art program. Toward this end, we incorporated all of the aforementioned characteristics of the prereferral intervention model, including an ecological perspective and a collaborative problem-solving version of consultation. We also borrowed salient features developed by several investigators who have implemented and studied the effects of prereferral intervention programs. Following the pioneering work of Cantrell and Cantrell (1976), for example, we constructed the MAT to reflect a behavioral approach to consultation. Additionally, like the work of Chalfant et al. (1979), the MAT project involves teams of special support personnel providing assistance to general educators.

However, the MATs do not merely reiterate other prereferral intervention programs. We believe our version of prereferral intervention is distinctive in four ways. First, it systematically employs a *multidisciplinary team* composed of a building-based school psychologist and a special educator as well as a general educator with a targeted difficult-to-teach student. Second, team members follow *written scripts* that are intended to contribute to proper use of behavioral consultation. Third, the MAT project was designed in part as a *component analysis* of three increasingly inclusive versions of behavioral consultation to identify a most effective *and* efficient process of consultation. Last, in contrast to many investigations of school-based consultative projects, our outcome measures included indices of *student performance* and *teacher behavior* as well as rate of teacher referrals to special programs.

Below is an extended discussion of these design features as well as a description of how we implemented the MATs in several middle schools of a large urban school district. This description will include information (a) on recruitment of building-based support staff, and subsequent in-service preparation of these professionals for their consultative duties, (b) on identification of classroom teachers and most difficult-to-teach students, and (c) on evaluation of the impact of the MATs' efforts. However, since the MATs were developed for a particular place and time, it is important that we first describe the setting to which the MATs were designed to conform. Some of these setting features, particularly attitudes about change and alternative practices, may be applicable to other situations.

SETTING

Two policies, one statewide and the other local, influenced the design of our prereferral intervention project. The first was Tennessee's newly initiated Career Ladder Program; the second was the way prereferral intervention was viewed officially in the district in which we planned to implement the project.

Tennessee Career Ladder Program

The Career Ladder law, SB 1, was enacted in March 1984 during a special session of the Tennessee Legislature. It is regarded as the most ambitious, controversial, and expensive component of former Governor Lamar Alexander's Better Schools Program. The law calls for a five-step ladder tied to more money for, and more rigorous evaluations of, general

and special educators and administrators in Tennessee's elementary and secondary public schools (Pipho, 1986). Arguments for this system included the assertion that Tennessee's most serious problems are per capita income (among the bottom 10 states in the United States) and rate of unemployment (among the top 10 states in the United States). Stronger job skills were seen as the key to more and better jobs; and stronger job skills required more effective schools and more capable teachers (Parish, 1983).

This logic won grassroots support for the Career Ladder Program as well as its passage in the state legislature. To help finance the merit system as well as other components of the Better Schools Program, the legislature increased the state sales tax by one penny. In 1985 this one-cent increase produced about $325 million in additional revenue, with elementary and secondary education receiving $165 million (Odden, 1986).

In contrast to overwhelming public support for the Better Schools and Career Ladder Programs, Tennessee's teachers and their state education association were, and continue to be, strongly opposed to them. At least three factors have contributed to their opposition. First, they were not involved through their professional organizations in the formulation of the programs (Pate-Bain, 1983). Second, the Better Schools package requires yearly criterion-referenced testing in several grades and pupil promotion based on these test scores. Since such testing tends to influence the nature of many educational goals and objectives as well as the selection of instructional materials, content, and activities, many teachers believe their professional autonomy has been seriously curtailed. Finally, and probably most important, many Tennessee teachers, like the majority of United States educators (Gallup, 1984), dislike a merit pay system. Their antipathy for incentives appears to be based on the beliefs that they will be evaluated unfairly and that merit pay will cause morale problems. Additionally, they were resentful that the Career Ladder Program initially permitted identification of only 15% of the workforce as master teachers, that is, professionals judged worthy of placement at the highest rung on the ladder (Pate-Bain, 1983). In fact, during the 1984–1985 school year, 65% of 3,100 Tennessee teachers who applied and were evaluated for the top two rungs of the career ladder failed to qualify.

Teacher unrest seemed uppermost in the minds of local school officials with whom we spoke in the fall of 1985 as we explored ways to implement the MAT project. Describing local teachers as feeling undervalued, overworked, misunderstood, and alienated, a middle school administrator counseled that if we wished to secure teacher cooperation, we could not ask much of them in terms of time and energy. This advice was repeated by several other officials in the school district's central office. The message was articulated more pointedly by building principals. Many communicated a fear of abetting a project that would be perceived by teachers as one more intrusive, disruptive, time-consuming evaluative exercise with which to contend. However, the principals also recognized that the MAT project addressed a major problem that they and their teachers inevitably would be required to confront, namely, an unprecedented number of retained, difficult-to-teach pupils, resulting from the new statewide policy requiring that promotion be tied to performance on criterion-referenced tests. If the MATs indeed could help teachers deal with such students, then the project would be highly valued. Nevertheless, several principals rejected the project outright. The others gave conditional consent: "If it's alright with my teachers, it's OK with me."

Special Education's Official View of Prereferral Intervention

Administrators in special education liked the MAT project for several reasons. First, they claimed to support in principle the preventive thrust of the project. Second, they applauded the fact that the MATs were designed to draw special and general educators together for the purposes of collaborative problem solving.

Such a feature, they said, was sorely needed in a school system in which special and general education operate so much apart. Relatedly, they asserted that many general educators have much to learn from special education and that, within the framework of the MATs, general education might develop a more positive regard for special education. Finally, they predicted that their teachers would enjoy consultation; it would provide many an opportunity to learn new, important skills and try something different.

However, two important facts served as brakes on their enthusiasm. First, they related that special education teachers in their district have been misused by principals who have required them to serve as aides in general education and in other positions having little to do with special education. To discourage such practice, the special education administrators said they repeatedly have argued that their teachers may be used only to further the educational development of handicapped pupils. Thus, although supportive of prevention as an idea, the administrators feared their support of special educators' participation on the MATs, which address the needs of nonhandicapped students, might blunt a major distinction they had worked so hard to sharpen.

The second reason, expressed implicitly by the administrators, related to the formula used by the state department of education to reimburse local school districts' special education costs. The reimbursement formula incorporates 10 service options that range in cost from $252.44 (for consultation to a classroom teacher) to $12,987.96 (for residential placement). Despite the panoply of services represented by this reimbursement formula, all must target a handicapped child. There is not one cent of reimbursement for the special education teacher who consults with a general educator who has requested help to address the needs of a difficult-to-teach *nonhandicapped* student.

In other words, the administrators literally could not afford to reduce the number of handicapped children with whom their teachers worked so they could participate in a large-scale prevention program of prereferral intervention. However, following several discussions, the administration gave permission for a limited number of special educators to participate in the project, provided that participation would be voluntary and that teachers understood there would be no concomitant reduction in direct caseloads.

Relation Between Setting and MAT Project

We took to heart what we learned from school officials about prevailing teacher attitudes, interdepartmental relations, and administrative policies. On balance, such descriptions did not auger well for our school-based consultation project: General educators did not appear to be of an overly generous disposition and, even if they had been, special educators and (we later learned) school psychologists had scant time to consult with these teachers. We came to a simple and, we believe, important conclusion. If the MAT project was to be effective it had to be *efficient*. We suspect that the importance of efficiency to consultation generalizes beyond our setting, a notion corroborated by Witt's (1986) research, indicating that teachers "are very concerned with the amount of time, personnel, and material resources that an intervention is likely to require" (p. 39). If, as we believe, there is widespread concern about the efficiency of consultation, it probably is because school districts tend to share many of the teacher attitudes, job descriptions for school psychologists and special educators, and reimbursement formulas that characterized our own setting.

In search of economy, we pursued several independent avenues. First, we selected a structured and explicit model on which to base our consultation approach. Second, we developed relatively prescriptive MAT materials and activities. Third, we attempted to present these materials and activities in an organized fashion. Fourth, as part of our project

evaluation, we designed an analysis of major components of the consultation process, hoping to distinguish indispensable from dispensable aspects of school-based consultation. Finally, we attempted to recruit special education teachers and school psychologists who were "quick studies" and hard workers. These and other procedural and substantive facets of our MATs are described below.

MATs: IMPORTANT DIMENSIONS

Behavioral Consultation

We placed much of our MAT activity in a framework of consultation because it and prereferral intervention share two very important attributes. First, consultation, like prereferral intervention, is basically an effort to prevent behavior and learning problems (Conoley & Conoley, 1982). As Lambert (1981) has noted, "If school psychologists are to become agents to promote the mental health and educational accomplishments of children, and . . . to prevent mental disorder and educational failure, the most promising strategy is the development of consultation skills" (p. 201).

Second, consultation and prereferral intervention are problem-solving ventures. Bergan (1977) writes, "Consultation typically involves an attempt to alter an existing set of circumstances in the direction of a desired set of circumstances. Moreover, it is generally not clear at the start of consultation how the needed alterations can best be effected" (p. 4). So, too, with classroom interventions aiming to prevent referrals to special education.

Behavioral consultation was chosen among alternative well-known consultation models, such as the mental health and the organizational development models, because it is comparatively straightforward, appears to be most explicit about the consultee, and often the student, as a problem solver who may participate as a co-equal in designing intervention strategies, and claims strong empirical support for its effectiveness. The effectiveness of BC has been evaluated experimentally more often than the success of alternative consultation models (Alpert & Yammer, 1983). Although some of this efficacy research suffers from conceptual and methodological limitations (Alpert & Yammer, 1983; Meyers, Pitt, Gaughan, & Freidman, 1978), there is steadily growing evidence from school-based investigations indicating its success in *increasing* pupils' attention, study behavior, completion of homework assignments, and mathematics and compositional response rates and *reducing* lateness, out-of-seat behavior, general disruptiveness, stealing, chronic absences, and digit reversals (e.g., Tombari & Davis, 1979).

Definition and characteristics. Behavioral consultation (BC), like the mental health and the organizational development models of consultation, involves a triadic network (consultant, teacher, and pupil) and indirect service. Unlike the other models, BC has roots in the learning theory tradition of Watson, Skinner, and Bandura. Not surprisingly, it emphasizes the role of environmental factors in controlling behavior. That is, it encourages exploration of antecedents and consequences of behavior in naturalistic settings to permit identification of variables influencing the frequency, rate, intensity, and/or duration of problem behavior. Behavioral consultants employ respondent, operant, and modeling procedures to change disturbing behavior.

In a similar vein, BC links decision making to empirical evidence. The model calls for the design and implementation of interventions to be based on behavioral data and empirically validated laws of behavioral change. Additionally, BC evaluations require focus on goal attainment and plan effectiveness. Finally, BC is conducted within a series of four well-defined, interrelated stages: problem identification, problem analysis, plan implementation, and problem evaluation.

Stages of behavioral consultation. The consultant guides the teacher through a majority of the stages of behavioral consultation in a succession of structured interviews in which specific objectives must be accomplished before consultation can proceed to subsequent stages. The major objectives of the first stage, problem identification, are to define the problem behavior in concrete, observable terms, obtain an estimate of the frequency or intensity of the behavior, and tentatively identify the environmental events surrounding the problem behavior. In the second stage, problem analysis, the goal is to validate the existence of a problem, discover factors that may influence problem solution, and develop with the teacher an intervention plan that directly addresses the problem. During the third stage, plan implementation, the consultant makes sure that the intervention plan is carried out as agreed and is functioning properly. Although plan implementation is primarily the responsibility of the teacher, the consultant monitors details of implementation. The goal of the final stage, problem evaluation, is for the consultant and teacher collaboratively to evaluate the effectiveness of the intervention and, if it has proved ineffective, to determine how it should be modified.

Component analysis: Variations of BC. An apparent basic and widespread presumption in the literature on BC is that all four stages constituting the model are important; none are indispensable (e.g., Gresham, 1982). Although Bergan and associates (e.g., Bergan & Tombari, 1976; Tombari & Davis, 1979) have indicated that the initial stage may be the most important to consultation outcomes, we are unaware of any systematic attempt to determine the relative value of the various stages or components of the BC model.

The absence of component analyses seems to reflect a more general dearth of process–outcome research in the consultation literature (e.g., Alpert & Yammer, 1983; Medway, 1982; Meyers et al., 1978; Witt & Elliott, 1983). This is unfortunate, since process–outcome research, including component analyses, can help identify dispensable facets of the consultation process, leading to approaches that are simultaneously effective and efficient. Operating in an environment relatively inhospitable to consultation, we were eager to develop efficient consultation procedures, not just for ourselves, but for the many school psychologists and special educators across the country conducting consultation despite an absence of institutional support. Toward this end, we undertook a component analysis of the BC model.

The importance of the various components of the BC model were explored by creating three increasingly inclusive versions. In the least inclusive variation, the consultant and teacher worked collaboratively on problem identification and analysis, but the consultant did not help the teacher implement the intervention developed during the problem analysis stage. Moreover, the consultant and teacher did not evaluate intervention effects in any formative fashion, precluding an opportunity to modify or fine-tune the intervention. In other words, our first version of the model incorporated only the first two of the model's four stages. The second variant of BC included the first two stages and also required the consultant to make a minimum of two classroom visits to assist the teacher with the intervention. However, like the first version, this second variation of the model did not include a formative evaluation stage. Thus, the second version comprised the first three stages of BC. Finally, our third and most inclusive version required the consultant and teacher to formatively evaluate intervention effects, and, therefore, incorporated all four stages of the BC model.

Written Scripts

Three of four BC stages (Stages 1, 2, and 4) are implemented during the course of formal interviews or meetings. (Stage 3, plan implementation, typically is conducted in the classroom.) Gresham (1982) has provided one of the more comprehensive descriptions of the substance to be covered during these meetings. Inspired by the Cantrells' Heuristic Report Form (Cantrell & Cantrell, 1977, 1980), we recast Gresham's materials into written scripts that guided much of our consultants' verbal behavior. Each of our three versions of BC had its own script. The

scripts provided consultants with an efficient means to create rationales and overviews for the meetings; to establish structure and maintain a logical and quick-paced flow; to obtain succinct descriptions of the classroom environment, qualitative and quantitative evaluations of most difficult-to-teach students, and logistical information such as days and times when the target child could be observed; and to check, and systematically double-check, that key information such as descriptions of the target pupil's behavior was sufficiently elaborate and precise to permit easy identification during the consultant's classroom observations.

In addition to promoting efficiency, we believe the scripts enhanced fidelity of treatment. That is, assuming (a) the scripts accurately reflected the BC model and (b) consultants faithfully followed the scripts, we could be confident that the model was implemented as intended. This fidelity of treatment issue was especially important because the majority of our consultants lacked formal consultation training and experience. This is not to suggest that scripts were without drawback. When read ploddingly or with disinterest, they could be quite deadly. Moreover, a couple of our more accomplished consultants disliked their prescriptiveness. Nevertheless, most consultants and teachers spoke very positively about them, raising the question whether beginning consultants might do well to work from scripts, improvising over time and finally discarding them when achieving sufficient mastery over the consultative process.

Outcome Measures

A wide range of outcome measures were used, reflecting a belief that proper evaluation of consultation and prereferral intervention requires a multisource, multimethod approach. This conviction is based partly on the fact that school consultation, by definition, involves several individuals playing very different roles and holding often contrasting perspectives and expectations. Similarly, the consultation process is multi-, not unidimensional, requiring qualitatively different measures to obtain appropriate information on its various components. Because we had money for research, we could employ a relatively large number of outcome measures. Practitioners, of course, do not typically have such support or opportunity. Consequently, they must choose carefully their methods of data collection. Nevertheless, we believe it is still possible for them to conduct a modest multisource, multimethod approach, which will increase the meaningfulness, or truthfulness, of their evaluative effort.

Our measures included the Revised Behavior Problem Checklist (Quay & Peterson, 1983), the Teacher Efficacy Scale (Gibson & Dembo, 1984), and the Stallings Observation Instrument (Stallings, 1983). Rather than discuss the data generated by use of these instruments, we limit our description of MAT effects to three additional measures that may be important and useful to practitioners: consultants' global evaluations, teacher ratings, and direct observations of pupil classroom behavior.

Consultant evaluations. During a debriefing interview following completion of MAT activities, consultants rated the effectiveness of the MAT from (a) their own perspective and (b) the point of view of each of their teachers. Consultants were given a four-point scale: 1 = *unqualified failure* ("The MATs made no impact on student or teacher behavior. It was really a waste of everyone's time"); 2 = *qualified failure* ("The MATs were responsible for minor positive changes in student or teacher behavior, but these changes were not really sufficient to make an important difference in the classroom"); 3 = *qualified success* ("The MATs resulted in real, if not dramatic, positive change in student or teacher behavior. It made a noticeable and welcomed difference to participants"); 4 = *unqualified success* ("The MATs led to dramatic positive change in student or teacher behavior. It made a very important difference in the classroom").

Teacher ratings. Teachers identified problematic social and/or academic behaviors of their most difficult-to-teach students. Then, using a Likert-type continuum, they rated each behavior in terms of *severity, manageability,* and *tolerableness.* The rating scales were incorporated into the written scripts and administered by the consultants prior to and following completion of consultation.

Classroom observations. An observation procedure was developed that combines features of (a) systematic time-interval recording and (b) anecdotal note taking on antecedents and consequences to the targeted classroom behavior. Consultants were instructed (by audio-tape and earphones) to observe on a rotating basis the target student and two randomly selected same-sex peers. Each target child and classmates were observed during two 30-minute sessions prior to MAT activity and two 30-minute intervals following MAT activity. Consultants were trained to a minimum level of .80 inter-rater agreement, which was maintained during pre- and postintervention observations.

This hybrid time-interval/anecdotal observation procedure (hereafter referred to as antecedent-behavior-consequence [ABC]) was developed with three objectives in mind. First, the time-interval aspect would quantify the seriousness of the target child's problem behavior as well as determine and quantify appropriate goals. Second, generation of time-interval data on a pre- and postconsultation basis represented an index of MAT effectiveness. Third, the anecdotal dimension of the ABC observation procedure would help consultants identify antecedent and/or consequent events surrounding problem behavior that might become the focus of intervention activity.

MATs: IMPLEMENTATION
Participants

Schools. For about 1 month, we spent much of our time in discussions with central administrators in the public school system in which we planned to implement the MAT project. These administrators, representing general and special education as well as school psychology, helped identify a pool of competent, hard-working, personable principals and building-based support staff. From central administration we also obtained for every school in the district data on size of enrollment, number of referrals to special education, Stanford Achievement Test (SAT) scores in reading and math, and percentage of black students enrolled.

Following conversations with principals, general education teachers, and building-based support staff, we recruited four inner city middle schools to serve as project schools. Next, five control schools were selected that matched project schools in terms of location (inner city), level (middle schools), average SAT reading and math scores, student enrollment, proportion of black students enrolled, and annual rate of referrals to special education. In comparison with all schools in the district, the nine project and control schools demonstrated lower SAT reading and math scores, a higher percentage of black enrollment, and a greater annual rate of referrals to special education.

Consultants. Associated with the four project schools were 10 school-based consultants. Five consultants were special education resource room teachers, two were school psychologists, and three were pupil personnel specialists (PPSs). The PPS was a newly created multidimensional position requiring the assessment skills of a psychologist, advising capacity of a school counselor, and family-work experience of a social worker. Among the PPSs, two were formally trained and experienced school psychologists. In addition to these school-based consultants, two graduate students with special and general education experience served as consultants, for a total of 12 consultants serving four project schools.

Teachers and pupils. Consultants in project schools helped recruit 24 fifth- and sixth-grade classroom teachers. In control schools, principals and project staff recruited an equal number of fifth- and sixth-grade educators. In each of the nine schools, classroom teachers were asked to identify their most difficult-to-teach, nonhandicapped pupil. Some of these students previously had been referred to, and were formally evaluated by, the district's Department of Psychology but were not certified for special programming. Others were more recently referred, and an evaluation had not yet been conducted. Nevertheless, a majority, despite their status as "most difficult-to-teach," had not been formally referred. In contrast to this experimental procedure of generating students to be helped through MATs, in actual implementation of MATs, teachers would make referrals for assistance as needed.

These 48 difficult-to-teach children were largely boys (71%), mostly black (65%), and approximately one grade below expectations in reading and math. These characteristics are similar to those describing pupils recommended by their teachers for evaluation (e.g., Lorion, Cowen, & Caldwell, 1974; Marston et al., 1984) and placement in special education (e.g., Rubin, Krus, & Balow, 1973). Additionally, 44% of the students were described as difficult-to-teach primarily because of "off-task" or "inattentive" behavior; 20% because of "poor academic work," despite capability to perform better; 15% because they "lacked academic skills;" 12% because of "poor interpersonal skills with adults;" 4% because of "poor interpersonal skills with peers;" and 4% because of "poor motivation." This description is in general accord with a composite characterization of students referred for possible special education placement by a large sample of classroom teachers in a study by Hutton (1985). (See Bahr, Fuchs, Stecker, Goodman, & Fuchs, 1988, for a detailed description of these difficult-to-teach children.)

Training

We conducted in-service and on-the-job training to prepare our consultants for their MAT responsibilities. The components of this training may be applicable in training school psychologists and other personnel to serve on MATs.

In-service training. Two all-day training sessions were conducted at our university for the school-based and graduate student consultants. During 14 hours consultants were trained in three areas. First, we discussed the problem-solving, collaborative, and data-based nature of BC. To improve understanding of these features, we asked consultants to role-play consultation in the context of several prepared vignettes. Corrective feedback accompanied this role-playing. Second, we trained consultants to employ the ABC observation procedure reliably. Videotapes of various nonstaged incidents of classroom conflict, scored by the ABC procedure prior to training, were used to train consultants to criterion. Third, we reviewed with consultants how to implement a broad range of behavior theory-inspired interventions, including token economies, contingency contracts, and self-management strategies. At the same time, we informed consultants that they were not bound to implement such interventions.

Each consultant received a packet of materials. The materials included (a) an agenda, (b) a two-page general description of BC, (c) brief guides to *specifying* and *analyzing* problem behavior, (d) a thick set of behavior management strategies, (e) a written script for each assigned teacher, (f) copies of all tests, questionnaires, and rating scales to be administered to teachers or pupils, (g) directions on using the ABC observation system, (h) ABC recording sheets, and (i) an audiotape to cue consultants' observations.

At the conclusion of our in-service training, we asked the 10 school-based consultants to evaluate anonymously the two-day in-service in respect to five dimensions: organization, clarity, amount of information, usefulness for consultation, and overall quality. On a 4-point scale (4 = *excellent*, 3 = *good*, 2 = *fair*, and 1 = *poor*), their rating for organization was 3.4; clarity, 3.2; amount of information, 3.6; usefulness for consultation, 3.8; and overall quality, 3.5.

On-the-job training. There was approximately a 10-day hiatus between completion of in-service training and initiation of MAT activity in the project schools. During this interval graduate students, including the two serving as consultants, visited the school-based consultants, verifying that the consultants possessed the necessary materials and an accurate understanding of the MAT sequence of activity, consultation scripts, and data-gathering procedures such as the ABC observation system. As necessary, missing materials were supplied and clarification on procedures was provided. Our impression is that this follow-up to the in-service training was very important. We believe it helped school-based consultants "get off on the right foot," and concretized our commitment to them and the project. We believe such follow-up activity in the schools is essential to the successful training of consultants, especially when they have scant background in this area.

Procedures

Sequences of consultants' activities. Table 1 displays sequences of salient consultation activities associated with our three versions of BC. In part, Table 1 graphically presents what already has been discussed. That is, Script 1 (least inclusive version) differs from Scripts 2 and 3 (more inclusive versions) in its omission of classroom visitation, whereas the uniqueness of Script 3 in relation to 2 is the more inclusive script's potential for a third classroom visit, fourth meeting, and fifth observation. Table 1 also indicates that Scripts 1 and 2 call for a 6-week consultation period, whereas Script 3 requires 5-8 weeks of consultation activity.

Multidisciplinary teams. An important distinctive feature of MAT activities, which is neither displayed in Table 1 nor described heretofore in the text, is that, irrespective of script, a multidisciplinary team met for every Meeting 2. The team comprised the classroom teacher, a school-based special educator, and either the building-based school psychologist or PPS. The presence of such a group at

TABLE 1
Sequence of Consultant Activities in Scripts 1, 2, and 3

Week	Consultant's Activity	Scripts[a]		
		1	2	3[b]
1	Meeting 1	X	X	X
	Observation 1	X	X	X
2	Observation 2	X	X	X
	Meeting 2	X	X	X
	Intervention begins	X	X	X
3	Classroom visit 1		X	X
4	Classroom visit 2		X	X
5	Observation 3	X	X	X
	Observation 4	X	X	X
	Intervention ends	X	X	X
6	Meeting 3	X	X	X
7	Modified intervention begins			?
	Classroom visit 3			?
8	Observation 5			?
	Modified intervention ends			?
	Meeting 4			?

[a]Scripts 1 and 3 represent our least and most inclusive versions of BC, respectively.

[b]Question marks in this column denote that consultants using Script 3 had an option to pursue the associated activities, depending on the evaluation of MAT effectiveness up to that point.

Meeting 2 reflects our beliefs that (a) the objectives for this meeting, including problem validation and analysis as well as the formulation of a classroom intervention, are relatively difficult and important to achieve, and (b) many heads are better than one or two, especially when they collectively represent diversity and richness in formal training and professional experience.

As Graden, Casey, and Christenson (1985) have made clear, it is possible for multidisciplinary teams to participate at numerous points in the prereferral intervention process. Teams may conduct an initial screening of requests for consultative services, identify specific areas of teacher concern, design and help implement possible classroom interventions, gather data to evaluate the efficacy of such implementations, and so forth. Why, then, did we use a team approach only in Meeting 2? Our reason was largely logistical. We were convinced that work demands on our school consultants precluded more frequent team gatherings.

If the demands on our consultants' time were less severe, it is likely we would have increased use of this approach.

Target behaviors and types of interventions. Approximately 60% of project teachers directed consultants to help them with students' off-task or inattentive behavior; about 20% of teachers targeted poor quality of work for planned interventions; and the remaining teachers wanted treatment plans to address poor relations with adults, poor relations with peers, and lack of academic skills.

A total of 22 of 24 planned interventions included delivery of some type of reinforcement contingent on display of desired behavior. In two cases, the nature of the classroom-based treatment was unclear. Among the 22 described interventions, 7 involved use of activity reinforcers, 4 included tangible reinforcement, and 3 made use of teachers' verbal praise. For 8 interventions type of reinforcement was not specified. Additionally, 17 of these 22 interventions included monitoring of pupil behavior; 5 did not. Among the monitored interventions, 5 teachers developed wall charts, 6 kept track of behavior on informally fashioned tally sheets, and 6 did not use a written record. Finally, teachers dispensed reinforcers in 17 of the 22 described interventions; an aide delivered reinforcement in one case; and 4 descriptions of interventions were unclear on this point.

Surprisingly, these planned interventions were very similar to each other. Teachers did not systematically use alternative, well-known behavioral strategies such as modeling, extinction, time-out, differential reinforcement, and shaping; there was no indication of group goal setting or use of group contingencies; and there was an absence of student self-monitoring and self-reinforcement. Even though there exists a broad array of empirically validated strategies from which teachers and consultants may choose, project teachers employed a small number of different types of interventions.

Finding the time for consultation. As described previously, our MAT project was implemented in an environment compar- atively "inhospitable" to consultation. Special educators' heavy caseloads of direct service, school psychologists' long backlogs of psychological assessments, and administrators' discomfort with preventive interventions all militated against "doing consultation." Given such conditions, an obvious question is, "How did consultation get done?"

All consultants stated they carefully scheduled times for prereferral intervention meetings, observations, and classroom visits that did not conflict with myriad school activities and obligations. Consultative meetings typically were reserved for before or after school, at lunch, or during teachers' planning time. Nevertheless, consultants reported rescheduling 25 of 76 meetings (33%) and 29 of 96 classroom observations (30%) because of *absences* of teachers, teachers' aides, consultants' aides, or students; because of *scheduling conflicts* brought on by breakdowns in communication, unplanned school activities, and teachers' forgetfulness; and because of *modifications of established timelines* such as the need to delay a second observation and second meeting because of failure to complete a first observation in timely fashion.

Each of the special education consultants said they asked their aides (if they had one) or another special education teacher or a general educator to cover their classes, freeing them for brief periods to attend to MAT activity. Two special educators employed a different strategy, asking a librarian and physical education teacher to extend class time. One special education teacher did some horse trading. She convinced the general educator with whom she was consulting that, in order for her to help plan and implement an intervention for a most difficult-to-teach nonhandicapped child, the general educator would have to agree to increase mainstreaming time for two handicapped pupils shared by both teachers. Securing the general educator's agreement not only reduced the special education teacher's direct caseload, thereby increasing opportunity for consultation, but helped to win for the two handicapped pupils additional mainstream experience, a year-long objective of the special educator.

Evaluation

By way of introduction to the report of evaluative findings, two brief comments are relevant. First, as discussed earlier, the discussion of MAT outcomes is confined to a subset of dependent measures — consultants' global evaluations of MAT success, teachers' pre- and post-MAT ratings of most difficult-to-teach pupils' targeted behavior, and pre- and post-MAT classroom observations of the same children and the same behavior. Second, our discussion of these data will be of a general nature; a more detailed, researcher-oriented exposition can be found elsewhere (see Fuchs & Fuchs, 1986; 1987).

Consultants' evaluations. On the four-point scale (1 = MATs were an unqualified failure; 2 = MATs were a qualified failure; 3 = MATs were a qualified success; and 4 = MATs were an unqualified success), consultants' mean evaluation of Script 1 (least inclusive version) was 2.0, of Script 2 (more inclusive version) was 2.8, and of Script 3 (most inclusive version), was 2.9. When taking the perspective of their consultees (that is, evaluating MAT success as they believed their teachers would), consultants assigned virtually identical mean scores to the scripts. Descriptively, such evaluations suggest that consultants and teachers were rather satisfied with the comparatively inclusive versions of BC, but were dissatisfied with the least inclusive variant. However, this difference in evaluations was not statistically significant.

Teachers' ratings. Teachers rated the severity, manageability, and tolerableness of their most difficult-to-teach pupils' target behavior on a pre- and post-MAT basis. These three ratings were aggregated to generate a single pre-MAT and post-MAT score for each student. Subtracting pre-MAT ratings from post-MAT ratings yielded the following average change scores: -.2 for control students, -.5 for Script 1 project pupils, -.9 for Script 2

pupils, and -1.0 for Script 3 pupils. In other words, teachers claimed that control students' problematic behavior decreased least; targeted behaviors of students in the most inclusive version of BC decreased most. Moreover, inferential statistical analyses indicated that the reported decreases in problem behavior associated with Scripts 2 and 3 were reliably greater than the decreases evidenced by pupils in control and Script 1 groups. Thus, teachers' ratings and the descriptive, rather than inferential, interpretation of consultants' evaluations, evidence a similar pattern: Relatively inclusive versions of BC seem to be regarded as effective and viewed with satisfaction; the least inclusive variant of BC appears to be perceived as ineffective and viewed with dissatisfaction.

Classroom observations. Observational data on difficult-to-teach pupils' problem behavior are both consistent and inconsistent with the emerging pattern in our findings. As expected, control students did not display a preintervention to postintervention decrease in targeted troublesome behavior; rather this group's behavior *increased* by 9%. Predictably, too, Script 2 pupils demonstrated a modest 6% decrease in problem behavior. However, the greatest percentage decrease in troublesome behavior (8%) was associated with the least inclusive variant of BC, or Script 1, which was the script that consultants and teachers viewed as least effective and least satisfying. Students involved with Script 3 activity surprisingly displayed no change in problem behavior from pre- to post-MAT observations. Differences among the groups' pre-to-post behavior changes "approached" (two-tailed $p = .11$), but did not "reach," the conventional threshold ($p < .05$) of statistical significance. Therefore, there was no reliable difference between the respective groups' observed behavior change.

DISCUSSION

We believe that there are at least three possible reasons for the apparent inconsistency between teacher ratings and classroom observations. First, teacher ratings may represent a forthright and precise estimate of students' classroom behavior; pupils associated with the two relatively inclusive scripts may have demonstrated, in fact, greater positive behavior change than those in the least inclusive script, but our four 30-minute classroom observation samples may have failed to detect this improvement. A second explanation starts with the somewhat different premise that the teacher ratings do not accurately reflect students' classroom behavior; that is, contrary to the ratings, children in Script 2 and 3 displayed the same preintervention-to-postintervention behavior change as students associated with Script 1. However, like the first explanation, this one assumes teacher ratings are truthful: Teachers participating in the more inclusive scripts honestly perceived a more positive transformation in their students than did teachers of children involved in the least inclusive script.

Yet a third reason begins with a presumption antithetical to that of the first; namely that the teacher ratings are less than completely honest and inaccurate. In other words, it is possible that the pupils' behavior did not improve and the teachers knew this but were reluctant to say so because they were afraid of offending their school-based colleagues who, in many instances, had worked very hard with and for them on the MAT. Presumably, teachers involved in relatively inclusive (i.e., more labor-intensive) scripts would have been more strongly oriented toward evasiveness than teachers associated with the least inclusive script. This "white lie" explanation is another way of stating that the obtained ratings were artifactual (see Sechrest & Phillips, 1979); that is, they represented an outcome of our *methodology*, rather than of our *experimental treatment*.

Having presented three different, but partially overlapping, explanations of our data, the inevitable question arises: Assuming these explanations represent all plausible interpretations, which is correct? Unfortunately, at this point, we do not know. As a result, we cannot present confidently a single set of implications or recommendations for practitioners and researchers. Instead, we feel obliged to discuss multiple sets of implications and recommendations, each one hinging on a different interpretation of the database.

Implications and Recommendations

Explanation 1. Explanation 1 promotes the verity of the teacher ratings and dismisses the observational data as unrepresentative and misleading. Accordingly, this view of our data indicates that, with respect to BC, "more is better." What does this mean? A salient characteristic distinguishing our least inclusive version from our two more inclusive variants of BC is that the more inclusive versions required consultants to visit teachers at least two times to assist with implementation of the classroom intervention. Explanation 1 posits that these visits contributed to greater positive change in student behavior, which is presumably what is reflected in the teacher ratings.

Simultaneously, this interpretation prompts the question whether school-based consultants typically make such visits. The importance of this question is underscored by the fact that many school psychologists and special educators have scant time for consultation and may view classroom visitation as desirable but unnecessary. Explanation 1 of our data contradicts this view, holding that such visits contribute to desired changes in pupil behavior.

Explanation 2. Unlike the preceding interpretation, Explanation 2 assumes that both teacher ratings and classroom observations are accurate. Although this second interpretation, like the first, supports the use of more inclusive versions of BC, this endorsement is not based on an expectation that student behavior will be positively affected. Rather, Explanation 2 argues that more inclusive variants of BC are more likely to positively change *teachers' perceptions* of students, which may or may not be linked to verifiable change in students' classroom behavior or academic performance. Lest some readers view teachers' attitude change as trivial in comparison to student behavior change, it must be emphasized that many practitioners and researchers (see, for example, Donaldson, 1980) can attest that attitude toward difficult-to-teach pupils often means the difference between willingness to modify classroom instruction and management to accommodate special learners and refusal to tolerate such students in the classroom.

Supporting the proposed causal connection between more inclusive versions of BC and positive change in teacher attitudes is the probability that our more complete versions encouraged teachers to think seriously about their difficult-to-teach pupils and, as a consequence, to become more knowledgeable about these children. According to person–perception theory (e.g., Adinolfi, 1971; Asch, 1946; Bieri et al., 1966; Bruner, Shapiro, & Tagiuri, 1958; Crockett, 1965), as one accumulates experience with, or knowledge about, another person, one's cognitive system with respect to that person becomes increasingly differentiated and articulated. This, in turn, reflects both growing awareness of the subtle differences in aspects of the other person and increasing capacity to respond differentially to such subtle differences. Fuchs, Fuchs, Dailey, and Power (1985) have demonstrated a close relation between cognitive complexity and positive attitude.

Explanation 3. Explanation 3, like Explanation 2, assumes that our observational data accurately reflect the failure of the classroom interventions to promote positive behavior change among most difficult-to-teach students. Earlier, we presented descriptions of these interventions consonant with this view. For example, among 22 interventions that used some type of reward system, 11 either did not include any form of teacher monitoring of student performance or did not require teachers to collect data during monitoring. How, one legitimately might ask, did the 11 teachers associated with these classroom treatments know whether, and if so when, to deliver reinforcement?

Whether or not more inclusive versions of BC were associated with greater positive changes in student behavior, we were not impressed with the conceptualization or execution of many classroom interventions. Our impressions were based on others' aforementioned descriptions as well as our own observations of these interventions. Their apparent low quality was surprising, since (a) we believed we had enlisted competent, hard-working school psychologists and special educators as consultants; (b) we trained the consultants for many hours and equipped them with pertinent materials; and (c) we organized them into multidisciplinary teams, believing that more heads, perspectives, and sets of skills were better than one.

Assuming our impressions to be correct, why were many interventions ineffective? Following numerous debriefings with consultants and teachers, we believe there are least two important reasons. First, despite having received training and materials, many consultants (and teachers) appeared insufficiently skilled to formulate and operationalize meaningful interventions. Second, consultants spent a good deal of time trying to engage teachers in collaborative consultation, when many of them simply wanted to be handed solutions to vexing problems. Both of these unanticipated and perplexing outcomes have influenced the nature of our project in Year 2, which we describe below.

Explanation 3, in contrast to Explanation 2, discredits also the veracity of the teacher ratings. According to this view, teachers associated with Scripts 2 and 3 indicated greater positive behavior change than those who used Script 1 because teachers in the more inclusive BC versions felt more indebted to the consultants, more compelled to tell them what they thought the consultants wished to hear. If there is truth to this explanation, teacher ratings should be viewed with a healthy dose of skepticism and, when used, should be supported by qualitatively different methods of data collection such as direct observation of behavior and/or collection of students' permanent products such as completed worksheets. How many school psychologists and special educators evaluate their consultation efforts solely on the basis of teachers' reports? How many investigators employ teacher ratings as the single outcome measure of their consultation research?

Future Directions for the MAT Project: Year 2

Inconsistency in our data and the uncertainty of our conclusions from Year 1 encouraged a reconceptualization of several facets of the MATs. Such "taking stock" resulted in several important changes that, we believe, may be of interest to practitioners and researchers involved in prereferral interventions.

Most importantly, in Year 2 we have attempted to strengthen project-related intervention by requiring use of contingency contracts and data-based monitoring procedures. These contracts between teachers and their targeted students stipulate six dimensions of the intervention: (a) the type and degree of the desired change in behavior or academic performance; (b) the activity (or activities) to which the contract applies; (c) how student behavior and academic performance will be monitored; (d) the nature of the reward; (e) when and by whom the reward will be delivered; and (f) whether the contract may be renegotiated. Contracts were selected as an intervention activity for two reasons. First, during Year 1, many of our consultants and teachers independently chose to implement contracts; second, recent surveys (e.g., Martens, Peterson, Witt, & Cirone, 1986) indicate they are viewed positively by large numbers of general educators.

Our data-based monitoring procedures involve either product inspection (for academic performance) or time interval recording (for classroom behavior). Building on the work of Meichenbaum (1977) and Meichenbaum and Asarnow (1979) as well as Hallahan and associates (e.g., Hallahan, Lloyd, Kosiewicz, Kauffman, & Graves, 1979; Hallahan, Marshall,

& Lloyd, 1981), we are exploring experimentally the effectiveness and efficiency of teacher monitoring versus student self-monitoring. (For more information on our student–teacher contracts and monitoring procedures, see Fuchs, Fuchs, Bahr, & Fernstrom, 1988).

Required use of contracts and data-based monitoring procedures, combined with continued use of written scripts, makes our consultation approach relatively directive in Year 2. We recognize that this prescriptiveness runs against the current conventional wisdom, which encourages, and may even admonish, school consultants to avoid use of heavy-handed prescriptions. Such procedures may "turn-off" consultants who view our directives as constraining, if not demeaning, and estrange teachers who are resentful of interventions that are imposed on them rather than formulated through a collaborative process to which they can lay claim.

On the other hand, many of our consultants seemed to have difficulty conceptualizing and operationalizing interventions for the classroom. A majority appeared to be in need of greater direction. Additionally, it is unclear just how nondirective or collaborative BC should be in school settings. Must the entire process, from problem identification through problem evaluation, reflect a distinctly nonprescriptive approach? Or is it possible that the degree of prescriptiveness should vary as a function of the phase in question? Perhaps consultants should be relatively directive during problem analysis or implementation and comparatively nondirective during problem identification. Contributing to our uncertainty is a consultation literature that appears to take on faith the assumption that nondirectiveness is desirable.

Despite our many questions, we believe we should, and *can*, end on a surer and more positive note. Year 1 of the MAT has been instructive in several ways. First, we have shown that even in a school system officially unsupportive of consultation prereferral intervention, including use of multidisciplinary teams, can be implemented. Finding time for such activity, however, was an unending challenge for project participants. That they succeeded more often than not is a tribute to their imagination, powers of persuasion, and commitment. Their collective fight to find time to consult dramatizes the importance of arming prospective consultants with strategies that will win support among administrators and teachers for consultation. Without knowledge of such tactics, all other information about the consultation process will ultimately mean little to practitioners.

Second, our use of written scripts, although unorthodox, succeeded in safeguarding the integrity of BC during implementation, expedited the consultation process, and functioned as a prompt to collect data in a timely manner. Also, as reported above, a majority of our consultants and teachers commented positively on the scripts. We recommend they be used as the training wheels of consultation: to be followed carefully by the neophyte, as a means of ensuring proper orientation and instilling confidence; to be discarded by the experienced consultant as unnecessary.

Third, our project illustrated operationalization of a component analysis of BC. As discussed above, its usefulness was reduced by the apparent fact that many interventions were relatively unsuccessful. Nevertheless, we remain steadfast in believing that BC, as well as other models of consultation, should be subjected to careful component analyses before practitioners are advised to implement the process lock, stock, and barrel. Since school psychologists and others engaged in consultation will always be pressured by central and building-based administrators to demonstrate efficiency, it is important to know whether short cuts can be taken without lessening the efficacy of prereferral intervention and other consultation processes.

ACKNOWLEDGMENTS

The Enhancing Instructional Program Options research project, described in this chapter, was supported by Grant No. G008530158 from the Office of Special Education in the U.S. Department of Education. This chapter does not necessarily reflect the position or policy of the U.S. Department of Education and no official endorsement by it should be inferred.

We wish to thank Mary Lynn Cantrell, Bill Erchul, Marilyn Friend, Ann Nevin, and Marty Tombari who provided wise counsel during the formative stages of this project and Jan Hawley, Kristin Palm, and Pam Stecker who helped us implement Mainstream Assistance Teams in 1985-86.

REFERENCES

Adinolfi, A. A. (1971). Relevance of person perception research to clinical psychology. *Journal of Clinical and Consulting Psychology, 37,* 167-176.

Algozzine, B. (1977). The emotionally disturbed child: Disturbed or disturbing? *Journal of Abnormal Child Psychology, 5,* 205-211.

Algozzine, B., & Ysseldyke, J. E., (1981). Special education services for normal children: Better safe than sorry. *Exceptional Children, 48,* 238-243.

Allington, R. (1980). Teacher interruption behavior during primary grade oral reading. *Journal of Educational Psychology, 72,* 371-377.

Alpert, J. L., & Yammer, D. M. (1983). Research in school consultation: A content analysis of selected journals. *Professional Psychology, 14,* 604-612.

Anderson-Inman, L. (1987). Consistency of performance across classrooms: Instructional materials versus setting as influencing variables. *The Journal of Special Education, 21,* 9-29.

Annual Report to Congress. (1984). *Sixth annual report to Congress on the implementation of Public Law 94-142: The Education for All Handicapped Children Act.* Washington, DC: U. S. Department of Education.

Asch, S. E. (1946). Forming impressions of personality. *Journal of Abnormal and Social Psychology, 41,* 258-290.

Bahr, M. W., Fuchs, D., Stecker, P. M., Goodman, R., & Fuchs, L. S. (April, 1988). *Difficult-to-teach pupils: Implications for prereferral intervention.* Paper presented at the annual meeting of the National Association of School Psychologists, Chicago.

Bergan, J. R. (1977). *Behavioral consultation.* Columbus, OH: Merrill.

Bergan, J. R., & Tombari, M. L. (1976). Consultant skill and efficiency and the implementation and outcomes of consultation. *Journal of School Psychology, 14,* 3-14.

Bieri, J., Atkins, A. L., Briar, S., Leaman, R. L., Miller, H., & Tripodi, T. (1966). *Clinical and social judgment.* New York: Wiley.

Bruner, J. S., Shapiro, D., & Tagiuri, R. (1958). The meaning of traits in isolation and in combination. In R. Tagiuri & L. Petrullo (Eds.), *Person perception and interpersonal behavior.* Stanford: Stanford University Press.

Cantrell, R. P., & Cantrell, M. L. (1976). Preventive mainstreaming: Impact of a supportive services program on pupils. *Exceptional Children, 42,* 381-386.

Cantrell, R. P., & Cantrell, M. L. (1977). Evaluation of a heuristic approach to solving children's problems. *Peabody Journal of Education, 54,* 168-173.

Cantrell, R. P., & Cantrell, M. L. (1980). Ecological problem solving: A decision making heuristic for prevention-intervention education strategies. In J. Hogg & P. J. Mittler (Eds.), *Advances in mental handicap research* (Vol. 1). New York: Wiley.

Chalfant, J. C., Pysh, M. V., & Moultrie, R. (1979). Teacher assistance teams: A model for within-building problem solving. *Learning Disability Quarterly, 2,* 85-96.

Conoley, J. C., & Conoley, C. W. (1982). The effects of two conditions on student-teacher problem descriptions and remedial plans. *Journal of School Psychology, 20,* 325-328.

Crockett, W. H. (1965). Cognitive complexity and impression formation. In B. A. Maher (Ed.), *Progress in experimental personality research* (Vol. 2). New York: Academic.

Curtis, M. J., Zins, J. E., & Graden, J. L. (1987). Prereferral intervention programs: Enhancing student performance in regular education settings. In C. A. Maher & J. E. Zins (Eds.), *Psychoeducational interventions in schools: Methods and procedures for enhancing student competence.* (pp. 7-25). Elmsford, NY: Pergamon.

Donaldson, J. (1980). Changing attitudes toward handicapped persons: A review and analysis of research. *Exceptional Children, 46,* 504-514.

Foster, G. G., Ysseldyke, J. E., Casey, A., & Thurlow, M. L. (1984). The congruence between reason for referral and placement outcome. *Journal of Psychoeducational Assessment, 2,* 209-217.

Fuchs, D., & Fuchs, L. S. (December, 1986). *Preliminary findings from the Mainstream Assistance Teams project.* Invited address presented at a colloquium sponsored by the Oregon School Psychology Association and University of Oregon's Visiting Scholar's Fund, Eugene, Oregon.

Fuchs, D., & Fuchs, L. S. (November, 1987). Mainstream Assistance Teams. In N. Safer (Chair), *Directive vs. nondirective approaches to prereferral intervention: Implications for school-based consultation.* Symposium presented at the annual meeting of the Teacher Education Division of the Council for Exceptional Children, Washington, DC.

Fuchs, D., Fuchs, L. S., Bahr, M. W., & Fernstrom, P. (April, 1988). *Mainstream Assistance Teams: Student-teacher contracts as prereferral intervention.* Paper presented at the annual meeting of the American Educational Research Association, New Orleans.

Fuchs, D., Fuchs, L. S., Dailey, A. M., & Power, M. H. (1985). The effect of examiners' personal familiarity and professional experience on handicapped children's test performance. *Journal of Educational Research, 78,* 141-146.

Gallup, A. (1984). The Gallup poll of teachers' attitudes toward the public schools. *Phi Delta Kappan, 66,* 97-107.

Gerber, M. M., & Semmel, M. I. (1984). Teacher as imperfect test: Reconceptualizing the referral process. *Educational Psychologist, 19,* 137-148.

Gibson, S., & Dembo, M. H. (1984). Teacher efficacy: A construct validation. *Journal of Educational Psychology, 76,* 569-582.

Graden, J. L., Casey, A., & Bonstrom, O. (1985). Implementing a prereferral intervention system: Part II. The data. *Exceptional Children, 51,* 487-496.

Graden, J. L., Casey, A., & Christenson, S. L. (1985). Implementing a prereferral intervention system: Part I. The model. *Exceptional Children, 51,* 377-384.

Gresham, F. M. (March 19, 1982). *Handbook for behavioral consultation.* Unpublished manuscript, Louisiana State University.

Hallahan, D. P., Lloyd, J., Kosiewicz, M. M., Kauffman, J. M., & Graves, A. W. (1979). Self-monitoring of attention as a treatment for a learning disabled boy's off-task behavior. *Learning Disability Quarterly, 2,* 24-32.

Hallahan, D. P., Marshall, K. J., & Lloyd, J. W. (1981). Self-recording during group instruction: Effects on attention to task. *Learning Disability Quarterly, 4,* 413.

Hutton, J. B. (1985). What reasons are given by teachers who refer problem behavior students? *Psychology in the Schools, 22,* 79-82.

Johnson, D. W., & Johnson, R. T. (1986). Mainstreaming and cooperative learning strategies. *Exceptional Children, 52,* 553-561.

Jones, R. L. (1972). Labels and stigma in special education. *Exceptional Children, 38*, 553-564.

Lambert, N. M. (1981). School psychology training for the decades ahead, or rivers, streams, and creeks — currents and tributaries to the sea. *School Psychology Review, 10*, 194-205.

Lietz, J. J., & Gregory, M. K. (1978). Pupil race and sex determinations of office and exceptional educational referrals. *Educational Research Quarterly, 3*, 61-66.

Lorion, R. P., Cowen, E. L., & Caldwell, R. A. (1974). Problem types of children referred to a school-based mental health program: Identification and outcome. *Journal of Consulting and Clinical Psychology, 42*, 491-496.

Marston, D., Mirkin, P. K., & Deno, S. L. (1984). Curriculum-based measurement of academic skills: An alternative to traditional screening, referral and identification. *The Journal of Special Education, 18*, 109-117.

Martens, B. K., Peterson, R. L., Witt, J. C., & Cirone, S. (1986). Teacher perceptions of school-based interventions. *Exceptional Children, 53*, 213-233.

Medway, F. J. (1982). School consultation research: Past trends and future directions. *Professional Psychology, 13*, 422-430.

Meichenbaum, D. (1977). *Cognitive behavior modification: An integrative approach.* New York: Plenum.

Meichenbaum, D., & Asarnow, J. (1979). Cognitive-behavioral modification and metacognitive development: Implications for the classroom. In P. C. Kendall & S. D. Hollon (Eds.), *Cognitive-Behavioral interventions: Theory, research, and procedures.* New York: Academic.

Meyers, J., Pitt, N. W., Gaughan, E. J., & Freidman, M. P. (1978). A research model for consultation with teachers. *Journal of School Psychology, 16*, 137-145.

Mosenthal, P. (1984). The problem of partial specification in translating reading research into practice. *Elementary School Journal, 85*, 1-28.

Odden, A. (1986). Sources of funding for education reform. *Phi Delta Kappan, 67*, 335-340.

Parish, J. (1983). Excellence in education: Tennessee's "master" plan. *Phi Delta Kappan, 64*, 722-724.

Pate-Bain, H. (1983). A teacher's point of view on the Tennessee master teacher plan. *Phi Delta Kappan, 64*, 725-726.

Pipho, C. (1986). Kappan special report: States move reform closer to reality. *Phi Delta Kappan, 68*, 1-8.

Quay, H. C., & Peterson, D. R. (1983). *Revised behavior problem checklist.* Herbert C. Quay, P. O. Box 248074, University of Miami, Coral Gables, FL 33124.

Reynolds, M. C., & Balow, B. (1972). Categories and variables in special education. *Exceptional Children, 38*, 357-366.

Ritter, D. (1978). Effects of a school consultation program upon referral patterns of teachers. *Psychology in the Schools, 15*, 239-242.

Rubin, R. A., & Balow, B. (1971). Learning and behavior disorders: A longitudinal study. *Exceptional Children, 37*, 293-299.

Rubin, R. A., Krus, P., & Balow, B. (1973). Factors in special class placement. *Exceptional Children, 39*, 525-532.

Salvia, J., & Ysseldyke, J. E. (1985). *Assessment in special and remedial education* (3rd ed.). Boston: Houghton Mifflin.

Sechrest, L., & Phillips, M. (1979). Unobtrusive measures: An overview. In L. Sechrest (Ed.), *Unobtrusive measurement today* (pp. 1-17). San Francisco: Jossey-Bass.

Shepard, L., Smith, M. L., & Vojir, C. P. (1983). Characteristics of pupils identified as learning disabled. *American Educational Research Journal, 20*, 309-331.

Singer, J. D., & Butler, J. A. (1987). The Education for All Handicapped Children Act: Schools as agents of social reform. *Harvard Educational Review, 57*, 125-152.

Slavin, R. E., Leavey, M. B., & Madden, N. A. (1984). Combining cooperative learning and individualized instruction: Effects on student mathematics achievement, attitudes, and behaviors. *Elementary School Journal, 84*, 410-422.

Stallings, J. (1983). *Stallings observation system.* Unpublished paper. (Available from J. A. Stallings, College of Education, University of Houston, TX.)

Tobias, S., Cole, C., Zibrin, M., & Bodlakova, V. (1982). Teacher-student ethnicity and recommendations for special education referrals. *Journal of Educational Psychology, 74*, 72-76.

Tombari, M., & Davis, R. A. (1979). Behavioral consultation. In G. D. Phye & D. J. Reschly (Eds.), *School psychology: Perspectives and issues* (pp. 281-307). New York: Academic.

Tucker, J. A. (1980). Ethnic proportions in classes for the learning disabled: Issues in nonbiased assessment. *The Journal of Special Education, 14*, 93-105.

Wang, M. C., Gennari, P., & Waxman, H. C. (1985). The adaptive learning environments model: Design, implementation, and effects. In M. C. Wang & H. J. Walberg (Eds.), *Adapting instruction to individual differences.* Berkeley, CA: McCutchan.

Wang, M. C., Reynolds, M. C., & Walberg, H. J. (1985). *Rethinking special education.* Paper presented at the Wingspread Conference on Education of Students with Special Needs, Racine, WI.

Weatherly, R., & Lipsky, M. (1977). Street level bureaucrats and institutional innovation: Implementing special education reform. *Harvard Educational Review, 47,* 171-197.

Will, M. (1986). Educating children with learning problems: A shared responsibility. *Exceptional Children, 52,* 411-415.

Witt, J. C. (1986). Teachers' resistance to the use of school-based interventions. *Journal of School Psychology, 24,* 37-44.

Witt, J. C., & Elliott, S. N. (1983). Assessment in behavioral consultation: The initial interview. *School Psychology Review, 12,* 42-49.

Ysseldyke, J. E., Algozzine, B., Regan, R., & McGue, M. (1981). The influences of test scores and naturally-occurring pupil characteristics on psychoeducational decision making with children. *Journal of School Psychology, 19,* 167-177.

Ysseldyke, J. E., Christenson, S., Pianta, B., & Algozzine, B. (1983). An analysis of teachers' reasons and desired outcomes for students referred for psychoeducational assessment. *Journal of Psychoeducational Assessment, 1,* 73-83.

Ysseldyke, J. E., & Thurlow, M. L. (Eds.). (1980). *The special education assessment and decision making process: Seven case studies* (Research Report No. 44). Minneapolis: University of Minnesota Institute for Research on Learning Disabilities.

Ysseldyke, J. E., & Thurlow, M. L. (1983). *Integration of five years of research on referral* (Research Report No. 143). Minneapolis: University of Minnesota Institute for Research on Learning Disabilities.

Ysseldyke, J. E., & Thurlow, M. L. (1984). Assessment practice in special education: Adequacy and appropriateness. *Educational Psychologist, 19,* 123-136.

Ysseldyke, J. E., Thurlow, M. L., Graden, J., Wesson, C., Algozzine, B., & Deno, S. L. (1983). Generalizations from five years of research on assessment and decision making. *Exceptional Education Quarterly, 4,* 75-93.

5

Institutionalization of a Consultation-Based Service Delivery System

**Naomi Lennox and
Irwin A. Hyman**
Temple University
Candice A. Hughes
Zurich, Switzerland

INTRODUCTION

There is ample evidence that demonstrates the efficacy of consultation procedures, but they are often difficult to implement in an educational setting (Fullan, Miles, & Taylor, 1980; Mannino & Shore, 1975; Medway, 1979). Two recent developments in New Jersey have served to bring the adoption and implementation of an indirect, consultation model of service delivery by child study teams closer to reality. The first was the addition of consultation as a specific role for child study team members in the 1984 revision of the New Jersey Administrative Code rules and regulations governing special education in the state (New Jersey State Department of Education, 1984). The second development was the recommendation contained in the report of the New Jersey Special Education Study Commission (1985) for a redefinition of the child study team as an educational support team whose primary role would be the provision of indirect, consultation-based services to children in both regular and special education programs. This commission, appointed in 1982 by the New Jersey Commissioner of Education, was charged with identifying and addressing the issues associated with prevailing national and state special education practices. In January 1986, the New Jersey Department of Education released a policy statement supporting the commission's recommendation, and indeed further sanctioned it by stipulating child study team involvement in district prereferral procedures. The impact of these two events was to both legitimize and publicize the consultation services delivery model as a primary focus for child study team members.

School districts seeking to implement a consultation service delivery system need to address several factors in the conceptualization, planning, and implementation of such efforts. First, change leaders must have knowledge and understanding of what educational change entails, with regard both to process and to the influences that are instrumental to its success. Second, the proposed change, or innovation, must be fully described and understandable to prospective users to facilitate its adoption and implementation. Finally, efforts to initiate innovative professional practice should be carefully planned, monitored, and evaluated.

The project described in this chapter evolved from a series of events that led to the utilization of both external and internal change agents in an effort to bring about needed changes in service delivery provided by the multidisciplinary teams in the district. Two distinct phases are described in the chapter: the preparatory phase, which covers the first 4 years of the project, and the institutionalization phase, which covers years 5 and 6. An important factor in this project was the collection each year of both quantitative and qualitative data that served to shape the project. The results of this data collection are presented in the project evaluation section. Finally, the last section provides a broad discussion of the organizational and personal factors that served to both facilitate and to inhibit the implementation of the consultation model in this urban school district.

BACKGROUND

The student population of the school district in which this project took place is approximately 14,250 and is composed of 75% black, 12% white, 12% Latino, and 1% other students. The number of students receiving special education, exclusive of speech therapy, amounts to 2,011, representing 14% of the total population. The district is serviced by 13 child study teams each consisting of a school social worker, school psychologist, and learning disabilities consultant.

This project developed from a rather unusual set of circumstances. The school district is typical of many midsized cities throughout the country that are struggling for economic survival. A declining tax base, racial tensions, and paralyzing political struggles brought the district to the attention of the State Department of Education (State Education Authority — SEA). In an action unprecedented in New Jersey, the SEA seized control of the policy and operational functions of the school board. Each department of the school district was assigned an SEA monitor who was responsible for overseeing its operations. At this time, a local college received a contract to conduct a needs assessment of the teachers. The results indicated that their number 1 priority was school discipline. Consequently, the director of special pupil services invited the National Center for the Study of Corporal Punishment and Alternatives in the Schools at Temple University to submit a proposal to address the district's needs in the area of discipline. This proposal was then submitted to the SDE as part of its application for special education funds.

Although the primary target was discipline, a secondary goal was systems change related to the delivery of child study team services.

This unique opportunity created a situation in which a variety of organizational, behavioral, and mental health consultation approaches to change could be utilized. The school district benefited from the input of graduate students in school psychology who were developing skills in consultation, program evaluation, and organizational change. The university benefited from the opportunity to work with experienced educators desiring a vehicle to bring about change.

The initial change model was based on the concept of parallel systems (Hyman, 1977). This model states that change is best achieved by working with those most interested in it, without any overt or covert pressure to recruit those who do not wish to participate. This model is consistent with a collaborative model of consultation (Caplan, 1970; Meyers, 1973).

Formative evaluation is an important element in parallel systems theory (Hyman 1972, 1977). It is assumed that the demonstrated effectiveness of an innovation will attract others who have been initially resistant to the innovation. Therefore, ongoing evaluation was built into the proposal in order to document positive change and to make corrections when needed. Another important aspect of this proposal was the multiplier effect, which was accomplished by having university consultants train school personnel who then became in-district trainers.

This 6-year project is described in terms of two phases: a preparatory phase and an institutionalization phase. The first 4 years were the preparatory phase and had as a focus the work of the university staff. The goal of the first year, which was the entry year, was to establish communication and build trust at the local school level. The focus for the second year was initiating and demonstrating the effectiveness of short-term consultation projects. Third year plans included continuing and expanding ongoing consultation projects and building trust with central office administrators. The fourth year was designed to train child study personnel in consultation approaches as preparation for the comprehensive implementation of the model.

Years 5 and 6 are considered the institutionalization phase of the project, as the focus was on the activities of the in-district staff. Plans for year 5 included the utilization of a consultation approach by three teams, continued training of staff in consultation, and the collection of data for formative evaluation. A long-term process is necessary as change efforts generally require at least 3 years before substantial results can be anticipated (Fullan et al., 1980).

Preparatory Phase

Year 1: Entry into the system. The first year of this project was devoted to establishing communication and trust. The project staff sent detailed questionnaires, based on the results of the needs assessment, that dealt with specific needs in the area of school discipline to every teacher and administrator in the district. School staff were then given the opportunity to indicate which areas of discipline were of most interest. Advanced graduate students were assigned to schools that expressed the desire to participate in the training project, and they worked with teachers using a consultation approach. One purpose of providing this service was to model the approach for the staff school psychologists in order to generate interest regarding a consultation model. Each student consultant was teamed with the local school child study team and was directly supervised by the university professor. Graduate student consultants were, in general, assigned to work with discipline problems and they acted in many cases as a prereferral service provider. Interestingly, it took great effort and persuasion to maintain a consultative rather than a diagnostic role as some school administrators tried to pressure the graduate student consultants into testing district students.

In order to initiate the multiplier effect, a "turnkey program" was established during the first year. (The term *turnkey* was suggested by one of the school administrators, who felt that these professionals would be the key to the success of the change effort in the district.) A course on school discipline was offered to all staff in the district. The curriculum of the course included the theory, research, and practice of school discipline. Fifteen child study team specialists and five teachers participated in the course during the first year. Classes met weekly after school hours in the district's administration building. The course was conducted by the university project manager. Most of the participants became involved out of interest in the topic, but some opted for district in-service credits, which could be used for advancement on the pay scale. An option of university graduate credit was also offered but not used by any participants. Toward the end of the year, participants were encouraged to become turnkeys by conducting projects and disseminating their knowledge during the next academic year.

Year 2: Initiating short-term consultation projects. During the second year, the scope of the project expanded in many directions. A major goal was to publicize the concept of the expanded role of child study specialists as consultants. The project continued to utilize graduate students to model the consultation role.

Several schools became centers for organization development efforts that went beyond individual teacher consultation. One junior high school focused on the teaching styles of individual teachers by using the Flanders System of Interactional Analysis (Amidon & Flanders, 1971). In another building, all teachers assessed classroom climate along the dimensions of authoritative–democratic leadership styles by using the Hyman A-D Scale (Hyman, 1964, 1986; Hyman & Lamberth, 1987). This scale measures teaching styles that foster internal versus external control and predicts the behavior of students in the absence of the teacher. Extensive resources were focused on these schools to avoid diluting the organizational change efforts.

The in-service course continued over the second year at two levels, again including teachers and child study personnel. Among the participants in the second year were teachers who developed school discipline codes, and participated in in-service training of peers. Two school psychologists in the original group participated as trainers with the university instructor during the second year. They were paid by the district for conducting this in-service. This group coalesced as the core for the turnkey program. In addition to the content of the course, the group began to discuss ways to implement organizational and individual consultation.

Year 3: Expanding consultation projects. A major goal during the third year was to establish the project as a clearly identifiable entity to all administrators in the district. This outcome was generally accomplished with the central office administration. However, only the five building-level administrators who originally requested services had become cognizant of the model by the beginning of the third year. Twenty other principals were essentially unaware of the project. The initial success of the program was a mixed blessing. Staff were assigned to several schools that were experiencing disciplinary problems but had not requested services. True to consultation theory, the project was unable to succeed in those buildings where endorsement by local administrators was lacking. In retrospect, the invitation of upper-echelon administrators who invited the project staff into the schools without the support of the local principals should have been resisted without more thorough discussion and coordination with building-level administrators. However, the need to broaden the project's base seemed to leave little choice at the time. These failure experiences constituted only a minor portion of the total efforts, but they reinforce the principle of collaborative efforts with gatekeepers.

During the first 3 years extensive annual reports were completed and submitted to central office administrators and to the State Department of Education. In addition, executive summaries were provided to building-level administrators. These reports contained comprehensive documentation regarding the various activities of the consultation project. Most impressive was one activity involving truancy at a junior high school for emotionally disturbed students. At the beginning of the project, this school had the highest rate of truancy in the district. After 2½ years of the organizational interventions, this school's truancy rate was the lowest of all the junior high schools. One of the activities generated from this school was the introduction of an automatic calling system to notify parents immediately when students were absent, which in turn resulted in a general increase in the communication between the school, teachers, and parents. Another outcome was the development of a computerized discipline reporting system (Berkowitz, Hyman, & Lally, 1984).

The state monitoring team left the district during the third year; therefore the trust that had been established between district and university personnel during the first 2 years was crucial for maintaining the project. Much effort was expended by the university consultants to establish their roles as outsiders who provided valuable services. As external consultants, they were able to accomplish goals that seemed unattainable to in-district staff. This was true in part because child study staff were viewed within the context of special education. Upper echelon administrators seemed unable to separate child study staff from the role of assessment, a perception clearly based on precedents established through funding legislation.

In the spring of the third year, the administration committed time and resources to the training of child study staff as consultants. As a result, a core group of turnkeys met twice a month for half-day training sessions from January to June. In addition to reviewing literature on discipline, teacher efficacy, observational systems, and an overview of consultation, the sessions also focused on planning the implementation of a limited consultation model during the fourth year of the project. The university project director encouraged staff to utilize an organization development model with targeted schools. However, district staff overwhelmingly favored consultee-centered consultation.

The original plan of the university project director was to use only participants who had been involved as turnkeys to implement the consultation model during the year. As predicted by the theory of parallel systems (Hyman, 1972, 1977), the success of the program resulted in interest by other staff, who subsequently asked to participate. The director of special pupil services decided to include staff who had not participated in any previous aspects of the project with the goal of expanding the project.

Year 4: Staff training for institutionalization. During the fourth year, the major goal of the project was training child study staff in various approaches to consultation. Sessions were similar to a university course in consultation and included lectures, readings, and discussions. A group of approximately twenty school psychologists, school social workers, and learning disability consultants met one-half day, twice monthly. Since there were many new people in the program, it was decided that the course would remain at a didactic level. Caution in attempting actual consultations was necessary for a variety of reasons: heavy diagnostic caseloads, limitations in supervisory time, and lack of appropriate procedures for implementation at a level that would assure success. Finally, many of the participants functioned on teams with other staff who were not part of this group. As all team members must be involved in making decisions regarding full evaluations, it was anticipated that this might create problems in case distribution and flow.

During the last few months of the school year, staff and department administrators discussed several plans to implement the consultation model. At the end of the school year, funding for the outside, university-based consultant was terminated. During the summer, the senior author, who was a participant in the training, assumed an administrative position in the department. Encouraged by the enthusiasm of the child study professionals to move from the traditional diagnostic role to a consultative one, and with the support of the director of special pupil services, a pilot implementation plan for consultation services was developed. The director's willingness to attempt this change was predicated on the assumption that all mandated responsibilities, such as the processing of new referrals, triennial reevaluations, and annual reviews would be completed within state time guidelines.

Institutionalization Phase

Year 5: Implementation of pilot consultation model. The decision to implement a pilot consultation model at this time was based on a number of factors, including concerns associated with special education programming, consumer satisfaction, the increasing dropout rate of special education students, and team morale. At the beginning of the fifth year the percentage of students in special education programs statewide was 11.8, quickly approaching the 12% guideline suggested by Public Law 94-142. In-district special education classes were being filled as early as October. Self-contained, in-district special education classes had been created yearly, at the rate of one or two a year, aggregating to a total of 100 classes. Not only were start-up costs for new classes a problem, but there was a serious lack of available space. Despite their best intentions, team personnel were forced to recommend placements in county and private out-of-district programs for newly classified students. These placements not only were costly to the district but may have been more restrictive than some students needed. In addition, other students, who might have benefited from self-contained classes were being served, at least temporarily, in resource rooms or supplementary instructional programs.

Special Pupil Services Department philosophy had always been to discourage unnecessary referrals and to organize special education to operate as a rotating process ("admit some, release some") but this rarely happened. For years department administrators had encouraged child study team members to move more students from special education programs back to the mainstream, but other than the issuance of occasional directives, no formal systemic procedure was instituted to facilitate this request. Consequently, less than 1% of the special education population had been declassified.

Finally, in reviewing the number of referrals for the previous year (the fourth year of the project), the project manager noted that 98% of referrals received were processed as full evaluations. The research of Christenson, Ysseldyke, and Algozzine (1982) found that 92% of students who were referred were evaluated and of those, 73% were subsequently placed in special education. On the basis of those findings, given the district's current rate of accepting approximately 200 referrals for evaluation yearly, it could be anticipated that 146 students might be added to the special education roles.

In addition to the obvious financial and practical problems encountered in serving the growing special education population, the Department of Special Pupil Services had serious ethical concerns regarding the process of classification and placement. The major concerns were related to the number of years students spent in special education, the lack of academic gain and continued school failure, the dropout rate of special education students, and the emergence of social and emotional problems as the students continued in the special education program. It was found that once students were classified and assigned to special education, they tended to continue in the program for the entirety of their school careers. In reviews of individual student files, it was noted that some students classified as perceptually impaired were in special education programs for 9 years or more, even though this is the mildest form of learning disability. In fact, some students initially classified in this category were reclassified as emotion-

ally disturbed upon reevaluation. In many cases, the disparity between ability and academic functioning appeared to widen the longer the student remained in special education. Teachers' expectations for students in special education appeared to be lowered, thus compounding the cyclical problem of never attaining the academic levels needed to return to the mainstream. It was also found that a significant number of special education students dropped out of school before graduation. Historically, 150 special education students would enter the high school but only 15 of this group would graduate.

Another factor in the decision to implement a districtwide consultation model was the department administrators' perception that this service delivery model would improve child study team services. Furthermore, consultation focusing on one problem child could lead to improved teacher functioning with similar children. Through consultation, the child study team specialists would become more familiar with ongoing student behavior in the classroom and with the services available in general education. This awareness could help in designing more practical recommendations for students in mainstream programs. In addition, positive interactions between child study team specialists and other school staff could lead to broader expectations with regard to department members' job functions. The traditional strictly diagnostic role seemed to generate the expectation that a deviant student would be removed from the classroom. Consequently, when the student was not removed, teachers were often frustrated.

Finally, the use of consultation would also address problems of staff morale, for both teachers and child study specialists. Principals and teachers had historically complained that child study staff rarely became involved in daily classroom problems. This was a realistic perception because child study staff had been alerted to guard against becoming crisis teams as this role interfered considerably with time management and delayed mandated assessment activities. Teachers' concerns, however, were serious and needed to be considered a substantive focus for team staff. Schmuck (1982) noted that teachers, students, and administrators will more likely be motivated and become more productive if their achievement, affiliation, and influence needs can be satisfied in their school life. It was hoped that by collaborating with a specialist and gaining control over persistent classroom problems, teachers would enhance their effectiveness. Similarly, it was anticipated that broadening the role of the child study staff would boost their morale. Increasing numbers of children had been classified and placed with little indication upon reevaluation that academic progress had been achieved. The knowledge that few children had made the gains necessary to return to the mainstream or be declassified was disillusioning.

Project goals and directions for the fifth year were developed to address the aforementioned concerns. These included (a) increasing teachers' efficiency and satisfaction, (b) improving students' social problem-solving and academic skills, (c) improving home and school relationships, (d) reducing the number of cases inappropriately processed for full evaluations and placement, and (e) increasing the movement of special education students to less restrictive settings.

Staff reorganization. Many of the child study staff felt that they had been utilizing various forms of consultation, but these activities were spontaneous, unsustained, and lacked an evaluative component. Understanding that systems are naturally resistant to change (Sarason, 1971), the project manager decided that a formal declaration was needed to mobilize and validate child study team efforts in consultation. In an effort to formalize the consultation approach during the fifth year and to incorporate an evaluation component, team responsibilities were reorganized. Previously, there were 10 teams divided into five geographic units, with two teams servicing each area. The teams had latitude in deciding how they assumed their responsibilities. To facilitate the consultation process, the units were reorganized into

A and B teams. A teams were responsible for evaluation, classifying, and placing new referrals and special education students transferring into the district and for serving the general education classes. B teams were responsible for reevaluating and monitoring special education students and servicing the special education classes in their catchment area. In addition, there were also four teams on special assignment who served two special education facilities, the high school, bilingual students, and a kindergarten intervention program. Two A and two B teams were defined as consultation teams. Ideally, in order to assess the effectiveness of the consultation role, experimental and control teams would be established by random assignment or careful matching on all significant independent variables. This was not possible in this situation. Instead, the consultation groups were matched according to the project manager's personal knowledge of the schools involved with respect to discipline problems, academic levels of the students in the general education area, and students' socioeconomic status (SES). A fifth team, the bilingual team, asked to be part of the project because of their former participation in the consultation training sessions.

Another problem that needed to be resolved before assuming a consultation mode was the existence of a quota system for teams to complete 66 full evaluation cases yearly. This quota had been initiated several years previously when the district was cited for noncompliance because of a backlog of cases. The director of special pupil services, who was supportive of the consultation project, authorized the removal of the quota system.

Staff training. The levels of training and experience with school consultation among team members varied. In keeping with the tradition already established by the external university-based consultant, a decision was made to implement an ongoing training program. The consultation teams met twice each month, once for ongoing case conferencing and once for skills development. These meetings were led by the project manager, who had extensive training in the area of consultation. During the case conference meetings, consultants discussed their unique situations, received peer support, and generated solutions for problems. Skills development included focusing on personality variables of consultants, resistance factors of consultees and consultants, communication skills, and behavioral consultation. A survey at the end of the school year indicated that the consultants felt that there were too many training sessions, and that they preferred the smaller case conference groups to the larger skills development sessions. Consequently, in the sixth year the meetings were condensed to six case conference meetings and four skills development meetings. The sessions lasted 2 hours each. In the fifth year of the project participants received approximately 40 hours of formal training and in the sixth year training was reduced to 20 hours. Unfortunately, this was probably not enough to expect major results to occur, and was considerably less than the 160 hours per year suggested by Fullan et al. (1980). In fact, it was felt that fewer than 24 hours of training could lead to a decline in the functioning of a consultation project, because problems are often generated that cannot be resolved in such a short time. Although the project manager was willing to devote the time, staff felt that the pressure to complete other duties precluded additional time commitments.

In addition to improving knowledge and skills, the monthly meetings provided a forum for the "collaborative energy" of the staff in which problems would be worked on in a productive manner. These meetings also allowed for project manager to support participants' efforts.

Consultation progress reports. The progress report form (see Figure 1) was developed to structure the consultation process. The form was oriented toward behavioral consultation and was arranged to provide step-by-step procedures for the consultant to follow. Referral problems were to be defined in behavioral terms. Consultees were encouraged to collect baseline data, set reasonable goals, and select intervention strategies based on the referral problem, and the consultee's and the consultant's knowledge, skills, and receptiveness. Evaluation of the intervention was to be determined by gathering postconsultation data using the original measures. The consultant and the consultee were asked to sign the form to establish collaborative responsibility for the process. Also included on the form was clarification of the level of intervention based on Meyers (1973) conceptualization. This dimension was included as a reminder for consultants to explore interventions on as many levels as possible.

Level I recognizes the modification of the behavior of a client or clients through the direct action of the consultant. The consultant intervenes directly by testing, interviewing, or counseling. Level II recognizes client change through an intervention provided by a consultee. The consultant's role is to work with the consultee to maximize intervention effectiveness. The goal of Level III is a change in the skills, knowledge, self-confidence, or objectivity of the consultee. It is assumed that a change in the consultee will result in benefits for the client or subsequent clients. The goal of Level IV is to improve the organizational functioning of the system as a whole, which should help both consultees and clients. Although not stated explicitly, there was a press in this project to produce more Level IV interventions as the intent was to influence the largest numbers of clients.

Consultants were asked to complete and submit progress reports to the project manager as soon as projects were completed. If interventions chosen were found to be ineffective, it was expected that the consultant would continue working with the consultee to design new intervention programs.

In attempting to model the collaborative process, the project manager allowed the consultants to choose the numbers and types of projects in which they wanted to become involved. The only directive was that at least one project be chosen for the year. Membrs of the A teams were to process all new requests for assistance as

FIGURE 1
Consultation Progress Report

	Date	Time Started	Time Finished	Total Hours
Consultee: _____	_____	_____	_____	_____
Position: _____	_____	_____	_____	_____
Class: _____	_____	_____	_____	_____
Consultant: _____	_____	_____	_____	_____

1. Identification of Problem:

2. Gathering Data:

Type   Person Responsible   Due Date

3. Setting Goals:

4. Selecting Intervention Strategies:

    Level   Strategy

5. Evaluation of Intervention:

Evaluation Measures   Person Responsible   Due Date

6. Conclusion:

    _____ Intervention Effective   _____ Intervention Ineffective
    _____ Terminate Services   _____ Set New Goals
                _____ Refer for Complete Evaluation

7. Comments:

_____   _____
  Consultee Signature   Consultant Signature

Level

I   — Direct service to student.
II — Indirect service to student through consultee.
III — Direct service to consultee.
IV — Service to organization.

"referrals for evaluation." The team was to decide after gathering initial data if the referral could be handled as a behavioral consultation case or if a full testing evaluation was indicated. The team also was to decide on the basis of the referral problem, which team member(s) would be the most appropriate to intervene. B teams were asked to focus their consultation projects on the needs of the special education student and teacher. A request for consultation services form was distributed to all special education teachers. There was some debate as to whether these forms should be processed through the principal's office. The group suspected that most teachers would be reluctant to ask for help if it came to the attention of the principal and decided to have the forms returned to the team directly. The form requested a short overview of the problem and an indication of the times the teacher was available for consultation. Although these forms were distributed to the special education teachers, there was little response. Unfortunately, because of limited resources, the reasons for the small number of referral requests could not be assessed at this time.

Year 6: Modification and expansion. The procedures of the previous year were maintained during the sixth year, but a reorganization of schools and special education classes forced the transfer of some consultation team personnel to new schools. As mentioned previously, the twice monthly meetings were reduced to one monthly meeting. At the end of the fifth year, some staff members not previously involved in the project expressed concern that it had produced an "elite" group of which they were not part. They suggested that involvement in the project, or at least the consultation training, be extended to all team personnel. This action was taken during the sixth year, but only two additional professionals joined the group. Project participants also requested that all principals and central office administrators be made aware of the intention of the department to move away from assessment, classification, and placement to more involvement in utilizing alternative interventions in the general education area. The project manager presented this information at an annual administrators' in-service at the beginning of the seventh year.

EVALUATION

In order to determine the efficacy of the consultation model, the formative evaluation component added during years five and six included measurement of the following:

1. Percentage of referrals accepted for complete evaluations.
2. Numbers and levels of consultation interventions.
3. Satisfaction of child study staff involved in the consultation project.

Although the importance of measuring the satisfaction of teachers and principals with the project was recognized, the project manager was wary of seeking it too early; before successes had been demonstrated. Therefore, consumer reactions were not sought at this time.

One of the goals of the consultation project was a reduction in the number of students for whom a full evaluation was the initial and only intervention by the child study teams.

Table 1 shows the number of referrals for service received by the department, the number processed for full evaluation, and the percentage processed for full evaluation from the fourth year to the sixth year. According to the records kept at that time, it appears that in 1983–1984 most referrals to child study teams were accepted automatically as full evaluations. However, this high number may be an artifact of the way records were maintained during those years. It is suspected that some consultation took place before initial referrals, with the result that only full evaluation cases were reported, but this practice did not appear to be widespread. Recording procedures for the subsequent years were modified so that all referrals for service were sent directly to the central office by the principal initially, and then disbursed to teams for prereferral conferences. Teams then noti-

TABLE 1
Percent of Referrals Processed as Full Evaluations

Units		1983–1984		1984–1985		1985–1986		1986–1987	
		N	%	N	%	N	%	N	%
Unit 1[a]	Referrals	51		51		93		100	
	Full evaluations	50	98	46	92	47	51[b]	59	59
Unit 2	Referrals	36		34		39		72	
	Full evaluations	35	97	27	79	22	56	56	78
Unit 3	Referrals	45		45		75		66	
	Full evaluations	45	100	43	96	49	65	44	67
Unit 4[a]	Referrals	34		47		36		47	
	Full evaluations	33	97	29	62	28	64	34	72
Unit 5	Referrals	40		59		72		65	
	Full evaluations	40	100	49	83	56	78	32	49
Unit 8 (bilingual)	Referrals	8		24		37		42	
	Full evaluations	8	100	21	88	23	62	34	81
Total	Referrals	214		260		352		400	
	Full evaluations	211	99	215	83	220	63	264	67

[a]consultation teams
[b]previously Unit 4a

fied the central office which cases were to be handled through consultation and which were to be processed for full evaluation. Generally, teams were encouraged to pursue a consultation approach for all referrals. Teams made decisions independently based on their perceptions of the student's needs, school circumstances, and their own skills in using consultation. At times, cases were presented at the training sessions for suggestions and direction. Although the data presented in Table 1 must be viewed within the aforementioned constraints, the percentage of referrals processed for full evaluation was reduced during the first 2 years of the institutionalization of the consultation project (1984–1985 and 1985–1986).

Units 1A and 4A were designated consultation teams. Unit 1A covered a geographical area that had the highest student transience rate, the lowest SES levels, and the most discipline problems in its schools. Unit 4A covered an area with more intact families and neighborhoods, moderate SES levels, and schools with the highest academic levels. The team servicing Unit 1A in the first year of the project did not volunteer, but was as-

signed to consultation. Only the psychologist had obtained consultation coursework in her preservice training program. This was also the first year that this group worked together as a team, and the first year that two of the members were assigned to this area. As can be seen from Table 1, there was little change in the numbers of referrals processed for full evaluation during 1984–1985.

Unit 4A members had had more experience with consultation. The psychologist held a doctorate in counseling psychology and the learning disability consultant had undertaken extensive coursework in psychology. Both had also been part of the initial training sessions run by the university project director. This team assumed the identity of a "consultation team." Unit 4A showed the significant reduction in referrals for evaluation from 97% in 1983–1984 to 62% in 1984–1985. Owing to a reorganization of special education classes and the child study staff in September 1985, the members of Unit 4A were transferred to Unit 1A. The team assigned to Unit 4A, which was still to be considered a consultation team, consisted of one participant experienced in consultation and two new participants. The team was able, however, to maintain a reduced percentage of testings for the 1985-1986 school year. During the sixth year of the project, Unit 1A, now consisting of a more experienced staff than Unit 4, showed a percentage drop from 92% to 51%.

The bilingual unit, Unit 8, was not officially designated as a consultation unit because they serviced the entire district and therefore did not have the time or opportunity to establish the collaborative relationships needed to initiate and maintain a consultation model. In addition, prereferral resources for the Spanish-speaking students were limited. This unit participated in consultation projects with the bilingual special education classes they monitored. However, they were motivated and experienced with consultation techniques, and were able to reduce the numbers of referrals processed for full evaluation from 100% in 1983-1984 to 63% in 1985-1986. Despite the fact that Units 2A, 3A, and 5A were not considered to be consultation units and were not included in the training sessions, there was also a reduction in the number of referrals processed for full evaluation by these units. The project manager suspected that department attention to the consultation project generated competition among the teams to reduce the

amount of full evaluations. Districtwide totals showed a reduction from 99% in the year preceding the institutionalization of the project to 83% during the first year, to 63% in the second year.

Intervention Levels

An analysis of interventions based on Meyers (1973) levels of consultation can be found in Table 2. Each project was counted as one entity even though they may have involved a series of activities. As might be expected, the greatest number of interventions were at Level II, indirect service to the student through a consultee (54% in 1984-1985 and 62% in 1985-1986). Formative statistics gathered in March, 1985 indicated an initial focus on Level IV interventions, most of which were in the area of in-service workshops at the school level. However, end-of-the-year data analysis revealed a greater span across all levels of interventions. It is possible that the schools involved had become satiated with workshops, the teams saw more benefit in working directly with teachers, or that more individual teachers requested services.

Following is an example of one project that generated interventions using a variety of approaches at four different levels (see Figure 2). The team was first contacted in January and worked on the

TABLE 2
Interventions by Levels of Consultation

	1984-1985		1985-1986	
	N	%	N	%
Level I Direct service to student	22	14	29	16
Level II Indirect service to student	86	54	114	62
Level III Direct service to teachers (and others)	31	19	33	18
Level IV Direct service to organization	21	13	7	4
Totals	160		183	

Note. N, total number of consultation interventions.

FIGURE 2
Project Designed for First-Grade Students Exhibiting Deficits in Letter Recognition Skills

Strategy	Level	Due Date	Results
1. Screen two students for emotional problems.	I	4/25	Full referrals processed 4/1
2. Hold consultation meetings with the parents of four students.	II	3/1	Two held, two parents did attend.
3. Arrange a parent group meeting to teach parents how to reinforce skills, and how to structure the home environment to facilitate studying.	III	3/1	Parent meeting held March, on-going group planned.
4. Analyze classroom communication using the Flanders system of interaction analysis (Amidon and Flanders, 1971).	III	2/15	Results of the Flanders analysis used in changing teacher behavior.
5. Arrange meeting between the principal, kindergarten teachers and first-grade teachers to discuss coordinating curriculum and teaching approach.	IV	3/1	Principal to arrange, not completed.
6. Arrange with Supplemental Instructor to vary program to give one period per day of language stimulation and letter recognition to five most needy of the students (without being classified).	IV	3/1	Supplemental Instruction began 3/1.

project through May. Eventually, five of the six strategies planned were completed, spanning three different levels. A first-grade teacher presented the team with several problems. Five to ten students seemed to lack basic letter recognition skills, had poor expressive language, and had not been taught or had not retained skills from kindergarten that are needed in first grade. It was suspected that there was a lack of reinforcement in the home for academic skills. Two of the students appeared to have emotional problems. The rest "clammed up and didn't dialogue" with the teacher. The goals set were to increase classroom discussion, increase spontaneous speech, improve oral language skills, increase letter recognition, increase support from the home, and improve coordination between the kindergarten and first-grade programs. Intervention strategies were planned by the psychologist and teacher. The single strategy not completed was one that was left for the principal to arrange, and may have been overlooked because of other priorities.

Activities utilized by teams at Level I included individual student counseling, group counseling, academic tutoring, observation, and referral to another specialist or agency. Interventions at Level II included behavior modification programs for the identified problem children carried out in collaboration with teachers, local administrators, lunch aides, and other school personnel, as well as parents. Level III activities focused on parent groups, several of which were organized and maintained on an ongoing basis. Most of the groups' discussion topics related to discipline, to realistic expectations based on development, to nutrition, and to restructuring family schedules and the home environment to facilitate the completion of homework or studying. At some meetings parents were taught how to practice academic skills with their children. The parents of special education students were pleased with discussions that explained their children's handicap and provided strategies to work with specific problems. The materials used at the parent meetings were developed or modified by the consultants. Attempts to use commercial materials, such as Parent Effectiveness Training (Gordon, 1970), proved to be unsuccessful, as many of the parents were not comfortable reading the texts. Level III interventions with teachers were usually based on data collected by consultant observations or the use of the Flanders Interactional Analysis System (Amidon & Flanders, 1971). In one particular situation, based upon the results of such an analysis, one teacher worked on increasing the acceptance and use of students' ideas, and praised and encouraged students in order to solicit student responses. Examples of Level IV activities included in-service training programs for school staff, and collaborating with principals to modify teachers' schedules to allow for meetings to coordinate curriculum and programming between grades, and to develop consistent teacher expectations within the same grade at the junior high school level. The in-services included programs on staff stress reduction, helping students prepare for districtwide testing, improving reading instruction, values clarification, and classroom management. Facilitating teachers' use of an established districtwide senior citizen volunteer program and developing a schoolwide peer tutoring program were also considered Level IV interventions. Some consultants also worked with central office administration to open resource rooms to nonclassified students.

Participant Satisfaction

Child study staff satisfaction with the project was surveyed at the end of each of the two years of the project (see Table 3). Staff generally felt that participation in the consultation project was satisfying and two-thirds felt that it did not take too much time away from other responsibilities. Case conference sessions focusing on individual cases were seen as more beneficial than the sessions focusing on theory and skills. During the fifth year of the project, over one-half disagreed that they could have participated more extensively. During the sixth year, a small

percentage felt they could have participated more fully, although 25% were undecided. As might be expected from their training, the majority of child study staff felt most competent working with teachers individually or with students in individual counseling situations. The areas in which staff felt least competent included working on an organizational level with principals and in modifying curriculum. It is interesting that in both years the group thought that their efforts had helped parents the most. Several staff commented that the most meaningful interactions occurred when teachers, parents, and students met together.

DISCUSSION

The project described in this chapter is notable in several respects. One of the most striking features is its longevity. The project is continuing into its seventh year, and has moved from a university-facilitated program to a district-based program. Services expanded from discrete pilot projects to institutionalized systemic changes.

Facilitators of Change

The organizational factors that appeared to promote this innovation were climate, leadership, structure, and resources. The need to seek program alternatives to prevent the numbers of special education students from growing was well documented. The leadership of the Special Pupil Services Department was committed to the use of consultation as the basis for service, and was willing to expend the energy and effort needed to change department procedures and provide training for staff. The use of an internal project manager was considered essential for the continuation of the innovation. The internal project manager was an administrator and, as such, had both authoritative powers such as reward and coercion (Martin, 1978), and knowledge of staff competencies, dynamics, and interrelationships. She was able to reorganize the structure and responsibilities of the child study teams to facilitate the consultation

TABLE 3
Survey of Staff Satisfaction with Needs Consultation Project

	1984–1985 (N = 13)			1985–1986 (N = 15)		
	A	U	D	A	U	D
1. Participation in the consultation project was satisfying.	77	23	—	75	25	—
2. Participation in the consultation project took too much time from other responsibilities.	31	8	61	31	13	56
3. The large group sessions focusing on theory and skills were beneficial.	69	23	8	63	25	12
4. The small group sessions focusing on individual projects/concerns were beneficial.	92	—	8	75	13	12
5. I was satisfied with my role in the consultation project.	62	23	15	62	19	19
6. I feel I could have participated to a greater extent.	46	—	54	56	25	19
7. I felt competent in the following consultation areas:						
a. Working with a single teacher.	85	15	—	100	—	—
b. Developing a behavior modification program.	46	46	8	44	44	12
c. Individual counseling	85	15	—	81	19	—
d. Group counseling and/or guidance.	62	38	—	56	38	12
e. Working with principals to effect changes.	46	38	15	44	50	6
f. Modifying curriculum.	—	31	23	31	31	38
8. I feel my efforts have helped:						
a. Students.	69	31	—	75	19	6
b. Teachers.	62	38	—	69	19	12
c. Principals.	38	62	—	50	38	12
d. Parents.	85	15	—	75	19	6

Note: Data represents a percentage distribution. A = agree; U = undecided; D = disagree.

model. The quota system was removed, training sessions were scheduled, and prereferral procedures were modified for consultation teams. Resources such as allowances for time, facilities to meet, and department support to mediate with principals were made available. In addition, transportation for parents to attend groups and other meetings was provided through the department.

Barriers to Change

Organizational factors that appeared to hinder the effectiveness of the innovation were the district's history of change, perception of the child study team role as being exclusively diagnostic, time constraints, assignment of consultants as opposed to volunteerism, and a lack of gain for the B teams. The track record of educational change in this district, related to the number of projects developed, the number implemented, and the number still in existence may have affected the enthusiasm of some of the consultants. Ironically, some of the personnel with the longest history of employment in the district, although voicing their doubts, were still very anxious to attempt something new, if only to alleviate the lack of challenge and futility of evaluation, classification, and placement activities. The generally accepted perception of the child study team as an assessment vehicle continued. Those teams that were able to involve themselves in schoolwide curriculum coordination, reading instruction, report card grading decisions, or other activities beyond the special education or mental health realm did so as a result of their own assertiveness. However, particularly in the case of in-service workshops, once the precedent of expanded services had been established, additional requests surfaced. Furthermore, as might be expected, constraints in allocating time needed to devote to consultation projects were voiced repeatedly by the consultants.

Another major obstacle was that not all consultants were volunteers. Some child study team members found themselves on consultation teams because of staff reassignment that was based on numerous other considerations. These participants were not necessarily as committed to the role of providing consultation as the other participants and often resisted use of the approach.

Two areas in which there appeared to be a lack of success were in moving students to less restrictive programs and in declassification of students. The A teams, who worked with prereferral cases, were more active than the B teams, who worked with special education students. When referrals were reduced, the gains for the A teams were apparent immediately. That is, testing was decreased. However, if B teams were successful and students were declassified, the open placements in their special education classes were filled immediately by other students needing service. Thus, B teams may not have received adequate reinforcement for their efforts.

Consultant Factors

The factors that appeared, from consultant interviews and discussions during the training sessions, to promote change were the consultants' knowledge and skills, attitudes and expectations, and motivation. The factors that presented themselves as obstacles were consultant anxiety over role change, resistance to collaboration with teachers, and externalization of blame. It was felt, however, that the underlying problem was a reaction to the change of role. Factors generating anxiety included uncertainty related to personal and departmental expectations, learning and applying new skills and changing from the familiar role of diagnostician to the less familiar role of consultant. The groups that became most

involved in the project were those whose members had backgrounds in counseling and school psychology, therapy, and behavior modification — generally the psychologists and social workers. To judge from observations at training sessions, the learning disability consultants seemed the least comfortable in a consultative relationship, and during the first year, at least, they preferred to work with students directly in a tutoring situation, or developing learning packets and lists of resource materials for teachers to utilize. During the second year there were more attempts to work directly with teachers on an individual basis. The most productive teams were the ones who perceived themselves as providing consultation rather than only diagnostic services. These also seemed to include some members who were more assertive and more willing to take risks. Self-confidence and risk-taking behavior may be important personality variables for consultants.

Consultants voiced concern over their new roles, particularly in several areas: defining consultation, establishing collaborative relationships, clarifying department expectations, entry problems, confrontation with teachers or principals, and uncertainty and rigidity in selecting and implementing interventions. A definition of what activities would be considered to be consultation, for the purposes of this project, was not developed by participants until the beginning of the seventh year. Initially, specialists tended to carry out all the consultation for the schools or classes they were monitoring and intervened from their own orientation rather than referring the cases to the most appropriate child study team member.

Another area in which negative beliefs appeared to play a role was in the specialists' expectations that the consultative project had to be successful. If there were some doubts, why start? Many of the consultants felt that they could never reorganize their time, and that they would never have enough time to counteract teacher resistance. Some expressed concern that students would do worse while they "fooled around" with consultation. Another tendency was to externalize blame. Consultants focused on their lack of previous training and their feeling that the system was not ready for consultation, that teachers would never change, that the Consultation Progress Report form was too complicated, and that there were too many other priorities.

Process Results

Several positive results of the project were suggested from the case conference sessions and from the input of administrative and teaching personnel as follows:

1. The expanded role of the child study team as a consultation team was recognized and validated.

2. Teachers appreciated opportunities to more closely work with team members.

3. There was a shift in the focus of child study team services from the traditional diagnostic medical model to an educational/instructional model. In addition, there was a shift from a reactive to a proactive approach.

4. An impetus and vehicle for child study team members to return to the classroom was provided, enabling specialists to become resensitized to problems that teachers face daily.

5. Greater awareness developed as well as more efficient and creative use of alternative programs already existing in the general education area.

6. More parents became involved. Many of the projects resulted in the development of ongoing parent groups, some of which addressed developmental and discipline issues and some of which actually improved parent academic skills so that they could help their own children more effectively.

7. There was greater awareness and use of programs and agencies available in the community.

8. A more positive public image for the department as a whole was created. As the project progressed, consultants increasingly were used as a resource for more problems in the general education area.

9. The project became a catalyst for activity. Being part of an innovation prompted organized efforts. Required attendance at monthly meetings in which activities were reviewed and discussed appeared to motivate members to continue efforts. Indeed, it was obvious in some cases that there was an increase of consultant activity during the week preceding the scheduled monthly meeting date.

10. Other child study personnel became motivated to be part of this project. As some successes in the project became known, additional staff wanted to be included. As a result, all teams were required to become part of the consultation project by the seventh year.

AREAS OF CONCERN

Internal vs. External Consultants

This project offers a retrospective view of the strengths and weaknesses of consultation that uses internal and external personnel. The external consultant provided extensive resources from the university that produced the capability for the start-up phases of the project. However, the external consultant only had expert power (Martin, 1978), whereas the internal project manager had the power to make systemic changes and to maintain the innovation.

The internal project manager must be prepared to accept the ultimate responsibility for maintaining the innovation. An outside consultant usually leaves, with a sense of accomplishment, at the most successful phase of a new program, when it is expected that it is able to maintain itself. The inside change agent must continue not only to modify the process as new difficulties arise but, more importantly, to sustain enthusiasm and effort.

Collaborative Modeling

There was a conscious effort on the part of the project manager to model the collaborative approach with the specialists. Consultants were given latitude in the number and types of projects with which they wanted to work, and in designing interventions. Reinforcement was offered for attempting rather than completing a successful project. It was stressed that consultation was a process and if an intervention was not successful, it only meant that the goals, strategies, reinforcement, and/or teacher objectivity had to be modified. The intent was to reduce anxiety so that consultants could choose a problem area and intervention level with which they felt knowledgeable and comfortable. This also encouraged consultant ownership of the individual project. It was also hoped that by eliminating an anticipation of guaranteed success, consultants would feel freer to be creative. The negative aspects of this approach were that some staff actually opted to work on only one project.

Training Program

A strategic aspect of this project was the ongoing training program. Most psychologists and other child study specialists working in the schools have not been formally trained in consultation techniques (Curtis & Meyers, 1985; Gutkin & Curtis, 1982; Martin & Meyers, 1980). As mentioned previously, the monthly meetings allowed consultants to share their problems and ideas and gain group support; and proved to be a catalyst for action as the more active members provided models for the less active. Problems were encountered in trying to address, simultaneously, the varied skill and concern levels of the consultants. Due to the reassignment of team members, the composition of groups became a mix of new and older members. However, the ideas and support of the experienced staff were helpful. Another positive outcome of the mixed groups was that the more experienced members appeared to gain confidence in their own competence in the process of helping their colleagues. It was also obvious that one 2-hour meeting per month was not sufficient to build skills and sustain effort.

CONCLUSIONS

The project described in this chapter suggests that a consultation approach can be effective in an urban district in reducing the percentage of referrals processed for full test evaluation, classification, and placement, and in expanding services to the general education area. Ongoing collaboration between an internal, district administrator change agent and an external, university-based consultant seems to be advantageous in accomplishing this goal. The internal consultant is needed to facilitate systemic change, protect and defend the innovation, and support and motivate the consultant staff. The external consultant can concentrate on training and evaluation, and monitor the objectivity of the internal change agent. Furthermore, an ongoing training program is vital for developing skills, building peer support, and addressing consultant resistance.

Future plans for this project include following up to determine if student problems initially resolved through consultation surfaced again in subsequent years, revising child study referral procedures to include a prereferral consultation conference, expanding the project to all teams in the district, and measuring consumer satisfaction.

REFERENCES

Amidon, E. J., & Flanders, N. A. (1971). *The role of the teacher in the classroom.* St. Paul, MN: Association for Productive Teaching.

Berkowitz, G., Hyman, I., & Lally, D. (1984). The development of a school-wide computerized discipline reporting system. Paper presented at a meeting of the National Association of School Psychologists, Philadelphia, PA.

Caplan, G. (1970). *The theory and practice of mental health consultation.* New York: Basic Books.

Christenson, S., Ysseldyke, J., & Algozzine, B. (1982). Probabilities associated with the referral to placement process. *Teacher Education and Special Education,* 5(3), 19-23.

Curtis, M. J., & Meyers, J. (1985). Best practices in school-based consultation: Guidelines for effective practice. In A. Thomas & J. Grimes (Eds.), *Best practices in school psychology* (pp. 79-94). Kent, OH: National Association of School Psychologists.

Fullan, M., Miles, M. B., & Taylor, G. (1980). Organization development in schools: The state of the art. *Review of Educational Research, 50*, 121-183.

Gordon, T. (1970). *Parent effectiveness training*. New York: Peter H. Wyden.

Gutkin, T. B., & Curtis, M. J. (1982). School-based consultation: Theory and techniques. In C. R. Reynolds & T. B. Gutkin (Eds.), *Handbook of school psychology* (pp. 796-828). New York: Wiley.

Hyman, I. (1964). *Some effects of teaching style on pupil behavior*. Unpublished doctoral dissertation, Rutgers University, New Brunswick, NJ.

Hyman, I. (1972). The school psychologist and change: Using the approach of parallel systems. *New Jersey Psychologist, 22*, 13-18.

Hyman, I. (1977). A bicentennial consideration of the advent of child advocacy. *Journal of Child Clinical Psychology, Winter*.

Hyman, I. (1986). Corporal punishment: Is it necessary? Part II. *Educational Oasis, 1*(3), 7-8.

Hyman, I., & Lamberth, J. (1987). Discipline climate of Oasis readers. *Educational Oasis, 2*(3), 10.

Mannino, F. V., & Shore, M. F. (1975). The effects of consultation: A review of empirical studies. *American Journal of Community Psychology, 1*, 1-21.

Martin, R. P. (1978). Expert and referent power: A framework for understanding and maximizing consultation effectiveness. *Journal of School Psychology, 16*, 40-55.

Martin, R. P., & Meyers, J. (1980). School psychologists and the practice of consultation. *Psychology in the Schools, 17*, 478-484.

Medway, F. J. (1979). How effective is school consultation? A review of recent research. *Journal of School Psychology, 17*, 275-281.

Meyers, J. (1973). A consultation model for school psychological services. *Journal of School Psychology, 11*, 5-15.

New Jersey Special Education Study Commission. (1985). *The turning point: New directions for special education*. Trenton, NJ: New Jersey Department of Education.

New Jersey State Department of Education. (1984). *New Jersey Administrative Code, Title 6. Education. Subtitle F. Division of Curriculum and Instruction. Chapter 28*. Trenton, NJ: New Jersey Department of Education.

Sarason, S. (1971). *The culture of the school and the problem of change*. Boston: Allyn & Bacon.

Schmuck, R. (1982). Organization development in the schools. In C. R. Reynolds & T. B. Gutkin (Eds.), *Handbook of school psychology* (pp. 829-857). New York: Wiley.

6

Linking Assessment to Intervention

**James E. Ysseldyke and
Sandra L. Christenson**
University of Minnesota

Historically, psychoeducational assessment has been *the* major activity of school psychologists. In spite of the fact that most school psychologists repeatedly express the opinion that their role and function ought to be broader (Goldwasser, Meyers, Christenson, & Graden, 1983; Martin & Meyers, 1980; Ramage, 1979), any detailed analysis of how most school psychologists spend their time shows the primary activity to be psychoeducational assessment. School psychology as a profession came into existence because schools needed professional psychologists (though they called them diagnosticians) who could assess students and make decisions about whether they were eligible for special education services. Although not all school psychologists spend the majority of their time in assessment activities, clearly many other people see them as assessors. Bardon (1982) described the perceptions of people about school psychologists:

> If you ask teachers or parents what school psychologists do, chances are good that you will get one of three responses: they will not know what a school psychologist is; they will say that school psychologists give tests to atypical children; or they will describe functions commonly attributed to psychiatrists or clinical psychologists. If you ask clinical or counseling psychologists what school psychologists do, they will most likely talk about testing of children for special education by an assortment of persons certified as school psychometrists. If you ask school psychologists what they do, you can expect to receive detailed information about the many functions school psychologists could perform, given an opportunity to do so. These functions will include virtually everything that can be done by professional psychologists of any kind or persuasion, but with emphasis on their performance in schools or with school-age children and their families. If you press further and insist that you be told what school psychologists actually do rather than what they could do if permitted, your respondents reluctantly will describe functions that are less encompassing than they would like them to be and inevitably involve substantial attention to the administration of individual tests to children referred by school personnel either for special education classification or because of untoward behavior or poor school performance in a classroom. (p. 3)

Over the past 10 years, much has been written about problems in traditional assessment methodologies and the importance of shifting assessment practices (Algozzine & Ysseldyke, 1986; Fuchs & Fuchs, 1986; Gallagan, 1985; Mann, 1971; Reynolds, 1975). Yet careful examination of these and other writings indicates a focus on the need for change rather than on careful delineation of specific directions. Professionals have spent considerable time admiring problems and listing reasons why change would be difficult. We now need to focus on the variety of ways in which professionals can do things differently in assessment, the major goal being to bring assessment into closer congruence with intervention. After all, as succinctly stated by the National Academy of Sciences Panel on Selection and Placement of Students in Programs for the Mentally Retarded: "The purpose of the entire process — is to improve instruction for children" (Heller, Holtzman, & Messick, 1982, p. x).

Over the past 5 years, in select locations, we have seen new, exciting alternatives developed and new, exciting practices put into use. Psychologists have begun to be engaged in prereferral intervention (Graden, Casey, & Christenson, 1985; Graden, Casey, & Bonstrom, 1985), instructional consultation (Rosenfield, 1987), curriculum-based assessment (Deno, 1985; Germann & Tindal, 1985; Marston & Magnusson, 1985), and direct assessment of academic performance (Howell, 1986). Yet there remain major disparities between the state of practice (what we do) and the state of the art (the optimal in what we know) (Ysseldyke, Reynolds, & Weinberg, 1984). School psychologists are the professionals in schools who know the most about learning theory and its implications for effective instruction. The imperative is to move in the direction of bringing this knowledge to bear in the classroom.

Clearly, assessment is an important activity of school psychologists. In this chapter we take a brief look at what is wrong with existing delivery systems with regard to assessment practices, and then describe promising alternatives. Specifically, we describe current assessment efforts as characterized by (a) a "search for pathology" in which the focus is on identification of within-student deficits or disorders, (b) a failure to account for the instructional environment, (c) an emphasis on educability, (d) instructional irrelevance, (e) overreliance on aptitude-treatment interactions, (f) failure to account for *how* students learn, and (g) overreliance on classification. In contrast with this approach, we describe assessment of students' instructional environ-

ments as one component in a set of new, alternative methodologies that are relevant to instructional assessment.

EXISTING SERVICE DELIVERY SYSTEMS — WHAT'S WRONG?

The quest for development of alternative systems for the delivery of school psychological services that is the subject of this volume implies that current delivery systems are less than optimal, maybe even in some cases unsatisfactory. In this chapter we posit that the majority of current practice in psychoeducational assessment is unsatisfactory and incomplete. We cite a number of major concerns or major difficulties that we and others have described previously in the professional literature.

1. *Traditional assessment practices are characterized by a "search for pathology."* In their text *Educational Handicap, Public Policy, and Social History*, Sarason and Doris (1979) described the psychoeducational assessment and decision-making process as a "search for pathology." To them, "Diagnosis is a pathology-oriented process activated by someone who thinks something is wrong with somebody else" (p. 39). Students are referred for psychoeducational evaluation when their teachers think there may be something wrong with them or when they "bug" their teachers. Assessment personnel administer tests for the purpose of confirming or disconfirming teachers' reasons for referral; they operate to search for within-student problems first cited by teachers. In brief, they search for pathology (Poland, Thurlow, Ysseldyke, & Mirkin, 1982; Ysseldyke, Algozzine, & Mitchell, 1982; Ysseldyke, Algozzine, Rostollan, & Shinn, 1981).

2. *Assessment focuses on the child or on within-student deficits, dysfunctions, or disabilities.* For the most part, assessment activities are directed at finding out what is wrong with children. And, for the most part, this consists of administering tests for the purpose of identifying within-student deficits, dysfunctions, or disabilities that are presumed to "cause" edu-

cational difficulties (Algozzine, Ysseldyke, & Hill, 1982; Mann, 1971; Ysseldyke, 1973; Ysseldyke, Regan, Thurlow, & Schwartz, 1981). Over the years psychologists have delineated and have attributed school failure to very many within-student characteristics (Mann, 1981; Ysseldyke & Christenson, 1987b; Ysseldyke & Mirkin, 1982). These include things such as "perceptual-motor or psycholinguistic deficits" (e.g., grammatic closure deficits or figure ground disorders); affective characteristics (temperament, self-concept, locus of control); motivational constructs; and individual difference variables (cognitive style, attitudes, anxiety, conceptual tempo, attribution patterns). For each of the traits, abilities, or characteristics psychologists and educators develop tests. This has enabled practitioners to profile students on lists of variables of presumed importance but of little relevance to instructional intervention. Brown and Campione (1986) indicated that in such efforts the "leap to instruction" is always problematic: The focus on within-student problems without considering those problems in a broader context limits development of appropriate instructional interventions.

3. *Diagnostic practice fails to account for the instructional environment.* Student behavior is a function of reciprocal interaction between the student and the instructional environment. Yet, in diagnostic practice, student behavior is often viewed as isolated performance on tests; there have been few attempts to account for the nature of the instructional environment. As Heller et al., (1982) noted, "To understand a child's learning problems, one must assess not only intellectual functioning and other aspects of the individual outside the intellectual domain but also the contribution of the child's educational environment to his or her performance in school" (p. xi). Diagnostic personnel recognize this fact! Yet, efforts to account for instructional environments have been limited to task analyses of curricula, a delineation of instructional or individual educational plan objectives, or instructional diagnosis (Englemann,

Granzin, & Severson, 1979). The instructional environment involves far more than curricula and curricular objectives. It involves documenting the appropriateness (not frequency of occurrence) of lesson demonstrations, student academic engaged time, feedback strategies, classroom management, guided practice, correcting errors, etc. Until recently, there has not been a systematic methodology for taking these factors into account.

Howell (1986) noted that classroom learning is an interactive process that at the very minimum, involves student, teacher, and setting. He states:

> If the purpose of evaluation is to affect the quality of this interaction, then evaluation must address each of these elements. To focus only on one element is to avoid the interactive nature of the learning process. . . . Additionally, if the ultimate goal of evaluation is to alter current instructional practice, not merely to describe or make predictions about it, the greatest amount of attention should be directed toward variables that have the most impact on the interaction and are easiest to alter. Frequently these "alterable variables" . . . are not student variables. (p. 325)

4. *Current assessment activities are directed at making decisions about educability rather than about teachability.* Most psychometric assessment activities have the purpose of helping the examiner decide whether a youngster is educable, or determine the student's "potential to learning." Emphasis is not put on delineating activities that will lead to successful instruction of difficult-to-teach students. Indeed, in developing the very first intellectual measures used in school, Alfred Binet was attempting to sort out those students for whom the outlook for academic success was not bright. Recent legislation has rendered the making of educability decisions moot. As Reynolds (1975) noted,

> We are in a zero demission era; consequently, schools require a decision orientation other than simple prediction; they need one that is oriented to individual rather than institutional payoff. In today's context the measurement

technologies ought to become integral parts of instruction designed to make a *difference in* the lives of children and not just a *prediction about* their lives. (p. 15)

5. *Commonly used assessment techniques are out of synch with the curriculum.* Howell (1986) has argued that much of current assessment is out of synch with students' curricula. As he states, "Traditionally employed techniques fail to link assessment to interventions because they are indirect, nomothetic, narrowly applied, and environmentally insensitive" (p. 325). He contends that treatments or interventions are subordinate to curriculum, and defines the curriculum as "what the student learns," a "sequenced, calibrated, and organized set of learning outcomes, or tasks, regularly called objectives" (p. 324). Howell (1986) and Ysseldyke and Algozzine (1984) argue that students come to the attention of diagnostic personnel when they fail to profit from the sequenced, organized set of experiences that school personnel have prepared for them. Assessment efforts, then, ought to be directed at reversing a student's pattern of inadequate progress. Instead, current assessment is not sensitive to progress through the curriculum, is not closely matched to curriculum, and is focused on within-student deficits that only presumably relate to curricular progress.

6. *Current practice relies on the use of aptitude–treatment interactions (ATIs) to select treatments.* The diagnostic-prescriptive methodology that characterizes current practice is based on the assumption that aptitudes interact with treatments to produce differential instructional outcomes for students (Reynolds, 1988; Ysseldyke & Salvia, 1974). That is, it is assumed that the score or scores that students earn on a norm-referenced test will tell us how to teach them. For students in general, and handicapped students in particular, there is little evidence for aptitude-treatment interactions (Ysseldyke, 1973). The concept is indeed compelling, but to date unsupported.

7. *Evaluation of products does not tell us how the student learns.* Examiners often attempt to make decisions about how best to teach youngsters by examining instructional products. Performance data do not tell us how students learn. Howell (1986), noting that "achievement is the product of learning, it is not learning itself" (p. 326), maintained that achievement is always a function of an interaction between the rate at which students learn material (a concept that Gettinger [1984] calls "time needed to learn") and the amount of available learning opportunity or instructional time. When a student is not achieving as expected, Howell claimed, it is due to inadequate learning rate or inadequate opportunity to learn. Therefore, he stated, we should intervene with students to develop corrective interventions that are based on increasing either learning rate or academic engaged time.

8. *The focus in current assessment is on classification; yet there are no reliable differences among groups.* Current assessment activities are directed at making allocation or eligibility decisions. The focus in assessment is on determining whether a student is handicapped and on allocating handicapped students to set-aside structures (resource rooms or self-contained classrooms) where they can be educated separately. Such classification efforts are fraught with major problems (Ysseldyke, 1987). Hobbs (1975) summed up a major review of research and practice in the classification of children by stating that the traditional approaches of schools to the classification and placement of children constituted "a major barrier to the efficient and effective delivery of services to them and their families" (p. 274). Scriven (1983) labeled classification practices in special education "scandalous," and the National Academy of Sciences Panel on Selection and Placement of Students in Programs for the Mentally Retarded (Heller et al., 1982) concluded that "we can find little empirical justification for categorical labeling that discriminates mildly mentally retarded children from other children with academic difficulties" (p. 87). There currently

is no defensible system for differential categorization or classification of mildly handicapped students (Ysseldyke et al., 1983).

9. *Very many nonhandicapped students are being declared handicapped.* Increasingly, educators have been able to demonstrate that very many nonhandicapped students are being declared eligible for special education services (Algozzine & Korinek, 1985; Algozzine & Ysseldyke, 1983; Shepard & Smith, 1981). In large part special education has become a dumping ground, a haven for the hard to teach and the tough to tolerate (Ysseldyke, 1986). Much of the increase in the numbers of students identified as handicapped has come in the ill-defined category of learning disabilities, which has increased 129% over the past 5 years.

The rapid increase in the numbers of students identified as mildly handicapped and the identification as handicapped of many students who are not has led to economic difficulties and to widespread criticism of classification practices. As a result, alternatives such as prereferral intervention (e.g., Graden, Casey, & Bonstrom, 1985) have been proposed.

THE CALL FOR CHANGE

The school psychology profession does not fail to recognize the difficulties in current assessment practice. Ysseldyke (1987) states:

> Classification of handicapped students is an activity at the root of nearly everything that occurs in special education. Students are classified and grouped for instructional purposes. Researchers conduct their investigations on categories of exceptional students. Groups of parents and professionals organize into associations for the purpose of advocating for specific types of handicapped students. Universities educate teachers of specific types of students and organize their professional preparation program based on disability labels. Given the prevalence of the use of classification practices, the neophyte observer could hardly help but conclude that there just must be good reasons for classifying

handicapped students. Yet, it is very difficult to find strong support for classification practices in the professional literature. (p. 234)

There are frequent calls for change. We review here the kinds of directions a variety of leaders in school psychology have suggested. It is noteworthy that these critics are calling for relatively major change and indeed for a reconceptualization of the entire assessment and decision-making process. As few as 10 years ago, those who advocated change were essentially recommending "band-aid" approaches. They proposed improvements in the technical adequacy of norm-referenced tests, research efforts designed to discover aptitude-treatment interactions, and improved classification efforts based on the use of multiple regression equations. We see now much more focus on instruction and on the relevance of assessment activities to instructional interventions. Indeed, the contemporary view is that improved instructional intervention is the *bottom line* in assessment.

Fuchs and Fuchs (1986) encouraged school psychologists to "employ assessment data objectively to (a) describe students and their instructional environments, (b) generate hypotheses concerning alternative instructional directions, and (c) evaluate and inductively develop ongoing instructional programs" (p. 320). They also called for assessment activities to be "ecologically sensitive" — saying that academic behavior should be understood in relation to environmental, especially classroom environmental, variables. Christenson, Abery, and Weinberg (1986) encouraged school psychologists to drop the use of the medical model and adapt an ecological perspective for guiding delivery of psychological services. That is, they encouraged psychologists to move away from a model in which the focus was on diagnosing within-student problems thought to cause academic difficulties. They encouraged movement toward conceptualization of problems as existing in interaction with school and home environment factors. Their comparison of school psychologists' activities under the two differing perspectives illustrates how an ecological perspective results in instructionally relevant decisions for students.

Lentz and Shapiro (1986) have stated that the linking of assessment to effective intervention requires an understanding of the academic ecology. They argued that assessment can be effectively linked to instructional intervention only if school psychologists assess the academic skills of a child directly, and "both conceptualize and analyze the relationship of academic problems to critical classroom environment factors" (Lentz & Shapiro, 1986, p. 346). They advocated assessment of the academic ecology and defined this as "a network of relationships among student and classroom environmental variables as they affect acquisition of new skills and student engagement in appropriate academic work" (p. 350). They argued that analysis of the academic environment is an indispensable part of an overall problem analysis leading to effective intervention. Assessment must provide information that facilitates intervention planning, not merely the classification of students as members of handicapped groups.

Rosenfield (1987) has argued for replacement of classification activities with instructional consultation. She held that in instructional consultation the focus is on "the quality and nature of the interaction, usually that of an instructional mismatch between an often vulnerable child, inadequate instruction, and a muddled conception of the task. It is the goal of the collaborative consultation process to hone in on analyzing the mismatch and facilitating a more productive interaction. Assessment is not for the purpose of classification, but for classroom instructional decision making" (p. 6).

Clearly, the times have changed. Assessment efforts directed at making classification decisions or simple predictions about students' performance in regular or special education cannot be defended. There is a recognized need for a shift from simple psychometrics to instructionally relevant decision-making. This shift has, quite frankly, been brought about more by legislation and litigation than research. But, in any event, there is clearly a new focus on instruction in new assessment and decision-making efforts.

Much of the call for change in assessment activities resulted from the recognition that norm-referenced testing tends to be a dead-end activity. Deno (1986) criticized diagnostic-prescriptive models (both those based on what Ysseldyke and Salvia [1974] call ability training and those based on what they call task analysis) as failing to provide school personnel with information on *how* to teach deficient skills. Deno noted that instructional plans (IEPs) based on either pupil performance on norm-referenced ability measures or on a diagnostician's task analysis of pupil performance are *instructional hypotheses*. He argued that school psychologists need to engage in formative evaluation of pupil progress in order to make and/or modify such instructional hypotheses. Deno (1986) recommended formative evaluation procedures that consist of direct and frequent measurement of pupil progress — individual rather than group measurements that are directly sensitive to the curriculum. He advocated curriculum-based measurement (CBM). Deno recommended a shift in assessment efforts from those that serve only "to classify and legitimate expenditure of funds" to those that lend themselves to active participation in the intervention process and that provide valid evidence for program effectiveness. He argued that "CBM and formative evaluation create an opportunity for school psychologists to become involved in formulating and documenting effectiveness of instructional interventions in direct and useful ways" (p. 373). He further argued that such activities "foster cooperation from teachers, because the data base on which decisions are made is relevant to the curriculum of the school" (p. 373).

Meyers and Lytle (1986) proposed process assessment techniques derived from recent work in cognitive psychology. They argued that school psychologists ought to assess the learning process rather than focus simply on the products or outcomes of learning. Included in process assessment are observation, procedures that incorporate intervention into the assessment process, testing the limits, verbal self-report techniques, monitoring the effectiveness of interventions, and "Think-Aloud Protocol Analysis."

There is much talk about a need for a major shift in assessment activities. Given all of the talk, why doesn't such a shift simply occur? There are several interrelated reasons for a failure to radically shift assessment efforts for students: some of which, including all of the factors related to systems change, involve simply a reluctance on the part of school personnel to change what they do. We think, however, that a primary reason there has been little change is that there has not been a methodology to facilitate or enable change. Until now there has been no systematic methodology that school psychologists could use to describe students' instructional environments and to develop interventions based on careful analysis of the qualitative nature of instruction. In the absence of a methodology by which to assess instructional environments school psychologists have been powerless in their efforts to resist simple solutions to complex problems — solutions in the form of long regression equations and neuropsychological assessment.

In the following sections we will describe the development of a methodology to enable school psychologists to gather data on the nature of students' instructional environments. The methodology is based on several factors that, in complex interaction, affect academic outcomes for students. Ysseldyke and Christenson (1987b) grouped these factors into three categories: *student characteristics, environmental factors, and instructional factors.*

STUDENT CHARACTERISTICS

Psychologists have spent considerable time, effort, and energy in isolating and describing the *student characteristics* that are related to instructional outcomes. In fact, it could be argued that psychologists have focused almost exclusively on student characteristics, without regard to the environmental and instructional factors that influence the manifestation of those student characteristics. Earlier, we conducted an extensive review of the literature in an examination of those student characteristics said to be or shown to be related to instructional outcomes. The factors most often cited in the professional literature are listed in Table 1. They include abilities and skills, cognitive and affective factors, and a large number of individual difference variables. Note that the focus on these characteristics has been intensive, and that there are tests or subtests designed to be used to measure each of the characteristics cited. There are measures of cognition, psychomotor abilities, psycholinguistic abilities, motivation, attention, learning style, cognitive style, locus of control, achievement motivation, cognitive or conceptual tempo, anxiety, attribution, and so forth. The history of efforts to identify student characteristics and to match such characteristics to instructional interventions (i.e., aptitude x treatment or trait x treatment interaction studies) has been primarily with nonhandicapped students (Bracht, 1970). The history of such efforts has been largely nonproductive, but especially in research with handicapped students (Ysseldyke, 1973).

A variety of *environmental factors* also are said to be or have been shown to be related to instructional outcomes. These are listed in Table 2. There are three categories of such variables: school district conditions, within-school conditions, and general family characteristics. There are reasonably well established relationships between each of these factors and instructional outcomes.

Very many *instructional factors* have been said to be or have been shown to be related to instructional outcomes for nonhandicapped students, and to a limited extent for handicapped students. These are listed in Table 3 and are described in an integrative review of instructional factors related to academic outcomes for students and implications for

TABLE 1
Student Characteristics Said to Be or Shown to Be Related to Student Outcomes

- Cognitive and affective entry behaviors
- Abilities (e.g., cognitive, psychomotor, psycholinguistic)
- Affective characteristics (e.g., temperament, self-concept, attention)
- Prior learning or knowledge
- Level of skill development
- Ability to understand instruction
- Motivation
- Task persistence
- Learning rate
- Time needed to learn
- Attentional set
- Individual differences in locus of control, achievement, motivation, cognitive style, conceptual tempo, anxiety, attribution patterns, attitudes, etc.
- Learning styles
- Cognitive types
- Naturally occurring pupil characteristics (race, sex, physical appearance, etc.)

TABLE 2
Environmental Factors Said to Be or Shown to Be Related to Student Outcomes

School district conditions
- Millage rate
- Teacher–pupil ratio
- Amount of emphasis on basic skills
- Amount of homework
- Amount of emphasis on test taking (including minimum competency testing)
- Process by which the curriculum is developed
- Attendance

Within-school conditions
- Class size
- School ambiance
- Extent of discipline problems
- Leadership from the principal
- Cooperative environment
- Collaborative staff relations
- Degree of structure
- Clarity of classroom rules and procedures
- Academic focus; high expectations

General family characteristics
- Status characteristics (SES, income level, educational level, occupation)
- Use of out-of-school time
- Peer group outside the school

TABLE 3
Instructional Factors Said to Be or Shown to Be Related to Student Outcomes

Planning procedures
- Sufficient time allocated to academic activities
- Quality of the teacher's diagnosis of student skill level
- Prescription of appropriate tasks that are clearly matched to student skill level
- Realistic, high expectations and academic standards
- Instructional decision-making practices (grouping, materials, ongoing diagnostic ability)
- Sufficient content coverage
- Design of instruction to include lesson presentation, practice, application, and review
- Kind of curriculum

Management procedures
- Efficient classroom management procedures
- Well-established and efficient instructional organization and routines
- Productive use of instructional time
- Positive, supportive classroom interactions

Teaching procedures
- The instructional sequence includes demonstration, prompting and provision of opportunity for practice
- Expectations (goals, objectives, academic standards) are communicated clearly
- Lesson presentation — Related factors
  - Extensive substantive teacher–pupil interaction, teacher questioning, signaling, re-explaining
  - Teacher-directed instruction (proceeding in small steps, careful structuring of learning experiences, etc.)
  - Clear demonstration procedures and systematic use of error correction procedures
  - High rate of accurate student response
  - Amount of guided practice prior to independent practice
  - Explicitness of task directions

- Practice — Related factors
  - Amount and kind of independent practice
  - Appropriateness of seatwork activities
  - Systematic application of principles of learning to instruction
  - High rates of academic engaged time (academic learning time; opportunity to learn)
  - Brisk, fast pacing (curriculum and lesson)
  - Degree of student accountability
  - Systematic, explicit feedback and corrective procedures

Monitoring and evaluation procedures
- Active monitoring of seatwork activities
- High success rates (on daily and unit tests)
- Frequent, direct measurement of pupil progress
- Progress through the curriculum depends on mastery criteria
- Curriculum alignment — the relationship between what is to be taught (goals), what is taught (instruction), and what is tested (assessment)

nstructing handicapped students (Ysseldyke, Christenson, & Thurlow, 1987).

ASSESSING STUDENTS' INSTRUCTIONAL ENVIRONMENTS

The notion that psychologists *ought* to assess or in some way account for the nature of the instructional environment is not new. For years those who have written about assessment have encouraged psychologists to spend as much time gathering data on students' instructional environments as they do gathering data on students. We have developed a methodology that would enable psychologists to do so — The Instructional Environment Scale (TIES) (Ysseldyke & Christenson, 1987a). We attempted to develop an instrument that could be used systematically to gather data on the extent to which the kinds of factors listed in Table 3 characterize a student's instructional environment. The instructional factors are important regardless of the curriculum or teaching program used. Analyzing a student's instructional environment is a complex task, in part, because evaluating the nature of instruction and teaching is imprecise. We based TIES on a comprehensive review of the literature, recognized the impreciseness in observing the instructional process, and chose data collection methods and TIES components that resulted in a practical and flexible method for describing a student's instructional environment. In this section we describe the purposes for administering TIES, the TIES data collection methods, and the TIES components.

Purpose in Using TIES

There are two major reasons for using TIES: "(a) to systematically describe the extent to which a student's academic or behavior problems are a function of factors in the instructional environment and (b) to identify starting points in designing appropriate instructional interventions for individual students" (Ysseldyke & Christenson, 1987a, p. 3). There are several applications of TIES. The scale is useful in gathering data as part of the prereferral intervention process and it is helpful in the process of instructional consultation. Ysseldyke and Christenson (1987b) have posited that TIES is helpful in putting content into the consultation process. They argued that often the focus in consultation is on the consultation process and that good instructional consultation requires that the consultant be able to gather data systematically on qualitative aspects of the instructional environment. TIES also is useful in developing individual educational programs and can be used to contrast alternative instructional environments for an individual student. Thus, school personnel could place a student in different instructional environments for periods of time and monitor the nature of those environments. Judgments could then be made about the instructional environment most conducive to student progress. TIES delineates the factors that are important to look at in making judgments about the adequacy of instruction. The scale is therefore useful in training teachers. Because TIES can be given on repeated occasions, it is also useful in the progress monitoring required under PL 94-142.

TIES Data Collection Methods

We believe that school personnel should use more than one data collection method in gathering information on the nature of students' instructional environments. The instructional environment is defined by a triangle, that is, the interaction of student characteristics and perceptions interacting with task characteristics and the teacher's instructional/management strategies. Personnel who analyze the instructional environment for an individual student must learn to "think" in terms of this triangle. Classroom observation, teacher interview, and student interview data are needed to understand the total instructional environment. First, the examiner observes the pupil in the classroom. Guidelines for selecting an appropriate setting, scheduling, conducting the observation, and recording data are described in the TIES manual. TIES uses a narrative recording procedure, and data on 12 components of effective instruction are recorded on the Data Record Form.

Data also are collected by means of teacher interviews and student interviews. One cannot understand some of the specific aspects of what is happening with respect to instruction without asking teachers about their instructional decisions and activities and without asking students about the extent to which they understand what they are being asked to do. Use of TIES requires the examiner to engage in a 20- to 30-min teacher interview and a 20-min student interview.

TIES Components

In selecting the components of instruction on which to gather data, we had to reduce our initial instrument, one designed to gather information on 22 components of effective instruction, to an instrument designed to gather data on 12 components. TIES is organized in such a way as to enable the user to gather information on planning procedures, management procedures, teaching procedures, and monitoring/evaluation procedures. TIES components in each of these areas, and ways to assess for their impact on student performance, are described below.

Planning procedures. Two of the components of effective instruction identified by TIES describe the extent to which appropriate instructional planning activities are part of the student's instructional environment: Instructional Planning and Teacher Expectations.

Instructional planning. Achieving the appropriate match between student characteristics and instruction delivered is undisputed as a necessary component of effective instruction. Bloom's mastery learning model (1985) underscores the importance of considering cognitive and affective entry behaviors when planning instruction. Good and Brophy (1984) clearly articulated that a primary task of the teacher must be to achieve an appropriate match — both on initial assignment of tasks and on modifications throughout instructional units. Such instructional planning is a major step in most teaching models (e.g., Squires, Huitt, & Segars, 1983).

In making judgments about instructional planning the examiner considers how accurately the student's needs have been assessed and how appropriately instruction is matched to the results of the instructional diagnosis. In making such judgments, the examiner considers the prior knowledge or prerequisite skills mastered by the student, the difficulty level of assigned materials, the student's success rate on assigned tasks, preferably over a 1- to 2-week period, and the student's academic engagement rate. A low engagement rate is seen not as a sign that a student lacks motivation but as a "red flag" signaling a poor instructional match. Such techniques as task analysis of the curriculum, diagnostic teaching, and monitoring of student success and task completion rates across different assignments are used to provide information on the various aspects of instructional match. In addition, the degree of congruence of the teacher's prediction of the student's success on independent seatwork and the student's actual success rate is a good indicator of the effectiveness of the instructional match; it is superior to teacher's ability to articulate the student's strengths and weaknesses (Denham & Lieberman, 1980).

Teacher expectations. Teacher expectations play a critical role in determining student outcomes. Establishment of high academic expectations and student accountability for meeting these expectations was one of the five key ingredients of effective instruction identified by Edmonds (1979) in school effectiveness research. Good and Brophy (1984) have written extensively about setting high, yet realistic, expectations for all students. Their research indicates that teachers' behavior affects students' expectations. For example, when teachers call on high achievers three to four times more than low achievers, the implicit assumption is that some students know the answer; others don't. Students view themselves as "smart," "average," or "dumb" as a result of the different opportunities to respond. In making judgments about this component, examiners look at the extent to which a teacher states realistic, yet high expectations for both the amount and accuracy of work to be completed by the individual student *and* whether the teacher's behavior conveys high expectations for the student. And they consider how clearly expectations, instructional goals, the teacher's intentions for the lesson, and task directions and demands are communicated to the student.

Management procedures. Student achievement is higher when settings are managed effectively. TIES includes one component in this domain: Classroom Environment.

Classroom environment. Effective classroom management, both behavioral rules and organizational routines, has been identified as a key to increasing students' engagement rates and their academic achievement (Good, 1983; Karweit, 1983). In making judgments about the classroom environment, examiners consider how efficiently and effectively the classroom is controlled, how positive and supportive the classroom atmosphere is, and how productively time is used. Examiners take into account a variety of factors including whether students are taught appropriate conduct; whether behavioral disruptions are "prevented" and whether, when they occur, they are handled promptly; whether there is a task-oriented, academically focused classroom; whether the teacher uses a "surveillance system" for redirecting unengaged students; and whether acceptance of and modification for individual learning differences is evidenced. Examiners are aware that efficient classroom management is a prerequisite for efficient teaching procedures. However, teachers may be effective at managing without employing effective instructional procedures.

Teaching procedures. Specific instructional procedures make a difference in the extent to which pupils profit from instruction. TIES includes five components in the area of teaching procedures: Instructional Presentation, Motivational Strategies, Cognitive Emphasis, Informed Feedback, and Relevant Practice.

Instructional presentation. There is consensus that the nature of instructional presentations has a significant effect on student achievement. Instructional presentation repeatedly is discussed as a factor influencing the quality of instruction (Carroll, 1963; Good, 1983; Rosenshine & Stevens, 1986), and it is believed that lesson development is the single most important aspect of instruction (Good &

Grouws, 1979). It is the essence of teaching.

In making judgments about this component, examiners take into account how clearly and effectively instruction is presented; whether directions contain sufficient information for the student to understand what kinds of behaviors or skills are to be demonstrated, and to what extent the student's understanding is checked before independent practice.

Examiners look at how the lesson is developed and whether it includes review, overview, explanation, demonstration opportunities, and practice; at the clarity of directions, particularly for independent seatwork activities; and at the way teachers or others check for student understanding at different points throughout the instructional process. The emphasis is on the notion of explicitness. During observation of the lesson, the following should become evident: *what* the skill is to be learned, *how* to apply the skill, *why* to use the skill, and *when* to use the skill. TIES users are encouraged to note the way in which student understanding is checked. Possibilities include accuracy of student responses (i.e., success rates), error pattern analysis, and student explanation of the process or operation involved. The critical point is that a student's assignments and curriculum materials (rather than norm-referenced tests) serve as the vehicles for checking for student understanding.

Motivational strategies. The importance of motivation for learning is undisputed in the educational and psychological literature. While extrinsic methods (e.g., contingency contract or rewards) have been used, intrinsic approaches recently have received primary attention. Users of TIES evaluate the implementation of motivational strategies by taking into account factors that influence student motivation. These include the extent to which the teacher shows enthusiasm for and interest in the material presented, the student understands the importance of assigned tasks, the lesson is presented clearly, instruction is designed to reflect the student's interests and experiences, instruction is matched to the student's skill level, extra motivational techniques are used when appropriate, and the student feels accepted by the teacher and in the classroom.

Cognitive emphasis. Students who understand how to solve problems and how to approach a task achieve more in school. Winne (1985) refers to the process of knowing how to think to solve problems as cognitive achievements. Although a relatively new research area, the study of student cognitions has led to the idea that a student's thinking processes mediate between teacher input and student achievement. In making judgments about this component, TIES users consider how much the teacher serves as a source of instructional support in modeling and directly teaching thinking processes and learning strategies. Examiners look for instances when the teacher "makes visible the invisible reasoning," and the student explains the process used to find an answer rather than just supplying the answer.

Informed feedback. Feedback and corrective procedures are an integral part of the mastery learning model (Bloom, 1985), and the importance of feedback is consistently stressed in the various models of school learning, in empirically documented teaching programs, and in the instructional psychology literature. For feedback to be effective, it must be task-specific and be explicit. In making judgments about informed feedback, TIES users look at the extent to which the student receives nearly immediate and relatively specific information on performance or behavior — that is, what makes the student's response correct or incorrect. They also examine both the extent to which correction is provided when the student makes mistakes and the timing of the correction. Students' achievement is improved when they have an opportunity to practice correct answers before moving to a new assignment or content area. Similarly, effective feedback provides the student with increased opportunity to respond during teacher–student interactions. When the student responds incorrectly, the teacher's use of prompts and cues to lead the student to the correct answer rather than calling on another student is important to improve student achievement. TIES users consider how the student receives feedback as well as the content of the feedback.

Relevant practice. Ample amounts of two kinds of practice — controlled (guided) or independent (seatwork) — need to be present to optimize student achievement. Practice has several purposes. Practicing a skill in varied ways builds different associations; this serves as the basis for generalization (Haring & Eaton, 1978). Practice also is important in bringing basic, essential skills to the point of automaticity (Rosenshine, 1983; Samuels, 1981). However, mere practice does not make perfect! Students must practice on academically relevant tasks with a high success rate. In assessing relevant practice, TIES users judge how adequately the student is afforded opportunity to practice with appropriate materials and the extent to which classroom tasks are important to achieving instructional objectives. In making such judgments, the kind, amount, and purpose of practice activities, student success rate, and monitoring of student performance vis-à-vis a set of objectives are used.

Monitoring and evaluation procedures. To facilitate student achievement, it is important that school personnel monitor student progress and use this information for subsequent instructional planning. There are four TIES components in the general area of monitoring and evaluation procedures: Student Understanding, Academic Engaged Time, Adaptive Instruction, and Progress Evaluation.

Student understanding. Good (1983) identified student perception of tasks and directions as critical to increasing engaged time and achievement. Research in the area of student cognition (e.g., Peterson, Swing, Stark, & Waas, 1984) has demonstrated that a student's understanding of a task and specific use of cognitive strategies to complete the task are directly related to student achievement. TIES users gather data on student understanding by interviewing students. They take into account how the student demonstrates an accurate understanding of what is to be done in the classroom. They make judgments about this by considering how well the student understands instructional goals, task directions, and the processes to be gone through in order to complete tasks.

Academic engaged time. Academic engaged time, a moderate predictor of student achievement (Borg, 1980; Karweit, 1983), is a necessary but not sufficient condition for student learning. Students must spend time on an academically relevant activity with high success not merely time on task. In making judgments about academic engaged time, TIES users take into account how actively the student is engaged in responding to academic content and how much the teacher monitors student engagement and redirects the student when it is needed to reinstitute engagement. Users consider factors that impede student academic engaged time (instructional mismatch, incomplete teaching, inadequate directions for seatwork) and the extent to which the teacher's monitoring of student attention emphasizes both task completion and learning vis-à-vis objectives.

Adaptive instruction. Adaptive instruction is viewed as a major means to enable mildly handicapped students to stay in mainstream settings and profit from their educational experiences. Adaptive instruction is evaluated by examining how readily the curriculum is modified to accommodate the student's specific instructional needs; adapting instruction involves a monitor adjust/component throughout teaching. TIES users judge adaptive instruction in terms of constraints on curriculum modifications set by teachers' limited willingness to adapt or by the rigidity of school district curricular objectives. Systematic evaluation of modifications has been used in making these judgments.

Progress evaluation. On the basis of extensive research on direct and frequent measurement systems, Mirkin, Fuchs, and Deno (1982) recommended the use of student performance data in making subsequent instructional decisions. The importance of monitoring student progress in order to provide correction and allow students the time needed to achieve mastery is underscored in Bloom's mastery learning model. In describing progress evaluation, TIES users appraise the amount of direct, frequent measurement of the student's progress toward completion of instructional objectives and gauge how extensively data on pupil performance and progress are used to plan subsequent instruction.

CONSIDERATIONS IN ASSESSING INSTRUCTIONAL ENVIRONMENTS

Assessing for intervention requires school psychologists to change the way they think about assessment and the way they approach assessment activities. An assessment-for-placement mentality dominates current assessment practice. Adopting an assessment-for-intervention perspective does not mean that school psychologists eliminate data collection procedures describing student characteristics and student's instructional needs. It does mean that school psychologists collect data on student characteristics *and* instructional characteristics in order to plan interventions to address students' instructional needs. Thus, assessment is characterized by an assessment–intervention–placement sequence of events; assessing the effectiveness of interventions occurs throughout teaching and provides information on how the student learns. Intervention planning prior to making eligibility decisions has the advantage of planning for students' needs in the mainstream classroom. In essence, intervention becomes the focus of all assessment activities.

A second set of considerations has to do with the use of TIES as an assessment instrument. We strongly believe that although TIES is based on a sound empirical basis, it should not be seen as a panacea. TIES is one viable means of assessing classroom environmental variables, but it is not the only method. Also, TIES is a new instrument, and like all other assessment instruments, there is a need for additional data on its use and effectiveness.

Changes in Thinking About Assessment

Assessing for intervention requires school psychologists to examine all factors that influence learning outcomes. Students' learning/behavior problems are conceptualized from an ecological perspective and as the result of an interaction of teacher, instructional, classroom, family, and student characteristics. The microscopic view of "testing the student" is shed for an approach that begins to account for the interaction of student characteristics with various environmental influences.

With an assessment-for-intervention perspective, the student's behavior is described in objective, specific, and behavioral terms — the emphasis is on what the student does, not on another individual's opinion or interpretation of student behavior. Referrals for vague terms like "learning-disabled," "motivational problems," or "poor academic performance" are discouraged. Teachers are guided to specify what their students do to suggest the conclusion that they are unmotivated.

The purpose of assessment is intervention, *not* merely behavioral description of the student. Collecting data on student characteristics is the prerequisite for identifying target points for intervention. Behavioral descriptions of the student are not used to "search for" or verify pathology. Attention is focused not on what to call or where to place the student, but on identifying the student's instructional needs for intervention planning. For example, consider a student who has expressive language difficulties and does not recall specific details, and who does not organize tasks, use of time, or papers in an efficient, orderly fashion. While many observers may characterize this description as a learning disability, assessing for intervention concentrates on how to meet

such a student's instructional needs (e.g., teaching organizational skills) rather than applying a label.

Specifying how a student's instructional needs are influenced (positively or negatively) in different environmental contexts is critical. This approach avoids statements such as "Nathan is unmotivated," and favors conditional statements such as "Nathan's task completion rates are 80-100% when the steps for task completion are numbered and sufficient guided practice opportunities are provided; when these instructional conditions are not met, task completion rates range from 40% to 55%." Simply stated, the purpose of assessment is not to admire the problem (whether it exists primarily in the home, student, or classroom), but to promote change and competent student responses within classroom settings.

Finally, assessment is conceived to be a dynamic, ongoing process that is modified and verified by the teaching act. The art and skill of assessment is identifying successful instructional/behavioral interventions. Assessment is composed of several stages: problem identification, data collection, intervention planning, and evaluation of the effectiveness of the intervention. Monitoring the effectiveness of interventions makes it possible to determine how a student learns.

Changes in Approach to Assessment

At a minimum, adopting an assessment-for-intervention orientation changes where school psychologists conduct assessments, what procedures are used to collect data, and the degree to which classroom teachers and support personnel interact. The primary location of assessment moves from what Bronfenbrenner (1977) described as "strange" — that is in a strange room, with a strange examiner, asking strange questions - to the student's classroom. Understanding a student's instructional experience and specifically the impact of different elements of the classroom context on student performance is essential for planning instructional/behavioral interventions.

This can be done only by moving from the "testing" room to the classroom.

Assessing for intervention involves the use of different and varied diagnostic procedures and techniques. Although norm-referenced testing is not excluded, procedures allowing for more direct assessment of the student's academic performance or behavior, such as interviewing, observation, diagnostic teaching, and curriculum-based assessment, are used more frequently. Observing and interviewing prior to administering norm-referenced or criterion-referenced tests have specific advantages. Observation provides an opportunity to understand the classroom context and to account for instructional factors that influence academic/behavioral difficulties for the student. Observing in classrooms is not new; observing with a systematic focus on the content of instruction, as provided by TIES, is new. Interviewing the teacher is essential to adequately define academic problems. Accurate problem identification (Bergan, 1977) is the most critical step in effective consultation and too often is omitted during assessment activities. Effective assessment practices do not use a standard battery of tests; rather they are planned on the basis of answers to two questions: (a) What decision must be made, and (b) what data must be collected to make the decision? Assessment becomes a process for addressing specific intervention needs. The selection of diagnostic procedures relies on accurate problem identification by interviewing the teacher.

Interviewing the student yields helpful information for selecting additional assessment procedures. Interviewing students about their assigned work allows for initial evaluation of student performance through examination of work samples, error pattern analysis, think-aloud procedures, calculation of success and task completion rates, and an opportunity to engage the student in a diagnostic teaching lesson particularly as it relates to the referral concern. Assessing for intervention does not lock the school psychologist into the administration of specific tests. It places the school psychol-

ogist in a decision-making role regarding the appropriate use of diagnostic procedures.

There are, at a minimum, two other advantages to observing and interviewing teachers and the referred student prior to developing a diagnostic plan. First, teachers often refer students to be "fixed" by specialists. The teacher interview establishes the theme that the psychologist (and other specialists) can work collaboratively to plan a course of action to address the teacher's concern. Second, interviewing and observation yields much instructionally relevant information about the student, especially about how the student's performance changes under varying environmental conditions. The focus on the student is not lost; however, there is a shift from attributing the problem to a deficit on the part of the student to understanding student performance in the context of his or her daily learning environment.

Finally, one way to use assessment data effectively for intervention planning is through consultation. Assessment and decision-making practices historically consist of reporting by each of several specialists on test results (Ysseldyke et al., 1983); seldom have assessment and decision-making practices involved consultation based on a problem-solving approach aimed at monitoring the effectiveness of instructional/behavioral interventions (Bergan, 1977; Graden, Casey, & Christenson, 1985). Although we believe that school psychologists need to be well informed about instructional interventions, we do not advocate an "expert" model of consultation. That is, school psychologists should not observe and interview with TIES and then write a list of recommendations or actions to be taken by the teacher. Rather, school psychologists need to work collaboratively with teachers to design and systematically implement and evaluate instructional/behavioral interventions. Collaboration is essential to determine what works for the teacher. Effective interventions are as good for the teacher as for the student.

Implications

One-half of the 4.3 million students currently identified as handicapped are learning-disabled, and there has been a 129% increase in students labeled learning-disabled over the past 5 years. *A change is needed.* We believe it is time for educators in general, and school psychologists in particular, (a) to systematically account for all factors that influence student achievement, not only to focus on what is wrong with the student; (b) to plan, implement, and evaluate systematically the effectiveness of interventions for students; and (c) to make instructionally relevant decisions, not simply placement decisions. These can be accomplished by changing assessment practices to improve instruction for children.

How can this change take place? First, it must be recognized that systems change slowly — and more slowly if new ideas are forced on individuals. It is important to introduce new methods along with currently used methods. As school psychologists learn new approaches, they may rely less, for example, on the norm-referenced approaches with which they are very comfortable. In brief, change is to be seen as a process, not an event.

REFERENCES

Algozzine, B., & Korinek, L. (1985). Where is special education for students with high prevalence handicaps going? *Exceptional Children, 51*, 388-397.

Algozzine, B., & Ysseldyke, J. E. (1983). Learning disabilities as a subset of school failure: The oversophistication of a concept. *Exceptional Children, 50*, 242-246.

Algozzine, B., & Ysseldyke, J. E. (1986). The future of the LD field: Screening and diagnosis. *Journal of Learning Disabilities, 19*(7), 394-398.

Algozzine, B., Ysseldyke, J. E., & Hill, C. (1982). Psychoeducational decision-making as a function of the number of devices administered. *Psychology in the Schools, 19*, 328-334.

Bardon, J. (1982). The psychology of school psychology. In C. Reynolds & T. Gutkin (Eds.), *The handbook of school psychology* (pp. 3-23). New York: Wiley.

Bergan, J. R. (1977). *Behavioral consultation.* Columbus, OH: Merrill.

Bloom, B. S. (1985). Learning for mastery. In C. W. Fisher & D. C. Berliner (Eds.), *Perspectives on instructional time* (pp. 73-93). New York: Longman.

Borg, W. R. (1980). Time and school learning. In C. Denham & A. Lieberman (Eds.), *Time to learn* (pp. 33-72). Washington, DC: National Institute for Education.

Bracht, G. H. (1970). Experimental factors related to aptitude-treatment interactions. *Review of Educational Research, 40*, 627-645.

Bronfenbrenner, U. (1977). Toward an experimental ecology of human development. *American Psychologist, 32*, 513-531.

Brown, A. L., & Campione, J. C. (1986). Psychological theory and the study of learning disabilities. *American Psychologist, 14*(10), 1059-1068.

Carroll, J. B. (1963). A model of school learning. *Teachers College Record, 64*, 723-733.

Christenson, S., Abery, B., & Weinberg, R. A. (1986). An alternative model for the delivery of psychology in the school community. In S. N. Elliott & J. C. Wilt (Eds.), *The delivery of psychological services in schools: Concepts, processes, and issues.* Hillsdale, NJ: Erlbaum.

Denham, C., & Lieberman, A. (1980). *Time to learn.* Washington, DC: National Institute for Education.

Deno, S. L. (1985). Curriculum-based measurement: The emerging alternative. *Exceptional Children, 52*(3), 219-232.

Deno, S. L. (1986). Formative evaluation of individual student programs: A new role for school psychologists. *School Psychology Review, 15*(3), 358-374.

Edmonds, R. R. (1979). Effective schools for the urban poor. *Educational Leadership, 37*, 15-27.

Englemann, S., Granzin, A., & Severson, H. (1979). Diagnosing instruction. *Journal of Special Education, 13*, 355-363.

Fuchs, L. S., & Fuchs, D. (Eds.). (1986). Linking assessment to instructional interventions. *School Psychology Review, 15*(3).

Gallagan, G. (1985). Psychoeducational testing: Turn out the lights, the party's over. *Exceptional Children, 52*, 288-298.

Germann, G., & Tindal, G. (1985). An application of curriculum-based assessment: The use of direct and repeated measurement. *Exceptional Children, 52*(3), 244-265.

Gettinger, M. (1984). Individual differences in time needed for learning: A review of the literature. *Educational Psychologist, 19*, 15-29.

Goldwasser, E., Meyers, J., Christenson, S., & Graden, J. (1983). A survey of the impact of PL 94-142 on the practice of school psychology. *Psychology in the Schools, 20*, 153-165.

Good, T. L. (1983). Classroom research: A decade of progress. *Educational Psychologist, 18*(3), 127-144.

Good, T. L., & Brophy, J. E. (1984). *Looking in classrooms* (3rd ed.). New York: Harper & Row.

Good, T., & Grouws, D. (1979). The Missouri mathematics effectiveness project: An experimental study in fourth-grade classrooms. *Journal of Educational Psychology, 71*, 355-362.

Graden, J. L., Casey, A., & Bonstrom, O. (1985). Implementing a prereferral intervention system: Part II. The data. *Exceptional Children 51*(6), 487-496.

Graden, J. L., Casey, A., & Christenson, S. L. (1985). Implementing a prereferral intervention system: Part I. The model. *Exceptional Children, 51*(5), 377-387.

Haring, N. G., & Eaton, M. D. (1978). Systematic instructional procedures: An instructional hierarchy. In N. G. Harris, T. C. Lovitt, M. D. Eaton, & C. L. Hanson (Eds.), *The fourth R: Research in the classroom* (pp. 25-40). Columbus, OH: Merrill.

Heller, K. A., Holtzman, W., & Messick, S. (1982). *Placing children in special education: A strategy for equity.* Washington, DC: National Academy Press.

Hobbs, N. (1975). *Issues in the classification of children.* San Francisco: Jossey-Bass.

Howell, K. W. (1986). Direct assessment of academic performance. *School Psychology Review, 15*(3), 324-335.

Karweit, N. L. (1983). *Time on task: A research review* (Report 332). Baltimore, MD: Center for Social Organization of Schools, Johns Hopkins University.

Lentz, F. E., & Shapiro, E. S. (1986). Functional assessment of the academic environment. *School Psychology Review, 15*(3), 346-357.

Mann, L. (1971). Perceptual training revisions: The training of nothing at all. *Rehabilitation Literature, 32*, 322-335.

Mann, L. (1981). *On the trail of process.* New York: Grune & Stratton.

Marston, D., & Magnusson, D. (1985). Implementing curriculum-based measurement in special and regular education settings. *Exceptional Children, 52*(3), 266-276.

Martin, R., & Meyers, J. (1980). School psychologists and the practice of consultation. *Psychology in the Schools, 17*, 478-484.

Meyers, J., & Lytle S. (1986). Assessment of the learning process. *Exceptional Children, 53*, 138-144.

Mirkin, P. K., Fuchs, L. S., & Deno S. L. (1982). *Considerations for designing a continuous evaluation system: An integrative review* (Monograph No. 20). Minneapolis: University of Minnesota, Institute for Research on Learning Disabilities.

Peterson, P. L., Swing, S. R., Stark, K. D., & Waas, G. A. (1984). Student's cognitions and time on task during mathematics instruction. *American Educational Research Journal, 21*, 487-515.

Poland, S. F., Thurlow, M. L., Ysseldyke, J. E., & Mirkin, P. K. (1982). Current psychoeducational assessment and decision-making practices as reported by directors of special education. *Journal of School Psychology, 20*, 171-179.

Ramage, J. (1979). National survey of school psychologists: Update. *School Psychology Digest, 8*, 153-161.

Reynolds, M. C. (1975). Trends in special education: Implications for measurement. In W. Hively & M. C. Reynolds, *Domain-referenced testing in special education.* Minneapolis: Leadership Training Institute/Special Education.

Reynolds, M. C. (1988). Putting the individual into aptitude treatment interaction. *Exceptional Children, 54*, 324-331.

Rosenfield, S. (1987). *Instructional consultation.* Hillsdale, NJ: Erlbaum.

Rosenshine, B. (1983). Teaching functions in instructional programs. *Elementary School Journal, 83*(4), 335-352.

Rosehshine, B., & Stevens, K. (1986). Teaching functions. In M. C. Wittrock (Ed.), *Handbook of research on teaching* (3rd ed., pp. 376-391). New York: MacMillan.

Samuels, S. J. (1981). Some essentials of decoding. *Exceptional Education Quarterly, 2*, 11-25.

Sarason, S., & Doris, J. (1979). *Educational handicap, public policy, and social history.* New York: Free Press.

Scriven, M. (1983). Comments on Gene Glass. *Policy Studies Review, 2*, 79-84.

Shepard, L., & Smith, M. L. (1981). *Evaluation of the identification of perceptual–communicative disorders in Colorado.* Final Report. Boulder, CO: Laboratory of Educational Research, University of Colorado.

Squires, D. A., Huitt, W. G., & Segars, J. K. (1983). *Effective schools and classrooms: A research-based perspective.* Alexandria, VA: Association for Supervision and Curriculum Development.

Winne, P. H. (1985). Steps toward promoting cognitive achievements. *Elementary School Journal, 85*(5), 673-693.

Ysseldyke, J. E. (1973). Diagnostic-prescriptive teaching: The search for aptitude-treatment interactions. In L. Mann & D. A. Sabatino (Eds.), *The first review of special education.* New York: Grune & Stratton.

Ysseldyke, J. E. (1986). Current U.S. practices in assessing and making decisions about handicapped students. *Australian Journal of Special Education, 10*, 13-20.

Ysseldyke, J. E. (1987). Classification of handicapped students. In M. Wang, M. Reynolds, & H. Walberg (Eds.) *Handbook of Special Education: Research and Practices, 1*, 253-272. London: Pergamon.

Ysseldyke, J. E., & Algozzine, B. (1984). *Introduction to special education.* Boston: Houghton-Mifflin.

Ysseldyke, J. E., Algozzine, B., & Mitchell, J. (1982). Special education team decision making: An analysis of current practice. *Personnel and Guidance Journal, 60*, 308-313.

Ysseldyke, J. E., Algozzine, B., Rostollan, D., & Shinn, M. (1981). A content analysis of the data presented at special education team meetings. *Journal of Clinical Psychology, 37*, 655-662.

Ysseldyke, J. E., & Christenson, S. L. (1987a). *The instructional environment scale.* Austin, TX: Pro-Ed.

Ysseldyke, J. E., & Christenson, S. L. (1987b). Evaluating students' instructional environments. *RASE, 8*(3), 17-24.

Ysseldyke, J. E., Christenson, S. L., & Thurlow, M. L. (1987). *Factors that influence student achievement: An integrative review* (Monograph No. 7). Minneapolis: University of Minnesota, Instructional Alternatives Project.

Ysseldyke, J. E., & Mirkin, P. K. (1982). The use of assessment information to plan instructional interventions. In C. Reynolds & T. Gutkin (Eds.), *The handbook of school psychology,* (pp. 395-409). New York: Wiley.

Ysseldyke, J. E., Regan, R. R., Thurlow, M. L., & Schwartz, S. Z. (1981). Current assessment practices: The cattle dip approach. *Diagnostique, 6*, 16-27.

Ysseldyke, J. E., Reynolds, M. C., & Weinberg, R. A. (1984). *School psychology: A blueprint for training and practice.* Minneapolis, MN: National School Psychology Inservice Training Network.

Ysseldyke, J. E., & Salvia, J. A. (1974). Diagnostic-prescriptive teaching. Two models. *Exceptional Children, 41*, 181-189.

Ysseldyke, J. E., Thurlow, M., Graden, J., Wesson, C., Algozzine, B., & Deno, S. (1983). Generalizations from five years of research on assessment and decision making: The University of Minnesota Institute. *Exceptional Education Quarterly, 4*(1), 75-93.

7

Curriculum-Based Measurement

Gerald Tindal
University of Oregon

Curriculum-based measurement (CBM) is a variant of curriculum-based assessment (CBA) developed and researched at the University of Minnesota by Deno and associates. The present review of the research on CBM and analysis of its applicability for practice in the schools should serve to demonstrate its vast potential as an important alternative assessment and evaluation system.

Generally, the CBM research completed to date has been conducted in public schools and simply represents systematic collection of data. Only a small percentage of the studies have employed experimental designs using random assignment to treatments, a practice that is difficult and questionable for practitioners in the public schools. In point of fact, although there is a need for much further investigation, most of this "research" can and should be done by practitioners in the field.

The theme of this chapter is that CBM provides an alternative paradigm for delivering educational programs and that the data-based decision-making perspective is its most important feature. As psychologists and teachers develop alternative programs and roles, they too must be data-based.

In implementing CBM, psychologists can perform a meaningful function by generating pertinent information useful in evaluating the impact of instructional programs. Consequently, it is important both to know the research behind CBM *and* to be capable of generating further

data on the impact of programs. Therefore, this chapter is heavily research-oriented. Investigations are reviewed with enough detail that the reader can not only focus on the final outcomes, but also be sensitized to the variables that are investigated and the manner in which they are implemented and evaluated.

Review of the literature on CBM reveals the need to tie together data across educational decisions to conduct an impact evaluation. At present, different data are generated for different decisions, with little relationship between the various data bases. For example, though considerable time is spent on initial assessments for eligibility in specialized programs, little empirical support exists for such programs (Carlberg & Kavale, 1980). Furthermore, given the mismatch between general achievement tests and curricula, little diagnostic data can be salvaged from such initial assessments (Freeman, Kuhs, Porter, Floden, Schmidt, & Schwille, 1983; Jenkins & Pany, 1978). Nor can labeling of students be considered helpful in determining instructional programs (Marston, 1987). Therefore, the information generated in the initial assessment is of virtually no worth other than to provide administrative vindication for allocation of resources. As a result, further data typically need to be collected by teachers to plan instructional programs; however, these data often are unsystematic and seldom are used to formatively evaluate instruction. And at present, almost no attention is given to the summative evaluation of programs. The net effect is that data collected during educational decision making are poorly integrated and incapable of being used for evaluating subsequent decisions.

The alternative to be proffered in this chapter is that data collected during initial assessment should be helpful in distinguishing low-achieving students who are quantitatively different from their peers *and* should have bearing on placing them in the curriculum, grouping them with other students, and developing progress-monitoring systems. Once such outcomes are accomplished, formative evaluation can then proceed, so as ultimately to build effective programs that are truly data-based. In the final analysis, however, data generated in the initial assessments should also be reestablished in order to determine overall program effects. In this manner, data are tied together across all of the educational decisions (Jenkins, Deno, & Mirkin, 1979).

In line with this reasoning, following a seven-point characterization of CBM, comparison with three other exemplary forms of CBA, and a discussion of the CBM validation studies, a review of CBM research is presented in three major sections: screening and eligibility decisions, formative evaluation of instructional programs, and summative evaluation of program outcomes.

CHARACTERISTICS OF CBM

Curriculum-based measurement can be defined as having the following seven characteristics. The first and most obvious characteristic, as the name implies, is a focus on sampling from the curriculum for the development of measurement items. The students' basal readers, spelling curriculum, or math programs are used to generate items on the measures. Second, CBM can be considered primarily in the context of basic skills assessment. All of the research conducted to date has involved reading, writing, spelling, and math computation problems. It is uncertain whether the results from this research can also be applied to other content areas or levels of knowledge (Roid & Haladyna, 1982).

The third important dimension of CBM is the employment of direct responding on the part of the student in the assessment process. As Hopkins and Antes (1978) noted, students make a selection-type response (in which both the problem and the answer appear on the test), or make a supply- or production-type response (in which only the stimulus is present on the test and the student needs to supply or produce the answer). Fourth, the metric for summarizing performance employs rate of correct responses rather than just accuracy of performance. Although a range of transformed scores may be derived eventually, the fact that all forms of measurement employ timed tasks implies that performance is basically rate-oriented. The fifth characteristic of CBM is the focus on repeated assessment, change in performance over time being considered the major outcome rather than level of performance at one moment in time. That implies an emphasis on slope of improvement rather than level of performance. A sixth important dimension of CBM is its applicability to making a range of educational decisions (Salvia & Ysseldyke, 1986) — screening and eligibility decisions, instructional planning and formative evaluation decisions, and finally, program impact and summative evaluation decisions. Finally, probably the most important dimension of CBM is that research supporting its implementation in applied settings has yielded empirical results establishing its impact.

These seven characteristics must be considered comprehensively, as constituting a system. Omission of any one of them would preclude use of the term CBM. To highlight this issue, the term curriculum-based assessment is reviewed, as developed in the field and appearing in the professional literature. Some of these issues are subtle, though their impact is considerable, particularly in reference to the final two characteristics, application for multiple decision-making and technical adequacy or impact evaluation.

CBM VERSUS OTHER VARIANTS OF CURRICULUM-BASED ASSESSMENT

Several authors have developed curriculum-based assessment procedures, but not withstanding their identification by a common term, the differences between them may be greater than their similarities. The following very brief review of the primary forms of CBA that appear in literature is keyed to the seven characteristics noted above. Two common and pervasive differences between CBA and CBM are the unknown applicability of many CBA procedures to multiple educational decisions and the lack of research on their technical adequacy and impact; few psychometric data have been completed with many CBA procedures.

Four different forms of CBA are considered that have each been developed or advocated at a particular university. The first, from the University of Illinois and the University of Vermont, may be the most similar in format to the type of testing that appears in most published curricula (mastery tests). The second, although infrequently referred to as CBA, comes from Precision Teaching, which was developed at the University of Kansas and the University of Washington. The third has been developed by Gickling at the University of Nevada and Hargis at the University of Tennessee. Finally, the version of CBA that is covered in depth in this chapter was first advocated by Deno and Mirkin (1977), of the University of Minnesota, and has been described in the November issue of *Exceptional Children* (1985) in a series of articles by Deno (1985), Marston and Magnusson (1985), and Germann and Tindal (1985).

University of Illinois/Vermont Approach

The forms of CBA developed at Illinois and Vermont are essentially the same in respect to development and utilization within a teaching consultation program. Idol, Paolucci-Whitcomb, and Nevin (1986) defined CBA as "a type of informal inventory in which test items are taken from or are similar to items from the curriculum used in the classroom" (p. 70).

Premised upon the principles of criterion-referenced testing, the system essentially employs three strategies: establishing a well-defined domain, selecting items for inclusion on the test, and utilizing a mastery criterion. This system is predicated on sampling items from the curriculum and has been typically employed in assessment of basic skills, though consideration is also given to levels of knowledge (i.e., comprehension). The procedures developed at these universities utilize a direct and overt response: Students are asked to read aloud and answer comprehension questions in reading, to compute math problems, and so forth. However, selection-type responses are also utilized in some of the formats, primarily in the assessment of content-specific knowledge. Most testing is based on repeated samples of behavior and utilizes both a rate or fluency metric (Idol-Maestas, 1983), though accuracy of performance is employed when assessment focuses on content area knowledge (Idol, Nevin, & Paolucci-Whitcomb, 1986). Little information is available on the application of this system in educational decisions beyond instructional planning and evaluation; nor is any information to be found on the technical adequacy or impact of employing such a system.

University of Washington: Precision Teaching Approach

Although not formally referred to as CBA, the procedures developed in the context of Precision Teaching are often so similar that they are confused with those described in this section. Originally developed by Lindsley (1964), these procedures also reflect many of the characteristics that serve as the foundation of CBM. Like the procedures developed at the University of Illinois, items closely tied to instruction are sampled in the assessments. Additionally, however, instructional tactics are developed around stages of learning: acquisition and fluency, with decision rules employed for determining when and what to change (Martin, 1980; White, 1985; White & Haring, 1980). Such assessment can therefore be considered truly curriculum-based. Measurement in Precision Teaching has a far broader focus than simply basic skills and has employed a diverse array of student responses, from independent living skills to a wide range of social and academic behaviors. The procedures typically use a production response, rate of responding, and repeated measurement. In fact, an emphasis is often placed on rate building, particularly in relation to the second phase of instruction, fluency. An assumption often made in this system is that behavior changes multiplicatively, necessitating the use of semilogarithmic charts. This characteristic has bearing on both the focus on rate of behavior and repeated measurement. As Tindal and Germann (1986) have summarized comparisons between Precision Teaching and CBM, two marked differences exist: (a) CBM has been applied to fewer skill areas although across a broader range of educational decisions, and (b) technical adequacy research and impact evaluation has been conducted with CBM.

University of Nevada Approach

The major premise from which Gickling (Gickling & Havertape, 1981; Gickling & Thompson, 1985) and Hargis (1987) operate is that instruction should be evaluated in reference to the relationship between what is known and what is unknown to the learner. They have developed strategies for determining a student's *instructional level* (at which the ratio of known to unknown is quite high). Below this point is the *frustration level* (where the ratio of known to unknown is quite low). The term *independent level* designates the point at which the ratio of known to unknown is very high (or even that performance is errorless). In developing materials for assessment, teachers are instructed to devise unique materials for each student at an instructional level. Indeed, this brand of CBA may ultimately be the most curriculum-based, each student being provided a unique curriculum. To date the focus has been only on reading and math, though the procedures obviously have relevance for other basic skills such as spelling and writing. In

reading, the measurement system would entail determining the words that a student can read and comprehend and developing a series of stories incorporating them. In math, the procedures would include the development of a series of computation worksheets, utilizing only those operations and procedures with which the learner is familiar. No literature exists for extrapolating the procedures to other content areas or levels of knowledge. As described in the Gickling and Havertape 1981 CBA manual, all measurement formats employ a production-type response. However, use of rate of behavior measures and repeated measurement over time are not specifically addressed. Rather, the focus of measurement is on accuracy of performance and pre–post testing is implied. The main educational decision for which this variant of CBA appears relevant is that of instructional planning, though with the use of posttesting, summative evaluation of program outcomes can also be established. No research has been completed that documents the technical adequacy of the measurement system. Only two studies have been completed that focus on impact evaluations from use of the system (Gickling & Armstrong, 1978).

University of Minnesota: Curriculum-Based Measurement (CBM)

The form of curriculum-based assessment investigated at the University of Minnesota emanated originally from the work of Deno and Mirkin. In their 1977 manual, Deno and Mirkin described a measurement system for use by special education resource teachers in a consultation process. With funding from the University of Minnesota Institute for Research on Learning Disabilities (IRLD), a series of validation studies was initiated to empirically investigate a variety of classroom measures. In the development of these measures, criteria were established as guidelines for the subsequent investigations. The major requisite of the system was the development of measures that were: reliable, valid, capable of frequent administration, adaptable to the development of alternate forms, easy to administer, inexpensive to produce, and conducive to easy training in their use (Deno, Mirkin, & Shinn, 1979).

ORIGINAL VALIDATION RESEARCH

Given these criteria, a series of studies were initiated by Deno, Mirkin, and Chiang (1982), Deno Mirkin, Lowry, and Kuehnle (1980), and Deno, Marston, and Mirkin (1982) to investigate the technical adequacy — the reliability and validity — of CBM measures in reading, spelling, and written expression. The strategy for conducting the research included the identification of various potential procedures within each content area and their validation with respect to several technically adequate published achievement tests.

Reading

In reading, students were directed to (a) read aloud words from a list randomly sampled from the basal reader; (b) read aloud passages randomly sampled from the basal reader; (c) orally define the meaning of words appearing in the basal reader; (d) provide the word(s) that had been deleted in a passage sampled from the basal reader; and (e) read words that were underlined in a passage taken from the basal reader (Deno, Mirkin, & Chiang, 1982). For all five measurement procedures, the number of words read correctly and incorrectly served as the dependent measures. The same students also were administered a number of achievement tests.

From this research, it was determined that counting the number of words read aloud in 1 min from either a word list or a passage in the basal reader served as a valid measure of a student's reading proficiency. The correlations between oral reading rate measures of performance (from a and b above) and the criterion measures (published norm-referenced achievement tests) ranged from .73 to .91, with most coefficients in the .80s. After the dependent measure was identified, research began on logistical considera-

tions, such as where to measure from (the domain of sampling), how long to measure (length of administration), and how to score (dependent measure) (Fuchs, Tindal, & Deno, 1984). Further research by Fuchs and Deno (1981) and Fuchs, Fuchs, and Deno (1981) established that this measurement system was also valid in monitoring performance in the curriculum and highly related to Informal Reading Inventories.

Spelling

In spelling, the same procedures were used to identify a system for measuring student performance (Deno et al., 1980). Several parameters of this measurement system were also investigated: the domain for sampling words, the length of test administration, and various scoring procedures — words spelled correctly and incorrectly, as well as correct and incorrect letter sequences (White & Haring, 1980) — and use of percentage versus rate of correct responses.

The number of words spelled correctly or the number of correct letter sequences spelled in response to a dictated word list (sampled from either spelling or reading curricula) were the most highly related to other published measures of spelling, the correlations ranging from .80 to .96. Furthermore, tests of 1, 2, and 3 min duration provided indices of spelling achievement consistent with the published tests of spelling achievement of longer duration.

Written Expression

In written expression, the research focused on five procedures for measuring performance: (a) total number of words written; (b) number of words spelled correctly; (c) number of large words written (words with seven or more letters); (d) number of uncommon words (those not appearing in a list of common words compiled by Finn, 1977); and (e) average number of words per T-unit, a syntactically complete phrase (Hunt, 1965). Additionally, the use of different stimuli for generating writing (pictures, story starters, and topic sentences) and various time limits were investigated.

The total number of words written and the total number of correctly spelled words, in response to either a story starter or a topic sentence, correlated well (.70 or higher) with published achievement tests (Deno, Marston, & Mirkin, 1982). Later research by Videen, Deno, and Marston (1982) established the criterion validity of correct word sequences as an index of quality of written expression that correlated highly with holistic ratings of quality. Marston and Deno (1981) demonstrated, by means of test-retest, split half, alternate form, and interjudge forms of reliability measures, that several of the measures of written expression — total words, correctly spelled words, mature words, and correct letter sequences — were reliable.

Math Computation

Though no research was conducted at the Minnesota IRLD in math, several districts that have adopted CBM procedures in the language arts also have implemented a system in math computation. The measurement system developed in math includes random sampling of computation problems for each operation (addition, subtraction, multiplication, and division), providing four separate measures, each 2 min in duration (Tindal, Germann, & Deno, 1983). Student performance is scored for the number of digits correct and number incorrect, as well as the number of problems computed correctly and number computed incorrectly. To date, no research has been completed on the criterion validity of these measures. The two field settings in which this measurement system has been implemented have generated some preliminary evidence for the discriminant validity of these procedures (Marston & Magnusson, 1985; Tindal, Germann, Marston & Deno, 1983).

General Research on Technical Adequacy and Summary

The work of Marston and Deno (1982) corroborated the criterion validity findings of the alternative measures of reading, spelling, and written expression. In addition, they examined the reliability of the measures (both test-retest and alternative forms) and found high coefficients (.80 to .90) for rate correct in reading and spelling, and moderate coefficients (.60) for written expression. Using a standard measurement task, Tindal, Marston, and Deno (1983) also determined that the reliability of the measures in reading, spelling, writing, and in most areas of math were high or moderately high (.70 to .95). In written expression and two areas of math, the coefficients were moderate (.55).

In conclusion, much of this research has established that these alternative measures of reading, spelling, writing, and math (a) are reliable and (b) are highly related to more accepted and commonly used measures of achievement in each of the respective areas. The results simply indicate that the rank ordering of students from low to high on CBM will closely reflect the same rank ordering that is attained when published achievement tests are used. Rarely, however, do practitioners simply need to rank order students. Rather, they must make a host of placement and program planning decisions about students. At the broadest level, students need to be placed into services delivery systems, ranging from compensatory programs to specialized environments. Although the initial CBM research focused on criterion validity, later research focused on using this data base for distinguishing students in various levels of specialized placements and in screening and determining eligibility for special education.

The question becomes one of making eligibility/placement decisions with CBM that produce the same results as are achieved with more traditional psychoeducational techniques. As an alternative to current practices, CBM can be evaluated by either the consistency of the decision/

outcome or the cost benefit from its use. The research to be reviewed next considers only whether the use of CBM results in the same type of decision, leaving the cost/efficacy issue to be calculated from a logical and practical point of view — examining the benefits from its use in terms of multiple-decision data bases. It is simply argued that if the same decision can be made in a fraction of the time, and if the data that are generated have application to more uses than placement of students into specialized environments (i.e., can also be used to place students into a curriculum, establish long-range goals, and organize formative monitoring systems), then the alternative practice is preferable. This research can be viewed from the two perspectives in which CBM has been used: (a) to study groups already classified and (b) to initiate the original classifications.

COMPARISON OF USE OF CBM FOR SCREENING AND ELIGIBILITY DETERMINATION

As reviewed by Shinn, Tindal, and Stein (1988), a number of studies have been completed on the use of CBM in screening students and in distinguishing groups of students. In the original validation research (Deno, Mirkin, & Chiang, 1982; Deno, Marston, & Mirkin, 1982; Deno, Mirkin, Lowry, & Kuehnle, 1980), comparisons of performance levels were made between students in resource rooms and regular classrooms. The major finding was that the reading, spelling, and writing levels of the students in the regular classroom were significantly greater than the performance of the resource room students at all grade levels.

In a study by Shinn, Ysseldyke, Deno, and Tindal (1986), direct measures in reading, spelling, and writing were administered to a subset of learning-disabled (LD) and low-achieving students who had been tested during the previous year on a wide range of commonly used psychometric tests (Ysseldyke, Algozzine, Shinn, & McGue, 1982). The results from the traditional published psychometric instruments revealed an extreme amount

of overlap in the scores of these two groups. In contrast, considerably less overlap was apparent on the CBM measures of reading, writing, and spelling. The average performance of LD students was significantly lower than their low-achieving counterparts on CBM measures and the distributions of the two groups were quite distinct and nonoverlapping.

Further comparisons between LD students and both Chapter 1 and regular education students have also been reported. Both Deno, Marston, Shinn, and Tindal (1983) and Marston and Deno (1982) found that primary grade LD students read significantly fewer words correctly than students in regular education. Furthermore, students receiving Chapter 1 services read significantly more fluently than those in special education in Grades 1 and 2. Subsequent research with students in intermediate grades that employed measures in all academic areas demonstrated that CBM consistently differentiated these three groups of students (Shinn & Marston, 1985). In reading, regular education students outperformed those in Chapter 1, who in turn outperformed those in special education. In math and written expression, the same results were found with two exceptions, in which only two comparisons were significant across the three groups. Likewise, Shinn, Tindal, Marston, and Spira (1987) found the performance of students in special education to be significantly lower than those in regular education or Chapter 1. Students at the 50th percentile in special education typically performed less favorably than the 3rd percentile of students in regular education and often less than the 20th percentile of students in Chapter 1. Furthermore, when level of reading performance was used to predict group classification, students were sorted into their respective groups with 97% accuracy.

In an analysis of students referred for special education Shinn, Tindal, and Spira (1987) found their performance to be significantly discrepant (lower) than the regular education norms, though when the scores were plotted in a distribution, many students who were referred had scores within the range of other regular education students not referred for special education. That is, for any student in special education, an equally poorly performing student was also present in regular education.

All of the research reviewed thus far has been based on the comparisons of students in intact groups: Students had been placed with non-CBM procedures, making it difficult to discern the applicability of using CBM in the initial placement. To investigate this application, a series of studies have been conducted on the use of CBM to screen students and to determine eligibility for special education.

Screening and Eligibility Research

In a study conducted by Marston, Tindal, and Deno (1984), an analysis was done on the percentages of students identified on the basis of various criteria for determining discrepancy from regular education students. From national incidence rates used as an informal criterion at the time of this study — it appeared that a discrepancy ratio (Deno & Mirkin, 1977) of -2.5 or greater resulted in percentages of students comparable to national rates. In grades 3-6, in the areas of reading, spelling, and written expression, the approximate percentage of students identified as manifesting discrepancy ratios of -2.5 ranged from 5.5% to 9%; the percentages when using ratios of -2.5 and -3.0 ranged from 3% to 6%. In the first and second grades, the percentages identified were much higher, suggesting a need to reconsider either the criteria used in determining eligibility or the domain from which the measurement items are sampled, since the distributions diverged greatly from normal.

Rather than using hypothetical data in which all students were sampled from regular education, Marston, Tindal, and Deno (1984) compared actual student performance from LD and non-LD groups and statistically reclassified them. They found that the direct measures of reading and written expression correctly identified 83% and 73%, respectively. In contrast, the use of the Peabody Individual Achieve-

ment Test (PIAT) (Dunn & Markwardt, 1970) and the SAT (Karlsen, Madden & Gardner, 1975) or the Test of Written Language (TOWL) (Hammill & Larsen, 1978) resulted in the correct placement of 86% and 80% in the areas of reading and written expression, respectively. The accuracy of classification by the Woodcock-Johnson Psychoeducational Battery (Woodcock & Johnson, 1978) was lower than the achievement measures in reading (62%) and comparable to the writing measure (74%). Thus, Marston et al. (1984) concluded that not only do the measures of fluency predict correct membership in special education about as accurately as the commercial measures of achievement, but both do quite well compared to more complicated procedures incorporating measures of ability.

Although the previous research employed CBM procedures in simulating eligibility decisions, no actual implementation was ever employed. One of the first studies to investigate the effects of using the CBM identification system in a school was completed by Marston, Mirkin, and Deno (1984). In this study, comparisons were made between screening and identification procedures based on CBM and the more typical procedure of teacher referral and ability-achievement measurement. Students in the CBM group were screened on CBM measures and subsequently placed into special education according to multiple criteria involving a comparison with CBM norms. Students in the standard procedure group, were referred by teachers and were tested on the Woodcock-Johnson Psychoeducational Battery (Woodcock & Johnson, 1978) and placed on the basis of the district's adopted criterion of a 20-point discrepancy. A third group served as control, and followed district procedures in a different school building.

The researchers found that, overall, the same numbers of students were referred by the two procedures. However, the number of students meeting the district guidelines was greater for the CBM procedures (80%) than the procedures actually mandated by the district (36%). No differences were found in the level of ability or the discrepancy of ability and achievement between any of the groups. Academic achievement appeared to be the most important consideration in teacher referrals. In the traditional system, teachers referred more males, whereas with the use of a CBM screening system, no significant differences in academic achievement were found in referrals as a function of student sex. Finally, more girls with social behavior problems were referred with the CBM procedures.

In another study employing CBM procedures to place students in special education, Tindal, Germann, and Deno (1983) compared the local rates of referral to state and national averages. In the classification of learning disabilities, the percentages were similar, with 4.10% identified in a rural Minnesota educational cooperative, 4.05% nationally, and 4.80% for the state of Minnesota. Approximately 1% more students were identified in this county as educable mentally retarded (EMR) than at the state or national levels. During the year of this research, the criteria used for differential classification of LD and EMR included both level of discrepancy and the number of areas in which discrepancies occurred. Students discrepant in one area at a level of 2.0 times less proficient than peers were identified as LD, whereas students discrepant in two or more areas at levels of 3.0 times or more less proficient than peers were identified as EMR. This classification system, however, was not inflexible; rather it was viewed as essentially a sociopolitical process based on very little scientific rigor (Tucker, Stevens, & Ysseldyke, 1983). Adjustments were made in the system to attain a level of identification in keeping with both the problems exhibited by the student population and the resources available to the school system.

In summary, there is empirical support for using a CBM system to determine eligibility for special education. The students identified as mildly handicapped (LD/EMR) are quite similar in many characteristics to those identified by using more traditional procedures involving assessment of ability and achievement. Furthermore, the measurement system

appears to be sensitive in discriminating current categories of exceptionality. Yet a number of interesting issues remain and require further systematic evaluation, much of which can be provided by practitioners in the field. As districts adopt or utilize CBM, particularly in the development of normative decision-making, it is imperative that new data be collected to ensure a sensible and supportive decision-making system. The following is a review of some of the research that needs more attention.

Investigating Alternatives in Screening and Classification

Many districts have employed CBM in the development of local norms, but a limited amount of research has been completed on the important parameters for such an application. For example, Tindal, Germann, and Deno (1983) determined that a minimum of 15–20% of the student population needs to be sampled to produce a stable index of normative performance. Magnusson (1986) examined the effects of using building norms versus district norms and concluded that the latter results in similar identifications and yet has the advantage of a greater number of students used for each normative index. This issue becomes important in large districts that have great diversity among the various schoolbuildings. Tindal, Marston, Deno, and Germann (1982) examined the effects of using different basal readers and found significant differences in the rates of performance between the programs; however, a comparison on a standard reading task did not replicate the same significant differences. This finding was not extended to determine the impact on identification of students for specialized programs.

Beyond these limited studies, few investigations have been completed on the norming process. Tindal, Germann, and Deno (1983) examined the distributions of norms and found them to be normal and regular, even though the low-performing students served in special education in the past had been excluded. This was true even at the classroom level with the use of only 40 students. It is not certain, however, what impact student selection strategies have on the norms and the subsequent identification rates. Most districts have included Chapter 1 students in the normative group but have excluded special education populations. Of course, this strategy raises the problem of comparisons within a truncated population, though little is known of the outcomes of this practice. Would more students be identified if the normative group included the low-performing students who have received special education in the past? What is the impact on the evaluation of outcomes at the end of the year? Is improvement more difficult to attain, given the slightly skewed norms in favor of higher-achieving students?

Another issue in the development of norms is related to the structure of the curriculum and the sampling procedures used for generating test materials. Some curricula may have review material in the beginning of the program, increasing the opportunity for students to generate higher scores. Although most districts have opted for three norming periods during the year, corresponding to fall, winter, and spring, little empirical evidence mandates such a practice. Certainly, in the early grades (first and second), change in performance is extreme over short periods of time. For example, most first graders enter schools in the fall as nonreaders. The distribution for letter or sound identification or basic consonant–vowel–consonant (CVC) word reading is extremely positively skewed and narrow. By winter, the distribution begins to normalize, and in the spring, a bell-shaped curve is often achieved (Tindal, Germann, & Deno, 1983). As a result, identification of special education students in the fall is extremely problematic, because it results in a tendency to overidentify. Furthermore, in the initial assessment of students, the choice of a normative period is critical. If a student is referred late in the fall and the norms from much earlier in the fall are used, the tendency to underidentify students exists.

Very little research has been completed on the criteria for classifying students. In part, this may be because the basic premise of CBM is antithetical to the concept of fitting students into a disability typology. However, in terms of practical procedures for determining administrative funding, it may be important to attend to such classifications. The only research to be completed (Tindal, Germann, & Deno, 1983) found that although the number of students identified as learning-disabled was similar to state and national averages, the number identified as educable mentally retarded was considerably greater than these averages.

EVALUATION OF INSTRUCTIONAL PROGRAMS

Although the field of school psychology has been narrowly involved in issues of classification and determination of eligibility, other roles for psychologists are suitable to the profession. Two very powerful and distinctive roles for which psychologists may be suitably trained are those of behavioral consultants and program evaluators. However, these occupations, though appropriate alternatives to traditional practice, presume familiarity with monitoring systems and data-based decision making.

Classification of students by CBM measures has received considerable attention; yet the measurement system was initially designed for evaluating instructional programs. Because CBM is premised on frequent measurement, the direction of this research has involved (a) documentation of growth and (b) the application of various decision-rules for determining whether an instructional program is sufficient or in need of modification. Both issues are addressed in this next section.

In consulting with teachers on program improvement, a critical dimension is the sensitivity of the measurement system for documenting change. Although the field of educational measurement has long used norm-referenced achievement tests to reflect performance changes from specific instructional programs, this fallible technique has been frequently criticized (Freeman et al., 1983; Jenkins & Pany, 1978). In an effort to develop an adequate measurement system, a considerable amount of research has been conducted with CBM on changes in performance levels over time.

Studies of Student Growth by Use of CBM

One form of validation of measurement systems is the occurrence of basic improvements in performance as children advance through the grades. In most such validation research, the emphasis is on the sensitivity of the measurement system to change, with less concern devoted to documenting the differential effects of specific interventions (cf. the experimental teaching project of Deno and Marston for data on this latter issue). Rather, this research is premised on the assumption merely that students are receiving instruction in schools; the exact nature of that instruction is left undocumented and uncontrolled.

In the original validation research on CBM, it was determined that growth over grades was consistent. This finding has been corroborated by Marston, Lowry, Deno, and Mirkin (1981) in reading, spelling, and written expression. Tindal, Germann, and Deno (1983) found growth among a large group of regular education students over 8 months. Furthermore, the findings for this sample were comparable to those obtained by Deno, Marston, Mirkin, Lowry, et al., (1982) for a sample from several regions of the United States. Both studies found growth both within grades and across grades on standard measurement tasks.

Although these findings indicate that CBM reflects improvement in basic skills over a large time frame, the minimum amount of time for reflection of growth in basic skills to appear is uncertain. Shinn, Ysseldyke, Deno, and Tindal (1986) found no differences between special education and Chapter 1 students in the slope of improvement over 5 weeks of measurement in reading, spelling, and written expression. Deno, Marston, Shinn, and Tindal (1983) found significant differences between LD and Chapter 1 students in slope over a 16 week period, but no differences apparent between these two groups in Grades 1 and 2. Finally, Marston, Deno, and Tindal (1983) found consistent growth both across grades and within each grade, over 10 weeks, in reading and written expression. Furthermore, the growth exhibited on the curriculum tasks was greater than that shown on the Reading Comprehension and Language subtests of the Stanford Achievement Tests.

Although this research provides peripheral validation data for CBM, the measurement system appears sensitive to general instructional effects; however, it provides very little guidance for practitioners who want to employ CBM in their school building or districts. One of the first issues to arise in developing a CBM system is the need to generate a sensible and sensitive domain from which to sample items for a measurement system. In some of the research into this question, sampling plans were developed by selecting material from the modal group in each grade. In other research, material was sampled across grade levels (Tindal, Germann, & Deno, 1983). What is not apparent, however, is that the sampling plan needs to be oriented around the use of the data and the type of decision to be made. Typically, for screening and eligibility, broader domains are sampled, whereas individual progress monitoring is based on more specific and narrow domains established from long-range goals. The next section reviews research that has been completed on the latter use.

Establishing Sensitive Domains for Monitoring Progress

Students are assessed in material in which they are expected to become proficient by the *end of the year* (Mirkin, Deno, et al., 1981). Selection of this material has been based on local norms, district curriculum standards, or any of several mastery criteria appearing in the literature. For example, in reading, an appropriate goal may be for the student to gain proficiency in material in which (a) peers are currently reading at a certain level of fluency, or (b) peers will eventually be reading at a certain level of fluency, or (c); it is possible that peers are not an appropriate standard. In this case, goals may be established for materials in which the student currently has minimal proficiency.

No CBM research has been completed that compares the different measurement systems with each other. However, some data have been collected on the effect of domain breadth on change in performance. In all of this research, instructional programs are left undocumented and uncontrolled; students in extant programs are the subject of the research, and the interest is more in overall reactivity of the measurement system and not in differential sensitivity to specific instructional programs. Nevertheless, the general content of most instructional programs was kept comparable across the domain comparisons.

Four studies have focused on differential sensitivity to change as a function of the domain from which items were sampled. Tindal and Deno (1981) and Fuchs, Tindal, and Deno (1984) found that change in student performance was optimal from a grade-level domain, in contrast to one sampling from a broader or from a more restrictive size. When students were measured from a pool of words that were grade-appropriate, the slope of improvement over time was greater than if they were tested on words sampled from across several grades or from within the instructional unit. In the latter procedure, the measurement system was more sensitive to change; however, both *slope* (change in performance over time) and *variability* (variation from day to day) showed increases, making it difficult to ascertain effects. Mirkin and Deno (1979) found that when reading samples were taken from independent and frustration levels, the effects of the experimental treatment were more obvious. As they stated, "formative evaluation of reading requires regular measurement on content external to daily instruction" (pp. 13-14). Finally, Mirkin, Deno, Tindal, and Kuehnle (1980) found the effect of daily achievement was significant for sampling procedures that incorporated words from a grade-specific list and less so for a sampling procedure that employed words from across several grades.

DATA UTILIZATION STRATEGIES

Although the growth research indicates that CBM is sensitive to change, the lack of documented and controlled instruction weakens the findings considerably. Indeed, more specific research is needed on the effects of specific programs on student performance and the establishment of treatment validity of instruction (Hoge, 1985) and reactivity of the measurement system to instructional variables (Tindal & Parker, 1987). The entire concept of CBM is, in fact, predicated on application to evaluating specific instructional programs, through the use of precise data and data-based decision guidelines. In most of this research, instruction has either been defined or rated in terms of major components such as interactive strategies, materials, motivational strategies, physical arrangements, and time.

Most of the decision rules research has focused on the decision of "when" to change a program, and less on "what" to change. It is typically assumed that by precisely and systematically outlining and delivering instruction, and concurrently measuring student performance, evaluation of successive modifications can be used to determine the best instructional tactics for any given student. This procedure is considerably different than most other systems, in that planning is a post hoc activity rather than a "front-loaded" procedure that emphasizes diagnostics and prescriptions. It is assumed that only by instructing students and evaluating the effects can program planning proceed in an empirical fashion (see Englemann, Granzin, & Severson, 1979, for a discussion of instructional diagnosis).

Two procedures have been outlined by Mirkin, Deno, et al. (1981) and described by Fuchs (1986) for use in this type of evaluation: short term measurement (originally referred to as progress measurement by Deno & Mirkin, 1977) and long term measurement. In the former procedure, measurement is based on the rate of mastery of successive units; in the latter, performance is expected to increase on a constant task. Short term measurement employs the same procedures as those used in the development of criterion-referenced tests, in which a domain is established, procedures are employed for sampling items from that domain, and mastery criteria are utilized for determining progress through the curriculum. In contrast, long term measurement samples from a larger domain and makes no assumptions about mastery; rather improvement is scaled as increased fluency on random parallel forms.

Two variations of long term measurement are further available: (a) goal-oriented, and (b) program-oriented (Deno & Fuchs, 1987). The emphasis of goal-oriented measurement is attainment of a goal. In contrast, program-oriented measurement, emphasizes isolating specific instructional strategies in a quasi-experimental fashion. In the former, evaluation is premised on future performance expectations; in the latter, evaluation takes careful note of previous levels of attainment.

The use of both decision-making strategies has been investigated in respect to the effect on student achievement. The next section describes both strategies for using curriculum-based measurement in: (a) short term measurement (formerly progress measurement), and (b) long term measurement (Fuchs & Fuchs, 1986).

Short Term Measurement

In short term measurement the teacher defines a long-range goal (LRG) and writes the short-term objective (STO) in terms of the rate of movement through the material toward that goal. This system (Figure 1) starts off from a comparison of current instructional placement with eventual attainment and calculates the number of units to be traversed over a fixed period of time. Following is an example of the LRG for this form of data utilization.

In 20 weeks (May 23, 1988) when presented with a story from the end of Ginn 720, Level D, John will read aloud at a rate of 100 words correct per minute with 4 or fewer errors.

Assuming that John was currently placed in the beginning of Level C and 10 stories were present in levels C and D, the following STO would be written:

Each week, when presented with successive stories from Units C and D of Ginn 720, John will master (read aloud at a rate of 100 words per minute with 4 or fewer errors) 1 story per week.

Measurement then proceeds by administration of a series of frequent curriculum-based measures, the test items being sampled from the lesson used for instruction. Once mastery is attained on that lesson (i.e., 100 words per minute with 4 or fewer errors), the student is advanced to the next lesson. Therefore, an important characteristic of this form of measurement is that the student is assessed over time from different materials that have been taught prior to the measurement, making comparison between successive measurements inappropriate. Because of this feature, a graph is plotted from mastery data, not directly from rates of performance. The purpose of the data utilization strategy is to increase the student's rate of movement through the lessons.

Long Term Measurement

In this form of measurement, the teacher is directed to establish a LRG and a STO that specifies improvement on an established domain from the LRG. In contrast to the short term measurement approach, in which the material for assessment changes over time, this form of assessment utilizes a constant set of materials to determine improvement over time. Rather than increasing the rate of movement through material, this data-utilization strategy focuses on improvement in performance on alternate forms of the same material over time. Following is an example of an LRG and STO from this perspective:

FIGURE 1
Graphic display of three forms of CBM instructional evaluation systems: Short term measurement, long term measurement with goal oriented criteria, and long term measurement with program oriented criteria.

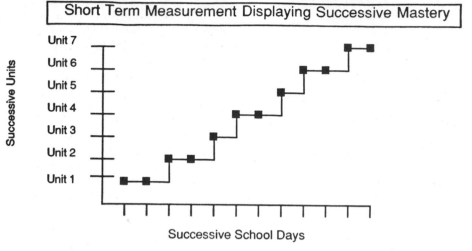

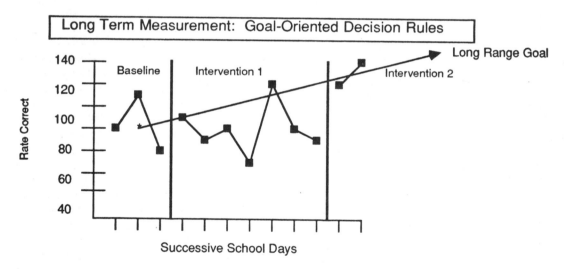

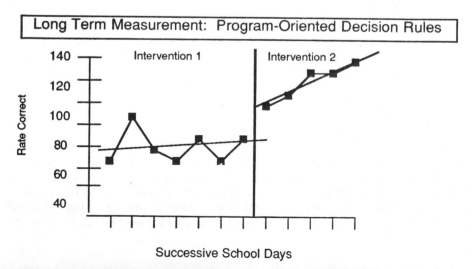

By May 23, 1988, when presented with a randomly selected passage from Ginn 720, Level D, John will read aloud at a rate of 100 words per minute with 4 errors or less.

Assuming that John is currently placed in the beginning of Level C, the teacher would assess from materials near the end of Level D, creating the following STO:

Each week, when presented a randomly selected passage from Ginn 720, Unit D, John will read aloud, at an average increase of 2 words read correctly per minute and no increase in errors.

Performance would reflect both increases and decreases, changing in part as a function of the material sampled for assessment and in part as a function of gradually increasing skill in reading. However, over time the slope of change should be generally upward.

DATA UTILIZATION RESEARCH

A number of studies have been completed in which CBM has been used to systematically monitor student progress and evaluate the effects of instructional programs. Generally, four major variables have been investigated: impact on structure of instruction and student achievement, data utilization in modifying instructional programs, instructional components analysis, and consumer satisfaction.

Structure of Instruction and Student Achievement

Through the findings of several interrelated studies, it has been found that frequent measurement does influence the structure of instruction and, on occasion, has also led to improved student achievement. Following are the major findings from some of these studies.

Fuchs, Deno, and Mirkin (1984) completed an experimental study in which two different data utilization strategies were employed, with teacher structure of instruction, accuracy of measurement, and student achievement

measured at three times during the year. In the experimental group, teachers established long-range goals using the procedures described by Mirkin, Deno, et al. (1981). These teachers measured approximately twice per week over the first 12 weeks, but more infrequently over the last 6 weeks; they also introduced more instructional changes initially, and fewer in the latter phases of the study. Student achievement on virtually all measures was significantly greater for students in this group than for those in a control group. Additionally, students in the experimental group were more knowledgeable about their learning both in terms of current levels of performance and projected goals.

Another study demonstrated a reliable relationship between the use of systematic data-based decision making and the structure of instruction (Fuchs, Deno and Mirkin, 1982). "Student scores across the three trimesters of the study increased for experimental group teachers, but decreased for contrast teachers" (p. 14). Furthermore, the teachers in the contrast group were more optimistic about the success of their program, but also more uncertain; yet, they were also less responsive to making changes in the goals of the program.

King, Deno, Mirkin, and Wesson (1983) found that teachers consistently employed initial measurement procedures and increased the amount of controlled practice in their structure of instruction. Teachers of experimental students were not proficient in evaluation and utilization of the data on an ongoing basis and the findings of achievement gains for their students were not significantly greater than those found with the control students.

Wesson, Deno, et al. (1982), using path analysis procedures for investigating the relationship between structure of instruction, measurement of student progress, and achievement in reading, found that all three constructs were stable over time. Measurement was found, however, to influence achievement, a finding consistent with the results of other studies (Jenkins, Mayhall, Peschka, & Townsend,

1974). No such influence of structure of instruction on achievement was found. Wesson, Deno, et al. (1982) stated that the novelty effects of measurement may need to be accompanied by more sophisticated data utilization eventually, if such effects are to be continued. Wesson, Skiba, Sevcik, King, and Deno (1984) found that gain in student performance on reading passages was significantly different for teachers who were high in implementation of data-based measurement procedures. "Apparently, the teachers made better instructional decisions using the technically adequate data and consistent rules regarding how to use that (sic) data" (Wesson, et al., 1983, p. 17). Finally, Sevcik et al. (1983) found that students taught with data-based measurement were more aware of working toward a goal and reported more optimism about reaching their goals. Although teachers who did not employ such data-based evaluations were initially optimistic but uncertain about the students' progress and success, they were far less optimistic near the end of the year.

Data Utilization

An important question in the use of curriculum-based procedures is: When teachers are frequently provided with student performance data, what is the effect of using various decision rules or guidelines for interpreting such data?

In general, it appears that use of systematic decision rules is usually more favorable than unsystematic judgments. In a major summary of data utilization effects using meta-analysis methodology Fuchs and Fuchs (1986) found that "when teachers were required to employ data-utilization rules, effect sizes were higher than when data were evaluated by teacher judgment (p. 205)." However, the research on this variable is not comprehensive enough to warrant making definitive statements. Often decision rules are implemented with minimal integrity. Collection and display of data do not necessarily set the occasion for use of those data to evaluate instructional programs. For example, Skiba, Wesson, and Deno (1982) determined that al-

though teachers can learn to administer the measurement systems and find the information practical and time-efficient, in their study very few changes in instructional programs resulted. More systematic training and monitoring is probably crucial in data utilization research and practice. Ideally, this system of student assessment would be used to actually ferret out the specific effects of certain instructional components. The following discussion describes some studies that help in understanding data utilization issues.

In one of the early reports on data utilization, Mirkin and Deno (1979) employed four different treatment groups in a reading study: daily measurement and data-based change, daily measurement and non-data-based change, pre–post measurement and non-data-based change, and no specific measurement frequency or change procedures. The most important conclusion was that "systematic formative evaluation most effectively contributes to student achievement when rules for the utilization of measurement data are included as part of the formative evaluation system" (p. 12).

In a separate study of data utilization strategies applied to spelling, Mirkin et al. (1980) compared daily measurement and data-based rules, daily measurement and teacher judgment, and weekly measurement and teacher judgment. They found that daily measurement was clearly superior to weekly measurement for a list of words from the students' grade level; however, on a common list from several grade levels, the findings were less clear. These findings were replicated across two successive treatment periods. In contrast, when data-based rules were compared with teacher judgment, no significant differences were found. Nevertheless, teachers who employed daily measurement *and* data-based rules showed greater student gains in both rate and accuracy of spelling performance over the gains found for teachers employing weekly measurement and teacher judgment.

Two types of data utilization strategies (assessment of long-term goals [LTG] and assessment of short-term goals

[STG]) and two frequencies of measurement (daily versus weekly) were compared by Tindal, Fuchs, Christenson, Mirkin, and Deno (1981). Differences between the two data utilization groups were not found on either of the posttests (a word list and a passage). Additionally, students measured daily made the same achievement gains as those measured weekly. In explaining these lack of differences, the authors noted that, generally, the teachers incorrectly implemented the procedures in both data utilization conditions. In contrast to the finding of no differences between data utilization strategies, Fuchs, Deno and Roettger (1983) found that a program-oriented decision-rule system resulted in greater achievement gains than that attained when a goal-oriented decision-rule system was used.

Finally, there do not seem to be differences in the number of instructional changes *between* short term monitoring and long term monitoring systems, according to a study by Fuchs, Wesson, Tindal, Mirkin, and Deno (1982). However, the number of changes was found to be significantly greater than for a no-data-utilization strategy, in which only one change was exhibited.

Instructional Components

Given that few studies have been completed on various instructional components, it is too early to make strong conclusions about this topic. Indeed, the nature of this variable is such that teachers should be regularly conducting this type of analysis as they determine optimal instructional programs for students in the least restrictive environment. Most of this research would employ single-case experimental designs. In one study of instructional factors, Deno, Chiang, Tindal, and Blackburn (1979) analyzed reading program components of a Child Service Demonstration Center in both an elementary and middle school resource room. Three primary comparisons were employed over a school year: graphing versus no graphing; use of decision rules with tokens versus praise; and finally,

concept teaching versus drill and practice. Using a dependent measure of the number of days taken to reach criterion, several significant findings were obtained. In the elementary school, graphing and decision rules with tokens were more effective than no graphing and decision rules with praise. In the middle school, concept teaching was more effective than drill and practice, but no other differences were found in graphing and decision rules with points or praise.

Another study to isolate an important instructional variable was reported by Fuchs, Fuchs, and Deno (1985). They found that "goal ambitiousness" was an important factor in the overall achievement of students. The "ambitiousness" of teacher goals was rated according to rigorously established quantitative criteria. Students of teachers who set very ambitious or moderately ambitious goals achieved significantly more on three different reading measures than students with teachers who set unambitious goals.

Teacher Preferences

For a system to be useful and receive widespread endorsement and implementation in the field, it is imperative that procedures be available for training and follow-up support. Manuals have been written for training teachers in data-based program evaluation (Mirkin, Fuchs, & Deno, 1982; Mirkin, Deno, Fuchs, Wesson, Tindal, Marston & Kuehnle, 1981); however, systematic investigation of its implementation in the field is needed. Several investigations completed at the Minnesota IRLD have focused on this variable, the general finding being that once teachers are trained, the procedures are found to be reasonable and are supported.

Curriculum-based measurement procedures are very time-consuming at first, although they can become very time-efficient after training and practice (Fuchs, Wesson, Tindal, Mirkin, & Deno, 1981). Training manuals are a necessary support material (Wesson, Mirkin, & Deno, 1982); however, on-site training may also be critical.

There is some evidence to suggest that teachers prefer short term over long term measurement. Teachers who followed students with short term measurement were found by Mirkin, Fuchs, Tindal, Christenson, and Deno (1981) to be more satisfied with student achievement. However, no differential achievement resulted from its use, and interestingly, fewer instructional changes were implemented in connection with short term than with long term measurement. Fuchs, Wesson, Tindal, Mirkin, and Deno (1982) also found that teachers generally preferred short term measurement though both data-utilization strategies were found to be equally effective in improving student performance. Furthermore, both strategies were more effective than the use of measurement without a data-utilization strategy.

Summary of Issues in Evaluating Instruction

Over a series of research efforts directed toward the utilization of student achievement data, the findings have not been uniformly consistent. At times, teachers implementing data-utilization procedures have been more effective in improving student achievement than teachers using infrequent and unsystematic strategies. Often no significant differences have been found between teachers using various forms of data-based evaluation and decision making. Presently, "scant evidence exists for the superiority of either data utilization procedure in producing greater student gains" (Deno & Fuchs, 1987, p. 11).

INVESTIGATING ALTERNATIVES IN INSTRUCTIONAL PLANNING AND EVALUATION

As school psychologists develop roles other than that of intelligence test administrator, it is imperative that consideration be given to the help that they can bring to the process of formative evaluation. School psychologists are uniquely prepared as measurement experts, providing the necessary link between the collection of data and its use in evaluating and modifying content. Many variables and procedures need to be explored: establishment of long-range goals and deployment of various measurement systems; adoption of various decision rules and their effect on structure of instruction and student achievement; use of data to systematically isolate effective instructional components; teacher and student knowledge of the effects and uses of various feedback and reporting systems.

The potential use of curriculum-based measurement in planning and evaluating instructional programs can be subsumed under two primary efforts: direct services in resource rooms and indirect services through consultation programs. The first area, in which much of the research has been completed, is in the development of empirically validated, individual educational programs (IEPs) in special education classrooms. Included here is the development of procedures for writing IEPs and monitoring programs through the use of data decision rules. The two applications reviewed earlier, short term and long term measurement systems, are examples of this line of research and practice. As much of this research has demonstrated, the findings are somewhat unstable or inconsistent. Some support exists for the use of curriculum-based assessment and evaluation strategies. Yet, more research needs to be completed on how CBM is used to evaluate and modify programs.

The second important area of research is the use of CBM in consultation, with program monitoring used to effect changes in the regular education environment through the use of classroom interventions. A host of evaluation questions can and should be addressed with specific students, though they can also be organized to evaluate general procedures. How should IEP goals be established? What are the optimal (most sensitive) measurement systems for evaluating progress toward IEP goals? How accurate are teachers and school psychologists in implementing systematic evaluation systems: What are the effects of different measurement systems on the structure of instruction? What is an optimal frequency of data review? Given systematic data collection, display, and evaluation systems, what effects are to be anticipated on the number and type of instructional changes? What type of data utilization guidelines are most easily implemented, including various forms of teacher judgment and decision rules? What is the relationship between teachers' preferences for certain data collection and evaluation strategies and student achievement?

Most of the studies on CBM have not attempted to isolate the effective variables responsible for achievement, making it difficult to determine whether improved performance is a result of the measurement procedure itself or the information generated as a result of the measurement procedures (and presumably, the changes made in the instructional programs). The frequent measurement of student performance with curriculum-based materials provides repeated practice in a controlled-stimulus situation, which may be the major source of improvement. Considerable evidence exists that supports the effectiveness of measurement and charting as a variable leading to increased student performance (Brandstetter & Merz, 1978; Jenkins, Mayhall, Peschka, & Townsend, 1974). The feedback provided to the student (i.e., performance graphs) may also account for improvement. Finally, gain in performance may occur because more accurate information becomes available to the teacher and instruction is subsequently modified. Combined, these various components are very powerful. Yet, the research must attend to the controlling variables in this paradigm and provide replicable findings.

SUMMATIVE EVALUATION OF PROGRAM OUTCOMES

Emphasis on formative evaluation is imperative both legally, in defining the least restrictive environment, and ethically, for its role in optimizing programs for individual students; however, a summative analysis of overall program effects is also necessary. As Tindal (in press) noted, systems-level evaluation is predicated on the need: (a) to simplify outcomes to a comprehensible level, (b) to document empirical support for programs, and (c) to establish stable and representative program outcomes.

Far more research has been conducted on the use of CBM in initial assessment and determination of eligibility for specialized programs than has been completed in the summary of overall program outcomes. Yet, given the standardized administration and uniform sampling plans for developing the measures, it is possible to use the same data base to evaluate the effects of the programs. For example, in the development of norms that are to be used in the calculation of discrepancies for referred students, changes in the relative position of these students in the various distributions can be computed, providing an index of effectiveness. The question is whether students who are placed in special education improve in their performance relative to the norm group, essentially becoming less discrepant from their peers. Three studies have been published that evaluate program effects in this manner.

In a study by Tindal, et al. (1982), students in special education were compared with a large sample of students in regular education at three times during the year (fall, winter, and spring). They found by means of a discrepancy index (Deno & Mirkin, 1977), that the special education students improved in their standing relative to regular education students over the year. However, no statistical tests were computed on changes in discrepancy.

In contrast, Shinn (1986), using the same methodology, found that students served in special education did not improve in their relative standing. Although he had used the same testing formats and time periods, he summarized his effects by using z-scores.

More recently, Tindal, Shinn, and Germann (1987) analyzed program effects for the same population investigated earlier by Tindal, et al. (1982). In a comparison of different metrics for determining program outcomes, they found no growth for either reading or spelling over the year with the use of z-scores, inconsistent growth across reading and spelling over the year with the use of the discrepancy index, and consistently significant growth over the year for both reading and spelling for raw scores and grade-equivalent scores. It should be noted that grade-equivalent scores were included for illustrative purpose only.

In all three of these studies, the approach for evaluating effectiveness was confined to a norm-referenced strategy. However, as reported in one other research effort, it is possible to assay effectiveness by means of learning rates. Marston and Magnusson (1986) compared the slopes of improvement of students served in regular education with the slopes obtained while they were subsequently served in special education, and found significant differences in favor of special education. In regular education, the average weekly slope of improvement in reading was .60 words read correctly (representing approximately one-half word increase per week), whereas in special education, the weekly slope of improvement was 1.15 words read correctly (representing more than one word increase each week).

At present, only these four studies have been completed on the use of CBM to evaluate overall program effectiveness (Marston & Magnusson, 1986; Shinn, 1986; Tindal, Germann, Marston & Deno, 1983; Tindal, Shinn & Germann, 1987). The research is quite inconclusive and reflects a range of options for summarizing effects. A number of metrics are available, some of which are absolute (level of performance, number of goals mastered), some relative (z-scores, percentile ranks, discrepancy indexes, etc.), and some time-series-oriented (rate of improvement). Yet little is known about how these different metrics reflect change and/or relate to each other.

Investigating Alternatives in Program Evaluation

CBM makes it possible to extend the range of decisions that can be addressed

with a single data base, providing a unique opportunity for evaluation data to be generated on the impact of decision making. Whereas assessment data traditionally are used solely for purposes of screening and eligibility determination, a more efficient and useful approach is to incorporate the results directly into an IEP. By using the initial-assessment data for monitoring progress toward IEP goals, both pupil and program evaluation can be conducted, such that a number of evaluation strategies become possible on the basis of either movement through a curriculum or improvement on a task.

It may be that in this role school psychologists are uniquely prepared and not only can, but must, become more involved. No other person in the public schools is more knowledgeable about measurement and evaluation. In this capacity, school psychologists would be helping make decisions about program options by basing placement in programs upon outcomes, not predictions of aptitude by treatment interactions (Deno, 1986).

With an emphasis on individualizing instructional programs, CBM can be used to collect empirical data on effective teaching (Brophy & Good, 1986). In actuality, by focusing on summative evaluation, it is anticipated that instructional programs would be initiated on the basis of CBM data. Then CBM would be used in systematically adapting instruction for individual students. To this end, however, program evaluation at the systems level is necessary.

SUMMARY AND IMPLICATIONS

This chapter has reviewed much of the research on CBM in reference to three major educational decisions — screening and eligibility for specialized programs, formative evaluation of program effects, and summative evaluation of program outcomes. The basic procedures for implementing CBM have been in place for almost 10 years now. Furthermore, since the initial research at the University of Minnesota Institute for Research on Learning Disabilities, many districts have adopted variations of the basic procedures or components of the system. Curriculum-based measurement has been *applied* to the full range of decision making, including screening, classification, placement, instructional planning, formative evaluation and modification of instruction, and program certification. Both the extensive research and successful applications suggest it indeed appears to be quite robust for implementation in such diverse circumstances. Yet considerable investigation needs to be completed to determine the implications and outcomes of using this type of measurement system in the delivery of educational services.

In presenting CBM as an alternative delivery system, I have taken the position that an appropriate role of school psychologists is not only to adopt more functional data collection methods in schools, of which CBM is just one variety, but more importantly, to adopt a critical and questioning position in the evaluation procedures for making educational decisions. In this perspective, blind adoption of CBM is unwarranted; the search for definitive tests is ill-founded; and the implementation of programs, whether assessment- or intervention-oriented, without concurrent data collection and evaluation, is presumptuous.

The basic paradigm of CBM provides an alternative to traditional assessment and evaluation procedures. The incorporation of elements of norm-referenced and criterion-referenced methodology allows evaluation to span several decisions, integrating placement data into program planning and evaluation. Furthermore, the roles of specialists are likewise integrated, providing a common base for regular and special education teachers as well as school psychologists to develop optimal programs for children who are not succeeding in the classroom. Finally, the system is oriented around student performance as the critical datum, removing the polemics from many current debates on the appropriate instruction of students. However, the system is also extremely accountable, making it difficult to avoid continuous evaluation and program

development. The research summarized in this chapter should represent a good start but, by all means, not a definitive statement on the status of CBM. Indeed, the main posture of such a system is to posit an experimental perspective in the teaching of children.

REFERENCES

Brandstetter, G., & Merz, C. (1978). Charting scores in precision teaching for skill acquisition. *Exceptional Children, 45,* 42-48.

Brophy, J., & Good, T. (1986). Teacher behavior and student achievement. In M. C. Wittrock (Ed.), *Handbook of research on teaching* (3rd ed. pp. 275-328). New York: Macmillan.

Carlberg, C., & Kavale, K. (1980). The efficacy of special versus regular class placement for exceptional children: A meta-analysis. *The Journal of Special Education, 14*(3), 295-309.

Deno, S. L. (1985). Curriculum-based measurement: The emerging alternative. *Exceptional Children, 52*(3), 219-232.

Deno, S. L. (1986). Formative evaluation of individual student programs: A new role for school psychologists. *School Psychology Review, 15*(3), 358-374.

Deno, S. L., Chiang, B., Tindal, G., & Blackburn, M. (1979). *Experimental analysis of program components: An approach to research in CSDCs* (Research Report No. 12). Minneapolis: University of Minnesota, Institute for Research on Learning Disabilities.

Deno, S. L., & Fuchs, L. (1987). Developing curriculum-based measurement systems for data based special education problem solving. *Focus on Exceptional Children, 19*(8), 1-15.

Deno, S. L., Marston, D., & Mirkin, P. K. (1982). Valid measurement procedures for continuous evaluation of written expression. *Exceptional Children, 48,* 368-371.

Deno, S., Marston, D., Mirkin, P., Lowry, L., Sindelar, P., & Jenkins, J. (1982). *The use of standard tasks to measure achievement in reading, spelling, and written expression: A normative and developmental study* (Research Report No. 87). Minneapolis: University of Minnesota, Institute for Research on Learning Disabilities.

Deno, S., Marston, D., Shinn, M. R., & Tindal, G. (1983). Oral reading fluency: A simple datum for scaling reading disability. *Topics and Teaching in Learning Disabilities, 2*(4), 53-59.

Deno, S. L., & Mirkin, P. K. (1977). *Data-based program modification: A manual.* Reston, VA: Council for Exceptional Children.

Deno, S. L., Mirkin, P. K., & Chiang, B. (1982). Identifying valid measures of reading. *Exceptional Children, 49*(1), 36–45.

Deno, S. L., Mirkin, P. K., Lowry, L., & Kuehnle, K. (1980). *Relationships among simple measures of spelling and performance on standardized achievement tests* (Research Report No. 21). Minneapolis: University of Minnesota, Institute for Research on Learning Disabilities.

Deno, S. L., Mirkin, P. K., & Shinn, M. R. (1979). *Behavioral perspectives on the assessment of learning disabled children* (Monograph No. 12). Minneapolis: University of Minnesota, Institute for Research on Learning Disabilities.

Deno, S. L., Mirkin, P. K., & Wesson, C. (1984). How to write effective data-based IEPs. *Teaching Exceptional Children, 16*, 99–104.

Dunn, L. M., & Markwardt, F. C. (1970). *Peabody Individual Achievement Test.* Circle Pines, MN: American Guidance Service.

Englemann, S., Granzin, A., & Severson, H. (1979). Diagnosing instruction. *Journal of Special Education, 13*, 355–363.

Finn, P. (1977). Computer-aided description of mature word choices in writing. In C. R. Cooper & L. Odell (Eds.), *Evaluating writing: Describing, measuring, judging.* Urbana, IL: National Council of Teachers of English.

Freeman, D. J., Kuhs, T. M., Porter, A. C., Floden, R. E., Schmidt, W. H., & Schwille, J. R. (1983). Do textbooks and tests define a national curriculum in elementary school mathematics? *Elementary School Journal, 83*(5), 501–513.

Fuchs, L. (1986). Monitoring progress among mildly handicapped pupils: Review of current practice and research. *Remedial and Special Education, 7*(5), 5–12.

Fuchs, L., & Deno, S. (1981). *The relationship between curriculum-based mastery measures and standardized achievement tests in reading* (Research Report No. 57). Minneapolis: University of Minnesota, Institute for Research on Learning Disabilities.

Fuchs, L. S., Deno, S. L., & Mirkin, P. K. (1982). *Direct and frequent measurement and evaluation: Effects on instruction and estimates of student progress* (Research Report No. 97). Minneapolis: University of Minnesota, Institute for Research on Learning Disabilities.

Fuchs, L., Deno, S., & Mirkin, P. (1984). The effects of frequent curriculum-based measurement and evaluation on pedagogy, student achievement, and student awareness of learning. *American Educational Research Journal, 21*, 449–460.

Fuchs, L., Deno, S. L., & Roettger, A. (1983). *The effect of alternative data-utilization rules on spelling achievement: An n of 1 study* (Research Report No. 120). Minneapolis: University of Minnesota, Institute for Research on Learning Disabilities.

Fuchs, L. S. & Fuchs, D. (1986). Curriculum-based assessment of progress toward long and short term goals. *Journal of Special Education, 20*, 69–82.

Fuchs, L., & Fuchs, D. (1986). Effects of systematic formative evaluation: A meta-analysis. *Exceptional Children, 53*(3), 199–208.

Fuchs, L., Fuchs, D., & Deno, S. L. (1981). *Reliability and validity of curriculum-based informal reading inventories* (Research Report No. 59). Minneapolis: University of Minnesota, Institute for Research on Learning Disabilities.

Fuchs, L., Fuchs, D., & Deno, S. L. (1985). Importance of goal ambitiousness and goal mastery to student achievement. *Exceptional Children, 52*(1), 63–71.

Fuchs, L., Tindal, J., & Deno, S. (1981). *Effects of varying domain and sample duration on technical characteristics of daily measures in reading* (Research Report No. 48). Minneapolis: University of Minnesota, Institute for Research on Learning Disabilities.

Fuchs, L., Tindal, G., & Deno, S. L. (1984). Methodological issues in curriculum based reading assessment. *Diagnostique, 9*, 191–207.

Fuchs, L., Wesson, C., Tindal, G., Mirkin, P., & Deno, S. (1982). *Instructional changes, student performance, and teacher preference: The effects of specific measurement and evaluation procedures* (Research Report No. 64). Minneapolis: University of Minnesota, Institute for Research on Learning Disabilities.

Fuchs, L., Wesson, C., Tindal, G., Mirkin, P. K., & Deno, S. L. (1981). *Teacher efficiency in continuous evaluation of IEP goals* (Research Report No. 53). Minneapolis: University of Minnesota, Institute for Research on Learning Disabilities.

Germann, G., & Tindal, G. (1985). An application of curriculum-based assessment: The use of direct and repeated measurement. *Exceptional Children, 52*(3), 244–265.

Gickling, E. E., & Armstrong, D. L. (1978). Levels of instructional difficulty as related to on-task behavior, task completion, and comprehension. *Journal of Learning Disabilities, 11*, 559–566.

Gickling, E. E., & Havertape, J. (1981). *Curriculum-based assessment (CBA).* Minneapolis: School Psychology Inservice Training Network.

Gickling, E. E., & Thompson, V. P. (1985). A personal view of curriculum-based assessment. *Exceptional Children, 52*(3), 205–218.

Hammill, D. D., & Larsen, S. C. (1978). *The Test of Written Language.* Austin, TX: Pro-Ed.

Hargis, C. H. (1987). *Curriculum-based assessment: A primer.* Springfield, IL: Thomas.

Hoge, R. D. (1985). The validity of direct observation measures of pupil classroom behavior. *Review of Educational Research, 55*(4), 469-483.

Hopkins, C., & Antes, R. (1978). *Classroom measurement and evaluation.* Itasca, IL: Peacock.

Hunt, K. W. (1965). *Grammatical structures written at three grade levels* (Research Report No. 3). Champaign, IL: National Council of Teachers of English.

Idol, L., Nevin, A., & Paolucci-Whitcomb, P. (1986). *Models of curriculum-based assessment.* Rockville, MD: Aspen.

Idol, L., Paolucci-Whitcomb, P., & Nevin, A. (1986). *Collaborative consultation.* Rockville, MD: Aspen.

Idol-Maestas, L. (1983). *Special educator's consultation handbook.* Rockville, MD: Aspen.

Jenkins, J., Deno, S. L., & Mirkin, P. (1979). Measuring pupil progress toward the least restrictive alternative. *Learning Disability Quarterly, 2,* 81-86.

Jenkins, J., Mayhall, W., Peschka, C., & Townsend, V. (1974). Using direct and daily measures to increase learning. *Journal of Learning Disabilities, 7*(9), 605-608.

Jenkins, J., & Pany, D. (1978). Standardized achievement tests: How useful for special education? *Exceptional Children, 44*(6), 448-453.

Karlsen, B., Madden, R., & Gardner, E. F. (1975). *Stanford diagnostic reading test (Green Level Form B).* New York: Harcourt, Brace, Jovanovich.

King, R. P., Deno, S., Mirkin, P., & Wesson, C. (1983). *The effects of training teachers in the use of formative evaluation in reading: An experimental–control comparison* (Research Report No. 111). Minneapolis: University of Minnesota, Institute for Research on Learning Disabilities.

King, R., Wesson, C., & Deno, S. L. (1982). *Direct and frequent measurement of student performance* (Research Report No. 67). Minneapolis: University of Minnesota, Institute for Research on Learning Disabilities.

Lindsley, O. (1964). Direct measurement and prosthesis of retarded behavior. *Journal of Education, 14*(7), 62-81.

Magnusson, D. (1986). *A comparison of school and district norms in making special education eligibility decisions.* Unpublished doctoral dissertation, University of Minnesota, Minneapolis.

Marston, D. (1987). Does categorical teacher certification benefit the mildly handicapped child? *Exceptional Children, 53*(5), 423-431.

Marston, D., & Deno, S. L. (1981). *The reliability of simple, direct measures of written expression* (Research Report No. 50). Minneapolis: University of Minnesota, Institute for Research on Learning Disabilities.

Marston, D., & Deno, S. L. (1982). *Implementation of direct and repeated measurement in the school setting* (Research Report No. 106). Minneapolis: University of Minnesota, Institute for Research on Learning Disabilities.

Marston, D., Deno, S., & Tindal, G. (1983). *A comparison of standardized achievement tests and direct measurement techniques in measuring pupil progress* (Research Report No. 126). Minneapolis: University of Minnesota, Institute for Research on Learning Disabilities.

Marston, D., Lowry, L., Deno, S., & Mirkin, P. (1981). *An analysis of learning trends in simple measures of reading, spelling, and written expression: A longitudinal study* (Research Report No. 49). Minneapolis: University of Minnesota, Institute for Research on Learning Disabilities.

Marston, D., & Magnusson, D. (1985). Implementing curriculum-based measurement in special and regular education settings. *Exceptional Children, 523*(3), 266-276.

Marston, D., & Magnusson, D. (1986). *The effectiveness of special education: A time series analysis of reading in regular and special education.* Unpublished manuscript. Minneapolis Public Schools, Department of Special Education.

Marston, D., Mirkin, P., & Deno, S. L. (1984). Curriculum-based measurement: An alternative to traditional screening, referral, and identification of learning disabled students. *Journal of Special Education, 18,* 109-118.

Marston, D., Tindal, G., & Deno, S. L. (1982). *Predictive efficiency of direct repeated measurement: An analysis of cost and accuracy in classification* (Research Report No. 104). Minneapolis: University of Minnesota, Institute for Research on Learning Disabilities.

Marston, D., Tindal, G., & Deno, S. L. (1984). Eligibility for learning disability services: A direct and repeated measurement approach. *Exceptional Children, 50*(6), 554-555.

Martin, M. A. (1980). *A comparison of variations in data utilization procedures on the reading performance of mildly handicapped students.* Unpublished doctoral dissertation, University of Washington, Seattle.

Mirkin, P. K., & Deno, S. L. (1979). *Formative evaluation in the classroom: An approach to improving instruction* (Research Report No. 10). Minneapolis: University of Minnesota, Institute for Research on Learning Disabilities.

Mirkin, P., Deno, S. L., Fuchs, L., Wesson, C., Tindal, G., Marston, D., & Kuehnle, K. (1981). *Procedures to develop and monitor progress on IEP goals.* Minneapolis: University of Minnesota, Institute for Research on Learning Disabilities.

Mirkin, P. K., Deno, S. L., Tindal, G., & Kuehnle, K. (1980). *Formative evaluation: Continued development of data utilization systems* (Research Report No. 23). Minneapolis: University of Minnesota, Institute for Research on Learning Disabilities.

Mirkin, P. K., Fuchs, L. S., & Deno, S. L. (1982). *Considerations for designing a continuous evaluation system: An integrative review* (Monograph No. 20). Minneapolis: University of Minnesota, Institute for Research on Learning Disabilities.

Mirkin, P., Fuchs, L., Tindal, G., Christenson, S., & Deno, S. L. (1981). *The effect of IEP monitoring strategies on teacher behavior* (Research Report No. 62). Minneapolis: University of Minnesota, Institute for Research on Learning Disabilities.

Roid, G. H., & Haladyna, T. M. (1982). *A technology for test-item writing.* New York: Academic.

Salvia, J., & Ysseldyke, J. (1986). *Assessment in remedial and special education.* Boston: Houghton-Mifflin.

Sevcik, B., Skiba, R., Tindal, G., King, R., Wesson, C., Mirkin, P., & Deno, S. (1983). *Curriculum-based measurement: Effects on instruction, teacher estimates of student progress, and student knowledge of performance* (Research Report No. 124). Minneapolis: University of Minnesota, Institute for Research on Learning Disabilities.

Shinn, M. R. (1986). Does anyone care what happens after the refer-test-place process? A systematic evaluation of special education. *School Psychology Review, 15,* 49-58.

Shinn, M., & Marston, D. (1985). Differentiating mildly handicapped, low achieving, and regular education students: A curriculum based approach. *Remedial and Special Education,* 31-38.

Shinn, M. R., Tindal, G., Marston, D., & Spira, D. (1987). Practice of learning disabilities as social policy. *Learning Disability Quarterly, 10*(1), 17-28.

Shinn, M. R., Tindal, G., & Spira, D. (1987). Special education referrals as an index of teacher tolerance: Are teachers imperfect tests? *Exceptional Children, 54*(1), 32-40.

Shinn, M. R., Tindal, G., & Stein, S. (1988). Curriculum-based measurement and the identification of mildly handicapped students: A review of the research. *Professional School Psychology, 3*(1), 69-85.

Shinn, M. R., Ysseldyke, J., Deno, S. L., & Tindal, G. (1986). A comparison of differences between students labeled learning disabled and low achieving on measures of classroom performance. *Journal of Learning Disabilities, 19*(9), 545-552.

Skiba, R., Wesson, C., & Deno, S. L. (1982). *The effects of training teachers in the use of formative evaluation in reading: An experimental–control comparison* (Research Report No. 88). Minneapolis: University of Minnesota, Institute for Research on Learning Disabilities.

Tindal, G. (in press). Evaluating the effectiveness of educational programs at the systems level using CBM. In M. Shinn (Ed.), *Applications of curriculum-based measurement to the development of programs for mildly handicapped students* (chap. 9). New York: Guilford.

Tindal, G., & Deno, S. L. (1981). *Daily measurement of reading: Effects of varying the size of the item pool* (Research Report No. 55). Minneapolis: University of Minnesota, Institute for Research on Learning Disabilities.

Tindal, G., Fuchs, L., Christenson, S., Mirkin, P., & Deno, S. L. (1981). *The relationship between student achievement and teacher assessment of short- and long-term goals* (Research Report No. 61). Minneapolis: University of Minnesota, Institute for Research on Learning Disabilities.

Tindal, G., & Germann, G. (1986). Models of direct measurement in the determination of eligibility, monitoring of student progress, and evaluation of program effects. *B.C. Journal of Special Education, 9*(4), 365-382.

Tindal, G., Germann, G., & Deno, S. L. (1983). *Descriptive research on the Pine County Norms: A compilation of findings* (Research Report No. 132). Minneapolis: University of Minnesota, Institute for Research on Learning Disabilities.

Tindal, G., Germann, G., Marston, D., & Deno, S. L. (1983). *The effectiveness of special education: A direct measurement approach* (Research Report No. 123). Minneapolis: University of Minnesota, Institute for Research on Learning Disabilities.

Tindal, G., Marston, D., & Deno, S. L. (1983). *The reliability of direct and repeated measurement* (Research Report No. 109). Minneapolis: University of Minnesota, Institute for Research on Learning Disabilities.

Tindal, G., Marston, D., Deno, S. L., & Germann, G. (1982). *Curriculum differences in direct repeated measures of reading* (Research Report No. 93). Minneapolis: University of Minnesota, Institute for Research on Learning Disabilities.

Tindal, G., & Parker, R. (1987). Direct observation in special education classrooms: Concurrent use of two observations and their validation. *Journal of Special Education, 21,* 43-58.

Tindal, G., Shinn, M., & Germann, G. (1987). The effect of different metrics on interpretation of change in program evaluation. *Remedial and Special Education, 8*(5), 19-28.

Tucker, J. A., Stevens, L., & Ysseldyke, J. E. (1983). Learning disabilities: The experts speak out. In J. Torgesen & G. M. Senf (Eds.), *Annual review of learning disabilities.* Chicago: Professional Press.

U. S. Department of Education. (1983). *Fifth annual report to Congress on implementation of P.L. 94-142.* Washington, DC: Department of Education.

Videen, J., Deno, S., & Marston, D. (1982). *Correct word sequences: A valid indicator of proficiency in written expression* (Research Report No. 84). Minneapolis: University of Minnesota, Institute for Research on Learning Disabilities.

Wesson, C., Deno, S., Mirkin, P., Sevcik, B., Skiba, R., King, R., Tindal, G., & Maruyama, G. (1982).

Teaching structure and student achievement effects of curriculum-based measurement: A causal (structural) analysis (Research Report No. 105). Minneapolis: University of Minnesota, Institute for Research on Learning Disabilities.

Wesson, C., Mirkin, P., & Deno, S. L. (1982). *Teacher's use of self-instructional materials for learning procedures for developing and monitoring progress on IEP goals* (Research Report No. 63). Minneapolis: University of Minnesota, Institute for Research on Learning Disabilities.

Wesson, C., Skiba, R., Sevcik, B., King, R., & Deno, S. L. (1984). The effects of technically adequate instructional data on achievement. *Remedial and Special Education, 5*(5), 17-22.

White, (. (1985). Decisions, Decisions. *B. C. Journal of Special Education, 9*(4), 305-320.

White, O., & Haring, N. (1980). *Exceptional Teaching.* Columbus, OH: Merrill.

Woodcock, R., & Johnson, R. (1978). *Woodcock-Johnson Psychoeducational Battery.* Circle Pines, MN: American Guidance.

Ysseldyke, J. E., Algozzine, B., Shinn, M., & McGue, M. (1982). Similarities and differences among low achievers and students labeled learning disabled. *Journal of Special Education, 16,* 73-85.

8

Curriculum-Based Measurement: District Level Implementation

**Douglas Marston and
Deanne Magnusson**
Minneapolis Public Schools

INTRODUCTION TO CURRICULUM-BASED MEASUREMENT

The recent emergence of curriculum-based assessment (CBA) as an alternative to traditional assessment methods reflects a current concern regarding traditional procedures frequently used by psychologists and educators. As Deno (1985) has noted, "Despite general agreement that we should routinely assess the student performance outcomes of instruction, general agreement regarding how this measurement must be done does not exist. The most widely accepted measures of achievement — commercially developed, standardized, and norm-referenced tests — are criticized because they are biased regarding curriculum content" (p. 219). In reviewing the problems of standardized testing that confront teachers and psychologists, Bersoff (1973) called for the development of an evaluation approach that addresses these needs when he wrote, "Within the framework for assessment that has been described, direct, continuous, naturalistic observation of behavior provides many of the advantages one seeks in evaluation. The advantages include precision, efficiency, immediate feedback and authenticity" (p. 898). Under the rubric curriculum-based assessment there are presently several options available to those interested in adopting such a model. The November 1985 issue of *Exceptional Children* was devoted to this topic and presented several CBA models (Gickling & Thompson, 1985; Blankenship, 1985; Peterson, Heistad, Peterson, & Reynolds, 1985; Deno 1985). In his review of these models, Tucker (1985) stated, "In curriculum-based assessment the essential measure of success in education is the student's progress in the curriculum of the local school" (p. 199). However, there are significant differences among the CBA models, as Deno (1986b) points out. The essential difference in the Deno model, known as curriculum-based measurement (CBM) is its reliance upon time series analysis of direct and repeated measurement procedures. For both the psychologist and the teacher, CBM can be viewed as an alternative that can either supplement or replace existing assessment systems (Marston, Mirkin, & Deno, 1984; Tindal & Marston, 1985). The Department of Special Education, Minneapolis Public Schools, currently is implementing CBM in its K-6 School Based Resource Program. This chapter describes the implementation of the curriculum-based measurement model.

The Failure of Traditional Testing Approaches

A discussion of alternative assessment systems is probably best initiated with an analysis of existing measurement strategies. A review of Buros's *Tests in Review* suggests that hundreds of psychological and educational tests and assessment procedures are available to educators. If so, one might then ask, "Why proceed any further and look for alternatives?" This is the question that confronted special education administrators in the Minneapolis Public Schools. In 1981 the department reviewed its assessment policies in relation to goals and objectives set for the Minneapolis Public School District. At the time a task force of educators, university faculty, and representatives of the state Department of Education established several priorities in the area of assessment for the district. Two of those objectives that had direct impact upon the Special Education Department were to

(1) . . . establish in all Minneapolis Public Schools a data-based management system to include continuous assessment of student progress in established objectives in mathematics, reading and writing. The system will provide virtually immediate turnaround of information to teachers to enable them to effectively manage instruction and provide frequent individual progress reports to students and parents. (p. 17)

(2) Revise procedures for identifying a student as mildly handicapped and in need of special education service to take into account comparison of the student's achievement and/or behavior to that of his/her peers. . . . To support this direction, develop an integrated system for curriculum and student management which will be common to both special education and the regular classroom. The system will include procedures for monitoring student progress and reporting to parents. (p. 53)

Consequently, administrators asked what tests could be used for these purposes. In their review, it became apparent that several problems with traditional testing approaches made it necessary to search for alternatives. These issues and their problematic nature are reviewed here.

APA Test Standards and Technically Inadequate Tests

Of primary concern to Minneapolis educators was the issue of technical adequacy. According to guidelines established by the American Psychological Association, the American Educational Research Association, and the National Council for Measurement in Education (1976), all tests used in education and psychology must be valid, reliable and have adequate normative data. In a review of assessment procedures and tests used in special education, Salvia and Ysseldyke (1981) listed 26 frequently used tests that were not technically adequate. These authors cautioned educators that using such instruments might negatively impact on the psychoeducational decision-making process in special education.

It could be argued that while there may exist technically inadequate tests in the area of special education, well-trained school psychologists, specialists, and teachers would not administer such measures. However, research evidence suggests the contrary. Ysseldyke, Algozzine, Regan, and Potter (1980) asked a group of 159 educators, psychologists, and specialists to review the case histories of children referred to special education and to then select assessment procedures necessary for identification and program planning. A content analysis of those instruments chosen for assessment indicated that 67% of the selected tests were not valid, 59% were not reliable, and 66% did not have adequately constructed norms. These authors concluded that, if the results indeed generalize to the field, there is a remarkable degree of uncertainty introduced into the special education decision-making system. As a result, the overall impact upon the delivery of services to handicapped children is significant and the benefits of such service may be greatly diminished.

Mismatch Between a Student's Curriculum and Test

A second problem associated with assessment is the extent to which the content of standardized achievement tests matches the classroom instruction provided to students. From this perspective, it is argued that achievement tests fail to adequately sample the curriculum taught the student. As a result, the various achievement tests available to educators differentially sample the many curricula used in our schools. Thus test scores do not truly represent pupil skill level since, to a large extent, they do not measure what the child has learned. Jenkins and Pany (1978), in a content analysis of five standardized tests of reading achievement and five reading curricula, found that expected grade scores for a given test varied widely as a function of the reading instruction. For example, second-grade pupils taught in Houghton-Mifflin were expected to score at the 3.2 grade level on the Peabody Individual Achievement Test (PIAT), but only 2.2 on this test when instructed in Ginn 360. Floden, Porter, Schmidt, & Freeman (1980) had similar results in math, and Lovitt and Eaton (1972) presented supporting data in reading when they examined the progress of learning-disabled students over a 9-month period. In the latter study, several pupils in a class made significant gains on the Wide Range Achievement Test (WRAT), and not on the Metropolitan Achievement Test (MAT). Conversely, several pupils in the same class made significant progress on the MAT, but testing with the Wide Range Achievement Test (WRAT) demonstrated little evidence of improvement. One of the conclusions these authors offered is that because standardized achievement tests fail to adequately sample the content the teacher is presenting, the tests give us invalid results with very little useful information for serving the handicapped child, a finding recently validated by Good and Salvia (1988).

Instructional Irrelevance of Standardized Tests

How helpful is standardized test information to special education resource teachers who must write individualized educational plans (IEPs) and plan intervention strategies? Thurlow and Ysseldyke (1982) examined this question by interviewing a total of 200 school psychologists and teachers. Given a list of commonly administered tests, including the Wechsler Intelligence Scale for Children-Revised (WISC-R), Bender Visual Motor Gestalt, and the WRAT, 100 psychologists typically rated the measures as useful for instructional planning. For example, 72% said the WISC-R was helpful, 64% endorsed the Bender, and 80% thought the WRAT aided program planning. When the 100 special education resource teachers were asked to evaluate the same lists of tests, a different perspective emerged. Only 10% thought the Bender was instructionally relevant, 30% rated the WISC-R as useful during the IEP planning process, and 10% said the WRAT contributed to developing effective instructional plans. The authors concluded that teachers of the handicapped are searching for assessment alternatives not provided by school psychologists. It is not surprising that when Keogh (1972) observed that the school psychologist's diagnostic contribution was limited, she also advocated that "a somewhat different model of school psychology be adopted if services to exceptional children are to be effective" (p. 144).

Cost of Using Standardized Tests: Can We Afford It?

Mirkin (1980) analyzed the cost effectiveness of the assessment process for students referred for special education services. In her analysis the average referral student required as much as 13–15 hours of professional time; and the potential cost could rise as high as approximately $1,800 for one student. If this condition existed in the Minneapolis K–6 Resource Program, given the approximately 800 referrals made each year, assessment costs would exceed $1.4 million.

Further illustration of the expensive nature of the testing process was provided by Goldwasser, Meyers, Christenson, and Graden (1983), who conducted a nationwide survey of the use of school psychologists' time. According to this study, school psychologists dedicate approximately 70% of their day to testing students for eligibility decisions. At 28 hr. per 40-hr. work week, this is indeed an expensive endeavor. School psychologists in a survey conducted by Smith (1984) indicated they desired a significant reduction of their assessment responsibilities and a corresponding increase in intervention and consultation.

Pre-Post Testing:
An Unreliable Assessment Design

Traditionally, psychologists have relied upon the pre-post test design for the purpose of measuring change or student learning. Unfortunately, the gain score analysis is problematic. Thorndike and Hagen (1978) pointed out that the reliability of difference scores may be quite low, especially if the two measures are highly intercorrelated. For example, two tests with exceptionally high reliabilities (i.e., .90) that are also highly correlated (r = .80) will result in a difference score reliability of .50, an unacceptable coefficient.

Salvia and Clarke (1973) illustrated this problem with discrepancy scores between the California Achievement Test and the California Test of Mental Maturity. These authors concluded that when a difference score from these two highly reliable tests is obtained, "the number of false negatives . . . will be about 50 percent" (p. 308).

Sensitivity to Pupil Growth

Measurement experts have also recently challenged the notion that standardized norm-referenced tests are adequately designed to measure learner outcome. Hively and Reynolds (1975) pointed out that most standardized, norm-referenced tests have been developed with the explicit purpose of measuring individual differences, a perspective that does not easily lend itself to the evaluation of pupil growth. Carver (1974) referred to this emphasis upon measuring pupil differences and abilities as the *psychometric* dimension of testing. In his review, he cited the necessity for designing *edumetric* tests, procedures that measure student learning. "Because the psychometric dimension has been focused on tra-

ditionally, many standardized tests are used to measure gain or growth without being developed or evaluated from an edumetric standpoint. The danger of this approach is that the psychometrically developed tests may not be sensitive to gain when in fact there is gain" (p. 518).

CBM AS AN ALTERNATIVE MODEL: MAJOR ASSUMPTIONS

Direct Measurement

A primary assumption of the CBM model is that assessment focuses upon direct observation of a student's academic skills and behaviors in their current curriculum of instruction. This differs from many standardized tests, which typically are composed of multiple choice items or "yes-no" questions from which one infers knowledge on the basis of the correctness of the response. Certainly, such a test format has provided educators with useful information about pupil performance; however, the precision of this model for measuring what a student actually knows has been questioned (Elliott & Piersel, 1982; Ysseldyke & Marston, 1982; Smith, 1980). For example, Tuinman (1971) has demonstrated with several measures of reading comprehension that it is possible to answer multiple choice items correctly without reading the corresponding passage. Lovitt (1967) posited that the validity of assessment can be significantly improved with an emphasis upon the direct measurement of academic behaviors of concern. Thus, the educator who wishes to determine the extent of a child's reading difficulty would directly evaluate the interaction of the reading text and the child's external responses. For example, in the domain of reading, the response of interest to many direct measurement proponents is oral reading.

Repeated Measurement

A second essential ingredient in the CBM model, and one that contributes most to its uniqueness, is the use of repeated measurement of pupil performance. From a measurement theorist's perspective, repeated behavioral sampling enhances an assessment's reliability, since it decreases the standard error of measurement (Nunnally, 1978; Thorndike & Hagen, 1978). In addition to increasing reliability, frequent assessment increases the validity of describing pupil change or progress. As a result of this increased accuracy of documenting student growth, the system can be used to monitor the effectiveness of educational interventions and progress toward goals. Repeated measurement serves well the notion that a "common metric" can indeed be established across the psychoeducational decision-making continuum.

Time Series Analysis

A third major element of the CBM model is time series analysis of the data display. Although direct and repeated measurement of pupil performance are necessary conditions for successful implementation of CBM, they are not sufficient to assure the effectiveness of the model. Essential to the process is graphing of the academic or behavioral data and analysis of students' learning rates in response to educational intervention. The importance of this point is highlighted by the research of Fuchs and Fuchs (1986), who demonstrated that when CBM scores are graphed rather than recorded, performance increases approximately .5 of a standard deviation unit.

Of some importance is the type of graph used for time series analysis. Some precision teaching proponents advocate the use of semilogarithmic paper (White & Haring, 1980), whereas others recommend equal-interval graphs. The Minneapolis Resource Program has regularly used equal-interval graphs, a practice supported by research (Marston, in press).

CURRICULUM-BASED MEASUREMENT: LEGAL AND EDUCATIONAL IMPLICATIONS

Public Law 94-142 and Curriculum-Based Measurement

Galagan (1985) pointed out that many standardized tests are improperly used, given the regulations of the Education for All Handicapped Children Act (EHA, PL 94-142). In a review of these inadequacies he states: "The pervasive employment of these legally deficient instruments loses all rationale in the face of emerging CBM measures. These measures are child- and curriculum-directed, entailing a genuine individual focus, and thus are more capable of identifying and addressing the specific educational needs of children and therefore the legal requirements of EHA" (p. 298). How does CBM fit the principles of PL 94-142? This section examines the relationship of CBM with three important components of PL 94-142: technical adequacy, least restrictive environment, and individualized educational plans.

Technically Adequate Assessment

An essential component in PL 94-142 is the mandate that educators administer only those assessment procedures that are technically adequate. Of major concern, therefore, is how well CBM measures conform to the APA test standards relating to validity, reliability, and standardization. Proponents of the CBM model described here have indeed attended to these issues and have documented CBM procedures as valid and reliable. In the preceding chapter, Tindal has presented the CBM research on these technical issues. With respect to standardization, the Minneapolis effort to develop local norms on a population of 8,160 students is described in a later section in this chapter.

Nondiscriminatory Assessment

PL 94-142 requires that all assessments for handicapped children be nondiscriminatory. Historically, however, special education has not adequately implemented assessment practices that account for cultural differences. In large part this is due to the use of standardized tests developed primarily for a white population. Shinn and Tindal (in press) argued that an alternative assessment is necessary if educators are indeed to take the nondiscriminatory requirement seriously. To this end they recommended an approach that extends beyond mere eligibility and includes instructional planning and program outcome.

> To ensure nondiscriminatory practices, an alternative measurement strategy must be based on the formal, continuous collection of data from the initial phase — prior to educational intervention — through the actual implementation of any program — to termination or review. With such a strategy, a determination can be made of both the student's eligibility for special education and the appropriateness of the program for that student. The critical issue in such a system is the development of an assessment system which can provide an accurate index for use in all the different educational decisions.

Shinn and Tindal (in press) argue that the CBM model should be considered a viable nondiscriminatory assessment alternative. The advantages of CBM cited by Shinn and Tindal include the following: CBM provides continuous data across decision areas; it can be used to evaluate the appropriateness of program placement; the data base is tied to the school curriculum; and local norms can easily be established within the CBM model.

Individual Educational Plans

PL 94-142 stipulates that an individual educational plan (IEP) be written for every student identified as handicapped. McLaughlin and Lewis (1986) reported that the law specifically requires

> (1) A statement of the child's present levels of educational performance;
> (2) A statement of annual goals, including short-term instructional objectives;
> (3) A statement of the specific special education and related services to be provided to the child, and the extent to which the child will be able to participate in regular educational programs;
> (4) The projected dates for initiation of services and the anticipated duration

of the services; and
> (5) Appropriate objective criteria and evaluation procedures and schedules for determining, on at least an annual basis, whether the short term instructional objectives are being achieved. (PL 94-142).

The CBM model and its approach to writing data-based IEPs easily fits these requirements. As Deno, Mirkin, and Wesson (1984) note, CBM data is "clearly tied to the goal, since the initial assessment data are used to determine the goal level and criteria" (p. 104). Using the procedures described by these authors, Minneapolis has adopted a data-based approach to writing IEPs.

EVOLUTION OF THE MINNEAPOLIS CBM MODEL

The recent implementation of CBM in Minneapolis did not occur overnight. Adoption of the model can be traced to several significant conceptual shifts in the philosophy of special education. In the past, the administrative arrangements for special education were designed to fit what Reynolds and Birch (1977) called the "two-box theory." In this perspective, there are two categories of students, two kinds of classrooms, and two types of teachers, "regular" and "special." As a result, two separate educational support systems evolved with separate administrative lines, teaching staffs, and funding. The results have often been deleterious to handicapped children. One problematic issue cited is the significant role assessment plays in this process. As Reynolds and Birch (1977) point out:

> Under the two box theory, a child who shows difficulty in a regular class is referred by the teacher to a psychologist and/or other specialist for study. If the child meets the standards for some category of special education (such standards often are defined by state regulations that specify the conditions for special categorical funding), placement is made in a special class or special school. Too often, psychological testing is the sole basis on which a final placement decision is made. (p. 30)

These authors concluded that assessment needs to be an ongoing process in which decisions about interventions with handicapped children can be made on a continued basis. While CBM, with its emphasis upon direct and frequent measurement in the student curriculum, can be utilized in school districts still subscribing to the two-box theory, it fits nicely into alternative service delivery models that stress alternative interventions. Over the past two decades delivery of services in the Minneapolis Special Education Department have evolved to the point where CBM can be effectively implemented. This necessary foundation upon which CBM can be implemented was influenced by three important educational trends: the cascade of services, noncategorical delivery of services, and data-based assessment.

Cascade of Services

The Minneapolis Public Schools, and the Department of Special Education in particular, have long been committed to serving handicapped children in the least restrictive environment. In the 1960s the Minneapolis Special Education Department, under the direction of Evelyn Deno (1970), developed a delivery of services model referred to as the cascade of services model (Reynolds & Birch, 1977). This approach to serving handicapped children incorporated much of the least-restrictive-environment principle into practice 10 years before it actually became part of PL 94-142. While there are many distinct features in the model, those characteristics congruent with the curriculum-based measurement model are the following (Reynolds & Birch, 1977):

> [That] children not be classified and given special placements on a permanent basis but, rather, that they be moved to special stations only for as long as feasible. Thus, no indelible labels are involved. The total number of children served over time in special settings greatly exceeds the number served at any given time. (p. 31)

A decentralization policy — to develop the capacity to conduct specialized forms of education in many settings, rather than in a few. (p. 39)

A joining of responsibilities for assessment, planning, and instruction in a single setting, as opposed to a policy of referral to special centers for child study and prescription. (p. 39)

Descriptions of students that are made mainly in terms directly relevant to instruction, rather than in terms of abstract categories, such as retarded or disturbed. (p. 39)

Noncategorical Delivery of Services

Building upon these ideas indispensable to the cascade of services model, the K-6 Resource Program, with a variance from our state Department of Education, has delivered services to mildly handicapped children on a noncategorical basis for the past 10 years. Pupils are not specifically labeled learning-disabled, educable mentally retarded, or emotionally disturbed. Rather, there has been an attempt to describe pupils and design instructional interventions in reference to their specific educational needs and not special education labels. The result of this initiative is to think of handicapped students not in terms of their placement category, but rather of a continuum of instruction or intervention that ranges from the least restrictive environment to more restrictive settings. Thus, the mildly handicapped pupils referred to frequently in this chapter are pupils with special needs who are served in their home school by the special education program for approximately 1-2 hr. each day.

The reaction of the State Department of Education to this approach to delivery of service has been positive and is congruent with the observations of Goldstein, Arkell, Ashcroft, Hurley, and Lilly (1975). These investigators, as part of the Project on the Classification of Exceptional Children, reported that noncategorical approaches eliminate overgeneralizations about students, reduce bias linked to labeling, discredit the notion that teaching failures are due solely to within-child disabilities, remove labels from explanatory constructs, and emphasize the need to examine the interplay of teacher and student during instruction. Further evidence that the noncategorical approach is a prominent alternative to traditional models is suggested by the recent statements of educational professionals (Reynolds, Wang, & Walberg, 1987), legal-based advocacy groups (Advocacy Center, 1986), and professional service agencies (National Coalition of Advocates for Students and the National Association of School Psychologists, 1985) supporting a restructuring of special education.

Need for Data-Based Assessment Model

A third significant trend that directed the Department of Education toward CBM was a commitment to a decision-making framework based upon a valid data base measuring student outcomes. Merely giving tests to students and reporting scores, in itself, was not viewed as exemplary practice. Instead, efforts were made to find an assessment system that provided a continuous source of information relevant to the needs of students. This philosophy emerges in a position paper written by the director and assistant director concerning assessment:

> Assessment, in educational settings, is an ongoing, multi-faceted process involving far more than the administration of a given test. Assessment is always an evaluative, interpretive appraisal of student performance. It provides information that should enable school personnel to make decisions regarding the students they service. (Kromer & Brown, 1979)

Often referred to as *data-based assessment*, it is convergence of this assessment paradigm with the concepts of the cascade of services model and noncategorical delivery of services that produced the foundation upon which CBM was implemented. In the remainder of the chapter we will focus upon a description of CBM, on how it is implemented across several decision areas, and on the implications of the model.

DESCRIPTION OF CURRICULUM-BASED MEASURES

The CBM system originally described by Deno and associates emphasized the use of materials prepared by teachers in the measurement of academic skills. For example, teachers are asked to randomly select stories from books or develop their own lists of spelling words. The primary purpose of this approach was to give the teacher flexibility in developing those measurement materials that are most important for monitoring progress. If the teachers have the skills to create their own assessments, it was reasoned, they would become less dependent upon tests that are inappropriate for measuring student goals.

While it has been our experience that teachers do have an appreciation of this independence, it was quickly recognized that time constraints limit teachers' ability to create their own CBM measures. Secondary to this need for considering time was the realization that inconsistencies in measurement materials might develop across the 35 elementary schools in the district. As a result, a team of curriculum specialists was assembled to develop the CBM materials for reading, spelling, written expression, math, and readiness for our 81 Special Education Resource Teachers (SERTs) and 18 tutors. The developmental work of these specialists over a 3-month period culminated in a package of assessment materials that could be used for all five academic domains across all psychoeducational decision-making areas from kindergarten to sixth grade.

Reading

The CBM measures used in the K–6 Resource Program were adapted from the research of Deno, Mirkin, and Chiang (1982) and created from the basal reading passages found in the district reading curriculum.

The CBM reading measure and its curriculum base. The reading curriculum currently used in the Minneapolis Public Schools is the Holt Reading Series (Weiss,

Steurer, Cruickshank, & Hunt, 1983). The Holt curriculum is a basal reading series composed of 15 books (Levels 2-16) at the elementary grades. Rather than have teachers randomly select stories or passages from basal readers, the Minneapolis team of curriculum specialists, with permission from the publisher, developed a package of reading passages to be used by all SERTs. At each level of Holt, 30 passages, with at least 200 words, were randomly selected and then typed onto separate pages. For each passage two laminated copies were created. The Student Copy, from which the pupil reads, contains the text. The Examiner Copy differs only in that cumulative word counts for each line, to aid in scoring, are found in the right hand margin. Lamination of reading materials is encouraged for two reasons: (a) Both copies are used repeatedly and will wear longer; and (b) the teacher may use a grease pen or felt marker on the Examiner Copy for recording scores, and after erasure, reuse the passage.

Procedures for administration. Before administration the examiner instructs the students to read aloud as they would if asked to do so by a teacher or parent. The students are advised that there is a 1-min. limit and that they must attempt each word. If a word is not correctly identified within 3 seconds, the reader is prompted to continue. It is emphasized that the reading is not a race and that if the examiner believes the pupil is rushing, he or she will be instructed to start over.

Scoring procedures. At the beginning of the 1-min. sample the student is told to "Begin." While listening to the student, the examiner crosses out words on the Examiner Copy that are pronounced incorrectly or omitted. Credit is given the student for words that are eventually self-corrected. At the end of 1 min. the examiner says "Stop" and counts the number of words read correctly. As illustrated in Figure 1, the student read 62 words correctly on the passage.

Spelling

Procedures for measuring pupil performance in spelling were derived from research conducted by Deno, Mirkin, Lowry, and Kuehnle (1980).

The CBM spelling measure and its curriculum base. The Minneapolis Public School system has developed its own spelling curriculum at each elementary grade level. This creation of district grade-appropriate word lists minimized the work of our team of curriculum specialists. With the use of list-making software designed for the Apple IIe the specialists were able to generate 15 lists at each grade level. Lists consisted of 20 words randomly selected from the spelling curriculum of each grade level.

Procedures for administration. Measurement of performance in spelling focuses upon how well students spell words dictated from a specific list. Using a "rolling dictation procedure," the examiner dictates a new word from the list every 7 sec, repeating it once during the 7-sec interval, during a total administration period of 2 min. By employing the standardized, 7-sec interval the spelling procedures can be group-administered, which reduces time necessary for testing and increases efficiency.

Scoring procedures. White and Haring's (1980) procedures for scoring Correct Letter Sequences are used to evaluate pupil performance on dictated words. In this approach each sequential combination of letters within a word are counted as correct or incorrect. The student's score is derived from the total number of Correct Letter Sequences written during the 2-min dictation period. In Figure 2 each caret denotes a correct letter sequence (the correct spelling of each word is in parentheses). In total there are 17 correct letter sequences.

Written Expression

Deno, Marston, & Mirkin (1982) examined the validity of several curriculum-based measures of written expression. The results of their research were

FIGURE 1
Example of a Third Grade Reading Passage Scored for Words Correct

Charlie tramped down the road, kicking a stone and	9
whistling a tramping song as he went. He looked at the	20
blue bells far away, and he listened to cowbells tinkling in	31
distant meadows. Sometimes he stopped to throw stones	39
at telephone poles, and sometimes he sat under a tree and	50
watched the clouds roll by.	55
Charlie kept tramping until it was almost sundown,	63
and then he picked a field to sleep in. He picked a field	76
where daisies grew and the grass and the clover smelled	86
sweet.	87

used in the development of Minneapolis CBM procedures for this academic domain.

The written expression measure and its curriculum base. At the time of CBM implementation there was not an existing district curriculum for written expression. However, the Story Starter approach to measuring written expression (Deno, Marston, & Mirkin, 1982) matched district objectives in this area. After reviewing the existing research on the topic, the team of curriculum specialists developed a set of 50 Story Starters for eliciting written compositions from students. In producing the Story Starters, the team controlled for age/grade appropriateness of content, high interest, and length of stimulus.

Procedures for administration. The written expression measures may be administered to the students individually or in groups. After the Story Starter is read to the pupil, the examiner explains that he or she has a minute to think of a story that would complete the initial statement. When that time has elapsed, the student is asked to start writing and is given 3 min to write a composition.

Scoring procedures. Once compositions are completed, the examiner counts the total number of words written correctly. It is this score that is used for screening, identification, and progress monitoring.

Math

Research on curriculum-based measurement in math was not conducted at the Institute for Research on Learning Disabilities (IRLD). However, both the Pine County Special Education Cooperative (Tindal & Germann, 1983) and the Minneapolis Public Schools (Skiba, Magnusson, Marston, & Erickson, 1985) have conducted validity research on CBM math measures that assure their technical adequacy.

The CBM math measure and its curriculum base. Math probes developed by the curriculum specialists were derived from the district math objectives set at

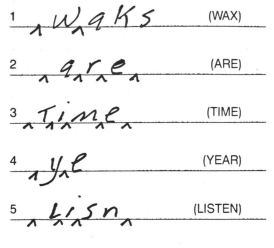

1   (WAX)
2   (ARE)
3   (TIME)
4   (YEAR)
5   (LISTEN)

FIGURE 2
Example of Correct Letter Sequence Scoring

each grade level in the Heath Mathematics curriculum (Rucker & Dilley, 1981). At each grade level emphasis was placed on the basic operations. For Grades 1-3 math probes, of increasing difficulty, matched to district objectives were generated for addition, subtraction, and mixed operations (combination of addition and subtraction problems). In Grades 4-6 probes were created for multiplication, division, and mixed operations (a combination of addition, subtraction, multiplication, and division).

Procedures for administration. Each math probe is administered for 2 min. At the beginning of each administration the students are told that they will be writing the answers to math problems. Students are encouraged to work quickly, but not to skip problems.

Scoring procedures. White and Haring's (1980) procedure for scoring math centers upon the number of digits written correctly in response to a problem. This procedure was adopted in Minneapolis and is used to score student performance on the math probes.

Readiness Skills

Although the initial use of CBM emphasized the academic domains of reading, spelling, written expression, and math in Grades 1-6, the team of specialists created a readiness measure. Referred to as Tool Movements, this assessment procedure measured student skills in copying letters and numbers. Tool Movements, however, did not completely meet our needs in the readiness areas for two reasons. First, in the areas of math and reading the CBM measures were not sensitive enough to discriminate low- and high-functioning pupils at the beginning of the first grade. Second, an increase in kindergarten referrals indicated a need for CBM readiness measures below first grade. Since the IRLD research on CBM did not extend to the readiness levels, Minneapolis developed and researched its own readiness measures (Marston, 1985).

The CBM readiness measures and their curriculum base. Our review of the district written expression objectives showed that specific skills in this area were not taught until the second grade. However, students were expected to have skills in holding, writing, and copying with a pencil. As a result, the team of curriculum specialists first developed two probes measuring Tool Movements. In the first probe students are asked to copy letters presented to them on a sheet of paper; in the second probe the students copy numbers. For the area of reading readiness pupils are measured on Letter and Word Identification. Letter Identification probes include a repeating pattern of the 26 letters in the alphabet. The Word Identification measure is composed of words found in both the Holt primer readers and the Dolch common word list. In math, an examination of district math readiness objectives and curriculum showed that pupils were expected to know the numbers 1-31. Based upon this information, the curriculum specialists designed the Number Naming probe to measure this skill area.

Procedures for administration. The Tool Movements measure contains two sections for measuring a student's skills in writing the 26 letters of the alphabet and the digits 0-9. On both tasks these symbols are presented visually, and the student is asked to copy the symbols during the 2-min administration time. The probe sheet measuring Letter Identification contains the 26 letters of the alphabet, which are repeated four times in random order. In a one-to-one testing situation, the student is asked to name each letter pointed to by the examiner during a 1-min interval. For the Word Identification probe the student is given 1 min to name the words on the Holt/Dolch list. Each of the three parallel forms of the list is composed of 100 words found in both the Holt, Levels 3 to 5, and the Dolch word list. Similarly, math readiness is assessed with Number Naming. Four sets of the numbers 1–31 are randomly arranged on the probe sheet, and the student identifies numbers on the sheet during a 1-min period.

Scoring procedures. On the Tool Movement probes, the student's letter and number formation must reasonably represent the visual stimulus. No credit is given for numbers or letters reversed. For the reading readiness measures the number of letters and words correctly identified are tabulated. On both tasks the student is credited for self-corrections. In Number Naming the examiner counts the correct responses. Two-digit numbers must be identified with the full name. For example, the correct response for "21" is "twenty-one," not "two–one."

Developing Local Norms

Developing the peer comparison component was a major task during the initial implementation of CBM and necessitated the generation of local norms. During the 1983–1984 academic year the CBM measures were standardized in reading, spelling, written expression, math, and Tool Movements. The first question confronting those responsible for implementation was the issue of school-based versus district norms. Since it was not possible to immediately compare performance levels of schools, it was decided that the development of school-based norms for each of 35 elementary

schools was consonant with the principles of the least restrictive environment. After consultation with measurement specialists from the University of Minnesota, a plan for standardization of the CBM measures in the Minneapolis Public Schools was initiated.

Assuming that students would progress on the academic measures during the school year and that the norms should reflect this improvement, standardization was scheduled for the fall, winter, and spring. Twenty students were randomly selected at every grade level, first through sixth, from each of the 35 schools. Subject selection produced 2,720 students who were tested each October, January, and April for a total standardization sample of 8,160. Within the randomly selected standardization sample, distribution of sexes was 50.4% female, 49.6% male.

The success of norming five academic measures on a standardization sample of 8,160 elementary students hinged on commitment from both regular and special education administrators, cooperation from the Minneapolis elementary building principals, and the dedication of a well-trained cadre of 15 SERTs, psychologists, and graduate students, who moved from school to school to complete the standardization process. For each norming period, testing was completed in approximately 3–4 weeks. Scoring and coding of the data for the computer analysis took an additional 2–3 weeks, with data summarization completed 8 weeks after norming began.

The evolution of the CBM model since the initial standardization has produced three significant changes. First, the Resource Program has moved from school to district norms. An examination of school means in reading demonstrated few significant differences across the six grade levels among the 35 elementary schools. Thus, school norms were eliminated in favor of district norms created from the original data base of 8,160 students. (A decision to initially use district norms would have reduced standardization costs considerably.) With a district norms format, only 100–150 randomly selected pupils per grade level

TABLE 1
Means and Standard Deviations for Curriculum-Based Measures in the Fall, Winter, and Spring

Curriculum measures	Grade	Fall Mean	Fall SD	Winter Mean	Winter SD	Spring Mean	Spring SD
Reading	1	18.93	36.06	51.69	49.82	71.34	39.37
Spelling		8.78	10.28	25.44	18.31	41.75	19.56
Math		5.07	5.11	16.71	8.94	25.04	11.44
Reading	2	51.30	41.23	72.78	43.85	82.06	38.72
Spelling		33.08	18.68	55.65	23.13	66.39	21.66
Math		23.37	10.59	27.31	12.69	33.38	15.02
Written expression		7.88	6.40	16.72	9.98	24.61	11.53
Reading	3	87.66	40.06	106.91	40.55	114.61	38.41
Spelling		60.35	23.29	81.41	24.75	81.80	14.32
Math		13.73	7.04	20.95	10.23	25.32	12.19
Written expression		19.26	9.92	27.83	11.94	31.22	12.37
Reading	4	105.49	42.50	114.59	40.67	118.31	42.78
Spelling		77.32	26.08	88.78	21.27	93.78	15.29
Math		23.47	9.65	28.78	12.30	34.06	13.31
Written expression		29.07	12.96	36.44	12.36	38.82	13.08
Reading	5	117.65	40.17	129.16	42.63	134.39	40.10
Spelling		90.55	24.31	100.96	20.26	100.73	20.11
Math		31.47	16.15	47.04	19.74	55.26	23.28
Written expression		37.08	14.72	44.61	13.65	44.20	13.73
Reading	6	115.16	39.38	120.15	37.35	131.25	39.07
Spelling		100.75	30.78	116.01	22.05	111.84	19.65
Math		58.35	27.70	72.97	29.05	84.14	32.71
Written expression		44.95	13.98	47.61	14.17	50.94	15.55

would have required testing, decreasing costs 66-77%. The means and standard deviations for each grade level for fall, winter, and spring are presented in Table 1.

A second modification that has occurred has been the movement from fall, winter, and spring norms to monthly norms. While the former format allowed for pupil progress during the year, SERTs indicated that it lacked precision during the transition months between periods, that is, December and March. By establishing test standardization techniques the initial data base was analyzed with regression methods solving both linear and polynomial equations for all measures. The result is a set of monthly norms now used by district personnel.

A third significant change in the evolution of the Minneapolis CBM standardization has been the development of new readiness measures. As pointed out in the previous section, the only readiness measure initially normed was Tool Movements, the copying of letters and numbers. Concerns expressed by Minneapolis SERTs about the need for more assessment at the kindergarten and first grade levels prompted further investigation of other procedures that might fit the CBM model. The result was the development and norming of Letter and Sound Identification probes, the Holt/Dolch list, and the Number Naming probes for both kindergarten and first grade. In total 1,800 pupils (900 from kindergarten and 900 in first grade) participated in the norming of CBM readiness measures during the second year of CBM implementation.

As the Minneapolis K-6 norms for curriculum-based measurement currently stand, a total of 10 academic measures are available with a total standardization sample in excess of 10,000 students. Given district projections for future major curriculum revisions, the CBM norms should be utilized for another 7-8 years before renorming. Whereas major test publishers revise tests on the average every 10-15 years, Minneapolis administrators have cut this cycle in half.

Training Staff in Administration, Scoring, and Interpretation

Crucial to the successful implementation of CBM is the provision of comprehensive training to staff in administering, scoring, and interpreting the measures. For Minneapolis, in-service training has been an ongoing process for a staff of SERTs and tutors that number nearly 100. New teachers coming into the program participate in two full days of training on how to administer and score the measures. The training is designed to educate SERTs on the philosophy and research behind CBM, followed by extensive experience in administration and scoring. For both areas new SERTs must exceed .90 reliability levels before training is terminated.

After the initial 2-day training session, SERTs continue training in the classroom, where they consult with a staff specialist on a weekly basis. It is in this situation that training in data interpretation is emphasized and becomes an integral part of the consultation process. The Minneapolis Resource leadership staff includes five lead teachers or resource specialists whose primary responsibility is to consult and provide ongoing training to approximately 16 SERTs and 4 tutors on a regular basis throughout the academic year.

IMPLEMENTATION OF THE CBM MODEL

Salvia and Ysseldyke (1981) posited that good assessment practice extends beyond identification decisions. Educators, they maintained, must concern themselves with a continuum of psychoeducational decisions, including screening, identification, program planning, progress monitoring, and program evaluation. In an attempt to build a common metric across this continuum, the Minneapolis K-6 Resource Program has implemented CBM procedures across all five of these decision areas.

Screening

The purpose of screening is to determine whether a referred student's academic performance is so significantly different from peer performance that further assessment is warranted. Currently there is increased emphasis upon implementing at least two prereferral interventions in the regular education classroom before referral. Assuming a child has not demonstrated progress on these interventions and referral is deemed appropriate, the referral process begins with screening. The student may be screened in the areas of reading, math, spelling, written expression, and/or readiness skills. Once the appropriate curriculum material is selected, the screening probes are administered on three separate days. The student's median performance on the curriculum-based screening is then compared with performance of the student's peers by calculating a discrepancy ratio (Deno & Mirkin, 1977). This index is the quotient of the grade level median divided by the student's median performance. For example, if our student is in the fourth grade and reads 38 words correctly during a November screening (fourth grade median is 108 words correct), her or his discrepancy ratio is 108/38 or "2.84 times discrepant."

When the discrepancy ratio is calculated, the screening results are presented to the Student Support Team (SST), a group of in-school educators who decide whether the pupil is eligible for further assessment to determine eligibility. According to K-6 criteria, the SST is encouraged to send on for further assessment for special education eligibility only those pupils who are more than "2 times discrepant." While the "2 times discrepancy" criterion is only a guideline, and not a requirement, it is of interest that over the past 3 years the SSTs have overridden the criteria in only 10-15% of the referrals. In an era when referral is often synonymous with eligibility (Algozzine, Christenson, & Ysseldyke, 1982), it would appear the CBM guidelines have increased the objectivity of the referral review process in Minneapolis. Further verification of the screening system as an effective means for evaluating the appropriateness of referrals has been provided by Deno, Marston, and Tindal (1985), who demonstrated that the performance of pupils not meeting the 2 times discrepant criterion is very similar to the typical performance of Chapter I pupils. The percentages of screened students meeting the 2 times discrepant screening guidelines, approximately 50-70%, and those students determined eligible by the Student Support Team for further assessment during the first 3 years of Minneapolis CBM implementation is presented in Figure 3.

Identification

Once the decision to assess is made, due-process safeguards are initiated.

Notification of the impending educational assessment, which requires written consent, is given to the parent(s). When permission is received, the assessment team has 30 school days to complete the evaluation. The identification process in Minneapolis is composed of two types of assessments, which are often simultaneous: survey level and specific level assessment.

Survey level assessment. Survey level assessment is the initial step of the identification process and is defined as the collection of samples of many student behaviors in a given academic area across different levels of that curriculum. Often referred to as "sampling back," the primary purpose is to determine the student's level of performance in that curriculum. For example, one may have a student read aloud from various levels of Holt, to examine composite or cumulative reading skills, or one may have a student complete

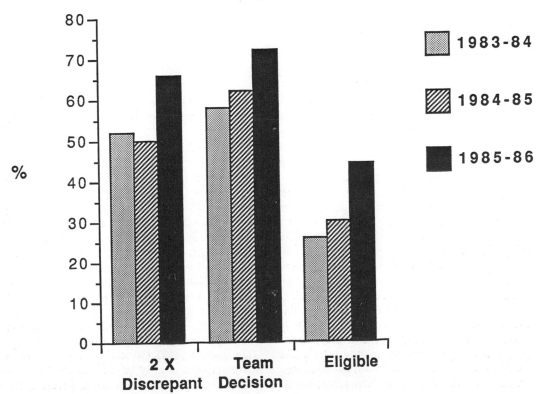

FIGURE 3
Percentage of Students Eligible for Assessment and Service

FIGURE 4
Survey Level Assessment for Reading

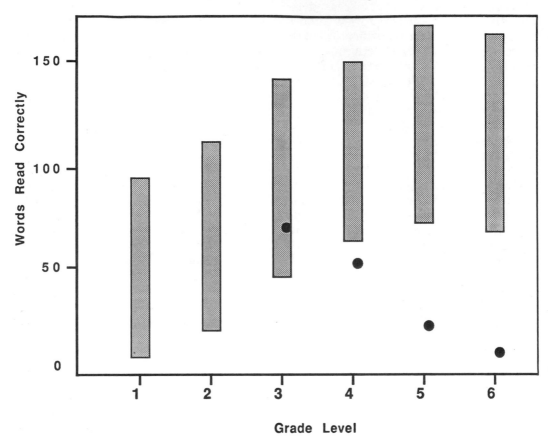

Grade Level

a page of mixed computational problems from Grades 3, 4, and 5. By comparing such general skills to the skills of typical students at different grades, one can specify how far the student is behind in the curriculum. This information is critical to making the eligibility decision. It is not sufficient that a student is discrepant from peers in academics to be eligible for service. They must also be significantly behind in the curriculum, which we have defined as at least 2 years.

An example of this process is presented in Figure 4, which displays the local norms developed from Minneapolis students reading from their grade level readers. The chart shows the typical range of words read correctly, plus or minus one standard deviation from the district mean, at each grade level. The data points in

Figure 4 represent Don's survey level testing on each set of grade level reading passages.

As can be seen, this sixth grade student is severely discrepant from grade level peers, having read only 12 words correctly. In sampling back to fifth grade material Don read 21 words correctly, which is still below the typical range of fifth graders. On fourth grade passages his performance improved to 51 correct words and was close to the normal range of fourth-grade pupils. Don's performance was most like third graders on third-grade material. His 64 words read correctly falls into the third-grade range, which extends from 42 words correct to 136. We can translate this into his being 3 years behind in the curriculum. By giving general survey level reading measures, we can obtain an idea of years behind. An analysis of these data also allows for the determination of IEP objectives that are measurable in the CBM system.

Interpretation of CBM survey level assessment data also identifies skills needing further testing. One of the difficulties that plague many criterion-referenced tests is that teachers often don't know which parts of the test to give. As a result, entire criterion-referenced batteries are administered at a considerable cost in time or are not utilized at all. Survey level testing, because of its general testing nature, samples many types of skills in a content area in a short period of time. By carrying out a careful process of error analysis of the survey level tests and by becoming familiar with the curricular demands at a given grade, a teacher may conduct concise assessments to document student skill areas that need a more thorough assessment. For example, Dave is a third grader with many spelling problems. Survey level assessment began by comparing Dave's spelling performance on second- and first-grade spelling words to the appropriate grade standard as in the example evaluating Don's performance. As a result, it was determined that Dave spells much like first graders do on first-grade words. During the survey level assessment, it was observed that he missed several words with the pattern CVC-e such as "bone" and "home." With a knowledge of the curricular demands, the SERT is then able to follow up these results with more detailed assessment and analysis of skill components with specific level assessment.

Six-week assessment plan. The Six-Week Assessment Plan (SWAP) involves the implementation of systematic interventions in order to serve the student in the least restrictive environment. The procedure utilizes the 30 school days allowed by federal law for the assessment of a student. The purpose of SWAP is to collect data to determine if any specific interventions in a student's educational program allows him or her to make appropriate progress in a regular education curriculum. Because the reliability of

most achievement tests, including CBM procedures, tend to be lower at the earlier grade levels, we emphasize use of the SWAP at kindergarten and first grade.

The SWAP is carried out by the regular education teacher with support and monitoring from the special education staff. After screening is completed and the SERT has identified the appropriate instructional level in the regular education curriculum in which a student can achieve progress, the SWAP is initiated. During this interval two regular education interventions are implemented: (a) Student outcome data are collected continuously, and (b) the effectiveness of the interventions is evaluated. Students who respond favorably to regular education modifications remain in regular education with assistance from Resource Program staff on a consultative basis. Those pupils who do not improve as a result of the two interventions during the 30 day period enter the Resource Program and an IEP is written for that particular academic or behavioral area.

An example of a SWAP is presented in Figure 5. In this example a fourth-grade student is referred for service in reading. The screening data indicated the child barely met the criteria, 2.2 times discrepant. After interviewing the classroom teacher, the SERT decided the student might benefit from a modification in the regular education curriculum. This particular student was placed in a Chapter I reading program for an extra 30 min per day and monitored in Holt Level 11, which is third-grade material. As illustrated in the graph, the pupil responded quite favorably to this change in instruction. The slope of the data indicate that the child is increasing reading performance at 4.5 words per week and that K-6 Resource Program help is not necessary at this time.

Specific skill assessment. Specific level assessment is a detailed examination of a student's skill. It is designed to more closely examine some of the conclusions reached during survey level assessment. Its purpose is extensive documentation of what a student can or cannot do with the

FIGURE 5
Six-Week Assessment Plan for K-6 Resource Program

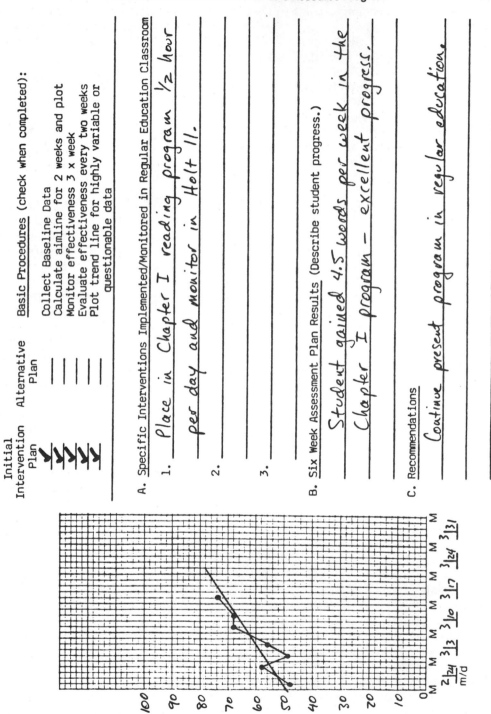

Number of Words Read Correctly

Initial
Intervention   Alternative
Plan   Plan   Basic Procedures (check when completed):

|||| |||| Collect Baseline Data
                                 Calculate aimline for 2 weeks and plot
                                 Monitor effectiveness 3 x week
                                 Evaluate effectiveness every two weeks
                                 Plot trend line for highly variable or
                                   questionable data

A. Specific Interventions Implemented/Monitored in Regular Education Classroom

1. Place in Chapter I reading program 1/2 hour
    per day and monitor in Holt II.

2. _____

3. _____

B. Six Week Assessment Plan Results (Describe student progress.)

    Student gained 4.5 words per week in the
    Chapter I program - excellent progress.

C. Recommendations

    Continue present program in regular education.

requirements of a curriculum as well as the identification of prerequisite skills necessary for success in the regular education curriculum.

While survey level assessment evaluates multiple skills, specific level tests single skills. For example, in math a fourth-grade survey level test may require a student to solve addition, subtraction, multiplication, and division problems, with and without regrouping, up to three digits. Assuming the student missed two of the four division problems involving basic division facts, the teacher would utilize specific level assessment techniques, giving the student a large sample of basic division facts. The teacher can then more reliably describe the student's skills.

Because specific level assessment analyzes the components of prerequisite skills, the outcome of the process provides further documentation of current performance and proper instructional placement within the curriculum. Should the student qualify for special education services, the process also supports the development of the instructional plan, a task-analyzed teaching strategy.

Results. The identification system in Minneapolis has had two significant results. First, this eligibility approach goes beyond most identification systems in that it provides specific information important to programming. Second, in the previous section it was shown that CBM measures in screening guided the referral review process through a more objective approach to examining referrals. Referral was not synonymous with eligibility. That trend continues in the identification phase. Returning to Figure 3, one can see that eligibility rates, about 25–45%, are much different from those reported by Algozzine, Christenson, and Ysseldyke (1982), where on the average 90% of referrals received special education service.

Program Planning

Using the procedures described by Deno, Mirkin, and Wesson (1984), Minne-

apolis has adopted a data-based approach to writing year-long goals for IEPs. Paramount in this system is the repeated measurement of pupil progress toward long-range goals in material of a constant level of task difficulty.

Setting the long-range goal. In developing long range goals (LRG) for Minneapolis IEPs we have utilized a behavioral approach to writing objectives and employ the Deno, Mirkin, and Wesson (1984) paradigm in which the condition, behavior, and criteria for the IEP are identified.

Condition: Establishing IEP goal material. The first step in setting an IEP goal is to determine the conditions for measurement. Specifically, the task is to decide from what academic material the goals are to be set. In reading, for example, the SERT must choose a basal level and set a goal in the material. Let's assume we are writing an IEP goal for a fifth grader whose reading instruction occurs in a second-grade reader. If the SERT were to set the IEP goal in fifth-grade reading material, it is likely that the pupil would find the reading level too difficult and not read many words correctly. Available research on this "floor effect" indicates that the monitoring system may not be sensitive enough to measure real pupil growth and that an easier level of the basal reader should be used for IEP assessment (White & Haring, 1980). However, if the SERT were to use the second-grade instructional level for measuring progress toward the IEP goal, it is quite possible that the student would read from material that has already been mastered. Coming up against a "ceiling effect," the student would read a high number of words correctly, leaving little room for growth to occur. Again a situation is created in which the monitoring system is insensitive to growth on the IEP.

To solve this problem Deno, Mirkin, and Wesson (1984) suggested a "sampling back" process. In this example, the SERT would listen to the pupil read fifth-grade material and successively easier levels, including grades 4, 3, and 2. These authors recommended that the IEP goal be set in material that is neither too difficult nor easy for the pupil, and that will be sensitive to academic gains. The guidelines used in Minneapolis for finding the appropriate goal level in reading are 10–30 words correct for first- and second-grade material, and 40–60 words correct for third-through sixth-grade material (Marston & Magnusson, 1985).

Behavior: What to measure. The academic areas to be measured on IEPs include reading, spelling, math, written expression, and readiness skills. The actual academic behaviors assessed are words read correctly for reading; correct letter sequences for spelling, correct digits in math, words written correctly in written expression; and tool movements, letter/word identification, and number naming for the readiness area.

Criteria: Developing IEP goals. How SERTs set IEP goals in the Minneapolis Resource Program is achieved in three ways. In the first instance, teachers have access to the normative data from kindergarten through sixth-grade and can estimate the typical performance of peers at any percentile level. For example, a SERT who wishes to set a goal for a pupil that is comparable with that of peers at the 30th percentile consults the "norms."

A second approach to setting goals is derived from the mastery research of Beldin (1970), Starlin and Starlin (1974), Starlin (1979), and Haring, Liberty, and White (Undated). Fuchs (1982) examined these mastery criteria for oral reading rates and concluded, "On the basis of technical and logistical considerations, it appears that absolute criteria, with rates between 50 and 70 words correct with seven or fewer errors, are among the best that have been studied" (pp. 69–70). In our review of these data we have employed this recommendation in setting the lower limits for reading goals. However, an examination of typical reading performance at the upper elementary grade levels (see Table 1) indicates a need to expand the mastery range. As a result, our reading mastery criterion for Grades 1 and 2 is 50–70 correct words and for Grades

3–6 the criterion is 70–100 words correct.

Third, we have empirically determined the average learning rates on IEPs for special education students (Marston & Magnusson, 1985) which are utilized for goal setting. In reading, the research shows that the typical Resource Program student gains knowledge of between 1.0 and 1.5 words per week. With this fact in mind, many SERTs will set IEP goals based upon a pupil's initial baseline rate plus the product of the number of weeks remaining in the year multiplied by 1.5 words per week.

The instructional plan. Once the long-range goal is set for the IEP, the SERT writes an instructional plan that describes the specific components of instruction in terms of the instructional objective, length of time, group size, instructional activity, and motivational strategy. For example, Don's SERT might set up an instructional plan that includes 5 min of oral reading in a 1:1 setting, 15 min of individual phonics worksheet activity, 15 min of silent reading, and 10 min of playing reading games on the microcomputer. The instructional plan is the SERT's documentation of what is happening in the resource room and is crucial to the successful progress monitoring of the pupil's IEP.

Progress Monitoring

Progress monitoring is the fourth decision area that is involved in CBM implementation. Within the CBM framework, SERTs are able to continuously monitor the effectiveness of their instructional interventions and student progress toward IEP goals, a process referred to as formative evaluation (Fuchs, Deno, & Mirkin, 1984). Most important to successful progress monitoring is time series analysis of the student performance data. This analysis provides SERTs with the mechanism by which they can determine the components of their instruction that improve reading performance. The graph presented in Figure 6 is an illustration of a pupil's reading performance during an academic year. Visual inspection of Phase A shows that instruction was not effective.

In actuality, this pupil's instructional plan corresponds to the example presented in the previous section. The pupil was receiving a total of 45 min of reading instruction, which included a variety of reading activities. Once the SERT had ascertained that the pupil was not making significant progress in reading, a change was made in the instructional program. This particular SERT chose to substitute a 30-min direct instruction lesson for the 15 min of phonics worksheets and 15 min of silent reading. As can be seen in Phase B, the pupil's reading performance increased dramatically.

Omitted in the above discussion is an explanation of how the SERT decided when the program needed changing. An integral component of time series analysis is the implementation of data utilization strategies during progress monitoring.

Data utilization strategies. Fuchs (1986) noted that although teachers may collect pupil data on a frequent basis, they often do not utilize the data to alter and improve instructional programs. This was the finding in a study conducted by Tindal, Fuchs, Mirkin, Christenson, and Deno (1981), who discovered that SERTs continued ineffective instructional interventions although CBM data indicated that their students were not progressing. The purpose of data utilization strategies is to circumvent this problem by providing teachers with sets of decision rules that determine when changes are to be made in instructional programs (White & Haring, 1980). The need for decision rules was made abundantly clear when Fuchs and Fuchs (1986) demonstrated that use of rules is correlated with a .5 standard deviation increase in student achievement. In Minneapolis, SERTs are employing two types of data utilization strategies: goal-oriented and treatment-oriented.

Goal-oriented decisions. The major distinction between the two strategies lies in the time reference of the criterion. In the goal-oriented approach decisions about instructional changes are based upon the relationship between the current level of performance and the IEP goal set at a *future* date. This relationship is defined by the IEP aimline, that line of progress on a graph that connects baseline performance with the specified goal or criterion. All judgments about instructional effectiveness are based upon looking forward to the prescribed goal and are described by whether performance is above or below the aimline. For example, in the initial stage of Phase B of Figure 7 the pupil's performance is typically at or above the aimline, suggesting that the instructional regime is effective. However, later in Phase B the pupil's performance has fallen below the aimline on four successive occasions. At this juncture, the goal-oriented decision rule dictates that a change in the program is to be implemented. A change, represented by the dark, vertical line, is illustrated in Figure 7, and Phase C instruction is initiated with continuing data collection.

Treatment-oriented decisions. The reference of the criterion is reversed in the treatment-oriented data utilization strategy, in which decisions about instructional effectiveness are based upon the success of the *past* treatment. In this approach effectiveness is evaluated by drawing the trend line or slope through the previous 9–12 data points of CBM data. The slopes drawn by the SERTs on the IEP graphs are calculated by White and Haring's (1980) quarter-intersect method. At this point the treatment-oriented approach offers two alternatives. If the rate of progress indicated from the slope line is higher than the previous period, minor modifications or additions to the program may be considered. However, if the slope indicates an undesirable rate of progress (e.g., a negative slope or slope lower than in the previous phase), major changes or modifications in the intervention should be considered. In phase B of Figure 8, the flat trend line indicates that the instructional program is not successful and a major change is to be made in the next phase. The slope in phase C, however, is increasing significantly and suggests only minor modifications for the upcoming phase D.

Exit criteria at the individual level. A student is terminated from special

FIGURE 6
Example of Monitoring of Progress in Reading

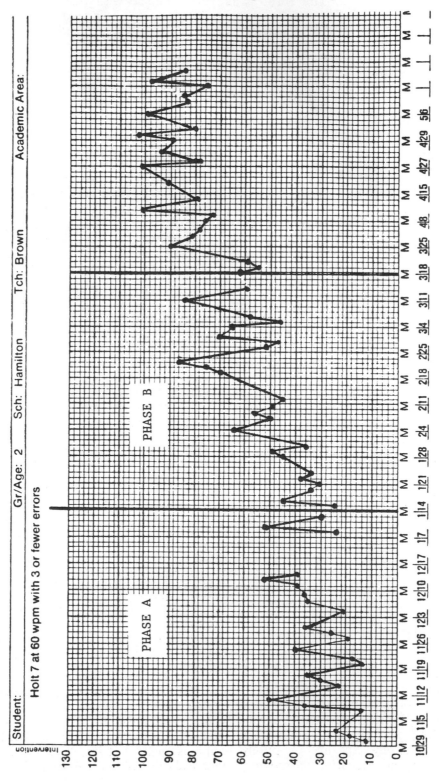

FIGURE 7
Performance Record under Goal-Oriented Data Utilization Strategy

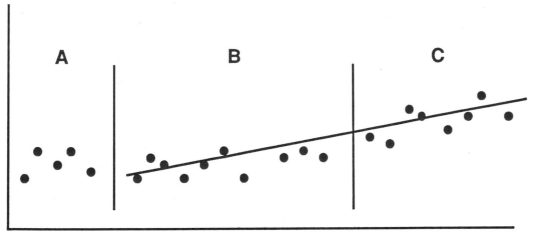

education service when reassessment and/or continuous assessment data indicate that her or his current levels of performance no longer reflect special education needs. Termination is determined by the Student Support Team in one of four ways.

1. The student has accomplished the goals listed on the IEP.
2. The goals on the IEP are determined to be no longer appropriate and service to the student can be delivered without special education.
3. Parents and/or students may decide by their own choice to discontinue service.
4. Reassessment results indicate that the student's current educational performance no longer qualifies him or her for a special education service.

The vast majority of students exiting from the Resource Program do so through the fourth option. Three times each academic year, in the fall, winter, and spring, SERTs review their entire caseload on grade level materials and determine pupil-peer discrepancy levels. Those students who are no longer two times or more discrepant from peers are brought up for review by the Student Support Team and typically are taken out of the K-6 program. Last year approximately 20% of our pupils returned to regular education classrooms,

whereas 4% were placed in a more restrictive environment in the special education delivery system.

Program Evaluation

The last psychoeducational decision-making area in which CBM is implemented is program evaluation. Whereas the first four areas discussed relate primarily to assessment at the individual level, program evaluation is concentrated on measuring outcomes at the systems level. When educational administrators are confronted with questions concerning program efficacy, there is a real need for program evaluation data. The Minneapolis K-6 Resource Program is organized so that all CBM data collected at the individual level, that is, referral and screening, identification, program planning, and progress monitoring, is aggregated across teachers and schools for program evaluation purposes. Two forms of program evaluation employed in the Resource Program are the Trimester Review and Program Comparison evaluations.

Trimester review. The caseload review data that SERTs collect in the fall, winter, and spring for exit purposes also doubles as program evaluation data. Every pupil is measured on grade level CBM materials in IEP service areas. The data are aggregated across teachers and summarized for the program. An example of data summarization from the 1984–85 academic year is found in Figure 9, where the average math performance of Resource Program pupils at each grade level in the fall, winter, and spring is charted.

As can be seen in Figure 9, the number of correct digits typically increases from fall to winter, and from winter to spring. In all cases these differences are statistically significant at or below p values of .05, except in second and third grade for winter to spring. For the program administrator such data are useful, for they demonstrate that the program at the systems level, in general, is effective. However, the administrator may want to more closely examine the situation at the second and third grades, which may indicate a need for in-service training. Whatever the case, data bases such as these can be compared across years, academic areas, and schools, providing the administrator with valuable information regarding severity of student needs, in-service training priorities, and allocation of resources to schools.

Program comparisons. Another option for program evaluation available to special education administrators is the comparison of the performance of Resource Program students with that of students placed in other educational programs. Figure 10 presents a comparison of the typical written expression performance of pupils enrolled in regular education, pupils receiving Chapter I intervention, and pupils referred for special education. For the latter group there are two subgroups: pupils who were not 2 times discrepant and were not eligible for services, and students whose performance was more than 2 times discrepant from peers. Of interest is the fact that Chapter I students and pupils not eligible for service are quite similar in performance levels. This is a finding that has been replicated across all the academic areas.

Summary of Decisions

This section has covered in detail the implementation of CBM across the psychoeducational decision-making continuum. As can be seen, it is possible to develop a common metric that can adequately guide our decisions about individual students and programs. Figure 11 summarizes the continuum with a brief description of the frequency of administrations, the duration of samples, and the level of measurement for the CBM process in screening, identification, program planning, progress monitoring, and identification.

FIGURE 8
Performance Record under Treatment-Oriented Data Utilization Strategy

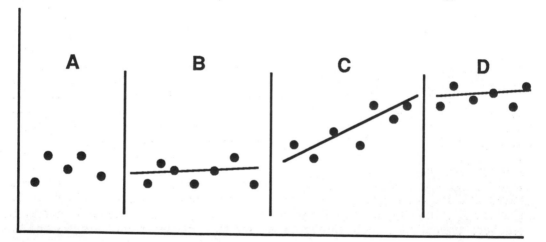

FIGURE 9
Program Evaluation Data: Average Math Performance of Resource Program Students in 1984–85

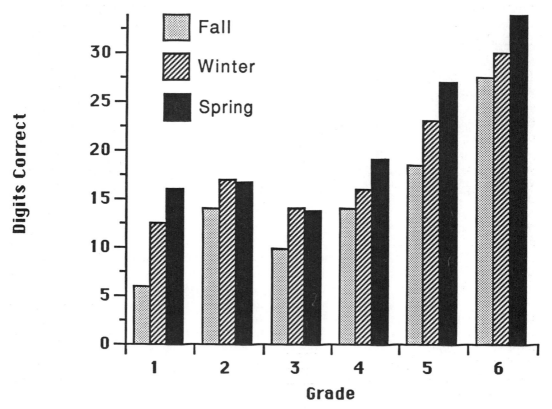

TRAINING AND RESEARCH WITH CBM IN MINNEAPOLIS

Experimental Teaching Project

Funded by a two-year federal training grant, the Experimental Teaching Project (ETP) was a collaborative effort between the University of Minnesota and the Minneapolis Public Schools that provided 55 SERTs with intensive training and experience in using curriculum-based measurements to create effective educational programs for handicapped children (Deno, 1986a). The project operated with three major assumptions. First, traditional approaches to prescribing educational treatments for student IEPs, whether they are modality-based or task analytic, usually fail because they are based on a diagnostic prescriptive system that is not technically adequate. Second, teachers typically fit their pupils to a standard program of instruction they have created, rather than design programs to meet individual student needs. Third, recent research on the technical adequacy of curriculum-based measures provides educators with an opportunity to continuously evaluate the effectiveness of instructional interventions and provides feedback concerning necessary adjustments. SERTs participating in the project were encouraged to examine their beliefs about what interventions worked best with handicapped students, to test their hypotheses by collecting CBM data over a 6-month period, and then to implement new, personally untried interventions when suggested necessary by the data. The primary goal of the training project was to get SERTs to expand their instructional horizons and begin to provide unique instructional opportunities for students when indicated by the time series data. Two interesting research findings emerged from this training project.

Teacher attitudes and beliefs about effective instruction. Before the beginning of Year 1 of the Experimental Teaching Project, all SERTs in the district were asked to complete questionnaires concerning their attitudes. At that time, there were no statistically significant differences on the variables between SERTs participating in the project, SERTs who were to participate in Year 2, or SERTs who chose not to participate. After 7 months of intensive training on how to use CBM data to make instructional decisions and how to make instructional changes along several dimensions (including curriculum, motivation, cognition, and use of tutors), a significant change in attitudes and beliefs had developed in the participants (Casey, Deno, Marston, & Skiba, 1986). By the end of Year 1 of the project, teachers had significantly greater knowledge about instructional interventions. More relevant was the finding that although this set of ETP teachers in-

creased their knowledge base about interventions, their certainty about the effectiveness of available instructional strategies decreased. The fact that participants became less dogmatic about their beliefs is important for two reasons. First, it would appear that the role of monitoring pupil progress with an objective data system changed teacher beliefs and helped motivate them to explore new instructional strategies. Second, it is argued here that this trend of expanding the instructional skills of SERTs will directly benefit the highly individual instructional needs of the handicapped child.

Effective instruction: What the data say. In addition to the primary findings related to training effects, secondary analysis of the student outcome data from the 2-year project also yielded information about the effectiveness of the various instructional strategies used by the SERTs. From Year 1 it was determined that the average slope of learning for pupils taught by participants was significantly higher in those instructional phases implemented

FIGURE 10
Average Written Expression Performance of Four Selected Groups of Students

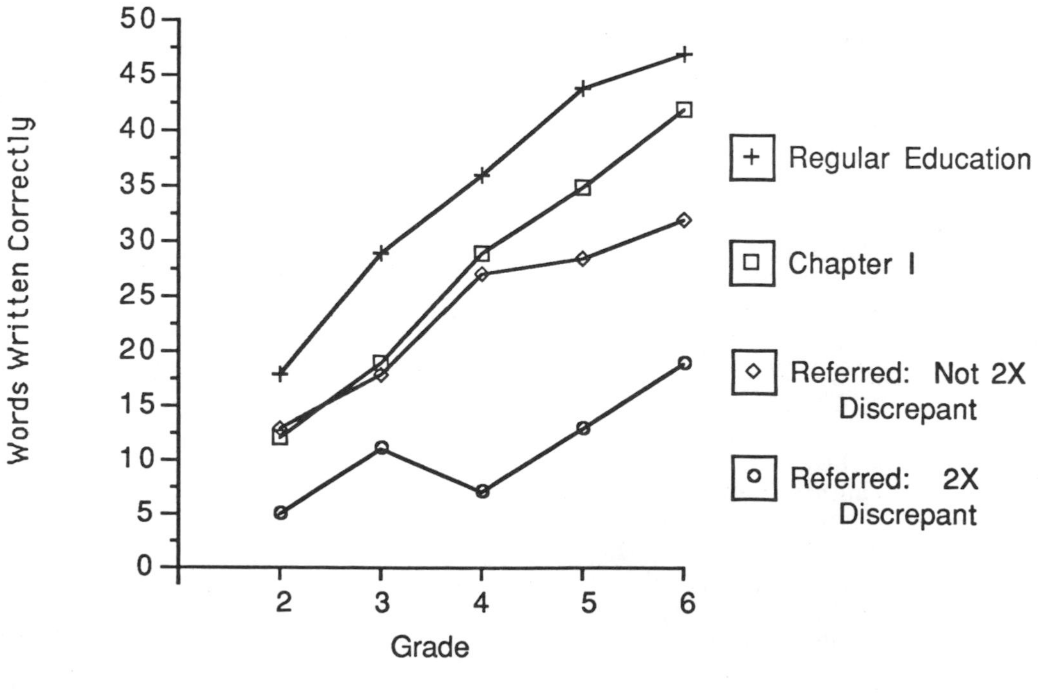

FIGURE 11
Frequency, Duration, and Level of Measurement for CBM Procedures

	Screening	Identification	Program Planning	Progress Monitoring	Program Evaluation
Reading Words Correct	The median of 9 one min. samples across 3 days in grade level mat.	Sampling back with one min. probes in Holt Basal Reader to determine "Years Behind"	Goal Setting in IEP material with Norms, Mastery or Peer Criteria	One minute samples monitored 2-3 times per week in IEP material: GO or TO decision rules * **	3 one minute, grade level passages each Fall, Winter, Spring
Spelling Correct Letter Sequences	The median of 3 two min. samples across 3 days on grade level lists	Sampling back with two min. probes across grades to determine "Years Behind"	Goal Setting in IEP materials with Norms or Peer Criteria	Two minute probe once per week on IEP spelling lists: GO or TO decision rules	Two minute Grade level spelling list each Fall, Winter, Spring
Written Expression Words Correct	The median of 3 three min. Story Starters across 3 days	Peer comparisons for determination of "Years Behind"	Goal Setting in IEP materials with Norms	Weekly 3 min. Story Starter: GO or TO decision rules	Three minute Story Starter each Fall, Winter, Spring
Math Correct Digits	The median of 3 two min. grade level probes across 3 days	Sampling back with two min. probes across grade levels for "Years Behind"	Goal Setting in IEP materials with Norms or Peer Criteria	Weekly 2 min. IEP probe: GO or TO decision rules	Three minute Grade Level Probe each Fall, Winter, Spring
Readiness Letter/Number Copying & Naming	The median of 3 one or two min. probes across 3 days	Six Week Assessment Plan with Tool Movements, Number and Letter Identification	Goal Setting in IEP materials with Norms	Weekly 1 or 2 minute probes: GO or TO rules	Probes administered Fall, Winter, Spring

* GO represents "Goal-Oriented" data utilization decision rules.

** TO represents "Treatment-Oriented" data utilization decision rules after initial training than before the project began. Therefore, it could be argued that frequent monitoring helped increase performance. Also of interest were the individual contrasts of different instructional strategies. An aggregation of the Year 1 data showed that students taught with a whole-word, or sight word approach, when compared to phonics instruction, progressed at a significantly higher rate (slope of 1.9 words per week versus .8 words per week). On the other hand, examination of learning rates of students taught with the language Experience (Stauffer, 1970) approach demonstrated that these pupils made gains significantly inferior to gains of students taught by other reading approaches, including free choice of reading material, high-interest/low-vocabulary reading material, and use of tokens (slope of .36 words per week for language experience vs. 1.01 words per week for the other approaches).

Study of Special Education Effectiveness

A secondary contribution of the CBM model is its ability to function as a reliable and valid measure of student outcomes for research studies in special education. Historically, educational research has been plagued with inadequate measurement methodologies that threaten both internal and external validity (Cook & Campbell, 1979). An example from special education is the meta-analysis research reported by Carlberg and Kavale (1980). After reviewing 50 special education efficacy studies, these authors reported that "special classes were found to be significantly inferior to regular class placement for students with below average IQs" (p. 295). Tindal (1985), however, pointed out that such conclusions are unwarranted because the metric for student outcomes used in many of these studies is technically inadequate.

The CBM model provides a more accurate means of measuring pupil's progress and the response to educational programs (Marston, Fuchs, & Deno, 1986; Fuchs, Deno, & Mirkin, 1984). For this reason, the effectiveness of special education was studied in Minneapolis with a multiple baseline, time series design (Marston, in press). During the academic year 220 low-achieving pupils taught in regular education but considered potential candidates for special education were monitored frequently in reading. In that year-long interval 15 pupils from this high-risk group entered the special education Resource Program. Since the educational interventions for these pupils could first be described as "regular education," and later as "special education," they represented an ideal opportunity to conduct a time series analysis comparing these two phases. The average length of regular education reading intervention (Phase A) was 10.5 weeks. Upon entering special education, these same students were taught reading in the Resource Program classroom (Phase B) for an average of 11.5 weeks. Each week during Phases A and B, student reading performance was monitored with CBM materials. The average growth of the students during Phase A regular education intervention was .6 words per week; during Phase B, special education intervention it was 1.1 words per week. Comparison of these slopes with repeated measures ANOVA showed the difference was statistically significant [$F(1, 10) = 8.4, p = 0.16$].

Study of Categorical Licensure for SERTs

The CBM model has also aided in the study of noncategorical services for handicapped children. Because Minneapolis operates a noncategorical approach to the instruction of special education pupils (i.e., LD teachers instruct EMR as well as LD pupils and EMR teachers instruct LD as well as EMR pupils), the district is an optimal setting for research on this timely issue. In an aptitude-treatment study conducted by Marston (1987), 12 LD-certified SERTs taught 38 LD and 24 EMR pupils. In addition, 12 EMR certified SERTs instructed 40 LD and 23 EMR students. It was hypothesized that if categorical services were of greater benefit than noncategorical services, then

LD pupils would progress more when taught by LD-licensed teachers than when instructed by EMR-licensed teachers. Conversely, EMR pupils would make more progress when taught by EMR teachers than their LD counterparts. When the performance of all students was assessed by CBM procedures, the results indicated there was no significant difference in the progress of the special education students with respect to licensure of their teacher. LD pupils taught by LD teachers made the same gains as LD students taught by EMR teachers. Conversely, EMR pupils gains were the same with LD and EMR teachers. The results of the study support the noncategorical approach to delivering special education services.

IMPLICATIONS OF CBM FOR SERVICE DELIVERY

Implementation of CBM obviously has had an impact on our district in many ways. What are the implications? How have roles changed? What are the major issues concerning the use of CBM? In the final section of this chapter we cover a variety of topics in addressing these questions.

Role of the Resource Teacher

A curriculum-based approach to special education services has changed the role of the Special Education Resource Teacher (SERT) in two ways — increased expectations of individual students and accountability for a teacher's instructional effectiveness.

In the past, students referred for LD special education services were assessed using norm referenced tests and assigned static IQ scores. In the traditional model, according to one SERT interviewed, change was not expected. The measurement of student progress was usually described in terms of student compliance to daily teaching activities. Further, transfer of skills to the district curriculum was never demanded or even expected by administrators. In the opinion of this SERT, teachers received reinforcement for "enduring" extended interaction with low

performing students and not for effective instruction. However, CBM with its continual emphasis upon improving instruction, has placed the expectation on teachers that students can learn in resource rooms and make significant progress.

With this expectation in place, SERTs feel more accountable for the effectiveness of instruction. CBM offers a method for documenting pupil progress and ultimately teacher effectiveness. In addition, decisions based on current performance in district curriculum has encouraged special education teachers to interface with regular education goals and objectives. As a result, many SERTs have increased their instructional repertoire of educational strategies in order to better meet the varying needs of students. As one SERT stated, "It has challenged SERTs as educators to become critical thinkers . . . to base student decisions and instructional interventions on objective data."

As explained in a later section, fifty-five of the Minneapolis SERTs participated in an intensive training program designed to instruct teachers on the critical elements of the CBM model and to encourage them to better utilize the collected data. Those teachers participating in Year 1 of that project, and surveyed one year after their participation, were asked to name the effects of implementing the CBM model. 53% of that sample stated they were more open to trying new interventions; 35% said they were more aware of student progress, or lack of it; and 18% reported being more "flexible." One interesting observation made by a SERT in reference to lack of progress was, "I blame the kid less."

The Role of the School Psychologist

During the first three years of implementation in the Minneapolis CBM model, a school psychologist has been assigned full time to responsibilities relating to the organization and the implementation of curriculum-based measurement in Minneapolis. Those responsibilities have included: organization of normative efforts, coordination of activities that led to the development of actual CBM measures, providing in-service training to SERTs, data analysis and research, ongoing consultation with SERTs on data utilization within the CBM model, and dissemination activities.

Other than the involvement of a full-time psychologist in CBM implementation, what has been the impact of CBM upon the role of the school psychologist in Minneapolis? Since implementation of CBM has primarily been the responsibility of the special education resource teachers, and not the psychologists, it has not directly affected the duties of Minneapolis psychologists. The school psychologists are still very much involved in assessment (other than CBM measures), consultation, direct treatment, and in-service training. However, it does appear that implementation of CBM, with its emphasis on a curriculum-based set of objective criteria for referrals and eligibility, has had some impact upon the practices of school psychologists in the district. Canter (1986) compared the time spent by psychologists on a variety of activities before CBM implementation (1981) and after implementation (1986). Several significant findings emerged from this report. First, in the area of assessment, time spent on testing is virtually the same in 1981 and 1986; about 35%. However, Minneapolis school psychologists are testing proportionately fewer students in 1986. Canter concluded that psychologists are reducing unnecessary testing and spending more time on those cases that demand comprehensive assessment. Second, Minneapolis school psychologists have increased their time in consultation activities regarding individual students and department programs from 12% in 1981 to 35% in 1986. Third, the district psychologists are also spending more time in direct treatment activities, 1.5% in 1981 and 6% in 1986.

In general, all three trends are viewed as improvements by a staff that prefers to spend more time in consultation and treatment activities. Whether these benefits can be directly attributed to the implementation of CBM remains an open question. What is not in doubt, however, is the fact that implementation of CBM

has given the Student Support Teams, for the first time, an objective set of criteria for purposes of making eligibility decisions.

Reynolds (1982), in his discussion of the impact of PL 94-142 on education, commented:

> Public education has changed: Student bodies have become more heterogeneous, new structures have begun to appear, and new functions and roles are demanded of teachers, building principals, school psychologists, and other specialists. Most of the changes derive from the mandated provision of services to populations that, heretofore, were considered marginal, that is the handicapped, minority, economically disadvantaged, bilingual, migrant, and other children and youth who have been systematically set aside or excluded from the mainstreams of society and the schools.

Obviously, in the changing ecosystem of education, the role of the school psychologist is affected. Although the change for school psychologists may be difficult, Reynolds suggested that this would be eased by "an in-depth analysis of the emerging rights of children and the new principles being applied to the education of 'marginal' children." To achieve this end, Reynolds (1982) has identified nine clusters of competency that school psychologists must possess to make a successful transition: consultation, individualized assessment, diverse social structures, individualized instruction, teaching psychological development, parent involvement, teaching basic skills, group management, and the law and judicial procedures. While all clusters are critical to improving services for handicapped students, it is individualized assessment of "marginal children" that receives much of Reynolds's attention.

> In general, assessment processes in the schools should be oriented to instructional decisions: that is, the assessments should help to design appropriate instructional programs for students. . . . Assessments should be mainly curriculum-based or behavioral. . . . In general, behavioral assessments should be based

heavily on direct observations rather than on presumed predispositional or underlying traits (p. 105).

Assessments of school progress should be highly specific to the domains of instruction and so designed that individuals have clear opportunities to become aware of their own progress.... (p. 106).

We have included these remarks because CBM implementation fits nicely with the model proposed by Reynolds. It is oriented to instruction, is data-driven, relates to the curriculum, and is behaviorally based. We agree with Reschly (1987), who concludes that the conventional testing model is inadequate: "The amount of time and energy now devoted to preplacement and reevaluations [in special education], which are dominated by determination of eligibility, represents excessively costly and ineffective use of resources." As school psychologists move away from the "gatekeeper" status to consultation and direct service, the CBM model will help guide their decision making on pupil progress and intervention effectiveness. It is our belief that as the role of the school psychologist changes, attraction to the CBM model will increase.

Role of the Administrator

From our perspective, the implementation of CBM has had a positive impact upon the role of the administrator. With an objective measurement system in place across all psychoeducational areas, current decisions regarding staff training needs, allocation of resources, and delineation of policies are supplemented with a comprehensive and consistent data base that monitors student outcomes and program effectiveness. Questions or concerns in any of these areas can easily be analyzed in reference to the CBM measures. For example, requests for increases in expenditures are more easily justified when one can verify an increase in the severity of problems in the served population. Pinpointing in-service training needs is facilitated by an analysis of achievement levels across academic areas. Building assignments for SERTs is a task

quickly accomplished by comparing school performance levels. For these basic administrative problems, and many more, the CBM measurement system has served the administrator well.

In addition, it is our belief that CBM would work well in combining the interests of interdisciplinary programs within schools. In their article about restructuring special and regular education, Reynolds, Wang, and Walberg (1987) made the point that schools are suffering from "disjointed incrementalism": numerous programs within schools developing their own eligibility, accountability, funding, and advocacy groups. Although such systems are well meaning, the net result can be "an extreme disjointedness" in which not all children find their needs completely served. A common data base and evaluation system, such as CBM, implemented across these domains would certainly reduce the number of children "falling through the cracks."

Measuring Ability

Frequently CBM proponents are questioned about the lack of emphasis upon the measurement of intelligence. Those who support traditional, categorical definitions of learning disabilities argue that it is necessary to determine the discrepancy between ability and actual achievement. Proponents of this approach have operationally defined intelligence scores as measures of children's educational ability and are quick to point out that such a process is absent in the CBM identification procedures, which measure only achievement.

The issue, while controversial, is not particularly problematic for those who espouse a CBM approach, because resolution of the matter resides solely in the purpose of assessment. Is the primary purpose of assessment to make classification or instructional decisions? If one intends only to measure individual differences and classify, the traditional psychometric model, as described earlier, will suffice. However, most educators yearn for more than classifying children with labels that are uncorrelated to successful interventions. When the objective is to identify the educational needs of children and prescribe effective instruction, the purpose of assessment is to make instructional decisions.

CBM proponents have long ago concluded that intelligence measures are not optimal measures for instructional decisions or children's potential in the achievement areas of reading, spelling, math, and written discourse. As an example, let us examine a child referred for a reading disability. One can only wonder if the best predictor of this pupil's reading ability is to ask him or her about specific facts relating to geography or history. The argument, of course, does not end here. One can continue to ask if copying figures, completing puzzles, answering math questions, reciting digits in reverse, doing analogies, and responding to intelligence test questions ad nauseam really gives us the best information about a child's potential in reading and about the best means for teaching this student. The major point to be made is that the best predictor of a child's expected achievement is not intelligence, but the child's achievement as it relates to instructional programs tried in the classroom. We believe that the CBM model, with the focus on learning rate more adequately measures a child's potential than do intelligence tests. Not only does the model emphasize the assessment of achievement, but it is based on the student's curriculum, is instructionally relevant, and provides a frequent measurement basis that guides the educator's decisions about a child's educational life.

Need for Intensive Teacher Consultation and In-service Training

An important reason for the successful implementation of CBM in Minneapolis is the extent to which in-service training was provided to district SERTs. Because the CBM model is fairly new, virtually none of the Minneapolis SERTs had preservice training or experience with systems of direct and frequent measurement and time series analysis at the time of implementation. As described in an earlier section, the provision of adequate in-service training on the principles and implementation of CBM is essential. While SERTs may at first feel disorganized and inefficient, recent research on training shows that teachers can quickly make the transition to CBM (Wesson, Fuchs, Tindal, Mirkin, & Deno, 1986).

The educational process, however, does not end with preschool workshops. A second important component is ongoing consultation with teachers. Learning how to administer and score CBM data is really the easy part; time series analysis and interpretation involves more sophisticated skills. In Minneapolis we have found that follow-up consultation has worked well in building skills in this area. One effective form of consultation has been the use of "chart share" sessions, in which SERTs meet in small groups of 5-10 teachers and talk about their cases and the data they have collected.

For those districts considering implementation of CBM, in-service training and consultation demand full attention and should be organized in such a way that SERTs learning the process can get quick feedback on performance. Although it could be argued that Minneapolis is a large district with extensive resources, we would point out that successful implementation of CBM has occurred in smaller settings such as Pine County (Minnesota) Special Education Cooperative, Sandstone, Minnesota, and Idaho Falls, Idaho. It is our recommendation that the district identify a team of lead teachers who have mastered the skills necessary to implement CBM, and then work with SERTs on a small-group and individual basis.

Cooperation With Regular Education Service Providers

When Assistant Secretary of Special Education and Rehabilitative Services, Madeleine Will, wrote of the difficulties in meeting the educational needs of students with learning problems, she described two directions in which educators must intervene (Will, 1986): "(1) Barriers to learning created in the regular classroom, and (2) barriers to learning created by special programs" (p. 5). In documenting the various problems within each delivery system, the message is very clear. For educators to deal effectively with the learning problems of an estimated 1.8 million students in this country, there must be a profound change in the way regular and special educators provide services to children and, ultimately, interact with one another.

Unfortunately, cooperation between regular and special education is often undermined by the predominant instructional strategy for children with learning difficulties, the "pullout approach." Will noted: "This approach is backed by a storehouse of good intentions — but it does not always work well because its vision is flawed. Although for some students the pullout approach may be appropriate, it is driven by a conceptual fallacy: that poor performance in learning can be understood solely in terms of deficiencies in the student rather than in the quality of the learning environment" (p. 16). It is argued that analysis of the learning environment is essential if both regular and special educators are to provide effective instructional interventions for handicapped students. One recommendation coming from the assistant secretary's report is the redefinition of individualized evaluation. "Evaluations should begin with the trained observations and informal assessments of the person best able to understand the difficulties of the student with learning problems — that student's classroom teacher. Teachers can be progressively trained — beginning at the entry level — to look for factors that impede the student's learning; to conduct curriculum-based assessments that describe what the student can and cannot do; and to determine the instructional strategies that are most promising for the individual student" (pp. 18-19).

Implementing Large-Scale Change: The Need for Coordination and Communication

Finally, for those considering implementation of CBM, we wish to briefly comment upon the necessity for coordination and communication. As most educators have probably experienced, the introduction of change can be fraught with frustration, stress, and anxiety. None of these factors were absent from the implementation of CBM in Minneapolis. The key to diminishing the effects of these variables, in our mind, is careful planning and coordination of activities, and continual communication with staff at all levels. Implementation of CBM in a program with 1,300 pupils and almost 100 teachers and tutors did not occur overnight. Administrators must be organized and committed, trainers and coordinators must possess a sound knowledge base, and teachers and psychologists must be motivated to institute changes in how they teach children and evaluate the results.

ACKNOWLEDGMENT

The authors wish to thank Drs. Keith Kromer and Judith Brown from the Department of Special Education of the Minneapolis Public Schools for their continued support.

REFERENCES

Advocacy Center for Elderly and Disabled. (1986). *Rights without labels.* New Orleans, LA: Author.

Algozzine, B., Christenson, S., & Ysseldyke, J. E. (1982). Probabilities associated with the referral to placement process. *Teacher Education and Special Education, 5*(3), 19-23.

American Psychological Association, American Educational Research Association, and National Council on Measurement in Education. (1976). *Standards for educational and psychological tests.* Washington, DC: American Psychological Association.

Beldin, H. L. (1970). Informal reading testing: Historical review and review of the research. In W. Durr (Ed.), *Reading difficulties: Diagnosis, correction, and remediation.* Newark, DE: International Reading Association.

Bersoff, D. N. (1973). Silk purses into sows' ears: The decline of psychological testing and a suggestion for its redemption. *American Psychologist, 28,* 892-899.

Blankenship, C. S. (1985). Using Curriculum-Based Assessment data to make instructional decisions. *Exceptional Children, 52,* 233-238.

Canter, A. (1986). *1986 time/task study.* Minneapolis, MN: Minneapolis Public Schools, Department of Special Education, Psychological Services.

Carlberg, C., & Kavale, K. (1980). The efficacy of special versus a regular class placement for exceptional children: A meta-analysis. *Journal of Special Education, 14,* 295-309.

Carver, R. P. (1974). Two dimensions of tests: Psychometric and edumetric. *American Psychologist, 29,* 512-518.

Casey, A., Deno, S., Marston, D., & Skiba, R. (1986). *Experimental teaching: Changing teacher beliefs about effective instructional practices.* Unpublished manuscript. Minneapolis, MN: University of Minnesota.

Cook, T. D., & Campbell, D. T. (1979). *Quasi-experimentation: Design and analysis issues for field settings.* Chicago: Rand McNally College Publishing Company.

Deno, E. (1970). Special education as developmental capital. *Exceptional Children, 37,* 229-237.

Deno, S. L. (1985). Curriculum-based measurement: The emerging alternative. *Exceptional Children, 52,* 219-232.

Deno, S. L. (1986a). *Experimental teaching: An approach to improving student achievement, changing teacher beliefs, and identifying effective practices* (Final report for Grant No. G008400649). Minneapolis, MN: University of Minnesota.

Deno, S. L. (1986b). Formative evaluation of individual student programs: A new role for school psychologists. *School Psychology Review, 15,* 358-374.

Deno, S. L., Marston, D., & Mirkin, P. K. (1982). Identifying valid measures of written expression for use in continuous evaluation of educational programs. *Exceptional Children, 48,* 368-371.

Deno, S. L., Marston, D., & Tindal, G. (1985). Direct and frequent curriculum-based measurement: An alternative for educational decision making. *Special Services in the Schools, 2,*(2/3), 5-27.

Deno, S. L., & Mirkin, P. K. (1977). *Data-based program modification.* Reston, VA: Council for Exceptional Children.

Deno, S. L., Mirkin, P. K., & Chiang, B. (1982). Identifying valid measures of reading. *Exceptional Children, 49,* 36-45.

Deno, S. L., Mirkin, P. K., Lowry, L., & Kuehnle, K. (1980). *Relationships among simple measures of spelling and performance on standardized achievement tests* (Research Report No. 21). Minneapolis, MN: Institute for Research on Learning Disabilities, University of Minnesota.

Deno, S. L., Mirkin, P. K., & Wesson, C. (1984). How to write effective data-based IEPs. *Teaching Exceptional Children, Winter,* 99-104.

Elliott, S. N., & Piersel, W. C. (1982). Direct assessment of reading skills: An approach which links assessment to intervention. *School Psychology Review, 11,* 267-280.

Floden, R., Porter, A., Schmidt, W., & Freeman, D. (1980). Don't they all measure the same thing? In E. Baker & E. Quellnalz (Eds.), *Educational testing and evaluation.* Beverly Hills, CA: Sage.

Fuchs, L. (1982). Reading. In P. K. Mirkin, L. Fuchs, & S. L. Deno (Eds.), *Considerations for designing a continuous evaluation system: An integrative review* (Monograph No. 20). Minneapolis, MN: University of Minnesota, Institute for Research on Learning Disabilities.

Fuchs, L. (1986). Monitoring progress of mildly handicapped pupils: Review of current practice and research. *Remedial and Special Education, 7,* 5-12.

Fuchs, L., Deno, S. L., & Marston, D. (1983). Improving the reliability of curriculum-based measures of academic skills for psychoeducational decision making. *Diagnostique, 8,* 135-149.

Fuchs, L., Deno, S. L., & Mirkin, P. K. (1984). The effects of frequent curriculum-based measurement and evaluation on pedagogy, student achievement, and student awareness of learning. *American Educational Research Journal, 21,* 449-460.

Fuchs, L. S., & Fuchs, D. (1986). Effects of systematic formative evaluation: A meta-analysis. *Exceptional Children, 53,* 199-208.

Galagan, J. E. (1985). Psychoeducational testing: Turn out the lights, the party's over. *Exceptional Children, 52,* 288-298.

Gickling, E. E., & Thompson, V. (1985). A personal view of curriculum-based assessment. *Exceptional Children, 52,* 205-218.

Goldstein, H., Arkell, C., Ashcroft, S., Hurley, O., & Lilly, S. (1975). Schools. In N. Hobbs (Ed.), *Issues in the classification of children.* San Francisco: Jossey-Bass.

Goldwasser, E., Meyers, J., Christenson, S., & Graden, J. (1983). The impact of PL 94-142 on the practice of school psychology: A national survey. *Psychology in the Schools, 20,* 153-165.

Good, R. H., & Salvia, J. (1988). Curriculum bias in published, norm-referenced reading tests: Demonstrable effects. *School Psychology Review, 17,* 51-60.

Haring, N., Liberty, K., & White, O. (Undated). *Instructional hierarchies research project: Handbook of experimental procedures* (Unpublished manuscript). Seattle: University of Washington.

Hively, W., & Reynolds, M. C. (Eds.). (1975). *Domain-referenced testing in special education*. Reston, VA: Council for Exceptional Children.

Jenkins, J., & Pany, D. (1978). Standardized achievement tests: How useful for special education? *Exceptional Children, 44,* 448-453.

Keogh, B. K. (1972). Psychological evaluation of exceptional children: Old handups and new directions. *Journal of School Psychology, 10,* 141-145.

Kromer, K., & Brown, J. (1979). *Special education assessment*. Minneapolis, MN: Minneapolis Public Schools, Department of Special Education.

Lovitt, T. (1967). Assessment of children with learning disabilities. *Exceptional Children, 34,* 233-239.

Lovitt, T., & Eaton, M. (1972). Achievement tests versus direct and daily measurement. In G. Semb (Ed.), *Behavior analysis in education*. Lawrence, KS: University of Kansas.

Marston, D. (in press). The effectiveness of special education: A time series analysis of reading performance in regular and special education settings. *The Journal of Special Education.*

Marston, D. (in press). Measuring academic progress of students with learning difficulties: A comparison of the semi-logarithmic chart and equal interval graph paper. *Exceptional Children.*

Marston, D. (1985). *Validity of curriculum-based readiness measures*. Unpublished technical report. Minneapolis, MN: Minneapolis Public Schools, Department of Special Education.

Marston, D. (1987). Does categorical teacher certification benefit the mildly handicapped child? *Exceptional Children, 53,* 423-431.

Marston, D., Fuchs, L., & Deno, S. L. (1986). Measuring pupil progress: A comparison of standardized achievement tests and curriculum related measures. *Diagnostique, 11,* 77-90.

Marston, D., & Magnusson, D. (1985). Implementing curriculum-based measurement in special and regular education settings. *Exceptional Children, 52,* 266-276.

Marston, D., Mirkin, P. K., & Deno, S. L. (1984). Curriculum-based measurement: An alternative to traditional screening, referral, and identification. *Journal of Special Education, 18,* 109-118.

Minneapolis Public Schools. (1982). *Five year plan*. Minneapolis MN: Minneapolis Public Schools.

Mirkin, P. K. (1980). Conclusions. In J. Ysseldyke & M. Thurlow (Eds.), *The special education assessment and decision-making process: Seven case studies*. Minneapolis: University of Minnesota Institute for Research on Learning Disabilities.

McLaughlin, J. A., & Lewis, R. B. (1986). *Assessing special students* (2nd ed.). Columbus, OH: Charles Merrill.

National Coalition of Advocates for Students and the National Association of School Psychologists. *Position statement: Advocacy for appropriate education for all children*. (1985). Boston: Author.

Nunnally, J. (1978). *Psychometric theory* (2nd ed.). New York: McGraw-Hill.

Peterson, J., Heistad, D., Peterson, D., & Reynolds, M. (1985). Montevideo individualized prescriptive instructional management system. *Exceptional Children, 52,* 239-243.

Reschly, D. J. (1987). Learning characteristics of mildly handicapped students: Implications for classification, placement, and programming. In M. C. Reynolds, M. C. Wang, & H. J. Walberg (Eds.), *The handbook of special education: Research and practice*. (Vol. 1). Oxford, England: Pergamon.

Reynolds, M. C. (1982). The rights of children: A challenge to school psychologists. In T. R. Kratochwill (Ed.), *Advances in school psychology* (Vol. 2). Hillsdale, NJ: Erlbaum.

Reynolds, M. C., & Birch, J. W. (1977). *Teaching exceptional children in all America's schools*. Reston, VA: Council for Exceptional Children.

Reynolds, M. C., Wang, M. C., & Walberg, H. J. (1987). The necessary restructuring of special and regular education. *Exceptional Children, 53,* 391-398.

Rucker, W., & Dilley, C. A. (1981). *Mathematics*. New York: Heath.

Salvia, J., & Clark, J. (1973). Use of deficits to identify the learning disabled. *Exceptional Children, 39,* 305-308.

Salvia, J., & Ysseldyke, J. E. (1981). *Assessment in special and remedial education*. (2nd ed.). Boston: Houghton-Mifflin.

Shinn, M., & Tindal, G. (in press). Using performance data in academics: A pragmatic and defensible approach to non-discriminatory assessment. In R. Jones (Ed.), *Psychoeducational assessment — A casebook*. Berkeley, CA: Cobb & Henry.

Skiba, R., Magnusson, D., Marston, D., & Erickson, K. (1985). *The assessment of mathematics performance in special education: Achievement tests, proficiency tests, or formative evaluation?* Unpublished manuscript. Minneapolis, MN: Minneapolis Public Schools, Department of Special Education.

Smith, C. R. (1980). Assessment alternatives: Non-standardized procedures. *School Psychology Review, 9,* 46-57.

Smith, D. K. (1984). Practicing school psychologists: Their characteristics, activities, and populations served. *Professional Psychology: Research and Practice, 15*, 798-810.

Starlin, C. (1979). Evaluating and teaching reading to "irregular" kids. *Iowa perspective* (Iowa Department of Public Instruction), *December*, 1-11.

Starlin, C., & Starlin, A. (1974). *Guidelines for continuous decision making.* Bemidji, MN: Unique Curriculums Unlimited

Stauffer, R. G. (1970). *The language-experience approach to the teaching of reading.* New York: Harper & Row.

Thorndike, E. K., & Hagen, E. (1978). *Measurement and evaluation in psychology and education.* New York: Wiley.

Thurlow, M., & Ysseldyke, J. E. (1982). Instructional planning: Information collected by school psychologists vs. information considered useful by teachers. *Journal of School Psychology, 20*(1), 3-10.

Tindal, G. (1985). Investigating the effectiveness of special education: An analysis of methodology. *Journal of Learning Disabilities, 18*, 101-112.

Tindal, G., Fuchs, L. S., Mirkin, P. K., Christenson, S., & Deno, S. (1981). *The relationship between student achievement and teacher assessment of short- or long-term goals* (Research Report No. 61). Minneapolis, MN: University of Minnesota Institute for Research on Learning Disabilities. (ERIC Document Reproduction Service No. ED 218 846)

Tindal, G., Germann, G., & Deno, S. (1983). *Descriptive research on the Pine County norms: A compilation of findings.* (Research Report No. 132). Minneapolis, MN: University of Minnesota Institute for Research on Learning Disabilities.

Tindal, G., & Marston, D. (1985). Approaches to assessment. In J. Torgeson & B. Wong (Eds.), *Learning disabilities: Some new perspectives.* Boston: Academic Press.

Tucker, J. A. (1985). Curriculum-Based Assessment: An introduction. *Exceptional Children, 52*, 199-204.

Tuinman, J. J. (1971). Asking reading dependent questions. *Journal of Reading, 14*, 289-292.

Weiss, B. J., Steurer, L. O., Cruickshank, S. B., & Hunt, L. C. (1983). *Holt Basic Reading.* New York: Holt, Rinehart, & Winston.

Wesson, C., Fuchs, L., Tindal, G., Mirkin, P. K., & Deno, S. L. (1986). Facilitating the efficiency of ongoing curriculum-based measurement. *Teacher Education and Special Education, 9*(4), 166-172.

White, O. R., & Haring, N. G. (1980). *Exceptional teaching* (2nd ed.). Columbus, OH: Merrill.

Will, M. C. (1986). Educating students with learning problems — A shared responsibility. *Exceptional Children, 52*, 411-416.

Ysseldyke, J. E., Algozzine, B., Regan, R., & Potter, M. (1980). Technical adequacy of tests used by professionals in simulated decision-making. *Psychology in the Schools, 17*, 202-209.

Ysseldyke, J. E., & Marston, D. (1982). A critical analysis of standardized reading tests. *School Psychology Review, 11*, 257-266.

9

Implementing Process Assessment

Joel Meyers and
Deborah Kundert
State University of New York at Albany

Process assessment is an alternative conceptualization of the diagnostic and assessment practices of school psychologists. It is a comprehensive model that has implications for alternatives in virtually all areas of assessment and diagnosis of concern to school psychologists, and it is a model that seeks to incorporate new and traditional approaches that are consistent with this model. Process assessment is similar to Ysseldyke's work in integrating assessment and intervention, and similar to Tindall's and Marston's work in supporting the use of curriculum-based assessment. Despite this overlap, process assessment has its theoretical roots in cognitive, metacognitive, and systemic theories about human behavior. This results in a philosophy and some techniques that are quite different from Ysseldyke's and Tindall's and Marston's methodologies. Although this chapter provides a comprehensive overview of process assessment to facilitate implementation by practitioners, a particular effort will be made to highlight the techniques that are unique to this approach.

In an effort to meet this goal, the chapter is divided into three major sections: (a) an introduction to process assessment and its rationale; (b) a detailed description of process assessment, including an overview of techniques consistent with the model; and (c) a discussion of strategies designed to facilitate implementation of process assessment in school systems.

OVERVIEW OF PROCESS ASSESSMENT AND THE UNDERLYING THEORY

Traditional techniques used to assess learning ability (i.e., IQ tests, achievement tests, perceptual-motor tests, etc.) have been questioned increasingly in recent years. The most common limitations attributed to these procedures include their bias toward racial and economic minorities, their inability to provide teachers with information of use in inducing educational change in regular and special classes, and their static assessment of achievement skills (e.g., Feuerstein, 1979; Hutson & Niles, 1974; Kratochwill, 1977; Thurlow & Ysseldyke, 1982). Too often evaluations are conducted primarily in response to teachers' requests to determine eligibility for special education. The reason for conducting a psychoeducational evaluation, however, should be to gather information about a particular student and to analyze the information in making crucial decisions about teaching and learning (Lerner, 1976). Sarason (1976) has noted that "there is a real theoretical and practical problem in how one goes from test data to what one should do for a child in the classroom" (p. 588). Process assessment has been proposed to resolve some of these problems.

One approach to overcome these limitations is to emphasize process measures rather than product scores. Process measures can provide information about information-acquisition processes, problem-solving strategies, learning processes, other cognitive skills, and behavioral functioning of students. Cognitive processes are used to learn, store, and retrieve information, and they include the strategies that transform and manipulate information between the time it enters memory as a stimulus and the time a response to it is made (Torgesen, 1979). Specific cognitive strategies that have been proposed include methods for organizing, analyzing, synthesizing, and retrieving information. Information about these types of processes can lead directly to suggestions designed to facilitate children's learning (Meyers, Pfeffer, & Erlbaum, 1985).

The emphasis on cognitive processes should not be confused with the perceptual process orientation that was prevalent in learning disabilities research in the 1960s. Perceptual processes are lower-order strategies that deal with interpretation of visual, auditory, and tactile stimuli received by the individual. This earlier process approach assumed that all learning had a sensorimotor foundation (see analysis by Wong, 1979), and the result was assessment instruments designed to assess these perceptual processes (e.g., Illinois Test of Psycholinguistic Abilities; Kirk, McCarthy, & Kirk, 1968), and related intervention programs that sought to improve academic performance by providing training in these perceptual skills (e.g., Frostig Training Program; Frostig & Horne, 1964). In contrast, process assessment focuses on problem-solving skills and strategies, particularly those that are connected directly to the academic or social task that is the focus of assessment.

The theoretical base for process assessment is drawn from recent research and theory in cognitive psychology that views the child as an active learner who participates in the educational process. This view suggests that the prior knowledge and experience, as well as the cognitive strategies, of the learner are important components of both teaching and learning (e.g., Baron, 1981; Resnick, 1976; Vygotsky, 1978; Weinstein & Mayer, 1986). One substantial element of this framework is that the child's knowledge and awareness of her or his own cognitive processes and strategies can be an important component of the learning process. This concept is referred to as metacognition, and it has been suggested that a productive approach to instruction can be to increase the child's knowledge and use of relevant strategies (Brown, 1980; Flavell, 1976).

Applying cognitive psychology to the educational process requires an expansion of cognitive theory to include a social perspective; this has been attempted by Turnure (1986). He has described five factors that are hypothesized to affect learning and problem solving, and he proposes a "pentrahedronal model" to illustrate the interactive effects of these five factors. They include (a) the characteristics of the learner (i.e., skills, knowledge, attitudes, strategies, etc.); (b) the nature of the materials (i.e., conceptual difficulty, sequencing of materials, physical structure, modality, etc.); (c) the learning activities (attention, rehearsal, elaboration, etc.); (d) the criterial tasks (i.e., recognition, recall, transfer, problem solving, etc.); and (e) the instructional agent (who may describe, question, model, reinforce, etc.). By considering the interactive effects of these factors there is an opportunity to go beyond the cognitive processes suggested by cognitive theory and the task analysis suggested by information-processing theories, and to include a consideration of the social environment through the instructional agent.

Further support for considering the impact of the social environment is found in ecological theory, which examines the influence of an individual's behavior on a particular environment, as well as the influence of the environment on the individual (Barker, 1968; Bronfenbrenner, 1981; Cantrell & Cantrell, 1985; Simeonsson, 1986). Ecological theory considers the individual's naturally occurring behavior, the environment immediately surrounding that behavior; and the ways the individual and the immediate environment are linked; this perspective is useful in considering the cognitive, affective, physiological, and structural components of the interaction between the learner and settings (Smith, 1983).

These theoretical perspectives influence process assessment's focus on the individual within a context rather than restricting assessment of the characteristics of the individual. Therefore, comprehensive assessment of the multiple factors assumed to influence learning and behavior is necessary (e.g., Gerken, 1985; Gresham, 1983; Mowder, 1983). Furthermore, based on this set of theoretical assumptions, process assessment assumes that a problem may be within the individual, the environment, a particular task, or the interaction of these factors. Instead of assuming that the individual has some deficit or disability, this approach assumes that children can learn and change, as there is a focus on strengths as well as weaknesses. In addition, it is assumed that children are active participants in learning rather than passive recipients, as the diagnostician seeks information about how, when, and where the student learns. This contrasts with the assumption that the individual has learned and that assessment should determine how much the individual has learned in comparison to same age peers. Thus, interventions resulting from process assessment seek to change: the individual within a specific context, the context or the task, and/or the expectations and/or attitudes of the system (i.e., school, family).

THE PROCESS ASSESSMENT MODEL

Assessing the Task, the Setting, the Child, and Their Interactions

The process assessment model views learning as a function of the task, the setting, the child's characteristics, and the interactions among these components (Meyers, Pfeffer, & Erlbaum, 1985; Smith, 1980; 1983). This framework requires a multidimensional approach to assessment in which many aspects of the three

individual components are examined as well as the interactions among these factors, rather than just assessing the child as has traditionally been done. In assessing many factors and their interactions, the school psychologist will consider a number of questions that are not asked systematically when assessment is focused primarily on the child's characteristics. This model is depicted by the diagram presented in Figure 1, which illustrates the focus on each of the three dimensions as well as the various possible interactions among these factors. The resultant multidimensional focus in process assessment provides a framework with the potential to influence the practice of psychoeducational assessment. By changing the questions asked to those that are meaningful to educators (e.g., how does this child learn?) and that attempt to promote effective interventions for children, school psychologists and other psychoeducational diagnosticians would increase their ability to provide significant help to children and schools.

Through use of this model, process assessment attempts to obtain information about how, when, and where a child learns, rather than determining how much a child has learned in comparison to his or her peers. By focusing on this broad range of interrelated factors, the school psychologist can generate hypotheses about the environmental conditions and task characteristics necessary to facilitate maximal learning, given the child's particular characteristics. The goal of assessment by this model is to modify the task and the environment in order to capitalize on the individual child's strengths (Hunt, 1969; Silberberg, 1971; Smith, 1980).

The unique aspects of the process assessment model concern the ways in which the child, the task, and the setting are viewed as interacting and the ways in which the examiner assesses each of these factors as well as their interactions. Although the model itself is more important than any specific technique, a familiarity with appropriate techniques helps to clarify the model and to illustrate approaches to implementing the model. Therefore, to increase the probability of

FIGURE 1
Process Assessment Model

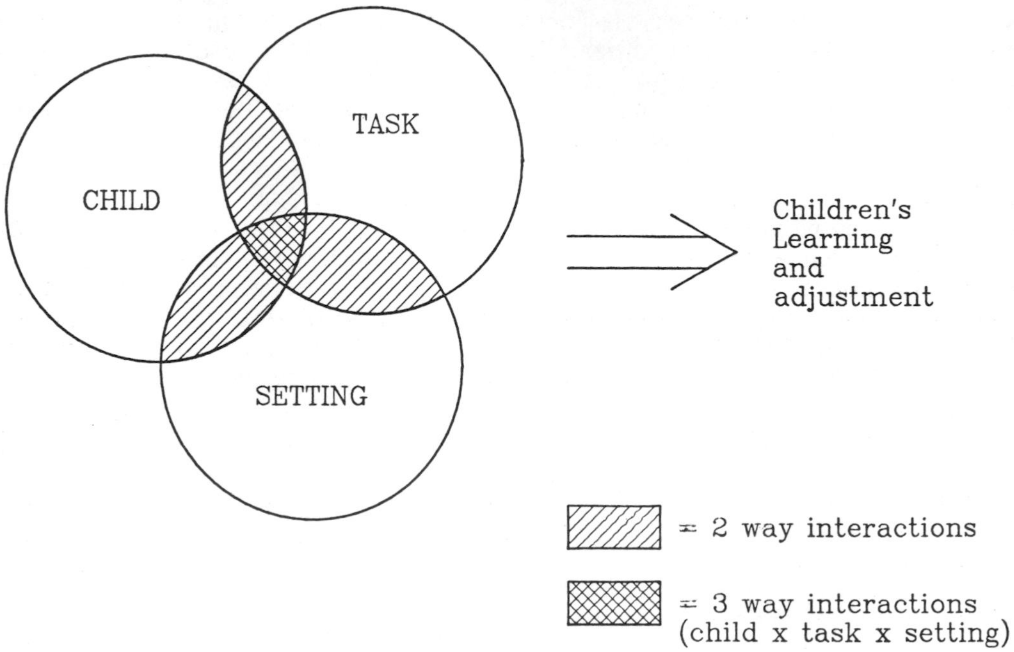

implementation and to ensure that there is a concrete and specific understanding of the various components of the model, the following discussion presents an overview of selected techniques that are consistent with the model.

The Child

Many of the assessment procedures that have been used traditionally by psychologists, such as tests of intelligence, academic achievement, and personality, all focus on particular global character-istics of the child under study, and generally these procedures do not con-sider environmental circumstances. The data obtained from such techniques do not lead directly to recommendations on how best to teach children. There are other approaches, however, to assessing the student's characteristics that have not been used on a regular basis by most practicing school psychologists. These include measures of learning style (e.g., Dunn, Dunn, & Price, 1983), study skills

(e.g., Brown & Holtzman, 1967), cognitive style (e.g., Karp & Konstadt, 1971), and learning strategies (e.g., Torgesen, 1977). Many of these measures of the child's characteristics focus on the process of learning or the way the child learns, rather than being limited to a consideration of scores that reflect only the results of past learning. Cognitive style, for example, has been defined as information-processing habits representing the individual's typical modes of perceiving, thinking, problem-solving, and remembering (Messick, 1976). Measures of cognitive style consider how individuals access information and solve problems, and differences in these infor-mation-processing skills are rarely consid-ered in traditional assessment practices or in developing educational programs (Saracho, 1984), despite their potential importance for educational planning (Keogh & Donlon, 1972; Lidz, 1987).

Field independence–dependence. The field independence–dependence di-mension is one of the more researched cognitive style variables, and has the potential to influence educational practice (Annis, 1979; Linn & Kyllonen, 1981). It is a continuum describing the degree to which an individual overcomes the influence of an embedding context. Field independence reflects an analytical, differentiated strategy of problem solving that is consistently used independently of the context, whereas field dependence reflects a global, diffuse strategy that is dependent upon context. Shade (1983) found that lower achievers were predominantly field-dependent, needed more explicit cues from the environment in order to solve problems, and had trouble providing their own structure to new situations. Field-independent students on the other hand were better able to provide structure for their own learning and to develop their own learning strategies (Witkin, Moore, Goodenough, & Cox, 1977). Furthermore, since field-independent students tend to be more intrinsically motivated than field-dependent students, who tend to be motivated by external factors, the latter children are more likely to be affected negatively by criticism than the former (Witkin et al., 1977). Field-independent students seem to prefer, and generally to do better in, math and science, whereas field-dependent students generally prefer, and do better, in the humanities and social studies (Good & Brophy, 1986). In general, field-dependent students prefer to learn in groups and to interact frequently with one another and with the teacher, whereas field-independent students may respond better to more independent and more individualized approaches such as contract systems or individualized projects (Good & Brophy, 1986).

The *Children's Embedded Figures Test* (Karp & Konstadt, 1971) is one frequently used standardized approach to assess cognitive style which differentiates between field dependent and field independent children. This is an individually administered test which involves a series of 27 chromatic test items. Thirteen of the test items have a 'tent' as the standard stimulus and 14 of the items have a 'house' as the standard stimulus. The child is instructed to find the previously seen standard stimulus (tent or house) embedded within a larger, more complicated figure. Scores are then used to place the child on the continuum of Field Independence–Field Dependence. Karp & Konstadt (1971) provide norms for children from ages 5–12, and they report reliability estimates ranging from .83 to .90. Other studies have reported reliability estimates ranging from .72 to .91 (i.e., Saracho, 1980; 1984; Saracho & Dayton, 1980), and there has been a growing body of research with this instrument (i.e., Saracho, 1980; 1984).

Think-aloud protocol analysis. Although the concept of cognitive styles has useful educational implications, it is conceptualized as a general cognitive process that is brought to bear on various tasks and situations. Since this approach measures an underlying process that is thought to be used on various tasks, it requires that inferences be drawn by the diagnostician in order to develop implications for performance on particular educational tasks such as reading or math. One way to minimize the need for such inferences is to use methods that assess the learning process in the context of the educational task, since these methods have more direct educational implications. One method that has been used to assess children's learning strategies on reading comprehension tasks is think-aloud protocol analysis (Lytle, 1982; Meyers & Lytle, 1986). The examinee thinks out loud while solving a problem so that the examiner can determine some of the student's characteristic problem-solving strategies. Think-aloud procedures have been used for some time to assess approaches to solving cognitive problems (e.g., Ericsson & Simon, 1980) and arithmetic problems (e.g., Brueckner, 1930; Kruteskii, 1976; Lankford, 1972, 1974), and recently they have been used to assess reading comprehension strategies (e.g., Bereiter & Bird, 1985; Christopherson, Schultz, & Waern, 1981; Garner, 1980; Garner & Reis, 1981; Johnston, 1985; Olshavsky, 1976/1977).

Think-aloud protocol analysis assumes that the individual's knowledge of her or his own cognitive processes may be a significant component of the learning process. This orientation is consistent with metacognitive theory, which suggests that it may be possible to facilitate instruction by increasing awareness of one's learning strategies (e.g., Flavell, 1976; Brown, 1980; Brown, Palincsar, & Armbruster, 1984). Think-aloud protocol analysis assesses students' problem-solving strategies by asking them to describe all of their thoughts while working on a task. By analyzing a transcript of the protocol reflecting their efforts to think out loud, the examiner attempts to determine their typical problem-solving strategies.

Think-aloud protocol analysis is an approach developed by Lytle (1982) to assess the "moves," "strategies," and "styles" used when attempting a reading comprehension task (Meyers & Lytle, 1986). Moves are the discrete responses that reflect what the reader does at a particular point to understand the reading material, strategies being the patterns of moves in response to doubt. Table 1 presents a coding system of all 24 possible moves, which fall into six major categories: monitoring doubt, signaling understanding, reasoning, elaborating the text, analyzing text features, and judging the text. The moves that constitute this system are defined in more detail elsewhere, with examples to facilitate scoring (Lytle, 1982; Meyers, 1985; Meyers, Palladino, & Devenpeck, 1987).

Think-aloud protocol analysis has been used in descriptive research studies as well as in clinical practice (Meyers & Lytle, 1986; Meyers, Palladino, & Devenpeck, 1987). Clinically, it has been used in conjunction with other assessment techniques for elementary school children referred, in part, because of reading problems. Typically two short passages of about 15–20 sentences are used. The passages are retyped so that each sentence is on a separate line and the entirety of each passage is covered with a blank piece of paper. The passages are selected so that they are relatively difficult for the child, and require strategic behavior. We have typically used fictional passages; however, other types of text could also be used (e.g., nonfiction, poetry, etc.), and

it may be particularly useful to include some material from the youngster's actual curriculum materials. There is not yet an adequate data base to indicate how such differences in text might affect the think-aloud process or strategic reading behavior, and this may be a productive direction for future research.

The procedure is to uncover the story one sentence at a time. The child is asked to say out loud all of his or her thoughts after reading each sentence. "Tell me what you are doing and thinking about as you try to understand the sentence. This is just like talking to yourself or thinking out loud." Then, metaphors are used to help the client develop an understanding of the task. For example, "It is just like a news broadcast in which you are the reporter, and you report each of your thoughts as they occur." The reader is also asked to report any efforts to understand the sentence in context of the entire passage, rather than in isolation. "After the first sentence you will tell me what you are thinking about to understand that sentence. After the second sentence you will tell me what you are thinking to understand two sentences. After the third sentence you will tell me what you are thinking about to understand those three sentences, and so on." The examiner underscores that the child *must* state all of the thoughts occurring when the passage is difficult to understand. This helps the examiner discover the sequence of moves that occur after a child's monitoring turns up a comprehension difficulty. Throughout the instructions, the examiner maintains a focus on one primary goal: to make the task clear to the child without influencing the nature of the child's responses. The examiner makes a verbatim record of the child's think-aloud responses.

Interpretation of the data obtained with this procedure is difficult since research is only beginning and there are no norms available. Therefore, data obtained with this technique must be interpreted cautiously, that is, as hypotheses requiring further investigation. The following steps may be used as guidelines for the process of interpreting data

TABLE 1
Reading Comprehension "Moves" Scored With Think-Aloud Protocol Analysis

Monitoring Comprehension Difficulties
1. Monitoring partial or no understanding of word or sentence
2. Monitoring conflicting meanings

Signaling Understanding
1. Report understanding
2. Paraphrase meaning
3. Inaccurate paraphrase
4. Summary

Elaboration
1. Imagery
2. Recall prior knowledge external to text
3. Refer to previous material in text
4. Refer to idea mentioned previously by reader
5. Add details to text without using imagery
6. Personal reaction

Reasoning
1. Hypothesis
2. Prediction
3. Question or search for evidence
4. Inference or use of evidence
5. Revise prior reasoning move

Analysis
1. Analyze words
2. Analyze sentences
3. Analyze paragraph function
4. Analyze stylistic aspects

Judging
1. Judging ideas
2. Judging text features

Note: Adapted from Lytle (1982).

derived from this approach. However, research is needed to ascertain the validity of these guidelines. (a) Calculate the relative frequencies of the six categories of moves as percentages of total moves. (b) Consider any category of move (other than monitoring, which is discussed below as a special case) used less than 5% of the time to be relatively infrequent, and any category used more than 20% relatively frequent. Consider 20–30% use as close to optimal. Use of a category more than 40% of the time may be significant. (c) Use of monitoring is interpreted separately, since the frequency of these moves should depend directly on the difficulty of the passage. The percentages cited above are applied for monitoring moves only when the passage is difficult for the client to understand. (d) There should be individual differences in relative use of styles; effective reading probably requires some flexibility in use. (e) The most effective readers are likely to make some use of reasoning and monitoring moves. (f) The final step in the process of interpreting these data is to consider sequences of moves. Particularly when the reader monitors comprehension difficulties, it is important to determine what the reader's subsequent moves are and whether there are identifiable patterns.

These guidelines only provide a framework for developing hypotheses about a client's approach to reading comprehension that must be confirmed through further analysis of the protocol and examination of other information about the child; any efforts to intervene with the child must be based on this information.

In the long run, the clinical utility of this procedure will be determined by its prescriptive validity. Evidence that this procedure does, indeed, lead to interventions that facilitate reading comprehension so far has been provided in the literature only through several case examples (e.g., Meyers, 1985; Meyers, 1988; Meyers & Lytle, 1986; Meyers, Palladino, & Devenpeck, 1987). Although the research has not yet been reported, an approach to teaching these strategies has now been developed, including several steps that can be used effectively with a small group of children; (a) Teach students the concept of strategies in reading comprehension as well as their potential importance. (b) Teach students to use the think-aloud procedure by having the teacher model this process first. (c) Introduce an individual move in subsequent sessions by defining the move, modeling its use, and then having the children use the move while thinking out loud. (This method is similar to "reciprocal teaching" [e.g., Brown, Palincsar, & Armbruster, 1984], in which the teacher and each student take turns using the move while thinking out loud; the other students observe this and suggest how they would have used the move in different ways.) (d) Have the students practice using the move during reading at school and using it at home prior to the next session, and have them report on their efforts to use the move.

The Task

Process assessment also uses task analysis techniques (i.e., Gagne & Briggs, 1979; Moyer & Dardig, 1978; Sloane, Buckholdt, Jensen, & Crandell, 1979; Smith, 1983; Sperry, 1974). Task analysis requires a detailed understanding of the task (Rosenfield, 1987) in respect to the prerequisite skills and behaviors assumed to have been mastered previously. Once

these have been clearly described, the examiner must do a detailed subskill analysis of the sequence of skills the learner must acquire to move form the current state toward the goal involved in the task. This technique requires the examiner to break down tasks into their discrete components and to develop concrete behavioral descriptions.

Task analysis should result in a detailed account of erroneously learned rules and missing skills as well as areas of strength (Aliotti, 1977), and in consonance with the process assessment model proposed here, this method helps discover what task attributes best match a student's abilities and learning styles. A weakness cited by Torgesen (1979) is that it does not indicate specifically how to instruct the student, as there is a breakdown in the process of moving from assessment to intervention. Process assessment does not stop with task analysis however; instead, it provides a consultative framework for using this information to develop and assess intervention plans, described later in this chapter.

Rosenfield (1987) suggested several ways to develop an effective task analysis that can be used as alternatives or in combination. These include the examiner performing the task, observing someone else do it, and checking the task analysis. Task analysis can be checked by using the following questions as guidelines. Are all subtasks stated in observable, measurable terms? Are any critical steps omitted, or can the major task be performed by mastering only the defined subtasks? Are all the subtasks necessary for the major task, or are any unnecessary tasks included? Are any subtasks so minute that they are unnecessary, and can any of these be combined without losing essential information? Are the subtasks arranged in logical order?

In addition to task ana.ys.s. scnool psychologists can use curriculum-based assessment (CBA) to determine the demands that curricular materials make on the students using them (see Tindall's and Marston's chapters in this volume). In addition to assessing individual student skills, curriculum-based assessment involves an analysis of the curricular materials that will be used by the student (Gickling & Havertape, 1981). CBA is important because of the wide variation between different curricula offered in various school districts, and even in various programs within a district. CBA can determine the demands made by a specific curriculum, as well as the child's performance in that particular curriculum. An example from an investigation of different spelling curricula can help to make the point. In an analysis of second grade spelling word lists from a popular spelling series, a low correspondence was found between high-frequency word lists and the word lists contained in the spelling series (Seretny & Kundert, 1987). In addition, little overlap between the two spelling word lists was noted. Further data analysis indicated variation in the average number of words per list and the average number of letters per word on the lists. It was concluded that the word lists of the spelling programs seem to be specific to the series chosen rather than related to any specific educational purpose, given the lack of commonality of the word lists. Systematic curriculum analysis provides school psychologists with information about the specific elements of the learning content, which tells the clinician what the student is expected to learn. This type of information, along with data about the student's performance on these materials, provides the specific information needed to plan effective instructional interventions for the student.

The Setting

A key component of this model is the attention given to the teaching environment. Despite the fact that the recent work on ecological and behavioral observation techniques has had promising results, practitioners still pay too little attention to these factors. The advent of Public Law 94-142 and the related increase in sensitivity to concerns about nondiscriminatory assessment have created a limited increase in the use of observation procedures by school psychologists (e.g., Goldwasser, Meyers, Christenson, & Graden, 1983), and there are now numerous collections of specific observation procedures available to school psychologists (e.g., Alessi & Kaye, 1983). However, the focus of these observations is still most frequently confined to the child's behavior rather than also including the environment (Meyers et al., 1985).

Standardized assessment typically holds the environment constant by using similar testing situations across cases in order to facilitate comparisons between the individual and the group. This orientation, however, may not capture the complexity of behavior. A more accurate view of the child may be provided if the examiner varies the environment systematically to highlight intraindividual comparisons. It is important for practitioners to assess children under a variety of environmental circumstances to promote useful intra-child comparisons for characteristics such as social behavior, academic performance, learning strategies, etc., as well as providing detailed assessments of the key environmental settings themselves (e.g., Meyers et al., 1985). Approaches are needed for assessing the environment that have acceptable psychometric properties, and in this context, the setting can be assessed by means of both behavioral procedures (e.g., Alessi & Kaye, 1983; Hall, Hawkins, & Axelrod, 1975; O'Leary, 1975) and ecological assessment techniques (e.g., Barker, 1968; Carlson, Scott, & Eklund, 1980; Gump, 1975).

The ecological approach relies on systematic observation of the individual in context, thus providing a measure of the contextual and functional influences of the environment. Ecological assessment is designed to emphasize natural behavior and minimize the use of inference in obtaining data. The observer tries to be unbiased, nonintrusive, and noninferential while collecting data. Two general methods are used in ecological observations: the specimen record and the chronolog. The specimen record requires narrative recording of observable behaviors (Simeonsson, 1986) to provide a verbatim description of behavior and speech. Based on the specimen record's narrative recording, the chronolog places the observed events in a time-referenced context (Scott, 1980). Once the chronolog is obtained, it is analyzed to provide more specific information about the patterns and sequences of the behavior (Scott, 1980). This approach to considering both the content and process of classroom activity provides a way to summarize the information that has been collected so that the interdependency of behavior and the environment can be understood.

The literature is filled with a variety of other examples of the ecological approach to assessment (e.g., Carlson, Scott, & Eklund, 1980; Gump, 1975; Kounin, 1970; Moos, 1979). One variation with particular relevance for this presentation is The Instructional Environment Scale (Ysseldyke & Christenson, 1987). This instrument, based on the assumption that learning and behavior are a function of the instructional environment, analyzes an individual student's instructional environment and uses observation and interviewing to obtain information. The purposes of this scale are to clarify presenting problems and to identify the starting points in designing appropriate instructional interventions for specific students (see Ysseldyke & Christenson in this volume for further discussion).

Child–Task–Setting Interactions

Once data have been gathered concerning the three separate factors of process assessment, the next step is to assess the interactions that occur among these factors. A variety of techniques that are consistent with the process assessment model can be used to assess such interactions, and these include diagnostic teaching (Ysseldyke & Salvia, 1974), paired associate learning technique (Kratochwill & Severson, 1977), learning potential assessment (Feuerstein, 1979), and trial interventions (Meyers et al., 1985). All of these approaches have the common goal of gathering data with direct implications for intervention.

Diagnostic teaching. Diagnostic teaching examines what the child knows, how new information is learned, and how the learning rate is affected by changes in stimuli and feedback (Kratochwill, 1977). Diagnostic teaching identifies the most effective instructional strategies for individual children (Ysseldyke & Salvia, 1974), and tries them out in the context of the clinical relationship between student and diagnostician, using materials that are directly relevant to the classroom. During diagnostic teaching, the diagnostician carefully monitors student performance while presenting different instructional approaches. Data are collected under each instructional condition to determine the most effective teaching technique (McLoughlin & Lewis, 1986). The specific steps in this procedure are the following:

1. identify relevant characteristics of the child (those that are related to the specific problem of interest);
2. specify the teaching objectives;
3. select the instructional strategy to lead the student to the objective;
4. select appropriate curricular materials;
5. test the strategy and materials to see if they work with the student. (Cartwright, Cartwright, & Ward, 1984, p. 384).

Diagnostic teaching works with materials that are directly related to the curricular demands of the classroom; other approachs (i.e., learning potential assessment and paired associate learning) are a step removed from the curriculum materials used in the classroom, but uses a similar test–teach–test format in the clinical setting in an effort to reach conclusions about the child's general approach to learning and related instructional strategies.

Paired associate learning. Paired associate learning requires the individual to memorize pairs of items in such a way that when one item of the pair is presented later its pair member is recalled. Paired associate learning is an attractive method to use in observing learning because the variables involved in the learning tasks can be examined and varied easily. These variables include the types of material to be learned, the number of items to be learned, the amount of time the items are presented, the number of trials needed to master the task, and the type of instruction provided. Paired associate learning tasks elicit mental activity of considerable ingenuity, especially in those who are efficient learners (Martin, Cox, Boersma, 1965) and it is a sensitive and effective way to assess children's learning (Stevenson, 1972). Careful analysis of the kinds of school learning that are required in the early grades, indicates that many of these closely approximate the paired associate learning paradigm in their formal structure (Rohwer, 1971). Examples of these are sight word learning, spelling, and associating names with places, and dates with events. It has been found that meaningful material is learned more easily than nonmeaningful material (Underwood & Schulz, 1960), that pairs of familiar items are easier to associate than pairs of novel items (Epstein, Rock, & Zuckerman, 1960), that the paired associate learning of nouns is easier when the nouns are concrete rather than abstract (Dean & Kundert, 1981; Paivio & Yuille, 1966), and that the paired associate learning of abstract material increases with age up to 18 years, presumably due to the increased facility with verbal mediation (Dean & Kulhavy, 1978). Furthermore Rohwer (1971) suggests that PAL is not affected by race or SES.

Dean and Kundert (1981) developed a paired associate learning task which consists of unfamiliar geometric designs as stimulus items (e.g., designs from the Bender-Gestalt, etc.) and high frequency abstract (e.g., idea, hope) and concrete (e.g., apple, chair) nouns as response items. Abstract geometric designs were used as neutral symbols, while high frequency abstract and concrete nouns were chosen as verbal response items. These two types of nouns appear in the expressive vocabulary of students of various ages, and therefore, are equally familiar. School work often involves the integration of familiar sounds with unfamiliar symbols, as does this paired associate learning task.

This paired associate learning task is presented by telling students that they will hear some words and see a picture that goes with each word. Students are informed that it is their task to remember the word that goes with each design because they will have to supply the correct word later. Two sample items are administered to ensure their understanding of the task. The task is administered using a cassette recorder. The examiner presents the appropriate card for each noun named on the tape. Six recorded random orders are presented to each student (three study trials, each followed by a test trial). Each design is presented for three seconds during the study trial and each noun is stated during this presentation. The test trials consist of the examiner showing the child each card for three seconds and the child is to respond with the noun that was paired with the figure in the study phase.

The use of paired associate learning tasks in assessment allows the clinician to observe learning-related behaviors which may be necessary for success in some classroom learning situations. These behaviors include the child's attention, the child's learning strategies (active vs. passive; systematic vs. trial and error), and the child's attitude toward learning new material. Moreover, when students are asked how they learn paired associate tasks, many are able to articulate their strategies clearly. Responses can range from undifferentiated strategies such as "I just keep saying the words", to descriptions of mediational devices (e.g., "Apples are round, the picture for apple is sort of round, so it was round apple."). These behaviors can be observed initially as the child performs the paired associate learning task for the first time. These observations can then be used as a basis for developing hypotheses about the child's learning which can be tested most effectively by attempting interventions or task modifications to explore learning further. These modifications can include visual versus auditory presentation of stimuli, performance in an individual setting versus the classroom, strategy instruction and/or the use of reinforcement strategies to increase learning (Kratochwill & Severson, 1977). Thus, paired associate learning tasks can be used to determine the individual learner's approach to these learning tasks, and to determine which kinds of learning materials are most suitable for the student (Levin, Rohwer, & Cleary, 1971). Despite its potential utility, clinicians must remember that it is an analogue observation technique that can be used to formulate hypotheses about how the student learns new information. These hypotheses must be tested out in the actual environment (see the later discussion of trial interventions) to determine whether the information may be of value in planning remedial activities for the classroom.

Learning potential assessment.
Learning potential assessment (Budoff & Friedman, 1964; Feuerstein, 1979) can be a useful approach to generating hypotheses about effective interventions that may be generalizable to a variety of situations. It is to be noted, however, this approach requires the diagnostician to use inference in order to draw conclusions about classroom learning. While it has received considerable attention in recent years, recent reviews suggest that more research is needed and that results from these techniques should be interpreted cautiously (e.g., Savell, Twohig, & Rachford, 1986). Learning potential assessment attempts to examine learning and problem-solving skills that are used to acquire new information, and this approach has been proposed by numerous authors as a potentially effective method of assessment (Lidz, 1987). It assesses thinking and learning by attempting to teach children how to perform a general learning task, such as is posed, for example, by the Raven's Progressive Matrixes, and then determining their ability to improve performance following a systematic learning experience (Babad & Budoff, 1974; Feuerstein, 1979). This strategy seeks to change a student's approach to learning while measuring (a) the extent to which the child's approach changes, (b) the difficulty with which the change is accomplished, and (c) the impact on learning by using a test–teach–retest procedure (Feuerstein, 1979). By

using this approach, information can be obtained on the following:

1. the ability to grasp principles underlying the initial tasks;
2. the amount and nature of effort required to teach the child the basic principles;
3. the extent to which newly acquired principles are successfully applied to the solution of problems;
4. the child's preference for presentation and instructional modalities; and,
5. the differential effects of different training strategies. (Smith, 1983, p. 324)

Trial interventions. Trial interventions are implemented in an effort to examine interactions between the characteristics of the child and those of the task and/or the setting. On the basis of a comprehensive understanding of data concerning the child, the task, and the setting, the diagnostician develops a variety of hypotheses about the child's level of and approach to learning as well as her/his personal development, motivation, and styles of relating to others. These hypotheses are translated into environmental modifications that are attempted on a limited basis in the relevant environmental setting, such as the home or the school, during the assessment process. By utilizing information concerning task and setting variables and attempting environmental modifications, the clinician formulates and tests hypotheses about interactions between child, task, and setting. Since trial interventions are attempted in the relevant setting, this approach uses interventions that are connected directly to the tasks and materials associated with the particular learning environment. Data resulting from trial interventions that point toward the potential efficacy of interventions attempted in the natural setting provide important support for the conclusions and/or recommendations resulting from a psychodiagnostic evaluation. Furthermore, the use of this approach during assessment involves the school and/or home in the assessment process, and this increases motivation to persist with these recommendations after assessment is completed.

AN EXAMPLE
ILLUSTRATING THE MODEL

Because process assessment involves a multifaceted approach to assessment that is implemented on an individual basis depending on the presenting problem, there is no typical assessment battery, nor should one be used. The following example is presented to help illustrate the model; it is underscored that this set of assessment procedures is just one of many possible examples of process assessment.

A fifth-grade girl named Frances was referred as a result of poor school performance, particularly in reading. The teacher was uncertain whether this youngster's academic difficulties were due to a learning disability. This school was in a middle-class suburban neighborhood in which the families generally supported education, and the children typically performed above grade level and scored above average on measures of intelligence. Classroom observations revealed a social youngster who seemed to prefer interacting with peers to performing academic tasks. As a result there were occasions when she was off task and talking to a neighbor, and she rarely volunteered to participate in the lesson. Nevertheless, she interacted appropriately with the teacher and consistently attempted to answer questions when they were directed to her. Despite her apparent effort, she was incorrect in her responses more often than her peers.

A Full Scale WISC-R IQ of 109 revealed at least average ability with no noteworthy strengths and weaknesses. The Key Math Diagnostic Arithmetic Test was used to provide a screening in math, which indicated average performance in all basic skills, confirming the teacher's classroom observations that this youngster displayed no academic problems in mathematics. The Woodcock Reading Mastery Test was used as one measure of reading in which performance included standard scores of 43 in Word Identification, 46 in Passage Comprehension, and 51 in Word Comprehension. An informal reading inventory supported these findings, suggesting that both decoding skills and passage comprehension were relatively weak when compared to the performance of her peers.

Observations of Frances's behavior during assessment seemed particularly important. Even though she was motivated to perform well and appeared to work hard, she made numerous careless errors that clearly compromised her performance. In addition, she was observed to become frustrated easily when confronted with tasks that she perceived as difficult, and this inhibited her logical problem-solving skills. Frequently Frances expressed performance anxiety with comments like "I hate this!"; "When will we be finished?"

It appeared that carelessness might be a major factor in explaining her poor performance on decoding tasks, and it was assumed that this same pattern might explain her poor comprehension. Consequently, it was determined that an analysis of her learning strategies might be useful; therefore, think-aloud protocol analysis was used to ascertain her strategic approach to comprehension tasks. This approach was implemented by asking Frances to think out loud while reading three short passages that were uncovered one sentence at a time. The initial analysis revealed a limited use of moves with primary reliance on paraphrasing (68% of the child's moves). There was absolutely no use of reasoning moves or the elaboration move in which the reader connects the meaning of the current sentence to previous material in the text. Moreover, in most instances (87.5% of the time) this youngster reported using only a single move in response to a sentence rather than combinations of moves (i.e., strategies).

Since the observations during testing (which were confirmed by teacher report) suggested that carelessness and anxiety were important factors influencing this child's performance, it was hypothesized that cognitive restructuring (e.g., Harris, Wong, & Keogh, 1985) could be used to control anxiety and to help reduce the number of careless errors. This hypothesis was examined by means of trial interventions that were attempted initially during the testing session with support provided by the classroom teacher. A brief training session was held during diagnosis in which the youngster was taught to check her work in an effort to reduce careless errors, and to use cognitive restructuring to control anxiety. Instruction for both error checking and cognitive restructuring included a brief statement of the rationale followed by the examiner's modeling of the procedure. After this introduction Frances was asked to practice the new skill. For example, the examiner explained why slowing down and checking one's work carefully can facilitate performance. Then the examiner performed a math problem while Frances observed. The examiner made several (purposeful) mistakes during this task which were each corrected by checking the work. Then Frances tried this on a math problem and a brief reading passage. She was instructed to continue using this technique in her schoolwork during the next week.

The brief training in cognitive restructuring was also initiated with an explanation. Using Frances's own words about how she "got mad" when she performed tasks she perceived as difficult, the examiner suggested that Frances use cognitive restructuring when she got mad during an academic task. The examiner modeled this process by pretending to get frustrated while performing an arithmetic problem, and then telling himself that he could solve the problem if he "stayed calm" and "kept working logically." Then the examiner asked Frances to practice this process on two difficult designs from the block design subtest of the WAIS-R. On the first task she was told to say these self-instructions out loud; on the second she was told to use the self-instructions silently. At the conclusion of this teaching process Frances was instructed to use these same techniques in her school tasks, and she was reminded to check her work. Trial interventions were attempted by asking the classroom teacher to reinforce these two strategies at least once every day for the remainder of the week.

Frances was retested 1 week later with portions of the Key Math, the Woodcock, and the WISC-R. Improvements in performance were observed in all subtests that were readministered, and this provided some support for the potential efficacy of these interventions, particularly given the brief nature of the intervention. Although these improvements may be explained, in part, as resulting from practice effects, the consistency of change on all subtests that were readministered was viewed as providing some support for the efficacy of these interventions. Not only were these changes reflected in her scores on these tests, but the clear change in her approach to these tasks provided additional support for the intervention. She worked more slowly and carefully and made fewer careless errors. Furthermore, she did not get frustrated as often as she had previously, and when she did she would pause briefly (as if she were using self-instructions) before returning to the task. The improvements in actual scores included: (a) Previous careless errors in the addition, subtraction, multiplication, and division computation problems of the Key Math did not occur at all upon retesting. (b) Word Identification improved from a standard score of 43 to 53. (c) Passage Comprehension improved from a standard score of 46 to 55. (d) Word Comprehension improved from a standard score of 51 to 58. (e) Block Design improved from a scaled score of 13 to 16. The use of trial interventions in this case went an important step beyond the initial use of norm-referenced measures. Rather than simply making recommendations regarding carelessness and anxiety we tried out these ideas first during assessment with reinforcement from the classroom teacher. By checking the validity of these recommendations the clinician had confidence in his recommendations. Furthermore, the teacher was enthusiastic about trying techniques that she and the psychologist had attempted successfully.

In addition, the results of this assessment suggested that teaching strategies to the child could facilitate reading and that it might be most appropriate to focus on comprehension rather than decoding, given that word attack weaknesses appeared to result from the impulsive response style, which also affected comprehension. The result was a recommendation that the reading specialist spend a few weeks tutoring Frances in comprehension strategies based on the think-aloud protocol analysis that had been completed. The result of ten weeks of tutoring (one session per week) was a 78% increase in the overall use of moves. This was reflected by three notable changes. First, there was an increase in reasoning moves from 0% to 28.2%. Second, there was an increase (0% to 15.6%) in the elaboration move, in which the reader connects the current sentence to previous material in the text. Third, there was a dramatic increase in the strategic use of patterns of moves. In the pretest Frances used combinations of more than one move only 12.5% of the time, whereas on the posttest she used strategic combinations of moves 62.5% of the time. After tutoring, the teacher was informed of these changes and asked to reinforce the use of these strategies during reading. Although there was no formal diagnostic testing of reading comprehension at the conclusion of tutoring, the teacher reported improvements in the fluidity of reading as well as comprehension, and she no longer felt that Frances required special help in school.

STRATEGIES TO FACILITATE IMPLEMENTATION OF PROCESS ASSESSMENT

Stage Model to Implement Process Assessment

Process assessment is an approach to problem diagnosis that is implemented in a unique manner to answer the specific referral question associated with each child. There is no particular test or test battery that is recommended with this approach. Instead, a range of options consistent with the model are available, and the examiner is encouraged to use those that are most appropriate for each case. There is, however, a set of general guidelines for implementing process assessment, derived from Sternberg (1981), that have been described else-

where by Meyers et al. (1985). These guidelines conceptualize three phases of assessment.

Phase I: Global methods. During the first phase of process assessment the examiner considers global methods of assessment in an effort to develop a broad background of information associated with characteristics of the child, the task, and the setting. The data that are gathered at this stage help to define the referral so that the examiner can formulate more specific questions and hypotheses for analysis in the later stages of assessment.

The various global methods include parent and family interviews, anecdotal observations at school, and process observations of the home setting or family interaction. This phase may also include the use of background information and prior records. Data from all of these sources are integrated to develop hypotheses and additional questions that provide the focus for the next phases of assessment.

Phase II: Focused data collection. The second phase emphasizes specific questions about the task, the child, and the setting. The task can be assessed at this phase by task analysis procedures such as those described earlier. It might also involve the collection of data with criterion-referenced procedures developed from the curriculum provided in the child's classroom.

The child's characteristics can be assessed during the focused data collection phase by many different procedures. For example, norm-referenced measures of intellectual, academic, and socioemotional functioning or nonstandardized approaches to assessment might be used to gather data about the child (e.g., Meyers et al., 1985; Smith, 1980). Frequently, this phase is designed to answer questions about motivational and learning styles with a particular focus on the youngster's strategic behaviors in a variety of situations or tasks. Think-aloud procedures and measures of cognitive style, for example, can be used to assess learning styles and cognitive strategies. Behavior rating scales, self-report measures, and informal observations can all be used to help answer questions about anxiety and motivational styles.

Focused data collection can answer questions about the setting or environment as well, and as noted earlier this could include the use of systematic procedures to observe the home, the family, and/or the school. Typically, behavioral (e.g., Bijou & Peterson, 1971) or ecological (e.g., Carlson et al., 1980; Gump, 1975) observation systems might be used for these purposes.

Phase III: Testing interactive hypotheses. Data are gathered in the first two phases of assessment to develop hypotheses about possible interventions. Generally this is based on diagnostic ideas about interactions that occur between the characteristics of the child and the task and/or the environment. This phase of process assessment relies on approaches such as diagnostic teaching and trial interventions. These approaches are used to determine whether there is reasonable support for the hypotheses that have been generated earlier in assessment. A general goal of this model is to make recommendations only when a data base is developed to support the potential efficacy of the recommendation.

Service Delivery Model Incorporating Process Assessment and Consultation[1]

One rationale for process assessment is that the frequently used traditional assessment techniques do little to help the child in the classroom. Psychoeducational assessment is not used typically to increase teachers' knowledge, understanding, and skills so that they can work more effectively with students. If assessment techniques are to have a meaningful impact on children in schools, it is crucial that the psychologist systematically implement steps to facilitate a clear translation of the data obtained during assessment. One way to facilitate this goal is to use models of assessment such as the one presented in this chapter so that data are gathered that lead directly to classroom intervention ideas for the child.

It is not likely, however, that simply shifting assessment models will accomplish this goal. Educational training for teachers does not provide an extensive theoretical and/or practical knowledge base for interpreting and translating psychological data into day-to-day classroom interventions. Nor does teacher training prepare teachers to understand the manner in which single test scores reflect a multitude of developmental and situational variables other than a child's intellectual and achievement levels. Furthermore, educators are frequently not aware that their own attitudes, expectations, interpersonal styles, and instructional approaches can affect the learning and adjustment problems of the students in their class. Despite the need to address these problems, most assessment models are not designed to intervene with these teacher-related factors in a systematic manner. Therefore, teachers can be expected to understand fully and deal effectively with their students' individual difficulties only if follow-up consultation is made available during assessment and after the evaluation has been completed.

Unfortunately, such consultative services are frequently precluded by the excessive amount of time psychologists must spend in assessment and paperwork. One factor contributing to these problems is that, historically, psychoeducational assessment and consultation have been viewed as separate processes. Rarely does the literature on assessment refer to consultation, and rarely does the literature on school consultation refer to psychoeducational assessment. In fact, the school psychology literature addressing consultation developed as a reaction to direct service techniques associated with the medical model. Since most traditional approaches to assessment in school psychology were identified with this orientation, consultation was frequently presented as a model that was an alternative to psychoeducational assessment. As a result, models of consultation have been implemented in schools without sufficient attention to the integration of consultation and assessment. This approach is illogical because effective consultation always requires some form of assessment. Models of assessment and consultation are needed that help to facilitate this integration in theory, research, and practice, and process assessment is one model of assessment that can be integrated readily with existing school-based models of consultation (e.g., see Curtis & Meyers, this volume; and Meyers, Parsons, & Martin, 1979) owing to its focus on the environment, the process of learning, and interventions.

The integration of process assessment with consultation in the school can be conceptualized by considering the three phases of process assessment (i.e., global data collection, focused data collection, testing interactive hypotheses) and incorporating consultation into the context of these phases. Consultation models used in the schools can be integrated with process assessment based on the stages of consultation, which include problem identification, problem definition, intervention, and evaluation (Meyers et al., 1979). Problem identification is the process of determining whether the child (i.e., child-centered consultation), the teacher (teacher-centered consultation), or the system (i.e., system-centered consultation) is the primary focus of the consultative intervention (see Curtis & Meyers, this volume; Meyers et al., 1979). By emphasizing roles of the teacher and the school as a system, rather than the child as an individual, consultation provides an opportunity to reach a maximum number of children and to achieve preventive goals (Curtis & Meyers, this volume; Meyers et al., 1979). Combining consultation with process assessment results in a service delivery system focused on assessment/consultation that has at least four distinct consultation stages during child-centered consultation that each generally require at least one consultation session. An overview of this model is presented in the flow chart in Figure 2.

Four stages of child-centered consultation. The first consultation stage associated with child-centered consulta-

tion occurs during Phase I of process assessment (global data collection) as the teacher and consultant meet in order to define the problem in the first consultation session. The consultant acquires generalized information about the child, the classroom setting, and the tasks, activities, or situations that present the student with particular difficulty. This stage is concluded as the consultant and others gather additional global data that are needed.

The second stage of child-centered consultation occurs in Phase II of process assessment, in which focused data collection becomes the primary goal. The consultant and teacher meet to analyze the global data gathered subsequent to the first consultation stage, and this analysis is used to plan the focused data collection that is to occur during the next stage.

Depending upon hypotheses about problem areas, target behaviors are selected and decisions made about procedures for observing the student's behavior systematically in a variety of classroom situations. As a result of the planning involved at this stage, the teacher(s) assess the child's ability and achievement level on various curricular tasks, using criterion-referenced measures as well as relevant classroom behavior. It is crucial to suggest practical approaches for data collection by teachers (i.e., time-limited approaches that can be implemented at convenient times for the teacher, etc.). At this point it may be appropriate for the consultant to arrange assessment sessions with the student. A variety of techniques can be used to discover the child's cognitive style, strengths and weaknesses, motivation, attentional capacities, cognitive strategies, work habits, emotional functioning, etc.

The consultation framework encourages active involvement of the teacher. Thus, in these first two stages the teacher provides direct input into decisions as to what data to gather and into the analysis of data gathered previously. This also increases the demand on the teacher to participate actively in the data-gathering process by using techniques such as classroom observation. Consistent with

FIGURE 2
Flow Chart Integrating School-Based Consultation with Process Assessment

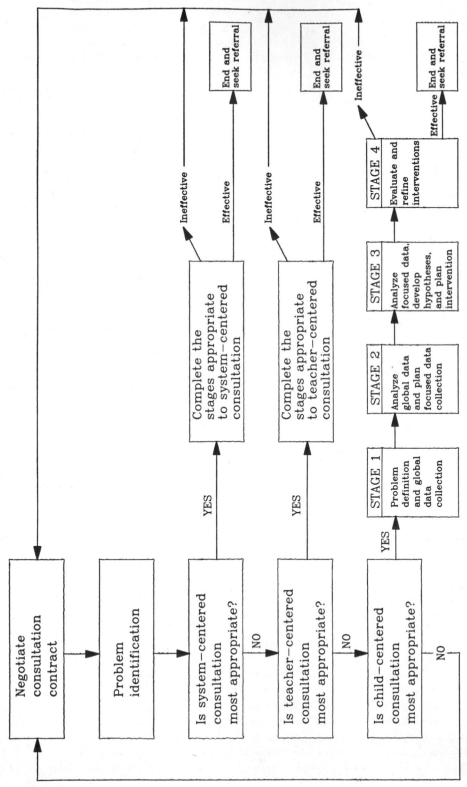

the consultation model there is a colla-borative interpersonal process that em-phasizes that the teacher and consultant are professional colleagues who will each contribute to problem solution (e.g., Curtis & Meyers, this volume). This collaboration is continued throughout this approach to assessment/consultation.

The third stage of child-centered consultation begins with the teacher and consultant sharing the focused data they have each gathered since the last meeting. During this stage the results are analyzed by the teacher and consultant in an effort to develop hypotheses concerning inter-actions between the characteristics of the child, the setting(s), and the task(s). This marks the beginning of Phase III, in which the consultant and teacher, by brain-storming, determine trial interventions to be attempted in the classroom and other appropriate setting(s). Subsequent to this session the teacher might implement trial interventions in the classroom and the consultant might implement diagnostic teaching or learning potential assessment procedures with the child.

The fourth stage of child-centered consultation is designed to evaluate and refine trial interventions as Phase III of process assessment is completed. The consultant and teacher analyze data gathered about the process of implement-ing these procedures as well as their efficacy. The process of implementation is assessed using formative evaluation techniques such as observations and interviews to determine any difficulties regarding implementation. Efficacy is assessed using tests and observation procedures directly related to the target behavior(s). As a result of these evalua-tions, a decision may be made to continue with the trial interventions as developed initially, or to modify these interventions.

There is no fixed time for each of the four stages of this assessment/consulta-tion process, but each stage typically requires as least one consultation session, which is often all that is needed. Each step is implemented in a flexible manner making every effort to meet the goals of consultation in the most efficient manner. Thus, while many approaches to data

gathering are referred to in the descrip-tion of each stage, it is not necessary that data be gathered for each of these factors in an invariant manner. While Stages 1 and 2 suggest that data are gathered concern-ing the characteristics of the task, the child, and the setting, there may be some situations where data gathering would focus on just one of these characteristics. By their participating jointly in the assessment/consultation process in these four stages there is a good chance that the teacher and consultant will develop intervention plans with a maximum opportunity to provide meaningful help to the child. The ideas developed for the classroom are likely to be realistic in that situation and the teacher is likely to be committed to working hard toward im-plementing plans after being actively involved in their development. Moreover, by incorporating child-centered consulta-tion into the assessment process, there is a greater opportunity for the consultant to develop other modes of consultation such as teacher-centered consultation and system-centered consultation (e.g., Curtis & Meyers, this volume; Meyers et al., 1979). In the long run, this integration of assessment and consultation services may help to provide better solutions to individual children's problems while opening greater opportunities for a range of preventive services including consulta-tion focused on the teacher, the classroom, and the school as a system.

Training Issues for Process Assessment

Assessment is a major component in the training of school psychologists, because it is one of the most common activities in their practice. Unfortunately, the heavy emphasis on training in assess-ment often results in the administration of a standard battery of tests with the overall goal of classifying and placing students in a special education class, while providing little or no information for planning interventions. A review of assess-ment textbooks (e.g., Salvia & Ysseldyke, 1985; Taylor, 1984) reinforces the dom-inance of test-based models for assess-ment that assume that learning problems are functions disabilities of the individual students rather than their interaction with the instructional environment (Sewell, 1981).

University training programs must explore the different models of assessment (e.g., Smith, 1983; Mercer & Ysseldyke, 1977), the assets and limitations of these models, the different assessment procedures associated with these models (e.g., curriculum-based, interview-based, observation-based, and test-based assessment, as well as informal assessment), and the specific approaches to planning interventions derived from assessment data. Consistent with Sewell's (1981) viewpoint, these varied goals of training view the individual students in the various contexts in which they function.

Training in these various skills could be done in specific courses on alternative approaches to assessment in which the emphasis is on the conceptual bases along with related assessment procedures. Alternative models could also be integrated into existing courses with units on the expanded focus as well as alternative techniques (e.g., Meyers, 1987). Training is needed also for practicing school psychologists, who frequently have opportunities for professional development through in-services at the local, state, or national level sponsored by professional school psychology organizations or university training programs. These approaches to in-service, however, may have limited effects, since they are focused more on presenting information in brief (i.e., half-day or one-day) workshops, rather than on developing knowledge and skills. A serious consideration of the theoretical base and the development of the related professional skills might more likely be possible in a series of workshops offered through a university over a period of time, or through extended in-service training at the school district level, which would provide an opportunity for specific feedback on cases relevant to training.

Although it is important to change assessment models as well as the practice of assessment by school psychologists, it is also necessary to educate the consumers of school psychological services about assessment and what it can and cannot do. Consumers include teachers, administrators, and parents. The increased emphasis on interventions rather than classification alone should enhance the usefulness of the assessment conducted by school psychologists (Reschly, 1980), and it is important that consumers be informed of these possibilities.

IMPLICATIONS OF THE MODEL

Many of the specific techniques suggested in this chapter are relatively new and have limited empirical support at this time. A good example is think-aloud protocol analysis. The procedure has been used in only two descriptive research studies that have been completed (Lytle, 1982; Meyers et al., 1987), and there is only anecdotal support for its utility as a basis for tutoring in about 20 cases. The existing data are promising, but there is a need for a great deal of research, and the results obtained with this technique during assessment should obviously be interpreted cautiously.

The most important goal of assessment is to develop effective interventions. Yet there is a widespread lack of prescriptive validity available for the assessment instruments used currently by school psychologists. In other words, there is not an adequate data base to indicate that the assessment techniques used frequently by school psychologists result in effective interventions for children. Although it is crucially important that research be conducted to document the utility of assessment in developing effective interventions, the lack of these data cannot be used as an excuse to avoid the development of interventions for children experiencing learning and adjustment problems. Process assessment is presented as a model that can be used to help develop interventions for such children, and the lack of empirical evidence of prescriptive validity suggests that the consultant must follow up to determine the effectiveness of particular interventions and must suggest modifications when necessary. At the same time, this model can be used as a stimulus for research into the prescriptive validity of the assessments conducted by school psychologists.

Given the need for additional research on various technical characteristics of numerous assessment techniques associated with process assessment, it is important to establish guidelines to evaluate the efficacy of this model. Nelson and Hayes (1985) offered some suggestions for evaluating assessment that have stimulated the following questions to serve as guidelines. (a) Do data from different sources provide support for the conclusions? (b) Is there evidence of generalizability from the clinical to the natural setting? (c) Is there evidence about how behavior varies across natural settings? (d) Do the data gathered answer the particular assessment questions? (e) Does behavior improve subsequent to assessment? When the answers to each of these questions is affirmative, there is strong evidence supporting the adequacy of the evaluation procedures used.

Bevan's (1981) keynote address to the Spring Hill Symposium, "The Future of Psychology in the Schools," suggested that school psychologists must develop a professional identity that differentiates them from technicians. He indicated that whereas professionals may be skilled in some areas, they are not dependent on particular skills and have the knowledge base to exercise professional judgment in solving difficult problems. There are many ways in which school psychologists can fall into the trap of behaving as technicians rather than professionals. This occurs when they rely on particular tests and standard batteries rather than conceptualizing the theories and the broad range of options available in psychoeducational assessment. It may happen when they rely too much on test scores rather than their professional skills in interpreting test scores, behavior observations, interview data, and so forth. It also occurs when school psychologists allow themselves to become part of systems that implement eligibility formulas blindly without allowing for professional input from those who have conducted the assessment (e.g., Manni, Winikur, & Keller, 1984; Ysseldyke

& Thurlow, 1983). The assessment model presented in this chapter does not rely on any one particular test, it is not dependent on test scores per se, and it does require professional judgment. Although it is legitimate to be concerned about potential bias or subjectivity resulting from professional judgment, it would be a mistake to rely on the rigid interpretation of test scores without allowing for professional interpretation of these scores. The guidelines for evaluating assessment can help to overcome potential problems associated with professional subjectivity, because in the long run, the efficacy of assessment and its interpretation must be judged by the resulting improvements in the learning and adjustment of children.

FOOTNOTE

[1]Thanks to Vicki Erlbaum, Randy-Ellen Koenigsberg and Beverly Speizer for their contribution to the development of this service delivery model.

REFERENCES

Alessi, G., & Kaye, J. (1983). *Behavioral assessment.* Washington, DC: National Association of School Psychologists.

Aliotti, N. C. (1977). Covert assessment in psychoeducational testing. *Psychology in the Schools, 14,* 438-443.

Annis, L. F. (1979). Effect of cognitive style and learning passage organization on study technique effectiveness. *Journal of Educational Psychology, 71,* 620-626.

Babad, E. Y., & Budoff, M. (1974). Sensitivity and validity of learning-potential measurement in three levels of ability. *Journal of Educational Psychology, 66,* 439-447.

Barker, R. G. (1968). *Ecological psychology.* Stanford, CA: Stanford University Press.

Baron, J. (1981). Reflective thinking as a goal of education. *Intelligence, 5,* 291-309.

Bereiter, C., & Bird, M. (1985). Use of thinking aloud in identification and teaching of reading comprehension strategies. *Cognition and Instruction, 2,* 131-156.

Bevan, W. (1981). On coming of age among the professions. In J. E. Ysseldyke & R. A. Weinberg (Eds.), *The Spring Hill Symposium on the future of psychology in the schools. School Psychology Review, 10,* 127-137.

Bijou, S. W., & Peterson, R. F. (1971). Functional analysis in the assessment of children. In P. McReynolds (Ed.), *Advances in psychological assessment* (Vol. 2, pp. 63–78). Palo Alto, CA: Science and Behavior Books.

Bronfenbrenner, U. (1981). *Recreating human ecology*. Evanston, IL: National College of Education.

Brown, A. L. (1980). Metacognitive development and reading. In R. J. Spiro, B. Bruce, & W. F. Brewer (Eds.), *Theoretical issues in reading comprehension* (pp. 453–481). Hillsdale, NJ: Erlbaum.

Brown, A. L., Palincsar, A. S., & Armbruster, B. B. (1984). In H. Mandl, N. L. Stein, & T. Trabasso (Eds.), *Learning and comprehension of text* (pp. 255–286). Hillsdale, NJ: Erlbaum.

Brown, W. F., & Holtzman, W. H. (1967). *Survey of study habits and attitudes*. New York: Psychological Corporation.

Brueckner, L. J. (1930). *Diagnostic and remedial teaching in arithmetic*. Philadelphia: Winston.

Budoff, M., & Friedman, M. (1964). "Learning-potential" as an assessment approach to the adolescent mentally retarded. *Journal of Consulting Psychology, 28*, 434–439.

Cantrell, M. L., & Cantrell, R. P. (1985). Assessment of the natural environment. *Education and Treatment of Children, 8*, 275–295.

Carlson, C. I., Scott, M., & Eklund, S. J. (1980). Ecological theory and method for behavioral assessment. *School Psychology Review, 9*, 75–82.

Cartwright, G. P., Cartwright, C. A., & Ward, M. E. (1984). *Educating special learners* (2nd ed.). Belmont, CA: Wadsworth.

Christopherson, S. L., Schultz, C., & Waern, Y. (1981). The effect of two contextual conditions on recall of a reading passage and on thought processes in reading. *Journal of Reading, 24*, 573–578.

Curtis, M. J., & Meyers, J. (1985). Best practices in school-based consultation. In A. Thomas & J. Grimes (Eds.), *Best practices in school psychology* (pp. 74–94). Kent, OH: National Association of School Psychologists.

Dean, R. S., & Kulhavy, R. W. (1978). Effects of language facility in learning. *American Educational Research Journal, 15*, 501–504.

Dean, R. S., & Kundert, D. K. (1981). Intelligence and teachers' ratings as predictors of abstract and concrete learning. *Journal of School Psychology, 19*, 78–85.

Dunn, R., Dunn, K., & Price, G. (1983). *Learning style inventory*. Lawrence, KS: Price Systems.

Epstein, W., Rock, I., & Zuckerman, C. B. (1960). Meaning and familiarity in associative learning. *Psychological Monographs, 74*, (4, Whole No. 491).

Ericsson, K. A., & Simon, H. A. (1980). Verbal reports as data. *Psychological Review, 87*, 215–251.

Feuerstein, R. (1979). *The dynamic assessment of retarded performers: The learning potential assessment device, theory, instruments, and techniques*. Baltimore: University Park Press.

Flavell, J. (1976). Metacognitive aspects of problem solving. In L. B. Resnick (Ed.), *The nature of intelligence* (pp. 231–253). Hillsdale, NJ: Erlbaum.

Frostig, M., & Horne, D. (1964). *The Frostig program for the development of visual perception*. Chicago: Follett.

Gagne, R., & Briggs, L. (1979). *Principles of instructional design* (2nd ed.). New York: Holt, Rinehart & Winston.

Garner, R. (1980). Monitoring of understanding: An investigation of good and poor readers' awareness of induced miscomprehension of text. *Journal of Reading Behavior, 12*, 55–64.

Garner, R., & Reis, R. (1981). Monitoring and resolving comprehension obstacles: An investigation of spontaneous text lookbacks among upper-grade good and poor comprehenders. *Reading Research Quarterly, 16*, 569–582.

Gerken, K. C. (1985). Best practices in academic assessment. In A. Thomas & J. Grimes (Eds.), *Best practices in school psychology* (pp. 157–170). Kent, OH: National Association of School Psychologists.

Gickling, E. E., & Havertape, J. (1981). *Curriculum based assessment*. Minneapolis, MN: University of Minnesota, National School Psychology Training Network.

Goldwasser, E., Meyers, J., Christenson, S., & Graden, J. (1983). The impact of PL 94-142 on the practice of school psychology: A national survey. *Psychology in the Schools, 20*, 153–165.

Good, T. L., & Brophy, J. E. (1986). *Educational psychology* (3rd ed.). New York: Longman.

Gresham, F. M. (1983). Multitrait-multimethod approach to multifactored assessment: Theoretical rationale and practical application. *School Psychology Review, 12*, 26–34.

Gump, P. V. (1975). Education as an environmental enterprise. In R. A. Weinberg & F. H. Wood (Eds.), *Observation of pupils and teachers in mainstream and special education settings: Alternative strategies* (pp. 109–121). Reston, VA: Council of Exceptional Children.

Hall, R. V., Hawkins, R. P., & Axelrod, S. (1975). Measuring and recording student behavior: A behavior analysis approach. In R. A. Weinberg & F. H. Wood (Eds.), *Observation of pupils and teachers in mainstream and special education settings: Alternative strategies* (pp. 193-215). Reston, VA: Council for Exceptional Children.

Harris, K. R., Wong, B. Y. L., & Keogh, B. K. (Eds.). (1985). Cognitive-behavior modification with children: A critical review of the state-of-the-art. *Journal of Abnormal Child Psychology, 13*, 329-476.

Hunt, J. McV. (1969). The early detection of potential learning disorders. *Academic Therapy, 4*, 12-15.

Hutson, B., & Niles, J. (1974). The missing link. *Psychology in the Schools, 11*, 188-191.

Johnston, P. H. (1985). Assessment in reading. In P. D. Pearson (Ed.), *Handbook of reading research* (pp. 147-182). New York: Longman.

Karp, S. A., & Konstadt, N. (1971). *Children's Embedded Figures Test.* Palo Alto, CA: Consulting Psychologists Press.

Keogh, B. K., & Donlon, G. M. (1972). Field dependence, impulsivity, and learning disabilities. *Journal of Learning Disabilities, 5*, 331-336.

Kirk, S., McCarthy, J., & Kirk, W. (1968). *Illinois Test of Psycholinguistic Abilities.* Champaign: University of Illinois Press.

Kounin, J. S. (1970). *Discipline and group management in classrooms.* New York: Holt, Rinehart & Winston.

Kratochwill, T. R. (1977). The movement of psychological extras into ability assessment. *Journal of Special Education, 11*, 299-311.

Kratochwill, T. R., & Severson, R. A. (1977). Process assessment: An examination of reinforcer effectiveness and predictive validity. *Journal of School Psychology, 15*, 293-300.

Kruteskii, V. A. (1976). *The psychology of mathematical abilities in school children.* Chicago: University of Chicago Press. (Translated from 1968 publication).

Lankford, F. G. (1972). *Some computational strategies of seventh grade pupils.* Charlottesville, VA: Center for Advanced Study, University of Virginia.

Lankford, F. G. (1974). What can a teacher learn about a pupil's thinking through oral interviews? *Arithmetic Teacher, 21*, 26-32.

Lerner, J. (1976). *Children with learning disabilities* (2nd ed.). Boston: Houghton Mifflin.

Levin, J. R., Rohwer, W. D., & Cleary, T. A. (1971). Individual differences in the learning of verbally and pictorially presented paired associates. *American Educational Research Journal, 8*, 11-26.

Lidz, C. (1987). *Dynamic assessment: Foundations and fundamentals.* New York: Guilford.

Linn, M. C., & Kyllonen, P. (1981). The field dependence-independence construct: Some, one, or none. *Journal of Educational Psychology, 73*, 261-273.

Lytle, S. (1982). *Exploring comprehension style: A study of twelfth-grade readers' transactions with text.* Unpublished Doctoral Dissertation, University of Pennsylvania.

Manni, J. L., Winikur, D. W., & Keller, M. R. (1984). *Intelligence, mental retardation, and the culturally different child.* Springfield, IL: Thomas.

Martin, C., Cox, D., & Boersma, R. (1965). The role of associative strategies in acquisition of P-A material: An alternative approach to meaningfulness. *Psychonomic Science, 3*, 463-469.

McLoughlin, J. A., & Lewis, R. B. (1986). *Assessing special students* (2nd ed.). Columbus, OH: Merrill.

Mercer, J. R., & Ysseldyke, J. E. (1977). Designing diagnostic-intervention programs. In T. Oakland (Ed.), *Psychological and educational assessment of minority children.* New York: Brunner/Mazel.

Messick, S., & Associates (1976). *Individuality in learning.* San Francisco: Jossey-Bass.

Meyers, J. (August, 1985). *Diagnostic diagnosed: Twenty years after.* Presidential address presented to the Division of School Psychology of the American Psychological Association at the annual convention in Los Angeles.

Meyers, J. (1988). Diagnosis diagnosed: Twenty years after. *Professional School Psychology, 3*, 123-134.

Meyers, J. (1987). Training dynamic assessors. In C. Lidz (Ed.), *Dynamic assessment: Foundations and fundamentals* (pp. 403-425). New York: Guilford.

Meyers, J., & Lytle S. (1986). Assessing the process of learning. *Exceptional Children, 53*, 138-144.

Meyers, J., Palladino, D., & Devenpeck, G. (1987, March). *Think-aloud assessment of reading comprehension: An empirical investigation of fourth and fifth grade students.* Paper presented at the annual meeting of the National Association of School Psychologists, New Orleans.

Meyers, J., Parsons, R., & Martin, R. (1979). *Mental health consultation in the schools.* San Francisco, CA: Jossey-Bass.

Meyers, J., Pfeffer, J., & Erlbaum, V. (1985). Process assessment: A model for broadening assessment. *Journal of Special Education, 19*, 74-89.

Moos, R. H. (1979). *Evaluating educational environments.* San Francisco: Jossey-Bass.

Mowder, B. A. (1983). Assessment and intervention in school psychological services. In G. W. Hynd (Ed.), *The school psychologist: An introduction.* Syracuse, NY: Syracuse University Press.

Moyer, J. R., & Dardig, J. C. (1978). Practical task analysis for special educators. *Teaching Exceptional Children, 11*, 16-18.

Nelson, R. O., & Hayes, S. C. (1985). Nature of behavioral assessment. In M. Hersen & A. S. Bellack (Eds.), *Behavioral assessment: A practical handbook* (2nd ed., pp. 3-37). New York: Pergamon.

O'Leary, K. D. (1975). Behavioral assessment: An observational slant. In R. A. Weinberg and F. H. Wood (Eds.), *Observation of pupils and teachers in mainstream and special education settings: Alternative strategies* (pp. 181-191). Reston, VA: Council for Exceptional Children.

Olshavsky, J. (1976/1977). Reading as problem solving: An investigation of strategies. *Reading Research Quarterly, 12*, 654-674.

Paivio, A., & Yuille, J. C. (1966). Word abstractness and meaningfulness, and paired-associate learning in children. *Journal of Experimental Child Psychology, 4*, 81-89.

Reschly, D. J. (1980). School psychologists and assessment in the future. *Professional Psychology, 11*, 841-848.

Resnick, L. B. (Ed.). (1976). *The nature of intelligence.* Hillsdale, NJ: Erlbaum.

Rohwer, W. D. (1971). Learning, race, and school success. *Review of Educational Research, 41*, 191-210.

Rosenfield, S. (1987). *Instructional consultation.* Hillsdale, NJ: Erlbaum.

Salvia, J., & Ysseldyke, J. E. (1985). *Assessment in special and remedial education* (3rd ed.). Boston: Houghton Mifflin.

Saracho, O. N. (1980). The relationship between teachers' cognitive styles and their perceptions of their students' academic achievement. *Educational Research Quarterly, 5*, 40-49.

Saracho, O. N. (1984). Young children's academic achievement as a function of their cognitive styles. *Journal of Research and Development in Education, 18*, 44-50.

Saracho, O. N., & Dayton, C. M. (1980). Relationship of teachers' cognitive styles to pupils' academic achievement gains. *Journal of Educational Psychology, 72*, 544-549.

Sarason, S. B. (1976). The unfortunate fate of Alfred Binet and school psychology. *Teachers College Record, 77*, 579-592.

Savell, J. M., Twohig, P. T., & Rachford, D. L. (1986). Empirical status of Feuerstein's "Instrumental Enrichment" (FIE) Technique as a method of teaching thinking skills. *Review of Educational Research, 56*, 381-409.

Scott, M. (1980). Ecological theory and methods for research in special education. *Journal of Special Education, 14*, 279-294.

Seretny, M. L., & Kundert, D. K. (1987, August). *Curriculum based assessment of spelling programs.* Paper presented at the annual meeting of the American Psychological Association, New York.

Sewell, T. (1981). Shaping the future of school psychology: Another perspective. *School Psychology Review, 10*, 232-242.

Shade, B. J. (1983). Cognitive strategies as determinants of school achievement. *Psychology in the Schools, 20*, 487-493.

Silberberg, N. E. (1971). Is there such a thing as a learning disabled child? *Journal of Learning Disabilities, 4*, 273-276.

Simeonsson, R. J. (1986). *Psychological and developmental assessment of special children.* Boston: Allyn and Bacon.

Sloane, H. N., Buckholdt, D. R., Jensen, W. & Crandell, J. (1979). *Structured teaching.* Champaign, IL: Research Press.

Smith, C. R. (1980). Assessment alternatives: Nonstandardized procedures. *School Psychology Review, 9*, 46-57.

Smith, C. R. (1983). *Learning disabilities: The interaction of the learner, task, and setting.* Boston: Little, Brown.

Sperry, V. B. (1974). *A language approach to learning disabilities.* Palo Alto, CA: Consulting Psychologists Press.

Sternberg, R. J. (1981). Testing and cognitive psychology. *American Psychologist, 36*, 1187-1189.

Stevenson, H. W. (1972). *Children's learning.* New York: Appleton-Century-Crofts.

Taylor, R. L. (1984). *Assessment of exceptional students: Educational and psychological procedures.* Englewood Cliffs, NJ: Prentice-Hall.

Thurlow, M. L., & Ysseldyke, J. E. (1982). Instructional planning: Information collected by school psychologists vs. information considered useful by teachers. *Journal of School Psychology, 20*, 3-10.

Torgesen, J. K. (1977). The role of nonspecific factors in the task performance of learning disabled children: Theoretical assessment. *Journal of Learning Disabilities, 10*, 27-34.

Torgesen, J. K. (1979). What shall we do with psychological processes? *Journal of Learning Disabilities, 12*, 514-521.

Turnure, J. E. (1986). Instruction and cognitive development: Coordinating communication and cues. *Exceptional Children, 53*, 109-117.

Underwood, B. J., & Schulz, R. W. (1960). *Meaningfulness and verbal learning.* Philadelphia: Lippincott.

Vygotsky, L. S. (1978). *Mind in society: The development of higher psychological processes.* Cambridge, MA: Harvard University Press.

Weinstein, C. E., & Mayer, R. E. (1986). The teaching of learning strategies. In M. C. Wittrock (Ed.), *Handbook of Research on Teaching* (3rd ed., pp. 315-327. New York: Macmillan.

Witkin, H. A., Moore, C. A., Goodenough, D. R., & Cox, R. W. (1977). Field dependent and field independent cognitive styles and their educational implications. *Review of Educational Research, 47*, 17-27.

Wong, B. (1979). The role of theory in learning disabilities research: Part I. *Journal of Learning Disabilities, 12*, 585-595.

Ysseldyke, J. E., & Christenson, S. (1987). *The instructional environment scale: A comprehensive methodology for assessing an individual student's instruction.* Austin, TX: Pro-Ed.

Ysseldyke, J. E., & Salvia, J. (1974). Diagnostic-prescriptive teaching: Two models. *Exceptional Children, 41*, 181-185.

Ysseldyke, J. E., & Thurlow, M. L. (1983). *Identification/classification research: An integrative summary of findings.* (Report Number IRLD-RR-142). Minneapolis, MN: University of Minnesota, Institute for Research on Learning Disabilities.

10

Adaptive Instruction: An Alternative Educational Approach for Students With Special Needs

Margaret C. Wang
Temple University Center for Research in
Human Development and Education

Maynard C. Reynolds
University of Minnesota

Lisa Levine Schwartz
University of Illinois

This chapter examines an alternative approach to serving students with special needs through a broadly restructured general education system. The core of this approach is using adaptive instruction to achieve what has long been a goal of special education programs: identifying and accommodating individual learning characteristics and needs.

CONTEXT FOR REFORM

Two Decades of Groundwork

Several major strands of activity undertaken over the past two decades represent important strides toward ensuring adequate and appropriate education for students with special needs. These include a recognition that reform aimed at improving the quality of educational services for students with special needs, and thereby maximizing their changes of schooling success, requires a renegotiation of the relationships between special and general education. Four areas are especially prominent for their contribution to current renegotiation efforts: development and testing of experimental service delivery models, legislative and judicial actions, reform through teacher educa-

tion, and programmatic developments in general education.

Experimental service delivery models. An agreement between the Bureau of Education for the Handicapped (the present Office of Special Education and Rehabilitative Services) of the United States Department of Education and the program office of the Education Professions Development Act opened the door to a series of experimental programs and service delivery models in the late 1960s. Many of these were designed to bridge the gap between special and general education. Several of the experiments involved a pullout service model for mildly handicapped students, incorporating various configurations of resource rooms and teachers, diagnostic–prescriptive teachers, and consulting teachers (Deno, 1973). During that period, school psychologists were concerned mainly with psychometrics and with the classification of students for the burgeoning special education programs. In later years, this preoccupation with testing and classification produced a reaction on the part of many school psychologists against service delivery models that preclude their involvement in instructionally meaningful diagnosis and prescription.

Legislative and judicial actions. Landmark court cases and legislation fueled the renegotiation movement in the 1970s. The consent decree of (PARC) *Pennsylvania Association for Retarded Children v. Pennsylvania* (1972), for example, made explicit the "least restrictive environment" (LRE) principle regarding the school placement of students with special needs. The Education for All Handicapped Children Act of 1975 (Public Law 94-142), and subsequent regulations of Section 403 of the Rehabilitation Act, confirmed and strengthened the LRE principle, thereby reinforcing the need to redefine the relationship between general and special education. Thus, the policy of the nation clearly began to call for providing education for handicapped children in regular classes and regular schools whenever feasible.

Reform through teacher education. The mid-1970s also saw a major reform effort to improve and broaden the preparation programs for mainstream teachers. Under the Deans Grant Project, 240 colleges and universities in the United States received federal funding support to strengthen their preparation programs for general education teachers (Grosenick & Reynolds, 1978; Sharp, 1982). The objective of these programs was to develop capabilities for accommodating students with special needs in regular classrooms and schools. While efforts such as the Deans Grant Project were significant for their impact in alerting the teacher education community to the mandates of PL 94-142, they did not address the substantive programmatic issue of how to adapt instruction to the needs of individual students, a critical feature of any approach to serving handicapped students in mainstream general education settings. Teacher preparation programs of the Deans Grant Project often consisted simply of lessons given by special educators on how to teach different categories of handicapped children.

The tendency to design reforms within the framework of the traditional special education categories continued through the 1970s. Under that approach, the adaptation of programs and services was limited mainly to relegating students with special needs to special education programs for varying amounts of time during the school day. The process of systematically pulling children out of general education classrooms produced an enormous amount of disjointedness in the experiences of both students and teachers as well as communication problems between general and special education teachers (Reynolds & Wang, 1983).

Programmatic developments in general education. As the reforms described thus far were being initiated from the special education perspective, research and development efforts in general education were making important inroads in improving instructional programs and classroom management practices. Programmatic developments such as the Adaptive Learning Environments Model (Wang, 1980; Wang, Gennari, & Waxman, 1985), the Houston Plan (Dollar & Klinger, 1975; Klinger, 1975; Meisgeier, 1976). Individually Guided Education (Klausmeier, 1975), and Team-Assisted Individualization (Slavin, 1983; Slavin, Leavey, & Madden, 1982) were all framed as alternative interventions for bringing together general and special education through adaptive instruction. They demonstrated the potential for combining the best of what had been learned from special education with the state of the art in effective adaptive instruction practices. Discussion in later sections of this chapter focuses on the design and evidence of effectiveness of the Adaptive Learning Environments Model (ALEM) as one such research-based approach to structuring general education programs in ways that accommodate students with special needs in the mainstream.

Demographic Trends

The numbers of children with special learning needs, including mildly handicapped students and others with poor prognoses for academic success, underline the importance of restructuring current educational systems. There is clear evidence of continuing increases in both the absolute numbers and the percentages of the school-age population who are handicapped or otherwise at risk. For example, 21.7% of the nation's children lived below the poverty line in 1983, compared to 14.2% in 1973 (Feistritzer, 1985). In the 1981 National Survey of Children, teachers indicated that 35.1% of the sampled school children from families with annual incomes of less than $10,000 needed remedial reading and that 16.7% of these children were slow learners or learning disabled. In contrast, 12.3% of the children from families with an income range of $20,000–35,000 were identified by teachers as needing remedial reading and 7.4% as slow learners or learning disabled (Child Trends, 1985).

Convergent with these statistics are the higher fertility and birth rates for poor women compared with those for other women. Additional demographic trends that correlate with greater numbers of students with special needs include increasing proportions of children who live with one or no natural parent and the increased survival of low-birthweight babies, who tend to have relatively high rates of congenital abnormalities or developmental delays (Zill, 1985). Of every 100 children born today, 12 are born out of wedlock, half to teenage mothers. Teenage mothers tend to have premature or low-birthweight babies, and these children often develop health and learning problems (Hodgkinson, 1985). Many of them become permanently disabled, needing a lifetime of medical care and supportive services (Hughes, Johnson, Rosenbaum, Simons, & Butler, 1987).

All of these factors point to intensified demands on categorical "special" school programs over the next decade. At the same time, the general school-age population is expected to grow from approximately 44 million in 1985 to 50 million in 2000 (U. S. Bureau of the Census, 1982).

The Challenge for Broad Educational Restructuring

Experience of the past two decades, along with predictions of continuing

increases in handicapped, economically disadvantaged, and other students with special needs, highlights the urgency of identifying systematic ways to effectively serve all students in the mainstream of general education classrooms. There is no distinct knowledge base to support the separate education of students by category of need. As noted by the National Academy of Sciences Panel on Selection and Placement of Students in Programs for the Mentally Retarded, there is little evidence of differences between special education programs and Chapter 1 programs for economically disadvantaged, low-achieving students (Heller, Holtzman, & Messick, 1982). Thus, the challenge is to structure a unified and well-managed general education system that includes a variety of coordinated "special" programs that effectively and efficiently provide for the needs of most, if not all, students. The adaptive instruction approach discussed below is one of a variety of alternative education approaches that aim to meet individual students' needs for instruction and related services within regular classroom environments. The discussion offers an illustration of the possibility of achieving such a unified system of education.

ADAPTIVE INSTRUCTION

Concept and Practice

Adaptive instruction refers to educational interventions that are aimed at accommodating the unique learning needs of individual students and enhancing each student's ability to develop knowledge and skills for mastering learning tasks. Adaptive instruction is grounded in the assumption that every class includes students with different interests, problems, and talents, and that whole-class instruction geared to the average student is bound to be too difficult for some learners and too easy for others. Thus, a major task is to identify and provide the diverse instructional supports required by individual students to efficiently and productively achieve given outcomes.

Over the last decade, instructional experimentation, combined with innovations in program development and implementation, has yielded a substantial research base to support the improvement of school effectiveness through adaptive instruction. Moreover, it is possible to derive from this research base a rather consistent list of features of programs that effectively provide for individual differences (Wang & Lindvall, 1984; Wang & Walberg, 1985). These programs have combined strategies and practices such as flexible scheduling, individual diagnosis and prescription, mastery learning, large- and small-group instruction, individual tutorials, and cooperative learning.

Observations in classrooms in which demonstrably effective, adaptive instruction programs are implemented provide a scenario that neither is the direct opposite of the conventional group-paced, teacher-directed approach (e.g., Brophy, 1979; Rosenshine, 1979), nor is strictly synonymous with open education or individualized instruction (e.g., Bangert, Kulik, & Kulik, 1983; Peterson, 1979). Although adaptive instruction calls for instructional planning based on the learning needs of the individual student, it does not prescribe that students work alone. Teacher and peer tutoring on a one-to-one basis, as well as cooperative learning and other group tasks, are often specified because they are assumed to be efficient for instructional management and because they are suited to the achievement of desirable outcomes such as group discussion, collaborative planning, social skills, and responsibility. A basic premise underlying the design of effective adaptive instruction programs is that a variety of educational objectives, instructional materials, and learning tasks is needed; furthermore, the implementation of different objectives and tasks requires a wide selection of teaching and learning strategies (Wang, 1980).

There is also considerable variety among adaptive instruction programs in the nature of specific program goals as well as the strategies and designs used to achieve the goals. However, adapting and combining different strategies in ways that best suit individual teachers, classes, and students seem to be characteristic of all adaptive instruction programs. Within any particular program, teachers vary their use of materials and procedures, and students are treated according to their unique learning needs and talents (Walberg & Wang, 1987; Wang & Lindvall, 1984; Wang & Walberg, 1985; Waxman, Wang, Anderson, & Walberg, 1985).

The Research Base

The implementation of adaptive instruction tends to be more complicated and challenging than the implementation of traditional, whole-class teaching. Nevertheless, research suggests both the feasibility of successfully operating adaptive instruction programs under a variety of circumstances and the effectiveness of such programs in terms of desired learning (e.g., Wang & Walberg, 1985, in press; Waxman et al., 1985).

Seven commonly noted features of adaptive instruction programs have been delineated by Wang and Lindvall (1984) based on their review of extant programs. These features are (a) instruction that is based on the assessed capabilities of each student; (b) materials and procedures that permit each student to make progress in mastering instructional content at a pace suited to his or her abilities and interests; (c) periodic evaluations of student progress that serve to inform individual students of their mastery; (d) students' assumption of responsibility for planning, monitoring, and evaluating their own learning and mastery; (e) availability of alternative activities and materials that help students efficiently and effectively acquire essential academic skills and content; (f) individual student choice of educational goals, expected outcomes, and activities; and (g) student cooperation and assistance in pursuing individual goals and in achieving group goals.

Consistent evidence of achievement is reflected in the findings from a recent synthesis of empirical studies of adaptive instruction programs that were reported in the literature between 1973 and 1982 (Waxman et al., 1985). The 38 studies included in this synthesis all met three criteria. Each study (a) was conducted in a general education classroom(s) in an elementary or secondary school; (b) produced either contrasted-groups or correlational results; and (c) produced sufficient quantitative data on the sample population for calculating effect sizes. (An effect size is defined by Waxman et al. as "a standardized estimate of where the treatment group stands in comparison with the control group distribution" [p. 229].) From the statistical data on a sample of approximately 7,200 students, 309 effect sizes were calculated to estimate the extent of positive student learning outcomes under the adaptive instruction programs. The mean of the study-weighted effect sizes for a variety of cognitive, affective, and behavioral outcomes was .45; the average score of students under the adaptive instruction programs was at the 67th percentile for all three categories of outcomes, compared to an average score at the 50th percentile for the control groups. To place these statistics in perspective, Waxman et al. noted that the mean effect size of .45 is more than twice the average effect size reported in syntheses of classroom research of the past few decades. The finding of an overall positive effect of adaptive instruction seemed constant when adjusted for grade, socioeconomic level, race, private or public school, and type of community.

In a recent observational study, Wang and Walberg (in press) addressed the need to greatly expand the data base on the relationships among program design features, implementation conditions, and program effects on classroom processes and student outcomes. The study was designed to analyze and characterize the features of adaptive instruction and to facilitate a better understanding of how different combinations of features and implementation conditions are integrated into working programs to produce classroom processes and outcomes commonly associated with effective instruction and learning.

Eight demonstrably effective programs were selected for study by Wang and Walberg. They were identified from a number of current, widely implemented programs or models of instruction that include the goal of making provisions for individual differences among students. The eight programs were the Adaptive Learning Environments Model (Wang, 1980; Wang, Gennari, & Waxman, 1985); the Bank Street Model (Gilkeson, Smithberg, Bowman, & Rhine, 1981); the Behavior Analysis Model (Ramp & Rhine, 1981); the Direct Instruction Model (Becker, Engelmann, Carnine, & Rhine, 1981); Individually Guided Education (Klausmeier, 1975; Klausmeier, Quilling, Sorenson, Way, & Glasrud, 1971); the Mastery Learning approach (Bloom, 1968); Team-Assisted Individualization (Slavin, 1983; Slavin et al., 1982); and the Utah System Approach to Individualized Learning (Jeter, 1980). Classrooms that represented exemplary implementation of these programs were identified by the program developers and served as the sample pool for the study. Data on seven categories of variables — program features, classroom processes, classroom climate, students' perceptions of self-responsibility, student achievement, teachers' attitudes, and students' socioeconomic status — were collected and analyzed for a total of 65 second-, third-, and fourth-grade classrooms.

The findings from the Wang and Walberg study suggest that programs that feature student choice, task flexibility, systematic teacher monitoring, peer tutoring, student-initiated requests for assistance from teachers, a wide variety of curriculum materials, and task-specific instructions produce high levels of self-management, frequent work in small groups, and more substantive interactions with teachers than just management-related ones. Overall, programs and classrooms in the study that featured the greatest use of strategies for individualizing instruction, as well as a clear delineation of task-specific directions, were associated with high levels of student responsibility.

On average, the programs that utilize predominantly adaptive instruction practices and strategies produced student achievement levels as great as, and often greater than, achievement levels under programs that are more characteristically teacher-directed and group-paced. Moreover, several of the sample programs with adaptive instruction features yielded additional results considered by many educators, parents, and students to be of great value. Among these outcomes were constructive student interaction with peers, independent work, individual diagnosis and prescription, cooperative learning, and exploration. Wang and Walberg (in press) also found that no single feature seemed to distinguish effective programs from less effective programs. Instead, it was the combination and coordination of several features in carefully implemented programs that appeared to produce a wide range of positive outcomes.

The results from studies such as those by Waxman et al. (1985) and Wang and Walberg (in press) contrast sharply with the findings that dominate the literature on effective teaching and school effectiveness (e.g., Brophy & Good, 1986). The latter research base has consistently been used to argue for the comparatively greater efficacy of the group-paced, teacher-directed approach. However, the two studies reported here lend much support for the position that adapting instruction to the learning characteristics and needs of individual students and fostering student autonomy can produce intended academic and social outcomes. In fact, features such as student choice, which is often described in the literature as ineffective (e.g., Bennett, 1976; Brophy, 1979), were found to facilitate learning.

Thus, there is a growing research base that supports technical advances in the implementation of adaptive instruction programs. The widely implemented instructional programs studied by Wang and Walberg (in press), for example, reflect increasingly refined views of individual differences, recent developments in cognitive psychology regarding instructionally relevant student characteristics, and state-of-the-art findings on classroom processes and student outcomes.

ADAPTIVE LEARNING ENVIRONMENTS MODEL

The Adaptive Learning Environments Model is an example of a research-based program of adaptive instruction that has been widely adopted by schools aiming to effectively serve in regular classes students with special learning needs (e.g., students classified in the various mild handicap categories in special education, students identified as low achievers or academically at risk, Chapter 1 students). The ALEM was designed as a general education program for enhancing schools' capability to accommodate individual differences in student learning (Wang, 1980). It has shown to be feasible and effective as an alternative intervention for providing the instructional and related service supports required by diverse student populations within the setting of the regular classroom. Over the course of nearly two decades of development, the ALEM has been implemented as a core general education program, a special education program, and a mainstreaming program for mildly or moderately handicapped students (e.g., students classified as learning disabled, educable mentally retarded, and socially and emotionally disturbed). It has also been used in conjunction with several compensatory education initiatives for economically disadvantaged students, such as Chapter 1 and the National Follow Through program.

The implementation and effectiveness of the ALEM in a variety of settings has been extensively documented. In addition to evaluation studies designed and conducted by the program developer (e.g., Wang, 1981; Wang & Birch, 1984a, 1984b; Wang, Gennari, & Waxman, 1985; Wang, Peverly, & Randolph, 1984; Wang & Walberg, 1983), informal and formal evaluations carried out by school and district personnel at numerous sites where components of the ALEM have been adopted have yielded substantial evidence of positive results (Wang, 1987).

Program Goals and Objectives

The overall goal of the ALEM is to establish and maintain school environments that accommodate individual needs and characteristics, thereby ensuring learning success for all students. Two basic premises underlie the program's design. The first is that students learn in different ways and require varying amounts of instruction and time to learn. The second premise is that the primary task of schools is to provide the instruction and related services each student needs to acquire basic academic skills, as well as to attain social and attitudinal goals such as positive self-perceptions of academic and social competence, a sense of responsibility for his or her own education and to the broader social community, and practical competence in coping with the social and academic demands of schooling.

The ALEM includes programming, management, and technical support for school administrators and instructional staff (Wang, 1980). It focuses on the systematic integration of features that theory, research, and practice have found to be instructionally effective and pedagogically meaningful for adapting schooling experiences to individual students. These features take into account what Glaser (1982) refers to as the "large practical variables": efficient allocation and use of teachers' and students' time, a practical classroom management system, systematic teacher feedback and reinforcement of students' learning behavior and progress, patterns of positive teacher-student interactions, instruction based on the diagnosed learning needs of individual students, and flexible administrative and organizational patterns that are responsive to program implementation and staffing needs. The incorporation of these variables in the design of the ALEM responds to the common concerns of teachers, educational researchers interested in day-to-day school operations, school administrators, and specialized and instructional support personnel (e.g., special education and Chapter 1 teachers).

The ALEM has been noted by many as an alternative program uniquely suited for mainstreaming and maintaining students with special needs in regular classes, where they can share equally with their general education peers all available learning resources and specialized services on a full-time basis (e.g., Cantalician Foundation, 1983; Epps & Tindal, 1987; Heller et al., 1982; Lloyd, 1988; Mayor's Commission on Special Education, 1985). In schools that have adopted the ALEM as an integrated approach to serving students with special needs, mildly handicapped students and others considered academically at risk are fully integrated socially and academically and show steady progress in their learning. The effective integration of students with special needs is a central objective throughout the planning, introduction, and maintenance of the program's implementation. It has been hypothesized that when instruction is tailored to individual needs and provided by regular and specialized staff for all students in the same setting, differences in learning are likely to be viewed as the norm rather than the exception; students who require special instructional help are less likely to perceive of themselves as exceptions or failures. Concomitantly, unique learning characteristics are no longer considered an acceptable rationale for school failure or for moving students to different and segregated environments. When mainstreaming occurs in this context, the need for remedial programs and tracking systems that employ special schools, special classes, and other pullout strategies can be sharply reduced (Wang, 1981).

Program Design Features

The ALEM has specific design features for providing adaptive instruction and for supporting program implementation. The major features that facilitate the adaptation of instruction to student differences are individualized progress plans, a diagnostic-prescriptive monitoring system, and the classroom instructional-learning management system known as the Self-Schedule System. The features that provide district-, school-, and classroom-level support for implementation of the ALEM are an adaptive program delivery system, the training sequence known as the Data-Based Staff Development Program, school and classroom organizational supports, and a family involvement component.

Features for the provision of adaptive instruction. *Individualized progress plans.* In ALEM classrooms, each student's educational experience is tailored to his or her particular learning characteristics and needs. Curriculum materials are modified when necessary for the development and implementation of individualized progress plans for each student. The plans are based on teachers' observation and information from diagnostic tests and records of student progress rates. This information is used by teachers to prescribe appropriate amounts and types of tasks for each student and to support students' learning through individual and group instruction.

The learning tasks included in the individualized progress plans are generally organized around two complementary curriculum components. The first, the prescriptive learning component, consists of highly structured tasks that foster mastery of basic skills in academic subject areas (e.g., reading, mathematics, science, social studies, spelling). The basic skills curricula developed by individual schools or school districts, as well as commercially published materials (e.g., basal texts) currently used in classrooms, constitute the core of the prescriptive learning component. Examples of learning tasks in this component are completing a written workbook assignment in a particular subject area, participating in a small-group teacher-guided science laboratory activity, and engaging in a one-to-one tutoring lesson with a teacher. The second curriculum component is the exploratory learning component. Tasks in this component are designed specifically to foster students' social and personal development, with a focus on enhancing their ability to plan and manage their own learning. These tasks also provide opportunities for basic skills enrichment. Examples of exploratory learning tasks are writing a script for a class play, creating a poster, and playing a game of chess.

Diagnostic–prescriptive monitoring system. The adaptive instruction process under the ALEM begins with the diagnosis of each student's entering level of skills and knowledge in the basic subject matter areas. The program's diagnostic–prescriptive monitoring system uses criterion-referenced assessments (e.g., curriculum-based assessment procedures built into the various basic skills curricula) to ensure that appropriate educational tasks are individually assigned and lead to successful learning. This system calls for ongoing monitoring of each student's progress through record-keeping procedures that incorporate paper-and-pencil or microcomputer formats to maintain up-to-date information. The role of diagnosis and prescription in the instructional cycle under the ALEM is illustrated by Figure 1, reproduced from Wang & Vaughan (1987a). Table 1 presents a list of resources that should be available to teachers for effective diagnosis, prescription, instruction, and monitoring and assessment of student learning (Wang & Vaughan, 1987a).

Self-Schedule System. An instructional objective integral to the ALEM is developing each student's ability to play an active role in her or his education. The Self-Schedule System (Wang, 1974a, 1976) is designed to foster students' sense of responsibility and ability to become increasingly self-instructive in managing their own learning. Because the cognitive and social demands of assuming self-responsibility for school learning vary in complexity and requisite abilities, students are guided through a progression of relatively simple tasks to more complex ones. Through a series of hierarchically organized exercises, they learn to schedule prescribed and self-selected activities in order to complete their learning tasks within specified periods of time. For example, one of the first steps in the hierarchy might be to choose which of two teacher-prescribed activities in the same subject should be done first; a subsequent step might be to complete both activities within an hour; and finally, students might progress to selecting two of five optional activities and deciding in what order to do the activities, along with all teacher-prescribed tasks, within a 3-hour period. As with the development of any skill, not all students move through the hierarchy of the Self-Schedule System at the same rate. Therefore, instruction in self-management skills is adaptive to individual differences.

In addition to managing their learning activities, students learn to work within the constraints of the classroom by observing rules, following directions, managing materials, and requesting help from, and giving assistance to, teachers and peers. As students become increasingly proficient in managing and monitoring their own learning, teachers are freed

from many routine management and instructional duties and are able to devote more time to instruction.

Features for supporting program implementation. *Adaptive program delivery system.* The ALEM's approach to effective program delivery is to complement and supplement the existing characteristics of particular schools. School personnel are encouraged and assisted to adjust ALEM implementation to their own improvement goals. The development of a school-specific program delivery system begins with a series of procedures to assess needs and plan implementation (Wang & Vaughan, 1987b). Based on needs assessments of school features such as student population characteristics, staffing patterns, curricula, operating practices, record-keeping procedures, and physical resources, a site-specific implementation plan for adopting the ALEM is developed.

FIGURE 1

Illustration of the role of diagnosis and prescription in the instructional cycle under the Adaptive Learning Environments Model. From *Handbook for the Implementation of Adaptive Instruction Programs: Module 4. Curriculum Resources for Individualizing Instruction* (pp. 4-5) by M. C. Wang and E. D. Vaughan, (1987). Philadelphia, PA: Temple University Center for Research in Human Development and Education. Copyright 1987 by the Temple University Center for Research in Human Development and Education. Reprinted by permission.

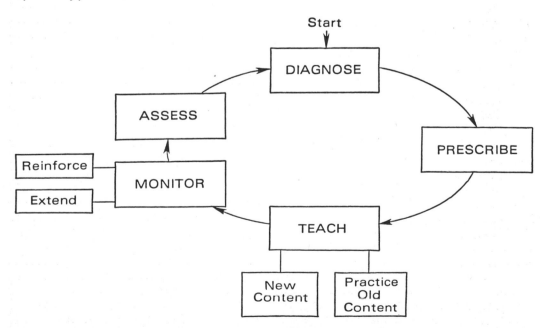

TABLE 1
Types of Curricular Resources Needed for Each Step of the Instructional Cycle

Step	Examples of Appropriate Resources
Diagnosis	Placement tests Diagnostic tests Pretests Work samples
Prescribing, teach- ing, and monitoring	Curriculum guides Teachers' manuals Textbooks Workbooks Skill sheets, worksheets, etc. Other available learning materials, e.g., kits, games, teacher- constructed learning tasks
Assessment	Skill sheets, worksheets, and other work samples Unit or lesson posttests Level tests Teacher-constructed tests

The plan, which includes an extensive-awareness program for all stakeholders (e.g., teachers, parents, school boards), eases the transition to the innovative educational approach and helps to ensure that the ALEM meets schooling needs and goals. Table 2 contains a checklist reproduced from Wang & Vaughan (1987b), of tasks for the development of a school-specific program delivery system.

Data-Based Staff Development Program. Research and experience consistently suggest that staff development programs that include ongoing training support are features of effective school improvement in general and of effective mainstreaming in particular. Preimplementation and ongoing support for the introduction and maintenance of the ALEM is provided through the Data-Based Staff Development Program (Wang & Gennari, 1983). The training sequence for school personnel has three levels. The first, basic training, provides an overview of the ALEM and working knowledge of the program's implementation requirements. The second level, individualized training, is keyed to particular functions of each staff role. The third level, in-service training, consists of an interactive process of program assessment, feedback, planning, and staff development. The Data-

Based Staff Development Program is the core of the "training-of-trainers" approach that is used to develop the competencies of local personnel for implementing the program in their own classrooms, schools, and districts. Local instructional leaders such as principals, building-level education specialists, and district-level staff development specialists receive systematic training in the functions of program development and implementation. The training prepares them for utilizing the structure of the Data-Based Staff Development Program to provide ongoing, in-service training support for classroom teachers and other instructional staff.

The Implementation Assessment Battery for Adaptive Instruction (Wang, Catalano, & Gromoll, 1983) is one of the major tools available for monitoring the degree of implementation and for identifying staff development needs. The Battery consists of a series of checklists, observation forms, and interview forms. It is routinely administered in ALEM classrooms to determine the presence or absence of critical program dimensions. There are 12 program dimensions: Arranging Space and Facilities, Creating and Maintaining Instructional Materials, Establishing and Communicating Rules and Procedures, Managing Aides, Diagnostic

TABLE 2
Checklist of Tasks and Implementation Planning Forms for the Development of Adaptive Program Delivery Systems

A. Identification of Program Classes

_____ Determine the number of classes that will participate in the program.

_____ Select grade levels and grade-level composition of classes.

B. Staffing

_____ Assign teachers to program classes.

_____ Select an education specialist.

_____ Identify resource and special personnel and define their roles in the program.

_____ Identify/hire paraprofessionals and/or arrange for other classroom aides.

C. Student Placements

_____ Assign regular education students to program classes.

_____ Make arrangements for placement of special needs students in the classes.

D. Scheduling

_____ Designate time, place, and personnel for curriculum preparation.

_____ Designate time, place, and personnel for pre-implementation training of staff.

_____ Construct a master schedule for the school compatible with program requirements.

E. Space, Facilities, and Materials

_____ Confirm that sufficient materials (i.e., textbooks, workbooks) are available.

_____ Identify/acquire supplemental instructional materials, if needed.

_____ Acquire necessary non-instructional materials.

_____ Allocate a room for the education specialist.

_____ Locate storage cabinets and other furniture for program classrooms.

F. Program monitoring and Evaluation

_____ Establish a system for monitoring program implementation and using the results for staff development.

_____ Identify appropriate measures of program effects (outcomes).

_____ Develop a schedule for collection of outcome data.

G. Communication and Dissemination of Information

_____ Develop a plan to inform stakeholders (e.g., parents, school board members) about the program.

_____ Establish an internal network for communication among program staff.

_____ Establish an external network for disseminating information to parents, community members, district administrators, and others about the program.

Note: From *Handbook for the Implementation of Adaptive Instruction Programs: Module 2. Needs Assessment and Implementation Planning* (pp. C–1 to C–2; D–1 to D–11) by M. C. Wang and E. D. Vaughan (1987). Philadelphia, PA: Temple University Center for Research in Human Development and Education. Copyright 1987 by the Temple University Center for Research in Human Development and Education. Reprinted by permission.

Testing, Record Keeping, Monitoring and Diagnosing, Prescribing, Interactive Teaching, Instructing, Motivating, and Developing Student Self-Responsibility. The items in the Implementation Assessment Battery for Adaptive Instruction are based on 108 performance indicators of these critical dimensions. The reliability and validity of the Battery have been established for a wide variety of school settings and for the identification of both teacher-specific and school-specific staff development needs (Strom & Wang, 1982; Wang & Gennari, 1983; Wang, Nojan, Strom, & Walberg, 1984; Wang & Walberg, 1983).

School and classroom organizational supports. Adapting instruction to the needs of individual students requires flexibility in school and classroom organizational patterns. At the school level, the ALEM encourages staffing patterns that promote effective program implementation. In schools where the ALEM is used as a mainstreaming program, the roles of instructional personnel are redefined to achieve an interface between general and special education services. The role of special education teachers, for example, includes consultation with general education teachers as well as the provision of direct instructional services for students with special needs in regular classes. General education teachers function as the primary instructors for both the general education students and the students with special needs in the ALEM classrooms.

Principals play an integral role in creating a supportive organizational climate for implementation of the ALEM. Findings from recent research show that effective schools tend to have principals who function mainly as instructional, rather than administrative, leaders (Fullan, 1981; Leithwood & Montgomery, 1982; MacPhail-Wilcox & Guth, 1983; Montgomery & Leithwood, 1983; Pinero, 1982). As instructional leaders, principals work actively with teachers to influence instructional strategies. They involve themselves in identifying and solving classroom problems; they participate in in-service activities; they conduct both formal and informal staff development sessions; they observe classrooms and provide feedback to teachers; and they work closely with teachers to identify instructional goals and the means to achieve them. Because adaptive instruction programs require flexible scheduling, restructuring of relationships among teachers, and ongoing training support, all of these instructional leadership functions take on increased importance.

At the classroom level, the ALEM encourages the use of multi-age grouping and instructional teaming as organizational patterns that maximize the implementation of adaptive instruction. Multi-age grouping provides the necessary flexibility to accommodate the differences of individual students, particularly those who make unusually slow or fast progress, without the social consequences of repeating or skipping a grade. It also offers opportunities for spontaneous and planned peer modeling and tutoring, which enable teachers to spend more time with students who require greater amounts of teacher assistance. Instructional teaming allows increased use of various grouping methods and encourages teachers to apply their own interests and talents to the provision of alternative learning experiences.

Family involvement. Learning occurs at home as well as in school. Given the limited amount of time in the school day, even students in the most effectively implemented educational programs can benefit from instructional reinforcement at home. Thus, the ALEM encourages an active program of family involvement to increase the communication and cooperation between school and home. Activities are designed to induce family members to support their children's learning in concrete ways. Initial awareness sessions are conducted to inform parents of the design and goals of the ALEM. As implementation of the program progresses, parents receive frequent formal and informal reports about their children's progress. Parents are encouraged to participate in designing and refining their children's educational plans and to provide home instruction in consultation with teachers. In addition, parents may work as volunteers in ALEM classrooms. Such activities ensure that families are knowledgeable about the school curriculum and about their children's learning plans and progress within the curriculum.

Summary of Major Findings on Program Implementation and Effects

The ALEM is supported by an ongoing program of research and evaluation. Findings from the past decade provide consistent evidence that high degrees of implementation of the ALEM can be attained in regular classrooms in a variety of school settings, and that effective implementation leads to positive changes in classroom processes. These changes, in turn, tend to result in intended academic and attitudinal outcomes (e.g., achievement gains, positive student attitudes toward learning, favorable attitudes on the part of school personnel and parents).

As noted earlier in this section, a variety of reports and publications have documented the research findings on the ALEM (e.g., Wang, 1982; Wang & Birch, 1984a, 1984b, Wang, Gennari, & Waxman, 1985; Wang, Nojan, Strom, & Walberg, 1984; Wang, Peverly, & Catalano, 1987; Wang, Peverly, & Randolph, 1984; Wang, Rubenstein, & Reynolds, 1985; Wang & Walberg, 1983). Highlights from three program evaluation studies are summarized here for illustrative purposes. The first was a study of five urban schools in which the ALEM was implemented as an alternative intervention for integrating mildly handicapped students in general education classrooms on a full-time basis (Wang, Peverly, & Randolph, 1984). The second study included suburban and rural schools with large concentrations of students from economically disadvantaged backgrounds (Wang & Birch, 1984b; Wang, Nojan, Strom, & Walberg, 1984; Wang & Walberg, 1983). The third study compared the effects of a full-time ALEM mainstreaming approach for special education students with a non-ALEM resource room approach by randomly assigning special education students to ALEM and non-ALEM classes (Wang & Birch, 1984a). Three categories of findings are discussed — the degree of program implementation, classroom processes, and student learning outcomes.

Degree of implementation. Degree of implementation data from ALEM classrooms are analyzed to examine the program's "implementability" — the extent to which it can be implemented effectively across school sites with varying characteristics and improvement needs — and the relationship between program implementation and specific process and product outcomes. Program implementation data are obtained by administering the Implementation Assessment Battery for Adaptive Instruction (Wang et al., 1983).

Overall, the research results to date support the implementability of the ALEM. The major patterns of findings include increases in the degree of implementation from the beginning to the end of the school year and from one school year to the next, and large percentages of teachers who maintain high degrees of program implementation. Such patterns have been consistently documented by school personnel where the ALEM has been implemented (e.g., Bright, 1987; Lowe, 1985; Winter, 1987).

Classroom processes. Analyses of classroom processes under the ALEM focus on the nature and patterns of interactions between students and teachers (student-initiated or teacher-initiated interactions, instruction-related or management-related interactions); the nature of students' interactions with their peers (constructive or disruptive); the settings in which learning activities occur (group or individual); the types of tasks on which students work (prescriptive or exploratory); and the manner in which classroom time is spent by students (on-task, distracted, or waiting for teacher help). The Student Behavior Observation Schedule (Wang, 1974b) is used to obtain these various categories of classroom process data.

One consistent finding across studies

of the ALEM is that there tends to be a significant relationship between the degree of implementation of the program's critical design dimensions and the nature of subsequent classroom processes. Specifically, high degrees of program implementation lead to the positive changes in classroom processes that were hypothesized by the researchers (Wang, Nojan, Strom, & Walberg, 1984; Wang, et al., 1987). These changes include increases in student-teacher interactions for instructional purposes and concomitant decreases in management-related interactions, increases in on-task behavior, decreases in student disruptive behavior, and increases in student-initiated learning activities.

There is also a consistent pattern in which the higher the degree of implementation, the greater the occurrence of such positive classroom processes. Analyses of data from classrooms characterized by overall high, average, and low degrees of implementation have shown a range of differences on the classroom process variables identified as intended program outcomes of the ALEM. Classrooms with lower degrees of implementation are associated with greater frequencies of management-related interactions between teachers and students. In classrooms with a high degree of implementation, the interactions among students are generally found to be more constructive and students spend more time working in group settings than working alone. Differences among classrooms of high, average, and low levels of implementation have also been found in types of activities in which students engage and the manner in which learning tasks are performed. Students in classrooms with high levels of implementation spend significantly more time on student-selected, exploratory learning tasks, exhibit higher rates of on-task behavior, and are less distracted (Wang & Walberg, 1983).

At one school where the ALEM was adopted as an alternative intervention for accommodating mildly handicapped students in general education classrooms, comparisons of classroom processes in ALEM mainstreaming classes and non-ALEM classrooms were made (Wang & Birch, 1984a). For the study, mainstreamed special education students were randomly assigned to either the ALEM classrooms full-time or to the school's special education resource room in the morning and to regular non-ALEM classrooms in the afternoon. Overall, the results show that the handicapped students in ALEM classrooms evidenced more positive changes in classroom processes over the course of the school year than did their peers in the resource room. By spring of their first year under the ALEM, the former students engaged less often in teacher-directed work, more frequently in independent work, and more often in on-task behavior. These findings are particularly noteworthy when the differences in adult-to-student ratio are taken into consideration. The non-ALEM resource room in the particular school where the study took place included 11 students, one special education teacher, and one instructional aide; the ALEM classrooms included an average of 45 students, with two regular classroom teachers, one aide shared by two classes, and consulting services from a special education teacher.

Student learning outcomes. Three categories of findings on student learning under the ALEM are summarized here. They are (a) student achievement in basic academic skills, (b) student attitudes, and (c) teacher and parent attitudes.

Student achievement in basic academic skills. Analyses of the impact of the ALEM on student achievement have included examining whether achievement under the program is comparable to national norms, and whether the achievement gains of ALEM students with special needs are comparable to the achievement gains of ALEM general education students and of non-ALEM special education students. The hypothesis underlying these investigations has been that if instruction is effectively adapted to the learning characteristics and needs of individual students, then all students in ALEM classrooms will make achievement gains. Data for analyses of student achievement have consisted of scores on standardized tests in mathematics and reading that were regularly administered by school districts.

Findings consistently suggest that achievement results for students under the ALEM are comparable with national norms and population norms (i.e., students with similar socioeconomic backgrounds). In studies of schools where the ALEM has been implemented in conjunction with the National Follow Through Program as a general education model for serving students from economically and educationally disadvantaged backgrounds, mean percentile scores in both mathematics and reading have actually exceeded the population as well as the national norms. For example, the ALEM students at the Follow Through schools have performed well above the reported norms for similar populations of students (Wang & Birch, 1984b; Wang & Walberg, 1983). Moreover, as many as 46% of the ALEM students have had achievement scores above the 75th percentile (compared to the national norm of 25%); as few as 10% have had scores below the 25th percentile (compared to the national norm of 25%).

When achievement results have been compared for general education students and for students with special needs in the ALEM mainstreamed classrooms, similar positive findings have been documented. Significant gains have been found for both groups of students. In one study (Wang et al., 1987; Wang, Peverly, & Randolph, 1984), at the end of the first year's implementation, the mean grade-equivalent gains in achievement for the ALEM general education students were 1.87 in math and 1.19 in reading. The mean grade-equivalent gains for the mainstreamed special education students were 1.08 in math and 1.04 in reading. While the gain scores for the mainstreamed special education students were not greater than the national norm of 1 year, they were significantly greater than the expected gains for students in the same school system who had similar special education classifications and who received instruction in self-contained special education programs. The average yearly achieve-ment gain for this latter group of students was 6 months.

Data from the same study showed that, after only 1 year of implementation, as many as 42.3% of the mainstreamed special education students in the ALEM classes had achievement scores that fell at or above the 75th percentile in mathematics; as many as 28.6% had scores at or above the 75th percentile in reading. Furthermore, the study provided evidence of ALEM's impact on the results for students with special needs. There was a dramatic increase in the percentage of these students who were recommended by their teachers for decertification (removal of the handicap classification). Decertification was recommended for about 30% of the mainstreamed students with special needs in the ALEM classrooms, compared with the average decertification rate of less than 3% for students with similar special education classifications enrolled in the school system's self-contained special education classes.

Student attitudes. The development and evaluation of the ALEM has incorporated the assumption that positive social and attitudinal outcomes are highly related to improved learning. It has been hypothesized that under adaptive instruction programs like the ALEM, students with special needs will develop positive perceptions of academic and social competence as well as overall feelings of self-esteem. In one study this hypothesis was tested by comparing the attitudes of general and special education students in a school's ALEM and non-ALEM classrooms (Wang, 1982). Data on students' perceptions of cognitive competence, social competence, and general self-esteem were obtained through the Perceived Competence Scale for Children (Harter, 1982).

Three major findings are noteworthy. First, the self-ratings of cognitive competence, social competence, and general self-esteem were significantly higher for the mainstreamed special education students in ALEM classes than for students with similar special education classifications in the non-ALEM classrooms. Second, general education students in the ALEM and the non-ALEM classrooms rated themselves at about the same levels in social competence and general self-esteem. Finally, the handicapped and general education students in the ALEM classrooms showed almost identical self-ratings on social competence and general self-esteem.

Teacher and parent attitudes. Under the ALEM, the attitudes of teachers and parents are considered important variables related to students' learning outcomes. Thus, research has included the development and administration of a variety of surveys and interviews to examine the attitudes of these important groups of stakeholders.

Findings from recent surveys of ALEM teachers and parents indicate highly positive attitudes (Wang, Peverly, & Randolph, 1984). More than 80% of the teachers agreed that they found the ALEM to be professionally rewarding, challenging, and stimulating; that they were able to get to know their students better through the program; and that students showed increased engagement and involvement in school work as a result of the ALEM. The general education teachers identified the individualized curriculum, the program's instructional-learning management system, and the data-based staff development approach as particularly important features in helping them to effectively serve the students with special needs in their classrooms. It is noteworthy that, although teachers generally felt they had to work harder under the ALEM than under their schools' conventional programs, they seemed to experience less frustration. More than 70% of the parents surveyed in this study agreed that the ALEM had been good for their children and they were pleased with how well their children were doing in school.

IMPLICATIONS FOR EDUCATIONAL RESTRUCTURING

The ALEM is one example of how systematic implementation of a compre-

hensive adaptive instruction program can enable schools to provide appropriate education that maximizes the chances of academic success for students with special needs. Other innovative programs and practices are noted throughout this volume and in a number of recent reviews of mainstreaming effects (e.g., Carlberg & Kavale, 1980; Epps & Tindal, 1987; Lloyd, 1988; Madden & Slavin, 1982; Nevin & Thousand, 1987; Wang & Baker, 1985-1986). Viewed collectively, these findings support the integration of students with special needs in general education classrooms. The establishment of cooperative linkages between general education instructional staff and specialized school personnel is a key component in the design of programs that aim to institutionalize the educational restructuring required to effectively serve students with special needs in regular classroom settings. In particular, the roles of general education teachers, special education teachers, principals, and school psychologists must be redefined to achieve an effective interface between general and special education. Examples of the features and implications of these redefined roles are discussed below, with special emphasis on the role of school psychologists.

In integrated classrooms such as those established under the ALEM, *general education teachers* are expected to implement complex instructional procedures for highly diverse student populations. Instead of pulling handicapped and other students with special needs out of the regular classroom for instruction in segregated settings for part of the school day, general education teachers serve all students in the mainstream. However, the increased instructional demands of this approach are offset considerably by support from special education teachers, school psychologists, and other staff people who work as members of the professional instructional team in the general education classrooms. Under these conditions, the work of the general education teacher can be demanding, yet also rewarding. For example, general education teachers from ALEM mainstream settings almost uniformly report that they work harder but feel less frustrated about what they can accomplish in their classrooms. Furthermore, they would not want to revert to former practices.

As noted above, *special education teachers* of mildly handicapped students spend increasing amounts of their day in general education classrooms under the kind of restructured system described in this chapter. Working together, special and general education teachers can become an efficient and powerful team that possesses full understanding of the curriculum and of instructional planning. The special education teacher is relatively free to operate on a cross-categorical basis and to concentrate on serving students who need the most intensive instructional help — whether or not the students have been formally identified by a handicap classification. Implied in the redefined role for general and special education teachers is the need to design preservice and in-service preparation programs in which these teachers join efforts to expand the schools' capabilities for providing effective adaptive instruction and relevant support services in regular classrooms.

In a restructured general education system, *school principals* can reclaim their role as both instructional and administrative leaders. Principals are called upon to lead the effort to reduce the disjointedness caused by formerly separate categorical programs. They provide staff development and other resource supports aimed at serving all students and all varieties of special needs in a unified way. Principals also assume increased responsibility and accountability for representing their schools' instructional approach to parents and other stakeholders, and for conducting frequent evaluations of program implementation and impact.

School psychologists can make a unique contribution to educational restructuring. Their specialized professional training and the functions typically associated with their work enable them to play a central role in three related areas: (a) providing support for instructional staff, parents, and others who are actively involved in the delivery of educational services for all students, but especially for students with special needs; (b) disseminating information about the state of the art to practitioners and administrators for the improvement of schooling practice; and (c) identifying individual students who require more than the usual educational support and providing information about their learning characteristics and needs for use in instructional planning.

Traditionally, and particularly since the enactment of PL 94-142 in 1975, school psychologists have been instrumental in identifying and classifying students who require special education and related support services; they have also contributed to marshaling, safeguarding, and delivering services for these students. Through effective monitoring, school psychologists have helped to ensure that all students who require more than the usual amounts of educational support actually receive it, that standards for accommodating individual student needs are upheld, and that resources are indeed directed to targeted students.

In the type of restructured general education system proposed here, school psychologists are also expected to play a pivotal role in linking assessment to the design of instructional interventions. In his recent article on the integration of instruction and testing, Glaser (1985) noted that, as a result of technological developments and advances in theories of learning and instruction, students and teachers in the twenty-first century will require a variety of information to make appropriate instructional decisions. He agrees with the prediction of Brown and Campione (1984, 1986) that "rather than attempting to identify a general underlying deficit, we will concentrate more precisely on helping the learner recognize incomplete or partial knowledge that can become a focus for more direct instruction attention" (Glaser, 1985).

The use of assessment to date has accomplished much in terms of identifying and securing services for students, and thereby advancing the provision of equal access to free and appropriate educational services for all children. However, assessment practices have fallen far short of ensuring schooling success for students with special needs. The current use of assessment typically fails to produce relevant information for instructional planning; it does not produce information for determining what services should be provided and how they can be most effectively delivered. School psychologists can make a critical difference in this area through the application of their knowledge and expertise in child development, in the design of learning environments, and in the identification of effective instructional strategies.

Thus, school psychologists may be viewed as both producers and users of new knowledge about learners, the learning process, and the ways in which information can be applied to improve instruction. They should no longer be expected to function simply as "gatekeepers" who select students for, or exclude them from, special services (e.g., programs for gifted students, special education programs, compensatory education programs). Instead, school psychologists in the restructured general education system would work closely with teachers and related school personnel (e.g., speech therapists, special education teachers) to identify the specific learning needs of individual students, develop instructional alternatives that improve students' motivation and learning in basic skills, and communicate effectively with parents and school instructional staff.

In conclusion, it is important to recognize that realizing the vision of educational restructuring proposed in this chapter is complicated by many programmatic, administrative, and fiscal roadblocks that continue to separate general education, special education, and other entitlement or compensatory education services (Reynolds & Wang, 1983; Wang, Reynolds, & Walberg, 1986). Experience with implementation of the ALEM as an alternate intervention for integrating students with special needs into regular classrooms has shown that it is possible to remove many of these roadblocks. For example, a waiver by the State Board of Education of Minnesota made it possible for a school district in the state to implement the ALEM as an experimental mainstreaming program without all of the constraints usually associated with the categorizing of students, teachers, and resources (Wang, Rubenstein, & Reynolds, 1985). Similar arrangements have been proposed for providing increased state and local autonomy to identify and adopt improved, coordinated programs for students currently served by a diversity of separate, categorical programs (Wang, Reynolds, & Walberg, 1986).

Despite the current roadblocks, there is increasing evidence of a nationwide movement toward establishing partnerships that can facilitate a renegotiation between general and special education (e.g., National Association of School Psychologists, 1986; Reynolds, Wang, & Walberg, 1987; Will, 1986). Important steps in this movement include (a) the recommendations that have been made by the Office of Special Education and Rehabilitative Services, United States Department of Education, for drawing from the state of the art and state of practice in special and general education to better serve as many students with special needs as possible in regular classrooms (Will, 1986); and (b) the dialogue that has been fueled by the joint position statement of the National Association of School Psychologists and the National Coalition of Advocates for Students (NASP, 1986) regarding "appropriate educational services for all students." Thus, the time seems ripe to join the forces of reform in general and special education to capitalize on what has been learned about providing effective instruction and improving the chances of lifelong success for all students.

REFERENCES

Bangert, R. L., Kulik, J. A., & Kulik, C. C. (1983). Individualized systems of instruction in secondary schools. *Review of Educational Research, 59,* 149-158.

Becker, W. C., Engelmann, S., Carnine, D., & Rhine, W. R. (1981). Direct Instruction Model. In W. R.

Rhine (Ed.), *Making schools more effective: New directions from Follow Through* (pp. 95-154). New York: Academic.

Bennett, N. (1976). *Teaching styles and pupil progress.* Cambridge, MA: Harvard University Press.

Bloom, B. S. (1968). Learning for mastery. *Education Comment, 1,* 2.

Bright, J. T. (1987). *Adaptive Learning Environments Model: The Randolph County West Virginia Follow Through Demonstration Training Project,* Randolph County, WV: Randolph County School District.

Brophy, J. (1979). Teacher behavior and its effects. *Journal of Educational Psychology, 71*(6), 733-750.

Brophy, J., & Good, T. L. (1986). Teacher behavior and student achievement. In W. C. Wittrock (Ed.), *Handbook of research on teaching* (3rd ed., pp. 328-375). Washington, DC: American Educational Research Association.

Brown, A. L., & Campione, J. C. (1984). Three faces of transfer: Implications for early competence, individual differences, and instruction. In M. Lamb, A. Brown, & B. Rogoff (Eds.), *Advances in developmental psychology* (Vol. 3, pp. 143-192). Hillsdale, NJ: Erlbaum.

Brown, A. L., & Campione, J. C. (1986). Psychological theory and the study of learning disabilities. *American Psychologist 41,* 1059-1068.

Cantalician Foundation, Inc. (1983). *Technical assistance and alternative practices related to the problem of the over representation of Black and other minority students in classes for the educable mentally retarded.* Buffalo, NY: Author.

Carlberg, C., & Kavale, K. (1980). The efficacy of special versus regular class placement for exceptional children: A meta-analysis. *Journal of Special Education, 14,* 295-309.

Child Trends, (1985). *The school-age handicapped* (NCES 85-400). Washington, DC: U. S. Government Printing Office.

Deno, E. N. (Ed.). (1973). *Instructional alternatives for exceptional children.* Minneapolis: University of Minnesota, Leadership Training Institute.

Dollar, B., & Klinger, R. (1975). A systems approach to improving teacher effectiveness: A triadic model of consultation and change. In C. A. Parker (Ed.), *Psychological consultation: Helping teachers meet special needs* (pp. 65-81). Reston, VA: Council for Exceptional Children.

Epps, S., & Tindal, G. (1987). The effectiveness of differential programming in serving mildly handicapped students: Placement options and instruc-
tional programming. In M. C. Wang, M. C. Reynolds, & H. J. Walberg (Eds.), *Handbook of special education: Research and practice: Vol. 1. Learner characteristics and adaptive education* (pp. 213-218). Oxford, England: Pergamon.

Feistritzer, C. E. (1985). *Cheating our children: Why we need school reform.* Washington, DC: U. S. Department of Education, National Center for Educational Information.

Fullan, M. (1981). School district and school personnel in knowledge utilization. In R. Lehming & M. Kane (Eds.), *Improving schools* (pp. 212-252). Berkeley, CA: Sage.

Gilkeson, E. C., Smithberg, L. M., Bowman, G. W., & Rhine, W. R. (1981). Bank Street Model: A developmental-interaction approach. In W. R. Rhine (Ed.), *Making schools more effective: New directions from Follow Through* (pp. 249-288). New York: Academic.

Glaser, R. (1982). Instructional psychology: Past, present and future. *American Psychologist, 37,* 292-305.

Glaser, R. (1985). Education and thinking: The role of knowledge. *American Psychologist, 39,* 93-104.

Grosenick, J. K., & Reynolds, M. C. (1978). *Teacher education: Renegotiating roles for mainstreaming.* Minneapolis: University of Minnesota, Leadership Training Institute.

Harter, S. (1982). The Perceived Competence Scale for Children. *Child Development, 53,* 87-97.

Heller, K., Holtzman, W., & Messick, S. (Eds.). (1982). *Placing children in special education: A strategy for equity.* Washington, DC: National Academy of Sciences Press.

Hodgkinson, H. L. (1985). *All one system: Demographics of education — Kindergarten through graduate school.* Washington, DC: U. S. Government Printing Office.

Hughes, D., Johnson, K., Rosenbaum, S., Simons, J., & Butler, E. (1987). *The health of America's children: Maternal and child health data book.* Washington, DC: Children's Defense Fund.

Jeter, J. (Ed.). (1980). *Approaches to individualized education.* Alexandria, VA: Association for Supervision and Curriculum Development.

Klausmeier, H. J. (1975). IGE: An alternative form of schooling. In H. Talmage (Ed.), *Systems of individualized education* (pp. 48-83). Berkeley, CA: McCutchan.

Klausmeier, H. J., Quilling, M. R., Sorenson, J. S., Way, R. S., & Glasrud, G. R. (1971). *Individually guided education in the multiunit school: Guidelines for implementation.* Madison: Wisconsin Resource and Development Center for Cognitive Learning.

Klinger, R. (1975). Epilog: After the fall. In C. A. Parker (Ed.), *Psychological consultation: Helping teachers meet special needs* (pp. 94-102). Reston, VA: Council for Exceptional Children.

Leithwood, K. A., & Montgomery, D. J. (1982). The role of the elementary school principal in program improvement. *Review of Educational Research, 52,* 309-339.

Lloyd, J. W. (1988). Direct academic interventions in learning disabilities. In M. C. Wang, M. C. Reynolds, & H. J. Walberg (Eds.), *Handbook of special education: Research and practice: Vol. 2. Mildly handicapped conditions.* Oxford, England: Pergamon.

Lowe, M. R. (April, 1985). *Review of Experimental Education Programs: Montevideo Public Schools ALEM Model.* St. Paul, Minnesota: Minnesota State Department of Education.

MacPhail-Wilcox, B., & Guth, J. (1983). Effectiveness research and school administration — Both sides of the coin. *NASP Bulletin, 67*(4), 3-8.

Madden, N. A., & Slavin, R. E. (1982). *Count me in: Academic achievement and social outcomes of mainstreaming students with mild academic handicaps* (Report No. 329). Baltimore: Johns Hopkins University, Center for the Social Organization of Schools.

Mayor's Commission on Special Education. (1985). *Special Education: A call for quality.* New York: Author.

Meisgeier, C. (1976). Discussion. In M. C. Reynolds (Ed.), *Mainstreaming: Origins and implications* (pp. 36-37). Reston, VA: Council for Exceptional Children.

Montgomery, D. J., & Leithwood, K. A. (1983). *Evaluating curriculum implementation: A criterial task for the effective principal.* Paper presented at the annual meeting of the American Educational Research Association, Montreal.

National Association of School Psychologists, (1986). *Position Statement: Advocacy for appropriate educational services for all children.* Boston: National Association of School Psychologists and National Coalition of Advocates for Students.

Nevin, A., & Thousand, J. (1987). Avoiding/Limiting special education referrals: Changes and challenges. In M. C. Wang, M. C. Reynolds, & H. J. Walberg (Eds.), *Handbook of special education: Research and practice: Vol. 1. Learner characteristics and adaptive education* (pp. 273-286). Oxford, England: Pergamon.

PARC (Pennsylvania Association for Retarded Children) v. Pennsylvania, 343 F. Supp. 279 (E.D. Pa. 1972).

Peterson, P. L. (1979). Direct instruction reconsi-dered. In P. L. Peterson & H. J. Walberg (Eds.), *Research on teaching: Concepts, findings, and implications* (pp. 57-69). Berkeley, CA: McCutchan.

Pinero, V. C. (1982). Wanted: Strong instructional leaders. *Principal, 61*(4), 16-19.

Ramp, E. A., & Rhine, W. R. (1981). Behavior analysis model. In W. R. Rhine (Ed.), *Making schools more effective: New directions From Follow Through* (pp. 155-200). New York: Academic.

Reynolds, M. C., & Wang, M. C. (1983). Restructuring "special" school programs: A position paper. *Policy Studies Review, 2*(1), 189-212.

Reynolds, M. C., Wang, M. C., & Walberg, H. J. (1987). The necessary restructuring of special and regular education. *Exceptional Children, 53*(5), 391-398.

Rosenshine, B. V. (1979). Content, time, and direct instruction. In P. L. Peterson & H. J. Walberg (Eds.), *Research on teaching: Concepts, findings and implications* (pp. 28-56). Berkeley, CA: McCutchan.

Sharp, B. L. (Ed.). (1982). *Deans Grant Projects: Challenge and change in teacher education.* Minneapolis: University of Minnesota, National Support Systems Project.

Slavin, R. E. (1983). *Cooperative learning.* New York: Longman.

Slavin, R. E., Leavey, M., & Madden, N. A. (1982, March). *Effects of student teams and individualized instruction on student mathematics achievement, attitudes, and behaviors.* Paper presented at the annual meeting of the American Educational Research Association, New York.

Strom, C. D., & Wang, M. C. (1982, March). *A validation study of a degree of program implementation assessment instrument.* Paper presented at the annual meeting of the National Council on Measurement in Education, New York.

U. S. Bureau of the Census. (1982). *Statistical abstract of the United States, 1982–1983.* Washington, DC: U. S. Government Printing Office.

Walberg, H. J., & Wang, M. C. (1987). Effective educational practices and provisions for individual differences. In M. C. Wang, M. C. Reynolds, & H. J. Walberg (Eds.), *Handbook of special education: Research and practice: Vol. 1. Learner characteristics and adaptive education* (pp. 113-128). Oxford, England: Pergamon.

Wang, M. C. (1974a). *The rationale and design of the Self-Schedule System* (LRDC Publication Series 1974/5). Pittsburgh: University of Pittsburgh, Learning Research and Development Center.

Wang, M. C. (1974b). *The use of direct observation to study instructional–learning behaviors in school settings* (LRDC Publication Series 1974/9). Pittsburgh: University of Pittsburgh, Learning Research and Development Center.

Wang, M. C. (Ed.). (1976). *The Self-Schedule System of instructional-learning management for adaptive school learning environments (LRDC Publication Series*, 1976/9). Pittsburgh: University of Pittsburgh, Learning Research and Development Center.

Wang, M. C. (1980). Adaptive instruction: Building on diversity. *Theory Into Practice, 19*(2), 122-128.

Wang, M. C. (1981). Mainstreaming exceptional children: Some instructional design considerations. *Elementary School Journal, 81*(4), 195-221.

Wang, M. C. (1982). *Effective mainstreaming is possible — Provided that . . . (LRDC) Publication Series*, (1982/13). Pittsburgh: University of Pittsburgh, Learning Research and Development Center.

Wang, M. C. (1987). Analysis of the impact of the dissemination component of the National Follow Through Program. In M. C. Wang and E. A. Ramp (Principal Investigators), *The National Follow Through Program: Design, implementation, and effects* (Vol. 1, Final Project Report for the project funded by the Office of Elementary and Secondary Education, U. S. Department of Education). Philadelphia: Temple University Center for Research in Human Development and Education.

Wang, M. C. & Baker, E. T. (1985-1986). Mainstreaming programs: Design features and effects. *Journal of Special Education, 19*(4), 503-521.

Wang, M. C., & Birch, J. W. (1984a). Comparison of a full-time mainstreaming program and a resource room approach. *Exceptional Children, 51*, 33-40.

Wang, M. C. & Birch, J. W. (1984b). Effective special education in regular classes. *Exceptional Children, 50*, 391-398.

Wang, M. C., Catalano, R., & Gromoll, G. (1983). *Training manual for the Implementation Assessment Battery for Adaptive Instruction*. Philadelphia: Temple University Center for Research in Human Development and Education.

Wang, M. C., & Gennari, P. (1983). Analysis of the design, implementation, and effects of a data-based staff development program. *Teacher Education and Special Education, 6*(4), 211-226.

Wang, M. C., Gennari, P., & Waxman, H. C. (1985). The Adaptive Learning Environments Model: Design, implementation, and effects. In M. C. Wang & H. J. Walberg (Eds.), *Adapting instruction to individual differences* (pp. 191-235). Berkeley, CA: McCutchan.

Wang, M. C., & Lindvall, C. M. (1984). Individual differences and school learning environments. In E. W. Gordon (Ed.), *Review of research in education* (pp. 165-225). Washington, DC: American Educational Research Association.

Wang, M. C., Nojan, M., Strom, C. D., & Walberg, H. J. (1984). The utility of degree of implementation measures in program evaluation and implementation research. *Curriculum Inquiry, 14*(3), 249-286.

Wang, M. C., Peverly, S. T., & Catalano, R. (1987). Integrating special needs students in regular classes: Programming, implementation, and policy issues. In J. Gottlieb & B. W. Gottlieb (Eds.), *Advances in special education.* (Vol. 6, pp. 119-149). Greenwich, CT: JAI Press.

Wang, M. C., Peverly, S. T., & Randolph, R. (1984). An investigation of the implementation and effects of a full-time mainstreaming program. *Journal of Remedial and Special Education, 5*(6), 21-32.

Wang, M. C., Reynolds, M. C., & Walberg, H. J. (1986). Rethinking special education. *Educational Leadership, 44*(1), 26-31.

Wang, M. C. Rubenstein, J. L., & Reynolds, M. C. (1985). Clearing the road to success for students with special needs. *Educational Leadership, 43*(1), 62-67.

Wang, M. C., & Vaughan, E. D. (1987a). *Handbook for the implementation of adaptive instruction programs: Module 4. Curriculum resources for individualizing instruction.* Philadelphia: Temple University Center for Research in Human Development and Education.

Wang, M. C., & Vaughan, E. D. (1987b). *Handbook for the implementation of adaptive instruction programs: Module 2. Needs assessment and implementation planning.* Philadelphia: Temple University Center for Research in Human Development and Education.

Wang, M. C., & Walberg, H. J. (1983). Adaptive instruction and classroom time. *American Educational Research Journal, 20*, 601-626.

Wang, M. C., & Walberg, H. J. (Eds.). (1985). *Adapting instruction to individual differences.* Berkeley, CA: McCutchan.

Wang, M. C., & Walberg, H. J. (in press). Exemplary implementation of eight innovative instructional models. *International Journal of Educational Research.*

Waxman, H. C., Wang, M. C., Anderson, K. A., & Walberg, H. J. (1985). *Adaptive education and student outcomes: A quantitative synthesis.* Pittsburgh: University of Pittsburgh, Learning Research and Development Center.

Will, M. C. (1986). Educating children with learning problems: A shared responsibility. *Exceptional Children, 52*(2), 411-416.

Winter, D. (1987). *Adaptive Learning Environments Model: The Waterloo Community Schools, Iowa Follow Through Demonstration Training Project.* Waterloo, IA: Waterloo School District.

Zill, N. (1985, June 25). *How is the number of children with severe handicaps likely to change over time?* Testimony before the Subcommittee on Select Education for the Committee on Education. U. S. House of Representatives, Washington.

11

Primary Prevention in the Schools: Methods for Enhancing Student Competence

Robert K. Conyne,
Joseph E. Zins, and
Stacey Vedder-Dubocq
University of Cincinnati

A long-standing, albeit not always primary or explicit, goal of our nation's schools has been the promotion of students' social and emotional development. Today, this goal is even more critical as children and adolescents face a myriad of potentially detrimental influences and circumstances. Among these are sexual abuse, teen and youth suicide, AIDS, substance abuse, parents' divorce, eating disorders, limited parental supervision, truancy, delinquency, illiteracy, family violence, single-parent homes, parents' alcoholism, psychological maltreatment, unemployment, psychiatric disturbance, dropping out of school, racism, school violence, and so on.

Schools provide what is perhaps the most accessible opportunity for addressing these complex, challenging problems. They are the only existing institution in which almost all children spend considerable amounts of time (Shaw, 1986). Moreover, as a main center of socialization, schools are in a position of encouraging the development of prosocial behaviors such as helping, cooperating, and caring, particularly through their capacity to create supportive, healthy environments (Harris, Eisenberg, & Carroll, 1982; Zins & Ponti, 1985). Such environments are illustrated in a number of ways, including positive teacher attitudes, peer-mediated and cooperative learning strategies, individualized learning environments, and other active involvement

processes (Astin, 1984; Johnson & Johnson, 1986a, 1986b; Remer, Niguette, Anderson, & Terrell, 1984).

The creation in the schools of "healthy environments" represents one key element of an educational and mental health intervention strategy, *primary prevention*, that recently has sparked a great deal of interest. Schools have been an especially popular setting for conducting primary prevention programs. For example, such programs have frequently been implemented to reduce or avert problems relating to health, sexual activity, social adjustment, and substance abuse (Weisheit, Hopkins, Kearney, & Mauss, 1984).

Briefly, primary prevention interventions are undertaken to prevent negative consequences from occurring later in students' lives. For instance, high-risk junior high school students have been taught a series of personal and social skills, yielding largely successful results in the prevention of tobacco, alcohol, and marijuana use (Botvin, 1983; Botvin & Dusenbury, 1987). Young children have been taught to avoid injuries on their way to school through programs directed toward seat belt use, pedestrian safety, and avoidance of abduction by strangers (Peterson, in press). The concept of helping people as soon as possible to avoid problems that might arise later on offers an efficacious alternative to the dominant and costly helping practice of remediating educational and psychological distress or malfunctioning *after* it has already taken root and is therefore more difficult to treat.

Primary prevention in the schools is a promising educational services delivery alternative for school psychologists and other special services staff. Many of the other alternatives discussed in this book, such as peer and cooperative learning, and social skills and behavioral interventions, can be implemented on a primary prevention basis (although they more frequently are applied on a remedial basis). Therefore, our goals are to sensitize school psychologists to the potential of primary prevention programs and to encourage them to become involved in such efforts. The involvement of school psychologists and other specialists in such activities simply makes good sense. As Shaw (1986) has observed:

> Counselors and school psychologists have two real advantages with respect to the provision of primary preventive services. First, they are already present in the schools; it is not necessary to develop and pay for a new professional to provide primary preventive services. ... Second, counselors and psychologists have a background of training that will make it possible for them to provide primary preventive services with a minimum of additional preparation. (p. 626)

Therefore, while some resource reallocation and retraining of personnel is required to implement such services, primary prevention programs in the schools do not add significantly to the present set of school functions, and in fact they parallel existing tasks. More importantly, evidence is mounting that an impressive number of primary preventive interventions provide substantive help to students and thus have the desirable side effect of making the jobs of teachers and administrators easier rather than more difficult (e.g., Aspy & Roebuck, 1977; Baker, Swisher, Nadenichek, & Popowicz, 1984; Gelfand, Ficula, & Zarbatany, 1986; Jason, Durlak, & Holton-Walker, 1984).

In this chapter, we first provide a conceptual model for understanding primary prevention in mental health.

Definitional clarity is fundamental to the subsequent implementation of effective services and programs. Next, various approaches to primary prevention are described. Finally, discussion of how to plan, implement, and evaluate primary preventive services in the schools is included, along with practical guidelines to follow. A number of examples of school interventions are provided throughout the chapter that illustrate concretely how primary prevention can be accomplished by school psychologists and related personnel. Although we have limited our discussion to students as targets of these interventions, teachers and other school personnel likewise could be the recipients of primary prevention efforts (see, for example, Blair, Collingwood, Smith, Upton, & Sterling, 1985).

PRIMARY PREVENTION IN MENTAL HEALTH

Major Dimensions

Considerable confusion has surrounded the concept of primary prevention in mental health (Klein & Goldston, 1977), and it has contributed to difficulties in converting the concept into practice. For this reason, we provide a clear conceptual framework so that practice can be well guided. Seven general dimensions characterize primary prevention in mental health. As will become clear, we view the mental health domain broadly, and regard it to be often closely interrelated with physical health.

Ecological Orientation. Practitioners involved in primary prevention efforts reject the total reliance on an individual or intrapersonal interpretation of student behavior; instead, they favor an ecological perspective. That is, primary preventionists tend to look to both human *and* environmental explanations and interventions (Conyne, 1985). Indeed, the interaction of people with environments is the basis of an ecological orientation.

Take, for example, the situation in a classroom in which most students appear lethargic and bored. One interpretation of this problem might be that "the students just don't care." This assumption represents a person-level explanation. An ecological perspective, on the other hand, encourages examination of all factors, including not only the persons involved, but environmental factors as well. Perhaps the real culprit in this example is not to be found in the students at all, but in the physical properties of the classroom if, at two o'clock during a blazing, hot, humid September, it provides an uncomfortable, cloistered, hothouse instructional setting.

In a word, primary preventive interventions are designed with persons *and* settings in mind. In fact, some observers have called for concentrating primary prevention efforts on high-risk settings instead of high-risk people (Price, Bader, & Ketterer, 1980).

Groups and populations as targets. Primary prevention interventions are intended for groups of people rather than individual students. The idea is to institute a program, such as social skills development, that benefits a maximum number of potentially affected students by strengthening them against or by eliminating hazards from their lives. This orientation reflects the public health influence on primary prevention, although that perspective often is applied less rigorously in the schools.

When possible, school psychologists seek to benefit targeted groups, organizations, neighborhoods, or communities through specific programs and services designed to prevent psychopathology or educational failure. To this end, competency-building workshops, physical fitness programs, implementation of social policies supportive of prenatal care, mass media educational campaigns, and organizational change efforts are conducted to keep vulnerable target members healthy.

Wellness. Primary prevention services and programs are directed at students who presently are "well." That is, these individuals are functioning adequately in their life situations, with no appreciable debilitating deficits. Of course, this level of functioning is difficult to assess with any degree of certainty. Essentially, however, on a broad level we are trying to distinguish between children who are "OK" from those in whom a particular deficit has been identified, who are "not OK." Generally, primary prevention in mental health is not intended for those currently maladjusted or seriously troubled. It is a before-the-fact intervention offered to students prior to identification or entrenchment of problems.

At-risk populations. Although the targeted students are considered to be doing well, they may still be "in harm's way." They may be at risk for developing some type of dysfunction at a future point, in consequence of a special vulnerability rooted in life circumstances that might have resulted from some precipitous combination of environmental and genetic variables. For instance, they might be poor, minority group members, and from single parent families — an aggregation of factors that leaves them particularly open to physical and psychological adversity. They might have been recent victims of a natural disaster, such as a tornado that destroyed their family's possessions, or the children of parents undergoing a divorce. They personally might be approaching a major transition point in their lives, such as moving from elementary to middle school, or from one neighborhood to another. Whatever the life circumstance, these presently well students may find themselves moving toward the possibility of disruption. This well-but-at-risk factor makes them candidates for primary prevention.

Proactive approach. As might be anticipated from the above criteria, students do not usually present themselves at the door of a primary prevention worker seeking help of some kind! Well people have a tendency to revel in their health, and even those at risk may be quite oblivious to their potential need for any help. In most cases, then, primary prevention programs take the form of outreach. The prevention staff engages in a proactive process of learning about potential needs, designing programs that address these needs (desirably in collaboration with members of the target group), and then implementing and evaluating the project so designed. This process contrasts with the reactive approach to delivery of services commonly found in most schools.

This proactive, intentional program development and evaluation process is examined at some length later in this chapter. Let it suffice for now to emphasize that primary prevention interventions are characterized by their intentional nature, their reliance on accurate needs assessment data, and on sound planning principles.

Empowerment. Rappaport (1981) touched a raw nerve for many psychologists when he dismissed certain forms of primary prevention (the "person-centered," which focuses on assisting groups of individuals to enhance their personal competence) as but another effort of the mental health establishment to take charge of the lives of the less fortunate. He decried what he saw as a top-down process of help-giving, whereby professionals *do something to* the recipients of the assistance. He envisioned in its place a collaborative, *working with* process between professionals and community members that is based on justice, the provision of life opportunities, and the strengthening and freeing of resources.

Other observers, such as Cowen (1985), look to the empowering qualities embedded in sensitively designed and conducted primary prevention efforts. For example, they hold that many competency enhancement programs, such as problem-solving or community organizing, in which people learn important life skills, possess the elements necessary to empowering people to reach higher levels of functioning. We tend to agree with this assessment. However, we are ever more aware of the potential of professional helpers to be power-robbing, rather than empowering — even in primary prevention efforts — for the reasons delineated in Rappaport's (1981) critique.

Direct and indirect methods. As we have seen, primary preventive interventions can be conducted with at-risk people or with at-risk settings. Furthermore, these interventions can be delivered directly or indirectly.

Direct methods, which are conducted face to face with students, are familiar to school psychologists and other special services staff. The helper meets with students and does something — counsels, teaches, organizes, advises, trains — that is meant to be directly beneficial to those clients.

Indirect methods are not used as often by many practitioners. However, they are being adopted with increasing frequency by those engaged in primary prevention as a means of extending helpers' impact. Greater numbers of students can be reached if the school psychologist can work through others or through technology. In the indirect approach, face-to-face interaction between the professional helper and those being assisted is sacrificed in order to multiply the helper's influence. Individual and organizational consultation, in-service training, and use of various media (e.g., pamphlets and computers) are prominent indirect modes in use today.

PRIMARY PREVENTION APPROACHES

Keeping in mind the dimensions of primary prevention discussed above, we can now consider a conceptual framework for primary prevention techniques, drawn largely from the work of Cowen (1985), that can aid both understanding and action. We also present some brief illustrations of school-based primary prevention efforts that correspond to the model.

Two broad approaches to delivery of school psychology services are used to accomplish primary prevention goals. These are the macrosocial approach, in which broad-scale social change is attempted, and the person-centered approach, in which competency enhancement is sought. Figure 1 contains a listing of these approaches and the variations contained within them. Throughout the review of the various primary prevention alternatives, it should be kept in mind that these programs are more effectively and efficiently implemented through the *collaborative* efforts of school personnel, parents, students, and community

FIGURE 1
Approaches to Primary Prevention

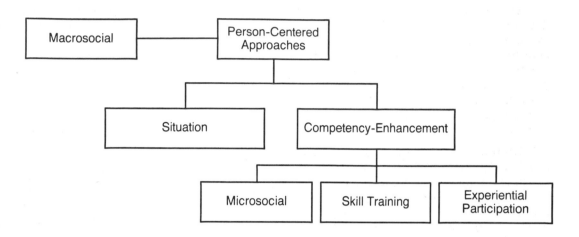

members. Furthermore, a major function of school psychologists in primary prevention efforts often is to act in a consultative capacity (Zins & Wagner, 1987), although their role is not limited to this modality.

Macrosocial-Focused Approaches

The macrosocial approach is the *sine qua non* of primary prevention in mental health, although it is not the major emphasis of this chapter. It is synonymous with large-scale social change efforts that are concerned with altering the widespread problems of the whole of society itself, including sexism, racism, ageism, injustice, handicappism, unequal distribution of wealth, poverty, limited opportunities, unemployment, and powerlessness (Albee, 1986; Rappaport, 1977, 1981). This approach contrasts with the microsocial, to be discussed later, which is concerned with bounded social entities such as a school or a church. From the perspective of macrosocial change, social pathogens, such as racism, are held responsible for the germination of dysfunction in students' lives. Consequently, it is held, basic system change is necessary to remove the very sources of distress.

How macrosocial change can be accomplished by school psychologists and other helpers is a complex question that cannot be addressed adequately within

the confines of this chapter. However, general means for accomplishing this goal have been suggested. These include serving as an advocate (Glidewell, 1984), a public policy influencer or developer (Sarason, 1984), a leader in professional organizations, an administrator of a human resource agency, a legislator or staff assistant, an expert witness (Task Force on Psychology, 1986), and an empowerer (Rappaport, Swift, & Hess, 1984). NASP efforts to advocate at the federal legislative level for implementation and funding of alternative educational services delivery systems, for "student rights without labels," and to abolish corporal punishment in the schools are concrete examples of such activities. Enactment of Public Law 94-142, which was instrumental in ensuring that appropriate educational services are to be provided to all students, was made possible, in part, by the efforts of large numbers of professionals and parents. Accordingly, from this perspective, it can be considered as another example of macrosocial change.

Assuming any of these responsibilities, some or all of which may seem, at first blush, to be unlikely roles for school services personnel, places the school psychologist in a position of changing or shaping the basic societal forces that contribute to student dysfunction. These are the kinds of involvements that Sarason (1984) labeled "missed opportunities" for psychologists and about which Albee (1986), in his article on a just society, stated:

> Psychologists must join with persons who reject racism, sexism, colonialism, and exploitation and must find ways to redistribute social power and to increase social justice. Primary prevention research inevitably will make clear the relationship between social pathology and psychopathology and then will work to change social and political structures in the interest of social justice. It is as simple and as difficult as that! (p. 897)

Although it can be overwhelming to consider researching and undertaking efforts to bring about these broad, societal changes, it must be remembered that such change is accomplished precisely through the efforts of concerned individuals. Each of us can be active in this regard, and collectively, we can exert significant societal influence.

Person-Centered Approaches

Person-centered approaches are used to build the competencies of targeted students so that they can function more effectively. An example is found in training high-risk adolescents in communication skills such as listening, questioning, and conflict management as an antidote to dropping out of school. The emphasis of the person-centered approach is on strengthening people against stressors, whereas the focus of the macro social approach is on eliminating major stressors from society.

The person-centered approach is composed of two main elements (Cowen, 1985): a situation focus, and a competency enhancement focus, both of which are used to strengthen the capacities of students.

Situation focus. The situation focus in person-centered change is reactive in the sense that primary preventive measures are enacted in response to some event or presenting life situation. The intent of this focus is to enhance children's capacities to cope more effectively with stressful life situations, events, and transitions, and to forestall an otherwise likely set of negative consequences. Thus, in the situation focus, the event or the anticipated event can be thought of as the antecedent triggering the primary preventive program.

Many examples exist of events and transitions that students may encounter throughout their school careers, some of which we have mentioned previously. There are certain life situations that have been shown to be inherently and predictably stressful. These include "transition periods" that most children will face at some point such as entrance into kindergarten, promotion to senior high school, geographic relocation, and the arrival of a new sibling (Zins & Ponti, 1985). Children also may experience other less predictable but inherently stressful life events and transitions such as the loss of a parent through death or divorce, hospitalization, the serious illness of a sibling, and adoption (Felner, 1984).

Other kinds of events also occur that are unexpected and often devastating. Among them are such tragedies as tornados and other natural disasters, and the all-too-common occurrence in modern society of rampages in which someone maims or kills a number of people. Still other examples are found in the lives of especially vulnerable populations. These children often can be identified demographically, and they face stressors involving long-standing situations such as living below the poverty level, being a member of a single-parent family on public assistance, suffering from a chronic illness, or having a parent who has alcoholism or a psychiatric disturbance. Although individual reactions to any of these stressful life events vary considerably (Bloom, 1977), there is growing evidence that they increase vulnerability to psychological, behavioral, and somatic disturbances as well as to school adjustment difficulties (Felner, Primavera, & Cauce, 1981; Rickel & Langer, 1985; Sterling, Cowen, Weissberg, Lotyezewsky, & Boike, 1985). There are, fortunately, a number of situation-focused primary preventive programs aimed at children and adolescents that have been conducted successfully. Several are briefly reviewed here.

Some preventive efforts to enhance the adaptive efforts of students experiencing school transition have focused on providing support groups of peers to facilitate coping and provide understanding of the new school's expectations and regulations (Bogat, Jones, & Jason, 1980). In another successful prevention program, Felner, Ginter, and Primavera (1982) promoted direct changes in the school environment to facilitate students' mastery of the tasks involved in school transfer. This program had two primary components. The first consisted of restructuring the role of homeroom teachers so that they served as the "primary administrative-counseling link" (p. 281) between students and their parents. They provided services such as helping students schedule classes, contacting parents regarding absences, and counseling students about personal or school-related problems. The second component involved reorganizing the school environment by scheduling all primary academic classes with the same peer group in an effort to facilitate the construction of social networks and increase a sense of belonging. Thus, the approach sought (a) to increase the amount of social support from teachers and peers, (b) to decrease the feelings of isolation and anonymity typically encountered in high school, and (c) to decrease the degree of chaotic change and complexity in the school environment.

Zins and Ponti (1985) described how "antecedent systematic desensitization" can be used effectively with young children entering school. Prior to the official opening of school in the fall, they suggested that children be accompanied by their parent(s) on a tour of the school building. The children would then be brought to their preassigned classrooms to meet their new teacher and to play with their classmates, while still in the presence of their parent(s) and teacher. Parent(s) then are faded out gradually once the children appear to be adjusted to the new setting, teacher, and classmates. This "anticipatory guidance" approach may take longer with some children, but the primary intention is to facilitate school adjustment prior to the chaotic time during which other, older students arrive. A similar approach might be used to help students make the transition from elementary school to junior high.

Separation and divorce of parents also have received considerable attention as potentially stressful life events. Research has clearly documented the negative effects that the divorce experience can have on children (e.g., Guidubaldi, Cleminshaw, Perry, & Mcloughlin, 1983). Most prevention programs in schools attempt to help students effectively adapt to the challenges and changes posed by parental divorce by providing a supportive atmosphere in which children can (a) share common experiences including divorce-related feelings and learn how to more effectively identify, express, and deal with these feelings; (b) clarify common misconceptions about divorce related to such issues as attribution, blame, and concerns about their future; (c) reduce feelings of isolation and stigma; and (d) learn problem-solving, communication, and anger-control skills (e.g., Pedro-Carroll & Cowen, 1985; Pedro-Carroll, Cowen, Hightower, & Guare, 1986; Stolberg & Garrison, 1985).

Competency enhancement. The competency enhancement focus in person-centered change is a proactive effort (Cowen, 1985). That is, these kinds of interventions are meant to be taken, not only before the fact, but also without reliance on any triggering events. This distinction between reactive and proactive efforts (Catalano & Dooley, 1980), when applied to competency enhancement, seems to be helpful conceptually, but quite difficult to make in practice.

Three variations of competency enhancement have been identified (Cowen, 1985). These are microsocial, skills training, and experiential participation.

The *microsocial* form of competency enhancement overlaps considerably with the macrosocial approach discussed earlier. The intent of both is to remove environmental barriers. The main difference is that of scope. In the microsocial form, the focus for environmental change is limited to groups, single schools, a neighborhood in a community, or some other bounded social entity. This contrasts with the macrosocial approach, which targets for change negative elements of the whole of society.

Microsocial change seeks to advance human competency by altering environmental conditions through a vast array of interventions that can be directed toward the five service areas typically provided by school organizations: assessment services, instructional services, related services, personnel development services, and administrative services (Maher, Illback, & Zins, 1984a).

Comer (1985) illustrated this approach quite well in his Yale–New Haven Primary Prevention Project. This program produced academic and social gains in racial and ethnic minority students through a continuing and interrelated series of environmental changes in the schools themselves. These changes included establishment of a representative governance group, a parent participation group and program, a mental health team and program, and an academic (curriculum and staff development) program. As Comer wrote, "The assumption is that the vast majority of children can acquire the psychological, social, and academic competencies needed to function adequately in and after school when the school environment is adequate" (p. 155).

Forman (1984) suggested using behavioral and cognitive behavioral staff (e.g., teacher) development approaches as a means to facilitate professional performance. Possible goals include increasing teachers' use of these methods to enhance student competence, and the use of these techniques to improve teachers' personal adjustment (e.g., stress reduction). This readily available technology can be of tremendous benefit in improving the functioning of the school organization.

Alternatively, classroom environments can be the focus of microsocial change efforts. Researchers have found that classrooms that are perceived to be high in order and organization, affiliation,

and innovation, promoted a more positive mood, greater peer popularity, and better adjustment among students (Wright & Cowen, 1982). Preventive efforts, therefore, can focus on training teachers to employ clearly defined rules and structure, and to use cooperative, interdependent teaching approaches (i.e., peer and cross-age tutoring) to enhance these environmental variables. Additional examples include establishing linkages with community and government agencies, information management, and coordinating regular and special education (see Maher, Illback, & Zins, 1984b, for additional discussion). In sum, it is clear that establishing healthy, prosocial environments can be accomplished through a wide variety of interventions.

Skills training is perhaps the major form of competency enhancement. The premise is that persons at risk can avoid encountering future dysfunction through training in age- and situation-appropriate skills. Once these skills are mastered and maintained, it is thought that they will then possess the resources necessary to coping more effectively with demands that they will face later in life.

Illustrative of the circumstances in which skills training can be usefully applied are the so-called milestone events that many or all individuals face in this culture: passing from home to school, entering adolescence, obtaining employment, getting married, becoming a new parent, and retiring. Each of them calls for a developmental adaptation. Thus, milestones represent a kind of developmental crisis point, the severity of which may be a function of the level of appropriate coping skills a person has attained, and the resources available in the immediate environment.

Another source of stressors that can give rise to a need for social skills training is the negative or limiting role models to which children too frequently are exposed. Advertisements, television (both programs and commercials), and popular press magazines, among other forms of media encountered daily, frequently do not portray healthy role models. Much of the content of the communications media is characterized by stereotyped sex role behaviors (Downs & Gowan, 1980), unrealistic representations of the handicapped (Donaldson, 1981), and portrayals of ethnic minorities as incompetent and unassertive (Barcus, 1983). Even though there has been greater sensitivity to these issues in recent years, these representations continue to be found too frequently.

Skills training programs (not all of which would meet the criteria for primary prevention, since they often are applied in a remedial fashion) are being increasingly made available "before the fact" to students who are about to pass through a certain point in their lives during which they likely will be exposed to potentially negative influences or limiting models. These include programs on preparation for childbirth, racial awareness, increasing sensitivity to the handicapped, interpersonal cognitive problem solving, study skills, stress management, and communication and assertiveness training. Several chapters in this volume address skills training programs (e.g., learning strategies, social skills) that could be implemented preventively. Two programs that we believe have tremendous potential are outlined briefly as examples of effective skills training programs.

Earlier we referred to the Life Skills Training program (Botvin, 1983; Botvin & Dusenbury, 1987), which is directed toward preventing substance abuse (alcohol, tobacco, and marijuana) and is based upon social learning (Bandura, 1977) and problem-behavior theories (Jessor & Jessor, 1977). Its goals include competency development in the areas of social skills, self-control, problem-solving, and study skills. There are three major components: (a) dealing with decision making and self-improvement, anxiety, and advertising; (b) considering the consequences of various health behaviors and the problems of resisting peer pressure; and (c) undertaking social skills training, including communication and assertiveness.

Elias, Clabby, and associates (Elias & Clabby, 1982; Elias, Clabby, Corr, Ubriaco, & Schuyler, 1982; Elias et al., 1986) have developed a comprehensive social skills program for elementary students that can be taught directly by teachers in regular classrooms. It involves introducing students to an eight-step problem-solving sequence that includes (a) focusing on one's own feelings in relation to problem situations, (b) putting feelings into words, (c) thinking about appropriate goals, (d) considering alternatives to attaining the goals and their potential consequences, (e) evaluating and choosing alternatives, (f) making plans for carrying out solutions, (g) anticipating and dealing with possible obstacles, and (h) developing positive expectations for addressing similar problems in the future.

Experiential participation constitutes the third form of competency enhancement. Rather than being the direct recipients of skills training, it is possible for students to experience competency enhancement through their own involvement as a helper. When such growth occurs, it can be viewed as a side-benefit and a kind of welcomed surprise, although in many instances such benefits are purposefully encouraged as an integral part of competency enhancement programs. Riessman (1965) has termed this phenomenon the "helper-therapy principle." Among the more widely adopted approaches are peer counseling, cross-age tutoring, and cooperative learning strategies. Several of these techniques are discussed at some length in other chapters of this volume (although not necessarily from a preventive point of view), but a brief summary of the major characteristics of cooperative learning can serve to illustrate this type of intervention.

Classroom instruction can be organized along a continuum of differentiated techniques that tend to enhance or to impede student interpersonal interactions and experiences that can contribute to goal attainment (Johnson & Johnson, 1986a, 1986b). In other words, teachers can exert tremendous influence regarding student patterns of interaction and interpersonal attraction. In *competitive* situations, students' goal achievements are negatively correlated. That is, a win-lose situation exists in which students work against one another to achieve a goal that only one or a few can attain. In *individualistic* situations, students work independently and there is no relationship among students in respect to goal attainment. Individual actions do not influence others' goal attainment, and students seek outcomes that are personally beneficial, ignoring as irrelevant the achievement of their classmates. These goal patterns inform a great deal of U.S. instructional practice today, and students come to school most commonly with competitive expectations.

An emphasis on *cooperative* interactions, however, links individual students so that there is a strong relationship between their joint interactions and goal attainment. They are encouraged to learn in pairs or small groups through helping each other master the assigned material. Students are taught that they can reach their learning goals only if other students in the learning group also are successful. Thus, students seek outcomes that are beneficial to all of those with whom they are cooperatively linked (Johnson & Johnson, 1986a, 1986b).

Research conducted by the Johnsons and others have found that such strategies result in higher achievement and retention of information (Johnson, Maruyama, Johnson, Nelson, & Skon, 1981). Additionally, increases have been found to occur in a variety of prosocial skills such as helping, sharing, and cooperating (Johnson & Johnson, 1983; Slavin, 1983) that were not necessarily specific goals of the program. This brief example demonstrates the potential value of experiential participation.

PROGRAM DEVELOPMENT

How can this conceptual framework for primary prevention in mental health be put into practice in the schools? The operational question is "How does one move from conception to implementation?" In answering this question, it is necessary to consider a systematic, planned approach to the translation of thinking to acting. Program development is an approach that can be particularly

helpful in accomplishing this task.

Program development is a practical process that begins with conceptualization of a program and other issues related to its creation, proceeds through program implementation, and ends with program evaluation. Essentially, a systematic problem-solving process that is cyclical and recursive is used. That is, program development includes the use of feedback throughout its several steps so that program designers and implementers (who may be the same or different people) are consistently kept informed about how the program is being conducted and with what effects. This continual information flow is important so that the program can be kept "on course," with any necessary modifications made along the way. Furthermore, collaboration among all parties involved in the program is essential — the program should not be done *to* organizational members; it should be implemented *with* them.

The systematic program development approach presented below is made up of three major steps and one recurring process. The steps are: planning, implementing, and evaluating. The recurring process is feedback, and it has to do with information that is produced about the program's implementation. Feedback is used by program personnel, as we mentioned earlier, to keep the program on target. An outline of these steps is contained in Table 1. Although we have organized the discussion according to these steps, in reality the steps are interrelated and interdependent. Our specific focus is on two of the three steps of the program development model: planning and evaluation. If these steps have been handled well, the implementation step should proceed almost automatically.

Planning, the first step of program development, contains five major substeps. As we briefly describe them, we provide some illustrations intended to provide guidance in actually performing such activities. Following the planning phase, we briefly address the second step, implementation. Finally, we review the third step, evaluation, and its two sub-

TABLE 1
Program Development Steps

Step 1: Planning	
A. Identify the generative base	
B. Assess needs and potential targets	
C. Set goals	↑
D. Select strategy	
E. Prepare for implementation	
Step 2: Implementation	Feedback
Step 3: Evaluation	
A. Formative evaluation	↓
B. Summative evaluation	
C. Dissemination and utilization of results	

steps. After this discussion, we show how the program development approach can be used in an actual primary prevention case. In addition, we recommend several other sources that provide more extensive information about the program development process in primary prevention (e.g., Conyne, 1987; Coursey, 1977; Cowen, 1984; Craig, 1978; Moore & Delworth, 1976; NIAAA, 1978; Price & Smith, 1985; Wilson & Yager, 1981). Also, Maher and Bennett (1984) have provided an excellent discussion of program planning and evaluation in schools that is applicable to primary prevention programs.

Step 1: Planning

Substep A: Identify the generative base. Generally, becoming familiar with the research and practical literature is a necessary first (or sometimes a second) step. This means studying what has been done in relation to primary prevention in the schools and in other settings (e.g., reviewing the *Journal of Primary Prevention, Prevention in Human Services, American Journal of Community Psychology,* and relevant books). What has worked? What has not been effective? Are there examples in the literature of particular competency enhancement programs that could be suitable for your setting? Are there illustrations of effective programs that have targeted adolescents and drug abuse, if that is an issue for you?

Knowing what has been done in the past and what has or has not worked gives one a tremendous advantage. It may even be possible to identify an effective primary prevention program that could be largely replicated in your own school, or that would take minimal modification to conduct. For instance, Botvin's Life Skills Training program (1983), and the social problem-solving programs of Weissberg and Gesten (Weissberg, Gesten, Leibenstein, Docherty-Schmid, & Hutton, 1980) and Elias and Clabby (1982) are readily applicable.

Substep B: Assess needs and targets. The next step is locally done. It involves the collection of information that allows program planners to authoritatively identify what needs exist, for whom, and in what settings.

In primary prevention, the most important question in determining needs is that of incidence. Incidence is an epidemiological term referring to the number of new cases of a problem or dysfunction that occur within a designated population. For example, for adolescent problem behaviors occurring following the drinking of alcoholic beverages (e.g., arrests, car accidents, blackouts, property damage, arguments, fights, school absences, poor grades, etc.), incidence is established by determining how many new instances of these problem behaviors occurred within a given period of time. Incidence is important to determine because one goal of primary prevention programs is to reduce or eliminate the number of *new* cases of a problem behavior or situation. If an accurate estimate of incidence can be obtained, then the program, when compared to stasis in a control situation, can be said to exert a primary preventive effect.

Substep C: Set goals: Once a local needs assessment is completed, program designers compare its results with the literature review already conducted. For instance, it may be shown that a high incidence of alcohol-related problems in a school under study mirrors the situation nationally, or in other similar schools, and that it therefore may make sense to consider the application of effective published programs on alcohol abuse prevention in the local setting.

First, however, specific goal setting must occur. The target population and setting must be identified as closely as possible. Is it boys only? What ages? Do black adolescents in the school experience the same kinds and amounts of alcohol-related problems as whites? Are there certain grades, or classrooms that should be selected? What about academic performance and drinking? What kinds of alcohol-related problems ought to be prevented (e.g., social ones, such as arguing and fighting)? What time period will be selected within which the program will be conducted? How will a reduction in incidence be ascertained (e.g., in numbers, in percentages, through some test of statistical significance)? Determining answers to these kinds of questions in the goal-setting step of program development should be based on the assessment information already collected.

Substep D: Select strategy. Once needs have been determined and goals established, it becomes possible to consider how the program will be designed to attain those goals. This "how" of the program is a matter of examining various program strategies.

Our experience suggests that many program planners rush to one strategy — usually their own pet one, or one that they have seen working in other situations —

and almost automatically or reflexively seek to use it again. However, emphasis should be placed on the generation of alternative strategies. Many successful planners use brainstorming, or some variation of it, in an effort to produce a maximum return on creative effort. Once a variety of possibilities have been suggested, planners move to determining the feasibility of each strategy. Feasibility can be established by examining several issues, including cost, resources available, time required, relationship to goals, consequences of taking a particular action, and so on. Sometimes a technique such as force field analysis can be very useful, as the forces in support of a strategy are plotted against the forces that restrain it. Finally, a strategy is selected that planners believe will most effectively and efficiently enable the organization to reach the established goals.

Substep E: Prepare for implementation. The operant word in this substep is "prepare," as no aspect of the program has yet been implemented. For example, responsibilities, time frames, places, resources, and means must be specified. Concrete answers are developed for the important questions of who will do what, with what resources, where, by when, and how? For instance, if a skills training workshop is a part of the overall program, it will be necessary to specify the goals for the workshop, its activities, their length, who will assume responsibility for each activity, what materials will be needed to conduct these activities, what spaces will be used for the workshop, what the workshop dates will be, how the workshop will fit sequentially within the total program, etc. The overall program needs to be planned at this level of detail.

Step 2: Implementation

Successful program implementation depends to a large extent on the efforts that were devoted to planning functions. If the target problem was identified accurately, if school personnel were involved in a collaborative planning process, and if the intervention was selected and designed thoughtfully, the likelihood of successful implementation and outcomes are enhanced significantly. Moreover, the importance of ensuring that program personnel attend to regularly obtained feedback about the program must be emphasized. The section on evaluation, to follow, expands on this point.

Although the steps suggested as part of the planning process will help to ensure successful implementation, there is no guarantee that various barriers to the program will not be encountered. These include issues such as an organizations' natural resistance to change, limitation of school psychologists' skills that might be encountered in accomplishing the program, the small number of quality primary prevention programs that are readily applicable, and the minimal amount of support that might be provided by administrators for reasons such as tight budgets. A detailed discussion of program implementation barriers that can be applied to primary prevention programs can be found in Maher and Bennett (1984) and Zins, Curtis, Graden, and Ponti (1988).

Step 3: Evaluation

The American Psychological Association has sponsored a Task Force on Promotion, Prevention and Intervention Alternatives in Psychology. This task force sought to identify the best prevention programs nationally and to disseminate their descriptions so that other practitioners and researchers could benefit from their findings. Of the hundreds of program descriptions submitted for review to the Task Force, only 14 were selected as "showcase" programs — those "that worked and had documented evidence of their effectiveness" (Bales, 1987, p. 18).

This issue of documented effectiveness is critical. Without demonstrable research evidence that a primary prevention program works, it is most difficult to be convincing to anyone, including yourself, that what happened actually did matter. Conversely, caution is needed when arriving at judgments about effectiveness and a realistic time perspective

must be allowed in which observable results can be generated (see Sarason, 1984).

Program evaluation in primary prevention is a complicated issue. Maher and Bennett (1984) noted that outcome assessment involves the following components: (a) evaluating goal attainment, (b) evaluating related effects, (c) evaluating consumer reactions, (d) evaluating cause and effect relations, (e) evaluating cost-effectiveness, (f) deciding about program change, and (g) communicating evaluation results. As in any other program evaluation, there are two main types of evaluation: formative and summative, which are followed by dissemination and utilization of the evaluation results.

Substep A: Formative evaluation. Formative evaluation consists of the steps that must be taken to assess the evolving relationship between what was planned for program implementation and what is actually occurring. In addition, this information must be fed back in a timely way to program personnel.

What might be examined in formative evaluation? The following queries would address several potential considerations: Are any workshops that were part of the plan actually being conducted? Were any canceled? Is the number of planned participants being realized? Are the activities being carried out as they were designed? Are the materials that were prepared appearing to be useful? Are participants completing the evaluation forms as requested? Is the time schedule holding up, or is delivery getting way behind, or way ahead? How are the group facilitators doing? Is the room selection working out satisfactorily? Are there any unanticipated events or conditions (e.g., assignment of a new principal to the school, or a natural disaster) that have affected delivery of the plan? Combinations of anecdotal observations (such as reflections made by participants) and numerical data (such as attendance figures) can be very useful in formative evaluation.

Substep B: Summative evaluation. While formative evaluation provides a sense of how a program is being delivered, summative evaluation provides information about the overall effect of a program. Program personnel will want to know if the incidence goals of the primary prevention program have been realized. For instance, was school vandalism decreased by 20% during the period of the program and did vandalism in the control school remain unchanged? Or: Did fewer students begin using tobacco during and following the program than in the control school?

Summative evaluation issues for primary prevention programs are similar to those of other kinds of applied research. That does not mean that the issues are easily resolved, however. It is most difficult to design and conduct programs following a sound research design in the real world as opposed to the laboratory.

Certainly it is always advisable to set primary prevention programs within a true experimental design, which usually involves at least randomization and a control group. However, doing so may not always be possible, particularly if it means denying a potenially effective intervention to a group of students. It then becomes necessary to seek the next best design. This may be a quasi-experimental design such as a nonequivalent control group, a time-series analysis, a multiple baseline, or intensive case studies (Campbell & Stanley, 1963).

Whatever research design is chosen, a number of challenging issues exist for the primary prevention researcher to consider, including the following: Are the dependent measures being used valid and reliable and do they sensitively relate to the program goals? Is there change in the target group compared to the status of a no-program control group? Are several data sources used for evaluation, or is there a reliance on just one? Are the changes that are being reported practically, as well as statistically, important? Are the changes found to be enduring over time and in different settings (Bloom, 1977)?

Other matters of concern, which are specific to primary prevention program research, involve determining whether the group being studied was healthy at present but at risk for some discernible problem consequence. In addition, it should be determined if the changes registered by the program indicated a reduction in incidence of the problem being studied.

Substep C: Dissemination and utilization of evaluation results. The results of the program evaluation are intended to be disseminated and utilized for decision making regarding future program directions. Summative evaluation data in particular must be shared both with decision makers (e.g., administrators, school board) and with school personnel involved in the primary prevention program. In addition, such information usually should be provided to other constituencies, including parents, students, and the taxpaying public.

Evaluation results can help primary interventionists to make decisions regarding program continuation, modification, and expansion. Too often, however, we have seen programs in which evaluative data were not obtained, were gathered as an afterthought, or were not utilized for decision-making purposes regarding future program activities.

In summary, a goal for primary prevention programs is to pass these kinds of evaluation hurdles and to record results that suggest that program goals were attained. Reaching that point requires program planners to have satisfactorily mastered every step of the program development process.

CASE ILLUSTRATION OF PROGRAM DEVELOPMENT

The following brief case illustration demonstrates important aspects of person-centered, microsocial primary prevention program development. Only the most important aspects of the program are described; because of space limitations, neither the program implementation nor the evaluation steps are covered in detail.

The impetus for the primary prevention program was an incident in which several senior high school students were severely injured in a high-speed car accident. Police investigations of the accident revealed that the students had been drinking alcohol and several were legally intoxicated at the time of the mishap.

The primary prevention program was implemented in a public school district located in a suburban area of a large midwestern city. Approximately 2,100 students attended the five schools in the district. Special services staff included a director of pupil personnel, a school psychologist, two speech and language therapists, three junior/senior high counselors, a school nurse, and a number of special education teachers. The district enjoyed a reputation of educational excellence locally and statewide, and most citizens of the community took pride in the schools. A substantial segment of the community did not have children in the public schools.

Step 1: Planning

Assessing needs and targets. In this case, this step occurred first. At the time of the accident, a needs assessment regarding a wide variety of education-related issues of potential concern to the community at large coincidentally had been conducted with parents and other community members serving as respondents. The results revealed that teenage drinking was perceived as widespread and was considered to be a significant problem. Teacher, parent, student, and police interviews and experiences confirmed these findings. Therefore, alcohol abuse by high school students was identified as a significant problem that warranted intervention, and a task force was appointed by the superintendent and school board to investigate possible plans of action. Representatives of these various constituencies (including the school psychologist, representative teachers, administrators, parents, and community members) agreed to serve on a task force with the goal of addressing the identified problem. Liaison also was established with various community organizations (e.g., juvenile

authorities, community mental health center) that dealt with this issue, since it was assumed that a variety of resources would be required to combat the problem.

Identifying the generative base. The task force reviewed the results of the survey as well as a number of potential options for addressing the issue of alcohol abuse. They spoke with other school personnel and community members in the immediate geographical area and throughout the state, and read materials that had been published by various organizations in order to prepare themselves for undertaking an appropriate intervention.

Goal setting. It was clear that the identified problem of alcohol abuse was not limited to the senior high level. Consequently, the task force believed that there was a need to place more emphasis on teaching *all* students problem-solving, decision-making, and social skills and to provide information on substance abuse from the time that pupils first entered school. Furthermore, it was hoped that the number of alcohol-related incidents, both in school and in the community, would decrease, but there was no expectation that all such occurrences would cease. An attempt was made to make the goals of the intervention as concrete as possible so that their attainment could be measured objectively (e.g., decrease in numbers of students involved in substance abuse incidents as reported by the city police, juvenile authorities, and school officials).

It also became apparent that the identified problem extended well beyond the school. Therefore, the additional community personnel (e.g., police officers, juvenile authorities, physicians, ministers, priests, etc.) with whom liaison previously had been established also were invited to become directly involved on the task force.

Selecting strategy. Several local professionals and out-of-state consultants with relevant expertise were identified and asked to assist in developing the organizational intervention. Although each had many good ideas to offer about specific programs to address the targeted problem, none were specifically applicable to the local situation. However, as a result of these discussions, a number of excellent ideas were generated. Eventually, it was decided to alter the school curriculum to include far more emphasis on problem-solving, decision-making, and social skills at all levels, and to include more educational efforts directed specifically toward substance abuse, beginning in the third grade. Various curricula were examined, but a decision was made to adapt different combinations of these programs to meet local needs. (Remedial efforts such as making counseling more readily available also were developed at this time to assist students already experiencing difficulties related to substance abuse.) In addition, it was decided that middle school homeroom teachers would hold discussions each day during homeroom period to discuss a wide variety of related issues (e.g., peer group and media pressure, self-concept, peer and family relationships).

The support of additional community members was also solicited. Religious leaders offered their assistance, which included their addressing related issues in sermons, in church bulletins, and with church groups. Stores selling alcohol also agreed (with some motivation supplied by the police department) to stepping up identification checks, and juvenile authorities agreed to more closely work with school personnel.

Preparing for implementation. Once a decision was made regarding the intervention plan, it was necessary to actually contract with various teachers to develop the revised curricula over the summer and to provide them with needed resources (e.g., reference materials, consultants, training); to inform the entire school community of the impending program; to schedule in-service training for teachers, particularly at the middle school level, regarding their roles; to purchase necessary materials; and to finalize specific evaluation plans.

Step 2: Implementation

Following more than 1 year of planning and numerous meetings with various constituencies designed to obtain their support, the program was implemented in several phases. The educational component was easiest to implement; it required less preparation, because there were a variety of curricular materials available that readily were adaptable to meet the district's needs. The social problem-solving components required more extensive preparation and in-service training and were therefore implemented later. Furthermore, given the finite resources of the district, it was felt that it would be better to undertake the change process in several steps rather than all at once.

Information regarding the program was also shared with the community at large. For example, articles were written for the local weekly newspaper and school newsletters, and talks were given to PTA groups at each school.

Step 3: Evaluation

Formative feedback was obtained at various key points in the implementation process. It was necessary, for instance, to ascertain that the educational component actually was added to the curriculum. Examination of lesson plans and observations by principals and the instructional supervisor were helpful in this regard. Teachers were provided with additional assistance and support if they encountered difficulty. It also was necessary to monitor the progress being made with regard to developing the problem-solving component, and the level of understanding and support within the community at large.

Summative evaluation data were collected at the end of each year, but because the program was an ongoing one, no definitive evaluation actually was conducted. Data such as incidents of alcohol-related offenses involving district students were collected (both in and out of school), self-report questionnaires were disseminated to students inquiring about their attitudes and behaviors related to alcohol, and parent and teacher surveys were conducted. These data suggested that the program was meeting some of its goals, but they also pointed to areas in need of modification (e.g., expansion of the program to address other issues such as pregnancy prevention). Overall, these results were helpful in deciding that the program should be continued, with some changes. A similar evaluation of the social problem-solving component was undertaken in later years.

CONCLUSIONS AND FUTURE DIRECTIONS

In this chapter, a conceptual model for understanding primary prevention was provided, as were numerous examples of school-based preventive programming. Our intent was to concretely illustrate how primary prevention programs can be implemented by school psychologists and other special services personnel. We emphasized that the main goal of primary prevention, that of forestalling adjustment and learning problems, can be advanced in a number of ways. These include reducing sources of stress in the environment and society at large, creating environments that optimize adjustment in all children and enhancing students' capacity to more effectively deal with life situations. These modes of prevention provide a positive, optimistic outlook regarding intervention, quite different from that offered in the traditional diagnostic-remedial approach. As Roberts and Peterson (1984) stated, "Prevention focuses on competence rather than deficit, on health rather than illness, and on factors that reduce vulnerability rather than those which lead to risk. It implies the ultimate circumvention rather than the treatment of dysfunction" (p. xi).

Despite the value that many school psychologists attribute to primary prevention (Strein, 1987) and the fact that a large number of student-related problems are amenable to a preventive approach (Zins & Wagner, 1987), school psychologists tend to expend too little of their effort in this direction (Alpert, 1985). The current focus of most service delivery systems on remediation seems to foster the reliance of special services providers on becoming involved with students only "when the problem becomes serious enough to warrant referral" (Zins & Ponti, 1985). The growing teenage suicide and pregnancy rates, for example, dramatically illustrate the need for a preventive rather than a remedial orientation to mental health services in schools. Waiting for referrals often is too late.

In keeping with NASP's call to expand services to meet the needs of all students, professionals are more than ever before being urged to incorporate preventive interventions into their services delivery models. Should special services providers in sufficient numbers not only delve into the literature to learn more about these promising approaches, but also actually incorporate such techniques into their daily functioning, such actions would have a major impact on the practice of school psychology and could lead to what Conoley (in press) called "a revolution in [school] psychological service delivery." We recognize that implementing primary prevention into the schools will not be easy, and that efforts at changing old, complacent modes of functioning inevitably will meet with resistance. However, if individual practitioners do not put forth the extra effort necessary to negotiate for such changes, to measure program effectiveness, to build public awareness regarding the merits of these programs, and to market prevention programs to administrators, public policy decision makers, consumers, and other school personnel, who will assume this critical responsibility?

There is widespread consensus regarding the desirability of schools as a prime institution for implementing primary prevention programs. However, there remains a dire need for additional research and training in this area. A brief perusal of the references at the end of this chapter suggests that school psychologists are not publishing such research, and that little research on school-based prevention is being published in journals directed toward school psychologists. Moreover, in our experience, few school psychologists and special services providers receive graduate coursework in primary prevention. In sum, the limited visibility that primary prevention receives within school psychology and related areas constitutes a major barrier to implementation of this approach. We hope that this chapter provides an impetus to encourage practitioners and researchers alike to expand their respective roles in advancing the application of primary prevention in the schools.

REFERENCES

Albee, G. (1986). Toward a just society: Lessons from observations on the primary prevention of psychopathology. *American Psychologist, 41,* 891-898.

Alpert, J. L. (1985). Change within a profession: Change, prevention, and school psychology. *American Psychologist, 40,* 1112-1140.

Aspy, D., & Roebuck, F. (1977). *Kids don't learn from people they don't like.* Amherst, MA: HRD Press.

Astin, A. (1984). Student involvement: A developmental theory for higher education. *Journal of College Student Personnel, 25,* 297-308.

Baker, S., Swisher, J., Nadenichek, P., Popowicz, C. (1984). Measured effects of primary prevention strategies. *Journal of Counseling and Development, 62,* 459-464.

Bales, J. (1987, April). Prevention at its best. *APA Monitor, 18,* 18-19.

Bandura, A. (1977). *Social learning theory.* Englewood Cliffs, NJ: Prentice-Hall.

Barcus, F. E. (1983). *Portrayal of minorities.* Newtonville, MA: Action for Children's Television.

Blair, S. N., Collingwood, T., Smith, M., Upton, J., & Sterling, C. (1985). Review of a health promotion program for school employees. In J. E. Zins, D. I. Wagner, & C. A. Maher (Eds.), *Health promotion in the schools* (pp. 89-98). New York: Haworth.

Bloom, B. (1977). Evaluating achievable objectives for primary prevention. In D. Klein & S. Goldston (Eds.), *Primary prevention: An idea whose time has come* (pp. 49-60). Rockville, MD: National Institute of Mental Health.

Bogat, C. A., Jones, J. W., & Jason, L. A. (1980). School transitions: Preventive intervention following an elementary school closing. *Journal of Community Psychology, 8,* 343-352.

Botvin, G. (1983). *Life skills training* (Teacher's manual). New York: Smithfield.

Botvin, G., & Dusenbury, L. (1987). Life skills training: A psychoeducational approach to substance abuse prevention. In C. A. Maher & J. E. Zins (Eds.), *Psychoeducational interventions in the schools* (pp. 46-65). Elmsford, NY: Pergamon.

Campbell, D., & Stanley, J. (1963). *Experimental and quasi-experimental designs for research.* Chicago: Rand McNally.

Catalano, R., & Dooley, D. (1980). Economic change in primary prevention. In R. Price, R. Ketterer, & B. Bader (Eds.), *Prevention in mental health* (pp. 21-40). Beverly Hills, CA: Sage.

Comer, J. (1985). The Yale-New Haven primary prevention project: A follow-up study. *Journal of the American Academy of Child Psychiatry, 24,* 154-160.

Conoley, J. C. (in press). Cognitive behavioral approaches and prevention in the schools. In J. N. Hughes & R. Hall (Eds.), *Handbook of cognitive-behavioral therapy in the classroom.* New York: Pergamon.

Conyne, R. (1985). The counseling ecologist: Helping people and environments. *Counseling and Human Development, 18,* 1-12.

Conyne, R. (1987). *Primary preventive counseling: Empowering people and systems.* Muncie, IN: Accelerated Development.

Coursey, R. (Ed.). (1977). *Program evaluation for mental health.* New York: Grune & Stratton.

Cowen, E. (1984). A general structural model for primary prevention program development in mental health. *Journal of Counseling and Development, 62,* 485-490.

Cowen, E. (1985). Person-centered approaches to primary prevention in mental health: Situation-focused and competence-enhancement. *American Journal of Community Psychology, 13,* 31-49.

Craig, D. (1978). *HIP pocket guide to planning and evaluation.* Austin, TX: Learning Concepts.

Donaldson, T. R. (1981). The visibility and image of handicapped people on television. *Exceptional Children, 46,* 41-47.

Downs, A. C., & Gowan, D. C. (1980). Sex differences in reinforcement and punishment on prime-time television. *Sex Roles, 6,* 683-694.

Elias, M. J., & Clabby, J. (1982). *Social problem solving curriculum for enhancing critical thinking skills.* New Brunswick, NJ: Rutgers University, Department of Psychology.

Elias, M. J., Clabby, J., Corr, D., Ubriaco, M., & Schuyler, T. (1982). *The improving social awareness–social problem solving project: A case study in school-based action research* (Action Research Workshop Report No. 4). New York: William T. Grant Foundation.

Elias, M. J., Gara, M., Ubriaco, M., Rothbaum, P., Clabby, J., & Schuyler, T. (1986). Impact of a preventive social problem solving intervention on children's coping with middle-school stressors. *American Journal of Community Psychology, 14,* 259-275.

Felner, R. D. (1984). Vulnerability in childhood: A preventive framework for understanding children's efforts to cope with life stress and transition. In M. C. Roberts & L. Peterson (Eds.), *Prevention of problems in childhood* (pp. 133-169). New York: Wiley.

Felner, R. D., Ginter, M., & Primavera, J. (1982). Primary prevention during school transitions: Social support and environmental structure. *American Journal of Community Psychology, 10,* 277-290.

Felner, R. D., Primavera, J., & Cauce, A. (1981). The impact of school transitions: A focus for preventive efforts. *American Journal of Community Psychology, 9,* 449-459.

Forman, S. G. (1984). Behavioral and cognitive-behavioral approaches to staff development. In C. A. Maher, R. J. Illback, & J. E. Zins (Eds.), *Organizational psychology in the schools* (pp. 302-322). Springfield, IL: Charles C Thomas.

Gelfand, D., Ficula, T., & Zarbatany, L. (1986). Prevention of childhood behavior disorders. In B. Edelstein & L. Michelson (Eds.), *Handbook of prevention* (pp. 133-152). New York: Plenum.

Glidewell, J. (1984). Training for the role of advocate. *American Journal of Community Psychology, 12,* 193-198.

Guidubaldi, J., Cleminshaw, A. K., Perry, J., & Mcloughlin, C. S. (1983). The impact of parental divorce on children: Report of the nationwide NASP study. *School Psychology Review, 12,* 300-323.

Harris, J., Eisenberg, N., & Carroll, J. (1982). Facilitation of prosocial behavior in children. In T. Kratochwill (Ed.), *Advances in school psychology* (Vol. 2, pp. 245-274). Hillsdale, NJ: Erlbaum.

Jason, L. A., Durlak, J., & Holton-Walker, E. (1984). Prevention of child problems in the schools. In M. Roberts & L. Peterson (Eds.), *Prevention of problems in childhood* (pp. 311-341). New York: Wiley.

Jessor, R., & Jessor, S. L. (1977). *Problem behavior and psychosocial development: A longitudinal study of youth.* New York: Academic.

Johnson, D., & Johnson, R. (1983). Social interdependence and perceived academic and personal support in the classroom. *Journal of Social Psychology, 120,* 77-82.

Johnson, D., & Johnson, R. (1986a). Impact of classroom organization and instructional methods on the effectiveness of mainstreaming. In C. J. Meisel (Ed.), *Mainstreaming handicapped children* (pp. 219-250). Hillsdale, NJ: Erlbaum.

Johnson, D., & Johnson, R. (1986b). Mainstreaming and cooperative learning strategies. *Exceptional Children, 52,* 553-561.

Johnson, D., Maruyama, G., Johnson, R., Nelson, D., & Skon, L. (1981). The effects of cooperative, competitive, and individualistic goal structures on achievement: A meta-analysis. *Psychological Bulletin, 89,* 47-62.

Klein, D. C., & Goldston, S. E. (1977). *Primary prevention: An idea whose time has come.* Washington, DC: National Institute of Mental Health.

Maher, C. A., & Bennett, R. E. (1984). *Planning and evaluating special education programs.* Englewood Cliffs, NJ: Prentice-Hall.

Maher, C. A., Illback, R. J., & Zins, J. E. (1984a). Framework for organizational psychology in the schools. In C. A. Maher, R. J. Illback, & J. E. Zins (Eds.), *Organizational psychology in the schools* (pp. 5-20). Springfield, IL: Charles C Thomas.

Maher, C. A., Illback, R. J., & Zins, J. E. (Eds.). (1984b). *Organizational psychology in the schools.* Springfield, IL: Charles C Thomas.

Moore, M., & Delworth, U. (1976). *Training manual for student service program development.* Boulder, CO: Western Interstate Commission for Higher Education.

NIAAA. (1978). *Planning a prevention program* (USDHEW Publication No. ADM 78-647). Washington, DC: U.S. Government Printing Office.

Pedro-Carroll, J. L., & Cowen, E. (1985). The children of divorce intervention program: An investigation of the efficacy of a school-based prevention program. *Journal of Consulting and Clinical Psychology, 14,* 277-290.

Pedro-Carroll, J. L., Cowen, E., Hightower, A. D., & Guare, J. C. (1986). Preventive intervention with latency-aged children of divorce: A replication study. *American Journal of Community Psychology, 13,* 111-124.

Peterson, L. (in press). Preventing the leading killer of children: The role of the school psychologist in injury prevention. *School Psychology Review.*

Price, R., Bader, B., & Ketterer, R. (1980). Prevention in community mental health: The state of the art. In R. Price, R. Ketterer, & B. Bader (Eds.), *Prevention in mental health: Research, policy, and practice* (pp. 9-20). Beverly Hills, CA: Sage.

Price, R., & Smith, S. (1985). *A guide to evaluating prevention programs in mental health.* Rockville, MD: National Institute of Mental Health.

Rappaport, J. (1977). *Community psychology: Values, research, and action.* New York: Holt, Rinehart, & Winston.

Rappaport, J. (1981). In praise of paradox: A social policy of empowerment over prevention. *American Journal of Community Psychology, 9,* 1-25.

Rappaport, J., Swift, C., & Hess, R. (Eds.). (1984). Studies in empowerment: Steps toward understanding and action. *Prevention in Human Services, 3,* 1-230.

Remer, R., Niguette, G., Anderson, G., & Terrell, J. (1984). A meta-system for the delivery of primary preventive interventions. *Journal of Counseling and Development, 63,* 30-34.

Rickel, A. D., & Langer, T. S. (1985). Short and long-term effects of marital disruption on children. *American Journal of Community Psychology, 13,* 599-611.

Riessman, F. (1965). The "helper" therapy principle. *Social Work, 10,* 27-32.

Roberts, M. C., & Peterson, L. (Eds.). (1984). *Prevention of problems in childhood.* New York: Wiley.

Sarason, S. (1984). Community psychology and public policy: Missed opportunity. *American Journal of Community Psychology, 12,* 199-207.

Shaw, M. (1986). The prevention of learning and interpersonal problems. *Journal of Counseling and Development, 64,* 624-627.

Slavin, R. (1983). *Cooperative learning.* New York: Longman.

Sterling, S., Cowen, E., Weissberg, R. P., Lotyezewski, B., & Boike, M. (1985). Recent stressful life events and young children's school adjustment. *American Journal of Community Psychology, 13,* 87-98.

Stolberg, A. L., & Garrison, K. (1985). Evaluating a primary prevention program for children of divorce. *American Journal of Community Psychology, 13,* 111-124.

Strein, W. (1987). Needs versus deeds: The unfilled research potential in school psychology. *Journal of School Psychology, 25,* 3-14.

Task Force on Psychology and Public Policy. (1986). Psychology and public policy. *American Psychologist, 41,* 914-921.

Weisheit, R., Hopkins, R., Kearney, K., & Mauss, A. (1984). The school as a setting for primary prevention. *Journal of Alcohol and Drug Education, 30,* 27-35.

Weissberg, R. P., Gesten, E. L., Liebenstein, N. L., Docherty-Schmid, K., & Hutton, H. (1980). *The Rochester social problem-solving (SPS) program: A training manual for teachers of 2nd-4th grade children.* Rochester, NY: University of Rochester, Primary Mental Health Project.

Wilson, F. R., & Yager, G. G. (1981). A process model for prevention program research. *Personnel and Guidance Journal, 59,* 590-595.

Wright, S., & Cowen, E. (1982). Student perception of school environment and its relationship to mood, achievement, popularity, and adjustment. *American Journal of Community Psychology, 10,* 687-702.

Zins, J. E., Curtis, M. J., Graden, J. L., & Ponti, C. R. (1988). *Helping students succeed in regular classrooms: A guide to developing intervention assistance programs.* San Francisco: Jossey-Bass.

Zins, J. E., & Ponti, C. R. (1985). Strategies for enhancing child and adolescent mental health. In J. E. Zins, D. I. Wagner, & C. A. Maher (Eds.), *Health promotion in the schools: Innovative approaches to facilitating physical and emotional well-being* (pp. 49-60). New York: Haworth.

Zins, J. E., & Wagner, D. I. (1987). Children and health promotion. In A. Thomas & J. Grimes (Eds.), *Children's needs: Psychological perspectives* (pp. 258-267). Washington, DC: National Association of School Psychologists.

12

Expanding Service Delivery Options in Regular Schools and Classrooms for Students With Severe Disabilities

Michael F. Giangreco
Cayuga-Onondaga Board of Cooperative Educational Services,
Auburn, New York and Syracuse University
Luanna H. Meyer
Syracuse University

This chapter presents an overview of the principles and practices of integrated educational programs for students with severe disabilities. After a brief historical overview, the major components of what are regarded to be the "most promising practices" in educational services for these students are summarized. The relevance of these components to the role of the school psychologist is emphasized, and suggestions are offered for modifying that role in critical areas through various professional activities to support integration of students with severe disabilities into regular schools and classes. The remainder of the chapter presents a conceptual framework for expanding service delivery options to typical schools and classes, and describes several innovative programs in the United States and Canada that exemplify these options. The chapter concludes with recommendations for future work needed to develop and validate integrated options that are both beneficial to children's growth and development and reflect societal values and systems capabilities.

HISTORICAL AND CURRENT CONTEXT

It has been many years since Burton Blatt published his pictorial essays of the daily lives of persons with mental retardation in U.S. institutions. *Christmas in Purgatory* (Blatt & Kaplan, 1966), *Exodus from Pandemonium* (Blatt, 1970), and *Souls in Extremis* (Blatt, 1973) exposed the substandard and inhumane conditions of facilities that had been constructed and established beginning in the nineteenth century across the United States. Institutionalization became a universally available service in every state. The books written by Blatt and others, visits to state institutions by prominent politicians, and finally litigation against those facilities on behalf of persons required to live and attend school in them reflected, and contributed to, a raised public and professional consciousness that something was terribly wrong. Yet the massive infusion of millions of dollars in each state to reform and rebuild these facilities has had limited impact; charges of neglect and abuse continue as institutions seem to persist unaltered in their basic inability to provide habilitation (Meyer & Putnam, in press). Furthermore, large congregate care facilities continue to exist in virtually every state. In fact, large institutions remain the *primary* locus of service to persons at certain ages with certain handicapping conditions — such as severe disabilities and severe behavior problems (Braddock, Hemp, & Howes, 1986).

Similarly, the first school services for students with severe disabilities were established in isolation from mainstream schools attended by nondisabled students in their own neighborhoods. Exclusion from the school altogether was followed by development of handicapped-only educational services, seldom administered by a local education agency. These programs were far more likely to be administered by private and advocacy organizations, state agencies, and/or separate educational cooperatives (Meyer & Putnam, in press). By the mid-1970s, a growing national consciousness regarding the educational rights of youngsters with severe disabilities had prompted the formation of a professional organization emphasizing the value of integration. This organization — which began as the American Association for the Education of the Severely and Profoundly Handicapped (AAESPH) and later changed its name to The Association for Persons With Severe Handicaps (TASH) — emerged as a major political force and became the forum for the development and validation of effective models of integration for these young people (Certo, Haring, & York, 1984). By 1987 there were no fewer than six books and hundreds of journal articles — including dozens of empirical studies documenting the positive effects of integrated programs for these students and none attesting to negative outcomes — that were widely available in the United States alone (for reviews of this material, see Halvorsen & Sailor, in press, and Meyer & Putnam, in press).

In addition to these philosophical and programmatic supports for the feasibility and validity of integrated educational programs, litigation in federal court lent further impetus to the call for integrated programming. In a case that extended over a period of several years, the city of Philadelphia finally accepted a court settlement requiring the establishment of integrated school services for its students with severe disabilities; this agreement further specified that various components of the "most promising practices" be included in the design and implementation of those services (see MacGregor, Janssen, Larsen, & Tillery, 1986, for a discussion of this case and its outcomes.) *Roncker v. Walter* (1983) in Ohio not only supported Neil Roncker's right to attend school with his nonhandicapped peers, but established the important principle of *portability*. According to this principle, the court ruled that any special education and related service judged to be portable — that is, of such a nature that they could be provided outside a segregated environment — must be provided in an integrated site.

Nevertheless, it is an unfortunate reality that the *Ninth Annual Report to Congress* (U.S. Department of Education, 1987) reveals that nearly 28% of U.S. children who are deaf-blind still attend school in a segregated public institution, and over 27% of those who are multihandicapped attend segregated, handicapped-only schools (See Table 1). It is disquieting that separate classes and separate schools continue to be the most typical service delivery options for students with those handicapping conditions most likely to represent severe disabilities — mental retardation, emotional disturbance, deafness, multihandicaps, orthopedic impairments, deaf-blind, and other health-impairments, including autism. Similarly, a special study commissioned in the State of Massachusetts and covering the period from 1975 through 1985 showed that proportionately more students were segregated today than 10 years ago at the time that Public Law 94-142 was passed (Massachusetts Advocacy Center, 1987).

PL 94-142 took effect in 1975 and mandated not only that free and appropriate education be provided for children with disabilities, but that this education be provided in the "least restrictive environment." Precise definition of the least restrictive environment was not included, other than the statement that "to the maximum extent appropriate, handicapped children, including children in public or private institutions or other care facilities, are educated with children who are not handicapped; and special classes, separate schooling, or other removal of handicapped children from the regular education environment occurs only when the nature or severity of the handicap is such that education in regular

TABLE 1
Number and Percentage of Children 3-21 Years Old Served in Different
Educational Environments During the School Year 1984-1985

Disability category		Regular class	Resource room	Separate class	Public separate school	Private separate school	Public residential facility	Private residential facility	Correction facility	Homebound/ hospital
						Educational environment				
Learning-disabled	#	296,599	1,113,411	382,397	20,426	14,224	559	1,034	2,920	1,561
	%	16.18	60.74	20.86	1.11	0.78	0.03	0.06	0.16	0.09
Speech-impaired	#	729,963	297,129	55,287	10,908	27,715	313	293	295	5,232
	%	64.76	26.36	4.91	0.97	2.46	0.03	0.03	0.03	0.46
Mentally retarded[a]	#	33,610	202,183	367,553	58,169	14,755	17,724	2,742	1,361	3,530
	%	4.79	28.82	52.39	8.29	2.10	2.53	0.39	0.19	0.50
Emotionally disturbed	#	44,152	128,198	124,875	32,129	17,979	6,337	9,019	5,965	5,957
	%	11.79	34.22	33.33	8.58	4.80	1.69	2.41	1.59	1.59
Hard of hearing and deaf	#	14,933	16,666	22,009	5,135	3,430	7,597	773	69	378
	%	21.84	23.48	31.01	7.24	4.83	10.68	1.09	0.10	0.53
Multihandicapped	#	1,940	9,629	30,734	12,596	6,994	4,378	1,750	252	3,490
	%	2.70	13.42	42.83	17.55	9.75	6.10	2.44	0.35	4.86
Orthopedically impaired	#	9,423	101,672	17,308	6,724	2,847	416	369	13	3,962
	%	18.21	20.63	33.46	13.00	5.50	0.80	0.71	0.03	7.66
Other health-impaired[b]	#	17,176	18,639	23,947	2,907	1,424	531	413	16	8,189
	%	23.45	25.45	32.70	3.97	1.94	0.72	0.56	0.02	11.18
Visually handicapped	#	9,254	8,406	5,344	1,151	926	2,788	296	59	211
	%	32.54	29.56	18.79	4.05	3.26	9.80	1.04	0.21	0.74
Deaf-blind	#	102	351	531	440	114	640	102	1	47
	%	4.38	15.08	22.81	18.90	4.90	27.49	4.38	0.04	2.02
All conditions	#	1,157,477	1,805,374	1,031,041	150,724	90,471	41,309	16,800	10,951	32,557
	%	26.69	41.63	23.77	3.48	2.09	0.95	0.39	0.25	0.75
All conditions excluding speech-impaired	#	427,514	1,508,245	975,754	139,816	62,956	40,996	16,507	10,656	27,325
	%	13.32	46.99	30.40	4.36	1.96	1.28	0.51	0.33	0.85

Note: Data as of October 1, 1986, from the Ninth Annual Report to Congress on the Implementation of the Education of the Handicapped Act, U.S. Department of Education, 1987.
[a] This includes the full range from mild to profound mental retardation.　　[b] Generally includes autistic.

class with the use of supplementary aids and services cannot be achieved satisfactorily." Elsewhere in the legislation, reference is made to the need to maintain a continuum of services — one that explicitly includes hospital as well as residential institutional settings. These references to the acceptability of removing children from regular classes and even regular schools on the basis of a determination of the severity of their handicapping conditions have sometimes become the rationale for the continued segregation of virtually all children with severe disabilities in isolated environments. We suspect these ambiguities in the legislation have created a situation in which the mandate to attempt to meet handicapped students' needs in the regular classroom — with appropriate adaptations and services — is ignored whenever the students involved have been judged to be "severely handicapped." Indeed, Reynolds, Wang, and Walberg (1987), in their discussion of the need for a reintegration of regular and special education, specifically suggested that this restructuring be applied to more than three-fourths of the clients of special education "but not to programs for children who are deaf, blind, severely disturbed, or deeply retarded in cognitive development" (p. 391).

Why not? What could be the philosophical and empirical rationale for the failure to consider the integration of *all* students into U.S. schools and classrooms? This book is about educational reform on behalf of children and youth with disabilities. It reflects a growing consensus that our efforts to address the needs of these children through "add on" and "pull out" special education and remedial programs will fail without systematic attention to the restructuring of our educational system. This restructuring involves a merger of special and regular education while enhancing the capability of schools to meet individual needs in a heterogeneous society (Reynolds, Wang, & Walberg, 1987; Stainback & Stainback, 1984). We concur with these developments, but offer a further challenge to that restructuring and reformation. Children with severe disabilities — all children, without exception — must be included in the planning and implementation of educational reforms. Unless they are included, changes that do occur will continue to allow for the ever lengthening list of exceptions that maintain the statistics in Table 1. Note, for example, that (excluding the category of children with speech impairments) only 13% of U.S. children with handicapping conditions receive special education services in the regular classroom full-time, whereas 30% continue to attend the separate special education classes challenged by Dunn 20 years ago (Dunn, 1968).

As long as we continue to allow "exceptions" to integration based upon categorical criteria such as "severity," integrated options and educational reform will remain an elusive goal in contrast to massive and well-established service delivery systems that now isolate and segregate these young people. As Gilhool and Stutman (1979) asserted:

> There is no cognizable reason under the statutes — that is, no *learning* reason and no *disability* reason — for handicapped-only centers, certainly not on the scale they now exist. If a child can come to a school at all, even to a self-contained class in a handicapped-only center, he can come to a self-contained class in a normal school. Any teaching techniques that can be used in a self-contained class can be used in a regular school building. There are few if any legitimate teaching strategies which require complete isolation of a child from interaction with other children, and the few such strategies that there may be apply to very few children and for very short periods of time. (p. 215)

The TASH Resolution on the Redefinition of the Continuum of Services (see Appendix 1) supporting these directions parallels the 1986 joint position statement of the National Coalition of Advocates for Student (NCAS) and National Association of School Psychologists (NASP) on appropriate educational services for all children. This resolution makes explicit the challenge to expand the restructuring of educational services to include all students, without prejudice. To do this, TASH calls upon the field both to advocate for such changes and to develop, implement, evaluate, and disseminate effective models and practices. This chapter will provide an overview of the most promising educational practices and illustrate how those practices indicators can be and are being applied in regular schools and regular classrooms for students with the most severe disabilities.

MOST PROMISING PRACTICES IN SEVERE DISABILITIES

In their now classic paper on the design of educational programs for students with severe disabilities, Brown, Nietupski, and Hamre-Nietupski (1976) articulated the "criterion of ultimate functioning." According to this criterion, program design and instructional planning must be referenced to the meaningful activities typical of current and future (adult) environments in the four domains of domestic living, work, leisure/recreation, and community. Since that early statement of principle, there have been numerous efforts to elaborate the components of this approach as well as empirically validate those components (see Horner, Meyer, and Fredericks, 1986, and Goetz, Guess, and Stremel-Campbell, 1987, as examples of collections summarizing many of these components). Sources are also available that summarize "appropriate," "best," or "most promising" practices (e.g., Bates, Renzaglia, & Wehman, 1981; Fox, et al., 1986; Horner, Meyer, & Fredericks, 1986; Meyer, 1985). Meyer (1985, 1987) identified "promising practices" that are posited as *Program Quality Indicators* (PQI). The PQI was socially validated through ratings of the relative importance of various program characteristics by six constituency groups having a vested interest in program quality, including behavior therapy experts, experts in severe disabilities, experts on the deaf–blind, mental retardation researchers, state-level directors of special education, and parents of children with severe disabilities (Meyer, Eichinger, & Park-Lee, 1987). Table 2 presents a summary of the major elements of these

promising practices and references them to the roles and activities of the school psychologist. The text that follows describes selected characteristics of quality service delivery that extend beyond what is currently the norm in the United States.

Integration and Normalization

Since the ultimate aim of educational programs is to prepare students with severe disabilities for maximal participation in integrated community environments, these students must not only learn to be as independent as possible, but also to cope with the highly interdependent nature of our society. People depend upon others (friends, spouses, roommates, fellow employees, paid service personnel, family members, employers, and so forth) on a daily and continuous basis according to various voluntary agreements that are negotiated either formally (paid contractual arrangement outside family and friendship networks) or informally (understandings among peers and family members) (Meyer & Eichinger, 1987). An increased focus on interdependencies as both outcomes of education and supports to persons with disabilities is consistent with the principle of normalization (Nirje, 1969). Wolfensberger (1972) defined normalization as the utilization of culturally normative means for establishing and maintaining behaviors and characteristics that are as culturally normal as possible.

As the focus of educational programs for persons with severe disabilities shifts from striving for exclusive independence toward an emphasis upon participation in normalized interdependencies, it becomes possible for all persons, regardless of their physical, cognitive, or social characteristics, to attain a meaningful social life. This may occur through partial participation in, and individualized adaptation to, activities in the immediate social environment, based upon the belief that persons with severe disabilities "can acquire many skills that will allow them to function, at least in part, in a wide range of least restrictive school and nonschool environments and activities." (Baumgart, et al., 1982, p. 19). The tenet of partial

TABLE 2
"Most Promising Practices" in Working With Students Who Have Severe Disabilities.

Most promising practices[a]		School Psychologist's Role and Potential Activities			
Dimensions	Components	Diagnosis & evaluation for student eligibility placement	Assessment and instructional planning	Consultaton and problem-solving	Program evaluation
Integration and normalization	Regular school class placements; Age-appropriate activities and curricula; Programmatic integration; Normalized behavior management; Social interactions with nondisabled peers	Advocate for placement in regular schools in proximity to nondisabled peers to maximum extent appropriate; Assess student's discrepancies from norms with emphasis upon supports needed for integrated education	Identify appropriate social and programmatic situations for integration	Assist school personnel & family in nonaversive behavior management; Work with regular education students to increase acceptance of peers with disabilities	Measure social adaptation of students over time; Assess generalized participation of students in community environments
Criterion of ultimate functioning	Ecological assessment directed to goal selection; Domain-referenced curricula; Criterion-referenced and community-based instruction; Heterogeneous instructional groupings	Reject use of developmental assessments which assign a "mental age" to students; Utilize domain-referenced student evaluation measures	Assist teachers in conducting ecological inventories in community environments; Coordinate input from various professionals to plan functional programs	Train regular education personnel in cooperative learning approaches (e.g., *Circles of Learning*)	Implement student outcome measures that are domain and criterion-referenced (e.g., SPAN); Advocate for graduate follow-up criteria such as integrated employment
Individualization and adaptations	Physical accessibility; Special equipment and prosthetic devices; Assessment adaptations; Curricular modifications; Integrated therapy approaches	Suggest adaptations/modifications needed to provide special education and related services to student in regular class; Utilize nondiscriminatory diagnostic and evaluation measures	Advocate at community site to adapt job activity to student abilities	Advocate at school level to appropriately adapt school disciplinary guidelines for individual student	Adapt student outcome measurement procedures to alternative form needs (e.g., for hearing impairments)
Data-based, systematic instruction	Behavioral principles and instructional practices; Task analysis; Motivation systems for learning and behavior; Data collection to monitor student progress & revise programs	Collect objective observation of student in natural environments as data source; Specify student performance characteristics relevant to remedial services	Assist teachers in design of relevant measures of student skills and behaviors	Consult with teachers and related services staff to problem-solve instructional difficulties	Implement data collection procedures for program use that have strong validity, reliability & utility
Staff and program development	Professional development and training; Training and supervision of paraprofessionals; Updating progress and services; Peer review and evaluation; Collaborative teaching/learning	Review and disseminate information on latest developments in diagnosis and evaluation	Design in-service training for paraprofessional staff; Offer examples of "research into practice" to revise programs	Coordinate school-based problem-solving team to address student needs	Utilize program evaluation tool to guide program development (e.g., PQI)

[a] Data in columns 1 and 2 are from "A validation of most promising practices in educational services for students with severe disabilities" by L. H. Meyer, J. Eichinger, & S. Park-Lee (in press), *Journal of the Association for Persons With Severe Handicaps, 12*, pp. 251–263. Copyright 1987 by the *Journal of the Association for Persons With Se-*

participation affirms that some level of participation in activities that are valued in society is inherently better than mastery of activities that are not valued, and that partial participation is clearly preferable to none at all. Participatory opportunities should be expanded through instruction, be longitudinal, and cause others to perceive the student as a more valuable, contributing, striving, and productive member of society.

Underlying the tenet of partial participation is the conviction that it provides opportunities for positive human interactions that would otherwise be unavailable if the person were merely a passive observer or did not participate at all. For example, during recess in elementary schools students typically are allowed to select games to play for a short period of time before returning to class. To integrate a youngster with severe multiple disabilities, a teacher would assist in identifying a variety of activities that would be of interest to both the child with a severe disability and nondisabled schoolmates. These activities might each embody components at which the student with disabilities could be proficient. In one such case, an electric race car track was adapted to allow a student with physical limitations to control one lane on the track through the use of a simple remote control switch (Giangreco, 1985, p. 54). Since the other lane was not altered, it could be used in the usual fashion by a nondisabled youngster at the same time. *The very activities that are appropriate for nondisabled individuals can be appropriate for those with severe disabilities — the difference is that at times our expectations about their participation in those activities must accommodate their characteristics.* Partial participation strategies can be applied in any curricular domain and hold the potential for both direct and indirect social, cognitive, and physical benefits. School psychologists can facilitate this process by bringing the principle of partial participation to the attention of school staff during planning meetings and by recommending adaptations that might facilitate prosocial interaction.

Functionality and Chronological Age Appropriateness

Functionality. Functionality and chronological age appropriateness are fundamental reference points for planning curriculum and activities for students with severe disabilities. The term *functional* simply means having direct, practical application in daily life. Functional activities typically are clusters of skills and actions that when grouped together allow a person to enter into such undertakings as making a purchase, pursuing a hobby, preparing a snack, engaging in work, or socially interacting with peers. A defining condition of functionality is engaging in activities in natural contexts. Three examples would be (a) practicing dressing skills before and after physical education class in the locker room, (b) dressing as part of a toileting routine in the privacy of a bathroom, and (c) removing and putting on outerware at one's locker when arriving and departing from school. The alternative of having students undress and redress behind a partition in the classroom at 9:30 a.m. because it is "time for dressing" on the schedule, is out of context. The need for sufficient teaching trials to learn functional skills can be addressed by designing additional natural situations for practice coordinated across home, school, and community settings. Concurrent simulated and natural environment teaching approaches (Nietupski, Hamre-Nietupski, Clancy, and Veerhusen, 1986) and paradigms such as "general case" strategies (Horner, McDonnell, & Bellamy, 1986) can also help to structure the necessary teaching/learning trials.

In contrast to functional activities, *nonfunctional* activities do not appear to have an immediate or future direct application in daily life (Giangreco, 1987). Pegboards, form boards, nesting blocks, and wooden stringing beads are some of the more common developmentally based activity materials inappropriately used with students with severe disabilities. Such activities are nonfunctional because their potential application in daily life is dependent upon generalization; but the assumption of generalization may lack validity with these students. For example, users of pegboards argue that their intention is to teach a generalized eye-hand coordination skill. Unfortunately, it is not reasonable to assume generalization will occur across activities, settings, people, natural cues, and so forth. Professionals who select nonfunctional activities may have a positive purpose in mind, but the same needs can be better addressed through the use of activities and materials that are functional for the individual. The school psychologist might ask, "If Jenny did develop generalized eye-hand coordination, in what ways would she functionally use that skill?" Staff would be encouraged to list a variety of activities based on an analysis of Jenny's daily and weekly routines that require the use of the eye–hand skills of interest (e.g., putting coins in vending machines, pay telephones, coin-operated washers and dryers, video games, banks, and parking meters; or using keys to lock and unlock one's home, locker, or bicycle). The psychologist could assist the staff in stating the goals and structuring the instruction to focus directly on the desired functional outcomes.

Chronological age appropriateness. Like partial participation and functional activities, the use of materials, activities, and interactions that are appropriate to the chronological age of persons with severe disabilities are more likely to foster positive social interaction with same-age peers. In the past, curricula for students with severe disabilities were based on developmental models that encouraged professionals and families to select activities that matched the "developmental age" of the student. This often resulted in clearly undesirable situations such as teenagers wearing Mickey Mouse bibs, being spoken to like infants, and being given toys such as rattles and teething rings. While acknowledging the importance of information about an individual's development, York and Williams (1977) point out that developmental sequences do not necessarily represent desirable teaching sequences, nor do they provide

for instruction on alternative or augmentative modes of attaining certain functions (e.g., use of a symbol board for communication; wheelchair for mobility). "Next appearing items" on developmental measures will seldom serve as appropriate instructional goals. If they are used in that way, children with severe disabilities will spend many years locked into learning skills long since mastered by much younger children. Rather than becoming "ready," students fall further and further behind as each year passes.

Developmentally-based curriculum goals may also stigmatize students. A study by Bates, Morrow, Pancsofar, and Sedlak (1984) validated the common-sense notion that age appropriateness has an impact on the perceptions of nondisabled persons. They found that a person with severe disabilities was perceived more favorably by others when engaged in functional, age-appropriate actions than in nonfunctional age-inappropriate situations.

Similarly to the problem-solving clarification process with the functionality issue, psychologists can assist staff in making the transition from age-inappropriate to age-appropriate materials and activities by acknowledging the positive intentions of staff and then helping them focus on the characteristics of the material or activity that need to be retained in a more age-appropriate alternative. For example, a 12-year-old with severe retardation, limited physical abilities, and impaired vision was inappropriately provided with a brightly colored rattle for leisure activity on the basis of the student's current motor development and the notion that he was interested in the bright coloration, the tactile contact, and the auditory stimulation. The psychologist can use this information in a problem-solving format to assist staff in determining potential alternative activities that reflect the student's motor needs and involve similar visual, tactile, and auditory characteristics (e.g., partial participation in hand-held electronic games). The school psychologist's knowledge of nondisabled students can facilitate this process since age-mates are a ready and extensive source of age-appropriate leisure suggestions.

This principle should be reflected in the location of classrooms and programs for students with severe disabilities as well as in the participation of those students in activities with their same-age peers. A past practice has been to locate classrooms for the full age range (including teenagers) on elementary school campuses on the assumption that this reflected a *developmental* match. Thus, a student with severe disabilities might be sent part-time into regular education classes with much younger children. Such age-inappropriate placements are sometimes rationalized because "developmentally" the student is deemed closest in functioning level to the younger students, for example, in grades K–2. However, placing disabled students with much younger children perpetuates the misguided notion that students with disabilities must be able to function at the same level as nondisabled students in order to fit into the regular education environment. Moreover, because if a student is significantly older than his or her classmates he or she may be exposed to activities and situations that will not necessarily facilitate interaction with age peers in school or other settings. Finally, as students with disabilities get older and continue to be placed with younger students according to developmental criteria, the age and size gaps become too wide for schools or parents to tolerate. At this point, students are unnecessarily banished to self-contained special education full-time so that integration eventually occurs only at the primary level. School psychologists can play an important role by recommending educational placements that allow students to move with their age peers through the school years.

In addition to positively affecting placement decisions made at initial individualized educational planning (IEP) meetings, and advocating age appropriateness and proximity to same-age peers, the school psychologist can become familiar with the integrated models that are available to support such placements, such as the *Circles of Learning* by Johnson, Johnson, Holubec, and Roy (1984). This model focuses on cooperative learning approaches within regular education that are designed for use with heterogeneous groups of students. School psychologists can play a vital role by providing ongoing consultative support to teachers and related service professionals working with integrated instructional programs.

Neighborhood schooling. Neighborhood schooling in the present context means attendance by students with severe disabilities in the same regular education school building they would attend if not disabled. Technically, exclusion may be a violation of civil rights, yet acute space problems that are due to increasing enrollment is a common rationale cited to justify out-of-district placement of students with severe disabilities. Although physical space is a concern, truly it should be a nonissue. In most districts, only students with disabilities are excluded from their neighborhood schools, which appears to be clear discrimination based upon handicapping condition. This would not be true if proportional numbers of nondisabled students were also bused to nondistrict sites. Generalized busing out of district would not be tolerated by the public and is so extreme that it probably would not even be suggested. Other solutions to space problems would be identified, such as capital improvements, portable classrooms, rearranging internal space, scheduling changes to facilitate space availability, multiple uses of space (e.g., the auditorium as a music room), elimination of unessential room use, or redistricting. While some of these ideas may be unpopular, undesirable, or short-term solutions, grudgingly they would be implemented in order to include *all* nondisabled children. It may be a statement of inertia, benign neglect, or a real or perceived lack of political clout, but in too many school districts the enthusiasm for including all students with disabilities pales by comparison.

Integrated locations and activities for students with severe disabilities in general-attendance schools typically have been limited to common-use areas such as the cafeteria, hallways, auditorium, and schoolyard or to specifically selected special subjects such as art, music, and physical education. Only recently are students with severe disabilities being placed into regular class with individualized educational programs for either part-time or full-time placement. Examples of such programs will be highlighted later in this chapter. There is overwhelming evidence to support the efficacy and value of the physical, social, and academic integration of students with severe disabilities into schools and programs with their nondisabled peers. Meyer and Putnam (in press) provide a comprehensive review of these efforts and outcomes such as positive social interaction, skill acquisition, and the development of friendships, as well as positive attitudes and acceptance of individual differences, including active parent and community support. Such benefits occur for children with disabilities and those who are nondisabled.

In a 1983 pilot integration project initiated in Ithaca, New York, five elementary-age students identified as having profound and multiple (physical and cognitive) disabilities and who attended a segregated (handicapped-only) school were each integrated into chronological-age-appropriate regular classes on a part-time basis (two to three times weekly) at nearby Northeast Elementary School. Following initial preparations and subsequent implementation of the project, a cross-sectional survey was sent to 140 families of nondisabled children from grades 2, 3, 4, and 5 who were participating in the project (Giangreco, 1984). Ninety-two families (66%) responded. Ninety-two percent of the families perceived that their child felt positively about the integration experience. Ninety-eight percent of the families "agreed" or "strongly agreed" that this integration experience was beneficial to their nondisabled child's personal and social development. Ninety-one percent of the families believed that the integration experience had a positive impact on changing their child's attitudes toward persons with disabilities, and 58% reported that the program also positively affected the attitudes of at least one other family member.

Unfortunately, while program data and parents' reports supported the positive effects of this effort on the performance of students receiving special education, the effects were lasting for only one of the students. Of the five children, only one was actually from the Northeast Elementary School neighborhood, since the segregated school was operated by an educational cooperative. When the program's initiator left the school system, the only child to continue in an integrated placement was the student from the Northeast Elementary neighborhood. Through his parents' cooperative efforts with school officials, this child's integration experience was increased to a half-time regular class placement, the home school district provided support by hiring a teacher assistant. This points out the importance of home district placement as it relates to continuity of program, advocacy, ownership, and parent involvement. While part-time integration into regular education environments is certainly a step in the right direction, it presents significant logistical problems compared to full-time regular-class placement, as accommodations have to be made with at least two completely independent schedules rather than one.

Criterion of Ultimate Functioning

The goal of having citizens with severe disabilities ultimately functioning as productively and independently as possible in integrated adult environments is the cornerstone of the "criterion of ultimate functioning" (Brown, Nietupski, & Hamre-Nietupski, 1976). Grouping and placement decisions made on behalf of children with severe disabilities, as well as the assessments that guide those decisions and instructional planning are profoundly affected by the tenets underlying the criterion of ultimate functioning. Critical components of this principle, including heterogeneous grouping and criterion-referenced assessment related to student outcomes and functional analysis of excess behavior, will be discussed in the following sections.

Heterogeneous grouping. It has been suggested that homogeneous tracking of students in both regular and special education retards academic progress, fosters low self-esteem, and promotes school misbehavior, especially for those in the average and lower ability groups (Oakes, 1985). In addition, homogeneous tracking is inherently separate and unequal.

In many school districts, homogeneous classes for students with severe disabilities are the only available placement option. Following placement, goals and objectives are generated for the student. While this approach is quite common, it is both illogical and inconsistent with the IEP process, since placement is supposedly designed to facilitate achievement of the goals and should reflect LRE guidelines.

Many school districts making the transition from segregated to integrated services display a tendency to move students to integrated sites by a hierarchical approach, the most capable and easily accepted students being transferred first. The logic of this approach is to allow schools to have an initial positive experience with integration. Receiving schools often can see the value in the inclusion of these relatively capable students. Such students represent few, if any, threats to the existing system. However, movement of these homogeneous groups leaves a corresponding homogeneous group of students behind whose behavior and needs are more challenging. When this hierarchical approach is employed, the later groups of students are at risk of being rejected when it is suggested that they arrive at the school en masse. This scenario can be avoided by transferring heterogeneous groups of students. The presence of a proportionally smaller number of more challenging students from the outset allows schools to adjust and respond to the range of students being integrated. Heterogeneous grouping pro-

vides opportunities for offering individualized instruction, enhancing self-perceptions, supplying appropriate models, and increasing student achievement. Grouping students heterogeneously while providing individualized supports safeguards against the educational, racial, and socioeconomic inequities that often plague homogeneous options. Thus, heterogeneous grouping can be an important component of an appropriate educational program.

Criterion-referenced assessment. In view of both the TASH priorities and those represented by the NASP position statement, it is critical that the primary role of the school psychologist shift from determining a child's diagnostic category and eligibility for special services to performing more functional assessments that can aid in the design of appropriate instruction as well as evaluate the effectiveness of that instruction. Evans and Meyer (1984) summarized the current trends in functional and criterion-referenced assessment procedures in special and remedial education, which parallel competency-based assessment in regular education. Their review provides a succinct overview of the issues and specific measures for students with mild to severe disabilities; therefore this general information will not be reported here. Since their review, further developments in two areas deserve mention: (a) the development of student outcome measures to evaluate the effectiveness of special education services, and (b) the development of useful and valid procedures to conduct functional analysis of excess behavior.

Student outcome measures. The various curricular reform efforts already summarized in this chapter share a basic goal: Educational programs for students with severe disabilities should enable them to achieve maximum independence and participation in current and future integrated environments, including home, school, workplace, and a variety of leisure and community settings. Thus, any measure of student outcomes should presumably document whether the student has achieved either mastery or meaningful participation in functional activity routines in each of the environmental domains. Yet the traditional measures available that might typically be used to evaluate students' progress (or even to determine diagnosis or initial placement needs) do not reflect everyday, functional routines. Instead such measures map the developmental mastery of relatively isolated skills in each of the traditional curricular areas such as language, motor, cognition, social-emotional, and self-help domains. The use of these measures with students with severe disabilities has included the assignment of a "mental age" to students that might be grossly discrepant from their chronological age. This contributes to the perpetuation of the use of preschool curricular content for students throughout their school careers, which in turn further reinforces the stereotypic notion that persons with severe developmental disabilities are similar to very young children. Whenever both the curriculum and outcome measures are developmentally oriented rather than being focused upon criterion environments and events, it is virtually ensured that students with severe disabilities will *not* have an opportunity to learn meaningful, age-appropriate activities likely to be of interest and use to them across the lifespan.

Alternative functional outcome measures need to be used that are capable of assessing student performance — and growth as a function of instruction — in criterion situations and environments (White, 1987). Evans and Brown (1986) and Evans, Brown, Weed, Spry, and Owen (1987) have developed and validated an outcome measure designed for this purpose that has several additional features critical to their assessment approach: (a) Functional life routines constitute the range of behaviors measured, some of which are considered to be fixed while others are substitutable. Fixed routines must be performed in a particular way to achieve a critical effect, whereas substitutable routines might be performed in various ways — any one of which achieves the critical effect. (b) Routines are characterized as either daily or episodic depending upon how often they are needed. (c) Each functional life routine is organized into core, extension, and enrichment components. Core components are those steps that are absolutely necessary to the performance of the routine. Extension components include such steps as preparing for, initiating, and terminating routines and are those elements that determine the degree of independence. Enrichment components are not central to the routines but are likely to affect the quality of their performance as well as whether the individual finds them enjoyable; these components include choice, communication, and social interaction.

Typically, assessment for planning or evaluation of outcomes has been based almost exclusively on core components — those steps that are absolutely necessary to the performance of the routine. This has led many professionals to embrace developmental models because they had difficulty visualizing persons with severe, multiple disabilities engaging in core components of functional activities in typical ways. Criterion-referenced models, like Evans and Brown's, provide a constructive conceptualization of participation that allows people to visualize various forms of participation even for persons with the most profound disabilities. For example, 9-year-old Steven has profound mental retardation, hydrocephalus, and spina bifida, is nonverbal and nonambulatory, has limited upper extremity control, and requires assistance to maintain all activities of daily living. Within the domestic curricular domain, preparation of lunch would be a functional routine. Many professionals might look at such an item and immediately discount it as "not applicable" because they have limited themselves to a restricted mind set regarding Steve's participation in meal preparation. In reality, his participation in meal preparation could be quite extensive. He could partially participate in the core skills through employment of the idea of substitutability via adaptation (e.g., given an adapted microswitch and appropriate interface for safety, he could participate in opening a can of condensed soup with an electric can opener, mixing the soup with water or milk in a blender, and heating the soup in a microwave oven and bread in a toaster). At the extension level, let us assume that Steve currently has shown he wants to pull out of an activity by crying — he could be taught to terminate his involvement in a more socially desirable fashion. At an enrichment level Steve can be given choices about what will be prepared for lunch and can engage in the social and communicative aspects surrounding activities that make them enjoyable. Such an expanded vision of participation and worthwhile outcomes provides much richer opportunities for families, friends, and peers to share common daily experiences than do many traditional approaches, which emphasize differences and result in increasing segregation and isolation.

Functional analysis of excess behavior. During the past year, several major professional organizations (e.g., NASP, American Association on Mental Retardation, Association for Retarded Citizens/ USA, TASH, which reaffirmed its 1981 resolution) have passed resolutions calling for the cessation of the use of corporal punishment and other aversives and emphasized the need to develop positive alternatives for use with persons with disabilities.

These alternatives have generally stressed the need to base intervention plans upon knowledge of the function served by problem behavior. Evans and Meyer (1985), for example, maintain that excess behavior can nearly always be found to serve one or more of several major purposes: (a) self-regulatory; (b) social-communicative; and (c) play or entertainment. Knowing the function of the behavior for the individual allows the interventionist to identify (and teach) an alternative, socially *positive* behavior or skill to replace it in the person's repertoire. Various functional assessment procedures to identify the functions of excess behavior have been described by Evans and Meyer (1985), Donnellan, Mirenda, Mesaros, and Fassbender (1984), and Touchette, MacDonald, and Langer (1985). A particularly

useful Motivation Assessment Scale (MAS) has been partially validated by Durand (in press) and Durand and Crimmins (1987). The MAS requires only minutes to complete by someone who knows the person well, and appears to be reliable and valid. As the school psychologist increasingly assumes the role of consultant to assist teachers and parents in addressing matters such as behavior problems, a tool such as the MAS that does not require that the consultant conduct the assessment directly, but does require mutual problem solving should be invaluable.

Individualization and Adaptation

Integrated therapy. Students with severe disabilities are frequently recommended to receive occupational, physical, and speech/language therapy as related services designed to increase their benefit from their educational programs, since no single discipline embodies the diverse skills required to meet their needs (Albano, Cox, York, & York, 1981; Hart, 1977; Hutchinson, 1978; Orelove & Sobsey, 1987; Sears, 1981). Segregated programs have been rationalized partly by the notion that therapy services must be centralized. Services in centralized settings were frequently delivered episodically (e.g., 2 times a week for 30 minutes) directly by therapists in isolation from the natural environment. Traditionally, this isolation has not only been physical, entailing removal of the student from the classroom in order to delivery services in a "therapy room" (Sternat, Messina, Nietupski, Lyon, & Brown, 1977). Therapy has also been programmatically isolated: That is, assessment, planning, intervention, and evaluation have infrequently or minimally been referenced to the general educational program, priority goals written on the individualized education plan, and students' identified management needs related to instruction (Giangreco, 1986a).

Physical and programmatic isolation are independent characteristics. Certain therapeutic techniques, situations, or student characteristics may call for short-term use of physically isolated therapy for reasons such as privacy (e.g., postural drainage prior to eating) or distractibility, and therefore they may be used appropriately in certain circumstances. Any time short-term isolation occurs because of distractibility, plans should be set forth detailing strategies for reintegration into the natural environment. Return to the natural environment often requires knowledge of instructional or behavioral strategies that are familiar to psychologists but may be less well known to persons from other disciplines. For example, if an occupational therapist or speech/language pathologist is teaching a child to eat independently, the regular school cafeteria may represent a highly distracting and even fear-producing setting. Rather than retreating to the safety and quiet of the classroom on a permanent basis, the psychologist could assist the team in devising a reintegration plan by using their knowledge of techniques such as chaining, shaping, fading, prompting, and systematic desensitization.

Conversely, programmatic isolation is clearly incongruent with PL 94-142 (Education for All Handicapped Children Act), which states that related services are to be provided *"as may be required to assist a handicapped child to benefit from special education."* In addition to the drawbacks of segregated programs discussed earlier, centralization for the purpose of providing therapy limits access to family members and other primary caregivers who must be familiar with therapeutic techniques, and long, static bus rides to and from centralized sites can undo the benefits of episodic, direct therapy. Furthermore, educational centralization and segregation of learners with severe disabilities for the purposes of receiving therapy perpetuates the misguided notion that these students attend school primarily to receive therapy. On the contrary, the purpose of related therapy services is to support the educational program.

For the above reasons, alternatives have focused on providing integrated therapy services delivered in general-attendance public schools (Campbell, 1987). Programmatically integrated therapy in educational settings refers to the incorporation of educational and therapeutic techniques employed cooperatively to assess, plan, implement, evaluate, and report progress on common needs and goals. Integrated therapy can be implemented directly by therapists or by indirect intervention, with the therapists serving primarily, yet not exclusively, as a consultant. An emerging research base documents the usefulness of this approach (Campbell, McInerney, & Cooper, 1984; Campbell, Place, & Gossett, 1986; Giangreco, 1986b; McEwen & Karlan, 1987).

Integrated therapy services are designed to result in more intensive, synthesized, and meaningful outcomes for service recipients. For example, an occupational therapist working in an integrated therapy mode observed an elementary special education teacher conducting a group lesson that ended with students doing classroom jobs (e.g., watering plants, erasing the chalkboard, washing the desks, collating homework). The therapist observed with the basic question in mind, "What can I offer from my area of expertise that can help this student participate more fully in this activity?" As the teacher worked with Jimmy — a child with profound multiple disabilities — to clean off his desk with a wet cloth, the therapist made several key observations that could be applied within the course of the lesson: (a) Jimmy had a variety of abnormal reflexes, including a severe assymetrical tonic neck reflex (ATNR), which sometimes caused him to get "stuck" in what is referred to as a "fencer's position." By turning to orient toward the teacher (a desirable social response), who was positioned beside him, Jimmy became caught in the ATNR. The therapist suggested that the teacher be positioned in front of Jimmy to lessen the probability of the ATNR occurring. (b) Jimmy also had a hypersensitive startle reflex that was elicited when the teacher became highly animated in her verbal praise. The therapist suggested that the teacher monitor her voice volume and intensity. (c) Jimmy also had abnormally high muscle tone, which inhibited his already compromised movement capabilities. The therapist was able to suggest a few simple muscle tone reduction techniques that could be infused in the lesson to facilitate participation (e.g., passive range of motion, manual vibration). (d) When holding the cloth, Jimmy exhibited a tight-fisted grip that was not intentional, but uncontrolled. The therapist decided to explore the use of hand splits that would maintain Jimmy's hand in a more neutral position and allow more purposeful grasping. In traditional therapy models, many of these same techniques would be employed, but in the isolation of a therapy room. Because of the temporal effects of many such techniques, their transfer value from isolated therapy to functional situations is limited.

In the integrated therapy model the therapist functions more in a technical assistance and problem-solving role. This does not mean that therapists work exclusively in indirect modes. In order for the therapist to make constructive suggestions, he or she must have direct knowledge of each student's characteristics. The therapist can then teach others (e.g., family members, teachers, aides, other therapists) the skills to assist the student in the educational context. The therapist retains accountability and continues to monitor the practice of those to whom skills have been taught. For more detailed discussion of related services, refer to Campbell (1987); Giangreco (1986a); and Giangreco, York, and Rainforth (1987).

CONCEPTUAL FRAMEWORK FOR EXPANDING SERVICE DELIVERY OPTIONS

Placement in the Regular Classroom

In addition to the environment, regular education can be characterized broadly by two components: (a) the program and (b) the supports. Environment in this context is the physical space in which learners receive their education, program is the curriculum and instruction provided to learners and is expressed in syllabi, scope and sequence charts, instructional practices, and so forth; it is operationalized in curricular goal statements, objectives, and lessons. Supports are resources such as teachers, therapists, psychologists, teacher aides/assistants, other school personnel, equipment, books, and materials. While there are relationships among these three components, analytically each can be considered separately from the others. Figure 1 presents a conceptual framework that offers four options for integration in regular education classrooms. These four options may be in operation independently, consecutively, or concurrently on a full-time or part-time basis for any particular student.

Integration Option A: Consultative/ resource supports and program similar to regular education. Integration Option A allows learners with disabilities to access substantively the same program as nondisabled students with consultative or resource supports provided to the regular education teacher. This option for integration is typically employed only for those students whose needs are similar to same-age, nondisabled peers. Thus, children with speech impairments or mildly disabled children whose discrepancies are minimal are likely to receive these kinds of services. This variation of integration is widely accepted as desirable and appropriate for such students.

Integration Option B: Program similar to regular education with extended supports. In Integration Option B, probably the next most frequently employed option, students pursue the regular education program with extended or individualized supports. This option is often used for learners who experience physical or sensory disabilities but can adequately participate in the regular education program at the same cognitive level as nondisabled learners (e.g., can pass local and state competency exams required for advancement and graduation with a high school diploma).

Integration Option C: Consultative/ resource supports similar to regular education with extended/individualized program. A third integration possibility,

FIGURE 1
Integration Options Within Regular Education Classroom Environments
Across the Dimensions of Support and Program.

Consultative Resource
Supports Similar to
Regular Education

Extended or
Individualized
Supports

Program Similar
to
Regular Education

A   B

Extended or
Individualized
Program

C   D

Option C, is less frequently employed. It calls for students with handicapping conditions to participate in the regular education program with consultative supports typically available to nonhandicapped learners while pursuing extended, modified, or otherwise individualized goals. There are a number of students with handicaps, including those with severe disabilities, who can fully or partially participate in a variety of regular education activities without extended supports. These students tend to be relatively cooperative and possess at least a rudimentary ability to follow directions. These opportunities are rare for students with severe disabilities because of the misconception that such a label necessarily implies the need for specialized supports to participate with nondisabled counterparts in typical activities. This phenomenon is merely an extension of the myth of special education, which has served to isolate this population. In this option, the student's teacher may be certified in regular education or dually certified (regular education/special education), but additional specialized staff serve a resource or consultative role to the teacher rather than providing direct services to the student.

Integration Option D: Extended/ individualized program and supports. Integration Option D is designed to provide extended or individualized supports to students who are pursuing individualized educational programs within the regular education environment. This option is meant to operationalize the section of the federal regulation that reminds us that we have a responsibility to provide "supplementary aids and services" within the regular education environment before considering removal from such settings. Unfortunately, most students identified as having severe disabilities are never afforded the opportunity to participate in regular education environments with the use of supplementary aids and services. Instead, they are immediately tracked into special education on the assumption that regular education environments can offer only regular education curricula with no adaptations or individualization of instruction.

Supports to Regular Education

If the integration of students with severe disabilities is to be successful, a variety of supports need to be available. Recently, emphasis has been placed upon the importance of the school principal as a leader in facilitating integration (Biklen, 1985; Northwest Regional Laboratory, 1985). To the surprise of school personnel, many of the resources needed to provide quality integrated education are already at the disposal of principals in general-attendance schools. These generic resources can be tapped, modified, or reallocated in creative ways. Planned staff development with regular education and special education staff jointly offers an ongoing mechanism for training and operationalizing quality programs (Meyer & Eichinger, 1987; Stile, Peters, & Piazza-Templeman, 1986). One of the keys to successful integration is coordinating regular education and special education resources to function as a single unit, with one mission, rather than as parallel or competing entities. The realization of such a union may be challenging, but the programs described in the next section, along with numerous other examples, provide evidence that such a goal is clearly attainable.

Through cooperative regular education/special education ventures, team approaches can be expanded to include both programs in ways that advance the learning and participation of students with disabilities and those who are nondisabled. For example, in the previously mentioned pilot integration project at Northeast Elementary School, a special education team consisting of a teacher, aides, and therapists planned jointly with regular education teachers in the conviction that integration could extend beyond improving social integration to include academic benefits for both

groups of students. The teachers experimented with the use of "curriculum overlapping," that is, the teaching of a heterogeneous group in such a way that students pursue individually determined objectives from different curricular domains within the context of a shared activity. In this case, the curriculum overlapping was typically carried out by one of the special education staff with a group that consisted of one youngster with severe multiple handicapping conditions and a group of three to five nondisabled students. For example, Joe was a fifth-grade age student with severe cerebral palsy and functioning in the profound range of mental retardation. The fifth-grade class he attended was studying the Civil War in their social studies unit. The teacher designed an activity using a stamp album with a set of postage stamps that commemorate historical events from that era to facilitate a review discussion with the nondisabled students on their recent readings and class activities related to this topic. This provided them with extra academic help and teacher feedback that would normally have been unavailable. At the same time, Joe was pursuing objectives related to the development of stamp collecting as an age-appropriate leisure skill. Thus, objectives were individualized and the two curricular areas (leisure skills and social studies) overlapped to generate benefits for a diverse group of students.

PROGRAM DESCRIPTIONS SUPPORTING REGULAR SCHOOL AND CLASS PLACEMENTS FOR STUDENTS WITH SEVERE DISABILITIES

Cayuga-Onondaga Board of Cooperative Educational Services (C-O BOCES), Auburn, New York

The C-O BOCES is a rural educational cooperative located in the Eastern Finger Lakes region of central New York state. Prior to the 1984-1985 school year, special education services delivered to students with severe handicaps by the C-O BOCES consisted of a center-based, handicapped-only program housed in a separate wing of an occupational center serving approximately 50 of its 110 students with the most severe disabilities, an educational program that was carried out at the center exclusively, and homogeneously grouped classrooms. Currently the C-O BOCES provides services to all of its 110 students with moderate to severe disabilities in integrated, chronological-age-appropriate public schools. Over 70% of these students are now educated within their home school districts — over 95% in heterogeneously grouped classes. In this case, heterogeneous grouping refers to the proportional inclusion of students with more severe disabilities in classes with those who are less disabled. In classes typically serving nine to 12 students, two to three of the students function in the severe or profound range of mental retardation and exhibit significant behavioral, physical, and/or sensory impairments. Classrooms are staffed accordingly to support student needs. This usually translates into a teacher, two or three aides, and recommended related services per classroom. It is the intention of the C-O BOCES Special Education Department to eliminate the homogeneous grouping of students with severe disabilities through two simple approaches: (a) All new incoming students will be placed in heterogeneous classes (either special class or regular class with support), and (b) students will continue to be dispersed.

Students in heterogeneous classes participate on a part-time basis in regular education classes (Integration Options B, C, and D from Figure 1) and in integrated community environments. At five elementary schools, this inclusion is facilitated through the dispersal of students, either individually or in small groups, into regular classes. While several students require supports and/or modified programs, others participate without additional supports. At two other schools, several students with severe disabilities historically have participated in a variety of special area subjects (e.g., physical education, art, chorus) in a dispersed

fashion without additional supports (Integration Option C).

One of the more unusual aspects of operationalizing age-appropriate placement is the establishment of a heterogeneously grouped class of students aged 18–21, with moderate to severe disabilities at Cayuga Community College in Auburn, New York (part of the State University of New York system). These students use a classroom space, and have access to the five-building campus and grounds and a variety of services. Students interact with nondisabled students and staff in a variety of common areas (e.g., cafeteria, student lounge, offices, locker rooms, library, nature trail, auditorium, athletic facilities, and work–study sites). The college administration has made a significant commitment to support the program through maintaining the rental agreement at a time when space availability is as pressing at the college as it is in area elementary and secondary schools. This support is partially based on the belief that the program not only benefits students with special educational needs, but also enriches the general college community (New York State Education Department, 1986). Students spend part of their time at the college receiving instruction and a significant amount of time off campus at community instructional sites learning skills related to domestic, leisure, vocational, and general community functioning (Giangreco, McKinney, Fitzpatrick, & Sabin, 1986). An ongoing vocational component includes in-classroom jobs at the elementary level and on-school-grounds jobs done with nondisabled peers at two middle schools in preparation for real work experience in a variety of settings for students attending two high schools and Cayuga Community College (Zacchei & Mirman, 1986). The community college is a highly normalized, age-appropriate site and is a natural decentralized extension in the educational program.

Although these improvements, developed through an educational cooperative, have upgraded services for students with disabilities, Biklen and his colleagues have pointed out the problems associated with integration efforts sponsored by educational cooperatives (Biklen, 1985). This raises the question of what roles educational cooperatives can serve in facilitating integrated, home school district placement of students with significant disabilities. During the 1985-1986 school year the C-O BOCES initiated a support service model for the purpose of assisting local school systems in providing appropriate educational programs for students with disabilities in their home school district through cooperative planning and assessing the resources available through the cooperative. Services provided under the proposal included consultation on educational assessment, IEP preparation and development, classroom planning, service options, staff training, educational evaluation, survey of physical accessibility, adaptations, and other services identified by the host district. This model is currently being examined for potentially more formalized application.

The support service model was initiated to assist the Jordan-Elbridge School district in serving a new student with severe, multiple disabilities in their home district. Traditionally, such students have been bused to regional programs and placed in homogeneous classes for students with severe disabilities. Owing to this school district's commitment to serving all students, they worked cooperatively with the BOCES to develop an individualized service delivery plan that included full-time regular class placement at an elementary school. Supports were provided by assignment of a consultant from C-O BOCES, involvement of the resource room special education teacher in the building, hiring of a teacher aide for the classroom to assist all students, and implementation of an integrated therapy model. Involvement of this youngster in the regular education classroom represented a combination of integration Options C and D as depicted in Figure 1. She required extended and individualized program content and at times could participate successfully without added supports although she required additional supports for other parts of her day. In subsequent years, additional school districts made use of these supports to varying degrees to retain students in home school district placements by using resources available through the support service model. This model, while in the infancy of its development, represents a potentially valuable role that can be played by educational cooperatives as services continue to become increasingly decentralized.

The Edward Smith School, Syracuse, New York

An integrated program for students with autism and other severe disabilities at the Edward Smith Elementary School in the City of Syracuse School District was initiated in 1980. The model was directly based upon Peter Knoblock's model at the Jowonio School, affiliated with Syracuse University (Knoblock & Lehr, 1986), and began in response to the need to provide continuity for Jowonio graduates as they reached the cutoff age for that program and would otherwise have most likely been referred to handicapped-only programs. Since that time, the Syracuse City School District has established programs for all of its students — including those with the most severe disabilities — in age-appropriate regular schools, but the Edward Smith program was unique: Children with autism were and are enrolled in regular same-age graded classrooms with their nonhandicapped peers.

Until last year, the program consisted of seven classes, one at each grade level (K-6), each of these classes consisting of 26-34 children of whom five or six were labeled autistic or, in some cases, multiply handicapped. Edward Smith School has a total enrollment of approximately 800 students, so at each grade level an additional three to four classrooms are *not* integrated but include only nondisabled students. During the 1986-1987 school year, however, the teachers in all the fourth grades voluntarily each enrolled one to two students with autism in his or her regular classroom. This pattern is being continued during the current year and is being considered for expansion to the other grade levels.

Fenwick (1987) provides a history of the program, an overview of its basic components, and a personal perspective based upon her years as one of the teachers at Edward Smith. In her discussion of the three alternative "models," or staffing patterns, variously used by the program, one particular approach is emphasized. In general, the program utilizes a combination of team teaching, (one teacher has special education certification and the other regular education) and teaching by personnel who are dually certified in special and regular education. In Fenwick's preferred model, two teachers divide their schedule and responsibilities across two classrooms, and special and typical children are enrolled in both. Teachers thus alternate between the rooms, but at any given time each teacher is responsible for all the children, both those who are not disabled and those with autism. Thus, the teacher conducting a lesson for a group of typical children also is teaching a child with autism, and must accommodate and adapt the group instruction accordingly. In contrast to other models in which teachers who are members of a team nevertheless identify more closely with either the typical or the special children, the above team approach, Fenwick argues, has more positive impact upon the ways in which autistic children are perceived by their peers, who see the teachers interacting equally with all the students.

Classroom environment and individualized instruction are similarly critical components of this integrated program. A school psychologist (who also serves other buildings), a social worker, and a coordinator provide additional support. Strong administrative leadership has also characterized the school, and the teachers meet as a group with the principal and the school psychologist approximately twice a month on instructional and behavioral issues. It is notable that in the Syracuse City School District, attendance at the Edward Smith School is viewed as most desirable by parents of disabled and nondisabled students alike.

Integration in Canada

"Each belongs" in regular classes, regardless of handicap, is the philosophical basis for the inclusion of all children in the Hamilton–Wentworth Separate School Board (HWSSB) in Hamilton, Ontario, including those with severe maladaptive or disruptive behaviors (Forest, 1986a). The Wellington County Separate School Board (WCSSB) in Guelph, Ontario, supports a similar educational goal, "to have every child's educational needs met in his/her home school in a regular classroom setting in accordance with their educational needs, be they of average ability, gifted, or in need of remediation. Each child's social, emotional, intellectual and physical needs must be addressed" (Forest, 1986b). Commitments of philosophy and policy at the level of the board of education and the superintendent are driving forces in these systems and others in Canada, especially when they are operationalized through ongoing implementation and support. For example, WCSSB has no special education classes, but offers a "needs-based program" to all students (Forest, 1984).

These and other schools in Canada have increasingly adopted variations on *education for community living (ECL)* (Forest, 1986b). ECL supports the merger of special and regular education, as proposed by Stainback and Stainback (1984). The ECL model is based on the premise that special education is obsolete and that there should be only one system of education for all children, which makes modifications and adaptations when necessary to meet the needs of individual students. ECL can be broadly characterized by a team approach; decisions based on total life environments; use of generic community resources; implementation by both certified professionals and noncertified staff with input from specialists; use of individually determined strategies; and high expectations for participation in community life. Support for progressive changes in Canada have been facilitated jointly by individuals and school districts as well as the Canadian Association for Community Living, institutions of higher education, and the G. Allan Roeher Institute (formerly the Canadian National

Institute on Mental Retardation).

The team aspect of service delivery in the WCSSB's elementary, junior high, and high schools is manifested in the form of school-based prescriptive teams. The individual school is the unit of service delivery for these teams. The services of the team are provided to students on the basis of program and service delivery needs, rather than label of disability. The school principal serves as the administrative head of the team, which consists of regular education teaching staff and "methods and resource" specialists who have training in special education and pupil personnel services. Additional support personnel external to the school unit are available on an as-needed basis. The school-based prescriptive team assumes accountability for planning and student progress. Methods and resource specialists work together with regular education staff; they are responsible for coordinating team activities and overseeing implementation of team recommendations. In this model, all members of the school community are responsible for the teaching of children who represent the full range of human capability. Such an approach bypasses a hierarchical system of special education whereby students with increasingly challenging needs are relegated to levels lower and lower on the educational totem pole and further from their own potentialities.

One of the most notable aspects of the Canadian programs reviewed, both in and out of schools, is the emphasis upon social interactions as the foundation for human growth. Ongoing networks of real relationships are developed through *support circles* (Snow & Forest, 1985) that focus on partnerships, interdependencies, and other normalized human interactions in contrast to paid professionals. Such support circles involve friends, relatives, co-workers, and so forth, and are often formed around two people, where an advocate speaks for the person challenged by a disability. It is the aim of support circles to grow large enough that they can meet support needs without placing undue pressures on members — which can occur when the circles are too small.

Support circles represent a grassroots approach to community support designed to provide benefits to all involved and to further empower persons who traditionally have been devalued in society.

At the time of this writing the Northwest Territories had initiated regular class placement for all students, and fully integrated options were being advanced in Ontario, the Maritime provinces, and to various degrees throughout Canada.

Regular Class Placement in Vermont

The State of Vermont has worked in cooperation with the Center for Developmental Disabilities (CDD) at the University of Vermont and local school districts to develop and implement quality services for students with severe disabilities in a variety of areas, such as curriculum, service delivery, social integration, communication, recreation and leisure services, and vocational preparation (Fox, Williams, & Fox, 1978; McKenzie, Hill, Sousie, York, & Baker, 1977; Reichle & Keogh, 1986; Williams, et al., 1986). Vermont programs not only are exemplary, but represent change on a broader scale and depict the interrelationships between the State Education Department, CDD, and local schools.

In 1983 the CDD received a 3-year federally funded grant to establish and evaluate a rural regional resource model for placing and educating school-age learners with severe handicaps in their home school district rather than in the traditionally operated regional education programs. One of the original school districts participating in the "Homecoming" project (as it was called) was the Franklin–Northwest Supervisory Union (FNSU) in Swanton, Vermont. In the FNSU as in the Ontario program, both affective and academic aspects of service delivery were emphasized. FNSU identified "desired student exit behaviors" as (a) positive self-image, (b) positive social skills, and (c) development of higher-level cognitive skills.

Through the development of core planning teams and a cooperative planning process, the establishment of access to consultants (Thousand, Fox, et al., 1986), and the provision of in-service training (Thousand, Nevin-Parta, & Fox, 1987), students with severe disabilities were integrated into regular classes in participating school districts. The core planning team was composed of a cross section of each local school's instructional staff (e.g., regular and special educators, speech pathologist, psychologist, principal). Each school's team was responsible for developing and implementing individual plans to address students' current educational needs and to carry out transition of students to regular class placements and post graduation services. For each student, the core planning team was expanded to include parents and the present and the next year's teachers. Depending on an individual student's needs, professionals with expertise in such areas as physical therapy and behavior management were added to the team. Teacher aides were also available to assist the regular education teacher. Generic resources for all students were made available to students with severe disabilities and, if needed, the schools could call on the State of Vermont Interdisciplinary Team for Intensive Special Education. This team provides interdisciplinary consultative support to school-age students with severe disabilities (Christie, 1984).

Of equal importance to the planning team was the availability of consultative services at the school district level from a professional with background and experience in developing integrated programs for students with severe disabilities. In some school districts special education teachers from the regional program were retrained to take on this new consultative role. The consultant provided in-service training, consultation, and technical assistance to the planning team and other school staff members.

By the fall of 1986, 56 students had been moved from regional special education programs to 26 local elementary, middle, and high schools (Williams et al., 1986). The project has demonstrated that students with severe handicaps can be educated within their local districts if they are provided with appropriate supports (Thousand et al., 1985). The program has been so successful that the State of Vermont has recognized the need to explore ways to educate *all* Vermont learners in their local schools. This is a primary goal of the state's plan for special education, approved by the State Board of Education (Riggen, 1985).

SUMMARY AND FUTURE DIRECTIONS

While many school districts throughout North America are engaged in notable endeavors directed toward alternative approaches to service delivery, this chapter has focused on a small number of examples representing a range of service delivery configurations in diverse settings. Although these programs are not yet typical, they do extend beyond homogeneous classes for students with severe disabilities in general attendance schools and reflect the characteristics outlined in Table 2 as most promising in this area. While these highlighted programs have received considerable regional or national attention because of their service delivery efforts, in each case the personnel associated with each program hesitated to embrace the label of "model program." Persons involved with these schools shared an enthusiasm for their efforts but pointed out that their programs were in need of ongoing improvements; they emphasized the need to individualize service delivery configurations to meet the unique circumstances present in different locations. Therefore, the examples cited herein are not presented as ultimate answers or "model programs" to be replicated directly. Rather, they are meant to provide examples of promising options, and of what can happen when schools become proactive. Fullan (1982, p. 410) reminds us that change is a process, not an event.

These examples were representative of various points along this continuum of change. Such glimpses of what can be may help us form a vision of future service configurations for all students that will offer equal access to quality education in neighborhood schools. While advancement needs to continue on many levels ranging from legislative, to funding mechanisms and preservice preparation, school psychologists as a group embody the skills and knowledge to provide impetus to the integration movement through a variety of activities. Clearly research and program development needs are numerous in this area and encompass a broad range of potential areas (e.g., nonaversive behavior management, instructional strategies for working with heterogeneous groups, refinement of social skills techniques, collaboration and negotiation strategies among personnel). On a more day-to-day level, psychologists in the United States can create an impact by applying their knowledge and skills in ways that are inclusionary, advance prosocial interactions, and are educational for all students, regardless of their learning characteristics.

We began this chapter by noting the discrepancy between the goals for integration and equality of opportunity that are espoused by a growing number of professionals and advocates and the attainment of those goals. While some regions and even states have made dramatic progress toward achieving integrated options for all students, others have not. Biklen (1988) has argued that we are undoubtedly naive in our belief that all educational decisions are informed by clinical expertise. Instead, there appears to be increasing evidence that separate services are being maintained to protect careers and current fiscal patterns. It may be that not all observers have similar values, yet the empirical evidence regarding the benefits possible as a result of well-planned integrated programs seems irrefutable. Perhaps the challenge of the next few years will be to expand our remedial perspectives from a relatively narrow focus upon helping children change, to developing and validating strategies to help *systems* change. As applied researchers and as clinical service providers, school psychologists could play a vital role in this new direction.

ACKNOWLEDGMENT

Preparation of portions of this chapter was supported in part by contract #300.82-0363, awarded to the University of Minnesota, and by Cooperative Agreement #G0084C3001, awarded to the Association for Persons with Severe Handicaps (TASH), with subcontracts to Syracuse University, by the Office of Special Education Programs, U.S. Department of Education. This material does not necessarily reflect the position or policies of the U.S. Department of Education, and no official endorsement should be inferred.

The authors wish to thank Wes Williams for his constructive input and editorial suggestions during the preparation of this chapter.

REFERENCES

Albano, M. L., Cox, B., York, J., & York, R. (1981). Educational teams for students with severe multiple handicaps. In R. York, W. Schofield, D. Donder, & D. Ryndak (Eds.), *The severely and profoundly handicapped child* (pp. 24-33). Springfield, IL: Illinois State Board of Education.

Bates, P., Morrow, S. A., Pancsofar, E., & Sedlak, R. (1984). The effect of functional vs. non-functional activities on attitudes/expectations of non-handicapped college students: What they see is what they get. *Journal of the Association for Persons With Severe Handicaps, 9*, 73-76.

Bates, P., Renzaglia, A., & Wehman, P. (1981). Characteristics of an appropriate education for severely and profoundly handicapped students. *Education and Training of the Mentally Retarded, 16*, 142-149.

Baumgart, D., Brown, L., Pumpian, I., Nisbet, J., Ford, A., Sweet, M., Messina, R., & Schroeder, J. (1982). Principle of partial participation and individualized adaptations in educational programs for severely handicapped students. *Journal of the Association for the Severely Handicapped, 7*, 17-27.

Biklen, D. (1985). *Achieving the complete school: Strategies for effective mainstreaming.* New York: Columbia University Teachers College Press.

Biklen, D. (1988). The myth of clinical judgment. *Journal of Social Issues, 44*(1), 127-140.

Blatt, B. (1970). *Exodus from pandemonium: Human abuse and reformation of public policy.* Boston: Allyn and Bacon.

Blatt, B. (1973). *Souls in extremis.* Boston: Allyn and Bacon.

Blatt, B., & Kaplan, F. (1966). *Christmas in purgatory: A photographic essay on mental retardation.* Boston: Allyn and Bacon.

Braddock, D., Hemp, R., & Howes, R. (1986). Direct costs of institutional care in the United States. *Mental Retardation, 24*, 9-17.

Brown, L., Nietupski, J., & Hamre-Nietupski, S. (1976). The criterion of ultimate functioning and public school services for severely handicapped students. In M. A. Thomas (Ed.), *Hey, don't forget about me: Education's investment in the severely, profoundly, and multiply handicapped* (pp. 2-15). Reston, VA: Council for Exceptional Children.

Campbell, P. (1987). The integrated programming team: An approach for coordinating professionals of various disciplines in programs for students with severe and multiple handicaps. *Journal of the Association for Persons With Severe Handicaps, 12*, 107-116.

Campbell, P., McInerney, W., & Cooper, M. A. (1984). Therapeutic programming for students with severe handicaps. *American Journal of Occupational Therapy, 38*, 594-602.

Campbell, P., Place, P., & Gossett, K. (1986). Comparison of two methods of teaching reaching behavior. Manuscript submitted for publication.

Certo, N., Haring, N., & York, R. (1984). *Public school integration of severely handicapped children.* Baltimore: Paul H. Brookes.

Christie, L. (1984). *Some questions and answers about I-Team services: State of Vermont interdisciplinary team for intensive special education.* Burlington, VT: University of Vermont, Center for Developmental Disabilities.

Donnellan, A. M., Mirenda, P. L., Mesaros, R. A., & Fassbender, L. L. (1984). Analyzing communicative functions of aberrant behavior. *Journal of the Association for Persons With Severe Handicaps, 9*, 201-212.

Dunn, L. M. (1968). Special education for the mildly retarded: Is much of it justifiable? *Exceptional Children, 35*, 5-22.

Durand, V. M. (in press). The Motivational Assessment Scale. In M. Hersen and A. S. Bellack (Eds.), *Dictionary of behavioral assessment techniques.* New York: Pergamon.

Durand, V. M., & Crimmins, D. B. (1987). *The Motivational Assessment Scale.* Albany, NY: O. D. Heck Development Center.

Evans, I. M., & Brown, F. A. (1986). Outcome assessment of student competence: Issues and implications. *Special Services in the Schools, 2*, 41-62.

Evans, I. M., Brown, F. A., Weed, K. A., Spry, K. M., & Owen, V. (1987). The assessment of functional competencies: A behavioral approach to the evaluation of programs for children with disabilities. In R. J. Prinz (Ed.), *Advances in behavioral assessment of children and families* (Vol. 3, pp. 93-121). Greenwich, CT: JAI Press.

Evans, I. M., & Meyer, L. H. (1984). Basic life skills. In J. E. Ysseldyke (Ed.), *School psychology: State of the art* (pp. 37-56). Minneapolis: National School Psychology In-service Training Network.

Evans, I. M., & Meyer, L. H. (1985). *An educative approach to behavior problems: A practical decision model for interventions with severely handicapped learners.* Baltimore: Paul H. Brookes.

Fenwick, V. (1987). The Edward Smith School Program: An integrated public school continuum for autistic children. In M. S. Berres & P. Knoblock (Eds.), *Program models for mainstreaming: Integrating students with moderate to severe disabilities.* Rockville, MD: Aspen.

Forest, M. (1984). Education update: The Wellington County Separate School Board at work. In M. Forest (Ed.), *Education integration: A collection of readings on the integration of children with mental handicaps into regular school systems* (pp. 71-75). Downsview, Ontario, Canada: National Institute on Mental Retardation.

Forest, M. (1986a). Education integration. *Entourage, 1*(1), 19-23.

Forest, M. (1986b). *Making a difference: What communities can do to prevent mental handicap and promote lives of quality: Vol. 3. Helping children live, learn and grow in their communities.* Downsview, Ontario, Canada: National Institute on Mental Retardation.

Fox, W., Thousand, J., Williams, W., Fox, T., Towne, P., Reid, R., Conn-Powers, C., & Calcagni, L. (1986). *Best educational practices '86: Educating learners with severe handicaps.* Burlington, VT: University of Vermont, Center for Developmental Disabilities.

Fox, W., Williams, W., & Fox, T. (1978). Program planning and development for the multi-handicapped in rural areas: Vermont's service delivery model. In A. M. Rehman (Ed.), *Serving the severely handicapped: Are we meeting PL 94-142 priorities?* (Vol. 2, pp. 75-90). Minneapolis: Minneapolis Public Schools.

Fullan, M. (1982). *The meaning of educational change.* New York: Columbia University Teachers College Press.

Giangreco, M. F. (1984). Northeast/BOCES integration project survey results. Unpublished document. Ithaca, NY: Tompkins-Seneca-Tioga Board of Cooperative Educational Services.

Giangreco, M. F. (1985). *Basic environmental control devices for persons with severe multiple handicapping conditions* (Code 115-M). Stillwater, OK: National Clearing House of Rehabilitation Training Materials. (ERIC Document Reproduction Service No. ED 258 418)

Giangreco, M. F. (1986a). Delivery of therapeutic services in special education programs for learners with severe handicaps. *Physical and Occupational Therapy in Pediatrics, 6*(2), 5-15.

Giangreco, M. F. (1986b). Effects of integrated therapy: A pilot study. *Journal of the Association for Persons With Severe Handicaps, 11,* 205-208.

Giangreco, M. F. (1987). *Cayuga-Onondaga assessment for children with handicaps (3rd Ed.).* Stillwater, OK: National Clearing House of Rehabilitation Training Materials.

Giangreco, M. F., McKinney, P., Fitzpatrick, M., & Sabin, C. A. (1986). *Initiating change at the local level: Delivery of services to students with moderate to profound handicapping conditions.* Auburn, NY: Cayuga-Onondaga Board of Cooperative Educational Services (ERIC Document Reproduction Service No. ED 276 182)

Giangreco, M. F., York, J., & Rainforth, B. (1987). *Providing related services to learners with severe handicaps in educational settings: Pursuing the least restrictive option.* Manuscript submitted for publication.

Gilhool, T., & Stutman, E. (1979). Integration of severely handicapped students: Toward criteria for implementing and enforcing the integration imperative of PL 94-142 and section 504. In *LRE: Developing criteria for the evaluation of the least restrictive environment provision* (pp. 215-216). Philadelphia: Research for Better Schools.

Goetz, L., Guess, D., & Stremel-Campbell, K. (1987). *Innovative program design for individuals with dual sensory impairments.* Baltimore: Paul H. Brookes.

Halvorsen, A. T., & Sailor, W. (in press). Integration of students with severe and profound disabilities: A review of research. In R. Gaylord-Ross (Ed.), *Issues and research in special education, Vol. 1.* New York: Columbia University, Teachers College Press.

Hart, V. (1977). The use of many disciplines with the severely and profoundly handicapped. In E. Sontag, J. Smith, & N. Certo (Eds.), *Educational programming for the severely and profoundly handicapped* (pp. 391-396). Reston, VA: Council for Exceptional Children — Division of Mental Retardation.

Horner, R. H., McDonnell, J. J., & Bellamy, G. T. (1986). Teaching generalized skills: General case instruction in simulation and community settings. In R. H. Horner, L. H. Meyer, & H. D. B. Fredericks (Eds.), *Education of learners with severe handicaps: Exemplary service strategies* (pp. 289-314). Baltimore: Paul H. Brookes.

Horner, R. H., Meyer, L. H., & Fredericks, H. D. B. (1986). *Education of learners with severe handicaps: Exemplary service strategies.* Baltimore: Paul H. Brookes.

Hutchinson, D. J. (1978). The transdisciplinary approach. In J. B. Curry & K. K. Peppe (Eds.), *Mental retardation: Nursing approaches to care* (pp. 65-74). St. Louis: C. V. Mosby.

Johnson, D., Johnson, R., Holubec, E., & Roy P. (1984). *Circles of learning.* Alexandria, VA: Association for Supervision and Curriculum Development.

Knoblock, P., & Lehr, R. (1986). A model for mainstreaming autistic children: The Jowonio school program. In E. Schopler & G. B. Mesibov (Eds.), *Social behavior in autism* (pp. 285-303). New York: Plenum.

MacGregor, G., Janssen, C. M., Larsen, L. A., & Tillery, W. L. (1986). Philadelphia's urban model project: A system-wide effort to integrate students with severe handicaps. *Journal of the Association for Persons With Severe Handicaps, 11,* 61-67.

Massachusetts Advocacy Center. (1987). *Out of the mainstream: Education of disabled youth in Massachusetts.* Boston: Author.

McEwen, I. R., & Karlan, G. R. (October, 1987). *Effect of position on communication board use by a student with cerebral palsy.* Paper presented at the 14th Annual Conference of the Association for Persons With Severe Handicaps, Chicago.

McKenzie, H., Hill, M., Sousie, S., York, R., & Baker, K. (1977). Special education training to facilitate rural, community-based programs for the severely handicapped. In E. Sontag, J. Smith, & N. Certo (Eds.), *Educational programming for the severely and profoundly handicapped* (pp. 96-108). Reston, VA: Council for Exceptional Children — Division of Mental Retardation.

Meyer, L. H. (1985). *Program quality indicators: A checklist of most promising practices in programs for students with severe disabilities.* Syracuse, NY: Syracuse University, Division of Special Education and Rehabilitation.

Meyer, L. H. (1987). *Program quality indicators: A checklist of most promising practices in educational programs for students with severe disabilities (Revised).* Syracuse, NY: Syracuse University, Division of Special Education and Rehabilitation.

Meyer, L. H., & Eichinger, J. (1987). Program evaluation in support of program development: Needs, strategies, and future directions. In L. Goetz, D. Guess, & K. Stremel-Campbell (Eds.), *Innovative program design for individuals with dual sensory impairments* (pp. 313-353). Baltimore: Paul H. Brookes.

Meyer, L. H., & Eichinger, J., & Park-Lee, S. (1987). A validation of most promising practices in educational services for students with severe disabilities. *Journal of the Association for Persons With Severe Handicaps.*

Meyer, L. H., & Putnam, J. (in press). Social integration. In V. B. Van Hasselt, P. S. Strain, & M. Hersen (Eds.), *Handbook of developmental and physical disabilities.* New York: Pergamon.

New York State Education Department. (1986). *Design for a comprehensive statewide service delivery system for severely handicapped children.* Albany, NY: Author.

Nietupski, J., Hamre-Nietupski, S., Clancy, P., & Veerhusen, K. (1986). Guidelines for making simulation an effective adjunct to in vivo community instruction. *Journal of the Association for Persons With Severe Handicaps, 11*(1), 12-17.

Nirje, B. (1969). The normalization principle and its human management implications. In R. B. Kugel & W. Wolfensberger (Eds.), *Changing patterns in residential services for the mentally retarded.* Washington, DC: President's Committee on Mental Retardation.

Northwest Regional Laboratory. (1985). *Effective Schools Research.* Seattle: Author.

Oakes, J. (1985). *Keeping track.* New Haven, CT: Yale University Press.

Orelove, F., & Sobsey, R. (1987). *Educating students with severe handicaps: A transdisciplinary approach.* Baltimore: Paul H. Brookes.

Rainforth, B., & York, J. (1987). Integrating related services in community instruction. *Journal of the Association for Persons With Severe Handicaps, 12*(3), 190-198.

Reichle, J., & Keogh, W. J. (1986). Communication instruction for learners with severe handicaps: Some unresolved issues. In R. H. Horner, L. H. Meyer, & H. D. B. Fredericks (Eds.), *Education of learners with severe handicaps: Exemplary service strategies.* Baltimore: Paul H. Brookes.

Reynolds, M. C., Wang, M., & Walberg, H. J. (1987). The necessary restructuring of special and regular education. *Exceptional Children, 53*, 391-398.

Riggen, T. (1985). *Special education long range plan.* Unpublished manuscript, Montpelier, VT: Vermont Department of Education, Division of Special & Compensatory Education.

Roncker v. Walter, 700 F. 2nd 1058 (6th Cir. Feb. 23, 1983).

Sears, C. (1981). The transdisciplinary approach: A process of compliance with PL 94-142. *Journal of the Association for the Severely Handicapped, 6*, 22-29.

Snow, J., & Forest, M. (1985). *Support circles: Building a vision.* Unpublished manuscript. Downsview, Ontario, Canada: G. Allan Roeher Institute.

Stainback, W., & Stainback, S. (1984). A rationale for the merger of special and regular education. *Exceptional Children, 51*(2), 102-111.

Sternat, J., Messina, R., Nietupski, J., Lyon, S., & Brown, L. (1977). Occupational and physical therapy services for severely handicapped students: Toward a naturalized public school service delivery model. In E. Sontag, J. Smith, & N. Certo (Eds.), *Educational programming for the severely and profoundly handicapped* (pp. 263-278). Reston, VA: Council for Exceptional Children, Division of Mental Retardation.

Stile, S., Peters, J., & Piazza-Templeman, T. P. (1986). Improving performance of school personnel: The teaching research inservice training model. *Performance and Instruction Journal, 25*(9), 22-24.

Thousand, J., Anderson, L., Reid, R., LeFebvre, D., LaRoche, S., Conte, N., Este, E., & Schattman, R. (1985, December). *Educating learners with severe handicaps in regular classrooms.* Paper presented at the twelfth annual conference of The Association for Persons with Severe Handicaps, Boston.

Thousand, J., Fox, T., Reid, R., Godek, J., Williams, W., & Fox, W. (1986). *The Homecoming model: Educating students who present intensive challenges within the regular education environment.* Burlington, VT: University of Vermont, Center for Developmental Disabilities.

Thousand, J., Nevin-Parta, A., & Fox W. (1987). Inservice training to support the education of learners with severe handicaps in their local public schools. *Teacher Education and Special Education, 10*(1), 4-13.

Touchette, P. E., MacDonald, R. F., & Langer, S. N. (1985). A scatter plot for identifying stimulus control of problem behavior. *Journal of Applied Behavior Analysis, 18*, 343-351.

United States Department of Education. (1987). *Ninth annual report to congress on the implementation of the education of the handicapped act (Vol. 1).* Washington, DC: U.S. Department of Education, Division of Educational Services, Special Education Programs.

White, O. R. (1987). [Book review of *Assessing severely and profoundly handicapped individuals*], *Journal of the Association for Persons With Severe Handicaps, 12*, 158-159.

Williams, W., Fox, W., Christie, L., Thousand, J., Conn-Powers, M., Carmichael, L., Vogelsberg, R. T., & Hull, M. (1986). Community integration in Vermont. *Journal of the Association for Persons With Severe Handicaps, 11*(4), 294-299.

Wolfensberger, W. (1972). *The principle of normalization in human services.* Downsview, Ontario, Canada: National Institute on Mental Retardation.

York, R., & Williams, W. (1977). Curricula and ongoing assessment for individualized programming in the classroom. In B. Wilcox, F. Kohl, R. T. Vogelsberg, B. Reguly, & M. Hagen (Eds.), *The severely and profoundly handicapped child: Proceedings from the 1977 statewide institute for educators of the severely and profoundly handicapped.* Springfield, IL: State Board of Education.

Zacchei, D. A., & Mirman, J. A. (1986). *Business education partnerships: Strategies for school improvement* (pp. 52-53). Andover, MA: Regional Laboratory for Educational Improvement of the Northeast & Islands.

APPENDIX 1: TASH RESOLUTION ON THE REDEFINITION OF THE CONTINUUM OF SERVICES

Children and adults with severe disabilities require specialized and individualized services that traditionally have not been made available in typical school and other community environments. Instead, access to such services has been tied to categorical placements which increasingly isolate persons with disabilities from relationships with their family, peers, and other citizens. In the past, the concept of a continuum of services has been used to foster the notion that persons with severe disabilities must earn the right to lead integrated lives in the community. TASH believes therefore that a redefinition of the continuum is vitally needed.

The Association for Persons with Severe Handicaps believes that specialized and individualized services can be readily and effectively provided in integrated settings, and need not preclude opportunities to develop peer and other social relationships which are so critical to the achievement of full participation in society.

TASH further believes that effective methodologies and models which can be applied in integrated settings now exist, and that the focus of new significant and systematic research and development efforts should now be upon the development, implementation, validation, and dissemination of such alternatives to outdated practices which segregate persons with disabilities from their families, peers and the community by requiring placement in handicapped-only and categorically-grouped services and settings.

Therefore, TASH calls for a redefinition of the continuum of services which emphasizes the attainment of the following characteristics and components:

1. The provision of specialized staff, resources, and services to meet individual needs in the regular classroom, neighborhood school, home and family, and community program and settings;
2. The substantive training and retraining of personnel, both special and generic service professionals — to prepare them for providing instruction to a variety of heterogeneous groups of learners;
3. The systematic shifting of service delivery design and services away from categorical, homogeneously grouped, and separate models to one which requires integration and thrives on a variety of grouping arrangements;
4. The philosophical and administrative merger of special and regular education and specialized and generic services into one service delivery system, evidenced by the integration of both professional staff and students; and
5. An unambiguous model of the Least Restrictive Environment which is marked without exception by integration into normalized community environments and proximity to family and peers who do not have disabilities and other citizens.

Furthermore, The Association for Persons with Severe Handicaps commits its resources and energies to support and promote such components of an integrated continuum of services, through advocacy, dissemination, research, training, and program development in collaboration with consumers, colleagues, families, professional training programs, research centers, and community services.

Passed by the Executive Board of The Association for Persons with Severe Handicaps (TASH), November 1986.

13

Provision of Psychological Services to Very Young Children and their Families

Caven S. Mcloughlin
Kent State University

The next professional frontier for school psychologists will be in providing and coordinating services to young children with handicaps who are below the traditional "preschool" age, and to their families. This service will certainly be provided in *nontraditional* settings, because infants at these ages have yet to attend formal school. Even without having received institutionalized "education," all infants are strong and active learners when parents act as competent instructors. In the case of the very young handicapped, however, school psychologists with appropriate education and experience are particularly well placed, because of their expertise in learning and psychology, to provide optimal, quality services so as to mitigate the effects of these children's handicapping conditions.

This chapter deals with services to children from infancy to age 3 years, with specific reference to recent determinations of the efficacy of intervention for young children with special educational needs. It is necessary to provide empirical justification for forays into early services, given that there remain recalcitrant pockets of disbelief about the utility and efficacy of such services. There is a wealth of data being accumulated by intervention researchers. These data suggest, for example, that there are significant economic incentives to investing in early intervention, and that the progress of children with handicaps is universally greater when they receive a program of structured instruction in heterogeneous populations alongside nonhandicapped agemates.

In as much as the field of early intervention is staffed by a relatively small number of professionals, including few psychologists, the urgent need for personnel preparation will also be considered. It is inevitable that any consideration of an emerging field will be speculative in respect to the many possible models for preparing a cadre of professionals to plan, coordinate, deliver, and monitor programs, without which it is certain that there never can be quality services. But an adequate staffing corps has yet to be developed. Thus, in contrast with the general theme of this book, which deals with services as alternatives to existing models, this chapter essentially considers services that today are virtually alternatives to nothing.

SIMILARITIES AND DIFFERENCES TO SCHOOL-BASED MODELS

In services to be provided to very young children there will be many similarities to today's typical school psychology model, but many differences as well. The similarities will be reflected in professional priorities, positive and optimistic relationships with colleagues and consumers, and in many of the philosophical and theoretical foundations driving practice. However, the work setting is likely to be very different. Since a primary intention is to promote optimal development in natural environments, services are unlikely to be delivered in schools. The content of what is provided also will evidence departures from traditional practice. Furthermore, although it is appropriate to think in terms of developing the school-aged child's independence through weaning from parents, this is clearly not indicated for the vulnerable infant. An emphasis on the contribution of parents to the education of handicapped infants will also likely be new to many practitioners; importance of parents' roles can no longer simply receive lip service. Unquestionably, parents are the logical, and economically the most viable, providers of services to infants and toddlers. Incorporation of parents into the service team is already, in many settings, a stated goal, but for infants *it must become a reality* if there is to be any impact.

It is self-evident that *school* psychology is an inappropriate term for describing the services provided to very young children. Nevertheless, the principles, concepts, and best practices of school psychology are equally appropriate to a variety of nonschool contexts, including the care of young children with special educational needs. For example, the seven-stage "appraisal process" modeled in the National School Psychology Inservice Training Network materials (Tucker, 1981), albeit with modifications to nomenclature, is as relevant to infants as it is to school-age children. While the primary care context may be different, the discipline's best practices are equally pertinent to matters of diagnosis, prescription, and intervention — whatever the client's age, and whatever the involvement of other related specialists.

The involvement of school psychologists in the care and treatment of children with special needs (and those at risk for developing handicaps, primarily by environmental variables) also has been termed "pediatric psychology." Some assumption of this label has been done by individuals who felt that through association they had "earned" the right to be considered coprofessionals with medical practitioners. However, owing to the guild and the professional disputes concerning the right to practice as a psychological subspecialist, the lack of an agreed subspecialty of pediatric psychology, and issues of liability and licensure, it is entirely appropriate for school psychologists working with very young children to avoid the pediatric prefix.

A continuing allegiance to the *school* label does nothing to limit the effectiveness of an exemplary psychological practitioner. In fact, given the potential for misinterpretation by consumers, and the current lack of comprehensive training for infant developmental psychological specialists, it seems professionally astute to forego the "pediatric" term until some greater professional maturity is achieved in this very specialized field. Personally, I think it disingenuous and sometimes plainly unprofessional to assume the title *pediatric* on the strength of one or even a few classes, or some passive related experiences.

There is at least one way in which alternative delivery systems are essential for serving young children with handicaps and their families. Since virtually all young children with handicaps are treated in settings other than schools (i.e., at home or in clinics, agencies, hospitals), service providers must be able to transfer their skills to those locations. This transfer, in itself, brings new challenges. Psychologists must collaboratively work alongside many other professionals, each of whom has very different specialized clinical and procedural insights into young children's care and treatment and perspectives on services to families.

We are soon to see an explosion in the provision of services to infants and toddlers, hence this is an especially opportune time for considering school psychologists' involvement in the instructional care of very young children with special educational needs. It may be reasonable to imagine that these future services will be based on the medical model. However, recent plans of state governments in reaction to federal incentives for providing infant/toddler services show that the largest single group of states identifying a specific lead agency have chosen public schools to coordinate and provide their services. In fact, those states with the longest experience of providing infant/toddler services overwhelmingly have opted for their state education agency (SEA) as their lead agency.

BACKGROUND TO RECENT LEGISLATION

Over the last two decades, the education of children with special educational needs has received significant new legislative support and federal funding. The public generally became aware of early intervention, or "infant stimulation" as it was then known, with the initiation of model programs developed as a result of Public Law 91-230, the Children's Early Education Programs Act. In 1972, PL 92-424 created the Headstart concept. In the following year, Public Laws 93-380 and 93-647 released federal funds for social services, and required that states prepare comprehensive plans to reflect the needs of every child with handicaps. The all-encompassing 1975 amendments to PL 94-142, Education of the Handicapped Act (EHA), cross-referenced all the then extant entitlements. It outlined families' rights, defined the constituents of program eligibility, drew attention to evaluation technology and procedures, and provided preschool incentive grants.

As all psychologists in educational settings are now aware, PL 94-142 mandated a right to a free appropriate public education to meet individual needs within the least restrictive environment. This mandate included the previously unserved (or inadequately served) group of preschoolers whenever consistent with state guidelines or a state court's requirement (PL 94-142, Section #612, 2 [B], 1975). Because compliance was far from complete, amendments were later enacted (PL 98-199) that revised and extended PL 94-142 so that state plans might include "all children from birth through five years of age" (PL 98-199, 97 Statute, 1366). Although states took various routes to meet this statute's requirements, relatively few enacted provisions for the implementation of comprehensive services from birth. For example, by 1985 only 21 states

had elected to require the "permissive" service option for any of their preschoolers with handicaps. This option allowed individual states to determine at what age and at what level of handicap services might begin.

In October 1986, the Education of the Handicapped Amendments were enacted to provide each state with financial incentives to "develop and implement a statewide, comprehensive, coordinated, multidisciplinary, interagency program of early intervention services for handicapped infants and toddlers and their families" (PL 99-457). Additionally, it provides financial assistance to states to strengthen services to handicapped children aged 3-5 years. All states have applied for these finances — and in so doing have become obligated to provide future services. One of the most directly noticeable consequences will be a dramatic increase in need for appropriately prepared personnel. The most pressing need will be for a leadership corps. In a survey of directors of state planning grants, Meisels (1986) determined that across the nation there will be an 80% shortfall in numbers of early childhood special educators by 1990 — the very year when states will be required to add to their responsibilities comprehensive services for handicapped children aged 3-5 years. And to this already massive shortfall will be added a need for personnel to serve infants and toddlers — for, again, all states have bought in to the concept of serving infants and toddlers through their application for federal incentive funds. Our professional task will be to contribute to the timely provision of appropriate quality services to the approximately one million children under the age of 5 years who, it is anticipated, will experience developmental disabilities (Reaves & Burns, 1982).

WHO NEEDS THESE SERVICES AND HOW ARE THEY TO BE PROVIDED?

The number of surviving low-birth-weight babies with medical complications has increased with every advance in medical technology. One consequence has been the increased number of infants experiencing severe and multiple handicaps who are in need of special services, as well as those medically fragile or environmentally at risk. For example, there are currently about 17,000 technology-dependent children in the United States. These children rely on ventilators, intravenous feeding, long-term drug therapy, and other forms of sophisticated medical devices and services. The number of children requiring such support could easily rise with the advent of AIDS and with the wider acceptance of aggressive medical interventions for children who otherwise would die.

Across the nation there are 124 children's hospitals and 2,831 pediatric units. Only a guess is possible at the number of "school psychologists" currently attached to these settings on a regular basis. However, any future review of our profession in the 1990s *should* show that psychologists with knowledge of the special instructional needs of very young children serve as members of children's hospital teams.

Trends in infant health care are towards increased use of outpatient services and shorter inpatient admissions. Consequently, there is an increased need for home care, hospice and respite care, day care for the medically fragile, and innovative programs to assist parents in caring for their young vulnerable and chronically disabled children in the home. There is an increased presence of infants in programming, and toddlers in preschools who have medically fragile and profound multiply handicapping conditions. In addition to shorter hospital stays, factors that contribute to this trend include an emphasis on providing home care so as to reduce the need for institutional care, and advances in the design of miniaturized, portable medical/prosthetic devices available to monitor treatments to children outside of direct-care medical facilities.

The primacy of the home requires that personnel attend to children's needs in natural settings, rather than in clinic environments; this in turn demands that service programs evolve to provide complex integrated services in as cost-efficient

a pattern as possible. Efficient service to children younger than kindergarten age, for example, requires that service providers be able to function in several environments — homes, clinics and hospitals, respite, a variety of daycare centers, etc. Services that traditionally have been provided in medical settings on an inpatient basis will, in the future, increasingly be offered by nonmedical specialists in home or educational settings. Personnel capable of accepting responsibility for coordinating and integrating services will, at least initially, be highly sought-after team members.

In the past, only cursory attention has been given to serving children in the home. At best, attention has been given to preparing parents as behavior change agents for their children. A more appropriate model recognizes the need to individualize services to families and to take care to reflect the structural, socioeconomic status (SES), cultural, educational, and personal preferences of the family unit. The particular needs of young children and their families dictate a different service pattern than that typically provided to older children with special needs. These differences are multifold:

- Because of these children's age, timely intervention is a greater need; transitions must be made with minimal delay or disruption to the children's progress;
- Strategies for assessment and treatment need specifically to be patterned to the children's age;
- Children's needs, when identified as special at an early age, are more likely to require the combined and parallel professional attention of medical and therapeutic personnel; and,
- Families of very young children with special needs are more likely to be the major focus for service.

Thus, a family's needs (rather than simply the needs of the target child) will dictate what services, and in what setting, the professional becomes involved. To this end, Section 677 of PL 99-457 requires for infants and toddlers (and persuasively suggests for preschoolers) that each family have an Individual Family Service Plan (IFSP) that constitutes a statement of the family's needs, strengths, and limitations, and a delineation of the services needed to meet that family's and child's unique requirements.

Families are complex, interrelated, dynamic units. Simply attention to, not to mention planned change for, one family member has impact on other family members. Consequently, the extended family, siblings, and significant others are also important influences (and recipients) of IFSP services. Fortunately, we have evidence that the very delivery of early intervention services can provide the family unit with the support, information, and education necessary to maintain an appropriate family milieu while concurrently fostering the development of the delayed youngster (Foster, Berger, & McLean, 1981). Yet the ultimate determiner of this service plan should be the parents.

> Parents have to be recognized as special educators, the *true experts* on their children; and professional people (teachers, pediatricians, psychologists and others) have to learn to be *consultants* to them. (Hobbs, 1975, p. 47; emphasis in original)

The impetus to focus attention on the needs of families, rather than solely on the child, has a multiplex rationale. As primary caretaker, the parent is the natural person to be the major change agent; the natural ecology of the home improves prospects for successful intervention; there are legal demands for the child to be served in the least restricting environment, and for very young children that is most easily defined as home; an ethical problem arises that, if left unattended, the complicating conditions could result in lifelong disabilities; finally a fundamental economic rationale arises from the fact that there can now be little doubt as to the long-range social and economic benefits that accrue from early intervention.

Early intervention is a rapidly developing arena of scientific inquiry, but it is a field in professional infancy. However, there are some empirical bases to guide good practice. Many studies have demonstrated that early intervention can be effective in maintaining, or even accelerating, development for handicapped and at-risk infants; that time spent in early "schooling" has a directly proportional effect on these children's development; and that early preschool intervention can reduce the need for later special educational intervention (Bronfenbrenner, 1975; Datta, 1979; Karnes & Teska, 1975; Lazar & Darlington, 1982; Ramey & Campbell, 1984). Meta-analyses of early intervention programs provide an empirical basis for believing that early intervention can have a positive impact on the lives of infants and young children, and on their families. However, there remains controversy regarding which program features enhance efficacy (see Dunst & Snyder, 1986, for comments on meta-analysis, and Strain & Smith, 1986, for questions on the findings; also see Casto & Lewis, 1984; Casto & Mastropieri, 1986a, 1986b, 1986c; Hanson, 1985; Mastropieri, White, & Fecteau, 1986).

Creating an environment for infants' maximal development is far from simple, and there are many fallacies associated with quick fixes. The fix-it method places emphasis on "curing" that which is perceived to be wrong in either the infant or the family. One parent expressed frustration with this type of model in stating, "I don't care if 400 people came to my house with terrific programs and worked with him day and night to make him as good as he can be. The bottom line is, *he can't be fixed*" (Kupfer, 1984, p. 23).

The growing awareness of the increasing numbers of infants who may develop problems secondary to an original medical (biological) impairment has contributed to a focus on "wellness" and prevention (e.g., Als, Tronick, & Brazelton, 1980; Anastasiow, 1981a, 1981b; Brazelton, 1982a, 1982b; DiVitto & Goldberg, 1979). This changing focus creates needs for multidisciplinary personnel skilled in areas related to family systems intervention.

Rather than a single way to "mend

the child," a potpourri of approaches and strategies has been found efficacious. In a review of the federal Handicapped Children's Early Education Program initiatives (HCEEP), Reaves and Burns (1982) noted the following summary findings. Approximately 55% of children served by a wide variety of HCEEP early intervention programs were later integrated, at least partially, into regular education settings alongside nonhandicapped children, and there was evidence of a significant return on dollars invested. For every federal dollar invested, some $18.37 was generated in programming funding for children and their families (similar fiscal savings were described in Berrueta-Clement, Schweinhart, Barnett, Epstein, & Weikhart, 1984; Schweinhart & Weikhart, 1980; Wood, 1981). Thus, the early intervention movement has gathered persuasive momentum as a result of replicated findings of multiple positive results of intervention, among them remediation of delays, development of skills, enhancement of parent-infant interactions, reduced costs of educational services, and positive outcomes for parents and other family members. In the earliest years of school psychologists' involvement in serving very young children, it is essential that professionals learn quickly how to access, translate, and utilize this developing knowledge base.

CURRENT SERVICE PATTERN

Who already provides services to young children? Immediately prior to the publication of PL 99-457 there were 7 states mandating services from birth to 6 years, 1 state mandating services from 2 years, 14 from age 3, 4 from age 4, and 15 from age 5 years (the children served typically were very young children with multiple or profound handicaps, and youngsters approaching kindergarten). During the 1984–1985 school year, the U.S. Office of Education (USOE) reported that 259,000 children 3-5 years of age received special education and related services, and 35,700 infants from birth through 2 years were similarly served. To meet the needs of these new consumers, the

numbers of several related services groups have increased; for example, there has been a threefold increase in speech pathologists in the past 15 years, 27% of whose caseloads now consist of under-fives, and an increase in the proportion of occupational therapists working with this group from 5.9% to 8.2%.

There are few reasons, however, to feel satisfied with the overall state of services for disabled infants born in this country. In the ranking of industrialized nations on infant mortality, the United States takes 19th place (Children's Defense Fund, 1988). Babies have a better average chance of surviving their neonatal period (i.e., to 28 days of life) in Singapore, Spain, or Hong Kong than in the United States. While the overall rate of deaths per 1,000 livebirths has dropped in the United States (from 14 per 1,000 in 1978, to 11 in 1985), in selected U.S. urban areas the mortality rate has *risen* (e.g., Milwaukee, Philadelphia, Pittsburgh, Boston). Each year 40,000 infants die during the neonatal period in this country. These babies disproportionately are born, along with 240,000 low-birth-weight (lbw; under 1500 gr.) to poor, young, and ethnic minority parents. According to the United States National Center for Health Statistics, in 1984, the latest year for which data are available, four women under the age of 15 gave birth to their fourth child, 18 gave birth to a third child, 251 gave birth to a second child, and 9,638 gave birth to a first child.

The absolute numbers of neither infant deaths or lbw babies have not dropped in the last 30 years. Yet this should not be surprising, if one believes that the investment relates directly to return. Since 1981, for example, there has been an 18% cut in federal funds (dollars held constant for inflation) for maternal and child health programs. The Children's Defense Fund 1985 report determined that in the first half of the 1980's, 26 of 33 states investigated had declining numbers of women receiving medical care in early pregnancy.

It may appear, at first blush, that these data have little practical relevance to the school psychologist, since the most direct response would demand involvement prior to birth. However, simply knowing these data might make it possible for the concerned school psychologist, like all service professionals, to draw the attention of appropriate policy makers so that fewer compromised babies will be entered into the early intervention sequence.

Many preschoolers and infants with handicaps have been receiving some services, but the challenging question is What proportion of children have been left unserved or underserved? The USOE estimated in 1986 that 70,000 of the nation's 100,000 infants with special needs were not receiving appropriate services. There are, of course, areas of relative wealth and poverty in service provision. For example, in Kansas approximately 1 in 3 children under age 6 who need help are getting some level of assistance; recent reports from California state that of the approximately 25,000 infants admitted to neonatal intensive care units (NICUs) over half (about 6% of California's newborns) required but did not receive early intervention services that would have reduced the likelihood of disability (the primary rationale cited for this shortfall was the limited number of appropriately credentialed personnel).

Where will school psychologists with training and experience in early childhood special education work? There is a broad array of early intervention possibilities: special education regional resource centers (a component specifically prescribed by PL 99-457); centers set up for case managership; nonprofit and philanthropically funded centers (e.g., Cerebral Palsy Association, Crippled Children Bureau, Easter Seals, etc.); residential programs; high-risk follow-up programs monitoring NICU graduates; private for-profit vendors and contract agencies; hospital-based programs; and publicly and privately funded preschool programs, with or without home-based services. This is not an exhaustive listing, consisting simply of some of the possibilities. In addition to roles emphasizing direct service, roles for the school psychologist in the nontraditional/alternative model for young children also include: (a) helping to seek and develop community and state support for programs by serving as a resource person to school districts, centers, and community agencies involved in planning services (which may involve the preparation of responses for grant funds competitions); (b) establishing programs in settings or communities where previously none existed; (c) serving as administrators/coordinators and leadership personnel for newly created programs.

FEDERAL PRESCHOOL AND EARLY INTERVENTION PROGRAMS MANDATED BY PL 99-457

There are several new components to PL 99-457, each of which needs separately to be addressed to understand its implications. Briefly noted, the major new initiatives of PL 99-457 are: reauthorization of the provisions of PL 94-142 to include a downward extension of all its rights and protections to handicapped children aged 3-5 years by school year 1990-1991; creation of a new state grant incentive program for infants and toddlers with handicaps (birth through age 2, including discretionary grants through HCEEP with full services within 4 years); a strengthening of PL 94-142 interagency provisions; creation of a national center on recruitment and employment in special education; and establishment of expanded authority on technology, media, and materials for persons with handicaps.

PL 99-457 rights reflect exactly the benefits embedded in "old" PL 94-142, and include a zero-reject model; a right to individualized and appropriate education at public cost; entitlement to nondiscriminatory testing, classification, and placement; service in the least restrictive placement; procedural due process; and decision making shared with parents. Preschool service models do not have to reflect the traditional educational model, in that the length of the instructional day, choice of center or home instruction, and attendance pattern are all at the states' discretion. This recognition of quality in alternative service models was specifically reflected in the committee report accepted by the 535 men and women on Capitol Hill who framed this legislation:

> The Committee also wishes to observe that there are currently a variety of effective special education models . . . being utilized across the country. Based on the unique needs of the particular child, these models range from part-day home-based to part- or full-day center-based services. (PL 99-457 Committee Report [#99-860, p. 20])

INFANT AND TODDLER PROGRAMS

PL 99-457 provides infants/toddlers with handicaps with new state-grant-supported early intervention programs (Part H-EHA). Definitions of eligibility include all infants and toddlers of ages from birth through 2 years who need early intervention services and who (a) experience delays in any of the developmental areas (cognitive, physical, language and speech, psychosocial, and self-help skills); (b) exhibit high probability of developmental delay because of a physical or mental condition; and (c) or are "at risk of having substantial developmental delay" (the definition of which is to be made at each state's discretion).

The legislation outlines requirements for a written individualized family service plan (IFSP) for each eligible child that will function like an IEP, except that it will be family-focused rather than limited to the child with handicaps. The written plan is to include information detailing the child's present levels of development; early intervention services necessary; dates for initiation of services; anticipated duration; family strengths and needs; major outcome expected for participants in programming; criteria, procedures, and timeline for evaluation; transition plans; and prescription of diagnostic medical and health services essential for the child to benefit from other specified early intervention services. A case manager must be nominated for every eligible child and family. The IFSP is to be developed by the parents in collaboration with the other members of the multidisciplinary team, and it must be evaluated at least

once yearly and be reviewed every 6 months. Services may begin, with parental consent, before the IFSP is signed.

Funds are already budgeted and obligated by Congress for infant/toddler programs. Unlike the funding for the 3-to-5 year age group, these funds are being distributed to states on the basis of a proportional census allocation, not on the numbers actually served in programs. To receive these financial incentives, in the first 2 years of a state's application all that is needed is for the state governor to designate a lead agency for overall administration of the program. All states did, in fact, make application for these funds. The governor must also establish a 15-member Interagency Coordinating Council representing relevant agencies, consumers, and providers. The council may also serve as the lead agency. By the third year, in order to receive continued funding, the state must have a public policy that stipulates eventual comprehensive access to all components of the statewide early intervention system for eligible infants and toddlers. In the fourth year the state must have developed a statewide system for providing services including multidisciplinary assessments, ISFPs, and case management services. In the fifth and succeeding years statewide provision and service must universally be available to all eligible children.

States must have a choice in designating a lead agency. Across the country the following agencies have been selected to represent states in providing programs to infants and toddlers: Education (SEAs, 18 states); Health (13); Human Services/Developmental Disabilities (6); Human Services/MH-MR (4); Human Services (2); Interdisciplinary Councils (3); other states elected one of each of the following: Department of Human Services, Mental Health, Governor's Office for Children and Youth, and Department of Public Welfare. It is particularly interesting that half of the states electing SEAs previously had a mandate or at least some optional services for infants (Campbell, Bellamy, & Bishop, in press).

Of the funds requested by states for programs, the following are the proportions allocated by categories for the initial year taken from states' proposed Part H–Infants and Toddlers spending plans: administration (salary, related costs, indirect costs, travel, etc.), 24%; Inter-Agency Coordinating Council (including staff, travel, etc.), 3.25%; costs to fiance the required 14 statewide components, 19.5%; provision of services for infants & toddlers, 48%. This last figure is of particular interest since the request for proposal for the initial year spending plan did not ask for or encourage expenditure on direct services. The initial year was viewed as a time for planning eventual service delivery. Particularly for states with limited experience in providing infant services, it may one day be seen to have been a mistake to start providing services prior to examining best practices.

There is no practical difference in the percentage distribution over alternative models between the spending plans of all states and the plans for states without prior mandated services for this population. Yet very different plans have been posited for the use of funds to serve infants/toddlers. The alternative models include regional distribution to infants on waiting lists (e.g., Pennsylvania); focus on specialized services (e.g., integrated care models in Delaware and in Massachusetts); and expanding services to previously unserved localities (e.g., North Carolina and Texas) (Campbell, Bellamy, & Bishop, in press).

There are 14 required components of each statewide early intervention plan. These include definition of developmental delay; timeline for implementation; multidisciplinary evaluation of the needs of infants/toddlers and families; use of IFSPs; system for child find; public awareness programs; central directory of services; comprehensive system of personnel development (CSPD); administrative procedures for the lead agency; contracting procedures; procedures for timely reimbursement of funds; procedural safeguards; training standards; and collection of data and reporting of standards. All these components need not be priorities for states. The components selected for the investment of state funds in the

initial year by more than 50% of the 30 states *without prior mandates* are definition; public awareness; IFSP; lead agency; CSPD; and data collection (Campbell, Bellamy, & Bishop, in press).

HOW IS EARLY INTERVENTION DIFFERENT?

As a result of the new federal preschool legislation certain rights and privileges for special needs preschoolers are now established. These changes to the statutes have brought a new interest in serving young children with handicaps. The role of the psychologist (and other discipline representatives) in providing these services has yet to be well defined. Thus, some of the issues involved in early intervention that differentiate it from traditional school-based provision are the topic of this section.

The several bases of support for early intervention for infants and toddlers (including those at risk for developing handicaps) and their families derive from developmental theories, empirical studies (both direct and inferential), expert opinion, and societal values and opinion. The major premises of early intervention are that initial learning patterns influence subsequent development; critical-period research is relevant; intelligence is responsive to environmental influences; handicaps cause spiraling progressive retardation; environment can be nurturing or depriving; early intervention can significantly enhance later remedial efforts; parents deserve special assistance in establishing constructive caretaking patterns; and early-intervention socioeconomic benefits can reduce later lifelong costs (e.g., Peterson, 1987).

However, arguments have been posed against early intervention. It is proposed that costs are too high for a minority service; that other educational priorities place early intervention at a lower priority; that sufficient and conclusive effectiveness data are lacking; that there is insufficient evidence that early intervention is any more effective than intervention at later stages; and that early intervention is primarily a "baby-sitting" service for infants with a questionable capacity to learn.

Professionals do have several *reasonable* concerns about the relatively "sudden" growth of interest and involvement in early intervention, among them the following:

- that local, state, and federal fiscal appropriation will be strained, insufficient, or unavailable;
- that a system only now consolidating service delivery patterns will be upset;
- that at-risk status may *overinclude* infants in special education;
- that, given contemporary naivete about infants, it may be propitious to avoid this arena (primum non nocere);
- that in respect to systems-level changes "we should do a better job now, not spread the net further," and "nobody can do it alone";
- that "turf issues" will arise among professionals; and
- that *underinclusion* of children from unassertive families is likely.

Nonetheless, our uncompromising perspective is that from early intervention clear benefits accrue to children, to parents, to siblings, to educators and other professionals, and to society.

Early intervention involves a blend of practices and values from early childhood education, special education, remedial therapies (speech, occupational, and physical), and compensatory education (see, for example, Antley & DuBose, 1981; McNulty, Smith, & Soper, 1983; Mowder & Widerstrom, 1986). Recent decades have created a changed perspective on what can be done with and for young children with handicaps. These adjustments in outlook for disadvantaged, handicapped, and other young at-risk children have arisen from advances in medical technology; the understanding that regardless of disability everyone can learn; the conviction that potential is best nurtured by support-responsive environments and sensitive caregivers; and the position that education is a civil right and society's responsibility. Early intervention is a field

that is noncategorical, requires a nontraditional system for identification and labeling, has its own particular service delivery approaches and curricular priorities, represents multidisciplinary involvement, and fully incorporates parents as coequal team members.

Early intervention generally includes a perspective and rationale that education is a right for *all* children; education encompasses *all* functional skills; children's readiness for learning can be cultivated; the curriculum should be fit to the child not vice versa; children should be educated in regular, integrated, nonrestrictive environments; and, finally, any failure to learn is the profession's responsibility, not the child's.

To write or talk about young children at risk for developmental delays requires that there be universal understanding of the concept. Thus, to define: Children are considered *at risk* when they have been subjected to certain adverse genetic, prenatal, perinatal, postnatal, or environmental conditions that are known to cause defects or are highly correlated with the appearance of later abnormalities (Peterson, 1987). Vulnerable infants and young children include those at established risk, at biological risk, and at environmental risk. Established risk refers to diagnosed disorders that entail a condition *known* to affect development (e.g., the congenital chromosomal anomalies associated with Down syndrome). Biological risk refers to prenatal, perinatal, and neonatal events that *may* affect later development (e.g., prematurity, low birth weight, abnormal perinatal neurological findings). Environmental risk refers to environmental influences that *could* affect development (e.g., parent substance abuse, adolescent pregnancy/parenting). These are, of course, not mutually exclusive conditions. The interaction among risk factors poses the most difficult problem for interventions.

Professionals serving the needs of young children with handicaps typically have a developmental orientation. They subscribe to traditional developmental principles, with some minor but significant deviation. Early interventionists acknowledge and reflect in practice the belief that orderly, predictable changes occur during the first 6 years of life. However, they recognize that even though all children proceed, at different rates, through similar sequences, children with handicaps cannot simply be thought of as slow-developing "normals"; a child's development is not necessarily uniform across domains; individual differences are discernible at an early age; domains are interrelated and cross-referenced; early development is best characterized by increasing levels of differentiation and integration; early developmental achievements pave the way for subsequent, more complex, learning; experience has a cumulative effect; and at certain periods young children show a maturational and psychological readiness for learning specific skills.

The following basic concepts are central to understanding the causative factors underlying impairments that are seen in our youngest population. Abnormalities of multiple causation are increasing, and those from single causes are decreasing; severe abnormalities/disabilities can be diagnosed earlier and more easily; the full impact of a condition is rarely discernible immediately; a particular pathological, genetic, or harmful environmental condition may cause different symptoms and degrees of impairment across individuals (variable expressivity); and the frequency with which a condition actually results in diagnosible abnormalities varies across individual children (variable penetrance) (Peterson, 1987).

Clear prenatal, perinatal, and postnatal risk factors exist. While these are not all directly remediable through later intervention, the psychologist should be aware of their existence and likely impact. The following circumstances signal an at-risk pregnancy: parents living in substandard, impoverished low-SES conditions; maternal age <15 or >40 years; mothers with a history of difficulties in prior pregnancies; and parents with a family history of congenital aberrations. Perinatal hazards that place a newborn at risk include prematurity and low birth weight; low growth rate; and asphyxia and

physical trauma resulting from birth injury. Postnatal conditions that threaten normal development include diseases and infections; ingestion of toxins; accidental or afflicted injury; postnatal nutritional anomalies; and substandard and depriving environments.

There are three basic principles that describe the relationship between at risk conditions manifest in early years and the diagnosis of handicap in school: At-risk does not invariably imply development of a handicapped status later in school, but simply increases the probability. Early treatment can stabilize conditions so that threatened outcomes are prevented or diminished. Finally, in as much as action can mitigate difficulties, a wait-and-see attitude is inappropriate. Equally important for the early intervention specialist to consider are the following three principles about developmental problems: Developmental irregularities in the formative years may not appear problematic once school begins; school environments create novel demands that make a child's strengths and weaknesses more apparent; and many young children show signs of emerging difficulties long before kindergarten screening.

There has been a significant change in orientation by early interventionists in the last two decades. The historical early intervention ethic held that early intervention is invariably effective; intervention should be started as soon as humanly possible; a high-intensity program should routinely be implemented; parents always should be involved in the program; and the individual therapist/teacher who best knows the child should determine which intervention practices to follow. Current assumptions and the contemporary ethic have been significantly modified such that it is now believed that intervention should come early, but not if there is unreasonable cost to parental bonding with the child; parents should participate in choosing their own level of involvement; the training experience should be individualized for the child and parents; and effectiveness should be aggressively monitored in the course of intervention.

These changes have arisen because

infancy research has yielded some surprises. We now recognize that what is logical is not *always* true (e.g., the 1950s practice of oxygen therapy for low-birth-weight infants caused retrolental fibroplasia). Traditional wisdom has told us that difficult-to-console babies are at a disadvantage compared to more temperamentally placid infants. However, a recent study suggests that there may be a hidden advantage in being "difficult to console" as an infant. But only for some infants. Mazaide and his colleagues (Mazaide, Cote, Boutin, Bernier, & Thivierge, 1987) reported details of 75, 4-month-old infants classified into "easy/average/difficult to console" groups (where difficult to console meant "less adaptable ... withdrawal from new stimuli, intense in their emotional reactions, difficult to soothe, negative in mood.") At 4.5 years children earlier classified as "difficult to console" had significantly higher IQs — but only those from middle or upper income families. Perhaps, the authors deduce, demanding babies from affluent homes get more active involvement from parents, thereby inducing exaggerated development, whereas less-privileged parents punish their irritable babies or otherwise impair their development.

However, not all conventional wisdom is faulty. For example, we know that groups of children of very low birth weight (vlbw) at 9 years of age, by comparison with matched controls, on average do have lower IQ scores, more school retention, lower math achievement, and visual motor and fine motor problems (source: A 1987 longitudinal follow-up study of $N = 46$ by Nancy Klein of Rainbow Hospital, Cleveland, Ohio, 1976 NICU cohort of <1,500-gm infants). There is clearly a neurologically less healthful prognosis for very low birth weight infants.

There also remain some puzzling outcomes from "infant stimulation." For example, we know that stroking/massage of low-birth-weight premature infants is equivalent to the infusion of growth hormones in its effects on growth, and that the use of waterbeds in NICU nurseries decreases apnea. However, despite the fact that both "stimulations" are kines-thetic, waterbeds have no effect on growth, and stroking does not lessen apnea!

We are becoming more aware of the problem of simplistic cause–effect thinking, particularly about findings relating to infants. Clearly, professional opinion can be dead wrong! And we are becoming alert that most easy, quick, uncomplicated "fixes" generally turn out to be wrong. Contemporary beliefs acknowledge that the world is complex, and that behavior is complex. If it were really simple to change behavior then this world would not really need professionals — and certainly not psychologists.

EVIDENCE FOR THE EFFECTIVENESS OF EARLY INTERVENTION

Data from early intervention research are not yet all in. There are clear limitations to existing early intervention efficacy research: Conceptual simplicity, inadequate data on service recipients, poorly designed service variables, flawed research designs, and restricted outcome measures. Consequently, there are more theories than proofs. However, several recent attempts at data compilation offer insight into the efficacy of early intervention.

The foremost contemporary investigations of the efficacy of early intervention include the meta-analysis developed by the Utah State Early Intervention Research Institute (EIRI), which reviewed in detail over 400 early intervention studies and identified over 2,500 effect sizes. With such a data set the careful reader will want first to know how the data were pooled. There are at least two ways of inappropriately summarizing past research: averaging the results of all studies, or selecting only those studies that match preexisting biases. The Utah approach used neither of these. Their system of interpretation, meta-analysis, is not a statistical technique — it is a perspective on aggregated data. It integrates numerous and diverse findings in a summary way to show the "attitude" of the data. Effect sizes are translated into standard deviations so that contrasts are possible across studies that have incorporated different outcome measures (e.g., comparison of an overall increase in self-help skills in one study with increases in mother–child interaction in a second study).

The Utah EIRI group reviewed the English language early intervention literature. The studies in the early childhood/special education literature were of two kinds. (a) Studies of an intervention versus nonintervention design characterized 90 studies of handicapped populations (24% of the total reviewed); 133 studies of disadvantaged populations (35%); and 32 studies of at-risk populations (8%; primarily premature births and low-birth-weight infants, and those with genetic complications). (b) An intervention A versus intervention B design characterized 42 studies of handicapped populations (12%); 69 studies of disadvantaged populations, (18%); and 11 studies of at risk populations (3%).

In summary, the Utah State University Early Intervention Research Institute findings provided (a) compelling evidence for positive *immediate* effects of early intervention with disadvantaged, handicapped, and at-risk infants; (b) moderate evidence of *medium-term* maintenance of early intervention's effects for disadvantaged youngsters; and (c) no firm evidence for *long-term* effects of early intervention with children with handicaps — beyond 1 year following cessation of treatment (Casto & Mastropieri, 1985; Casto & White, 1983; White & Casto, 1984).

For this chapter, a selected sample of this data set is briefly examined. This selection is the data set of the University of Massachusetts Early Intervention Collaborative Study (EICS), which yielded a reinterpretation of the Utah EIRI data. It used a filter mechanism to select from the 400+ Utah EIRI-identified studies to select research investigations on the basis of two criteria: (a) The infants studied had entered into early intervention programs prior to 36 months of age, suffered biological disability, and were home-raised (53 studies total); (b) studies were of the A versus B or control/contrast group types, with no major threats to validity (31 studies total with 91 effect sizes). Thus,

these data focus on the noninstitutionalized, biologically traumatized, very young children of the broader study, who were the subjects of the "strongest" subset of research studies. These infants are closest to the population at the focus of this chapter.

In the 1987 Massachusetts EICS reinterpretation of the EIRI data the 91 effect sizes derived from the 31 studies produced a mean effect (m.e.) of .62 *SD* (range = –0.94 to +2.0 *SD*). The outcome measures evaluated in the 91 effect sizes were IQ/DQ (51% of research studies); motor skill (15%); language (12%); parent–child interaction (3%); social-emotional (<1%); and family functioning (0%). Thus, we can readily see that although psychologists speak loudly to the need for due consideration of the effect of the family on the infant with handicaps, the vast majority of research has focused exclusively on intellectual, motor, and language outcomes.

In brief, we can see that the strongest effects (m.e. = 1.17) are demonstrated in studies of improvements in linguistic competence (although these represent the smallest number of studies). IQ/DQ (m.e. = .62) and motor skill (m.e. = .43) improvements also are significantly related to intervention. The most *practically* significant fact discernible from these data is the paucity of studies investigating the outcome of early intervention in terms of anything other than three vary basic measures.

Data on mean effects for programs by population served show fairly conclusively that young children served in heterogeneous populations fare better than children served in single-handicap groupings. Nevertheless, there remains evidence, somewhat less persuasive, that children with moderate and severe handicaps served in single-category groupings experience some (less powerful) gains from intervention. It is also evident that the greater the degree of curriculum structure incorporated into the early intervention activities, the greater the power of the outcome.

Two aspects of parent involvement were considered: the level of parent involvement along a continuum from *extensive* to *none*; and the type of parent involvement in programming and intervention activities (in terms of the degree to which the child is served separately from the parent, or whether these services are combined in a single activity focus). The data clearly demonstrated that the greatest effects are attributable to extensive involvement of parents (although this was not deemed a prerequisite to successful intervention services). This finding is contrary to the Utah EIRI interpretation in as much as the Utah group did not find a relationship between parent involvement and the degree of children's success. The reason for this difference may be that the EICS data analysis of younger children specifically was designed to compare studies that planned parent involvement with those that did not have extensive parent involvement, rather than to see whether such a feature would spontaneously be manifested in the finding, which was the basis on which the Utah EIRI study was designed. A more beneficial outcome was evidenced for children whose parents received services in parallel with their own receipt of services.

In summary, some tentative conclusions can be made about the characteristics of early intervention programs that are associated with greatest impact on children's development. It appears that the optimal arrangement is service to heterogeneous populations (i.e., to children with a range of disabilities) that entails a program modeled on a structured intervention plan, with full and meaningful integration of parent participation in decision making and service.

As to the specific effects that have been demonstrated by early intervention for children with handicaps, the following can be tentatively concluded: (a) Children make gains in early intervention programs, but this does not necessarily signal a causal relationship. (b) Most professionals and parents agree that early intervention programs facilitate development. (c) There is a desperate need for more scientifically interpretable studies of early intervention evaluation with young children with handicaps, since there are few

such studies because of ethical, methodological, and practical problems they encounter. (d) Finally, "pragmatic significance" is probably more powerful than statistical significance (for example, self-feeding skill outweighs $p < .001$ in virtually anything; see, among others, Bricker, Bailey, & Bruder, 1984; Dunst & Rheingrover, 1981; Odom & Fewell, 1983; Strain, 1984; White & Casto, 1984).

In contrast to the tentative conclusion above, we definitely can posit that the query Does early intervention work? is the wrong question. The correct kinds of questions are: What kinds of interventions have what types of effects? Delivered by which professionals? On what varieties of infants? In what sorts of settings? (Anastasiow, 1986; Bricker, 1987; Meisels, 1985a, 1985b; Strain & Smith, 1986).

SKILLS NEEDED FOR SPECIALIST PERSONNEL FOR DIRECT SERVICES FOR INFANTS AND THEIR FAMILIES

The vast majority of community services for at-risk or handicapped infants and their families rely on interdisciplinary teams (of a variety of configurations) to provide infant assessment/intervention and family services. Interdisciplinary service emphasizes a holistic view of the children to be served, the importance of the family as coequal team partners, and recognition that the family is the only "durable thread" in these children's lives. That a variety of models of service delivery are required to appropriately serve infants living in rural and urban/suburban communities is clear (Swift & Fine, 1982). Professionals must not only be prepared in a specific discipline (e.g., psychology, therapy, education) or with a *particular* "professional" model, but must also be trained to provide direct services for the infant and family in coordination with a number of medical, therapeutic, educational, and counseling/social work personnel who are likely to be involved in infant and family services (Campbell, 1982; Fewell, 1983). Model approaches to the provision of services to infants with handicaps are based on teams (Hanson,

1984), each team member of which is skilled in a particular discipline and, if well trained, experienced in the application of those skills to infant assessment, development, and programming. Unfortunately, professional training that is carried out within a particular discipline often does not facilitate acquisition of the "teaming" and "coordinating" skills necessary to work effectively in interdisciplinary teams (Bricker, 1976; Hanson, 1984; Orlando, 1981).

Teaming Skills

That families and infants require some sort of coordinated and interdisciplinary assistance is an essential principle in provision of quality services for families and their infants (e.g., Anastasiow, 1981a, 1981b; Campbell, 1982; Fewell, 1983; Hanson, 1984). Yet many professionals, including psychologists, because of their separate preparation programs, have not been trained in an interdisciplinary fashion (e.g., Bricker, 1976; Connor, Williamson, & Sieppe, 1978). Not only may professionals in particular disciplines have failed to gain expertise in certain areas needed to program for families and their infants with handicaps, but they also may lack teaming skills as well as those necessary to coordinate services for families (Haynes, 1976). Furthermore, current models of teaming (e.g., interdisciplinary, transdisciplinary) are inherently rooted in a diagnostic–prescriptive approach to infant intervention, and they lack emphasis in areas related to families. Skills in providing support for families in the care of their infants must be taught to professionals within an integrated team approach (e.g., Carney, 1983; Campbell et al., in press; Zeitlin, 1981).

The literature in programming for infants supports the need to train professionals not only in specialized skills appropriate for a particular population or age group, but also in the communication skills required to interact effectively and in a coordinated fashion both with parents and with other professional discipline (e.g., Bailey & Bricker, 1984; Bailey &

Wolery, 1984; Hanson, 1984). Federal and state agencies providing services to vulnerable young children also encourage team structures as the basis for infant programming (Beckman & Burke, 1984). Nevertheless, despite the fact that best practice entails the implementation of coordinated interdisciplinary services, training priorities for personnel preparation traditionally have separated the training of educators, including psychologists, from that of related services personnel.

Current services for this population are provided, for the most part, by educational, psychological, and related services personnel who have limited professional preparation in relevant areas. This is inevitable since quality assurance through specialty training and licensure has been virtually absent. Personnel may have licenses or certificates to practice their respective disciplines, but little or no specific expertise in working with infants and their families.

Dissociation between the so-called medical and educational/therapeutic regimens has been of sufficient concern that the American Academy of Pediatrics has developed a national in-service training program (Project Bridge) designed to educate physicians about infants with handicaps as well as to train interdisciplinary personnel (Spencer, 1984). There is, unfortunately, no existing parallel to this in the field of child psychology. However, in September, 1987, the National Association of School Psychologists (NASP) adopted a Position Statement on Early Intervention in the Schools that encourages university programs, professional associations, public schools, and other continuing education unit providers to introduce appropriate professional development experiences into their programs. In 1988 NASP began sponsoring Regional Institutes on preschool services. The nationwide implementation of such a training program would make psychologists substantially more aware of the needs of families and their infants with handicaps.

Personnel Needs

The increasing, and soon to be urgent, need for personnel reflects the growing appreciation of the benefits of early intervention and the development of mandates to serve infants and preschoolers with handicaps. Professionals from a variety of psychological, educational, therapeutic, medical child development, and family/social service disciplines are needed to serve infants and toddlers with special needs. It is self-evident that a state cannot move from partial to comprehensive services without educating a professional cadre to provide these services. Furthermore, more quality programs that do more than offer expensive caretaking cannot be created unless personnel are available for hire with skills appropriate to treatment of infants. Young children and their parents are entitled to receive services from professionals trained to meet their unique needs.

Each of the professionals who may be involved with families and infants requires additional training to acquire skills specific to infants with handicaps. Participation in controlled in-service training is required by professional organizations (for example, American Medical Association, AOTA, APA, APTA, ASHA, NASP) to ensure the maintenance and updating of skills necessary to continue professional certification. In-service training provides the primary vehicle for currently employed psychologists and other related services personnel to develop skills to be applied with specific population groups, such as infants. Psychologists may need some update in the skills necessary to work within a family systems approach; most will also need to learn about infant development, assessment, programming, care, and management (e.g., Mallory, 1983; McCollum, 1982; Peterson, 1987).

It is impossible to estimate accurately the numbers of new personnel that must be trained to provide comprehensive services. However, it is clear that personnel needs are great. Collaboration with colleges and universities in developing locally appropriate training programs (Swift & Fine, 1982) will be necessary to address the following problems: (a) current staff training is inadequate; (b) the lack of trained professional personnel is the greatest inadequacy in service delivery; and (c) the lack of personnel to ensure quality services is a significant barrier to enacting a comprehensive service system for infants with handicaps and their families.

COORDINATION AND COMMUNICATION

New approaches to providing services for families and their infants with handicaps are being advocated by parents and professionals (e.g., Blacher, 1984; Kaiser & Hayden, 1984; Kupfer, 1984; Turnbull & Turnbull, 1985; Vincent, 1984). Parents of children who have been enrolled in early intervention programs are beginning to speak up about the effects of participation in those programs on both the family and the child (Vincent, 1984). Parents are questioning the personal and financial sacrifices made by themselves and other family members, and are requesting public services that support the integrity of the family while enhancing the growth of their infants (e.g., Kupfer, 1982; Jones, 1985). Families are speaking out about the negative effects of professional expectations that have required them to be therapists, teachers, and nurses for their children in order to qualify as "good parents" while these requirements have not merited their inclusion as coequals in the decision-making team for their infants.

Professionals have responded by looking into the need for new models of service delivery for families and their infants with handicaps (e.g., Blacher, 1984; Ludlow, 1981; Turnbull & Turnbull, 1978a, 1978b, 1985). Models that support the family and enhance the capabilities of families to care for their infants with handicaps have been advocated as a method for decreasing the negative impact of current service models on the family system (e.g., Field, 1983; Hanson, 1984; Kaiser & Hayden, 1984). The emergence of new models of services will require training and retraining of personnel who are currently working with infants with handicaps, as well as those soon to serve this population. Families will need to learn to express their needs, obtain desired resources, and use professionals in ways that benefit both the family and the child with handicaps. Professionals will need to learn to provide resources that help and support families in the care of their infants, rather than to simply prescribe solutions to be followed by families. Only through changes in attitudes and beliefs and in knowledge and skills can parents and professionals join together in partnership to provide quality services that best serve families with infants who are handicapped.

Many of the difficulties reported by families in caring for their infants derive from poor coordination between services and among professionals (Bell, 1981; Bray, Coleman, & Brackmen, 1981). Many infants who sustain handicaps will have been cared for in a hospital NICU but will later receive services exclusively through community-based resources. Families are frequently discharged from a NICU with infants requiring follow-up by physicians in a variety of specialties (surgery, orthopedics, neurology, pediatrics) and by other medical practitioners in various specialties (e.g., respiratory therapy, other therapies, apnea monitoring, nutrition), in addition to any community-based programs to which families may be referred. However, there is little coordination in transition between the medical services provided in early infancy and the community services that later may be required. Case managership and service coordination is demonstrably a central component of quality services — and fortunately a required component of PL 99-457.

In the absence of professionals who undertake the appropriate coordination with community services, families are left to provide their own coordination among specialists and between medical and educational groups (e.g., Jones, 1985; Vadasy, Fewell, Meyer, Schell, & Greenberg, 1984); this is a source of stress for many families with infants (Beckman-Bell, 1981). Families with additional wants (e.g., food, housing, etc.) are at even greater risk for high stress levels attrib-

utable to the pressing family needs (e.g., Bronfenbrenner, 1978).

PSYCHOLOGISTS' CONTRIBUTION TO QUALITY SERVICES

Because interaction among client, family, and service providers is a primary component of effective intervention for very young children with handicaps, and because parents are best situated as providers of this interaction, the preferred intervention model attempts to balance complementary needs. This approach emphasizes the dual assessment of the family's and the child's needs, as well as the evaluation of family dynamics, with a view to identifying physical and social resources (Adelman, 1982; Paget, 1985; Paget & Nagle, 1986). The psychologist's intervention focuses on providing parents instruction in developmentally appropriate activity — by providing emotional support to the family, exchanging information with the family, facilitating use of community resources, encouraging parent–child interaction, sharing child development information, helping parents select appropriate children's materials, promoting a playful learning environment, creating understanding that development is sequential, and helping parents develop interactional strategies that promote infant learning.

Such an approach enables parents to retain control, avoids professional authority-lay parent misunderstanding through reciprocal communication, and deals with parent priorities by respecting their aspirations for their children. It builds on parents' strengths in interactions with their children, involves parents in planning activities, respects parents' idiosyncratic styles of interaction with their children, provides instruction on tested strategies for interacting as well as content of interaction, and provides parents with alternatives in their child-care intervention sessions. Above all, it enhances parents' self-esteem in interactions with their children by powerfully illustrating and validating for them their central role in their children's development.

Parent education/instruction is a component specific to the intent of PL 99-457. But before parents are to receive instruction a needs assessment is required — from their perspective. A most basic design element is to ask parents "What do you want from the education system for your young child with handicaps?" Probably more parents know what they want and what they need than most professionals would credit. In answer to this question one parent of a child with handicaps (admittedly one who had professional experience in working with disabled adults) brought up the following desiderata: Service providers' work should reflect (a) the principle that "no matter how handicapped, every child can learn"; (b) guarantee integration between education and therapies; (c) use a curriculum that teaches to the child's *functional* needs, not strictly according to the milestones of nonhandicapped infants/toddlers; (d) incorporate data-based instruction, with decisions on adjustment of curriculum made on the basis of objective information; and (e) from day one plan for a transition to the next environment.

However, if we are to take seriously this parent's aspirations in respect to the next environment, we also need to be aware of what the next environment *is*, and what it involves for the child. We need to have a contemporary picture. For example, in an analysis of 25 kindergarten classrooms, the University of Pittsburgh EIRI (Strain, 1987) discovered that only 15% of class time is devoted to active instruction, that there is less than a 1% chance of praise for children's positive behavior, and more than a 60% chance of punishment for negative behavior. Also, we have confirmed that less-successful children have an even smaller chance of being praised, and greater likelihood for punishment. Teachers' expectations as to standards of performance routinely exceed age-expectations. Clearly, this is far from an ideal next environment for the child with disabilities.

Approaches to parents need revision if their partnership is to be made real. In the past, parents have all too frequently been unfairly subjected to stereotypical characterization. Parents have variously been labeled unrealistic, nuisances, dependency builders, uncooperative, uncaring, and incompetent. They have also been the victims of platitudes and double-talk ("I agree with your philosophy, but . . ."), passing the buck ("I agree with you but I'm not the one to make this decision . . . you'll need to talk to . . ."), insinuation that the expert knows best ("According to our research . . . the data say . . .; we have found . . ."), and blaming ("These things take time . . .; you must be patient . . .; you're too involved . . .; other parents haven't found that . . .").

There are some unifying assumptions and action plans about families that, if reflected in professional practice, enhance the prospect of finding creative solutions to the difficulties of very young, handicapped children and their families. Services must include a commitment to integrated programming. Members of multidisciplinary teams serving such clients must

ACCEPT the belief that families are an integral part of integrated team planning and decision making.

AFFIRM the value of family/professional collaboration.

ACCLAIM the positive benefits that can accrue from effectively designed family participation in the interdisciplinary process.

ACTIVATE alternatives for families and professionals to work together within their roles as partners.

ALLEVIATE the anxiety and hostility that is sometimes caused by family/professional conflicts, through mediation and negotiation.

ACCENTUATE the importance of family/professional teamwork in the interdisciplinary process.

CONCLUSIONS

The field of early intervention in school psychology is in its infancy. The most pressing current problem is not solely *how to provide alternative services,* but *who is going to provide them.* The need for adequately prepared professionals is almost overwhelming. There are simply not enough preparation vehicles (whether universities, professional institutes, or in-service options), and there is not yet a national plan for provider training. Even so, the major problem in imparting this "new" knowledge is not simply the absence of graduate classroom-learning opportunities, but more importantly the limited access to hands-on experience through supervised practica. Given the recognized incentive to provide comprehensive services to the most vulnerable members of our citizenry, it appears inevitable that many children with desperate needs are soon to have these needs addressed by sincere, but weakly prepared and content-naive "professionals."

Information in this chapter has been freely incorporated into the section *How is early intervention different?* of Nancy L. Peterson's highly recommended 1987 text *Early Intervention for Handicapped and At-Risk Children.* Peterson's treatise is clearly the most comprehensive and readable source of information currently available for the school psychologist wishing to become familiar with this new field.

REFERENCES

Adelman, H. S. (1982). Identifying learning problems at an early age: A critical appraisal. *Journal of School Psychology, 11,* 255-261.

Als, H., Tronick, E., & Brazelton, T. B. (1980). Stages of early behavioral organization: The study of a sighted infant and blind infant interaction with their mothers. In T. M. Field (Ed.), *High-risk infants and children: Adults and peer interactions.* New York: Academic.

Anastasiow, N. (1981a). Early childhood education for the handicapped in the 1980s: Recommendations. *Exceptional Children, 47,* 276-284.

Anastasiow, N. (1981b). The needs of early childhood education for the handicapped: A song for the 80s. *Journal of the Division for Early Childhood, 2,* 1-7.

Anastasiow, N. J. (1986). The research base for early intervention. *Journal of the Division for Early Childhood, 10,* 99-105.

Antley, T. R., DuBose, R. F. (1981). *A case for early intervention: Summary of program findings, longitudinal data, and cost-effectiveness.* Unpub-

lished manuscript. Seattle, WA: University of Washington, Experimental Education Unit.

Bailey, D. B., & Wolery, M. (1984). *Teaching infants and preschoolers with handicaps.* Columbus, OH: Merrill.

Bailey, E. J., & Bricker, D. (1984). The efficacy of early intervention for severely handicapped infants and young children. *Topics in Early Childhood Special Education, 4*(3), 30-51.

Beckman, P., & Burke, P. (1984). Early childhood special education: State of the art. *Topics in Early Childhood Special Education, 4*(1), 19-32.

Beckman-Bell, P. (1981). Child-related stress in families of handicapped children. *Topics in Early Childhood Special Education, 1*(3), 45-54.

Bell, P. J. (1981). Characteristics of handicapped infants: A study of the relationship between child characteristics and stress as reported by mothers. *Dissertation Abstracts International, 41,* 4356A-4357A. (University Microfilm No. 81-04, 366)

Berruetta-Clement, J. R., Schweinhart, L. J., Barnett, W. S., Epstein, A. S., & Weikhart, D. P. (1984). *Changed lives: The effects of the Perry Preschool Program on youths through age 19.* Ypsilanti, MI: High/Scope Press.

Blacher, J. (1984). *Severely handicapped young children and their families: Research in review.* New York: Academic.

Bray, N. C., Coleman, J. M., & Brackmen, M. B. (1981). Critical events in parenting handicapped children. *Journal of the Division for Early Childhood, 3,* 26-33.

Brazelton, T. (1982a). Joint regulation of neonate-parent behavior. In E. Tronick (Ed.), *Social interchange in infancy: Affect, cognition and communication.* Baltimore: University Park Press.

Brazelton, T. (1982b). Assessment in early infancy as an intervention. In A. Waldstein (Ed.), *Issues in neonatal care.* Chapel Hill, NC: Western States Technical Assistance Resource (WESTAR), and Technical Assistance Development System (TADS).

Bricker, D. (1976). Educational synthesizer. In M. Angel-Thomas (Ed.), *Hey don't forget about me.* Reston, VA: Council for Exceptional Children.

Bricker, D. (1987). Impact of research on social policy for handicapped infants and children. *Journal of the Division for Early Childhood, 11,* 98-105.

Bricker, D., Bailey, E., & Bruder, M. (1984). The efficacy of early intervention and the handicapped infant: A wise or wasted resource? In M. Wolraich & D. Routh (Eds.), *Advances in Developmental and Behavioral Pediatrics* (Vol. 5). Greenwich, CT: JAI Press.

Bronfenbrenner, U. (1975). Is early intervention effective? In M. Guttentag & E. Streuning (Eds.), *Handbook of evaluation and research*. Beverly Hills, CA: Sage.

Bronfenbrenner, U. (1978). Is early intervention effective? In B. Friedlander, G. Sterritt, & G. Kirk (Eds.), *Exceptional infant: Assessment and intervention*. New York: Brunner/Mazel.

Campbell, P. H. (1982). Individualized team programming with infants and young handicapped children. In D. McClowry, A. M. Guilford, & S. Richardson (Eds.), *Infant communication: Development, assessment, and intervention*. New York: Grune and Stratton.

Campbell, P. H., Bellamy, T., & Bishop, K. K. (in press). Statewide education systems: An overview of the new federal program for infants and toddlers with handicaps. *Journal of Special Education*.

Carney, I. H. (1983). Services for families of severely handicapped preschool students: Assumptions and implications. *Journal of the Division for Early Childhood, 7*, 78-85.

Casto, G., & Lewis, A. C. (1984). Parent involvement in infant and preschool programs. *Journal of the Division for Early Childhood, 9*, 49-56.

Casto, G., & Mastropieri, M. A. (1986a). The efficacy of early intervention programs: A meta-analysis. *Exceptional Children, 52*, 417-424.

Casto, G., & Mastropieri, M. A. (1986b). Strain and Smith do protest too much: A response. *Exceptional Children, 53*, 266-268.

Casto, G., & Mastropieri, M. A. (1986c). Much ado about nothing: A reply to Dunst and Snyder. *Exceptional Children, 53*, 277-279.

Casto, G., & White, K. (1983). The efficacy of early intervention programs with environmentally at-risk infants. *Journal of Children in Contemporary Society, 17*, 37-48.

Children's Defense Fund. (1988). *The health of America's children*. Washington, DC: Children's Defense Fund.

Connor, F., Williamson, G., & Sieppe, J. (1978). *Program guide for infants and toddlers with neuromotor and other developmental disabilities*. New York: Teacher's College Press.

Datta, L. E. (1979). Another spring and other hopes: Some findings from national evaluations of Project Head Start. In E. Zigler & J. Valentine (Eds.), *Project Head Start: A legacy of the war on poverty*. New York: Free Press.

DiVitto, B., & Goldberg, S. (1979). The effects of newborn medical status on early parent–infant interaction. In T. M. Field (Ed.), *Infants born at risk: Behavior and development*. New York: Spectrum.

Dunst, C. J., & Rheingrover, R. M. (1981). An analysis of the efficacy of infant intervention programs with organically handicapped children. *Evaluation and Program Planning, 4*, 287-323.

Dunst, C. J., & Snyder, S. W. (1986). A critique of the Utah State University early intervention meta-analysis research. *Exceptional Children, 53*, 269-276.

Fewell, R. R. (1983). The team approach to infant education. In S. G. Garwood & R. R. Fewell (Eds.), *Educating handicapped infants: Issues in development and intervention*. Rockville, MD: Aspen.

Field, T. M. (1983). Interactions of preterm and term infants with their lower- and middle-class teenage adult mothers. In T. M. Field (Ed.), *High-risk infants and children: Adult and peer interactions*. New York: Academic.

Foster, M., Berger, M., & McLean, M. (1981). Rethinking a good idea: A reassessment of parent involvement. *Topics in Early Childhood Special Education, 1*(3), 55-65.

Garner, J. B. (1987). *Effective family participation in integrated team planning* (Limited distribution monograph). Cuyahoga Falls, OH: MidEastern Ohio Regional Resources Center, and Family Child Learning Center.

Hanson, M. J. (Ed.). (1984). *Atypical infant development*. Baltimore: University Park Press.

Hanson, M. J. (1985). An analysis of the effects of early intervention services for infants and toddlers with moderate and severe handicaps. *Topics in Early Childhood Special Education, 5*(2), 36-51.

Haynes, U. (1976). The national collaborative infant project. In T. Tjossem (Ed.), *Intervention strategies for high-risk infants and young children*. Baltimore: University Park Press.

Hobbs, N. (1975). *The futures of children: Categories, labels, and their consequences*. (The Jossey-Bass Behavioral Science Series). San Francisco: Jossey-Bass.

Jones, M. (1985). *How to care for your chronically ill child*. New York: Harper and Row.

Kaiser, C. E., & Hayden, A. H. (1984). Clinical research and policy issues in parenting severely handicapped infants. In J. Blacher (Ed.), *Severely handicapped young children and their families: Research in review*. New York: Academic.

Karnes, M. B., & Teska, J. A. (1975). Children's response to intervention programs. In J. J. Gallagher (Ed.), *The application of child development research to handicapped children*. Reston, VA: Council for Exceptional Children.

Kupfer, F. (1982). *Before and after Zachariah: A family story of a different kind of courage.* New York: Delacorte.

Kupfer, F. (1984). Severely and/or multiply disabled children. *Equals in this partnership: Parents of disabled and at-risk infants and toddlers speak to professionals.* Washington, DC: National Center for Clinical Infant Programs.

Lazar, I., & Darlington, R. (Eds.). (1982). Lasting effects of early education: A report from the Consortium for Longitudinal Studies (Summary report, DHEW Publication No. OHDS 80-30179). *Monographs of the Society for Research in Child Development, 47*(2-3, Serial #195).

Ludlow, B. (1981). Parent-infant interaction research: The argument for earlier intervention programs. *Journal of the Division for Early Childhood, 3*, 34-41.

Mallory, B. L. (1983). The preparation of early childhood special educators. *Journal of the Division for Early Childhood, 7*, 32-40.

Mastropieri, M. A., White, K., & Fecteau, F. (1986). Introduction to special education textbooks: What they say about the efficacy of early intervention. *Journal of the Division for Early Childhood, 7*, 32-40.

Mazaide, M., Cote, R., Boutin, P., Bernier, H., & Thivierge, J. (1987). Temperament and intellectual development: A longitudinal study from infancy to four years. *American Journal of Psychiatry, 144*(2), 144-150.

McCollum, J. (1982). Teaching teachers to teach: A framework for preservice program planning. *Journal of the Division for Early Childhood, 6*, 52-59.

McNulty, B., Smith, D. B., & Soper, E. W. (1983). *Effectiveness of early special education for handicapped children.* Denver: Colorado Department of Education.

Meisels, S. J. (1985a). The efficacy of early intervention: Why are we still asking this question? *Topics in Early Childhood Special Education, 5*(2), 1-11.

Meisels, S. J. (1985b). Why are we still asking this question? *Topics in early childhood special education, 5*(2), 1-11.

Meisels, S. J. (1986, November). *National profile of early intervention policy: Where do we go from here?* Paper presented at the meeting of the Division of Early Childhood, Council for Exceptional Children, Louisville, KY.

Mowder, B., & Widerstrom, A. H. (1986). Philosophical differences between early childhood and special education: Issues for school psychologists. *Psychology in the Schools, 23*(2), 171-175.

Odom, S. L., & Fewell, R. R. (1983). Program evaluation in early childhood special education: A meta-evaluation. *Education Evaluation and Policy Analysis, 5*, 445-460.

Orlando, C. (1981). Multidisciplinary team approaches in the assessment of handicapped children. *Topics in Early Childhood Special Education, 1*(2), 23-30.

Paget, K. D. (1985). Preschool services in the schools: Issues and implications. *Special Services in the Schools, 2*, 3-25.

Paget, K. D., & Nagle, R. J. (1986). A conceptual model of preschool assessment. *School Psychology Review, 15*, 154-165.

Peterson, N. (1987). *Early intervention for handicapped and at-risk children: An introduction to early childhood-special education.* Denver: Love.

Ramey, C. T., & Campbell, F. A. (1984). Preventive education for high risk children: Cognitive consequences of the Carolina Abecedarian Project. *American Journal of Mental Deficiency, 88*, 515-523.

Reaves, J., & Burns, J. (1982, November). *An analysis of the impact of the handicapped children's early education program.* (Final Report 2 for Special Education Programs, U.S. Department of Education, Contract No. 300-81-0661). Washington, DC: Roy Littlejohn Associates.

Schweinhart, L., & Weikart, D. (1980). *Young children grow up: The effects of the Perry Preschool Program on youths through age 15.* Ypsilanti, MI: High/Scope Educational Research Foundation.

Spencer, P. (1984). *Enhancement of the decision-making capacity of multidisciplinary teams working with young handicapped children.* Washington, DC: Project Overview, American Academy of Pediatrics.

Strain, P. (1987). *Early childhood research institute: Final report, executive summary.* Pittsburgh, PA: Western Psychiatric Institute and Clinic, University of Pittsburgh.

Strain, P. S. (1984). Efficacy research with young handicapped children: A critique of the status quo. *Journal of the Division for Early Childhood, 9*, 4-10.

Strain, P. S., & Smith, B. J. (1986). A counter-interpretation of early intervention effects: A response to Casto and Mastropieri. *Exceptional Children, 53*, 260-265.

Swift, J., & Fine. B. (1982). Neuromotor assessment of infants. In M. Lewis & L. T. Taft (Eds.), *Developmental disabilities: Theory, assessment, and intervention.* Jamaica, NY: Spectrum.

Tucker, J. (1981). *Sequential stages of the appraisal process: A training module.* Minneapolis: University of Minnesota, National School Psychology Inservice Training Network.

Turnbull, A. P., & Turnbull, H. R. (1978a). *Parents speak out: Views from the other side of the two-way mirror.* Columbus, OH: Merrill.

Turnbull, A. P., & Turnbull, H. R. (1978b). *Parents speak out: Then and now.* Columbus, OH: Merrill.

Turnbull, A., & Turnbull, H. (1985, October). *Efficacy of early intervention.* Paper presented at the meeting of the Division of Early Childhood, Council for Exceptional Children. Denver, CO.

Vadasy, P., Fewell, R., Meyer, D., Schell, G., & Greenberg, M. (1984). Involved parents: Characteristics and resources of fathers and mothers of young handicapped children. *Journal of the Division for Early Childhood, 8,* 13-25.

Vincent, E. (1984). Family relationships. *Equals in this partnership: Parents of disabled and at-risk infants and toddlers speak to professionals.* Washington, DC: National Center for Clinical Infant Programs.

White, K. R., & Casto, G. (1984). *An integrative review of early intervention efficacy studies with at-risk children: Implications for the handicapped* (Publications of the Early Intervention Research Institute). Logan, UT: Utah State University.

Wood, P. (1981). Cost of services. In C. Garland, N. Stone, J. Swanson, & G. Woodruff (Eds.), *Early intervention for children with special needs and their families: Findings and recommendations.* Monmouth, OR: WESTAR.

Zeitlin, S. (1981). Learning through coping: An effective preschool program. *Journal of the Division for Early Childhood, 4,* 53-61.

14

Alternative Service Delivery in Preschool Settings: Practical and Conceptual Foundations

David W. Barnett
University of Cincinnati
Kathleen D. Paget
University of South Carolina

Preschool educational and psychological services are at a critical juncture. For years, preschool services have played a relatively minor role in the practice of school psychology. However, with the recent passage of Public Law 99-457, preschool psychological services to handicapped and at-risk children will expand substantially. There has never been a better time to examine the role of the school psychologist with young children.

This chapter first introduces practices and procedures generally applicable for effective services to high-risk children, and for those with learning and behavior problems. Because of the many unknowns in educational and psychological service delivery, the empirical foundations for early intervention are of critical importance, and are discussed in the second section. The third section appraises traditional professional practices with respect to their potential impact on alternative services. The final sections discuss the realities of practice and the training implications of alternative service delivery.

PRACTICAL FOUNDATIONS OF ALTERNATIVE SERVICE DELIVERY

The foundations of alternative service delivery are those of intervention design (Barnett & Carey, in press; Paget, in press). The foundations serve as guides or templates for preschool psychological practices and encompass interrelated steps that psychologists are likely to follow in successfully applying problem-solving principles to preschool screening, assessment, and intervention without unnecessary labeling (National Association of School Psychologists, 1987). The foundations discussed are based on an interactive systems perspective whereby major emphasis is given to supporting and enhancing the skills of caregivers.

An Ecological and Family Basis

A major contribution from the ecological or systems perspective is that problems can be potentially resolved through a range of alternative strategies: by modifying the problem behavior, changing the expectations of the persons encountering the behavior, or altering the situation (e.g., Cantrell & Cantrell, 1985). In addition to the analysis of the problem situation, attention is also drawn to the analysis of system strengths — healthy, adaptive mechanisms and coping strategies. The professional attempts to understand the network of relationships within and between settings. A general principle is that problems belong to systems, not individuals. Other major views include the evaluation of unintended as well as intended effects from interventions, and the focus on long time spans in evaluating the overall benefits and risks associated with interventions (Willems, 1977). While both home and school ecologies are of interest, we focus on families in the next paragraphs.

The assessment of family realities is an important first step (MacPhee, Ramey, & Yates, 1984). Like other environments, the family environment presents both "risks or opportunities" for development (Garbarino, 1982, p. 3). While family situations often fall short of various ideals (e.g., single or foster parents), many strategies and alternative social arrangements potentially lead to the development of competence for children given the presence of key elements in the social environment (Garbarino, 1982). Several major points of analysis are discussed next.

Although parents may receive technical assistance in the course of an intervention, it should be provided in a way that is likely to encourage independent problem solving and relationship building through natural means (e.g., Guralnick & Bennett, 1987; Dunst & Trivette, 1987). Thus, critical attention is given to outcomes that foster strength in families.

Because of their effects on parent–child relationships and experiences, parental stress (e.g., Abidin, 1986) and coping may be important targets in assessment and intervention design. Stressors encountered early in life have the potential for both beneficial and harmful consequences. "There may be *sensitization* to the effects of later stressors but also there are *steeling* effects involved in overcoming stress and adversity" (Rutter, 1981, p. 347). Factors that buffer the effects of stressful events such as divorce, disease, and loss of employment may be associated with inherited resilience, but they may be also related to the availability of at least one caregiver who provides: (a) a relationship characterized by warm, reciprocal, and supportive interaction; (b) the continuity of experiences; and (c) the active promotion of competence (e.g., Werner & Smith, 1982).

Another related approach is based on the analysis of learning and mediational contexts provided by families that hold opportunities likely to encourage growth and competence of children. A full range of experiences in the family system can be evaluated to identify ways to transform events into learning experiences (e.g., Laosa & Sigel, 1982). Methods of control, punishment (e.g., Mancuso & Handin, 1985), and underlying parental belief systems (McGillicuddy-Delisi, 1985) may influence learning and behavior outcomes.

One of the most widely researched techniques for the assessment of early learning environments is the Home Observation for Measurement of the Environment (HOME) scale (Bradley & Caldwell, 1979; see Gottfried [1984] for a major review). HOME variables show modest but significant correlations with development, and serve to summarize important aspects of early learning environments: (a) emotional and verbal responsivity of the caregiver(s), (b) avoidance of restriction and punishment, (c) organization of the physical and temporal environment, (d) availability of play materials, (e) degree of maternal involvement, and (f) opportunities for variety in daily stimulation. The moderate nature of these correlations are not entirely due to the limitations of the variables, but also result from measurement difficulties, especially in discerning the impact of subtle and/or infrequent events not readily reflected in observations. Furthermore, environmental influences are often different for individual children within the same family (Plomin, 1987).

For reasons that fit the challenges of preschool services and ecological principles, we focus attention on the analysis of roles. Preschool psychologists must assume a number of assessment and intervention roles and shift emphasis from child to adult behaviors as needed. Caregivers should receive primary attention as change agents. Thus, the greatest challenge is "in the management of ecological systems defined by individual exceptional children" (Hobbs, 1975, p. 461).

Screening from an Alternative Service Delivery Perspective

Screening is most beneficial when it encourages parent, teacher, interagency, and interdisciplinary collaboration. Furthermore, screening may be conducted in a way that reflects ecological strategies. With this end in view, one of the first steps in screening is organizational development (Adelman, 1982; Barnett, 1984) in order to prepare systems and individuals for diverse roles. Often it will be a primary focus.

There are many challenges to be met by systems approaches to screening. Mental health professionals frequently work with families in crisis, but it may appear that caregivers have insufficient resources, skills, and motivation to provide guidance and nurturance at the moment of crisis. Also, some parents may be quite hard to reach (Wahler, 1980), and attendance and compliance with parent training programs does not guarantee success (Dumas & Albin, 1986).

Furthermore, preschool teachers must have adequate resources to assist with screening and assessment, and to serve as change agents for a wide variety of problem behaviors. Preschools are often the first settings in which the social and educational consequences associated with severe developmental disabilities, maladaptive behaviors, and risk status can be subjected to comprehensive analysis. Yet personnel preparation is often minimal (e.g., O'Connell, 1983) and may not meet the background requirements necessary for appropriate assessment and intervention.

Despite the difficulties, we argue that mental health and educational screening should focus on (a) family circumstances, since other factors in the caregivers' experience may preclude the adequate expression of the parental role; (b) the range and quality of personal, social, and educational learning experiences that are provided in the home and at school; and (c) the child's overall adaptation to preschool settings in respect to the ongoing assessment of preacademic skills and social behavior. In contrast, traditional screening measures focus attention on children's skills at one point in time. Although the screening of children is essential in many areas (e.g., hearing, vision, medical), the caregivers' behavior is the primary consideration for many young children.

Assessment-Intervention Design for Alternative Service Delivery

Steps in ecological assessment and intervention. A number of ecological interviews have been described that provide useful guidelines for practitioners (e.g., Hartman, 1978; Wahler & Cormier, 1970). They should be conducted within a framework of family systems theory (e.g., Paget, 1987). We describe one in some detail rather than provide a comprehensive review.

The eco-map (Hartman, 1978), depicted in Figure 1, can be helpful in evaluating family and community systems, and possible sources of family support. It can be developed with family members as a part of an interview process. The eco-map can help portray the often complex networks and stresses of contemporary families such as divorce, separation, shared custody, foster care, adoption, nontraditional childrearing patterns, and alienation of the family from external support systems and community life. Sources of stress such as illness can be depicted, as well as changes that occur during the course of the assessment-intervention process.

A primary value of the eco-map is the visual impact of the technique. It makes possible the organization and presentation of factual information, perceptions of significant relationships, and other variables.

The symbols are easy to follow (Figure 1). Squares represent males; circles represent females. When helpful, ages are placed within the figures. Connecting lines are drawn between family members: dashed lines for "tenuous connections," Xs representing "conflicted or stressful connections." Arrows are drawn where appropriate, along the lines indicating "flow of energy," "nurturance," "supplies or

FIGURE 1
An Example of An Ecological Assessment Technique

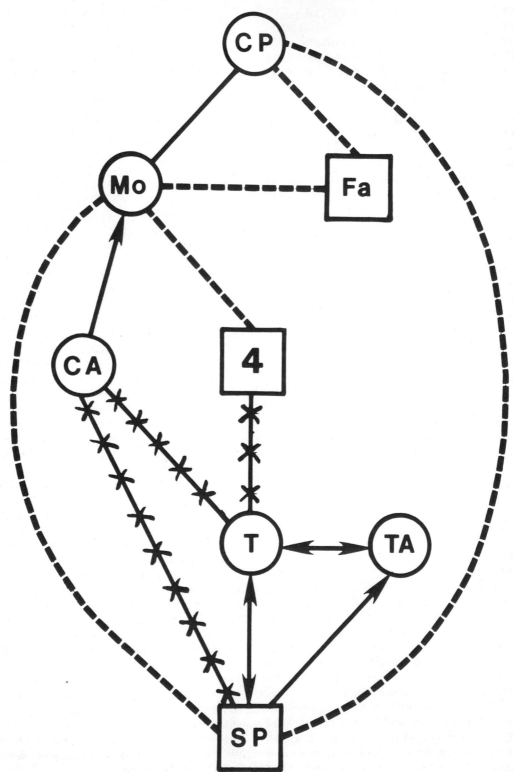

support." Arrows can be drawn in both directions if the relationships are mutual or reciprocal. "An almost empty eco-map helps the client objectify and share loneliness and isolation" (Hartman, 1978, p. 471). Even more important, the eco-map can be used to help identify the possibility of new resources.

Figure 1 depicts a crisis situation in which a 4-year-old autistic boy without language or self-care skills was integrated into a preschool setting by a community agency (CA) functioning from a strong advocacy position. Furthermore, the child exhibited a number of maladaptive behaviors. Initial consultation focused on the teacher's concerns about the overall adaptation of a severely handicapped child to a regular preschool classroom. The teacher (T) and assistant (TA) felt ill prepared to work with the child [4]. While the relationship of the mother (Mo) and father (Fa) was described as tenuous, the mother was being counseled by a clinical psychologist (CP). The school psychologist is represented by [SP]. In a later phase, procedures and resources to enable adaptation to school were maintained while the focus shifted to parent skill training. Parental concerns were directly addressed, and included expanding learning experiences in mother-child play, language development, and self-care. The eco-map may be reconfigured in conjunction with the phases of intervention design (Barnett, in press).

The rationale and scope of behavioral assessment and intervention. Because behavioral assessment is fundamental to interventions with preschool children, we do not view it as an "alternative" to other assessment approaches (e.g., Nelson & Hayes, 1986). Ecological principles yield a means of identifying the suitability of change agents and loci, and the behavioral paradigm provides a powerful technology for change.

The focus of behavioral assessment is to select significant targets for change (Kanfer, 1985), and to measure the effects of well-designed, specified, and executed interventions. The analysis is based on the interaction of behavior, person variables, and environmental variables. Often it is difficult to find specific causes for behaviors, and the focus then shifts to one of identifying strategies to enable growth or success. General assessment methods include (a) obtaining frequency measures of behaviors or events (e.g., hitting); (b) recording behaviors in defined categories (e.g., skill sequences, appropriate-inappropriate behaviors); (c) recording behaviors within intervals of time (e.g., rates or occurrences of behavior); and (d) recording the duration of responses (e.g., crying).

Many contemporary behaviorists include the study of covert processes and subjective experiences (e.g., Kendall, 1985). Central concepts include the analysis of *self-regulatory systems* and *metacognition*, both terms encompass major trends in assessment and intervention design (Bandura, 1986; Meichenbaum, 1986). Metacognitive processes (Reeve & Brown, 1985) involve (a) understanding what is required by a task, (b) understanding one's capabilities, (c) employing strategies in planning, and (d) self-monitoring and coordinating problem-solving activities. The development of internally regulated processes often requires the use of external means such as modeling, prompting, and reinforcing of problem solving behaviors.

Although research on self-regulation has been mixed (Billings & Wasik, 1985; Bornstein, 1985), specific methods can be used to enhance self-regulation training (e.g., Guevremont, Osnes, & Stokes, 1986). As to professional practice, the techniques that encourage self-regulation and independent problem solving can be combined with other behavioral procedures. For example, time-out may be successfully applied to tantrums or aggressive behaviors. In combination, alternative problem-solving behaviors can be taught, encouraged, and reinforced. Furthermore, instances of maladaptive behavior can be charted in a manner suitable for sharing with many preschool children, and contingencies can be established for reinforcing improvements and instances when conflicts are avoided.

Recommended practices in cognitive, language, behavioral, and affective assessment and intervention. Research trends support the importance of naturalistic interventions. Naturalistic interventions are based on the analysis of actual roles, routines, skills, and interests of caregivers (Barnett & Carey, in press). The interventions are also revealed by the natural teaching styles of successful caregivers (Sigel, 1982; White, Kaban, & Attanucci, 1979).

To achieve naturalistic interventions, skill deficits can be recast through an analysis of specific cognitive and/or social behaviors required to adapt to various environments. Furthermore, attention can be given to the planning activities of teachers and parents, and to interventions that may be adapted to evident styles of parenting and teaching.

The caregiver role includes selecting learning events and focusing the attention of children on those that are important. The range of learning events, both pleasant and unpleasant, includes intentionally provided experiences, but also the framing of subtle or serendipitous occurrences. The potential learning outcomes of most events include cognitive, behavioral, language, and affective skills. Personal and social learning cannot be readily separated from the processes involved in early cognitive and language learning. Attitudes towards oneself, social competence, and social responsibility (e.g., attitudes and acts towards others) are taught, modeled, and valued, and they arise out of interactions with others. "Contingent verbal responsiveness . . . is perhaps the greatest single influence on early cognitive development" (MacPhee, Ramey, & Yates, 1984, p. 349). The most important aspect is adaptive caregiver-child communication (e.g., Hart & Risley, 1982). Therefore, one of the tasks of a preschool psychologist is to assist caregivers in exploring the possibilities of an expanded and deliberate role in cognitive and social modeling, and planning of learning activities. Furthermore, behaviors that are used to elicit and mediate children's responses are targets of assessment and intervention.

Play and early peer relationships have pervasive developmental implications and can be assessed through interviews and observation. Interventions include the active structuring of experiences that incorporate cognitive, language, social, and motor learning in peer groups (Guralnick, 1981; Hecimovic, Fox, Shores, & Strain, 1985). Interventions also can be tied to caregiver skills in managing individual play, and more broadly to family recreation that requires family cohesion and purpose.

In summary, preschool psychologists need to explore numerous and sometimes subtle events with the goal of assisting caregivers with their role in designing and executing learning experiences. Caregivers, especially those in difficult circumstances, may underestimate the power of brief moments of shared experiences for child development. There is no "magic" time for learning; walks, mealtime, and bedtime all can be utilized. "[Teaching] need not necessarily be a self-conscious, deliberate activity but can be embedded within daily routines" (Sigel, 1982, p. 49). Even negative events can be tapped for their learning potential through verbally mediated discipline, whereby appropriate behaviors are directly taught, modeled, rehearsed, prompted, and reinforced. Other analyses suggest that major benefits of relatively brief, school-based early childhood programs may be attributable to indirect effects on parental attitudes and parent-child interactions (Lazar, 1983).

The above *naturalistic* analysis can be extended to formal intervention design. Planning can be directed to the identification of (a) a range of treatment options based on research, and (b) naturally occurring approximations to these successful strategies by caregivers. Thus, partially successful strategies and emerging skills of the caregivers are of potential importance.

Interviews and observations may reveal that caregivers have a grasp of skills that are consistent at least in some ways with researched interventions, but that they are not aware of the importance and logical expansions of their behaviors. The value of the behavior and the subsequent skills may need to be taught or encouraged. Thus, interventions can be based at least in part on behaviors that are close to being mastered, and on research. In addition, it is likely that the acceptability of interventions, and the self-efficacy of caregivers as change agents, can be enhanced through this approach.

Two research-based examples illustrate the use of naturalistic means. First, restitution and positive practice overcorrection (e.g., Azrin & Besalel, 1980; Foxx & Bechtel, 1983) may be based on naturally occurring caregiver strategies for teaching both socially appropriate behaviors and natural consequences of specific behaviors. For example, a child who exhibits noncompliant or disruptive behavior is then required to perform a task in excess of what was originally requested, both in respect to practicing positive behaviors and restoring the environment. Important conditions are that: (a) the additional task must be similar or related to the original task or behavior; (b) the overcorrection should occur immediately after the misbehavior if possible; (c) the duration of the overcorrection should be longer than the period of initial refusal; (d) the child must be engaged actively in the positive practice overcorrection task; and (e) appropriate alternative behaviors should be reinforced when not applying overcorrection. The use of a verbal cue may also be important. Since overcorrection is considered to be aversive, safeguards and established procedures should be followed, and positive interventions should be tried first. However, the overcorrection procedures can be applied effectively to a wide range of children's behavior problems.

A second example of a naturalistic intervention, especially applicable to pervasive language difficulties in preschool populations, was described by Hart and Risley (1980, 1982). Termed "in vivo language intervention," incidental teaching was used to increase compound sentences in spontaneous speech. Simply, adult attention is focused on the child's language productions, and elaboration is encouraged on topics originated by the child. The process is described as "loose" training that follows the child's attention.

Test- and curriculum-based assessment. When traditional tests are employed, intervention-based questions that guide interpretations and recommendations help orient the process to goals related to change. Many measures have predictive value, although their interpretation should be conditioned by the literature on the modifiability of skill development. Global performance measures may assist in identifying attained developmental levels (Vygotsky, 1978), and promote an understanding of emerging skills through adaptive testing or planned testing of limits procedures. Three areas can be estimated: (a) skills measured independently of assistance, (b) skills the child is close to mastering, and (c) skills that become manifest through aided performance — conditions under which the highest levels of performance will be maintained at a specific point in time.

Questions for test-based assessment that are designed to aid the planning of interventions include the following. (a) What is the range of skill development? (b) What skills are necessary in solving inadequately performed tasks? (c) What component skills did the child demonstrate? (d) What problem-solving steps or knowledge did the child seem to be missing? (e) How could these be adequately assessed? (f) How could the child acquire those skills? (g) What difficulties seem to exist with respect to learning processes (e.g., attentional, retentional, productive, motivational)? (h) Are there deficits in related skills (e.g., language, motor) that affect the level of performance? (i) How did the performance in testing compare with the child's performance in other environments or at other times? (j) What are the child's current optimal performances (e.g., with assistance; through N = 1 experiments)?

With high-risk populations it may not be sound to use traditional test-based techniques for the identification of relatively high-incidence learning problems. The technique of choice would be systematic ongoing evaluation of children in a well-constructed curriculum (e.g., Haywood, Brooks, & Burns, 1986; Neisworth & Bagnato, 1986) whereby children are referred who are not progressing adequately. Curriculum based-measurement reveals individual competence and rate of progress in comparison with peers following the same school curriculum. The principles can be applied readily to preschoolers. LeBlanc, Etzel, and Domash (1978) described a *functional* curriculum for young children that emphasizes teacher behavior, peer behavior, instructionally relevant assessment strategies, including self assessments by young children, and empirically tested alternative teaching strategies. "A functional curriculum is one that continuously matches instructional conditions to each child's learning ability for each task to be learned" (p. 373).

In summary, assessment and intervention design for alternative service delivery is based on interrelated practices in ecological problem-solving, behavioral assessment, and researched interventions. Furthermore, a functional preschool curriculum enables instructionally relevant screening, assessment, and intervention. In the next section, we review the underlying empirical basis for the delivery of psychological and educational services to preschool children.

EMPIRICAL FOUNDATIONS OF EARLY INTERVENTIONS

There have been several important reviews of the effectiveness of early intervention (e.g., Casto, 1987; Gallagher & Ramey, 1987; Guralnick & Bennett, 1987; Odom & Karnes, 1988; Strain, 1984; White 1985–1986). It is a complex literature, and one that is bound to increase substantially in the next few years. The central issues involve (a) avoiding the consequences of biological and/or social adversities, (b) minimizing their impact, and (c) enhancing the development of children with identified handicaps through early intervention (e.g., Guralnick & Bennett, 1987).

Typically, large-scale projects such as Head Start (Zigler & Valentine, 1979), Abecedarian (e.g., Ramey & Campbell,

1984), and Hi/Scope (Berreuta-Clement, Schweinhart, Barnett, Epstein, & Weikart, 1984) have suggested that early intervention has considerable *promise* of effectiveness. The projects illustrate design components for major facilities and programs. However, the results of large scale experimental programs cannot serve as the only foundation for alternative service delivery. They are difficult to replicate because the efforts and resources needed for planning, program execution, and evaluation are so great and because the excitement of innovations may not transfer entirely to replications. Furthermore, there is a need to provide appropriate interventions within educational programs for at-risk and handicapped populations because the needs of these children will vary in significant ways. Most important, major efforts should include interventions within normal preschool settings. Numerous questions remain, and many research problems plague the field (Marfo & Kysela, 1985).

In evaluating the effectiveness of early intervention efforts, it is important to recognize also that intervention design is in its infancy. There are complex technical difficulties in the identification process, especially with those children traditionally termed mildly handicapped or at-risk. Therefore, samples of children sometimes have not been well defined. In addition, descriptions of interventions often have lacked the detail necessary for replication, or if well described, have lacked measures of treatment integrity to determine if interventions were actually executed as planned. Control groups are difficult to establish, especially for low incidence handicapping conditions. The developmental trajectories of children with seemingly similar handicapping conditions may vary substantially because of unknown but important differences in children, as well as unspecified differences or changes in caregivers' behaviors.

Empirical Bases for Alternative Service Preschool Practices

The empirical foundations for alternative preschool practices include developmental research, large scale demonstration projects, and, especially, the substantial early intervention research base suggested by single case studies (Guralnick & Bennett, 1987). The elements of single case designs include measures of stability, level, and trend of behavior; the introduction of an intervention while maintaining the measurement procedures; and the examination of behavior with respect to the intervention. The results of single case studies are of interest because the characteristics of the individual children typically are well described, as are the corresponding interventions.

In reviewing this literature, one is struck by the impressive number of data-based intervention studies conducted by practitioners (see Paget, in press). Now, among the important components of alternative delivery systems is a systematic consideration of the range of treatment options for problem behaviors of individual children based on interventions of demonstrated validity and/or replicated case studies. Points of analysis include the characteristics of children and settings, components of the intervention, observational systems, loci of interventions (Glenwick & Jason, 1984), and the clinical significance of reported behavior change. Gaps in the research base are also important, and single case designs are appropriate for the occasions when the usefulness of an intervention is unknown. Often lacking are a child-systems approach for the appropriate contextualization of assessment-intervention plans, and methods to enhance utilization, maintenance, and generalization of interventions. The components of alternative service delivery, based on key ecological and behavioral principles, are designed to help with these problem areas.

In summary, although support exists for early intervention, much further research is needed. Important foundations stem from a child-systems approach that focuses on caregivers' skills, and procedures related to single case experimental designs.

TRADITIONS IN PRESCHOOL SERVICE DELIVERY: A CRITICAL APPRAISAL

In many respects, professional practices at the preschool level lack a consensus viewpoint. Many traditions are not based on sound theory or the most significant developmental constructs. This section reviews potential problem areas for preschool psychology services.

Complexity of Developmental Changes

Change is the major characteristic of childhood: "Children are biologically and cognitively designed for adaptation and change" (Achenbach, 1982, p. 655). Historically, major developmental theorists such as Freud and Piaget provided strong arguments for the significance of early developmental experiences, the predictability of stages and sequences of development, the considerable stability of patterns that emerge at about age 6 years, and the continuity of early developmental patterns in the later years. Substantial evidence now exists for both the importance of the early years for development and for the capacity for substantial change through adulthood (Lerner, 1987; Rutter, 1984). Rutter (1984) states: "The concept of continuity implies meaningful links over the course of development — not a lack of change" (p. 62). Along with inherited characteristics and lawfulness in development, evidence also can be found for significant variation in developmental trajectories.

For example, Hindley and Owen (1978) found substantial variability in measured intelligence, in that 25% changed 20 IQ points *or more* between the ages of 3 and 17, and 50% changed by more than 10 IQ points. In a different study, children's IQs changed an *average* of 28.5 points between approximately the same ages, and one in seven changed 40 IQ points (Kopp & McCall, 1982). We state these findings not to draw attention to IQ, but to the potential developmental (and decision-related) implications of these results in considering this measure as a global developmental indicator. There is increased stability for more severely impaired children, but the stability may be overestimated for individuals (Kopp & McCall, 1982). Most important for professional practice is the identification of factors that determine malleability — those that alter or maintain patterns of development.

One of the major factors in understanding both constancy and change in human development relates not only to child variables, but to the continuities in interactions of the child with family members (e.g., Langner, Gersten, Wills, & Simcha-Fagan, 1983), peers, and members of social institutions. Sroufe and Rutter (1984) suggested that "disordered behavior ... does not simply spring forth without connection to previous quality of adaptation, or without changing environmental supports or altered environmental challenges" (p. 22). Whereas studies show that some children "survive" difficult early environments and experiences (Werner & Smith, 1982), the outcomes of development can be enhanced for at-risk and handicapped children. Some childhood syndromes are strongly associated with later adjustment problems but others are not, and it is often difficult to predict the course of individual outcomes (e.g., Robins, 1979). Changes in personal and social development are multiply determined by psychosocial, biological, and accidental events (Bandura, 1986; Rutter, 1984).

Although development is influenced broadly by many interacting variables, there are empirically established links that exist between specific parent and childhood syndromes. For example, parental depression may alter the care and monitoring of behavior, and childhood experiences (e.g., Zahn-Waxler, Cummings, Ianotti, & Radke-Yarrow, 1984). Maternal depression can be viewed also as a potential outcome of difficult and unrewarding parent–child interactions that can be magnified by other stressors.

A second example of an empirically established link between parent and childhood syndromes is associated with aggressive, antisocial children. The central idea of a research program that now spans several decades is that antisocial behavior stems at least in part from deficits in parenting skills rooted in a reciprocal process by which family members "train" each other to elicit coercive behaviors (Patterson & Bank, 1986; see also an alternative view by Wahler & Dumas, 1986). Achenbach (1985) also has suggested possible links between aggressive and depressive disorders.

Wahler's research (Wahler & Dumas, 1986; Panaccione & Wahler, 1986; Wahler, 1980) has emphasized the need to consider the mother's social and family systems in addition to the mother-child relationship and child behavior. Further research is needed in establishing the impact of the father's psychological status with respect to associations between parent and child syndromes (e.g., Lamb, 1986).

Utility of Early Development Constructs

Developmental theories warrant appraisal proportionate to the degree to which they guide the assessment–intervention process. "The value of a theory is ultimately judged ... by the power of the methods it yields to effect psychological changes" (Bandura, 1986, p. 4). This is an important criterion for professional psychologists working with at-risk young children or those with handicapping conditions, because some theories and constructs may lead to less effective strategies for helping than others.

Researchers often have objectives and criteria for success that are different from those of practitioners. For example, temperament is a developmental construct associated with broad and relatively stable characteristics of behavior (e.g., Thomas & Chess, 1977). Frequently, inherited links are suggested. Although statistically associated with diverse and important indicators of adjustment, the magnitude of the relationships found through the use of available measures do not usually lend themselves to application at the level of the individual child (e.g., Paget, Nagle, & Martin, 1984), and environmental interventions still are implicated (e.g., Plomin, 1987). Nevertheless, temperament serves as a "reminder" that children exhibit behaviors that possibly are influenced by inherited factors. Since they thus represent natural expressions of personality, it is often necessary to modify interventions to incorporate this potential reality (Barnett & Zucker, in press).

Application of developmental psychology involves changing the course of maladaptive behavior. The central constructs used in facilitating change are different from those typically associated with many developmental theories, or those measured by traditional scales. The foundations rest on research associated with normal development, research that focuses on developmental changes, and research based on experimental and naturally occurring interventions (e.g., adoptions).

The following constructs underlie assessment and intervention design from the social and cognitive learning viewpoint. First, the concept of the reciprocal-influence process is used as the basic principle for the analysis of complex behavior, in which interactions of person variables with covert processes, overt behavior, and environmental factors all have potential importance in assessment-intervention design (Bandura, 1986). (The relative importance of the variables and interactions cannot be determined on an a priori basis.) Second, cognitive and symbolic processes play a central role in learning and performance. Third, self-regulation is stressed. Fourth, life events, not necessarily test items, are the direct focus of analysis. Finally, Bandura (1981) has proposed self-efficacy as a broadly integrative developmental construct central to the study of behavioral change. Self-efficacy reflects personal beliefs about competency. Self-efficacy has the potential for influencing the child's and parents' (and teachers', and psychologist's) choices of activities, their persistence in solving difficult tasks, their thoughts, and their emotional reactions. Self-efficacy has its origins in infancy, is derived from environmental interactions, and later is extended and modified through the influence of peer groups.

Preschool Screening, Assessment, and Service Delivery

Preschool screening and assessment should be linked to educational and psychological services. The challenges of preschool service delivery (Barnett, 1986; Paget, 1985) include various developmental theories that tend to lead practitioners in divergent and untested directions; an explosion of research in cognitive and social development that has not found its way into application; uneven training of preschool personnel; a confusing array of service delivery alternatives that defies straightforward program-level evaluation (e.g., Anastasiow, 1978; Clark-Stewart & Fein, 1983); and controversial instruments and procedures used in the process of identifying young handicapped and at-risk children. Each step in problem solving is delimited by (a) theoretical and conceptual issues that guide the process, (b) the difficulty of the adjustment problem and/or child's circumstances, (c) the available resources, and (d) the adequacy of the assessment procedures used.

Judging the technical adequacy of preschool developmental scales entails resolution of a set of difficult issues that have many points of analysis (Barnes, 1982; Bracken, 1987; Paget & Bracken, 1983; see also the discussion of rating scales and checklists by Evans & Nelson, 1986). In addition to a wide range of differences in assessment and intervention philosophies, large gaps exist in the psychometric data available on preschool instruments. Few validity studies examine key facets of the problems: (a) whether the constructs that underlie the scales are adequately developed; (b) whether the scales can be interpreted with confidence for *individual* children; (c) whether there are significant benefits over alternative screening procedures; and (d) whether the results have clear utility for intervention design.

Relatedly, the reliability of decisions is an important consideration. Findings are often specific to the instrument and time of testing (e.g., Poth & Barnett, 1988). Different methods should converge on outcomes (e.g., "a child is eligible or is not eligible for services"; "a specific intervention is or is not advisable"). However, outcomes are likely to differ because of the natural variability of behavior, as well as the variability introduced by instruments and raters. *Decision reliability* is critical to the evaluation of assessment procedures, and may be surprisingly low even with techniques that meet established conventions for reliability and validity. Many preschool screening programs may be associated with high error rates when all factors are considered.

Screening through the use of traditional developmental scales for learning and behavior problems in high-risk groups may be less advantageous in many cases than making referral decisions based on alternatives that include parent and teacher consultation and curriculum-based procedures. First, some issues stem from the problems of base rates, defined by the percentages of persons with characteristics of interest in a population; if base rates are either very high or very low (e.g., numbers of children at risk in a population), screening procedures are expensive and prone to error. Second, the screening procedures may be unrelated to intervention design. Third, the screening procedures will miss children who are functioning well at present but who are existing in precarious circumstances. Fourth, children who experience developmental delays, but have supportive and knowledgeable caregivers and are situated in appropriate environments, may be unnecessarily screened. In contrast, alternative service delivery procedures may be used effectively for screening and intervention design.

In summary, there is a need for new assessment practices for young children. Simply increasing the *number* of assessment techniques is not a helpful strategy and serves to *reduce* accuracy at the same time that professional confidence is *increased* (Arkes, 1981; Mash, 1985). The loosely defined multifactored model of assessment implied by PL 94-142 ("No single procedure is used . . .") requires systematic case-by-case planning for individual children (Barnett & Carey, in press; Paget & Nagle, 1986) that contrasts

with the use of traditional test batteries.

IDEALIZED VERSUS REAL-WORLD ISSUES

The realities of practice also merit attention. Presently, one of the most difficult issues facing practitioners is the tenuous link between various theoretical perspectives, research-based interventions, and the challenges and difficulties of real-world practice. There are many facets to these issues, but perhaps the most fundamental is the lack of resources and support needed to fully implement interventions that are consistent with "model" practices in many situations.

Alternative services should be based on a coherent theoretical model, on appropriate research, and on a workable practitioner model. Given the absence of rules, formulas, and cookbook procedures, the best that can be offered is the foundations of assessment and intervention design, knowledge of exemplary interventions and practices that are applicable to young children and caregivers, problem-solving methods, and the creative, sensitive, and careful implementation and evaluation of professional plans. Professional practices may involve approximations to various ideals, but appropriate scientific methods can be applied (e.g., Barlow, Hayes, & Nelson, 1984).

TRAINING IMPLICATIONS OF ALTERNATIVE SERVICE DELIVERY

The training issues based on preschool alternative service delivery concepts are considerable. They include the specialized nature of training, and practical experiences related to assessment and intervention.

There is a need for specialists who are trained in preschool service delivery. However, although some may choose to specialize, preschool training in alternative service delivery can be integrated into other training experiences at the certification level. Much of the coursework is identical, and it can build upon skills learned in parent and teacher consultation and in other facets of professional practice related to assessment and intervention design.

Among the benefits of incorporating preschool training into professional school psychology training, even for those who do not plan to work with young children, is that is gives trainees first-hand knowledge of primary prevention and early intervention efforts — long neglected topics in our field. Second, for those who plan to work with adolescents, there is an increasing number of referrals from young parents in crisis. Because of the nature of preschool settings, there is a greater likelihood that consultants will be interacting with young parents who are in the initial stages of reacting to the knowledge of developmental disability, handicap, or risk. Early consultations have an emotional intensity often not found in later stages of adaptation, and training experiences should deal directly with significant realities such as parental depression, anger, and coping.

There is a growing literature regarding the curriculum and practicum components of training programs in early intervention. A program described by Mallory (1983) is consistent with the model proposed in this chapter, with its emphasis on the acquisition of skills within an ecological and developmental framework. The goal of the program is to prepare graduates to understand the nature of developmental dysfunction as it is caused by, or is sustained in, various ecological settings. The program also emphasizes both individual and systems-focused intervention strategies.

Mallory (1983) recommends that a training program contain a clinical component and a "liaison" component. The former provides students with specific diagnostic and prescriptive skills to be applied in both clinical and community/family settings. The latter provides skills in systems or ecological interventions (e.g., Hutton & Dokecki, 1977). In this second component, students learn to utilize systems-oriented intervention strategies to forge linkages among resources available to young children and their families.

While preschool coursework facili-tates training, the primary consideration is the provision of a practicum or internship site for the acquisition of preschool service delivery skills. Whether based in schools or other agencies (e.g., Head Start centers) several factors are helpful. First is an extension of the usual time frame for the assessment-intervention process that enables trainees to capture the variability in behavior that is characteristic of young children, and to help develop, implement, and evaluate an ecologically valid intervention plan for a child, parent, and teacher. Trainees should be allowed to play a number of different roles rather than assume a narrowly defined set of assessment responsibilities.

CONCLUSIONS

There are both positive and negative considerations that support alternative service delivery. Out of necessity, "alternatives" are needed in providing educational and psychological services to young children. Models of service delivery include home-based child-oriented, home-based parent-oriented, center-based child-oriented, and center-based parent-oriented programs (Linder, 1983). Philosophically, normalization is a central guiding rule for service decisions and it is nowhere more appropriate than with preschoolers. Thus, alternatives are needed to restrictive placements.

Alternative service delivery is also directly linked to the fundamentals of assessment and intervention design, rather than on traditional diagnostic categories. The essentials are straightforward and derive from the analysis of the current situations of child and caregivers as a starting point, with corresponding objectives, interventions, and needed resources developed that are likely to enable successful adaptation. The outcomes of the intervention are monitored over long time periods and are modified as necessary. These are also the concepts that underlie intervention assistance programs; the outcomes of the collaborative problem-solving process are well-planned and executed interventions prior to potentially restrictive changes in educational placements (Graden, Casey, & Christenson, 1985). With an expanded parental role, and multidisciplinary emphasis, such practices can be applied to preschool settings.

Many of the "negative" justifications for alternative preschool educational services are well known, and are subsumed by labeling issues. Basic are the philosophical and technical difficulties inherent in classification schemes (Garber, 1984; Hobbs, 1975). Although labeling may be necessary at some level for administrative purposes, and is implicit even in alternative services ("the child is at risk and requires services"), the problems with categorization are intensified with young children.

First, classifications or labels, as well as measures from which they are derived, should be reliable and valid, and have clear utility. However, there are no agreed upon criteria for defining the traditional categories in special education related to young children's learning and behavior problems. Second, there has been a lack of correspondence between categorical services for mildly handicapped children and the development of instructional strategies of demonstrated effectiveness. Third, interventions are imperative before some classification decisions are made because successful interventions may alter diagnostic status. Furthermore, a wide range of services may be necessary to support likely interventions. Even though problems may be serious, or longstanding, these factors alone do not predict the limits to successful interventions.

The challenges to preschool psychological services are numerous but so are the potential benefits. Although research in child development remains the foundation, new research is needed that focuses on assessment and intervention design in a preschool context. Likely strategies include child–systems assessment techniques derived from ecological principles, sequential decision strategies rather than diagnostic decisions, and the intervention foundations associated with single case experimental designs. A critical appraisal of the wide range of professional practices associated with service delivery to young children, their families, and teachers is necessary.

REFERENCES

Abidin. R. (1986). *Parenting stress index — Manual* (2nd ed.). Richmond, VA: Pediatric Psychology Press.

Achenbach, T. M. (1982). *Developmental psychopathology* (2nd ed.). New York: Wiley.

Achenbach, T. M. (1985). *Assessment and taxonomy of child and adolescent psychopathology.* Beverly Hills, CA: Sage.

Adelman, H. S. (1982). Identifying learning problems at an early age: A critical appraisal. *Journal of Clinical Child Psychology, 11,* 255-261.

Anastasiow, N. J. (1978). Strategies and models for early childhood intervention programs in integrated settings. In M. J. Guralnick (Ed.), *Early intervention and the integration of handicapped and non-handicapped children* (pp. 5-20). Baltimore: University Park Press.

Arkes, H. R. (1981). Impediments to accurate clinical judgment and possible ways to minimize their impact. *Journal of Consulting and Clinical Psychology, 49,* 323-330.

Azrin, N. H., & Besalel, V. A. (1980). *How to use overcorrection.* Austin, TX: Pro-Ed.

Bandura, A. (1981). Self-referent thought: A developmental analysis of self-efficacy. In J. H. Flavell & L. Ross (Eds.), *Social cognitive development: Frontiers and possible futures* (pp. 200-239). New York: Cambridge University Press.

Bandura, A. (1986). *Social foundations of thought and action: A social cognitive theory.* Englewood Cliffs, NJ: Prentice-Hall.

Barlow, D. H., Hayes, S. C., & Nelson, R. O. (1984). *The scientist practitioner: Research and accountability in clinical and educational settings.* New York: Pergamon.

Barnes, K. E. (1982). *Preschool screening: The measurement and prediction of children at-risk.* Springfield, IL: Thomas.

Barnett, D. W. (1984). An organizational approach to preschool services: Psychological screening, assessment, and intervention. In C. A. Maher, R. J. Illback, & J. E. Zins (Eds.), *Organizational psychology in the schools: A handbook for professionals* (pp. 55-82). Springfield, IL: Thomas.

Barnett, D. W. (1986). School psychology in preschool settings: A review of training and practice issues. *Professional Psychology: Research and Practice, 17,* 58-64.

Barnett, D. W. (in press). Professional judgment: A critical appraisal. *School Psychology Review.*

Barnett, D. W., & Carey, K. T. (in press). Intervention design for young children: Assessment concepts and procedures. In B. A. Bracken (Ed.), *The psychoeducational assessment of preschool children* (2nd ed.). New York: Grune & Stratton.

Barnett, D. W., & Zucker, K. B. (in press). *The personal and social assessment of children.* Boston: Allyn & Bacon.

Berreuta-Clement, J., Schweinhart, L., Barnett, W., Epstein, A., & Weikart, D. (1984). *Changed lives.* Ypsilanti, MI: High/Scope Press.

Billings, D. C., & Wasik, B. H. (1985). Self-instructional training with preschoolers: An attempt to replicate. *Journal of Applied Behavior Analysis, 18,* 61-67.

Bornstein, P. H. (1985). Self-instructional training: A commentary and state-of-the-art. *Journal of Applied Behavior Analysis, 18,* 69-72.

Bracken, B. A. (1987). Limitations of preschool instruments and standards of technical adequacy. *Journal of Psychoeducational Assessment, 5,* 313-326.

Bradley, R. H., & Caldwell, B. M. (1979). Home observation for measurement of the environment: A revision of the preschool scale. *American Journal of Mental Deficiency, 84,* 235-244.

Cantrell, M. L., & Cantrell, R. P. (1985). Assessment of the natural environment. *Education and Treatment of Children, 8,* 275-295.

Casto, G. (1987). Plasticity and the handicapped child: A review of efficacy research. In J. J. Gallagher & C. T. Ramey (Eds.), *The malleability of children* (pp. 103-113). Baltimore: Brookes.

Clark-Stewart, K. A., & Fein, G. G. (1983). Early childhood programs. In P. H. Mussen (Ed.), *Handbook of child psychology* (pp. 917-999). New York: Wiley.

Dumas, J. E., & Albin, J. B. (1986). Parent training outcome: Does active parental involvement matter? *Behavior Research and Therapy, 24,* 227-230.

Dunst, C. J., & Trivette, C. M. (1987). Enabling and empowering families: Conceptual and intervention issues. *School Psychology Review, 16,* 443-456.

Evans, I. M., & Nelson, R. O. (1986). Assessment of children. In A. R. Ciminero, K. S. Calhoun, & H. E. Adams (Eds.), *Handbook of behavioral assessment* (2nd ed., pp. 601-630). New York: Wiley.

Foxx, R. M., & Bechtel, D. R. (1983). Overcorrection: A review and analysis. In S. Axelrod & J. Apsche (Eds.), *The effects of punishment on human behavior* (pp. 133-220). New York: Academic.

Gallagher, J. J., & Ramey, C. T. (Eds.). (1987). *The malleability of children.* Baltimore: Brookes.

Garbarino, J. (1982). *Children and families in the social environment.* New York: Aldine.

Garber, J. (1984). Classification of childhood psychopathology: A developmental perspective. *Child Development, 55,* 30-48.

Glenwick, D. S., & Jason, L. A. (1984). Locus of intervention in child cognitive behavior therapy: Implications of a behavioral community psychology perspective. In A. W. Meyers & W. E. Craighead (Eds.), *Cognitive behavior therapy with children* (pp. 129-162). New York: Plenum.

Gottfried, A. W. (Ed.). (1984). *Home environment and early cognitive development: Longitudinal research.* Orlando, FL: Academic.

Graden, J. L., Casey, A., & Christenson, S. L. (1985). Implementing a prereferral intervention system: Part I: The model. *Exceptional Children, 51,* 377-384.

Guevremont, D. C., Osnes, P. G., & Stokes, T. F. (1986). Preparation for effective self-regulation: The development of generalized verbal control. *Journal of Applied Behavior Analysis, 19,* 99-104.

Guralnick, M. J. (1981). The social behavior of preschool children at different developmental levels: Effects of group composition. *Journal of Experimental Child Psychology, 31,* 115-130.

Guralnick, M. J., & Bennett, F. C. (Eds.). (1987). *The effectiveness of early intervention for at-risk and handicapped children.* New York: Academic.

Hart, B., & Risley, T. R. (1980). In vivo language intervention: Unanticipated general effects. *Journal of Applied Behavior Analysis, 13,* 407-432.

Hart, B. M., & Risley, T. R. (1982). *How to use incidental teaching for elaborating language.* Austin, TX: Pro-ed.

Hartman, A. (1978, October). Diagrammatic assessment of family relationships. *Social Casework,* 465-476.

Haywood, H. C., Brooks, P., & Burns, S. (1986). Stimulating cognitive development at developmental level: A tested, non-remedial preschool curriculum for preschoolers and older retarded children. In M. Schwebel & C. A. Maher (Eds.), *Facilitating cognitive development: International perspectives, programs, and practices* (pp. 127-147). New York: Haworth.

Hecimovic, A., Fox, J. J., Shores, R. E., & Strain, P. S. (1985). An analysis of developmentally integrated and segregated free play settings and the generalization of newly acquired social behaviors of socially withdrawn preschoolers. *Behavioral Assessment, 7,* 367-388.

Hindley, C. B., & Owen, C. F. (1978). The extent of individual changes in I.Q. for ages between 6 months and 17 years, in a British longitudinal sample. *Journal of Child Psychology and Psychiatry, 19,* 329-350.

Hobbs, N. (1975). *The futures of children: Categories, labels, and their consequences.* San Francisco: Jossey-Bass.

Hutton, R. E., & Dokecki, P. R. (1977, August). *A critique of mental health services: The case for the liaison perspective.* Paper presented at the annual meeting of the American Psychological Association, San Francisco.

Kanfer, F. H. (1985). Target selection for clinical change programs. *Behavioral Assessment, 7,* 7-20.

Kendall, P. C. (1985). Toward a cognitive-behavioral model of child psychopathology and a critique of related interventions. *Journal of Abnormal Child Psychology, 13,* 357-372.

Kopp, C. B., & McCall, R. B. (1982). Predicting later mental performance for normal, at-risk, and handicapped infants. In P. B. Baltes & O. G. Brim, Jr. (Eds.), *Life span development and behavior* (Vol. 4, pp. 33-61). New York: Academic.

Lamb, M. (Ed.). (1986). *The father's role: Applied perspectives.* New York: Wiley.

Langner, T. S., Gersten, J. C., Wills, T. A., & Simcha-Fagan, O. (1983). The relative roles of early environment and early behavior as predictors of later child behavior. In D. F. Ricks & B. S. Dohrenwend (Eds.), *Origins of psychopathology: Problems in research and public policy* (pp. 43-70). Cambridge, London: Cambridge University Press.

Laosa, L. M., & Sigel, I. E. (Eds.). (1982). *Families as learning environments for children.* New York: Plenum.

Lazar, I. (1983). Discussion and implication of findings. In Consortium for Longitudinal Studies, *As the twig is bent. . . . Lasting effects of preschool programs* (pp. 461-466). Hillsdale, NJ: Erlbaum.

LeBlanc, J. M., Etzel, B. C., & Domash, M. A. (1978). A functional curriculum for early intervention. In K. E. Allen, V. A. Holm, & R. L. Schiefelbusch (Eds.), *Early intervention — A team approach* (pp. 331-381). Baltimore: University Park Press.

Lerner, R. M. (1987). The concept of plasticity in development. In J. J. Gallagher & C. T. Ramey (Eds.), *The malleability of children* (pp. 3-14). Baltimore: Brookes.

Linder, T. W. (1983). *Early childhood special education: Program development and administration.* Baltimore: University Park Press.

MacPhee, D., Ramey, C. T., & Yates, K. O. (1984). Home environment and early cognitive development: Implications for intervention. In A. W. Gottfried (Ed.), *Home environment and early cognitive development: Longitudinal research* (pp. 343-369). Orlando, FL: Academic.

Mallory, B. L. (1983). The preparation of early childhood special educators: A model program. *Journal of the Division for Early Childhood, 7,* 32-40.

Mancuso, J. C., & Handin, K. H. (1985). Reprimanding: Acting on one's implicit theory of behavior change. In I. E. Sigel (Ed.), *Parental belief systems: The psychological consequences for children* (pp. 143-177). Hillsdale, NJ: Erlbaum.

Marfo, K., & Kysela, G. M. (1985). Early intervention with mentally handicapped children: A critical appraisal of applied research. *Journal of Pediatric Psychology, 10,* 305-324.

Mash, E. J. (1985). Some comments on target selection in behavior therapy. *Behavioral Assessment, 7,* 63-78.

McGillicuddy-Delisi, A. V. (1985). The relationship between parental beliefs and children's cognitive level. In I. E. Sigel (Ed.), *Parental belief systems: The psychological consequences for children* (pp. 7-24). Hillsdale, NJ: Erlbaum.

Meichenbaum, D. (1986). Metacognitive methods of instruction: Current status and future prospects. In M. Schwebel & C. A. Maher (Eds.), *Facilitating cognitive development: International perspectives, programs, and practices* (pp. 23-32). New York: Haworth.

National Association of School Psychologists (1987). *Position statement on early intervention services in the schools.* Washington, DC: Author.

Neisworth, J. T., & Bagnato, S. J. (1986). Curriculum-based developmental assessment: Congruence of testing and teaching. *School Psychology Review, 15,* 180-199.

Nelson, R. O., & Hayes, S. C. (Eds.). (1986). *Conceptual foundations of behavioral assessment.* New York: Guilford.

O'Connell, J. C. (1983). Education of handicapped preschoolers: A national survey of services and personnel requirements. *Exceptional Children, 49,* 538-540.

Odom, S. L., & Karnes, M. B. (Eds.). (1988). *Early intervention for infants and children with handicaps: An empirical base.* Baltimore: Brookes.

Paget, K. D. (1985). Preschool services in the schools: Issues and implications. *Special Services in the Schools, 2,* 3-25.

Paget, K. D. (1987). Systemic family assessment: Concepts and strategies for school psychologists. *School Psychology Review, 16,* 429-442.

Paget, K. D. (in press). Early behavioral interventions: Grasping the complexities. In J. C. Witt, S. N. Elliott, & F. M. Gresham (Eds.), *Handbook of behavior therapy in education.* New York: Guilford.

Paget, K. D., & Bracken, B. A. (Eds.). (1983). *The psychoeducational assessment of the preschool child.* New York: Grune & Stratton.

Paget, K. D., & Nagle, R. J. (1986). A conceptual model of preschool assessment. *School Psychology Review, 15,* 154-165.

Paget, K. D., Nagle, R. J., & Martin, R. P. (1984). Interrelationships between temperament characteristics and first-grade teacher-student interactions. *Journal of Abnormal Child Psychology, 12,* 547-559.

Panaccione, V. F., & Wahler, R. G. (1986). Child behavior, maternal depression, and social coercion as factors in the quality of child care. *Journal of Abnormal Child Psychology, 14,* 263-278.

Patterson, G. R., & Bank, L. (1986). Bootstrapping your way in a nomological thicket. *Behavioral Assessment, 8,* 49-73.

Plomin, R. (1987). Behavioral genetics and intervention. In J. J. Gallagher & C. T. Ramey (Eds.), *The malleability of children* (pp. 15-24). Baltimore: Brookes.

Poth, R. L., & Barnett, D. W. (1988). Establishing the limits of interpretative confidence: A validity study of two preschool developmental scales. *School Psychology Review, 17,* 322-330.

Ramey, C. T., & Campbell, F. A. (1984). Preventative education for high-risk children: Cognitive consequences of the Carolina Abecedarian project. *American Journal of Mental Deficiency, 88,* 515-523.

Reeve, R. A., & Brown, A. L. (1985). Metacognition reconsidered: Implications for intervention research. *Journal of Abnormal Child Psychology, 13,* 343-356.

Robins, L. N. (1979). Follow-up studies. In H. C. Quay & J. S. Werry (Eds.), *Psychopathological disorders of childhood* (pp. 483-513). New York: Wiley.

Rutter, M. (1981). Stress, coping, and development: Some issues and some questions. *Journal of Child Psychology and Psychiatry, 22,* 323-356.

Rutter, M. (1984). Continuities and discontinuities in socioemotional development: Empirical and conceptual perspectives. In R. N. Emde & R. J. Harmon (Eds.), *Continuities and discontinuities in development* (pp. 41-68). New York: Plenum.

Sigel, I. E. (1982). The relationship between parental distancing strategies and the child's cognitive behavior. In L. M. Laosa & I. E. Sigel (Eds.), *Families as learning environments for children* (pp. 47-86). New York: Plenum.

Sroufe, L. A., & Rutter, M. (1984). The domain of developmental psychopathology. *Child Psychology, 55,* 17-29.

Strain, L. A. (1984). Efficacy research with young handicapped children: A critique of the status quo. *Journal of the Division for Early Childhood, 9,* 4-10.

Thomas, A., & Chess, S. (1977). *Temperament and development.* New York: Brunner/Mazel.

Vygotsky, L. S. (1978). In M. Cole, V. John-Steiner, S. Scribner, & Souberman, E. (Eds.), *Mind in society: The development of higher psychological processes.* Cambridge, MA: Harvard University Press.

Wahler, R. G. (1980). The insular mother: Her problems in parent-child treatment. *Journal of Applied Behavior Analysis, 13,* 207-219.

Wahler, R. G., & Cormier, W. H. (1970). The ecological interview: A first step in out-patient child behavior therapy. *Journal of Behavior Therapy and Experimental Psychiatry, 1,* 279-289.

Wahler, R. G., & Dumas, J. E. (1986). "A chip off the old block": Some interpersonal characteristics of coercive children across generations. In P. S. Strain, M. J. Guralnick, & H. M. Walker (Eds.), *Children's social behavior: Development, assessment, and modification* (pp. 49-91). New York: Academic.

Werner, E. E., & Smith, R. S. (1982). *Vulnerable but invincible: A study of resilient children.* New York: McGraw-Hill.

White, B. L., Kaban, B. T., & Attanucci, J. S. (1979). *The origins of human competence.* Lexington, MA: Heath.

White, K. R. (1985-1986). Efficacy of early intervention. *Journal of Special Education, 19,* 401-416.

Willems, E. P. (1977). Steps toward an ecobehavioral technology. In A. Rogers-Warren & S. F. Warren (Eds.), *Ecological perspectives in behavioral analysis* (pp. 39-61). Baltimore, MD: University Park Press.

Zahn-Waxler, C., Cummings, E. M., Ianotti, R. J., & Radke-Yarrow, M. (1984). Young offspring of depressed parents: A population at risk for affective problems. In D. Ciccheti & K. Schneider-Rosen (Eds.), *Childhood depression* (pp. 81-105). San Francisco: Jossey-Bass.

Zigler, E., & Valentine J. (1979). (Eds.). *Project Head Start: A legacy of the war on poverty*. New York: Free Press.

15

Effective Classroom Management and Instruction: A Knowledge Base for Consultation

David C. Berliner
Arizona State University

In the business world there are various professionals who regard the discovery that a major system is not working well, as a great opportunity. Trouble-shooters, problem-solvers, creative entrepreneurs — consultants of all kinds — try to identify problems and then attempt to ameliorate them. In the process, of course, they create a market for themselves. It is my contention that problems exist in our system of education that can be ameliorated through the services of school psychologists. New roles, new markets if you will, exist for school psychologists if they choose to pursue them. And a new knowledge base for school psychologists to use in their work also exists, giving them an advantage over less qualified professionals who might see the same educational problems as signs of opportunity for promoting their services. Throughout this chapter these two themes will recur: That a need exists for a special kind of consultant in the classroom and that school psychologists, if they learn a new body of scientific knowledge, are uniquely qualified to take on that role.

PROBLEMS IN EDUCATION

The New Teacher

In recent years the many inadequacies of preservice and in-service teacher education, as they relate to new teachers, have been well and often documented. Four of these problems can also be recast as opportunities for those who have psychological training and who work in schools.

Inadequate teacher preparation. The time spent by novice teachers in preparing to teach is not adequate. In many universities all but a few of the courses of those preparing to teach high school are taken outside of the colleges of education. Those preparing to teach at the elementary level also take the great majority of their courses outside of the teacher education program. These cutbacks in teacher preparation courses occurred because of the public's belief that scientifically based pedagogical knowledge was scanty and that whatever knowledge did exist was of little value (Berliner, 1984). The trend to cut back on pedagogical preparation coincided with a great burst of productivity from the educational research community. Now that considerable amounts of scientifically based pedagogical information is available (e.g., Wittrock, 1986; Berliner and Rosenshine, 1987; Richardson-Koehler, 1987) there is almost no time left in teacher education programs to communicate this information. This problem, the failure to adequately communicate scientific knowledge — *primarily psychological knowledge* — in preservice teacher education programs opens up an opportunity for psychologically trained personnel within the schools. School psychologists, if they choose to master this body of knowledge, could help transmit this knowledge and thereby ameliorate certain common pedagogical problems.

Among the population of new teachers will be an even needier group than those who come out of teacher education programs, namely, those who receive certification through an alternative means. Because many state legislatures have viewed teacher education as of little value, they found it cheaper to circumvent it than improve it. Legislation has passed in a number of states that allows persons with college degrees in a subject matter field to teach classes without much pedagogical preparation. They can bypass completely the teacher preparation programs of the colleges and universities. This is particularly true in the areas of the curriculum where the greatest personnel shortages exist in the schools, in the mathematics and science courses at the secondary level. Ignorance of both the existence of useful pedagogical knowledge and the complexity of public school classroom teaching is shown by such legislation. And a good deal of arrogance is shown by those who take advantage of such legislation, who believe that they can virtually walk in off the street and teach 32 hard-to-teach students with little pedagogical preparation. Although we may decry the ignorance and the arrogance that is associated with this legislation, what is most relevant to the professional school psychologist is that school districts are employing an increasing number of such ill-trained individuals to teach. Someone is going to have to provide such personnel with help, by observing them and consulting with them in their classrooms. Most of these people will need even more help than the ordinary new teacher, fresh from a teacher education program. To simply abandon both of these types of new teacher — the minimally trained and the untrained — is an act of professional cruelty. School psychologists who already are proficient in the methodology of consultation, can, if they choose to, play a big role in addressing this national problem. They would be doing something very useful for individual novice teachers, while simultaneously (and perhaps more importantly for the profession of school psychology) redefining and enlarging the role of the school psychologist.

The plight of novice teachers. One area in which the newly developed scientific knowledge about pedagogy is applicable is the problems of the first-year teacher. It is not unusual for the numbers of students in the novice teacher's classes to be at least the equivalent of those in the classes of highly experienced teachers. In addition, because experienced teachers with seniority often get the most choice assignments, the novice teacher often has classes that are filled with more of the hard-to-teach students than are assigned to the classes of more experienced teachers. Thus a novice teacher faces a high likelihood of encountering in their first year some of the most difficult teaching conditions that they are ever likely to face. It is not surprising, therefore, that the dropout rate for beginning teachers is very high during their first few years on the job. Approximately 50% of the beginning teachers in some districts leave the profession within 5 years. This is not only a waste of scarce training dollars and the students' study time while they are in college, but a major contributor to the teacher shortage that we are experiencing in some areas. The problems of the novice teacher can be greatly alleviated by making available to them well-trained and empathic consultants, an assignment for which school psychologists should be well qualified.

The slow acquisition of pedagogical skill. In addition to the likelihood of inadequate preparation for teaching and an undesirable first-year teaching assignment, novice teachers also face the challenge, similar to that faced by other professionals trying to learn a complex field, that the solutions to some problems are learned very slowly through experience and reflection about that experience. We have learned that many of the problems of pedagogy that confront novices early in their careers are not solved easily, if at all. Huberman (1985), for example, inquired of a group of experienced teachers about the point in their careers at which they were able to solve 18 problems that had been specified by novice teachers as causing them the most difficulty. It was noted by the majority of experienced teachers that it required a long time, often 5 or more years, to solve problems of handling discipline, dealing effectively with slow and rapid learners, sustaining the interest of poorly motivated students, providing a variety of materials that students like to work with, and establishing a set of requirements for the classroom. In fact, of the original 18 problems, only five were adequately solved by the majority of experienced teachers in less than 3 years!

Competency in the organization of instruction and the management of classrooms is acquired over a considerable period of time. Lengthy and extensive experience is needed for a novice to gain the skills of an expert teacher. Kolodner (1983) has discussed the evolutionary development of expert kinds of knowledge in the domain of medical diagnosis, but this analysis applies to teaching as well:

> Two things happen in that evolution. First, knowledge is built up incrementally on the basis of experience. Facts, once unrelated, get integrated through occurrence in the same episodes. Second, reasoning processes are refined, and usefulness and rigidity of rules is learned. . . . Because experience is vital to the evolution from novice to expert, experience is organized in long-term memory, and guides reasoning processes. . . . When a person has only gone to school and acquired book knowledge, he is considered a novice. After he has experience using the knowledge he has learned, and when he knows how it applies both to common and exceptional cases, he is called an expert. . . . Experience serves to turn unrelated facts into expert knowledge. (p. 498)

Because of the slow acquisition of skill in teaching, new teachers may need instructional mentors during their first few years on the job. Instruction, classroom organization, and classroom management are areas of pedagogy in which psychologists have made major contributions. The consultation with new teachers to help them with pedagogical problems in these areas should be done by the existing psychological staff in the schools. The professional school psychologist is equipped more than most to read, interpret, and communicate this scientific psychological knowledge.

The inadequacies of staff development. The problems of beginning teachers — inadequate preparation, difficult conditions of teaching in the first year, and the need for extensive experience to learn classroom organization and management skills — could be addressed by sensible staff development programs within the school or district. The obvious need for some kind of help for beginning teachers would be taken care of in this way. But professional development programs are usually inadequate (Fenstermacher and Berliner, 1985). They are underfunded and mistargeted. It is the rare staff development program that receives a significant amount of a district's operating budget for the personal and professional growth of its staff. And it is the rarest of programs that is individualized — is targeted to the needs of the individual teacher and the individual classroom, which is what beginning teachers need most. Here an opportunity exists for consultative, individualized help for beginning teachers.

Working with new teachers. The problems facing new members of the teaching profession are embedded in the fabric of our educational system. These problems can be seen as a cause for national despondency, or as a great opportunity for some individuals to have a powerful impact on the socialization and development of novice teachers as they launch their careers. Simply stated, new teachers need a knowledgeable as well as a compassionate colleague to help them master the complexities of classroom teaching. I believe that school psychologists are uniquely qualified to take on this kind of role, to redefine what they do in schools, if they choose to.

Furthermore, in the decade ahead, it is estimated that 1,000,000 new teachers will enter the profession. That is a potential market of 1,000,000 clients for psychologically trained personnel, *if* those individuals possess the knowledge about classroom teaching requisite to providing services. My vision is of a school or clinical educational psychologist taking on a consultation role, with *classrooms* as clients. The school or clinical educational psychologist would work over lengthy periods of time with new teachers, providing individualized staff development based on the rich yield of contemporary research on teaching. Berliner (1985a) has provided a full description of the role that can be played by such an individual and the effects such consultation can have.

The Teacher At Risk

A second group of teachers in need of the kind of help that a consulting school psychologist with knowledge of classroom teaching, organization, and management could provide are those whose classrooms are considered to be "at risk." This is a new concept, but one that originated with school psychologists and that should, therefore, make the most sense to school psychologists, though it may be too politically controversial an issue to pursue.

School psychologists have worked for some time with at-risk populations, individual students who, from actuarial data or teacher referral, are regarded as likely to perform inadequately, drop out of school, show personality problems, and so forth. It makes sense to identify and treat as early as possible students for whom dire consequences are predicted. Using the same logic, my students and I wondered if whole classrooms could be at risk in the same actuarial sense. Did we know enough to measure in economical ways the classroom performance of teachers and to reveal classrooms in which students were not likely to perform well? That is, could we identify classrooms that were at risk, for numerous reasons. They could be classes to which very hard-to-teach children have been assigned. They could be overcrowded classrooms or classrooms with inadequate instructional materials. Or they could be classrooms

with teachers who are in need of help, just like those that are new to the teaching profession. In the same way that school psychologists hope for early identification of children who are at risk, we searched for ways to find classrooms that were at risk. From a cost-benefit standpoint it would make more sense to find 30 at-risk children associated in a classroom and try to treat them as a group than to find one here and one there as we look at individual data. I have demonstrated in two small pilot studies with school psychology graduate students at the University of Arizona the feasibility of an inexpensive system for identifying at-risk classrooms early enough so that something might be done about them.

In our first study we used a standardized achievement test, the California Achievement Test (CAT), as the outcome measure and several predictor variables including time management, student success, teacher behavior, and classroom climate. Despite the fact that this was a small and poorly controlled study, with a minimum of training for observers and with only a few classroom observations per teacher, the results were impressive. Our multiple correlations ranged from .30 to .80 on the eight different subtest scores of the CAT. As much as 60% of the variance of achievement could be accounted for by our predictors (Lynn, 1980).

We repeated our little study 2 years later. Once again the California Achievement Test was used as the outcome measure. A set of time management variables, variables related to student success, and classroom process variables were again used as predictors. Once again the ability to predict classroom achievement was demonstrated. In this study (Ellis-Schwabe, 1986), the multiple correlations for prediction of gain scores on the various CAT subtests ran between .54 and .78. The variance accounted for ran from about .30 to .60. In general, the two studies were quite similar, though sample sizes were small (around 25 classes per study) and both instrument and observer reliability were not high (Berliner, 1987).

We designed these two small and very imperfect studies with practical goals in mind. We wanted to know whether simple classroom observation instruments could be developed from what we know about instructional time and related variables. We wanted also to find out whether only brief training might be provided for classroom observers and whether only a small number of classroom observations would be necessary in order to predict classrooms that might be at risk. That is, we wondered if, in actual school settings, we could obtain validity coefficients of sufficient magnitude that we could predict who would be the more effective and who the less effective teachers. Validity coefficients do not have to be high to be useful. A multiple correlation of .30 or even less will allow considerable accuracy of prediction at the extremes of the score distribution, though not in the middle. Thus, if one wants only to pick out the top and bottom 5%, 10%, or 15% of the cases (say, the most and least effective teachers), one could be quite accurate even with relatively low correlations between predictor and criterion measure.

We consider the less effective teachers in our assessment system, the bottom 10-20% of teachers on the composite predictors, to be in charge of classrooms that are at risk. These would be the teachers who, it is predicted, will have low aggregate classroom performance on standardized tests. We think such classrooms could be identified through observations with existing instrumentation — say, before January 1 of an academic year — and possibly be helped before the predictions become reality. The form of help would vary, of course, depending on the apparent source of the problems. An analysis and consultation with the teacher involved could lead to a recommendation for using teaching aides, for instituting time management systems, for instituting family intervention with one very hard-to-teach child, for learning classroom discipline techniques, and so forth. Classrooms are likely to be at risk for different reasons (as are children), and thus remediation is likely to take different forms (as it does with children). To help teachers a knowledgeable classroom consultant trained in

psychology will be needed to identify what the problems are and what some likely solutions might be.

Existing school psychology techniques for consultation with students and parents can be adapted easily to this form of consultation with teachers about classroom instruction and management (e.g., Bergan, 1977). We have certainly demonstrated the *technical* feasibility of identifying at-risk classrooms. We must note, however, that the technical aspects of a program to code classroom behavior, including concern about issues of reliability and validity, analysis and interpretation of results, and planning of remedial programs, are nowhere near as problematic as are the political problems that might be encountered by trying to set up such a program. Just as there is concern about the labeling of youngsters as learning-disabled, slow, at-risk, and so forth, there is also the problem of labeling a classroom at-risk, in need of help, likely to have low mean standardized test performance, and so forth. Teachers and their professional groups are likely to reject any attempts to institute a system of identifying at-risk classrooms. But the technical methods for doing so are available and could be used by school psychologists to help districts identify those classrooms most in need of remedial services from principals, central office personnel with expertise in curriculum and instruction, or school psychologists trained in classroom consultation techniques.

Regardless of how teachers become clients selected to receive consultation — whether they are inexperienced or otherwise less effective, or even if they are skilled but are experiencing problems with a particular student — the kind of knowledge that is needed for classroom consultation is pedagogical knowledge, focused on classroom organization and management. We have simple but powerful ways to think about guiding consultation in these areas that derive from a knowledge base that simply did not exist 20 years ago.

THE KNOWLEDGE BASE FOR CLASS-ROOM CONSULTATION

In the area of classroom organization and management we have learned an enormous amount in the last few years. Our *findings*, our *concepts*, our *technology*, and our *theory* can help teachers solve many of their problems. What we need is a delivery system for all this research, such as can be provided by school psychologists who are knowledgeable about and interested in improving classroom teaching and learning. Helping people learn to use new skills in situ is a desirable goal for any training program. I believe that staff development, teacher training, or pedagogical consultation that takes place *in* the classroom, is much more likely to lead to successful implementation of some of the scientific findings we have about effective teaching than any other means of dissemination.

Findings

Let us talk first of findings, which include the isolated bits of information that every science accumulates. One example of a finding would be the accumulation of knowledge about the effects of "wait time" (Rowe, 1974), the elapsed time from the end of a teacher's thought-provoking, higher-order question, say in science or social studies, until the moment that a student begins to respond. That time is generally .8 sec. When it is increased to about 3 sec, the following seven phenomena have often been found to occur:

1. The length of student responses increases.
2. The number of alternative explanations given by students increases.
3. The number of students who fail to respond decreases.
4. The complexity and cognitive level of student responses increase.
5. The number of unsolicited but appropriate student responses increases.
6. The number of student-to-student interactions increases.
7. Student achievement (in mathematics and science) goes up.

These powerful main effects, with no harmful side effects, have been observed in at least 16 replications (Tobin, 1987). Nevertheless, this simple, scientifically derived, and well-validated teaching technique is not ordinarily seen in common use in classrooms. Many U.S. teachers may have somehow learned about this finding through their in-service or pre-service training but have not had the chance to integrate it into their teaching practice. If they are daring enough to even try this technique in their classes they often realize that a slowdown in the pace of instructional activities may take place. This slower pace causes a conflict, since the maintenance of a brisk pace of instruction is also an important consideration for classroom teachers. So of the few who do try this technique, many are likely to abandon it. Classroom consultation would be helpful in discussing ways to use this technique.

Other replicable findings also exist, that also are not in every teacher's repertoire. One such finding is about teacher monitoring. *Monitoring* is the name given to a broad set of teacher behaviors that includes walking around the classroom and checking students' output as they do seatwork; keeping vigilant while correcting papers or running a small group; and other activities that display close attention to the ways students are spending their time. High rates of monitoring correlate with academic achievement in the elementary grades. (Denham & Lieberman, 1980; Rosenshine & Stevens, 1986). This is not at all surprising, since many elementary classrooms make heavy use of individual seatwork assignments to accomplish the work of school. As much as 40-60% of the school day may be spent by a child in such solitary activities. Thus, a teacher who is vigilant, who monitors more, is likely to be a more successful teacher. New teachers and teachers in at-risk classrooms do not always show an understanding of this simple finding.

Yet another replicable finding deals with teachers' "structuring" activities. These include previewing and reviewing at the start of lessons, using advance organizers, providing directions, setting objectives and communicating expectations, explaining why certain things are studied, etc. Teachers who employ such structuring techniques as they start to teach a lesson have classes that generally achieve more on standardized tests (Denham & Lieberman, 1980; Rosenshine & Stevens, 1986). Their students seem to gain a cognitive advantage in information processing by the cueing and scaffolding that is provided by advance organizers, reviews, and previews. The provision of clear directions and reasons why something is important has motivational consequences as well. Students apparently feel better about what they are doing when they can be clear about what is expected, when they know what they should be doing and why they are doing it. But structuring is not in common use in classrooms throughout the United States.

Another replicable finding has to do with "pacing," or "content covered per unit of time." Teachers who find ways to cover more of the curriculum generally have students who achieve more (Brophy & Good, 1986; Berliner, 1985b). Their students are likely to have been exposed to and perhaps even have practiced more of the skills required to do well on a standardized achievement test. Furthermore, students do not become discipline problems as frequently in classes that make use of fast-paced instruction (Brophy & Good, 1986). The differences in the pace of instruction across different classrooms is enormous. With students of approximately equal ability we have recorded differences across classrooms in the amount of instruction covered per unit of time in ratios of 10 to 1. Surely some classroom consultation on pacing and content coverage can improve instruction and achievement.

Study of how success rate affects the performance of young students has led to another replicable finding. Children, up to about the fourth or fifth grade, seem to need very high rates of success, perhaps giving 70%, 80%, or 90% correct answers while doing worksheets, or when answering questions during classroom recitation, or when doing homework problems (Brophy & Good, 1986; Denham & Lieberman, 1980). Changing a classroom environment that is failure-oriented, in which children are succeeding only part of the time, into a success-oriented environment is not easy. Such factors as the heterogeneity of the classroom, the variety of learning materials that are available, the pace of instruction, and other complex factors all play a role. Nevertheless, despite this complexity, some teachers manage to provide classroom learning environments that allow for a good deal of student success, and other teachers do not. A classroom consultant armed with this concept and experience in other classrooms can, perhaps, help change a classroom that is not providing enough success experiences for young students.

This listing of findings, replicable bits of knowledge that contribute to make better classroom learning environments, continues to grow. We could discuss the use of "praise," ordinarily applied incorrectly, but powerful when used effectively (Brophy, 1981). We could discuss how tests and grades motivate students when used judiciously, or how corrective feedback or use of student ideas all affect achievement in reliable ways (Berliner, 1985b). The point is that anyone who would hope to consult about teaching and learning in the classes of teachers who are either new or at risk, *must* learn the contemporary body of research findings. (Major reference works include Berliner and Rosenshine, 1987; Richardson-Koehler, 1987; and Wittrock, 1986.)

Concepts

We have more than empirical findings to offer a classroom consultant. We also have *concepts* of great utility for understanding the processes of classroom instruction. These are concepts that help us to organize our world better, they help us by allowing us to name things, by giving us a technical vocabulary that we can then use with colleagues as we describe classroom phenomena. A rich array of concepts need to be easily accessed by consultants if they are to help teachers understand, organize, and control the myriad phenomena impinging on them as they perform their work in classrooms.

The first of these organizing concepts we can discuss is the simple notion of *allocated time*. It turns out that allocated time is a positive predictor of achievement because there is enormous variation in the amount of time allocated for instruction in each classroom. In different elementary school classrooms, allocated time can range from as little as 16 min a day to as much as 50 min a day for mathematics instruction, and from 45 to 137 min a day in reading instruction. Time allocated to a content area of geometry, such as isoceles triangles, can range from 0 time to 10 hours per student in different classrooms. Thus, some classrooms have 2 or 3 or 10 times more time allocated for instruction than other classrooms (Berliner, 1979).

Allocated time as a concept for organizing what we see and how we think about classes is a very important concept. When a parent or some newspaper criticizes the schools because students are not learning how to write, or the students do not comprehend well, or they are not performing well in science, the simplest question for a consultant to ask is whether somebody allocated enough time for writing, reading comprehension, or science activities. If educators are not allocating sufficient time, then students don't have the opportunity to learn the skills the public wants them to have. Students cannot be expected to perform well on standardized tests if they have not had the opportunity to learn those things that are measured by the tests. In fact, unless teachers allocate sufficient time to particular areas of the curriculum, we should not ordinarily expect, for example, that students will ever learn about such things as multiplying fractions, the United Nations charter, Chaucer, or the anger of colonists over the Stamp Act. Allocated time is a very useful concept for thinking about *what* and *how much* instruction is actually offered to students. Just as the management consultants in industry can help executives allocate their time more productively, the classroom consultant can help teachers allocate their time in more sensible ways than might presently be the case. Allocated time is a rich concept for thinking about instruction, as well as a scarce resource to be used wisely.

A second concept that enhances our technical vocabulary is *engaged time*. Engaged time, or time on task, or attention, is also a positive predictor of achievement (Denham & Lieberman, 1980; Brophy & Good, 1986). It is usually measured by determining the percentage of students in a classroom doing the work assigned during an observation period, and then averaging these percentages over all the observations obtained. Enormous between-classroom variation in rates of engagement have been found (Berliner, 1979; Fisher & Berliner, 1985). We may find a 40% or 50% time-on-task level in one classroom while next door, perhaps with children of the same socioeconomic group, we may see a 90% time-on-task level. Those differences represent an enormous disparity in the amount of curriculum the children are exposed to. We have learned, unfortunately, that some elementary classrooms do not even deliver 100 hr of time on task over the course of the school year, in reading and mathematics combined! This happens because the school year really is not a year but is in fact 9 months; the 9 months are not a full 9 months, but are really 180 days of instruction. However, the 180 days of instruction must be reduced by the number of days on which there are plays, field trips, strikes, bus breakdowns, snow days that are not made up, mental health days for teachers, real illnesses of teachers and students, etc. Also the week before Christmas and the week at the end of the school year are not genuine instructional weeks. We might end up, if we are lucky, with 140 *real* instructional days. If mathematics is taught 30 min a day, which is very common in, let's say, second grade, we end up with a total allocated time for mathematics of 70 hr for the year. With a low engaged time rate, say 50%, the *delivered* curriculum is only 35 hr! All the mathematics for the year totals 35 hr. Reading may be twice that value, about

70 hr, and the whole year may sum to about 100 hr of engaged time in these two important academic areas of the elementary school curriculum. It should be obvious, therefore, that the concept of engaged time is an important one for thinking about instructional activities in classrooms. New teachers and at-risk teachers do not always handle engaged time well. They do not always have the management skills to control it and they may not have any way to monitor it. Without their awareness, large blocks of classroom time go by, unfilled by time spent on educationally significant tasks.

Time may be the single most important resource over which schools have control. Rossmiller (1982), for example, in a 3-year longitudinal study, found that for low-ability students, the variance accounted for in reading or mathematics achievement by a set of time variables was 73%! Even for the highest-ability students, 10% of the variation was accounted for by time variables. Concepts of the ways schools use and expend time, separate from the empirical status of time variables and achievement, are important for thinking about curriculum and instruction. Time variables are the metric by which we can measure and judge whether we are doing what we are trying to do as educators. That is, in a fundamental way, time is the metric by which our philosophies of education can be measured. Educational philosophy *must* have duration if it is to have any classroom manifestation and not be mere empty words. Consultants working at the classroom level with new and at-risk teachers can serve an important role by helping these teachers take their beliefs about schooling, teaching, and learning — their educational philosophy — and providing them with data about the implementation of their beliefs, as reflected in some kind of time metric.

Another concept of great utility is *curriculum alignment*, or overlap, as it is sometimes called. The concept refers to the alignment or overlap between what is taught and what is tested. Schools, we think, are vastly *under*estimating their students' performance by using tests mismatched to the curriculum (Freeman et al., 1980). Research informs us, for example, that if a school district is unfortunate enough to have chosen the Stanford Achievement Test as a criterion measure and uses the Addison-Wesley fourth-grade Mathematics Curriculum Series, there will be only an estimated 47% overlap. That is, items on the test will have been found to correspond to items in the text about 47% of the time. That means, of course, that 53% of the items on that test will have been unfamiliar to the students unless the teachers have taken extraordinary action. Even in the best case, with the Scott-Foresman series and the Metropolitan Achievement Test, the overlap is only about 70%. This indicates that about 30% of the items on the test were likely to be unfamiliar to students. Psychologically trained classroom consultants are aware of the basic assumptions that undergird fair testing programs. An elementary assumption necessary to fairness in achievement testing is that test takers have been exposed to the curriculum materials from which items on the test were drawn. With knowledge of basic testing practices and concepts such as curriculum alignment in mind, classroom consultants can help many new and at-risk teachers fill the gaps between the tests and curriculum. If that is done, students are almost always likely to achieve more on achievement tests.

My favorite concept, used frequently in my own classroom consultations, is one my colleagues and I invented. It incorporates some other concepts and findings, and is called *academic learning time*, or ALT (Fisher et al., 1980). We defined ALT as that part of classroom time that is allocated to a curriculum content area in which students are *engaged* and *successful*, and during which the *activities or materials they are involved with are related to outcomes that are valued*. The variable of ALT can be reliably measured in hours, minutes, and seconds by well-trained classroom observers. When ALT is high, students have had sufficient opportunity to learn those things highly related to instructional outcomes that are valued. The variable of ALT has turned out to be an interesting predictor of effectiveness. Teachers who produce high levels of ALT in the content areas of reading or mathematics generally have students who score higher in those curricular areas. When an attempt is made to account for variance in achievement in a content area, after the entering ability of students is partialed out, the residual variance is often well accounted for by ALT.

For example, in second grade, the amount of residual variance in achievement accounted for by the variables that make up ALT was 17% in the reading content area of decoding blends; for learning syllables and word structure it was 14%. In learning word problems and in learning to use money in second-grade mathematics, the amount of residual variance accounted for by ALT was 7% and 12%, respectively. In general, across a large number of curriculum content areas in second- and fifth-grade classrooms, the ALT variables predicted around 10% of the residual variance. The ALT variables are, in essence, a classroom measure of the teachers provision of the opportunity to learn. Thus, it is no wonder that ALT is consistently associated with effectiveness. The two small studies, mentioned previously, that were designed to identify at-risk classrooms, used ALT and related variables as the focus of the classroom observations. The concept of ALT is a rich one for consultation with new teachers and teachers in at-risk classrooms because in this single concept we can incorporate a good deal of empirically verified knowledge about its constituent sub-concepts. When a class is not doing well, a consultant called in to help, if armed with the concept of ALT, can immediately begin to examine important aspects of classroom life. The consultant examines the allocations of time, measures the engagement rates of students, estimates the level of success students are experiencing, and decides whether what they are involved with is connected in some logical way to the outcomes that are valued and/or will be tested. ALT can be measured in minutes accrued in reading comprehension, factoring, or Newtonian laws and the results can be evaluated. Low levels of ALT are not likely to lead to high achievement. Increasing the teachers' management skills to increase attending rates, or slowing the pace of instruction to raise the level of success, or changing the curriculum to emphasize what will be on an anticipated achievement test, all become remediation options after analysis of a classroom using the concept of ALT as a guide. Conceptually and empirically it is a good guide for thinking about classroom instruction.

One of the more interesting new concepts for organizing a consultant's thoughts about classrooms is the notion that the classroom really functions as an *economic system*. It is a system in which "there is an exchange of performance for grades." This is the basis of the "deal" that is sometimes made between teachers and students, a way that some teachers survive in at-risk classrooms. If the students do not go too bonkers, the teachers will reward them with a decent grade. An economic pact comes into existence. This concept has some utility for explaining, perhaps, why some classrooms are so dull (Doyle, 1983).

This concept also helps explain how new teachers, particularly, can become socialized to the existing instructional system. Armed with imagination, new ideas, and a desire to be different from the existing staff, new teachers may try to introduce teaching practices that capitalize on the creativity of their students. Imagine a high school biology teacher trying to teach a unit on "The Pond" as a process-oriented curriculum unit, involving lots of discussion, inference making, and conjecture. Suppose, however, that the goals of the lessons are unclear and therefore the ways of obtaining grades are also unclear. What is called for is creativity, patience, and faith by the teacher and the students that the process itself will yield something useful; the teacher is providing an invitation to explore. But under such conditions the students could become troublesome. They may not react well to this lack of structure, the lack of certainty about their grades. Under ordinary conditions they know what to do to get the grade they want.

They understand the implicit (if not explicit) contract that they have entered into with their teacher. But in an unstructured environment they might start asking: "How long does our assignment have to be?" "Can we work on it together?" "Will this be on the test?" "How many pages do you want?" and so forth. With their loss of clarity about how to exchange performance for grades, they attack the teacher to regain some control. They turn a creative teaching act into a structured exercise, one with surety and safety for themselves. By pulling down the lesson, by asking inane questions and giving silly answers to the teachers questions, they force the teacher to return to a much more predictable teaching style. They help to drive the kinds of lessons that depend upon creativity, spontaneity, and the process of discovery, out of the classroom. They communicate to the teacher that he or she better get back to the place where students can say: "If I do this assignment, I am pretty sure I'll get this grade."

If the familiar criticism that teachers are noncreative is true, the fault for that may lie in the kind of society we have and the expectations parents have regarding their children's grades. It may be that teachers literally cannot enter ambiguous curriculum areas without endangering students' economic security. This conception of schools and classrooms is very provocative, I think, and assuredly applicable to some schools and classrooms that I know. Rich concepts such as that of using an economic frame to describe classrooms provide us with enormously powerful ways to organize our experience. This is, I believe, a generative concept. Armed with such concepts, informed consultants can observe classrooms in a way that lay people cannot, can analyze what is seen in a more sophisticated way, and can recommend actions that have a higher probability of remediating problems.

Let us describe one more concept, now receiving a great deal of attention. It is the concept of the *routine*, something many of us are finding to be important in explaining differences between expert teachers and those who are novices or are otherwise in difficulty. Within most

teaching tasks or activities there are many routines or scripts. A management routine might be identified when the teacher says, "Pass the papers to the right." Another, more cognitive, routine, is seen when a student during an oral response is reminded to specify the steps used to get an answer. The routines are shared, scripted, virtually automated units of action. Behavioral routines and scripts often allow students and teachers to devote their attention to other, perhaps more important, matters inherent in the lesson.

Leinhardt and Greeno (1986) examined the performance of an opening homework review by an expert teacher. The expert teacher was found to be brief, taking about one-third less time than a novice. In addition, she was able to pick up information about attendance and information about who did and who did not do the homework. She was able to get all the homework corrected and she elicited mostly correct answers throughout the activity. She identified who was going to need help in the subsequent lesson and she did so at a brisk pace and without ever losing control of the lesson. Routines were used to record attendance, to handle choral responding during the homework checks, and for hand raising to get attention. The expert used clear start-up and finishing signals.

Interviews with the expert revealed how the goals of the lesson, the time constraints, and the curriculum itself were blended to direct the activity. A script for conducting the lesson existed at all times. In contrast, when a novice was observed while carrying out an opening homework review, she was not able to get a fix on those who had and those who had not done the homework, she had problems with taking attendance, and she asked ambiguous questions that led to inadequate assessment of the difficulty level of the homework. At one time the novice teacher lost control of the pace, and never did learn which students were going to have more difficulty later in the lesson. The novice teacher showed a lack of familiarity with well-practiced routines. There seemed to be no habitual way to act. Students, therefore, were unsure of their roles. As noted above, students have a preference for surety.

Studies about routines and scripts used by experts help us to understand, therefore, what constitutes a bug-laden routine or an incomplete script, such as might be used by novice teachers or those having management and instructional problems in their classrooms. Leinhardt and Greeno (1986), for example, found that well-scripted routines, such as one for visual scanning, were important characteristics of a successful opening homework review by expert teachers. Brooks and Hawke (1985), comparing experienced/effective teachers with inexperienced/ineffective teachers of mathematics in the seventh grade, found almost the same characteristics when they studied class period openings. They concluded from their study that

> If you had to prescribe to a junior high school teacher an apparently effective method for opening a class period, the scenario would be as follows: Develop a routine opening that features visual scanning, a quick call to order in a businesslike tone of voice, a method of roll taking that is time efficient, an opening verbal sequence that includes behavioral and academic expectations, anticipate areas of confusion in explanations, and call for questions before signaling the beginning of the first activity. Threats to an efficient opening appear to include: the absence of an effective day-to-day behavioral routine, a slower call to order in a nonbusinesslike tone of voice, the absence of visual scanning, a procedure for taking roll that is time consuming, the inability to anticipate confusion and the absence of advanced organization. (p. 5)

These studies give us some information about what beginning teachers and teachers of classrooms that are at risk might want to think about when they plan for or engage in activities such as lesson openings and opening homework reviews. Dozens of other teaching activities are also carried out by means of these well-learned routines. These forms of pedagogical behavior are important to understand if

one is to understand how instruction is carried out in the classes of experienced/ expert teachers in contrast to those who are less experienced and less expert. Possession of a powerful concept such as "routines" and the related concepts of "scripts," "buggy algorithms," and the like can enable consultants to understand how some individuals control the complexity inherent in classroom teaching. Scores of such concepts exist, including some that help teachers effectively run small groups in their classes (Marland, 1977), and others that allow us to understand classroom management and the control of off-task behavior and student misbehavior (Kounin, 1970).

Technology

The technology, or the scientifically derived tools for teaching and learning that we have invented, must also be mastered by a classroom consultant. Technology in medicine, in the form of pharmaceuticals, surgical techniques, noninvasive systems to examine internal organs, and artificial body parts, has given that field part of its much deserved reputation. Technology is the application of scientific knowledge to solve problems. Obviously, a consultant to classrooms needs knowledge of available educational technology and an assurance that it does, indeed, function as it should. In the last decade we have created such technology.

Technology now exists for producing cooperative behavior among students and between students and teachers (Slavin, 1983). These techniques have also given rise to higher self-esteem for the learners, as well as improved academic classroom behavior and, even more astounding, higher academic achievement. These recent experiments in cooperative learning environments have involved thousands of students in thousands of classrooms. In the process we have learned how certain cooperative teaching techniques can help to integrate handicapped children into the mainstream of the classroom, help to integrate minority members into the majority culture, and help to produce more nearly equal performance among students of different social classes. Such technology has been developed and field-tested only in the last 10 years. This is the kind of technology that many new teachers and teachers having difficulty need to be taught to use.

In classroom management, also, we have new technology. This is the area that the press and the public love to criticize teachers about, and it is the area that teachers have the most fear about when they begin to teach. We have made unbelievable strides in the last decade, having learned many of the techniques used by teachers that lead to smooth-running, on-task, cheerful classrooms. That work was first reported only in 1970 by Jacob Kounin. It was investigated by others through the 1970s and was turned into teacher-training materials at the University of Texas and Utah State University during the early 1980s (Borg and Ascione, 1982; Emmer, Evertson, Sanford, Clements, & Worsham, 1984; Evertson et al., 1984). Those materials, based on sound empirical research, have been field-tested by such organizations as the American Federation of Teachers. The recommendations for teachers are as simple as "Stand at your door on opening day, because . . . " and as complex as deciding when to intervene in a behavior problem — a decision about timing that is complex and based on very imperfect information. In New York and other urban areas the results of using these techniques have been amazing. Teachers who previously had failed to meet the criteria of good management were, for the first time in their professional lives, in complete control of their classes. One 20-year veteran of the New York City schools opined that the training produced nothing short of a miracle.

Our technology also includes heuristics for teaching in explicit areas of the curriculum, such as mathematics. Rosenshine and Stevens (1986) have codified the many and diverse findings of different researchers and have presented them as six teaching functions to be performed for promoting student achievement. If in mathematics, for example, you first start with review, second present new material,

third do guided practice, fourth provide corrections and feedback, fifth give independent practice, and sixth provide for weekly and monthly review sessions, then your students are likely to achieve well (See Good, Grouws, & Ebmeir, 1983). This is instructional technology, an ordering of activities that when applied sensibly results in higher student achievement. And yet it is technology that is not in the hands of many new teachers and teachers in at-risk classrooms.

Let us look at one last example of recently created technology: "outcome-based" or "mastery" strategies (Spady, 1984). In Red Bank, New Jersey, in 1978 the average eighth grader scored 1.5 years *below* grade level in reading on the Metropolitan Achievement Test. In 1983, the eighth graders were 1.5 years *above* grade level. In mathematics, from 1978 to 1983, the eighth grade class was measured as going from a mean of 1.5 years *below* grade level to a mean of almost 2.5 years *above* grade level. That is, in 5 years of a special program the mean achievement level in mathematics went up four grade levels on the Metropolitan Achievement Test. A similar program was found in an elementary school in New Canaan, Connecticut. The overall results show that about 15% of the graduating sixth graders in that school finished half of algebra 1. About 60% of the sixth graders and 30% of the fifth graders scored at the 99th percentile on the mathematics section of the Metropolitan Achievement Test in mathematics. In the entire school, in 7 years, only about two students per year scored under grade level on the standardized achievement tests. The programs that were in use in these very different schools were outcome-based, mastery-type programs.

Assuredly there are costs involved in the use of any technology — in this case, philosophical arguments about the possible inappropriateness of mastery programs — and they must be considered seriously. But because there are impressive data to support the usefulness of these programs we must examine this kind of outcome-based technology very carefully and be proficient enough in it ourselves to consult intelligently about it.

There are still other technologies available. Some adaptive instructional programs consistently build student responsibility (Wang, 1980; Wang, Reynolds, & Schwartz, this volume). Other packaged instructional material for teachers to use in computer environments are now available as well, and they show good results with the children hardest to teach (Pogrow, 1987). Research-based technology is increasing, but the dissemination of its findings is not good. Perhaps even more important is that there are virtually no personnel assigned to helping teachers who want to try to use such technology. Taking on the risk of technological change requires a safe and a supportive environment. This technical support can be provided by psychologically trained personnel at the school.

Theory

We have theory as well as empirical findings, concepts, and technology to help us in understanding the dynamics of the classroom. Dozens of the findings, concepts, and technologies that have emerged from correlational and experimental studies of teacher effectiveness seem to be related in a simple theory about classroom instruction (Berliner, 1987). That theory predicts that most teaching variables influence student achievement by affecting one of the components of Academic Learning Time, described previously to include allocated time, engaged time, success, and the congruence of the tasks with the outcome measures. I believe we can understand the findings that keep emerging from research on effective teaching by asking how they affect the ALT components, which are known correlates of achievement. Put another way, we are proposing that consultants apply a theory of classroom instruction built around the concept of ALT that enjoins teachers to provide their students with better opportunities to learn what it is they are supposed to learn by attending to time variables and student success variables, and by matching the curriculum and the outcome. Let us test, just briefly, the way

such a simple theory might be put to use.

When we replicate a finding, say, the one about "pacing," and determine that it is causally related to achievement, we can demonstrate our ability to *control*. This is but one of the goals of science. When we demonstrate that more-effective teachers are likely to maintain a faster pace through the curriculum than their colleagues, we satisfy another goal of science, *prediction*. When we hypothesize that the reason the variable called pacing is a consistent predictor of achievement is that it regulates the amount of opportunity students are provided for learning the things that they are to be held responsible for learning, we realize a third goal of science, *understanding*. We see then how our theory, concerned with learning opportunities and related to time variables, accounts for the existing data relating to pacing.

We noted before that "structuring" is a variable that has been found to be a predictor of teacher effectiveness. Teachers who share the goals of a lesson with students, provide clear directions at the start of a lesson, and provide introductions, advance organizers, reviews, summaries, and so forth are usually more effective than teachers who do not engage in such activities. These findings let us predict. To understand *why* structuring acts as it does is a bit harder. In line with our theory, however, we would hypothesize that structuring works because of a number of factors. Clear directions by a teacher reduce error rates because students are aware of what they are to be doing. Intelligible short directions also ensure higher engaged time. Since students know what they are to be doing they cannot easily act befuddled and cannot honestly remain unengaged. Summaries and reviews help keep error rates down by providing students with a way of checking what they have done. The summaries and reviews also expose students to key ideas and information, possibly increasing the congruence of the curriculum studied with anticipated achievement tests. Reminding students about why they are doing certain tasks decreases their feelings that tasks are mindless, thus increasing motivation to learn and producing higher rates of engaged time in class, and possibly higher allocations of uncommitted time to the tasks. A simple theory relying on the concept of ALT helps us in understanding how this reliable predictor might work.

We have stated that "monitoring" is a variable that correlates with achievement. Teachers who do such monitoring generally have classes that achieve more. Monitoring probably "works" because it acts to keep error rates down and engagement rates up. Teachers who wander about their classrooms can catch students' mistakes before they are practiced for too long, and can also keep off-task behavior to a minimum simply by their presence in an area. Thus, monitoring is a predictor of achievement by affecting ALT variables and therefore affecting the students' opportunity to learn.

This kind of analysis could go on: Cooperative learning increases motivation to learn, thus increasing time-on-task; outcome-based instruction works because of the very tight tie between curriculum and outcome measures. But by now the basic elements of our understanding of effective teaching practices should be clear. Teacher behaviors, classroom processes, and school-level variables that affect ALT probably affect a student's opportunity to learn. Thus, we not only can predict teacher effectiveness; in my opinion, we now also *understand* how many of the findings related to effectiveness must function. The roots of this theory, of course, are in J. B. Carroll's (1963) model of school learning. This simple adaptation of his theory, however, is a powerful one. It has already guided us in development of systems to identify at-risk classrooms, and it can also guide classroom consultants in their work with new teachers and with teachers having problems in management and instruction.

CONCLUSIONS

Professionals assigned to helping teachers implement effective classroom interventions must be caring and knowledgeable people, willing to work in class-rooms over a lengthy period of time. To be knowledgeable means to have learned a body of findings, to have understood a set of concepts, to have gained experience in using new technology, and to have assimilated certain theories to guide classroom observation. If school psychologists incorporate this body of knowledge into their professional training and continuing education programs, they will be prepared to play an important additional role in the schools, that of the classroom consultant.

Naturally, there are barriers that tend to prevent school psychologists from taking on this role. Legally they are called upon to perform certain functions, often relating to psychological testing and developing special education programs for children with special needs. But in my experience children with special needs are not always randomly distributed across classes. They often are found in greater numbers in some classrooms than others. These are the classrooms of teachers who have not fully perfected their skills, perhaps because of inexperience, perhaps because of placement in difficult teaching assignments. When school psychologists provide services to children without regard for the classroom learning environment, treatment can prove to be inadequate. Thus it is recommended that the classroom environment be more of an object of attention and study by school psychologist than it is now.

It is a great luxury to sit in the back of a classroom and observe what goes on. From that position things can be seen that the classroom teacher is unaware of, because the classroom teacher is so busy. Thus, to get involved in classroom observation almost always leads to a desire to provide classroom help. Mastery by school psychologists of the body of pedagogical knowledge that now exists will provide them richer concepts with which to interpret what they observe in these classes, as well as findings, technology, and theories to share with teachers of a sort that could improve the instructional and affective dimensions of the classrooms. The current training of school psychologists does not usually include coursework on these subjects, and the job descriptions of school psychologists do not usually mention these duties. But professions change, particularly as new roles open up. Thus, electrical engineers become computer scientists, nurses become midwives, biologists become chemists, and chemists become biologists.

I am convinced that there is a new role to be played in the schools, that of classroom consultant, to ameliorate the problems of new teachers and teachers in classes that are at risk. School principles sometimes take on this role, but often reluctantly and not consistently. School district central office personnel sometimes take on this role, but often they are more concerned with curriculum than instruction and management.

The knowledge base for the role of consultant to classes is primarily psychological and the method of communication is primarily consultative. From my perspective as an academic educational psychologist, rather than a practicing school psychologist (meaning a perspective that may be naive, ahistoric, poorly informed about the licensing requirements in different states, unaware of the constraints on school psychologists, uninformed about their current case loads, etc.) it appears to me to be a role to be filled most easily by school psychologists. If school psychologists choose to take this role the profession has a chance to transform itself and to end up woven more tightly into the fabric of school life than I believe it is now. And scientific psychology will have more impact on society, as I believe it should.

REFERENCES

Bergan, J. R. (1977). *Behavioral consultation.* Columbus, OH: Merrill.

Berliner, D. C. (1979). Tempus educare. In P. L. Peterson & H. J. Walberg (Eds.) *Research on teaching: Concepts, findings, and implications.* Berkeley, CA: McCutchen.

Berliner, D. C. (1984). Making the right changes in preservice teacher education. *Phi Delta Kappan, 66,* 94-96.

Berliner, D. C. (1985a). The clinical educational psychologist: Scientist and practitioner. In J. R. Bergan (Ed.), *School psychology in contemporary society.* Columbus, OH: Merrill.

Berliner, D. C. (1985b). Effective classroom teaching: The necessary but not sufficient condition for developing exemplary schools. In G. Austin & H. Garber (Eds.), *Research on exemplary schools.* New York: Academic.

Berliner, D. C. (1987). A simple theory of classroom instruction. In D. C. Berliner & B. Rosenshine (Eds.), *Talks to teachers.* (pp. 93-110). New York: Random House.

Berliner, D. C. & Rosenshine, B. (Eds.). (1987). *Talks to teachers.* NY: Random House.

Borg, W. R., & Ascione, F. R. (1982). Classroom management in elementary mainstreaming classrooms. *Journal of Educational Psychology, 74,* 85-95.

Brooks, D., & Hawke, R. (1985, April). *Effective and ineffective session-opening teacher activity and task structures.* Paper presented at the meetings of the American Educational Research Association, Chicago.

Brophy, J. E. (1981). Teacher praise: A functional analysis. *Review of Educational Research, 51,* 5-32.

Brophy, J. & Good, T. L. (1986). Teacher behavior and student achievement. In M. Wittrock (Ed.), *Handbook of research on teaching* (pp. 328-375). New York: Macmillan.

Carroll, J. B. (1963). A model of school learning. *Teachers College Record, 64,* 723-733.

Denham, C. & Lieberman, A. (Eds.). (1980). *Time to learn.* Washington, DC: National Institute of Education.

Doyle, W. (1983). Academic work. *Review of Educational Research, 53,* 159-199.

Ellis-Schwabe, M. A. (1986). *Prediction of classrooms that are at risk: Implications for staff development.* Unpublished dissertation, College of Education, University of Arizona, Tucson.

Emmer, E. T., Evertson, C. M., Sanford, J. P., Clements, B. W., & Worsham, M. E. (1984). *Classroom management for secondary teachers.* Englewood Cliffs, NJ: Prentice-Hall.

Evertson, C. M., Emmer, E. T., Clements, B. S., Sanford, J. P., Worsham, M. E., & Williams, E. L. (1984). *Classroom management for elementary teachers.* Englewood Cliffs, NJ: Prentice-Hall.

Fenstermacher, G. D., & Berliner, D. C. (1985). A conceptual framework for evaluating staff development. *Elementary School Journal, 85,* 281-314.

Fisher, C., & Berliner, D. C. (1985). *Perspectives on instructional time.* New York: Longman.

Fisher, C., Berliner, D. C., Filby, N., Marliare, R., Cahen, L. S., & Dishaw, M. (1980). Teaching behaviors, academic learning time, and student achievement: An overview. In C. Denham and A. Lieberman (Eds.). *Time to Learn.* Washington, DC: National Institute of Education, Education Department.

Freeman, D., Kuhs, T., Porter, A., Knappen, L., Floden, R., Schmidt, W., & Schwille, J. (1980). *The fourth grade mathematics curriculum as inferred from textbooks and tests* (Report No. 82). East Lansing, MI: Michigan State University, Institute for Research on Teaching.

Good, T., Grouws, D. & Ebmeir, M. (1983). *Active mathematics teaching.* New York: Longman.

Huberman, M. (1985). What knowledge is of most worth to teachers. *Teaching and Teacher Education, 1,* 251-262.

Kolodner, J. L. (1983). Towards an understanding of the role of experience in the evolution from novice to expert. *Journal of Man–Machine Studies, 19,* 497-518.

Kounin, J. (1970). *Discipline and group management in classrooms.* New York: Basic Books.

Leinhardt, G., & Greeno, J. G. (1986). The cognitive skill of teaching. *Journal of Educational Psychology, 78,* 75-95.

Lynn, D. (1980). Predicting at-risk classrooms. Unpublished manuscript, University of Arizona.

Marland, P. W. (1977). *A study of teachers' interactive thoughts.* Unpublished dissertation, University of Alberta, Alberta, Canada.

Pogrow, S. (1987). *Higher Order Thinking Skills (HOTS) Newsletter.* Tucson, AZ: College of Education, University of Arizona.

Richardson-Koehler, V. (1987). *Educators' handbook.* White Plains, NY: Longman.

Rosenshine, B., & Stevens, R. (1986). Teaching functions. In M. C. Wittrock (Ed.), *Handbook of research on teaching (3rd ed.)* (pp. 376-391). New York: Macmillan.

Rossmiller, R. A. (1982, September). *Managing school resources to improve student achievement.* Paper presented at the State Superintendent Conference for District Administrators, Madison, WI.

Rowe, M. B. (1974). Wait-time and rewards as instructional variables, their influence on language, logic, and fate control: Pt. 1. Wait-time. *Journal of Research in Science Teaching, 11,* 81-94.

Slavin, R. E. (1983). *Cooperative learning.* White Plains, NY: Longman.

Spady, W. G. (1984). Organizing and delivering curriculum for maximum input. In *Proceedings of three state conferences: Making our schools more effective.* San Francisco, CA: Far West Laboratory for Educational Research and Development.

Tobin, K. G. (1987). The role of wait-time in higher-cognitive-level learning. *Review of Educational Research, 57,* 69-95.

Wang, M. C. (1980). Adaptive instruction: Building on diversity. *Theory into Practice 19*(2), 122-128.

Wittrock, M. (Ed.). (1986). *Handbook of research on teaching (3rd ed.).* New York: Macmillan.

16

Direct Instruction

Douglas Carnine,
Alex Granzin, and
Wesley Becker
University of Oregon

With the current recognition of the serious limitations of most psychoeducational testing procedures (Galagan, 1985), school psychologists have become more actively involved in assisting classroom teachers with behavioral and instructional interventions. In many instances, a lack of teaching experience combined with a very limited familiarity with effective instructional practices has placed school psychologists at a considerable disadvantage in their attempts to function as instructional consultants. There is some evidence, however, that training programs for school psychologists are beginning to recognize the importance of providing their students with an adequate background in the area of effective teaching practices. For example, school psychology students at the University of Oregon are now required to complete an instructional practicum in a special education setting and are offered the opportunity to complete additional coursework in instructional consultation. Both the practicum and the consultation coursework emphasize instructional skills and materials that have been demonstrated to be effective in a variety of settings. Although instruction is a complex process with a massive literature, it is somewhat comforting to realize that there is a body of convergent findings that suggest that it is possible to specify the characteristics of both good instructional materials and good teaching.

The introduction of the term *direct* *instruction* by Rosenshine (1976) marked a significant turning point in the specification of effective teaching practices. Rosenshine analyzed a large body of educational research to determine which instructional practices were consistently associated with higher academic achievement scores. He noted that such scores are demonstrated when teachers observe the following practices.

1. Devote substantial time to active instruction.
2. Break complex skills and concepts into small, easy-to-understand steps and systematically teach in a step-to-step fashion.
3. Provide immediate feedback to students about the accuracy of their work.
4. Conduct much of the instruction in small groups to allow for frequent student-teacher interactions.

Additional support for these findings has come from a variety of sources (Bennett et al., 1976; Brophy and Evertson, 1976; Brophy & Good, 1986; Fisher et al., 1980; Soar, 1973; Stallings and Kaskowitz, 1974). Although different authors have focused on somewhat different sets of characteristics, the findings have been consistent, particularly with respect to the importance of students being involved in academic activities (academic engaged time).

This chapter is devoted primarily to the discussion of a particular set of curricular materials and instructional practices that embody both the principles of direct instruction as specified by Rosenshine and the principles of instructional programming that have been specified by Engelmann and Carnine (1982). This set of teaching strategies and instructional presentations is referred to as Direct Instruction and is based on carefully scripted programs designed by Siegfried Engelmann and colleagues and published by Science Research associates (SRA). The most well known of these programs are the nine DISTAR programs (three levels each in reading, arithmetic, and language). DISTAR Reading has recently been replaced by a six-level reading basal program (Reading Mastery). A six-level spelling basal (Spelling Mastery), and a two-level composition program (Expressive Writing) have also been published. A six-level language program and a six-level mathematics program are being planned. Other programs have been written for remedial students: Corrective Reading (comprehension and decoding skills with three levels each), Morphographic Spelling, and a Corrective Mathematics series that covers addition, subtraction, multiplication, division, fractions, equations.

This chapter will provide a review of the assumptions and general features of Direct Instruction and then proceed to a discussion of research on implementation of Direct Instruction programs, investigations of specific instructional variables, and the development of new programs.

ASSUMPTIONS OF DIRECT INSTRUCTION

The Direct Instruction approach is built upon the following premises, which derive from applied behavior analysis and logical analyses of knowledge systems:

- Operant (voluntary) behavior is learned.
- Learning is a function of environmental events.
- The teacher can control environmental events to make learning happen.

- Learning rate is largely a function of teaching technology.
- If you can find ways to teach more in less time, the children will gain relative to those taught less.
- Thinking and related covert cognitive processes can be taught first as overt (usually verbal) processes.
- Program sequences derive logically from the nature of the skills and knowledge to be taught — not the individual. This implies that it is possible to teach all children with the same program sequence, although several different sequences could work equally well.
- Task sequences to teach concepts and operations should be designed to permit only one interpretation wherever possible.
- If the sequence permits only one interpretation consistently, only that interpretation can be learned.
- Transfer of skills to related (but different) tasks and situations must be planned for in the teaching program.
- Generalization to new examples not used in the teaching will occur only where there are specific cues (discriminative stimuli) present in the new examples that were the essential features of the examples already taught. Again, there is no magic.
- Instructional processes require careful monitoring and feedback systems to ensure quality control.
- If the student fails, do not blame the student; diagnose the teaching history. The teaching sequences control what can be learned.

COMPONENTS OF DIRECT INSTRUCTION

Common to the various Direct Instruction programs developed under Engelmann's directions are (a) pretested scripted lessons, (b) teacher-directed small-group instruction for part of each lesson, (c) teaching procedures, (d) motivating procedures, (e) training procedures, and (f) formative evaluation.

Scripted Presentations

A program is a series of tasks to be taught. The instruction takes the form of frequent interchanges between the teacher and the students. To ensure that what is intended is delivered, daily lessons are designed in script form, showing the teacher what to do and what to say during these interchanges. Scripted lessons make it possible to implement effective instruction by using aides, where necessary, as teachers after only one or two weeks of preservice training. The use of scripted lesson plans has been criticized as restricting the teacher's initiative. However, some important values derive from the use of scripts. We are concerned with designing disseminable procedures for improving instruction. Scripts permit the use of explicitly pretested examples and explanations. (The procedures that govern the creation of instructional examples and explanations are discussed below.) The teacher knows that if the students have the prerequisite skills, the teaching sequence will work. The teacher does not have to spend time experimenting with various possible illustrations, choosing appropriate language, and analyzing possible teaching sequences. Thus, the training requirements for a given program can be formalized in detail and executed.

Scripted lessons also facilitate the effective use of direct observation. A school psychologist observing the behavior of a student receiving such instruction is able to focus on a narrow range of critical instructional variables that are likely to have a significant impact on student performance. In addition, a variety of direct observation instruments have been developed (Gersten, Carnine, Zoref & Cronin, 1986) specifically to facilitate the collection of data on both teacher and student behavior during the course of direct instruction. A school psychologist can walk into any room and within a few seconds be explicitly oriented as to what should be going on and thus can evaluate what in fact is going on and provide appropriate help. Finally, the use of standardized teaching sequences allows for the development of program-based tests that are directly related to the process of instruction and that do not introduce extraneous response requirements or formats not typically encountered in the instructional setting. This congruence between instructional procedure and program-based tests further simplifies the school psychologist's analysis of a particular student's behavior by identifying a specific task or groups of tasks that are problematic.

Scripted presentations are not necessary or even desirable in all areas or levels of education, but they most certainly can serve an important role when dealing with competencies that all children should have. They may also play an important role in teacher training.

Small Groups

Small groups have many advantages. They are more efficient than one-on-one instruction and provide for more adult direction, prompting, reinforcement, correction, and individualization than are found in large-group instruction. They also permit an emphasis on oral communication, which is frequently a problem for children from non-English-speaking and economically disadvantaged backgrounds. Finally, small groups provide a setting in which repetitious practice on important building blocks can be made fun and in which other students can be used as models. Although we have most often worked with groups of five to fifteen students, at advanced levels and with less-disadvantaged students larger groups have been used effectively.

Teaching Procedures

Teaching procedures change with the development of student skills. Some of the more distinctive features of Direct Instruction (e.g., choral responding on signal with rapid pacing in small-group instruction) occur primarily in the early levels of the DISTAR program. Signals facilitate attention and keep some children from cuing on what the others say (Carnine, 1981). Rapid pacing keeps the students interested and allows more material to be covered in a fixed time (Carnine, 1976). As the students develop skills, more activities are built into the programs. By tying workbook or other seat-work activities closely to what has been taught (so that the students can do them) and by carefully monitoring their work, the commonly observed low productivity of seat-work time can be avoided. With careful programming, it is also possible to anticipate the kinds of errors students will make and to prepare the teacher to correct them with effective procedures.

For the school psychologist, the specification of critical teacher behaviors dramatically simplifies the process of observation and can assist in the identification of target behaviors during the process of instructional consultation. Given the complexity of the interactions that typically occur during instruction, it is vital that the school psychologist have a good understanding of which behaviors on the part of teachers are most likely to increase or diminish the effectiveness of a given instructional presentation. For a more detailed discussion of the relationship between specific teaching procedures and the process of instruction see Carnine and Silbert's text *Direct Instruction Reading* (1979).

Motivating procedures. It is common knowledge that students who have skill deficiencies tend to avoid schoolwork. It is therefore important to build strong motivational procedures into teaching programs for basic instruction with children who are behind and in remedial programs. With Direct Instruction, a variety of strategies are aimed at facilitating motivation. These include (a) rapid confirmation of correct responses; (b) frequent use of praise; (c) use of races against the teacher to help to consolidate skills; (d) use of intentional mistakes by the teacher to teach students to think for themselves, to learn that they are smart, and to challenge authority; (e) use of story lines that introduce humor, plots, and absurdities that catch the students' attention; (f) giving of points for good learning performance that lead to a grade and/or special activities or treats; and (g) use of goals and charts of progress. The advanced programs use charting of student progress and point-contract systems tied to grades to aid motivation. School psychologists utilizing applied behavior analysis to design motivational programs for individual students will find that these motivational procedures provide an ideal framework.

Training Procedures

With scripted programs, it is possible to train teachers to deliver instruction in much the same way that actors learn to deliver their lines. Directed practice is given that uses the general strategy of model, lead, and test (Carnine and Fink, 1978). A supervisor shows the teachers what to do by pretending the teachers are students and the supervisor is the teacher. Then the teachers teach the tasks to the supervisor. Finally, the teachers carry out the instruction on their own, with pairs of teachers taking turns being teacher and student. Preservice workshops are usually followed by actual classroom observation, classroom demonstrations, and in-service workshops. The training requirements for various programs vary from one to two full days of training. This may be followed up by several hours of in-service training during the year.

Training teachers to use effective techniques is a crucial aspect of the Direct Instruction model. And the training does not come about through lectures, discussions, or conferences. In Direct Instruction, expert teachers are trained to work as coaches with other teachers. The coaches model and observe teachers as they try new teaching techniques. The coaches give feedback, have the teachers try again, and come back at later times to see if the teachers are properly executing a new technique. Even with intensive coaching, most teachers take more than a year to learn techniques such as reminding students how to apply a strategy learned previously (Gersten, Carnine, Zoref, & Cronin, 1986).

However, it is clear that even individuals with little or no teaching experience can learn to be highly effective teachers with such training. It is also important that school psychologists and other teacher consultants realize that the volume of training that typically accompanies the introduction of most new instructional programs is woefully inadequate. Thus school psychologists acting as instructional consultants must be prepared for consulting relationships that are more extended than those that are typically associated with the completion of a typical individual psychoeducational evaluation.

Formative Evaluation

Direct Instruction places a strong emphasis on the use of formative evaluation during the course of program development and program implementation. There is a growing body of literature that attests to the importance of formative evaluation both in the design of programs and the practice of teaching (Fuchs, 1986; Gersten, Carnine, & White, 1984; Lovitt, 1981; White & Haring, 1980; Fuchs, Deno, & Mirkin, 1984).

A variety of formative evaluation procedures are utilized in Direct Instruction. Criterion-referenced tests to monitor student (and teacher) performance are built into (or available for) each Direct Instruction program. Items on these criterion-referenced measures are designed to correspond to specific instructional tracks so that the remedial implications of the failure of a particular item are clear. Student performance on specific classes of items can be easily utilized to define areas in which additional instruction is required. Teachers can also utilize the results of these measures to identify areas in which there may be weaknesses in the instruction being provided. For example, if all students in a beginning reading group are having difficulty passing the blending items on the criterion-referenced test, then the teacher should give some attention to the manner in which blending tasks are being presented.

In addition to student performance on criterion-referenced tests administered throughout the course of the program, student progress is measured in terms of content covered. Content covered is typically measured in terms of lessons, where it is expected that a high-ability group will cover from 1.2 to 1.5 lessons per day and the lowest group is expected to cover at least 0.7 lessons per day.

Both criterion-referenced tests and content covered are program-specific measures and may not be adequate for measuring progress towards long-term goals. Recently a variety of authors have indicated the importance of long-term goal monitoring, noting that such monitoring is better correlated with performance on global achievement tests than the short-term monitoring that is typified by periodic program-based tests. As Fuchs (1986) has indicated, such long-term monitoring typically takes the form of measuring student performance on a large pool of related measures having approximately the same level of difficulty. For example, a series of passages from a basal reader might be identified as test items. Student progress would then be evaluated by monitoring the students' oral reading performance on these passages.

The careful analysis of content that is typical of Direct Instruction facilitates the design of program-based tests that have clear remedial implications. Use of these measures in conjunction with long-term monitoring creates a sensitive evaluation system that can provide immediate and specific information on student progress.

RESEARCH ON DIRECT INSTRUCTION

Taken as a whole, research findings from a number of sources within and outside the United States, that have looked at students at different ages and with different needs attest to the potential of Direct Instruction to contribute to students' competence and confidence.

Findings from Follow-Through Researchers

The National Follow Through Project included a large-scale longitudinal study of over 20 different approaches to teaching economically disadvantaged students in kindergarten through third grade. At the project's peak 7,500 low-income children from 170 communities participated each year. A wide range of low-income communities were represented.

The evaluation of Follow Through was conducted by two impartial, independent agencies. The basic data for the Follow Through Evaluation were collected by Stanford Research Institute and analyzed by Abt Associates (Stebbins, 1976; Stebbins, Pierre, Proper, Anderson, & Cerva, 1977). A paper on the Abt findings, a critique of those results (House, Glass, McLean, & Walker, 1978), and rebuttals by several groups were published in the same issue of the *Harvard Education Review*. (See also Bereiter & Kurland, 1981–1982.) Many points of the House et al. (1978) critique are valid, particularly those citing limitations of research designs in which students are not randomly assigned to the experimental or control groups. However, the major findings of the national evaluation of Follow Through (summarized below) stand in spite of its shortcomings, in part, because of the consistency of the findings over time and across different school districts.

Results: Normative performance. The Abt III and IV Reports provide median grade-equivalent scores by site and by sponsor for four MAT measures: Total Reading, Total Math, Spelling, and Language. The means for these data, by model (converted to percentiles) for students entering kindergarten, are presented in Figure 1. (Scores for entering first-grade students, who had one less year of instruction, are lower.) Figure 1 displays percentiles on a one-fourth standard deviation scale. With this display, differences among sponsors of one-quarter standard deviation or more are easily detected and a norm reference is provided. The 20th percentile, which represents the average expectation for disadvantaged third graders without special help, was chosen for a baseline in drawing the graphs in Figure 1.

The major objective of the Direct Instruction Follow Through Program was to bring the achievement levels of disadvantaged primary students up to the national median. Figure 1 indicates that Direct Instruction students are close to or at national norms on all measures.

A second objective in Follow Through was to determine whether the particular approaches had differential effects or if providing extra funds and outside input from experts produced comparable results. Four sponsors have reading programs that are making some headway toward average reading performance by the end of third grade (Direct Instruction, Behavior Analysis, Bank Street College, and Responsive Education). For Total Math, Direct Instruction is at least one-half of a standard deviation ahead of all the others. For Spelling, the Behavior Analysis program is the only program other than Direct Instruction that approaches national norms. For Language (usage, punctuation, and sentence types) the Direct Instruction program is three-fourths of a standard deviation ahead of all other programs. On all four measures, the approaches apparently differ substantially in effect.

The sponsors are ordered in Figure 2 according to overall rank on percentage of significant outcomes.[1] The first four programs are the only programs with more positive than negative outcomes on some measures. Direct Instruction is the only model that shows consistently positive outcomes across measures. The more open-ended and child-centered programs show consistently negative outcomes. These findings from formal tests were replicated in interviews with parents. Haney (1977) found that parents of children receiving Direct Instruction felt their children received a better education in the primary grades than did parents of children taught by any other approach.

These findings concerning Direct Instruction deserve particular attention. First, Direct Instruction students achieved well not only in basic skills, as defined by Abt, but also in cognitive skills — reading comprehension, math problem solving, and math concepts. Second, Direct Instruction students' scores were quite high in the affective domain, suggesting that competence enhances self-esteem and not

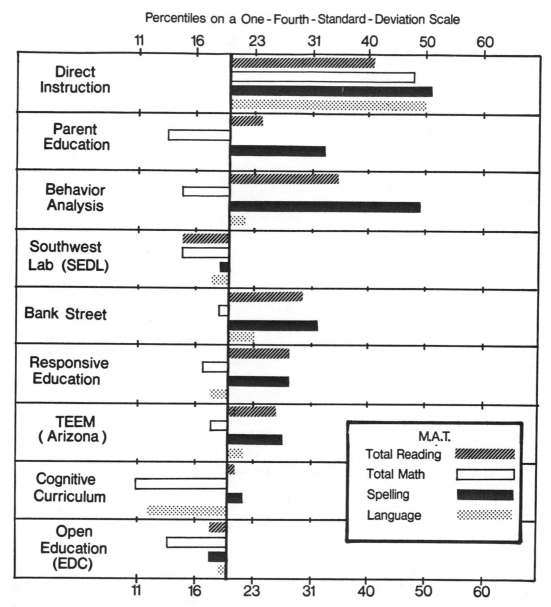

FIGURE 1
Percentile Scores on Four Standardized Test Measures for Nine Major Follow-Through Sponsors

Percentiles on a One - Fourth - Standard - Deviation Scale

vice versa. Other sponsors stressed developing students' self-esteem; yet neither academic nor self-esteem scores was noteworthy.

The affective findings from the Abt report are particularly noteworthy, though the measures suffer from low reliability (Stebbins et al., 1977).

the performance of FT [Follow Through]

children in Direct Instruction sites on the affective measures is an unexpected result. The Direct Instruction model does not explicitly emphasize affective outcomes of instruction, but the sponsor has asserted that they will be the consequence of effective teaching. Critics of the model have predicted that the emphasis on tightly controlled instruction might discourage children from freely express-

FIGURE 2
Percent of Significant Outcomes on Three Types of Measures for Nine Major Follow-Through Sponsors

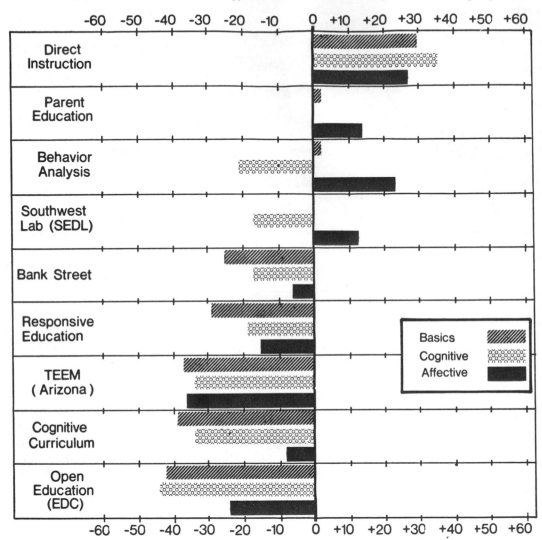

ing themselves, and thus inhibit the development of self-esteem and other affective skills. In fact, this is not the case. (Abt IVB, p. 73)

Findings From the Direct Instruction Follow Through Sponsors

Sponsor-Data collected by the sponsors of the Follow Through evaluation of Direct Instruction support the following conclusions.

1. A greater measurable and educationally significant benefit is present at the end of third grade for those who began Direct Instruction in kindergarten than for those who began in first grade (Becker & Engelmann, 1978; Gersten, Darch, & Gleason, in press).

2. Significant gains in IQ are found, which are largely maintained through third grade. Students entering the program with IQs of more than 111 do not lose during the Follow Through years, though one might expect some repeated regression phenomenon. The low-IQ children, on the other hand, display appreciable gains, even after the entry IQ has

been "corrected". Students with IQs below 71 gain 17 points in the entering kindergarten sample and 9.4 points in the entering first-grade sample; gains for the children with entering IQs in the 71–90 range are 15.6 and 9.2 points, respectively (Gersten, Becker, Heiry, & White, 1984).

3. Studies of low-IQ students (under 80) show that the program is clearly effective with students who have a higher probability of failure. As indicated in Figures 3 and 4, these students gain nearly as much each year in reading (decoding) and math, as the Direct Instruction students with higher IQs — more than a year per year on the Wide-Range Achievement Test in reading (WRAT) but year for year on MAT Total Math (Gersten, Becker, Heiry, & White, 1984).

4. Follow-up studies of Direct Instruction and comparison students were carried out in five districts. All the significant differences favored the Direct Instruction students: five on academic measures, three on attendance, two on college acceptance, and three on reduced retention rates (Gersten & Keating, 1987).

5. The model generalizes across both time and populations. The Department of Education has a Joint Dissemination Review Panel that validates educational programs as exemplary and qualifies them for national dissemination. During the 1980–1981 school year, the last of the 12 Direct Instruction Follow Through projects were submitted for validation. Of the 12 districts 11 had 8–10 years of data on successive groups of children — replication over time. The schools sampled a full range of students: large cities (New York, San Diego, Washington, DC), middle-sized cities (Flint, MI; Dayton, OH; E. St. Louis, IL); rural white communities (Flippin, AR; Smithville, TN); a rural black community (Williamsburg, SC); Latino communities (Uvalde, TX; E. Las Vegas, NM); and a Native American community (Cherokee, NC). One hundred percent of the projects were certified as exemplary in reading and mathematics for the primary grades, thus providing replication over 8–10 years in a dozen quite diverse communities.

Research on Direct Instruction Preschools

Other researchers have conducted evaluations of Direct Instruction preschool programs for four- and five-year olds. One large longitudinal evaluation was conducted by the Seattle public schools. A report was co-authored with Weikart's High/Scope Foundation (Schweinhart & Mazur, 1987). The 2,883 economically disadvantaged children who participated in Seattle's Direct Instruction preschool program

> achieved better educational placements than a comparable control group ... only 11% of these youngsters left high school before graduation, which is a dropout rate two-thirds the size of the control group's 17% dropout rate. . . . [The program] had more than twice the percentage of students in gifted education and a rate of placement at or above the age-appropriate grade that was 10 percentage points higher than that of the control group (Schweinhart & Mazur, 1987, pp. 18–19).

The findings on placement in gifted programs is particularly noteworthy. The percentage for Direct Instruction students was about the same as for the district as a whole, 8% versus 9%. Yet 95% of the Direct Instruction students were minority, whereas less than 50% of the students in the district as a whole were minority.

A final study was conducted by Weisberg at the University of Alabama (Carnine, Carnine, Kary & Weisberg, in press). The 108 children, virtually all from low-income backgrounds (34% of the children received public assistance and 14% were in foster homes), received instruction over a 9-year period. The first finding was that students who received 2 years of instruction, as 4-year-olds and 5-year-olds, scored significantly higher on standardized reading achievement tests than did students who had only 1 year of instruction. The correlation between number of lessons completed and reading achievement was .92 ($p > .0001$), an extremely strong correlation.

The second finding stemmed from a comparison of students in Direct Instruc-

FIGURE 3
Yearly Gains in Decoding for Students According to IQ

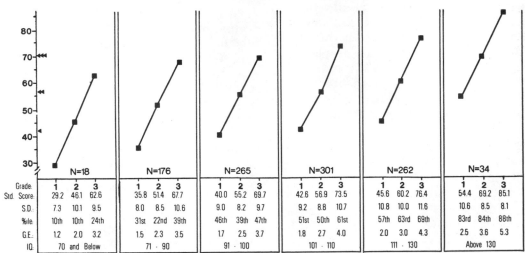

		N=18			N=176			N=265			N=301			N=262			N=34	
Grade:	1	2	3	1	2	3	1	2	3	1	2	3	1	2	3	1	2	3
Std. Score:	29.2	46.1	62.6	35.8	51.4	67.7	40.0	55.2	69.7	42.6	56.9	73.5	45.6	60.2	76.4	54.4	69.2	85.1
S.D.:	7.3	10.1	9.5	8.0	8.5	10.6	9.0	8.2	9.7	9.2	8.8	10.7	10.8	10.0	11.6	10.6	8.5	8.1
%ile:	10th	10th	24th	31st	22nd	39th	46th	39th	47th	51st	50th	61st	57th	63rd	69th	83rd	84th	88th
G.E.:	1.2	2.0	3.2	1.5	2.3	3.5	1.7	2.5	3.7	1.8	2.7	4.0	2.0	3.0	4.3	2.5	3.6	5.3
IQ:	70 and Below			71 - 90			91 - 100			101 - 110			111 - 130			Above 130		

◄ Grade 1 National Median
◄◄ Grade 2 National Median
◄◄◄ Grade 3 National Median

tion, cognitive development, Head Start, and no preschool programs. Students were given the standardized achievement test for first grade at the beginning of first grade, the end of first grade, and the end of second grade. At each time, the Direct Instruction students scored significantly higher than the students in all the other groups. Especially provocative was the writing done by some of the students, such as the story in Figure 5, written by a 5-year old student. (Kathryn was the teacher's name.)

Research on Handicapped Students

Two review papers (Gersten, 1981; Maggs & Maggs, 1979) have summarized many studies of Direct Instruction conducted with handicapped populations. Maggs and Maggs (1979) reviewed 20 studies conducted in Australia with moderately and severely retarded, mildly retarded, learning-disabled, and regular elementary students. Over 1,000 students and 80 teachers were involved in the studies.

The results demonstrate the Direct Instruction programs have been effective across settings and populations when independently evaluated against norm-referenced and criterion-referenced dependent measures. In addition, the results exceeded the usual expectations held for these populations in relation to academic and intellectual achievement. (Maggs & Maggs, 1979, p. 26)

Other research, in the United States, has applied some of the principles of Direct Instruction to reading instruction for learning-disabled (Lloyd, Cullinan, Heins, & Epstein, 1980) and minimal brain dysfunction children (Stein & Goldman, 1980) and to training in nonacademic curriculum for severely handicapped populations — community living skills (Close, Irvin, Taylor, & Agosta, 1981) and vocational education (Horner & Bellamy, 1978).

CURRICULUM DESIGN

We have seen that there is a large body of evidence that attests to the effectiveness of the Direct Instruction programs. However, school psychologists are typically not at liberty to specify student placement in a particular instructional program. Nevertheless, school psychologists can assist more effectively in the

FIGURE 4
Yearly Gains in Math for Students According to IQ

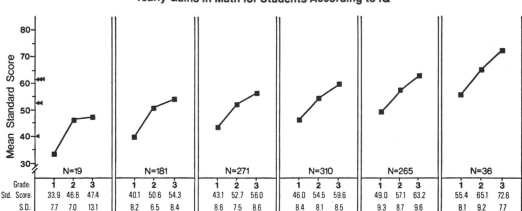

Grade:	1	2	3	1	2	3	1	2	3	1	2	3	1	2	3	1	2	3
Std. Score:	33.9	46.6	47.4	40.1	50.6	54.3	43.1	52.7	56.0	46.0	54.5	59.6	49.0	57.1	63.2	55.4	65.1	72.6
S.D.:	7.7	7.0	13.1	8.2	6.5	8.4	8.6	7.5	8.6	8.4	8.1	8.5	9.3	8.7	9.6	8.1	9.2	7.7
%ile:	30th	22nd	11th	50th	41st	29th	66th	51st	34th	78th	59th	44th	88th	70th	58th	94th	88th	81st
G.E.:	1.6	2.2	2.3	1.9	2.5	2.8	2.0	2.7	3.0	2.2	2.9	3.4	2.4	3.1	3.7	2.9	3.9	4.9
IQ:	70 and Below			71 - 90			91 - 100			101 - 110			111 - 130			Above 130		

◄ Grade 1 National Median
◄◄ Grade 2 National Median
◄◄◄ Grade 3 National Median

design and implementation of individual educational programs if they are aware of the most critical features of quality instruction.

Direct Instruction assumes that learning is primarily the product of instructional communication, that is, what the teacher presents to the student, rather than the characteristics of the learner. The principles of instructional communication deal with the range of generalizations implied in the presentation of a specific set of examples. If a communication is vague or ambiguous, it conveys more than one possible generalization or discrimination. Some students will learn any generalization that is implied by the communication, whether or not it is the intended generalization. For example, when students learn to rename in subtraction, they often ignore numeral location and make errors like these:

$$
\begin{array}{r} 72 \\ -\ 15 \\ \hline 63 \end{array}
\quad \text{or} \quad
\begin{array}{r} 94 \\ -\ 27 \\ \hline 73 \end{array}
$$

These errors are reasonable generalizations implied by earlier instruction in addition, where numeral location is irrelevant. When renaming is introduced it's no surprise that they ignore numeral location, and subtract the smaller number from the larger. Similar examples can be drawn from language arts instruction.

The Direct Instruction analysis deals not only with modes of communication, but also with systems of knowledge classification. Ideally, the classification of any skill should indicate not merely something about its structure but also how it is to be communicated. In other words, there should be a parallel between the structure of the concept or skill taught and a communication formula for teaching it. The two objectives of organizing different types of knowledge are (a) to provide an exhaustive system for classification of any cognitive operation, from simple discriminations to complex operations, and (b) to link the classification system with instructional procedures, so that all concepts within a particular class or category can be processed through variations of the same communication form.

The Direct Instruction model assumes that knowledge can be classified into one or more of these four categories: (a) basic

FIGURE 5
Story written by Five-Year Old Low Income Student in Direct Instruction Preschool

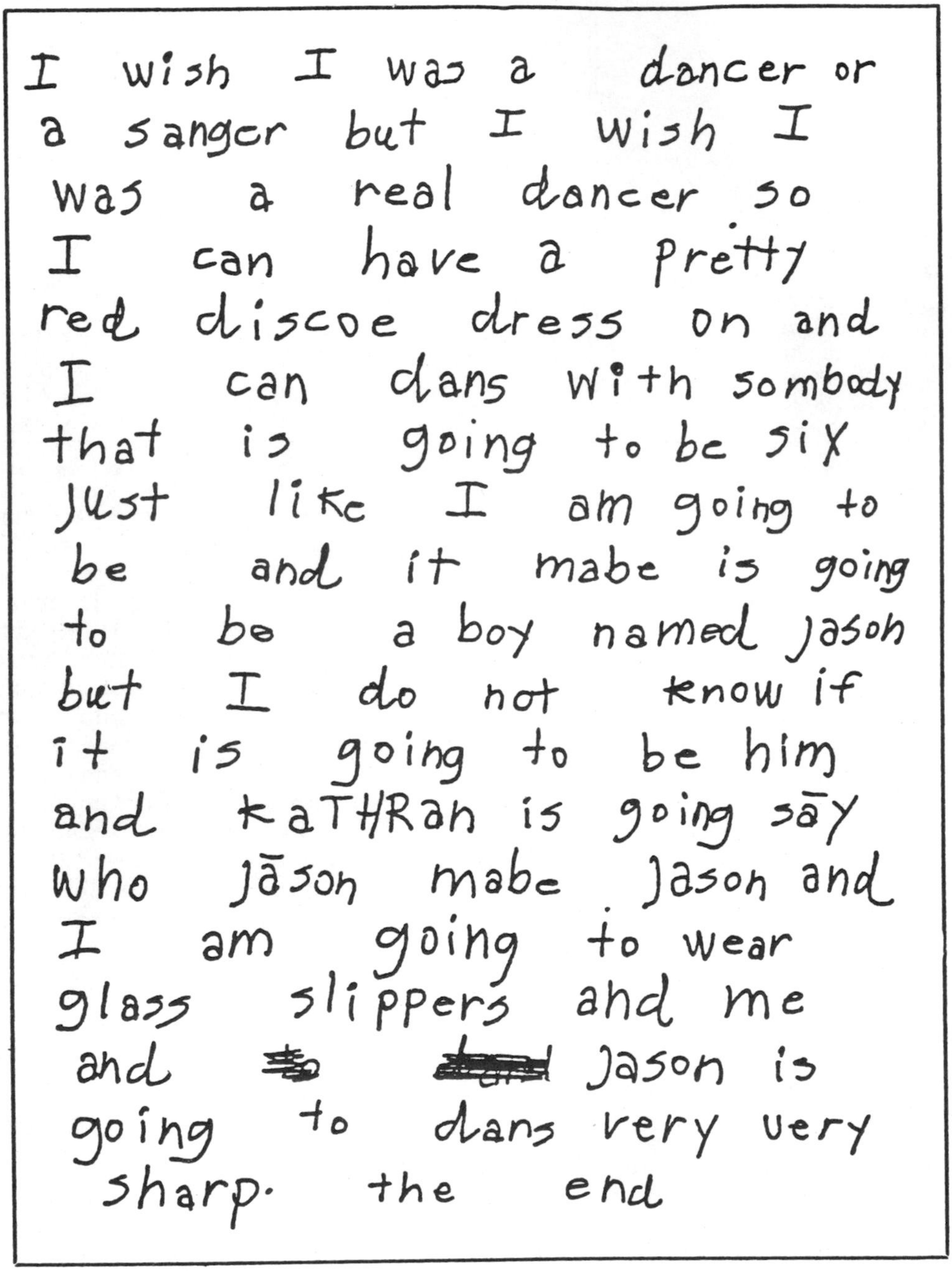

I wish I was a dancer or
a sanger but I wish I
was a real dancer so
I can have a pretty
red discoe dress on and
I can dans with sombody
that is going to be six
just like I am going to
be and it mabe is going
to be a boy named Jason
but I do not know if
it is going to be him
and kaTHRan is going say
who Jason mabe Jason and
I am going to wear
glass slippers and me
and ~~so~~ ~~girl~~ Jason is
going to dans very very
sharp. the end

concepts, (b) rules, (c) cognitive routines, and (d) fact systems.

The four major categories subsume over 20 classes of knowledge and over a dozen principles for constructing communications. The discussion that follows illustrates only a few of these classes and principles. A complete exposition, as well as additional research references, are found in *Theory of Instruction* (Engelmann & Carnine, 1982).

Basic Concepts

Basic concepts cannot be reduced to simpler forms, and they cannot be clarified through verbal explanation. Basic concepts have to do with specific meanings of words like hotter, steeper, red, under, back, truck, door, sit, horizontal, and girl. To communicate any basic concept, examples must be presented, some of which show what the concept is (positive examples) and others what the concept is not (negative examples). To test the effectiveness of such a presentation a test must be provided on examples other than those demonstrated or modeled by the teacher.

The following discussion illustrates, drawing on research studies, several principles from communication formulas for basic concepts, such as comparatives and prepositions. Each principle is illustrated through the teaching of the preposition *over* and is presented in the form of a question that a school psychologist might ask when observing instruction designed to teach basic concepts.

Does the demonstration present a range of positive examples? It is impossible to convey a basic concept like *over* through the presentation of only one concrete example. A corollary is that it is very difficult to convey only one interpretation if only positive examples are used.

Does the demonstration present negative examples? Positive examples are not to be used exclusively. In teaching the concept *over*, for example, the teacher could hold the pencil to the side or under a table to create negative examples. If negative examples are not provided, students are more likely to treat a range of undemonstrated negative examples as positive (Williams & Carnine, 1981).

Are the differences between negative examples and positive examples clear? A negative example logically rules out a maximum number of misinterpretations when it is least different from some positive example. Failure to illustrate such minimum differences may result in higher error rates when test items outside the original instruction are presented. In fact, Carnine (1980), using five separate example sets, found a significant linear trend between the similarity of positive and negative examples and correct responses on a transfer test. This finding suggests that the greater the number of possible interpretations, the greater the probability that some students will learn an interpretation other than the one intended.

Does the demonstration use juxtapositions effectively? Juxtapositions may be used for showing differences. When minimum-difference examples are juxtaposed and treated differently, the intended interpretation becomes obvious. This principle would be applied in teaching *over* by having the teacher hold a pencil over the table and labeling it *over*, then moving the pencil slightly to the side of the table and labeling it *not over*. In two studies Granzin and Carnine (1977) presented a set of examples to primary students, but altered the order of example presentation, which allowed them to compare the effects of minimum-difference juxtapositions of positive and negative examples with random difference juxtapositions. Training was completed in significantly fewer trials for the minimum-difference juxtaposition groups in both studies.

Does the demonstration indicate the range of positive variation? Range of positive variation also must be considered. According to the principle for showing the range, if juxtaposed positive examples differ greatly and are treated in the same way, appropriate generalization is implied. In teaching *over*, the teacher would move the pencil to many different places above the table. A study conducted by Carnine (1980) tested this principle by varying the range of positive examples in teaching students to convert fractions to decimals. The findings indicated that students receiving a demonstration of fraction to decimal conversion that were presented with the widest variation in positive examples made significantly fewer errors on a transfer test than a group receiving an equal number of demonstrations with a more restricted range of examples.

Does the demonstration utilize continuous conversions? Continuous conversions occur when one example is transformed into the next without any interruption. They are assumed to increase the obviousness of the difference between positive and negative examples. For *over*, a teacher moves the pencil to generate positive and negative examples, rather than presenting different pictures of positive and negative examples. Gersten, White, Falco, and Carnine (1982) compared continuous and noncontinuous conversions sequences in four different studies, two with preschoolers and two with handicapped children. In all four studies, the same positive and negative examples were presented continuously and noncontinuously for diagonal or convex. The continuous conversion groups met the criteria of performance in significantly fewer trials than the noncontinuous conversion groups. Continuous conversion is logically superior to noncontinuous conversion because if an example is converted into the next, only the "active" dimension of the presentation is manipulated. A number of features remain unchanged from example to example. If a change from negative to positive results, whatever details remain the same are irrelevant to the change in label. The detail that changes is therefore shown to be critical.

Does the demonstration utilize precise, consistent communication? Consistent instructions prompt the learner to discover how the examples are the same. If this interpretation is correct, communications that are not precise in treating examples of the same concept in the same way will not communicate as early as presentations that are precise. For example, imprecise communications for *over* would include instructions such as "Hold your hand over the table", or "What flies over trees?" or "Tell me something that's not over my desk."

When Williams and Carnine (1981) compared the performance of preschoolers taught a simple positional discrimina-tion with a fixed set of positive and negative examples, they found that the groups of students asked to do the same thing to all examples reached criterion in half as many trials as the group that was presented with a variety of response options.

The preceding analysis of demonstrations used to teach basic concepts is not exhaustive; however, it should provide a basis for critical evaluation of instructional practices that are commonly used in both regular and special education classrooms to teach the most fundamental units in the knowledge hierarchy.

Rules

Rules involve relationships between concepts. Students might understand the concepts but not the relationship between the concepts. A learner might understand *get hotter* and *get bigger*, but not the relationship *if solid things get hotter, they get bigger*.

A suggested procedure for teaching the relationship is first to ask about the outcome implied by the relationship and then ask, "How do you know?" The answer to this second question makes overt the relationship between the two concepts.

Ross and Carnine (1982) demonstrated the importance of using such a questioning strategy when teaching new relationships to young children. They also found that without specification of a rule most children failed to discover the relationship, even though the range of examples thought to be required to induce the generalization was provided and even though a large number of practice examples was provided.

If a learner is highly sophisticated, the presentation of a rule without any applications should be sufficient to imply how the rule would be applied to any specific examples; however, to make the communication perfectly clear for less sophisticated students, the presentation of the rule should be followed by application to a range of examples that demonstrate sameness of response. Carnine, Kameenui, and Maggs (1982) verified this when teaching the following rule to first and second graders: "the lower you eat on the food ladder, the more protein you get."

Cognitive Routines

Cognitive routines are invented to help learners process complex problems. The routine is necessary for communications to be consistent with a single generalization or interpretation. It serves as a bridge, a mnemonic that shows the naive learner precisely what to do in solving problems of a given kind. Once the learner has mastered the routine and has applied it to various problems, the overt instruction on the routine is systematically removed and the learner is prompted to carry it out covertly. Instruction on cognitive routines allows students with special needs to learn more complex skills in a school year and to make fewer errors.

The reason for teaching cognitive operations in an overt way is to make them more like physical operations. The physical environment provides feedback to the learner for all applications of physical operations but not on cognitive operations. Physical operations include fitting jigsaw pieces together, throwing a ball, "nesting" cups together, swimming, and buttoning a coat. When the learner performs any physical operation, the physical environment provides feedback, which often takes the form of contingencies such as preventing the learner from continuing or providing some unpleasant consequence for inappropriate actions. For example, if the learner does not carry out the operation of tucking correctly when going into a forward roll, the physical environment may provide the learner with unpleasant consequences. Since the physical environment "interferes" only when the operation is not being performed correctly, the "response" from the physical environment carries a precise message: Some behavior must change.

Another important feature of physical operations is that all actions that account for achieving the goal of the operation are overt. Hence, analysis of the task is simple. However, to generalize the principles of physical operations to cognitive ones is misleading.

For any cognitive operation, no necessary overt behaviors account for its completion. Reading does not entail overt actions that account for successful comprehension. This point is extremely important. *Cognitive operations do not exist in the same sense that physical operations do.* Since the physical environment does not specify overt behaviors for cognitive operations, the communication of cognitive operations remains imprecise and inadequate unless we invent adequate communications. To do this, we design operations or routines that do what the physical operations do. The test of an adequate design is this: Can any observed outcome be totally explained by the overt measures the learner has taken? If the answer is yes, the cognitive routine is designed so that adequate feedback is possible.

In a study comparing overt procedures with covert procedures, Carnine (1977) taught two groups of preschoolers to read a set of regularly spelled words. They were later tested on generalization to both regularly spelled and irregularly spelled words (none of which appeared in training). One group received instruction on component skills and instruction on performing a sounding-out operation for identifying words. The other group received only look–say practice on the words in the training set. The sounding-out group reached the training criterion faster, performed significantly better on the transfer test, and averaged over three times as many correct word identifications as the look–say subjects. The study clearly implies that if overt procedures are applied to identifying the various elements that cause one word to be different from another (the individual letters), the instruction will more precisely communicate generalizable word-attack skills.

Additional support for the importance of making the steps in cognitive routines overt has been provided by a series of studies that involved a broad range of tasks including the identification of faulty arguments (Patching, Kameenui, Carnine, Gersten, & Colvin, 1983), problem solving (Fielding, 1980), and responding to general comprehension questions on complex reading passages (Carnine, Kameenui, & Woolfson, 1982). These studies strongly suggest that clarifying instruction by making the steps overt in complex cognitive routines is critical not only for the naive learner during initial instruction in reading but also for much more sophisticated students approaching difficult tasks such as the logical analysis of arguments.

Given that students must eventually function without Direct Instruction, we might expect that routines initially presented in overt form might be utilized in a covert fashion when students work independently. The assumption of the present analysis is that teaching an overt operation does not imply that learners will perform the steps of the operation covertly unless they are presented a variant of the overt operation that can be performed covertly. The effectiveness of teaching students how to utilize overt routines covertly has been demonstrated in a variety of contexts (Paine & Carnine, 1981; Carnine, Carnine, & Gersten, 1984).

Many other studies have investigated various aspects of cognitive routines, in study skills (Adams, Carnine, & Gersten, 1982), comprehension (Carnine & Kinder, 1985), word problems (Darch, Carnine, & Gersten, 1984), and math computation (Kameenui, Carnine, Darch, & Stein, 1986). The analyses of cognitive routines are explained in detail in *Direct Instruction Reading* (Carnine & Silbert, 1979) and *Direct Instruction Mathematics* (Silbert, Carnine, & Stein, 1981).

There are a number of additional factors that are critical in designing instruction in cognitive routines. Making the steps in the routine overt will be of little value if the routine is not applied to a broad range of examples. More critically, communications must demonstrate clearly the important commonalities across related problem types and provide specific feedback to students on their application of the routine. Limited space does not allow us to develop more fully application of these design principles to specific instructional examples. A more thorough exposition can be found in Engelmann and Carnine (1982).

In summary, the Direct Instruction analysis assumes that cognitive routines are best designed if they (a) teach preskills first, (b) are made up of overt steps, (c) are applied to a broad range of examples, (d) provide feedback, and (e) are eventually made covert, that is, are internalized by the learner.

Fact Systems

If a primary purpose of content area textbooks is indeed to "inform" and if it is agreed that this informing should be done efficiently, it seems necessary to examine different ways of efficiently "informing" the students. This is especially true when one acknowledges the "inconsiderate" words, cohesive ties, syntactic links, and intrasentential anaphora facing students in many passages in content area textbooks (Armbruster, 1984). It can be argued that the "inconsiderateness" of content area textbooks not only makes it difficult for a reader to extract critical points of information from the text, but it also short-circuits the reader's ability to develop a more complete schema of the text. The perception that content area textbooks are designed to inform and should do so efficiently, coupled with the view that these texts are "inconsiderate," suggests that perhaps a different examination of content area texts is in order.

One very promising approach is "instructional graphics," in particular, graphic organizers. These formats for organizing information rely on the use of lines, arrows, geometric shapes, and spatial arrangements that describe the text content, structure, and key conceptual relationships typically found in a content area text. (See Figure 6.) In the case of graphic organizers, the arrangement of ideas, facts, concepts, and ideational relationships are presented visually and in parallel with a text. The explicit purpose of a graphic organizer for content area texts is to highlight for the reader the interrelationships of ideas and the logical connections between higher-order concepts and lower-order concepts. The

FIGURE 6
Graphic Organizer for Teaching a Fact System Involving Terrain, Vegetation, Animals, and Industries

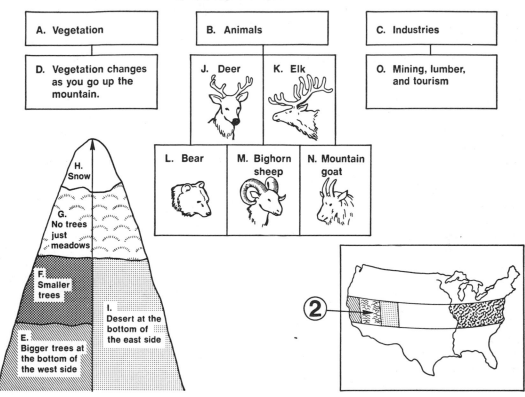

assumption is that a reader informed about the hierarchical arrangements of information in a text is more likely to understand the overall meaning of the text as well as the relationship of individual concepts and facts to each other. To acquire the information, the reader is required to study the visual or graphic arrangement of the information as it is visually depicted.

Initial research into the effectiveness of using graphic organizers in teaching material from content area texts (Darch & Carnine, 1986; Darch, Carnine, & Kameenui, 1986) suggests that the application of such strategies can markedly improve student performance. However, further research will be necessary in order to provide teachers with a specific set of procedures for the application of graphic organizers in existing instructional contexts.

Although the complexity and volume of the findings reported here may initially appear to be overwhelming, the simplicity and elegance of the analysis recommends it to those practitioners, such as school psychologists, who are faced with evaluating student performance in instructional contexts. The simplicity of the Direct Instruction analysis of curriculum can be illustrated by restating the two major goals that have served as the foundation of this analysis: (a) to provide an exhaustive system that permits classification of any cognitive operation; and (b) to link the classification system with instructional procedures, so that all concepts within a particular class or category can be processed through variations of the same communication form.

When such an analysis is utilized, a more precise and potentially more useful analysis of student performance can be conducted — an instructional assessment that takes into consideration not only variables peculiar to the learner (intelligence, skill level, memory, etc.) but also those equally critical variables related to curriculum and teaching techniques.

NEW DIRECTIONS

Underlying the many studies on Direct Instruction is the crucial role of the teacher. The precision and specificity of Direct Instruction, the complexity of the curriculum analysis, the emphasis on increasing the amount of academic engaged time, and the heavy teacher responsibility for student success — all of these make it very demanding to be a Direct Instruction teacher. During the last 4 years we have been looking at ways to make the role of the teacher more manageable, by exploiting the capabilities of various technologies: computer-assisted instruction, low-cost networking, and videodisk courses. The curriculum design procedures described earlier take advantage of the capabilities of the technologies to improve overall instruction.

Videodisk Courses

Videodisk technology allows an interactive format that is not possible with conventional audiovisual materials. The teacher can jump to a particular demonstration within a few seconds. After showing a dynamic demonstration, the disk stops automatically, with a series of questions for students to answer. The question screen remains frozen until the teacher judges that the students have had time to formulate their answers.

Videodisk technology also dynamically presents experiments and demonstrations that are difficult or expensive to conduct in the classroom. Vivid visual demonstrations are associated with nearly every concept that is presented, rendering them easily understood. Computer graphics, sound effects, brisk pacing, highlights, and other techniques also help maintain students' attention.

Each videodisk course published by Systems Impact in Washington, DC (1985-

1987), is presented to an entire class of students on a large monitor. It has a specific system for helping teachers diagnose and remedy students' learning difficulties. This system is incorporated in six steps that are utilized in connection with all concepts introduced in the program:

1. During the initial explanation of a concept, the narrator on the videodisk asks questions that students answer orally.
2. Immediately following the initial explanation students write answers to a series of problems. Students get feedback after working each problem. The last problem serves as an informal test. If more than 20% of the students miss it, the teacher plays an explanation from the disk. This pattern of demonstration followed by practice is repeated for each concept presented in a lesson.
3. Students do homework (without supervision).
4. The next lesson begins with a quiz covering the one or two major concepts introduced in the previous lesson. The screen gives the disk address for a remediation if one is needed.
5. Every fifth lesson is a test. Again, teachers diagnose student errors and select remedies from the disk on the basis of student performance.
6. After being tested, a concept is reviewed every few lessons.

This instructional design, videodisk technology, and six-step mastery learning procedure make it easier for the teacher to present essential content in a visually compelling manner. Current research with special education teachers is finding that the videodisk course is easy to use and a very effective instructional tool (Kelly, Carnine, Gersten, & Grossen, 1986). Courses like "Understanding Chemistry and Energy" are particularly helpful to less confident teachers, since the academic content is presented in a clear fashion from which students will learn. Moreover, the course provides an in-class, daily model of effective teaching practices.

Computer-Assisted Instruction

Health promotion. Computer simulations can track complex interactions in ways that would overwhelm a teacher. For example, Woodward, Carnine, and Gersten (in press) taught learning-disabled students problem-solving strategies for profiles of health-related facts concerning heredity, disease, nutrition, exercise, stress management, drinking, smoking, life styles, and so on by means of a computer simulation. The problem-solving strategy required students to prioritize and change undesirable health habits, check stress level, and maintain health habit changes over time. The mastery learning procedure required students to successfully apply the strategy to simpler profiles before more complex ones were introduced. The careful teaching of prerequisite content, combined with instruction on explicit problem-solving strategies, produced proficiency in health promotion analysis in more than two-thirds of the 15 handicapped students. Only two of 15 nonhandicapped seniors in a health class exhibited this same level of problem-solving sophistication.

Reasoning skills. One of the advantages of computer-assisted instruction is the capability to give fairly extensive, individualized feedback to students when they make mistakes. Collins, Carnine, and Gersten (1987) conducted research on process feedback, which related student errors to previously taught rules. The computer assisted instruction program taught individual remedial and learning-disabled students to draw syllogistic conclusions and to critique arguments. Students learned step-by-step procedures for constructing and critiquing arguments. Process feedback led to significantly higher scores on the posttest and a transfer test, yet students did not take significantly more time to complete the program.

In a later study (Collins & Carnine, in press), the performance of four groups of students was compared: learning disabled high school students, general education high school students, college students in an introductory logic class, and college preservice education students. On the constructing-arguments subtest, the learning disabled students were quite proficient, being comparable to their general education peers and to the logic students. The college preservice education students scored significantly lower than the other three groups. On the critiquing-arguments subtest, the logic students scored significantly higher than the other three groups.

The capacity of computers to keep track of student responses over a long period of time and to adjust instruction on a large sample of items according to type and frequency of error has also been exploited in instructional programs designed to teach vocabulary (Johnson, Gersten, & Carnine, 1987).

Low-Cost Networking

The studies cited above illustrate a variety of technologies, curriculum design principles, and mastery learning procedures that contribute to the effectiveness of instructional programs. However, efficiency is another important program attribute. If technology can free the teacher by providing instruction, a significant efficiency is realized. Consider vocabulary instruction. Students taught under a program developed by Beck, Perfetti, and McKeown (1982) learned an average of 85–104 words presented, but it required 2250 minutes — considerably more than that typically devoted to vocabulary instruction in secondary schools.

In contrast, the computer-assisted program in the Johnson et al. study (1987) taught about 30 words, but a teacher was not required to instruct. Similarly, the reasoning skills program did not require a teacher. Although the computer simulation and videodisk courses required a teacher, the technology still made the instruction much more efficient. For example, in one study a teacher presented the content of the *Mastering Fractions* program on overheads rather than on the videodisk. The students learned as much from the overhead presentation as did other students (randomly assigned) who learned from the videodisk course. However, the teacher who used the overheads required a half-time assistant to create and manage the overheads (Hasselbring, Sherwood, & Bransford, 1986).

Other research we have conducted has focused more exclusively on a low-cost networking system as a means of increasing efficiency. The technology was *Teacher Net*, a system that instantly gives both teachers and students feedback on performance by networking eight or more keyboards to a single IBM computer (Carnine, 1984). In a study by Golden (1986), learning-disabled secondary students responded on their own keypads to questions interspersed throughout a series of instructional sessions on reading comprehension. Responses were immediately scored and summarized by Teacher Net for the teacher. Consequently, the teacher was able to immediately adjust her class presentation to address the difficulties experienced by individual students. These students had higher posttest scores than comparison students taught the same comprehension curriculum without Teacher Net. Other studies using Teacher Net have found comparable time savings in providing computer-assisted video instruction, test administration, scoring of independent work, and calculating grades (Woodward, Carnine, Gersten, Moore, & Golden, 1987).

The new directions in technology have a common theme — helping teachers become better professionals. The applications range from clerical to supportive to stand alone instruction. All these roles are necessary and technology can help with each.

SUMMARY

The findings presented here establish a strong case both for the use of Direct Instruction and for the application of direct instruction principles in the process of instruction. Of critical importance is the finding that school psychologists and other school personnel have access to innovative materials and teaching practices that are of demonstrated effectiveness. Although school psychologists are seldom placed in the position of directly teaching students, they often assist in designing and evaluating student programs. They act as advocates for children who are experiencing limited academic success; in that capacity they can fruitfully search for explanation of such failure in that they take into account not only student characteristics but also the process of instruction.

However, for school psychologists to act as effective instructional consultants they must be adequately trained. Given the current rather extensive devotion of resources to assessment, this might seem to represent a somewhat insurmountable task. It is encouraging, then, to note that Direct Instruction programs have an extensive history of effective implementation at the paraprofessional level. The ease with which these programs are implemented and the growing but generally convergent literature on Direct Instruction make it possible for students to master a set of principles that guide program design, implementation, and evaluation.

Using these principles and more general skills in consultation, school psychologists can place themselves in a position to have a significant impact on the quality of instructional programs. Furthermore, the effective application of the principles discussed in this chapter can help to restore a balance to analysis of learning problems. That is, an equivalent amount of attention can be devoted to an analysis of the process of instruction without assuming that all failure is the result of student deficiency. It has been argued elsewhere (Engelmann, Granzin, & Severson, 1979) that to search for student pathology without first analyzing the quality of instruction being provided is folly; we find little reason to challenge that argument at this time.

FOOTNOTE

[1]The major findings of the Abt Report are given in a series of tables, one for each sponsor. For each measure, a covariance adjusted comparison was made with a *local* comparison group and with a *pooled* national comparison group. When the mean

for the Follow Through students exceeded the non-Follow Through mean by at least one-fourth of a standard deviation on a given measure, and when the difference was statistically significant, this was considered an educationally significant outcome, and a plus (+) was placed in the table. When non-Follow Through exceeded Follow Through by the same criteria, it was considered to be a significant negative outcome, and a minus (-) was placed on the table. When the results fell between these limits, the difference was considered null and the table left blank. The number of pluses for each sponsor for each of the three types of measures was counted (for the cognitive academic skills, the Raven's Progressive Matricies test, which is not an academic measure, was excluded). Then the number of minuses was subtracted, and the result was divided by the number of comparisons. Both local and pooled comparisons were included. Decimals were converted to percents by multiplying by 100.

REFERENCES

Adams, A., Carnine, D., & Gersten, R. (1982). Instructional strategies for studying content area texts in the intermediate grades. *Reading Research Quarterly, 181*(4), 406-418.

Armbruster, B. B. (1984). The problem of "inconsiderate text." In G. G. Duffy, L. R. Roehler, & J. Mason (Eds.), *Comprehension instruction: Perspectives and suggestions* (pp. 202-217). New York: Longman.

Beck, I. L., Perfetti, C. A., & McKeown, M. G. (1982). Effects of long-term vocabulary instruction on lexical access and reading comprehension. *Journal of Educational Psychology, 74*, 506-521.

Becker, W. C., & Engelmann, S. (1978). *Analysis of achievement data on six cohorts of low-income children from 20 school districts in the University of Oregon Direct Instruction Follow Through Model* (Technical Report 78-1). Eugene, OR: University of Oregon.

Bennett, N., et al. (1976). *Teaching styles and pupil progress.* Cambridge, MA: Harvard University Press.

Bereiter, C., & Kurland, M. (1981-1982). A constructive look at Follow Through results. *Interchange, 12*, 1-22.

Brophy, J. E., & Evertson, C. M. (1976). *Learning from teaching: A developmental perspective.* Boston: Allyn & Bacon.

Brophy, J., & Good, T. (1986). Teacher behavior and student achievement. In M. Wittrock (Ed.), *The third handbook of research on teaching* (pp. 328-375). New York: Macmillan.

Carnine, D. W. (1976). Effects of two teacher presentation rates on off-task behavior, answering correctly, and participation. *Journal of Applied Behavioral Analysis, 9*, 199-206.

Carnine, D. W. (1977). Phonics versus look-say: Transfer to new words. *Reading Teacher, 30*(6), 636-640.

Carnine, D. W. (1980). Relationships between stimulus variation and the formation of misconceptions. *Journal of Educational Research, 74*, 106-110.

Carnine, D. W. (1981). High and low implementation of direct instruction teaching techniques. *Education and Treatment of Children, 4*(1), 42-51.

Carnine, D. (1984). Mainstreaming computers. *Educational Leadership, 41*(8), 77-82.

Carnine, D., Carnine, L., Karp, J., & Weisberg, P. (in press). Kindergarten for economically disadvantaged children: The Direct Instruction component. In B. Day (Ed.), *Options for early childhood education*, Alexandria, VA: Association for Supervision and Curriculum Development.

Carnine, D. W., & Fink, W. T. (1978). Increasing the rate of question-asking and use of signals in direct instruction trainees. *Journal of Applied Behavior Analysis, 11*, 34-56.

Carnine, D. W., Kameenui, E. J., & Maggs, A. (1982). Components of analytic assistance: Statement saying, concept training, and strategy training. *Journal of Educational Research, 75*, 374-377.

Carnine, D. W., Kameenui, E. J., & Woolfson, N. (1982). Training of textual dimensions related to text-based inferences. *Journal of Reading Behavior, 14*(3), 335-340.

Carnine, D., & Kinder, D. (1985). Teaching low-performing students to apply generative and schema strategies to narrative and expository material. *Remedial and Special Education, 6*(1), 20-30.

Carnine, D. W. & Silbert, J. (1979). *Direct instruction reading.* Columbus, OH: Charles Merrill.

Carnine, L. M., Carnine, D. W., & Gersten, R. M. (1984). Analysis of oral reading errors made by economically disadvantaged students taught with a synthetic-phonics approach. *Reading Research Quarterly, 19*(3), 343-356.

Close, D. W., Irvin, L. K., Taylor, V. W., & Agosta, J. (1981). Community living skills instruction for mildly retarded persons. *Exceptional Education Quarterly, 2*, 75-85.

Collins, M., & Carnine, D. (in press). Evaluating the field test revision process by comparing two versions of a reasoning skills CAI program. *Journal of Learning Disabilities.*

Collins, M., Carnine, D., & Gersten, R. (1987). Elaborated corrective feedback and the acquisition of reasoning skills: A study of computer-assisted instruction. *Exceptional Children, 54*(11), 254-262.

Darch, D., & Carnine, D. (1986). Approaches to teaching learning disabled students literal comprehension during content area instruction. *Exceptional Children, 53*(3), 240-246.

Darch, D., Carnine, D., & Gersten, D. (1984). Explicit instruction in mathematics problem solving. *Journal of Educational Research 77*(66), 350-359.

Darch, C., Carnine, D., & Kameenui, E. (1986). The role of visual displays and social structure in content-area instruction. *Journal of Reading Behavior, 18*(4), 275-295.

Engelmann, S., & Carnine, D. (1982). *Theory of instruction.* New York: Irvington.

Engelmann, S., Granzin, A., & Severson, H. (1979). Diagnosing instruction. *Journal of Special Education, 13*(4), 355-363.

Fielding, G. (1980). *A comparison of an inquiry-oriented and a direct instruction approach to teaching legal problem solving to secondary school students.* Unpublished doctoral dissertation, University of Oregon.

Fisher, C. W., Berliner, D., Filby, N., Marliave, R., Cohen, L., & Dishaw, M. (1980). Teaching behaviors, academic learning time, and student achievement: An overview. In C. Denham & A. Lieberman (Eds.), *Time to learn.* Washington, DC: U.S. Government Printing Office.

Fuchs, L. S. (1986). Monitoring progress among mildly handicapped pupils: Review of current practice and research. *Remedial and special Education, 7*(5), 5-12.

Fuchs, L. S., Deno, S. L., & Mirkin, P. K. (1984). The effects of frequent curriculum-based measurement and evaluation on pedagogy, student achievement, and student awareness of learning. *American Educational Research Journal, 21*, 449-460.

Galagan, J. E. (1985). Psychoeducational testing: Turn out the lists, the party's over. *Exceptional Children, 52*(3), 288-299.

Gersten, R. (1981). *Direct instruction in special education settings: A synthesis of evaluation research (Technical Report,* 81-2). Eugene, OR: University of Oregon.

Gersten, R., Becker, W. C., Heiry, T. J., & White, W. A. T. (1984). Entry IQ and yearly academic growth of children in Direct Instruction programs: A longitudinal study of low SES children. *Educational Evaluation and Policy Analysis, 6*(2), 109-121.

Gersten, R., Carnine, D., & White, W. A. T. (1984). The pursuit of clarity: Direct instruction and applied behavior analysis. In W. L. Herward, T. E. Heron, D. S. Hill, & J. Trap-Porter (Eds.), *Focus on behavior analysis in education* (pp. 38-57). Columbus, OH: Merrill.

Gersten, R., Carnine, D., Zoref, L., & Cronin, D. (1986). A multifaceted study of change in seven inner city schools. *Elementary School Journal, 86*(3), 257-276.

Gersten, R., Darch, C., & Gleason, M. (in press). The effectiveness of academic kindergartens for low income students: Analysis and discussion. *Elementary School Journal.*

Gersten, R., & Keating, T. (1987). Improving high school performance of "at risk" students: A study of long-term benefits of direct instruction. *Educational Leadership, 44*(6), 28-31.

Gersten, R., White, W., Falco, R., & Carnine, D. (1982). Enhancing attention of handicapped and non-handicapped students through a dynamic presentation of instructional stimuli. *Analysis and Intervention in Developmental Disabilities, 2*, 305-317.

Golden, N. (1986). *Effectiveness and efficiency of Teacher Net in facilitating lectures for learning disabled secondary students.* Unpublished doctoral dissertation, University of Oregon.

Granzin, A. C., & Carnine, D. W. (1977). Child performance on discrimination tasks: Effects of amount of stimulus variation. *Journal of Experimental Child Psychology, 24*, 322-334.

Haney, W. (1977). Reanalysis of Follow Through parent and teacher data. Boston: Huron Institute.

Hasselbring, T., Sherwood, B., & Bransford, J. (1986). *An evaluation of the Mastering Fractions level one instructional videodisk program:* (Technical Report). Nashville, TN: The Learning Technology Center at Vanderbilt University.

Horner, R. H., & Bellamy, G. T. (1978). A conceptual analysis of vocational training with the severely retarded. In M. Snell (Ed.), *Systematic instruction of the moderately, severely, and profoundly handicapped.* Columbus, OH: Merrill.

House, E. R., Glass, G. V., McLean, L. D., & Walker, D. F. (1978). No simple answer: Critique of the Follow Through evaluation. *Harvard Educational Review, 48*, 128-160.

Johnson, G., Gersten, R., & Carnine, D. (1987). Set size and review procedures in CAI vocabulary instruction. *Journal of Learning Disabilities, 20*(4), 206-213.

Kameenui, E., Carnine, D., Darch, D., & Stein, M. (1986). Two approaches to the development phase of mathematics instruction. *Elementary School Journal, 86*(5), 633-650.

Kelly, B., Carnine, D., Gersten, R., & Grossen, B. (1986). The effectiveness of videodisk instruction.

Lloyd, J., Cullinan, D., Heins, E. D., & Epstein, M. H. (1980). Direct instruction: Effects on oral and written language comprehension. *Learning Disability Quarterly, 3*, 70-76.

Lovitt, T. C., (1981). Notes on behavior modification. *Journal of Special Education, 15*, 395-400.

Maggs, A., & Maggs, R. K. (1979). Direct instruction research in Australia. *Journal of Special Education Technology, 3*, 26-34.

Paine, S., & Carnine, D. (1981). Covertization in teaching multiplication skills to elementary students. *Education and Treatment of Children, 5*(2), 93-107.

Patching, W., Kameenui, E., Carnine, D., Gersten, R., & Colvin, G. (1983). Direct Instruction in critical reading. *Reading Research Quarterly, 18*, 406-418.

Rosenshine, B. (1976). Recent research on teaching behavior and student achievement. *Journal of Teacher Education, 27*, 61-64.

Ross, D., & Carnine, D. W. (1982). Analytic assistance: Effects of example selection, subject's age, an syntactic complexity. *Journal of Education Research, 75*, 294-298.

Schweinhart, L. J., & Mazur, E. (1987). *Prekindergarten programs in urban schools*. Ypsilanti, MI: High/Scope Foundation.

Silbert, J., Carnine, D., & Stein, M. (1981). *Direct Instruction mathematics*. Columbus, OH: Merrill.

Soar, R. S. (1973). *Follow Through classroom process measurement and pupil growth (1970–71): Final Report*. Gainesville, FL: University of Florida, Institute for Development of Human Resources, College of Education.

Stallings, J., & Kaskowitz, D. (1974). *Follow Through classroom observation evaluation 1972-73*. Menlo Park, CA: Stanford Research Institute.

Stebbins, L. (Ed.) (1976). *Education experimentation: A planned variation model* (Vol. IIIA). Cambridge, MA: Abt Associates.

Stebbins, L., St. Pierre, R. G., Proper, E. L., Anderson, R. B., & Cerva, T. R. (1977). *Education as experimentation: A planned variation model* (Vol. IVA-D). Cambridge, MA: Abt Associates.

Stein, C. L'E., & Goldman, J. (1980). Beginning reading instruction for children with minimal brain dysfunction. *Journal of Learning Disabilities, 13*, 219-222.

White, O. R., & Haring, N. G. (1980). *Exceptional teaching* (2nd ed). Columbus, OH: Merrill.

Williams, P., & Carnine, D. (1981). Relationship between range of examples and of instruction and attention in concept attainment. *Journal of Educational Research 74*, 144–48.

Woodward, J., Carnine, D., & Gersten, R. (in press). Teaching problem solving through a computer simulation. *American Educational Research Journal*.

Woodward, J., Carnine, D., Gersten, R., Moore, L., & Golden, N. (1987). Using computer networking for feedback. *Journal of Special Education Technology, 8*(4), 28-35.

17

Effective Reading Interventions in the Regular Classroom

Francis E. Lentz, Jr.
University of Cincinnati

INTRODUCTION

Most children referred for special education evaluation are referred for unsatisfactory progress in reading; this makes regular classroom reading interventions a primary target for alternative service delivery. Furthermore, most referred children are likely experiencing unsatisfactory progress in reading *in spite of the use of existing extraclassroom resources for reading remediation.* Thus, acceptable alternative efforts need to have both a high probability for success and be able to be implemented within the regular classroom context and resources. In order for consultants to meet these reading needs, they must be thoroughly familiar with the existing data on applicable reading interventions.

Use of effective reading interventions in the regular classroom should serve several important functions. Given the primacy of reading problems in referrals to special education, regular classroom remediation could reduce the necessity of actual special education placement for mildly handicapped children. There is little evidence that demonstrates that the *needs* of low achievers differ from the needs of most mildly handicapped children, or that indicates such needs can only be met in special education (Lentz & Shapiro, 1985). In addition to the issue of placement, there are large numbers of children who are not successful in reading and who will not legally qualify for special education, yet who certainly deserve

services (Curtis, Zins, & Graden, 1987; Lentz & Shapiro, 1985). Finally, efficacious regular classroom reading interventions are needed to improve the success of special education students who are at least partially mainstreamed. Unfortunately, while reading assessment has often been discussed in the school psychology literature, the presentation of interventions is rare (e.g., Elliot & Piersel, 1982). It is fully recognized that reading is one of the most complex skills that school-children are expected to acquire; however, there is a rapidly expanding literature that suggests that manipulation of the learning environment and certain low-cost and relatively simple instructional procedures can pay large dividends in student progress (Lentz & Shapiro, 1985).

In the following discussion the generic elements of reading interventions in the regular classroom are outlined (these elements are also applicable to other academic areas), empirically documented reading interventions that are feasible for regular classrooms are reviewed, and the role that school psychologists and other consultants can play in planning and implementing reading interventions are examined.

REQUIREMENTS FOR REGULAR CLASSROOM READING INTERVENTIONS

A number of criteria must be met if consultants are to effectively assist regular classroom teachers with reading interventions. These criteria are intended as a general guide to the consultant who becomes involved in reading interventions in the regular classroom.

1. *Interventions in the regular classroom must be of relatively low cost to the classroom teacher.* It is highly unlikely that teachers will be willing to implement or to continue interventions that are extremely complicated or excessively time-consuming (Witt, 1986). The classroom teacher is probably already spending some extra time with most children who are failing reading sufficiently to have been referred. It would seem desirable that a special intervention not greatly exceed this time; furthermore, teachers may be even more willing to continue interventions that actually reduce the "extra" time and frustration.

2. *Interventions must produce improvement in functional classroom reading behaviors.* The selection of efficacious target behaviors for classroom interventions is critically important (Kratochwill, 1985; Hoge and Andrews, 1987). However, intervention results must be apparent within the classroom reading curriculum; interventions must produce positive changes in reading behaviors that are functional within the regular requirements of the reading curriculum and that the teacher can observe (Treiber & Lahey, 1983). After all, the teacher will have observed specific deficits that were disturbing enough to result in referral; intervention must address these observations. There is clear (although not voluminous) evidence, by the way, that targeting student behaviors related to performance within curriculum activities significantly improves achievement test scores (Hoge & Andrews, 1987).

3. *The resources needed for change must be available in the regular classroom.* Current funding patterns clearly require that change agents and materials be available within the parameters of the regular classroom. Likewise, the role of the consultant is unlikely to involve direct treatment of the student, but rather be that of resource developer; the intervention will ultimately need to be maintained within the limits of the regular classroom and executed by regular classroom personnel.

4. *More molar interventions should be the rule.* If students require extensive instruction in many fine-grained or complex skills, it is unlikely that regular class resources will be fully sufficient. For example, current research on the use of learning strategies to improve reading skills and performance is quite positive but requires skilled extraclassroom trainers (Deshler, Alley, Warner, & Schumaker, 1981). However, there are numerous examples of highly successful interventions that address more general classroom behaviors, for example, reinforcing completion of assigned classwork and peer tutoring within curriculum-based activities (Greenwood, Delquadri, & Hall, 1984).

5. *Special service personnel need to be familiar with classroom reading curricula and with curricular requirements for student behavior.* Classroom consultants can no longer assume that students' problems are not related to curricular requirements, or that problems reside totally within students (Lentz & Shapiro, 1986). Teachers will perceive changes as valid only if they are manifested in functional classroom behavior. Therefore consultants must clearly understand classroom demands and behaviors if they are to be effective in service delivery.

6. *Assessments of reading problems must address the student's performance within the particular classroom environment and produce data that are clearly linked to intervention planning.* This intervention orientation to assessment (see Lentz and Shapiro, 1986; Marston & Magnusson, this volume; Shapiro, 1987; Tindal, this volume; Ysseldyke & Christensen, this volume) allows analysis of existing student skills in relation to the curriculum and within the idiosyncrasies of the classroom. Assessment of classroom variables is crucial precisely because it is highly likely that important classroom variables will need to be changed (Lentz & Shapiro, 1986).

7. *Consultants must be aware of the generic elements of effective reading interventions.* Rather than a "bag of tricks," effective interventions contain a set of identifiable generic elements. This allows idiosyncratic problems to be addressed by initial interventions that have a good chance of success. Although it is true that we are never sure of the exact likelihood of success in academic intervention (Deno, 1985), it would also appear true that we have an excellent idea about the generic elements of effective academic remediation.

INTERVENTION PLANNING

Reading interventions in the regular classroom are implemented through a problem-solving process of consultation (Bergan, 1977; Curtis & Meyers, this volume; Gutkin & Curtis, 1982; Lentz & Shapiro, 1985; Shapiro & Lentz, 1985). The steps in this process can be delineated for reading specifically as follows: (a) Assessment is conducted to identify the operational problems in reading (assessment could include direct classroom observation, interviews, examination of permanent products, and curriculum-based measures). (b) Analysis is made of assessment data to determine what factors are contributing to the failure of the student to meet reading expectations in the classroom. The deficits could be the result of such variables as lack of student motivation (poor work contingencies or misdirected teacher attention), interfering behaviors, or actual skill deficits (e.g., poor fluency, inadequate sight word vocabulary). (c) An intervention is planned that will address the functional components identified through assessment. Intervention planning includes setting a specific goal, establishing a monitoring system, and considering the elements of strong reading interventions. (d) A change agent is chosen to implement the intervention. There are at least four readily available change agents — teacher, peers, the referred child, and parents or siblings. Each of these agents could have prime responsibility for teaching new behaviors or managing current ones. The

idea of several change agents means that most identified needs of children with reading problems can be addressed by someone *other than the teacher.* (e) The intervention is implemented, progress monitored, and interventions changed on the basis of progress or performance data.

Assessment Requirements

Identification of the problem in terms of classroom behavior. Regardless of particular theoretical orientation, problem-solving consultation begins with structured interviews of teachers that are critical in defining the reading problems and in identifying additional assessment requirements for intervention planning (Shapiro & Lentz, 1985; Shapiro, 1987). Effective remediation requires that the consultant assist the teacher in identifying the *behaviors* of the student that have generated the referral; and that the identification of such behaviors occur within behaviors required by the reading curriculum (Shapiro, 1987; Treiber & Lahey, 1983).

While this may seem relatively simple, it may be quite difficult to operationalize some reasons for referral in a manner that will be useful for designing interventions. For example, problems reported in such formulations as "visual processing difficulty," "can't remember from day to day," or "reading comprehension" are difficult to match with appropriate interventions. More useful examples for the purpose of selecting interventions would include more specific identification of behaviors such as doesn't complete independent seatwork at 80% accuracy; can't answer questions about a passage that the student has just read; can't answer questions about a passage read by another student; can't do vocabulary matching in the workbook; can't write workbook answers to questions about the current basal story; doesn't follow workbook directions, etc. The student behaviors that have been observed by the teacher and that are of concern must be eventually changed by an intervention (Lentz, in press) or the reasons for referral will continue to remain for the teacher to observe. Problems may be complex, encompassing many areas of reading performance. However, if an effective solution is to be planned, then clarity and specificity about the problem is absolutely critical at the initial stage. "Snipe hunts" for ephemeral internal process difficulties will only delay or prevent the realization of solutions in regular classrooms (Ysseldyke & Mirkin, 1982).

Finally, research literature makes it very clear that many even quite severe reading problems result less from students' lack of skills (skill problems) than from their failure to exhibit behaviors that are within their repertoires. Furthermore, students who do not practice or perform new skills will eventually show skill deficits. *Skill* problems will require interventions that produce new behavior; *performance* problems may require interventions involving manipulation of "motivation" through contingency management. Without observable operational definition of presenting reading problems, it is impossible to untangle the issue of skill versus performance and thus to plan interventions that are clearly linked to useful assessment information.

Identification of problem elements in the classroom environment. Table 1 provides a set of elements in a classroom ecology that may be related to the existence of reading problems (Lentz & Shapiro, 1986), and that therefore may need to be altered during the course of an effective intervention. The elements in this functional classroom environment are variables that research suggests are functionally related to academic progress and that must be *assessed* during the problem-solving process. For example, contingent teacher attention or praise during students' work, rewards for accuracy or completion, and teacher goal setting/progress monitoring can be evaluated through interviews and/or direct observation (Lentz & Shapiro, 1986). These classroom circumstances can be modified to increase effective student engagement with reading work and improve achievement. Also, environmental assessment is required to adequately

distinguish whether the reading difficulties result from skill deficits or performance problems.

Assessment of reading skills problems. Given the emphasis on identifying reading problems in relationship to classroom curricula, some form of curriculum-derived assessment of possible skills deficits may be required. Chapters 7 and 8 in this volume provide an extensive examination of such procedures by means of timed probes of oral reading of text, basal word lists, or lists of phonemes. Reading probes have been suggested as a way to place a child in reading material that is suited to ability, to set goals for interventions, and to be used in progress monitoring during an intervention. Such probes are highly useful for these purposes; however, other kinds of classroom performance can be used in planning and evaluating reading interventions. Of particular value may be accuracy and completion of daily classwork, periodic curriculum-based mastery tests, or other behaviors such as silent reading, oral response to questions, and homework completion.

Two issues are very important in the assessment of reading performance. First, the end result of assessment of student skill or performance must be the selection of targets for direct intervention, and/or selection of a metric that allows interventions to be monitored and altered in a timely fashion. Probes and/or regular classroom performance can be used for these purposes.

Second, reading interventions in the regular classroom are likely to require that students stick to a large extent to curriculum materials with which other students in the classroom are being taught. It seems likely that children referred for reading problems will already be placed in the lowest level of reading materials in their classroom (the lowest group). Although special education programs will place children into materials at an "instructional" level, such placement is unlikely in the regular classroom. It remains unclear if there are optimum levels for instructional efficacy (although

TABLE 1
Environmental Variables Related to Reading Performance

Environment during classwork

Instruction
    Models/prompts
    Pacing
    Praise
    Error correction
Opportunities to respond
Response rate
Contingencies
    Teacher attention
    Peer attention
    Accuracy feedback
Class structure
    Grouping
    Pattern of contacts
Competing behaviors

Pre- or postwork practices

Instructions
Contingencies for accuracy or completion
Performance feedback

Teacher planning/evaluation

Note: Adapted from Lentz and Shapiro, 1986.

there are various strategies for such placement; see Deno, 1985), and at least one highly successful regular classroom intervention program advocates for (and demonstrates success in) attempting remediation in the student's current materials (Greenwood, Delquadri, & Hall, 1984). Therefore, for logistical ease, it is recommended that if a child is already in the lowest level of materials, remediation should be attempted within the child's current placement level. This means that goals and progress monitoring systems should be set within classroom materials. Irrespective of placement, any child with a reading problem must be eventually successful in materials used in the regular classroom.

Elements of Effective Reading Interventions

The end result of an assessment oriented towards intervention planning

must be the selection of an intervention that matches the analyzed problems. For example, if assessment indicates that a child cannot do well in reading group, on individual seatwork, and on unit reading tests because he/she is not fluent, doesn't have an adequate sight word vocabulary, and has poor word attack skills, then the intervention must be oriented towards helping the student acquire new skills and fluency. On the other hand, if the assessment indicates that the student's skills are sufficient (at least at some minimal level) to be successful in meeting classroom requirements, but that the child just doesn't perform to capacity, then the intervention is likely to be oriented towards increasing accurate performance through procedures such as contingency management, rather than teaching new skills. I have often seen teachers assume that a student's failure to meet classroom reading requirements results from a skills deficit, when in fact that was not the case.

Interventions such as peer tutoring were implemented, with poor results. The results were poor not because peer tutoring is not a good procedure, but because it is effective in helping children gain fluency in reading or acquire new skills, but not necessarily effective with performance problems. Thus the match between problem and intervention is always critical.

Although one can never be *certain* that a selected intervention for reading problems will be effective, the process of planning a structured intervention should be guided by an understanding of what variables are part of "strong" reading interventions. Research has delineated the instructional and/or classroom variables that are related to effective reading remediation. Table 2 provides the elements that should always be included in any reading intervention. The actual nature of any of these variables can and should vary across interventions for different types of problems; however, the planner should always carefully consider how each variable will be manifested in any intervention.

Opportunities to respond. Recent research has strongly indicated that students having problems with reading are not actively engaged in making useful reading responses during classroom instruction or practice activities (Hall, Delquadri, Greenwood, & Thurston, 1982; Stanley & Greenwood, 1983). Whether conceptualized as *academic engagement* (Rosenshine, 1980) or *opportunities to make responses* (Greenwood, Dinwiddie, et al., 1984), it is clear that students must be involved in making active responses to reading material that is related to the objectives in classroom curricula. This active responding appears to be necessary both in work directed towards acquiring new reading behaviors, and in practice addressed to improving fluency of reading behaviors that have been *acquired* at an initial level.

The types of response opportunities that are to be provided during remediation will depend on the nature of the student's reading problem. For example,

if the student cannot answer certain types of questions about text that has been read silently, then as one part of the intervention opportunities to make "comprehension" responses must be provided. If the student lacks fluency in reading, then opportunities to practice oral reading can be highly effective in increasing reading fluency (Hall et al., 1982).

Additionally, it appears that certain students require more opportunities to respond than others in mastering reading-related skills (Gettinger, 1984). Thus appropriate materials must clearly be provided that incorporate increasing opportunities for student response beyond that usually provided within normal classroom activities, and/or by manipulating variables that improve student responses to regular classroom opportunities. In the first case, the intervention must include provision of new materials that elicit responses, or provide additional opportunities for response in the regular materials. In the second case, contingencies (controlled by the student or by others) must be arranged to increase responses and response accuracy within regular activities.

As a final note concerning provision of opportunities to respond, it appears to be more efficient to plan instruction or practice frequently for shorter periods than to provide infrequent but massed sessions (Mayhall & Jenkins, 1977).

Contingencies for reading responses. Altering reinforcement for accurate or increased reading responses has been shown to be amazingly effective in improving reading in regular and special classrooms (e.g., Ayllon, Layman, & Kandel, 1975; Billingsley, 1977; Jenkins, Barksdale, & Clinton, 1978; Holt, 1971). For example, making access to desired activities contingent on certain levels of accuracy during daily seatwork has radically improved performance on independent reading seatwork (Aaron & Bostow, 1978). Likewise, reinforcement during the teaching of new reading skills appears crucial to help accelerate students' rates so that they can catch up to classroom expectancies. In this regard,

TABLE 2
Elements of a Strong Reading Intervention

1. Frequent opportunities to respond

2. Contingencies for reading responses
   a. Accuracy
   b. Completion
   c. Improvement over previous behavior

3. Error correction procedures

4. Progress feedback to the student

5. Instruction of new skills includes:
   a. Opportunities to respond
   b. Prompts to respond
   c. Models
   d. Fading of assistance
   e. Reinforcement

Rosenberg, Sindelar, and Stedt (1985) demonstrated that teacher's praise for on task behavior and correct responding, or only for correct responding, was effective in improving acquisition of new reading skills. Praise given for both was more effective than for responding alone, and may have served the function of increasing attention during presentation of new material. Copeland, Brown, and Hall (1974) had the school principal in their study praise work during tutoring for sight words and showed significant increases in acquisition of new words. It seems logical that students who have chronically failed at reading will respond better to experiences that produce positive outcomes.

Although it is to be hoped that reading will become intrinsically interesting to students with reading problems, the initial use of extrinsic rewards, with planned fading of such explicit contingencies, will increase the efficiency of interventions. Reinforcement is too often ignored in the formulation of otherwise sound remedial plans; this may result in slow progress and eventually cut teachers' interest in maintaining interventions.

Error correction and progress feedback. Any reading intervention must contain some plan for correcting students' mistakes, and for providing structured feedback to students about their progress.

Research data suggest that some forms of error correction in reading are more effective than others. If a pattern of errors has already occurred, then some form of error drill is likely to be most effective (Jenkins, Larson, & Fleisher, 1983; Rosenberg, 1986; Singh, 1987). On the other hand, there are procedures to model correct responses *before* students fall into repeated error. In this regard, Hendrickson, Roberts, and Shores (1978) showed that antecedent modeling of new sight words during practice was more effective than modeling the correct word *after* the student had already responded incorrectly.

A basic principle is that errors should be corrected as soon after they occur as possible. Given that this is not usually feasible in regular classrooms, the consultant must carefully plan for error correction to occur quickly, perhaps by utilizing a classroom change agent other than the teacher (see Paine, Radicchi, Rosellini, Deutchman, & Darch, 1983, for excellent ideas for quick error correction procedures).

Just as error correction is important for gaining new skills (or practicing those previously learned), students' progress will be enhanced by providing them frequent information about their progress. For example, having students graph their progress or providing feedback graphs concerning changes in target behavior has been shown to improve the rate of progress (Thorpe, Chiang, & Darch, 1981; Jenkins, Mayhall, Peschka, & Jenkins, 1974). Students' involvement in goal setting, self-graphing, and decisions about whether goals are being met are ways to build progress feedback into reading interventions. Similarly, public feedback about classroom performance can increase accuracy and completion (e.g., Van Houten, Hill, & Parsons, 1975).

Structured procedures to teach new skills. Inasmuch as interventions should be effective as quickly as possible and should be highly efficient relative to the time invested, any intervention involving teaching new behaviors should be carefully structured. Structured interventions include the use of teacher models of new responses, procedures to prompt student responses if necessary, procedures to fade teacher prompts so that students can eventually exhibit the new behavior independently, and use of reinforcement (often in the form of descriptive praise) for correct or approximated responses (see Carnine, this volume).

Consultant as Resource Manager

The classroom teacher is only one of many possible persons (teachers, peers, parents, siblings, or the students themselves) who can manage reading interventions in the regular classroom. Consultants for reading problems may have heard teachers lament, "But I just don't have time" more often than they would like. The proper reply is "OK, let's look at another person to manage the intervention." In this regard, the school consultant becomes not only a consultant for intervention planning and remediation but one who develops resources for remediation — for example, establishing a bank of tutors trained in a general reading package; teaching children self-management; teaching teachers to train tutors, etc. By assuming this role, consultants can help overcome resistance, have a wider impact, and more efficiently manage the time of at least two professionals, themselves and the teacher consultees.

READING INTERVENTIONS

Many reading interventions have either been implemented in regular classrooms, or have been implemented in special classes and could easily be used with regular class remedial readers. No attempt has been made here to complete an extensive literature review; rather the literature cited is illustrative, or provides empirical support for the efficacy of procedures.

Two general types of reading interventions are examined – those that teach new skills or are directly related to both acquisition of skills and improvement of fluency; and those directly related to increasing accurate responding during instruction with classroom materials. For both, examples using all change agents are provided. It must always be kept in mind that interventions should only be designed *following* assessment and problem analysis. Furthermore, interventions must be carefully matched to the conditions contributing to the particular child's reading problem *as elucidated* by assessment data.

Teaching New Skills and Improving Fluency

Intervention that has as its purpose the acquisition of new reading skills or improved fluency should be planned around the goal of resolving the reading problems *as seen by the teacher in the classroom.* In short, the decision is that a student's reading problems have *resulted* from skills or fluency deficits in relationship to *the current curriculum placement.* Low-cost programs designed to correct skills/fluency deficits have been demonstrated for all of the classroom change agents (as to teacher-controlled interventions, they seem less likely to be accepted by teachers, who frequently are already busy with many concurrent demands for their attention; hence the teacher-implemented instructional interventions discussed below are somewhat specialized and are likely to be employed in the course of normal instruction.)

Peers as reading tutors. The literature on the use of peer tutors for children with reading problems is extremely positive (e.g., Epstein, 1978; Hall et al., 1982; Kalfus, 1984; Osguthorpe & Scruggs, 1986). Oral reading rates, achievement test scores, acquisition of sight words, and phonics skills have all been improved. Good tutoring packages provide greatly increased opportunities for student response (Hall et al., 1982), effective error correction procedures, structured use of prompts, and utilization of praise or other contingencies for improved skills. Although relatively unstructured reading tutoring has been effective (Kalfus, 1984), structured reading tutoring with structured training of tutors is highly recommended for several reasons. First, it allows consultant and teacher to have knowledge of the intended form of the intervention, and makes the remediation plan more explicit. Second, it allows inclusion of all the elements that research suggests pay off in the remedial process (see the discussion above). Third, tutors can also be trained as data collectors, thus relieving the teacher of yet another burden during the problem solving process. My experience suggests strongly that training tutors is perhaps the most critical element of successful peer programs. A comprehensive chapter in this volume (Chap. 18) has been devoted to peer tutoring, and the reader is referred there for additional information concerning tutoring programs.

A reading tutoring program designed to improve general reading fluency and sight word vocabulary (adopted from Greenwood, Delquadri, & Hall, 1984) provides a good illustration of a wide-ranging tutoring program *within* the regularly assigned reading curriculum. This program is intended for children who exhibit poor oral reading skills, who do not readily acquire new basal words, and who show a deficit sight word vocabulary in their current book placement. This program fits the requirements for low-cost reading interventions in several ways.

First, it emphasizes work with materials with which the child is expected to perform, and it has a general focus on reading problems (Greenwood, Delquadri, & Hall, 1984). Second, the teacher's daily requirement is to ensure that materials are ready for the tutor (the tutor could also perform this), monitor the course of tutoring, and perhaps manage contingencies. Finally, the consultant's role is likely to be initial training of tutors (or training the teacher to train), or managing a pool of tutors that can be used when demands are recognized through the consultative arrangement.

A summary of the procedures employed in this remedial tutoring package is listed in Table 3. The procedure provides for intensive opportunities for the child to make responses in regular materials; it provides for an immediate error correction procedure; it provides intensive drill on missed words, and allows the child's daily performance to dictate which sight words are drilled most frequently; it can provide additional contingencies for increases in rate, more correct reading, and mastery of previously unknown sight words; and it provides an ongoing assessment of words appearing in the child's current basal reader that have not been mastered. Additionally, the tutor can be trained as a data collector and progress monitor; in this process the target child receives continuous (daily) progress information from the graphing of performance.

Curriculum-based and standardized achievement test data from Greenwood, Delquadri, & Hall, (1984), Greenwood, Dinwiddie, et al. (1984), and Sindelar (1982) indicate that tutoring procedures similar to those of the preceding example, using the regular classroom curriculum, can be highly effective in remediating poor reading skills. There are several issues about the use of this type of package that are important to consider. The first is to tutor with materials in which students are currently placed *regardless* of their reading entry skills. Even students whose reading rates would seem to indicate that their current reading book placement is too high (presumably the lowest reading

TABLE 3
Sequence of Procedures in a Wide-Range Reading Tutoring Package

(Tutor gets tutoring package containing flash cards, materials for oral reading, graphs)

1. Drill with previously made sight word flashcards each "pass" through drop words identified on first try.

2. Model errors, require tutee to repeat; praise corrects.

3. Mark back of flash cards, words identified correctly the first "pass" with a plus, others with a minus.

4. Move mastered words to special pocket in tutoring packet (mastered equals three days in a row with the first try being correct).

5. Read for one minute in story; correct mistakes by modeling and asking for tutee to repeat.

6. Have tutee make flash cards for any words missed; drill these once (you can go back and repeat the sentence containing missed word).

7. Repeat oral reading cycle _____ number of times.

8. Drill new flashcards as you did the original flashcards (do not mark the backs).

9. Compute reading probe rate from first minute oral reading sample.

10. Count sight words mastered.

11. Determine contingency earned (if applicable).

12. Tutor and tutee graph rate and words mastered.

group in the classroom) have been effectively tutored within their current book (Greenwood, Delquadri, & Hall, 1984). Reading tutoring programs using extraclassroom materials have also been shown to be highly effective (Trovato & Bucher, 1980), but they require additional logistical efforts. Second, because this tutoring package emphasizes the normal classroom curriculum, generalization problems (the issue of whether student performance within one curriculum or setting will generalize to another) are minimized (e.g., Anderson & Redd, 1980).

Peers have also been used to teach children more narrowly defined reading skills. For example, Jenkins et al. (1974) and Heron, Heward, Cooke, and Hill (1983) trained peer tutors to teach children new sight words from their basal reading curriculum. Both involved structured training in using prompts, correcting errors, and using praise. In addition, Heron et al. (1983) trained tutors to plot words that had been learned on a gamelike progress chart. In both cases, the inter-

ventions were successful. Heron et al. (1983) used first grade tutors of sight words with first grade target children; Young, Hecimovic, and Salzberg (1983) taught kindergarten children to tutor others in letter recognition. It appears that even very young children can become effective tutors; this certainly widens the possible number of tutors for school personnel consulting about reading problems.

Parents/grandparents as reading tutors. Parents have been used as tutors in several published reading interventions. Gang and Poche (1982) targeted phonic skills, Wedd and Fowler (1984) used parents to teach prereading skills to preschoolers needing remediation, and Hall et al. (1982) taught a parent to teach sight words and a grandparent to tutor a variety of skills, including reading. Each of the procedures included standard training of tutors, structured practice, standard error correction procedures, and contingent praise; two also used parents as data collectors. Additionally, there is no reason parent volunteers could not be trained in one of the more broad-range procedures discussed previously; the content of effective instruction is identical irrespective of the change agent involved.

Both Gang and Poche (1982) and Hall et al. (1982) examined parent/grandparent tutoring behavior before training and found clear evidence that adults are not necessarily natural tutors. In fact, in at least one case, pretraining tutors engaged in practices that may have been detrimental to student learning. These data strongly indicate the serious problems that may be created by just asking parents (or any other potential tutor) "to help" without providing training in good tutoring practices. I have often found teachers who have already "tried" parent or peer tutoring without good effects. These cases were always informal, nonstructured interventions.

Teacher-controlled interventions for skills and fluency problems: Concentrated drill. This procedure involves identifying sight words that the child cannot read or reads only hesitantly. One possible source for these words may be the basal words from a child's current reading story; this source could be especially important for children whose failure to learn sight words as they are introduced is a concern. Sheets are made up with each of the target words on each row, in random order. After initial orientation for the student (read from left to right, try all words), the teacher (or tutor) models the first row and asks the student to match each word to one word in subsequent rows. Then the child reads the rest of the words for approximately 1 min, followed by praise, modeling of errors, and the child's drill of errors. Note that the first reading also provides a built-in assessment procedure and allows monitoring of intervention process. The process is repeated one or two more times. Sterling, Goetz, and Sterling (1984) demonstrated that this procedure is highly effective both for acquisition of new sight words and for gaining fluency in reading. It incorporates all the elements of good reading interventions, and increases opportunities for responding to a much higher level than would characterize normal instruction. Total time is less than 5 mins (best done each day), and this process could easily be managed by a peer or parent volunteer.

Teacher-controlled interventions for skills or fluency problems: Previewing. Adding structure to practices that already are in relatively common use has been shown to increase students' oral reading rates and accuracy, and improve comprehension accuracy (thus allowing them to attain normal classroom rewards for good performance). Previewing (Rose & Sherry, 1984) usually involves having someone read a story aloud while target children follow along silently. Variations include having the teacher "model" good reading for the first part of a basal story, followed by having the children take a turn at reading aloud (Smith, 1979); discussing the story and introducing new words by modeling them (Singh & Singh, 1984); or having the target children listen to a tape of sight words or of someone reading the story they themselves are about to read (Freeman & McLaughlin, 1984; Rose & Beattie, 1986). All of these interventions are intended to reduce the children's error rates during subsequent reading and to increase fluency. When taped word lists (Freeman & McLaughlin, 1984) are used, the goal can also involve acquisition of new sight words. Oral reading of the material with target children following the text silently appears to be much more effective than having them just silently preview the material (Rose, 1984; Rose & Sherry, 1984). While oral previewing led by the teacher may be the most effective, students can listen to tapes (Rose & Beattie, 1986) or can listen to a peer doing the previewing. In these cases, the managers of the instructional intervention would be peers or the target children themselves.

Children for whom such interventions are appropriate are those who are referred (at least in part) for poor oral reading (in respect to accuracy and/or rate) during reading group or whose independent seatwork does not appear to benefit from the reading group experience.

Errorless learning procedures used by tutors or teachers. Procedures involving errorless learning can be incorporated into either teacher- or peer-managed instruction. Typically used in the teaching of either sight words or phonics with mildly handicapped children, errorless learning is highly appropriate for children who are not acquiring new responses by traditional means (trial and error instruction such as that used in flash card drill). The most common errorless learning procedures involve the use of delayed prompting (time delay) (Bradley-Johnson, Sunderman, & Johnson, 1983; Schimek, 1983). In delayed prompting the instructor presents the stimulus (a flash card, for example) immediately modeling the correct response. The children model the instructor, and gradually the instructor's model is delayed (usually from 0 up to 6 sec). The children begin to anticipate the model, thus acquiring the correct response with few or no errors. When contingencies are built in, more reward is usually offered for anticipation than for subsequent modeling. Antecedent modeling without delay has also been effective with difficult-to-teach children (Thorpe & Borden, 1985; Hendrickson et al., 1978).

Summary: Skills and fluency. Once a particular skills problem has been identified, consultants can assist by helping select an instructional manager that the teacher will accept as not too great a burden on his or her time. If other change agents are chosen, the teacher's prime role is then to observe the intervention for fidelity to the original plan, monitor progress data, and support the change agent. The results of the interventions discussed above have been extremely positive; the performance of children who are reading so poorly that they are referred can be remediated in the regular classroom. Unfortunately, there are few data that allow us to pick the likely failures prior to intervention; thus, there would seem to be little to lose by attempting remediation of skills problems in the regular classroom.

The interventions directed at skills or fluency remediation all involve arranging opportunities for children to learn new behaviors or to gain fluency. There also are a number of reading interventions that have been used to increase the engagement of children with practice assignments (performance interventions). While the difference between the two types of interventions is not always precise, it is useful in discussing interventions to distinguish between skills and performance problems, because children who do not practice reading during practice exercises are likely to develop fluency, skill, or maintenance problems.

Increasing Students' Reading Performance

Although many students exhibiting reading problems require interventions oriented towards skill deficits, it is clear that many children, for various reasons, simply do *not perform* when in fact they have the requisite skills. Even for problems that are usually conceptualized as complex skills deficits, such as reading comprehension, the provision of positive or negative consequences for performance has been highly effective (e.g., Jenkins, et al., 1978). When the assessment and problem analysis have determined that a child's problems of inaccurate or incomplete performance of assigned reading work do not result from skills deficits, the intervention must involve arranging antecedent or contingent events around the expected performance. As in the case of reading skills deficits, any of the potential classroom change agents can be involved.

Teachers as change agents in cases of performance problems in reading. Unlike some interventions for skills problems, interventions for performance problems do not necessarily involve much teacher time. Teachers must have mechanisms for scoring the targeted work, planning reinforcing activities, and monitoring progress; however, the burden of instructing new skills is not present. Teacher-controlled contingencies can be as simple as planning to use praise in a more structured manner during reading seatwork or reading group. On the other hand, it could involve allowing the student to engage in some desirable activity contingent upon completing work to some accuracy criterion.

There are a number of examples of making desirable events contingent on specific levels of accurate responding. Hay, Hay, and Nelson (1977) had a teacher praise correct responding during independent seatwork in reading (along with a star on a "good work" card), and demonstrated impressive improvement in the percentage of assignments that children completed correctly. Children classified as hyperactive were reinforced with tokens for accurate responding in reading workbooks (answers to questions, vocabulary exercises, and daily tests) and increased percentage of correct responses from an average of less than 50% to above 80% (Ayllon & Roberts, 1974; Ayllon et al., 1975). Taking away points for being off task was also shown to be effective in improving reading performance with children classified as hyperactive (Rapport, Murphy, & Bailey, 1982). This example is notable because these children, currently often conceptualized as attention deficit-disordered, were also taking Ritalin with little effect on their academic performance. Token reinforcement was shown clearly more effective than Ritalin in regard to both hyperactive behavior and academic performance. A final example: A student considered functionally illiterate was provided free time contingent on improvement in academic activities (reading among them) and these contingencies were effective in improving his performance (Trice, Parker, & Furrow, 1981).

Even for problems in reading comprehension contingencies have proven highly effective, *without interventions that are skill-oriented*. Both handicapped and nonhandicapped children with severe comprehension problems were rewarded for accurate answers about text material (Jenkins et al., 1978; Lahey, McNees, & Brown, 1973; Rosenbaum and Breiling, 1976). In these cases, accuracy drastically improved; Lahey et al. (1973) increased comprehension to levels exhibited by children on grade level with no reported problems. Likewise, reversals in letter identification were successfully and immediately remediated when correct responding was rewarded with tokens exchangeable for pennies (Deno & Chiang, 1979). Such problems have been popularly associated with processing deficits, although in this case they proved amenable to manipulation with positive contingencies.

In implementing contingency-type interventions for reading problems, there are several issues to consider in addition to the standard ones. The first step is to identify the performance measure that will be targeted. Second, a procedure must be developed to score the targeted work immediately after it is turned in. Children can be taught to self-correct, or peers can be used. It must be remembered that the contingencies should be for independently completed, accurate work. Problems on which a child has received help should not be counted as correct in determining if the contingency is met. Also, the consultant and teacher must decide that the student's reading skills are adequate to allow him or her to do the work. If there are inadequate skills to complete independent work, the practice assignment is inappropriate. Provision of reward for work that *cannot* be done by the student may well *increase* inappropriate behavior (Center, Deitz, & Kaufman, 1982). Finally, there must be a clear assessment of what events the student would find reinforcing. Too often teachers may employ contingencies that they think are reinforcing, when in fact the activities mean little to the student (for example, the use of stickers contingent on good work). Likewise, praise is *not* reinforcing for all students; the teacher and consultant must be very careful with this part of the assessment to determine what *is* reinforcing.

Teacher-controlled contingencies can also be provided for completion of reading modules or other independent work. Kelley and Stokes (1982) actually paid high school dropouts in an alternate school for completing reading assignments in an individualized curriculum for attainment of a GED. Contracts were established with each student and the results were excellent; in fact, student attendance was better when they were paid for work completed than when they were paid for attending.

A final type of teacher-controlled contingency for reading performance is the use of public feedback about performance to improve accuracy and completion of reading assignments. A system has been developed by Van Houten and associates (e.g., Van Houten et al., 1975) that involves specific time limits for performance on reading comprehension and vocabulary exercises, student self-correction of work, public posting of scores, and praise for improved performance (students were praised for exceeding their own previous performance). In a comprehensive evaluation of this package, children's accuracy in comprehension was found to have nearly doubled and completion of word meaning problems to have significantly improved. Once developed, this intervention could be easily managed for more than one student. It is interesting that this procedure also seemed to increase the number of positive peer comments to children about reading improvement.

Peers as change agents in cases of reading performance problems. Just as with skill interventions, peers can serve as change agents in correcting reading performance problems. Training is obviously key, and perhaps more care must be taken in managing such interventions, because a role of the peer in this case is to provide contingent rewards for good performance. In a classroom for hyperactive children, tokens were provided by the teacher to students for both completion of reading modules, and for helping other students complete their work (Robinson, Newby, & Ganzell, 1981). The combined package was extremely effective in increasing completion of daily assignments and in improving scores on standardized vocabulary tests.

Self-management of reading performance problems. Teaching children to manage their own behaviors is an oft-

stated goal of education. In remediation of reading problems, typical self-management procedures include self-monitoring of on-task behavior during academic seatwork (e.g., Kneedler & Hallahan, 1981), monitoring on-task behavior during oral reading group (Hallahan, Marshall, & Lloyd, 1981), and involvement of the student in setting criteria for reinforcement (e.g., Billingsley, 1977). Self-management of reading might be selected as an intervention when the assessment has revealed that the student can perform required tasks and when it is felt that results will be better if intervention is self-managed than if teacher-managed or the student is the only available change agent.

Hallahan and his associates (Kneedler & Hallahan, 1981) have posited self-monitoring of on-task behavior as important for children who have deficits in attention and who thereby do not profit from arranged independent practice. While most of their research has been with academic subjects other than reading, their procedures illustrate this type of intervention. Basically, children are trained to discriminate when they are on-task or off-task, to determine if they are on-task at the moment a recorded tone sounds, and to record their decision. Typically, no external rewards are used (other than praise), although research has been conducted in classrooms with structured contingency management systems in place. In general, their results indicate that self-monitoring increases the percentage of time students are on-task, that there are often effects on work accuracy or completion, and that the use of the structured tone can be faded (Kneedler & Hallahan, 1981). The effects on academic performance of self-monitoring are variable and not as striking as more direct interventions (see also Snider, 1987, for a critique), but the intervention is very "cheap" in terms of teacher or consultant time and may have perceived benefits in terms of promoting student responsibility.

Hallahan et al. (1981) taught three learning-disabled boys to self-monitor on-task behavior during oral reading group with a procedure similar to that described above. The results were positive and the effects were maintained after the external cues and other procedures were withdrawn. Although no effects on reading performance were measured, this procedure would seem ideal for a child whose lack of attention during reading group is affecting acquisition of new skills and/or reading fluency.

Billingsley (1977) looked at whether student-established goals or teacher-set goals would be more effective during an intervention to increase reading fluency. Effects were very mixed across students, although both types of goal setting led to reading improvement. To the extent possible, children should always be involved in goal setting and progress monitoring. When children can see their progress towards a goal, their rate of progress will often improve (e.g., Jenkins et al., 1978). For example, Piersel and Kratochwill (1979) had children with reading problems chart their progress in completing units of an SRA reading lab or completion of phonics worksheets; the results indicated greatly increased reading progress. Design of similar self-monitoring or charting interventions requires preparing graphs, training students to graph and interpret their own data, structuring teacher praise around meeting goals, and establishing some sort of self-correction procedure.

Parents as change agents in cases of reading performance problems. For many children, parents control reinforcers that are more powerful than those available to school personnel, and their enlistment in interventions may be highly important. A second reason to involve parents is philosophical and revolves around the general issue of productive parent involvement with children's problems in the school. Because of the nature of most programs for reading that will be discussed, involving parents can also provide to them frequent positive information concerning their child's progress, instead of the usual "only contact parents when there is trouble" procedure.

Establishing a home/school contingency program for reading performance problems involves several steps (Brough-ton, Barton, & Owen, 1980). First is the decision that the problem is performance and not skills. Second, the teacher and/or consultant needs to arrange for a parent conference during which the problem is explained, the desire for parental involvement is expressed, the type of work that the student is expected to do is examined, and some system of daily communication is arranged. A variety of home–school notes have been used that range from very general ("John had a good day in reading") to elaborate reporting of percentage of correct responses in several activities. There does not appear to be any special advantage to any one communication system; the critical issue is that everyone understands what is being communicated (Broughton et al., 1980.

In the parent conference the teacher arranges to send home a "good note" whenever the child meets the desired performance criteria; the parent agrees to provide some desirable activity contingent upon receiving a good note. Notes about bad performance also can go home, but I suggest trying only positive notes at first so as to promote appropriate behaviors and prevent intrafamily squabbles. One potentially important rule about notes is that "no note equals did not meet performance criteria" so that potential problems with losing notes are obviated. The parent should agree not to lecture, inquire about reasons for no note, or punish the child. The reasons for these features are both philosophical and practical — on the one hand protracted arguments about schoolwork may well be detrimental to progress, and on the other hand positive interventions are generally more desirable.

Following the parent conference the procedure should begin immediately (if the child is not present, another conference should be held). It is suggested that home/school communication forms be copied and that the responsibility for having the teacher complete the notes be eventually given to the child.

Excellent results have been found with home school programs for reading. For example, Jenkins et al. (1978) used parents to reinforce increased comprehension performance on the part of children identified as "the worst reading comprehension children in the school." With no additional instruction, the performance of these children in answering comprehension questions about assigned readings increased to very acceptable levels. Lordeman and Winett (1980), Trice, Parker, Furrow, and Iwata (1983), and Witt, Hannafin, and Martens (1983) also demonstrated successful home–school programs for improving reading performance of problem children.

Summary: Reading performance. Each of the identified change agents can be used to manage interventions designed to improve student performance on reading tasks. The type of task may range from comprehension exercises to phonic worksheets; the interventions essentially result in keeping the child engaged with appropriate reading activities. In this sense, opportunities to respond are maintained at a high level, and reading progress is enhanced. The decision about which change agent to employ will depend on a number of factors including the teacher's preference, the teacher's willingness to commit time to the intervention, and decisions about the likely efficacy of different types of interventions with particular children.

Training Change Agents

Training potential change agents for different regular classroom reading interventions involves the use of identical procedures, whether the trainee is a peer, the referred student, or a parent tutor. The following steps are taken from virtually all of the studies in which training was conducted. I have found that following these steps nearly always results in well-trained and competent tutors, contingency managers, etc. It cannot be emphasized enough that failure in the training of reading change agents will usually result in ineffective or poor interventions.

Step 1. Identify all the steps/behaviors that you expect the change agent to exhibit (write them down). Ensure that any necessary materials have been prepared.

Step 2. Meet with the trainee and explain her or his role, the purpose of the intervention, and the expected outcomes. Obviously, this discussion will differ with the age of the trainee.

Step 3. Using the trainee as the tutored student, role-play the procedure, discussing each step and answering questions. If there is more than one student, allow all to see the role-play.

Step 4. Have the trainee now assume the role of the tutor and begin to go through the procedure. The role of the adult trainer is to prompt, model when necessary, and praise good attempts. With older students, a written checklist will prove highly useful as they perform all the steps in the procedure to be learned.

Step 5. Continue practice, fading assistance from the trainer, until the trainee can go through the procedure independently. A general rule of thumb is that the trainer should see independent performance at least twice before allowing the trainee to operate independently. Finally, the trainer can use the procedural checklist to document the outcome of training.

For most of the procedures discussed in this chapter (tutoring, self-management, etc.), change agents can be trained in one or two half-hour sessions. There also are several general rules for potential tutors (and these should be practiced): many positives for the tutee; no negatives, including facial expressions, rolling of the eyes, etc.; all information during tutoring is confidential. It is suggested that these rules be discussed very frequently to prevent problems.

Once training is complete, someone needs to monitor accurate performance occasionally, providing praise and recognition for the change agent. Likewise, it is suggested that regular meetings between tutors and the managing adult be scheduled so that any problems can be prevented; again, recognition of the change agent's efforts will enhance the entire process.

CONCLUSIONS

Although reading is a complicated process and can present complicated problems, there are a number of interventions of documented effectiveness that can be implemented in the regular classroom. If the consultant follows the problem-solving process, attends to the elements of strong reading interventions, and collects progress data and uses it, success in interventions is much more probable than with loosely structured interventions for loosely defined reading problems. There are of course unanswered questions when it comes to fully evaluating regular class reading interventions that are arranged by consultants. The first involves a relative lack of data around the process of implementing successful "real life" reading interventions. Further research is badly needed so that consultation about reading problems can be made most effective. Second, it is unclear what type of reading problems are not remediable with the resources of the regular classroom. Current identification procedures for special education are simply not helpful; useful predictive data would greatly enhance the whole process. Third, special service personnel who intend to consult about reading problems must contend with "competition" from other sources and possible turf conflicts, even when other sources have not been effective with a particular child. However, given the large number of students needing help in reading, there should be more than enough problems to be helped by various specialists. In spite of these problems, classroom consultants are urged to become involved in this most critical of school based problems; we can gain knowledge and skills to make a real contribution to the success of countless schoolchildren.

REFERENCES

Aaron, B., & Bostow, D. (1978). Indirect facilitation of on-task behavior produced by contingent free-time for academic productivity. *Journal of Applied Behavior Analysis, 11,* 197.

Ayllon, T., Layman, D., & Kandel, H. (1975). A behavioral-educational alternative to drug control of hyperactive children. *Journal of Applied Behavior Analysis, 8,* 137-146.

Ayllon, T., & Roberts, M. (1974). Eliminating discipline problems by strengthening academic performance. *Journal of Applied Behavior Analysis, 7,* 71-76.

Andersen, B., & Redd, W. (1980). Programming generalization through stimulus fading with children participating in a remedial reading program. *Education and Treatment of Children, 3,* 297-314.

Bergan, J. (1977). *Behavioral consultation.* Columbus, OH: Merrill.

Billingsley, F. (1977). The effects of self- and externally-imposed schedules of reinforcement on oral reading performance. *Journal of Learning Disabilities, 10,* 20-30.

Bradley-Johnson, S., Sunderman, P., & Johnson, C. (1983). Comparison of delayed prompting and fading for teaching preschoolers easily confused letters and numbers. *Journal of School Psychology, 21,* 327-335.

Broughton, S., Barton, E., & Owen, P. (1980). Home-based contingency systems for school problems. *School Psychology Review, 10,* 26-36.

Center, D., Deitz, S., & Kaufman, M. (1982). Student ability, task difficulty, and inappropriate classroom behavior. *Behavior Modification, 6,* 355-374.

Copeland, R., Brown, R., & Hall, R. (1974). The effects of principal-implemented techniques on the behavior of pupils. *Journal of Applied Behavior Analysis, 7,* 77-86.

Curtis, M., Zins, J., & Graden, J. (1987). Prereferral intervention programs: Enhancing student performance in regular education settings. In C. Maher & J. Zins (Eds.), *Psychoeducational interventions in the schools: Methods and procedures for enhancing student competence* (pp. 7-25). Elmsford, NY: Pergamon.

Deno, S. (1985). Curriculum-based measurement: The emerging alternative. *Exceptional Children, 52,* 219-232.

Deno, S., & Chiang, B. (1979). An experimental analysis of the nature of reversal errors in children with severe learning disabilities. *Learning Disabilities Quarterly, 2,* 40-45.

Deshler, D., Alley, G., Warner, M., & Schumaker, J. (1981). Instructional practices for promoting skill acquisition and generalization in severely learning disabled adolescents. *Learning Disabilities Quarterly, 4,* 415-421.

Elliot, S. N., & Piersel, W. C. (Eds.). (1982). Reading: Assessment and intervention. *School Psychology Review, 11,* 219-305.

Epstein, L. (1978). The effects of intraclass peer tutoring on the vocabulary development of learning disabled children. *Journal of Learning Disabilities, 11,* 63-66.

Freeman, T., & McLaughlin, T. (1984). Effects of a taped-words treatment procedure on learning disabled students' sight-word oral reading. *Learning Disabilities Quarterly, 7,* 49-54.

Gang, D., & Poche, C. (1982). An effective program to train parents as reading tutors for their children. *Education and Treatment of Children, 5,* 211-232.

Gettinger, M. (1984). Measuring time needed for learning to predict learning outcomes. *Exceptional Children, 51,* 244-248.

Greenwood, C., Delquadri, J., & Hall, R. (1984). Opportunity to respond and student academic performance. In W. Heward, T. Heron, J. Trap-Porter, & D. Hill (Eds.), *Focus on behavior analysis in education* (pp. 58-88). Columbus, OH: Merrill.

Greenwood, C., Dinwiddie, G., Terry, B., Wade, L., Stanley, S., Thibadear, S., & Delquadri, J. (1984). Teacher- versus peer-mediated instruction: An ecobehavioral analysis of achievement outcomes. *Journal of Applied Behavior Analysis, 17,* 521-538.

Gutkin, T., & Curtis, M. (1982). School-based consultation: Theory and techniques. In C. Reynolds & T. Gutkin (Eds.), *The handbook of school psychology* (pp. 796-829) New York: Wiley.

Hall, R., Delquadri, J., Greenwood, C., & Thurston, L. (1982). The importance of opportunity to respond in children's academic success. In E. Edgar, N. Haring, J. Jenkins & C. Pious (Eds.), *Mentally handicapped children: Education and training* (pp. 107-141). Baltimore: University Press.

Hallahan, D., Marshall, K., & Lloyd, J. (1981). Self-recording during group instruction: Effects on attention to task. *Learning Disabilities Quarterly, 4,* 407-413.

Hay, W., Hay, L., & Nelson, R. (1977). Direct and collateral changes in on-task and academic behavior resulting from on-task versus academic contingencies. *Behavior Therapy, 8,* 431-441.

Hendrickson, J., Roberts, M., & Shores, R. (1978). Antecedent and contingent modeling to teach basic sight vocabulary to learning disabled children. *Journal of Learning Disabilities, 11,* 524-528.

Heron, T., Heward, W., Cooke, N., & Hill, D. (1983). Evaluation of a classwide peer tutoring system: First graders teach each other sight words. *Education and Treatment of Children, 6,* 137-152.

Hoge, R., & Andrews, D. (1987). Enhancing academic performance: Issues in target selection. *School Psychology Review, 16,* 228-238.

Holt, G. (1971). Effect of reinforcement contingencies in increasing programmed reading and mathematics behaviors in first grade children. *Journal of Experimental Child Psychology, 12,* 362-369.

Jenkins, J., Barksdale, A., & Clinton, L. (1978). Improving reading comprehension and oral reading: Generalization across behaviors, settings, and time. *Journal of Learning Disabilities, 11,* 607-617.

Jenkins, J., Larson, K., & Fleisher, L. (1983). Effects of error correction on word recognition and reading comprehension. *Learning Disabilities Quarterly, 6,* 139-145.

Jenkins, J., Mayhall, V., Peschka, C., & Jenkins, L. (1974). Comparing small group and tutorial instruction in resource rooms. *Exceptional Children, 40,* 245-250.

Kalfus, G. (1984). Peer mediated intervention: A critical review. *Child and Family Behavior Therapy, 6,* 17-43.

Kelley, M., & Stokes, T. (1982). Contingency contracting with disadvantaged youths: Improving classroom performance. *Journal of Applied Behavior Analysis, 15,* 447-454.

Kneedler, R., & Hallahan, D. (1981). Self-monitoring of on-task behavior with learning-disabled children: Current studies and directions. *Exceptional Educational Quarterly, 2,* 73-82.

Kratochwill, T. (1985). Selection of target behaviors in behavioral consultation. *Behavioral Assessment, 7,* 49-61.

Lahey, B., McNees, M., & Brown, C. (1973). Modification of deficits in reading for comprehension. *Journal of Applied Behavior Analysis, 6,* 475-480.

Lentz, F. (1988). On-task behavior, academic performance, and classroom disruption: Untangling the target selection problem in classroom interventions. *School Psychology Review, 17,* 243-257.

Lentz, F., & Shapiro, E. (1985). Behavioral school psychology: A conceptual model for the delivery of psychological services. In T. Kratochwill (Ed.), *Advances in school psychology* (Vol. 4, pp. 191-222). Hillsdale, NJ: Erlbaum.

Lentz, F., & Shapiro, E. (1986). Functional assessment of the academic environment. *School Psychology Review, 15,* 346-357.

Lordeman, A., & Winett, R. (1980). The effects of written feedback to parents and a call-in service on student homework submission. *Education and Treatment of Children, 3,* 33-44.

Mayhall, W., & Jenkins, F. (1977). Scheduling daily or less than daily instruction: Implications for resources programming. *Journal of Learning Disabilities, 10,* 159-163.

Osguthorpe, R., & Scruggs, T. (1986). Special education students as tutors: A review and analysis. *Remedial and Special Education, 7,* 15-26.

Paine, S., Radicchi, J., Rosellini, L., Deutchman, L., & Darch, C. (1983). *Structuring your classroom for academic success.* Champaign, IL: Research Press.

Piersel, W., & Kratochwill, T. (1979). Self-observation and behavior change: Applications to academic and adjustment problems through behavioral consultation. *Journal of School Psychology, 17,* 151-161.

Rapport, M., Murphy, H., & Bailey, J. (1982). Ritalin vs response cost in the control of hyperactive children: A within-subject comparison. *Journal of Applied Behavior Analysis, 15,* 205-216.

Robinson, P., Newby, T., & Ganzell, S. (1981). A token system for a class of underachieving hyperactive children. *Journal of Applied Behavior Analysis, 14,* 307-315.

Rose, T. (1984). The effects of two prepractice procedures on procedures for enhancing student competence in oral reading. *Journal of Learning Disabilities, 17,* 544-548.

Rose, T., & Beattie, J. (1986). Relative effects of teacher-directed and taped previewing on oral reading. *Learning Disabilities Quarterly, 9,* 193-199.

Rose, T., & Sherry, L. (1984). Relative effects of two previewing procedures on LD adolescents' oral reading performance. *Learning Disabilities Quarterly, 7,* 39-44.

Rosenbaum, M., & Breiling, J. (1976). The development and functional control of reading-comprehension behavior. *Journal of Applied Behavior Analysis, 9,* 323-333.

Rosenberg, M. (1986). Error-correction during oral reading: A comparison of three techniques. *Learning Disabilities Quarterly, 9,* 182-192.

Rosenberg, M., Sindelar, P., & Stedt, J. (1985). The effects of supplemental on-task contingencies on the acquisition of simple and difficult academic tasks. *Journal of Special Education, 19,* 189-203.

Rosenshine, B. (1980). How time is spent in elementary classrooms. In C. Denham & A. Lieberman (Eds.), *Time to learn* (pp. 107-126). Washington, DC: National Institute of Education.

Schimek, N. (1983). Errorless discrimination training of diagraphs with a learning disabled student. *School Psychology Review, 12,* 101-105.

Shapiro, E. (1987). *Behavioral assessment in school psychology.* Hillsdale, NJ: Erlbaum.

Shapiro, E., & Lentz, F. (1985). Assessing academic behavior: A behavioral approach. *School Psychology Review, 14,* 325-338.

Sindelar, P. (1982). The effects of cross aged tutoring on the comprehension skills of remedial reading students. *Journal of Special Education, 16,* 199-206.

Singh, N. (1987). Overcorrection of oral reading errors. *Behavior Modification, 11,* 165-181.

Singh, N., & Singh, J. (1984). Antecedent control of oral reading errors and self-corrections by mentally retarded children. *Journal of Applied Behavior Analysis, 17,* 111-119.

Smith, D. (1979). The improvement of children's oral reading through the use of teacher modeling. *Journal of Learning Disabilities, 12,* 39-42.

Snider, V. (1987). Use of self monitoring of attention with LD students: Research and application. *Learning Disabilities Quarterly, 10,* 139-151.

Stanley, S., & Greenwood, C. (1983). How much "opportunity to respond" does the minority disadvantaged student receive in school. *Exceptional Children, 49,* 370-374.

Sterling, E., Goetz, E., & Sterling, T. (1984). Acquisition and maintenance of basal and organic words. *Behavior Modification, 8,* 495-519.

Thorpe, H., & Borden, K. (1985). The effect of multi-sensory instruction upon the on-task behaviors and word reading accuracy of learning disabled children. *Journal of Learning Disabilities, 18,* 279-286.

Thorpe, H., Chiang, B., & Darch, D. (1981). Individual and group feedback systems for improving oral reading accuracy in learning disabled and regular class children. *Journal of Learning Disabilities, 14,* 332-334.

Treiber, F., & Lahey, B. (1983). Toward a behavioral model of academic remediation with learning disabled children. *Journal of Learning Disabilities, 16,* 111-116.

Trice, A., Parker, F., & Furrow, F. (1981). Written conversations with feedback and contingent free time to increase reading and writing in a non-reading adolescent. *Education and Treatment of Children, 4,* 35-41.

Trice, A., Parker, F., Furrow, F., & Iwata, M. (1983). An analysis of home contingencies to improve school behavior with disruptive adolescents. *Education and Treatment of Children, 6,* 389-399.

Trovato, J., & Bucher, B. (1980). Peer tutoring with or without home-based reinforcement, for reading remediation. *Journal of Applied Behavior Analysis, 13*, 129-141.

Van Houten, R., Hill, S., & Parsons, M. (1975). An analysis of a performance feedback system: The effects of timing and feedback, public posting, and praise upon academic performance and peer interaction. *Journal of Applied Behavior Analysis, 8*, 449-457.

Wedd, J., & Fowler, S. (1984). "Read me a story mom": A home tutoring program to teach prereading skills to language-delayed children. *Behavior Modification, 8*, 245-266.

Witt, J. (1986). Teachers' resistance to the use of school-based interventions. *Journal of School Psychology, 24*, 37-44.

Witt, J., Hannafin, M., & Martens, B. (1983). Home-based reinforcement: Behavioral covariation between academic performance and inappropriate behavior. *Journal of School Psychology, 21*, 337-348.

Young, C., Hecimovic, A., & Salzberg, C. (1983). Tutor-tutee behavior of disadvantaged kindergarten children during peer teaching. *Education and Treatment of Children, 6*, 123-135.

Ysseldyke, J., & Mirkin, P. (1982). Assessment information to plan instructional interventions. A review of the research. In C. Reynolds & T. Gutkin (Eds.), *The handbook of school psychology* (pp. 395-409). New York: Wiley.

18

Using Peers as Instructional Agents: Peer Tutoring and Cooperative Learning

Mary Katherine Hawryluk
Rutgers, the State University of New Jersey
Diane L. Smallwood
South Brunswick (NJ) Public Schools

In recent years, the failure of educational programs to meet the needs of children at all levels of ability has been well documented (National Commission on Excellence in Education, 1983). There is general consensus that traditional approaches have been insufficient in meeting current demands on schools and school personnel; yet effective solutions are less evident. It is apparent, however, that efforts to enhance the learning and development of students will have to draw largely on resources already available in our schools. For this reason, educators and related professionals must consider strategies for capitalizing on and reallocating existing human, material, and financial resources.

This chapter emphasizes the potential of peers as a human resource that may be systematically developed and utilized in existing instructional programs. Because teacher-led instruction typically allows for only one student to respond at a time, use of peer groups or dyads may be an effective means of increasing student involvement in learning activities. Moreover, peers appear to be more effective teachers than adults for some types of material, because children are better able to discern each other's signs of confusion, differentiate easy and difficult content, and use language that other children understand (Allen & Feldman, 1973; Buckholdt, & Wodarski, 1978).

The purpose of this chapter is to provide psychologists and other school personnel with an understanding and appreciation of peer-assisted learning as a valuable component of alternative service delivery systems. An overview of basic concepts is followed by a summary of research on two broad categories of peer-assisted learning — peer tutoring and cooperative group learning. In the second part of the chapter, guidelines for designing and implementing peer-assisted learning activities are outlined. Particular attention is given to issues for school psychologists in consultative or program development roles.

OVERVIEW OF PEER-ASSISTED LEARNING

The term *peer-assisted learning* (PAL) refers to instructional methods in which two or more students engage in structured interactions to accomplish a specified learning task. These interactions are planned and guided by a teacher or other staff member and are designed to promote attainment of academic or social-emotional goals for some or all of the students involved (Miller & Peterson, 1987). This definition encompasses two broad approaches to PAL: peer tutoring and cooperative group learning.

In peer tutoring, students work on academic tasks in dyads, in which one student serves as the instructor (tutor) and the other as the learner. Tutoring typically occurs on a regular basis (e.g., daily or twice a week) over a designated time period (e.g., 10 weeks or a semester). Lessons and materials for tutoring sessions usually are structured by the tutored student's teacher and regular contact between the tutor and teacher makes possible prompt feedback on the tutor's instructional skills and learner's progress. Typically, the tutor and learner roles are stable, with the more competent or older student always providing instruction. In some programs, however, partners alternate roles midway through each tutoring session (e.g., Delquadri, Greenwood, Whorton, Carta, & Hall, 1986).

The methods used in peer tutoring include directed learning, with individually prepared lessons and materials based on identified learning objectives, and programmed learning, which provides a highly structured sequence of learning activities based upon criterion-referenced objectives (Jenkins & Jenkins, 1981). Specific materials and strategies are developed by either the professional staff or the tutor, working in close consultation with the learner's classroom teacher. Peer tutoring has been applied successfully with a variety of tutor-learner combinations (Feldman, Devin-Sheehan, & Allen, 1976; Osguthorpe & Scruggs, 1986), including older students tutoring younger children, handicapped peers alternating in tutor-learner roles with each other, handicapped children tutoring younger students, and nonhandicapped children tutoring same-age handicapped peers.

Cooperative group learning (CGL) encompasses diverse instructional approaches in which students collaborate in groups on academic tasks with the dual goal of promoting each group member's learning of designated material, and attaining some reward or recognition based upon the entire group's performance (Johnson & Johnson, 1975, 1986; Sharan, 1980). Cooperative learning groups typically are heterogeneous in composition, being composed of low-, medium-, and high-ability students, and being balanced with regard to student race/ethnicity and sex.

CGL can best be understood in comparison with individualistic and competitive learning. When *individualistic* methods are used, students work alone on learning tasks, with evaluation and rewards based on predetermined performance criteria. For example, students may study lists of spelling words on their own and receive individual grades based upon the percentage correct on a weekly quiz. Performance criteria used in individualistic approaches may be the same for all class members or may be tailored to individual skill levels. In *competitive* learning approaches, students also work alone on academic tasks, but performance is evaluated and rewarded in comparison to that of other students. Grading curves are illustrative of competitive learning (Johnson & Johnson, 1975).

In individualistic approaches, little task-related interaction occurs among students, and each student's grade or reward is completely independent of that attained by other students. Task-related interaction also is limited in competitive learning situations, but evaluations and grades are not independent. Rather, there is "negative interdependence" among students, such that one student's attainment of rewards (e.g., high grades) reduces the rewards available to other students. Students compete with one another for available rewards, and there always are "winners" and "losers." In contrast, the relationship among students in CGL has been described as "positive interdependence," wherein students interact extensively to ensure learning success and attainment of rewards by each group member (Johnson & Johnson, 1980, 1986).

The ways in which student cooperation and interdependence have been incorporated into classrooms are as varied as the teachers implementing such methods. Groups may compete against each other for rewards or recognition. Similarly, students may work on individually tailored and paced tasks within a group context, receiving tutoring and support from other group members.

As shown in Table 1, most CGL approaches can be classified as either group tutoring or group investigation

TABLE 1
Description of Illustrative Cooperative Group Learning Methods

Group Tutoring Methods

1. Student Team Learning (Slavin, 1980)

   Students are divided into teams of five to eight students. Following initial teacher instruction, team members tutor one another in material, using teacher-developed worksheets. Then teams compete against each other to demonstrate mastery of material. In all team learning methods, individual student learning is measured and contributes to a group score. The team with the highest winning score is recognized through newsletters, privileges, rewards, etc. Team learning approaches described in the literature include Student-Team-Achievement-Divisions (STAD), Jigsaw II, and Teams-Game-Tournaments (TGT), as well as Team-Assisted Individualization (TAI), which combines individually paced instruction with cooperative group tutoring.

2. Learning Together (Johnson & Johnson, 1975)

   Students are divided into heterogeneous groups of two to six and given one set of learning materials to work on. Emphasis is on sharing and support among group members. Mastery of material is measured by individual tests/grades or group products.

3. Jigsaw (Aronson, Blaney, Stephan, Sikes, & Snapp, 1978)

   Students are divided into heterogeneous groups and each group member is given only one part of the lesson (e.g., one part of a reading assignment) printed separately on a card or sheet. Students meet with counterparts from other groups to review material thoroughly and then go back to their groups to teach other members the material. Mastery is determined through individual tests and grades. (Jigsaw II, a team learning approach referred to above, is based upon this method.)

Group Investigation Methods

1. Group Investigation (Sharan & Hertz-Lazarowitz, 1980)

   Students are divided into groups, each group responsible for investigating a particular subtopic related to a general area of study. Groups plan methods of gathering pertinent information, usually resulting in division of labor among members. Each group then plans and presents a report or project to the class. Ultimately, each class member is expected to learn all material presented in each group. Individual testing may be used to measure mastery. Quality of the investigation process used by each group is also emphasized.

2. Co-op Co-op (Kagan, 1985)

   Similar to Group Investigation, but more structured in that specific steps are followed in dividing the general area of study into subtopics and then dividing the subtopics into minitopics. Each group member is responsible for researching a minitopic and presenting to other group members. Then the group integrates information into a presentation for the class. Individual mastery of material is measured; in addition, it is recommended that individual student's contributions to the group effort be evaluated and recognized.

(Sharan, 1980). In tutoring groups, learning goals typically involve acquisition of rote material (e.g., spelling words, history facts) or technical skills (e.g., arithmetic operations). After a teacher's presentation of a lesson, students drill one another in the material to be learned. This may occur in the form of reciprocal tutoring dyads or each group member may teach all other members a particular aspect of the lesson. Each student's learning may be measured through quizzes or tournaments, but individual performance ultimately contributes to a group score. Group investigation methods typically are used to promote creative or critical thinking. For example, each group member may explore one aspect of a research topic (e.g., military tactics of World War II); students then share information and integrate it into a group product or project (e.g., written report, oral presentation, dramatization), with grading based in part or solely upon the group product.

PEER TUTORING AND COOPERATIVE GROUP LEARNING: COMMON ELEMENTS AND DIFFERENCES

Peer tutoring and CGL share many characteristics, but have somewhat different applications and structures. This section summarizes essential similarities and differences between the two approaches, with emphasis on applications in alternative service delivery systems.

Learning Goals and Tasks

At a fundamental level, all PAL methods address the goal of enhanced student learning and achievement. Typically, learning goals associated with peer tutoring center on acquisition of factual information and basic skills, whereas CGL strategies have been applied to a broader range of goals and tasks. As noted previously, group tutoring is likely to focus on mastery of rote knowledge; group investigation is more often used to promote divergent or critical thinking (Sharan, 1980). Common to both CGL and peer tutoring is the assumption that academic performance should improve through increased review of material or more active engagement in academic tasks.

Student Characteristics and Needs

The focus of CGL is on performance of all students. Peer/cross-age tutoring focuses primarily on learner achievement, although a side effect often seems to be enhanced academic performance by tutors. Both strategies have been used with students at all age/grade and ability levels. In recent years, however, peer tutoring has been applied most often with students displaying learning difficulties or other school adjustment problems (Ehly, 1986; Jenkins & Jenkins, 1981). CGL typically has been used on a classwide basis and hence has been less problem-focused than peer tutoring.

Student Interactions and Relationships

The most salient distinction between peer/cross-age tutoring and CGL is reflected in the relationship between students who work with one another. In CGL, work partners interact as equals, each being responsible for promoting the other's learning. Although group members may have varied learning abilities or achievement levels, differences are not formally highlighted; in fact, learning tasks and reward criteria typically are designed to compensate for status differences among students. In cross-age tutoring, by contrast, the relationship between work partners is not symmetrical or coequal. Rather, the older student, assumed to be more competent, enacts the role of instructor for the younger learner. The tutor directs and manages interactions and the learner follows directions. Relationships between partners in same-age peer tutoring vary from program to program. In some cases, the relationship resembles cross-age tutoring, with more competent students providing instruction to less able youngsters; in other cases, peers have equal status, alternating tutor and learner roles. The latter approach is similar to CGL, although reward structures may be based solely upon individual, rather than dyadic, performance.

Time and Location

CGL activities occur in the context of a class session and are part of the instructional plan for a particular subject or unit. While peer tutoring sometimes is implemented as part of a class curriculum, more typically tutoring is designed to supplement classroom instruction. Partners meet during a free period or before or after school hours to review material covered in class.

Teacher's Role

In both peer tutoring and CGL, the classroom teacher assumes three essential responsibilities. First, as the primary instructor, the teacher plans lessons and provides initial instruction in skills or concepts to be learned. Second, as instructional manager, the teacher designs learning materials and provides ongoing supervision of students as they work together. Finally, in both CGL and peer tutoring, the teacher evaluates student progress and provides feedback or rewards accordingly.

RESEARCH ON PEER-ASSISTED LEARNING

From an alternative service delivery perspective, both academic and social/affective outcomes of PAL are critical. In addition to academic failure, emotional and behavioral problems are frequently the basis for referral to the special education system (Ysseldyke, Pianta, Christenson, Wang, & Algozzine, 1983). Even when low-performing students are not placed in special education, they may experience repeated frustration and failure in learning situations, in consequence experiencing lowered self-esteem and reduced motivation. Furthermore, research has consistently shown that mainstreamed handicapped students are not well accepted by peers and do not show gains in self-esteem unless specific strategies are used to facilitate social integration (Madden & Slavin, 1983b). For both low-achieving and handicapped students, therefore, alternative service delivery approaches must include educational practices designed to help students profit from academic instruction and socialization opportunities in the regular classroom.

The summary of research provided in this section highlights findings and conclusions most pertinent to applications of PAL as a component of alternative service delivery systems. Much of the empirical research on peer tutoring and CGL has occurred in applied settings, as part of ongoing instructional programs, and methodological problems associated with applied educational research may limit reliability and validity of findings. The specific technical issues include lack of appropriate control groups; failure to control for variables that may mediate success, such as amount of instructional time, effects of teacher attention, or other context factors; limited attention to subject selection variables; and inadequate long-term follow-up.

Cooperative Group Learning

A vast body of empirical evidence, compiled primarily by two prominent research groups, documents the effects of CGL strategies on achievement, interpersonal relationships, and emotional adjustment. Roger and David Johnson and colleagues at the University of Minnesota, known for the Learning Together model (Johnson & Johnson, 1975), have conducted numerous investigations and reviews comparing cooperative, competitive, and individualistic learning. Robert Slavin and colleagues at the Johns Hopkins University Center for the Social Organization of Schools have focused much of their research on student teams and interteam competition (e.g., Student–Team–Achievement–Divisions, Teams–Games–Tournaments, Team-Assisted Individualization). Complementing the efforts of these two groups is an emerging body of research on student interaction patterns in small learning groups (e.g., Webb, 1982; Peterson & Janicki, 1979).

Impact of CGL on student achievement. A substantial amount of research indicates that achievement outcomes in CGL are at least equivalent, and usually superior, to those obtained with other methods. Meta-analysis of 122 CGL studies (Johnson, Maruyama, Johnson, Nelson, & Skon, 1981) has indicated that significantly higher achievement and better retention of material is achieved by using cooperative methods rather than individualistic and competitive learning. These differences applied to all age groups and academic subjects, for a diverse range of learning tasks including concept formation, verbal and spatial problem solving, memory, and prediction. The only learning tasks in which CGL was not superior to other methods were rote decoding and correcting. Although some authors (Cotton & Cook, 1982; Slavin, 1983) have questioned the conclusions of Johnson et al. (1981) about the superiority of cooperative learning, other reviews and investigations (e.g., Sharan, 1980; Webb, 1982) have yielded similar results: When CGL is used, student achievement and participation generally are enhanced.

Achievement outcomes associated with CGL have been attributed in part to the nature of the learning process when students work in groups. Reviewing, summarizing, and questioning activities that occur when group members drill one another may be more extensive and intensive than in individual study, enhancing recall of material, awareness of whether mastery has been achieved, organization of material, and understanding of concepts and information (Yaeger, Johnson, & Johnson, 1985; Webb, 1982).

Alternative explanations for achievement outcomes in CGL have focused on motivational factors. Involvement with peers in learning groups may be sufficiently enjoyable and reinforcing that students put forth more effort (Johnson & Johnson, 1986), or group incentive structures and peer pressure may prompt students to study harder and perform more successfully. Slavin (1983) emphasizes the importance of *individual accountability* combined with group reward to promote higher achievement. These findings are crucial in light of some teachers' reluctance to base rewards on group performance.

The utility of CGL in the context of alternative service delivery is predicated upon its effectiveness with low-achieving and maladjusted students in the regular classroom. Evidence on this issue is limited but promising. In an analogue study, Cosden, Pearl, and Bryan (1985) found no differences in performance of learning-disabled students paired with nondisabled peers under individual or cooperative conditions. Classroom studies of CGL have shown higher overall achievement for students at all ability levels compared with individualistic methods (Yaeger et al., 1985), higher math achievement on the part of mildly handicapped students when Team-Assisted Individualization is used (Slavin, Madden, & Leavey, 1983), and enhanced reading vocabulary achievement among socially isolated low achievers (Lew, Mesch, Johnson, & Johnson, 1986).

The degree of heterogeneity within cooperative groups may influence achievement outcomes (Webb, 1982); however, it may be that group composition is most influential during initial interaction and that after groups have gained experience working together, differences in heterogeneity are not related to achievement (Webb, 1984).

Although student ability has been the most frequently researched influence on achievement in CGL, other determinants of learning have been identified. Of particular interest are studies indicating that the amount and kind of student interaction may be critical factors in learning success. For example, individual achievement has been positively correlated with receiving explanations from other group members and negatively related to not receiving explanations when needed (Peterson & Janicki, 1979; Webb, 1982). Passive behavior (i.e., watching but not participating) and off-task behavior also appear to be negatively related to achievement (Webb, 1982). In addition, teachers' structuring of students' interactions through assignment of listener/presenter roles seems to facilitate immediate and long-term retention (Yaeger et al., 1985).

Impact of CGL on social and emotional adjustment. The most frequently researched affective outcome of CGL is enhanced interpersonal relationships among students. Compared with individualistic and competitive instructional methods, CGL has resulted in more cooperative and altruistic attitudes toward peers, increased helping behavior among classmates, increased feelings of being liked and supported by peers, more frequent cross-racial friendship choices, and increased acceptance of mainstreamed handicapped students by nonhandicapped peers (Sharan, 1980; Madden & Slavin, 1983a; Johnson, Johnson, & Maruyama, 1983; Johnson & Johnson, 1980).

Findings on acceptance of handicapped students have been mixed, but generally promising. Madden and Slavin (1983a), for example, reported significantly less rejection (on sociometric measures) of mildly handicapped students as potential workmates in cooperative learning than in individualistic situations. Other investigators have reported greater acceptance of handicapped students as work partners or friends when cooperative methods are used in nonacademic activities (e.g., sports) and in learning situations (Johnson & Johnson, 1980). Moreover, cross-handicap relationships fostered by cooperative learning experiences in the classroom may generalize to nonstructured class situations (e.g., free study time) and even to out-of-class school activities (Johnson, Johnson, Warring, & Maruyama, 1986).

Closely related to peer acceptance outcomes of cooperative learning are gains in prosocial skills. Students involved in CGL were observed to make more positive statements about peer performance and ability (Crockenberg & Bryant, 1978). And Lew et al. (1986) found that CGL, combined with reinforcement for collaboration, promoted more adaptive interpersonal behavior by social isolates as well as entry into relationships with more competent peers.

Affective gains associated with CGL have included enhanced self-perceptions as well as more positive attitudes toward school and learning. Students in CGL have shown higher levels of self-esteem and healthier processes for drawing conclusions about self-worth (Johnson & Johnson, 1986; Madden & Slavin, 1983a). In classes using CGL, students have expressed more positive views of classroom climate and greater liking for school (Wright & Cowen, 1985; Zahn, Kagan, & Widaman, 1986). When group investigation approaches were used consistently, students rated classroom social climate as more positive than when these methods were used sporadically (Sharan, 1980). CGL may also result in enhanced achievement motivation and more positive attitudes toward the subject being taught (Johnson & Johnson, 1986).

Although there is strong empirical and theoretical support for use of CGL to improve students' social and emotional outcomes, certain factors that mediate these outcomes must be considered. Although evidence is limited, two variables appear to influence social and affective outcomes, especially for lower-achieving students. The first is the relationship among student groups in a classroom. Empirical data indicate greater benefits for cross-racial and cross-handicap relationships when learning groups cooperate than when they compete, as is often the case in team learning approaches (Johnson & Johnson, 1984; Johnson et al., 1986). When groups compete, lower-achieving students may be less accepted by group members who perceive them as impediments to attainment of group goals (i.e., winning).

Group success is a second important influence on social and affective outcomes of CGL. In analogue situations, lower-performing students have shown enhanced self-perceptions and satisfaction with learning when their group successfully attained its goal. In unsuccessful groups, low performers made much harsher judgments of their own ability and were less satisfied with the experience, and high performers were more likely to blame and reject low performers (Ames, 1981). Although further research is needed, it seems important for teachers to monitor patterns of success and failure. If low-achieving students are frequently members of unsuccessful groups, the impact on self-esteem and attitudes toward learning may be no more positive, and perhaps even more negative, than in competitive situations.

Peer Tutoring

Because "peer tutoring" encompasses numerous instructional paradigms, it is important to clarify the usage of several terms. As an adjunct to teacher-led instruction, peer tutoring may supplement classroom learning, the partners meeting outside of regular class periods, or it may be incorporated into the instructional program as a classwide activity. Approaches are identified as "supplemental" or "classwide" when such distinctions are relevant. Tutoring also may be structured to provide for either same-age or cross-age peer interaction. Classwide approaches are limited to same-age dyads in most cases, but supplemental tutoring may be either same-age or cross-age. Findings specific to either format are identified accordingly. The generic term "peer tutoring" refers to reciprocal student interactions within any of the above paradigms.

Impact of peer tutoring on student achievement. Tutoring can be successfully applied at all age/grade levels, from preschool (Hamblin & Hamblin, 1972; Stokes & Baer, 1976) through secondary and college levels (Cloward, 1976; Vassallo, 1973), and involve students at all levels of ability and performance, including learning-disabled (Delquadri et al., 1986; Scruggs & Osguthorpe, 1986), mentally retarded (Wagner & Sternlicht, 1975), low-achieving (Cloward, 1976), and behaviorally disordered children (Maher, 1984). Learning goals and instructional content for peer tutoring typically focus on enhancement of learners' performance in basic academic skills (i.e., decoding, computation, spelling). Although the explicit purpose of most tutoring programs is enhancement of tutored students' academic skills, the results often are investigated from the perspective of tutor gains as well.

In a review of studies comparing peer tutoring with teacher-led instruction, Gerber and Kauffman (1981) noted that under specified conditions, peer tutoring and teaching may be equally effective, and that combinations of tutoring and teaching may be more effective than teacher-led instruction by itself. They emphasized, however, that insufficient evidence exists to compare cost effectiveness of teacher-led instruction with widescale peer tutoring programs.

Variables that appear to contribute significantly to academic outcomes for tutored students include reinforcement contingencies and schedules, tutor train-ing, organization of learning objectives and instructional materials, selection/matching of tutoring partners, classroom environment (Gerber & Kauffman, 1981), and frequency and duration of tutoring sessions (Jenkins & Jenkins, 1981). Specific tutor or learner characteristics do not appear to be related to learning outcomes (Gerber & Kauffman, 1981).

Rewarding good performance within tutoring dyads may enhance learning. Three forms of reinforcement can be used in peer tutoring: rewarding whole classrooms on the basis of group contingencies, rewarding tutors for quality teaching, and rewarding learners for accurate or improved performance (Gerber & Kauffman, 1981). Both tangible rewards (i.e., tokens or grades) and social reinforcers (i.e., attention or praise) are effective in peer tutoring, and training tutors in delivering reinforcement may improve learning (McGee, Kauffman, & Nussen, 1977).

Regardless of subject area, learner performance is facilitated by well-organized, hierarchical, and sequential instruction (Gerber & Kauffman, 1981; Jenkins & Jenkins, 1981). Use of a mastery-based model of tutoring (presenting new material only after previous content has been mastered) also may facilitate learning (Jenkins & Mayhall, 1979; Robertson, 1972). Materials structured to elicit brief, unambiguous responses may allow tutors to discriminate correct from faulty responses more readily, permitting accurate and efficient feedback (Melaragno, 1976). Daily 30-minute sessions appear more effective than longer, biweekly sessions (Mayhall & Jenkins, 1977).

Explanations for academic gains by tutored students typically have focused on the positive effects of increasing engaged academic time or providing additional opportunities to respond to learning tasks (Hall, Delquadri, Greenwood, & Thurston, 1982). Support for such hypotheses is provided by recent empirical studies (Greenwood et al., 1984; Delquadri et al., 1986) that indicate classwide peer tutoring produces greater student participation and higher test scores than do comparable teacher-directed activities.

Improved academic performance by

peer tutors has been reported less consistently than gains by tutored students, but there is evidence that the teaching role, by reinforcing previously acquired knowledge and concepts, advances tutors' academic achievement. In two experiments within special education settings, Scruggs and Osguthorpe (1986) observed significant academic gains by both tutors and learners. In a large-scale urban program using low-achieving students as tutors, gains in tutors' academic achievement surpassed those by their partners (Cloward, 1976). Jenkins and Jenkins (1981) provide two generalizations about the cognitive effects of tutoring: (a) Tutors demonstrate greater personal academic gains when given responsibility for creating or organizing instructional materials and techniques than when only implementing programmed tutoring, and (b) improved academic performance of tutors themselves is most evident when tutoring is in subjects in which they are somewhat deficient themselves.

Impact of peer tutoring on social and emotional adjustment. In addition to academic benefits, peer tutoring often results in positive changes in social behavior or school adjustment (Jenkins & Jenkins, 1981; Strodtbeck, Ronchi, & Hansell, 1976). Cross-age tutoring may provide learners with opportunities to experience greater success in learning situations, receive academic help without having to confront an "authority figure," learn more positive social behaviors through modeling, and receive encouragement and support from an older friend (Lippitt, 1976). Gains in tutored students' academic skills and collaboration with a higher-status peer have been associated with more positive school attitudes, as well as increased self-confidence and higher self-esteem (Cohen, 1986; Feldman et al., 1976).

Empirical studies have demonstrated psychological benefits associated with the role of tutor as well. Allen and Feldman (1976) reported that tutors rated themselves more competent in cognitive and academic skills after teaching other children. Maher (1984) observed greater completion of academic assignments and fewer disciplinary referrals among handicapped adolescents who tutored younger handicapped students. Other advantages of acting as tutor may include collaborative interactions with adults, opportunities to feel responsible or needed, higher status within peer groups, and a chance to develop or practice helping skills (Lippitt, 1976).

A number of variables that influence the nature and quality of peer tutoring interactions have been identified. Allen and Feldman (1976) reported greater satisfaction of tutors with the teaching role and more positive attributions about a partner's likability when tutored students performed well. Garbarino (1975) found that students expecting a monetary reward were less effective teachers and displayed more negative reactions to their partners than tutors with more intrinsic motivation. Preferences for same-sex tutoring partners have been reported (Allen & Feldman, 1976), although gender effects with regard to tutoring outcomes have not been obtained (Feldman et al., 1976). When tutors are required to evaluate and grade their partners' efforts, confidence in teaching skills and enjoyment with tutoring may be lowered (Allen & Feldman, 1976).

It is important to recognize that negative psychological effects also may be derived from peer tutoring. Perceptions of inferior status or performance associated with the learner role may adversely affect self-concept and school attitudes (Cohen, 1986). In addition, both tutors and learners may experience fear of failure or nonacceptance (Lippitt, 1976). Overall, however, peer tutoring relationships can provide an appropriate structure for academic and social learning.

IMPLEMENTING PEER-ASSISTED LEARNING IN SCHOOLS: GUIDELINES FOR PRACTICE

Clearly, a technology exists for utilization of PAL methods in classroom settings. In order to provide a viable alternative to traditional special education classification and placement, however, that technology must be applied systematically and integrated effectively into the general education program. Whether PAL strategies are implemented on a school or district-wide level, in a single classroom, or with only a few students, school professionals face a number of conceptual issues and logistical decisions pertinent to program success. This section examines key issues involved in using PAL as a component of alternative services delivery and delineates guidelines for practice based upon the authors' own experience and perspectives gleaned from the literature. Strategies to facilitate success are considered with regard to each of four phases of program development: establishing readiness, initial planning and design, program implementation, and evaluation.

A central premise of this discussion is that school psychologists can and should take an active role in introducing and supporting use of PAL as an alternative instructional method. Efforts in this vein may require a combination of direct participation in planning and scheduling instructional activities, and indirect involvement in the form of teacher training and consultation, program monitoring, and follow-up "trouble shooting." The guidelines presented in this section include strategies for the direct-service professional (most often the classroom teacher) responsible for day-to-day implementation of a particular PAL activity, as well as ways in which consulting personnel (e.g., school psychologists) can support use of such strategies.

Establishing Readiness for PAL

The notion of readiness for educational innovation may be defined in terms of both attitudinal factors, such as awareness or understanding of the new approach, and availability of essential resources to support the program (Maher & Bennett, 1984). As applied to PAL, readiness refers to preliminary acceptance of concepts, rationales, and methods pertaining to use of peers as agents of instruction and acquisition of technical skills and knowledge required for effective

use of peer-mediated instruction. Readiness should be assessed and promoted differentially for administrators, classroom teachers, students, and parents.

Administrative readiness. An appropriate starting point for introducing PAL into regular education curriculum is the administrative staff, with particular emphasis on support from the building principal. The principal is the individual who can sanction procedural adjustments needed to support a particular PAL program, such as release time for teacher or student training, scheduling modifications that allow students to tutor one another and to communicate regularly with teachers, and changes in allocation and design of physical space for instruction (e.g., so that students may work in group arrangements in a classroom). Administrators also play a key role in encouraging regular use of PAL methods (Johnson & Johnson, 1982).

Teacher readiness. The multidimensional role for teachers in structuring, facilitating, and monitoring PAL requires considerable organization and flexibility. In planning CGL activities, for example, teachers must take into account such factors as group size and composition, student role assignments, relationships among groups, and criteria for grading and rewards (Johnson & Johnson, 1986). Peer tutoring methods require efficient scheduling, as well as ongoing supervision of tutor and learner performance. Other teacher skills include competence in developing suitable instructional materials, providing group instruction as a basis for CGL or peer tutoring, and facilitating effective interaction among students. Clearly, teachers' readiness for PAL is dependent upon thorough training in these methods, most often in the form of in-service education with follow-up consultation and supervision.

An additional critical dimension of readiness is attitudes toward concepts and techniques encompassed by PAL. Teachers must be willing to modify classroom routines in order to incorporate PAL into lesson plans on a regular basis. Perhaps even more critical, teachers must be able to relinquish some degree of control to students. Shared responsibility for the instructional process is an essential component of PAL, yet often difficult for teachers and administrators to accept (Lippitt, 1976). Another attitudinal issue that can impede effective use of CGL is teachers' reluctance to assign group grades or rewards.

Strong administrative support is likely to influence teachers' reactions to and willingness to implement PAL methods. In addition, in-service training that includes simulated cooperative group activities can provide teachers with direct personal experience with different dimensions of PAL (Johnson & Johnson, 1982). Finally, personal contact with colleagues who have used PAL successfully may make its nontraditional components seem more acceptable.

Student/parent readiness. Students' and parents' apprehensions regarding PAL often are based on misconceptions about the nature or purpose of peer learning methods and about teachers' expectations for student performance. A common source of resistance to CGL, for example, is the belief that higher-functioning students may be penalized by group-based grades. In both peer tutoring and CGL, parents and students may believe that instruction time spent with less adept youngsters will detract from the learning of more skilled students. At the same time, lower-ability students and their families may fear social rejection as a consequence of the "public" nature of performance in a peer learning context. In this vein, advance preparation of students and parents for PAL is essential. It is particularly important that students and parents be made aware of the variety of learning approaches to be used in the classroom (including individualistic methods) and of the importance of individual as well as group performance in teachers' grading criteria. With students, such preparation occurs largely through oral and written instructions from the teacher explicating expectations and performance criteria in the PAL context. Parents' understanding of PAL may be enhanced through discussions at PTA meetings, articles in school district newsletters, letters sent home prior to initiation of a PAL program, and personal contacts.

Initial Design and Development of PAL Programs

Once some degree of "readiness" for peer-assisted methods is established, a focus of planning turns to introduction of a particular PAL program or strategy. Tasks to be accomplished at this point include selection of PAL methods best suited to identified goals and objectives, decision making about how PAL will be integrated into classroom instruction, and preparation and training of all participants.

Selecting a PAL approach. Decisions concerning the specific PAL method to be used should be based upon an analysis of learning goals and tasks, the number and characteristics of students to be addressed, and the resources available (Bohlmeyer & Burke, 1987). Preferences for classroom based or supplemental interventions also play a role in the choice between peer tutoring and CGL, as well as in designing the format of same-age tutoring programs.

Integrating PAL with other instructional methods. Even the staunchest advocates of PAL approaches do not contend that these methods can or should be used exclusively. Peer tutoring usually serves as a vehicle for structured practice and reinforcement of lessons presented by the classroom teacher. The teacher's responsibility, therefore, is to coordinate classroom instruction and peer tutoring schedules to ensure that tutoring activities and materials are targeted at recent classroom lessons.

With regard to CGL, the task for teachers is to determine the balance of cooperative, competitive, and individualistic methods suited to learning goals and context (Johnson & Johnson, 1975). A science teacher, for example, might decide to use group investigation approaches for lab activities and research projects and individualistic learning structures for teaching and measuring factual material. In the authors' experience, preliminary decisions about the relative proportion of cooperative and other learning approaches should be made during the initial design phase for two reasons. First, such decisions are essential for effective planning of instructional units and daily lessons. Second, resistance to cooperative learning on the part of students, parents, or administrators often can be defused by pointing out that this is one of several instructional approaches being used, constituting a specified proportion (e.g., 25%) of the learning experience.

Preparing teachers. The teacher plays a central role in providing initial instruction in material to be learned, structuring learning tasks to be carried out in the context of a peer-assisted approach, developing needed materials (e.g., worksheets) for peer tutors or learning groups, monitoring student progress and behavior, and facilitating student interaction and collaboration (Johnson & Johnson, 1986; Miller & Peterson, 1987). Training and preparation of teachers during initial program development should be aimed at understanding of the purpose and essential features of the PAL method being used, skill in planning lessons and preparing materials for student use, and competence in teaching interactional and problem-solving behaviors to students. Training activities should include classroom aides or other personnel likely to be involved in implementation.

When only a few teachers are involved in introduction of a particular PAL method, the most efficient and feasible approach to preparation and training may be consultation (e.g., by a school psychologist), complemented by reading of teacher manuals and other practitioner-oriented materials (e.g., Ehly, 1986; Jenkins & Jenkins, 1981; Johnson & Johnson, 1975; Slavin, 1980). When several teachers are involved, a series of in-service training sessions may be useful. Whether provided through individual consultation or group training, teacher preparation should include (a) didactic instruction in

basic elements of PAL methods, (b) simulation exercises that familiarize teachers with both student and teacher roles, (c) modeling of strategies for social skills training and conflict resolution with students, and (d) discussion of anticipated difficulties that may impede implementation. In the authors' experience, this last component is extremely important in helping teachers feel comfortable with and committed to the PAL program. Inadequate attention to teachers' reservations may result in half-hearted attempts at implementation or premature abandonment of the program when difficulties arise.

Student preparation. Needless to say, the success of PAL is dependent upon student responsiveness to the attitudinal and behavioral demands of this instructional approach. Peer tutors must be skilled in developing and presenting instructional material, providing explanations and corrective feedback to their partners, recognizing responses as correct or faulty and delivering reinforcement, redirecting off-task behavior, monitoring their own verbal and nonverbal responses to learner behavior, and communicating with the teacher about tutoring sessions and learner progress (Ehly & Larsen, 1980; Jenkins & Jenkins, 1981). Equally important is an understanding of the special characteristics and learning needs of the tutored student. Prior to implementation of tutoring it is highly recommended that tutors be formally trained in these skills by means of didactic presentations about the peer tutoring process; practice in delivering instruction, recognizing correct responses, providing reinforcement, and charting learner progress; group troubleshooting discussions; and individual meetings to provide relevant information about the learner (Ehly & Larsen, 1980; Gerber & Kauffman, 1981; Jenkins & Jenkins, 1981; Maher, 1984).

Two opposing philosophies are evident in selection and matching of tutoring partners. One approach uses academically competent students as tutors for same-age or younger peers. Older, more capable students are easier to train, require minimal supervision, and in most cases are more effective in managing their partners' behavior (Jenkins & Jenkins, 1981). Furthermore, competent tutoring, an important ethical consideration, is easier to assure when academically capable students serve as tutors (Gerber & Kauffman, 1981). An alternative approach assigns handicapped or low-achieving students as cross-age tutors for younger children (Cloward, 1976). The latter method typically is based upon program goals that prioritize academic or social gains for tutors. Avoiding the pairing of students with mutually aversive behavior also is important to successful tutoring (Gerber & Kauffman, 1981).

In cooperative learning, important student competencies include communication skills (i.e., explaining, question asking, listening), ability to organize group tasks and allocate responsibility, group problem solving and conflict resolution skills, and understanding of group and individual performance and reward criteria. Some authors have advocated formal training of students for CGL (Aronson, Blaney, Stephan, Sikes, & Snapp, 1978), but others contend that group contingencies for collaborative behavior are sufficient to promote appropriate interaction (Lew et al., 1986). In the authors' experience, class sessions focusing on communication skills and systematic problem solving are beneficial.

Parent preparation. When peer tutoring activities single out individual students, parental consent should be obtained. Prior to any request for consent, parents should be provided with a clear explanation of the program, reasons for their children's involvement, and safeguards against possible negative effects. Because cooperative learning strategies and classwide peer tutoring involve all students in a given setting, individual contact and consent is not needed. However, sending a letter to parents prior to initiating CGL may help avoid parental misconceptions about methods or grading policies. In such a letter, it is particularly helpful to describe the extent to which cooperative learning will be used relative to other types of instructional approaches.

Implementing PAL Programs

The success with which PAL methods are introduced and implemented in a classroom or school system is dependent upon both student and teacher behavior. It is essential that the students involved interact with one another in ways that promote attainment of designated academic and social/emotional goals. Equally important is continued teacher motivation and commitment, precluding premature abandonment of the program.

Facilitating student interaction. Teachers and other school personnel play an essential role in promoting positive learning-focused interaction between students involved in PAL. In peer tutoring programs, initial tutor training is an important first step in this regard. Once tutoring begins, however, systematic supervision and monitoring of tutoring dyads is critical (Gerber & Kauffman, 1981). Research indicates that tutoring programs using daily, structured supervision may be more effective than those without this element (Mayhall et al., 1975). Essential components of such supervision include meetings with the tutor following each tutoring session to review material covered and learner progress, periodic observation of tutoring pairs, modeling and role-playing of effective tutoring behavior for the tutor, corrective feedback to the tutor regarding teaching and interactive behavior, and immediate intervention to assist tutoring pairs with conflict resolution.

Also essential to successful implementation of peer tutoring are carefully structured lessons that are understandable to the tutor and relatively easy to implement, with clear instructions for each part of the session. Since increased involvement in development of lessons and materials results in higher academic gains for tutors (Cloward, 1976), responsibility for planning instruction should be shared with tutors as much as possible.

A final consideration for peer tutoring

programs involves reinforcement or recognition for tutors to maintain participation and interest. This is of particular importance in cross-age tutoring that takes place outside of regularly scheduled class time, since tutors may have to forego participation in other equally desirable activities. A combination of intrinsic and extrinsic reinforcers, including personal attention and praise from teachers, group planning sessions, letters of commendation, or regularly scheduled reinforcement events (i.e., luncheons, parties, awards, meetings) can be effective in maintaining the interest and involvement of cross-age tutors (Jenkins & Jenkins, 1981).

The task of facilitating student interaction and productivity in CGL may be even more complex than in peer tutoring. In tutoring, the focus is on pairs of students with fairly explicit role assignments (i.e., teacher and learner). Cooperative learning, however, usually involves several students (as many as eight) in each learning group, and depending on the approach used, members may assume a number of different roles (e.g., teacher, listener, recorder, researcher) at different points in the learning task. Successful student interaction in cooperative groups requires a sense of interdependence among group members with regard to group goals and rewards, skill in attending to and limiting off-task behavior, and ability to organize responsibilities, materials, and time (Johnson & Johnson, 1986).

Recently, several authors have suggested guidelines for teachers in implementing cooperative learning methods (Johnson & Johnson, 1986; Lew et al., 1986; Miller & Peterson, 1987; Yaeger et al., 1985). Included among these guidelines are recommendations pertaining to ways of structuring cooperative groups and tasks, reminders to students about the importance of collaboration, contingencies for collaborative behavior, intervention to facilitate resolution of group conflict, and strategies for prompting students to examine and improve their interactive patterns and productivity.

Among the recommended strategies for CGL, the most difficult to implement may be those pertaining to facilitation of group problem solving and conflict resolution. Teachers must provide sufficient structure and guidance to help groups identify ways of resolving difficulties, but they should resist the temptation to tell students how to solve problems. In this vein, training students in explicit problem-solving methods (e.g., Gesten & Weissberg, 1986) may be useful in providing a language system for teacher prompts as problems arise in groups.

Although the literature has emphasized the role of classroom teachers in facilitating student interaction in PAL programs, other school personnel also may be involved. When peer tutoring involves students from several classes, it may be most efficient for a pupil personnel professional, such as a school psychologist, to coordinate the program, assuming responsibilities for matching tutoring dyads, initial tutor training, and ongoing supervision. When this occurs, however, regular communication and close collaboration with teachers is essential.

In CGL, the classroom teacher takes primary responsibility for guiding student interaction. In some cases, however, the school psychologist might collaborate with the teacher in initial training of students in problem solving and communication skills. Supplementary coaching outside the classroom might also be provided by the psychologist to handicapped students or other youngsters with deficits in social skills (Johnson & Johnson, 1986).

Maintaining teacher motivation and commitment. When teachers are novices in the use of PAL methods, early implementation problems may be especially discouraging. If students are resistant or simply have difficulties learning new behaviors required to participate in PAL, teachers may question whether the time needed to promote student cooperation is worthwhile. Negative reactions from parents, administrators, or colleagues also may prompt teachers to forego the new program in favor of more traditional methods.

Supportive consultation may help teachers approach these problems from a systematic problem-solving perspective, leading to experimentation with alternative solutions. When several teachers in a school building or system are involved in implementing similar PAL programs, periodic meetings to exchange ideas and concerns may be helpful. One of the authors used monthly discussion groups as a vehicle for supporting junior high school teachers as they began to implement cooperative learning methods. These meetings provided an opportunity for teachers to share difficulties and to obtain suggestions from colleagues about effective solutions as well as lessons in which CGL had been most successful. Two cautions about colleague support systems should be made, however. First, group discussions can turn into "gripe" sessions that dampen rather than foster commitment to the program. Second, an element of competition and defensiveness can emerge as teachers describe their successes and difficulties. Hence, such meetings should be facilitated by a professional skilled in promoting group cohesion and problem solving. Other forms of teacher support include opportunities to observe in colleagues' classes and attendance at workshops outside of the district.

Evaluating PAL Programs

Evaluation efforts associated with PAL should be both formative (process-oriented) and summative (outcome-oriented). Throughout the initial implementation and maintenance of educational programs, it is essential to determine to what extent (a) instructional activities have been implemented as planned, (b) learning activities/methods are appropriately matched to student needs and abilities, (c) participants (i.e., school personnel and students/parents) are satisfied with instructional tasks, methods, and materials, and (d) intended learning outcomes have been attained. Valid and reliable information is needed about the first three issues, which are addressed through formative evaluation, before meaningful conclusions may be drawn from data related to learning outcomes.

An effective approach to formative evaluation is to pose questions about educational programs/activities that may be answered through collection of qualitative and/or quantitative data (Maher & Bennett, 1984). Table 2 presents general questions related to PAL and issues specific to peer tutoring and CGL. These questions provide a general framework for formative evaluation of PAL activities that may be supplemented with more focused concerns pertinent to local program components.

Assessment of PAL outcomes should include measures of both academic and social/emotional performance. In evaluating peer tutoring programs, it is pertinent to review the performance of tutors and learners with regard to specific academic gains, study skills, and affective variables such as motivation, school attitudes, self-concept, and self-efficacy. Determining outcomes of CGL should include attention to individual and group performance, as well as measures of academic content and concepts acquired through group learning activities. Affective variables relevant to CGL outcomes include changes in frequency and quality of student cooperation, indicators of motivation, changes in degree of acceptance of group members, and interpersonal skills, including group problem solving and conflict resolution.

Evaluation data can be obtained through a variety of methods, including: review of student and teacher records, direct observation of PAL activities, structured interviews or surveys, and sociometric measures. Sources of evaluation information include school administrators, teachers, students, and parents, as well as permanent products of learning activities.

ETHICAL CONSIDERATIONS

Several ethical issues with respect to using peers as instructional agents merit attention. First, and most important, PAL activities must benefit all participants, not just targeted individuals or subgroups. Moreover, an effort should be made to ensure that instructional activities provide not merely a generalized positive effect, but clearly address identified

TABLE 2
Formative Evaluation Questions for Peer-Assisted Learning

General Issues

To what extent have PAL activities been implemented as planned?

How have school administrators, classroom teachers, students, and parents perceived/reacted to PAL?

What proportion of total instructional time is devoted to PAL?

How much teacher time is required for preparation of activities and materials associated with PAL?

How are specific PAL techniques selected/adapted for classroom use?

What techniques were used to prepare students for PAL activities?

Have specific goals and goal indicators been identified for PAL activities?

To what extent are students actively engaged in learning during PAL activities (i.e., proportion of total instructional time that student is on-task)?

What methods were used to assess student outcomes?

Cooperative Learning

What types of cooperative learning activities have been used?

How do students resolve conflicts within learning groups?

How often and in what ways do teachers intervene for the purpose of conflict resolution?

What are the predominant interaction patterns observed in student work groups?

How does the teacher interact with student groups?

How were students assigned to cooperative learning groups?

What is the range of heterogeneity in student learning groups with respect to ability level and/or other status characteristics?

What criteria are used to determine individual/group rewards?

How do students respond to group rewards and/or grading policies?

Peer Tutoring

How were students selected for participation in peer tutoring?

What factors were considered in matching tutor–learner dyads?

How were tutoring sessions scheduled and where do tutoring dyads meet?

What strategies were used to train tutors?

How were tutoring goals and instructional materials identified?

What methods were used to assess tutor outcomes?

What types of reinforcement were used and how did learners respond?

What interaction patterns were observed within tutoring dyads?

How did teachers monitor peer tutoring activities?

---

learning needs (Gerber & Kauffman, 1981). Second, school personnel must be competent in the application of peer-assisted learning to specific classroom uses, and must provide appropriate training for students prior to implementation of PAL methods. Finally, there is a need to ensure that PAL procedures are integrated appropriately into the overall instructional program (Greenwood, 1981).

REFERENCES

Allen, V. L., & Feldman, R. S. (1973). Learning through tutoring: Low achieving children as tutors. *Journal of Experimental Education, 42,* 1-5.

Allen, V. L., & Feldman, R. S. (1976). Studies on the role of tutor. In V. L. Allen (Ed.), *Children as teachers: Theory and research on tutoring* (pp. 113-129). New York: Academic.

Ames, C. (1981). Competitive versus cooperative reward structures: The influence of individual and group performance factors on achievement attributions and affect. *American Educational Research Journal, 18*, 273-287.

Aronson, E., Blaney, N., Stephan, C., Sikes, J., & Snapp, M. (1978). *The jigsaw classroom*. Beverly Hills, CA: Sage.

Bohlmeyer, E. M., & Burke, J. P. (1987). Selecting cooperative learning techniques: A consultative strategy guide. *School Psychology Review, 16*, 36-49.

Buckholdt, D. R., & Wodarski, J. S. (1978). The effects of different reinforcement systems on cooperative behaviors exhibited by children in classroom contexts. *Journal of Research and Development in Education, 12*, 50-68.

Cloward, R. D. (1976). Teenagers as tutors of academically low-achieving children: Impact on tutors and tutees. In V. L. Allen (Ed.), *Children as teachers: Theory and research on tutoring* (pp. 219-229). New York: Academic.

Cohen, J. (1986). Theoretical considerations of peer tutoring. *Psychology in the Schools, 23*, 175-186.

Cosden, M., Pearl, R., & Bryan, T. H. (1985). The effects of cooperative and individual goal structures on learning disabled and nondisabled students. *Exceptional Children, 52*, 103-114.

Cotton, J., & Cook, M. (1982). Meta analyses and the effects of various systems: Some different conclusions from Johnson et al. *Psychological Bulletin, 92*, 176-183.

Crockenberg, S., & Bryant, B. (1978). Socialization: The "implicit curriculum" of learning environments. *Journal of Research and Development in Education, 12*, 69-77.

Delquadri, J., Greenwood, C. R., Whorton, D., Carta, J. J., & Hall, R. V. (1986). Classwide peer tutoring. *Exceptional Children, 52*, 535-542.

Ehly, S. (1986). *Peer tutoring: A guide for school psychologists*. Washington, DC: National Association of School Psychologists.

Ehly, S. W., & Larsen, S. C. (1980). *Peer tutoring for individualized instruction*. Boston: Allyn & Bacon.

Feldman, R. S., Devin-Sheehan, L., & Allen, V. L. (1976). Children tutoring children: A critical review of research. In V. L. Allen (Ed.), *Children as teachers: Theory and research on tutoring* (pp. 235-252). New York: Academic.

Garbarino, J. (1975). The impact of anticipated reward upon cross-age tutoring. *Journal of Personality and Social Psychology, 32*, 421-428.

Gerber, M., & Kauffman, J. M. (1981). Peer tutoring in academic settings. In P. S. Strain (Ed.), *The utilization of classroom peers as behavior change agents* (pp. 155-187). New York: Plenum.

Gesten, E. L., & Weissberg, R. P. (1986). Social problem-solving training with children: A guide to effective practice. *Special Services in the Schools, 2*(4), 19-40.

Greenwood, C. R. (1981). Peer-oriented behavioral technology and ethical issues. In P. S. Strain (Ed.), *The utilization of classroom peers as behavior change agents* (pp. 327-360). New York: Plenum.

Greenwood, C. R., Dinwiddie, G., Terry, B., Wade, L., Stanley, S. O., Thibadeau, S., & Delquadri, J. C. (1984). Teacher-versus peer-mediated instruction: An ecobehavioral analysis of achievement outcomes. *Journal of Applied Behavior Analysis, 17*, 521-538.

Hall, R. V., Delquadri, J., Greenwood, C. R., & Thurston, L. (1982). The importance of opportunity to respond in children's academic success. In E. Edgar, N. Haring, J. Jenkins, & C. Pious (Eds.), *Mentally handicapped children: Education and training* (pp. 107-140). Baltimore, MD: University Park.

Hamblin, J. A., & Hamblin, R. L. (1972). On teaching disadvantaged preschoolers to read: A successful experiment. *American Educational Research Journal, 9*, 209-216.

Jenkins, J. R., & Jenkins, L. M. (1981). *Cross age and peer tutoring: Help for children with learning problems*. Reston, VA: Council for Exceptional Children.

Jenkins, J. R., & Mayhall, W. F. (1979). Development and evaluation of a resource teacher program. Reprinted in E. L. Meyen (Ed.), *Basic readings in the study of exceptional children and youth, 11*, 607-617.

Johnson, D. W., & Johnson, R. T. (1975). *Learning together and alone*. Englewood Cliffs, NJ: Prentice-Hall.

Johnson, D. W., & Johnson, R. T. (1980). Integrating handicapped students into the mainstream. *Exceptional Children, 47*, 90-98.

Johnson, D. W., & Johnson, R. T. (1984). Effects of intergroup cooperation and intergroup competition on ingroup and outgroup cross-handicap relationships. *Journal of Social Psychology, 124*, 85-94.

Johnson, D. W., & Johnson, R. T. (1986). Mainstreaming and cooperative learning strategies. *Exceptional Children, 52*, 553-561.

Johnson, D. W., Johnson, R. T., & Maruyama, G. (1983). Interdependence and interpersonal attraction among heterogeneous and homogeneous individuals: A theoretical formulation and a meta analysis of the research. *Review of Educational Research, 53,* 5-54.

Johnson, D. W., Johnson, R. T., Warring, D., & Maruyama, G. (1986). Different cooperative learning procedures and cross-handicap relationships. *Exceptional Children, 53,* 247-252.

Johnson, D. W., Maruyama, G., Johnson, R. T., Nelson, D., & Skon, L. (1981). Effects of cooperative, competitive, and individualistic goal structures on achievement: A meta-analysis. *Psychological Bulletin, 89,* 47-62.

Johnson, R. T., & Johnson, D. W. (1982). Staff development for the social integration of handicapped students into the mainstream. In P. A. Roy (Ed.), *Structuring cooperative learning experiences in the classroom.* Edina, MN: Interaction Book Co.

Kagan, S. (1985). Co-op Co-Op: A flexible cooperative learning technique. In R. Slavin, S. Sharan, S. Kagan, R. Hertz-Lazarowitz, C. Webb, & R. Schmuck (Eds.), *Learning to cooperate, cooperating to learn* (pp. 437-462). New York: Plenum.

Lew, M., Mesch, D., Johnson, D. W., & Johnson, R. T. (1986). Positive interdependence, academic and collaborative skill group contingencies, and isolated students. *American Educational Research Journal, 23,* 476-488.

Lippitt, P. (1976). Learning through cross-age helping: Why and how. In V. L. Allen (Ed.), *Children as teachers: Theory and research on tutoring* (pp. 157-168). New York: Academic.

Madden, N. A., & Slavin, R. E. (1983a). Effects of cooperative learning on the social acceptance of mainstreamed academically handicapped students. *Journal of Special Education, 17,* 171-182.

Madden, N. A., & Slavin, R. E. (1983b). Mainstreaming students with mild handicaps: Academic and social outcomes. *Review of Educational Research, 53,* 519-569.

Maher, C. A. (1984). Handicapped adolescents as cross-age tutors: Program description and evaluation. *Exceptional Children, 51,* 56-63.

Maher, C. A., & Bennett, R. E. (1984). *Planning and evaluating special education services.* Englewood Cliffs, NJ: Prentice-Hall.

Mayhall, W. R., & Jenkins, J. R. (1977). Scheduling daily or less-than-daily instruction: Implications for resource programs. *Journal of Learning Disabilities, 10,* 159-163.

Mayhall, W. R., Jenkins, J. R., Chestnut, N., Rose, F., Schroeder, K., & Jordan, B. (1975). Supervision and site of instruction as factors in tutorial programs. *Exceptional Children, 42,* 151-154.

McGee, C. S., Kauffman, J. M., & Nussen, J. (1977). Children as therapeutic change agents: Reinforcement intervention paradigms. *Review of Educational Research, 47,* 451-477.

Melaragno, R. J. (1976). The tutorial community. In V. L. Allen (Ed.), *Children as teachers: Theory and research on tutoring* (pp. 189-197). New York: Academic

Miller, J. A., & Peterson, D. W. (1987). Peer-influenced academic interventions. In C. A. Maher & J. E. Zins (Eds.), *Psychoeducational interventions in schools: Methods and procedures for enhancing student competence* (pp. 91-100). Elmsford, NY: Pergamon.

National Commission on Excellence in Education. (1983). *A nation at risk: The imperative for educational reform.* Washington, DC: U. S. Government Printing Office.

Osguthorpe, R. T., & Scruggs, T. E. (1986). Special education students as tutors: A review and analysis. *Remedial and Special Education, 7*(4), 15-25.

Peterson, P. L., & Janicki, T. C. (1979). Individual characteristics and children's learning in large group and small group approaches. *Journal of Educational Psychology, 71,* 677-687.

Robertson, D. J. (1972). Children learn from children. In S. Sebesta & C. Wallen (Eds.), *Readings on teaching reading* (pp. 277-283). Chicago: Science Research Associates.

Scruggs, T. E., & Osguthorpe, R. T. (1986). Tutoring interventions within special education settings: A comparison of cross-age and peer tutoring. *Psychology in the Schools, 23,* 187-193.

Sharan, S. (1980). Cooperative learning in small groups: Recent methods and effects on achievement, attitudes and ethnic relations. *Review of Educational Research, 50,* 241-271.

Sharan, S., & Hertz-Lazarowitz, R. (1980). A group investigation method of cooperative learning in the classroom. In S. Sharan, P. Hare, C. Webb, & R. Hertz-Lazarowitz (Eds.), *Cooperation in education* (pp. 14-46). Provo, UT: Brigham Young University Press.

Slavin, R. E. (1980). *Using student team learning.* Baltimore, MD: Center for Social Organization of Schools, Johns Hopkins University.

Slavin, R. E. (1983). When does cooperative learning increase student achievement? *Psychological Bulletin, 94,* 429-445.

Slavin, R. E., Madden, N. A., & Leavey, M. (1983). *Effects of Team Assisted Individualization on mainstreamed academically handicapped students.* Baltimore, MD: Center for Social Organization of Schools, Johns Hopkins University.

Stokes, T. F., & Baer, D. M. (1976). Preschool peers as mutual generalization-facilitating agents. *Behavior Therapy, 7,* 549-556.

Strodtbeck, F. L., Ronchi, D., & Hansell, S. (1976). Tutoring and psychological growth. In V. L. Allen (Ed.), *Children as teachers: Theory and research on tutoring* (pp. 199-218). New York: Academic.

Vassallo, W. (1973). Learning by tutoring. *American Education, 9*(3), 25-28.

Wagner, P., & Sternlicht, M. (1975). Retarded persons as "teachers": Retarded adolescents tutoring retarded children. *American Journal of Mental Deficiency, 79,* 674-679.

Webb, N. M. (1982). Student interaction and learning in small groups. *Review of Educational Research, 52,* 421-445.

Webb, N. M. (1984). Stability of small group interaction and achievement over time. *Journal of Educational Psychology, 76,* 211-224.

Wright, S., & Cowen, E. L. (1985). Effects of peer teaching on student perceptions of class environments, adjustment, and academic performance. *American Journal of Community Psychology, 13,* 417-431.

Yaeger, S., Johnson, D. W., & Johnson, R. T. (1985). Oral discussion, group to individual transfer, and achievement in cooperative learning groups. *Journal of Educational Psychology, 77,* 60-66.

Ysseldyke, J. E., Pianta, B., Christenson, S., Wang, J. J., & Algozzine, B. (1983). An analysis of preferral interventions. *Psychology in the Schools, 20,* 184-190.

Zahn, G. L., Kagan, S., & Widaman, K. F. (1986). Cooperative learning and classroom climate. *Journal of School Psychology, 24,* 351-362.

19

An Instructional Model for Teaching Students How to Learn

Donald D. Deshler and
Jean B. Schumaker
University of Kansas

A sizable number of mildly handicapped and other low-achieving students are excluded from the mainstream instruction of the regular classroom. In some instances, this exclusion is explained by the students' placement in alternative classes (e.g., a special education class, a Chapter 1 class, or some other remedial or low-track placement); in many other cases, however, students may be physically placed in mainstream classes but still experience "functional exclusion" from the educational experiences offered there. In other words, despite mainstream placement, these students receive little benefit from the experience because of the mismatch between their proficiency as learners and the demands of the mainstream setting (Schumaker & Deshler, 1984). The lack in these classes of effective accommodations that meet these students' needs further exacerbates the problem. Hence, as these students move through the educational system, the mismatch between their skills and the demands of mainstream educational experience becomes even greater. In too many instances, these students completely distance themselves from a public school education by dropping out of school altogether (Levin, Zigmond, & Birch, 1983).

The reasons that certain groups in the student population are functionally excluded by the educational system from beneficial learning in mainstream classes are varied and complex. Research conducted over the last decade on low achievement and failure in public schools has identified five major reasons for this exclusion.

First, these students are not taught the necessary and appropriate skills and strategies that will enable them to cope effectively with the curricular demands of the mainstream classroom. Middle and secondary school teachers, whose overriding instructional goal is the delivery of content, unfortunately assume that students have mastered these skills and strategies in earlier grades. Data have indicated, however, that learning-disabled and other low-achieving students reach the secondary grades without these skills (e.g., Sinclair & Ghory, 1987; Deshler, Schumaker, Alley, Warner, & Clark, 1982).

Second, such attempts as are made to teach deficient students the skills needed for success in mainstream classes fall far short of their intended goal. Limited instructional time is devoted to the endeavor, skills are targeted on the basis of low scores on achievement tests rather than a careful analysis of the curricular demands a student is expected to meet, students are not required to master the skills, and generalization of the skills to mainstream classes is not programmed (Deshler & Schumaker, 1986; Haring & Eaton, 1987). In short, the traditionally used "band aid" approach does little to cure a gaping wound.

Third, mildly handicapped and low-achieving students are functionally excluded from mainstream education because in most mainstream classes, content is not delivered in a fashion that (a) enhances the student's ability to *understand* what is taught and (b) facilitate the student's ability to *remember* the key points of each lesson. Although the educational literature is replete with evidence on how learning can be enhanced through the systematic application of key instructional principles such as the use of advance organizers (Lenz, Alley, & Schumaker, 1987), the careful organization of materials (Kierstead, 1986), the concretization of information (Walberg, 1986), and structured overviews and reviews of information (Rosenshine & Stevens, 1986), content teachers at the secondary level tend to apply these principles sporadically and relatively infrequently (Bulgren, Schumaker, and Deshler, 1987; Kea, 1987; Putnam, 1988). Possible explanations for the infrequent use of these procedures include the fact that most teacher-preparation programs involve limited training on *how* to teach content materials; that is, teacher trainees spend most of their time in college specializing in a specific content area and do not master the needed skills to teach that content. A second explanation is that the instructional principles mentioned above have not been translated into specific instructional routines that can be easily applied by classroom teachers in mainstream classrooms. Teacher-training programs tend to familiarize prospective teachers with principles and techniques in isolation; these principles and techniques are rarely integrated into comprehensive routines that can be used day in and day out by classroom teachers.

A fourth contributor to the ineffective mainstreaming of mildly handicapped and low-achieving students is the reluctance of teachers to coordinate their instructional efforts on behalf of these students. Most schools, especially secondary ones, are so compartmentalized that it is difficult for teachers to operate as a team or to coordinate their instruction on behalf of particular students. In short, teachers often operate in isolation from each other (Cusick, 1983), despite the fact that recent research suggests that the performance of mildly handicapped students in mainstream settings can be enhanced if teachers cooperatively plan and execute educational plans for these students (Schmidt, Deshler, Schumaker, & Alley, in press).

A final factor contributing to the functional exclusion of these students from the mainstream is a failure by students themselves to assume responsibility for mastering and using critical learning strategies that will enhance their ability to acquire, organize, store, and express curricular information. In other words, a key determinant of students' success in the mainstream environment is the degree to which they feel and accept a vested interest in overcoming deficiencies in their learning and performance repertoires.

The five factors described above suggest that the effective mainstreaming of mildly handicapped and other low-achieving students is dependent on the design and implementation of a comprehensive instructional model that addresses all of these factors. The purpose of this chapter is to describe some of the work that has been completed at the University of Kansas Institute for Research in Learning Disabilities (KU-IRLD) during the past 10 years to facilitate the mainstreaming of mildly handicapped students. As a result of this work, an instructional model called the Strategies Intervention Model (Schumaker, Deshler, & Ellis, 1986) has evolved.

EVOLUTION AND OVERVIEW OF THE STRATEGIES INTERVENTION MODEL

The initial work at the KU-IRLD began with a series of epidemiological studies that were conducted to identify the learning characteristics of learning-disabled and other low-achieving adolescents (Deshler et al., 1982). Specifically, the research showed that these students tend to reach an achievement plateau while in 10th grade (e.g., the average reading performance plateaus at the fourth-grade level) and do not appear to improve their performance substantially after the seventh grade. They also tend to be ineffective and/or inefficient in approaching and completing academic tasks. In some instances, the poor performance of these students seems attributable to strategic deficiencies; that is, many of them have difficulty designing their own strategies for novel learning tasks (Warner, Schumaker, Alley, & Deshler, in press).

In addition to focusing on the characteristics of the students, initial research at the KU-IRLD also homed in on the instructional approaches being employed by public schools to provide these students remedial services (Deshler, Lowrey, & Alley, 1979). The results of a national teacher survey revealed that the two most popularly employed intervention approaches were the remediation of basic skill deficiencies (e.g., instruction in the decoding of words or computation of arithmetic problems) and academic tutoring (i.e., assisting students with classroom assignments to "keep them afloat" in their mainstream classes). Little or no time appeared to be devoted to teaching students how to succeed independently in their mainstream classes.

In light of these findings, research was also conducted to identify the demands that students are expected to meet to be successful in secondary mainstream classrooms (Putnam, 1988; Schumaker & Deshler, 1984; Schumaker, Sherman, & Sheldon-Wildgen, 1982). This research has indicated that students have to be able to use a broad array of strategies including reading and interpreting large amounts of information in printed materials (e.g., textbooks), memorizing and storing information for tests, and expressing learned information in class assignments or on tests.

The major conclusion that emerged from these three lines of epidemiological research was the following: In order for mildly handicapped and other low-achieving students to effectively cope with mainstream demands, they need an instructional program that directly addresses both the realities of their learning deficiencies and the realities of the requirements for successful performance in the mainstream. Since the traditionally used remedial and tutorial approaches did not appear to be fitting this bill, a new instructional model, the Strategies Intervention Model (SIM) was designed. Four main goals are associated with this model: (a) to make students independent learners and performers by teaching them to use specific learning strategies when responding to academic demands; (b) to make students skilled in the use of specific social strategies such that they can interact appropriately with others in a variety of situations; (c) to empower students to earn a standard high school diploma; and (d) to enable students to make a successful transition from secondary to postsecondary life. The main thrust of this instructional model is to teach low-achieving and mildly handicapped students how to strategically analyze and complete tasks. In short, the primary emphasis is on teaching students how to learn and how to perform academic, social, or job-related tasks in order to cope with immediate demands as well as to generalize these skills to similar tasks in different settings under different conditions throughout their lives.

KEY COMPONENTS OF THE STRATEGIES INTERVENTION MODEL

The SIM (depicted in Figure 1) has five features that have been found to be central to effectively preparing mildly handicapped and other low achievers to be strategic learners in the mainstream. First, instructional interventions for these students take place in multiple settings (i.e., in mainstream classroom(s) and support settings) under the guidance of specialists in those settings (i.e., the mainstream teacher(s) in the content classroom and learning specialist(s) in the support setting). Second, the roles of all those involved in the instructional process (mainstream teacher(s), and support teacher(s) and students) need to be clearly specified. Third, mechanisms for ensuring effective cooperative planning and regular feedback among instructional staff are essential. Fourth, generalization and maintenance of the use of targeted strategies by students in the criterion environment (i.e., mainstream classrooms) must be an explicit goal of the instructional program. Fifth, support systems involving school administrators, family members, and agencies external to the classroom must be available to promote student success and adjustment in mainstream environments. The critical attributes of these five features will become apparent as the roles of the participants are discussed below.

The Teacher's Role in Support Service Class(es)

There are four major roles to be performed by the support service teacher or learning specialist. The most critical role of this teacher is to teach specific strategies to mildly handicapped and other low-achieving students by using a specified instructional methodology. The academic strategies taught by this teacher are the ones included in the Learning Strategies Curriculum (see Figure 2). The curriculum is organized in three major strands that correspond to the major demands of the secondary curriculum.

One strand in the Learning Strategies Curriculum includes strategies that help students acquire information from written materials. The Word Identification Strategy (Lenz, Schumaker, Deshler, & Beals, 1984) is aimed at the quick decoding of multisyllabic words. Three other strategies are aimed at increasing a student's reading comprehension. The Visual Imagery Strategy (Clark, Deshler, Schumaker, Alley, & Warner, 1984) is used to form a mental picture of events described in the passage. The Self-Questioning Strategy (Clark et al., 1984) is used to form questions about information that has not been provided by the author and to find the answers to those questions later in the passage. The Paraphrasing Strategy (Schumaker, Denton, & Deshler, 1984) is used to paraphrase the main idea and important details of each paragraph after it is read. The Interpreting Visual Aids Strategy (Lenz, Swanson, & Agudelo, in press) is used by students to gain information from pictures, diagrams, charts,

tables, and maps. Finally, the Multipass Strategy (Schumaker, Deshler, Alley, & Denton, 1982) is used for attacking textbook chapters by conducting three passes through the chapter to survey it, to obtain key information from it, and to study the critical information.

Another strand in the Learning Strategies Curriculum includes strategies that enable students to identify and store important information. The Listening and Notetaking Strategy (Robinson, Deshler, Schumaker, & Denton, in press) enables students to identify organizational cues in lectures, to note key words, and to organize key words into outline form. The FIRST-Letter Mnemonic Strategy (Nagel, Schumaker, & Deshler, 1986) and the Paired-Associates Strategy (Bulgren & Schumaker, in press) provide students with several options for memorizing key information for tests.

The final strand of the Learning Strategies Curriculum includes strategies for facilitating written expression and demonstration of competence. Four strategies have been designed to enable students to cope with the written expression demands of secondary schools. The Sentence Writing Strategy (Schumaker & Sheldon, 1985) provides students with a set of steps for using a variety of formulas when writing sentences. The Paragraph Writing Strategy (Schumaker & Lyerla, in press) helps students organize and write several types of paragraphs. The Error Monitoring Strategy (Schumaker, Nolan, & Deshler, 1985) is used to detect and correct errors in written products. The Theme Writing Strategy (Schumaker, in prep.) is used to organize and write a five-paragraph theme. An Assignment Completion Strategy (Whitaker, 1982) is used by students to schedule time and organize themselves to complete assignments on time. Finally, the Test-Taking Strategy (Hughes, Schumaker, Deshler, & Mercer, 1988) enables students to effectively take classroom tests.

The task-specific strategies described above are not meant to be a complete set of learning strategies required for school success by poor learners; rather, they are representative of the types of learning be-

FIGURE 1
Strategies Intervention Model

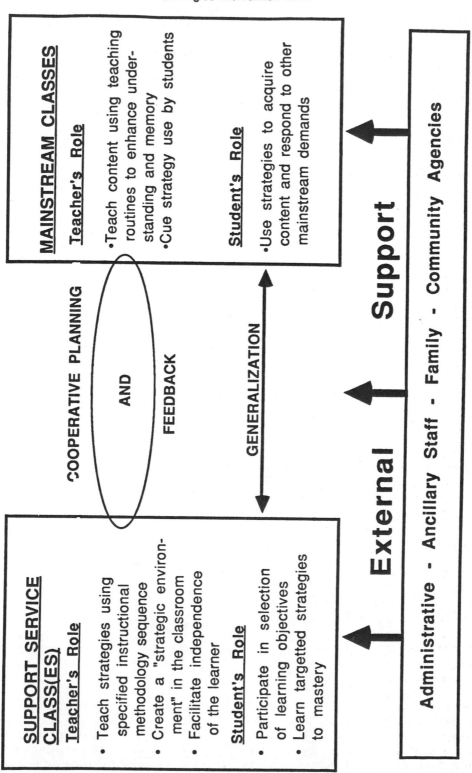

FIGURE 2
Learning Strategies Curriculum

ACQUISITION	STORAGE	EXPRESSION AND DEMONSTRATION OF COMPETENCE
Word Identification	First-Letter Mnemonic	Sentences
Paraphrasing	Paired Associates	Paragraphs
Self-questioning	Listening and Notetaking	Error Monitoring
Visual Imagery		Themes
Interpreting Visual Aids		Assignment Completion
Multipass		Test Taking
SOS		

haviors required by students to respond successfully to curriculum demands. They have been identified and developed after a careful review of the literature on the demands of secondary settings (Schumaker & Deshler, 1984). The Learning Strategies Curriculum is in the form of a series of instructor's manuals. Each manual includes guidelines, scripts, cue cards, and activities for teaching one of the strategies to students.[1]

In addition to teaching the academic strategies of the Learning Strategies Curriculum, support-setting teachers also need to teach other strategies to students. Included in the program are social strategies such as resisting peer pressure, negotiating, and giving negative feedback (Hazel, Schumaker, Sheldon, & Sherman, 1982; Hazel, Schumaker, Sherman, & Sheldon-Wildgen, 1981; Schumaker, Hazel, & Pederson, 1988), and transitional strategies such as problem solving and goal setting (Knackendoffel, Schumaker, Hazel, & Deshler, in press). The purpose of these strategies is to enable students to interact effectively, to solve day-to-day problems, to motivate themselves to learn, and to make successful transitions to postsecondary life.

In light of the number of areas in which students demonstrate deficiencies in the strategies named above, as well as the complexity of most of the strategies taught in Strategies Intervention Model programs, research has shown that the strategies must be systematically taught to students in an intense and direct fashion. To enable students to master these strategies, a teaching methodology, based on sound instructional principles, has been developed (Deshler, Schumaker, & Lenz, 1984; Deshler, Alley, Warner, & Schumaker, 1981). This methodology has two major phases: the acquisition phase and the generalization phase.

The purpose of the acquisition phase of the teaching methodology is to give students the knowledge, motivation, and practice necessary to apply a strategy successfully in the support setting. To this end, the acquisition methodology includes seven steps. In the Pretest step, students are tested to determine their current learning habits regarding a particular task. Then they are individually informed of their strengths and weaknesses and make a commitment to learn a new strategy to remedy their weaknesses. In the Describe step, the new strategy is described to the student. It is broken down into component steps, rationales for learning the strategy are given, the types of results students can expect to achieve are described, and situations in which the strategy can be used are delineated. Also in this step, students write their own goals regarding how fast they will learn the new strategy. In the Model step, the new strategy is modeled for the students from start to finish by the teacher while thinking aloud. Students are progressively involved more and more in subsequent demonstrations of the strategy until they are taking part, as a group, in guided practice activities.

In the Verbal Rehearsal step, the students use verbal rehearsal to learn to name all the steps of the strategy in order. In the Controlled Practice and Feedback step, students individually practice the new strategy to a specified criterion performance in controlled materials (i.e., materials in which the complexity, length, and difficulty levels have been reduced). In the Grade-Appropriate Practice and Feedback step, students individually practice the skill to a mastery criterion (both accuracy and speed are emphasized) in materials and situations that closely approximate those encountered in mainstream classes and other natural environments within the community. In the Posttest step, students take a test to determine if their performance has progressed to a point that allows them to cope with demands in the target area. Reinforcement and corrective feedback are given after each performance throughout the Verbal Rehearsal, Practice, and Posttest Steps.

The teacher in the support setting is also responsible for implementing the generalization phase of the teaching methodology. Instruction for generalization must be a framework in which all instruction is couched rather than a finite phase through which a student passes

(Deshler, Schumaker, & Lenz, 1984; Ellis, Lenz, & Sabornie, 1987); therefore care has been taken to program generalization techniques throughout the seven acquisition steps described above. For example, antecedent generalization techniques (Ellis et al., 1987) are programmed into the first acquisition step by enlisting the student's commitment to learn a particular strategy to be used in mainstream classes. Throughout the remaining six acquisition steps, the student experiences concurrent generalization techniques (Ellis et al., 1987) such as the use of multiple exemplars, daily reminders about where the strategy can be used, and actual application of the strategy to mainstream class assignments and materials.

Once the use of a strategy has been mastered by a student, subsequent generalization (Ellis et al., 1987) begins. Here, three generalization steps are applied. During the Orientation generalization step, students are made aware of the variety of contexts within which the learning strategy can be applied. Thus, the support service teacher has a discussion with the students about the different mainstream classes where the strategy can be applied and about the cues that the students will likely encounter in different settings that should remind them to use the strategy. In addition, a discussion is held regarding ways in which the strategy can be adapted to better meet the unique requirements of given class situations. During the Activation generalization step, students are given ample opportunities to practice the strategy in different materials and in different settings that have not been encountered during strategy acquisition and to receive specific feedback on their mainstream classroom assignments with the goal of increasing the degree to which the students can automatically apply the strategy to novel tasks. The final step of the generalization methodology is Maintenance. The purpose of the maintenance step is to conduct periodic probes to determine whether the student is continuing to use the strategy in a variety of settings with fluency. These maintenance probes occur at intermittent intervals over

a sustained period of time (e.g., a semester or even an entire academic year).

Thus, a major role for the support service teacher is to orchestrate instruction in specified strategies by using a validated sequence of acquisition and generalization methods. Mastery of the strategies and their subsequent generalization to mainstream environments requires deliberate programming on the part of the support service teacher throughout the instructional process.

Another major role of the support service teacher is to create a "strategic environment" in the classroom. Theoretically, as students are being taught to use a task-specific strategy, they are being exposed to a host of behaviors (through both the modeling of the teacher and a variety of instructional activities) that should teach them to be strategic learners and performers. Unfortunately, teachers spend only a portion of each class period directly instructing students in task-specific strategies (Carlson, 1985). The remainder of a class session is spent doing such things as giving directions, reviewing assignments, giving feedback, helping students solve personal or other school-related problems, and general classroom organization and management activities (Kea, 1987).

Many of these instructional tasks can be performed in a "strategic" fashion in which the teacher thinks aloud (thus modeling the use of metacognitive or cognitive strategies) or requires the students to complete routine tasks in a strategic fashion (Pressley, Goodchild, Fleet, Zajchowski, & Evans, in press; Levin, 1986). By programming the application of strategic thinking throughout the class hour, a teacher can create a "strategic" environment. For example, a teacher could model the use of metacognitive and cognitive strategies when she/he is helping students prepare for a history test (note in this example how the emphasis is on *how* to learn the content and not the content per se). Rather than quickly and *silently* reviewing some possible ways of preparing for the test in his head and then telling the students how he would solve the problem (an approach typically used), a teacher who is actively programming a "strategic" environment would think aloud so students could understand exactly how a good learner goes about solving a problem.

In the instance of preparing for an upcoming history test (the problem), the teacher might say, "Let's see, for the history test on Thursday, you're probably going to have to know these five things that contributed to the settlement of the midwest (barbed wire, six shooter, steel plow, windmill, and sod houses). Those are the kinds of things Ms. Exby usually wants to know on her tests. Now how would I go about learning these five things? Maybe I would try to use the first letter of each item in the list to see if that will help me learn the list. That's B, S, S, W, S. Boy, there are no vowels that will help me spell a word with those letters. I'm not going to use that strategy. . . . I know! I'll try to form a visual image in my mind to help me remember them. Okay, I can see a man with a holster around his waist and a six shooter in the holster. He's standing in front of his sod house. He looks out over his property, and he sees a shiny barbed wire fence glistening in the sun as it surrounds his land. He has to prepare all of his property for planting, so he gets behind his steel plow and begins plowing his land. As he is plowing the land, he forgets to watch where he is plowing, and he bumps into the windmill that sits in the middle of his property! Now, let's see if I can remember that image and the five things: a six shooter, a sod house, some barbed wire, a steel plow and a windmill. I've got them; that's the strategy I'll use to remember the five things that helped settle the midwest. I think I'd be able to do well on this test."

In the above scenario, the teacher used a host of metacognitive and cognitive strategies. Specifically, he started by analyzing the problem. Next, he selected a specific cognitive strategy that he thought would help him solve the problem. He tried using the first strategy, but rejected it when he monitored the difficulty inherent in its use. He then selected another effective strategy (visual imagery), used it, and monitored its effective-

ness. Finally, he made a self-coping statement regarding his ability to deal successfully with the curriculum demand.

When teachers deliberately attempt to infuse strategic functioning into all parts of their instruction as in this example, students get multiple exposure to what is involved in effective learning and performing (Pressley, Johnson, & Symons, 1987). Repeated exposure to strategic behavior is important for students who lack these behaviors in their repertoires. Teachers need to consciously program the use of different metacognitive and cognitive strategies into the majority of their interactions with students. With a little forethought and practice, such routine tasks as taking roll, giving directions, and reviewing assignments can all be approached from a strategic perspective. To the extent that teachers do this, they will be enhancing the transformation of low achievers into more strategic, successful learners and performers.

Another critical role in SIM for teachers in the support setting is to deliberately facilitate independent functioning by the learner. Traditional approaches to dealing with low-achieving and mildly handicapped students tend to encourage them to be passive and dependent learners (Deshler, Schumaker, Lenz, & Ellis, 1984). In contrast, there are three guidelines followed by SIM teachers that encourage independent behavior by their students. First, they deliberately involve students in planning their own instructional programs. An instructional package entitled "The Educational Planning Strategy" (Van Reusen, Bos, Schumaker, & Deshler, 1987) is used to teach students to inventory their learning strengths and weaknesses, to identify instructional objectives they would value accomplishing, and to set short- and long-term goals. In addition, it is used to teach students a set of behaviors for advocating for themselves in educational planning sessions, such as an individual education plan (IEP) conference. The intent of teaching students this planning strategy is to effectively involve them in the educational planning process so that they feel ownership in their educational program and a vested interest in its implementation. In conjunction with this planning strategy, students are taught how to chart their performance daily, to monitor and evaluate their work, and to use a self-reinforcement system for achieved goals. The collective intent of each of these instructional tactics is to transform these students into active learners who are not dependent on adults to make all decisions for them within the educational setting.

A second guideline SIM teachers follow to promote independence is to avoid tutoring students in assignments from their content classes (e.g., history, health, science, etc.) because this tutoring process causes students to become very dependent on their teacher's assistance, and they usually acquire no skills or strategies for functioning independently when assistance from the support service teacher is not available. Furthermore, because most support service teachers are not certified to provide instruction in all of the content areas, their effectiveness in this area is open to question. Rather than tutoring students to provide them with a short-term solution, SIM teachers spend the majority of their time teaching their students strategies that will enable them over the long haul to function independently over a broad array of study areas.

A third guideline SIM teachers follow is to incorporate into their instructional routines what Kea (1987) has called "behaviors that facilitate independence." These behaviors are defined as any act by the teacher that requires the student to think or act on his or her own or to motivate himself or herself. Examples of such behaviors would include: verbal prompts to independent thinking (e.g., Student: "I can't find the answer to this question." Teacher: "Where do you think would be the most likely place to look for it?"); structuring initiation of independent work (i.e., the teacher expects students to begin work immediately after entering the room); prompting independent thinking on goal setting (e.g., Teacher: "Do you think your previous goal was set too high or too low?"); promoting independent

thinking on self-evaluation (e.g., Teacher: "What do you think of your progress so far?"); and promoting individual performance within a group (e.g., Teacher: "John, will you role-play your phone conversation with the apartment manager?").

A final critical role of the support service teacher involves taking responsibility for the cooperative planning process with mainstream teachers in whose classes the served students are enrolled, because the mainstreaming of mildly handicapped and other low-achieving students appears to be enhanced if mechanisms for ensuring cooperation and feedback among instructional staff are in place (Schmidt et al., in press). When teachers operate independently rather than collaboratively while planning and delivering instruction (Cusick, 1983), instruction often tends to be fragmented and disjointed. This can be frustrating for even the normal achiever in school, but for a student saddled with a learning problem, it can be devastating. This is especially true when instruction is not coordinated between support service staff and mainstream teachers. Often, owing to the absence of cooperative planning, instruction offered in the support service class usually is unrelated to the demands and expectations in the mainstream setting, and in turn, instruction in the mainstream setting does not encourage the use of skills and strategies learned in the support class.

While cooperative planning and regular feedback among teachers make sense, there are numerous reasons why it is difficult to implement, including scheduling difficulties, lack of time, and lack of specific procedures to facilitate the process. To address the last concern, Knackendoffel, Schumaker, and Deshler (in press) have developed and validated a set of "Teaming Techniques" designed to provide support service teachers with the tools they need to gain information and work cooperatively with mainstream teachers.

Since knowing *what* to teach becomes a critical concern for special education personnel at the secondary level, one Teaming Technique, called "Targeting

Demands," was developed so that support teachers could easily determine the demands of mainstream settings. Previously the determination of what to teach was based on formal assessment results and the day-to-day pressures of helping the student pass tests in the regular class. Given their new role as learning specialists, support service teachers must know the specific demands placed upon each of their students in content classes. This information can then be used to both prioritize the skills and strategies that need to be taught to the student to match the demands of the mainstream classrooms and to determine when and in which studies students can be mainstreamed. The Targeting Demands Technique involves both an interview with the content teacher and examination of materials used in the content class to determine the demands of the class. Teachers complete a summary worksheet on each class on which they determine from the information obtained from the content teacher which learning strategies need to be taught. Support service teachers can then use the information gathered from a class or a combination of classes to prioritize instructional needs.

Another Teaming Technique, called "Problem-Solving Skills" was developed because special education teachers are often asked to consult with mainstream teachers to solve a variety of problems after handicapped students have enrolled in their classes. Problem-Solving Skills, and their accompanying communication skills, are crucial to a team approach if workable solutions are to be achieved. The self-instruction packet that has been developed to teach these skills to special educators includes an overview of interpersonal communication skills and follows with a detailed problem-solving procedure for working with mainstream teachers. Teachers learn to define problem behaviors, help classroom teachers generate alternatives and choose a realistic solution, develop a plan of action, and finally, develop a monitoring system and specify the criteria for success. Teachers learn to use this process to improve their communication with educators in the main-

stream and to jointly arrive at workable solutions to problems that face learning-disabled students in the regular classroom.

An additional Teaming Technique is called "Negotiating Win–Win Solutions." This strategy enables support teachers to negotiate with others in the schools to fulfill their role as advocates of exceptional students. Special education teachers learn to negotiate successfully with other teachers and administrators by first specifying a goal rather than a position for their negotiations. They plan for a successful negotiation session by outlining the interests of the other negotiators and then searching for areas of mutual gain based on shared interests. Teachers are instructed in how to plan in advance for the negotiation and then how to conduct the negotiation session to maximize their chances of obtaining mutually satisfying solutions. This process can be used by special educators to clarify their instructional role, to gain release time for cooperative planning, to gain cooperation from other teachers to accommodate exceptional students in the mainstream, and to settle a wide variety of other situations that face support service teachers.

The last Teaming Technique, called "Coaching for Professional Change" enables support service teachers to promote changes in the way instruction is delivered in the mainstream class. Special education staff often suggest that mainstream teachers try new approaches or strategies to deliver content in the regular classroom. Unfortunately, change is difficult even in the best of situations unless it is undertaken systematically. Even the simplest teaching routine might be ignored or implemented in a faulty manner unless mainstream teachers are coached through the process. The Coaching for Professional Change Technique is designed to enable support service teachers to present new teaching routines to other professionals. It is based on the premise that sharing instructional methodology is a process rather than a single act or event in which a teacher merely tells another teacher about a teaching routine that might be useful. Through instruction in this strategy, support service teachers are shown how to set the stage for collaboration, how to introduce the teaching routine, how to gain a commitment from mainstream teachers to try the routine, and finally, how to provide feedback and to assure maintenance and adoption of the teaching routine.

To summarize, the role of the support service teacher in a SIM program is complex. This teacher is required to use a specialized set of curriculum materials in conjunction with an instructional methodology in such a way as to ensure mastery and generalization of specified strategies. In addition, the teacher needs to create a strategic environment so that the student is constantly experiencing new and various examples of the application of strategic functioning. Also, the teacher needs to ensure the independent functioning of students in learning settings. Finally, the support service teacher is responsible for ensuring that the cooperative planning process with mainstream teachers is successful by using a series of "Teaming Techniques" designed to foster cooperative planning.

The Student's Role in Support Service Class(es)

There are two major roles for students assigned to support services (see Figure 1). One role is the active selection of the learning objectives for themselves in the support setting. A key philosophical underpinning of the SIM is to provide students with a major voice in specifying the instructional goals toward which they will work. The support service teacher provides students with as much information as necessary to enable them to make good decisions. For example, the teacher defines for the students what the support teacher's role is (i.e., to teach certain learning, social, and transitional strategies, etc.) and what the role is *not* (e.g., it does not include the provision of tutorial services); the teacher shares with students information about the demands they will need to meet in different mainstream classes and postsecondary settings; and

the teacher indicates approximately how long it may take students to master targeted objectives. As discussed previously, students are taught the Educational Planning Strategy (Van Reusen, et al., 1987) to assist them in how to go about targeting desired instructional areas as well as advocate effectively for their selected areas of intervention with participants in an educational decision-making meeting (e.g., an IEP). Thus, in an SIM program, students choose what they will learn and set goals for how fast they will learn it after they have been given enough information to enable them to make these choices.

The second major role for students in the support service setting of an SIM program is to learn the targeted strategies to mastery. In other words, after decisions have been made as to *what* to learn and *how fast* to learn it, a student's main responsibility is to learn to use the targeted strategies with a high level of fluency and proficiency in dealing with the requirements of the mainstream environment. As students become more and more proficient with a strategy, they become responsible for using it for mainstream assignments within the support service setting and becoming ready to use it in other settings.

Teachers have found that it is very important to clearly define these two roles for students so they can understand exactly why they are receiving support services and the importance of their active participation in the entire process. A secondary purpose of this explanation is to lay the groundwork for the students to see the relationship between their mastery of specific strategies in the support setting and their subsequent success in mainstream classes. A key element to effective strategy instruction is for students to understand the link that exists between strategy application and academic progress.

The Teacher's Role in Mainstream Class(es)

A content teacher who has responsibility for teaching a mainstream class (e.g., U.S. history) to groups of students that include some low-achieving and mildly handicapped learners plays a vital role in the success or failure of these students in meeting the expectations associated with the course. Recent research has clearly demonstrated that mildly handicapped and low achievers can experience success in responding to the demands of the mainstream curriculum if content teachers fulfill their role as outlined in Figure 1 (Bulgren, Schumaker, & Deshler, 1987; Deshler, Schumaker, Bulgren, Hudson, & McKnight, in press; Lenz, Alley, & Schumaker, 1987; Schumaker, Deshler, Hudson, & McKnight, in press). One facet of this role is to teach content to their classes through the use of specific teaching routines so as to enhance the understanding and memory of that content by all students. In other words, researchers have found that if content teachers carefully structure and organize the information that they present, learning by all students, especially low achievers, will be enhanced.

One way of structuring content to facilitate learning is to use different understanding and memory devices. These devices are teaching techniques designed for use by mainstream teachers to enable students in secondary mainstream classrooms to better understand and remember content-related information. The Devices for Understanding (Schumaker et al., in press) are based on the premise that new information is more easily understood and remembered when it is fit into the cognitive framework of the student's background knowledge (i.e., prior knowledge and previous personal experience). The Devices for Understanding consist of a series of examples (e.g., photographs, timelines, personal stories, anecdotes, current events, demonstrations) and comparisons (e.g., analogies, similes, synonyms, antonyms, role-plays, debates) that can be used to relate new information to previous and familiar knowledge and experiences. Classroom teachers apply the Devices for Understanding by preplanning the use of selected examples and comparisons based on the information to be presented and

a personal knowledge of the students' interests, knowledge, and experiences. Each time an example or comparison is utilized, a prescribed three-step procedure is carried out to enhance the understanding of the information presented. In the first step, teachers *cue* students that they are going to use a Device for Understanding; during the second step, they use or do the device as they present the content information; and during the third step, they *review* the key information and the device used to enhance its understanding. Devices for Understanding promote a more active student role in learning through increased student participation and make subject content more easily understood and personally meaningful to students. The Devices for Memory (Deshler et al., in prep.) augment the Devices for Understanding by providing students with specific techniques for memorizing certain kinds of information. Techniques for learning lists of information, pairs of facts, and sequences of events are presented in conjunction with information introduced through the use of Devices for Understanding. The three-step "cue–do–review" procedure is also used with the Devices for Memory.

Lenz et al. (1987), for example, developed an advance organizer procedure for use by mainstream teachers. At the beginning of each class period, teachers introduced the day's lesson by using an advance organizer that incorporated one or more of the following behavioral components: (a) informing the students of the purpose of the advance organizer; (b) identifying the topic of the learning task; (c) identifying the subtopics related to the learning task; (d) providing background information; (e) clarifying the task's physical parameters in terms of actions to be taken by the teacher; (f) clarifying the task's physical parameters in terms of actions to be taken by the student; (g) stating the concepts to be learned; (h) clarifying the concepts to be learned; (i) motivating students through the use of rationales; (j) introducing or repeating new terms or words; (k) providing an organizational framework for the learning task; and (l) stating the outcomes desired. Lenz et al. found that these procedures substantially affected LD students' retention of information presented in their content classes *if* the students were taught by their support teachers to attend to and use the advance organizers presented by their mainstream teachers.

A second example of a teaching routine that can be used by mainstream teachers is one that deals with what Armbruster (1984) calls "inconsiderate textbooks." The purpose of this routine is to point out to students good and poor features of their textbooks and to systematically introduce the key features and content of a chapter to the class. The acronym used to depict the key steps of this routine is TRIMS (T = title, R = relationship of the chapter to other parts of book, I = introduction including chapter goals and objectives, M = main parts of the chapter, S = summary). This routine is used by the content teacher every time a new textbook chapter is introduced to the class. As the teacher introduces the chapter by using the TRIMS procedure, the class is actively engaged in learning through a questioning process and the completion of a structured study guide. Teachers devote approximately 30 minutes per chapter to the TRIMS teaching routine. Studies have been carried out in which all students who previously had been failing chapter tests moved into the passing range when this procedure was used on a regular basis in their mainstream classes. Most of the other students' grades on chapter tests improved as well (Schumaker et al., in press).

Another teaching routine that has been successfully used by mainstream teachers is one designed by Bulgren, Schumaker, and Deshler (1988) to facilitate the teaching of concepts in content classes. A basic component of this routine is the use of a one-page "concept diagram" that enables teachers to plan and present a key concept in a lesson. A completed diagram contains the key information to be presented including the concept name, its definition, its salient characteristics, and examples and nonexamples of the concept. As teachers present the lesson to students through an interactive process, they fill in designated areas on a blank concept diagram. Students also fill in a blank diagram for note-taking purposes. The interactive process in which students are engaged involves the identification of critical features of the concept and testing membership of suggested examples in the concept class. This teaching routine has been shown to significantly improve the performance of LD students, low achievers, and normal achievers on tests about the concept information and on regular chapter tests (Bulgren, Schumaker, & Deshler, in press).

Each of the teaching routines described above has been designed to meet three basic criteria for successful application in mainstream classrooms: (a) It must be easy to use by mainstream teachers so that it does not markedly alter their established instructional procedures; (b) it must be sufficiently powerful to favorably impact on the performance of low-achieving students with regard to classroom requirements; and (c) it must be perceived as a valuable and acceptable teaching routine by normal achievers in the classroom. Each of these routines meets these criteria.

A second major role for the mainstream teacher is to cue students to use, in the mainstream class, the task-specific learning strategies that they have mastered in their support service class. A key element in having students successfully generalize any skill or strategy is to have them practice its use in different settings under different circumstances from that in which it was first learned. Research has shown that if a regular class teacher cues students to use a previously learned strategy, they will use the strategy and improve their performance in the class (Schmidt, et al., in press).

In order to give effective cues to students mainstream teachers need the following information: (a) a general idea of what the task-specific strategy is; (b) specific situations in their classes to which the strategy can be applied; and (c) procedures for how to effectively cue students to use the strategy in meeting class requirements. The cueing procedure used by the mainstream teacher is quick and easy to implement. For example, if a student has learned to use the Error Monitoring Strategy (Schumaker et al., 1985) to detect and correct errors in written classroom assignments, the mainstream teacher would merely need to ask the student to use "WRITER" *before* he or she begins work on a certain writing assignment.

A related and equally important role of the mainstream teacher is to reinforce students for successfully using strategies in the mainstream class. Stokes and Baer (1977) underscored the importance of reinforcing learners for application of skills in the natural setting as a key element in promoting generalization and maintenance of the skills. Thus, mainstream teachers need to tell students that they are pleased with their use of the strategies in their classes.

The Student's Role in Mainstream Class(es)

Students must have a clear understanding of how important it is for them to deliberately look for opportunities to apply strategies they have mastered in their support service class to help them meet demands in the mainstream setting. In order for students to be successful learners, they must be *active* learners who accept responsibility for their progress. Among the specific things students can do to be effective in the mainstream are: (a) to deliberately choose before class, a specific strategy to use during the class; (b) to prompt themselves, through self-talk, to use a strategy to cope with a specific mainstream demand; (c) to keep alert for cues that will suggest that they should use a particular strategy; (d) to use cue cards to refresh their memories about the strategies as needed (for an example cue card, see Van Reusen et al., 1987); (e) to adapt and modify task-specific strategies to better meet the unique requirements in their mainstream classes; and (f) to integrate several task-specific strategies into a "package" that will allow them to deal with the complete

set of demands placed on them in a given setting. In short, a major part of teaching students to effectively generalize strategies to mainstream settings is teaching them that they play a key role in determining the amount of success they will achieve. They must actively use the strategies they have been taught in their support class to acquire the content information and respond to other assignments in their mainstream classes; this will greatly increase their chances of getting a passing grade.

EXTERNAL SUPPORT SOURCES

It is frequently assumed that the main inputs in addressing problems presented by mildly handicapped learners are the instructional materials and teaching procedures used in the support setting. While these ingredients are certainly necessary, they are by no means sufficient. In short, success in both the support service and mainstream classroom is directly related to the amount of external support given to teachers. Work on the SIM in recent years has underscored the importance of four sources of external support: administrative support, ancillary staff support, family support, and community support.

In the absence of strong *administrative support*, it is highly unlikely that the SIM will flourish. During the past 4 years, affiliates of the KU-IRLD have trained approximately 25,000 teachers to use the SIM. Unquestionably, the sites with the highest rates of program implementation and student achievement are those that have active and strong administrative support. Several types of administrative support seem important in promoting successful SIM implementation. First, administrators must voice support and expectations for teachers with regard to fulfilling their unique roles as defined in this model. Second, they must provide teachers with the required materials and sufficient time for appropriate training, preparation, and cooperative planning. Third, administrators must be willing to make the necessary trade-offs and accept the consequences of supporting the implementation of this model; for example, they must not expect support service teachers to tutor students in content subjects to keep them afloat in the mainstream classes. Fourth, they must become actively involved in monitoring the instructional effectiveness (not just the disciplinary and management effectiveness) of teachers participating in this effort, and they must reinforce these teachers accordingly (Cusick, 1983).

Additionally, the support from *ancillary* staff (e.g., counselors, school psychologists) is central in obtaining important structural changes that will facilitate student growth. As an example, correctly arranging students' class schedules is a very important factor in facilitating cooperative planning among teachers and placement of students in appropriate classes. The school counselor or scheduling officer's willingness to "hand-schedule" (in lieu of computer-scheduling) students' enrollment can go a long way in realizing the success that students can experience.

Similarly, school psychologists can do much to promote the successful operation of an SIM program by taking an active role in several areas. First, school psychologists must expand the focus of their assessment efforts to include a profiling of the different setting demands students are expected to meet in mainstream classrooms and other school activities. The data collected through an assessment of these domains will allow teachers in support settings to make sound instructional decisions regarding target areas for intervention. Second, as contributors to IEP and other educational planning meetings, school psychologists should be aware of the importance of having all members of the committee (teachers, parents, and students) actively participate in the decision-making process. Providing opportunities for participation in such meetings is central to obtaining the necessary commitment and support by the key participants (mainstream and support service teachers, parents, and the student). The school psychologist should view his or her role in such meetings as a conveyor of information, problem solver, and facilitator. Third, the school psychol-

ogist can do much to promote cooperative planning and other interactions among the instructional staff involved in this model. Cooperative planning between support service and mainstream teachers is particularly challenging because of the schedule conflicts that arise during a typical school day (e.g., planning periods or lunch periods that don't match). Because of school psychologists' more flexible schedules, they can facilitate the efforts of different staff members in cooperative planning by being middle men or by encouraging a reluctant staff member to interact with other teachers on behalf of targeted students. Fourth, given their familiarity with the students being served through this model (e.g., their successes and challenges) as well as their familiarity with the specific needs of the instructional staff to more effectively serve the assigned students (e.g., the need for more instructional materials or supplies, etc.) school psychologists can do much to communicate valuable information to school administrators to garner the necessary support for this program. Finally, and perhaps most importantly, the school psychologist can play some very important roles relative to instruction with targeted students. For example, they can deliver strategy instruction in one-to-one or small-group settings (Weinstein & Mayer, 1986) or they can team with the mainstream teachers in efforts to increase the effectiveness of their presentation of subject matter. This teaming relationship can be established, for example, in the form of a peer coaching arrangement (Joyce & Showers, 1982). In brief, school psychologists can do a great deal to support and facilitate processes that are critical to the implementation of a SIM program.

Other potentially significant sources of external support for the SIM program are the families of the students being served by the program. Handicapped students report that they rely on their family as one of their most important supports (Deshler, Alley, Warner, Schumaker, & Clark, 1980). Many parents also report a desire to take a very active role in the educational progress and life adjustment success of their children (Dinkmeyer & McKay, 1976) even though they feel inadequately prepared to do so (Turnbull & Turnbull, 1986). While families feel a responsibility to assist their handicapped children in meeting the school's academic requirements, they also see their children as needing assistance in such areas as acquiring independent living skills, social skills, and other coping behaviors (Hazel, Walther, Nolte, Schumaker, & Deshler, in press).

Conceivably, active parental and family support for mildly handicapped students can serve to extend the services provided in the school. Unfortunately, while there is often a high level of *desire* to assist family members with handicapping conditions, parents and siblings often lack the specific knowledge and skills to do so effectively. There is an obvious need to train family members in the necessary skills to create a significant support system within the home (Hazel, Schumaker, & Deshler, 1986). Current KU-IRLD research efforts are focusing on developing methods for training parents to facilitate homework sessions, to encourage the use of appropriate social skills, and to reinforce instruction provided in the school.

Another important source of external support is that provided by community citizens and agencies. The difficulty of the transition from secondary to postsecondary education is well documented (Knowlton & Clark, 1987). The movement into meaningful jobs (i.e., ones that serve as entry points for career paths and/or pay more than a minimal wage) or postsecondary training programs following high school is a transition that requires significant planning and the mobilization of resources external to the school (Schumaker, Hazel, & Deshler, 1985). To establish this needed support, KU-IRLD researchers have developed a program that consists of the following components. First, starting in their ninth-grade year in school, students are made aware of the many factors they must consider as they prepare for adult life (i.e., independent living responsibilities, choosing and gaining access to postsecondary training,

successfully completing postsecondary training, and getting and maintaining a meaningful job). This is accomplished, in part, by completing a Transition Curriculum (Knackendoffel et al., in press). Second, students are made aware of the types of support services available to them through a community agency (e.g., a mental health center) that has teamed with the school district to provide transitional services to young adults who have left high school (Moccia, Schumaker, Hazel, & Deshler, in press). The goal associated with the Transition Program administered by this agency is to provide the student protegé with a personal support system external to the school and family but central to the community setting. A major part of these services is the matching of students in their junior year with volunteer mentors from the community who possess background experience or interests that are applicable to the student's. Mentors serve in a broad array of roles vis-à-vis their protegés. Among the most salient are the following: role model, sounding board, advocate, problem solver, teacher, and friend. In addition to the mentor program, the introduction and familiarization of students with a community agency (such as a mental health facility) through their high school years is an important element in establishing a community support base for these students once they leave high school.

The initial results of this mentoring program have been positive and indicate the importance of this element as an external support for these students. Specifically, of a sample of 33 mildly handicapped students who worked with their mentors, 31 are now out of high school and could be contacted, 13 are employed, 13 are employed *and* have entered postsecondary training, 4 are in postsecondary training only, and 1 is not employed and not in a postsecondary training program. Of the 46 students who have entered the program while in high school, only four have dropped out of school (Moccia et al., in press). These data vary significantly from those reported by Levin et al. (1983).

In short, as the SIM has evolved over the past 10 years, the importance of the existence and operation of support agents or services external to the classroom has become increasingly clear. To the extent that these elements are present, the chances of mildly handicapped students being successfully integrated into the mainstream educational curriculum and making a transition to a productive postsecondary life are increased. The school psychologist, because of his or her unique competencies and scheduling flexibility, can play an important role in promoting the active functioning of several of these external supports.

SUMMARY

Meeting the needs of mildly handicapped students in public schools is a great challenge. How these students should be served best has been the subject of much recent debate. Included in this exchange have been several charges about the failure of special education services to meet the needs of mildly handicapped students and statements about the desirability of returning these students solely to mainstream settings. Although the progress noted on behalf of these students through "traditional" service arrangements for mildly handicapped students has been discouraging, KU-IRLD research has clearly underscored the fact that if teachers' roles are clearly defined, if the intervention content (e.g., task-specific strategies highly related to curricular demands) is clearly specified, if validated instructional procedures that produce both acquisition and generalization are employed, if teachers regularly work together to plan on behalf of at-risk students, and if sufficient external supports are in place to complement classroom instruction, significant gains and success can be realized by the students.

The overriding objective of a program that incorporates all these factors is to intensively intervene with at-risk students so as to promote the generalization and automatic application of strategies for coping in the mainstream setting *shortly* after the intervention in the support service setting begins and not at some unspecified time in the future. Unfortunately, proponents of traditional special services for the mildly handicapped population *hope* for eventual success rather than commit themselves to a specific time frame in which goals are regularly measured. In the absence of explicit, ambitious, and regularly evaluated instructional goals, students will benefit only marginally, if at all, from education in support service settings. The Strategies Intervention Model has been structured to ensure that students gain maximum benefit from instruction provided in support class settings.

REFERENCES

Armbruster, B. B. (1984). The problem of "inconsiderate text." In G. Duffy, L. Roehler, & J. Mason (Eds.), *Comprehension instruction: Perspectives and suggestions.* New York: Longman.

Bulgren, J. A., & Schumaker, J. B. (in press). *Learning strategies curriculum: The paired-associates strategy.* Lawrence: University of Kansas, Institute for Research in Learning Disabilities.

Bulgren, J., Schumaker, J. B., & Deshler, D. D. (1988). *The effectiveness of a concept teaching routine in enhancing the performance of LD students in secondary mainstream classes* (Research Report). Lawrence: University of Kansas, Institute for Research in Learning Disabilities.

Bulgren, J. A., Schumaker, J. B., & Deshler, D. D. (1987). Effectiveness of a concept teaching routine in enhancing the performance of LD students in secondary level mainstream classes. *Learning Disability Quarterly,* Fall, 319-331.

Carlson, S. A. (1985). The ethical appropriateness of subject-matter tutoring of learning disabled adolescents. *Learning Disability Quarterly, 8,* 310-314.

Clark, F. L., Deshler, D. D., Schumaker, J. B., Alley, G. R., & Warner, M. M. (1984). Visual imagery and self-questioning: Strategies to improve comprehension of written materials. *Journal of Learning Disabilities, 17*(3), 145-149.

Cusick, P. A. (1983). *The equalitarian ideal and the American high school.* New York: Longman.

Deshler, D. D., Alley, G. R., Warner, M. M., & Schumaker, J. B. (1981). Instructional practices for promoting skill acquisition and generalization in severely learning disabled adolescents. *Learning Disabilities Quarterly, 4*(4), 415-421.

Deshler, D. D., Alley, G. R., Warner, M. M., Schumaker, J. B., & Clark, F. L. (1980). *An epidemiological study of learning disabled adolescents in secondary schools: Use of support systems in and out of school.* (Research Report No. 19). Lawrence: University of Kansas, Institute for Research in Learning Disabilities.

Deshler, D. D., Lowrey, N., & Alley, G. R. (1979). Programming alternatives for LD adolescents: A nationwide survey. *Academic Therapy, 15,* 355-358.

Deshler, D. D., & Schumaker, J. B. (1986). Learning strategies: An instructional alternative for low-achieving adolescents. *Exceptional Children, 52,*(6), 583-590.

Deshler, D. D., Schumaker, J. B., Alley, G. R., Warner, M. M., & Clark, F. L. (1982). Learning disabilities in adolescent and young adult populations: Research implications (Part I). *Focus on Exceptional Children, 15*(1), 1-12.

Deshler, D. D., Schumaker, J. B. Bulgren, J., Hudson, P., & McKnight, P. (in press). *A training manual for teaching mainstream teachers how to facilitate the memory of classroom lectures.* (Curriculum material). Lawrence: University of Kansas, Institute for Research in Learning Disabilities.

Deshler, D. D., Schumaker, J. B., & Lenz, B. K. (1984). Academic and cognitive interventions for LD adolescents (Part I). *Journal of Learning Disabilities, 17*(2), 108-117.

Deshler, D. D., Schumaker, J. B., Lenz, B. K., & Ellis, E. S. (1984). Academic and cognitive interventions for LD adolescents (Part II). *Journal of Learning Disabilities, 17*(3), 170-187.

Dinkmeyer, D., & McKay, G. (1976). *Systematic training for effective parenting: Parents' handbook and leader's manual.* Circle Pines, MN: American Guidance Service.

Ellis, E. S., Lenz, B. K., & Sabornie, E. J. (1987). Generalization and adaptation of learning strategies to natural environments: Part I: Critical agents. *Remedial and Special Education, 8*(1), 6-20.

Haring, N. G., & Eaton, M. D. (1987). Systematic instructional procedures: An instructional hierarchy. In N. G. Haring, T. C. Lovitt, M. D. Eaton, & C. L. Hansen (Eds.), *The fourth R: Research in the classroom.* Columbus, OH: Merrill.

Hazel, J. S., Schumaker, J. B., & Deshler, D. D. (1986). *The development and evaluation of an intervention program for families with learning disabled youths.* (Grant No. GO 8635203). U.S. Department of Education.

Hazel, J. S., Schumaker, J. B., Sheldon, J., & Sherman, J. A. (1982). Application of a group training program in social skills to learning disabled and non-learning disabled youth. *Learning Disability Quarterly, 5,* 398-408.

Hazel, J. S., Schumaker, J. B., Sherman, J. A., & Sheldon-Widgen, J. (1981). *ASSET: A social skills program for adolescents.* Champaign, IL: Research Press.

Hazel, J. S., Walther, C., Nolte, M., Schumaker, J. B., & Deshler, D. D. (in press). Research study. Lawrence: University of Kansas, Institute for Research in Learning Disabilities.

Hughes, C., Schumaker, J. B., Deshler, D. D., & Mercer, C. (1988). *The learning strategies curriculum: The test-taking strategy.* Lawrence, KS: Excel Enterprises.

Joyce, B. R., & Showers, B. (1982). The coaching of teaching. *Educational Leadership, 40,* 4-10.

Kea, C. D. (1987). *An analysis of critical teaching behaviors employed by teachers of students with learning disabilities.* Unpublished doctoral dissertation. Lawrence: University of Kansas.

Kierstead, J. (1986). How teachers manage individual and small group work in active classrooms. *Educational Leadership, 44*(2), 22-25.

Knackendoffel, A., Schumaker, J. B., & Deshler, D. D. (in press). *A training manual for teacher collaborative/consultation skills in problem-solving to special education teachers.* (Curriculum material). Lawrence: University of Kansas, Institute for Research in Learning Disabilities.

Knackendoffel, A., Schumaker, J. B., Hazel, J. S., & Deshler, D. D. (in press). *Effective transitions through goal setting and life planning.* (Curriculum material). Lawrence: The University of Kansas, Institute for Research in Learning Disabilities.

Knowlton, H. E., & Clark, G. M. (1987). Transition issues for the 1990s. *Exceptional Children, 53*(6), 562-563.

Lenz, B. K., Alley, G. R., & Schumaker, J. B. (1987). Activating the inactive learner: Advance organizers in the secondary content classroom. *Learning Disability Quarterly, 10*(1), 53-68.

Lenz, B. K., Schumaker, J. B., Deshler, D. D., & Beals, V. L. (1984). *The learning strategies curriculum: The word identification strategy.* Lawrence: University of Kansas.

Lenz, B. K., Swanson, J. T., & Agudelo, T. (in press). *The learning strategies curriculum: The interpreting visual aids strategy.* Lawrence, KS: Excel Enterprises.

Levin, E. K., Zigmond, N., & Birch, J. W. (1983). *A follow-up study of 52 learning disabled adolescents.* Paper presented at AERA, Montreal.

Levin, J. R. (1986). Four cognitive principles of learning-strategy instruction. *Educational Psychologist, 21*(1 & 2), 3-17.

Moccia, R. E., Schumaker, J. B., Hazel, J. S., & Deshler, D. D. (in press). *A training manual for preparing mentors to aid mildly handicapped adolescents to make successful transitions to adult life.* (Curriculum material). Lawrence: University of Kansas, Institute for Research in Learning Disabilities.

Nagel, D., Schumaker, J. B., & Deshler, D. D. (1986). *The learning strategies curriculum: The FIRST-letter mnemonic strategy.* Lawrence, KS: Excel Enterprises.

Pressley, M., Goodchild, F., Fleet, J., Zajchowski, R., & Evans, E. (in press). The challenge of classroom strategy instruction. *Elementary School Journal.*

Pressley, M., Johnson, C. J., & Symons, S. (1987). Elaborating to learn and learning to elaborate. *Journal of Learning Disabilities, 20*(2), 76-88.

Putnam, M. L. (1988). *An investigation of the curricular demands in secondary mainstream classrooms containing mildly handicapped students.* Unpublished doctoral dissertation. Lawrence: University of Kansas.

Robinson, S., Deshler, D. D., Denton, P., & Schumaker, J. B. (in press). *The learning strategies curriculum: The listening and notetaking strategy.* (Curriculum materials). Lawrence: University of Kansas, Institute for Research in Learning Disabilities.

Rosenshine, B., & Stevens, R. (1986). Teaching functions. In M. C. Wittrock (Ed.), *Handbook of research on teaching.* New York: Macmillan.

Schmidt, J. L., Deshler, D. D., Schumaker, J. B., & Alley, G. R. (in press). The effects of four generalization procedures on LD adolescents' written language performance in the mainstream class. *Journal of Reading, Writing, and Learning Disabilities International.*

Schumaker, J. B. (in press). The learning strategies curriculum: The theme writing strategy. Lawrence: University of Kansas, Institute for Research in Learning Disabilities.

Schumaker, J. B., Denton, P. H., & Deshler, D. D. (1984). *The learning strategies curriculum: The paraphrasing strategy.* Lawrence: University of Kansas, Institute for Research in Learning Disabilities.

Schumaker, J. G., & Deshler, D. D. (1984). Setting demand variables: A major factor in program planning for LD adolescents. *Topics in Language Disorders, 4*(2), 22-44.

Schumaker, J. B., Deshler, D. D., Alley, G. R., & Denton, P. H. (1982). Multipass: A learning strategy for improving reading comprehension. *Learning Disability Quarterly, 5*(3), 295-300.

Schumaker, J. G., Deshler, D. D., & Ellis, E. S. (1986). Intervention issues related to the education of LD adolescents. In J. K. Torgeson & B. L. Wong (Eds.), *Learning disabilities: Some new perspectives.* New York: Academic.

Schumaker, J. B., Deshler, D. D., Hudson, P., & McKnight, P. (in press). *A training manual for teaching mainstream teachers how to facilitate understanding of classroom lectures* (Curriculum material). Lawrence: University of Kansas, Institute for Research in Learning Disabilities.

Schumaker, J. B., Hazel, J. S., & Deshler, D. D. (1985). A model for facilitating post-secondary transitions. *Techniques, 6*, 437-446.

Schumaker, J. B., Hazel, J. S., & Pederson, C. S. (1988). *Social skills for daily living.* Circle Pines, MN: American Guidance Services.

Schumaker, J. B., & Lyerla, K. (in press). *The learning strategies curriculum: The paragraph writing strategy* (Curriculum material). Lawrence: University of Kansas, Institute for Research in Learning Disabilities.

Schumaker, J. B., Nolan, S., & Deshler, D. D. (1985). *The learning strategies curriculum: The error monitoring strategy.* Lawrence: University of Kansas, Institute for Research in Learning Disabilities.

Schumaker, J. B., & Sheldon, J. (1985). *The learning strategies curriculum: The sentence writing strategy* (Curriculum material). Lawrence: University of Kansas, Institute for Research in Learning Disabilities.

Schumaker, J. B., Sherman, J. A., & Sheldon-Wildgen, J. (1982). Social interaction of learning disabled junior high students in their regular classrooms: An observational analysis. *Journal of Learning Disabilities, 15*, 355-358.

Sinclair, R. L., & Ghory, W. J. (1987). *Reaching marginal students: A primary concern for school renewal.* Chicago: McCutchan.

Stokes, T. F., & Baer, D. M. (1977). An implicit technology of generalization. *Journal of Applied Behavior Analysis, 10*, 349-367.

Turnbull, A. P., & Turnbull, H. R. (1986). *Families, professionals, and exceptionality — A special partnership.* Columbus, OH: Merrill.

Van Reusen, A. K., Bos, C., Schumaker, J. B., & Deshler, D. D., (1987). *The educational planning strategy.* Lawrence, KS: Excel Enterprises.

Walberg, H. J. (1986). Syntheses of research on teaching. In M. C. Wittrock (Ed.), *Handbook of research on teaching.* New York: Macmillan.

Weinstein, C. E., & Mayer, R. E. (1986). The teaching of learning strategies. In M. C. Wittrock (Ed.), *Handbook of research on teaching.* (3rd Edition, pp. 315-327). New York: Macmillan.

Warner, M. M., Schumaker, J. B., Alley, G. R., & Deshler, D. D. (in press). *An epidemiological study of school identified LD and low-achieving adolescents on a serial recall task: The role of executive control. Learning Disabilities Research.*

Whitaker, K. K. (1982). Development and field test of an assignment completion strategy for learning disabled adolescents. Unpublished master's thesis, University of Kansas, Lawrence.

FOOTNOTE

[1]Some of these materials (i.e., those associated with the *Learning Strategies Curriculum*) are available only through training sessions led by trainers associated with the KU-IRLD. For more information contact Dr. Frances L. Clark, Coordinator of Training, University of Kansas-IRLD, 223 Carruth-O'Leary Hall, Lawrence, KS 66045.

20

Developing Effective Behavioral Interventions

Ann Casey
Iowa State University
Russ Skiba
Indiana University
Bob Algozzine
University of Florida

Teaching is the systematic presentation of content assumed necessary within curriculum areas of instruction. Teachers must be familiar with content they are presenting; for most of them, this is the least of their worries. What worries teachers is the behavior of their students which interferes with content presentations. In addressing the overriding need to control behaviors that disrupt and interfere with teaching, teachers rely heavily on behavioral intervention.

The goals of behavioral intervention are to increase appropriate or adaptive behavior and to decrease inappropriate or maladaptive behavior. Contingent attention for appropriate responses, tangible rewards, and negative consequences for inappropriate responses are commonly used methods for achieving the twin goals of behavioral intervention. Recently, feedback and cognitive-behavioral approaches have become topics of interest for those who practice behavioral interventions in classroom environments.

There is ample evidence that behavioral interventions work. Evaluation of the effectiveness of behavioral interventions has been closely tied to behavioral assessment practices. All behavioral interventions require some direct contact with students. These approaches provide an excellent opportunity for school psychologists to work with students in a role other than psychoeducational assessment. To be successful, though, these interventions require indirect contact as well. School psychologists need to work with parents and/or teachers in implementing successful behavioral programs.

WHAT DRIVES BEHAVIORAL INTERVENTION?

The twin goals of behavioral intervention are to increase appropriate or adaptive behavior and to decrease inappropriate or maladaptive behavior. The underlying assumption of any behavioral intervention is that students' behavioral problems represent either deficits in adaptive behavior, or excesses of behavior that prove maladaptive in the students' environment. If a student is unable to carry out a required task or behavior because of deficits in prerequisite skills, the task of instruction may be to supply the lacking skills. In contrast, a student may be capable of performing a target skill or behavior but may for some reason lack the motivation to perform at a level commensurate with ability. Talking to friends or cutting up in class may simply be more fun than doing math. In the face of a lack of motivation the first step of instruction is to supply stimuli designed to increase the likelihood of an appropriate response, usually by arranging antecedent or consequent conditions in the environment.

If the student's skills appear to be sufficient, the task of instruction clearly is to arrange the classroom ecology and/or consequences of behavior to maximize the likelihood of performance of already learned behaviors. Haring and Phillips (1972) noted that in some classrooms an open book and instructions from the teacher are adequate cues to start many students studying, but for others the same cues will result in disruptive behavior designed to avoid what may be viewed as a highly aversive task. Many students who have a history of failure in academic settings, begin to develop complex repertoires of behavior designed to avoid academic work.

Common Behavioral Intervention Practices

Three approaches have most often been used in behavioral intervention to manage classroom behavior: redirecting teachers' attention toward positive, rather than negative behaviors; providing tangible rewards for appropriate behavior; and providing some form of negative consequence for inappropriate or disruptive classroom behavior. There is a wide body of literature supporting the efficacy of these procedures in classroom management. The key to success is to use consequences in a consistent manner. Assuring consistent contingent consequences requires teachers' confidence that their efforts will pay off. School psychologists and others can help by providing moral support to follow-through.

There is strong evidence that increasing teachers' attention to instances of appropriate behavior can be an effective behavior management strategy in the classroom. Occasional conflicting findings, however, suggest the need to identify the effective components of social reinforcers in the classroom. Effective reinforcement of appropriate behavior must be delivered contingently, and must specify the rewarded behavior and include nonverbal components that demonstrate to the

student that the praise is sincere and credible.

For students who fail to respond to social contingencies such as praise, tangible reinforcers (token economies, activity reinforcement, or edible treats) have proven to be a powerful addition to the repertoire of behavior management. Furthermore, group reinforcement contingencies have been shown to be as effective, and occasionally more effective, than individual contingencies. In a review of the literature, Litow and Pumroy (1975) concluded that group contingencies are effective and interdependent group contingencies (the entire group must perform the contingent behavior before any individual is reinforced) are most effective. Nevin, Johnson and Johnson (1982) found group contingencies to be superior to individual contingencies in increasing the rate of correct academic performance and in decreasing the negative social interactions of small groups of resource room and low-achieving students. The results of a meta-analysis of single-case-design investigations of classroom behavior management (Skiba, Casey, & Center, 1986) indicated that although both individual and group contingencies are effective in improving classroom behavior, group reinforcement contingencies are somewhat more effective in controlling the behavior of students with problems.

Together with the literature on positive teacher attention, investigations of tangible reward systems provide extensive evidence of the effectiveness of reinforcement in the classroom. In a comprehensive meta-analysis of reinforcement procedures Lysakowski and Walberg (1981) found that the general affect of reinforcement on classroom learning is moderately large and fairly robust. In addition, their findings indicated that students in special education are in general more influenced by reinforcement than are other students. No difference in effectiveness was found between tokens, activity reinforcers, and social attention.

Recent research has provided consistent and fairly convincing evidence that some form of negative consequences may be necessary in order to maintain appropriate classroom behavior among students with severe behavior problems (Pfiffner, Rosen, & O'Leary, 1985; Rosen, O'Leary, Joyce, Conway, & Pfiffner, 1984; Walker, Hops, & Fiegenbaum, 1976). Still, the use of behavior reduction procedures remains the focus of considerable controversy. If such procedures are to be used, they should be used in such a way as to maximize positive effects and minimize intrusive or deleterious side effects. Findings from experimental studies with animals and from the child development literature suggest several important considerations in implementing any negative consequence. First, timing is extremely important: The longer the delay between the behavior and the consequence, the less effective the intervention is likely to be (Parke & Walters, 1967; Walters, Parke, & Cane, 1965). Second, the consequence should be administered consistently, preferably after every expression of the target behavior (Deur & Parke, 1970). Third, since effectiveness in the use of negative consequences appears to increase as the degree of cognitive structure is increased (Cheyne & Walters, 1969), students should be told the specific nature of the inappropriate behavior that brought on the consequence. In observational studies, specific criticism by teachers appears to be positively correlated with students' achievement as measured by achievement tests (Anderson, Evertson, & Brophy, 1979), whereas general criticism is negatively related to achievement (Stallings, 1985). Finally, research showing that negative consequences are more effective when administered by someone who has a positive relationship with the child (Parke & Walters, 1967) — as well as general ethical considerations — dictate that negative consequences must be implemented only in the context of a well-planned positive program. Providing a positive program also increases the effectiveness of negative consequences by providing an alternative response that can be learned in place of the maladaptive behavior. A more complete listing of the effective procedures is provided in several excellent reviews in the areas of reprimands (Van Houten,

1983), response cost (Walker, 1983), and time-out (Brantner & Doherty, 1983). A number of comprehensive treatments on ethical considerations in the use of decelerative consequences are also available (Gast & Nelson, 1977; Martin, 1975; Wood & Braaten, 1983).

Emerging Behavioral Intervention Trends

An impressive body of evidence has been generated that demonstrates the effectiveness of behavioral interventions in the management of behavior problems in the classroom. Recent research on the acceptability of behavioral interventions (Kazdin, 1981; Witt & Martens, 1983; Witt, Martens, & Elliott, 1984) indicates that teachers' willingness to use behavioral procedures in the classroom is based on more than just treatment effectiveness. Treatment acceptability appears to be a complex interaction of the severity of the behavior being treated, the effectiveness of the procedure and the ease with which the procedure can be implemented. Although exchangeable reinforcers and negative consequences have been shown to be effective in the management of classroom behavior, they also differ, in some cases dramatically, from the daily routines of many classrooms. For less disruptive behavior or in situations where a more intrusive intervention is not practical, a less structured alternative may be preferable. Recent advances in the areas of feedback and cognitive behavior modification (self-management, self-instruction, and self-reinforcement) may provide such alternatives.

Corrective and supportive feedback. Reinforcement of student behavior serves both a motivational and an informational function. In situations in which the presence of an explicit reinforcer may not be desirable, merely providing information or feedback to students can be an effective intervention. Lobitz and Burns (1977) compared the effectiveness of public and private feedback in increasing the on-task behavior of a fourth grader rated by the teacher as the most disruptive student in the class. A public feedback procedure, in which the teacher announced a rating of the student's behavior to the class at five-minute intervals, was successful in reducing the student's off-task behavior to a rate commensurate with the rest of the class. Dougherty and Dougherty (1977) reported the use of a home-school report card procedure in reducing disruptive behavior. Simply providing a written report on behavior, sent home nightly, was sufficient to improve students' behavior without the addition of an explicit reinforcer. Feedback may also be given by peers. Kerr, Strain, and Ragland (1982) found that having students with behavioral disorders comment on whether their peers had achieved their daily behavioral goals and applaud those who had, increased the attainment of their goals. Bellafiore and Salend (1983) reported on the effectiveness of a peer confrontation model for inappropriate classroom behavior.

Although feedback (providing information about performance) can be distinguished theoretically from reinforcement (providing information plus a contingent reward for improvements in performance), it may be more difficult to distinguish between feedback and social reinforcement in practice. Teachers' announcements to the class every five minutes might prove highly reinforcing (or highly punishing) to the target student, depending on the nature of those announcements. Similarly, applause from one's peers can be a powerful social reinforcer above and beyond its informational value. Still, such procedures are less intrusive than full-scale token economies and may indeed be the treatment of choice for a mild misbehavior in regular classrooms (Drabman & Lahey, 1974).

Cognitive-behavioral approaches. The role of cognition in effecting behavior change has received much attention in the past decade. Cognitive-behavioral approaches are those that incorporate both a cognitive and a behavioral element. Much of the literature in cognitive-behavior therapy focuses on adult applications that are substantively different from applications for use with children. Whereas adult cognitive-behavior therapy typically focuses on changing irrational thought patterns, the major application of cognitive-behavior therapy with children has been the use of self-instructional training (Kendall, 1984). However, Bedrosian (1981) suggested that many of the adult techniques can be modified successfully for use with adolescents.

Meichenbaum and Goodman (1971) introduced a cognitive-behavioral strategy for use with impulsive children, who continue to be the focus of much of the work being done today in this area (Kendall & Braswell, 1984). Briefly, the approach is posited on the theory that impulsive children suffer cognitive deficits and, thus, fail to evaluate their choices and do not think through a matter before acting. The intervention, then, involves teaching the student self-control and problem-solving techniques. The student must first learn a strategy that will stop the impulsive behavior, after which problem-solving strategies can be employed. Meichenbaum and Goodman (1971) provided an excellent example of the technique.

> Okay, what is it I have to do? You want me to copy the picture with the different lines. I have to go slowly and carefully. Okay, draw the line down, down, good; then to the right, that's it; now down some more and to the left. Good, I'm doing fine so far. Remember, go slowly. Now back up again. No, I was supposed to go down. That's okay. Just erase the line carefully . . . Good. Even if I make an error I can go on slowly and carefully. I have to go down now. Finished. I did it! (p. 117)

Aggression is the other behavior that is often the focus of cognitive-behavioral interventions (Camp & Ray, 1984). However, aggressive behavior appears less amenable to treatment than impulsive behavior (Kendall & Braswell, 1984; Meyers & Cohen, 1984). Spivak, Platt, and Shure (1976) suggested that aggression in some children is related to deficits in alternative and means–end thinking. Children with deficits in alternative thinking have difficulty in generating alternative solutions to problems and often are "stuck" when a problem remains unsolved. Deficits in means-end thinking are analogous to going on a trip without an itinerary or map. A student may have a goal in mind, but have no idea about how to proceed, have given no thought to obstacles that might arise, or have failed to plan how these might be avoided. Thus, interventions are developed to provide such students with these skills. Some of these techniques include the following: use of a coping model, self-instructional training, relaxation training, practice in alternative thinking and decision making, and perspective-taking training (Kennedy, 1982).

Although there have been successful cognitive-behavioral treatment programs with young children, DiGuiseppe (1981) suggested that children need to have attained a certain level of cognitive development in order for some interventions to be effective. For example, some children do not understand the difference between fact and opinion, which could be an important distinction in some cognitive-behavioral interventions. The major drawback with these kinds of self-instructional training programs is that the self-instructions are usually highly specific to a particular behavior, and thus there is low generalization to other behaviors (DiGuiseppe, 1981). This is not to say that school psychologists should refrain from using cognitive-behavioral interventions with young children, but they may need to be much more directive and employ higher degrees of modeling and follow-up procedures when working with younger students.

As suggested earlier, adolescents may benefit from cognitive-behavioral treatments that are similar to those used with adults. Bedrosian (1981) listed a number of cognitive distortions that are common in adolescence. These distortions center around topics of physical appearance, sexuality, competency and peer status, and autonomy. The focus of a cognitive-behavioral intervention would be on changing these dysfunctional beliefs. The school psychologist's role is to investigate these cognitions and then to challenge them by using a variety of cognitive-behavioral techniques such as empirical disputing. In this technique, the school psychologist would question the evidence the student had to support the dysfunctional belief. Other options could include decatastrophizing: asking the student "What if . . . ?"; or using guided association: encouraging the student to examine his or her worst fear by asking "and then what?"

While impulsivity and aggression have been the behaviors most often targeted in cognitive-behavior therapy with elementary-age children, Kendall (1984) suggested that some of the techniques used with adolescents and adults could be useful with withdrawn and depressed children as well. The treatment of choice for the withdrawn is self-instructional training, which focuses on inhibiting behaviors. When it appears that a withdrawn child is distorting and misperceiving social situations, the school psychologist should focus on the identification and removal of any dysfunctional cognitions the child might hold.

Problems related to social skills are a third area in which a cognitive-behavioral intervention can be appropriate. Teaching children interpersonal problem-solving skills has been seen as a major strategy for preventing later maladaptive behavior.

Spivak et al. (1976) found that overly aggressive and inhibited four- and five-year-olds were more deficient than adjusted youngsters in posing alternative solutions to interpersonal problems and in consequential thinking. Thus, they developed a program of cognitive problem-solving that addressed these deficits. Their research in this area has been very promising. Weissberg and Gesten (1982) described a social-problem-solving curriculum developed for the Rochester (NY) schools. In addition to teaching component cognitive problem-solving skills, the program emphasizes a sequential process for students to learn. This process consists of six major steps: (a) problem definition, (b) goal statement, (c) impulse delay, (d) generation of alternatives, (e) consideration of consequences, and (f) implementation. Children are taught to integrate the process into their daily lives through role-play procedures. Perhaps the key for any kind of social-problem-solving program is that it be immersed in the curriculum. Teachers must be prepared to cue students on when to use the process; they must reinforce students for their efforts; and they must be prepared to review techniques with students as needed.

In the preceding section a wide variety of behavioral interventions were described, but the presentation is in no way exhaustive. However, from the preceding sample of possible interventions it should be possible to develop an effective intervention program by drawing on the Reference section when further information is necessary.

A Review of Behavioral Intervention Effectiveness

The application and removal of positive and negative consequences is the treatment of choice when modifying transgressions that interfere with classroom instruction. A significant body of literature supports the use of these and other behavioral interventions for increasing appropriate, adaptive behavior and decreasing inappropriate, maladaptive behavior, including reviews of the literature on the effectiveness of the various interventions.

The traditional practice of reviewing research in a narrative fashion has come under increasing criticism in recent years (Jackson, 1980; Light & Pillemer, 1984), the reasoning being that subjective biases may vary by reviewers, increasing the likelihood that different reviewers will come to a different set of conclusions regarding the same body of literature. On the other hand, simply listing or describing the results of individual investigations precludes firm statements and conclusions regarding the relative efficacy of different treatment approaches. Consequently, in order to identify the most effective treatment approaches, it is necessary to review the results of quantitative syntheses (meta-analyses) of the research literature.

Quantitative reviews of behavioral interventions in educational settings consistently have shown that they range from moderately to highly effective. In a meta-analysis of reinforcement procedures in classrooms Lysakowski and Walberg (1981) reported an average effect size (ES) of 1.20; that is, on the average, experimental subjects in between-group investigations of reinforcement exhibited improvement greater than one standard deviation more than untreated controls. In a meta-analysis of group-design research investigating interventions for students with behavioral disorders Skiba and Casey (1985) reported a somewhat smaller average effect size (ES = .93) than Lysakowski and Walberg, but found that interventions derived from behavioral or cognitive-behavioral theory were significantly more effective for students with behavior disorders than were interventions based on other theoretical orientations. Skiba et al. (1986) reported a quantitative synthesis of single-case studies investigating positive reinforcement and feedback approaches in the management of classroom behavior for either regular or special education students. That analysis reported a mean effect size for positive reinforcement and feedback approaches of 1.88, indicating that students' performance during treatment was almost two standard deviations superior to their performance prior to treatment in the baseline phase. In a summary of quantitative reviews of educational interventions, Bloom (1984) reported that only peer tutoring evidenced a higher average effect size than reinforcement-based approaches.

It is unclear to what extent the results of meta-analyses can be used to determine the relative efficacy of different behavioral interventions. Examination of the results of three quantitative reviews that have compared various behavioral interventions reveal few significant differences among the interventions themselves. Lysakowski and Walberg (1981) found no difference in effectiveness between tokens, tangible reinforcers, and social attention, but they discovered that behavioral procedures were most effective for students in special settings. The results of

Skiba and Casey (1985) suggest that for students labeled behavior disordered interventions based on behavioral theory are more effective than procedures founded on other theoretical orientations in controlling disruptive classroom behavior. In the synthesis of single-case-design research by Skiba et al. (1986), in contrast, no consistent main effect differences were found between procedures by setting, type of procedure, or type of behavior, although activity reinforcers were superior to other interventions when only immediate changes in behavior were taken into account.

The failure to find consistent main effect differences is in fact not particularly surprising. The nature of the populations involved may make it unlikely that any single intervention will be the treatment of choice for all populations or all behaviors in all settings. Rather, treatment effectiveness is likely to be highly dependent on ecological and subject characteristics. Thus, even though they failed to find any significant overall differences among procedures, Skiba et al. (1986) found that different procedures varied in their effectiveness depending on the setting or arrangements in which they were administered. When administered on an individual basis, for instance, feedback procedures provided slightly more effective than positive reinforcement in behavior management. When group contingencies were in force, however, reinforcement proved far superior to feedback in the studies included in the meta-analysis.

PROBLEMS IN THE USE OF BEHAVIORAL INTERVENTIONS

Although the overall picture is positive, there are problems to be addressed by those who advocate the use of behavioral interventions. How well treatment effects are maintained in environments and under circumstances other than those of training are of interest to practitioners and researchers alike. Similarly, those who implement behavioral interventions are concerned with continuing to demonstrate that their efforts are effective and with improving measures of their effectiveness.

Improving Generalizability

Even relatively nonintrusive procedures often represent a departure from typical educational programming. As such they raise concerns about the degree to which generalization of effects will be achieved when the treatment is discontinued or when students are returned to a less structured environment. The paradox has special force in work with handicapped populations. More severely disruptive behavior will presumably require more highly structured programming in order to control and/or treat the disruptive behavior. Yet there is little reason to expect that such procedures will maintain their effects across time (Wildman & Wildman, 1975), or the very reason that the greater the extent to which departures from typical instruction are required to control disruptive behavior, the less likely that treatment gains will generalize without explicit programming.

Thus, there has been an increased focus in recent years on explicit programming that will ensure the maintenance of the treatment gains of behavioral intervention across time or settings. One of the better-researched approaches is the practice of equating stimulus conditions; that is, making the stimulus situations in the training and target environments as similar as possible. Stokes and Baer (1977) suggested that programming common stimuli, such as the same curriculum, in both settings will increase the chance that those stimuli will come to control responding in both settings. Similarly, Hundert (1982) has suggested that the special classroom be made as similar to the mainstream classroom as possible by, for instance, fading from small-group to large-group instruction as quickly as possible. Wildman and Wildman (1975) recommended fading from tangible to social reinforcers in order to more closely approximate the conditions of the regular class.

Transition might also be facilitated by changing characteristics of the mainstream classroom so as to increase the chances of success for students being mainstreamed. Walker, Hops, and Johnson (1975) trained regular education personnel in behavior management techniques, increasing the success rate of students being reintegrated into the mainstream. It may also be possible to train students to modify their environments. Stokes, Fowler, and Baer (1978) taught preschool children to recruit teacher praise for their appropriate behavior. Such an approach might be useful for mildly handicapped students in mainstream settings that typically provide rather low rates of reinforcement.

Evaluating Effectiveness

In selecting among effective behavioral interventions, professionals too often have been guilty of searching for a panacea — an intervention that will be effective with all students. Instead, it should be assumed that some interventions will be effective for some students and not for others. The only way to know for sure whether an intervention will be effective for an individual student is to implement it and measure the effect on the student's performance. In short, teachers and support services personnel should treat all of their interventions as hypotheses to be tested. In this model, the implementer of an intervention acts as a researcher who is interested in testing promising hypotheses about what might be an effective strategy for a given student.

This model of hypothesis testing is the basis for single-case-research design. Single-subject designs, in which assessment of the behavior prior to the introduction of the intervention (baseline) is followed by measurement of behavior under the treatment condition, are a hallmark of behavioral procedures. By carefully alternating the phases, one can identify increases or decreases in behavior that covary with the introduction or removal of treatment (Baer, Wolf, & Risley, 1968). For researchers, such ongoing measurement provides empirical evidence that it is indeed the treatment, and not an intervening variable, that has caused

changes in behavior (Campbell & Stanley, 1963). For practitioners, the frequent progress review afforded by the methodology of behavioral assessment encourages fine-tuning of the student's educational program so as to maximize educational progress and minimize side-effects. Thus, the single-subject assessment design methodology used to measure the effects of behavioral intervention seems particularly well suited to the requirements for individualization of educational programs in special education (Sindelar & Wilson, 1984). The intent here is not to present overwhelmingly complex research designs, but to provide a rationale for measuring behavior on a frequent basis and to provide some ways in which this can be done. We are not suggesting that formal research be undertaken but we are advocating the evaluation of intervention plans. Treating intervention as experimentation requires two things: frequent measurement, and use of the data generated from these measurements to decide whether the intervention should be continued, modified, or dropped.

How are data gathered? Time-series methodology requires the use of continuous measurement to examine the effects of interventions on students' performance over time and relies on the students' serving as their own controls. The most simple research design available to determine if an experiment is effective is an AB design: A represents data collected during the baseline (pretreatment) phase: B represents data collected during the intervention phase.

For example, assume that the target student is a second-grade boy who completes little of his seatwork assignments because of a variety of misbehaviors he exhibits during this unstructured time. The teacher and school psychologist have hypothesized that by increasing the amount of his seatwork completed, the misbehaviors would automatically decrease. In order to test this hypothesis, they first devised a measurement system, percentage of the assignments completed, and kept track of this behavior on a daily basis for seven school days. These data constituted the A or baseline phase. Given their hypothesis, the intervention they developed consisted of ignoring all misbehavior and reinforcing attention to and completion of seatwork assignments. The reinforcement was both verbal and tangible. The teacher gave the student stickers for every three completed assignments. The data for this "experiment" are shown in Figure 1. Prior to the start of the intervention it was decided that progress would be reviewed in two weeks. After two weeks of intervention, the behavior did not increase to a level acceptable to the teacher. Thus, the intervention was changed to include elimination of the misbehavior.

While a simple AB design does not control for most threats to internal validity, it may be sufficient for many purposes in education. Since our goal is to improve student functioning, we do not always care whether we can say with certainty that it was the intervention that improved the behavior as long as the behavior improved. The simple phase-change design includes AB designs as well as BC designs, where B is a first intervention and C is a second. No baseline is taken in the BC design. The simple phase change is designed to answer simple questions such as whether a treatment works or whether one treatment works better than another (Barlow, Hayes, & Nelson, 1984).

The withdrawal (sometimes called reversal) design provides some additional control. After the initial AB sequence, the treatment is withdrawn and then reintroduced. In the ABAB design, if the behavior in the second baseline phase returns to pretreatment levels and then increases after the reintroduction of the treatment, fairly good evidence exists that the intervention was responsible for the effects. While demonstration of control over the intervention may be very worthwhile, there are a number of reasons why practitioners choose not to use this design. Ethical issues can arise over the removal of an intervention that has been effective. Furthermore, some behaviors cannot be "reversed." That is, the student has learned a new skill, perhaps in an academic area, that cannot be unlearned. However, the design can be useful, particularly in cases in which withdrawals naturally occur (school vacations, etc.). The practitioner should take advantage of these data for evaluative purposes.

FIGURE 1. An AB Design

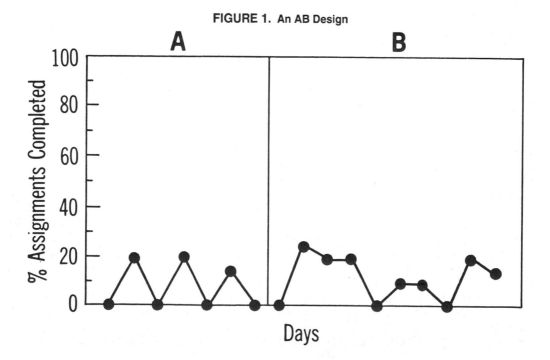

Perhaps the most frequently used designs in the research literature are complex phase changes. Following introduction of more than one intervention, each one is compared with the others as well as with the baseline data. The simplest of these designs is ABAC, where B and C are two different intervention procedures. The changing-criterion design also belongs in this category. This kind of design is often useful when the criteria for acceptable performance are gradually increased. Both kinds of designs can be useful to practitioners who are interested in identifying effective interventions for particular students.

Probably the design that is least used in practice but may have the most utility is the alternating treatment design (ATD). The ATD consists of rapid and random alteration of two or more conditions (Barlow & Hayes, 1979). There are no phases in an ATD. In the typical ATD, two interventions are introduced on alternating days. By graphing the data for each treatment, it is possible to determine if one intervention is better than the other in producing the desired results. A representation of this design is shown in Figure 2.

In this example, the teacher was unsure about which approach would be best for a student who was experiencing attention difficulties. The teacher contrasted a contingent teacher attention intervention with a self-monitoring procedure. While the teacher attention approach seemed to be superior, it was thought that it might be worthwhile to compare it with yet another approach to determine if the student's attending could be increased even further. These data were relatively easy to evaluate because there was no overlap in the data. (When data overlap, the amount of convergence and overlap are the data of interest in making an evaluation.)

Barlow, Hayes, and Nelson (1984) have listed a number of advantages to the alternating treatment design: (a) It does not require withdrawal of treatment; (b) comparison can be made more quickly; (c) one can proceed without a formal baseline period; and (d) it is insensitive to back-

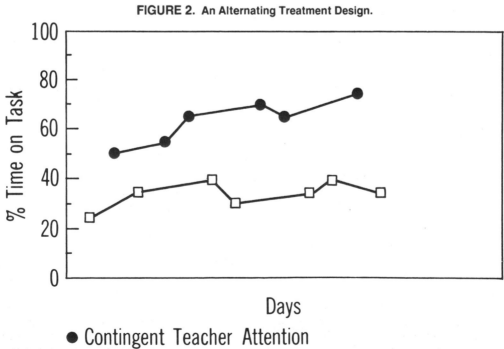

FIGURE 2. **An Alternating Treatment Design.**

● Contingent Teacher Attention
□ Self-monitoring

FIGURE 3. A Multiple Baseline Design.

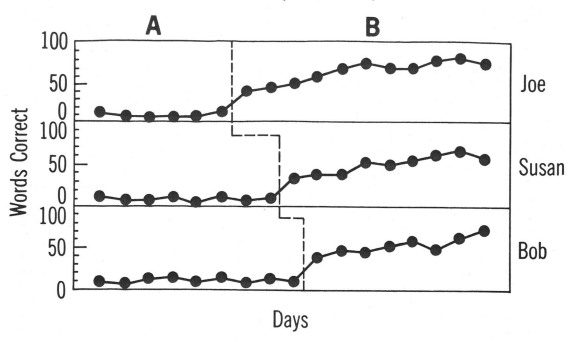

Days

ground trends such as maturation. While treatment interference could be a problem depending on the interventions chosen, this is not a major concern if the treatments are randomly alternated. This design could be very useful in instances in which it is not certain which approach will prove to be the most effective for a particular child. In addition, this design can be used to document the effect of a single treatment with several behaviors or with a behavior in several settings.

The multiple baseline design is another very useful method of determining intervention effectiveness. Simply stated, the multiple baseline design is really a variation on an AB design. Several AB "experiments" are grouped together, the B phases being introduced at different times. A clear effect of the intervention is evident if performance changes when the intervention is applied (Kazdin, 1982). This design combines both within- and between-series comparisons. It can be used to compare the effect of one intervention in many settings, one intervention implemented with several students, or one intervention with several behaviors. The hallmark of this design is that the inter-

vention is introduced at different points so that each successive baseline is longer than the first. How the data in a multiple baseline design might look is demonstrated in Figure 3. A multiple baseline design is a good choice when one wants to determine the effectiveness, for example, of a particular intervention strategy used with a small group of students all of whom are exhibiting the same target behavior. Another example for use is with mainstreamed students for whom one wants to test implementation of an intervention across settings. There are potential problems with this design, such as interdependence among the baseline data, but it is another tool that can be very useful in evaluating effectiveness of intervention strategies.

How are data evaluated? All of the above designs for evaluating intervention effectiveness require the use of continuous (frequent) measurement. How are all of these data points used to make a judgment about effectiveness? In spite of the considerable discussion about visual versus statistical analysis of time series data (De Prospero & Cohen, 1979; Jones,

Vaught, & Weinrott, 1977; Parsonson & Baer, 1978), we suggest that at the present time statistical analysis is not practical for most practitioners. This may change in the near future, given the increasing use of microcomputers that are capable of generating means and slopes of time series data. However, for now, visual analysis of graphed data is an acceptable alternative. The major risk involved is that visual analysis will tend to underestimate an effect. However, Parsonson and Baer (1978) argued that what is desired is effects of a magnitude sufficient to be perceived by the naked eye, and they question the practical significance of data that may be statistically significant but not visually evident.

If visual analysis is to determine if there was an effect, we must first use good graphing techniques. In developing a graph, it is important to keep in mind the following: The x and y axis should be in proportion to one another; each axis should be labeled with the temporal unit on the x axis and the dependent measure on the y axis. A vertical line should divide each phase from the next: Connect continuous data points but do not connect points between phases. In analyzing graphed data there are several points to consider. It is desirable that there be a stable baseline period prior to implementing the intervention: When there is a trend in the baseline data, it is much more difficult to discern whether an intervention has had an effect. A lot of variability in the data from day to day is also not desirable, and one might want to investigate possible sources of the variability. However, both of these cases are somewhat beyond the practitioner's control. In the educational setting these problems are likely to be due to student characteristics, and thus the data at hand must serve as the basis for analysis. In deciding whether the intervention had the desired effect, the less overlap in data points between phases the more convincing the data. In addition, there need to be a sufficient number of data points in each phase to determine if there is a clear trend.

Three variables are of key importance in analyzing graphed data: slope (trend),

level (mean response), and variability. When looking for changes in data from one phase to the next we need to consider all three variables. In general, with behaviors we wish to increase, the statistical goal is to increase both the slope and level of measure of the behavior as well as decrease the variability, an indication that the student is responding more consistently. The levels of desired performance can be set by those who are implementing the interventions and they are the ones who need to specify the criteria for acceptable behavior change.

GUIDELINES FOR IMPLEMENTING BEHAVIORAL INTERVENTIONS

The breadth of the literature on behavioral procedures for use in the classroom is such that space does not permit a listing of individual procedures for specific problems. A number of fine resources are available to the practitioner interested in specific program ideas (Alberto & Troutman, 1986; Algozzine, 1983; Axelrod, 1983; Lovitt, 1984). It is possible, however, to offer guidelines, based on successful applications of behavioral technology, that may increase the likelihood of successful intervention.

1. *Define the behavior in objective and measurable terms.* Without a clear definition of the target behavior, it is difficult if not impossible to develop an appropriate intervention and to determine its effectiveness. It is worth spending the time necessary to determine a clear, complete, and measurable definition of the behavior.

2. *Analyze the problem carefully.* As much as possible, behavioral interventions should be tailored to the student, setting, and problem behavior. Analyzing elements in the environment that are shaping or maintaining the inappropriate behavior makes any plan more likely to succeed. Out-of-seat behavior that is maintained by attention to peers, for instance, might be best addressed through an intervention that reinforces appropriate in-seat behavior with opportunities for peer interaction. If the same behavior appears to be meant to attract the teacher's attention, how-

ever, praise or "extra time with the teacher" might be a suitable reward for appropriate behavior.

3. *Measure the student's behavior before, during, and after an intervention.* Disruptive or disordered behavior can only be identified in comparison with a student's peers. Behavioral observation is necessary to determine whether, and to what extent, the student's behavior is discrepant from peer behavior. Once an intervention is chosen, measurement is necessary to determine whether the treatment is having its intended effect. Immediate and dramatic changes in behavior might be hoped for, but they do not often occur. By graphing behavior, the intervener can detect slight improvements in behavior that might not have been otherwise noticed. This could provide impetus for continuing an intervention that requires more time to take effect rather than dropping a seemingly ineffective one. Finally, measurement is necessary to determine when the goal of the intervention has been reached, and whether the gains produced by the intervention are maintained when the treatment is removed. For the purpose of assessing the extent of behavior change, memory is rarely as accurate as data.

4. *Be contingent, specific, and immediate.* One of the more strikingly consistent findings in behavioral research has been the importance of implementing contingent, specific, and immediate consequences, whether those consequences are positive, negative, or neutral. Recent research has indicated that students with behavior problems may well be acting out in reaction to a history of inconsistent consequences (Wahler & Dumas, 1986). For these students, punishment for misbehavior may well be preferable to the uncertainty of not knowing what might happen next. Making the contingencies — the "rules of the game" — clear is extremely important in providing a secure environment for such youngsters. Defining the target behavior precisely (and in a way that the student understands it) whenever a positive or negative consequence is carried out is also important in making

expectations clear to the student. Finally, immediate administration of the intervention contingent upon the defined behavior again clarifies the rules for the student, as well as ensuring that the consequence will not be delivered for the wrong behavior.

5. *Choose the least intrusive level of intervention that is likely to be effective.* By law, education must be provided in the least restrictive environment. One might well extend that principle to interventions planned for the regular classroom by choosing the least intrusive interventions possible. If effective in controlling a student's behavior, feedback may be preferable to a token economy, as its effects may generalize better over time or settings. Although some writers have suggested that this principle means always starting with the least intrusive intervention and working gradually toward more structured interventions, such a recommendation faces the problem of habituation. Faced with interventions that gradually become more and more intrusive, a student may become accustomed to more and more intense levels of behavioral programming without significantly changing the targeted behavior. Such a cycle can be frustrating for both student and teacher. Rather, it may be best to carefully consider all possible options in light of the severity of a student's behavior, and choose the least intrusive intervention that is likely to be effective: Time-out would probably be too severe an intervention for turning in one's seat; praising and ignoring would not likely be the intervention of choice for aggression toward peers or teachers.

6. *Program a "fair pair."* The tendency to use only negative consequences in regular classrooms has been well documented. Simply finding more effective methods of using those negative consequences is something of a perversion of the behavioral approach. While teachers might initially find themselves reinforced by the effectiveness of those techniques, a management system based primarily on negative consequences is bound to lead to frustration and hard

feelings for both students and teachers. The goal of any management system, rather, should be to emphasize the positive, creative aspects of both teaching and learning. At the very least, the addition of any negative component in an intervention should always be accompanied by the introduction of an additional opportunity to earn a positive reward. If the ultimate goal of education is for students to experience the joy of learning, what better way to reflect that message than through an abundance of positive programming.

7. *Plan for generalization and maintenance of treatment effects from the outset.* Special programs or interventions are typically set up for students for whom the regular classroom routine is not working. There seems to be little reason to expect that changing a student's circumstance temporarily will have any lasting effect on behavior if the student is simply put back into the same routine at the close of the behavioral program. Therefore any behavioral program, from time-out or response cost to feedback, should be gradually faded so that the difference between the condition of the program and of the ongoing environment is minimized. Plans for fading the program should be specified as soon as the intervention is defined. Failure to plan for generalization is simply to trust in luck; if luck fails, a great deal of time and effort might be wasted.

ENHANCING THE EFFECTIVENESS OF BEHAVIORAL INTERVENTIONS

School psychologists and related services personnel can enhance their roles in the schools by becoming skilled in the use of behavioral interventions. Unfortunately, the development of these skills alone is not enough to ensure that behavioral interventions will be implemented properly. Only in a minority of cases are school psychologists the direct providers of behavioral interventions for students. Even in those cases, the students will need to learn to apply their new skills or behaviors in the classroom. In order to plan for the generalization of these skills, the school psychologist must work with the classroom teacher and engage the teacher's support for continuing the intervention.

Thus, in the majority of cases, the classroom teacher or parent is the primary intervener. While the school psychologist may have excellent skills in designing behavioral interventions, the chance of successful implementation of these interventions is minimal without the exercise of another skill, that is, consultation. Too many times, school psychologists have developed wonderful behavioral plans for students, only to complain that it was unsuccessful because the teacher did not implement it correctly or did not implement it at all. The onus for failure was placed on the teacher. It would be safe to say that in many of these cases the school psychologist has gone into the classroom and "told" the teacher what to do, with little or no input from the teacher. In this model, school psychologists view themselves as the expert in behavioral interventions, and thus, believe their wisdom is beyond reproach and that the intervention plan should be followed without question. The likelihood of implementation of behavioral interventions can be increased if the teacher is involved in the process of determining the intervention plan.

Consultation is a key skill required in the design and implementation of behavioral interventions. There are several consultation models used in school systems, but behavioral consultation is specifically appropriate to the present discussion because the elements of behavioral consultation are consistent with the principles of applied behavioral analysis. In using this model, continuity is preserved between the intervention and the process used to develop it. While the discussion that follows focuses only on the use of behavioral consultation for behavioral interventions, there is nothing inherent in the model that limits its use to this area. Behavioral consultation can also be applied to academic interventions. Consult Bergan (1977) for a detailed description of the behavioral consultation process.

Importance of Following Through

Tombari and Davis (1979) have suggested that the major challenge facing the behavioral consultant is influencing the consultee to carry out the procedures developed during the consultation process. They suggest that consultants' ineffectiveness and consultees' lack of skill and motivation may be important reasons why teachers often do not follow through. Consultant skill is clearly seen as an important variable in successful behavioral intervention, and training in this area is highly recommended for school psychologists. Lack of skill and motivation on the part of the teacher is another matter. Consultants can provide skills training to teachers in a variety of ways such as modeling, role-playing, and instructing. This still is no assurance, though, that behavioral interventions will be implemented properly. It is important, then, to assess whether the teacher has the skills to implement the intervention. If not, then some kind of skills training should be provided by the consultant. Further strategies are required for successful implementation and include the use of feedback, prompting, and modeling (Tombari & Davis, 1979).

Motivation of teachers to implement behavioral programs may require ingenuity on the consultant's part. Perhaps the best strategy is to assume the teacher is motivated and express the assumption in the interviewing process through use of phrases such as "I know you want to change this behavior." This can reinforce the important role the teacher must play in the intervention process. In addition, the consultant may wish to be prepared for common objections to behavioral interventions. Following is a list of some objections and possible responses:

1. "Reinforcement is bribery." Response: Bribery implies the unethical use of rewards in an effort to corrupt someone. We are suggesting nothing unethical nor are we trying to corrupt. Rather, we are targeting a behavior that needs improvement.

2. "Kids should work for intrinsic reasons and not be given tangible rewards." Response: Our goal is exactly that, but it is a gradual process of shaping and of pairing reinforcements, which may initially require the use of more tangible rewards.

3. "If I reward one student, all the others will want to be rewarded, too." There are a variety of responses one could make. You could suggest group contingencies or the use of covert reinforcement so that other students do not know, or simply explain that children usually know when other children may require something "extra" to improve their behavior. The other students could be reinforced for their independence and lack of reliance on this something "extra."

4. "This intervention doesn't focus on why Johnny is behaving this way. Don't you want to talk with him?" Response: We are not unconcerned with why people behave the way they do, but it most likely won't be helpful to us in dealing with your particular concerns here in the classroom. For example, Johnny may have a very unsatisfactory home life that is contributing to his behavior problems in school. However, we must deal with what we have control over, and that is the school environment.

Although problem evaluation is stressed in the behavioral consultation model, we maintain that establishing a means for follow-up is more than evaluation — it is a good social skill. Teachers need to know that they are not alone in the intervention process. The consultant needs to demonstrate interest and concern in the intervention as it is occurring. We suggest that consultants who regularly check in with teachers during the implementation phase will more likely see their recommended interventions implemented successfully than those who do not. Furthermore, if the intervention is not working, consultants who have scheduled follow-up appointments will be able to assist the teacher in modifying the plan before too much time with an unsuccessful intervention has passed, possibly causing the teacher to be less the enthusiastic about trying another intervention. With the special education reform movement under way (Reynolds, Wang, & Walberg, 1987), there will be an increasing need for school psychologists and other support services personnel to provide consultation to assist in the development of appropriate interventions for students in the regular classroom. Toward this goal, behavioral consultation provides a systematic means of directing and participating in programs that increase appropriate behavior and decrease inappropriate behavior that often interfere with success in educational settings.

REFERENCES

Alberto, P. A., & Troutman, A. C. (1986). *Applied behavior analysis for teachers* (2nd ed.). Columbus, OH; Charles E. Merrill.

Algozzine, R. (1983). *Problem-behavior management.* Rockville, MD: Aspen.

Anderson, L. M., Evertson, C. M., & Brophy, J. E. (1979). An experimental study of effective teaching in first grade reading groups. *Elementary School Journal, 79, 193–223.*

Axelrod, S. (1983). *Behavior modification for the classroom teacher* (2nd ed.). New York: McGraw-Hill.

Baer, D., Wolf, M., & Risley, T. (1968). Some current dimensions of applied behavior analysis. *Journal of Applied Behavior Analysis, 1,* 91-97.

Barlow, D. H., & Hayes, S. C. (1979). Alternating treatments design: One strategy for comparing the effects of two treatments in a single subject. *Journal of Applied Behavior Analysis, 12,* 199-210.

Barlow, D. H., Hayes, S. C., & Nelson, R. O. (1984). *The scientist practitioner: Research and accountability in clinical and educational settings.* New York: Pergamon.

Bedrosian, R. C. (1981). The application of cognitive therapy techniques with adolescents. In G. Emery, S. Hollon, & R. Bedrosian (Eds.), *New directions in cognitive therapy.* New York: Guilford.

Bellafiore, L. A., & Salend, S. J. (1983). Modifying inappropriate behaviors through a peer-confrontation model. *Behavioral Disorders, 8,* 274-279.

Bergan, J. R. (1977). *Behavioral consultation.* Columbus, OH: Charles E. Merrill.

Bloom, B. S. (1984). The two sigma problem: The search for methods of group instruction as effective as one-one tutoring. *Educational Researcher, 13,* 4-16.

Brantner, J. P., & Doherty, M. A. (1983). A review of timeout: A conceptual and methodological analysis. In S. Axelrod & J. Apsche (Eds.), *The effects of punishment on human behaviors* (pp. 87-132). New York: Academic.

Camp, B. W., & Ray, R. S. (1984). Aggression. In A. Meyers & W. E. Craighead (Eds.), *Cognitive behavior therapy with children.* New York: Plenum.

Campbell, D. T., & Stanley, J. C. (1963). *Experimental and quasi-experimental designs for research.* Chicago: Rand-McNally.

Cheyne, J. A., & Walters, R. H. (1969). Intensity of punishment, timing of punishment, and cognitive structure as determinants of response and inhibition. *Journal of Experimental Child Psychology, 7,* 231-244.

DeProspero, A., & Cohen, S. (1979). Inconsistent visual analysis of intrasubject data. *Journal of Applied Behavior Analysis, 10,* 573-579.

Deur, J. L., & Parke, R. D. (1970). Effects of inconsistent punishment on aggression in children. *Developmental Psychology, 2,* 403-411.

DiGuiseppe, R. A. (1981). Cognitive therapy with children. In G. Emery, S. Hollon, & R. Bedrosian (Eds.), *New directions in cognitive therapy.* New York: Guilford.

Dougherty, E. H., & Dougherty, A. (1977). The daily report card: A simplified and flexible package for classroom behavior management. *Psychology in the Schools, 14,* 191-195.

Drabman, R. S., & Lahey, B. B. (1974). Feedback in classroom behavior modification. Effects on the target and her classmate. *Journal of Applied Behavior Analysis, 7,* 591-598.

Gast, D. L., & Nelson, C. M. (1977). Time out in the classroom: Implication for special education. *Exceptional Children, 47,* 461-464.

Haring, N. G., & Phillips, E. L. (1972). *Analysis and modification of classroom behavior.* Englewood Cliffs, NJ: Prentice-Hall.

Hundert, J. (1982). Some considerations of planning the integration of handicapped children into the mainstream. *Journal of Learning Disabilities, 15,* 73-80.

Jackson, G. B. (1980). Methods for integrative reviews. *Review of Educational Research, 50,* 438-450.

Jones, R. R., Vaught, R. S., & Weinrott, M. (1977). Time-series analysis in operant research. *Journal of Applied Behavior Analysis, 10,* 151-166.

Kazdin, A. E. (1980). Acceptability of alternative treatments for deviant child behavior. *Journal of Applied Behavior Analysis, 13,* 259-273.

Kazdin, A. E. (1981). Acceptability of child treatment techniques. The influence of treatment efficacy and adverse side effects. *Behavior Therapy, 12,* 493-506.

Kendall, P. C. (1984). Cognitive processes and procedures in behavior therapy. In C. M. Frank, G. T. Wilson, P. C. Kendall, & K. D. Brownell (Eds.), *Annual review of behaior therapy: Theory and practice* (Vol. 10, pp. 123-163). New York: Guilford.

Kendall, P. C., & Braswell, L. (1984). *Cognitive-behavioral therapy for impulsive children.* New York: Guilford.

Kennedy, R. E. (1982). Cognitive-behavioral approaches to the modification of aggressive behavior in children. *School Psychology Review, 11,* 47-63.

Kerr, M. M., Strain, P. S., & Ragland, E. V. (1982). Teacher mediated peer feedback treatment of behaviorally handicapped children. *Behavior Modification, 6,* 277-290.

Light, R. J., & Pillemer, D. B. (1984). *Summing up: The science of reviewing research.* Cambridge, MA: Harvard University Press.

Litow, L., & Pumroy, D. (1975). A brief review of classroom group oriented contingencies. *Journal of Applied Behavior Analysis, 8,* 341-347.

Lobitz, W. C., & Burns, W. J. (1977). The "least intrusive intervention" strategy for behavior change procedures: The use of public and private feedback in school classrooms. *Psychology in the Schools, 14,* 89-94.

Lovitt, T. C. (1984). *Tactics for teaching.* Columbus, OH: Charles E. Merrill.

Lysakowski, R. S., & Walberg, H. J. (1981). Classroom reinforcement and learning: A quantitative synthesis. *Journal of Educational Research, 75,* 69-77.

Martin, R. (1975). *Legal challenges to behavior modification: Trends in schools, corrections, and mental health.* Champaign, IL: Research Press.

Meichenbaum, D. H., & Goodman, J. (1971). Training impulsive children to talk to themselves: A means of developing self-control. *Journal of Abnormal Psychology, 77,* 115-126.

Meyers, A. W., & Cohen R. (1984). Cognitive-behavioral interventions in educational settings. In P. C. Kendall (Ed.), *Advances in cognitive-behavioral research and therapy* (Vol. 3, pp. 131-167). New York: Academic.

Nevin, A., Johnson, D. W., & Johnson, R. (1982). Effects of group and individual contingencies on academic performance and social relations of special needs students. *Journal of Social Psychology, 116,* 41-59.

Parke, R. D., & Walters, R. H. (1967). Some factors influencing the efficacy of punishment training for inducing response inhibition. *Monographs of the Society for Research in Child Development, 32*(2), (Serial No. 109).

Parsonson, B. S., & Baer, D. M. (1978). The analysis and presentation of graphic data. In T. Kratochwill (Ed.), *Single subject research: Strategies for evaluating change.* New York: Academic.

Pfiffner, L. J., Rosen, L. A., & O'Leary, S. G. (1985). The efficacy of an all-positive approach to classroom management. *Journal of Applied Behavior Analysis, 18,* 257-261.

Reynolds, M. C., Wang, M. C., & Walberg, H. J. (1987). The necessary restructuring of special and regular education. *Exceptional Children, 53,* 391-398.

Rosen, H. S., O'Leary, S. G., Joyce, S. A., Conway, G., & Pfiffner, L. J. (1984). The importance of prudent negative consequences for maintaining the appropriate behavior of hyperactive students. *Journal of Abnormal Child Psychology, 12,* 581-604.

Sindelar, P. T., & Wilson, R. J. (1984). The potential effects of meta-analysis on special education practice. *Journal of Special Education, 18,* 73-80.

Skiba, R. J., & Casey, A. (1985). Interventions for behaviorally disordered students: A quantitative review and methodological critique. *Behavior Disorders, 10,* 239-252.

Skiba, R. J., Casey, A., & Center, B. A. (1986). Nonaversive procedures in the treatment of classroom behavior problems. *Journal of Special Education, 19,* 443-458.

Spivak, G., Platt, J. J., & Shure, M. B. (1976). *The problem-solving approach to adjustment.* San Francisco: Jossey-Bass.

Stallings, J. (1985). Implementation and child effects of teaching practices in follow through classrooms. *Monographs of the Society for Research in Child Development, 40*(7-8), (Serial No. 163).

Stokes, T. F., & Baer, D. M. (1977). An implication technology of generalization. *Journal of Applied Behavior Analysis, 10,* 349-367.

Stokes, T. F., Fowler, S. A., & Baer, D. M. (1978). Training preschool children to recruit natural communities of reinforcers. *Journal of Applied Behavior Analysis, 11*, 285-303.

Tombari, M., & Davis, R. (1979). Behavioral consultation. In G. D. Phye & D. J. Reschly (Eds.), *School psychology: Perspectives and issues*. New York: Academic.

VanHouten, R. (1983). Punishment: From the animal laboratory to the applied setting. In S. Axelrod & J. Apsche (Eds.), *The effects of punishment on human behavior* (pp. 13-44). New York: Academic.

Wahler, R. G. & Dumas, J. E. (1986). Maintenance of factors in coercive mother-child interactions: The compliance and predictability hypotheses. *Journal of Applied Behavior Analysis, 19*, 13-22.

Walker, H. M. (1983). Applications of response cost in school settings: Outcomes, issues, and recommendations. *Exceptional Education Quarterly, 3*, 47-55.

Walker, H. M., Hops, H., & Fiegenbaum, E. (1976). Deviant classroom behavior as a function of combinations of social and token reinforcement and cost contingency. *Behavior Therapy, 7*, 76-88.

Walker, H. M., Hops, H., & Johnson, S. M. (1975). Generalization and maintenance of classroom treatment effects. *Behavior Therapy, 6*, 188-200.

Walters, R. H., Parke, R. D., & Cane, V. A. (1965). Timing of punishment and the observation of consequences to others as determinants of response inhibition. *Journal of Experimental Child Psychology, 2*, 10-30.

Weissberg, R., & Gesten, E. (1982). Considerations for developing effective school-based social problem-solving (SPS) training programs. *School Psychology Review, 11*, 56-63.

Wildman II, R. W., & Wildman, R. W. (1975). The generalization of behavior modification procedures: A review with special emphasis on classroom applications. *Psychology in the Schools, 12*, 432-448.

Witt, J. C., & Martens, B. K. (1983). Assessing the acceptability of behavioral intervention used in classrooms. *Psychology in the Schools, 20*, 510-517.

Witt, J. C., Martens, B. K., & Elliott, S. N. (1984). Factors effecting teachers' judgments of the acceptability of behavioral interventions: The involvement, behavior problem severity, and type of intervention. *Behavior Therapy, 15*, 204-209.

Wood, R. H., & Braaten, S. (1983). Developing guidelines for the use of punishing interventions in the schools. *Exceptional Education Quarterly, 3*, 68-75.

21

Effective Social Interventions

Howard M. Knoff
University of South Florida

As a formal component of the regular classroom curriculum, the instruction, reinforcement, and remediation of students' positive social interaction have been largely ignored. In reaction to recent proposals for sex education in our schools, some parents have held that public schools should be in the business of education as more traditionally defined, not the business of teaching children how to behave and how to interact socially. And, in support of the "back to basics" movement, others have argued that the time spent on teaching effective social interaction is wasted, resulting only in less time spent on reading, writing, and arithmetic.

However, we do know that inappropriate classroom behavior and interaction disrupt the learning process, and that inadequate social skills cause some children to be rejected by their peers and other children to be referred for special psychological attention. In fact, some studies (see Good, 1983, for a comprehensive review) suggest that teachers sometimes spend more time dealing with discipline problems and classroom transitions than with actual instruction. Other studies (Cowen, Pederson, Babigian, Izzo, & Trost, 1973; Reisman, 1985; Roff, Sells, & Golden, 1972; Ullman, 1957) link children's poor peer relations, peer rejection, and social isolation to psychiatric disorders, delinquency, dropping out of school, developmental disruptions or delays, and subsequent mental health difficulties during adulthood. Clearly,

effective social interaction is necessary to forming effective friendships and maintaining appropriate social development; enhanced interaction may be prerequisite to some children's academic progress and success. Thus, without exception, every school in this country must acknowledge the impact of children's social skills on their educational and social–emotional development. Indeed, the planned use of social skills programs and interventions on a daily and system-wide basis constitutes an alternative service that can be organized and implemented in the regular classroom setting for all students.

For special education students, the development of social interaction skills has been equally ignored, especially in programs that emphasize academic progress and remediation to the exclusion of social and adaptive behavior and interpersonal coping. For example, it is well known that, compared with their typical peers, learning-disabled (LD) students are less well liked, demonstrate significantly fewer problem-solving skills, choose less socially acceptable responses, have difficulty understanding the thoughts and feelings of others, and participate less often in school activities. Furthermore, their social problems often continue into adulthood (see Schumaker & Hazel, 1984a, 1984b, for a review). Because of these characteristics, White, Schumaker, Warner, Alley, and Deshler (1980) suggested that the development of learning-disabled students' social skills are as important as their academic skills, and they advocate social skills training as important to their future employability and their satisfactory accomplishment in the community, at work, and in the family. Yet social skills intervention with learning-disabled students seems more prevalent in the research literature than apparent in the typical classroom. And preventive programs that provide training for "at-risk" learning-disabled students designed to increase their chances of remaining in the regular classroom are virtually nonexistent.

For disruptive students who manifest acting-out, defiant, or socially aggressive behavior in the regular classroom, similar situations exist. In the absence of preventive social interaction programs and in the face of teachers and/or administrators who are unprepared, unwilling, or unable to implement effective interventions, these students often are referred for special education evaluations and placement. Thus, for some of these students, the *system's* deficiencies are overlooked as the system identifies the *student* as the problem and places him or her in a class for the behaviorally disordered or emotionally disturbed. At other times, children with poor social skills are placed in classes for the behaviorally disordered only to receive *academic* programs rather than those emphasizing social skills interventions. This practice decreases a child's opportunity to learn those skills that would allow a return to the regular classroom (where there are more appropriate peer models and opportunities for prosocial reinforcement), and increases the potential that the child will remain in special education for an undue period of time.

Thus, effective social interaction and interventions that teach effective social interaction can significantly influence the educational placement and prospects for successful mainstreaming of special education students (Gresham, 1981), as well as improve their academic and interpersonal success (Cartledge & Milburn, 1986; Schumaker & Hazel, 1984a, 1984b; Strain, Cooke, & Apolloni, 1976). That is, for some students placed in special education classrooms, the instruction and development of appropriate social skills should speed their reintegration into the regular classroom where other needed academic or supportive services can be provided. In addition, enhanced social interaction should increase the chances that students referred for, but not yet placed in, special education will remain in the regular classroom as long as their educational weaknesses are not too severe and the classroom is able to adapt to these weaknesses with approaches and services that maximize their academic progress and success.

At a secondary level, students' effective social interactions and interpersonal successes also can influence their attributions of locus of control, their feelings of self-control, and positive self-concepts. Special education students, for example, who have positive and effective social skills are more likely to feel responsible for their own successes, to demonstrate and maintain greater degrees of self-control, and to express satisfaction with themselves, their accomplishments, and their future prospects (Bryan & Bryan, 1986; Glenwick & Jason, 1984). Social intervention, then, may break the negative self-concept pattern that causes many students to fail interpersonally despite the fact that they possess both the necessary skills and the behavioral repertoires that can ensure success.

To summarize, the ability to behave and interact appropriately is generally a *necessary condition* (a) for keeping a prospective special education student in the regular classroom, and (b) for considering the special education student for mainstreaming into that setting. If the system and the regular classroom teacher are able to adapt to a given child's educational needs and style, and the student evidences ongoing academic motivation and progress, the *necessary and sufficient conditions* for successful services in the regular classroom are fulfilled. *The educational difficulties of the mildly handicapped children can and should be addressed in the regular classroom as much as possible; their inability to interpersonally and intrapersonally cope with the demands of the regular classroom and peer group should become, with the advent of alternative services and classroom-based programs, the predominant factor in making a special class placement.* Thus, *all* special education students should receive routine and substantial programming in social interventions so that they can return (as quickly as possible) to, or stay (as successfully as possible) in, the regular classroom. And, *all* special education students, regardless of the severity of their handicaps, should receive social intervention programming, commensurate with their social–emotional and cognitive development, in explicit individual educational plan (IEP) goals and activities. In this way, all special education students can maximize their individual potential by receiving services in the least restrictive educational settings during their school years and in the most normalized community settings during their adult years.

In an effort to help professionals to understand and implement effective social intervention strategies, this chapter will (a) define and analyze social competence and social skills, (b) discuss the specific skills that maximize social and interpersonal effectiveness, (c) review the intervention approaches and techniques that facilitate the development of such skills, and (d) describe selected social skills and problem-solving programs and the intervention components that make them successful. Maintaining students in the regular classroom setting will be especially emphasized throughout, as will the notion of primary, secondary, and tertiary preventive services. Finally, integrated within these discussions will be intervention approaches for aggressive or acting-out and for withdrawn or isolated children.

SOCIAL COMPETENCE AND SOCIAL SKILLS DEVELOPMENT

The definition of relationship between social competence and social skills development are much debated in the professional literature. Some researchers, such as Foster and Ritchey (1979), suggest that social competence is the more comprehen-

sive of the two, providing a conceptual "umbrella" that includes social skills. Others (e.g., Anderson & Messick, 1974; Zigler & Trickett, 1978) note that the absence of a precise definition of social competence for school-aged children makes it difficult to identify objective, reliable, and externally validated assessment criteria, and that some definitions of social skills are equally as global and imprecise (Asher, Oden, & Gottman, 1977; Asher, Singleton, Tinsley, & Hymel, 1979; Gottman, 1977).

For the present discussion, a definitive resolution to the debate is not necessary. What *is* important is that any social behaviors targeted for intervention be specific, observable, and measurable for purposes of evaluating accountability and documenting efficacy. To facilitate this requirement, two representative definitions of social skills are offered (Ladd & Mize, 1983; Rinn & Markle, 1979). Rinn and Markle (1979) define social skills as:

> a repertoire of verbal and nonverbal behaviors by which children affect the responses of other individuals (e.g., peers, parents, siblings, and teachers) in the interpersonal context. This repertoire acts as a mechanism through which children influence their environment by obtaining, removing, or avoiding desirable and undesirable outcomes in the social sphere. Further, the extent to which they are successful in obtaining desirable outcomes and avoiding or escaping undesirable ones without inflicting pain on others is the extent to which they are considered socially skilled. (p. 108)

Ladd and Mize (1983), utilizing a cognitive-social learning theory model, define social skills as:

> children's ability to organize cognitions and behaviors into an integrated course of action directed toward culturally acceptable social or interpersonal goals . . . [and their ability] to continuously assess and modify goal-directed behavior so as to maximize the likelihood of reaching one's goals. (p. 127)

Rinn and Markle's (1979) definition emphasizes an overt ecological/behavioral perspective that addresses the interdependence of children's social skills (i.e., the influence of one child on another), as well as the need for specific behaviors in their repertoires such that they can initiate appropriate interpersonal interactions. Ladd and Mize's (1983) definition broadens the first definition by including children's cognitions (i.e., their attitudes, attributions, beliefs, expectations, and self-statements) in the conceptualization, assessment, and development of social skills. This addition reinforces the reciprocal determinism perspective of behavior (Bandura, 1977), which states, in part, that children's cognitions do influence their social skills behavior and vice versa. For example, a child's belief that he or she cannot possibly interact successfully with a new group of peers — expecting to be rejected by them — can affect the interactive skill, confidence, and assertiveness of any approach to the group, and even whether an approach is made in the first place. Ladd and Mize's definition also emphasizes that social skill efforts are ongoing, continuous, and in a constant state of adaptation and flux.

A third definition developed by Michelson, Sugai, Wood, and Kazdin (1983) integrates many of the components discussed above into a single, comprehensive definition of social skills, which states that:

1. Social skills are primarily acquired through learning (e.g., observation, modeling, rehearsal, and feedback).

2. Social skills comprise specific and discrete verbal and nonverbal behaviors.

3. Social skills entail both effective and appropriate initiations and responses.

4. Social skills maximize social reinforcement (e.g., positive responses from one's social environment).

5. Social skills are interactive by nature and entail both effective and appropriate responsiveness (e.g., reciprocity and timing of specific behaviors).

6. Social skill performance is influenced by the characteristics of the environment (i.e., situational specificity). That is, such factors as age, sex, and status of the recipient affect one's social performance.

7. Deficits and excesses in social per-

formance can be specified and targeted for intervention. (p. 3)

On the basis of the three definitions above and their ecological, behavioral, and cognitive–social learning emphases *and* of the relationship between social skills and social competence, it is suggested that social competence involves a child's more global, comprehensive ability to function, positively and effectively, in social situations. These social situations may entail various settings and many individuals. They arise in the context of specific ecological conditions and histories and are defined in part by the child's current developmental and maturational status.

Social skills are the more discrete techniques and processes that collectively determine one's social competence. They can be behaviorally learned, preventively and remedially, and their development and reinforcement can be made incompatible with undesirable behaviors such that the latter can be significantly altered or eliminated. Children's social skills also must be assessed, developed, and evaluated in the context of their specific environments. Assessment and intervention should be made in cooperation with the other individuals in the environments, should acknowledge their interactions over time and the development and maturation of the children involved, and should incorporate approaches that have documented success and prescribed procedures. That is, social skills assessments and interventions are best accomplished within a multisetting, multisource, multimethod process. Finally, social skills assessments and interventions must be socially valid. This important characteristic will be discussed briefly below followed by an identification of some specific social skills that tend to maximize children's success in the regular classroom and three important ways to behaviorally categorize children who manifest significant social skill needs.

Social Validity and Social Skill Intervention

Assurance of the social validity (Kazdin, 1977) of social skills intervention requires identification of the social competencies and skills, appropriate to the specific ecosystem or environment and to the ages of the children in that environment, that truly result in a child's prosocial development and appropriate interpersonal interaction. Social validity, then, involves choosing the "right" prosocial behaviors for a specific child and circumstance, intervening appropriately such that meaningful and lasting behavior change occurs, encouraging the change so that others in the environment see it and agree that it is significant, and building in generalization processes such that this behavior change continues developmentally and extends to other settings and persons. The identification process first begins at a theoretical level as those who work with children hypothesize and specify prosocial skills for various environmental conditions and social situations. It continues at an applied level when specific children are evaluated in respect to these skills and intervention programs are developed, implemented, and evaluated by methodologically sound approaches and procedures.

In this process, three points are critical. First, many social interventions reported in the research literature have been accomplished in experimental schools or settings. Because these settings (and researchers) often have greater stimulus control over identified and extraneous variables, have better trained and supervised staff and/or more advantageous student–staff ratios, and have more explicit goals and objectives geared to social intervention success, they may not represent the typical special or regular education classroom. The results of these studies, therefore, may not generalize to these nonexperimental school settings, and the social intervention targets and strategies may not be applicable or socially valid. This must be determined on a case-by-case and study-by-study basis; certainly, there is no wisdom in utilizing interventions that do not work in real life even though they have been successful in laboratory situations.

Second, some studies in the research literature report results that are statistically significant yet functionally meaningless. For example, an intervention that results in a child's manifesting four more prosocial approaches to peers over baseline may be statistically significant, yet functionally irrelevant if there are 20 approach opportunities per day that are missed. The "improved" approach behavior in this example is not socially valid; that is, it does not occur in sufficient frequency to cause a noticeable or functional change in the child's actual environment or behavioral repertoire. Practitioners must test this aspect of a social intervention's validity continually.

Finally, social interventions must effect changes that are recognized and considered significant by adults and peers who routinely interact with the child. That is, behavior change is valid only when others perceive the change as constructive, meaningful, and lasting. This point is very important, because there are no fixed, universal criteria by which to judge the effectiveness of social change at the present time (Hops, 1983). Furthermore, there are times when a child's behavior has indeed changed, only to be ignored or go unrecognized by peers. This occurrence has engendered some new conceptualizations in social intervention research, for example, the use of contingencies to reinforce social reciprocity between children referred for social interaction problems and their nonreferred peers (Strain, Odom, & McConnell, 1984) and the use of nonhandicapped peers who actually do the social intervention training with their referred peers (Strain & Odom, 1986).

SOCIAL SKILLS AND BEHAVIORAL CATEGORIES FOR REGULAR CLASSROOM INTERVENTIONS

While there are a number of developmental scales that list critical socialization skills that emerge at various chronological ages or maturational milestones, few studies have empirically validated these scales or their social skill hierarchies and developmental chronologies, or have demonstrated the existence of pivotal social skills that are necessary and sufficient for social competence and interpersonal success at specific ages or as precursors for the development of more complex skills. In general, most studies have identified social skill targets pragmatically and with an eye toward social validity, that is, through classroom observation of behavior designated as socially appropriate or inappropriate in children at narrowly defined age levels. Others, however, have chosen specific social skills and then validated these choices by demonstrating a target child's increased social effectiveness with those skills after a prescribed intervention. Despite the absence of a comprehensive empirical foundation, a number of social skills are consistently mentioned as critical to children's social success (Gottman, Gonso, & Rasmussen, 1975; Gottman, Gonso, & Schuler, 1976; Gresham & Nagle, 1980; Kelly, 1981; LaGreca & Mesibov, 1979; Oden & Asher, 1977): (a) smiling and laughing; (b) verbal greeting and social initiations or inviting skills; (c) appropriate physical appearance and grooming; (d) conversational skills, including the ability to ask and answer questions appropriately and to give and receive positive social reinforcement; (e) complimenting or praise-giving skills; (f) sharing and cooperation skills; (g) play skills, including the ability to orient appropriately and maintain proximity to peers; (h) appropriate affective responsiveness and the ability to perceive and accurately interpret others' affective responses; and (i) role-taking skills such that a child is able to identify with the feelings or perceptions of a peer or significant other.

These social skills have been investigated primarily across four types of children who may most need social skills training (Ladd & Asher, 1985): socially withdrawn and isolated children, children with low levels of peer acceptance or popularity, children who are generally accepted but have no close friends, and exceptional children who have learning or social-emotional difficulties that interfere with their ability to learn, remember, and use social skills. In general, the social skills listed above have discriminated these four

at-risk groups from other children who do not have social skills difficulties, and research has demonstrated that these skills can be taught successfully to the many children represented in these groups (Cartledge & Milburn, 1986; Gresham, 1981).

From a preventive mental health perspective, Strayhorn and Strain (1986) have organized these skills into three "broad-band" competency areas:

> (a) the ability to be kind, cooperative, and appropriately compliant, as opposed to having a prevailing habit of being hostile and defiant; (b) the ability to show interest in people and things, to be appropriately outgoing, to socialize actively, as opposed to being withdrawn, fearful, and shy; and (c) the ability to use language well, to have a command of a wide range of vocabulary and syntax such that ideas may be both comprehended and expressed with facility. (p. 288)

There are two additional points inherent in the existence of these competencies. First, social skills can be organized into discrete, isolated "narrow-band" skills areas (e.g., the nine specific skills above) and then into more integrated "broad-band" competencies (i.e., the three competencies above). This suggests that interventions that focus on narrow-band skills may need to include strategies that integrate and generalize these skills into one or more of the broad-band competencies. This ultimately may maximize the effects of the entire intervention program, because the broad-band competencies necessarily receive more ongoing and general attention during a typical day, thus they and their specific component skills will receive more opportunities for practice, reinforcement, and strengthening in many settings and circumstances.

The second important point relates to Strayhorn and Strain's (1986) preventive mental health emphasis, which reminds us that social skills training can address primary, secondary, and tertiary prevention needs, despite the fact that educators often find themselves most needing and using tertiary social skills interventions. Briefly, primary prevention focuses on community or system-wide programs of problem resolution; secondary prevention focuses on programs for identified individuals who are at-risk for a particular problem or circumstance; and tertiary prevention involves direct service interventions attempting to prevent existing problems from continuing. As will be described below (see Chapter 11 as well), numerous researchers have utilized primary prevention programs to provide students in entire school districts or school buildings with social skills and problem-solving mechanisms designed to facilitate positive interpersonal interaction and ongoing social growth. Others have targeted smaller, at-risk groups for social skills intervention, attempting to provide secondary prevention mechanisms that will interrupt these children's development from "potential problems" to "active problems" in need of immediate attention and tertiary intervention. If more pilot projects in primary and secondary social skills interventions were attempted in our communities and school districts, perhaps the usefulness of proactive social skills planning would be immutably recognized, and the number of situations in which students (and teachers and classrooms) are referred *in crisis* would significantly decrease. At that point, these districts would leave their "band-aid" approaches to service delivery behind, and would join the school systems across the country that already have recognized social skills interventions in the regular classroom.

Patterns of Social Skills Difficulties

Regardless of the type of preventive intervention required, children manifesting social skills difficulties present different behavioral patterns that require different and often individualized intervention approaches. From the current social skills literature, three basic patterns of social difficulties can be identified: social skill deficits, performance deficits, and self-control deficits (Gresham, 1981; Ladd & Mize, 1983). *Social skill deficits* occur when children do not have (i.e., have never learned or been exposed to) the

necessary skills to interact appropriately with peers or adults in different social situations or environments. These children often lack the conceptual knowledge that defines appropriate social behavior, they are unable to analyze specific situations to determine what social goals are appropriate, they do not have the applied skills and behaviors necessary to succeed interpersonally in social situations, and they are unable to discriminate the social subtleties that suggest one interactional approach over another (Ladd & Mize, 1983). Remedially, social knowledge, analysis, and skill must be *taught* to these children, and then practiced and reinforced in varied settings and situations so that the behaviors become automatic, appropriate to specific situations, and generalized across persons, settings, and circumstances. These interventions, like all interventions to address these three behavioral patterns, should build upon and extend the child's existing social skills knowledge, be consistent with his or her developmental status, and target skills that are socially valid in the existing environment for the particular circumstances.

Performance deficits occur when children have the necessary knowledge and skill to interact appropriately in diverse situations, yet they fail to perform accordingly. This may occur because of situation-specific characteristics that interfere with behavioral responses (e.g., the presence of a peer group that reinforces an antisocial response), anxiety or other affective responses that successfully compete with appropriate responses, lack of motivation or environmental incentives, poor generalization processes, or some other interfering antecedent or consequent conditions. It also may take the form of behaviors (e.g., aggressive behavior, conduct-disordered behavior) that are incompatible with and preclude the performance of prosocial behavior. Remediation here should involve the adaptation, alteration, or manipulation of antecedent or consequent conditions such that appropriate behavior is manifested and reinforced and can be programmed for generalization.

Self-control deficits involve children's inability to control their own aggressive or impulsive behavior such that they are unable to exhibit prosocial behaviors. Self-control deficits can result from a lack of, or an inefficient, learning history that leaves a child without the ability to control behavior or impulses, or from situational circumstances that interfere with previously learned behaviors and strategies. In the latter case, children often know what social behaviors are appropriate and expected, yet they are unable to monitor and evaluate their behavior and its effects on others or to make necessary behavioral changes and adaptations. In essence, then, these children's poor self-control makes their isolated pro-social interactions functionally irrelevant. Intervention with these children often focuses on aggression and impulse control techniques that help the individual (a) to shortcircuit any out-of-control behavior, (b) to evaluate individual situations and plan appropriate social responses, and (c) to carry out these responses, and (d) carry out subsequent self-evaluation (always) and self-reinforcement (when successful).

With the identification of these three patterns of social skills problems, the specification of those social skills that most facilitate regular classroom success, and the definitions of social skills and social competence, a review of the many tested and proven social skills interventions is now in order.

SOCIAL INTERVENTIONS

There are many review articles in the research literature addressing social interventions; so many that, because of space limitations, a full review of their contents and critical points is impossible. Table 1, however, summarizes these review articles along with each review's target populations and recommended intervention techniques. Many of these techniques are discussed below along with prototypical studies that demonstrate their utility. Exhaustive explanations of the basic behavioral techniques that often underlie these social skill intervention techniques will not be provided here; the reader is referred to other chapters in this book and elsewhere that cover these techniques and their implementation in individual, systemwide, prereferral, consultation, and other circumstances.

Environmental Interventions

In an ecological context, it is important to note that not all interventions geared to changing a target child's behavior need to be child-focused. Analysis of the antecedent behavior and consequence conditions may uncover an environmental cause of the problem behavior or social skills deficit. In these cases, intervention that changes the environment would be the most parsimonious means of obtaining a significant and lasting behavior change. From an alternative service delivery perspective, the availability of environmental interventions also is important in that successful interventions in the regular classroom (a) will end the behavior-related need for (otherwise inappropriate) special education placements for some children, and (b) will discourage the mindset that child-focused interventions in special education settings are the only means that will work with children manifesting social skills problems.

Among the common environmental interventions that promote prosocial behavior are changing a child's classroom schedule or altering the classroom instruction or curriculum; changing the student's seat in the classroom or other aspects of the physical environment; utilizing peers, other people, or activities in the classroom or school and/or parents or significant others as social or intervention supports; and changing environmental consequences to reinforce appropriate behavior or extinguish inappropriate behavior. Often these interventions are attempts to bring a target child closer to situations and individuals who will support and reinforce prosocial behavior in a natural way, and away from environmental conditions that encourage antisocial behavior or no social behavior at all. These interventions, therefore, can be used with socially immature and socially withdrawn children and with children who have social skills deficits or behaviors that are incompatible with positive social development.

Environmental interventions are rarely used in isolation, yet they often exemplify sound preventive approaches toward prosocial behavior. For example, Tremblay, Strain, Hendrickson, and Shores (1981) noted that among typical preschoolers simple classroom games and free-play activities (e.g., make-believe, dress-up) were likely to facilitate multiple interactions and potentially prevent children's social withdrawal. Huber (1976) suggested that noncompetitive games (and environments) may be helpful both in decreasing aggressive students misbehavior (i.e., incidents that arise when they lose, strike out, or are eliminated as part of the rules) and in encouraging isolated or hesitant children's social interaction (because of the decreased pressure to win or be a significant contributer and the increased emphasis on group outcomes and group benefits). Good and Brophy (1978) suggest a number of classroom organizational strategies that prevent classroom discipline problems while encouraging appropriate social interactions.

Fundamental Behavioral Approaches

While many social skills interventions involve fairly complex behavioral approaches and combinations of approaches, the more fundamental behavioral techniques such as shaping, chaining, extinction, and fading are still very useful and should be seriously considered before more time-consuming approaches are tried. Some social skill deficits (for example, in areas known to be critical to social success, such as smiling, laughing, greeting, grooming), can be addressed successfully by comparing their current approximations with task analyses of the desired behaviors and by using simple shaping and chaining approaches with appropriate tangible or social reinforcements. Morris (1976) has written behavioral programs at this molecular skill level for many prosocial behaviors, beginning with appropriate eye contact and extend-

ing through more complex interactive patterns. Naturally these isolated skills do need to be integrated with more complex social behaviors and generalized so that more comprehensive patterns of social competence result.

Allen et al. (1964) and Buell, Stoddard, Harris, and Baer (1968) reported two classic examples of the application of some fairly basic behavioral approaches (reinforcement with attention and prompting) that significantly affected children's social behavior (in these cases, social withdrawal). In the former study, a 4-year-old girl's lack of peer interaction was changed by making adult attention (a reinforcer for her) contingent on her approaches to and eventual group play with same-aged peers. Here, the child exhibited a performance deficit, and clearly no more complex or intrusive intervention was needed to successfully encourage her prosocial, interactive behavior. In the latter study, a 3-year-old's immature and virtually nonexistent peer interaction, a consequence of her not using outdoor play equipment, was successfully changed by use of a simple prompting procedure, rather than a more complex approach. This intervention required a teacher only to place the child on some outdoor equipment and to provide contingent social reinforcement as long as the child stayed on the apparatus. As in the first study, this girl was exhibiting a performance deficit; again a fairly simple intervention, which could be adapted for older students, was most successful.

Behavioral Approaches Using Differential Reinforcement

The differential reinforcement approaches — differential reinforcement of low rates of behavior (DRL), of other behavior (DRO), and of alternative behavior (Alt-R) — are used most generally when a child's aggressive or inappropriate behavior needs to be reduced at the same time that a prosocial substitute needs to be taught or strengthened (Sulzer-Azaroff & Mayer, 1977, 1986). For example, a DRL contingency might be used with children

TABLE 1
Summary of the Reviews in the Current Literature Focusing on Social Skills Training and
Intervention, Their Foci, and the Intervention Approaches Covered

Reviewer and Date	Target Population Reviewed	Intervention Considered
Urbain & Kendall (1980)	School-aged children	Social-cognitive problem-solving approaches: Problem-solving training studies Verbal-mediation self-control studies Perspective-taking problem-solving studies
L'Abate (1980)	School-aged children and beyond	Social skills training curricula: Assertiveness approaches Communication approaches Effectiveness approaches Encounter approaches Enhancement approaches Enrichment approaches Fair-fighting approaches Mediation approaches Microcounseling approaches Problem-solving approaches Structured learning therapy approaches Sexuality approaches Values clarification approaches
Zigmond & Brownlee (1980)	Learning-disabled adolescents	Social skills training: Social perception/perspective-taking approaches Behavioral rehearsal approaches Modeling approaches Survival skills curricular approaches
LaGreca (1981)	Learning-disabled children	Social skills training components: Studies comparing normal vs. LD children's social behaviors Studies comparing normal vs. LD children's social perceptions (role-taking skills and comprehension of nonverbal communications)
Strain & Fox (1981)	School-age children	Peer social initiations and the modification of social withdrawal
Gresham (1981)	Handicapped children	Social skills training: Studies involving the manipulation of antecedent conditions Studies involving the manipulation of consequent conditions Studies involving modeling techniques Studies involving cognitive-behavioral techniques
LeCroy (1982)	Adolescents	Social skills training Studies involving the following approaches: Instructions and self-instructions Modeling Role-playing Behavioral rehearsal Relaxation Self-monitoring Coaching Feedback and videotaped feedback

(Table 1 continued)

Reviewer and Date	Target Population Reviewed	Intervention Considered
Swetnam, Peterson, & Clark (1982)	Young children	Preventive and therapeutic social skills approaches: Early intervention approaches Comprehensive preventive programs Dyadic interventions
Kennedy (1982)	Aggressive children	Cognitive–behavioral approaches: Problem-solving approaches Approaches toward generating alternative solutions Decision-making approaches Perspective-taking approaches Impulse inhibition approaches
Stainback, Stainback, & Strathe (1983)	Severely handicapped students	Generalization of positive social behavior Article reviews the: Selection of target behaviors and consequences Effects of multiple training settings Effects of multiple trainers Effects of environmental variables Use of handicapped and non-handicapped students during training Impact of multiple social responses
Gresham & Lemanek (1983)	School-age children	Cognitive–behavioral social skills training procedures: Reviews studies related to six methodological issues: Age of subjects Training procedures (symbolic modeling, coaching, combined techniques, self-control training) Outcome measures Research design Evidence for generalization Social validation
Schumaker, Pederson, Hazel, & Meyen (1983)	Mildly handicapped adolescents	Social skills curricula and social learning approaches
Ladd & Mize (1983)	School-age children	Cognitive–social learning approach to behavior change
Goldstein & Pentz (1984)	Aggressive adolescents	Social learning approaches: Modeling Role-playing Performance feedback Transfer and maintenance of training
Beck & Forehand (1984)	Preschool and school-age children	Social skills training based on behavior modification approaches: Contingent reinforcement studies Peer-mediated approach studies Modeling studies Treatment packages Methodological considerations Clinical implications and analyses

(Table 1 continues next page)

(Table 1 continued)

Reviewer and Date	Target Population Reviewed	Intervention Considered
Pellegrini & Urbain (1985)	School-age children with diverse emotional, social skill, and acting out problems	Interpersonal cognitive problem-solving approaches: Remediation studies Secondary prevention studies Primary prevention studies
Spivack & Shure (1985)	School-age children	Interpersonal cognitive problem-solving approach

to decrease incessant talking that is interfering with acceptance by their peers and simultaneously to teach and reinforce acceptable listening and reflecting skills; a DRO contingency might reinforce a child's ability to deal acceptably with a peer's confrontive behavior by other than physical or aggressive means; and an Alt-R contingency might extinguish a child's socially isolated behavior by reinforcing conversational and other prosocial initiations. These three procedures collectively demonstrate that many unwanted behaviors may be eliminated from a child's behavioral repertoire *constructively and without aversive or punishment procedures*. This is especially important in the regular classroom, where the consideration of punishment approaches may suggest the teacher's inability to control the child, the child's inability to conform to explicit classroom norms and rules, and a need for a special education referral and an alternative setting. Thus, these differential procedures not only directly impact on children's effective social behavior, but they also indirectly serve to make alternative services in the regular classroom more feasible and more acceptable.

While a number of exemplary studies could be cited in this area (see Gresham, 1981; and Homer & Peterson, 1980, for reviews), none of the most effective social interventions involve only a DRL, DRO, or Alt-R procedure. These procedures are used most often within a comprehensive intervention package and interlocking treatment program. Thus, it is commonplace to see a DRO component, for example, within a social skills training package. This makes sense, because most children who have performance or self-control deficits need to discontinue one type of behavior and increase an alternative, sometimes incompatible prosocial behavior. Educators are encouraged to seriously consider these differential approaches whenever a social intervention is needed. While they may appear routine, they do make a significant contribution to an intervention program.

Aversive Behavioral Approaches

Once again, the aversive behavioral approaches (e.g., verbal reprimands, response cost paradigms, time-out processes, overcorrection techniques; Sulzer-Azaroff & Mayer, 1977, 1986) are used primarily to decrease behaviors that interfere with the performance of, or the learning and reinforcement of, prosocial behavior. These approaches are effective — for example, Kazdin and Frame (1983) cite literature that suggests that overcorrection strategies reduce aggressive behavior more rapidly and comprehensively than extinction and positive reinforcement approaches — yet they should not be implemented casually, capriciously, or without the consultation and supervision of a trained professional. Briefly, verbal reprimands consist of a teacher's negative comments and attention that ideally identify a student's inappropriate behavior while suggesting more appropriate, prosocial behavior. Soft, private reprimands have been found to be more effective with elementary-age students (O'Leary, Kaufman, Kass, & Drabman, 1970), but teachers must be careful to determine when students are looking for any type of attention, positive *or* negative, because verbal reprimands in this situation might actually reinforce inappropriate behavior.

Response cost procedures involve a child's loss of a reinforcer or potential reinforcer in consequence of performance of a preidentified inappropriate behavior. That is, the child is penalized a specified number of points or rewards or privileges following instances of an antisocial or undesired behavior and the penalty is so aversive that the child ultimately discontinues this behavioral pattern and replaces it with a more adaptive one. Response cost procedures can produce a strong and rapid reduction of unwanted behavior with minimal side effects (e.g., escape, avoidance, or aggression), they have the potential for persistent and long-lasting effects, and they are convenient and fairly easy to implement individually and with other behavioral approaches (Kerr & Nelson, 1983; Sulzer-Azaroff & Mayer, 1977, 1986). They have been effectively used to decrease aggressive statements by predelinquent boys, classroom rule violations, and other antisocial behaviors across many settings and populations (Kazdin, 1972).

Time-out procedures may occur when a child exhibits some preidentified, undesirable behavior and consist of having the child placed a few feet from ongoing activity (contingent observation), removed from the activity but not the classroom (exclusion time-out), or removed entirely from the classroom setting (seclusion time-out). In all cases, time-out involves the child's loss of any opportunity to receive positive reinforcement for the duration of the procedure; thus, stopping the unwanted behavior, so that positive reinforcement becomes a goal for the student. Time-out procedures are most effective when the student fully understands the contingencies, when the time-out setting is not positively reinforcing to the student, when time-out periods are kept brief (i.e., 1–5 minutes), and when the teacher can apply the technique quickly and consistently (Kerr & Nelson, 1983; Sulzer-Azaroff & Mayer, 1977, 1986). Time-out has been effective in decreasing behaviors that interfere with positive social interactions; however, it must be emphasized that this technique only creates a condition of client receptivity —

children learn social skills only through positive approaches that teach, reinforce, and maintain discrete skills that generalize into global competencies.

Overcorrection is a mild punishment approach that attempts to highlight and stop a child's undesired behavior by forcing him or her to overcorrect the results of that behavior (restitutional overcorrection) and/or to overpractice a more acceptable behavioral option that can take its place (positive-practice overcorrection). More concretely, the restitutional overcorrection of a child's damage to school property might involve the repair of the damage in question *and* an additional 10 hours of repairs to other damaged areas around the school under a janitor's supervision. A positive-practice overcorrection intervention for a child's ridicule of a physically handicapped child might involve a verbal apology and 10 hours of "community service" in a special education classroom helping and interacting positively with these individuals. Overcorrection approaches can produce rapid and long-lasting behavioral change when applied immediately, consistently, and with relevant overcorrection activities. They also have the potential to decrease specific inappropriate behaviors while other, more appropriate social behaviors are at least practiced if not established.

Cognitive Behavioral Techniques and Self-Control Training

Cognitive behavior modification and self-control training techniques often are important components of the social skills and problem-solving intervention packages discussed below. Nonetheless, they can be used individually and with great effectiveness to curb children's impulsive and disruptive behavior and to structure and sequence alternative, prosocial, nonaggressive responses, first internally or subvocally, and then overtly and behaviorally. Historically, Meichenbaum (1977) is most associated with the cognitive behavior modification or *self-mediational* techniques most relevant to social interventions: self-instruction, self-monitoring, self-reinforcement, and self-evaluation. Generically, all of these self-mediational techniques begin with an adult model who demonstrates a skill or task (e.g., impulse control or the ability to share a toy or activity) to a specific child and end with the child performing the task as guided by his or her own internal speech. In total, Meichenbaum's basic procedure consisted of the following:

1. An adult model performed a task while talking to himself out loud (cognitive modeling);
2. The child performed the same task under the direction of the model's instruction (overt, external guidance);
3. The child performed the task while instructing himself aloud (overt self-guidance);
4. The child whispered the instructions to himself as he went through the task (faded, overt self-guidance); and finally
5. The child performed the task while guiding his performance via private speech (covert self-instruction). (pg. 32, 1977)

Children who are performing a target task or skill, Meichenbaum says, should (a) define the specific problem or task, (b) attend to the problem and its solution by using self-instruction and self-monitoring techniques, (c) apply self-reinforcement for acceptable behavior or successful task completion, and (d) use self-evaluation to facilitate coping skills, self-correction, and future planning. This "think-aloud" approach to social intervention also has been successfully used by Bash and Camp (1986).

These self-mediational techniques have been used successfully to decrease aggressive and disruptive behavior, to improve socially immature and inadequate behavior, to reduce social withdrawal behavior, and to teach more adaptive and appropriate social responses across a wide range of specific behaviors and populations (Gresham, 1981; Kerr & Nelson, 1983). Across a number of studies, however, it appears that the most socially valid behavior change and the most meaningful generalization have occurred when the entire self-mediational/cogni-

tive process was used or when the entire process was used with other, complementary behavioral techniques. For example, when used alone, self-evaluation did not appear to meaningfully reduce disruptive students' acting-out nor to effectively generalize positive behavior change to other classroom settings. Yet when used with token reinforcement approaches, self-evaluation was effective in controlling disruptive behavior, and the overall social intervention program was more successful (Gresham, 1981).

Kendall and Braswell (1985) also advocate self-mediational strategies to decrease children's impulsivity and to increase their academic and social success in the classroom. Using a variety of cognitive behavioral approaches strategically interfaced with many of the fundamental behavioral approaches above (e.g., social reward contingencies, response cost), they have documented a great deal of success in the social interventions area. By expanding these intervention programs to include cognitive restructuring techniques (Bernard & Joyce, 1984; Ellis & Bernard, 1983; Meichenbaum, 1977) — by which children learn to alter the irrational or inaccurate beliefs, assumptions, attitudes, and expectations that often counteract positive behavioral patterns and adaptive, prosocial interactions — an assortment of very powerful social interventions, with impressive past successes and enormous future applications, becomes apparent.

SOCIAL SKILLS AND PROBLEM-SOLVING PROGRAMS

Social Skills Training Programs

Social skills training programs most often involve integrated curricula that identify a number of interdependent skills that, taught sequentially, can result in a child's improved interpersonal and prosocial functioning. While there are many social skills training programs available (see Table 1), they all use the same basic underlying behavioral and psychological processes: modeling, shaping, coaching, guided rehearsal, and generalization

(Cartledge & Milburn, 1986; Ladd & Asher, 1985). With minimal adaptation, these programs can address the wide range of social problems exhibited by students — social skills, performance, and self-control deficits and withdrawn, immature, and acting-out behaviors.

Modeling and guided rehearsal strategies form the foundation of most social skills programs. These approaches generally require that a student be able (a) *to attend*, for example, to a specific model, a particular social skill, or a subtle interpersonal cue that can help an appropriate interpretation of a social situation; (b) *to retain* demonstrated social skills such that new learning can occur and be practiced or to retain interpersonal experiences such that positive interactions can be built upon and negative interactions can be corrected and avoided in the future; (c) *to motorically reproduce* the behaviors and skills required for successful social interaction at appropriate times, in appropriate situations, and at the optimal frequencies, durations, and/or intensities; (d) *to be motivated* to perform positive social skills both during the learning process and afterwards, without the excessive prompting or complicated external reinforcement contingencies that undercut personal behavioral responsibility; and (e) *to demonstrate* the skills appropriately across time, setting, and associates (Bandura, 1977). Most social skills programs begin with a target student, individually or in a small group, and a controlled setting such as a private classroom or office. There the social skills programs are taught to mastery by modeling, by shaping, when specific skills or skill components are not yet in the child's behavioral repertoire, by coaching, and by guided rehearsal. As appropriate, controlled practice and reinforcement opportunities are provided in classroom and other settings, such that successful change and generalization occurs. Ultimately, the child should exhibit adaptive and prosocial behavior spontaneously and without external supervision.

While more detailed discussions of the social skills training processes are available elsewhere (see Cartledge & Milburn, 1986; Michelson, et al., 1983; Strain, Guralnick, & Walker, 1986, for comprehensive treatments), a brief discussion of coaching and guided rehearsal procedures, and a summarizing overview, are in order. Coaching, as contrasted with modeling, is a direct instructional method that uses verbal instructions to guide a child through a particular social skill or interactive behavioral pattern. At times, this may involve a psychologist "shadowing" the child and whispering the appropriate verbal or behavioral responses needed in a particular situation. At other times, a more intricate and planned process might be necessary. Oden and Asher (1977), for example, successfully used coaching to help socially isolated third- and fourth-grade students to make friends with same-aged peers by providing them verbal instructions, followed immediately by opportunities to practice the skills taught, followed finally by a post-play review and feedback session with each target child. The verbal instructions in their study primarily consisted of social skills concepts and examples that would help the target children to understand how peer-group participation, cooperation, discussion, and helpfulness could be enjoyable and useful. Oden (1986) is now investigating the effects of certain independent variables (e.g., coaching style, the number of children per coaching group, age, and sex) on the coaching process, research that hopefully will further improve our effective use of coaching procedures.

Guided rehearsal is an extension of behavioral rehearsal (see Goldfried & Davison, 1976) in which a child practices a modeled or taught skill in a structured role-play format. This process may involve the child in (a) covert responding (imagining the behavioral components necessary to put into practice the particular social skill and his or her ability to perform those components effectively); (b) verbal responding (describing these components and their enactment and considering various behavioral alternatives, resolutions, and consequences in problem situations that might involve the particular social skill); (c) motor responding (formally role-playing the situations, discussing and evaluating one's performance, and then replaying the scene, incorporating the suggestions from the evaluation/discussion phase); and (d) completing a final evaluation process, prior to practicing the skill in a real classroom situation, which may utilize self-evaluation, self-reinforcement, and other self-mediating mechanisms (Bandura, 1977). Clearly, guided rehearsal may be considered an integrated component of a comprehensive modeling process, and there may not always be a fine distinction between it and the coaching process. Nonetheless, there are differences, and it remains for future research to clarify whether they are functional or insignificant and whether a process integrating the two would be most effective in the long run.

Before describing a few social skill training program examples, it may be instructive to summarize a 10-step social skills teaching process (Northrop, Wood, & Clark, 1979) that most social skills programs follow in whole or in part. The basic steps in this process are (a) positive approaches to students (instructor makes opening statement — a greeting or descriptive phrase that includes no punishing statements); (b) detailed descriptions by instructor of inappropriate behavior; (c) descriptions of appropriate behavior; (d) rationales for the appropriate behavior (instructor describes consequences, both good and bad, that could result from appropriate and inappropriate behavior): the link to the real world (reason for performing behavior) the long-term payoff; (e) modeling of desired, appropriate (perhaps including the inappropriate) ways to perform the defined social skill; (f) student practice of the desired behaviors in role-playing (instructor should develop the role-play scene to include necessary social stimuli, for example, from other peers, adults); (g) feedback, both positive and negative, from instructor on student's performance; (h) additional practice by student (instructor suggests specific behavior changes and improvement to be included; might use cues); (i)

praise for accomplishments; and (j) "homework" practice assignments that the student is to attempt in another setting, at another time, or with different people — instructor should reemphasize the desired behaviors and rationales to be employed (pp. 87-88).

Despite these common teaching processes, it still is important to note that all social skills programs have critical differences. Before using a particular social skills program, psychologists and other professionals must evaluate its technical adequacy, its effectiveness and utility, the comprehensiveness and clarity of its manual and audiovisual supports, and its appropriateness for its intended populations. Social skills programs should be strategically chosen; they should not be used only because of convenience or simplicity.

Examples of social skill training programs. Cartledge and Milburn (1986) provide an excellent appendix that describes a number of social skills training programs, among them the DUSO program (Developing Understanding of Self and Others) for kindergarten through fourth-grade students, the TAD program (Toward Affective Development) for third-grade through sixth-grade students, and the Accepts Program, which targets handicapped children and their integration into less restrictive settings. These programs run the gamut from regular to special education students, from preschool ages through adolescence. While an analysis of each of these available programs is impossible in this chapter, yet another program, Skillstreaming or Structured Learning, will be used as a prototypical example of an effective social skills program.

Structured Learning. Structured Learning (SL; Goldstein, Sprafkin, Gershaw, & Klein, 1979, 1986) is a planned integrated social skills curriculum that utilizes modeling, role-playing, feedback, and transfer-of-training procedures (the latter, to encourage generalization from the training setting to real-life situations) to teach new and adaptive social skill behaviors to children with social interaction difficulties. Providing explicit directions, the SL curriculum specifies who should participate in the social learning process; how many sessions should be planned, along with their length and spacing; who can lead an SL group; and how the sessions should be organized. To date, SL has been used effectively in regular education classrooms, special education classrooms, residential centers, state mental hospitals, and juvenile offender correctional centers with aggressive, emotionally disturbed, and passive-resistant elementary school and adolescent-aged individuals (see Goldstein & Pentz, 1984, for a review).

For adolescents, the SL curriculum is organized into six major skill areas: (a) Beginning Social Skills (e.g., listening, starting a conversation), (b) Advanced Social Skills (e.g., asking for help, apologizing), (c) Skills for Dealing With Feelings (e.g., knowing your feelings and understanding those of others), (d) Skill Alternatives to Aggression (e.g., negotiating, responding to teasing), (e) Skills for Dealing with Stress (e.g., dealing with embarrassment, responding to failure), and (f) Planning Skills (e.g., setting a goal, making a decision). While the specific skills within each area are introduced and practiced through a modeling, role-playing, feedback, and transfer-of-training process, the curriculum also attends to such training dynamics as the trainer-trainee relationship, SL training group processes, skill selection and sequencing, and the importance of making the entire process positive and constructive. Overall, the SL curriculum represents a well-conceived, well-documented, and empirically based approach to social skills development. It utilizes the components necessary for effective and socially valid behavior change, and it attends very clearly to the importance of skill transfer and generalization, the functional determinants of a successful intervention program.

Social Problem-Solving Training Program

Social problem-solving (SPS) skills training programs, also referred to in the literature as interpersonal problem-solving approaches (IPS) and interpersonal cognitive problem-solving training (ICPS), have been touted as a fourth general social skills training approach alongside contingency management, modeling, and coaching (Pellegrini & Urbain, 1985). SPS programs, in general, address the resolution of children's interpersonal problems and conflicts by presenting an organized problem-solving approach (e.g., problem identification, goal identification, generation of solutions, anticipation of consequences, solution selection, means-ends thinking, implementation, and evaluation) that helps children to conceptualize conflict situations, plan appropriate and effective solutions, and implement those solutions behaviorally. Social problem-solving approaches emphasize primarily *covert thinking processes*, although a number of recent SPS programs have also incorporated affective and behavioral skills components. This cognitive emphasis, however, is what makes SPS programs different from social skills programs, even though social problem-solving is clearly an important component of any child's social competence.

A number of sources reviewing SPS research and programs are currently available (e.g., Gesten, Weissberg, Amish, & Smith, 1987; Pellegrini & Urbain, 1985; Spivack & Shure, 1985; Urbain & Kendall, 1980). In fact to date, there have been more than 50 child-focused studies based on SPS interventions, ranging from preschool children to adolescents, from self-contained emotionally disturbed students to typical students in the regular classroom, and from inner-city children to suburban children. Significantly, a number of these studies have focused on primary and secondary prevention programming, and in general most of these studies, especially the most recent ones, have reported significant improvements in children's problem-solving skills and in peer and teacher ratings of their popularity and behavior. There have been some notable nonsignificant and/or negative results, however. Some of these results, though, may be attributed to poor methodology, others to the complexity of implementing a comprehensive SPS curriculum over a lengthy period of time with environmental conditions that are not always stable. At this point, SPS research is moving from a molar level, to determine whether an entire curriculum results in significant cognitive and behavioral changes in children, to a more molecular level, at which specific variables or conditions within the instructional process, the SPS participants, or the intervention environment are being studied to assess their differential effects on SPS success and generalization (Gesten et al., 1987).

Below three SPS programs are briefly reviewed. Again, these programs were chosen to exemplify those available to psychologists and educators. All three have exceptional research support, which the reader should pursue from the original sources.

Spivack and Shure's Interpersonal Cognitive Problem-Solving (ICPS). Spivack and Shure developed one of the first interpersonal cognitive problem-solving (ICPS) training programs (Spivack & Shure, 1974; Shure & Spivack, 1978; Spivack, Platt, & Shure, 1976), originally for disadvantaged inner-city black preschoolers who were experiencing inhibited or impulsive/aggressive behaviors. Consisting of a 46-lesson curriculum implemented by their preschool teachers, the curriculum was provided in daily 15–20 min. sessions consisting of discussions, role-play, and other structured activities. While the basic curriculum has been extended upwards through the elementary school ages and sideways to include emotionally disturbed populations and parents, the ICPS program consistently focuses on the development of five broad skill areas: the ability (a) to recognize and be sensitive to interpersonal problems, (b) to generate alternative solutions to these problems, (c) to use "means-ends" thinking to develop step-by-step approaches to problem resolutions, (d) to consider the consequences of one's actions to oneself and others, and (e) to understand how others feel. At its roots, however, the ICPS

program's primary goal is to teach children to think.

Spivack and Shure's ICPS program continues to receive substantial programmatic and research attention. While many studies have reported favorable results, more multivariate and methodologically sound research is needed. Clearly, the ICPS program like any social problem-solving program must be carefully matched to the population and setting where it will be used. The reader is referred to Spivack and Shure (1985) for the most updated overview of this seminal ICPS program.

Bash and Camp's Think Aloud Program. The Think Aloud program was developed initially to improve self-control in young aggressive boys, and now constitutes an organized curricular program focusing on the cognitive and social problem-solving skills of elementary school children (Bash, 1978; Bash & Camp, 1986; Camp & Bash, 1978). Developed primarily from the work of Meichenbaum (1977) and Shure and Spivack (1978), the program is based on training students to actively work through their problem situations by asking four questions: (a) What is my problem? or, What am I supposed to do? (b) How can I do it? or What is my plan? (c) Am I using my plan? and (d) How did I do? In helping students to answer these questions, the training program systematically teaches students (a) to focus on their specific problems; (b) to brainstorm possible solutions as a group, to evaluate the consequences and effects of each solution, to choose the most appropriate solution for the specific problem situation, and to thoroughly plan the step-by-step process of implementing the solution effectively; (c) to continually ask themselves, during the plan's implementation, if they are using it correctly and with the desired effect; and (d) to evaluate themselves after completing the plan across dimensions like plan completion, effort, efficiency, on-task behavior, and satisfaction with the results. Throughout the learning process, students practice all of these steps and processes by *thinking or talking about them out loud.*

Ultimately, the student is taught to internalize this overt talk such that they are truly *thinking* about problems and problem-solving by using the same techniques as in the think-aloud mode.

The Think Aloud curriculum consists of nine interpersonal lessons that include aspects of (a) identifying and sharing emotions, (b) recognizing physical causality, (c) recognizing emotional causality, (d) considering what might happen next, (e) asking is it a good idea or not a good idea? and (f) problem-solving. When determining if a problem solution is appropriate, students are additionally taught to ask: Is it safe? Is it fair? How does it make you and others feel? Does it solve the problem? Initial research has been very positive (e.g., Bash & Camp, 1986), yet this research has the same limitations and future needs as all of the SPS approaches and curricula.

Weissberg and Gesten's Social Problem-Solving Curriculum. Weissberg and Gesten's SPS curriculum (Weissberg et al., 1980) began as a pilot project to teach conflict resolution skills to second and third graders and expanded into a 34-lesson preventive program, based on an adapted SPS curriculum, that has been used with typical kindergarten students, preadolescent boys in outpatient therapy, and most recently with preadolescent seriously emotionally disturbed students. Integrating affective, cognitive, and behavioral dimensions of problem-solving and using teacher trainers to implement the program in the classroom, the SPS curriculum uses highly structured 20- to 30-min. lessons that are reinforced by various review and maintenance activities and numerous in-class illustrations that model the resolution of interpersonal conflicts through social problem-solving. Collectively, these lessons are organized into five major units (Feelings in ourselves and others, Problem sensing and identification, Generation of alternative solutions, Consideration of consequences, and Integration of problem-solving behavior), and the entire SPS process involves eight component skills and social problem-solving steps: (a) Identification of Feelings

("Look for signs of upset feelings"); (b) Problem Identification ("Know exactly what the problem is"); (c) Goal Identification ("Decide on your goal"); (d) Impulse control ("Stop and think before you act"); (e) Alternative Solution Generation ("Think of as many solutions as you can"); (f) Consequential Thinking ("Think ahead to what will probably happen next after each solution"); (g) Solution Selection ("When you think you have a really good solution, try it!"); and (h) Overcoming Obstacles and Recycling the Process ("If your first solution doesn't work, try again!") (Gesten & Weissberg, 1986; Gesten et al., 1987).

The SPS approach is especially important in that it specifically has a preventive focus. That is, it attempts to reach and train students *before* they have interpersonal difficulties that result in referrals or services that take them out of the regular classroom and normal curriculum. To date, a series of programmatic research studies at the second-grade through fourth-grade levels have indicated that the SPS curriculum can successfully teach social problem-solving skills, that these skills do generalize to real-life situations, and that these skills do relate to adjustment gains and improved adjustment ratings by teachers and peers (Gesten et al., 1987; Weissberg & Gesten, 1982). The entire SPS curriculum has extensive and explicit documentation relative to its various skills and components, and its instructional format addresses such implementation concerns as program structure, training issues, and the supervision of trainers. It clearly has great potential as an alternative service delivery program.

SUMMARY AND FUTURE DIRECTIONS

In essence, most if not all of the social interventions discussed in this chapter can be used whenever a child is manifesting social competence, social skills, aggression, acting-out, withdrawn, socially isolated, and/or problem-solving difficulties. Thus, these various programs can become alternative service delivery interventions, depending on where, when, and how they are implemented. If these interventions are used during prereferral, preventive, and/or consultative interactions so as to permit placement or retention in the regular classroom or the least restrictive possible setting (and not, in contrast, to "prove" that a child needs placement or retention in a more restrictive setting), then they can be considered alternative service delivery interventions. This intervention perspective becomes more of a systemic and conceptual mindset — a concerted effort to serve children's individual psychoeducational needs within the general education system. The social interventions discussed, then, must be integrated within this mindset; except for the intervention programs that focus explicitly on primary and secondary prevention, none of the interventions above require the processes integral to the alternative service context.

With respect to future directions, Ladd (1984) has identified a number of critical issues specific to social skills training that, when generalized to the entire social intervention area, may significantly influence both research and field-based interventions in the years ahead. Briefly, he addressed the purposes of social skills training and our ability to justify their use with children, the question of who will most benefit from social skills training, what components should be used in the social skills curriculum or process, and what procedures and techniques should be incorporated into the training process. Generalized to the entire social intervention area, the following questions need to be addressed and clarified in future research: (a) When should social interventions be used with children, who should decide when they are necessary, and what should the goals of the intervention program entail from both an alternative service delivery perspective and a remedial/special educational perspective? (b) Who will most benefit from social intervention technology and which intervention approach will best serve which clients and under what ecological circumstances? (c) What are the critical affective, behavioral, and cognitive components that lead to social competence

in children across the school-aged spectrum and across the various psychological and behavioral disturbances; which social interventions best address which components in this developmental and/or remedial process; and what criteria should be used in the selection and evaluation process? (d) What intervention methodologies and implementation processes will maximize social intervention success, social validity, and generalization; what research methodologies will best evaluate these interventions such that their differential successes might be documented, and be established as reliable and valid; and what individual, systemic, and ecological characteristics are critical to ensuring positive and lasting results in practice?

Social development and intervention, as noted in the introduction, often are not considered when evaluating children who are having difficulties in the regular classroom. Even when they are considered and used, social interventions must be socially valid and lasting, comprehensive yet realistic. This chapter has provided only an introduction to the social intervention technology. In many ways, it has provided a "review of the literature reviews." There are many social interventions that have documented success under both experimental and field-based conditions. Yet, there is a great deal more research and specificity needed. Readers are encouraged to pursue this area and its vast literature, and to participate in advanced training, in practice, and in appropriate supervision. Social interventions can make a difference. They can become a crucial component of the alternative service delivery process. They can help children to remain and receive optimal services in the regular classroom, with their same-aged peers.

REFERENCES

Allen, K. E., Hart, B. M., Buell, J. S., Harris, F. R., & Wolf, M. M. (1964). Effects of social reinforcement on isolate behavior of a nursery school child. *Child Development, 35,* 511-518.

Anderson, S., & Messick, S. (1974). Social competency in young children. *Developmental Psychology, 10*, 282-293.

Asher, S. R., Oden, S. L., & Gottman, J. M. (1977). Children's friendships in school settings. In L. G. Katz (Ed.), *Current topics in early childhood education* (Vol. 1, pp. 33-61). Norwood, NJ: Ablex.

Asher, S. R., Singleton, L. C., Tinsley, R. R., & Hymel, S. (1979). A reliable sociometric measure for preschool children. *Developmental Psychology, 15*, 443-444.

Bandura, A. (1977). *Social learning theory.* Englewood Cliffs, NJ: Prentice-Hall.

Bash, M. A. (1978). *Think aloud classroom resource manual* (Grades 1-2). Denver, CO: Denver Public Schools.

Bash, M. S., & Camp, B. W. (1986). Teacher training in the think aloud classroom program. In G. Cartledge & J. F. Milburn (Eds.), *Teaching social skills to children: Innovative approaches* (2nd ed., pp. 187-218). New York: Pergamon.

Beck, S., & Forehand, R. (1984). Social skills training for children: A methodological and clinical review of behavior modification studies. *Behavioral Psychotherapy, 12*, 17-45.

Bernard, M. E., & Joyce, M. R. (1984). *Rational–emotive therapy with children and adolescents: Theory, treatment strategies, preventative methods.* New York: Wiley.

Bryan, T., & Bryan, J. (1986). *Understanding learning disabilities* (3rd ed.). Palo Alto, CA: Mayfield.

Buell, J. S., Stoddard, P., Harris, F. R., & Baer, D. M. (1968). Collateral social development accompanying reinforcement of outdoor play in a preschool child. *Journal of Applied Behavior Analysis, 1*, 167-173.

Camp, B. W., & Bash, M. A. (1978). *Think aloud group manual* (rev. ed.). Denver, CO: University of Colorado Medical Center.

Cartledge, G., & Milburn, J. F. (1986). *Teaching social skills to children: Innovative approaches* (2nd ed.). New York: Pergamon.

Cowen, E. L., Pederson, A., Babigian, H., Izzo, L. D., & Trost, M. A. (1973). Long-term follow-up of early detected vulnerable children. *Journal of Consulting and Clinical Psychology, 41*, 438-446.

Ellis, A., & Bernard, M. E. (1983). *Rational–emotive approaches to the problems of childhood.* New York: Plenum.

Foster, S. L., & Ritchey, W. L. (1979). Issues in the assessment of social competence in children. *Journal of Applied Behavior Analysis, 12*, 625-638.

Gesten, E. L., & Weissberg, R. P. (1986). Social problem-solving training with children: A guide to effective practice. *Special Services in the Schools, 2*, 19-39.

Gesten, E. L., Weissberg, R. P., Amish, P., & Smith, J. (1987). Social problem-solving training: A skills based approach to prevention and treatment. In C. A. Maher & J. E. Zins (Eds.), *Psychoeducational interventions in schools: Methods and procedures for enhancing student competence* (pp. 26-45). New York: Pergamon.

Glenwick, D. S., & Jason, L. A. (1984). Locus of intervention in child cognitive behavior therapy. In A. W. Meyers & W. E. Craighead (Eds.), *Cognitive behavior therapy with children* (pp. 129-162). New York: Plenum.

Goldfried, M. R., & Davison, G. C. (1976). *Clinical behavior therapy.* New York: Holt, Rinehart, & Winston.

Goldstein, A. P., & Pentz, M. (1984). Psychological skill training and the aggressive adolescent. *School Psychology Review, 13*, 311-323.

Goldstein, A. P., Sprafkin, R. P., Gershaw, N. J., & Klein, P. (1979). *Skill-streaming the adolescent: A structured learning approach to teaching prosocial behavior.* Champaign, IL: Research Press.

Goldstein, A. P., Sprafkin, R. P., Gershaw, N. J., & Klein, P. (1986). The adolescent: Social skills training through structured learning. In G. Cartledge & J. F. Milburn (Eds.), *Teaching social skills to children: Innovative approaches* (2nd ed., pp. 303-336). New York: Pergamon.

Good, T. L. (1983). Classroom research: A decade of progress. *Educational Psychologist, 18*, 127-144.

Good, T. L., & Brophy, J. (1978). *Looking in classrooms.* New York: Harper and Row.

Gottman, J. M. (1977). Toward a definition of social isolations in children. *Child Development, 48*, 513-517.

Gottman, J., Gonso, J., & Rasmussen, B. (1975). Social interaction, social competence, and friendship in children. *Child Development, 46*, 709-718.

Gottman, J., Gonso, J., & Schuler, P. (1976). Teaching social skills to isolated children. *Journal of Abnormal Child Psychology, 4*, 179-197.

Gresham, F. M. (1981). Social skills training with handicapped children: A review. *Review of Educational Research, 51*, 139-176.

Gresham, F. M., & Lemanek, K. L. (1983). Social skills: A review of cognitive-behavioral training procedures with children. *Journal of Applied Developmental Psychology, 4,* 239-261.

Gresham, F. M., & Nagle, R. J. (1980). Social skills training with children: Responsiveness to modeling and coaching as a function of peer orientation. *Journal of Consulting and Clinical Psychology, 18,* 718-729.

Homer, A. L., & Peterson, L. (1980). Differential reinforcement of other behavior: A preferred response elimination procedure. *Behavior Therapy, 11,* 449-471.

Hops, H. (1983). Children's social competence and skill: Research practices and future directions. *Behavior Therapy, 14,* 3-18.

Huber, F. (1976). A strategy for teaching cooperative games: Let's put back the fun in games for disturbed children. In N. J. Long, W. C. Morse, & R. G. Newman (Eds.), *Conflict in the classroom: The education of emotionally disturbed children* (pp. 266-272). Belmont, CA: Wadsworth.

Kazdin, A. E. (1972). Response cost: The removal of conditioned reinforcers for therapeutic change. *Behavior Therapy, 3,* 533-546.

Kazdin, A. E. (1977). Assessing the clinical or applied importance of behavior change through social validation. *Behavior Modification, 1,* 427-452.

Kazdin, A. E., & Frame, C. (1983). Aggressive behavior and conduct disorder. In R. J. Morris & T. R. Kratochwill (Eds.), *The practice of child therapy* (pp. 167-192). New York: Pergamon.

Kelly, J. A. (1981). *Social skills training.* New York: Springer.

Kendall, P. C., & Braswell, L. (1985). *Cognitive-behavioral therapy for impulsive children.* New York: Guilford.

Kennedy, R. E. (1982). Cognitive-behavioral approaches to the modification of aggressive behavior in children. *School Psychology Review, 11,* 47-55.

Kerr, M. M., & Nelson, C. M. (1983). *Strategies for managing behavior problems in the classroom.* Columbus, OH: Merrill.

L'Abate, L. (1980). Toward a theory and technology for social skills training: Suggestions for curriculum development. *Academic Psychology Bulletin, 2,* 207-228.

Ladd, G. W. (1984). Social skill training with children: Issues in research and practice. *Clinical Psychology Review, 4,* 317-337.

Ladd, G. W., & Asher, S. R. (1985). Social skill training and children's peer relations. In L. L'Abate & M. A. Milan (Eds.), *Handbook of social skills training and research* (pp. 219-244). New York: Wiley.

Ladd, G. W., & Mize, J. (1983). A cognitive-social learning model of social-skill training. *Psychological Review, 90,* 127-157.

LaGreca, A. M. (1981). Social behavior and social perception in learning-disabled children: A review with implications for social skills training. *Journal of Pediatric Psychology, 6,* 395-416.

LaGreca, A. M., & Mesibov, G. B. (1979). Social skills intervention with learning disabled children: Selecting skills and implementing training. *Journal of Clinical Child Psychology, 8,* 234-241.

LeCroy, C. W. (1982). Social skills training with adolescents: A review. *Child and Youth Services, 5,* 91-116.

Meichenbaum, D. (1977). *Cognitive-behavior modification: An integrative approach.* New York: Plenum.

Michelson, L., Sugai, D. P., Wood, R. P., & Kazdin, A. E. (1983). *Social skills assessment and training with children: An empirically based handbook.* New York: Plenum.

Morris, R. J. (1976). *Behavior modification with children: A systematic guide.* Cambridge, MA: Winthrop.

Northrop, J., Wood, R., & Clark, H. B. (1979, June). *Social skill development in children: Application of individual and group training.* Invited Workshop, Association for Behavior Analysis, Fifth Annual Convention, Dearborn, MI.

Oden, S. (1986). Developing social skills instruction for peer interaction and relationships. In G. Cartledge & J. F. Milburn (Eds.), *Teaching social skills to children: Innovative approaches* (2nd ed., pp. 246-269). New York: Pergamon.

Oden, S., & Asher, F. R. (1977). Coaching children in social skills for friendship making. *Child Development, 48,* 495-506.

O'Leary, K. D., Kaufman, K. F., Kass, R. E., & Drabman, R. (1970). The effects of loud and soft reprimands on the behavior of disruptive children. *Exceptional Children, 37,* 145-155.

Pellegrini, D. S., & Urbain, E. S. (1985). An evaluation of interpersonal cognitive problem solving training with children. *Journal of Child Psychology and Psychiatry and Allied Disciplines, 26,* 17-41.

Reisman, J. M. (1985). Friendship and its implications for mental health or social competence. *Journal of Early Adolescence, 5,* 383-391.

Rinn, R. C., & Markle, A. (1979). Modification of skill deficits in children. In A. S. Bellak & M. Hersen (Eds.), *Research and practice in social skills training* (pp. 107-129). New York: Plenum.

Roff, M., Sells, S. B., & Golden, M. M. (1972). *Social adjustment and personality development in children.* Minneapolis, MN: University of Minnesota Press.

Schumaker, J. B., & Hazel, S. (1984a). Social skills assessment and training for the learning disabled: Who's on first and what's on second? Part I. *Journal of Learning Disabilities, 17,* 422-431.

Schumaker, J. B., & Hazel, S. (1984b). Social skills assessment and training for the learning disabled: Who's on first and what's on second? Part II. *Journal of Learning Disabilities, 17,* 492-499.

Schumaker, J. B., Pederson, C. S., Hazel, J. S., & Meyen, E. L. (1983). Social skills curricula for mildly handicapped adolescents: A review. *Focus on Exceptional Children, 16,* 1-16.

Shure, M. B., & Spivack, G. (1978). *Problem-solving techniques in childrearing.* San Francisco: Jossey-Bass.

Spivack, G., Platt, J. J., & Shure, M. B. (1976). *The problem-solving approach to adjustment: A guide to research and intervention.* San Francisco: Jossey-Bass.

Spivack, G., & Shure, M. B. (1974). *Social adjustment of young children: A cognitive approach to solving real-life problems.* San Francisco: Jossey-Bass.

Spivack, G., & Shure, M. B. (1985). ICPS and beyond: Centripetal and centrifugal forces. *American Journal of Community Psychology, 13,* 226-253.

Stainback, W., Stainback, S., & Strathe, M. (1983). Generalization of positive social behavior by severely handicapped students: A review and analysis of research. *Education and Training of the Mentally Retarded, 18,* 293-299.

Strain, P. S., Cooke, T. P., & Apolloni, T. (1976). The role of peers in modifying classmates' social behavior. *Journal of Special Education, 10,* 351-356.

Strain, P. S., & Fox, J. J. (1981). Peer social initiations and the modification of social withdrawal: A review and future perspective. *Journal of Pediatric Psychology, 6,* 417-433.

Strain, P. S., Guralnick, M. J., & Walker, H. M. (Eds.). (1986). *Children's social behavior.* Orlando, FL: Academic.

Strain, P. S., & Odom, S. L. (1986). Peer social initiations: Effective intervention for social skills development for exceptional children. *Exceptional Children, 52,* 543-551.

Strain, P. S., Odom, S. L., & McConnell, S. (1984). Promoting social reciprocity of exceptional children: Identification, target behavior selection, and intervention. *Remedial and Special Education, 5,* 21-28.

Strayhorn, J. M., & Strain, P. S. (1986). Skills for preventive mental health. In P. S. Strain, M. J. Guralnick, & H. M. Walker (Eds.), *Children's social behavior* (pp. 287-330). Orlando, FL: Academic.

Sulzer-Azaroff, B., & Mayer, G. R. (1977). *Applying behavior-analysis procedures with children and youth.* New York: Holt, Rinehart, & Winston.

Sulzer-Azaroff, B., & Mayer, G. R. (1986). *Achieving educational excellence using behavioral strategies.* New York: Holt, Rinehart, & Winston.

Swetnam, L., Peterson, C. R., & Clark, H. B. (1982). Social skills development in young children: Preventive and therapeutic approaches. *Child and Youth Services, 5,* 5-27.

Tremblay, A., Strain, P. S., Hendrickson, J. M., & Shores, R. E. (1981). The validity of role play tests for assessing social skills in children. *Behavior Therapy, 12,* 202-216.

Ullman, C. A. (1957). Teachers, peers, and tests as predictors of adjustment. *Journal of Educational Psychology, 48,* 257-267.

Urbain, E. S., & Kendall, P. C. (1980). Review of social-cognitive problem-solving interventions with children. *Psychological Bulletin, 88,* 109-143.

Weissberg, R. P., & Gesten, E. L. (1982). Considerations for developing effective school-based social problem-solving (SPS) training programs. *School Psychology Review, 11,* 56-63.

Weissberg, R. P., Gesten, E. L., Leibenstein, N. L., Doherty-Schmid, K., & Hutton, H. (1980). *The Rochester social problem-solving (SPS) program: A training manual for teachers of 2nd–4th grade children.* Rochester, NY: University of Rochester.

White, W. J., Schumaker, J. B., Warner, M. M., Alley, G. R., & Deshler, D. D. (1980). *The current status of young adults identified as learning disabled during their school career* (Research Report No. 21). Lawrence, KS: University of Kansas Institute for Research in Learning Disabilities.

Zigler, E., & Trickett, P. K. (1978). IQ, social competence, and evaluation of early childhood intervention programs. *American Psychologist, 33,* 789-798.

Zigmond, N., & Brownlee, J. (1980). Social skills training for adolescents with learning disabilities. *Exceptional Education Quarterly, 1,* 77-83.

Part III:

Facilitating the Development and Operation of Alternative Service Delivery Systems

22

Improving School Psychology Services Through Strategic Marketing and Planned Change

Robert Illback
Fort Knox Community Schools and Spalding University

Most observers would agree that there is no generically "correct" role for the school psychologist, and practitioners have for years been encouraged to adapt practice to the specific circumstances of the work site (Bardon & Bennett, 1974). Nonetheless, there remains a high degree of predictability to the practice of school psychology in most settings (Meacham & Peckham, 1978). Increasingly, there is concern within school psychology that narrow and traditional conceptions of role and function may be unresponsive to the broad-based needs and desires of potential consumers of school psychology services (Illback & Maher, 1984).

Clearly, the scope of practice for the profession of school psychology is dictated to a significant extent by legal and professional mandates, which can interfere with the provision of more responsive and comprehensive services to children, and there certainly is evidence that school systems are slow to change and to adopt innovations (Fullan, Miles, & Taylor, 1980). However, it also appears that the profession of school psychology as a whole has been reluctant to adopt the perspective that roles and functions should be largely determined by the needs and wants of consumers of services.

The National School Psychology Inservice Training Network in *School Psychology: A Blueprint for Training and Practice* (1984), described remedial and special education as a "nonsystem," predicted major changes in the structure of these service delivery systems, and advocated concurrent changes in the profession of school psychology. The document further delineated 16 domains of school psychology leadership and function in the schools that can serve as the basis for practice (e.g., class management, basic academic skills, parent involvement, assessment, research). Although there is controversy about the organization and coverage of these domains (Lambert, 1986), it is notable for the purposes of this discussion that the areas described appear to be oriented toward the needs of children in schools, rather than based on narrow, traditional service delivery models.

This chapter begins with the assumption that a fundamental problem within the profession of school psychology is the absence of a *marketing orientation*. Many school psychology service activities are essentially outgrowths of modes of functioning that were appropriate in an earlier era, but are no longer responsive or relevant to the needs and wants of current consumers. There is in fact evidence that consumers of services are not entirely satisfied with what is being provided (Gilmore & Chandy, 1973; Hughes, 1979), and that the needs of consumers in schools are changing (Good & Weinstein, 1986; Wang, 1987). As education undergoes global reform, and special and remedial education in particular become more oriented to effective instructional design and practice (Brophy, 1986), school psychologists will of necessity experience changes in roles, responsibilities, and relationships. By taking a marketing perspective on practice, and through the use of specific marketing concepts and strategies, school psychologists can become more responsive to the clientele they serve.

In addition to assessing the desires of its target markets and communicating more effectively with these markets about its product, the profession of school psychology also must become more effective in setting the conditions for effective practice through proactive means. At the individual level, this would require developing relationships with key decision makers in the school community, such as administrators, school board members, and parents. At the state organization level (which will serve as the focus of much of this chapter) a program of planned change involving public relations and legislative action is required.

The dual elements of strategic marketing and planned change are essential ingredients of any effort to alter the practice of school psychology. Moreover, the concepts and methods of strategic marketing and planned change are essential at both the individual and state organization levels. And for any marketing or planned change initiative to be maximally effective, efforts at the two levels must be coordinated.

MARKETING PERSPECTIVES IN SCHOOL PSYCHOLOGY

As key marketing and legislative action concepts are introduced, case examples are provided from the Commonwealth of Kentucky, which for the past 6 years has been active in marketing school psychology services, both at the individual and at the state level. As a state in which school psychology certification was not established until 1979 and in which school psychology services have never been mandated, there remains a strong need (a) to be proactive in communicating with actual and potential markets about services and (b) to alter the conditions that have limited the

growth and development of the profession in the state through legislative and political initiatives.

Notably, barriers to growth and development in Kentucky have been broken down through specific activities, many of which will be described here. Although Kentucky remains significantly underdeveloped economically relative to other states, it is possible that in consequence of the strategic marketing and legislative action plan that has been carried out by the Kentucky Association for Psychology in the Schools (KAPS), the profession will find itself better positioned in the Kentucky educational marketplace to take advantage of opportunities and withstand the threat of fiscal retrenchment than in more well-developed states.

Need for an Alternative Orientation Toward Services

There are a number of convergent factors that make the need for a marketing orientation to the practice of school psychology imperative. A central problem recognized for some time in the profession is consumer dissatisfaction with current services, a strong indicator of which is the increased use by schools of contracted psychological services. Through contracting, the scope of services are subject to become compartmentalized and narrowed, limiting the amount of interaction between other educators and school psychologists. The net effect is that school psychologists become more closely associated with paper compliance functions and less involved with instructionally relevant interventions, leading to even further limitations of professional purview. This indicates a problem of perception by consumers and decision makers, and therefore represents a marketing problem. It necessitates efforts by the profession not only to limit the use of contractual services, but more fundamentally to address the problem of how school psychology services are perceived in the marketplace.

It is also noteworthy that the institutional context in education appears to be undergoing meaningful changes. Since the publication of *A Nation at Risk* (National Commission on Excellence in Education, 1983), there has been a spate of educational reform reports and recommendations, and in response most states have adopted measures to change (and hopefully improve) their educational systems. Many challenges and opportunities have arisen from these changes, and many new problems will occur as a result. For example, through research on effective schools, there appears to be an increased emphasis on constructs such as the assessment and development of basic academic skills, academic engaged time, and higher-order thinking. School psychologists thus have been encouraged to engage in curriculum-based assessment and intervention (Shapiro & Lentz, 1985). The advent of these techniques represents a tremendous marketing opportunity for the growth and enhancement of the profession; however, it also can be seen as a threat in that these approaches are by no means exclusive to the domain of psychology.

Increased competition among providers of school psychology services is another factor with which school psychologists are confronted. As financial resources diminish, social and educational demographics shift, and demands for educational services in other areas increase, it appears likely that even in states that have been relatively immune to direct competition, rivals for service delivery dollars will emerge. In Kentucky, for example, a number of professional groups currently find themselves competing for limited instructional support roles and monies, including school psychologists, school counselors, school social workers, educational diagnosticians, and special education administrators.

The manner in which school psychology as a profession responds to these challenges and opportunities will be dictated to a great extent by its orientation toward the services it provides. It is not theoretical orientation but the manner in which services are conceptualized that is at issue. Some school psychologists tend to view their work from a *production* orientation, with a focus on efficiency in production and distribution. Emphasis is placed on such activities as keeping up with the referral rate and producing reports or rendering individual services sufficiently to meet quotas or preconceived expectations of productivity. Other school psychologists have a *product* orientation in which providing high-quality offerings that are deemed good for the public is the primary focus. The emphasis is on making more sophisticated diagnoses, writing quality reports, and conforming to professional standards and norms. Practitioners who are primarily involved with trying to stimulate the interest of clients in existing offerings, by promoting the school psychology services program regardless of responsiveness to consumer needs or wishes, can be said to have a *sales* orientation.

In contrast to the prior approaches, a *marketing* orientation emphasizes strategies that are client-centered, the services being conceptualized and designed with primary reference to consumer needs and wants (Kotler, 1975). It should be noted that these various orientations are not mutually exclusive, nor should it be implied that one is always preferable to another. Rather, the profession as a whole must evolve an orientation that incorporates more elements of the marketing perspective.

Elements of Marketing

Kotler (1975) provided an authoritative definition of marketing in human services organizations that contains four major elements: (a) the analysis, planning, implementation, and control of carefully formulated marketing programs, (b) designed to bring about voluntary exchanges of benefits with target markets for the purpose of achieving organizational objectives, (c) relying heavily on the design of the organization's offerings in terms of the target market's needs and desires, (d) using effective pricing, communication, and distribution to inform, motivate, and service the markets.

Analysis, planning, implementation, and control of marketing. This element implies that marketing is a crucial aspect of any human services program. There is a tendency in the human services arena to emphasize the content of human services programs without recognizing that communication about the program often determines the program's success or failure. In fact, many human services professionals, including school psychologists, tend to eschew marketing aspects as unprofessional or otherwise unsavory. In part, these individuals may be confusing a *sales* orientation (described earlier) with a marketing orientation. An alternative perspective to marketing is that in order for clients to profit fully from services, they must perceive the services as important and feel positive about potential outcomes. This would suggest that marketing should be considered to be a systematic part of school psychology services planning.

Exchanging values. A marketing perspective also involves appreciation of communication and exchange relationships with others, suggesting the need to identify the groups or markets with whom the practitioner exchanges values. Internal markets for the individual practitioner may include the school organization, the student population, school administrators, teachers, other special services personnel, paraprofessionals, and board of education members. External markets may include parents and families of students, professional associations, mental health service providers, physicians, and colleagues employed elsewhere. At the state level, internal markets will include segments of the profession within the state; external markets may include affiliated organizations and associated fields, the Department of Education, the State Board of Psychology, and local education agencies (school districts).

Service providers and service organizations interact continuously with various markets, exchanging values in the process. In some transactions, the practitioner represents the school organization in exchanges with staff, for example, when a teacher submits a referral for consultation or psychoeducational assessment;

the organization responds by assigning a school psychologist to handle the case. The underlying assumptions are that psychological services will be of value to the teacher in resolving the problem at hand, and that the services and resolutions will occur within the confines of organizational policies, procedures, and constraints. In other transactions, the practitioner is part of the profession of school psychology in exchanges with the school organization. The values exchanged between the school psychology staff member and the organization involve salary and fringe benefits, security, social rewards, and sense of accomplishment in exchange for the practitioner's time, effort, and support of implicit and explicit organizational goals.

At the state level, value exchanges also occur, although they may be more subtle and more complex. For instance, a state school psychology organization, communicating with the public at large about the value of school psychology services, is likely to emphasize values such as proper identification and treatment, professional competence, and assistance to parents in return for increasing public support (financial and otherwise) for school psychology services in the community. To provide a more specific example, there has been an effort in Kentucky to associate the need for additional school psychology services with key elements of the educational reform movement by emphasizing dropout prevention, substance abuse prevention, and redress of problems of over- and under-identification of certain categories of handicapped pupils, problems which have received considerable media coverage. A direct exchange of values is implied.

Market needs and desires. The above example also serves to illustrate the third element of marketing delineated by Kotler, the critical relationship between services provided by the organization and the target market's needs and desires. In the marketing perspective, to the extent that services provided correlate with market needs, the offerings of the organization are seen as more relevant, and the institution is therefore more likely to thrive. In school psychology, there are numerous legal, ethical, and professional standards to which individual practitioners and professional organizations look for guidance about practice. These standards tend by and large to determine the nature of services and the methods or procedures by which services are delivered. While there is undoubtedly a relationship between these standards and the needs of consumers, it is important to note that the profession rarely makes determinations about service delivery on the basis of a systematic assessment of the needs and wants of the clients. This may cause school psychological services to be judged irrelevant by major segments of the potential market.

In Kentucky, considerable discussion has occurred within the school psychology leadership about important issues and trends in education in the state. These discussions have led to specific actions that have resulted in a greater perception of the profession's relevance. For example, public statements about the offerings of the profession in hearings, regulatory meetings, conferences, and affiliated association committees have purposefully emphasized these trends and issues. Additionally, written documents such as position papers and guidelines for practice have sought to make timely use of these concerns. These strategies will be discussed in more detail later in the chapter.

Technology of marketing. The final element of Kotler's definition pertains to the technology of marketing, including techniques for pricing, communication, and distribution. These techniques are often viewed by professionals in narrow terms, and are associated with the baser aspects of advertising and promotion. Such techniques are seen as attempts to mold public opinion in unfair or manipulative ways, perhaps toward simplistic or unhealthy ends, and are therefore deemed unethical.

A more appropriate attitude would be to view marketing strategies and techniques as necessary methods to inform, motivate, and service human services markets. In this context, the profession of school psychology can be seen as having a responsibility to the public to discern what services the public wants and desires, to deliver those services effectively, to educate the public about available services, and to insure that the public perceives services as effective and relevant.

Market Demand and School Psychology

School psychology programs are exposed to a range of marketing problems, depending on situational variables. An analysis of the nature and scope of the problems faced by the service delivery program, whether it be at an individual or a state level, can provide a basis for planning a marketing program, as well as for improving and developing the program. Kotler (1975) provided a framework for conceptualizing marketing problems in respect to aspects of demand.

A condition of *negative demand* exists when a major part of the market dislikes the offerings of the program and seeks to avoid it. This situation would be manifested if a group of teachers should feel extremely negative about school psychology services and seek to boycott these services by not sending in referrals, or at the state level, by lobbying against these services. This problem suggests the need for a marketing campaign designed to change beliefs and attitudes about school psychology services, or at the very least, to neutralize and confine the resistance.

A related problem is the condition of *no demand*, in which targeted clients feel uninterested or indifferent toward services. For example, there may be little interest in the community for services because citizens are unaware that services exist or are unsure about their purpose. In Kentucky, this condition existed in that school psychology services were so new that very few teachers, parents, or administrators had any experience with them; therefore they could not distinguish them from other related services (e.g., school counseling). A situation of no demand implies the need for marketing to focus on matching needs and interests of relevant client groups with products and services offered by the program.

Latent demand refers to the situation in which clients share a desire for something that cannot be satisfied by current offerings. For example, when teachers are desirous of specific consultation and intervention planning to assist with classroom problems, and the school psychology staff is not prepared to offer these services, a condition of latent demand exists. In Kentucky, as in most states, there is reason to believe that teachers are in need of classroom assistance, particularly in light of increasing placements of pupils with special needs in general education classrooms. Yet current regulations and practices are not conducive to such activities, creating a marketing problem defined by the need to develop new products and services to satisfy this demand.

When there are gradually diminishing requests for certain offerings of a program, a situation of *falling demand* exists. For example, in a particular school building, requests for consultation services for students with academic or behavioral problems may be diminishing in comparison with requests for "testing services." Or, school psychology services in general may no longer be in heavy demand, as other programs compete to address the needs of teachers, administrators, and parents. The marketing problem created in this instance implies a need for reversal of the trend through creative *re*marketing.

Irregular demand can be equally vexing; it occurs when seasonal, daily, or hourly variations in the need for services complicate time and task management. This is a condition familiar to school psychologists who have peak and slow periods for referrals and whose time scheduling becomes a nightmare in consequence of the relative unpredictability of demand for various kinds of services. Whereas in January, for example, a building's referral rate may drop off precipitously, at the end of the third marking period, the school psychologist often becomes swamped with referrals.

Different marketing problems also result from conditions of *full demand* and *overfull demand*. In the former, there is a need to maintain an appropriate level of demand for services; in the latter, requests for services significantly exceed the operational capabilities of the program. When school psychologists finally achieve an appropriate level of referrals, for example, efforts can be applied to retaining this demand level to insure predictability and stability in the program. On the other hand, when the referral rate skyrockets, there is a tendency to discourage requests for service from certain market sectors (e.g., spurious or borderline referrals). Vigilance in servicing markets at appropriate levels is the hallmark of full demand. "Selective demarketing" characterizes activities occurring in periods of overfull demand.

Before a marketing program was developed, an initial analysis of the situation in Kentucky revealed a number of problems associated primarily with conditions of no demand and latent demand, and to a lesser extent, negative demand. In 1979, there were only a limited number of practitioners in the schools, most of whom were concentrated in suburban areas of Lexington, Louisville, and Cincinnati. At the school district level, there was minimal awareness of the fact that the certification category even existed, much less of what services school psychologists could provide. The state professional organization consisted of a relatively small number of practitioners, trainers, students, and persons from related fields, most of whom were dedicated but isolated. There were no viable funding mechanisms available in the state for school psychology services, other than federal flow through funds. The major educational organizations in the state were not even aware of the existence of the professional organization, and were unaffiliated with other organizations. School psychologists had no access to decision-making processes within the Department of Education or the legislative assembly. Nor did they have very many meaningful contacts or representation in related professional groups or committees. Limited opportunities for professional development existed for school psychologists, and there were no written standards or guidelines for school psychology in the schools.

In sum, school psychology in Kentucky was a very small minority group within educational professions with no representation and no public recognition. It was, in fact perceived negatively by some role groups, partly owing to stereotypes attributable to problems created by non-school psychologists delivering psychological services in schools, and partly owing to the perceived threat to related pupil services groups (see Mason and Remer, 1979, for an analysis of these social and political aspects of school psychology in Kentucky). On the other hand, tremendous potential for growth and development existed as a function of the significant unmet educational and child mental health needs across the Commonwealth, creating a vacuum into which school psychology could move. On the basis of a marketing analysis of these conditions, KAPS determined to launch a concerted marketing campaign on a number of fronts to fill this vacuum. In doing so, the organization faced a number of persistent problems.

Problems in Marketing School Psychology Services

School psychologists, like other human services practitioners, are faced with certain idiosyncratic problems in marketing their services. The first is that the clientele of school psychology services is large and varied. While it can be argued that the ultimate client must always be the child, it is often difficult to separate the needs of the child from those of the family, other staff members, the administration, and the community at large. But frequently the needs and wants of these groups are in conflict. From a marketing perspective, this raises a number of crucial questions, such as: What market do we want to target? Who is our primary client? What data do we need to present to document the need for our services? What types of data will be convincing? What are the accountability demands of the various

groups who control our destiny?

In addition, there typically is great confusion among various potential client groups about school psychology services, and these groups often cannot appropriately differentiate them from related services. For school psychologists interested in marketing their services, the relevant questions then become: What information do clients need to know about school psychology services in order that demand will be increased? What concerns do potential clients have about these services? How can we communicate to potential clients how we are different from counselors, clinical psychologists working in the community, educational diagnosticians, or similar groups? What rationales (e.g., legal, professional, instructional) can be offered to potential clients for establishing school psychology service programs in the school?

Another problem in the marketing of school psychology has to do with the time and effort required to mount such an effort. Most practitioners are so tied up with daily routine that they cannot mobilize the resources required to engage in systematic, strategic marketing. At the state organization level, this is especially problematic in that literally hundreds of hours of coordinated efforts are required from what is usually an all-volunteer work force. Problems of communication, geography, financial resources, and a myriad of other factors can conspire to defeat such initiatives, necessitating a high level of commitment and preseverance.

Finally, the most pervasive problem, lack of knowledge about marketing strategies, remains. As has been shown, school psychologists may underemphasize the marketing aspects of service delivery, in part because of a lack of familiarity with concepts and methods associated with this orientation.

These inherent problems can be overcome at both the individual and state organization levels through careful consideration and planning, hard work, and persistence. Especially important is a willingness to accept that many initiatives will later appear naive and amateurish, even though others will appear sophisticated and effective. The essential message of this section is the need (a) to bring focus to the central concepts about the profession that will be marketed to the target groups, (b) to develop a sound, long-term plan for implementing the marketing program, and (c) to begin, learning from inevitable miscalculations.

IMPLEMENTING STRATEGIC MARKETING IN SCHOOL PSYCHOLOGY

Marketing can be seen as a management process in which the leadership of an organization (a) conceives a strategic direction, and (b) through coordinated efforts, targets resources to move the organization in that direction. As a management process, strategic marketing involves elements of planning, implementation, and control, including activities such as finding attractive opportunities in the marketplace, determining availability of resources to take advantage of these opportunities, delineating organizational goals in relation to the opportunities, developing marketing strategies, designing and implementing marketing strategies, and insuring that effective and efficient means are used to carry out the marketing program (McCarthy, 1981).

Understanding Target Markets

In order to properly design a program of offerings in a human services organization, it is crucial to obtain a thorough knowledge of the professional environment in which the program is found. In this regard, school psychology service programs can be described in relation to the local, regional, and national factors in education that shape the marketplace. For example, the practice of school psychology over the past decade has been greatly influenced by the advent of Public Law 94-142, the Education for all Handicapped Children Act of 1975. In addition, local and state-level funding patterns and traditions tend to create opportunities and threats to the profession. The development of new technologies in education (e.g., assessment devices, computeriza-

tion) are further examples of environmental conditions that can profoundly affect the profession.

A *market analysis* in school psychology involves describing the major factors in the marketplace that are operating and determining trends that may have important implications for the profession. The particular opportunities or threats that flow from this analysis are then derived. Opportunities are defined as arenas in which school psychology is likely to enjoy a particularly competitive advantage. Threats are defined as unfamiliar trends or environmental disturbances that could lead to negative effects on support for school psychology services (Kotler, 1975).

A marketing opportunity presented itself in Kentucky in 1984 with the election of a new state superintendent of public instruction. Particularly in the areas of special education and student services, a period of fluidity and rapid change ensued as new ideas were being considered and leadership was changing. This situation allowed the profession to redefine itself and market some new concepts about the need for additional services and about the importance of broad-based delivery systems. Similarly, a threat to school psychology emerged in the marketplace in 1985 with considerations of new regulations for the role and function of school counselors, especially in relation to individual testing services. The identification of this threat led to a marketing strategy designed to minimize its impact.

Market segmentation involves dividing a market into distinct target groups with different needs, preferences, perceptions, attitudes, and behaviors. Each market segment may require different services and different marketing strategies and goals. For example, the market in schools constituted by the students can be segmented on the basis of the type and amount of service provided, psychoeducational needs, classification category, degree of psychological impairment, school location, or similar variables. In this manner, a school psychologist assigned to two buildings might identify a range of subgroups within this student population, each with different needs, such as children classified as educationally handicapped (e.g., learning-disabled, behavior-disordered), educationally disadvantaged children (e.g., children eligible for Chapter I programs), children at high risk for learning and behavior problems (e.g., first graders who do poorly on readiness screening tests), and children with underdeveloped social skills (e.g., highly passive children).

The market made up of teachers can similarly be segmented along a variety of dimensions. Teachers with minimal experience are likely to have needs that differ from those of long-term, successful staff members. Teachers who instruct special needs learners will have some problems different from those facing teachers who provide instruction in regular classrooms. Other variables by which teachers could be segmented include instructional style, classroom organization, and curriculum.

State school psychology organizations are also regularly involved in market segmentation. Market segments at this level may include the special education division within the state department of education (SDE), the pupil services department of the SDE, the state legislature, the certification/licensure apparatus, parent groups, and other professional associations (e.g., school administrators, teacher groups).

After defining present and potential markets in school psychology, a two-way flow of communication with all segments of the market can be initiated to learn what is valued by each and what each wishes to exchange. In Kentucky, care has been taken to develop relationships with various agencies within the state department of education. With the Division of Student Services, the focus of the communication has been on broad-based school psychology services, emphasizing the needs of all students and the importance of collaboration with other pupil services role groups. Key issues that face the Division of Student Services include dropout prevention, substance abuse, and minimum competency testing, and therefore these issues have been specifically addressed in developing the relationship. With the Office of Special Education,

emphasis has been placed on more narrow roles and functions that derive specifically from Kentucky Administrative Regulations pertaining to special education in general, and provision of related services specifically. Key issues that currently face this office include the over- and under-identification of certain categories of handicapping conditions and the funding of related services; this difference in issues of concern dictates a somewhat different approach than that used with the Student Services Division.

Through systematic interactions over time about key issues, the needs, preferences, perceptions, and attitudes of the market can be monitored so that marketing strategies can be targeted to them. Also, the volume and frequency of demand for services can be forecast by market segment, and projections about the amount of time that can be allotted to particular tasks or markets can be determined. Thus, market analysis, market segmentation, and related market research lead to more productive exchanges of values.

Transacting With Target Markets

Once the target market(s) are delineated and understood, the task for the school psychologist or state organization becomes one of transacting effectively in support of strategic objectives. Transactions at both levels can take various forms, including personal selling and publicity, advertising, political action, coalition building with related groups, and similar activities. For the purposes of this chapter, market transactions will be discussed within two broad categories: (a) influencing market perceptions through public relations, and (b) influencing the legislative/political environment through legislative action.

Public relations. Public relations is a loosely defined set of activities that coalesce around what is commonly called the 4 Ps of marketing: *P*roduct, *P*romotion, *P*lace, and *P*rice. In this regard, school psychologists must first define their *product*, which can be seen as any activity that satisfies a market need or want, including services, programs, procedures, or ideas. Once the potential products available to the marketplace are clear, emphasis is placed on *promotion*, on persuasive communication between the practitioner or state organization and the markets. Persuasive communication at a personal level may include informal discussions with the teaching staff about services, publication of a purpose statement or a service offerings description, or presentations at faculty and departmental meetings. At a state organization level, persuasive communication may include publication of a flyer about school psychology services, personal contacts with key decision makers, liaison activities designed to link school psychology services to key issues or problems, and the development of public service announcements for use in the media.

Place involves the accessibility or availability of goods and services to markets. In school psychology, this is a crucial issue, in that teachers, parents, and other clients may not always feel that school psychology services, including traditional assessment services, are available to them. In order for school psychologists to be perceived as accessible, they must be seen regularly at the building level and be easily reached. A useful approach in this regard might be to make available a regular block of time during which teachers can meet individually to talk about classroom problems, for example. Accessibility entails not only physical proximity but also psychological accessibility, to the extent that clients feel comfortable in approaching the school psychologist and discussing problems or otherwise making use of service offerings. At the state organization level, accessibility means being present at state and regional meetings where problems and issues are discussed, ensuring representation on various boards and committees, and building coalitions to influence and coordinate organizational responses to various concerns.

Finally, *price* has to do with the direct and indirect costs of services. For the individual practitioner of school psychol-

ogy, the direct costs of services are often obscured by the fact that services are not delivered on a fee-for-service basis. Nonetheless, there is a cost to the school organization that is associated with the time and effort expended in relation to each type of service offering and instance of service delivery. Indirect costs to consumers of services may include the discomfort of having someone in the room to observe, the complications associated with implementing an intervention plan, disruption to classroom or home routines, anxiety attached to being scrutinized or learning new skills, and the possible loss of status or prestige that may accrue as a function of acknowledging problems. Hopefully, these are balanced against the prospect of receiving meaningful and effective services designed to improve the presenting situation.

In Kentucky, an extensive set of public relations and liaison activities have been carried out at the state level through KAPS. All have been directed toward achieving the strategic goal of influencing market perceptions of the profession of school psychology in the state. A partial list follows:

Comprehensive School Psychological Services Handbook — Developed a resource book for superintendents, special education directors, school psychologists, and others offering guidelines, suggestions, rationales, and information relating to school psychology programs at the local district level; written and designed to portray these services in a positive light, and published by the Kentucky Department of Education.

School psychology brochure — Published and distributed thousands of brochures across the Commonwealth describing comprehensive school psychological services to parents, teachers, and others at the grass roots level.

Formal affiliation with school administrators — Established affiliate status with Kentucky Association of School Administrators, an umbrella organization for principals, counselors, superintendents, and pupil services organizations; linkage with this group greatly influenced public perception of school psychology.

Formal liaison with other professional groups — Affiliated with state Council of Administrators of Special Education, Council for Exceptional Children, Kentucky Psychological Association, Kentucky Association for Counseling and Development, Kentucky Coalition for the Handicapped, Kentucky Mental Health Coalition, and Kentucky Education Association, among others. This enabled greater visibility and input.

School Psychology Week proclamation — Established yearly proclamation by governor of School Psychology Week coincident with annual convention; publicized through press releases, buttons, posters, and individual selling by school psychologists throughout the state.

School psychology booth — Contracted with professional designer to create a booth for use as exhibit at various conventions, fairs, and related occasions; emphasizes large pictures of children interacting with school psychologists with the slogan "KAPS is for Kids"; staffed by volunteers at meetings who have numerous copies of brochures, handbooks, and similar material to hand out; individual contact and discussion is the most crucial element of this technique.

Public service announcements — Used modified versions of National Association of School Psychologists (NASP) public service announcements in major media markets in state.

Awards and recognition program — Created awards and recognition program for individual practitioners in five areas: consultation, assessment, organization development, research and program planning, and interventions; publicized nominees and winners to local newspapers; involved superintendents in recognition.

Professional development activities — Established annual convention, quarterly workshops, and Summer Institute throughout the state; sought to attract participants from variety of professional groups by broadening themes and inviting key persons.

Posters, pins, t-shirts, and pencils — Developed a variety of promotional items for distribution designed to highlight school psychology services, essentially conversation starters.

Legislative actions. Legislative action cannot be separated from public relations and liaison activities in practice, since both are essential components of the same social influence process. Clearly, public relations efforts can set the conditions for effective legislative efforts by creating a positive perception of the profession. Similarly, perceptions created about the profession as a function of legislative initiatives can support and enhance public relations campaigns.

Legislation initiatives can be described at both the individual and professional organization levels. At the individual level, school psychologists can be seen as engaged in what is equivalent to legislative activity when they seek to modify board of education policy, when they assist in rewriting district and building procedures for case management, or when they serve on committees or boards in the community. At the state level, legislative activity may include service on department of education committees and advisory panels, committee work and leadership through state professional organizations, development of legislation, lobbying, and testimony at regulatory hearings.

A further subdivision of legislative activities can be described in terms of the various environments that are influenced through these activities. The *organizational environment* at the individual level of practice consists of the school in its organizational aspects embedded in the context of the community. At the state level, the organizational environment is more complex, and may involve many professional groups, various special interest groups, and a range of interrelated agencies and departments. In order to create change, entry must be gained into these organizational milieus and methods for influencing their processes must be derived.

Another way to conceptualize legislative activity is to situate it in the *legal or regulatory environment*. At the local level this may be defined in terms of policies, procedures, and practices, codified or otherwise. At the state level, the regulatory environment is once again more complex, including statutes, administrative regulations, policy determinations, written guidelines, legal opinions, accreditation standards, consent agreements, and reports of boards and commissions. All of these in combination establish the conditions for practice at the local level, creating both opportunities and limitations. Planned change efforts in the regulatory arena require considerable forethought and carefully crafted interventions, often aimed at creating more favorable language in regulatory documents.

Finally, the *fiscal environment* governs much of the decision making in other spheres. At the local level, school psychologists need to be informed about the fiscal basis for their programs, and seek a firm foundation that can allow for both security and flexibility. For example, when school psychology service programs are supported by soft money funds, they are vulnerable to shifting trends. Additionally, practice under these conditions may be severely limited by the funding source and expectations regarding the products that are to be delivered. An important strategic goal under these circumstances is to ascertain the sources of revenue for the district and seek to place the funding basis for the program on a different foundation (e.g., local funds rather than federal funds).

At the state level, fiscal issues may revolve around the method the state uses to allocate funds to local school districts, such as formulas based on total school population, numbers and types of children with special needs, and/or support for special services. Each state has its own method for making these determinations, and a clear understanding of the structure being used can lead to interventions aimed at creating a more favorable fiscal environment for the profession.

In Kentucky, a number of legislative activities have been carried out in coor-

dinated fashion, again all tied to the strategic direction that had previously been agreed upon. A sampling of some of these activities in Kentucky includes the following:

Experimental school psychology program — Developed proposal for an experimental funding program for 25 school psychology positions that would be awarded to districts that commit to supporting one-half of the funding base and provide a comprehensive program as defined by the afore-mentioned *Handbook;* obtained funding through the 1986 Legislative Assembly of $400,000, including a substantial professional development and program evaluation component; presently being implemented, with the expectation that it will be expanded for the upcoming biennium.

Related services funding — Supported and lobbied for generation of additional unit funding of related services positions (such as school psychologists) for local districts based on number of identified pupils with special education needs; passed by the 1986 General Assembly, awaiting funding battle in the upcoming (1988) General Assembly.

Revisions to Kentucky Administrative Regulations — Actively sought to be represented on committees engaged in regulatory rewrites, especially those pertaining to assessment and consultation.

Certification revisions — Testified extensively and coordinated organizational responses to proposed changes in qualified examiner status of counselors, psychometry certification, educational diagnostician certification, administrator certification, and attempts to reduce proliferation of new professional specialties.

Accreditation standards — Lobbied for a more precise and rigorous set of standards for school psychology services at the local level.

Pupil discipline — Published a position statement in opposition to corporal punishment in the schools.

Academic competition — Testified on the emerging concept of academic competition leagues; helped to establish guidelines that focused on appropriate competition and sound instructional practice.

Minimum competency testing — Testified and lobbied against adoption of the Kentucky Essential Skills Test, a locally developed and hastily constructed instrument of undetermined validity, which relies on extrapolated national norms and seeks to create "educational reform" and "accountability" through narrow assessment of basic academic skills.

SUMMARY

This chapter has emphasized the importance of strategic marketing and planned change approaches to promotion of the profession of school psychology. The successful promotion of alternative service delivery programs in school psychology will require attention not only to content changes, but also to the process of change and the perceptions of consumers of school psychology services. Consequently, school psychologists, individually and collectively, must (a) identify the needs and wants of the various markets they serve, (b) conceive a strategic direction, (c) segment and target services to specific markets in relation to present needs, and (d) plan, implement, and evaluate transactions with target markets through public relations and legislative action.

REFERENCES

Bardon, J. I., & Bennett, V. C. (1974). *School psychology.* Englewood Cliffs, NJ: Prentice-Hall.

Brophy, J. (1986). Teacher influences on student achievement. *American Psychologist, 41,* 1069-1077.

Fullan, M., Miles, M. B., & Taylor, G. (1980). Organization development in schools: The state of the art. *Review of Educational Research, 50,* 121-183.

Gilmore, G. E., & Chandy, J. (1973). Teachers' perceptions of school psychological services. *Journal of School Psychology, 11,* 139-147.

Good, T. L., & Weinstein, R. S. (1986). Schools make a difference: Evidence, criticisms, and new directions. *American Psychologist, 41,* 1090-1097.

Hughes, J. N. (1979). Consistency of administrators' and psychologists' actual and ideal perceptions of school psychologists' activities. *Psychology in the Schools, 16,* 234-239.

Illback, R. J., & Maher, C. A. (1984). The school psychologist as an organizational boundary role professional. *Journal of School Psychology, 22,* 63-72.

Kotler, P. (1975). *Marketing for nonprofit organizations.* Englewood Cliffs, NJ: Prentice-Hall.

Lambert, N. M. (1986). Engineering new designs for school psychological service delivery: A commentary on *School psychology: A blueprint for training and practice. Professional School Psychology, 1,* 295-300.

Mason, E., & Remer, R. (1979). Politics in school psychology: A case study. *Journal of School Psychology, 17,* 74-81.

McCarthy, E. J. (1981). *Basic marketing: A managerial approach.* Homewood, IL: Irwin.

Meacham, M. L., & Peckham, P. D. (1978). School psychologists at three-quarters century: Congruence between training, practice, preferred role and competence. *Journal of School Psychology, 15,* 195-206.

National Commission on Excellence in Education. (1983). *A nation at risk: The imperative for educational reform.* Washington, DC: Government Printing Office.

National School Psychology Inservice Training Network. (1984). *School psychology: A blueprint for training and practice.* Minneapolis, MN: Author.

Shapiro, E., & Lentz, F. (1985). Assessing academic behavior: A behavioral approach. *School Psychology Review, 14,* 325-338.

Wang, M. C. (1987). Individual differences and effective schooling. *Professional School Psychology, 2,* 53-66.

23

Influencing Program Change at the District Level

Mary Henning-Stout
Austin College and Red River Clinic
Sherman, Texas
Jane Close Conoley
University of Nebraska-Lincoln

Schools are complex social structures. To function effectively, they rely upon individuals who are capable of and willing to work within the organization. Effectiveness is maximized when these individuals also participate in activities that keep their schools responsive to internal and external pressures for change.

As with all social structures, schools have rules, mores, and taboos. The members of the school system must perform in accordance with these organizational rules. They must also have strategies for changing ineffective rules. Rules vary from system to system and are central to the relative effectiveness of the school's performance. While schools require cooperation to accomplish important system functions, there seems to be a pervasive inability among school employees to collaborate in effective ways (Schmuck, 1982). This difficulty is never more apparent than when the system is faced with a mandate or opportunity to change in some way. Awareness of a particular school's "culture" — its history, its community context, its explicit and implicit rules — is central to determining how to interact with the system to influence change (Sarason, 1982).

The focus of this chapter is on how school psychologists and other special service professionals can influence change at the district level. This type of involve-ment by school psychologists represents quite a departure from the test-and-place role that has typified the profession (Bardon, 1982). In fact, many school psychologists and other professionals may imagine such a role to be impossible, given their current work situations. However, the growing calls for schools to be accountable and effective increase the relevance of system-wide intervention for organizational development. In training and practice, more special service professionals will find that the school system is in need of (and, ideally, responsive to) consultation at the district level for development of programs that are both educationally and economically effective.

In the culture of the schools, special service professionals tend to focus their attention on individuals. Individually administered tests and individualized educational plans are hallmarks of special education. District policy and programming may significantly affect service providers' attempts to respond to children's needs. At the same time, district activity may appear to be beyond the influence of those professionals.

District-wide directives are common phenomena in the public school systems. For example, in the same week, the following policies might be announced: (a) Psychologists must increase the number of assessments they accomplish in a week; (b) special education teachers must document weekly contacts with parents; (c) speech therapy groups must increase in size to cover the case load of a therapist who is on a year's leave. Professionals providing special services in the schools must have effective ways of responding to and influencing such policy and the resulting programs. Although the idea of system-level influence may seem far removed from child service, the success of alternative service delivery systems for children depends both on good ideas and effective district-level adoption and implementation.

There is no single guaranteed recipe for successful intervention at the district level of a school system (Illback & Zins, 1984). Given the complex organization of the schools, this lack of "cookbook" answers is understandable. Special service personnel interested in facilitating change must be observers who collect information and insights about the school system. They must be informed in the theory of organizational development and its application (see Maher, Illback & Zins, 1984, and Schmuck & Runkel, 1985, for excellent summaries of the application of organizational development in the schools). In addition, these professionals will find that they draw on all other skills they have developed as service providers (e.g., assessment, consultation, program development, and evaluation).

In this chapter we propose a model for instituting change at the district level. Following a discussion of the problem of change in the schools and the skills relevant to facilitating that change, we provide a detailed analysis of a "collective investment" approach to organizational programming. This model is proposed as a vehicle for program development that is flexible enough to take into account the complexities of the system in which it is applied.

PROBLEMS OF DISTRICT LEVEL CHANGE AND HOW TO FACE THEM

Change can simply be defined as any alteration in a system. The extent of change tolerated is determined by the system's norms and social rules. Buying a new copy machine for an elementary school represents a change. Implementing a new program for sex education represents another change. Eliminating the grade level system would represent yet another change. Any of these changes in a school district would have an impact on the system as a whole. The addition of a new copy machine will have considerably less impact than the implementation of a new sex education program in some districts. The elimination of the grade level system would greatly affect the district and would be likely to have a ripple effect into larger and related educational systems.

The effect of any change is mediated by the values of the system in which the change occurs. Neglect of this fact represents the single most significant factor in the failure of new educational programs (Sarason, 1982). Because the values of a system are perpetuated by the people who populate it, the change agent in the school district must be particularly attuned to the needs and attitudes of all the district's employees.

> The biblical metaphor of seeds falling onto hard ground seems particularly appropriate here. For innovative ideas to become innovations in a particular system, the people in the system must be prepared to accept them, especially through participatory decision making. (Conoley, 1981, p. 3)

For real change to occur, the vehicles for change must be presented in a manner consistent with the values of the people within the system. At times, several versions of a program may be necessary because subgroups within a system differ in their values. Differences among system participants are not signs of system dysfunction. In fact, variation in outlook is an unavoidable and positive attribute of any complex system. As people within a system specialize, their goals and perspectives change. Administrators, teachers, clerical staff, and maintenance crews will all have somewhat different priorities and will be motivated by different incentives. The key to facilitating district-level change is awareness of not only the differences but also the commonalities that bind the many subsystems together.

Every human system, by definition, has some common purpose, some identity that characterizes it as unique. The goal of serving children is shared by most school system personnel. The desire to be seen as effective and as contributing to community welfare is another commonly shared goal. As Fullan (1982) has observed, any change will have different meanings for different members of the changing organization. Change cannot occur unless the members of the system involved are invested in the change, regardless of their reasons for being invested.

How can the special service professional play a role in this change? As either internal or external agents, service providers have the opportunity to enhance their value to the district as liaisons between district administration and school building faculty, staff, and students. This rather marginal, boundary role (Illback & Maher, 1984) increases their opportunities to do system-level consultation.

For example, school psychologists may be grouped with administrators or faculty, or they may have some other subgroup affiliation. Despite these associations, they must not be aligned exclusively with any particular group and in fact they provide their best services when maintaining alliances with all subgroups within the district. As they work closely with administrators, teachers, staff members, students, and parents, school psychologists can gain insight into the implicit values of the system as a whole as well as those of each subgroup. By having good relationships with each of these groups, school psychologists and other special service practitioners can more effectively facilitate the change process by serving as agents for linking the system's human resources (Havelock, 1973).

In the course of developing relationships with the different subgroups in a system, school psychologists are faced with the problem of presenting themselves as effective agents of change. The popular view of school psychologists as psychometric specialists restricts this presentation (Bardon, 1982). Complete consideration of the issues that surround changing what is expected of school psychologists and how they are perceived is an enormous task (witness the length of this volume). Psychologists attempting to influence district programming and change must be political. They are aware of their relationships with the powerful, potentially powerful, and comparatively weak segments of the system; they appreciate the dynamic nature of that power relationship; and they work to maintain open, trusting communication with each subgroup. This is not a simple task.

To be effective change agents, school psychologists and other special service professionals can draw on their training and experience in the school system. When working at the district level, they bring to bear their unique collection of knowledge about the system, coupled with techniques in organization development, to facilitate the development of workable programs for district-wide implementation. In this role, special service professionals are system-aware advocates, working with and within the system of the school district to aid in positive educational programming for school children.

ONE APPROACH TO INFLUENCING DISTRICT PROGRAMMING

The procedures outlined below were developed with the contributions of special service personnel and the school district, as well as the nature of systemic change, in mind. This "collective investment" approach is an attempt to respond to Sarason's (1982) observation that those who program change in schools tend to divide the members of the school system into three groups: (a) those who favor the change ("the good guys"), (b) those who are opposed to the change ("the bad guys"), and (c) those who are assumed to have no interest in the change, and are therefore ignored. The model presented here is based on the notion that, for a program to work, all who will be involved in it should be included at all stages of its development and implementation. Aspects of this approach appear in work by J. P. Burke and Ellison (1985), Conoley and Conoley (1982), Havelock (1973), Illback and Zins (1984), Parsons and Meyers (1984), Schein (1969), and Schmuck and Runkel (1985).

Perhaps the notion of system-wide participation seems a bit idealistic, or even unrealistic. But as Conoley and Gutkin (1986) have suggested,

> Both practitioners and educators (in school psychology) balance real and ideal notions about their roles and functions in the ways they spend their days in schools and in how they build their graduate programs. The challenges are not only to know what the realities of the field are, but also to know how to continually strive toward more perfect situations. Neither challenge is trivial. (p. 457)

The notion of involving in the planning of change those who are to implement the change is not a new idea and has been the focus of significant research in industrial/organizational psychology (e.g., Bowers, Franklin, & Pecorella, 1975; W. Burke, 1978; Franklin, 1976). The application of such theory in the schools has been explored and found to be useful for working within educational systems (for excellent theory development see Maher, Illback, & Zins, 1984, and Schmuck & Runkel, 1985; for a comprehensive review of the literature on organizational development in schools see Fullan, Miles & Taylor, 1981). One way in which participant involvement in planning for change is actualized is illustrated in the consultation literature. Collaborative consultation in the schools has been given impressive theoretical and research support (see, e.g., Conoley & Conoley, 1982; Gutkin & Curtis, 1982; Parsons & Meyers, 1984; Raffaniello, 1981). This approach to consultation suggests that teachers will be most able to facilitate behavior change in the classroom if they are involved in the problem solution and plan generation processes.

The approach suggested here for influencing district change draws heavily on theories of organizational development and models of collaborative consultation. When working for a change at the district level in a school system, providers of special services will be most successful if they employ strategies from both of these areas for interacting simultaneously with the system as a whole, with subgroups within the system, and with individual members of the subgroups.

The proposed collective investment model has been designed to afford a flexible perspective from which to balance the realities faced and the ideals possible within a given organization (school district). From both practical and pedagogical standpoints, the notion of collective involvement seems central to the success of an organization's programming. The approach presents practical, *realistic* ways to go about facilitating such involvement, while stimulating movement toward the ideal of having participants invested in, and therefore committed to, the success of a program. This framework, as illustrated in Figure 1, can be readily applied to influencing change at the district level.

The collective investment approach is characterized by three stages: need identification, preparation for change, and program implementation and evaluation. The proposed model is activated by the identification of a need in the system. The need may be identified by anyone in the system, but it must be brought to the attention of some powerful individual or group before programming for change can be initiated. The group initially identifying the need may be one not of formal power but of emergent power in the system. Whether the concern arises from established or emergent power sources, tracing the origin of the concern can be a helpful first step in influencing change. By determining the source of need identification, individuals and groups can be identified who are potential change activists and whose values and agendas must be considered when structuring a program for district-wide change.

FIGURE 1
The Collective Investment Model of Program Development and Implementation

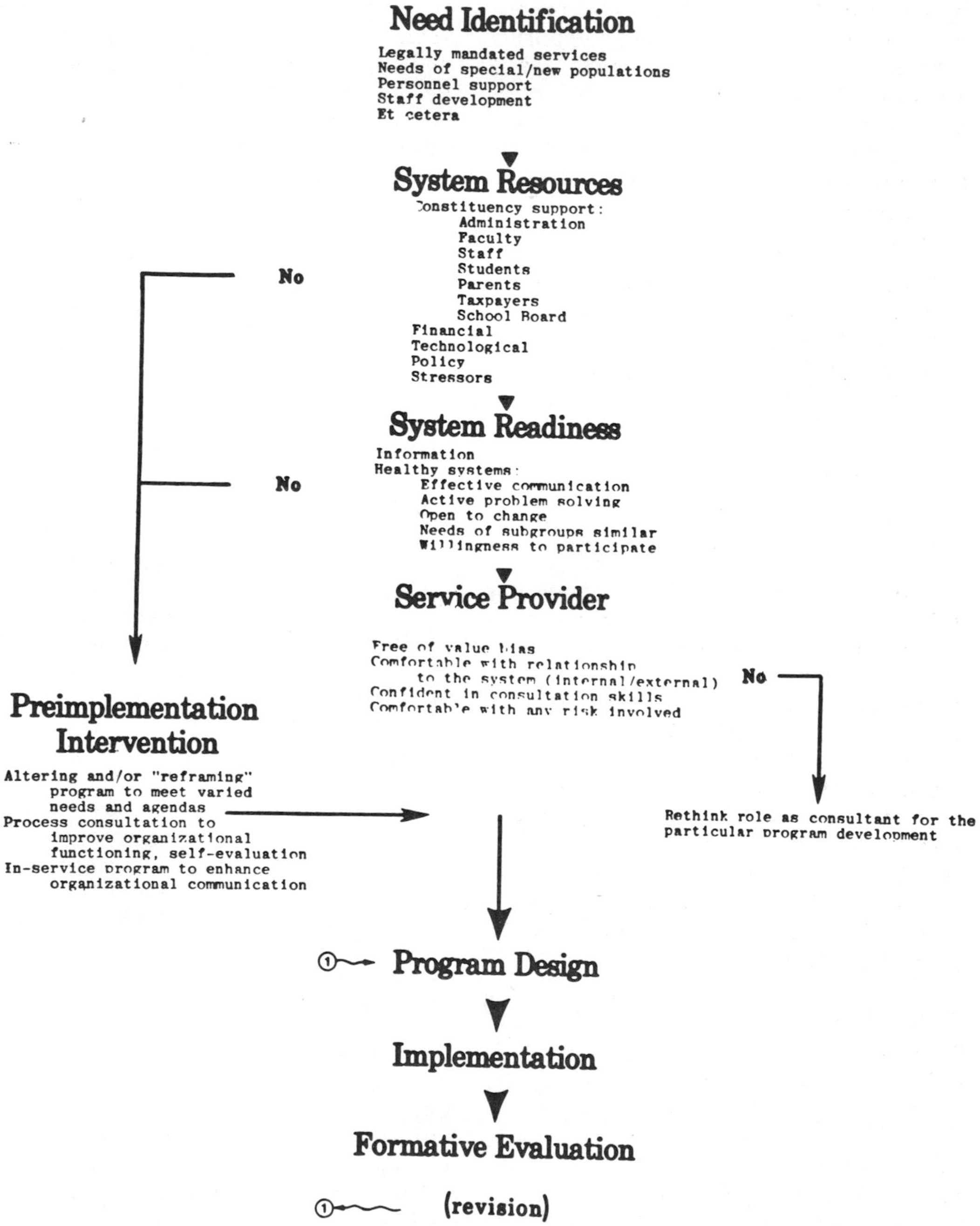

Need Identification

Legally mandated services
Needs of special/new populations
Personnel support
Staff development
Et cetera

▼

System Resources

Constituency support:
    Administration
    Faculty
    Staff
    Students
    Parents
    Taxpayers
    School Board
Financial
Technological
Policy
Stressors

No

▼

System Readiness

Information
Healthy systems:
    Effective communication
    Active problem solving
    Open to change
    Needs of subgroups similar
    Willingness to participate

No

▼

Service Provider

Free of value bias
Comfortable with relationship
    to the system (internal/external)
Confident in consultation skills
Comfortable with any risk involved

No

Preimplementation Intervention

Altering and/or "reframing"
    program to meet varied
    needs and agendas
Process consultation to
    improve organizational
    functioning, self-evaluation
In-service program to enhance
    organizational communication

Rethink role as consultant for the
particular program development

① ↝ ## Program Design

▼

Implementation

▼

Formative Evaluation

① ↜ (revision)

The second stage of the proposed model consists of assessment in three broad areas prior to program implementation: the resources of the system, the readiness of the system, and the characteristics of the service providers. This is the most crucial stage of the collective investment approach. Although a specific need must be identified for the change process to be activated, assessment and facilitation of the system's preparation for change is vital to maximizing the possibility that substantive change can occur. As a part of the proposed model, certain activities are suggested for anticipating and overcoming barriers to change so that the system is prepared for successful implementation of a new program.

The final stage of the collective investment approach to district programming includes both program implementation and evaluation. In order for a program of change to be effective, it must be responsive to the needs of the system. These needs include those identified prior to program development, those that arise as the program is put in place, and those not yet discovered. As the program is being implemented, there must be evaluation measures built in for assessing its effectiveness. Issues of communication among implementers and overseers of the change process are of central concern in this stage of the proposed model.

The proposed collective investment model, as represented in Figure 1, is purposely incomplete in its explicit listing of actions to take, given particular barriers to the change process. This incompleteness is consistent with the reality that all systems are different and that the particular combination of system and service provider will dictate what deficiencies emerge as most potent and what steps need to be taken to remediate these problems. Characteristic of this model is a constant need to recall that each program must be designed with regard to the particular district's characteristics.

In addition, the sections of this model are by no means discrete. The procedures and awareness characterizing one phase of the approach might also occur in other phases. This seeming redundancy is inherent in the responsive nature of this approach, which is designed to guide simultaneous response to multiple considerations for change.

Need Identification

Needs arise for a variety of reasons and from a variety of sources in the schools. There could be a need for developing a program to meet the requirements of a legal mandate. The myriad programs developed in response to PL 94-142 are examples of responses to such a need. A need might emerge for an innovative response to a situation involving only a small portion of the school population. For example, when a new population immigrates to an area, a need for sympathetic awareness of cultural diversity arises. In contrast, a need might develop from a situation that has existed in a school district for some time. For example, the role of the school in community education of adults is not a new need, but is one for which new programs are being developed in many districts across the country. The identification of some need is required to activate the change mechanism proposed in the collective investment approach. The service provider's first task is to help the system assess the need.

The process of needs assessment is a familiar one in many organizations. The more broadly and acutely a need is felt, the more likely a solution will be created. Needs assessment is likely to indicate the priority placed by an organization on its identified needs. A systematic assessment of needs helps to identify which needs should be targeted for immediate action.

Excellent sources for advice on how to conduct needs assessment are available to special service personnel (e.g., Guba & Lincoln, 1982; Hunter & Lambert, 1974; Nickens, Purga, & Noriega, 1980), as are additional sources on the construction of interviews and questionnaires (e.g., Oppenheim, 1966; Payne, 1951). The professionals who carry out the assessment process should plan to have respondents identify specific needs, rank them for importance, forecast what changes would have to occur for each need to be met, and indicate what resources are necessary for meeting each need. To ensure a collective investment in the process, some guidelines should be considered:

1. Every subsystem within the school system has needs. Each group must believe that its needs are being considered and responded to if its members are either to engage in the assessment activities or support the implementation of a new program.

2. Although school systems have the encompassing goal of educating children, each unit within the system has unique needs. The search for a "common good" is very difficult in systems with fixed resources. For example, the presence of an aide might make mainstreaming behaviorally impaired children more successful, but the funds used for aides might have been used to hire a teacher with a needed specialty. A needs assessment can create expectations for action. Although such expectations are important and vital for change to occur, the possibility that some group's needs will not be met must be made explicit at the start of a needs assessment process.

3. The results of the needs assessment should be translated back to the staff and to the decision makers. Staff members often complain about filling out questionnaires and then seeing no change. The people who fill out the questionnaires should at least be informed of the results.

4. When a list of needs is formulated, the needs on that list must then be placed in priority. Representatives of the groups who completed the needs assessment (or everyone who responded, if the numbers are manageable) must meet to set these priorities and begin planning. The priority of each need and the intended and unintended consequences of a change to meet the needs must be considered.

Preparation for Change

After a specific need is identified, the practitioner employing the proposed collective investment model enters the most important phase of that process: Assessing the status of the organization in order to influence program change at the district level (J. P. Burke & Ellison, 1985; Illback & Zins, 1984; Schmuck & Runkel, 1985). Such an assessment represents an immense task.

In the "real life" experience of special service professionals in a school district, programming to meet identified need is often expected to be developed and implemented immediately. The time necessary to make the assessments and preparations described below may seem nonexistent. However, when reading these suggestions, keep in mind that the successful service provider is one who, from the moment of employment, begins to note the subtle and overt behaviors of the organization. Assessment of the system's resources, its readiness for change, and the characteristics of its special services staff should be quickly and efficiently accomplished when professionals have remained aware of their district's patterns of functioning (routine and idiosyncratic).

System resources. One important step in assessing a district's preparedness for change is to determine the resources available for program development. The most important resources to consider are the people who work within the district. In addition to the needs assessment accomplished to identify the area of change, subgroup and individual support for a particular program idea should be determined. What are the values held by each subgroup with respect to the proposed program? How involved would they expect to be in the program if it were to be implemented? What is the morale status of the subgroups in the system? This assessment can include both formal (questionnaires) and informal components (chats in break rooms, incidental conversations).

Additional assessment should be made of the explicit and implicit values of the district. What policies, currently in effect, would tend to facilitate or detract from the success of the proposed program? What programs have succeeded and failed in the past? This information, coupled with that obtained through assessing the values of the subgroups in the district can allow for development of specific preimplementation intervention.

Through gathering information about the "personality" and "behavioral patterns" of the system, the service professional should gain important insight into the distribution of power within the district. Often the formal organization of a system does not accurately reflect the actual power structure. Careful assessment of the history of change activity in the district can help to shed some light on the sources of power as they affected the success or failure of past programs. Where did the earlier ideas under examination originate? Did the administration actively control the programs, or simply serve as a rubber stamp? What and who stood in the way of failed programs? All of this information, gathered in a friendly, nonevaluative fashion, contributes significantly to the special services professional's understanding of the system's human resources.

Prior to developing a district program, the extent of financial and technological support should be assessed. Are there sufficient financial resources available and is the system willing to allocate them to funding the program? Does the system have access to the technology necessary for the program's success (e.g., computer facilities, audiovisual equipment, efficient communication systems)? Should technology or funding be lacking, steps should be taken to determine either how these resources can be acquired or how the program can be made to fit into the constraints represented by limited resources. For assessing technology and funding, good working relationships with administrators and awareness of resources available from the district, community, or government are important.

Finally, school psychologists and other special services professionals involved in district-level program planning should be aware of the stressors currently impinging on the system. Is the district in financial stress and how does this stress affect openness to change? Are there significant population changes (e.g., large numbers of immigrants to be incorporated into the system)? What recent state and federal legislation is affecting the district? These stressors and distractors may need to be addressed before any sort of program implementation can occur.

System readiness. Once the status of system resources is assessed, the next area of concern is the readiness of the system for introduction of change. A large portion of assessing readiness will have already been accomplished by the canvassing of subgroups regarding their needs, attitudes, and values related to the proposed program. Once the need is identified for specific programming, the variation in perception of the urgency and reality of the need by the affected subgroups must also be assessed (Fullan, 1982). With this information, additional insight can be gained into the match between the values and change agendas of the subgroups. Some level of agreement among these agendas is necessary for program success and can be facilitated with preimplementation intervention.

The following is an example. Suppose a school psychologist and a special educator have seen a need for change in the referral process. These professionals were interested in changing procedure so that consultation in the classroom would occur prior to referral for testing. Their idea was prompted by a perception that regular education teachers tried few, if any, program modifications before referring children for special education assessment. In addition, the psychologist noted that many of the children she tested were "slow learners" — not specifically disabled children. The special education teacher suspected that many of the activities he performed to adapt the instruction for children in his resource room could be accomplished in the regular program.

They felt that by implementation of a prereferral consultation process many problems could be solved without testing and/or placement in special education. Prior to making a proposal for this program change, the school psychologist and special educator conducted a needs assessment to measure the relative consensus in subgroups' perceptions of need for, and in their attitudes toward, the program change (Illback & Zins, 1984). They talked with special and regular education teachers, administrators at the building and district levels, special and regular education students, and parents to assess each group's attitudes toward the proposed change.

Following this informal information gathering, the professionals designed a questionnaire to distribute among larger numbers of the four identified subgroups. In this manner, they learned that parents and regular education teachers were opposed to the program, which they saw as potentially reducing the teacher's control in the classroom. Administrators favored the program because it represented a way to save money for the district by potentially lowering the numbers in special education classes. Special educators were split in their opinions, some seeing such change as leading to more effective and appropriate service to students, some perceiving a threat to the continuation of their positions. Students, also, were both for and against the program. Some students felt that children having trouble should be given the opportunity to remediate without special education, whereas others felt that troubled children should be taken out of the regular classroom so they would no longer be disturbances.

With these results, the school psychologist and special educator had sufficient information to enter the preimplementation intervention stage of the proposed collective investment model. They had made a useful assessment of the relative support their program would have from the different subgroups and could see that implementation without regard to subgroup attitudes and needs would result in program failure. (For studies illustrating the actual implementation of prereferral consultation, see Graden, Casey, & Bonstrom, 1985; Graden, Casey & Christenson, 1985; and Gutkin, Henning-Stout, & Piersel, 1986.)

As illustrated above, the subgroups' values need not be in exact concordance. A program can succeed if all participants agree that implementation of the program will serve to enhance their individual situations. For example, a change in the referral system might ultimately be accepted by all subgroups as matching their particular needs. Special education teachers might be assigned children more appropriate to their classrooms. Regular education teachers might find that the program provides them with increasingly effective classroom management skills. Students and parents might support the program because of the opportunity to help remediate learning or behavioral problems without removal of students from the regular classrooms. Administrators might see this program as enhancing organizational collegiality and, at the same time, providing economic benefit, since less testing and placement would be necessary. Finally, school psychologists might value the program for affording them more time for the provision of alternative services.

In addition to being acceptable to each of the affected subgroups, the program must not offend any prevailing system-wide values (Conoley & Conoley, 1982; Davis, 1984). If such a deficiency is present, efforts can be taken to modify the discordant value positions, or the program can be altered to fit with existing mores. The most significant block to successful program implementation is a fundamental fear of change.

If such a fear exists, chances are great the broader community would share and, therefore, perpetuate that aversion to novelty (Sarason, 1982). This state of affairs poses an interesting problem for the change agent. If a program seems necessary to a district, the school psychologist must determine how to work at translating the program into a form that fits with the district values.

The therapeutic literature (e.g., Watzlawick, Weakland, & Fisch, 1974) describes a process called *reframing* that may be useful to practitioners interested in such translation. In essence, the reframing strategy involves pointing out how a proposed change can help meet the variety of goals sought by individuals and groups. Reframing allows individuals to see change from various perspectives. Some will prefer their own "frames" and not be persuaded, but others may see that their own values and goals are included in the proposed program.

Along with assessing subgroup agendas and system values relative to change, the organization's ability to solve problems and the effectiveness of communication within the organization should also be measured. These characteristics of organizational effectiveness can be assessed by gathering historical information on ways in which various problems have been approached in the past. Interviewing subgroup representatives about the way problems are dealt with in the district would provide insight into the problem-solving ability of the system from a variety of perspectives. Because the development of a new program represents an effort to "solve a problem," to meet some district need, the district's problem-solving ability is central to the program's success.

The effectiveness and pattern of communication within a school district can be assessed. One way is through monitoring a week's communiques. Who sends memos to whom? What seem to be the lines of communication among members of different subgroups? For example, do the parents go directly to the principal instead of the teacher? Do the teachers have access to district administrators or must they rely on the principal or some other administrator as liaison? Do the students have vehicles for voicing their concerns, and to whom are these concerns voiced? Often, the success of a new program is subverted if the subgroups involved in the program have no effective ways to communicate with each other.

Characteristics of special service personnel. Service providers working to influence district programming must also be aware of their own skills, personal values, and needs. They must know themselves and understand how closely their values and needs match with those of the district (J. P. Burke & Ellison, 1985); they must ask if their values are in any way reducing the effectiveness with which they are able to facilitate program development most useful to the district.

This question has two distinct and apparently contradictory aspects. One of the greatest challenges to special service professionals working to influence organizational programming is to give up the role as expert/savior, and to work instead as facilitator of organizational effectiveness. If they enter the system with a personal agenda for what sort of programs should be implemented and disregard the needs and abilities of the system, they will find that the programs are ineffective (Sarason, 1982).

Instead, special service personnel should work to build relationships with all subgroups of the system, thereby establishing themselves as resources for change. Presenting oneself as a resource instead of an expert has been described as having "referent" power (Martin, 1978). A change agent with referent power fits most effectively in the proposed collective investment model. These individuals function as catalysts for change, as "process helpers," "resource linkers" (Havelock, 1973), and "boundary role professionals" (Illback & Maher, 1984). They do not impose leadership on the system, but realize that leadership cannot be effective unless the support of the followers is strong.

At the same time, the service provider must be aware of system values or habits that might block successful program implementation. This awareness involves a "value judgment" on the part of the special services professional. While service providers must resist imposing their personal agendas on the organizations within which they work, they are professionally obligated to judge which organizations are failing to function effectively. Among the service provider's obligations as a consultant to the district on program change is to "hold up a mirror" to the organization and help identify organizational habits that inhibit effective programming. The service provider's awareness and confrontation of organizational "self-sabotage" is known as process consultation (Schein, 1969).

This point is aptly illustrated by the experience of a school psychologist interested in promoting the effectiveness of a recent state mandate for teacher assistance teams. These teams were intended to help teachers with child-related problems. They were to be made up of teachers in individual school buildings who could request consultation with special service staff from throughout the district. The school psychologist was frustrated by the attitudes of her peers in response to this mandate. While the state school psychology organization had frequently called for psychologists to expand their roles from diagnostics to intervention, many school psychologists were avoiding interaction with these teacher assistance teams.

The school psychologist gave a workshop at the state school psychology convention entitled "Who's Stopping Us Now?" Workshop participants were asked to inventory their roles and functions from their own perspectives and the perspectives of their consumers (district personnel). They were also asked to generate descriptions of their ideal functioning. The process revealed that psychologists knew that teachers and principals wanted their active involvement in cases under consideration by the teacher assistance teams. They discovered that, even though a discrepancy between real roles (mainly limited to diagnostics) and ideal roles (including intervention) was inevitable, there were ways in which they could become more flexible in making their services available while continuing to meet needs of their districts.

During the action planning phase of the workshop, the participants were confronted with how their unwillingness to participate in the teacher assistance teams was obstructing their reaching identified ideal roles. Through the workshop process, the psychologists were forced to face the choice of identifying themselves as diagnostic specialists or expanding their roles by actively responding to the new state mandate. The school psychologist leading the workshop had successfully balanced her personal values with the organizational mirroring necessary to stimulate change in the state organization.

Like this school psychologist, professionals working at the district level must refrain from imposing their own agendas while at the same time watch for and interrupt habits in the organization that block successful programming — a judgment that cannot be made without reference to one's understanding (values) regarding effective organizational functioning. Some level of influence (i.e., imposition of values) is inevitably brought to bear in any individual's involvement in a system. By virtue of choosing to work with a system, one has an impact (Schmuck and Runkel, 1985). The challenge is to rely upon professional knowledge about improving the effectiveness of an organization without imposing personal values and agendas on the program development process when they do not match those of the district.

In addition to assessing personal values relative to any given situation, service providers must determine their level of comfort with their relationship to the system. As Pipes (1981) has suggested, status within or outside the organization can have various implications. An internal consultant has "intimate knowledge" (Pipes, p. 13) of the system and may be somewhat blinded to the organizational self-sabatoge mentioned above. The external consultant has "status" (Pipes, p. 13) beyond that of a familiar internal staff member, but also runs the higher risk of being seen as an antagonist rather than a facilitator and of being unaware of complex and subtle system dynamics.

Either position (internal or external) has built-in strengths and weaknesses. The practitioner's position relative to the district does not guarantee success or failure for any program. Curtis and Metz (1986) reported on a systems level intervention that depended on the cooperation of both internal and external personnel. They highlighted how the daily presence of the internal consultant was invaluable to program success. This case and one reported by Wenger (1986) might bolster internal consultants' confidence that they can promote program change within their own organizations.

Finally, service providers must be confident with their consultation skills and comfortable with any risk involved in working with program change proposed by the district (J. P. Burke & Ellison, 1985). Consultation skill is central to a change agent's successful interaction at the district level; this skill cannot be applied effectively if the service provider is threatened by the nature of the program change. If participation in district programming compromises personal or professional ethics, for example, the service provider might choose not to participate or might work toward modification of the proposed program. This issue is closely related to that of the match between service provider and district values. If any of these questions regarding service provider characteristics is answered in a discordant fashion, reconsidering one's involvement in the program development is appropriate.

Preimplementation interventions. Where barriers to change are found in the assessment of the district's resources, its readiness for change, and the characteristics of special service personnel, interventions to move toward readiness for programming should occur. These interventions would be of two primary types: (a) process consultation (Schein, 1969) and (b) in-service programs with a variety of different groups at different levels of readiness.

The needs and values of district subgroups must match those of the proposed program before that program can be successful. If there is inconsistency in the needs of the subgroups, this information can be communicated to administrators. Administrators may be surprised to learn that their agendas for the district are significantly opposed by the people in the system who are expected to implement programs based on those agendas. With that awareness, administrators might be willing to become involved in groups of representatives of each district subgroup with the goal of coming to agreement regarding the nature of programs to be implemented.

The effectiveness of such groups would be facilitated by a service provider's involvement as a process consultant (see Schmuck & Runkel, 1985, and Schein, 1969

for descriptions of this consultation model). The aim of process consultation is to facilitate organizational self-evaluation and enhance organizational effectiveness. In process consultation, the consultant analyzes the interactive patterns in the group and points out how these patterns are facilitating and inhibiting the group's movement toward its goal.

With process consultation, the service provider can help the group explore the interaction between the structure of the organization and the individuals involved (Illback & Zins, 1984). If the structure of the organization is such that the participants' needs and values are not taken into consideration during development of programs, the likelihood that the programs will fail is greatly increased. Process consultation with representative groups can improve district problem-solving by enhancing organizational communication and providing a new vehicle for approaching district problems (i.e., subgroup representation in groups established initially to assess the problem at hand and propose alternative solutions).

The problem analysis and alternative solutions generated by these representative groups must not be definitive. That is, if district programming decisions were left to small groups (even if representative), those decisions would not have the investment of the full constituency — the individuals who would be affected by, and determine the ultimate success of, the programs to be implemented. The work of these representative groups can be taken to the larger subgroups by the group representatives themselves and by the school psychologist, who can design in-service programs to introduce program concepts reframed to fit with the various subgroups' needs. In-service programs held within subgroups can include information sharing, small-group discussion of the proposed program and its relevance/ utility to individuals, surveying of participants' attitudes toward the program given the new information, and discussions.

Larger in-service programs could be held to facilitate communication among subgroup members regarding the proposed program. This type of in-service programming can be useful for developing what Neigher and Fishman (1984) refer to as interorganizational linkages — communication links among the various subgroups of the district system. This enhanced communication is another key variable in the success of district programming.

Summary of preimplementation activity. Once a need is identified, but prior to introducing any new program, the availability of district resources for supporting that program must be determined. When methods have been developed for accomplishing such an assessment, they can be applied in subsequent program development processes. In the same manner, system readiness can be enhanced with preimplementation intervention strategies such that all facets of the organization are more effective and, therefore, more receptive to change. Such readiness, however, would seem to be contingent upon continued process consultation to support organizational effectiveness (Schein, 1969), given the dynamic nature of those human systems (and the unavoidable reality of unforeseen "roadblocks" to that effectiveness).

With each new program, with each new system, special service personnel must assess their personal positions relative to the situation faced. With increased experience in these consultative/program development situations at the district level, school psychologists can become more proficient at recognizing situations with which they do not "fit," and more capable of facilitating district development even when their own ideals do not match with values of the district.

District Level Change and the Stages of Consultation

A slight digression is in order here to draw an analogy between consultation theory and the process discussed in the collective investment approach. It is helpful to recognize the connection between the general model for consulting with classroom teachers (Gutkin & Curtis,

1982) and the activity involved in influencing district programming. Table 1 illustrates how consultation skills are useful for personnel working at the district level.

The preimplementation process just reviewed matches well with Gutkin and Curtis's (1982) first two steps in consultation. Need identification and assessment define and clarify the problem for which the district seeks a solution. Assessment of the district's resources and readiness for change, and evaluation of the special service professional's relation to the district and the proposed program represent analysis of the systemic context in which the problem exists.

Gutkin and Curtis's remaining steps match with the program development, implementation, and evaluation phases. As we return to our discussion of these stages of the collective investment approach, we will refer to Gutkin and Curtis's model as a way of organizing the ideas we present in respect to a service strategy with which many readers are familiar (i.e., classroom consultation).

Implementing and Evaluating a New Program

Once the district is ready for a program, the implementation process can begin. This process includes program development, program implementation, and program evaluation and is discussed with reference to the collective investment model proposed above.

Program development. Up to this point, the proposed model for district change has allowed for the identification and publicizing of needs, the promotion of investment in working to satisfy those needs, and the assessment of organizational changes necessary for supporting new programs. These activities must occur before the specifics of a program can be established.

Program development might be conceptualized as a series of "what" questions (Apter & Conoley, 1984). With the needs well defined, program developers can focus on a specific outline of goals. What

TABLE 1
The Steps of Consultation as Steps for Program Development

Consultation		Program development
1. Define and clarify the problem.	◊	Assess the need for the program. Determine who will be involved in the program's implementation.
2. Analyze the forces imping-ing on the problem.	◊	Assess system resources and stressors. Determine the relative investment individuals are willing to make in the program.
3. Brainstorm alternative strategies.	◊	Develop the program by taking it through revision until the needs of all system subgroups' needs can be met.
4. Evaluate and choose among alternatives.	◊	Agree on a final program format for implementation.
5. Specify consultee and con-sultant responsibilities.	◊	Determine which subgroups will be responsible for which facets of program implementation.
6. Implement the chosen strategy.	◊	Implement the program.
7. Evaluate the effectiveness of the action and recycle if necessary.	◊	Build in formal and infor-mal formative evaluation measures. Make small (fine-tuning) changes and regularly scheduled pro-gram revision to meet system's changing needs

Note. Left-hand column from "School-based consultation: Theory and techniques" by T.B. Gutkin and M.J. Curtis, in *The Handbook of School Psychology* (p. 808) edited by C.R. Reynolds and T.B. Gutkin, 1982, New York: Wiley. Copyright by John Wiley and Sons, Inc. Reprinted by permission

goals are possible? Which are short-term and which are long-term? Which of the goals appear impossible? How important are these? What people should be involved in the actual writing of the program? What other already existing programs might support the new program? What are the constraints to program development? What will indicate that the program is a success? What will indicators of failure be?

Sarason (1982) suggested that con-stituent power must not be overlooked; the people who are affected by a program are "as much the implementers as the objects of change" (p. 293). The constit-uency of a school district includes the students, parents, educational personnel at all levels of the organization, school board members, and taxpayers. In most district programs, all of these subgroups are affected and should be involved in the change process.

Information gained about the needs and values of the different subgroups that has been gathered during the preimplementation phase of district programming, can be helpful in determining who should be involved in developing a program. Again, employing the example above of introducing a change in the referral process to include consultation prior to referral for testing, a number of subgroups should be involved in the decision-making process regarding this program change: regular and special educators, parents, administrators, students, school psychologists, and diagnosticians (if a part of that particular system). These individuals would have been involved in the preimplementation process and would have reached some agreement as to the collective goal of the program change.

Various drafts of a program description might be disseminated among interested parties for feedback concerning whether the goals and program features outlined are consistent with their agendas. Although the circulation of program priorities is a time-consuming task, it improves the probability of success. As with so many other tasks, initial effort has long-term payoff.

Program implementation. Only after the "what" questions associated with the new program have been investigated, should "how" questions be introduced. Once the "whats" are well known, the "hows" can be explored. This separate focus is very important. Often, the universe of alternatives is not explored by program developers because they move too quickly into *how* to do something. Solutions are generated before the complexity of the problem is well understood.

The school psychologist and special educator of our continuing example regarding prereferral consultation would be well advised to keep open minds on strategies to meet the needs they identi-

fied. While they considered prereferral consultation to be the ideal solution, the process of collective investment may suggest other alternatives to meet the same needs they have recognized. If the need and the goals are well defined, many "hows" can be tried and evaluated.

The stages of program development (what) and implementation (how) match the third and fourth consultation steps of Gutkin and Curtis (1982) (see Table 1). The program developers must brainstorm program features and evaluate potential strategies for those most likely to encourage collective investment and program success.

Special service professionals involved in district change should work with each subgroup to develop "how to" ideas. The solutions generated by each group can be shared among other groups. The feedback concerning possible program strategies might also contain a description of the roles people in the district are willing to play in the new program (see Gutkin & Curtis, 1982, and step 5 in Table 1).

Once a list of possible solutions is generated by people interested in the new program, specific interventions must be chosen (see Gutkin & Curtis, 1982, and step 6 in Table 1). These strategies will probably require modification and refinement before they can be implemented. There must be a way to accomplish each of the major program goals. Program developers must also pay attention to the evaluation methodologies they will use. How will information be collected to monitor the program implementation and check on the program outcomes? How does the evaluative information relate to program goals?

For example, if district personnel want to reduce the number of children they place in special education classes and increase their regular educators' skills in dealing with mildly handicapped children, there are many possible strategies. They could rely on systematic in-service training with faculty members on the components of effective instruction (Gettinger, 1987). Or they could train classroom observers in Ysseldyke and Christenson's (1986) system for characterizing the instructional environments created for target students. District administrators could provide teachers with individual feedback on how closely their classrooms approximate ideal instructional environments. Or they could set up building-level teacher assistance teams to solve problems with, and provide support to, teachers prior to formal referral of students for testing. The possible "hows" are very numerous and will be limited only by imagination, carefully defined goals, and the real-life constraints of a particular system.

Program evaluation. By completing the "what" step and the "how" step in program change, program developers have the basis for formative and summative evaluation. Formative evaluation involves ongoing monitoring of a program to ensure it is being implemented as planned, that short-term goals are being met, and that unforeseen problems are being considered and solved with program modification.

This phase of district programming matches with Gutkin and Curtis's (1982) final step in the consultation process. At this stage, effectiveness of the program is monitored and earlier stages of the program development process are repeated if necessary for adjusting the program to enhance its effectiveness. Primarily, the formative evaluation occurring at this stage allows for continual fine-tuning of the program. For example, suppose program developers decided that faculty members required in-service training to facilitate the success of a prereferral process. Did the in-service occur? This small element would be part of a formative evaluation ensuring that the much discussed strategies were implemented as planned.

Summative evaluation compares the outcomes of a program against the goals and needs that prompted the program development process. Have the goals been met? Is the need being addressed? If a goal of prereferral consultation was an increase in the collegiality among teachers, an evaluation plan must contain an element to investigate whether building climates or staff interaction have improved following the introduction of the innovation.

The need for an evaluation strategy should be recognized before the program is implemented. The "whats" and "hows" of evaluation deserve attention during the program planning times. By anticipating evaluation needs, critical measurement points are not lost and necessary feedback can be gathered.

For example, to ascertain if a prereferral consultation is successful, the developers might decide to measure the following:

1. Special education referral rates for 2 years prior to program implementation and 2 years after implementation;
2. numbers of children sent to the principal's office for discipline for the year before implementation and the year after;
3. results of a school climate indicator filled out just before program implementation and after 2 years of implementation;
4. perceptions of teachers who used the prereferral consultation program as to its effectiveness in assisting them in coping with difficult classroom situations;
5. perceptions of teachers who did not use the program concerning the reasons for their lack of involvement and suggestions they might have to improve the program;
6. perceptions of the teacher assistance team members as to the effects of team membership on their professional development, their data regarding usage of the team, and observational data they collected reflecting children's change after classroom teachers implemented the team suggestions.

Just these few measurement possibilities make clear that prior to implementation decisions must be made concerning evaluation. The most important outcomes should be considered. The most easily accessible data should be used if they serve as indicators of program effectiveness. The intrusiveness of data collection should be considered. Will evaluating the program be more trouble than implementing it?

Evaluating the program asks the question "did?" Did the program implementers do as was planned? Were timelines met? Did the program reach goals that were identified? Do the constituencies involved think their needs were met? The answers to "did" questions help to monitor movement toward meeting program development and implementation concerns. Positive and negative results are useful in reconceptualizing original goals and needs. Evaluation results are also helpful for intensifying or fading program features, choosing new program strategies, and presenting information to the consumers and implementers of the program.

Although a distinction can be drawn between formative and summative evaluation, the distinction is a rather arbitrary one. All evaluative information should be formative for as long as the program continues. Evaluative data are useful only inasmuch as they improve the program implementation and/or provide information to decision makers concerning the worth of a particular approach. (This rather sweeping axiom is, by the way, why many school psychologists have become disenchanted with standard norm-referenced testing. An evaluation process that does not improve a child's program *or* evaluate the effectiveness of his or her special program is considered by many to be a waste of precious time to the psychologist. See Lentz & Shapiro, 1986, for alternatives.)

All of this evaluation information serves a formative function (Davis, 1984). The information gathered can be applied to continual fine-tuning of the program. A self-adjusting feedback loop can be established to ensure that the program is increasingly effective in serving the needs it was designed to meet. The fine-tuning can be done without disrupting the program as a whole. Sometimes, these small adjustments can be individualized to accommodate a teacher or administrator (for example) whose needs relative to the program are slightly different from those addressed by the program. Periodic larger-scale program revisions can be considered on a less frequent basis, as indicated by the initial program description (e.g., biannually at first; annually; then on an as-requested basis).

Barriers to Program Success

Although special service professionals who want to promote alternative service options for children must work at district levels (and beyond) to accomplish their goals, there are significant roadblocks to such work. Some of these barriers are to be found in the special service professionals, others in the people around them, and still others in the structure of the school district. The preimplementation segment of the collective investment model is designed specifically to circumvent such barriers to successful programming. Yet even with the most thorough preimplementation activity, roadblocks can arise.

Personal roadblocks. Courage, assertiveness, patience, persistence, vision, flexibility, and tact are only a few of the attributes needed by individuals interested in facilitating system change. Most of these skills can be learned. Change agents who recognize a personal or skill deficit can correct the problem or enlist the aid of a colleague with skills, attitudes, and knowledge that complement their own.

Those who feel most skilled in working with individuals may be hesitant to "take on" an entire system. They may need some additional training or they may need to apply to working at the district level what they already know about successfully influencing individual change. Not having done something before is not a good excuse for not doing something now.

The key personal roadblock to developing a new repertoire of service skills is a feeling of being victimized by the system. School staff who believe that "you can't beat (or even influence) city hall" find it difficult to assume responsibilities for district-level change. They may defensively label those who attempt to influence district policy as naive or idealistic. They may warn of the dangers of rocking the boat or point to other, more pressing tasks.

Roadblocks from others. Familiar patterns are often comfortable ones both for special services professionals and for their colleagues and administrators. Lerner (1985) pointed out that when individuals begin a change process, they are often met with "countermoves" from the people around them. People may intentionally or unintentionally make change difficult by labeling it as "not our job." They may identify change as too disruptive to the usual flow of events, too demanding of effort from them, too restrictive of their access to resources currently available, and so on. Such reactions from others have less to do with the content of a particular change than with the process of change itself. If these barriers continue to arise, the prospective change agent must face the fact of the system's lack of preparation for change and revert to the preimplementation activities designed to diminish these barriers.

Structure of the organization. Especially in large districts, there may be a differentiation of roles such that only a few people are expected to contribute to system-wide change. These individuals may be identified as program developers or evaluation experts. Districts are fortunate, of course, to have differentiated staff. The danger is that people who occupy specific niches may not be allowed to move into anyone else's territory.

The newest management theories promote role flexibility and active participation of staff from all levels in organizational decision making (e.g., Lewis, 1985). Nonetheless, people with ideas outside of the usual structure must be very careful to involve the right people and show appropriate concern for going through channels. This kind of strategy is aversive to many would-be change agents, but is often necessary to get needs and goals met.

Finally, there is the barrier of time. Most programs are hastily conceived. The people who will implement the program are not consulted and the universe of possible strategies for effective programming is not explored. Very little attention is given to evaluation plans. In this context, the fact that any new programs

take hold and facilitate positive changes is amazing. Often the press to generate a new idea or provide a service immediately results in many wasted hours. Poorly defined goals lead to ambiguous role definitions that promote staff insecurity and eventual disillusionment with the program.

Taking time to assess organizational readiness and implement necessary preintervention strategies, although cumbersome, leads ultimately to the most efficient and relevant programming. Allowing time for a program to show its effects is also important. Sarason (1986) has noted that educators and taxpayers alike expect results too quickly from public education. Teaching and learning are complex operations embedded in hugely complex institutions. Promising rapid changes in outcomes (e.g., test scores, dropout rates, teacher competencies) associated with longstanding processes (e.g., poverty, discrimination, teacher training institutions, school cultures) is misleading.

SUMMARY

In this chapter we have explored the issues related to influencing change at the school district level. We have proposed a model for enhancing the success of such influence. Our observation of school districts and other complex organizations leads us to believe that such influence is possible, necessary and valuable.

That's the good news. The bad news is that, enmeshed as school psychologists and other special service professionals are in school systems, it is difficult for them to imagine different ways of functioning. Often, system-level intervention is unfamiliar territory. At the same time, special services professionals in the schools often do not realize the generalizability of their training and experience with more direct or individual service. Those skills can be applied through the collective investment approach to yield an enriching influence on district policy and programming.

To conclude, we offer the following suggestions for potential agents of change in school districts:

1. Remember that there are really no individual or isolated acts in a social system. Every act has a ripple effect throughout the system. System-level consultation only formalizes that common-sense truth.

2. Establish some small goal for a policy or procedural change that you imagine will benefit the children and families you serve.

3. Practice the program development steps offered in this chapter on something small and manageable in order to gain experience for more ambitious efforts.

4. Practice understanding the needs and motivations of administrators and teachers as well as children. Empathy toward the adults in the school system reveals many innovative ideas and ways to accomplish them.

5. Keep yourself tuned in to the subtleties of district functioning. Try always to increase your insight into the ways the system is open and closed to change. Recognize your barriers and develop creative ways for getting around them.

6. Make your skills in program consultation well known to teachers, principals, and district administrators. Extra effort at the beginning will be necessary for establishing a new role. (This means that initial efforts at program development and implementation will undoubtedly be done on *your* time. Volunteer!)

7. Build constituencies. Program consultants are both facilitators and innovators. You will need contacts, people who know and trust you. You will need a positive history in the system. If you are known as a talented and reliable direct service provider, your chance to expand your role will be enhanced.

8. Be patient, but goal-directed. Waiting around for an opportunity will be ineffective. Actively searching for an opportunity and making an initial effort a big success will open up new possibilities.

REFERENCES

Apter, S. J., & Conoley, J. C. (1984). *Childhood behavior disorders and emotional disturbance.* Englewood Cliffs, NJ: Prentice-Hall.

Bardon, J. I. (1982). The psychology of school psychology. In C. R. Reynolds & T. B. Gutkin (Eds.), *The handbook of school psychology* (pp. 3-13). New York: Wiley.

Bowers, D. G., Franklin, J. L., & Pecorella, P. A. (1975). Matching problems, precursors, and interventions in OD: A systematic approach. *Journal of Applied Behavioral Science, 11*, 391-409.

Burke, J. P., & Ellison, G. C. (1985). School psychologists' participation in organizational development: Prerequisite considerations. *Professional Psychology: Research and Practice, 16*, 521-528.

Burke, W. (Ed.). (1978). *The cutting edge: Current theory and practice in organization development.* La Jolla, CA: University Associates.

Conoley, J. C. (1981). The process of change: The agent of change. In J. C. Conoley (Ed.), *Consultation in schools: Theory, research, procedures* (pp. 1-10). New York: Academic.

Conoley, J. C., & Conoley, C. W. (1982). *School consultation: A guide to practice and training.* New York: Pergamon.

Conoley, J. C., & Gutkin, T. B. (1986). Educating school psychologists for the real world. *School Psychology Review, 15*, 457-465.

Curtis, M. J., & Metz, L. W. (1986). System level intervention in a school for handicapped children. *School Psychology Review, 15*, 510-518.

Davis, B. G. (1984). How many? How much? How well? The role of program evaluation in school management. In C. A. Maher, R. J. Illback, & J. E. Zins (Eds.), *Organizational psychology in the schools: A handbook for professionals* (pp. 365-384). Springfield, IL: Charles C Thomas.

Franklin, J. (1976). Characteristics of successful and unsuccessful organization development. *Journal of Applied Behavioral Science, 12*, 471-492.

Fullan, M. (1982). *The meaning of educational change.* New York: Teachers College Press, Columbia University.

Fullan, M., Miles, M. B., & Taylor, G. (1981). Organizational development in schools: The state of the art. *Review of Educational Research, 50*, 121-183.

Gettinger, M. (Ed.). (1987). Research in effective teaching: Implications for school psychologists [Special Issue]. *Professional School Psychology, 2*(1).

Graden, J. L., Casey, A., & Bonstrom, O. (1985). Implementing a prereferral intervention system: Part II. The data. *Exceptional Children, 51*, 487-496.

Graden, J. L., Casey, A., & Christenson, S. L. (1985). Implementing a prereferral intervention system: Part I. The model. *Exceptional Children, 51,* 377-384.

Guba, E. G., & Lincoln, Y. S. (1982). The place of values in needs assessment. *Educational Evaluation and Policy Analysis, 4,* 311-320.

Gutkin, T. B., & Curtis, M. J. (1982). School-based consultation: Theory and techniques. In C. R. Reynolds & T. B. Gutkin (Eds.), *The handbook of school psychology* (pp. 796-828). New York: Wiley.

ヿutkin, T. B., Henning-Stout, M., & Piersel, W. C. (1986). Impact of school-based consultation on patterns of service delivery. Unpublished manuscript.

Havelock, R. G. (1973). *The change agent's guide to innovation in education.* Englewood Cliffs, NJ: Educational Technology Publications.

Hunter, C., & Lambert, N. (1974). Needs assessment activities in school psychology program development. *Journal of School Psychology, 12,* 130-137.

Illback, R. J., & Maher, C. A. (1984). The school psychologist as an organizational boundary role professional. *Journal of School Psychology, 22,* 63-72.

Illback, R. J., & Zins, J. E. (1984). Organizational interventions in educational settings. In C. A. Maher, R. J. Illback, & J. E. Zins (Eds.), *Organizational psychology in the schools: A handbook for professionals* (pp. 21-49). Springfield, IL: Charles C Thomas.

Lentz, F. E., Jr., & Shapiro, E. S. (1986). Functional assessment of the academic environment. *School Psychology Review, 15,* 346-357.

Lerner, H. G. (1985). *The dance of anger.* New York: Harper and Row.

Lewis, J. (1985). *Excellent organizations: How to develop and manage them using theory Z.* New York: J. L. Wilkerson.

Maher, C. A., Illback, R. J., & Zins, J. E. (1984). Applying organizational psychology in schools: Perspectives and framework. In C. A. Maher, R. J. Illback, & J. E. Zins (Eds.), *Organizational psychology in the schools: A handbook for professionals* (pp. 5-20). Springfield, IL: Charles C Thomas.

Martin, R. P. (1978). Expert and referent power: A framework for understanding and maximizing consultation effectiveness. *Journal of School Psychology, 16,* 49-55.

Neigher, W. D., & Fishman, D. B. (1984). Linking schools to community and government: Strategies for collaboration. In C. A. Maher, R. J. Illback, & J. E. Zins (Eds.), *Organizational psychology in the schools: A handbook for professionals* (pp. 422-453). Springfield, IL: Charles C Thomas.

Nickens, J., Purga III, A., & Noriega, P. (1980). *Research methods for needs assessment.* University Press of America.

Oppenheim, A. N. (1966). *Questionnaire design and attitude measurement.* New York: Basic Books.

Parsons, R. D., & Meyers, J. (1984). *Developing consultation skills.* San Francisco: Jossey-Bass.

Payne, S. L. (1951). *The art of asking questions.* Princeton, NJ: Princeton University Press.

Pipes, R. B. (1981). Consulting in organizations: The entry problem. In J. C. Conoley (Ed.), *Consultation in schools: Theory, research, procedures* (pp. 11-34). New York: Academic.

Raffaniello, E. M. (1981). Competent consultation: The collaborative approach. In M. J. Curtis & J. E. Zins (Eds.), *The theory and practice of school consultation* (pp. 44-54). Springfield, IL: Charles C Thomas.

Sarason, S. B. (1982). *The culture of the school and the problem of change* (2nd ed.). Boston: Allyn and Bacon.

Sarason, S. B. (1986, August). *Time, perspective, and educational change.* Paper presented at the annual meeting of the American Psychological Association, Washington, DC.

Schein, E. (1969). *Process consultation: Its role in organizational development.* Reading, MA: Addison-Wesley.

Schmuck, R. A. (1982). Organization development in the schools. In C. R. Reynolds & T. B. Gutkin (Eds.), *The handbook of school psychology* (pp. 829-857). New York: Wiley.

Schmuck, R. A., & Runkel, R. J. (1985). *The handbook of organization development in schools* (3rd ed.). Palo Alto, CA: Mayfield.

Watzlawick, P., Weakland, J., & Fisch, R. (1974). *Change: Principles of problem formation and problem resolution.* New York: W. W. Norton.

Wenger, R. D. (1986). A longitudinal study of indirect service case. *School Psychology Review, 15,* 500-509.

Ysseldyke, J., & Christenson, S. (1986). *The Instructional Environment Scale.* Austin, TX: Pro-Ed.

24

Programmatic Change Strategies At the Building Level

Louis J. Kruger
Tufts University

All too often people attempt to change what they cannot and fail to try to change what they can. One typical exercise in frustration is to attempt to correct a "personality defect" of a colleague; highly persistent and well-intentioned efforts to alter someone's personality can fail miserably when that person is unmotivated to change. The other type of mistake, failure to pursue change when it is indeed possible, often occurs when the problem involves groups or organizations. Because group problems by definition involve many individuals, it might seem plausible that their resolution is beyond the control of the school psychologist. This assumption is erroneous and anachronistic. Programmatic change can and does occur in schools. Moreover, the school psychologist can be the primary architect of these changes. The term *program*, as used here, refers to a system of staff, materials, and procedures intended to improve or resolve a problem that a group of students have in common.

The use of the word *architect* to describe the school psychologist as a change agent is not incidental. As defined in at least one dictionary, an architect is one who "plans and achieves a difficult objective." Though programmatic change is possible, it is nonetheless not an easy task. It requires careful planning, a team approach, and the availability of resources (e.g., appropriate materials). Much like an architect, a school psychologist needs a blueprint for action to expedite the planning and implementation of the program. Just as an executive of a large corporation would be foolhardy to allow an architect to begin construction of an office building without a clear and logical blueprint, so too would a school administrator be ill-advised to allow programmatic change to occur without a written program design.

To continue the analogy, both the school psychologist and architect need to creatively blend concerns about practicality and utility with scientific knowledge. The architect, for instance, needs to be aware that more space allocated for one office may entail less space for other rooms on the same floor. Similarly, a school psychologist should be aware that proposing that school staff be involved in activities related to the new program may imply less time for their other activities. Just as an architect would be incautious to spend hundreds of thousands of dollars on an experimental procedure for supporting tons of weight that lacked scientific grounding, so too would a school psychologist be unwise to propose a program for students that lacked empirical support in the professional literature.

Finally, the extent to which both the architect and school psychologist are involved in creative endeavors must not be underestimated. Programs described in journals or books should not be merely adopted "as is" by a school. All schools in their overall contexts are unique, and sometimes the variations make a difference in how change should occur in a school. The guidelines for bringing about programmatic change that are provided in this chapter can do no more than provide a general framework for implementation. There is no algorithm for the specific manner in which program components should be combined.

ARGUMENTS FOR PROGRAMMATIC CHANGE AT THE BUILDING LEVEL

One argument for programmatic change stems from the limitations of treating all problems as isolated entities. For example, a school psychologist can rush to assist a handicapped student become more socially integrated with peers only to learn that several handicapped students in other classrooms are confronted with the same type of problem. Among other options, the school psychologist can (a) remain highly involved with the first student and put the other students on a waiting list, (b) approach each student as an individual case and become concurrently involved with all of them, or (c) explore alternative perspectives and begin planning a group program that might not only help the presently handicapped students become more socially integrated, but also help future students with this problem. The first option, high involvement with only one student, has the obvious disadvantage, albeit temporary, of not attending to the needs of the other students experiencing similar problems. The second option, attempting to simultaneously implement individualized interventions, might be overly ambitious and impractical. In contrast, the group program alternative can have at least three advantages. It can be time-efficient. For example, a program . that has similar goals (e.g., greeting one's peers in socially acceptable ways) and activities (e.g., social skills training) for each student can help conserve the time of service providers. The group program also can be viewed as a preventive approach to school problems. After a social integration program has been developed, it can be implemented at the beginning of each school year prior to the possible occurrence of difficulties between handicapped and nonhandicapped peers.

Finally, the perennial implementation of such a program can allow for periodic evaluations and modifications so that the program can be improved on a routine basis. However, there are limitations to this programmatic approach. Though individual problems are often group problems as well, this is not always the case. At times, the idiosyncratic or acute nature of a student's problem demands a primarily individualized approach.

A second reason why school psychologists at the present time should seriously consider being involved in programmatic change is that opportunities for such change may be increasing. Reports critiquing the current state of affairs in public schools have recently appeared (e.g., National Commission on Excellence in Education, 1983). These reports may help to establish a climate of greater receptivity to programmatic change. A third factor possibly contributing to the increased opportunities for school psychologists to engage in programmatic change is the higher visibility such a role has in the school psychology literature. For example, two of the most prominent school psychology texts in the last several years, *The Handbook of School Psychology* (Reynolds & Gutkin, 1982) and *Best Practices in School Psychology* (Thomas & Grimes, 1985) both include chapters concerning building level change. Furthermore, it appears that practicing school psychologists are also beginning to view programmatic change as part of their role. For example, the results of a recent survey of school psychologists (Hartshorne & Johnson, 1985) indicated that program development and consultation with administrators ranked in the lower half of the top ten of actual and preferred functions. Nonetheless, other school personnel may not share the school psychologists' perception that programmatic change is an important aspect of the school psychologist's role. Indeed, school psychologists may need to negotiate with school personnel in order to be perceived as legitimate agents of programmatic change. In this regard, Robinson, Cameron, and Raethal (1985) presented a case study of the process by which two school psychologists renegotiated their roles to include provision of indirect services, such as consultation and program development. The authors argued that systematic application of a consultative problem-solving model enhanced their assumption of their new roles. Activities relevant to this model were (a) development of a contract that delineated goals to be achieved by the program(s), as well as the responsibilities of school personnel involved with the program(s); (b) data-gathering for the purpose of clarifying the problem(s) to be resolved; (c) careful diagnosis of the nature and scope of the problem(s) to be addressed; and (d) providing school personnel with feedback about the information obtained from the data-gathering and diagnostic activities.

PREREQUISITE ATTITUDES, KNOWLEDGE, AND SKILLS FOR THE SCHOOL PSYCHOLOGIST AS CHANGE AGENT

Attitudes

Though conditions for programmatic change may be improving, it is nonetheless important for the school psychologist to be equipped with appropriate attitudes, knowledge, and skills before embarking on a change effort. Three specific attitudes may be particularly important: (a) a strong sense of self-efficacy, (b) positive but realistic expectations for change, and (c) a high degree of commitment to the change effort.

Self-efficacy has been defined as a person's belief that important outcomes will be attained by means of personal effort (Bandura, 1977). Self-efficacy of school personnel had been found to be an important variable in predicting whether programmatic change will persist over time (Berman & McLaughlin, 1978). Germane to the present discussion is the distinction between performance self-efficacy and organizational self-efficacy (Fuller, Wood, Rapoport, & Dornbusch, 1982). Whereas performance self-efficacy is the extent to which a person expects to directly influence important outcomes relative to his/her own work duties (e.g.,

increased teacher satisfaction with psychological reports), organizational self-efficacy denotes the degree to which a person perceives that he/she can indirectly produce important organizational outcomes (e.g., higher school attendance rates) by influencing others. Attaining a high degree of organizational self-efficacy may be difficult in schools where there is little routine contact among professionals from different disciplines. Nevertheless, both types of self-efficacy are important to the school psychologist contemplating programmatic change. To be perceived as a credible initiator of programmatic change, it is important that other school personnel perceive the school psychologist as having a strong sense of performance self-efficacy. In addition, to successfully implement a group program the school psychologist must be able to influence the actions of others. Perceiving oneself as being able to influence others may be an important antecedent to actually influencing them.

Another attitude needed in initiating programmatic change is *positive but realistic expectations for success*. Moreover, it is critical that the school psychologist communicate these expectations to the others involved. Building positive expectations with staff has been found to be related to the successful implementation of programs (e.g., Maher, 1984). But expectations should also be realistic in regard to what can be accomplished. Weick (1984) has argued that if problems are conceived as too massive, dysfunctionally high levels of arousal occur and the problems defy rational approaches to resolution. In order to avoid this difficulty, Weick maintains we should define problems on a smaller scale and initially be satisfied with attaining subgoals. A subgoal is an outcome of moderate importance. Attaining a series of subgoals can, if appropriately conceived, "add up to" a large accomplishment. For example, as an initial step to introducing a consultation approach to improving school discipline, a school psychologist might first begin to spend less time directly counseling students and more time discussing discipline problems with teachers. This change, coupled with subsequent efforts, might initiate a long-term process of introducing the consultation approach.

The third important attitude to possess is a high degree of *commitment to the change effort*, although this does not mean that a certain degree of adaptability is not necessary. Not all obstacles can be anticipated and planned for. Therefore, the school psychologist, or any change agent, must be able to persevere in the face of setbacks and resistance. One must be able to distinguish temporary setbacks from more serious obstacles that pose a threat to the overall change effort. In addition, one must be able to discern when perseverance is not generating the anticipated results. For example, an attempt to implement a token economy in a school's three self-contained classrooms might be repeatedly blocked by a school principal who steadfastly believes that children should not be "bribed by rewards" in order to learn, all attempts to dissuade the principal from this belief having failed. At this point the school psychologist must decide whether the cost of persevering (e.g., alienating the principal) is becoming prohibitively high. The comedian W. C. Fields very aptly summarized the relationship between perseverance and efficient use of time and effort: "If you at first don't succeed try, try again. If after that you still don't succeed, forget it. Don't make a big fool of yourself." Thibaut and Kelly's (1959) exchange theory provides one framework for determining the appropriate extent of commitment to a change effort. For these authors, each action has a reward-cost value (outcome) attached to it. These outcomes are evaluated against two types of standards: a comparison level (CL) and a comparison level for alternatives (CL-ALT). A CL reflects the outcomes a person believes he/she deserves. A CL-ALT involves comparing current outcomes for specified actions (e.g., program development actions) with outcomes associated with alternative actions (e.g., making preplacement evaluations). According to this framework, the staff with the highest degree of commitment to the change effort will be those who perceive the anticipated outcomes of program development and implementation as (a) higher than or equal in value to those outcomes they deserve (CL), and (b) higher in value than outcomes that might be achieved through nonprogram activities (CL-ALT). In short, if a staff person believes that time (a) would not be efficiently spent on program activities, and (b) would be efficiently spent on nonprogram activities, that person's commitment to the program will be low.

Knowledge of School as an Organization

In addition to the aforementioned attitudes, knowledge of the school as an organization is critical for the change agent. First, it is important for the school psychologist to be aware of the *school's ongoing routines.* Since any programmatic change in a school involves adding, deleting, or adapting current programmatic regularities (Sarason, 1982), foreknowledge about what regularities might be affected, and to what extent, are prerequisite to implementation. For a program to be successfully implemented and maintained over time, it is essential that it be compatible with existing routines, some of which are naturally more important than others. For example, given the current "back to basics" movement in education, a drug education program that encroaches upon student time spent on the 3 Rs might be viewed less favorably than one that can be integrated into the health education curriculum. In this example, one type of program is viewed as more accommodating than others to a new project.

Another organizational factor to consider when designing a group program is *how closely the school's personnel and departments work with each other.* Weick (1976) has suggested that schools are loosely coupled systems, that is, the degree of interdependence among the school's personnel and departments is relatively weak. For instance, a school psychologist and guidance counselor may have offices in the same building, but the effects of their duties on each other, as well as their collaboration, may be minimal. In loosely coupled schools it may be of relatively little importance to consider the impact the program might have on nonprogram staff, but in schools characterized by a high degree of interdependence, it might be pivotal. Weick (1976) speculated that a loosely coupled school may be especially well suited to small, localized change efforts (e.g., a program tailored to the needs of students in one particular classroom), whereas a more tightly coupled school may provide opportunities for schoolwide program changes.

The school's *degree of interdependence with the external environment* also should be considered prior to initiation of change. In some schools, for instance, there are mechanisms for parents' review and approval of new program proposals. In these schools, it is imperative for the school psychologist or other program development staff to discuss with the parents the purpose, nature, and scope of a proposed program.

The *size of the school* with respect to the number of staff and students is another organizational factor to be aware of before undertaking a change effort. In schools with a small staff and student body, there is (a) greater pressure for staff to take on more and diverse roles, (b) greater effort required by each staff member, (c) less evaluation of differences among staff, and (d) a greater sense of functional importance of each to the organization (Barker, 1978). The effects of large schools are the converse of those delineated for small schools. These consequences present both problems and opportunities for programmatic change in small and large schools. In small schools, for example, though staff may tend to have a greater sense of self-efficacy, they may be reluctant to become involved in a new program because of the diverse demands of their current role. Conversely, in large schools, though staff may not be as likely to feel overtaxed by diverse role demands, they may be less optimistic about the extent to which they can affect change in the organization.

Additionally, the school psychologist as change agent should be aware that *schools are slow to embrace innovations.* Sarason (1982) has maintained that the strongest pressure for change in schools has originated from forces outside the school, such as Public Law 94-142. Also, most schools have no formal mechanism for altering existing programmatic regularities. To meet this limitation a mechanism such as the quality circle might be introduced. The quality circle is made up of a small group of workers who are trained in, and employ a variant of, the generic problem-solving process. Quality circles emphasize voluntary participation, use structured data collection procedures, and meet routinely to resolve work-related problems. A quality circle for school psychologists, for instance, might address the problem of how they can devote more time to counseling services. However, despite the promise of the quality circle for resolving work-related problems (see, e.g., Wood, Hull, & Azumi, 1983) few schools have adopted it or similar mechanisms for altering existing regularities. Thus, new programs will seldom be implemented rapidly. Schools' halting moves to implement new programs suggest that the school psychologist who attempts to initiate change should maintain a long-term relationship to the target school (not to mention considerable patience!).

Knowledge of the Professional Literature

In addition to knowing the school as an organization, the school psychologist bent on introducing change should be familiar with the professional literature in regard to the major components of any proposed program. If the use of cooperative learning groups is being proposed for the purpose of promoting increased social integration of minority students in the classroom, the school psychologist should be aware of (a) the extent of empirical support for using cooperative learning groups for that purpose, (b) possible negative effects of such an intervention, (c) limitations of research findings with respect to the intervention, (d) theoretical assumptions implicit in using such an intervention, and (e) guidelines for implementing cooperative learning groups.

However, practitioners often are reluctant to review professional literature for this information. A recent survey of psychotherapists (Morrow-Bradley & Elliot, 1986) indicated that only 10% of those surveyed found theoretical or practical literature the most useful way to educate themselves about their work, and only 4% believed that reading research was the best means of educating themselves. Respondents were critical of research that ignored the complexities of the setting within which practice occurs. A parallel problem has been reported with respect to teachers' failure to make use of educational research (Zahorik, 1984). Regardless of whatever difficulties may be attendant to reviewing and applying the professional literature to practice, school psychologists should ground their change efforts in the professional literature in order to avoid common pitfalls and wasting time reinventing the wheel. Though professional experience and advice from colleagues can be important sources of knowledge, program development and implementation are complex tasks and a familiarity with the relevant published literature can only enhance school psychologists' competence as change agents.

Planning Skills

Development and implementation of group programs involve judicious management of available resources, including financial and human resources and physical settings, techniques and methods, and materials. Judicious allocation of these resources requires planning. And an essential, but often overlooked planning skill is the *ability to clarify program-related problems*. These problems are highly complex and demand that the school psychologist take an active role in defining their nature and scope. Typically, there is a wide range of possibly appropriate approaches for understanding and improving service delivery, and new approaches are continually being identified. Moreover, there are no consensually recognized criteria for choosing among these approaches. For example, the problem of physical violence in a school conceivably could be addressed by a number of different (and possibly overlapping) approaches, including anger-control training, a comprehensive system of reinforcers and punishments, and social problem-solving training. When many types of programs can seemingly address the same problem, it becomes exceedingly important to clarify the problem in a systematic manner, and not to make the mistake of developing an inappropriate formulation of the problem. According to Dunn, Mitroff, and Deutsch (1981), one possible safeguard against inappropriate formulation of problems is taking multiple perspectives. An example might help elucidate this point: After comparing the percentage of her school's students who are in special education with those of similar schools in the same state, a principal declares to the school psychologist, "Too many of our students are in special education. See what you can do about it." Several different problem-solving perspectives are possible. The school psychologist might want to clarify (a) what prereferral interventions (if any) are used in the school, (b) what decision-making criteria are used in admitting students to and releasing students from special education, and (c) what procedures or approaches are used to mainstream special education students into regular education classes. There are, of course, other possible perspectives applicable to the problem. Nonetheless, school psychologists should not attempt to develop service delivery programs without first clarifying whether in fact they face a service delivery problem and if so, what kind of service delivery problem. How the problem is defined has implications for program development. For example, if the aforementioned principal's complaint about too many special education students is related to poorly defined admittance criteria, the solution might be to define the criteria more clearly and not directly intervene with students.

Another important planning skill is the ability to write in a clear, succinct, and jargon-free manner about proposed programs. School psychologists, with their training and practice in psychological report writing, can be important contributors to documents delineating the essential components of a proposed program. The importance of putting plans in writing cannot be overstated. A well-written plan provides a focal point for discussion and helps insure that program staff and other interested parties have a common understanding of the proposal. Moreover, a well-written plan can be a means of persuading school administrators that your proposed program should be seriously considered for implementation. A multiple plan should be developed, including elements for (a) training staff, (b) designing the program, (c) facilitating implementation, and (d) evaluating the program. For example, a written design for a program should specify the goals of the program, the group of students to receive services, what methods or techniques will be used, and when the program activities will occur. The outline below was used to develop an evaluation plan for an enrichment program in an inner city middle school. (This outline does not reflect the entire range of areas that could be evaluated with respect to the program.)

1.0 Description of the enrichment program to be evaluated — including information about the students, the educational context, and the purpose and objectives of the program.

2.0 Purpose and goals of the evaluation plan — in regard to the enrichment program, the program's coordinator particularly wanted information about the manner in which specific elements of the program were being implemented, as well as satisfaction of parents and others with the program.

3.0 Data to be collected about the program's implementation.
   3.1 Special projects and field trips — including dates, sites, durations, frequencies, and content associated with these activities.
   3.2 Extent to which different goals were emphasized — as reflected in time spent on different types of instructional content.
   3.3 Staff input about program's design — who gave input, how frequently, and how input was given.

4.0 Data to be collected about people's reaction to program.
   4.1 Reactions of program and nonprogram staff to various program elements.
   4.2 Reactions of program's students to various program elements.
   4.3 Reactions of parents to various program elements.

5.0 Resources needed for collecting evaluation data.
   5.1 Human — for example, program coordinator and staff.
   5.2 Time — instrument development, recording implementation data, collecting data about people's reactions, and summarizing data.
   5.3 Data collection instruments — recording logs for implementation data and questionnaires for reaction data.
   5.4 Physical resources — for example, paper and pencils.
   5.5 Financial — for example, photocopying costs.

6.0 Guidelines for collecting data — who is responsible for collecting different types of data, when data collection activities will occur, and what specific types of data will be collected.

7.0 Guidelines for summarizing data.
   7.1 When data summarization will occur and who will summarize data.
   7.2 What types of summarization procedures will be used — frequency counts, means, etc.

8.0 Guidelines for making judgments about the program.
   8.1 When judgments will be made and who will make them.
   8.2 Criteria for determining problematic program elements — for example, a mean rating of 3.5 (on 1-7 scale, where 7 = *extremely satisfied* and 1 = *not at all satisfied*) or lower from parents in response to a question about their satisfaction with their contact with program staff.

9.0 Disseminating data evaluation results.
   9.1 In what ways results will be communicated — for example, written and oral reports.
   9.2 Who will receive results — parents, program staff, school administrator, etc.

10.0 Routine assessment of the evaluation plan — specific aspects to be assessed, for example, staff time devoted to evaluation activities.

11.0 Training that staff needs in order to carry out evaluation activities.

12.0 Secure storage of evaluation data.

Another important planning skill is *ability to adapt the initial program plan.* Programs are never perfectly designed. In this regard, soliciting feedback from program staff can help school psychologists successfully modify their programs to mesh with contextual realities. In a program for which the author was a consultant, each participating teacher was assigned the responsibility of "mentoring" one high school student, who was at risk of failing one or more courses. However, after implementation, teachers began to feel overwhelmed by this responsibility. As a result, the program was modified so that two teachers were assigned the task of mentoring one student. These teacher dyads seemed to function as an effective support mechanism for the participating teachers. In this example, adapting the mentoring aspect of the program seemed essential to reducing the stress experienced by the teachers.

Enriching tasks in order to make them more satisfying or intrinsically meaningful to program staff can also be considered part of planning. Three means of enriching tasks are (a) selecting the "right task" for the "right individual," (b) providing a meaningful rationale for why certain tasks need to be performed, and (c) using feedback from staff to redesign tasks. An example of selecting the right task for the right individual is asking a person who has excellent interpersonal skills to help resolve program-related interpersonal problems. One strategy that can help make tasks more intrinsically meaningful to staff is to provide them with well-thought-out rationales for why these tasks must be accomplished. Using feedback from staff not only can result in tasks that are more consistent with the program's goals, but also can communicate to staff that their feedback and ideas are valued by others.

Interpersonal Influence Skills

It is also important for the school psychologist contemplating programmatic change to be able to influence others to perform up to potential. One way to motivate others is to provide, or arrange to provide, *appropriate reinforcement* for program staff. The school psychologist as program manager must be aware that the reinforcement procedure employed should be tailored to the particular staff person. The same procedure may function as a positive reinforcer for one person, and function as punishment for another person. For example, in an attempt to positively reinforce two program staff members' contributions, a school psychologist publicly praises their efforts. One of them is pleased with this public recognition and subsequently is further motivated to perform ably; the other is embarrassed, and subsequently decreases productivity to avoid future public attention. Thus, the praise functioned as positive reinforcement for the first staff member, but as punishment for the other.

Another method of improving staff's performance is through *performance feedback.* Simply put, performance feedback is the provision of information about past performance. Positive feedback, that is, information about past successes, is recalled more accurately than negative feedback, and relatively frequent feedback (e.g., weekly) is more likely to have a positive impact on future performance than relatively infrequent feedback (e.g., bimonthly) (Ilgen, Fisher, & Taylor, 1979). Furthermore, it appears that performance feedback has relatively specific effects (Frederiksen, Richter, Johnson, & Solomon, 1982). In other words, the beneficial effects of feedback on one task behavior might not generalize to other tasks. For example, informing a staff person that he/she appropriately implemented a training workshop for teachers in classroom behavior management does not necessarily mean that this positive feedback will improve that person's motivation to regularly attend staff meetings.

Oftentimes, performance feedback is used in conjunction with goal setting, that is, *setting goals for work-related activities* assigned to a particular staff person. A recent meta-analytic study of goal setting (Tubbs, 1986) suggested support for the effectiveness of the following goal setting practices: (a) setting specific goals as opposed to vague goals or no goals, (b) having staff participate in setting their own goals, and (c) providing performance feedback in tandem with goal setting. Program responsibilities, for instance, might involve a staff person in teaching a social problem-solving curriculum to elementary students. In this case, one specific performance goal collaboratively set by the staff person and school psychologist might be implementation of the curriculum activities in their appropriate sequence during 95% or more of social problem-solving instructional periods. In addition to the goal setting, the school psychologist can provide the instructor with periodic feedback about the extent to which he/she is attaining the goal.

Establishing rapport can be another important way to influence program staff positively. Of the several bases of social power identified by French and Raven (1959), referent power most closely approximates establishing rapport as a means of motivating others. Referent power is used when attempts to influence others are based on the interpersonal relationship or mutual identification among staff. Some teachers are wary of the advice of school psychologists because they believe the school psychologist does not appreciate or understand the daily demands of being a teacher. Establishing rapport with teachers can help the school psychologist effectively communicate the message that their job demands are understood and appreciated. The school psychologist can attempt to influence staff members who are extremely mistrustful of school psychologists by enlisting the support of other staff who have a good rapport with the mistrustful ones. This type of influence process is delineated in Figure 1. In this illustration, the school psychologist is attempting to influence teacher B (who is mistrustful of the school psychologist) through the actions of teacher A (who has a good rapport with

both the school psychologist and teacher B).

The school psychologist also should be adept at *resolving interpersonal conflicts.* Interpersonal conflicts can occur among program staff, or between program staff and other school personnel. If not resolved, these conflicts can dramatically impair staff members' ability to work with each other constructively. Maher (1985) had identified several activities that might reduce interpersonal conflict. These activities include (a) obtaining consensus about the nature of the conflict from disputants, (b) requesting from disputants alternative solutions to conflict, (c) analyzing possible negative and positive consequences of each solution, (d) selecting the best solution and assessing disputants' satisfaction with the solution selected, (e) developing a written conflict solution plan and obtaining a consensus on a plan of action, and (f) evaluating success of conflict solution plan.

Finally, in their capacity as change agents, school psychologists should not be reluctant to exercise the appropriate level of authority in attempting to *provide direction for staff.* If the school psychologist is too passive, important program development and implementation time lines might not be adhered to. In this regard, the school psychologist should be aware of four E's that relate to directing staff: (a) Examine what tasks must be accomplished; (b) Engage the program staff's attention; (c) Explicit communication is required about roles, responsibilities, and relationships; and (d) Expectations for performance are set by means of goal setting. In regard to examining what tasks must be accomplished, it is important that the selected tasks be attractive to staff and have a high likelihood of facilitating attainment of program goals. To engage the staff's attention, formal mechanisms should be developed so that the program staff can discuss program issues. For example, the author was involved in one project in which a steering committee of program members met on a weekly basis to discuss

FIGURE 1

FIGURE 1

A school psychologist attempts to influence Staff Person B through Staff Person A. (Arrows indicate intended direction of influence process. "+" denotes relationship characterized by rapport; "–" denotes relationship characterized by mistrust.)

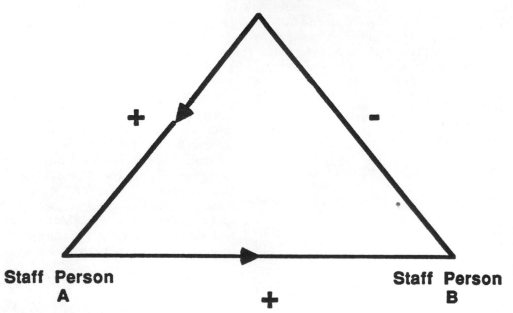

School Psychologist

Staff Person A

Staff Person B

short-term goals and implementation problems. Explicit communication about roles, responsibilities, and relationships can help reduce interpersonal conflicts and work-related stress by providing clear work guidelines for staff. Setting expectations for performance has been discussed above in the context of goal-setting.

THE PARTICIPATION APPROACH TO PROGRAMMATIC CHANGE

The participation approach assumes that the most ethical and efficacious manner to carry out a change program is to involve a group of people who can collaborate as a team in order to systematically plan and evaluate programmatic solutions. Miles's (1965) distinction between human relations and human resources approaches to participation can help clarify the meaning of participation. A human relations approach stresses participation of group members only for the purpose of gaining their cooperation; members are not viewed as being capable of making substantive contributions to the

problem-solving process. In contrast, th human resource approach emphasizes that the members have something valuable to add to the problem-solving process In the latter approach, participation is not "illusory" but actually involves the members as important problem-solving and informational resources. In this chapter, the participation approach to programmatic change refers to the more optimistic, human resource perspective of what staff can contribute to important decisions.

Potential Advantages of the Participation Approach

If staff collaborate in developing the program, they will have a greater sense of ownership of it. This sense of ownership increases the likelihood that the program will be implemented as planned and maintained over time. In this regard, staff (teacher) participation in project decision-making was found to be an important strategy in the success of federally funded school programs (Berman & McLaughlin,

1978). The participation approach can also facilitate group problem solving of service delivery problems. In solving such complex problems, groups tend to be better than individuals working alone (Shaw, 1981). Hypotheses advanced to explain the superiority of group problem solving include (a) the greater interest in the task stimulated by group membership, (b) the summative effect of individual contributions, (c) the group rejection of poorly conceived solutions, and (d) the greater amount of information available in the group context. Acknowledgment of this superiority frequently occurs at meetings where the human resources approach to participation is employed. The author, for example, has often heard comments from team leaders such as, "That's something (a team member's point) that didn't occur to me. I'm glad we got together to discuss this issue."

Division of labor is another potential advantage of the participation approach. Tasks can be divided among participants so as to capitalize on each individual's unique expertise and experience. School social workers, for example, can use their rapport with parents to lead discussion groups with parents about proposed programs. Another possible strength of the participation approach is that it can serve, especially in loosely coupled schools, to bring together school personnel, who typically do not work with one another into collaboration, from which they further develop their professional knowledge and skill by observing and learning from each other. Finally, the participation approach to programmatic change, consistent with values of the larger democratic society, can provide a vehicle for democratic decision making in the change process.

Factors to Consider When Initiating the Participation Approach

One factor to consider when initiating a participation approach to planned change is the *degree of emphasis on task issues*. On the basis of his research with groups, Bales (1958) has argued that an effective group attains a quasi-equilli-brium between task issues and group maintenance issues. Group maintenance involves (a) communicating praise and acceptance to other members, (b) mediating interpersonal conflicts, (c) attempting to reduce tension within individuals and the group, and (d) devising compromise decisions that might be acceptable to all group members. Oftentimes work groups emphasize task issues to the near exclusion of maintenance ones, thus precipitating intrapersonal or interpersonal obstacles to task accomplishment. As a general rule of thumb, it is advisable to reserve a portion of group meeting time (but not the lion's share) to discuss maintenance issues. It has been the author's inclination to discuss maintenance issues at the beginning of meetings. The assumption is that if maintenance issues can be identified and resolved at the beginning of the meeting, then they will be less likely to interfere with the task-oriented discussion. However, two caveats should be mentioned about this process. First, the leader needs to be able to accurately assess what maintenance issues should be discussed with the entire group, and which ones should only be discussed privately with one or two members. Second, the leader has to be able to assess when the maintenance discussion is generating diminishing returns and attention should shift to task issues.

Another factor to consider when implementing the participation approach to programmatic change is the *phases of a group's development*. Just as knowledge of developmental norms for children can be used as a guide for assessing delayed or deviant development, so can knowledge of the benchmarks of group development be used to assess faulty group development. On the basis of their review of the research, Tuckman and Jensen (1977) have posited a five-stage model of group development. Although it may be useful to think of these stages as occurring sequentially, they often overlap in time and are recycled throughout a group's life.

1. Forming. Initially, group members must resolve issues about coming together and forming a cohesive unit. During this

stage, members have an opportunity to get to know one another before beginning task activities. Though some members may become impatient and immediately want to begin work on a task, the forming stage is an opportunity for the leader to build a cohesive team. The leader wants to prevent members from remaining on the periphery of the group and encourage all members to actively participate.

2. Storming. This stage involves the development of subgroups that precipitate conflict over how tasks should be accomplished. During this stage, members may jockey for power within the group. Scapegoating of members, in particular scapegoating of the leader, may occur. It is important that leaders not personalize these reactions to their authority. Moreover, leaders should try to resolve authority issues during this time so that they don't continue to hamper the group's work activities.

3. Norming. After the group has resolved its major conflicts, norms and roles for appropriate member behavior are developed. Consistent with the aforementioned participation approach is collaboration by the entire membership in the development of group norms. If members perceive that they have had an important part in determining the norms and roles, they are more likely to conform to them. The leader should avoid imposing norms on members, because members may develop negative feelings about norms and only conform to them when closely supervised.

4. Performing. During this stage, the group is highly involved in performing tasks and attaining work-related goals. The work of this stage represents the group's raison d'etre. Clearly, the leader should want the group to spend the bulk of its time in this stage. If the leader has been successful in navigating the group through the first three stages, the group can have a productive and lengthy performing stage.

5. Adjourning. During this final stage, group members begin to withdraw from work tasks and say good-bye to each other. This is an easy stage to ignore, because at this time the group has finished most,

if not all of its work. It is tempting to approach this stage in a laissez-faire manner and let members take leave of each other in whatever way they please. However, if the leader approaches this stage in such a manner, there is the risk that members may feel that their efforts were unappreciated. Therefore, the leader should structure times for providing feedback to members and for members to withdraw from the association in a constructive way.

An understanding of Tuckman and Jensen's model might be especially helpful to the novice group leader, who might, for example, be less likely to panic when a moderate amount of interpersonal conflict occurs during the storming stage.

Another factor to consider in the participation approach is the *extent to which team members participate.* Though it is not clear to what extent disproportionate participation occurs on teams involved in programmatic change, it has been found to be a problem on multidisciplinary preplacement evaluation teams. In particular, the research (e.g., Trailor, 1982) points to higher participation by school psychologists and relatively lower participation by classroom teachers. Therefore, the school psychologist should be careful not to overparticipate during meetings, while encouraging classroom teachers to take an active role. Assessing and addressing members' concerns can help resolve participation problems. For example, the author once led a work team on which one of the members initially underparticipated and arrived at meetings late. Individual conversations between the leader and this member revealed that he disagreed with some of the program's procedures. Nonetheless, he agreed to try to implement these procedures for a trial period. Fortunately, during this trial time, he became sufficiently convinced of the utility of the procedures that he became a more active team member.

"Groupthink" (Janis, 1982) is another possible factor to be aware of in a team endeavor. Groupthink results from strong pressures toward uniformity in thinking that severely limit the range of decision-making options that a group considers. Janis presents several interesting historical examples of groupthink and their unfortunate consequences. One of Janis's arguments is that group cohesiveness, by itself, is neither good or bad. Rather, cohesiveness without the members' critical reflection about the group's process, and in particular about the decision-making process, can result in poor decisions. One of the most common examples of groupthink occurs when members refuse to tactfully challenge a group leader's suggestions, even when the suggestions strike the members as counterintuitive. One possible safeguard against groupthink is to gain consensus on using a structured decision-making procedure (one such procedure, the nominal group technique, is presented later in this chapter).

DEVELOPING AND IMPLEMENTING A SERVICE PROGRAM FOR STUDENTS

The process of developing and implementing a program in a school can be delineated through responses to the following interrelated questions: Is there a need for programmatic change? Should programmatic change be attempted? What specific characteristics of the school might impede or support programmatic change? How can a school's readiness for change be improved? How can an appropriate program be selected? How can implementation be promoted?

Is There a Need for Programmatic Change?

Though this may seem to be an obvious question, it is an important one to address. School psychologists are not exempt from impulses to unwittingly jump on bandwagons. Only problems that affect one or more groups of students can be appropriately addressed by a (group) intervention program; problems that are idiosyncratic to a particular student or staff member do not require systems level intervention.

An important safeguard against developing a program for which there is no need is to systematically design and implement a needs assessment. As Bell, Nguyen, Warheit, & Buhl (1978) noted, several generic questions should be addressed in the needs assessment: (a) What do people want to know about the problem? (b) What data should be gathered? (c) Where (or from whom) can the data be collected? (d) What data collection methods should be used? (e) How will the data be analyzed? (f) What are the most appropriate means for presenting the data? (g) How can the findings be used to inform programmatic decision-making?

A case example might help elucidate how these questions might be used in a needs assessment. Because of the brevity of the example, the complexity of the issues involved cannot be fully discussed (for a more detailed discussion about conducting needs assessments, see Maher & Bennett, 1984). The author wanted to design a program to address the apparent problem of verbal aggression between students at a middle school. However, the first step was to determine whether relevant others, especially school personnel, were concerned about the verbal aggression. From interviews with staff and students, it was determined that people did believe verbal aggression was a serious problem. Next, a questionnaire was developed and disseminated to staff to assess the nature and scope of the problem across different school settings. (Though observation can be considered a more direct method of assessing verbal aggression, staff resistance to direct observation and time constraints precluded its use.) Because data were to be presented to school personnel, who had varying degrees of familiarity with statistics, data analysis procedures focused on reporting means and frequency counts. The findings were presented at a monthly staff meeting, and were used to justify the designing of a new counseling program at the school.

Should Programmatic Change Be Attempted?

Though a need for change may exist, the prospects for successfully implementing change vary along a continuum from very good to very poor, in as much as some schools are much more receptive to change than others. Therefore, a fundamental question should be: Should change be attempted in this school at this time?

Kanter (1983) identified several factors that seemed to characterize relatively uninnovative organizations; organizations not hospitable to programmatic change. First, less innovating organizations tended to have rigid hierarchies and chains of command that are rarely challenged. This factor might be exemplified in the following sequence of events: (a) a principal of a high school informs the assistant principal of a new policy, (b) the assistant principal informs the department heads, (c) the department heads inform the teachers they supervise, and (d) the teachers inform their students of the policy. Moreover, there is little meaningful dialogue between personnel from nonadjacent levels in the hierarchy. Such communication patterns do not make fertile ground for program development and implementation.

A second organizational factor that can inhibit programmatic change is "nickel and dime" decision-making at the top of the hierarchy, for example, a principal insisting on selecting the specific reading passages on which students will be tested. Principals preoccupied with making these types of decisions probably have less time to devote to more administrative tasks, such as setting the conditions for programmatic change to occur. A third factor identified by Kanter is poor lateral communication. This factor is similar to Weick's (1976) notion of loose coupling. The gravest form of poor lateral communication arises where teachers see the classroom as a "fortress" and will not tolerate any encroachment into their personal territories. Fourth, less innovative organizations frequently have limited resources for carrying out change. Though an initial lack of resources for programmatic change can be problematic, often school personnel can obtain these resources by means of grant writing or other activities. Even more inimical to programmatic change than an initial lack of resources is a school administration that stifles staffs attempts to acquire needed resources. A fifth factor that can inhibit innovation is limited organizational vehicles with which to promote change. A hypothetical elementary school, for example, may have only one staff meeting each month, at which suggestions for programmatic change are vociferously opposed. Clearly, these meetings are not an appropriate vehicle for initiating programmatic change. A final factor cited by Kanter as being inimical to innovation is an organization's excessive reliance on outside consultation. Exclusively involving outside consultants to plan curriculum changes may create a "culture of inferiority" among classroom teachers within the school, thereby deterring teachers from developing their own suggestions for change. In addition, overreliance on outside consultants may impede efforts to ensure that the program is maintained and adapted over time.

Though the presence of the above factors in a school may make the successful implementation of a program difficult, Kanter suggests that it is possible to "innovate against the grain." However, there are clear risks for the school psychologists who attempt to implement a program in a school that is resistant to change. Previously friendly co-workers may become distant or even hostile, and one's job may be jeopardized. Moreover, attempting to innovate in an environment inimical to planned change can present the school psychologist with difficult ethical dilemmas. For example, a proposed program might be likely to improve career guidance services for students. However, implementing the program might cost the school psychologist the credibility with the principal requisite to recommending other needed changes. Despite the risks and the obstacles, Kanter identifies four types of persons who seem to be able to initiate change in an uninnovative environment. One of these is referred to as the "honeymooner." This is someone who is new to an organization, and who therefore might be given more latitude about violating the implicit norms in regard to initiating change. However, if one proceeds too quickly with change the honeymoon can come to an abrupt halt. A second type is the "lone ranger." The lone ranger is "half hero and half outlaw," who is loyal to the organization but is willing to circumvent some of the organization's regulations to improve its functioning. A third type of prospective change agent who might succeed in implementing a new program in a school that resists change is the "waterwalker." This is the person who seemingly can do no wrong and do just about everything right for the organization. Because of a previous record of successes, this would-be innovator is allowed to initiate change projects that no one else in the organization can. The final type is the "dissident subculture member," whose change initiatives must be supported by a small group of staff who share the dissident's view of how change should occur in the organization. This small group can form the "critical mass" needed for change, if its members are sufficiently adept at influencing others (Orlich, 1979).

Finally, Kanter identifies several factors characteristic of the more innovating organizations. These include (a) broadly defined job roles, (b) periodic nonroutine job assignments, (c) job assignments that intersect and allow for collaboration among co-workers, (d) strong autonomy for the individual professional, (e) a willingness to invest resources both toward the implementation of programs and toward promoting staff's welfare, (f) a broad administrative mandate for change, and (g) the existence of a culture of pride. Because it is often not cited in the literature on organizational change, the culture of pride as a factor in facilitating change deserves further discussion. In such a culture, competence and innovation are esteemed. Individual's successes are openly acknowledged, and this helps to foster staff members' belief that they are part of a successful organization. Kanter asserts

that a "self-reinforcing upward cycle" of "performance stimulating pride stimulating performance" occurs in the more innovating organizations. In such organizations, working a few extra hours a week is not a problem for staff; they are dedicated to promoting the organization's goals.

What Specific Characteristics of the School Might Impede or Support Programmatic Change?

If it is decided that programmatic change has a reasonable likelihood of success at a particular school, the next step is to assess what specific characteristics of the school might support or impede the change effort. One framework that can be used to assess these characteristics is identified by the acronym AVICTORY (Davis & Salasin, 1975). The letters in the acronym denote the following questions about organizational readiness for change:

Ability. What resources are available for program development and implementation?

Values. Are the attitudes and beliefs of key personnel compatible with the proposed changes?

Information. Do key personnel understand the reasons for the proposed changes?

Circumstances. What stable conditions in the organization or external to the organization will impede or support the change effort?

Timing. What temporary conditions might impede or support the change effort?

Obligation. Do key personnel feel committed to support program development and implementation?

Resistance. What are the sources and the extent of resistance to proposed changes?

Yield. Do key personnel believe that the change effort will have positive outcomes?

Illback and Hargan (1984) provided a case example of how these AVICTORY characteristics of an organization can be assessed with respect to implementing a microcomputer program for special needs children. They constructed a questionnaire with a five-point Likert-type scale (1 = Disagree, 5 = Agree) to assess readiness. For instance, in regard to the Values characteristic, school personnel were asked how much they agreed with the following statements:

1. Microcomputers can play a valuable role in delivering instruction to special needs children.
2. People in this organization will support the implementation of a microcomputer project for special needs children.
3. This organization has a history of supporting change and innovation for special needs children.
4. My immediate supervisor values the use of microcomputers in the classroom with special needs children.

How Can a School's Readiness for Change Be Improved?

The data from the readiness assessment can be used to inform program planners about how to intervene to facilitate readiness for program development and implementation. For example, if an obstacle is low Obligation as reflected in a lack of support from an important group (e.g., teacher, parent, student, or administrator), presentations can be tailored to address the particular concerns of that group. A program intended to integrate educable mentally retarded students into regular classrooms might be opposed by teachers. These teachers might be concerned that they will receive little or no additional technical assistance on how to instruct the handicapped students. In this instance, program staff can inform teachers about what assistance will be available to them. There may be Resistance to implementation as a result of aversive program elements. For instance, concern may be voiced about the amount of paperwork required by the program. Because of this concern, program staff might write a grant proposal that includes a provision for a clerical staff member. Another obstacle to implementation may be staff who lack knowledge or skill to carry out necessary activities

(Ability). One possible strategy for intervening with this potential obstacle is to incorporate a staff development component into the program. Unfavorable Circumstances, such as interpersonal or intrapersonal problems, may interfere with implementation. Implementation-threatening interpersonal problems can occur between students and program staff, among staff, and between individuals of important support groups, such as administrators and parents. The aforementioned conflict management skills can be helpful in minimizing this type of obstacle. Sometimes face-to-face meetings mediated by an impartial third person can help dispel irrational beliefs that might be at the root of the conflict. The author once served as a consultant to a school attempting to implement a program for mainstreaming emotionally disturbed students. A few program staff members assumed that an administrator's lack of direct involvement in program planning signified his disapproval of the program. However, when tactfully confronted about this, he revealed that his lack of involvement was because of urgent administrative tasks. In addition, he stated that he was enthusiastic about the program's potential. Though less likely to threaten the overall success of implementation, intrapersonal problems can make implementation more difficult. Moreover, some individual's problems may be of a highly intractable nature and necessitate referral to an outside mental health professional.

How Can an Appropriate Program Be Selected?

It is important for the school psychologist to resist the temptation to impulsively implement a program suggested by the school principal, or a program recently read about in the latest issue of a professional journal. Instead, the school psychologist and other staff initially should consider several alternative programs for possible implementation. The alternatives considered should be based upon the purpose and goals of the change effort, which can be derived from the data collected during the problem clarification activities. One procedure that can facilitate exploring a full range of alternative programs is referred to as "brainstorming" (Osborn, 1963). In brainstorming, the group defers judgments about the appropriateness of programs until after all possible alternatives have been generated. The assumption is that premature critical evaluation may limit the number of options generated.

In addition to brainstorming, several other decision-making guidelines can be of assistance in selecting the program to be implemented. One of these guidelines is to keep attention on the purpose and goals for which the program is being designed. When considering possible program alternatives, planning teams sometime begin to drift and consider programs that are increasingly distant from the original service delivery purpose and goals. If the purpose is to promote prosocial peer interaction among students, then the methods and activities of the proposed program alternatives should be consistent with improving peer interaction. Another guideline to consider in evaluating alternatives is to examine nonobvious risks and nonobvious advantages of each alternative. In other words, teams should evaluate initially preferred alternatives with respect to potential risks, and evaluate initially rejected alternatives with respect to potential advantages.

A third suggestion is to obtain information about resources needed for implementation. The lack of such information can make it difficult to assess the relative practicality of the different alternatives. For instance, in considering implementation of an after-school peer-tutoring program intended to improve reading skills, it might be advantageous to know if students have time to participate in the program. Acknowledging contextual factors is a fourth important guideline in evaluating alternatives. To continue the previous example, even if students have time to participate in an after-school program, administrators may not support such a program. Some administrators may be opposed to using students as "surrogate staff." A fifth decision-making suggestion

is not to search for the perfect alternative, but instead to "satisfice" (Simon, 1976). Simon argues that people have "bounded rationality," that is, they have a limited ability to process information and foresee the consequences of various alternatives. Therefore, it is often inefficient for a team to spend considerable amounts of time searching for the ideal alternative; rather, teams should be satisfied with an alternative that seems to hold promise for substantially improving the present state of affairs.

Finally, teams should use a structured decision-making procedure. As Pfeiffer (1980) noted about multidisciplinary preplacement evaluation teams, merely bringing together several professionals does not insure that the most appropriate decisions will be made. Kaiser and Woodman (1985) have proposed that a modified version of the nominal group technique (NGT) be used by multidisciplinary teams in schools. As outlined by Kaiser and Woodman, the NGT involves several steps:

1. Each member individually generates a written list of alternatives. (This step is similar to brainstorming.)
2. Each member is asked to provide alternatives to the group, until all alternatives are recorded.
3. All alternatives are discussed in sequence with respect to their advantages and disadvantages.
4. Independently, members rate each alternative for possible implementation.
5. The highest-rated alternatives are combined into one chart for the purpose of displaying overall ratings to the group.
6. In a optional step, each member is allowed time to discuss one of the highest-rated alternatives.
7. Finally, the group selects an alternative to be implemented. This selection can occur by awarding points to each of the highest-rated alternatives on the basis of their perceived practicality, utility, and propriety.

In regard to Step 7, propriety refers to how appropriate the proposed programs are with respect to ethical concerns, and legal and local school regula-

TABLE 1
Example of Chart That Can Be Used to Assist Selection of Program to Be Implemented

Program	Criteria for Selection			Total Rating
	Utility	Practicality	Propriety	
Social skills training	3 3 3 3 2 3	3 3 2 2 3 3	3 2 3 3 3 3	50
Peer counseling	3 3 3 2 3 2	2 2 2 2 3 2	2 3 3 2 2 2	43
Group counseling	3 2 2 2 2 2	2 2 2 3 2 2	3 3 3 3 3 3	44

Note: Ratings based on a 3-point scale: 3 = high, 2 = moderate, 1 = low. Each number under Utility, Practicality, and Propriety columns represents one team member's rating.

tions. Practicality addresses whether needed resources are available, and whether a proposed alternative is compatible with ongoing school routines. Utility refers to the anticipated student outcomes of a proposed program. A visual aid, such as a chart, can be used during Step 7. In Table 1, hypothetical data are presented in the form of a chart. Six team members have rated three proposed programs. The proposed programs are intended to ameliorate the problem of verbal aggression between students. Prior to ratings, members share information about resources needed to implement the proposed programs and clearly define the purpose and goals to be attained. In Table 1, ratings reflect several team members' relative misgivings about the practicality of the peer counseling and professional group counseling alternatives. Though professional group counseling has very high propriety ratings, it is rated lower with respect to expected utility. The only alternative that received consistently high ratings relative to all three criteria was the social skills training program.

How Can Implementation of a Program Be Promoted?

One important way to promote implementation is to *communicate the nature and scope of the program persuasively* to nonprogram staff and parents.

Prior to any formal group presentations, however, sanctions for proceeding with the project should be obtained from those personnel who exercise either legitimate or informal power with the school. Next, consensus should be reached about (a) when and where presentations will occur, (b) who will be the audience, and (c) what, specifically, will be presented. Often, the initial formal presentation is given at a staff meeting, where almost all key personnel are present.

In regard to this type of presentation, several suggestions might be helpful (MacLachlan, 1983/1984). Open the presentation by giving people a reason for listening. Gain parents' attention by informing them how the proposed program is intended to improve the welfare of their children. At a group meeting with nonprogram staff, for example, ask the audience to say what they see as possible advantages and disadvantages of the proposed program. Build on points of agreement and develop a common frame of reference. For example, if parents believe discipline is a problem in their children's school, presenters can indicate how their proposed program (to reduce verbal aggression, for example) might also improve the discipline problem. Key points should be reiterated, since reiteration improves long-term recall, and points that are reiterated may be judged as having greater veracity. (However, reiteration can be boring and it should be limited to a small number of instances and be relieved by variation in phraseology and interesting examples.) Jargon-free language should be used. Rather than tell a group of teachers that one goal of a proposed program is to improve students' social initiation skills, a presenter might say, "One goal for our proposed program is to improve the way students greet each other. Students sometimes actually start fights because they don't know how to say hello appropriately. Yesterday, for instance, Mark W. greeted George M. by walking up to him and playfully punching him in the arm. Not surprisingly, George mistook the gesture and became angry at Mark."

During the next part of the group discussion, ask participants their formative opinions on the proposed program. As Kurt Lewin (1947) noted, positive reactions voiced in a group can serve to intensify each person's support for a program. After participants express their opinions, the presenters can summarize the participants' opinions and state possible implications. Possible implications can range from future verbal support for the program to actual program involvement.

One problem that might have to be addressed prior to implementation can be termed *underdeveloped technology;* that is, the present status of the science and art of applied psychology may be inadequate to address the students' problems. When this obstacle is evident, staff should consider adapting empirically validated interventions. For example, program staff in a high school decided that in order to successfully mainstream seriously emotionally disturbed adolescents, it was important for classroom teachers to be trained in life-space interviewing (see, e.g., Brendtro & Ness, 1983). However, the literature reviewed by the school psychologist revealed no reports of teachers being trained in life-space interviewing. Therefore, program staff decided to adapt instructional strategies that were effective in developing teachers' behavior modification skills to the training of teachers in life-space interviewing.

Problems occur not only prior to implementation, but during implementation as well. Hannafin and Witt (1983) suggested that several types of system level problems can occur during program implementation. One of these is *ineffective interaction among system components.* This type of problem might occur when there is no forum for staff to exchange information, such as progress reports, with one another. If two or more staff members are working with the same students, for example, it is critical that they have the opportunity to meet on a regular basis to plan and modify a consistent approach to their interventions. Another type of problem that might arise during implementation is the *omission of important program elements.* For instance, suppose that in attempting to mainstream students into regular classrooms from private schools no one is assigned the role of liaison person; because of this omitted program element, several persons perform the liaison function, but in a haphazard and time-inefficient manner. A third problem identified by Hannafin and Witt is *inadequate articulation of program components.* For example, a teacher is trained to carry out social skills training in the classroom as part of a primary prevention program. However, the boundaries of her or his training responsibilities are not clearly articulated. Because of this lack of clarity, the teacher questions the students about family secrets, which in turn precipates an angry reaction from several parents. A fourth possible systems level problem is *insufficient monitoring of implementation.* Once implemented, a program can easily veer off its intended course. Without monitoring, the discrepancy between intended and actual implementation is difficult to ascertain. Furthermore, not all discrepancies between intended and actual implementation are undesirable; some changes might result in improved services to students. Staff members' recording of their activities on structured forms is one practical means of monitoring implementation. Finally, a program can be *improperly coordinated.* A weekly meeting that is well attended by program staff does not, by itself, insure that staffs' program duties will be successfully coordinated. It is also important to avoid poor agenda setting, such as spending too much time on relatively unimportant issues or day-to-day crises which can seriously limit opportunities to discuss how members can work more efficiently as a team.

CONCLUSIONS

Developing and implementing a change program for a group of students is a complex endeavor, but it is arguably not intrinsically more difficult than designing and implementing an intervention for an individual student. Perhaps it is the abstract nature of the target of change that makes programmatic change seem exceedingly complex. We can physically touch and see another person, but not a program. An attempt has been made to put some "flesh and bones" on this abstract topic by providing guidelines for planning and implementing intervention programs in the schools. Though this chapter and others in this book can offer potentially useful information, in the final analysis, much learning must occur by doing. If change is needed in your school, attempt to initiate it. However, keep in mind W. C. Fields's sage advice about not squandering your time and effort.

REFERENCES

Bales, R. F. (1958). Task roles and social roles in problem-solving groups. In E. E. Maccoby, T. M. Newcomb, & E. L. Hartley (Eds.), *Readings in social psychology,* (3rd ed.) (pp. 437-447). New York: Holt, Rinehart & Winston.

Bandura, A. (1977). *Social learning theory.* Englewood Cliffs, NJ: Prentice-Hall.

Barker, R. G. (Ed.). (1978). *Habitats, environments and human behavior.* San Francisco: Jossey-Bass.

Bell, R. A., Nguyen, T. D., Warheit, G. T., & Buhl, J. M. (1978). Service utilization, social indicator, and citizen approaches to human services need assessment. In C. Attkisson, W. Hargreaves, M. Horowitz, & J. Sorensen (Eds.), *Evaluation of human service programs.* London: Academic.

Berman, P., & McLaughlin, M. W. (1978). *Federal programs supporting educational change: Vol. 8. Implementing and sustaining innovations.* Santa Monica, CA: Rand.

Brendtro, L. K., & Ness, A. E. (1983). *Re-educating troubled youth: Environments for teaching and treatments.* New York: Aldine.

Davis, H., & Salasin, S. (1975). The utilization of evaluation. In E. Streuning, & M. Guttentag (Eds.), *Handbook of evaluation research* (Vol. 1, pp. 621-666) Beverly Hills, CA: Sage.

Dunn, W. N., Mitroff, I. I., & Deutsch, S. J. (1981). The obsolescence of evaluation research. *Evaluation and Program Planning, 4,* 207-218.

Frederiksen, L. W., Richter, W. T., Johnson, R. P., & Solomon, L. J. (1982). Specificity of performance feedback in a professional service delivery setting. *Journal of Organizational Behavior Management, 3*(4), 41-53.

French, J. R., & Raven, B. (1959). The bases of social power. In D. Cartwright (Ed.), *Studies in social power* (pp. 150-167). Ann Arbor: University of Michigan, Research Center for Group Dynamics, Institute for Social Research.

Fuller, B., Wood, K., Rapoport, T., & Dornbusch, S. M. (1982). The organizational context of individual efficacy. *Review of Educational Research, 52,* 7-30.

Hannafin, M. F., & Witt, J. C. (1983). System intervention and the school psychologist: Maximizing interplay among roles and functions. *Professional Psychology: Research and Practice, 14,* 128-136.

Hartshorne, T. S., & Johnson, M. C. (1985). The actual and preferred roles of the school psychologist according to secondary school administrators. *Journal of School Psychology, 23,* 241-246.

Ilgen, D. R., Fisher, C. D., & Taylor, M. S. (1979). Consequences of individual feedback on behavior in organizations. *Journal of Applied Psychology, 64,* 349-371.

Illback, R. J., & Hargan, L. (1984). Assessing and facilitating school readiness for microcomputers. *Special Services in the Schools, 1*(1), 91-105.

Janis, I. L. (1982). *Groupthink: Psychological studies of policy decision and fiascoes* (2nd ed.). Boston: Houghton Mifflin.

Kaiser, S. M., & Woodman, R. W. (1985). Multidisciplinary teams and group decision-making techniques: Possible solutions to decision-making problems. *School Psychology Review, 14,* 457-470.

Kanter, I. L. (1983). *The change masters: Innovation and entrepreneurship in the American corporation.* New York: Simon and Schuster.

Lewin, K. (1947). Frontiers in group dynamics: Concept, method, and reality in social science; social equilibria and social change. *Human Relations, 1,* 5-41.

MacLachlan, J. (1983/1984). Making a message memorable and persuasive. *Journal of Advertising Research, 23*(6), 51-59.

Maher, C. A. (1984). Implementing programs and systems in organizational settings: The DURABLE approach. *Journal of Organizational Behavior Management, 6*(3), 69-98.

Maher, C. A. (1985). Resolving problems of mainstreaming: Effects of training educational administrators in interpersonal problem-solving with staff members. *Special Services in the Schools, 1*(4), 83-89.

Maher, C. A., & Bennett, R. E. (1984). *Planning and evaluating special education services.* Englewood Cliffs, NJ: Prentice-Hall.

Miles, R. E. (1965). Keeping informed: Human relations or human resources. *Harvard Business Review, 43,* 148-163.

Morrow-Bradley, C., & Elliot, R. (1986). Utilization of psychotherapy research by practicing psychotherapists. *American Psychologist, 41,* 188-197.

National Commission on Excellence in Education. (1983). *A nation at risk: The full account.* Washington, DC: United States Office of Education.

Orlich, D. C. (1979). Federal education policy. The paradox of innovation and centralization. *Educational Researcher, 8*(7), 4-9.

Osborn, A. E. (1963). Applied imagination. *Principles and procedures of creative problem-solving* (3rd ed.). New York: Scribners.

Pfeiffer, S. I. (1980). The school-based interprofessional team: Recurring problems and some possible solutions. *Journal of School Psychology, 18,* 388-394.

Reynolds, C. R., & Gutkin, T. B. (Eds.). (1982). *The handbook of school psychology.* New York: Wiley.

Robinson, V. M. J., Cameron, M. M., & Raethal, A. M. (1985). Negotiation of a consultative role for school psychologists: A case study. *Journal of School Psychology, 23,* 43-49.

Sarason, S. B. (1982). *The culture of school and the problem of change* (2nd ed.). Boston: Allyn & Bacon.

Shaw, M. E. (1981). *Group dynamics: The psychology of small group behavior* (3rd ed.). New York: McGraw-Hill.

Simon, H. A. (1976). *Administrative behavior: A study of decision-making processes in administrative organization* (3rd ed.). New York: Macmillan.

Thibaut, J. W., & Kelley, H. H. (1959). *The social psychology of groups.* New York: Wiley.

Thomas, A., & Grimes, J. (Eds.). (1985). *Best practices in school psychology.* Washington, DC: National Association of School Psychology.

Trailor, C. B. (1982). Role clarification and participation in child study teams. *Exceptional Children, 48,* 529-530.

Tubbs, M. E. (1986). Goal setting: A meta-analysis examination of the empirical evidence. *Journal of Applied Psychology, 71,* 474-483.

Tuckman, B. W., & Jensen, M. A. (1977). Stages of small-group development revisited. *Group and Organizational Studies, 2,* 419-427.

Weick, K. E. (1984). Small wins: Redefining the scale of social problems. *American Psychologist, 39,* 40-49.

Weick, K. E. (1976). Educational organizations as loosely coupled systems. *Administrative Science Quarterly, 21,* 1-19.

Wood, R., Hull, F., & Azumi, K. (1983). Evaluating quality circles: The American application. *California Management Review, 16,* 37-53.

Zahorik, J. A. (1984). Can teachers adopt research findings? *Journal of Teacher Education, 35,* 34.

25

Evaluating the Effectiveness of Alternative Educational Delivery Systems

Randy Elliot Bennett
Educational Testing Service

Alternative systems, effectiveness, and *evaluation* mean different things to different people. Thus, any chapter on these topics might best start with some discussion of what these terms mean.

To define *alternative systems of educational services* it is first necessary to establish what such systems are alternatives to. One simple way of viewing the functioning of school systems generally is in terms of the structure proposed by Maher and Bennett (1984). Their structure breaks the school system into five major components: assessment, instruction, related services, personnel development, and administration. Assessment, instruction, and related services are provided directly to students; personnel development and administration are indirect functions. Assessment can be viewed as the process of gathering information about individual students for educational decision making; instruction facilitates the development of academic, vocational, and social skills; and related services are meant to provide the supports needed for students to benefit from instruction. Personnel development helps school staff members (and sometimes parents) achieve and maintain competencies needed to perform their jobs. Finally, administration coordinates the provision of services.

Within each of these five areas, services can be rendered in alternative ways. For example, assessment services traditionally have been made available only upon referral of a student by a regular education teacher. These services have consisted of the administration by a multidisciplinary team of formal and informal measures, perhaps an interview with the parents and teacher of the referred student and an observation of the student in the classroom. On the basis of these activities, the team reaches a decision about the student's status.

An alternative to this assessment system might require the classroom teacher to seek consultative aid from the school psychologist before making a formal referral. This aid could center on modifications in instructional or management techniques that might improve the student's functioning in the regular classroom. In this context, behavioral or curriculum-based assessment might be provided to suggest whether these modifications were successful or if other modifications should be tried. Should the data suggest that repeated curricular or management modifications have failed to enable the student to succeed in the regular classroom, comprehensive multidisciplinary assessment and placement in a special education setting might follow.

For the purposes of this chapter, an alternative educational delivery system, or program, is one of the several approaches to providing a service. The alternative generally is considered innovative and is an attempt to improve upon traditional practices. It is typically more than a technique, method, material, or piece of equipment. Rather, it is an organized configuration of resources — personnel, facilities, methods, materials, policies, and procedures — aimed at achieving a particular purpose.

It should be obvious that alternative programs can, and have been, developed in each of the five service areas. New approaches to assessment, such as curriculum-based assessment, computerized adaptive testing, and expert assessment systems, are being experimented with in various environments (see Bennett & Maher, 1986, for an overview). Instructional innovations (e.g., IBM's *Writing to Read* program) are also being tested and in some cases adopted. Because of the rapidly decreasing cost and increasing capability of computer technology, the related services area has seen a virtual explosion of alternatives (Bennett, 1986). Finally, both personnel development and administration have begun to consider new approaches to old tasks: training by videodisk and computer simulation, and information management and exchange by means of telecommunications technology (Bennett, 1982, 1984, 1986).

What is *effectiveness?* In one sense, effectiveness relates to the importance of the problem a program addresses: If the program is addressing an important problem, it is often considered "worthwhile" in much the same way as a program intended to help the homeless is said to be "for a good cause." Effectiveness can also be defined in respect to program design or structure. That is, a program can be considered to have value if it has explicit goals, is based upon theoretically sound assumptions, and incorporates meaningful activities. How a program operates is yet another conception of effectiveness. Smooth, efficient operation is often associated with effectiveness. Finally, the most common (but least operationally used) notion of effectiveness turns on program outcomes or results. If the program goals are achieved, if the program produces better results than alternatives, it is considered effective.

Clearly, each of these definitions of effectiveness incorporates something of importance. Equally clear, however, is that no one of these definitions can stand on its own. A program may address an important problem, but in an inefficient manner; or, it may operate smoothly but fail to achieve results. Even if it achieves results, and yet its design is poor (i.e., it is based on theoretically questionable assumptions), the case for generalizability to other populations and target sites is greatly weakened: If the results can't be explained, how can the conditions under which the program will operate effectively be predicted? Effectiveness, then, is a multidimensional concept, one that refers to various aspects of a program.

What is *evaluation? Evaluation,* a process employed in designing or modifying a program (Maher & Bennett, 1984), involves gathering information about the various aspects of a program so that judgments about it can be made. Evaluation provides information for judgments about the need for the program, the appropriateness of the program goals, the strengths and weaknesses of different options, the manner in which the program is carried out, and the ultimate success of the effort. This information becomes the basis for improvement of the program.

Why is it important to evaluate the effectiveness of alternative educational delivery systems? Any proposed alternative educational system must in some specific, important way be better than the existing one, since there are substantial costs to inaugurating alternative systems that must be justified *before* such systems are implemented on any large scale. These costs take the form of the time and expense involved in planning and implementing a new program and of the loss of continuity in school operations that occurs when an existing program is replaced with a new one. But perhaps the heaviest potential costs would be those incurred if the alternative should prove to be *worse* than the status quo and just as hard, once it is started, to stop. While evaluation might not prevent such a sad occurrence, it should reduce its likelihood.

A FRAMEWORK FOR EVALUATING ALTERNATIVE EDUCATIONAL SYSTEMS

Analytical frameworks, although

helpful for organizing one's thoughts about a particular question, are necessarily idealized and somewhat artificial: The world is never quite as simple as a framework might suggest it should be. Still, such schemata do serve a heuristic purpose by lending an explicit structure that can be examined and applied when appropriate.

Figure 1 presents a framework for conceptualizing the evaluation of alternative educational systems that is based on the planning and evaluation concepts of Maher and Bennett (1984); it displays the five service areas on its vertical dimension and the four evaluation concerns on its horizontal axis. The content of evaluation — the methods, activities, procedures, and results — is denoted by the intersection of these two dimensions.

Several points should be noted about the framework. First, it implies the need for an integrated conception of effectiveness that includes consideration of problem importance, program design, implementation, and outcome. Through an integrated conception, a broad picture of a program can be painted that provides more useful information than that based on any single conception.

Second, through its inclusion of the five areas that compose the school's operations, the framework recognizes the need to apply evaluation to all its operational components not just instructional ones.

Third, the content of evaluation may vary according to both the type of program being evaluated and the evaluation concern being addressed. Judging the value of the problem addressed by a program requires methods different from those appropriate to assessing the program's results; similarly, the methods for determining the outcomes of an instructional innovation (e.g., tests, observations) differ from those for assessing the results of a new administrative record-keeping system (e.g., document analysis).

Finally, the framework implies that evaluation is a team effort. It requires the participation of individuals knowledgeable about evaluation, but also of persons familiar with the program. The involvement of the latter group helps ensure that evaluation responds to the needs of users, to those responsible for developing and improving the alternative education effort.

Problem Evaluation

Judgments about the problem to be addressed by the program should be sought from representatives of various groups, but certainly from those affected by the problem and those who are responsible for dealing with it. If not already included in these groups, other constituencies to consider might include community members, parents, school administrators, and teachers. As a group, the judges should be reasonably open-minded and respected by the school community. Otherwise, their opinions will carry little weight.

Judgments will necessarily be somewhat subjective. But to the extent that broad agreement across judges is obtained, confidence in the objectivity of judgments is increased. Objectivity is important because judgments should depend more on the nature of the problem than on who is doing the judging. Agreement by a number of judges suggests that the problem has a clear value definition (or lack thereof): that different judges drawn from those same constituencies would likely react similarly.

That a group of generally respected judges agrees that the problem is important suggests that a more thorough look at the program is in order. If, however, the group's opinion is that the problem is trivial, then the purpose of the program itself is called into question. In this case, spending resources to carry out any further evaluation of the program is probably uncalled for.

Evaluating the Program Design

The program design provides the basic structure for the alternative system. It indicates the program's purpose, target population, resources (staff, materials, facilities, activities), and expected outcomes (Maher & Bennett, 1984). Ob-

FIGURE 1

A framework for conceptualizing the evaluation of alternative systems of educational services. Adapted from *Planning and Evaluating Special Education Services* (p. 10), by C. A. Maher and R. E. Bennett, 1984. Copyright 1984 by Prentice-Hall. Reprinted by permission. Englewood Cliffs, NJ: Prentice-Hall.

SERVICE AREA	PLANNING AND EVALUATION PROCESS			
	Problem Assessment	Program Design	Program Implementation	Outcome Assessment
Assessment				
Instruction	*PLANNING*			
Related Services		*AND*		
Personnel Development			*EVALUATION*	
Administration				*CONTENT*

viously, the design must be explicit if it is to be evaluated. Ideally, the design should be in written form and provide enough detail to give persons not familiar with the program a reasonable picture of it.

One approach to assessing the quality of the design is adversarial evaluation (Worthen & Owens, 1978). This approach calls for the selection of two teams, one of which argues for the design and the other against it. Adversarial evaluation both forces assessments of the program to be backed up with evidence and requires cross-examination of the validity of that evidence. Thus it can be helpful in bringing to light not only real short-comings but also criticisms that true adversaries may eventually raise (see Wood, Peterson, DeGracie, & Zaharis, 1986, for an interesting adaptation of this model).

The program design can be evaluated on the basis of five criteria suggested by Provus (1972). The first test is for *clarity*, the extent to which the design is understable and its components objectively measureable. Second, the design is inspected to guarantee its *comprehensive-*

ness, that it fully describes the program's purpose, implementation, and expected outcomes. Third, it is checked to ensure *internal consistency*, that the components are logically interrelated. *Compatibility* with the problem addressed, with existing support conditions, and with other related programs is reviewed next. Finally, *theoretical soundness* is considered in terms of the degree to which the design describes a program that is consistent with current professional knowledge and principles of good practice.

Evaluating Program Implementation

Implementation evaluation, or monitoring, serves to document whether the program is being carried out as planned and, if not, why not. Implementation evaluation can reveal operational problems that, unless corrected, will prevent the alternative from succeeding, or functional modifications not described in the design that should be added to it.

Questions addressed by implementation evaluation might include the following:

1. Did the program begin on time? Was all essential equipment on hand and in working order?

2. Does the staff assigned to the program have qualifications similar to those called for in the design? If not, does this discrepancy appear to be affecting the operation of the program?

3. Were staff adequately trained in the use of program methods, materials, equipment, and activities? Do they appear to use these methods, materials, equipment, and activities correctly when carrying out the program?

4. Are the goals articulated by program staff consistent with those specified in the design?

5. Are the activities called for in the design being carried out? If not, why not?

6. Has special equipment continued to operate adequately? If not, has it been promptly replaced or repaired?

7. Is the appropriate target audience being served? If not, why not? Has target audience attendance been adequate? Has significant attrition occurred?

8. Has the actual cost of the program been consistent with the budgeted amount?

The criteria against which most implementation results are measured are the design specifications. When operation is not consistent with the design, it should be determined whether it is the operation or the design that needs to be modified.

Implementation evaluation often makes heavy use of observation, interview, and product review. For an innovative assessment project built around curriculum-based assessment (Deno, Marston, & Tindal, 1986), observation of staff performing the assessment, interviews with them to ascertain how well they understand the purposes and procedures, and analysis of assessment protocols and staff interpretations of them might be carried out.

Evaluating Program Outcomes

Outcome evaluation is, without doubt, the most complex of the four types of evaluation. It requires the greatest time and effort and the most specialized expertise, and it poses the most serious practical challenges. For these reasons, the outcome evaluations conducted in schools are often of limited scope and, as a result, of equally limited value.

Outcome evaluation presupposes that questions about implementation have been answered. Without implementation results outcome evaluation makes no sense: If the program has not been properly implemented (if the computers haven't arrived or are constantly in need of repair), why look to see if the program has produced any results?

As with effectiveness, the notion of outcome has various definitions. One notion of outcome is the degree to which program goals were achieved and the extent to which this achievement can be tied to the program and not to the other likely sources.

A second notion of outcome involves related effects — that is, the extent to which the program has produced harmful or beneficial unintended results. A program may achieve its goals but produce side effects so harmful that it simply cannot be continued (consider pharmaceutical drugs for some dramatic illustrations). The opposite situation has also been known to occur: Programs have failed to achieve their stated goals, but produced beneficial side effects, so much so as to be continued with a new emphasis on the previously unintended results.

Third, outcome can be conceptualized in terms of consumer reaction (Wolf, 1978). Program consumers include not only the target audience, but also groups that receive benefits less directly: parents, program staff, and the school community. The basic question asked of consumers is, "In your view, is the program effective?" Consumer reaction is an important outcome in its own right. After all, program consumers (in particular, parents and community members) foot the bill for education; how these individuals are affected cannot be ignored.

Fourth, cost-effectiveness constitutes a common view of outcome. This conception of outcome is rarely formally operationalized in schools because of the complex economic, educational, and methodological issues it raises. However, in periods when resources are shrinking, allocating limited funds to programs that produce the greatest impact becomes critical. Hence, at some level, consideration of cost-effectiveness becomes essential.

OUTCOME EVALUATION: SPECIAL CONSIDERATIONS

As noted, program outcomes are generally the most complex manifestations of effectiveness to evaluate. Yet when carefully conducted, outcome evaluations provide the critical information for program development and improvement that many consider the bottom line in determining program worth. Special considerations for evaluating the outcomes of alternative programs are discussed below. The discussion generally is framed in the context of goal attainment, which is often judged to be the most crucial outcome. However, it should be noted that the treatment generally applies to evaluations of other outcomes: related effects, consumer reaction, and cost-effectiveness. (For information on evaluating these and other program characteristics, the interested reader should consult Maher and Bennett, 1984.)

Timing the Outcome Evaluation

It is of primary importance that outcome evaluation not be attempted until the alternative program has had sufficient time to stabilize. Programs come to stability from one of two prior states. The more common of these states varies from mildly confused to chaotic (equipment arrives late, teacher training carefully scheduled for summertime winds up taking place during the school year), and as a result the integration of the program into the classroom routine is slow and labored. While implementation evaluation should be documenting these difficulties so that they can be identified and corrected, assessing outcomes at the conclusion of the first year in this circumstance is pointless: In effect, the program has yet

to be delivered. It makes much more sense to work with program staff to help identify and put into place improvements, and to schedule outcome evaluation, assuming all goes well, for the following year.

While most new programs of any considerable size and degree of complexity do not run smoothly in the first year, some seem to be characterized by just the opposite condition. Equipment arrives on time, training is delivered without a hitch, and staff and students enter the school year enthusiastic about the innovation. Student and teacher attendance increases and it is clear that the students are learning. The critical question, however, is: "How long will it last?" Are these beneficial effects due to the novelty of the program, or due to intrinsic, stable program characteristics? If the outcome evaluation is conducted too early in the program life cycle, the answer will not be apparent. Worse, positive evaluation results might encourage a decision to extend the program to other district schools and populations, a move that could be seriously in error.

Experimental Designs for Outcome Evaluation

In addition to timing, the strength of the evidence resulting from outcome evaluation is central. One foundation of this strength lies in the evaluation design — that is, the data-gathering structure for evaluating the program. Without question the strongest designs, those producing the most trustworthy evidence, are experimental ones (Campbell & Stanley, 1963). Experimental designs are characterized by direct control of the independent variable (the program); rather than working with an existing program and a given alternative, experimental designs presuppose some control over what the alternative and existing programs are; where, when, and with whom they will operate; and so on. Control of the alternative and existing programs is important because hypotheses about how critical differences between them affect important outcomes can be tested directly. If outcomes occur as predicted, the evidence for a causal link between the critical difference (e.g., the addition of word processing to an English composition class) and the observed effect (e.g., improved writing ability) is all the more believable.

A second characteristic of experimental design is random assignment, the placement of subjects in different treatment groups such that every member of the population from which subjects are drawn has an equal chance of being chosen for that assignment (Kerlinger, 1973). The purpose of random assignment is to increase the probability of balanced treatment groups, that is, groups that are equal in all characteristics that might affect how they respond to the treatment. Examples of such characteristics include age, developed ability, achievement level, motivation, and sex. When enough subjects are available (most authorities specify at least 30 in each group), random assignment tends to create relatively equal groups. Without random assignment (or with small groups), the validity of results is not as strong and erroneous decisions about the effectiveness of alternative programs are more likely to be made.

While experimental designs are the most powerful evaluation structures, they are used infrequently in schools. This is often because administrators, teachers, and parents are hesitant to provide potentially beneficial programs to some students but not to others and because schools are usually composed of intact groups (i.e., classes) that cannot be broken up without great difficulty. But, once institutionally sanctioned, new programs are virtually impossible to stop; therefore the most trustworthy evidence needs to be gathered before a decision to institutionalize an alternative program is made. This means that if at all possible, an experimental design is generally the one of choice.

Given their practical disadvantages, how can experimental designs be implemented in schools? Powers and Alderman (1979) described experimental designs built around the notion of withholding treatment *temporarily*. In each design, data are gathered on two randomly constituted groups, each working toward the same goals: the experimental group (the one in the innovative program) and the control group (the one in the traditional program). Data are collected before the program begins and after it ends. These two data points can be used in various ways to estimate the effect of the alternative program (e.g., comparing posttest scores across groups, given equal pretest scores; comparing pretest–posttest differences).

Three of the designs described by Powers and Alderman are particularly relevant to the evaluation of alternative educational programs: delayed treatment, program structure, and program popularity. In the first model, delayed treatment, schools offer special programs to groups of students on a rotating basis. For example, many secondary schools are beginning to offer computer mathematics courses designed in part to give students a better conceptual understanding of mathematics through the use of the computer (Bitter, 1987). Such courses may be offered in both the fall and spring semesters. In this case, students can be randomly assigned to semesters, the delayed group being enrolled in a traditional math course, which serves as control for the group taking computer mathematics.

Program structure can also provide a control. In some schools, an alternative treatment constitutes only a part of the curriculum to be covered in a given semester. So, for example, seventh-grade social studies might include using database management programs to help students develop an appreciation for historical facts and relationships. Students might enter information into the programs and sort and search that information in various ways intended to highlight important results. Database systems might be applied at various times during the term and with a variety of social studies content. For example, one class might use these programs early in the semester to learn about the presidents of the United States; a second class might learn this content through traditional means but use the systems later for a unit on westward expansion. The evaluation comparisons would be between the classes at the beginning of the semester and after the presidents unit (and perhaps again after the westward expansion unit). Assigning students at the beginning of the semester to classes having different plans as to subjects to which these tools will be applied and timing of implementation offers a natural set of controls.

For many innovative programs, there will be more potential participants than available places. In these situations, program popularity can serve as control. For example, consider that a school district has instituted a new program to teach reading through direct instruction. Because of its experimental nature, the program is limited in size: Students are considered for the program by parent request and assigned to it at random; those who apply but are not selected serve as controls and are taught reading through traditional methods.

While these three approaches to random assignment may be workable in some situations, there will still be many instances in which random assignment simply is not practical. Where a substantial number of classes are available for participation in the evaluation, classes (instead of individual students) might be assigned randomly to treatment and control groups. Where this is not possible, less powerful, though still informative, quasi-experimental designs will need to be implemented. Two such designs are the comparison group and time-series designs.

Quasi-Experimental Designs

Comparison group design. The comparison group design involves comparing students in the innovative program with similar individuals in a traditional one designed to achieve the same goals. To the degree possible, both programs should be similar except on the dimensions intended to differentiate them. This similarity should extend to the individuals participating in the programs; characteristics that could cause differences in the ability to profit from the programs should be balanced (e.g., general ability, maturational rate, specific skills taught by the program, parental support, participation in other related programs). Without similarity across the innovative and traditional programs, outcome differences may simply arise from unperceived differences in the individuals assigned to them or in other program characteristics. In most instances, some unintended differences between programs will occur. As a consequence, it is critical to identify these factors and attempt to rule them out as likely explanations for any observed disparities in the performance of the groups.

As an example, consider a school district that wants to evaluate the effectiveness of a curriculum-based assessment (CBA) system in helping teachers make decisions about teaching writing and mathematics basics to individual students newly identified for special education. Because random assignment of teachers or students to traditional and innovative assessment programs is not administratively feasible, the school psychologist and consulting evaluator supervising the evaluation have decided to implement curriculum-based assessment in one school and use another similar school as a comparison. Background information on the two schools, their students, and teachers have been reviewed to assure similarity. At the comparison school, teachers are asked to base instructional plans on assessment results collected through the classification process and through their own classroom assessment routines. The outcomes on which the two programs are to be compared include writing and mathematics achievement (since CBA systems are meant to help students learn more effectively, increased achievement seems a reasonable goal) and teachers' perceptions of the utility of the assessment system. Measures of these variables are collected at the beginning and end of the year and include, for students, work products (e.g., short compositions, math homework assignments), standardized test results, and behavioral measures (e.g., the number of math problems computed correctly in a given time period). In addition, the implementation of each program is monitored to determine if the programs are being properly conducted and if they differ in unintended ways. At the end of the year, the programs are compared in regard to student achievement and teacher satisfaction to see if the CBA system has provided any benefit over the traditional program.

Time-series design. In the time-series design, only one group is assessed. However, this group is assessed repeatedly — prior to, during, and sometimes after implementation of the alternative program. The group, in essence, serves as its own control. Marked changes in outcome data from baseline (during which the traditional program was operative) to time periods following the implementation of the alternative offer evidence to support the alternative's role in causing the observed outcomes. Here, too, external events occurring over the course of the program need to be appraised and logically ruled out as competing causes of program effects.

A school district wanting to test the effectiveness of a prereferral intervention system can serve as an example of the application of the time-series design. The system is intended to insure that teachers refer for evaluation only those children with learning and behavior problems that cannot be served effectively within the regular classroom. The primary goal of the alternative system, therefore, is to reduce the number of inappropriate referrals to special education. To measure this variable, a school management team consisting of the principal, a school psychologist, and a master teacher render a judgment on the appropriateness of each referral. In addition, structured observations are made to determine if undue class disruption (an unintentional side effect) is caused by trying to service more students in the regular classroom. Because schools composing the district vary widely on important background characteristics, a comparison group design is not feasible. Instead, measures of referral appropriateness and classroom functioning are taken

for several months while the existing program remains in place (this program allows teachers essentially to make unrestricted referrals). These measures continue to be taken periodically after the prereferral intervention program commenced. At the end of the year, the number of referrals and the results of the structured observations are plotted by month. These plots are then examined to see if the number of inappropriate referrals or the level of class disruption is related to the change in referral programs.

For more information on evaluation designs, the interested reader should consult Campbell and Stanley (1963), Maher and Bennett (1984), Powers and Alderman (1979), and Stecher (1987).

Evaluating the Size of Effects

When is an alternative program to be judged more effective than a traditional one? And, more to the point, how much better must it be to justify institutionalizing it? These are not easy questions to answer, for as noted earlier much depends on how effectiveness is conceived. All other things equal (e.g., costs, consumer reaction, related effects), it is logical to think that an alternative program is better than the traditional one to the degree that it shows greater goal attainment. To be greater, the difference between the two programs on goal attainment measures must be statistically significant. This indicates that the difference is a reliable result — that is, that it would likely occur again with different samples of students randomly drawn from the same population.

But small differences in goal attainment, even if significant, should not necessarily lead to institutionalizing an alternative: New programs commonly require large amounts of time and effort to install so that the payoff, in terms of goal attainment, must be substantial to justify this investment. This cutoff point undoubtedly will vary from one situation to the next, as potential costs and benefits change. One general guideline, suggested by Cohen (1969), can be of use. Cohen considers the *minimum* difference necessary for a meaningful effect in the social sciences to be 0.2 standard deviation units (a measure of group variability), where the standard deviation units are those of control group performance. But this is truly a minimal cutoff: on the WISC-R scale, this would translate to a difference of only 3 IQ points (assuming a control-group standard deviation of 15).

EVALUATING EVALUATION

As for other educational programs, the effectiveness of the effort to evaluate alternative educational systems can itself be evaluated. Devoting some attention to the evaluation's effectiveness is critical: Without that attention, problems may not be identified, faulty information may be reported, and erroneous conclusions may result.

While the notion of *effectiveness* advocated in this chapter can be applied to evaluation, a more conventional conception is in terms of utility, feasibility, propriety, and accuracy (Joint Committee on Standards for Educational Evaluation, 1981). Utility can be regarded as the extent to which the evaluation serves the practical information needs of important audiences. The qualifications of the evaluators, the relevance of the evaluation information to the needs of the audiences, the clarity and timeliness of the report, and the identification of where, how, and what values entered the evaluation process all contribute to evaluation utility.

Feasibility considerations are intended to insure that the evaluation is realistic, prudent, diplomatic, and frugal. Evaluation procedures should be practical so as to minimize disruption. The different positions of interested groups should be kept in mind so that their cooperation can be obtained and efforts to sabotage the evaluation or misuse its results can be avoided. Finally, the evaluation should be cost-effective: If the evaluation costs more than the potential positive or negative effects of the program, something is seriously amiss!

Evaluation propriety refers to the legal and ethical ramifications of the activity. The rights and welfare of human subjects should be protected, reporting should be complete and fair, and conflicts of interest should be openly and honestly identified so that they do not compromise evaluation processes and results.

Accuracy primarily is a measure of the extent to which the information gathered and reported is technically adequate. Technical adequacy implies consideration not only of instrument reliability and validity, but also of the extent to which the program and the context in which it operates was sufficiently considered. Evaluation purposes, procedures, and data analysis methods should be described, conclusions explicitly justified, and safeguards (e.g., independent reviews) inserted to insure objective reporting.

Evaluations should be quality efforts. Periodically assessing evaluation activities with reference to these standards should help insure this quality.

INVOLVING SCHOOLS
IN EVALUATION EFFORTS

While evaluation should be a quality enterprise, anyone who has worked with schools in an evaluation capacity knows that getting officials to support evaluation *under any circumstances* is oftentimes a difficult task. Interest in evaluation seems to come about only when it is required by a funding agency, paid for by someone else, or consistent with the political ends of the school administration. This resistance to evaluation should be of little surprise, for schools have for years been exposed to evaluations that were of low quality in the sense that they provided very little information of direct local use. These evaluations have been conducted primarily as required parts of federally funded programs (for example, Title I) and have served to justify the allocation of these funds (David, 1981; vanderPloeg, 1982).

How does one get schools interested in conducting more frequent high-quality evaluations? Selling evaluation in the schools is little different from selling anything else. To be sold, evaluation must be presented as a cost-effective solution to an important problem. To what problem? The problem of how to develop and improve alternative programs so that they are better than the programs they are intended to replace. In what way might the alternative be better? It might be better by addressing a reconceptualized problem, one that is similar to but more important or remediable than the problem originally defined by the traditional program.[1] It also might be better by incorporating a more explicit and thorough design that states goals, methods, activities, and a theoretical rationale. Third, it might be better in its implementation, running more smoothly. Finally, it might produce superior outcomes (higher levels of goal attainment, no negative related effects, positive consumer reaction) and for lower or equal costs. Developing programs that are *better* is the primary goal of the conceputalization of evaluation presented here.

On the other side of the coin, evaluation is an insurance policy. It insures (to a reasonable degree) against costly mistakes: spending money on programs that prove little better than existing ones or, worse, institutionalizing a program that produces less than the current one and is just as hard to terminate. Furthermore, should the alternative program still turn out to be a costly mistake, the fact that information was systematically gathered and evaluated before making the original decision may be the only defense against unsympathetic criticism.

Changing attitudes toward evaluation will take time; after all, such attitudes took time to develop. Through the inclusion of school staff in evaluation planning, quality evaluations should result that respond to staff information needs and that produce among staff a sense of involvement and ownership. These are the only evaluations that schools should be expected to, and probably the only ones they are likely to fund and to cooperate with fully.

SUMMARY

Alternative education programs can exist in any of the five service areas that compose school structures: assessment, instruction, related services, personnel development, and administration. Effectiveness refers to the value of the problem addressed by a program, the quality of the program design, the efficiency of its implementation, and the level and nature of its outcomes. Evaluation is a process employed in designing or improving a program. The effectiveness of alternative education delivery systems should be evaluated because such systems must be designed and improved, and because such systems must be shown to be substantially better than existing systems if the cost of installing the alternative is to be justified.

The evaluation of alternative educational delivery systems can be accomplished by means of a conceptual framework that includes both the different functional segments of the school district and the program elements that constitute effectiveness. This framework recognizes that evaluation (a) must look at a system comprehensively, (b) can be applied to program alternatives regardless of service area, (c) may vary according to the type of program being evaluated and the evaluation concern addressed, and (d) is a team effort.

Outcome information is generally regarded as critical to any assessment of a proposed alternative program. Important considerations in conducting such evaluations are timing (i.e., after the alternative has had a chance to stabilize) and the trustworthiness of evidence. The trustworthiness of evidence is enhanced to the degree that experimental evaluation designs can be utilized.

Evaluations themselves can and should be evaluated so that the quality of evaluation efforts is assured. Evaluations can be evaluated in terms of utility, feasibility, propriety, and accuracy.

Involving schools in evaluation is most readily achieved by conducting user-centered evaluations: quality evaluations that respond to the concerns school staff and program consumers have about the alternative system, and that provide needed information for a reasonable cost.

REFERENCES

Bennett, R. E. (1982). Applications of microcomputer technology to special education. *Exceptional Children, 49,* 106-113.

Bennett, R. E. (1984). Myths and realities in automating special education information management. *Journal of Learning Disabilities, 17,* 52-54.

Bennett, R. E. (1986). A framework for studying the use of computers in special education. *Journal of Special Education Technology, 8*(2), 44-52.

Bennett, R. E., & Maher, C. A. (Eds.). (1986). *Emerging perspectives on assessment of exceptional children.* New York: Haworth.

Bitter, G. G. (1987). Planning a computer-education curriculum. In R. E. Bennett (Ed.), *Planning and evaluating computer education programs* (pp. 79-101). Columbus, OH: Charles Merrill.

Campbell, D. T., & Stanley, J. C. (1963). *Experimental and quasi-experimental designs for research.* Chicago: Rand McNally.

Cohen, J. (1969). *Statistical power analysis for the behavioral sciences.* New York: Academic.

David, J. L. (1981). Local uses of Title I evaluations. *Educational Evaluation and Policy Analysis, 3,* 27-39.

Deno, S. L., Marston, D., & Tindal, G. (1986). Direct and frequent curriculum-based measurement: An alternative for educational decision making. In R. E. Bennett and C. A. Maher (Eds.), *Emerging perspectives on assessment of exceptional children* (pp. 5-27). New York: Haworth.

Heller, K. A., Holtzman, W. H., & Messick, S. (Eds.). (1982). *Placing children in special education: A strategy for equity.* Washington, DC: National Academy Press.

Joint Committee on Standards for Educational Evaluation. (1981). *Standards for evaluations of educational programs, projects, and materials.* New York: McGraw-Hill.

Kerlinger, F. N. (1973). *Foundations of behavioral research.* New York: Holt, Rinehart, and Winston.

Maher, C. A., & Bennett, R. E. (1984). *Planning and evaluating special education services.* Englewood Cliffs, NJ: Prentice-Hall.

Powers, D. E., & Alderman, D. L. (1979). Practical techniques for implementing true experimental designs. *Evaluation Quarterly, 3*(1), 89-96.

Provus, M. (1972). Discrepancy evaluation. Berkeley: McCutchan.

Stecher, B. (1987). Evaluating the outcomes of computer-education programs. In R. E. Bennett (Ed.), *Planning and evaluating computer education programs* (pp. 163-194). Columbus, OH: Charles Merrill.

vanderPloeg, A. J. (1982). ESEA Title I evaluation: The service of two masters. *Educational Evaluation and Policy Analysis, 4,* 521-526.

Wolf, M. M. (1978). Social validity: The case for subjective measurement *or* How applied behavior analysis is finding its heart. *Journal of Applied Behavior Analysis, 11,* 203-214.

Wood, K. C., Peterson, S. E., DeGracie, J. S., & Zaharis, J. K. (1986). The jury is in: Use of a modified legal model for school program evaluation. *Educational Evaluation and Policy Analysis, 8,* 309-315.

Worthen, B., & Owens, T. (1978). Adversarial evaluation. *Journal of School Psychology, 16,* 39-48.

FOOTNOTE

[1] A wonderful example of this comes from the report of the National Academy of Sciences Panel on Selection and Placement of Students in Programs for the Mentally Retarded (Heller, Holtzman, & Messick, 1982). Charged with investigating the causes of overrepresentation of minority children in classes for the mentally retarded, the panel quickly recognized that disproportion per se was not a problem. Rather, they felt that disproportion signaled underlying conditions that might be problematic. Therefore, they reconceptualized the problem in terms of discovering these underlying conditions. As a result, the panel's recommendations dealt not with how to eliminate or reduce disproportion, but instead with how to redress the inequitable conditions that underlay it, in particular the validity of assessment for placement and the quality of instruction.

26

Alternative Delivery Systems: Legal and Ethical Influences

Daniel J. Reschly
Iowa State University

The current educational delivery system in place in the United States today was created by legal provisions. The alternative delivery systems recommended in this monograph will also come into existence by virtue of legal provisions. This chapter will provide discussion of the origins and mechanisms of current legal influences, as well as an analysis of the basic principles that govern the provision of special services to handicapped students. Opportunities for revision of current practices within existing legal guidelines will be identified whenever possible. The basic characteristics of legal influences will then be discussed in order to create the background for consideration of changes in the present delivery system. The legal provisions that would allow, encourage, or mandate such changes will be analyzed.

Ethical guidelines will also be discussed, but only in general terms. The lesser emphasis on ethical guidelines reflects the judgment that ethical standards have relatively weak influence on the delivery system and the specific behaviors of individual professionals. (Reschly, 1980a).

Legal action in courts and legislative bodies has created a revolution in the educational rights of handicapped students. Profound changes prompted by legal action began in the early 1970s; these changes continue today and are likely to develop further in the future. By the mid-1970s lawyers were regarded as the "new heroes of special education" (Hobbs,

1975a, p. 172). This estimate is not as general today because the legal influences have become increasingly complex and more divisive as progressively more complicated issues have been addressed or resolved through legal action (Fleig & Reschly, 1985). Some of the complicated issues considered in recent legal action include (a) alleged IQ test bias (*Larry P.*, 1979, 1984, 1986; *Marshall*, 1984, 1985; *S-1*, 1986); (b) extended school year services for the severely handicapped (*Armstrong v. Kline*, 1979; Stotland & Mancuso, 1981); (c) catheterization as a related service required by federal law (*Tatro v. Texas*, 1984); (d) interpretation of "appropriate education" to mean a program that merely confers benefits rather than best professional practices (*Board of Education v. Rowley*, 1982); and (e) recovery of attorney's fees for parents who prevail at hearings or in court (*Smith v. Robinson*, 1984; Handicapped Children's Protection Act, 1986). Each of these issues is complex, legally and educationally. Yet each had to be considered and resolved through court and/or legislative action. The nature of this legal action and its impact on these and related issues will be considered to explain the legal context in which delivery system changes must be developed.

Given the broad variety of alternatives discussed in other chapters of this volume, the question arises of what features of those alternatives can be implemented within current legal provisions? What legal changes are necessary in order to allow, encourage, or mandate desirable changes in the existing delivery system?

LEGAL AND ETHICAL INFLUENCES: ORIGINS AND MECHANISMS

Four sources of legal influences and the various mechanisms to ensure compliance have significantly influenced the current delivery system. Together they reflect the layers of legal provisions that influence the delivery of services to children and youth and guarantee various rights to handicapped students (Reynolds & Wang, 1983).

Origins of Legal Influences

Legal influences originate from four sources: constitutional law, state and federal legislation, federal and state regulations implementing legislative principles, and case law. The recent history of the development of services for students classified as handicapped has been markedly influenced by all four sources.

Constitutional law. Two key provisions in the United States Constitution served as the basis for class action court suits about 15 years ago that established the educational rights of handicapped students (see later subsection on case law). These principles were *equal protection* from the Fourteenth Amendment and *due process* from the Fifth and Fourteenth Amendments. These principles were applied to cases filed on behalf of handicapped students who had been excluded from participation in public school programs owing to their handicapped conditions and to cases alleging misclassification of minority students as handicapped. The courts ruled that denial of educational services to handicapped students was in violation of equal protection of the law, meaning that persons were treated unequally by the governmental unit (a school district) without sufficient cause or justification. Furthermore, the exclusion of handicapped students and the classification of normal minority students as handicapped were done without due process protections. That is,

the decisions were made without providing parents or other representatives of the student (a) appropriate information prior to the decision; or (b) opportunities to challenge the decision, to examine the bases for the decision, to provide additional information, or to obtain an impartial review.

State and federal legislation. A second important source of legal influence is legislation enacted at the state and federal levels. Legislation generally establishes broad principles that must be carried out by governmental agencies, private institutions, or individuals. The current delivery system is based on state and federal legislation. The basic principles in current state and federal legislation, particularly those pertaining to students classified as handicapped, are discussed in a later section.

Federal regulations and state rules. Federal and state regulations are a third origin of legal influences. They are interpretations of the basic principles established in legislation. The purpose of the regulations is to carry out the intent of the legislative body. Typically, regulations are far more detailed than the original legislation. An example of the typical relationship between legislation and regulations is provided in Table 1. In Table 1, the original legislation concerning establishment of the Protection in Evaluation Procedures provisions of the Education of the Handicapped Act (EHA) of 1975 are reprinted, followed by the EHA regulations intended to implement the intent of congress. Clearly, these regulations go considerably beyond the legislation. However, that is appropriate if the further provisions are consistent with the intent of the legislative body. Determining intent is part of what makes legal influences ambiguous and evolutionary.

The fact that regulations typically require considerably greater detail than the legislation they are designed to implement may introduce requirements that were not in the original legislation. Regulations most often are developed by the department or agency in the executive branch that is responsible for implement-

TABLE 1
EHA PEP Regulations and EHA Legislation

EHA LEGISLATION, SECTIONS 1412(5) (c) and 1414(a)(5)

Section 1412(5)(c)

The state has established that "(c) procedures to assure that testing and evaluation materials and procedures utilized for the purpose of evaluation and placement of handicapped children will be selected and administered so as not to be racially or culturally discriminatory. Such materials or procedures shall be provided and administered in the child's native language or mode of communication, unless it clearly is not feasible to do so, and no single procedure shall be the sole criterion for determining an appropriate educational program for a child."

Note. Section 1412(5)(c) is cited as justification for each of the PEP Regulations.

Section 1414(a)(5)

"A local agency or an intermediate educational unit which desires to receive payments under Section 1411(d) of this title shall submit an application to the appropriate state agency. Such application shall — . . . (5) provide assurances that the local educational agency or intermediate educational unit will establish, or revise, whichever is appropriate, an individualized education program for each handicapped child at the beginning of each school year and will then review and, if appropriate revise, its provisions periodically, but not less than annually."

Note. Section 1414(a)(5) is cited as justification for only one of the PEP Regulations, 300.533, and it appears relevant to only one subsection of 533(b), which pertains to the development of an individualized educational program.

EHA REGULATIONS, CFR 300.530 - CFR 300.534: PROTECTION IN EVALUATION PROCEDURES (PEP)

Reg. 300.530. General

(a) Each State educational agency shall insure that each public agency establishes and implements procedures which meet the requirements of Regs. 300.530-300.534.
(b) Testing and evaluation materials and procedures used for the purposes of evaluation and placement of handicapped children must be selected and administered so as not to be racially or culturally discriminatory. (20 U.S.C. 1412(5)(c))

Reg. 300.531. Preplacement Evaluation

Before any action is taken with respect to the initial placement of a handicapped child in a special educational program, a full and individual evaluation of the child's educational needs must be conducted in accordance with the requirements of Reg. 300.532.
(20 U.S.C. 1412(5)(c))

Reg. 300.532. Evaluation Procedures

State and local educational agencies shall insure, at a minimum, that:
(a) Tests and other evaluation materials:
  (1) Are provided and administered in the child's native language or other mode of communication, unless it is clearly not feasible to do so;
  (2) Have been validated for the specific purpose for which they are used; and
  (3) Are administered by trained personnel in conformance with the instructions provided by their producers;
(b) Tests and other evaluation materials include those tailored to assess specific areas of educational need and not merely those which are designed to provide a single general intelligence quotient;
(c) Tests are selected and administered so as best to ensure that when a test is administered to a child with impaired sensory, manual, or speaking skills, the test results accurately reflect the child's aptitude or achievement level or whatever other factors the test purports to measure, rather than reflecting the child's impaired sensory, manual, or speaking skills (except where those skills are the factors which the test purports to measure);
(d) No single procedure is used as the sole criterion for determining an appropriate educational program for a child; and
(e) The evaluation is made by a multidisciplinary team or group of persons, including at least one teacher or other specialist with knowledge in the area of suspected disability.

(table 1, continued)

(f) The child is assessed in all areas related to the suspected disability, including, where appropriate, health, vision, hearing, social and emotional status, general intelligence, academic performance, communicative status, and motor abilities.
(20 U.S.C. 1412(5)(c))

Comment. Children who have a speech impairment as their primary handicap may not need a complete battery of assessments (e.g., psychological, physical, or adaptive behavior). However, a qualified speech-language pathologist would (1) evaluate each speech impaired child using procedures that are appropriate for the diagnosis and appraisal of speech and language disorders, and (2) where necessary, make referrals for additional assessments needed to make an appropriate placement decision.

Reg. 300.533. Placement Procedures

(a) In interpreting evaluation data and in making placement decisions, each public agency shall:

(1) Draw upon information from a variety of sources, including aptitude and achievement tests, teacher recommendations, physical condition, social or cultural background, and adaptive behavior;
(2) Insure that information obtained from all of these sources is documented and carefully considered;
(3) Insure that the placement decision is made by a group of persons, including persons knowledgeable about the child, the meaning of the evaluation data, and the placement options; and
(4) Insure that the placement decision is made in conformity with the least restrictive environment rules in Regs. 300.550–300.554.

(b) If a determination is made that a child is handicapped and needs special education and related services, an individualized education program must be developed for the child in accordance with Regs. 300.340–300.349 of Subpart C.
(20 U.S.C. 1412(5)(c); 1414(a)(5))

Comment. Paragraph (a) (1) includes a list of examples of sources that may be used by a public agency in making placement decisions. The agency would not have to use all the sources in every instance. The point of the requirement is to insure that more than one source is used in interpreting evaluation data and in making placement decisions. For example, while all of the named sources would have to be used for a child whose suspected disability is mental retardation, they would not be necessary for certain other handicapped children, such as a child who has a severe articulation disorder as his primary handicap. For such a child, the speech-language pathologist, in complying with the multisource requirement, might use (1) a standardized test of articulation, and (2) observation of the child's articulation behavior in conversational speech.

Reg. 300.534 Reevaluation

Each state and local educational agency shall insure:

(a) That each handicapped child's individualized education program is reviewed in accordance with Regs. 300.340–300.349 of Subpart C, and
(b) That an evaluation of the child, based on procedures which meet the requirements under Reg. 300.532, is conducted every three years or more frequently if conditions warrant or if the child's parent or teacher requests an evaluation.
(20 U.S.C. 1412(5)(c))

---

ing the legislation. The regulations usually are formulated and then submitted to the public and to professional associations for comment and review, reformulated one or more times on the basis of comment and review, and finally submitted to the legislative body for final approval. In most instances, the final approval is provided by a committee assigned responsibility for implementation of the legislation, not by the entire legislative body.

Case law. Case law is a fourth source of legal influence. Case law originates when a person or group seeks resolution to a dispute over the application of constitutional law, state or federal statutes, or federal or state regulations, through litigation or administrative law hearings (discussed later as mechanisms of legal influence). The outcomes of these legal proceedings, for example, injunction or judicial opinion, create case law. Case law has been crucial in all phases of the establishment of the current legal system governing provision of educational services to handicapped students.

Two fundamentally different kinds of

cases have been and continue to be crucial influences at all levels, from administrative law hearings in a local school district to cases decided ultimately by the United States Supreme Court. On one hand there are the right-to-education cases, which originally sought access to an appropriate education for handicapped students (*Mills v. Board of Education*, 1972 [Mills]; *Pennsylvania Association for Retarded Children v. Pennsylvania*, 1972 [PARC]). Right-to-education cases continue today, now directed primarily toward refinement of the concepts of appropriate education and least restrictive environment. The other kind of case has been based on alleged misclassification of minority students as handicapped. These cases established basic due process rights as well as requirements regarding nondiscriminatory assessment, use of valid and reliable assessment procedures, multifactored assessment, group decision making, and so on. Early cases established those rights (*Diana*, 1970; *Guadalupe*, 1972); recent cases have refined the meaning and applications of those rights (*Larry P. v. Riles*, 1986; *Marshall v. Georgia*, 1984, 1985; *S-1 v. Turlington*, 1986).

Case law is evolutionary and usually ambiguous. Case law is the primary means by which the meaning, breadth, and scope of basic principles from various sources of legal influences are defined; for example, culturally and racially nondiscriminatory assessment and decision making in diagnosis and placement of students is a basic principle that was firmly established, first by cases filed under constitutional law provisions and then through federal and state legislation, followed by federal and state regulations. But many ambiguities still remain to be clarified. Does *nondiscriminatory* mean a prohibition of IQ tests? The federal courts have issued contradictory rulings on that question and the United States Supreme Court may ultimately decide (Reschly, 1987a). Even that result may be ambiguous, because case law always applies specifically to a particular situation or set of facts, and only by inference to other situations.

Case law establishes precedents that may be binding on subsequent cases, but there can be enormous differences in impact depending on the level of the legal proceeding and the legal status of the hearing or court. Administrative hearings at the local level typically have no direct influence on other hearings. In contrast, federal district court decisions carry the weight of law within their respective districts; they become law in several districts if upheld on appeal to a federal appeals court; they become law throughout the United States when decided by the United States Supreme Court. In considering the progression of broadening influence by successively higher courts, it is sometimes comforting to recall Bersoff's (1982) explanation that the Supreme Court is not supreme because it is best. It is supreme because it is last.

Revisions. Opportunities to change the four kinds of legal influences vary dramatically. Constitutional law is extremely difficult to change because it requires a change in the United States Constitution. There have been fewer than 20 such changes since the Constitution was enacted (along with the original 10 amendments) about 200 years ago. However, *interpretation* of the constitution does change through case law. State and federal legislation are also relatively difficult to change, since concurrence of two legislative bodies as well as approval of the chief executive (president or governor) are usually required. In contrast to constitutional law and federal and state statutes, regulations and rules are relatively easy to change. They typically are changed by the same process as that by which they were established.

Change in regulations, owing to their relative susceptibility to change and greater responsiveness to public comment and professional association advocacy, is usually the most appropriate and effective means to influence the service delivery system. The potential for changing rules and regulations, particularly at the state level, will become more apparent when the broad variations among states, all in compliance with federal legislation and regulations, are discussed later.

Mechanisms of Legal Influence

There are a variety of mechanisms through which legal influences are implemented. These mechanisms include several kinds of court proceedings as well as various executive branch functions such as monitoring compliance and providing financial support.

Litigation and Hearings. The first judicial mechanism is the *injunction*, which can be issued when a court is convinced that harm would result if current procedures or activities were allowed to continue. An extremely influential use of the injunction was the *Larry P. v. Riles*, 1972, 1974 injunctions by a federal district court that banned the use of IQ tests with black students if those students were classified as mildly mentally retarded. A trial in this case was held in 1977–1978.

A second court mechanism is the *consent decree*. A consent decree is a settlement negotiated between plaintiffs and defendants in a suit and then approved by the court. The consent decree has the effect of law on the parties to the dispute. One of the most important consent decrees in the history of educational services for handicapped students was PARC (1972), which committed the Commonwealth of Pennsylvania to far-reaching changes in the availability, funding, and program characteristics of educational services for handicapped students. A number of other consent decrees in the early 1970s (*Diana*, 1970; *Guadalupe*, 1972; *Mills*, 1972) had substantial influence on subsequent state and federal legislation.

Judicial opinions are perhaps the most important of the court mechanisms. Judicial opinions are developed after a trial in which the parties to the dispute have presented various kinds of evidence, written briefs, and oral arguments. Judicial opinions have the effect of law in the area or region within the court's jurisdiction. Judicial opinions appealed to higher courts have the effect of broadening the applicability of the decision if they are upheld.

Several judicial opinions rendered since the late 1970s have exerted profound influences on the provision of services to handicapped students. For example, in *Rowley* (1982) three courts, a federal district court in New York, a United States Circuit Court of Appeals, and the United States Supreme Court, issued opinions concerning the meaning of "appropriate education" in federal legislation guaranteeing educational rights to handicapped students. The *Rowley* decision has influenced the provision of services throughout the United States because it ultimately was decided by a United States Supreme Court ruling. This decision, incidentally, defined *appropriate* as education from which the student is deriving benefits, rather than the best, most desirable, or even most effective educational services or methodology.

A final form of influence is the *administrative hearing* which is established in federal and state statutes as part of the due process protections. Administrative hearings, in the context of public education, are designed to resolve disputes between parents and local or state agencies. Due process hearings can be initiated by students, by representatives of students (usually parents), or by an educational agency. An impartial hearing officer then conducts a hearing in which both sides have the opportunity to present evidence, examine witnesses, and enter oral and written arguments. Hearings allow parents and others to carefully scrutinize the recommendations of school officials, including key decisions regarding classification, placement, and programming. Administrative hearings are a potentially significant influence on the delivery system in that students or their representatives can strongly advocate for provision of particular kinds of services in specific settings. An example of this kind of influence is the recent upsurge of hearings throughout the United States relating to providing services to severely handicapped children and youth over an extended school year (*Armstrong v. Kline*, 1979). There have been numerous hearings on this issue that in turn have prompted the development of additional rules from state departments of education clarifying policies concerning educational services beyond the traditional school year. Although the results of administrative hearings do not have the same effect as judicial opinions, they generally are seen to influence policy trends, particularly within the state.

Compliance monitoring and financial incentives. The major mechanism by which legislation and accompanying regulations and rules are implemented is compliance monitoring and financial incentives. Compliance monitoring of legislative mandates is typically carried out by professionals on the staff of the executive branch department responsible for implementing the pertinent legislation. Compliance monitoring usually involves visits to the service agency (e.g., a local school district) during which various sorts of information are gathered and compared to regulations and rules, various persons such as teachers and parents are interviewed, and a random sample of records is reviewed and other observations are made. Failure to comply with rules and regulations usually leads to some kind of official citation that requires a satisfactory response from the delinquent agency. Satisfactory response may take the form of an appeal of the citation or description of changes designed to ensure compliance in the future. Financial support can be withdrawn or delayed as a result of noncompliance.

Compliance monitoring is one of the most effective means of ensuring implementation of a particular delivery system. Of course, depending on developments relating to policy at the state and federal level, it could be a strong force toward either continuation of the present system or development and implementation of various alternatives. Compliance monitoring has a significant influence on the meaning and implementation of rules and regulations. In many instances, it appears to go beyond the provisions stipulated in

published rules and regulations and beyond apparent legislative intent. For example, the last section of the federal regulations pertaining to reevaluation (reprinted in Table 1) has frequently been interpreted by officials responsible for compliance monitoring as requiring retesting in all of the areas for which tests were given in the original evaluation. This interpretation has led to absurd practices such as readministering IQ tests to profoundly retarded teenagers. Nothing in the regulation mandates retesting. Furthermore, the regulations to which the reevaluation provision refers specifically uses the term "where appropriate." Challenges to interpretations that are neither in the best interest of students nor consistent with an effective delivery system need to be made through local, state, and national associations.

Much of what can go wrong with the implementation of legislation occurs at the level of compliance monitoring. Persons responsible for monitoring have an unenviable task in that they have a relatively small amount of time and limited staff resources to determine whether an agency is in compliance with a vast array of rules or regulations, most of which are ambiguous (see below). In order to reduce ambiguity in the decisions that must be made, there is an understandable tendency to specify precise details, such as retesting. This precision undoubtedly improves objectivity and reliability across situations and monitors, but it may also be inconsistent with the purpose of the regulations. The regulatory purpose in the example above is to ensure appropriate classification, proper placement, and effective programming. Some retesting has an obscure relationship to those broad purposes. Much of what is right with the current system has to do with laudable principles guaranteeing rights; some of what is wrong occurs through compliance monitoring using very detailed schedules that go beyond and, occasionally, defeat the purposes of the general principles.

Compliance monitoring is one of the most difficult dilemmas associated with the current system. Clearly, compliance monitoring is a two-edged sword. On one hand, it is a mechanism whereby powerful influences are exerted, principally through the possible loss of financial support. On the other hand, trivial aspects of services may be imposed through detailed monitoring schedules with the effect of inducing rigidity into a system that becomes increasingly unresponsive to the needs of individual students. The dynamic tension between ensuring compliance and ensuring sufficient flexibility to meet individual student needs is a dilemma that must be addressed in efforts to improve the delivery system. Further discussion of this question is provided in the section on prereferral interventions.

Reciprocal Influences

There are multiple reciprocal influences among the origins and mechanisms of legal influence (Figure 1). The major breakthroughs in assuring the rights of handicapped students to educational services arose from consent decrees settling federal district court cases filed as class action suits on behalf of handicapped students that were based on the equal protection and due process constitutional provisions. Early placement bias litigation using these same protections also was settled by consent decrees (*Diana*, 1970; *Guadalupe*, 1972) or court injunction (*Larry P.*, 1972, 1974).

These consent decrees had a profound influence on federal and state legislation enacted in the early to middle 1970s. Several specific statements in the Protection in Evaluation Procedures Provisions (see Table 1) are identical to phrases that appeared in the consent decrees in *Diana* (1970) and *Guadalupe* (1972). The principles concerning rights to educational services, due process protections, placement in the least restrictive environment, and individualized programming from *Mills* (1972) and *PARC* (1972) appear in virtually the same form in subsequent state and federal legislation.

The third phase in the expression of reciprocal influence of legislation and litigation has been apparent in diverse litigation since 1975. The second-genera-

tion right-to-education and placement litigation cases have been filed using legislation that, in turn, had been prompted by earlier litigation. These cases typically are filed using the EHA principles (1975). The second-generation court cases can be seen as efforts to clarify the meaning of general principles such as right to appropriate education and least restrictive environment (Reschly, 1987a).

A fourth phase in the legislation-litigation cycle is suggested in Figure 1. Currently, we see increasing interest in reforms of the present system. These reforms also involve the effects of litigation and legislation and can be expected, in turn, to prompt a fifth phase of reciprocal influences in the future.

Responsiveness to Authoritative Sources and Scientific Reports

There are a variety of other influences on litigation and legislation that are important to recognize as potential contributions to the development of alternative delivery systems. Both court decisions and legislation are influenced by social trends, position statements by authoritative sources, and major scientific reports (Reschly, Kicklighter, & McKee, 1988). These kinds of influences on litigation are particularly apparent in two recent placement litigation decisions (*Marshall*, 1984, 1985; *S-1*, 1986). Both cases involved lengthy trials in which plaintiffs and defendants generally agreed upon the importance of certain authoritative sources, particularly the American Association on Mental Deficiency (AAMD) *Classification in Mental Retardation* (Grossman, 1983) and the recommendations of a blue ribbon panel established by the National Academy of Sciences (NAS) (Heller, Holtzman, & Messick, 1982). The NAS panel was charged with the responsibility of examining the problem of overrepresentation of minority students in special class programs for the mildly retarded. One of the major recommendations of the panel called for far greater involvement of regular education in the development of a variety of alternatives for students with learning or

FIGURE 1
Reciprocal Influences of Litigation and Legislation

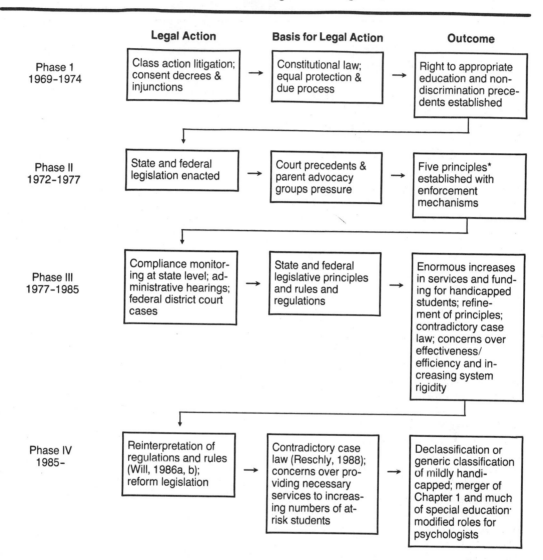

	Legal Action	Basis for Legal Action	Outcome
Phase 1 1969–1974	Class action litigation; consent decrees & injunctions →	Constitutional law; equal protection & due process →	Right to appropriate education and non-discrimination precedents established
Phase II 1972–1977	State and federal legislation enacted →	Court precedents & parent advocacy groups pressure →	Five principles* established with enforcement mechanisms
Phase III 1977–1985	Compliance monitoring at state level; administrative hearings; federal district court cases →	State and federal legislative principles and rules and regulations →	Enormous increases in services and funding for handicapped students; refinement of principles; contradictory case law; concerns over effectiveness/efficiency and increasing system rigidity
Phase IV 1985–	Reinterpretation of regulations and rules (Will, 1986a, b); reform legislation →	Contradictory case law (Reschly, 1988); concerns over providing necessary services to increasing numbers of at-risk students →	Declassification or generic classification of mildly handicapped; merger of Chapter 1 and much of special education modified roles for psychologists

*The five principles are (a) appropriate educational services for handicapped students at public expense; (b) placement in the least restrictive environment; (c) individualized education program; (d) due process; (e) protection in evaluation procedures.

behavior problems. These principles of responsibility (Heller et al., 1982, pp. 94–95) emphasize the development of a variety of regular education programs as a prerequisite to, and for many students as an alternative to, special education classification and placement. These principles are reprinted in Table 2.

The NAS and AAMD examples reflect the influence on litigation of a report from a very prestigious scientific association and a classification manual from an authoritative professional association, respectively. Legislation is similarly affected, although it is sometimes more difficult to identify specific influences

TABLE 2
Principles of Responsibility from National Academy of Sciences Report on
Special Education Placement (Heller et al., 1981, pp. 94-95)

1. It is the responsibility of teachers in the regular classroom to engage in multiple educational interventions and to note the effects of such interventions on a child experiencing academic failure before referring the child for special education assessment. It is the responsibility of school boards and administrators to ensure that needed alternative instructional resources are available.

2. It is the responsibility of assessment specialists to demonstrate that the measures employed validly assess the functional needs of the individual child for which there are potentially effective interventions.

3. It is the responsibility of the placement team that labels and places a child in a special program to demonstrate that any differential label used is related to a distinctive prescription for educational practices and that these practices are likely to lead to improved outcomes not achievable in the regular classroom.

4. It is the responsibility of the special education and evaluation staff to demonstrate systematically that high-quality, effective special instruction is being provided and that the goals of the special education program could not be achieved as effectively within the regular classroom.

5. It is the responsibility of the special education staff to demonstrate, on at least an annual basis, that a child should remain in the special education class. A child should be retained in the special education class only after it has been demonstrated that he or she cannot meet specified educational objectives and that all efforts have been made to achieve these objectives.

6. It is the responsibility of administrators at the district, state, and national levels to monitor on a regular basis the pattern of special education placements, the rates for particular groups of children or particular schools and districts, and the types of instructional services offered to affirm that appropriate procedures are being followed or to redress inequities found in the system.

---

because, unlike judicial opinions, the source for particular ideas typically goes uncited in legislation. However, the principles reflected in the NAS report are likely to have been a major influence in recent changes in New Jersey legislation (*Plan to Revise Special Education*, 1986) and revisions in state rules requiring prereferral interventions (*Louisiana Pupil Appraisal Handbook*, 1983; *Florida Resource Manual*, 1985). Use of authoritative sources and the reports of prestigious scientific associations are among the more effective methods individuals and groups can employ in advocating for changes in the delivery system.

Ethical Considerations

The principles of professional ethics provided by two major professional associations concerned with alternative delivery systems, the American Psychological Association (*Ethical Principles of Psychologists*, 1981); and the National Association of School Psychologists (*Principles for Professional Ethics*, 1984), are designed to protect the interests of

clients through the promotion of appropriate conduct by their members. However, ethical principles typically are quite ambiguous and often extremely difficult to apply in specific situations (Bersoff, 1975; Reschly, 1980a). Certain characteristics of the current delivery system provoke especially perplexing ethical problems. Perhaps the most frequently encountered ethical dilemma is the problem of deciding whether to classify as handicapped a student who is experiencing learning and/or behavioral difficulties. Classification decisions with students who have relatively minor handicaps, particularly those who do not express behavioral patterns attributable to physical or biological etiologies, are especially perplexing. In many instances, a stringent application of classification criteria would render the individual ineligible for needed services, whereas a less stringent application could lead to a classification as handicapped. Depending on whether the person is classified as handicapped, may determine whether a variety of services will be provided and may subject the client to whatever stigma may be associated with the diagnosis. The dilemma is clear. Appropriate resolution is far from clear, in large part because it is impossible in most instances to determine with certainty whether the services provided will be sufficient to offset the disadvantages associated with being so classified.

In the situation just described it is extremely difficult to determine how key ethical principles are to be applied. There is no argument about the ethical cannon concerning making decisions in the best interest of the client. However, whether it is in the best interest of the client to classify or not to classify, is far from clear. Much of the rationale for providing an alternative delivery system is related to problems resulting from the requirement that students must be called handicapped in order to receive services.

LEGAL BASIS FOR COMPENSATORY, REMEDIAL, AND SPECIAL EDUCATION

Federal legislation has established three general programs in all states and in virtually every district that are intended to improve educational opportunities for students with learning and/or behavioral problems. These three programs are Head Start, designed for preschool students above the age of 3 years; Chapter 1, intended for school-age students who are economically disadvantaged and achieving below grade or age expectations; and special education programs intended for students with various kinds of handicaps. These programs are supported to varying degrees by federal funding. The characteristics of these programs and the students served by them are particularly important because one trend in the current special education reform movement contemplates combining such programs (Reynolds, Wang, & Walberg, 1987).

Head Start

Head Start, the first major federal compensatory education program, was established by the Economic Opportunity Act (EOA) (1964), and was first imple-

mented in 1965. Head Start goals have always been broad, including social and emotional development, physical well-being, general intellectual development, motivation, and academic success. Children are admitted to Head Start programs if their families meet income guidelines and if a program is available in their community. Most communities have Head Start programs.

Considerable debate has occurred over the past 20 years concerning the effects of Head Start. Although this debate is beyond the scope of this chapter, one outcome of such programs is quite relevant. Students who have participated in Head Start are less likely than non-Headstart low-income children to be placed in special education programs for the mildly handicapped during their school age years (Lazar & Darlington, 1982). This outcome, as well as the Head Start goal of improving educational achievement for students at risk for school-related problems, supports a closer relationship between Head Start and preschool special education programs. One of the most important recent changes in federal special education legislation (passed in 1986) was extension of the EHA mandate to preschool handicapped students.

Chapter 1

The Chapter 1 program is the largest federally funded compensatory education program. The forerunner of Chapter 1, Title 1, was established by the Elementary and Secondary Education Act (1965). Slight changes were made when the program was changed to Chapter 1 in the Educational Consolidation and Improvement Act (1981). Generally, Chapter 1 is designed to provide remedial educational services to economically disadvantaged students with achievement difficulties. The Chapter 1 allocation of resources is complex. Federal grants are distributed to states and districts on the basis of the numbers of economically disadvantaged students (Leinhardt & Bickel, 1987). Districts then establish programs according to numbers of economically disadvantaged students in attendance at different centers. However, students at a specific center are typically assigned to Chapter 1 remedial instruction on the basis of group-administered standardized achievement tests. Although some may not meet income guidelines (Carter, 1984), students are supposed to be educationally deprived in order to receive the more intensive Chapter 1 services. According to Leinhardt and Bickel (1987), Chapter 1 serves about 4.5 million children and is funded in the $4 billion range. It is important to note that Chapter 1 monies are distributed according to income characteristics of populations in states and districts, not according to individual student characteristics.

Special Education for the Mildly Handicapped

Special education programs for the mildly handicapped developed slowly over the first 70 years of this century, then rapidly after 1972, in large part as a result of key court cases (see previous section) that led to mandated legislation at the state and federal levels. The federal Education of the Handicapped Act (1975) provided financial incentives if the state enacted special education legislation that met certain basic requirements (see discussion in the following section). EHA is perhaps best understood as a grant-giving statute (Bersoff, 1982), because states receive monies if basic requirements are fulfilled. These requirements must be met by states and local districts. The federal Office of Special Education and Rehabilitation Services monitors state compliance on a regular basis.

It is important to note that special education involves a mixture of programs and kinds of students. One of the most complex features of special education is the intermingling of the mildly and the more severely handicapped (Reschly, 1987b). Briefly, the mildly handicapped exhibit significant learning or behavioral problems, but do *not* have any underlying biological anomalies; their handicaps are relatively temporary in that they typically are most apparent during the school-age

years, during which time special services are required, but they are frequently not classified officially as handicapped during their adult years. In contrast, the more severely handicapped typically have learning and behavioral problems that have a *physical etiology;* their handicaps are usually identifiable during their preschool years and are life-long conditions. This distinction is important because the special education reform movement and the alternative service delivery systems discussed in this volume are primarily concerned with the mildly handicapped, *not the more severely handicapped.* Mildly handicapped students classified as learning-disabled (LD), mildly mentally retarded (MMR), or emotionally disturbed (ED), constitute about 80% of the population of students classified as handicapped (Algozzine & Korinek, 1985). Mildly handicapped students are similar in many respects to students receiving compensatory educational services in Head Start and remedial/compensatory services in Chapter 1 (Kavale, 1980; Leinhardt & Bickel, 1987; Leinhardt, Bickel, & Pallay, 1982; Reschly, 1986).

Similarities and Differences

In respect to legal requirements and student characteristics there are important similarities and differences between programs for economically disadvantaged and mildly handicapped students. Some of the critical similarities are the following: (a) Both have a strong emphasis on reading and math instruction, particularly at the elementary grade levels. (b) Both rely heavily on pull-out interventions (that is, instruction occurs outside the regular classroom) (Carter, 1984). (c) Economically disadvantaged students are more likely to be placed in both programs (Kavale, 1980). (d) Students in the two programs have similar educational problems. (e) The same instructional techniques are effective with students in both kinds of programs (Leinhardt & Bickel, 1987; Leinhardt et al., 1982).

On the other hand, there are some significant differences between Chapter 1 and special education programs for the mildly handicapped. The following are the most important of these differences. (a) Problems exhibited by students in Chapter 1 programs are assumed to be of environmental origin, poverty-related, and correctable through additional educational opportunities, whereas, in contrast, the problems exhibited by mildly handicapped students are assumed (often erroneously) to originate within the person and a biological cause may or may not be assumed. (b) Eligibility for individual students is much simpler in Chapter 1 programs (a combination of income and achievement levels), whereas in special education programs there are complex eligibility guidelines that are very expensive to apply to individual cases. (c) There is greater parental involvement in special education programs in conjunction with complex due process procedures; in contrast, parental involvement is encouraged in Chapter 1, but not required. (d) Additional monies for Chapter 1 are far less available — less than $1,000 per student (Carter, 1984) — than for handicapped students placed in special education programs (approximately $2,000–$5,000). (e) Much greater stigma is attached to special education, since the etiologies are often assumed to reside with the individual, rather than the environment. (f) Special education programs for handicapped students are mandatory, whereas low-achieving, economically disadvantaged students may not have access to Chapter 1 programs, depending on characteristics of their service center and district. (g) Special education pull-out instruction is much more likely to be based on a written individualized program, delivered individually, whereas Chapter 1 pull-out instruction is more likely to be delivered to small groups of children who have similar achievement difficulties. (h) Special education for the mildly handicapped is more likely to involve social skills objectives, in addition to academic objectives; Chapter 1 almost always focuses exclusively on academic skills. (i) LD and MMR students are usually farther below regular classroom averages than are Chapter 1 students. (j) Finally, some special education students are placed in self-contained classes where they receive nearly all of their educational program.

Perhaps the most critical difference between special education for the mildly handicapped and Chapter 1 involves entitlement. The special education entitlement is governed or controlled by an eligibility determination system that is enormously complex, often requiring expenditures of hundreds of dollars to determine whether a student is eligible for the program (Shepard, 1983). Once eligibility is established, an appropriate program must be provided. In contrast, determining eligibility for Chapter 1 is very inexpensive, but not all eligible students receive Chapter 1 instruction. Furthermore, there are a host of additional requirements concerning special education programs, but relatively sparse requirements concerning Chapter 1 programs. One of the most important issues in efforts to develop alternative systems will be the degree to which certain desirable features of special education programs will be retained and attempts will be made to implement these features more broadly. Due process procedural protections, written individualized programming, multifactored assessment, and multidisciplinary team decision making are very important but also quite expensive. Part of the differential in per-student costs between EHA and Chapter 1 programs is related to these additional features. If all of these legal requirements are extended to Chapter 1 students, costs could increase significantly, perhaps double. If none are retained and existing Chapter 1 and EHA systems are combined, several advocacy groups, particularly parents of students classified now as learning-disabled, are likely to strongly resist any changes because of perceived threats to the public awareness of LD problems, to current legislation and funding, and to the implementation of legislative mandates. The critical issue will be to establish legal requirements that allow and encourage cost-efficient, effective methods to provide services, and at the same time preserve previous advances in parents' and students' rights. Some of the possibilities for accomplishing these objectives through flexible interpretation and slight revisions in existing EHA legal requirements are discussed in the next section.

OPPORTUNITIES FOR ALTERNATIVE SYSTEMS AND EHA LEGAL PROVISIONS

More attention is devoted here to the legal requirements of EHA, and opportunities it provides for the development of alternative systems, because although both EHA and Chapter 1 serve slightly over 4 million children, roughly $13 billion is expended on programs for the handicapped, whereas $4 billion is budgeted for Chapter 1 programs. Furthermore, the EHA legal requirements are of special interest, being based on several layers of legal influence, including court mandate, state and federal legislation, and federal regulations and state rules. And even though most of the funding for special education programs originates in state and local monies, it should be noted here that the federal share of costs being only about 10%, the requirements attached to EHA are implemented in every state and have exerted substantial influence on state legislation and rules.

Individual students first must be identified as handicapped as a prerequisite to receipt of services under EHA; (identification is a mandatory feature in EHA and, arguably, the single most important issue that must be resolved in order to develop alternative delivery systems). The services provided to handicapped students thus identified are governed by five major principles expressed in EHA legislation and regulations and applied throughout the United States. The critical EHA principles are (a) the guarantee of appropriate educational services at public expense; (b) the provision of due process procedural protections governing classification, placement, and programming; (c) mandatory application of rule in placement in the least restrictive environment; (d) protection in evaluation procedures provisions that are designed to ensure fairness in classifica-

tion and placement; and (e) an individualized educational program developed according to certain specifications. The potential influence of each of these legal principles on the development of alternative delivery systems is discussed in subsequent sections.

The Link Between Identification and Appropriate Education

Special education classification represents a kind of Faustian bargain. Students (and their parents) are guaranteed appropriate educational services if they agree to being classified (labeled) as handicapped. This appropriate education guarantee at public expense is realized through a variety of other requirements such as the development of an individualized educational program and placement in the least restrictive environment. But classification is prerequisite to access to special education monies that support the educational services carried out according to the EHA principles.

The mandated link between classification and guaranteed appropriate education is set out in several federal regulations (EHA, 1975, 34 CFR, part 300). In Regulation 300.5, 11 kinds of handicap (e.g., mentally retarded, deaf/blind, specific learning disability) are listed with definitions for each. Handicapped children must be evaluated according to the Protection in Evaluation Procedures provisions (Table 1) and must be certified as needing special education and related services as a result of the handicapping condition. Subsequent regulations provide further specification on the link between handicapped classification and appropriate educational programming. In Regulation 300.145, there is a prohibition of comingling of funds, that is, combining monies intended for the handicapped with funds intended to support other kinds of educational services. Regulation 300.141 requires states to seek recovery of funds expended by districts on behalf of children who have been erroneously classified or are ineligible to be classified as handicapped. Subsequent regulations, 300.182 and 300.194, restrict the use of funds to defray the excess costs associated with educating handicapped children. These regulations also require state departments of education to withhold monies from local educational agencies if the latter fail to comply with EHA. Clearly, current federal regulations, as well as state legislation and rules, mandate that special education monies be restricted to students with identified handicaps. These requirements represent an obvious barrier to combining current special education and compensatory/remedial educational programming. However, this barrier may not be insurmountable.

The purposes of classification are well known and will be mentioned only briefly (extensive discussion of issues in classification has been provided by Hobbs, 1975a, 1975b). The major purposes of a classification system are (a) to facilitate communication about basic phenomena essential to conducting research, developing and assessing the effects of treatment programs, and exchanging information among scholars, practitioners, and advocates; (b) to enable parents and professionals to focus public attention on problems and to advocate for legislation and funding; (c) to appropriate money based on needs; (d) to ensure accountability for disbursement of funds (i.e., monies can be reserved for students who meet certain criteria); (e) to protect against misclassification of normal students as handicapped; and (f) to organize and deliver appropriate programming based on the students' diagnoses/classifications (this assumed or hoped-for benefit of classification has been questioned in recent years). Each of the above purposes is an important component of the justification for some kind of handicapped child classification system. The most important justification is probably financial accountability. A major concern of parent advocacy groups and legislators is that without a classification requirement funds would not necessarily be expended on students with serious problems, and the purposes of providing additional educational resources for students with learning or behavior difficulties might be undermined. Alternative

means to account for expenditures must be developed if significant changes are to occur in the current classification/placement legal requirements.

Funding according to counts of eligible students is one means of ensuring accountability. (Other means have been discussed by Gallagher, Forsythe, Ringelheim, & Weintraub, 1975). Funding mechanisms could be based, in addition to numbers of handicapped students, on numbers of professional personnel or on the unit cost of particular kinds of special programs (e.g., for a resource teaching program or a special class). Any of these alternatives would provide a means to ensure that monies were expended according to intended purposes, but would eliminate the need to classify individual students as handicapped. The use of these funding alternatives appears to have declined in recent years, perhaps because of the EHA requirement that federal monies be allocated according to an annual count of eligible handicapped students.

There are many problems associated with funding special education programs according to the number of individual students certified as handicapped. Many of these problems are discussed in considerable detail in other chapters of this volume and will be mentioned briefly here.

One of the most serious problems with child-count allocations of resources is that the numbers of students needing remedial/compensatory services is far larger than the available resources . Even though special education funding has increased rapidly since 1975, and the percentage of students classified as handicapped has grown from about 6% to about 11%, many more students, a total of 20-25% according to Leinhardt et al. (1982), have achievement problems and need remedial educational programs. The very expensive per-student costs prohibit extension of special education to all the students who need these services. Hence these financial considerations in the face of large total numbers of students needing services strongly influence the movement supporting alternative delivery systems.

In addition to the fiscal problem,

there are further concerns with the efficiency and usefulness of some of the components of the current special education process. At present, approximately $1,000, and often more, is spent to determine whether a referred student is eligible to be classified as handicapped. These expenditures involve processing referrals, formation of multidisciplinary teams, carrying out multifactored assessments, staffing, and selection of placement options. This expenditure occurs whether or not the student is ultimately deemed handicapped and eligible for special education. Expenditure for determination of eligibility in Chapter 1 programs is approximately 1/100th of that for special education, about $10 per student (Shepard, 1983).

A further concern is that the kind of information gathered in order to make classification decisions typically has little relevance to instruction or intervention. Classification nearly always involves norm-referenced decisions. In contrast, intervention decisions require criterion-referenced information (Reschly, 1980b, 1987a).

Perhaps the most serious problem with the current funding system is that a forced separation of regular and special education is imposed. The imposition of a separate system is particularly inappropriate because the vast majority of handicapped students, about 80% (*Seventh Annual Report*, 1985), spend the majority of the school day within regular education. This forced separation also divides responsibilities and diminishes the degree to which regular education personnel see themselves as primarily responsible for developing interventions to overcome specific learning or behavioral problems.

Forced separation of programs also stifles innovative efforts to use existing resources more efficiently and effectively. Wang and Reynolds (1985) provided a valuable discussion of the contradiction inherent in the present funding system. Innovative programs that either prevent or remediate problems exhibited by handicapped students ultimately lose state and federal financial support be-cause the students, after effective interventions, are no longer certified officially as handicapped. Thus, the Catch 22 is that successful program outcomes lead to elimination of the successful program. Readers interested in further discussion of this problem are referred to other chapters in this volume, as well as Wang and Reynolds (1985) and Wang, Reynolds, and Walberg (1987).

However, there is some flexibility in application of current federal regulations. Creative use of this flexibility can provide considerable opportunity to design interventions for students with learning and behavioral problems without spending large sums of money on classification/placement activities and perhaps without restricting those interventions to handicapped students. Several areas of flexibility can be seen in varying practices among different states and in innovative plans recently developed and currently being established.

States have considerable latitude in determination of the nature of the handicapped child classification system. They do not have to use the 11 categories specified in federal regulations. Considerable variation exists across the states in names, definitions, and classification criteria. For example, a wide variety of terms are used for mental retardation, for example, mental disability, mental handicap, and significantly limited intellectual capacity (Patrick & Reschly, 1982). Despite these variations the Office of Special Education and Rehabilitation Services has approved all of the state programs as in compliance with EHA requirements. Furthermore, the choice of classification criteria to be associated with different handicapping conditions is a state prerogative, and there are significant differences among the states. For example, there are two states that do not require classification according to the 11 handicapping conditions specified in federal regulations or any other list of handicapping conditions as such. These states, Massachusetts and South Dakota, do require local districts to determine whether students are handicapped, but they do not require specification of a particular label. However, these two states, as well as all the others, annually report to the federal government a child count that uses the 11 categories specified in the EHA regulations. Just how this child count is done in the two states mentioned above has never been clear, but the critical point is that there is considerable flexibility in handicapped classification. In any case, it would appear that a state could adopt the recommendations of Hobbs (1975a) and draw a fairly general distinction between mildly handicapped and severely handicapped, making more detailed classification of students only as to the kinds of services that are needed. In this circumstance a state would be required to determine whether a student is handicapped, as is done now in South Dakota and Massachusetts, but would not have to expend vast sums of money deciding whether students are "really" mentally retarded in contrast to learning-disabled. A reform plan enacted by the New Jersey legislature (*Plan to Revise*, 1986) identifies students as "mildly handicapped" without assigning a specific label. Accountability for funding will be based on the very general determination of eligibility as well as a designation of the kinds of services provided. This approach appears to be quite similar to the Hobbs (1975a) recommendations, as well as to the more recent formulations of Reynolds and Lakin (1987).

Recent policy statements from the Office of Special Education and Rehabilitation Services (Will, 1986a, 1986b) have endorsed the development of alternative programs for serving mildly handicapped students. These programs entail combining existing programs, as indicated in a key definition in the Will (1986b) paper: "The term learning problem is used broadly to address children who are having learning difficulties, including those who are learning slowly; those with behavioral problems; those who may be educationally disadvantaged; and those who have mild specific learning disabilities, and emotional problems" (p. 1). This definition, as well as the accompanying papers (Will, 1986a, 1986b), amply justifies development of innovative approaches to providing services to children with learning problems. And Will's definition clearly indicates that "children with learning problems" includes all of the students now classified as mildly handicapped, students eligible for Chapter 1 and Head Start, and students with other kinds of learning and behavioral problems as well. Alternative delivery systems for serving students with learning problems, including the combining of funds and programs, are now encouraged by the Federal Department of Education on a pilot basis. Formal "wavers for performance" (Reynolds et al., 1987) will probably be required, but innovative programs now are not only clearly permitted, but are encouraged by recent federal policy statements.

Two further possibilities *within* the current legal requirements deserve further emphasis here. First, there is the possibility of determining eligibility for services through application of behavioral assessment and curriculum-based measures. These measures appear to be a justifiable means of determining whether students are likely to be eligible for traditional handicapped child classifications, and they have added benefit of being far more closely related to interventions (Deno, 1985; Shapiro & Lentz, 1985). Given the considerable flexibility that *presently* exists, there would appear to be no insurmountable barrier to a state's developing a cross-categorical classification system for mildly handicapped students, meaning that students no longer would be classified as learning-disabled or mildly retarded, but rather would merely be certified as "eligible for services for the handicapped." The population would not change much, if at all, because students who score lowest on curriculum-based measures are the same students currently classified as mildly handicapped by the elaborate, expensive, and largely irrelevant (to interventions) assessment procedures required by current eligibility criteria (Deno, Marston, Shinn, & Tindal, 1983; Shinn & Marston, 1985; Shinn, Tindal, Spira, & Marston, 1987). This change would accomplish two critical things: (a) Classification would be based on functional skills rather than traits such as intelligence; and (b) Eligibility information would have relevance to intervention.

One further program entirely consistent with current regulations is the establishment of prereferral interventions involving cooperative efforts by classroom teachers and support services personnel such as school psychologists (Graden, Casey, & Bonstrom, 1985; Graden, Casey, & Christensen, 1985; Grimes & Reschly, 1986; Reschly & Casey, 1986). These prereferral services attempt to resolve learning or behavioral problems without resorting to the expensive and often cumbersome handicapped child classification/placement system. The prereferral services are definitely in compliance with the EHA regulations governing the expenditures of federal monies for support services personnel at the state and local level. Some states (e.g., Louisiana and Florida) mandate the provision of prereferral services. The mandated services include the development, implementation, and evaluation of one or more interventions designed to resolve the learning or behavioral problems *prior to* referral of the youngster for consideration of classification and placement in special education.

Identification and appropriate education: Summary. Current legal provisions require students to be classified as handicapped in order to receive services supported by special education funding. The accountability purposes of current classification requirements need to be recognized in efforts to reform the system; specifically, other means to ensure accountability need to be developed in order to ensure resources are expended effectively and efficiently. There is some flexibility, however, in current legal requirements, although it is often not utilized at the state and local level. Current EHA legal requirements allow for a variety of approaches to classification of students as handicapped, recognize a variety of kinds of classification criteria, and permit the development of different approaches to services (including prereferral interventions). It appears that further flexibility

in interpretation of classification requirements is being encouraged by recent federal policy statements (Will, 1986a, 1986b). This flexibility, along with slight revisions in current legal requirements, could lead to significant changes in the provision of services to students with learning and behavioral problems *without* massive changes in the layers of legal stipulations that currently protect the rights of handicapped students.

Due Process Procedural Protections

The EHA due process protections attempt to ensure procedural fairness throughout the classification, placement, and programming decision-making process. These due process protections include informed consent, access to information used by the school in decision making, rights to challenge information and to obtain an independent evaluation, and the right to an impartial hearing. Bersoff (1978) provided an insightful discussion of the different levels of implementation of the due process rights. Due process rights are important in the discussion of alternative delivery systems because they occasionally have been misconstrued to prevent alternative services such as prereferral intervention.

A basic question faced by many practitioners is, What can be done without informed consent? If a parent provides informed consent for referral to special education, does that mandate preplacement evaluation? These questions have become problems in states where narrow roles for support services providers exist along with a strong tradition of providing eligibility evaluations for all referrals. To clarify these questions, it is helpful to consider the purposes of the due process procedural protections and to specify the events that trigger these protections.

The primary purpose of due process is to ensure fairness in decision making. The question is, What kind of decision? Due process protections were instituted to ensure, in the present context, that students are not railroaded into special education programs and that parents can influence critical decisions about classification, choice of placement option (e.g., part-time resource program vs. full-time special class), and programming (e.g., objectives on individualized programs and services received in order to accomplish those objectives). The critical purpose of due process has to do with special education classification and placement.

There appear to be two moments at which informed consent from parents becomes necessary: (a) the initial consideration of special education classification and placement and (b) treatment of a child in a way that differs substantially from the way other students in the classroom are treated. "Substantially different" might be defined as differential treatment that is apparent to a casual observer. Consultation of the kind envisioned by Graden and co-workers (Graden, Casey, & Bonstrom, 1985; Graden, Casey, & Christensen, 1985) and others might or might not trigger the need for informed consent. Consultation with a child's teacher and unobtrusive behavioral observation in the classroom do not involve, typically, consideration of special education eligibility or treatment that is sufficiently different so as to focus attention on an individual. Thus, much of what is usually done as part of prereferral interventions would not run up against the informed consent provisions connected with EHA. In addition, other activities related to prereferral interventions, such as interviewing other educational personnel (e.g., previous teachers), review of educational records, and examination of samples of daily work, could be carried out without the informed consent required by EHA regulations. It is important to emphasize here that individual assessment procedures carried out with a student outside of the classroom, individual counseling sessions, or any procedure involving determination of special education eligibility must be delayed until informed consent from a parent is obtained.

The confusion over the purposes and elements of due process has sometimes led special services personnel to the following self-defeating reasoning. First, they may decide that all services, including

consultation with teachers, must be delayed until informed consent is obtained from parents. Second, the informed consent procedure used by the district that authorizes consideration of special education eligibility may also commit the district, and its personnel, to completing a preplacement eligibility evaluation within a certain time period, often specified as 30 days. Then, with the eligibility evaluation mandated, support services persons decide that they must carry out individual evaluations including extensive testing, development of reports, and staffing procedures. Then, if the student is found to be eligible, special education placement typically follows, in which case problem solving with the classroom teacher may be viewed as irrelevant. This self-defeating sequence of events has been used by some as a rationalization for not carrying out prereferral intervention.

There are a variety of ways to revise the system so that informed consent does not mandate a special education eligibility evaluation. One obvious way is to routinely provide to classroom teachers services that involve consultation, review of records, and unobtrusive observation of students and thus do not require informed consent. The second, and better method, is to develop two levels of informed consent requests. One level would inform parents that their child was experiencing various kinds of difficulties and that consultation with support services persons is recommended. Limits on this consultation might be further specified (e.g., prohibition of individual assessment outside of the classroom). In this instance, the parents are asked to agree to consultation or some other form of prereferral intervention without authorizing either a preplacement evaluation or any kind of special education service. The second kind of informed consent might be related to special education eligibility evaluation which is the aim of most current informed consent procedures.

The due process procedural protections and the many different ways of implementing those protections (Bersoff, 1978) illustrate one of the most important principles concerning the influence of legal requirements, namely, that there usually are a variety of ways to comply with such requirements. Compliance needs to be directed toward development of the most appropriate ways to serve students, communicate with parents, and efficiently utilize precious resources such as the time of support services personnel. A due process procedure that mandates a number of subsequent steps that may not be required or appropriate is inconsistent with all of the purposes of informed consent. The different procedures for implementing the informed consent requirement provide further illustration of the flexibility that exists within the current EHA requirements. This flexibility needs to be utilized to expand the range of services to students, a goal entirely consistent with the purposes of due process.

Least Restrictive Environment

Placement in the least restrictive environment (LRE) is one of the most important principles in the EHA legal provisions. The LRE regulations require "that to the maximum extent appropriate, handicapped children . . . are educated with children who are not handicapped" (EHA, 1975, CFR 300.550). The LRE regulations require that a continuum of alternative placements be provided and utilization of placements outside the regular classroom must be justified by the severity of the child's handicap and the impossibility of providing the needed services within the regular classroom.

The LRE regulations would appear to provide strong support for alternative delivery systems that place strong emphasis on the development of a variety of alternative options within regular education. Of course, the least restrictive alternative of all, and therefore entirely consistent with EHA, is for students eligible to be classified as handicapped to remain *unidentified* and to receive the services they need within regular education. But again, there arises the dilemma of classification: the LRE protections are provided as rights to students who are classified as handicapped.

Current LRE regulations do not need to be changed or reinterpreted in order to carry out various reforms embodied in the alternative delivery systems. In fact, the LRE protections could be interpreted as requiring the development of a variety of alternatives within regular education, with or without classification of students as handicapped in order to receive those services.

Individualized Educational Program

An extensive series of regulations govern the development and implementation of individualized educational programs (IEP) for handicapped students. These provisions appear as CFR sections 300.340–300.349 (EHA, 1975). The components of the IEP, the participants in meetings related to the IEP, and annual review are specified in these regulations. The IEP rights, like other EHA rights, come to bear by virtue of classification of a student as handicapped and in need of special education services.

The IEP regulations, like the LRE regulations discussed above, appear to be entirely consistent with the various proposals for alternative delivery systems, particularly those approaches that emphasize acquisition of academic skills within an existing regular education curriculum. A critical issue in the development of alternative delivery systems will be the degree to which the IEP requirements of EHA are maintained for individual students. IEPs are expensive devices: They require considerable professional time in initial development and maintenance; the various meetings are time-consuming and expensive; and the delineation of general goals and specific objectives might be redundant with the goals and objectives that are already specified for the regular education curriculum. The degree to which the IEP regulations are incorporated into alternative delivery systems should be determined by the extent to which the regular education curriculum is used with individual students. If the regular education curriculum is not the basis for most of the goals and objectives established for individual handicapped students, IEPs of the form developed to meet EHA regulations should be developed. On the other hand, if the goals and objectives are taken directly from the regular education curriculum, the EHA regulations concerning IEPs probably should be simplified.

Protection in Evaluation Procedures

The Protection in Evaluation Procedures provisions (PEP) appear as CRF sections 300.532–300.534. The PEP regulations generally specify nondiscrimination, an individual preplacement evaluation, basic standards that the evaluation procedures must meet, standards for placement procedures, and reevaluation at least every 3 years. The entire PEP regulations are reprinted in Table 1 in order to illustrate the relationship between regulations and legislation.

The PEP protections clearly reflect a concern for preventing misclassification. However, the kind of misclassification that is of greatest concern is not entirely apparent simply from reading the regulations. The legislative history of EHA reflected a fear of misclassification of normal students as handicapped. In all likelihood, there was not as much concern about failure to classify eligible students as non-handicapped. The latter problem may become more serious with the implementation of alternative delivery systems that attempt to avoid classification of students as handicapped. The EHA regulations establishing the link between classification as handicapped and provision of services (Regulation 300.5) establish a two-pronged test: (a) The student must meet the eligibility criteria, and (b) The student must "need special education and related services" because of the effects of the handicapping condition. One could argue that effective alternative services within regular education would prevent the need for special education and related services, therefore rendering the student ineligible to be classified as handicapped according to the EHA regulations.

The PEP protections of EHA would appear to have relatively little influence on alternative delivery systems, because these provisions, particularly those relating to valid measures and demonstration of specific educational need, are supportive of the major features of most alternative delivery systems. Other PEP provisions, such as those requiring a multidisciplinary team and a multifactored assessment that includes areas such as intelligence and adaptive behavior, are most relevant to the implementation of classification criteria in various areas such as mental retardation. In contrast, if the classifications are changed significantly or eliminated through system reform, the need to assess some of the related areas, such as intelligence, would clearly be lessened, if not eliminated.

Summary

The EHA regulations have enormous influence on the provision of services to students with learning and behavioral problems. A significant number of those students are now classified as mildly handicapped. However, a significantly greater number, perhaps twice as many, need the kinds of services provided in EHA and state-mandated special education programs, but they do not meet stringently applied eligibility criteria. Alternative delivery systems that would sever the link between classification as handicapped and provision of needed services would, potentially, provide services to far more students and avoid the current problems with classification of students as handicapped. These classification activities are difficult to carry out, quite expensive, and bear little relationship to interventions.

The EHA principles that need to be reinterpreted and/or revised in order to carry out alternative delivery systems are those requiring classification of students as handicapped in order to gain access to the appropriate education rights and the due process provisions, particularly where the latter are narrowly interpreted as requiring informed consent in order that alternative services can be provided within regular education. The other EHA principles, LRE, IEP, and PEP have less direct influence on the development of alternative delivery systems.

CHARACTERISTICS OF LEGAL INFLUENCES

Six major characteristics of legal influences that impinge on alternative delivery systems can be identified to summarize the content to this point and to establish the context for suggested changes in legal provisions affecting education of students with special needs. These characteristics are as follows.

Reciprocal Influences

The legal system is influenced by various reciprocal forces of two sorts. First, the different legal origins and mechanisms have reciprocal influences. For example, litigation based on constitutional principles had a profound influence on legislation which, in turn, has led to further litigation. The second kind of reciprocal influence has to do with social forces and societal trends. The legal system has an influence on social forces and trends and, in turn, is influenced by social forces and trends. For example, the changing attitudes about racial segregation as well as social science evidence concerning the influence of segregation on psychological and educational development had a profound influence on the landmark *Brown v. Board of Education* (1954) decision. The *Brown* decision is also credited with influencing the court cases in the early 1970s that established the educational rights of handicapped students. The latter cases were also strongly influenced by the civil rights movement of the 1960s as well as the publication of research indicating the educational benefits that could be derived from special education programs by handicapped students.

Dynamic and Evolutionary

A second characteristic of these legal influences is that they are dynamic and evolutionary. Legal influences are rarely static. There is always the possibility of the reinterpretation of a particular legal provision or constitutional protection that would significantly touch on the provision

of services to students with special needs. Several such interpretations have been cited in this chapter.

Relative and Ambiguous

Legal principles are nearly always ambiguous, particularly as they relate to a specific situation, with relative rather than absolute meanings. The LRE principle involves a complex relationship between the particular characteristics of an individual, a set of potential placement options, and the degree to which appropriate services can be provided within various settings. There is no such thing as a single "least restrictive" placement for all children and what is regarded at any time as least restrictive can be further influenced by the development of technology or other advances in knowledge about the education of handicapped students. Furthermore, the LRE principle has been interpreted more broadly recently than it was 10 years ago, soon after EHA was implemented. Then, separate centers of instruction in local school districts for severely handicapped students were generally accepted as consistent with the LRE principle. Educational services at those centers coupled with living in the local community were certainly less restrictive than were the institutional placements that were common prior to EHA implementation. Recently, LRE has been interpreted to prohibit the use of separate school attendance centers for handicapped students during federal and state compliance monitoring. The literal formulation of the LRE principle in EHA has not been changed since 1975. The *interpretation* of that principle has changed and what was accepted formerly as least restrictive is not acceptable now.

Different Levels of Implementation

In addition to the relative, ambiguous meaning of particular legal principles, there also are different levels of implementation. The best description of different levels of implementation was provided in Bersoff's discussion of due process protections (Bersoff, 1978), in which an insightful account was provided of the different levels of implementation, ranging from surface compliance to full implementation consistent with the spirit and intent of the legislation and, perhaps, even going beyond what might have been contemplated by the authors of the legislation and regulations. There nearly always are different levels of implementation concerning any legal principle.

Unanticipated Consequences

The extension of legal principles to new situations or the reinterpretation of legal protections often has unanticipated and far-reaching consequences. An example is the *Armstrong v. Kline* (1979, 1980) decision, which ruled that state laws restricting the school year to some arbitrary limit, such as 180 days, were unacceptable limitations on the right to an appropriate education for handicapped students. This case was filed on behalf of severely handicapped students who were believed to regress significantly in skill performance as a result of summer recess. An unanticipated effect of this court decision was the necessity of developing measures to determine which students would experience a significant regression of skills over a summer recess. Such measures were not developed at that time and there was very little to apply from research. This unanticipated consequence prompted a considerable amount of further effort on the part of special educators, school psychologists, and others (Browder & Lentz, 1985). Numerous other unanticipated consequences of legal changes were discussed in Reschly (1983, 1987a). Each of the major EHA principles has had significant influences on the development of assessment instruments and procedures.

Compliance Through Professional Standards and Best Practices

Owing to the nature of legal influences, compliance is often difficult to achieve. This is true even when individuals are making good-faith efforts to conform with both the spirit and the letter of the

legal provisions. Perhaps the best way to achieve compliance is *not* through attempts to follow the exact letter of regulations or to rely on rigid interpretations, but rather to apply best professional practices and to implement authoritative professional standards. Various professional groups have developed statements concerning best practices and professional standards in recent years. These resources have been extremely influential in recent court decisions. The *Marshall* and *S-1* trials (*Marshall*, 1984, 1985; *S-1*, 1986) appeared to have been significantly influenced by the utilization of the American Association on Mental Deficiency *Classification in Mental Retardation* (Grossman, 1983), regarded by both plaintiffs and defendants in those cases as the principal authoritative source on mental retardation classification. These trials were also markedly influenced by the NAS report (Heller et al., 1982), particularly the principles of professional responsibility reprinted in Table 2.

LEGAL PROVISIONS FOR A BETTER DELIVERY SYSTEM

The current delivery system has been described herein as a legal entity; alternative delivery systems will also be created by legal provisions. There are two basic ways changes in the current delivery system might come about through legal provision. The first and most feasible, but somewhat limited means is to use more flexible interpretations of key principles in current legislation. The advantage of this approach is that the existing layers of legal provisions do not have to be changed significantly and the hard-fought gains in legislation and regulations are not threatened directly. Although it is nice to think about starting afresh, it is very unlikely that substantial change in legislation at the state and federal levels could be accomplished in the foreseeable future. Changes that are likely to take place will have to be restricted within the confines of current legislation.

Considerations of change in legal provisions need to take into account the relative ease with which each of the levels of legal influence can be modified. Constitutional law is extremely difficult to change, but state rules and compliance monitoring schedules are modified more easily.

Criteria for Good Legal Provisions

It is important to identify at the outset what legal provisions should accomplish and the characteristics of a good legal system for the development of services. At the risk of sounding trite, the most important single criterion is that the legal provisions foster the development of services that meet children's needs. Children's needs are varied; the legal system needs to reflect these wide variations. In general needs are related to acquisition of skills along dimensions that are critical to normal functioning during the childhood, adolescent, and adult years: some key domains are social, intellectual, academic, and vocational. Significant problems in one or more of these areas may require the development of special services in order to overcome deficits or to develop compensatory mechanisms.

The current system appears to be reasonably well developed in terms of the *dimensions* of behavior that are addressed. The major problem in the current system is the imposition of a dichotomy, handicapped versus nonhandicapped, on the very broad continuum of skills that exist along the key dimensions. The total number of students needing special services is difficult to estimate because of the effects of relatively lenient or more stringent criteria. Leinhardt et al. (1982) estimated that 20-25% of all students had discrepancies ranging from average to sufficiently severe as to require special services. These discrepancies extend from moderately below average to markedly below average performance, which might be measured roughly as a standard score of 90 down to 65 or a percentile rank of 25 down to 1 (assuming a standard score scale with a mean of 100 and standard deviation of 15).

Performance on most relevant dimensions such as reading or mathematics varies continuously from the upper to the lower bound of this range. There are fine gradations between similar points on these scales. Differences of 5 to as much as 10 points are not very important, but differences of 20 or more points are usually quite important. The critical point is that there are fine gradations on these continua with no natural demarcations. Classification criteria stated in terms of these continuua are inherently arbitrary. The arbitrariness is felt most sharply with the imposition of the dichotomy, handicapped or not handicapped, on a continuous scale such that small differences, sometimes as trivial as one or two points, make a large difference in classification, resources, and programming. Thus, a student with an achievement score that is more than one standard deviation below the population average may be treated quite differently than a student with an achievement score that falls slightly less than one standard deviation below average. The former may be deemed eligible for the classification of learning disability and the latter deemed ineligible, when in fact there are no substantive differences between the levels of performance.

The problem, in short, is a classification system that implicitly regards children's problems as dichotomies (i.e., handicapped or not handicapped) when their needs vary continuously. The relevant competencies range continuously along the key dimensions in fine gradations from below average to markedly below average. A sensible classification system must reflect the nature of children's development on these key dimensions and should provide for finely graduated eligibility based on degree of need. Rather than all-or-none decisions, handicapped or not handicapped, there could be fine gradations of eligibility based on the number of dimensions on which the individual is performing below average and the degree of discrepancy from average levels of performance on each of these dimensions. For example, students with large discrepancies on more than one dimension would receive more intensive services than students with small discrepancies on a few or only one dimension.

Such a classification system would allocate resources accordingly.

In addition, a good classification system should (a) direct resources to students needing services; (b) foster the development of services that match specific needs; (c) include quality control mechanisms to ensure effective interventions evaluated on the basis of outcomes of services rather than on process or amount of instruction provided; (d) maintain cost efficiency and accountability for expenditures; (e) allow the development of a variety of alternatives based on students' needs; and (f) utilize regular education to the greatest extent possible.

The current delivery system does not meet these criteria to the degree that would be desirable. Numerous instances in which the current system could be improved have been suggested throughout this chapter. Two of the most serious problems with the current system have to do with directing resources to students needing services and attaining cost efficiency. An alternative system that allocated resources and directed expenditures according to services needed and degree of discrepancy on relevant dimensions would accomplish these goals more effectively.

Desirable and Necessary Legal Changes

The most important change required by the current system is to sever the link between classification of students as handicapped and the provision of services. This link needs to be made more flexible and based on finely graduated increments of intervention depending on students' needs. These finely graduated increments might be expressed in terms of combinations of minutes of service required per day, the number of dimensions for which services are needed, degree of discrepancy from regular curriculum objectives, and the kind of professional or paraprofessional services employed. The system should allow maximum flexibility for unique combinations of variables related to specific needs for services. Each of these variables could be weighted according to some rational scheme and monies could

be allocated according to costs of the different kinds of services delivered. Financial accountability would be maintained, perhaps even improved, because expenditures could be audited directly, based on services received by students. This system would require substantial changes in state and federal legislation — a difficult, but not impossible, scenario.

Changes Within Current Legal Provisions

The kinds of changes envisioned in the previous section may not take place for an extended period of time. However, much can be done within the present system to achieve alternative delivery systems. The key principles established now in EHA can be interpreted in ways that foster the development of alternative delivery systems. Already there are many significant variations among states, all of which are regarded as in compliance with EHA. It is important for each of us to draw upon this flexibility, perhaps with the attitude: "If Louisiana can do it (perhaps referring to their prereferral interventions requirements), then Iowa (or New York or Oregon) can do it." Significant reforms in the way classification decisions are made, the delivery of appropriate programs for handicapped students in the context of regular education, and other features of alternative delivery systems have been implemented already in one or more states. These reforms need to be implemented more broadly.

Establishment of a significantly changed legal system where the link between classification as handicapped and the provision of services is eliminated will become increasingly possible as reforms within the present system are implemented, evaluated, and shown to be effective. Maximum utilization of current opportunities will make more likely the achievement of fundamental changes in legal provisions. It is important that we not simply wait passively for massive changes, but rather work toward reforms to the greatest extent possible. These reforms can be carried out best through a combination of individual action at the local level (Grimes, 1981) and the action of corporate bodies such as local, state, and national professional associations. The influence of state associations on monitoring schedules and state rules has been significant in many instances. The critical steps in exerting this kind of influence are (a) to identify ways that the interests of children can be served better; (b) to express the need for change in a reasonable and articulate fashion; (c) to gather support for that change through resolutions endorsed by professional associations and parent advocacy groups; and (d) to exert consistent and persistent efforts to persuade decision makers to revise monitoring schedules and state rules. These kinds of changes will create the climate in which more fundamental legal changes, such as severing the link between classification as handicapped and the provision of services, can be accomplished.

REFERENCES

Algozzine, B., & Korinek, L. (1985). Where is special education for students with high prevalence handicaps going? *Exceptional Children, 51,* 388-394.

Armstrong v. Kline, 476 F. Supp. 583 (E.D. Pa. 1979). Aff'd CA 78-0172 (3rd Cir., July 15, 1980).

Bersoff, D. N. (1975). Professional ethics and legal responsibilities: On the horns of a dilemma. *Journal of School Psychology, 13,* 359-376.

Bersoff, D. N. (1978). Procedural safeguards. In L. Morra (Ed.), *Due process: Developing criteria for evaluating the due process procedural safeguards provisions of Public Law 94-142* (pp. 64-142). Washington, DC: U.S. Office of Education, Bureau of Education for the Handicapped.

Bersoff, D. N. (1982). The legal regulation of school psychology. In C. R. Reynolds & T. B. Gutkin (Eds.), *The handbook of school psychology* (pp. 1043-1074). New York: Wiley.

Board of Education v. Rowley, 102 S Ct 3034 (1982).

Browder, D. M., & Lentz, F. E. (1985). Extended school year services: From litigation to assessment and evaluation. *School Psychology Review, 14,* 188-195.

Brown v. Board of Education, 347 U. S. 483 (1954).

Carter, L. F. (1984). The sustaining effects study of compensatory and elementary education. *Educational Researcher, 13,* 4-13.

Deno, S. L. (1985). Curriculum-based measurement: The emerging alternative. *Exceptional Children, 52,* 219-232.

Deno, S. L., Marston, D., Shinn, M., & Tindal, G. (1983). Oral reading fluency: A simple datum for scaling reading disability. *Topics in Learning and Reading Disabilities, 2*(4), 53-59.

Diana v. State Board of Education, C. A. No. C-70-37 (N. D. Cal., July, 1970) (consent decree).

Economic Opportunity Act of 1964, P. L. 88-452, 78 Stat. 508 (1964).

Education of the Handicapped Act, (1975) PL 94-142, 20 U. S. C. 1400-1485, 34 C. F. R. Part 300. (As Amended to October 8, 1986).

Educational Consolidation and Improvement Act of 1981, PL 97-35, 95 Stat. 367 (1981).

Elementary and Secondary Education Act of 1965, P. L. 89-10, 79 Stat. 27 (1965).

Ethical Principles of Psychologists. (1981). Washington, DC: American Psychological Association. (Reprinted in the *American Psychologist, 1981, 36,* 633-638.)

Fleig, G. S., & Reschly, D. J. (1985). Special education and the law. In L. Sametz & C. S. McLoughlin (Eds.), *Educators, children and the law.* (pp. 84-109). Springfield, IL: Thomas.

Florida Resource Manual for the Development and Evaluation of Special Programs for Exceptional Students, Volume 1-B: Florida Statutes and State Board of Education Rules — Excerpts for Programs for Exceptional Students. (Revised Edition, July, 1985). Tallahassee, FL: Department of Education.

Gallagher, J. J., Forsythe, P., Ringelheim, D., & Weintraub, F. J. (1975). Funding patterns and labeling. In N. Hobbs (Ed.), *Issues in the classification of children* (pp. 432-462). San Francisco: Jossey-Bass.

Graden, J. L., Casey, A., & Bonstrom, O. (1985). Implementing a prereferral intervention system: Part II. The data. *Exceptional Children, 51,* 487-496.

Graden, J. L., Casey, A., & Christensen, S. L. (1985). Implementing a prereferral intervention system: Part I. The model. *Exceptional Children, 51,* 377-384.

Grimes, J. P. (1981). Shaping the future of school psychology. In J. Ysseldyke & R. Weinberg (Eds.), *The future of psychology in the schools: Proceedings of the Spring Hill Symposium. School Psychology Review, 10,* 206-231.

Grimes, J. P., & Reschly, D. J. (1986). *Relevant Educational Assessment and Intervention Model (RE-AIM).* (Project proposal funded by the United States Department of Education.) Des Moines, IA: Iowa Department of Education, Bureau of Special Education.

Grossman, H. J. (Ed.). (1983). *Classification in mental retardation.* Washington, DC: American Association on Mental Deficiency.

Guadalupe Organization v. Tempe Elementary School District No. 3, No. 71-435 (D. Ariz., January 24, 1972) (consent decree).

Handicapped Children's Protection Act, P. L. 99-372, 97 Stat. 1357, 1986.

Heller, K., Holtzman, W., & Messick, S. (Eds.). (1982). *Placing children in special education: A strategy for equity.* Washington, DC: National Academy Press.

Hobbs, N. (1975a). *The futures of children.* San Francisco: Jossey-Bass.

Hobbs, N. (Ed.). (1975b). *Issues in the classification of children (Vols. 1–2).* San Francisco: Jossey-Bass.

Kavale, K. (1980). Learning disability and cultural-economic disadvantage: The case for a relationship. *Learning Disability Quarterly, 3,* 97-112.

Larry P. v. Riles, 343 F. Supp. 1306 (N. D. Cal. 1972) (preliminary injunction). Aff'd 502 F. 2d 963 (9th Cir. 1974); 495 F. Supp. 926 (N. D. Cal. 1979) (decision on merits) Aff'd (9th Cir. No. 80-427 Jan. 23, 1984). Order Modifying Judgment, C-71-2270 RFP, September 25, 1986.

Lazar, I., & Darlington, R. (1982). Lasting effects of early education: A report from the Consortium for Longitudinal Studies. *Monographs of the Society for Research in Child Development, 47* (Serial No. 195).

Leinhardt, G., & Bickel, W. (1987). Instruction's the thing wherein to catch the mind that falls behind. *Educational Psychologist, 22,* 177-207.

Leinhardt, G., Bickel, W., & Pallay, A. (1982). Unlabeled but still entitled: Toward more effective remediation. *Teachers College Record, 84,* 391-422.

Louisiana Pupil Appraisal Handbook (1983).

Marshall et al., v. Georgia. U. S. District Court for the Southern District of Georgia, CV482-233, June 28, 1984; Affirmed (11th Cir. No. 84-8771, Oct. 29, 1985).

Mills v. Board of Education, 348 F. Supp. 866 (D. D. C. 1972).

Patrick, J., & Reschly, D. (1982). Relationship of state educational criteria and demographic variables to school-system prevalence of mental retardation.

American Journal of Mental Deficiency, 86, 351-360.

Pennsylvania Association of Retarded Children v. Commonwealth of Pennsylvania, 343 F. Supp. 279 (E. D. Pa. 1972).

Plan to Revise Special Education in New Jersey. (1986). Trenton, NJ: State Department of Education, 225 W. State St., CN 500, Trenton, NJ 08625.

Principles for Professional Ethics. (1984). Washington, DC: National Association of School Psychologists.

Reschly, D. (1980a). Assessment of exceptional individuals: Legal mandates and professional standards. In R. Mulliken & M. Evans (Eds.), *Assessment of children with low incidence handicaps* (pp. 8-23). Washington, DC: National Association of School Psychologists.

Reschly, D. (1980b). School psychologists and assessment in the future. *Professional Psychology, 11,* 841-848.

Reschly, D. (1983). Legal issues in psychoeducational assessment. In G. Hynd (Ed.), *The school psychologist: Contemporary perspectives* (pp. 67-93). Syracuse, NY: Syracuse University Press.

Reschly, D. J. (1986). Economic and cultural factors in childhood exceptionality. In R. T. Brown & C. R. Reynolds (Eds.), *Psychological perspectives on childhood exceptionality: A handbook* (pp. 423-466). New York: Wiley Interscience.

Reschly, D. J. (1987a). Assessing educational handicaps. In A. Hess & I. Weiner (Eds.), *Handbook of forensic psychology* (pp. 155-187). New York: Wiley.

Reschly, D. J. (1987b). Learning characteristics of mildly handicapped students and implications for classification, placement, and programming. In M. C. Wang, M. C. Reynolds, & H. J. Walberg (Eds.), *The handbook of special education: Research and practice* (Vols. 1-3, pp. 35-58). Oxford, England: Pergamon.

Reschly, D. J. (1988). Special education reform: School psychology revolution. *School Psychology Review, 17,* 465-481.

Reschly, D. J., & Casey, A. (1986). *Behavioral consultation.* Ames, IA: Iowa State University, Department of Psychology, Project RE-AIM.

Reschly, D. J., Kicklighter, R. H., & McKee, P. (1988). Recent placement litigation. Part III: Analysis of differences in *Larry P., Marshall,* and *S-1. School Psychology Review, 17,* 37-48.

Reynolds, M. C., & Lakin, K. C. (1987). Noncategorical special education for mildly handicapped students: A system for the future. In M. C. Wang, M. C. Reynolds, & H. J. Walberg (Eds.), *The handbook of special education: Research and practice* (Vol. 1, pp. 331-336). Oxford, England: Pergamon.

Reynolds, M. C., & Wang, M. (1983). Restructuring "special" school programs: A position paper. *Policy Studies Review, 2*(Special No. 1), 189-212.

Reynolds, M. C., Wang, M. C., & Walberg, H. J. (1987). The necessary restructuring of special and regular education. *Exceptional Children, 53*, 391-398.

S-1 v. Turlington, Trial on Merits, May 19-June 4, 1986, Order on Motion to Dismiss, No. 79-8020-Civ-Atkins, U. S. District Court, Southern District of Florida, October 9, 1986.

Seventh Annual Report to Congress on the Implementation of Public Law 94-142: The Education for All Handicapped Children Act. (1985). Washington, DC: Office of Special Education, United States Department of Education.

Shapiro, E. S., & Lentz, F. E. (1985). Assessing academic behavior: A behavioral approach. *School Psychology Review, 14*, 325-338.

Shepard, L. A. (1983). The role of measurement in educational policy: Lessons from the identification of learning disabilities. *Educational Measurement: Issues and Practice, 2*, 4-8.

Shinn, M., & Marston, D. (1985). Using curriculum-based measures to identify mildly handicapped students. *Remedial and Special Education, 6*(2), 31-45.

Shinn, M. R., Tindal, G. A., Spira, D., & Marston, D. (1987). Practice of learning disabilities as social policy. *Learning Disability Quarterly, 10*, 17-28.

Smith v. Robinson, 468 U. S., LW 5179 (1984).

Stotland, J. T., & Mancuso, E. (1981). U. S. Court of Appeals decision regarding *Armstrong v. Kline:* The 180 day rule. *Exceptional Children, 47*, 266-271.

Tatro v. Texas, 481 F. Supp. 1224 (ND Tex. 1979). Reversed in *Tatro v. Texas*, 625 F. 2d 557 (CA5 1980). Affirmed in *Tatro v. Texas*, 703 F. 2d 823 (CA5 1983). Affirmed in part and Reversed in part, *Irving Independent School District v. Tatro*, U.S.C. 1984.

Wang, M. C., & Reynolds, M. C. (1985). Avoiding the "catch 22" in special education reform. *Exceptional Children, 51*, 497-502.

Wang, M. C., Reynolds, M. C., & Walberg, H. J. (Eds.). (1987). *The handbook of special education: Research and practice* (Vols. 1-3). Oxford, England: Pergamon.

Will, M. C. (1986a). Educating children with learning problems: A shared responsibility. *Exceptional Children, 52*, 411-415.

Will, M. C. (1986b). *Educating students with learning problems — A shared responsibility.* Washington, DC: United States Department of Education, Office of Special Education and Rehabilitation Services.

Part IV:

Reactions
and Conclusions

27

Alternative Educational Delivery Systems: Implications for School Psychology

Maynard C. Reynolds
University of Minnesota

The work of the schools and of school psychologists takes shape from research and maxims based on the wisdom of practice but also from the values, policies, and economics of particular places and times. The occasion for producing this book acknowledges that we are in a period — in late twentieth century — of broad and important changes that cause needs for alternative models of practice (Graden, Zins, Curtis, & Myrick, this volume) in school psychology and special education. This chapter provides one person's view of the context within which alternatives are developing. Partly, the chapter reflects my reading of the earlier parts of the book, which I found to be an interesting and rewarding task, but also a personal set of perceptions, beliefs, and commitments.

A BIT OF HISTORY

School psychologists, no doubt, are worn thin on references to Binet's work as a beginning point in the history of their field; so I'll be brief about it and cover only what is essential to my argument. The practical aim of Binet's work in the early part of the twentieth century was to predict which children would likely not progress well in academic studies. The Binet tests provided such prediction at a higher level than ever before accomplished; indeed, there has been but little improvement in the early predictive procedures, even to this day. Binet's approaches spread to the United States

and many other parts of the world and became the major basis on which pupils with low IQs were set aside in special classes.

Over succeeding decades, the new testing technology permitted millions of pupils earlier termed academic "laggards" (Davies, 1959) to be labeled "morons" and later "educable mentally retarded" (EMR), and then to be removed from the ordinary or regular classes in favor of special education classes. As Cronbach (1967) put it, "When ability tests became available they were used by the schools — to put it bluntly — to decide which pupils should be allowed to drop by the wayside or to vegetate in a undemanding slow classroom" (p.24). Later a special category of students was created for those predicted to succeed academically but for whom the prediction was in error (in the "under-achieving" direction). These were termed "learning-disabled" (LD). Again, it was the availability of the Binet test and predictive scheme, or some variation of it, that permitted the definition of LD, now the largest category of exceptionality.

Procedures for "selecting out" some students from regular classes and schools by the kinds of psychometric methods just described were never based on evidence demonstrating value for the children involved; rather, it was simply that they were predicted to perform poorly or, in fact, were performing poorly in regular classes. Special education programs have rarely been evaluated carefully; even less has the complicated system of separating children into various categories for allocation in the huge and growing "second system" of education been based on evidence of value (see Ysseldyke & Christenson, this volume). Special funding systems that pay off on the input side (that is, expand funding whenever a child is labeled and placed in a special education program) have served to perpetuate the largely unevaluated approaches. Whether the program does any good for the students is unrelated to funding.

School psychologists in their role as administrators of individual normative tests, are key figures in the allocation of pupils to the various programs. Pupils who score low on IQ tests or who exhibit a big negative discrepancy between their predicted and actual academic progress are allocated to special classes or resource rooms.

I have intended, so far, to refer to so-called mildly retarded and learning-disabled pupils. Many of the students labeled emotionally disturbed (ED) or behavior-disordered (BD) are included in much of what I say below, but the history of that field follows a somewhat different course, not detailed here. Suffice it to say that problems of classification have been very substantial in the ED/BD category just as in other parts of special education; and, in fact, there is much overlap among those labeled as EMR, LD, and ED.

THE POLICIES CHANGE

With the Pennsylvania Association for Retarded Children case (PARC, 1971) and kindred closely following court decisions and Public Law 94-142 in 1975, much of what is described above was changed. At least policies were changed, even though changes in practice are still incomplete and proceeding quite awkwardly. Many school psychologists understand now that they were party to a system that was rejection-oriented and of doubtful value in serving some children and their families. There were serious moral and technical flaws in common modes of practice. For the most part, the roles of psychologists in the schools were limited within very

narrow parts of the range of their potential contributions.

The major policy change in the 1970s was the declaration that the programs that are provided to "handicapped" children should offer advantages to them. If IQ tests were used to send children off to special classes, it would be a responsibility of persons making the placement to show that the children learn more advantageously in the special classes. Under PL 94-142, this kind of accountability was established for individual pupils. Specific educational plans were required for each "handicapped" child and reviews of progress were mandated to ascertain that planned programs are appropriate, which means that they are succeeding or should be changed again.

Under the new policies education was required to be adaptive rather than selective (rejection being the other side of that coin). The least restrictive environment (LRE) principle was established; it creates an explicit bias in placement decisions in favor of holding children in regular schools and classes whenever it is feasible. Moreover, the LRE principle amounted to a call for professionals to go to work on expanding the power of mainstream school environments to serve children with exceptional needs (Stainback & Stainback, this volume). One of the emerging approaches to strengthening the mainstream that has had good leadership by school psychologists is prereferral intervention and consultation (see Fuchs & Fuchs, this volume, and Curtis & Meyers, this volume).

The effect of the new policies is to challenge school psychologists to engage not just in straight-on measurement functions, as in administering IQ tests and calculating expectancy-achievement discrepancies, but to focus on the interpretation of measurements and other data in the context of decisions about school placement and instructional enhancements. For example, deciding that a child is mentally retarded, on the basis of measurement functions, and letting that become the basis for school placement is no longer acceptable practice. In the famous Larry P. case (1972) the presiding judge, commenting on IQ tests, said, "Whatever the general scientific merits of the tests, therefore, defendants have failed to show a valid, legal justification for their use for black EMR placement" (p. 103). The alternative programs must be evaluated generally and in particular for each child; and validity questions should run to placement decisions not just to tests.

In sum, the old system for rejecting children from mainstream educational structures was turned on its head. No longer could pupils be "referred" out of regular classes simply because they were difficult, inconvenient to teach, or predicted to perform poorly. Referral out of the mainstream now required evidence that a "distinctive" and positively defined program was needed and would be provided and, moreover, required evidence that the "distinctive" program would likely offer advantages to the child. The traditional rejection-oriented system was declared unacceptable. The whole system of education for mildly handicapped students was seen to be in disrepair. Growing numbers of children had problems, but new solutions were required. We came into a new era.

PREVAILING PRACTICES ARE NOT ADEQUATE

It became apparent that much of the prevailing practice of special education and school psychology could not be justified when examined in some detail and in light of today's policies. Classification procedures for mildly handicapped pupils were (and remain) seriously flawed technically (Ysseldyke & Christenson, this volume). Classification of children was excessively tainted by aspects of rejection and segregation (Reschly, this volume). We had been unrealistic about the distinctiveness of the several separate categories of exceptionality. Separation of children into many different programs, often requiring dispatching systems for sending children back and forth between regular classes and resource rooms, had contributed to the growing disjointedness of school programs and to a wasteful "procedural-

ism" in special programs (Reynolds, Wang, & Walberg, 1987). We had let simplistic ideas about categories of children penetrate also to levels of specialized teacher preparation and licensing, the structuring of professional and advocacy groups, and even our professional literature. We had permitted "special" school programs to be withheld from children until their problems were serious and severe, even in the face of evidence showing that early interventions often reduce the rates at which serious problems develop (see Barnett & Paget, this volume; Conyne, Zins, & Vedder-Dubocq, this volume).

These problems, especially those relating to classification of children as handicapped, have been recounted repeatedly over more than a decade. Hobbs (1980) led a broad study of classification problems in the early 1970s and concluded that systems of classification used by special educators and school psychologists were a "major barrier to the efficient and effective delivery of services to them [exceptional children] and their families" (p. 274). On appeal by the Office of Civil Rights, the National Academy of Science (NAS) appointed a special panel to study placement practices in special education. A key recommendation in the NAS report was that "it is the responsibility of any placement team that labels and places a child in a special program to demonstrate that any differential label used is related to a distinctive prescription for educational practices . . . that lead to improved outcomes" (Heller, Holtzman, & Messick, 1982, p. 94). Recently, a major review of research and practice led by Wang, Reynolds, and Walberg (1987–1988) came to similar conclusions: Present-day special education practices relating to the separation of mildly handicapped pupils into various categories and removing them from the mainstream of the schools is not justified and is wasteful in the extreme. The inefficiencies of the present system are especially problematic because of the increasing numbers and proportions of children in the schools who have special problems and needs (Reynolds & Lakin, 1987).

REACTIONS TO THE CHALLENGE

The chapters of this book tell a mainly positive story of serious efforts to revise practices in special education and school psychology to meet the new challenges. But not all behavior in the present situation is positive. The changes required will be difficult to accomplish. Many people will resist and resent efforts for change. At the risk of appearing somewhat facetious, I shall describe some of the less positive reactions to the situation.

The Medicine Man Model

For some educators and psychologists it is highly threatening to give up present practices. Even if there is little or no evidence in favor of them, they prefer to go on with the traditional refer-test-place practices, leaving school programs comfortably in place with minimal change. Some people feel so committed to traditional ways of doing their work and feel that the general public is so fixed in expectations about their work that they think it would be unkind and a disservice to make changes. By extension it might seem even harmful, and unprofessional, to make changes. The first duty of the professional is to "do no harm"! There are billions of dollars involved in present operations, and thus high levels of forbearance (continuing practices even in the face of negative appraisal) have their rewards.

The Blinker Model

A pattern of behavior closely related to the Medicine Man Model is the Blinker Model. Blinkers are sometimes placed to the outside of a horse's eyes to limit peripheral vision. Here the reference is to people who prefer not to know about the Hobbs, NAS, Wang-Reynolds-Walberg reports or other research findings and summaries that may disturb their assumptions and practices. They prefer the know-nothing approach — straight ahead with little attention to new data. This permits them to disregard any evidence that casts doubt on their practices and to go on "doing psychologicals" (WISC-R, Bender, and WRAT?) and special education in the same old way. No boat rocking here.

The Huckster Model

Another approach in the face of major challenges is to hit the street with "six easy steps" to solve the problem. This takes practice outside of quality assurance channels. It involves a lot of selling and pretense as "specialist," sometimes with innocence, and sometimes not. "In 20 minutes we can tell you what your learning style is and how you should be taught" — or so it goes. What might be a decent research hypothesis is rushed into practice, often attended by much cachet and great reward!

A FRAMEWORK FOR REFORM

In thinking positively about the challenging situation we face, a useful concept for me is that of *order of dispositions*. The concept has a rich history in analytic philosophy; here I will present it in only a limited educational context. The central idea is that a given state or condition can often be understood in terms of a series or orders of predispositional states. Iron is magnetizable, as some other metals are not, because it has certain properties or conditions that might be termed a disposition to magnetizability.

A child who is having difficulties in academic learning can be diagnosed strictly at the "level of the lesson" or at a curriculum level. In such a case one would analyze the learning task, measure the child's present levels of competence and performance in the essential components of the task, and perhaps monitor responses in learning trials under various conditions of instruction.

The diagnosis of learning problems frequently goes beyond the curriculum level to presumed dispositional states. A widely used definition of learning disability, for example, requires a finding of significant discrepancy between ability (or "capacity") and achievement in a basic area (such as reading), *plus* evidence of "disorder in one or more of the basic psychological processes involved in understanding or in using language...." (*Federal Register*, Dec. 29, 1977, p. 65083). The reference to "capacity" and "basic psychological processes" moves the definition beyond the curriculum level to a presumed predispositional state.

In schools, it is common to move from a curriculum level to a psychological order of disposition. The most common predispositional attribute studied by school psychologists is intelligence. On the basis of IQ tests psychologists often tell teachers what can be "expected" of (predicted for ?) individual children. From there, the psychologist may go on to tell teachers about aspects of the child's personality, motivation, and specific cognitive abilities. All of this gives detail to presumed dispositional states, not directly at a curriculum level, but presumably of importance in arranging the curriculum and instruction. Much of the classification of pupils for special education has been based on evidence at this "one order removed" level. Teachers have complained for decades that much of what psychologists tell them about what to "expect" about children is useless; nevertheless practice has gone one.

The situation frequently takes a still further step in "remove" from curriculum level by calling in a neuropsychologist, physician, or other professional specializing in organic disabilities. The analysis and classification then moves beyond psychology in the ordering of dispositions. Cruickshank (1972) illustrated this process when he said all learning disabilities (first-order or curriculum level) are "essentially and almost always the result of perceptual problems [second-order, or psychological] based on the neurological system" [third-order, or organic] (p. 383). Sometimes, school systems adopt classification and placement practices based mainly on such third-order analysis: Thus, for example, children may be classified and given special placement as neurologically impaired, brain-injured, minimally brain-injured, or neurologically impaired-educationally handicapped children (Reynolds, 1979).

Definitions and classificatory procedures that cut across several orders of disposition are enormously complex and usually difficult to justify on the basis of clear evidence of relevance to instructional issues. It is the tendency to conduct diagnostic and classification processes at one or more orders of disposition removed from the level of curriculum that has caused much of the controversy about placement processes in special education — as in the Larry P. and kindred cases.

What is happening now, with considerable justification, is a return to the "level of the lesson" for both diagnosis and instructional planning. Thus we see a surge of interest in curriculum-based assessment (see Tindal, this volume; Marston & Magnusson, this volume). Also, there is a strong turn to instructional issues, not to the level of simple predictions about how rapidly children might be "expected" to learn, but rather to manipulable variables that can be arranged to influence better learning — especially by pupils who, under ordinary circumstances, do not learn efficiently. This is the turn to the "effectiveness" variables (see Carnine, Granzin, & Becker, this volume; Deshler & Schumaker, this volume; Casey, Skiba, & Algozzine, this volume; Hawryluck & Smallwood, this volume; Berliner, this volume).

In proposing a return to the "level of the lesson" for diagnosis and planning — rather than to dwell on dispositional analysis — I do not intend to depreciate the role of school psychologists in the educational process for, indeed, much of the work at the level of the lesson is being led by psychologists. Consider for example, the work of Anderson (1985), Bereiter and Scardamalia (1987), Brown and Day (1983), and Berliner (this volume). There is always the possibility, of course, that researchers will establish clear relationships between dispositional states and instruction that will require revisions in the views I express here.

The "level of the lesson" is where the work of teachers is engaged in deliberatel; causing learning and improved performance. Gradually, if programs are successful, students become aware of their own learning and grow in deliberate management of their own learning and performance. In the ideal case, students gradually become strategic or metacognitive and self-regulatory about their own learning, and less dependent upon management by teachers (Deschler and Shumaker, this volume). The argument that I advance is that both teachers and psychologists should be drawn to analysis and function at the levels of the lesson and of metacognition and to a much lesser degree than has been true in the past, to underlying predispositional states. At least, this should be the strategy, I believe, until we have much better evidence than is available now about the relevance of predispositional states to instructional and curricular improvement.

Many additional positive ideas and strategies are proposed in earlier chapters of this volume. I wish to mention only one additional domain, which is concerned with the professionalization of teaching and the implications of that change for school psychologists. Many colleges, state licensing boards, and school leaders are deeply involved these days in the revision of teacher preparation programs — at both preservice and in-service levels. Much of what appears to be occurring on the positive side in such revisions will be based on psychological research and theory. Thus, it is of utmost importance, I believe, that school psychologists concerned with improving educational practices should join in and support efforts for improvement in teacher education at this time. It is quite clear that how well exceptional children — or any children, for that matter — are understood and taught will, as always, depend upon the quality of their teachers. Listed below are some of the topics being discussed in the teacher reform movement that school psychologists should be aware of as they assist in teacher education:

- Principles of learning and of instruction including motivation, reinforcement, explanations, advance organizers, corrective feedback, task analysis, schema theory, etc.

- Representation, organization, and

transformations of knowledge for teaching purposes at various developmental levels.

- Classroom management — setting rules and expectations, preventing disruptive behavior, creating positive learning environments, dealing with crises, etc.

- Teaching students to be self-regulating and strategic about learning and performance.

- Taking into account individual differences among students.

- Creating positive interdependencies (cooperative structures) among students in diverse groups.

- Evaluating learning and instructional effectiveness.

- Setting procedures for skill development — as in high automaticity in reading, math, and motor skills.

There is a signal here for school psychologists, first, to establish their own mastery of knowledge in these domains and, second, to help lead the way in revisions of teacher preparation. Teachers who are competent in these several domains and who are well supported by school psychologists and other specialists will most assuredly gain in their capacity to serve children in the schools.

CONCLUDING NOTE ON PATIENCE

The kinds of transformation in the schools envisioned in this volume and commented upon in this chapter will not come quickly. It would be unwise to change suddenly all the expectations and rules relating to teachers, school psychologists, and special education. It would inflict a cruelty upon many people to order an abrupt return of all (or most) students in programs for the handicapped back to the mainstream or to make any such major moves in practical programs. It is necessary, I think, to develop and follow a strategy that is at once strong and persistent, but also patient and properly timed. There are myriads of rules and regulations emanating from federal, state, and local authorities that govern much of special education practice. Much of that regulatory operation is flawed, but it cannot be changed easily or quickly.

Some of us have thought that a decent and practical strategy might be to encourage selected local school districts and states — those where there is evidence of readiness to change (they have ideas, energy, respect for data) — to move ahead on what we've called a "waiver for performance" basis (see Wang, Levine, & Reynolds, this volume). The idea is that governmental authorities would grant "waivers" of some rules and regulations so that new forms of education could be tried experimentally, but with the proviso that the programs would be evaluated very carefully; thus, the "for performance" part of the waivers, meaning evaluative data would be required (Reynolds & Lakin, 1987; see also Bennett, this volume). It seems quite obvious, I believe, that if traditional methods of delivering special education are inefficient and sometimes even harmful, we should change the rules at least for experimental purposes. Then, as new forms of education are evaluated and found to be successful, the findings can be synthesized and new approaches to policy and broader changes in school operations can be considered.

There is urgent need to accelerate experimental efforts for improvement in the delivery of special education and to move to a broad new round of policy reformation. This whole volume speaks of this challenge. School psychologists have more to lose than most other professions if we fail in these efforts, and more to contribute to experimental trials for new approaches. This is because school psychologists are key figures as gatekeepers among school programs. Also, much of the knowledge base for reform will come from psychology and should be delivered by school psychologists.

There are times when practices in the professions, policies of the society, and moral principles collide. This is such a time for school psychology. There is an opportunity for a very interesting professional life over the next decade for those who take up the challenge represented by this set of facts and this timely book.

REFERENCES

Anderson, J. R. (1985). *Cognitive psychology and its implications* (2nd ed.). San Francisco: Freeman.

Bereiter, C., & Scardamalia, M. (1987). An attainable version of high literacy: Approaches to teaching higher order skills in reading and writing. *Curriculum Inquiry, 17*(1), 9-30.

Brown, A. L., & Day, J. D. (1983). Macrorules for summarizing texts: The development of expertise. *Journal of Verbal Learning and Verbal Behavior, 22*, 1-14.

Cronbach, L. J. (1967). How can instruction be adapted to individual differences: In R. M. Gage (Ed.), *Learning and individual differences* (pp. 23-39). Columbus, OH: Merrill.

Cruickshank, W. M. (1972). Some issues facing the field of learning disabilities. *Journal of Learning Disabilities, 5*, 380-383.

Davies, S. P. (1959). *The mentally retarded in society.* New York: Columbia University Press.

Federal Register, (1977, Dec. 29).

Heller, K. A., Holtzman, W. H., & Messick, S. (Eds.). (1982). *Placing children in special education: A strategy for equity.* Washington, DC: National Academy Press.

Hobbs, N. (1980). An ecologically oriented service-based system for the classification of handicapped children. In E. Salzinger, J. Antrobus, & J. Glick (Eds.), *The ecosystem of the "risk" child* (pp. 66-76). New York: Academic.

Larry P. v. Riles. (1972). Civil Action N.L.-71-2270, 343 F. Supp. 1306 (N.D. CA).

PARC (Pennsylvania Association for Retarded Children) v. Pennsylvania. (1971). 334 F. Supp. 1257 (E.D. PA).

Reynolds, M. C. (1979). On the implications of mainstreaming in the U.S.A. *McGill Journal of Education, 14*(3), 317-325.

Reynolds, M. C., & Lakin, K. C. (1987). Noncategorical special education for mildly handicapped students: A system for the future. In M. C. Wang, M. C. Reynolds, & H. J. Walberg, (Eds.), *Handbook for special education: Research and practice* (Vol. 1). London: Pergamon.

Reynolds, M. C., Wang, M. C. & Walberg, H. (1987). The necessary restructuring of special and regular education. *Exceptional Children, 53*, 391-398.

Wang, M. C., Reynolds, M. C., & Walberg, H. J. (Eds.). (1987-1988). *Handbook for special education: Research and practice* (Vols. 1-3). London: Pergamon.

28

Alternative Educational Delivery Approaches: Implications for School Psychology

Jack I. Bardon
University of North Carolina at Greensboro

For well over 30 years the literature on school psychology has criticized the narrow and limited role the field plays in the schools and proclaimed both the desire and the intention to be of greater use. At the same time, school psychology practitioners have continued to respond to schools' needs for services that mainly have been determined by federal laws translated into rules and regulations at the state level, which invariably have been concerned with the identification and classification of children with special educational needs. The field has responded simultaneously to two pressures: to create an expanded and more comprehensive kind of school psychology and to meet the demands of a service delivery system in special education not of its own making and often incompatible with its own views and assumptions about how children learn and how best to educate them in schools. The dissonance between these two forces has been unpleasant but, ultimately, productive. No one can question that school psychology has made enormous progress, even in comparison with other practitioner specialties in psychology. It has succeeded in raising its training and practice standards, attracted increasingly able students to the field, organized at state and national levels, provided professional identity for its practitioners, advocated for the rights of students and parents, and contributed to the corpus of applied knowledge on how

children can learn and be managed in schools.

CONTRIBUTIONS OF THIS VOLUME

This book, stimulated by an elegant position statement titled "Advocacy for Appropriate Educational Services for All Children," published by the National Association of School Psychologists (NASP) and the National Coalition of Advocates for Students (NCAS), moves the field of school psychology ahead in important ways. In its entirety, it expresses the maturity of the field as well as the maturity of special education. It does not argue particularly for the centrality of school psychology in educational service delivery. Rather, it concentrates on how alternative ways of offering educational services to children in schools might be accomplished. It is task-oriented rather than self-oriented; concerned more with children and better schools than with how school psychology can promote itself. While the book is appropriately critical of current school psychology practices, it is also realistic in its assessment of the enormous difficulties involved in effecting changes both in the specialty and in the schools.

The various chapters provide divergence among contributors about how change might take place and about what leaders in school psychology and special education believe are the assumptions underlying good education and the approaches that might be taken to improve education for all children. It advocates for diversity, experimentation, and cooperation among educators and specialists in education. It recognizes the increasing importance of ecological and systems principles as fundamental requisites for understanding schools and how they operate. The book acknowledges that laws and legislators, as well as officials who implement laws and legal regulations, have a lot to do with how children are educated and how educators function. Most authors realize that a great concept translated into action sometimes creates problems not anticipated in the burst of enthusiasm surrounding the new, bright idea.

Some of the present authors propose that what really works best is the combination and coordination of different features of different programs; that nothing works for everyone. Programs that seem relatively simple and clear at conception become more complicated over time and their underlying problems become exposed. It is easier to start a program than to sustain it, and it is not even very easy to start one! Alternative ways of offering educational services to children in schools must remain experimental and be seasoned with experience, evaluated, and modified to fit the individual needs and subcultures of communities in which schools are located. Even strategically and systematically planned programs are likely to take new forms as plans evolve and continuing action is taken. Change is evolutionary.

Throughout the chapters, the authors in one way or another show understanding of the problems inherent in trying to make changes in relatively stable systems, in which tradition, habit, complacency, and fear of the unknown and untried are pervasive. Segmentation of schools into special and regular education is seen as a problem to be overcome if all children are to receive appropriate education. But it is also understood that resistance can be expected from both regular and special educators and from groups advocating for special groups of children now categorized in at least eleven different ways. People fight hard for what they struggled mightily

to get and will not easily give up newly acquired powers, rights, and privileges. The need for involvement of those affected by change is recognized.

In addition, it is noted that changes in special services, special education, and school psychology practice are intimately intertwined with other changes in education — in fact, in our entire sociopolitical economic complex. Attitudes toward change itself and the direction of that change are profoundly influenced by national leadership, by the mood of the country, by the stock market, by power politics, by who gets what from whom, by proprinquity, by happenstance, all interacting in intricate ways beyond our current understanding and ability to influence definitively. Yet, throughout the book there is a sense of optimism that change can take place, that the attempt to intrude into this welter of complicated dynamics influencing change is worth the effort.

The book takes the position that there are ways of offering services to pupils in schools that are likely to be better than those now offered. In taking this position, the editors and authors know that there is some danger that the benefits accrued through enaction of Public Law 94-142 may be jeopardized. Change must be advocated, and criticism of current special education procedures must be levied, but the fundamental and revolutionary changes in conceptions of student and parent rights that are the bases for recent legislation about special education must also be preserved.

CHANGE AND THE CHANGE PROCESS IN SCHOOL PSYCHOLOGY

One part of the change process not sufficiently acknowledged in this volume, in my opinion, is the change needed within school psychology itself if it is truly to be part of the advocacy movement that prompted the creation of this book. School psychology as a field is not immune to the tendency to resist change. There are understandable and almost lawful discrepancies among the different ways in which persons in a field like school psychology function.

At one end of the professional discipline is its literature. Its scholars, advocates, conceptual leaders, researchers, and critics speak for the future. They attempt to look ahead to societal needs, identifying problems to be resolved and issues that need addressing. They try to state what *should* be. They conduct research to expose the problems of the field and recommend changes in practice and training, though mostly in practice.

At the other extreme of the discipline are its practitioners; those who daily work in the schools and who must deal with the crises of schooling, the details of interprofessional interaction, the forms and paperwork created by attempts to resolve problems at national and state levels. These practitioners are already "trained." They have completed their formal educational programs for the most part. Continuing education is not often a requirement and is usually chosen as a way to augment or enhance current practice methods and to resolve problems presented in everyday work: They must meet the demands imposed on them by their schools. By exposure and experience practitioners are expert at what they do, but new approaches and ideas are *not* what they do. And since many are comfortable with what they are doing, resistance to futuristic views is not uncommon or unexpected. Criticism of the field is likely to be construed as criticism of *them.*

In between are educators and trainers of school psychologists, who are likely to be critical of many aspects of practice and attracted to the new ideas presented in the literature. In fact, they are most often among those producing the research and ideas leading to changes in the field. However, like practitioners, they are also part of systems that are fixed and difficult to change. Like practitioners, they too have become expert in certain aspects of the field. Movement to alternative ways of teaching and preparation of new course content and format take time and energy. Altered relationships among training programs and schools and among departments and programs in the universities

— plus the difficulty of getting anything changed in a university — promote resistance to changes that require major alterations in program content and methods. Faculty in training programs will tend to select only those ideas and methods that already fit the program's point of view. These will be adopted, taught, written about, and advanced. Changes in the field that require major reconstruction and reconsideration of training methods and course content will, naturally, be cautiously approached and probably resisted at least initially.

Yet this book speaks to significant changes in the conception of the field itself, as well as changes in special education and regular education and the relationships among them. If I am correct in my synthesis of what is presented in the various chapters, the shift suggested to make school psychology more useful to schools and to provide a best fit of the specialty to the directions advocated are at least these:

- More attention must be given to what parents, teachers and administrators need to know in order to help children learn and be managed in schools.

- More attention must be given to instruction, school curriculum, and what actually takes place in classrooms and other learning environments.

- Integration of children with special needs in regular educational settings requires environmental assessment as well as individual assessment.

- A search for pathology is misplaced. The emphasis should be on educability.

- Local norms and individualized tailoring of assessment to educational functioning are necessary.

- What takes place in classrooms includes not only academic instruction but instruction in life and social skills as well.

- Childrens' educational and related problems must be addressed early. Problems should be identified and interventions planned before damage is done, so that instruction takes place in ways most likely to be successful.

- Individualized education in groups is the wave of the future. Assisting with this complex interplay between individualized student instruction and group interaction is needed.

- School psychologists probably can most usefully contribute their expertise by indirect services.

- Evaluation of educational efforts and accountability (providing justification and evidence of effective psychological services) will determine whether school psychological services continue and are used well.

- School psychologists will less often function as solo performers. They must live and work in interdisciplinary and collaborative arrangements with others who also have important services to offer. School psychologists' uniqueness in this intergroup arrangement is yet to be demonstrated if current roles are changed and old approaches to assessment and intervention are replaced with alternative approaches.

These directions, stated and implied by many of the book's authors, will be resisted by some practitioners and trainers. Some will continue to believe that what they are doing and teaching is as important and useful as any new ideas proposed. Some will be confused by lack of clarity about their obligations, as the new approaches to enhance the education of all children through individualized instruction in group settings, with a wider range of ability, under revised structural school organization are not yet in common use, not having been demonstrated to be valid, reliable, and trusted. Others will say that change is not needed until schools themselves change; that what we do now is what is asked for and needed. And still others will say we do not know enough yet to permit school psychologists to organize this basic psychological knowledge so that it can be brought more closely to bear on practitioners' problems. Among school psychologists, as among special educators and regular educators, there are differences that are inherent in medical versus educational models of practice and in views about the dichotomous versus continuous nature of children with special educational needs.

Alternative educational delivery approaches and required changes in school psychological services will not occur easily and without dissension and debate. Yet it is my view that the changes implied throughout the book will take place in due time. The survival of school psychology as a distinct specialty in psychology and in education depends on its practitioners' ability to understand these changes and work toward incorporation of the specialty into this exciting educational movement. From my perspective, the most influential persons in school psychology who can help change the field's perception of its own role are the school psychology educators and trainers. As they promote new ideas and concepts, participate in the development and publication of the new research, methods, and materials, and influence the new generation of school psychologists entering the field, they have a central place in changing the field. The next most influential forces involved in promoting change are the national and state associations concerned with school psychology. Through their newsletters, position statements, workshop offerings, convention programs, legislative and advocacy activities, and professional networks they not only can help their practitioner members to accept change but can help in promoting and shaping national and state legislation to change the nature of the educational enterprise itself toward the goals stated in this book.

The practitioners in the field are, as always, in that difficult position of having to carry out their regular functions while they work toward altered roles and functions. For them the intention to be part of this movement is essential. Their part in bringing about change involves doing their current jobs well, *intending* to introduce change when it is possible to do so, and working toward helping others in their school districts understand the benefits of new directions as well as the problems of current assessment and intervention approaches. Their task is the most difficult assignment of all in this change process in school psychology. They will need continuous support and encouragement from their organizations and from their colleagues in the field.

OVERCOMING BARRIERS TO CHANGE

The various alternative delivery systems already under way here and there and the well-researched experimental programs discussed in this volume provide testimony that there are many ways to offer services to children who do not learn easily. The current monolithic special education structure is more cumbersome and costly, and less effective than many would like to believe. What is especially impressive is that some educators and school psychologists have found ways to break through the system, to overcome the barriers to change, and to use what is known in psychology and related disciplines to develop promising alternative ways to educate children.

For those who have been in the field for a decade or more it is sufficient to think back to the mid-1970s to realize that many of the ideas for service delivery presented in this book are dramatically innovative. They not only are surprisingly creative in and of themselves, but they capitalize on the development of ways of thinking about how learning and teaching take place, the nature of intelligence, how pupil personnel service workers can function, what psychology has to offer, and the very nature of schools themselves. Prereferral assessment and intervention, cooperative learning, adaptive learning, curriculum-based assessment, process assessment, direct instruction, peer instruction, strategic interventions, varieties of behavioral interventions, and other service delivery approaches and models presented in this book are but examples of how reconceptualization of schooling and of the relationship between assessment and intervention lead to appropriate new ways to help teachers to teach and pupils to learn.

A problem with any one of these alternative delivery approaches, alluded to in some of the chapters, is that it can too easily become cultish; that it can be seen by its creators and by those who learn

well how to work with it as the definitive solution to special education problems or to the link between assessment and educational intervention. What we do not need at this time is internecine battles among different ideologies, points of view, and pet projects all vying for attention and dominance. Rather, as strongly suggested in this volume, we need a period of time in which many different approaches are tried, evaluated, improved, and disseminated, with special attention to what kinds of service delivery models and methods work best in particular kinds of educational settings under particular kinds of circumstances, and what kinds of educators and pupil personnel service workers can carry them out at what degree of efficiency and at what cost to the taxpayers. We are reminded throughout this volume, and have learned over the past decade at least, that services are not deemed satisfactory if they merely work but rather if they work well enough while meeting other practical requirements. Considerations of cost effectiveness, territoriality, good fit to school structure and function, time and energy required, and threats to existing organizations and persons must also be considered.

School psychology can become a leader in the attempt to redirect attention to normalization and individualization of teaching as critical educational concepts by avoiding internal disputes about which programs are better than others. Leadership involves seeking unity in the field at every possible level — national, state, and local — on the value of trying new ways to offer services to pupils with special needs, stressing the importance of applying multiple methods of service delivery and evaluation of these services, and taking a developmental view of the change process. As one author points out, small wins accumulate.

Very few consequences of a change process continue in force as anticipated. Once Public Law 94-142 was in place, it immediately began to take on a life of its own, in which the rules, regulations, and problems of implementation often became more of a preoccupation than the purposes for which this revolutionary legislation was created. Public Law 99-457, which amends the Education of the Handicapped Act to extend its benefits to handicapped children aged 3-5 years in school year 1990 — 91, will undoubtedly turn out to have attributes and problems not readily predictable from a reading of the intent of the law.

School psychology can promote the changes now under way in regular and special education by being mindful of the change process itself. The process is encouraged when a scholarly, evaluative position on the changes taking place, rather than a strident "me too" position is taken; when efforts and attention remain focused on purposes more than procedures; when participation occurs in many ways at many levels. Developing, trying out, evaluating, and refining instruments, procedures, and service delivery models that meet both the spirit and intent of the laws and regulations supporting new ways to teach and organize in schools can make a difference. But school psychology can also take leadership by continuing to point out and document problems that interfere with purposes. Leadership also involves advocating for human rights in education while maintaining a flexible position on how implementation of these rights might be realized. Behavior on the part of practitioners that models this flexibility can greatly help the change process.

IMPLICATIONS FOR THE PRACTICE OF SCHOOL PSYCHOLOGY

Many of the authors of chapters in this book offer advice on how school psychology practice can best implement the purposes stated in the NASP/NCAS Position Statement on Advocacy for Appropriate Educational Services for All C ildren. Their recommendations reflect a strong desire to shift the focus of practice from normative assessment to "something else." Here are brief, sometimes overlapping, extracts of suggestions made in various chapters, paraphrased in my own words:

- Stop trying to be an expert/savior and work for organizational effectiveness.

- Consultation skills are increasingly important, especially process consultation.

- School psychologists need to stay in one place long enough to be influential.

- Problem identification is a particularly important function for school psychologists. Instead of accepting what others say, school psychologists should seek to find basic problems and help others work on them.

- Assessment strategies should shift from crisis diagnosis to long-term data collection based on pupils' developmental functioning. In other words, engage in the psychological equivalent of a health check-up, in contrast to emergency room services.

- The critical datum for school psychologic practice is student performance.

- School psychologists should be decision makers and processors, helping others to decide what instruments, methods, and programs to use and evaluating efforts to improve student performance and behavior.

- The purpose of school psychology practice should be improved intervention more than labeling and personality description.

- Training of teachers should be part of what school psychologists do.

- Coordination of programs and collaboration with others in mutually determined activities are important roles.

- Understanding the processes of learning and teaching and relating them to curriculum and classroom management are the basic knowledge and skills that school psychologists should seek to develop.

- Indirect service delivery through working with teachers and parents is the emphasis needed.

- Serving as a knowledgeable practitioner to help others know about best practices in making critical school decisions is useful.

- A broader conception of intelligence should be implemented through diverse means of assessing ability to function.

- The school psychologist's role involves advocating, identifying, assisting, designing, training, preventing, consulting, coordinating, measuring, implementing, adapting, disseminating, and utilizing the most promising practices currently known and available.

- A keen awareness of the needs of others is needed.

- Marketing services as well as offering them is encouraged.

- School psychologists are "brokers" who are involved in collaborative problem solving.

Quite a list! What can be distilled from this impressive array of activities and purposes? There is a strong plea for school psychologists to function as professionals rather than as technicians. The background education and training of school psychologists must be rigorous and broad if they are to serve as psychological resources in the many ways psychology can address the problems of schooling. There is no single function that is dominant over others. Instead, school psychologists are asked to participate in finding problems and helping to address them, whatever they may be. In this sense school psychology is seen as the general practice of psychology in the schools, but with an important difference. The emphasis on knowing what schools do, what teachers do, what happens in classrooms, and on the psychological components of learning and teaching differentiates the school psychologist who is described by various authors in this book from other psychologists and from other pupil personnel workers, regardless of the particular functions stressed by different authors. The method of service delivery most often cited is that of consultation. Indirect service delivery is suggested as the way to use the services of a professional who cannot possibly see every child who needs attention and who must, of necessity, concentrate efforts at a level at which most people will derive the most benefits from the services offered.

If we are to take the advice of the authors in this volume, we will need to continue to upgrade school psychology education and training. School psychology

education and training curricula and the nature of supervised practice will have to be reconsidered by training programs. School psychologists in the field will need to engage in intensive continuing education of a kind somewhat different from that now offered. If we are to heed these authors, and others in the field who also advocate for changes in the specialty, a major second-order change in what school psychology is all about is needed. A move toward a more sophisticated, educationally oriented specialty with strong applied research skills as well as practice skills is indicated. This orientation is in process in many sectors of school psychology but by no means is it generally accepted. The long-standing historically based tradition of school psychology as child clinical psychology in the schools has deeply influenced the field and probably best describes current practice and the orientation and training of most practitioners presently working as school psychologists.

This volume calls for and describes new service delivery models and approaches, but it also calls for new school psychology models and approaches if school psychology is to participate in changes in special and regular education that emphasize serving *all* children. School psychology's commitment to the NASP/NCAS position statement will have to be matched by a commitment to change within the field itself.

RESEARCH NEEDED TO IMPLEMENT ALTERNATIVE EDUCATIONAL DELIVERY APPROACHES

The ever-present problem of how to translate research into practice remains as a special problem for practitioner psychologists. A review of the book's chapters suggests that the significant problems that need to be researched in order to successfully implement new methods in schools and to encourage others to change — to try new approaches and accept new ideas — are not always those currently addressed by much of the research in psychology that is related to educational practices. Current research methodology does not always provide the means to satisfactorily address significant practice problems. Among the questions raised by this book are the following:

- Why do many pilot programs remain pilot? Why do they not continue after an initial period, even when successful in reaching their intended goals?

- What is it about some pilot programs that do permit them to break through and become integrated with ongoing practices or replace them? What factors in the program, people, processes, or environment allow them to proceed?

- What more do we need to know about children with special needs? In what ways are these children similar and different and how do these similarities and differences affect how they learn and how they are successfully taught?

- How do you change people's minds? How do you educate teachers and administrators to be flexible, deal well with abstractions, and match behavior with principles and educational goals?

- How do programs develop? What are the steps in the process by which program development and change take place?

- How can evaluation be done in schools so that it retains its quality and at the same time takes into consideration how schools actually function so that resistance to evaluation is minimized?

- How do we assess the instructional environment?

- How do we inject into curriculum-based assessment the necessary test standard requirements we expect of other kinds of psychological assessment? How do we improve the technical aspects of the data base used in academic performance measurement and assessment?

These kinds of questions often defy empirical analysis or else can be addressed empirically only by dealing with such small components of the problems involved that ecological, holistic qualities germane to the basic questions are not adequately or usefully addressed.

On the other hand, it is possible to cite examples of research projects that already have helped us to deal with some of the questions raised by this book. For instance, James Ysseldyke and his associates have helped to dispel extant myths about categorical education and the process of team functioning, which can lead to willingness to consider new ways of helping children with special educational needs. Margaret Wang and her associates have demonstrated that a complex, multimethod educational approach can be evaluated and that it can be made to work. Donald Deshler and his associates have provided, tested, and disseminated an instructional model for teaching students how to learn that is accepted by some school districts and is implementable by teachers and related service personnel. Other examples abound.

The research questions raised and the examples, above, of research and demonstration programs providing acceptable research information lead to a dilemma and, at the same time, offer promise that some answers can be found to the practical questions required to make alternative service delivery work. The dilemma is that the current research models we are taught are not always sufficient or pertinent to deal with the practical questions we ask. While we strive for scientific rigor, increasingly use more refined statistical procedures, and are convinced that internal and external validity are needed in good research, we too often attend to problems we can address rather than to those we must try to resolve. Our published literature is selective. It reports those studies that have been done right but does not always publish studies about problems we must know more about.

The promise is that the environment in which research is conducted and published is also changing, especially in educational research. Single-case experimental designs are increasingly respectable and especially useful in our efforts to understand individuals and individual programs in particular educational situations. Ethnographic and case study research in education are becoming more sophisticated and adaptable to school settings and problems. Qualitative research is no longer frowned upon. Respectable journals are discussing qualitative research and appear to be accepting a broader range of research-based studies. Expository articles and phenomenological descriptions appear now and then. Interdisciplinary research is promoting the mixing and merging of different research constructs and methods. Heuristic inquiry conducted in practice settings can lead to researchable hypotheses and questions, shaping the more researchable questions to be more carefully studied. School psychologists are among those asking the difficult questions, coming up with useful hunches, trying out ways of helping people, and attempting to find out how their efforts can be evaluated.

These kinds of applied research procedures and approaches are more closely tied to the problems faced in practice. They allow room for error while the questions themselves get clearer and the answers get closer to the fundamental questions. Closer working relationships between school psychology practitioners in the schools and school psychology educators and trainers and educational psychologists, who are in the best position to use the insights and ideas of the practitioner, form the basis for more substantial and rigorous research studies. Practitioners could contribute much if they began to view themselves as contributors to research by asking good questions and offering research-productive "good guesses" about what is working for them and why they think it is happening.

CONCLUSIONS

The challenge today for school psy-chology is to take seriously the changing nature of regular and special education and to dedicate itself to assisting with appropriate educational services for all children; indeed, for all persons regardless of age. The challenge for the field of school psychology and for its practitioners and educators is to consider how to retool for the future. Change in education is taking place right now, probably to a greater extent than at any other time in our lives. While we cannot predict what particular directions it will take and what problems the fact of change will create, we are in a position to influence that change by what we do and also by what we fail to do. As psychology itself becomes more complex, as new specialties develop and science and practice struggle to find ways to complement each other, the future of the field now called school psychology may well depend on how it conceives of itself; how it views its purposes and its special place in psychology and in education.

The import of this book is that it should foster among school psychologists a realization that there are alternatives to present-day psychological functioning in schools. There are other ways to educate children. There are better ways to teach and learn. Many of the alternative educational delivery approaches presented in the book are not carried out by school psychologists. In truth, many do not even include school psychologists as part of the coordinated efforts involved. The field itself and its practitioners must decide collectively and individually whether they want to be part of the change. That decision can be made by default or by concerted action. A momentous choice faces the field.

Ce qui se passe à
CUBA

RESTE À CUBA!

Catalogage avant publication de Bibliothèque et
Archives nationales du Québec et Bibliothèque et Archives Canada

Dubois, Amélie

Ce qui se passe à Cuba reste à Cuba !

ISBN 978-2-89585-703-7

I. Titre.

PS8607.U219C372 2015   C843'.6   C2015-941489-X

PS9607.U219C372 2015

Les Éditeurs réunis bénéficient du soutien financier de la SODEC et du Programme de crédits d'impôt du gouvernement du Québec.

Nous remercions le Conseil des Arts du Canada de l'aide accordée à notre programme de publication.

Financé par le gouvernement du Canada
Funded by the Government of Canada

Édition :
LES ÉDITEURS RÉUNIS
www.lesediteursreunis.com

Distribution au Canada :
PROLOGUE
www.prologue.ca

Distribution en Europe :
DNM
www.librairieduquebec.fr

 Suivez Amélie Dubois et
Les Éditeurs réunis sur Facebook.

Imprimé au Canada

Dépôt légal : 2015
Bibliothèque et Archives nationales du Québec
Bibliothèque et Archives Canada

AMÉLIE DUBOIS

Ce qui se passe à CUBA

RESTE À CUBA!

LES ÉDITEURS RÉUNIS

De la même auteure

Oui, je le veux... et vite !, Les Éditeurs réunis, 2012.

Ce qui se passe au Mexique reste au Mexique !, Les Éditeurs réunis, 2012.

Ce qui se passe au congrès reste au congrès !, Les Éditeurs réunis, 2013.

Le gazon... toujours plus vert chez le voisin ?, Les Éditeurs réunis, 2014.

SÉRIE « CHICK LIT » :

Tome 1. *La consœurie qui boit le champagne*, Les Éditeurs réunis, 2011.

Tome 2. *Une consœur à la mer !*, Les Éditeurs réunis, 2011.

Tome 3. *104, avenue de la Consœurie*, Les Éditeurs réunis, 2011.

Tome 4. *Vie de couple à saveur d'Orient*, Les Éditeurs réunis, 2012.

Tome 5. *Soleil, nuages et autres cadeaux du ciel*, Les Éditeurs réunis, 2013.

Tome 6. *S'aimer à l'européenne*, Les Éditeurs réunis, 2014.

 Amélie Dubois

 ame_dubois

www.ameliedubois.com

La vie est courte, l'art est long,
l'occasion fugitive, l'expérience trompeuse,
le jugement difficile...

– Hippocrate

... je dirais même TRÈS difficile pour certaines!

– Amélie Dubois

PROLOGUE

(À lire en s'imaginant, hum..., la suave voix virile de Charles Tisseyre...)

Fort populaire auprès des touristes depuis la fin des années 1990, l'île de Cuba – et en particulier la station balnéaire de Varadero – constitue la destination favorite du «tout-inclusif-voyageur-québécois». Rêvant à la fois de mer turquoise digne de la Polynésie française et de prix compétitifs comme à Old Orchard Beach, bon nombre de gens y trouvent leur compte. Troquant les hôtels modernes pour des complexes désuets datant des années 1970, les vacanciers acceptent en toute connaissance de cause de – possiblement – se mesurer à un système de climatisation défectueux ou encore à un robinet de salle de bain qui explose. Certains habitués disent même voyager avec quelques outils dans leurs bagages, «juste en cas que...». Ceci dit, la nourriture peu savoureuse, et ce, d'un bout à l'autre de la péninsule tropicale, procure au vacancier la chance inouïe de terminer ses vacances avec cinq livres en moins. Quel bonheur! Sachez que le voyageur à Cuba s'en sort toujours vivant en avalant çà et là quelques morceaux de tomates vertes et de concombres ainsi que des pommes de terre frites – quand il n'y a pas de pénurie, ce qui arrive d'ailleurs fréquemment.

Le vacancier typique, adepte du rapport qualité-de-la-plage–prix, acceptera volontiers de partager ses astuces personnelles sur les blogues de voyage. Certains conseilleront par exemple de ne pas toucher aux rideaux de douche souvent souillés pour ne pas attraper de vilains champignons, alors que d'autres suggéreront d'offrir illégalement une bière

les marchés aux puces regorgeant de marchandise redondante et hors de prix afin de rapporter à la maison des articles inutiles qui feront office de ramasse-poussière jusqu'au prochain ménage du printemps.

gratuite au vieux Cubain en habit hawaïen vendant des *peanuts* sur la plage depuis vingt ans en échange d'une photo cocasse avec lui. Quel souvenir original !

Le transport dans la ville de Varadero étant facilité grâce aux fameux autobus deux étages à cinq pesos la journée, les vacanciers peuvent déambuler dans

Mais de retour de leur périple, les photos caribéennes aux teintes bleu vert incroyables rappelleront aux vacanciers que « sur la côte ouest du Mexique, les plages sont pas belles, pis qu'à Punta Cana, c'est ben trop cher ! » Ils se promettront donc de retourner l'année suivante à Varadero... et ce, pour la huitième fois en huit ans...

Caroline pousse du bout des doigts trois mouchoirs de papier chiffonnés et humides jonchant la table devant elle. Puis, changeant finalement d'idée, elle se lève pour aller les déposer dans une petite corbeille vide qui se trouve tout près de l'entrée. Debout face à la grande porte opaque, elle renifle un grand coup, soupire, puis se retourne. La pièce toute blanche et exiguë où elle se trouve est dénuée de fenêtre, mais elle s'avère tout de même artificiellement lumineuse en raison d'un généreux éclairage au néon encastré au plafond. Résolue à poursuivre, Caroline reprend place sur sa chaise. Très concentré, un des deux hommes assis devant elle termine d'inscrire de l'information sur la première grande feuille huit pouces et demi par quatorze d'une pile cumulant une dizaine de pages. Il marque une pause pour s'assurer que l'écriture a bien traversé le papier carbone permettant de dupliquer ses écrits sur les quelques copies subséquentes. Comme tout semble conforme, il poursuit sa tâche.

Gentil, le deuxième type rassure un peu Caroline, qui s'essuie le nez une fois de plus, l'air abattu.

— Madame, beaucoup de gens font des bêtises en voyage. Certains consciemment, d'autres pas. J'espère que cela vous servira de leçon. Comme je vous l'ai dit plus tôt, nous sommes tenus au secret professionnel dans votre cas, mais sachez que vous n'êtes pas la première à vous retrouver dans ce genre de situation nébuleuse.

— Que je sois la première à me faire prendre ou pas, ça ne change pas grand-chose au final. Seigneur...

L'homme qui écrivait depuis déjà un petit moment termine enfin. Il vérifie le document à nouveau. Comme il semble satisfait du résultat, il tend la pile de feuilles à son collègue. Celui-ci en inspecte minutieusement le contenu avant de confirmer :

— C'est complet, je pense. Il faut seulement terminer d'inscrire les informations techniques de la fiche d'identification. Nous avons déjà votre nom complet et votre adresse de résidence à Gatineau. Il manque juste votre profession.

— Professeure au secondaire, en français.

— La matière n'est pas vraiment nécessaire, je pense, ronchonne le type, sévère, en ayant l'air de trouver que celle-ci livre beaucoup trop de détails compte tenu de l'information demandée.

— Je considère que je pratique un métier honorable, vous savez. Une enseignante se doit d'avoir des principes éthiques. Vous comprendrez que je n'aurais jamais pu cautionner une affaire de même de mon plein gré...

— Ah, madame, écoutez... En vingt-sept ans de métier, j'ai appris que peu importe le style de vie de quelqu'un, son métier ou ses revenus, tout le monde peut déraper un jour ou l'autre dans sa vie...

— Bah... Pfft..., réplique la pauvre Caro qui n'ose contredire ce fait indéniable.

— L'adresse de votre lieu de travail, s'il vous plaît?

— POURQUOI? crie Caroline, maintenant prise de panique.

— C'est uniquement pour remplir le formulaire, ne vous inquiétez pas.

Caroline hésite un moment, comme si elle n'en croyait pas un mot. Elle toise un instant les deux types devant elle. Son regard se pose en alternance sur le badge de l'Agence des services frontaliers du Canada que porte l'agent de droite et sur l'insigne affichant son nom complet – Jacques Potvin. Caroline se résout à obtempérer, mue inconsciemment par un respect de l'autorité bien ancré dans sa personnalité. Elle livre l'information demandée avec lenteur, telle une dictée, question de lui laisser le temps de prendre le tout en note. Réflexe archaïque d'enseignante de français.

— Voilà, je pense que c'est tout pour le moment. L'inspecteur Biron viendra vous voir bientôt.

— Ah ouin, c'est Biron qui travaille à matin? T'es certain? fait le deuxième homme, pas convaincu de ce que son collègue vient d'avancer.

— Me semble que oui...

Les deux hommes se lèvent en échangeant un regard confus, le premier agent ayant suscité un doute considérable dans la tête de l'autre.

— Je pensais que c'était plutôt Laliberté? Me semble que je l'ai croisé tantôt...

Toujours préoccupés quant aux ressources humaines présentes en cette période achalandée du temps des Fêtes, ils semblent tous deux se foutre royalement de l'état d'âme de la pauvre Caroline qui reste en plan, toujours assise sur sa chaise trop droite, l'ai démuni et la larme à l'œil. Ainsi ignorée, elle pleurniche :

— Moi, je fais quoi?

Les deux agents frontaliers – qui se dirigeaient tout bonnement vers la porte – se tournent avec stupéfaction, comme si, tel le Messie, elle venait d'apparaître.

— Euh... Vous restez ici pour le moment. Quelqu'un viendra sous peu.

Sans que Caroline ait le temps de demander plus d'éclaircissements, les deux hommes sortent de la pièce. Par-dessus le bruit des pentures de la porte se refermant sur les deux ombres qui s'éloignent déjà, Caroline entend :

— Non, non, je te dis. Je pense vraiment que c'est Biron qui travaille aujourd'hui.

— Ah ben... Je pensais qu'il était parti avec son beau-frère à Fort Lauderdale...

Clac! fait la porte dans un bruit de serrure métallique. Un frisson lui parcourant l'échine, Caroline agrippe le gobelet de café en carton qu'on lui a offert il y a une heure. Elle avale une gorgée du breuvage froid un peu de travers, ce qui la fait grimacer d'écœurement. Tout à coup, elle constate qu'elle vient ainsi de déposer son ADN sur le réceptacle et son cœur s'affole l'espace d'un instant... Elle revient illico de son délire en relativisant qu'elle ne se trouve tout de même pas dans un épisode de *CSI Miami*. Quoique... Tandis qu'elle se livre à ses réflexions paranoïaques, un des néons au plafond clignote comme s'il allait s'éteindre à tout jamais.

JOUR 8

AÉROPORT MONTRÉAL-TRUDEAU
SALLE 303 – **7 H 52**

— Me semble que ça sent le renfermé ici ? s'indigne Vicky en plissant le nez avec dégoût.

Les deux employés qui se tiennent devant elle, un tout petit homme ne mesurant pas plus de cinq pieds cinq pouces et un plus grand et plus corpulent lèvent instinctivement le museau dans le but d'avaliser ou de démentir les propos de la voyageuse.

— Je ne sens rien, toi? dit le type de droite, alias le petit, qui ressemble étrangement à Laurel du populaire duo comique Laurel et Hardy.

— Non, moi non plus, avoue le plus costaud.

— Dommage, ajoute Laurel, un peu déçu de ne pas être en mesure de corroborer les dires de la séduisante voyageuse à qui il doit faire remplir une déclaration d'événements.

— De toute façon, c'est pas important..., minaude Vicky qui, bien entendu, a remarqué dès son arrivée que ledit Laurel s'avérait sensible à ses charmes.

— On va terminer cette portion d'interrogatoire, si vous permettez. Donc, votre adresse à Gatineau est celle de votre résidence permanente? demande le gros douanier, plus austère que son acolyte.

— Ouais, petite vie de petite vie. J'aimerais bien ça, posséder une résidence où il fait plus chaud l'hiver, mais mon salaire de petite prof sous-payée ne me permet pas – et ne permettra jamais d'ailleurs, il faut le préciser – de me payer une résidence secondaire en Californie...

— Ah ouais, hein..., s'intéresse Laurel, qui semble tout à coup succomber à une envie profonde de s'investir conjointement dans le projet de vie de Vicky de posséder une résidence à Los Angeles.

Rêveur, il la contemple en souriant sottement, les visualisant – lui en Speedo, elle en monokini – près de la piscine de leur copropriété de luxe. Son collègue, sans doute son supérieur, lui passe alors les papiers avec élan afin qu'il quitte son fantasme et revienne un peu sur terre. Comme Laurel fixe toujours intensément Vicky, en bavant presque à l'idée de planifier l'agencement intérieur du mobilier de leur future résidence commune, Hardy ramène finalement les papiers vers lui afin de poursuivre l'entretien :

— Donc, votre métier ?

— Professeure d'arts plastiques au secondaire.

— Écoutez, je ne pense pas qu'il soit nécessaire de mentionner la matière…, s'impatiente Hardy, toujours l'air grognon.

— Ça sent vraiment drôle ici, réitère Vicky en s'éventant le visage d'une main.

— Il manque juste l'adresse de votre école et je crois que ce sera complet.

Vicky lui fournit l'information sans broncher.

— On reviendra vous voir pour la suite.

— Quelle suite ? Je commence à être tannée…

— La suite des procédures, répond le type en se levant, aussitôt imité par son collègue lunatique.

— Aaaah, je comprends. «La suite»…, raille Vicky, déçue de ne pouvoir obtenir plus de détails.

Les deux hommes quittent la salle. Laurel sort le dernier, en jetant un ultime regard coquin en direction de Vicky qui lui envoie la main avec nonchalance, souriant faussement juste avant de rouler des yeux en direction des tuiles cartonnées du plafond.

JOUR 8

AÉROPORT MONTRÉAL-TRUDEAU
SALLE 322 – 7 H 52

Katia toise non subtilement l'agent frontalier de droite, qu'elle a trouvé très à son goût dès la seconde où il est entré. Elle lui envoie une œillade charmante tandis que le second agent – au dos un peu voûté – remplit le document la tête penchée vers la table. Professionnel, et surtout pas dupe, l'agent convoité ne répond pas à son avance. Son visage reste de glace et il détourne plutôt la tête vers la sortie.

— Ceci est bien l'adresse de votre résidence ? s'assure le type en lui lisant rapidement l'information.

— En fait, j'ai quatre maisons, dont une à Vegas, une à L.A., une dans le West Side à New York... Mais bon, la résidence où je passe le plus de temps, c'est celle de Gatineau ! Par choix, bien sûr ! déconne Katia.

Devant les deux regards sévères qui la tambourinent tel un marteau-piqueur, Katia réalise rapidement que sa blague n'était pas si drôle, compte tenu de la démarche officielle en cours.

— On vous demanderait de faire preuve d'un peu de sérieux, madame, la sermonne l'agent de gauche, toujours armé de son stylo à bille.

— Bon... Ouiiii, c'est bien mon adresse.

— Nous avons déjà l'adresse de votre lieu de travail. Quel métier y exercez-vous ?

— Je suis prof.

— De quoi ?

— Ben là, ça doit pas être un détail SI important, me semble. Voulez-vous bien me dire ça serait quoi le rapport avec l'enquête ? les houspille Katia juste pour le plaisir de se montrer déplaisante à son tour.

— Toutes les informations et tous les détails ont leur importance, madame, ainsi que votre transparence dans la démarche.

— Anglais. Prof d'anglais. Habituellement, avec le deuxième cycle, mais les quatre premières années de ma carrière, j'ai enseigné au premier cycle. Personnellement, j'aime mieux les plus vieux. Ils écoutent des vidéoclips de chanteuses américaines à moitié à poil sur YouTube toute la nuit, donc ils sont comme meilleurs en anglais, tsé. Voulez-vous d'autres détails ?

Les agents frontaliers, qui ont décelé son attitude pince-sans-rire et désinvolte, la fixent froidement pendant un long moment pour lui signifier qu'ils saisissent très bien qu'elle se moque d'eux.

— Quoi? Vous m'avez dit «TOUS les détails». Aaaah... J'ai le cerveau en compote, je suis fatiguée, avoue Katia avec une once de repentir, ne voulant tout de même pas être mise en état d'arrestation pour avoir fait la fanfaronne.

— Nous pouvons comprendre, concède l'agent de droite, qui apprécie tout de même secrètement le cran de chien de son interlocutrice.

— Donc, c'est complet, je pense bien, conclut celui de gauche. Je vais aller consulter le reste de l'équipe.

Il ouvre l'appareil de communication accroché à sa ceinture avant de franchir la porte, laissant ainsi Katia seule avec l'agent qu'elle trouve de son goût. D'emblée, celle-ci esquisse son sourire le plus ravageur en envoyant avec candeur ses cheveux vers l'arrière. De marbre, le séduisant agent fuit de nouveau son regard.

JOUR 8

AÉROPORT MONTRÉAL-TRUDEAU
SALLE 315 – 8 H 08

Épuisée et toujours recluse dans la pièce sans fenêtre, Caroline tombe dans la lune en fixant un trombone abandonné au sol près d'une des chaises de l'autre côté de la table. Le bruit de la poignée qui tourne la ramène brutalement à la réalité. Un homme en uniforme ouvre toute grande la porte et demeure en retrait tandis qu'il laisse pénétrer Vicky et Katia.

À la vue de ses amies, Caroline bondit hors de sa chaise tel un clown éjectable sortant de sa boîte à surprise. Vicky fonce alors droit sur elle pour la prendre dans ses bras. Katia bat des mains avec enthousiasme comme si elle débarquait chez Caro pour le réveillon :

— *Hello ! Long time no see !*

Posté en sentinelle dans le cadre de porte, l'homme leur annonce :

— Malheureusement, à cause du temps des Fêtes et du nombre élevé de voyageurs franchissant la frontière, l'inspecteur qui doit approuver toutes les déclarations est présentement occupé à un cas plus urgent. Je dois donc vous faire patienter ici pour un moment. Ça peut être un peu long. Vous disposez d'un téléphone de communication interne s'il y a un problème ou si vous désirez aller aux toilettes.

Il referme la porte qui se verrouille automatiquement en émettant son fameux cliquetis s'apparentant à celui d'une cellule de prison.

— Ayoye, un des gars qui m'a interrogée était vraiment trop *cute*, je vous jure ! Oufffff ! balance Katia en prenant place nonchalamment sur une des trois chaises présentes dans la pièce.

— Eille, pas moi! Un petit et un baquet bête comme ses pieds, rien de très intéressant, se désole Vicky en s'assoyant à son tour devant Caroline.

— Moi, le *cute* portait malheureusement une bague de gars très marié, mais je suis sûre qu'il me trouvait à son goût pareil, ajoute Katia d'une voix mêlant conviction et désolation.

— OK! Vous autres, là, comme d'habitude, vous pensez juste à *cruiser*! rugit Caroline.

— Pour ma part, je pense à rien pantoute... Je suis brûlée, souligne Vicky en descendant son bassin sur l'assise peu rembourrée de la chaise afin d'appuyer l'arrière de sa tête contre la partie supérieure du dossier.

Elle effectue ensuite des bruits de poisson avec sa bouche, témoignant ainsi de son état cérébral oisif. Katia, qui s'étire les bras de chaque côté du corps, imite la position à l'allure confortable de son amie, puis elle fait claquer sa langue au palais. Silence.

— LES FILLES? crie Caroline.

L'air franchement agacé par son attitude paniquée, Katia se redresse un peu pour la regarder.

— Caro, on en a parlé hier. De toute façon, ils ont bien dû te le redire aussi: on ne risque rien. C'est juste pour leur dossier intergouvernemental. Comment ça s'appelle? Interpol?

Caroline ironise, les baguettes en l'air:

— Parfait ! Tout va bien, quoi ! On est présentement incarcérées par Douanes Canada sans pouvoir contacter notre famille et sans avoir accès à nos téléphones... mais tout va bien !

— Ouin, c'est vrai, j'aimerais ça qu'ils nous redonnent nos affaires. Peut-être qu'on peut leur demander ? Au moins, si on peut capter le WiFi gratuit de l'aéroport, on aura quelque chose à faire, comme jouer à Candy Crush, approuve Vicky en reluquant avec désolation sa manucure défraîchie.

Caroline s'insurge de nouveau en secouant la tête :

— L'autre qui veut jouer à Candy Crush...

— Bon, les filles, j'ai une grave confidence à vous faire. Je vous ai pas tout dit pendant le voyage et, contrairement à vous deux, je vais pas attendre la nuit des temps pour me confesser..., débute une Katia angoissée.

— AAAAAH ! Honnêtement, à ce stade-ci, je me fous royalement de tes histoires de cul du voyage ou de n'importe quoi d'autre. On dirait que vous prenez la situation à la légère, les filles. Êtes-vous inconscientes ou quoi ? réplique Caroline du tac au tac, tout en croisant les bras en signe de frustration.

— Bon ! Relaxe, Caro... Tant pis d'abord, vous le saurez pas..., envoie Katia, un peu offusquée de se faire ainsi fermer le clapet.

— Les filles ? Il y a d'abord eu le Mexique, il y a deux ans, ensuite le congrès de débiles à Québec... Et là, encore une fois, tout tourne au drame ! C'est QUOI notre maususse de problème ?

— Le congrès, c'était pire, sérieux !

— Voyons !? On dirait que vous ne réalisez pas pantoute la gravité de la situation !

— Hier, j'ai vraiment capoté. Mais là, on peut rien faire d'autre que d'attendre. C'est LA chose à faire quand on n'a pas de contrôle sur une situation, rationnalise Vicky, bien fière de sa grande capacité à effectuer un lâcher-prise.

— C'est même pas de notre faute, en plus… En tout cas, pas trop de notre faute, mettons, nuance Katia.

— Eille, vous me découragez pas à peu près, s'offusque Caro en les dévisageant.

— On est des victimes, au fond. Hein ? se réjouit presque Vicky en poussant un peu Katia du bras.

— Avoue, Caro, que c'est vrai ? On est arrivées décidées et super motivées à ne pas commettre les mêmes erreurs que pendant notre voyage au Mexique. Mais bon… On a été malchanceuses, c'est tout !

— «Pas faire les mêmes erreurs», mon œil, oui, s'oppose Caroline, les bras soudés contre sa poitrine.

— On a essayé très fort, du moins…

Après une attente interminable pendant laquelle le trio a serpenté à pas de tortue entre les cordons de foule, la femme en poste à l'enregistrement des passagers remet à chacune des filles une carte d'embarquement. Vicky lui sourit en déclarant :

— Poids des bagages qui respecte la limite permise, pas de retard pour s'enregistrer, ça va vraiment bien notre voyage, hein ? C'est gé-ni-al !

La femme maigrichonne au menton tout aussi pointu que son nez lui renvoie un sourire forcé lui signifiant qu'elle n'a rien relevé d'exceptionnel dans son énumération. Sous son regard inquisiteur et sévère doublé d'un signe de tête expéditif, les filles se déplacent pour la laisser poursuivre son travail auprès des autres voyageurs. Un chaos infernal règne à l'aéroport Montréal-Trudeau, transformé en une véritable fourmilière depuis le début des vacances de Noël.

— Non mais, avoir un AIR DE CUL, c'est-tu un préalable si tu veux travailler pour une compagnie aérienne ? peste Katia en parlant assez fort pour que ladite femme l'entende.

— Chut ! Katia, arrête…, implore Caroline, honteuse du comportement immature de son amie.

La femme, qui fait semblant de n'avoir rien entendu, sourit tout à coup plus gentiment à la petite famille qui avance vers le comptoir avec autant de bagages que s'ils déménageaient carrément à Cuba pour six ans.

— En tout cas, les filles, on se l'est dit, hein ? Maintenant, on sait dans quoi on s'embarque. Pas question de refaire les mêmes erreurs, souligne Caroline en rangeant avec soin son passeport dans son sac à bandoulière.

— Ouais, on a de l'expérience maintenant ! Quoique j'aimerais quand même vérifier le contenu de ton bagage à main avant de passer les contrôles de sécurité, la prie Katia en faisant mine d'inspecter le sac de Caro.

— Non, pas besoin. J'ai été sur le site de Douanes Canada et j'ai imprimé la liste des objets interdits. Pas de danger, cette fois. Regardez, les filles, je vais même jeter ma bouteille d'eau, parce que je sais que je n'ai pas le droit de l'apporter ! les rassure Caro en se déplaçant à grands pas chassés vers une poubelle, la tête haute comme si elle s'apprêtait à recevoir une distinction spéciale du Gouverneur général du Canada soulignant son geste de prévention admirable.

— Hoooon ! Bravo, Caroline ! C'est vrai que, là, on sait à quoi s'attendre. J'ai même placé trois tubes de crème solaire dans ma valise, précise Vicky, l'air tout aussi digne que son amie d'obtenir un prix.

— Dans mon cas, j'ai emporté autant de condoms que la dernière fois parce que ma vie affective, c'est de la marde. Il faut qu'il se passe de quoi, mentionne Katia en devenant un peu songeuse.

— Ouin, pauvre toi. Mais moi, je suis supposée commencer mes règles genre demain ou après-demain. Ark ! C'est tellement pas le temps, se résigne une Caroline bien désappointée.

— C'est poche, en effet..., approuve Vicky qui est subitement coupée par Katia qui rage.

— Non mais, *dompée* par texto la veille de Noël, qui dit mieux ? Ma vie amoureuse, c'est du gros n'importe quoi, se désole Katia d'une voix forte comme si elle s'adressait à l'ensemble des gens présents à l'aéroport. Il y a un truc qui cloche entre Noël et moi...

— Il était bizarre depuis le début, ce gars-là, Kat, lui fait remarquer Vicky.

— Oui, mais avoir su, je me serais préparé un « ami de Noël » en *back up*. J'haïs tellement ça aller dans mes *partys* de famille toute seule.

— Toi, c'est plus ça qui t'écœure...

— Mes tantes, je suis plus capable, sérieux ! « T'es encore toute seule, ma belle Katia ? Eh que c'est donc compliqué, l'amour, à votre âge... » Pis elles ont le culot de me dire ça alors que mes oncles somnolent sur le divan à 20 h après avoir mangé trop de tourtière. Leurs super maris, qui ne leur ont probablement pas fait l'amour de façon noble depuis l'Expo 67. « Wow, c'est vraiment mieux de votre bord, hein ! » que je me dis à chaque fois.

— Ouin... Moi, par contre, je n'ai pas apporté de condom pour ce voyage-ci. Mais comme Marc tarde à officialiser notre relation après plus d'un an de fréquentation, je me suis dit : «Je ne couche pas avec personne par respect, mais je *frenche*-rien-que...»

— Je «*frenche*-rien-que»? prononce Caroline en détachant chaque syllabe, pas certaine de comprendre cette nouvelle expression.

— Je fais juste *frencher* : je «*frenche*-rien-que»!

— C'est bon ça! J'aime ça! approuve Katia, heureuse d'avoir trouvé une complice pour ses futures soirées de chasse aux mâles en sol cubain.

Plus ou moins d'accord avec son plan, Caroline s'abstient de tout commentaire et se dirige plutôt vers la grande file de voyageurs faisant le pied de grue entre les cordons de foule longitudinaux menant au contrôle de sécurité. Elle bâille alors à s'en déboîter la mâchoire, se frottant un peu les yeux.

— Sérieusement, c'est le *fun* de partir pour le jour de l'An, mais je suis comme brûlée des *partys* des Fêtes. Je vais relaxer en voyage cette fois, je vous le jure, annonce Caroline.

— C'est quoi l'idée de faire décoller des avions en pleine nuit, aussi...

JOUR 8
AÉROPORT MONTRÉAL-TRUDEAU
SALLE 315 – 8 H 24

Avachies de façon peu gracieuse dans leurs chaises respectives, les trois filles poursuivent leur discussion.

— Quand je repense à mon projet de «je *frenche*-rien-que»…

— Ha! ha! ha! Tu vois, ça, je trouve ça quand même drôle! s'amuse enfin Caroline.

— Pourquoi, dans la vie, les choses ne se passent jamais comme on s'y attend? fait remarquer Vicky, gravement découragée par la vie de façon générale.

— Pour pas que ce soit plate! Pour vivre des affaires…, souligne Katia.

— «Vivre des affaires…» Laisse faire! Je m'en serais passé, avoue Caroline, qui semble tout de même plus calme que lorsque les filles sont venues la rejoindre dans la salle 315.

— Tout semblait si bien parti au départ. C'est fou pareil comment le vent peut tourner vite, des fois.

— «Vivre des affaires…» Pfft! répète Caroline en balançant sa tête vers l'arrière.

JOUR 1
CUBA
AÉROPORT DE VARADERO

Les filles attendent parmi les voyageurs qui essaient tant bien que mal de faire la file indienne devant les austères cabines de douane du petit aéroport. Les rangs sont très désordonnés; c'est la cohue. Pas très loin, deux Cubains en uniforme vert pâle discutent nonchalamment, les jambes bien écartées, assis sur deux chaises de bois qui semblent avoir été installées à la va-comme-je-te-pousse au beau milieu de la place. Ils semblent tous deux bien à l'aise avec le chaos ambiant. L'un d'eux envoie même un semblant de baiser dans les airs en direction de Katia qui s'était tournée vers eux un peu par hasard.

— Je rêve ou le douanier vient de m'envoyer un genre de bec soufflé dégueu?

Caroline prête peu d'attention à son commentaire, davantage étonnée du fonctionnement un peu particulier des douanes cubaines.

— Coudonc... Ça leur tentait pas de mettre des cordons pour diriger la foule, eux? Les files d'attente sont tout croches, y'a même des gens qui dépassent!

— Voyons? Le douanier qui *cruise* les passantes! Me semble que c'est inadéquat.

— Regardez-moi ça, cette organisation bizarre: on parle avec un douanier caché dans un trou et ensuite on passe par une porte qui se débarre automatiquement. On dirait des portes de toilettes publiques. Ça fait pas très sérieux! En plus, ils prennent une photo de nous, comme si on était des criminels.

Vicky, qui ajuste le bas de son chandail à manches courtes afin d'être jolie sur photo en toutes circonstances, pousse du pied son bagage à main posé au sol et affirme :

— Ouf! C'était vraiment une bonne idée de se changer en vêtements d'été dans l'avion. J'ai déjà chaud.

— Ouais, ma tante m'a conseillé de faire ça. De cette façon, tu crèves pas de chaleur pendant le transport pour te rendre à l'hôtel.

Les filles se retrouvent enfin de l'autre côté des fameuses «portes de toilette» et commentent leur expérience :

— Elle ne m'a rien demandé, à part si j'étais allée en Afrique récemment, affirme Vicky.

— C'est à cause de l'Ebola, en déduit Katia qui fait à présent la queue devant le contrôle de sécurité où les passagers doivent placer leurs bagages à main dans une machine à rayons X.

Vicky regarde droit devant en attendant son tour et chuchote :

— Me semble que ça fait un peu «guédaille», la façon dont les femmes sont habillées...

Les douaniers, regroupés autour des appareils de façon aléatoire, voire désordonnée, bavardent en espagnol à voix forte comme s'ils se trouvaient à une bamboula de quartier plutôt qu'à un contrôle douanier. Les femmes portent toutes un uniforme beige composé d'un chemisier de style militaire rehaussé de badges colorés et d'une jupe assez courte. Leurs jambes sont toutefois recouvertes de bas résille affriolants ressemblant à ceux des danseuses de cabaret des années 1920. De plus, leur visage lourdement fardé semble indiquer qu'elles seraient davantage des femmes aux mœurs légères que des figures d'autorité.

Déchiffrant les directives floues mimées par un employé qui rigole avec sa collègue, les filles placent leurs effets personnels dans des bacs de plastique gris que la machine à rayons X *vintage* avale rapidement.

Ayant franchi l'étape de la sécurité avec brio, Katia, Caro et Vicky se dirigent vers le troisième et dernier carrousel de bagages où un petit groupe de voyageurs attendent déjà leurs valises.

Debout devant un tapis roulant tout aussi rustique que le reste de l'équipement de l'aéroport de Varadero, les filles observent tout autour en souriant, savourant le dépaysement qui les enveloppe comme un doux voile exotique. La section des arrivées internationales ressemble davantage à un établissement accueillant les avions de vols domestiques au fin fond du Québec. Deux douaniers assis sur des chaises au milieu de l'aire ouverte éclatent de rire. Une Cubaine – danseuse de cabaret roussâtre à la repousse noire comme le jais – leur crie un truc qui semble très drôle, et les deux gars «pénoches» éclatent de rire encore plus fort. En termes d'ambiance latino décontractée, on ne pourrait faire mieux. Partout autour, les Cubains en habit couleur « safari en Afrique » discutent entre eux, rigolent et s'amusent tandis que les vacanciers récupèrent leurs effets personnels. Une musique lascive retentit dans les haut-parleurs, question de signaler aux touristes que l'atmosphère est à la fête, et ce, dès leur arrivée à destination[1].

Repérant sa valise sur le tourniquet, Katia l'annonce aux filles :

— Ma valise est là !

— La mienne aussi, scande à son tour Caroline.

Elles extirpent leurs mallettes de l'engin déglingué. Katia tire sur la poignée rétractable de sa valise à roulettes avant de rappeler joyeusement à la troupe :

— On est là, les filles ! Yéééé ! Et juste pour le prix d'un seul forfait divisé en trois ! Ouuuuh !

— C'est fou pareil ! Gagner un voyage pour deux... Malade ! apprécie Vicky. Là, c'est vrai que ça fait un voyage pas cher ! Quatre cents dollars chacune et voilà, merci, bonsoir !

— On ne dira pas de quelle façon on a gagné le prix, par contre..., insiste Caroline, toujours éthiquement préoccupée par ce détail.

---

1. Imaginez si, à l'aéroport Montréal-Trudeau, on accueillait les touristes au son d'un disque de la Bottine souriante ? « Son p'tit porte-clés tout rouillé, tout rouillé/Son p'tit porte-clés tout rouillé gaiement... »

— Mais surtout, surtout, surtout : j'aurai une chambre pour moi toute seule... *Oh my God!* fantasme Katia en levant des yeux pieux pour en remercier le ciel.

Les trois voyageuses restent un moment devant le carrousel de métal en attendant l'apparition de la valise de Vicky. Après dix longues minutes, le mécanisme cesse subitement de tourner en émettant un bruit de ferraille comme s'il venait de rendre l'âme. La totalité des touristes sont sortis, à l'exception d'un homme âgé en fauteuil roulant que deux Cubaines semblent avoir pris en charge. Sur le tapis de caoutchouc noir, seuls une repoussante malle brune recouverte d'étiquettes jaunes et un sac de sport Nike sont demeurés non réclamés.

— Ben voyons, tout le monde semble avoir sa valise sauf moi. Pourquoi avoir arrêté le truc ? s'inquiète Vicky.

— Je sais pas. On va aller s'informer à quelqu'un...

Katia s'approche de deux hommes absorbés par leur pause-rigolade et leur fait part de la situation en anglais :

— Excusez-moi. Il nous manque une valise et...

Perplexe, l'un d'eux lève les deux mains bien haut en guise de non-compréhension de la langue d'usage employée par Katia et lui désigne du menton une porte plus loin. En haut de celle-ci, on peut lire : «*Equipaje extraviado – Lost and found*». Toujours aux commandes du volet «communication», Katia s'y dirige d'un pas preste puis interrompt une femme qui, assise derrière un petit bureau, papote sur son téléphone cellulaire. Elle lui présente le collant de l'étiquette de bagages qui a été apposé derrière la carte d'embarquement de Vicky par la préposée à Montréal. La femme s'empare du carton, puis elle compose un numéro sur un téléphone noir près d'elle. Pendant ce temps, Caroline et Vicky, se tenant tout près de l'embrasure de la porte, aperçoivent un homme qui pénètre dans l'établissement par les portes automatiques menant à l'extérieur et qui crie assez fort quelque chose d'incompréhensible en espagnol. Un autre homme tout près du tourniquet hurle à son tour une ritournelle en direction du bureau responsable des bagages où se trouvent les filles. La femme comprend que celui-ci s'adresse à elle, donc elle se lève pour faire un signe de la main à l'homme en question. Elle lui gueule sa réponse, un bras en l'air. Toujours au même moment, un hispanophone habillé en civil arrive près des filles pour leur demander :

— *¿Taxi? ¿Hotel?*

— *No taxi.* Valise. Euh… *Suitcase. Malete?*

— *Aaaah si, maleta*[2]… *¿Después taxi*[3]*?*

La femme, maintenant debout devant le bureau, reprend le téléphone qui sonne. Elle lève son index droit en direction des filles :

— *Un momento por favor*[4].

---

2. Valise.
3. Ensuite, taxi ?
4. Un moment s'il vous plaît.

— Voyons, tout le monde parle en même temps, panique Caroline, confuse face à cette conversation polyglotte de niveau olympique.

— Eille, s'ils ont perdu ma valise, je me suicide, pleurniche Vicky au bord du désespoir.

— Ben non, du calme. *¡No problemo!*

La femme lâche enfin le combiné, puis sort du bureau pour crier à nouveau quelque chose au type près de la porte, qui semble attendre le verdict. Elle se tourne ensuite vers l'autre hispanophone près du carrousel pour lui communiquer à son tour de l'information concernant la valise perdue.

— *¿Taxi?* réitère le troisième homme qui désire à tout prix être l'heureux élu qui conduira éventuellement les vacancières vers leur destination de rêve.

— Simonaque, on peut-tu être plus clair, s'il vous plaît?! s'impatiente Katia en bon français et en perte de contrôle totale du volet «communication».

— On n'a pas besoin de taxi, un bus nous attend, explique Vicky en français en direction du chauffeur qui répond par une expression embrouillée signifiant qu'il n'a rien saisi.

— *Si, si, maleta y despuès taxi*[5].

---

5.   Oui, oui, la valise et ensuite le taxi.

La femme du comptoir d'information explique quelque chose en espagnol au chauffeur de taxi qui finit par baisser la tête avant de s'éloigner, bredouille.

— Bon?! fulmine Katia, tout aussi dans le brouillard que l'ensemble du groupe.

Comprenant l'urgence de rassurer les touristes complètement perdues, la femme annonce en anglais:

— Nous avons égaré vos bagages, mais l'autobus pour vous rendre à l'hôtel doit partir…

— QUOI? rugit Vicky, furieuse.

La femme poursuit en levant une main afin de prier Vicky de se calmer:

— … donnez-nous le nom complet de votre hôtel et nous irons vous la livrer aussitôt que nous la retrouverons.

— QUAND? Où elle est, ma valise?

— On ne sait pas, mais ce ne sera pas long.

— «Pas long», comme dans «tu vas passer la moitié de tes vacances sans tes vêtements» ou «pas long» comme dans «tu n'auras même pas le temps de boire un "piña Canada" que ta valise sera arrivée»? demande Vicky à Katia comme si celle-ci était désormais une gestionnaire de crise spécialisée en perte de bagages à l'étranger.

— Bientôt, bientôt! la rassure Katia, avec le ton d'une citoyenne engagée venant tout juste de se lancer en politique municipale.

L'employé près de la porte brait une nouvelle fois à l'intention des retardataires toujours présents dans le terminal. Katia confirme à la femme le nom complet de l'hôtel et les filles se dirigent vers la porte, pressées par les Cubains tout autour qui leur font de grands signes avec les bras.

— C'est-tu une arnaque, ça, vous pensez? panique Vicky en jetant un regard derrière elle tout en marchant. Ils vont se diviser le contenu de ma valise, c'est ça?

— Impossible, Vicky! Cuba, c'est super touristique. Ils feraient jamais ça, rationalise Caroline.

— Une chance qu'on s'est changées. Au moins, t'as des vêtements courts pour aujourd'hui, souligne Katia.

Caroline seconde l'affirmation de son amie.

— Ouin! Sinon, on va t'en prêter. Inquiète-toi pas.

— Eille, c'est le boutte de la marde en esti! Je prends soin de respecter la limite de poids pour les bagages, pis ils trouvent le moyen de les perdre!

En arrivant tout près des doubles portes automatiques, les filles aperçoivent, à travers les grandes vitres, les autocars nolisés qui s'avèrent effectivement prêts à partir. L'homme qui les escorte les presse à nouveau de la main comme si le feu était pris quelque part. Les deux premières portes s'ouvrent et un puissant jet d'air chaud ébouriffe les filles au passage. Lorsque les deux autres portes s'ouvrent sur l'extérieur, une masse d'air frisquet les happe de plein fouet.

— Ben voyons donc ! Fait donc ben frette ? ! se surprend Caroline en regardant ses amies avec ahurissement.

— Cibole ! Quessé ça ?

— *What the fuck ?* beugle Katia. Étiez-vous allées voir la météo sur Internet ?

— Non ! Dans ma tête, on s'en venait dans le Sud... J'étais donc certaine qu'il ferait chaud, avoue Caroline.

— « Le Sud », mon œil, oui ! Ç'a aucun sens ! Il faisait pas très chaud quand je suis venue il y a cinq ans, mais jamais aussi froid que ça.

Malgré tout, les profs en vacances continuent de suivre l'homme qui les a prises en charge. Il gesticule depuis cinq minutes comme si le retard des filles avait occasionné une situation urgente. La température ambiante de treize degrés Celsius et le taux d'humidité élevé donnent l'impression qu'il doit faire tout au plus cinq degrés.

— *¡Muy frio[6] !* commente leur guide tout en ayant l'air de trouver la situation météorologique peu clémente franchement cocasse.

— « Frio », ce n'est pas le mot. « Glacio », oui ! En fait, je pense qu'il faisait plus chaud à Montréal, se désole Caroline en frissonnant.

---

6. « Très froid » *in spanish. Combien de gens ont déjà vécu ça dans le Sud ? Moi, si !*

— *¡Frio! ¡Frio! ¡Ja! ¡ja! ¡ja!* s'amuse encore plus le Cubain en voyant les filles réagir si négativement.

— *¿Cerveza?* clame un autre Cubain en levant à la hauteur de leurs yeux son cabaret rempli de canettes de bière.

Les filles l'ignorent, un peu étonnées de se faire offrir ainsi de l'alcool à trois mètres du terminal.

— *¡Ja! ¡ja! ¡ja!* rigole encore le type tout en présentant de la main l'autocar dans lequel elles doivent monter.

— En plus, il trouve ça drôle, lui! Eille, le casque de bain, c'est pas une croisière en Alaska qu'on voulait faire! s'énerve Katia.

Sans surprise, après avoir placé les deux valises dans la soute sous le véhicule, celui qui les escortait frotte ses doigts ensemble en attente de son pourboire.

— Ne-non, là! Vous avez perdu ma valise, il fait aussi frette qu'en Sibérie, pis tu trouves ça drôle... facque de la marde, pour ton *tip*! Sèche! balance Vicky en passant devant lui, la main en l'air, avant de grimper le petit escalier.

— *¡Hola!* les accueille le chauffeur, heureux.

— *Hola, hola,* répond Vicky laconiquement, son enthousiasme n'ayant pas tenu le coup face aux événements désolants qu'elle vient de vivre en rafale.

Dans l'autocar bondé, plusieurs voyageurs ensommeillés adressent aux filles un sourire jaune de fausse compassion, ignorant la situation qui justifie leur retard. Heureusement, la représentante de la compagnie de voyages, micro en main, se montre plus indulgente et surtout plus chaleureuse. Elle leur demande en anglais :

— Tout va bien ?

Katia en profite pour passer un message clair aux gens autour :

— Non, il nous manque une valise. On n'était pas parties faire une virée de *shopping*, là...

— Aaah, ça arrive parfois. Vous l'aurez probablement demain au plus tard, précise la jeune femme qui baragouine un français cassé.

— *Anyway*, pas trop besoin de linge court ici !

Aussitôt les filles assises dans l'avant-dernier banc, le chauffeur démarre. Le véhicule franchit à peine trois mètres de distance qu'une femme hispanophone s'extirpe avec vigueur du dernier banc, comme munie d'un ressort. Vicky, qui ne l'avait pas vue, fait un saut :

— Hey ! Cibole...

— *¿Cerveza? Tres dollares canadienses o dos por cinco*[7], propose la vendeuse itinérante qui trimballe une chaudière de plastique remplie de glace et de canettes de bière.

---

7. « Bière ? Trois dollars canadiens ou deux pour cinq. » (À Varadero, on offre ça pendant le transport !)

— *¿Dos por cinco?* Amènes-en une caisse, oui! Pis ça presse! envoie Katia en sortant son argent.

— Tu vas boire une bière si tôt le matin? demande Caro, dont l'intonation de voix est digne du Jugement dernier.

— Pour nous, c'est plus tellement le matin… De toute façon, il est toujours quatre heures quelque part dans le monde, comme on dit!

— *¡Bienvenidos a Varadero!* annonce avec motivation la représentante à l'avant à l'aide de son micro.

— Bienvenue, mets-en…, chiale Vicky en relevant un peu le col de son chandail pour se tenir au chaud.

JOUR 8

AÉROPORT MONTRÉAL-TRUDEAU
SALLE 315 – **8 H 33**

L'intensité lumineuse à l'extrémité d'un des longs néons au plafond vacille toujours, laissant ainsi croire qu'il pourrait cesser de fonctionner à tout moment. Les trois filles le fixent, comme pour voir s'il s'éteindra ou pas. L'éclairage tressaute un peu, puis se remet finalement à briller à sa puissance maximale.

— Maususse qu'il faisait frette pareil, hein?! se souvient Caroline.

Vicky seconde le propos de son amie :

— Avant de partir, on se disait naïvement : « On s'en va dans le Sud, ça va être la canicule totale. » Eille, une grosse baloune qui t'explose en pleine face ! Boum ! Suuu-per !

— Mais bon, c'est pas juste ça qui a ennuagé notre arrivée là-bas, disons…

— On était pourtant tellement motivées à pas commettre les mêmes gaffes que lors de notre voyage au Mexique. C'est fou, la puissance du karma, analyse Vicky en hochant la tête.

— On n'a pas été motivées longtemps, je trouve, spécifie Caro.

— Mais au moins la motivation était là au départ, c'est ça l'important ! se réjouit Katia, tout de même fière de leur performance générale.

Caroline semble plus ou moins d'accord.

— Dans la vie, Katia, l'important, ce n'est pas ce que tu dis, mais bien ce que tu fais…

JOUR 1

CUBA, VARADERO
COSTA AZUL DEL MAR RESORT

Après avoir fait le tour de la péninsule et vu des touristes descendre à neuf hôtels différents, les filles débarquent enfin de l'autobus d'un pas exaspéré. Katia, qui a bu des bières sans tenir compte du fait qu'il n'y avait pas de toilettes dans l'autobus, laisse ses amies en plan pour foncer vers le lobby à la recherche de cabinets. Vicky et Caro s'empressent de récupérer les deux valises du trio qui attendent déjà sur le trottoir tandis que l'aube pointe doucement le bout de son nez.

À son retour, Katia, qui semble désormais se contre-foutre de la température glaciale autant que du temps perdu pendant le transport interminable entre l'aéroport et le Costa Azul del Mar, improvise quelques pas de danse sur le pavé menant à l'entrée du complexe hôtelier.

— *La cucaracha, la cucaracha, la lala lalalala!*

— Bon, elle est déjà soûle, elle! Trois bières en une heure, je comprends…, note Caroline qui ne peut réprimer un sourire en coin.

— *¡No problemo!* C'est la bière Cristal! C'est comme de l'eau de source, dans le fond! Faut s'hydrater, dans le Sud! Tellement, que j'ai failli le faire dans mes culottes, d'ailleurs. Il faudrait songer à fournir des toilettes dans les autobus en échange de cette hydratation…

— Pas certaine que nous sommes autorisées à utiliser le mot «Sud» en ce moment! Même après deux bières, il fait toujours aussi frette! Mais bon, je suis bien contente d'être ici finalement, même s'il me manque ma valise, synthétise une souriante Vicky en admirant le panorama paradisiaque qui s'illumine peu à peu en suivant l'ascension du soleil au loin.

— *Party!* Moi, je vais pas me coucher, hein! annonce Katia. Il est peut-être juste six heures du matin, mais j'ai vu sur Internet qu'il y avait un bar ouvert vingt-quatre heures sur le *résore*[8]. Si on se couche, *anyway*, on va se sentir décalées après.

— Allons au moins aux chambres porter nos affaires, suggère Caroline en tentant de repérer le lobby au loin.

— Ah, justement! À ce sujet, le bain de votre chambre fait demander si tu prévois boire des «noix de gastro», parce que si c'est le cas, il va sacrer son camp au plus vite! déconne Katia en frappant doucement Vicky sur le bras.

— Et moi, je vais déménager dans la chambre de Katia! ajoute Vicky.

— Ah! ah! aaaah! Très drôle. Non, je vais m'abstenir. J'apprends de mes erreurs, MOI! leur fait remarquer Caro en laissant sous-entendre des accusations pas très claires.

— Bon, vite! Ce voyage-là manque vraiment de boisson! s'égosille Katia en s'élançant vers le lobby.

Étant donné leur précédente expérience au Mexique, Vicky et Caroline entrent dans leur *habitacíon* sur le qui-vive, appréhendant d'y trouver un bordel incroyable. La chambre de Katia se trouve juste en face de la leur, de

---

8. Important de toujours prononcer le mot *resort* de cette façon. C'est de la francisation «correcte»! ☺

l'autre côté du corridor. Les portes respectives des deux pièces grandes ouvertes, les filles commentent à voix haute leur exploration des lieux.

— C'est propre! C'est beau! On a un oiseau en serviettes sur notre lit avec des fleurs rouges d'Hawaï! apprécie Caro.

— Moi aussi, c'est *cool*! leur crie Katia tout en effectuant un rapide tour du propriétaire.

— Pas de touffe de poils pubiens sur les oreillers... Ben coudonc! Tout se passe à merveille!

Vicky rappelle, d'une voix tout de même pas si emballée:

— Un instant. Il fait moins mille degrés pis j'ai pas de valise... Ça se passe pas SI bien, je trouve...

— AAAAAHHHHH! s'écrie alors Caroline en reculant de plusieurs pas.

En regardant dans la même direction qu'elle, c'est-à-dire sur le plancher, au pied du deuxième lit, Vicky demande:

— Quoi?

Elle n'y voit rien.

— J'ai vu une coquerelle!

— QUOI? panique à son tour Vicky. OÙ ÇA?

— Ben voyons? Qu'est-ce qui se passe? s'inquiète Katia qui entre dans leur chambre en trombe.

— Une coquerelle!!! Une coquerelle!! Elle s'est faufilée sous le lit, je l'ai vue!

— AH! CALVAIRE! gueule Vicky qui bondit sur le lit en question pour ainsi éviter le pire.

— T'es certaine? s'informe Katia, le doute inscrit en profondeur sur ses traits. C'est quand même propre...

— OUI! Je l'ai vue! Était grosse de même, soutient Caroline en désignant entre ses doigts quelque chose mesurant environ dix centimètres.

Paniquée comme si un tigre du Bengale se trouvait dans la chambre, Caroline décide finalement d'imiter Vicky et elle se hisse d'un grand bond sur le premier lit.

— Ben là, les filles? Elle vous mangera pas, quand même...

Vicky s'indigne:

— Veux-tu l'amener dans *ta* chambre? Lâche-toi lousse! Eille, je ne suis certainement pas venue ici pour faire du camping sauvage et dormir avec des bibittes...

— Vous êtes vraiment bébé lala. Attendez, je vais regarder...

Katia, tout de même secrètement un peu craintive de ce qu'elle pourrait y découvrir, se penche en petit bonhomme pour inspecter le dessous du lit sur lequel Vicky trépigne toujours, l'air d'analyser la structure du plafonnier pour s'y accrocher si jamais cela s'avérait nécessaire.

— Y a rien, conclut Katia, maintenant à quatre pattes sur le plancher de tuiles.

— Y a rien, y a rien! Je l'ai vue, je vous dis! plaide à nouveau Caroline, hystérique comme jamais.

— Il faut appeler quelqu'un en renfort! Des exterminateurs, peut-être? s'illumine Vicky.

— Il faut changer de chambre! conclut plutôt Caroline.

Vicky approuve sa suggestion en hochant frénétiquement la tête.

— Du calme. Du calme. On ne peut rien faire. Elle va ressortir par où elle est entrée, c'est tout. Vous n'en aurez même pas connaissance, les rassure Katia, toujours désireuse d'aller boire un verre au plus vite.

— T'es sûre que tu vois rien?

— Venez constater par vous-mêmes.

Les filles descendent alors de leur estrade de protection en mettant précautionneusement un pied par terre comme si elles craignaient de réveiller un tyrannosaure aux dents bien affilées.

Prenant son courage à deux mains, Caro respire un grand coup et elle se penche la première. Vicky l'imite. Au même moment, Katia pousse un cri:

— BOOOOUUUH!

Les filles font un saut vertigineux. La petite comique éclate de rire.

— T'es vraiment conne !

— Vous voyez qu'y a rien. Bon ! On va visiter ? propose Katia, tout sourire.

— Ouin...

— Moi, si je la revois, je retourne direct au Canada, chiale Caroline.

— Il faudrait se rhabiller en long avant d'aller explorer les alentours...

— Ouin, c'est vrai, approuve Katia en retournant à sa chambre.

Après avoir pris quelques verres au resto-bar ouvert vingt-quatre heures près de la plage, les filles se rendent à la réception pour s'informer de la marche à suivre pour réserver une table dans un des nombreux restaurants à la carte du complexe hôtelier. La Cubaine en poste leur explique la marche à suivre. Grosso modo, les clients doivent se déplacer jusqu'à un comptoir de services ouvert seulement entre 16 h et 18 h afin d'inscrire leur nom et numéro de chambre sur une liste. Le lendemain, entre 8 h et 10 h, ils doivent se rendre dans un autre lieu afin de récupérer un carton de réservation qu'il faut présenter à l'entrée du restaurant choisi. Katia lève son mojito bien haut pour souligner son indignation et elle critique le système en place avec véhémence :

— Simonaque!? C'est vraiment compliqué pour rien, leur affaire. On n'a pas juste ça à faire, en vacances. Non, mais, tant qu'à y être, demandez-nous d'apprendre à danser la macarena la tête en bas en jonglant avec des caniches pour pouvoir réserver au resto, ce serait plus simple!

— Je vais m'en occuper, moi, ça me dérange pas, offre Caroline, bienveillante.

— On pourra même pas y aller ce soir, ça veut dire? C'est plate, fait remarquer Vicky.

— On va soudoyer un membre du personnel. Voyons donc! C'est un tout compris, on va pas capoter pour un maudit carton! Laissez-moi ça entre les mains, les filles, décide Katia.

— Évidemment, tu connais bien ça, toi, «la manipulation de membres du personnel», la taquine Caroline.

Celle-ci resserre un peu son foulard autour de son cou avant de commenter:

— Il fait un peu moins froid, c'est toujours ça de gagné.

— Au moins, il neige pas, ironise Vicky.

— Ah oui, on a oublié de demander à la madame de la réception s'il est censé faire chaud à un moment donné, dans son pays «chaud», tsé..., poursuit Katia.

— J'y pense, il doit bien y avoir des jacuzzis quelque part? s'enflamme Vicky.

— Oui! Bonne idée! On va se réchauffer!

— On peut aller manger au buffet avant ? J'ai faim, dit Caro.

— *Go !* C'est pas loin, justement... Par là, je pense.

En arrivant au buffet central du complexe hôtelier, les filles observent les alentours. La pièce à aire ouverte, mais recouverte d'un toit, est vaste et le vent frisquet pénètre de partout. Compte tenu de l'heure hâtive, peu de personnes y sont installées. Dans un bruit d'ustensiles qui s'entre-choquent, les serveurs préparent les tables afin d'accueillir le gros de la clientèle qui inondera bientôt le buffet pour déjeuner. Des oiseaux volant un peu partout à la recherche de miettes de n'importe quoi caquettent gaiement comme pour dire « bonjour » aux nouvelles venues. Katia, déjà en mode chasse-aux-mâles-alpha, reluque les hommes présents.

Elle se justifie même auprès de ses amies :

— Faut quand même que je me trouve un *prospect* au plus sacrant...

— Le *cruising* de bonne heure de même, c'est pas l'idéal, je pense, fait remarquer Caroline en se déplaçant vers une table.

— Pas de temps à perdre ! Ils doivent pas servir de boisson à cette heure-ci, par contre, se désole Katia en focalisant maintenant son attention sur un éventuel service de bar.

Affamées, les filles prennent d'assaut les longues tables en inox regorgeant de nourriture. Katia fait deux pas de côté pour contourner un homme et sa femme qui filment passionnément le buffet[9]. Ladite femme s'adresse à elle :

— Avez-vous vu ça, toute le beau manger ?

— Ben oui, toi…, répond Katia en haussant les sourcils.

En revenant à leur table, l'assiette bien remplie, Katia partage son expérience hilarante avec ses amies :

— Le couple là-bas m'a dit être en train de filmer « toute le beau manger »…

— « Le manger », mon Dieu, c'est assez *vintage* merci comme expression.

Les filles commencent à déguster leur déjeuner en silence. Caroline prend quelques bouchées et fronce les sourcils. Vicky effectue aussi une drôle de mimique en brassant un peu les œufs brouillés dans son assiette.

— Euh, c'est moi ou tout goûte la même affaire ? souligne Caroline.

— Oui, et c'est froid.

— Mes œufs et mon jambon ont la même saveur étrange… Ah tiens, mes fèves aussi…

---

9.   Les gens qui filment le buffet dans les tout compris, perso, je trouve ça vraiment très drôle ! (Pauvres téléspectateurs qui visionneront le tout…)

Caroline prend encore quelques bouchées tandis que Katia beurre une rôtie. Caroline laisse finalement tomber sa fourchette sur la table en s'exclamant :

— Sérieux, c'est dégueulasse ! Un goût d'huile passée date ou je sais pas quoi...

Katia abonde dans le même sens :

— Eille, même le beurre goûte bizarre ! Il est comme jaune fluo en plus...

— Il faut mettre du sel et du poivre en masse, je pense !

— Bonne idée !

Katia agrippe la salière sur la table et la remue vigoureusement au-dessus de son plat. Elle a beau la secouer avec l'énergie du désespoir, rien n'en tombe.

— Voyons ?

Elle dévisse le couvercle afin de défaire à l'aide de la pointe de son couteau le sel amalgamé à cause de l'humidité. Elle maintient le petit contenant de verre au-dessus de son assiette puis elle gratte. Le sel, qui se libère finalement d'un seul coup, tombe en une grosse galette qui se répand dans son assiette.

— Bon... simonaque !

— Il faudrait vraiment trouver le moyen d'aller dans un resto à la carte ce soir. Il paraît que c'est toujours meilleur que le buffet.

— Ouin, il paraît que «le beau manger» est mieux, en effet…

JOUR 8

AÉROPORT MONTRÉAL-TRUDEAU
SALLE 315 – 8 H 39

En y repensant, Caroline bat énergiquement des mains de chaque côté de son corps en sortant un peu la langue, puis elle déclare:

— C'était quelque chose, hein? Je pense que j'ai jamais mangé mal de même de ma vie!

— Pour vrai, j'ai perdu dix livres, j'en suis certaine. Voilà bien le seul avantage de ce maudit voyage-là, précise à son tour Vicky.

— Avec ce qui s'est passé, c'est bien certain qu'on a perdu dix livres. Surtout depuis hier, à cause du stress, exagère Caroline.

— Tu dis, et il faut que je voie un médecin au PC! Ça semble pas se passer pantoute mon affaire, les filles, souligne avec désolation Vicky en se tortillant un peu sur sa chaise.

— Pauvre toi, c'est pas drôle. Je ne comprends pas que ça ne guérisse pas, sympathise Katia.

— Et moi, je dois réserver ma coiffeuse au plus vite. Pour faire changement, tsé..., pleurniche Caroline, la moue bien pendante en se prenant le côté de la tête.

— Toute cette histoire-là, c'est la faute à la mouffette, aussi. Sans lui, ça ne se serait jamais passé de même.

— Aaaah! la maudite mouffette à marde...

JOUR 1
CUBA, VARADERO
COSTA AZUL DEL MAR RESORT

En arrivant près de l'aire de détente où un gentil employé leur a indiqué la présence de spas, les filles en remarquent deux, bien mis en valeur par de petits podiums en céramique aqua. Hélas, les bains à remous sont déjà remplis – le temps peu clément ayant donné à plusieurs touristes l'idée de venir s'y réchauffer. Emmitouflée dans la serviette de plage de l'hôtel, Vicky s'approche de Katia pour lui chuchoter :

— Ton maillot est bien trop grand du top pour que je parade devant tout le monde arrangée de même. On voit presque mes seins par les côtés. T'as vraiment des plus grosses boules que moi...

— Pas grave. T'enlèves ta serviette, tu entres dans le spa à toute vitesse et hop! le tour est joué, lui répond Katia qui peine à avancer sans renverser les quatre verres de mojito trop pleins qu'elle trimballe.

— J'ai lu récemment dans le journal que les spas publics étaient plein de coliformes fécaux, souligne Vicky.

— Hon... Pour vrai ? fait Caroline, tout à coup écœurée.

— Ben non ! Maudit que t'es dédaigneuse, Vic...

Un jeune G.O. cubain qui passe en courant dans le petit chemin avec un ballon dans les mains aborde les filles au passage :

— *¡Hola! ¿Bolleyboll?*

— Hein ? s'enquiert Vicky en se tournant vers lui.

— Il veut qu'on aille jouer au volleyball, mais avec son accent, il y a trop de «B» dans son mot, on dirait, explique Katia.

— Euh, *no, gracias...*

Tout sourire, il continue sa course dans une motivation sportive admirable en lançant le ballon dans les airs.

— Voyons, lui ? C'est un peu précoce comme proposition, laisse-nous le temps d'arriver, cibole !

Au-devant de la troupe, Caroline a continué d'avancer vers les bains et elle semble à présent se demander lequel des deux est le moins bondé. En la voyant hésiter de la sorte, un gars dans la vingtaine avancée qui arbore une chevelure originale – sa tignasse noire est tranchée au milieu par une liasse de cheveux blond platine – se pousse un peu vers sa voisine pour céder la place aux nouvelles arrivantes.

— Venez ici! les encourage-t-il en les invitant de la main.

— Ah, c'est gentil, apprécie Caroline en délaissant sa chaude serviette pour se glisser à la vitesse de l'éclair dans le bain fumant.

Ses deux amies se joignent à leur tour au groupe qui mijote en toute quiétude. Caroline se pousse subrepticement contre le gars à la coiffure excentrique pour faire comprendre aux gens présents que les nouvelles venues l'accompagnent. Avec agilité, et afin de se libérer une main pour dénouer sa serviette, Katia pose deux de ses petits verres de plastique au sol. Pendant ce temps, Vicky effectue une manœuvre aussi discrète que rapide pour enlever aussi la sienne, désireuse d'éviter de s'exposer trop longtemps en public avec le maillot de bain trop grand de Katia. En voulant se glisser dans l'eau en même temps, les deux filles entrent en collision, faisant en sorte que Vicky manque de perdre pied. Sous l'impact, Katia renverse dans l'eau la moitié du contenu des deux verres qu'elle tenait toujours. Caroline sursaute et lâche un «Hip!» sonore tout en levant sa main pour retenir le dos de Vicky et ainsi lui éviter un amerrissage éclaboussant.

Simplement heureuse d'avoir épargné la moitié de ses cocktails, Katia sourit avec béatitude en s'assoyant.

— J'ai sauvé l'essentiel! En passant, Caro, t'as pas le droit de dire «Hip!», c'est trop matante.

— Ah ouin?

— Ça fait «matante qui fume des Craven "A" *king size*, qui boit des rhums coco et qui fait l'étoile au lit», tu comprends?

— Je vois pas trop le rapport, non. J'aime ça, les «rhums coco», moi...

— En passant, il faut prononcer «ronnnnne coco» en roulant le «r». Mais de toute façon, arrête-moi ça! C'est un *drink* de matante. À notre âge, on est comme dans un entre-deux; on n'est plus des p'tites jeunesses, mais on ne doit pas agir trop en matantes non plus. Il faut donc éviter ce genre de comportement en public.

Saisissant un des verres de Katia posés par terre, Vicky approuve:

— Elle a raison, c'est important!

— Eille, vous êtes «sickement» crampantes, vous autres! réagit le gars aux cheveux bicolores, qui les écoutait de biais en se faisant sécher les dents.

— Sans farce, on est vrai-ment drôles, surtout elle! renchérit Katia en désignant Caroline.

— Elle est un peu «ron coco[10]» des fois, mais elle est bien comique, ajoute Vicky.

Après les présentations d'usage, les filles apprennent que Dave, leur voisin de circonstance, vient de Montréal,

---

10. Expression se déclinant en adjectif qualificatif lorsqu'on parle d'une matante.

mais qu'il habite maintenant à Toronto. Sa personnalité authentique et franche le pousse à annoncer d'emblée qu'il est homosexuel. Sa gestuelle semble d'ailleurs abonder dans le même sens. Il s'enfile à grandes gorgées du rhum brun pur, sans glace, comme s'il buvait simplement son café matinal.

« Trop malade, un nouvel ami gai ! Depuis le temps que j'en rêve ! », se réjouit intérieurement Vicky.

« Ah wow ! Il a donc bien l'air gentil », apprécie Caroline.

« Cool ! Il boit le matin ! », pense quant à elle Katia.

— Tu voyages tout seul ?

— Oui, je suis ici depuis déjà quatre jours. Il me reste juste trois jours…

— En tout cas, si tu connais un truc pour nous faire entrer illégalement au resto de fruits de mer ce soir, dis-le. On vient d'arriver cette nuit, donc on n'a pas eu la chance de réserver…

— Ah pas de problème, j'y suis allé deux fois. Je connais bien le gars à la porte. « Tsé, Yo l'ami ! Tu me reconnais ? »

— Ah ouin, pour vrai ? Super, alors ! s'enthousiasme Caroline.

Un toast énergique rehausse ce moment de réjouissance groupale. Pendant ce temps, un couple qui trottine à petits pas de Chinois approche des spas en filmant les environs. La femme, qui semble carrément animer une émission de voyage au canal Évasion, commente avec maladresse le décor l'entourant.

— Donc… nous avons ici des spas… avec de l'eau… de l'eau chaude… et des gens aussi… Et il y a des arbres autour, bien des palmiers, plutôt et…

Reconnaissant le couple qui filmait le buffet plus tôt, Katia adopte un air pédagogique à souhait et chuchote en direction de Dave et des filles :

— Regardez. Par exemple, elle, là-bas… Elle est très, très « ron coco ». Comprenez-vous ?

La femme cinquantenaire, qui porte fièrement, par-dessus son col roulé blanc, un chandail à manches courtes représentant une femme en bikini, poursuit sa présentation des lieux tandis que son mari semble avoir un plaisir fou à braquer sa lentille attentive sur chacun des détails qu'elle énumère. Fidèle à la thématique vestimentaire conjugale, le cinéaste en herbe porte quant à lui un t-shirt montrant un monsieur très musclé vêtu d'un Speedo.

— Les gens se baignent, oui… On voit les gens, les gens en vacances…

Dave se redresse alors un peu et il crie en direction de la dame :

— Eille, t'es « ron coco », toé !

Les yeux ronds de stupéfaction, Caroline lui reproche :

— Chut ! Chut ! Chuuutt ! Voyons ? Qu'est-ce que tu fais là ?

— Pardon ? fait la femme interloquée en arrêtant illico son tournage pour répondre à la personne qui semble s'adresser à elle.

Katia rigole en s'immergeant dans l'eau jusqu'au menton, son verre maintenu bien haut.

— Yo ! Rien ! Laisse faire, lance Dave en levant le bras en direction de la pauvre dame qui, en plus d'être « matante », est maintenant confuse.

Il se tourne ensuite vers les filles pour leur dire en riant :

— *Cheers !*

Une dame plus âgée, qui se trouve aussi dans le bain avec eux, semble insultée que Dave se soit moqué de la pauvre femme. Les lèvres serrées ensemble telles les pinces d'un homard, elle le fixe avec morgue. Se sentant ainsi dévisagé, il lui adresse un beau sourire et la rassure avec grande classe :

— Yo ! *Cheers,* toé si !

— …

Dave, qui termine d'un trait son verre de rhum, se lève en demandant aux filles si elles désirent autre chose à boire.

— Avec grand plaisir! Même chose pour moi! Mojito! accepte Katia en levant son verre, trop heureuse de ne pas devoir sortir d'une eau si confortable pour aller faire le plein.

— Moi aussi, tiens, approuvent en simultané Caro et Vicky.

Serviable, il se lève et quitte le bain, mais revient finalement sur ses pas et couine d'une voix stridulante: «Câliiiin?!» avant de se pencher pour enlacer les épaules de Vicky et de Katia par-derrière. Celles-ci ricanent en se laissant faire, trouvant leur nouvel ami bien attachant. Avant de partir pour de bon, il apostrophe Vicky et la taquine:

— «*Frenche*-rien-que» pas pendant que je suis parti, là, hein?!

— Promis! rigole Vicky.

Elles sourient toutes à belles dents en le regardant s'éloigner. Comme les filles discutaient avec lui depuis un bon petit moment, la situation amoureuse de chacune avait été passée au peigne fin par Dave-le-curieux. Le sujet des amours d'autrui semblait le passionner à outrance. Les doigts et les orteils bien ratatinés, deux enfants qui se trouvaient dans le spa en sortent. Ainsi moins à l'étroit, les filles prennent leurs aises en écartant bras et jambes au maximum.

— Aaaaaah! souffle Katia, qui fait maintenant l'étoile dans le bain à remous.

— Faut que je me tienne loin des jets, mes seins vont sortir du maillot, souligne avec anxiété Vicky en replaçant une fois de plus les minces triangles de tissu qui ondulent dans tous les sens à chaque agitation aquatique.

— Il est drôle, mais un peu étrange, notre nouvel ami, vous trouvez pas ? demande Caroline.

Au même moment, deux hommes assez grands apparaissent dans le petit chemin. À leur vue, Katia ignore la question de son amie puis elle lève le regard par-dessus ses lunettes de soleil afin de mieux les examiner. Pas certaine de la netteté de sa vision, elle abaisse carrément ses verres fumés sur le bout de son museau.

— Oh *bo-boy* ! apprécie-t-elle en les relevant finalement pour rendre sa manœuvre d'observation plus discrète.

— Lâche pas, Kat ! T'es subtile comme un dix roues, lui souligne Vicky.

Les deux vacanciers approchent et semblent à leur tour s'interroger à savoir s'ils prendront place dans le bain de droite ou dans celui de gauche. Katia – assise au milieu des deux filles – tire violemment le bras de Vicky pour la traîner de l'autre côté afin de libérer l'espace près d'elle. Sous l'impulsion, le haut de bikini de Vicky se déplace et on aperçoit son sein droit pendant une fraction de seconde.

— Ben là ?! Déshabille-moi donc, un coup parti..., rechigne Vicky en tentant désespérément de replacer son haut de maillot fuyant.

— *No problemo*, on les a déjà vues, tes boules, *anyway*, murmure Katia.

De retour à son plan de séduction, elle s'adresse aux deux arrivants avec un enthousiasme frôlant l'hystérie :

— Aaaallo ! Bienvenue, bienvenue !

Ainsi cordialement invités dans le bain des filles, les deux gars sourient avec entrain en entreprenant leur projet de dévêtissement[11]. Avide de ne pas manquer une seconde du spectacle, Katia pivote à cent quatre-vingts degrés pour profiter pleinement d'une vue panoramique sur leurs futurs voisins de bassin qui enlèvent pantalon long et chandail. Un couple tout près d'eux rit sous cape en voyant la touriste peu timide reluquer la scène avec autant de ferveur. Honteuse, Caroline lui adresse un signe d'exaspération muet en levant les bras tandis que Vicky, qui rigole dans sa barbe, lui tire la cheville sous l'eau. N'ayant rien remarqué de la scène de voyeurisme dont ils font l'objet, les deux hommes en maillots forment un tas avec leurs vêtements et les disposent sur une chaise longue située à proximité, avant de se glisser dans l'eau en souriant à Katia qui arbore le visage séraphique d'un archange tout droit descendu du ciel.

Tout le monde se présente rapidement, à tour de rôle. De belle apparence, l'homme le plus âgé des deux – probablement dans la jeune quarantaine – prend la parole :

— Moi, c'est Mike. Voici mon fils, Cédric.

— Aaah ! Et votre femme se repose sur la plage avec un bon livre, je suppose ? lui balance Katia, sa subtilité

---

11. Du verbe «dévêtisser», bien évidemment. À paraître dans *Le Petit Dubois illustré*.

s'apparentant maintenant à celle d'un Boeing 747 qui explose dans un champ de fraises.

— Non, c'est un voyage père-fils. Je suis divorcé depuis six ans, répond l'homme, les yeux plissés d'amusement et nullement dupe de la stratégie limpide d'investigation de la vacancière aux faux airs angéliques.

— OK, *good*, *good*, se réjouit délicieusement Katia en proposant un toast aux deux hommes qui tiennent entre leurs doigts agiles ce qui semble être un simple gobelet de café.

— Fait pas chaud, hein ? débute Vicky, les deux mains toujours rivées aux cordons de son maillot en guise de prévention.

— En effet, on est arrivés cette nuit. Savez-vous si c'est froid comme ça depuis longtemps ?

— Aucune idée. On est arrivées sur le même vol que vous, répond Vicky.

— Hein ? Curieux ! On vous a JAMAIS vus. Pourtant..., s'étonne Katia en se grattant le côté de la mâchoire.

— Ben oui, hein, pourtant..., continue Mike en lui décochant un regard rempli de sous-entendus. On a eu un peu de retard à l'arrivée, par contre. On a dû patienter au moins vingt minutes à cause de trois filles qui ont failli rater le transport...

Comme si leur mésaventure figurait en tête de liste des grandes réussites marquantes de sa vie, Katia s'exclame en levant son verre :

— Eille! C'était nous autres, ça!

— Oui, je sais, lui répond Mike en haussant le menton, taquin.

S'ensuit une discussion de groupe tout ce qu'il y a de plus socialement adéquate. Mike, qui habite à Saint-Jérôme, est entrepreneur en construction et son fils étudie au cégep en génie mécanique dans le but de s'inscrire en ingénierie à l'université par la suite.

— Saint-Jérôme! Wow! Tchin-tchin! se réjouit d'emblée Katia, qui, s'imaginant déjà un éventuel rancard avec Mike, trouve le lieu pas si loin de Gatineau.

— Tu connais la région? demande Mike.

— Euh... de nom seulement. Mais on dit que c'est VRAIMENT beau! exagère Katia, qui ne connaît de la ville que la sortie sur l'autoroute 50 pour rejoindre la 15 Nord.

Trouvant que son amie en met beaucoup plus que le pauvre client en demande, Caroline lui assène subtilement un coup de pied sous l'eau.

— Ayoye! marmonne Katia, les lèvres presque fermées, surprise par l'assaut sous-marin.

De retour avec les verres de tout le monde, Dave saute dans le spa avec beaucoup trop d'ardeur, faisant ainsi remuer tout le bassin. Le contenu des quatre verres se déverse un peu dans la flotte au passage.

— Hip! ne peut s'empêcher de s'écrier Caroline.

— Héééé! s'époumone à son tour Vicky, qui a encore failli voir sa poitrine exposée au grand jour.

Des feuilles de menthe fraîche et quelques morceaux de lime ondulent à la surface de l'eau.

— Attention! Les verres sont déjà mini, faut pas en renverser, se désole Katia en lui volant un mojito désormais rendu aux trois quarts.

Dave, qui constate alors la présence de nouveaux vacanciers près des filles, avance le visage vers Mike pour lui dire de très près, en employant le même ton langoureux que Katia:

— Aaaallooo!

«Eille, les cheveux de mouffette, laisse mon *prospect* tranquille», songe Katia en défiant le jeune homme coloré d'un regard de combattant extrême de la UFC.

Dave entame alors une conversation avec Mike, en faisant comme si les filles n'étaient pas là:

— Eux autres, c'est des matantes «ron coco» qui font l'étoile au lit et qui «*frenchent*-rien-que», elles me l'ont dit tantôt!

— Ark! Pas rapport! On le connaît même pas, lui, rectifie Katia en regardant Mike.

— Menteuse, on est *full* amis, on soupe même ensemble ce soir! se réjouit la mouffette en sapant une bonne gorgée de rhum pur.

— Vous soupez où? demande Mike.

— Au resto de fruits de mer. Vous autres ?

— On va essayer de rentrer au *steak house*, mais on va aller prendre un verre à la discothèque de l'hôtel après, envoie Cédric qui semble tout à coup complice du flirt évident entre Katia et son paternel.

— *Good! Good!* Nous autres aussi…, renchérit Katia en secouant la tête.

JOUR 8

AÉROPORT MONTRÉAL-TRUDEAU
SALLE 315 – **8 H 57**

Un agent des services frontaliers inconnu, qui vient tout juste de surgir dans la pièce, observe les filles d'un air navré. Il explique :

— Excusez-nous du délai, mesdames, mais le responsable n'est toujours pas de retour. C'est la folie ici. Ça ne devrait pas être trop long.

Vicky soupire et ose demander :

— Est-ce qu'on peut ravoir nos affaires ? Nos bagages à main au moins.

— Je vais voir ce que je peux faire.

L'agent ressort aussi vite qu'un courant d'air. Clac ! fait froidement la porte de leur salle de détention.

Les filles continuent de papoter.

— Sérieux, la mouffette, je l'ai aimée, genre, cinq minutes, gros max! se remémore Katia.

— Moi, deux minutes…, précise Vicky.

— Je n'ai jamais vu quelqu'un ne pas avoir de filtre social de même, souligne Caroline. Son comportement était tout le temps inadéquat.

— Et quand il devenait trop soûl, son manque de retenue était quatre fois pire. Un vrai bizarre, fait remarquer Vicky.

— C'est pour ça qu'au départ, je me sentais pas coupable pantoute de l'utiliser pour aller souper ce soir-là… Quelle arnaque, finalement!

— Le souper… Aaaaaah, mon Dieu! réagit avec émotion Vicky.

JOUR 1
CUBA, VARADERO
COSTA AZUL DEL MAR RESORT

Les filles passent un après-midi paisible à alterner entre les spas et les chaises longues disponibles sous la paillote, emmitouflées dans leur serviette. Malgré la fraîcheur, elles apprécient le décor enchanteur qui les entoure; la simple vue des palmiers se balançant au vent et le parfum des embruns marins ont réussi à dissiper la fatigue et le stress attribuables à leur début de voyage mouvementé.

À présent douchées et bien propres, Katia, Caro et Vicky se dirigent vers le restaurant où Dave doit déjà les attendre.

— Je suis si contente que ma valise soit enfin arrivée! Ç'a pas été long, finalement, se réjouit Vicky.

— Ouin, mais ça change pas grand-chose: on doit encore porter notre linge sale d'hier, parce qu'il fait toujours moins huit mille degrés et qu'on n'a pas d'autres vêtements chauds! fait remarquer Katia, déçue de ne pas pouvoir être un peu plus *sexy* dans sa tenue de soirée.

— Yo! Les «ron coco», les interpelle Dave en les voyant approcher dans le sentier.

En arrivant près de lui, Katia, agacée, lui explique:

— Ne-non, t'as rien compris. On n'est PAS des «ron coco», justement. C'est ça le gag.

— Câlin? la relance celui-ci en s'approchant des filles pour former à nouveau un cocon d'amour.

Motivées par l'attrait du potentiel repas sans réservation, les filles se laissent faire en riant un peu jaune. Comme Dave semblait discuter avec l'hôte à la porte au moment de leur arrivée, Caroline lui demande avec discrétion:

— Comment ça fonctionne?

— C'est vingt pesos cubains chaque, répond Dave en étendant la main.

— Comment ça, il faut payer ?

— C'est de même. Pour avoir une place sans réservation, il faut sortir la sauce. Yo !

— Je pensais que tu disais que tu pouvais nous faire entrer ?

— Pour vingt pesos, oui.

— Avoir su…, se désole Vicky.

— Ah, les filles, on est rendues, c'est pas grave, tempère Caroline en sortant quelques billets de son sac à main.

Vicky fait de même en soupirant, visiblement offusquée par la tournure des événements.

Le groupe pénètre dans la salle en suivant le maître d'hôtel. Caroline s'extasie devant les nappes blanches empesées et Vicky s'émerveille à la vue des lampions et des fleurs fraîches sur chaque table. Tout a été soigneusement disposé afin de créer l'illusion d'un restaurant chic. En prenant place à une table qui semblait effectivement réservée pour les clients qui paient un «léger» supplément, les filles scrutent le menu.

— Ici, faut prendre la totale : l'assiette de fruits de mer tout en haut de la page. Trop *sick* ! J'ai pris ça le premier soir, indique Dave le faux Samaritain.

— Ah bon, super! C'est vrai que ça a l'air bon : queue de langouste géante, cocktail de crevettes... Miam! J'en reviens pas que tout ça soit compris dans le plat!

— Ça doit être parce que c'est un pays communiste ; tout est moins cher, je suppose, dit Vicky.

Au moment de passer la commande, tout le monde adopte la suggestion de Dave sauf lui. Il choisit les pâtes aux légumes, le seul mets sans fruits de mer du menu.

— Tu prends pas la super assiette?

— Non...

Les filles échangent un regard furtif qui signifie : «Il est un peu *weird*, lui!» mais elles changent vite de sujet. Un serveur en tenue de gala apporte la carafe de vin blanc que le groupe s'est commandée. Les filles se désolent de sa qualité et recrachent presque le contenu de leur verre sur la nappe immaculée.

— Le vin est chaud... et vraiment pas bon! Ouache!

— Ça goûte le jus de pomme mal fermenté, c't'affaire-là! Un bon petit vin de messe, quoi! commente Vicky en faisant la grimace.

— Oublie ça, même le curé n'en voudrait pas! Faut juste se pincer le nez pour le boire. *¡Viva Cuba!* conclut Katia, toujours prête à affronter les pires éventualités pour se maintenir dans un état d'ivresse acceptable.

La mouffette, qui parle un peu en lettres attachées compte tenu de son état d'ébriété avancé, entame alors un discours émotif faisant l'éloge de son père, qui était si merveilleux, mais qui a quitté la maison familiale lorsque Dave avait à peine dix ans. Les filles l'écoutent, tout de même attendries, malgré le fait qu'elles considèrent le sujet un peu délicat pour être ainsi raconté de long en large à des inconnues en vacances. Pendant près d'une demi-heure, il leur relate en détail un séjour à la campagne avec son père, suivi d'un voyage au Nouveau-Brunswick, pour ensuite enchaîner avec trois soirées du temps des Fêtes où son père s'était déguisé en père Noël, mais avait oublié de mettre la barbe...

Complètement ennuyées – l'empathie s'étant peu à peu évaporée au fil du monologue de Dave – les filles l'observent gesticuler avec entrain en espérant que les plats arrivent au plus vite.

Au moment où il quitte la table pour se rendre aux toilettes, Vicky commente :

— Il me gosse donc ben, sérieux ! C'est désolant, la situation avec son père et tout, mais je suis arrivée ici de bonne humeur, et là, je suis en dépression profonde...

— C'est pas des farces, j'ai le goût de demander mon assiette *take out* pour me pousser dans un autre pays avec ! exagère Katia avant de caler une généreuse gorgée de vin, suivie d'une longue grimace.

— En plus, il ne nous a absolument servi à rien, il a fallu payer ! rappelle Vicky.

— Les filles... c'est vraiment triste, son histoire d'abandon. Il a sûrement besoin d'en parler, compatit Caroline, définitivement plus altruiste que ses comparses.

— Eille, on est à Cuba en vacances, pas dans le train de Josélito Michaud. Ne-non, on mange, pis on se sauve en courant par une fenêtre. Je suis pu capable! décide Katia.

Le repas qui arrive enfin fait miroiter aux filles l'espoir ultime de mettre fin aux histoires pathétiques de Dave. Les grandes assiettes ovales garnies de crevettes, de langoustes, de pétoncles bien juteux, d'un ramequin de moules à la crème et d'une montagne de riz couronnée de tranches de citron coupées en tourbillon semblent à première vue très appétissantes. Les filles attaquent sans plus attendre ce festin dément. La mouffette, qui revient des toilettes – après y avoir passé trop peu de temps, selon Katia –, poursuit d'emblée et avec ferveur son ennuyeux discours, et ce, avant même de prendre le temps de se rasseoir.

— Facque là, c'était trop *sick*. Une fois, à Pâques, mon père...

Caroline le coupe sans ménagement en relâchant sa fourchette avec dépit. Pendant la chute de l'ustensile, du riz volant atterrit sur sa voisine, Vicky.

— Mon repas est dégueulasse, sérieux!? On dirait que ça goûte la même chose que la bouffe du buffet de l'hôtel!

— Hé, lance-moi pas du riz! la réprimande Vicky en balayant de la main les grains sur son pantalon, avant de poursuivre. Je suis d'accord, c'est vraiment pas bon. Les crevettes sont pas cuites, on dirait.

— Regardez ! On dirait que mes moules sont comme élastiques, remarque Katia en étirant le mollusque mollasson droit devant ses yeux. Ça veut dire que c'est trop cuit ou pas assez ?

— Je sais pas trop. Mais il faut manger au moins un peu si on ne veut pas tomber dans les pommes, se résigne Caroline en reprenant sa fourchette.

Après s'être forcées à engloutir au moins le tiers de leur assiette, les filles terminent rapidement les verres de vinasse – qui leur paraît étonnamment moins infecte qu'à leur arrivée – avant de se lever. Leur manœuvre groupale coupe Dave en plein milieu d'un souvenir touchant de son père qui lavait toujours sa voiture dans la cour en caleçon...

— Bon bien, bye, Dave ! Bonne soirée ! lui envoie Katia pour du coup l'expédier K.-O. au plancher sans plus de délicatesse.

— Je vous suis ! Yo ! Je vais terminer mon histoire en route...

— Euh... pas vraiment. Ben, c'est qu'on s'en va entre filles sur la plage, invente Vicky en fixant à tour de rôle ses deux complices pour les encourager à poursuivre dans la même veine.

— Je suis comme une fille, vous savez ! soutient la mouffette en dansant sur place comme un canard sans aucune raison valable.

— Non, il faut qu'on discute en privé. Euh… Oui, c'est ça, hein ? Il faut qu'on se parle, c'est super important, tente Katia au bord du désespoir.

— J'aime ça parler, moi !

— Ouais, ça, on le sait…, murmure Katia entre ses dents.

Leur serveur apparaît alors pour leur refiler un bout de papier. Les filles sont évidemment surprises de voir qu'on tend vers elles ce qui semble être une facture alors qu'elles se trouvent dans un tout compris. Katia s'empare du morceau de papier et, après en avoir pris connaissance, le propulse sur la table avec véhémence.

— C'est quoi ? tente de comprendre Vicky.

— Ç'a pas d'allure, ils veulent nous charger vingt-cinq pesos chacune pour le repas ! crache Katia tout en faisant signe au serveur de s'approcher.

— Hein ? Ben voyons, c'est pas possible ! On a déjà payé pour entrer ici, s'offusque Caro.

L'homme en livrée se penche vers Katia et lui montre le menu en désignant du doigt l'endroit où c'était bien indiqué que l'assiette royale était disponible advenant un «léger» supplément. Katia plisse des yeux comme jamais dans sa vie pour arriver à lire la note minuscule en bas de la page. Elle fait ensuite des efforts inouïs pour garder son calme, mais on voit bien qu'elle bout d'une rage contenue. Elle aimerait balancer des tonnes d'injures ordurières à la tête de l'employé, qui ne semble pas du tout désolé de la situation. Elle déverse donc le tout sur Dave :

— Coudonc, toi, chose! T'aurais pas pu nous avertir que l'assiette de fruits de mer coûtait le prix du voyage?

Dave mime le gars surpris qui ne comprend pas pourquoi on le blâme.

— Ben là, yo! C'était marqué dans le menu...

— C'correct... on va s'en souvenir pour l'avenir, hein, les filles? tempère Caro qui veut éviter un éclat public.

— Franchement! Faut ben venir dans un «tout inclus» pour payer quarante-cinq piastres pour un souper de marde de même! dit Vicky.

— Ah, j'en ai une bonne pour vous! Une fois, au restaurant, mon père..., se souvient Dave tandis que les filles paient le serveur.

Ne sachant plus comment s'en débarrasser, Katia improvise une ultime planche de salut:

— Écoute, on va se voir plus tard à la discothèque, d'ac? Bye!

Katia saisit chacune des filles par un bras pour déguerpir presque au trot sans même savoir où elles s'en vont.

À la sortie, les filles tournent rapidement dans le petit sentier sinueux du complexe hôtelier en regardant à tout moment derrière comme si elles étaient poursuivies par l'armée cubaine en grand déploiement.

— Je comprends qu'il voyage tout seul, lui. Il est vraiment lourd de sa personne! rugit Katia, hors d'elle.

— Il est tellement lourd! Il nous pèse, oui! rigole Vicky, trouvant l'expression franchement adéquate.

— Les filles…, les morigène Caroline, qui trouve tout de même que le pauvre jeune homme fait bien pitié au fond.

— Sérieux, faut changer de *résore,* sur-le-champ! décide Katia, comme si la possibilité de déménager leurs pénates vers un autre hôtel s'avérait tout à fait envisageable.

— Changer de continent, je pense! Moi, au début, je me disais, «C'est *cool*! Un ami gai pour nos vacances!». Gros ouache, finalement, confesse Vicky.

Caroline se tâte le ventre avec la main, tout en ralentissant un peu le pas.

— Ouf! Ça brasse un peu, mon affaire.

— Ah non, pas un autre épisode de *turista*?! Ha! ha! se moque un peu Vicky avant de se prendre le ventre à son tour. Hein? Moi aussi, on dirait…

— J'avoue que, moi aussi, ça gargouille. Mais il ne s'agit quand même pas d'une urgence de niveau «bain»! confesse Katia, qui ne peut s'empêcher d'éclater d'un rire franc.

— Bon, on passe à la chambre? Je pense que je vais me prendre des Imodium préventifs…, annonce Caroline.

— Ouin, moi je veux me brosser les dents et voir si la coquerelle géante n'a pas mangé nos bagages…

Caroline regarde l'heure sur sa montre avant de se tourni-coter avec nervosité une couette de cheveux du bout du doigt.

— Il faudrait vraiment que j'appelle Éric, il doit telle-ment s'inquiéter...

— Oui, c'est clair, approuve Vicky.

— Ils vont sûrement nous redonner nos affaires bientôt. De toute façon, ils n'ont aucune raison de nous en priver. On n'est quand même pas en transit pour la prison Tanguay! fait remarquer Katia. On devrait même exiger qu'ils nous redonnent nos sacoches tout de suite.

— On n'est pas ENCORE en route pour la prison de femmes, tu veux dire...

— Franchement, Caro!

— Sérieusement, les filles, il ne faudrait jamais, au grand jamais, que la commission scolaire apprenne ce qui s'est passé...

— Pas de danger. Comment veux-tu qu'ils le sachent? demande Vicky.

— Moi, ils m'ont vraiment spécifié que le contenu de nos dépositions demeurait secret et qu'il ne serait divulgué qu'aux autorités, se souvient Katia.

— Oui, moi aussi, avoue Caroline.

— Puis, de toute façon, si on considère toutes les personnes bizarres qu'on a rencontrées durant le voyage, il y a pas de chance que ça s'ébruite ! Je pense pas garder contact avec beaucoup de monde, ajoute Vicky.

— Pour de vrai, ça n'a aucun bon sens ! Je pensais pas qu'autant de gens *fuckés* dans la tête pouvaient se retrouver au même endroit, au même moment. Sans farce, pensez-y deux minutes..., s'étonne Katia, avant d'exploser d'un rire tonitruant.

— Pas de bon sens, comme tu dis ! Au moins, s'ils étaient apparus dans notre séjour de façon graduelle, ç'aurait été moins frappant, me semble, réfléchit Vicky.

— Eh non, le karma nous les réservait tous pour le premier jour... ou presque ! Bang !

JOUR 1

CUBA, VARADERO
COSTA AZUL DEL MAR RESORT

Après une dizaine de minutes de marche et quelques minutes d'égarement dans les dédales obscurcis de la station touristique, les filles aboutissent à la discothèque. Katia semble bien heureuse de constater que ce n'est pas très grand. La pièce carrée comprend deux niveaux : un bar muni d'un grand comptoir entouré de plusieurs tabourets, puis un palier, plus bas, faisant office de piste de danse. Un écran géant désuet présente le vidéoclip d'une chanson latine crachée par de grands haut-parleurs de plus de deux mètres de hauteur. Katia se réjouit intérieurement du fait que l'espace à aire ouverte lui permettra de repérer facilement le beau Mike dans la foule grouillante.

Alors qu'elle fait la queue au bar pour commander à boire, Caroline est surprise par deux jeunes hommes qui arrivent en embuscade près d'elle. Ils se positionnent en statue à ses côtés et la fixent, tout sourires. Visiblement pas originaires de l'Amérique, les deux gars semblent provenir du nord de l'Europe. Malgré le fait que leurs cheveux sont fort courts, voire presque rasés, on peut tout de même en déduire qu'ils sont d'un blond très pâle. De petite taille et plutôt rondelets, les deux types ne disent pas un mot, mais leur langage corporel laisse croire qu'ils désirent ardemment entrer en relation avec la belle Caroline. Pour se montrer polie, celle-ci les salue. Ils hochent la tête, bienheureux de son accueil. En fait, le duo oscille la tête de côté sans arrêt en fixant l'enseignante de français. Un malaise palpable s'installe illico. Katia, qui voit la scène de biais, décide de s'immiscer :

— Allo ! D'où venez-vous ? leur demande-t-elle en anglais.

— *Russia*, baragouine un des gars sans fournir plus de détails.

Les énergumènes détournent leur regard de Katia, puis ils se remettent de plus belle à hocher la tête en détaillant Caroline.

— Bon…, ajoute celle-ci en guise de réponse en toisant Katia, l'air de la supplier d'improviser quelque chose pour dissiper l'embarras.

— Vous êtes arrivés quand? poursuit Katia sans trop les regarder, plutôt occupée à tenter d'attirer l'attention d'un serveur dans le but de se commander à boire.

Ils ne répondent pas à sa question et haussent les épaules.

— Ben là? Ils savent même pas quand ils sont arrivés ou quoi? chuchote Caroline.

— Écoute. Soit ils sont paquetés raide, soit ils parlent pas un mot d'anglais. On va vérifier… Vous aimez vos vacances? tente de nouveau Katia en même temps qu'elle lève la main vers un serveur.

Aucune réponse. Les têtes se remettent en branle. L'un d'eux exécute un sourire disgracieux un peu tordu, laissant paraître son état d'ébriété visiblement très avancé.

— Nos deux hypothèses sont bonnes, je pense!

À quelques mètres d'elles, Vicky, qui attend aussi son tour au bar, pivote la tête tout autour comme une hirondelle surstimulée. Elle se tourne finalement vers ses amies qui semblent en discussion avec deux garçons. Curieuse, elle approche:

— Qu'est-ce qui se passe? Vous avez de nouveaux amis?

— Caro se fait *cruiser* par deux Russes soûls comme des bottes qui parlent pas l'anglais. Ça pourrait devenir très divertissant, analyse Katia.

— Ah wow! Chanceuse!

Vicky fixe un instant les deux gars qui ballottent toujours la tête comme si leur cou bougeait à l'aide d'une bille rotative bien huilée. N'ayant pas besoin de se soucier de sa langue d'usage pour être discrète, elle demande aux filles à voix haute et devant eux:

— Pourquoi ils font ça avec leur tête au juste? Ils ont le Parkinson?

— À ce stade-ci, on le sait pas encore. On dirait des *bobbleheads* qu'on place en haut du tableau de bord des autos, remarque Katia, très concentrée et en pleine analyse du comportement étrange des deux Russes.

L'air de penser qu'ils se sont assuré une touche avec les filles étant donné leur observation attentive, les deux *bobbleheads* effectuent un toast énergique avec leur bière Cristal avant de la caler goulûment comme on le ferait avec un verre de lait après une pointe de gâteau au chocolat trop sucré. Le plus rondelet des deux en renverse même sur le devant de son chandail.

— Super! Je me sens vraiment valorisée de me faire *cruiser* par deux Russes muets soûls morts, s'apitoie Caroline, un peu écœurée par le gars qui tente tant bien que mal d'essuyer la bière qui lui coule encore sur le menton et dans le cou.

Katia détourne la tête et se désole :

— Je vois Mike nulle part...

— Il n'est peut-être pas encore arrivé..., prétend Vicky.

— Aaaah ! Mais regardez donc ce qu'on a ici, par contre..., s'émoustille Katia, le regard coquin, en posant un doigt sur ses lèvres tout en mirant quelque chose au loin.

Les filles en déduisent que Katia dévisage sans subtilité un danseur cubain bien baraqué qui arrive comme un cheveu sur la soupe au beau milieu de la piste de danse. Sa camisole à l'effigie de l'hôtel témoigne qu'il est, sans l'ombre d'un doute, en service. De plus, plusieurs voyageurs qui se déhanchent avec suavité le saluent au passage. La bouche un peu entrouverte, Katia l'étudie un moment telle une lionne qui salive en repérant au loin une gazelle aux cuisses bien dodues. Elle annonce aux filles avec conviction :

— Voilà un petit dossier facile, droit devant. J'ai de l'expérience. Je vais aller tâter le terrain[12] d'avance au cas où ça marcherait pas avec le beau Mike. Un genre de *back up*, tsé ! Grrrrr !

Katia abandonne son verre sur le comptoir et fonce droit sur l'adonis aux abdos bien saillants sous son survêtement

---

12. Autrement dit, « aller lancer une carotte cubaine ou deux » (pour les lectrices de la série *Chick lit*)...

moulant. Arrivant à proximité de lui sur la piste de danse, elle lui adresse un sourire séducteur avant d'envoyer ses cheveux vers l'arrière dans une rotation de tête sensuelle digne d'être visionnée au ralenti, puis elle lui tend la main telle une princesse d'Espagne désirant recevoir un baise-main. Ses deux amies, restées en plan au bar, l'épient un moment et ne peuvent réprimer un roulement des yeux jusqu'au plafond. Le jeune Latino, enchanté d'avoir trouvé si aisément une partenaire de danse à ce point disponible et motivée, l'entraîne aussitôt dans un mérengué. Hélas, moins de deux secondes plus tard, une touriste blonde et élancée comme une cigogne arrive tout près du couple entortillé comme deux bretzels. Elle repousse sans ménagement Katia de l'épaule et de la hanche afin de se frayer un chemin pour se pendre littéralement au cou du jeune homme. Sans plus de transition, le couple nouvellement réuni débute alors une danse lascive. Obnubilé par sa seconde prise de la soirée, le type ne se retourne même pas vers la pauvre Katia, abandonnée comme un vieux coton. Bredouille et ainsi exclue, celle-ci rebrousse chemin en ne daignant même pas jeter un dernier regard dans leur direction.

En revenant près de ses amies, elle explose :

— EILLE !? L'avez-vous vue, la *bitch* de blonde conne ?

Caroline sourit dans sa barbe. Vicky aussi. Les *bobble-heads*, fidèles au poste, branlent toujours du chef, l'air d'imiter les deux idiots dans le film *A Night at the Roxbury*.

— C'était juste trop impoli, voyons ! Je dansais avec lui, elle a ben vu ! crache Katia, en beau fusil.

— C'est étrange, elle me fait penser à quelqu'un lors d'un certain voyage au Mexique..., ose Caroline en détournant le regard.

— Quoi? Je poussais pas les autres filles en sauvage de même!

— Ben..., doute Vicky.

Heureusement, Mike fait diversion en se faufilant au bout du bar avec son fils.

— Pfft! *Anyway*, c'est LUI que je veux, bougonne Katia, tout de même heureuse de le voir enfin surgir.

— Moi, faudrait que je me trouve quelqu'un pour «*frencher*-rien-que», confie Vicky.

— Nous avons justement deux magnifiques *bobble-heads* pleins de bière disponibles ici, à ma droite, lui mentionne Caroline avec l'insistance d'une vendeuse à la commission.

— Bof! Je te les laisse...

— Ça sent bizarre, vous trouvez pas? demande Caroline, le nez en l'air. Ah! ben oui, c'est la mouffette qui vient d'entrer dans la place...

Katia, qui cherchait désespérément les filles depuis plus de dix minutes, les retrouve enfin à l'autre extrémité du bar, seules et dissimulées dans un coin sombre à l'abri des regards. En se joignant à elles, Katia constate que ses copines sont crampées en deux tellement elles rient.

— Coudonc, ça fait trois jours que je vous cherche ! Qu'est-ce que vous faites ?

— Nous autres ? On rit notre vie, c'est ça qu'on fait, explique vaguement Vicky, qui peine à reprendre son souffle.

— Pis on est dans le jus à part de ça ! ajoute Caro en mettant sa main devant sa bouche pour s'esclaffer à nouveau.

— Comment ça ? s'amuse Katia, même si elle ne comprend encore rien à rien.

— Premièrement, on s'est sauvées de la mouffette qui court après nous depuis tantôt pour nous parler de son père. Moi aussi, il m'énerve, finalement ! Ensuite, on vient de rencontrer un gars qui est venu *cruiser* Vic. On l'a affectueusement surnommé le « soufflé de Drummond ». Un genre de culturiste. C'est vraiment drôle, je n'ai jamais vu un gars pas de contenu de même. En plus, il se donne des airs de philosophe songé des temps modernes, tu vois le genre ? Sinon, les deux sosies russes de Michael J. Fox en pleine crise d'épilepsie semblent à tout coup nous retrouver PARTOUT dans le bar pour venir se brasser la tête pas trop loin. On dirait qu'on a été catapultées dans un pays lointain rempli de caricatures. On rit tellement ! explique Caroline sans même reprendre sa respiration.

— Il est où, votre soufflé de Drummond ? On dirait que j'ai le goût de trouver ça drôle, moi aussi !

— Chut, il arrive justement…, lui indique Vicky en tournant un peu la tête, question de se la jouer discrète.

— Allo! amorce Katia en s'empressant de lui tendre la main, impatiente de rire de lui à son tour.

Les présentations se résument à l'essentiel. Le gars – sans aucun doute adepte de stéroïdes – déclare aussitôt à Katia, l'air très inspiré, le pouce et l'index de la main droite joints ensemble vers le ciel :

— Tsé, euh… j'expliquais à tes amies que, dans la vie, il faut en profiter et laisser faire la vie à mener la nôtre[13]…

— Laisser faire quoi? ne peut s'empêcher de demander Katia.

— «Faire la vie à mener la nôtre», répète le gars avec langueur, la main désormais à plat sur le torse comme s'il récitait un discours touchant lors d'une fête commémorative tenue à la mémoire des anciens combattants.

-Aaah! OK! OK! Je comprends, là, rigole Katia qui vient tout juste de recevoir un coup de coude discret dans les côtes de la part de Vicky qui a de plus en plus de difficulté à masquer le fait qu'elles se paient sa tête.

Comme s'il le faisait exprès, il poursuit :

— Parce que dans la vie, si tu la vis pas ta vie, hein, qui va vivre ta vie à ta place? Hein, qui?

---

13. *What?!*

— Ben oui, qui ? C'est ça qu'on se demande en se levant tous les matins, nous autres, hein, les filles ? relance Katia, qui se marre intérieurement.

— Tous les matins de notre VIE, on se le demande, ironise à son tour Vicky.

— Ta vie ben, c'est TA vie, tsé, conclut le type musclé, convaincu d'ainsi livrer l'épilogue savoureux d'une allocution digne d'un cours universitaire de deuxième cycle en philosophie moderne.

Vicky rabaisse un peu le niveau de la conversation aristocratique en cours en s'informant auprès de Katia :

— Et toi ? Ta rencontre avec le beau Mike ?

La mouffette, qui, telle une fusée, surgit alors de nulle part, entend la fin de la question de Vicky. Excité, il sautille derrière les filles et tape deux petits coups dans ses mains en déclarant :

— Yo ! Tu «trippes» sur le gars du spa de ce matin ? Je l'savais ! Il est là-bas, je vais aller lui dire pour t'aider !

Sans qu'elles puissent l'en empêcher, il part au triple galop rejoindre Mike et son fils, tous deux assis au bar, *tranquillos*.

— Quoi ? Il est pas sérieux, lui… Il NIAISE, j'espère ?! s'inquiète Katia, abasourdie, en écartant largement les bras en direction de ses amies tout en continuant d'espionner Dave qui gambade en effectuant des sauts de kangourou vers le bar.

Les filles le suivent des yeux jusqu'à ce qu'il arrive à destination et se poste près de Mike. Il désigne ensuite sans plus attendre Katia de la main avec autant de subtilité qu'un élève de maternelle dans une cour d'école.

— Esti, je vais le tuer à mains nues, je pense…, réagit Katia qui serre les dents en se prenant la tête de honte avant de la pivoter en direction opposée pour faire semblant de rien.

— Il a tellement pas rapport avec son implication, lui. Je te jure, c'est de pire en pire, son affaire, confirme Vicky.

— J'ai l'air trop conne! Il m'énarve tellement, sérieux… Regardez-le! Il est tout content!

Un peu en retrait, le soufflé de Drummond ne comprend qu'à moitié ce qui se passe. Il décide tout de même d'y mettre son grain de sel. Il approche très près de Katia, leur visage n'étant séparé que par son doigt qui effectue des allers-retours entre son nez et le sien, mais sans la toucher. Il lui intime avec force:

— Regarde-moi, regarde-moi, regarde-moi! Dans la vie, rien n'arrive pour rien et la vie sait quoi faire et…

— Laisse faire avec tes «la vie par-ci, la vie par-là», je t'ai pas sonné, chose! répond froidement Katia en se reculant un peu en signe de non-ouverture à sa morale confucianiste.

Elle pivote sur elle-même, question de courir auprès de Mike afin de sauver les meubles – du moins ce qu'il en reste. Dans son mouvement de rotation, elle tombe nez à nez avec les deux Russes revenus en douce à proximité des filles afin de se renverser d'autre bière sur la poitrine en escomptant les charmer.

— Ah non, simonaque, tassez-vous, vous autres! On vient de débarquer dans un vrai cirque ou quoi?

Le culturiste, bien décidé à livrer son message spirituel jusqu'au bout, place sa jambe en travers du chemin de Katia malgré l'intention évidente de celle-ci de poursuivre sa route.

— Le cirque, ou bien le *cercle* de la vie…, conclut-il avec suspense en hochant la tête, bien sérieux, tout en dégageant sa jambe de la trajectoire de la pauvre Katia qui n'en peut plus.

Les yeux exorbités, elle ouvre grand la bouche en se tournant vers ses amies. Elle fait ensuite mine de s'arracher les cheveux de la tête. Amusées de voir Katia si dépassée par les événements, ses deux collègues se prennent le ventre à deux mains tellement la situation les amuse.

JOUR 8

AÉROPORT MONTRÉAL-TRUDEAU
SALLE 315 – **9 H 11**

Au son des filles qui se dilatent la rate en se remémorant cette scène singulière, la tension redescend encore d'un cran dans la salle d'interrogatoire à l'ambiance glaciale.

— C'était comme une *joke*. Un coup monté. Si quelqu'un m'avait dit à ce moment-là : «Il y a des caméras là-bas, vous vous êtes fait prendre à *Surprise sur prise dans le Sud*», je l'aurais cru, je pense, se rappelle Katia.

— Eille, j'ai jamais ri autant de ma vie! Tout ça en une seule soirée, en plus. Tout le monde était comme vraiment à côté de la *track*, se souvient Vicky.

— On aurait pu appeler cette journée-là : «La rencontre des énergumènes du *résore*», complète Caroline.

Katia enchaîne en se remémorant un autre fait cocasse :

— Oui, ou encore, la journée «Parlons de température». Tout le monde n'avait que ce sujet de conversation, c'était tellement drôle. On a découvert un phénomène social très intéressant. Vous souvenez-vous, au buffet, le matin...?

JOUR 1

CUBA, VARADERO
COSTA AZUL DEL MAR RESORT

Katia, qui sélectionne aléatoirement les composantes de son déjeuner dans les plats de service en inox du buffet, se fait aborder par une femme :

— Ouin, ben, c'est pas chaud pour la pompe à l'eau, le Sud!

— Ben non, hein..., répond-elle sans entrain.

— Ah non, pas chaud, pas chaud...

JOUR 8
AÉROPORT MONTRÉAL-TRUDEAU
SALLE 315 – **9 H 12**

Caroline poursuit leur récapitulation :

— Au jacuzzi, aussi...

JOUR 1
CUBA, VARADERO
COSTA AZUL DEL MAR RESORT

Pendant que les filles se détendent en compagnie de Mike et de son fils, un couple dans le spa voisin se lève pour quitter les lieux. Au passage, la femme s'adresse à eux :

— En tout cas, nous autres, on pensait qu'il ferait plus chaud. On va retourner voir les prédictions sur le site de MétéoMédia à l'ordinateur du lobby. Ce matin, on annonçait plus chaud pour demain et après-demain...

— Ah, on espère ! répond Caroline, toujours polie.

— Si on vous recroise, on vous le dira !

JOUR 8

AÉROPORT MONTRÉAL-TRUDEAU
SALLE 315 – **9 H 13**

Vicky enchaîne à son tour en partageant sa propre expérience sur le sujet :

— Au petit bar de la plage aussi…

JOUR 1

CUBA, VARADERO
COSTA AZUL DEL MAR RESORT

Vicky, qui attend les mojitos qu'elle a commandés depuis un bon moment, sourit à un couple de voyageurs assis au bar. L'homme lui dit :

— On dirait que le ciel s'éclaircit ; il va faire beau demain !

— Ah, peut-être bien…

— Oui, regardez là-bas, la prie le gars en lui montrant une éclaircie à travers la masse épaisse de nuages gris pâle.

— Aaaah, OK, oui, concède Vicky à l'opposé du bar, tout en se penchant presque à quatre pattes pour voir l'horizon sans que sa vue ne soit obstruée par le toit du bâtiment.

JOUR 8

AÉROPORT MONTRÉAL-TRUDEAU
SALLE 315 — **9 H 14**

— Dans les sentiers aussi... Vous souvenez-vous ? demande Caroline.

— Moi oui, approuve Vicky.

JOUR 1

CUBA, VARADERO
COSTA AZUL DEL MAR RESORT

Les trois filles foulent le pavé du chemin pour aller se préparer à la chambre en vue de leur repas gastronomique au restaurant de fruits de mer. Elles croisent une femme seule avec sa fille et lui sourient au passage. La mère adopte une expression faciale dépressive digne de celle de Passe-Partout lors de ses confessions à la fin de chaque émission, puis leur déclare :

— Bonjour... C'est humide sans bon sens, hein ? C'est pour ça qu'il fait froid, je pense.

— Oui, c'est ça, l'humidité..., l'appuie Katia tout en roulant les yeux avec discrétion.

— C'est ben, ben, ben plate... Venir dans le Sud et avoir ce genre de température là. On trouve ça ben dommage, nous autres, hein, ma pitoune ?

— Nous autres aussi. Bonne fin de soirée...

JOUR 8

AÉROPORT MONTRÉAL-TRUDEAU
SALLE 315 – **9 H 15**

— Elle était tellement débinée, la pauvre madame...

— Même le soufflé de Drummond avait quelque chose à dire là-dessus à la discothèque..., envoie Vicky en riant.

JOUR 1

CUBA, VARADERO
COSTA AZUL DEL MAR RESORT

À l'écart de Katia qui discute plus loin avec Mike, les yeux dans les yeux, les filles se tournent vers le monsieur muscles qui semble une fois de plus vouloir partager une déclaration d'importance planétaire.

— Dans la vie, tu sais jamais quelle température il va faire...

— Ben oui, toi, parle-moi d'une affaire bizarre, réagit Vicky en adressant un clin d'œil à Caro.

— C'est fascinant! en rajoute Caro, avant de se détourner pour rire comme une gamine.

JOUR 8
AÉROPORT MONTRÉAL-TRUDEAU
SALLE 315 – **9 H 16**

Les trois filles secouent la tête de découragement.

— Non mais, c'est typiquement québécois de parler de température de même ou quoi? On a jasé avec des Français, des Cubains et des Canadiens anglais durant le voyage… et ils ne parlaient pas AUTANT du sujet, analyse Vicky, trouvant toujours le phénomène inexplicable.

— Même Mike, assis au bar en train de s'enfiler des *shooters*, a eu envie d'en parler. Je lui ai coupé ça assez raide sec, merci! Du genre: «Euh, je pense qu'on a mieux à faire que s'improviser météorologues…»

— En effet!

— J'aimerais souligner que Mike et son fils furent les seuls hommes normaux de tout le voyage! Sans compter le gars qui est venu nous reconduire à l'aéroport, bien sûr, déclare Vicky.

— Hish… Hon, hon, hon…, s'étouffe presque Katia avant de rire jaune.

— On l'a rencontré juste le deuxième jour, lui? L'aviez-vous vu avant, vous autres? Je veux dire, le premier jour..., s'informe Caroline, l'air de s'autoposer la question.

Katia fronce les sourcils, songeuse:

— Je pense que je l'ai vu assis au bar de la plage le premier jour. Mais tsé, les Cubains se ressemblent tous, de loin, donc c'était peut-être pas lui.

Vicky tente à son tour de se souvenir. Elle conclut finalement:

— Non, moi, il me disait rien quand il nous a abordées ce jour-là...

JOUR 2
CUBA, VARADERO
COSTA AZUL DEL MAR RESORT

Vicky et Caroline dorment paisiblement dans leur chambre lorsque quelqu'un cogne à la porte.

— Hein? maugrée Vicky, encore très endormie.

— *Holaaaa... ¿Mini barrr?* propose une voix hispano-phone très sensuelle en roulant à outrance la sonorité du dernier «r» avant d'y ajouter un semblant de petit cri à la Michael Jackson.

Désirant faire d'une pierre deux coups, le Cubain se tourne alors vers la porte de la chambre de Katia, juste en face, et il y cogne avant de répéter la même offre avec autant d'intonation.

— *Holaaa... ¿Mini barrr?*

Katia, qui se réveille aussi, lève sa tête échevelée en grognant :

— *What?*

Endormie, Caroline se dirige vers la porte, convaincue qu'il s'agit d'une mauvaise blague. Ne comprenant pas du tout de quoi il retourne, Katia fait de même, un peu en maudit de se faire niaiser de la sorte. Elle ouvre la porte à vive allure et s'informe, bête comme ses pieds :

— *What?*

Le pauvre Latino répète pour la troisième fois :

— *Holaaa... ¿Mini barrr...?*, en mimant une moue sensuelle, la langue un peu sortie comme s'il offrait plutôt un service aux chambres de cunnilingus cubains.

— Quessé ça ?

— De quoi y parle, lui ? On veut pas prendre un verre à cette heure-ci !? ne comprend pas Caroline, tout aussi ébouriffée que son amie qui lui fait face dans l'embrasure de la porte de sa chambre.

— *¿Mini barrrrr?*

— *No, mini bar!* crache Katia, les nerfs en boule.

— *Si, mini barrrrr, ahi*[14]..., insiste l'employé tout en désignant de l'index le meuble sur lequel repose le téléviseur.

— Hein?

Voyant que les filles ne comprennent visiblement rien à rien, il pénètre dans la chambre de Caroline et Vicky et tire sur une des portes latérales du meuble qui laisse voir un petit réfrigérateur. Il l'ouvre pour leur montrer que celui-ci renferme quelques boissons gazeuses, deux bouteilles d'eau et deux bières en canette. Il explique:

— *Mini barrrrr...*

— Sérieux, s'il répète une autre fois «minibar», je l'étampe avec mon oreiller, menace Vicky qui remet l'arme potentielle sur sa tête pour avoir un peu de paix.

Constatant que le frigo est encore plein, l'homme de service se dirige vers la porte en disant aux filles:

— *Mañana, mini barrrrr, siiii*[15]...

Katia, debout de l'autre côté du corridor, met Vicky au défi:

— Il vient de le redire. Faut que tu le cognes avec ton oreiller, tu l'as dit! Prends-toi une bonne *swing* baseball!

— Je dors, ça me tente plus.

---

14. Oui, minibar, ici.
15. Demain, minibar, ouiii.

— ¡*Buenos díaaaaas*! fait le gars sur un ton démesurément suave en poursuivant sa route, poussant son chariot dans le corridor.

— Eille, je comprenais tellement rien à son offre! Je savais même pas qu'on avait un frigo dans la chambre.

— Moi non plus. Je pensais que c'était un genre de service de bar aux chambres. Je me disais: «À cette heure-là? Parle-moi d'un hôtel de débauche!», avoue Caroline.

— Oui, mais c'est quoi l'idée aussi de parler avec un ton de *gogo-boy* hispanophone en chaleur? souligne Vicky qui l'imite ensuite: «Miniiii barrrrrr»! Voyons donc?!

— C'est vraiment n'importe quoi! Bon, on va se lever, je pense...

Les filles, confortablement installées sous un *palapa* sur la plage, admirent le panorama en prenant un verre de bière Cristal. La journée, tout de même plus chaude que la veille, reste pour le moins frisquette. La température atteint environ seize degrés sous un ciel opaque tantôt foncé, tantôt plus clair, ce qui détonne avec le décor paradisiaque de la mer bleu turquoise. Le soleil apparaît de temps à autre derrière les grassouillets nuages qui bedonnent dans le firmament cubain, venant ainsi réchauffer les minces espoirs des quelques braves voyageurs venus affronter la rigueur du climat, les deux espadrilles dans le sable.

Malgré le temps froid, les filles tenaient mordicus à enfiler leur maillot – juste au cas où – sous leurs vêtements longs. Vicky a enroulé sa serviette de plage autour de ses jambes pour avoir plus chaud. Caroline, quant à elle, la maintient autour de ses épaules tel un châle de grand-mère.

— Regardez, les filles, je me mets de la crème solaire quand même! C'est juste de la quinze, mais au moins... souligne Vicky en s'enduisant le visage.

Sa fierté est palpable à distance. Elle ne se fera pas prendre deux fois...

— Bravo! On est très fières de toi! la félicite Katia comme si elle s'adressait à un enfant de trois ans.

— Aaah wow! un catamaran! Regardez! Voilà l'activité qu'il faudrait faire! s'excite mémé Caroline en montrant un bateau sur le point de s'amarrer à quelques dizaines de mètres d'elles.

— Moi, j'aimerais voir La Havane, rappelle Vicky.

— On pourrait faire les deux excursions. Au prix qu'on a payé le voyage..., propose Katia.

Les filles lèvent les yeux pour observer le catamaran de grosseur moyenne transportant plus de vingt touristes habillés jusqu'au cou, qui approche tranquillement de la berge. Trois Cubains supervisent le retour à bon port de l'impressionnante embarcation. L'un d'eux saute à l'eau muni d'une grosse corde pour tenter de faire accoster adéquatement le bateau. Malgré le temps frais, les vacanciers à bord paraissent faire la grosse vie. Certains sont étendus dans de grands cordages et d'autres sont debout à regarder les hommes travailler tout en sirotant une bière. Vicky remarque un détail :

— Les gens ont des masques de plongée. On dirait une excursion de *snorkeling* ! Ah oui, on y va !

— Hish, ça devait pas être chaud, chaud, me semble, remarque Vicky.

— Ils doivent prêter des combinaisons thermiques exprès. De toute façon, on s'entend qu'on va oublier l'activité culturelle, cette fois-ci. Les cigares et le faux village traditionnel, on a déjà donné au Mexique ! ajoute Katia.

— Ça me tente, de la plongée en apnée ! Jouer les sirènes des mers et voir plein de beaux poissons, wow ! se réjouit Vicky. Il est censé faire plus chaud dans les jours à venir en plus. Depuis ce matin, au moins deux cents personnes nous l'ont confirmé.

— Je sais pas comment ça fonctionne, les excursions... On s'informera à la réception tantôt.

Un Cubain d'une quarantaine d'années passe alors devant les trois vacancières accompagné de sa petite fille. La belle chouette d'environ trois ans avance maladroitement dans le sable, l'air de reculer un pas sur deux. Sa tignasse garnie de tresses rehaussées de billes bleu pâle et blanches lui confère un air croquable exotique à souhait.

— Regardez la petite puce ! Trop belle ! s'extasie Caroline en tentant de demeurer discrète.

— Ah mon Dieu! Qu'elle est *cute*!

— Allo! Ça va bien? les salue l'homme dans un anglais impeccable.

Cordial, il se présente alors aux trois filles:

— Sylvio, bien enchanté.

Les filles déclinent leur prénom à tour de rôle en toisant la charmante fillette. Celle-ci pose une main au bout de la chaise longue de Vicky en dévisageant les touristes avec curiosité, ses grands yeux foncés en amande remplis d'interrogation.

— Voici Camila, ma petite dernière.

— Vous avez d'autres enfants? demande Caroline, ravie d'échanger avec un papa cubain.

Celui-ci extirpe d'emblée un portefeuille de sa poche arrière pour lui présenter fièrement sa famille, comptant deux autres enfants en bas âge.

— C'est votre femme? Elle est très jolie, le complimente Caroline en détaillant le cliché familial avec intérêt.

Elle farfouille à son tour sur son téléphone intelligent afin de présenter son fils et Éric à leur interlocuteur.

Comme le gars ne porte pas l'uniforme classique des employés du complexe, Katia s'informe:

— Travaillez-vous ici?

— Bah... disons que je suis dans l'administration...

Ne comprenant pas trop son hésitation à répondre et la gêne que la question semble lui avoir causée, Katia avance la tête comme si elle désirait ainsi lui faire comprendre qu'une explication plus élaborée serait appréciée. Cependant, Vicky coupe court à la conversation pour lui soutirer une information de nature plus concrète :

— Sylvio, où doit-on s'inscrire pour faire une balade en catamaran ?

— Pour le *snorkeling* ? C'est tout près de la réception, en face du bar du lobby. Vous allez voir, il y a un kiosque d'information concernant toutes les activités offertes à Varadero et aux alentours.

La bambine tire sur son pantalon et lui adresse quelques mots en espagnol. Sylvio se penche un peu pour lui répondre.

— Mon Dieu que c'est comique, un enfant qui parle espagnol ! souligne Caroline.

— On veut aller à La Havane aussi ! Est-ce une station balnéaire ou juste une ville ? demande Vicky à Sylvio, pas certaine de ce détail.

— Une ville, je pense, devine Katia en attendant la réponse de Sylvio. Tout le monde parlait de cet endroit quand je suis venue ici, il y a cinq ans...

— C'est une ville, la capitale de Cuba. Elle est située à un peu moins de deux heures de route d'ici. Vous devez absolument voir ça !

En français, Katia se confie à ses amies :

— Sérieux, c'est un peu loin. Pas certaine que j'ai le goût de faire autant de route pour aller visiter une grosse ville toute la journée...

— Ouin, il faut y aller en autobus? se questionne Caroline, trouvant aussi la mer, la plage et les palmiers définitivement plus enchanteurs comme décor.

Sylvio, qui pressent leur ambivalence sans même comprendre leur langue d'usage, décrit :

— La Havane, c'est un joyau, une des plus belles villes du monde entier. C'est pittoresque, plein de couleurs... Tout le monde adore! On tombe amoureux de La Havane comme de son premier ami de cœur...

— Tant que ça? Ah oui, je veux vraiment y aller! impose Vicky.

— Oui, en plus, l'endroit est en bordure de la mer, donc entouré d'eau.

— OK, on verra alors, tergiverse Katia, pas certaine quant à son intérêt réel pour la potentielle expédition.

Comme sa progéniture baragouine à nouveau quelque chose en pliant un peu les genoux d'impatience, Sylvio roule des yeux en direction des filles, un sourire en coin. Il prend la main de sa fillette et s'apprête à quitter la plage.

— Quand une princesse demande la lune à son papa, il doit la lui donner tout de suite!

— Pas de problème, à plus tard!

En observant l'homme qui s'éloigne, les filles commentent :

— Il est fin, lui, et pas *crosseur* comme certains que l'on ne nommera pas ! soulève d'emblée Katia, en mémoire d'un passé amoureux mexicain fort lointain.

— C'est quoi sa *job*, au juste ? se questionne Caroline, pas certaine d'avoir saisi la signification de sa réponse floue.

— Dans « l'administration », pas d'uniforme de l'hôtel... Sérieusement, les filles, l'hôtel lui appartient peut-être, genre ? Ou peut-être à sa famille ? suppute Katia, bonne détective.

— Peut-être. En plus, il se promène avec sa fille à l'hôtel. Pas certaine que les membres du personnel puissent emmener leurs enfants pendant les heures de travail, souligne avec pertinence maman Caroline.

Un Québécois dans la trentaine, vêtu d'un maillot de bain et d'un chandail kangourou, avance vers les filles. Sans le vouloir, il coupe court à leur conversation analytique concernant le statut professionnel de Sylvio.

— Salut, les filles, ça roule ?

— Ouais, merci !

— Je me présente, je m'appelle Mathieu, mais tout le monde m'appelle Matt, facque, appelez-moi comme vous voulez. L'un ou l'autre, ça me dérange pas ! Je suis certain que vous êtes des filles super *willing*, donc je vous fais part de l'idée du siècle. On est un petit groupe là-bas et on veut organiser un genre de jeu sur la plage. En fait, pour commencer, il faudrait aller demander des œufs au buffet… S'ils ne veulent pas nous en donner une douzaine, ben il faudrait aller en acheter en ville en taxi. Ensuite, le jeu est comme une *game* de soccer, mais avec un Frisbee. Les buts sont aux quatre coins, par contre. On sait pas si l'hôtel a un Frisbee en stock, mais bon, sinon on ira au marché en taxi en acheter un en même temps que les œufs, mettons. Donc là, il y a deux équipes, et on place les œufs dans notre maillot de bain, vous autres dans le *top* ou le bas, c'est comme vous voulez. L'important est qu'il ne faut pas qu'ils cassent! Donc là, on accumule des points selon les passes réussies et dans quel but on compte. Ça pourrait être un point ce coin-là, deux points l'autre, cinq points le troisième et dix points le dernier, genre… Pis, dans le fond, c'est pas grave si les œufs se brisent, mais chaque fois on perd un point, ou deux, selon le cas. Pis on peut aller se laver dans la mer, facque, pas de trouble…

Le front ondulé comme la frange d'une Africaine passant la porte de son fidèle coiffeur un samedi matin, les trois filles figent – autant de confusion quant à l'activité en tant que telle que d'étourdissement quant au propos vomi avec tant de rapidité par Matt l'hyperactif. Vicky se déplisse le front la première, l'air soudainement prise d'une urgence. Elle se lève et quitte le plateau sans s'expliquer.

Mathieu se tourne vers les deux participantes potentielles restantes :

— Pis? Ça vous tente?

— Ben, euh… Pfft…, souffle Katia, peu enjouée face au projet fort laborieux décrit par Mathieu.

— Moi, euh…, hésite à son tour Caroline en resserrant sa serviette autour de ses épaules, ambivalente quant à la façon de refuser poliment l'étrange invitation.

Silence. Malaise. Une volée de goélands marins passe dans le ciel. Les filles ne savent pas quoi dire pour ne pas vexer Mathieu et anéantir toute sa belle motivation.

— Écoutez, on va ramasser ce dont on a besoin et je vous fais signe quand ça commence, OK?

— On verra rendu là! conclut Caro en riant à contrecœur.

Le gars s'éloigne au moment où Vicky revient. Matt sollicite au passage deux autres filles étendues sur des transats. Vicky reprend place parmi ses amies et commente en faisant une grimace:

— C'était donc ben compliqué son affaire, lui! J'ai rien compris!

— N'importe quoi! C'est pas mêlant, j'en saigne du nez! Voir si on devrait se casser le bicycle de même en voyage pour organiser un simple jeu! Le «bolleyboll», me semble que c'est un beau classique qui se démode pas, ajoute Katia.

— Les points, les œufs, les buts, le Frisbee, je comprenais rien, mais je me disais juste: «Arkkk, ça me tente vraiment pas…», spécifie Caroline qui se blottit dans le fond de sa chaise longue, prise d'un frisson.

— Son projet me rejoint pas pantoute, comme on dit! rigole Vicky.

— Toi, ça va? T'es partie vite, me semble, demande Katia.

— Ouin, correct... Disons que j'ai pas dix minutes pour me rendre aux toilettes quand ça me pogne, mais rien de grave comparé à Caro au Mexique. Ha! ha! Je me sens comme ça depuis les fruits de mer d'hier soir...

— Moi aussi, confesse Katia. J'ai l'estomac à l'envers depuis le souper.

— Ah, vous voyez, moi, c'est tout le contraire... Je pense que deux Imodium préventifs, c'était trop. Je me sens toute ballonnée, fait Caro en se palpant le ventre à deux mains.

— Je te paie une noix de gastro si tu veux, ça va te débloquer solide! se marre Katia.

— Bon, on change de sujet..., insiste Vicky.

La femme au chandail imprimé d'une femme *sexy* en maillot de bain et son mari, complètement absorbés par leur plan-séquence interminable de la plage, passent devant l'emplacement des filles.

— Allo! fait la femme. Il fait un peu plus chaud, hein?

— Ben oui! Allo! répondent les filles en chœur en réalisant tout à coup qu'elles se trouvent sous les projecteurs.

Elles envoient machinalement la main à la caméra en souriant pour être charmantes. Le couple de cinéastes en herbe poursuit sa route, l'air bienheureux des scènes recueillies au passage. Les filles observent le couple qui s'éloigne et s'échangent un regard blasé.

Tout à coup, le G.O. motivé croisé la veille traverse la plage en joggant. Tout aussi survolté que la journée précédente, il les questionne au passage :

— *¿Bolleyboll? ¿Sí?*

— Ah bon ! Justement ! Voilà l'autre, encore.

— *No, gracias*, refuse poliment Katia avant de dire à ses amies : Vous voyez, ç'a beau être un classique, ce jeu-là me tente pas plus...

JOUR 8

AÉROPORT MONTRÉAL-TRUDEAU
SALLE 315 – **9 H 21**

— Chaque fois que je les voyais passer avec leur caméra, eux autres, les fesses me serraient comme par réflexe. «Chat échaudé craint l'eau froide», comme on dit, avoue Caroline.

— Les gens avec des caméras, ça peut être lourd de conséquences, en effet, approuve Vicky, avec un sourire tendu.

— Ces deux-là n'ont rien fait d'autre du voyage, fait remarquer Caroline.

— Je plains leurs familles, qui devront se taper un montage beaucoup trop long de leur «aventure» cubaine. Imaginez, le buffet, filmé à chaque repas, pendant sept jours... Pire qu'un supplice grec! dit Vicky.

Katia, bien songeuse, fixe la surface du bureau. Elle semble se creuser la tête. Vicky remarque bien entendu son état d'esprit.

— À quoi tu penses?

— Le gars... On dirait que c'est irréel. Je revois les scènes dans ma tête et ça ne colle pas, on dirait.

— Dur à croire pour toi, hein?

— À ce moment-là, je me doutais de rien du tout, pour vrai. Le reste du voyage non plus, d'ailleurs. Je n'aurais jamais pu imaginer que..., affirme Caroline.

— Oui, mais toi, t'es un peu naïve de nature, Caro. C'est pas nouveau! émet Vicky.

— Comment ça, «naïve»?

— C'est pas méchant ce qu'elle dit, c'est juste que t'as tendance à trouver les gens gentils d'emblée, sans trop te poser de questions, explique Katia pour étayer la pensée de son amie.

— Ah, parce que tu te doutais de quelque chose, toi, Vicky ? T'avais pas l'air. T'as rien dit…, se défend Caroline, convaincue du contraire.

— OK ! Il faut que j'avoue que non… mais… j'aurais dû. D'habitude, j'ai un bon sixième sens…

JOUR 2

CUBA, VARADERO
COSTA AZUL DEL MAR RESORT

En pénétrant dans l'aire de buffet, les trois comparses prennent d'assaut les grands comptoirs garnis de nourriture avant même de choisir une table. On y retrouve divers plats de viandes et de poissons en sauce, des pommes de terre pilées préparées à base d'un mélange en poudre, de grosses fèves blanches dans une sauce tomate bien rouge et des légumes variés provenant assurément de boîtes de conserve. Une femme d'origine cubaine taille des lanières dans une grosse pièce de porc braisé pour les clients. Plus loin, un homme fait sauter des pâtes tandis qu'un dernier îlot offre des charcuteries, des fromages, des pains et diverses salades et marinades afin de rehausser un peu le niveau de fraîcheur culinaire. On retrouve aussi d'autres réceptacles contenant des aliments plus typiquement nord-américains, dont des frites et de la pizza déposées sous un réchaud muni d'une seule lampe, la deuxième étant brisée depuis cinq jours.

Ambivalentes et presque craintives, les filles remplissent peu à peu leur assiette en déambulant en mémères autour des plats proposés. Tandis qu'elles choisissent une table, Katia analyse l'assiette de son amie :

— T'as pris les patates pilées ! Moi aussi !

Une fois réunies et attablées, elles commencent à manger.

— Moi, j'ai pris plein de fromage. Il y en avait de toutes sortes : du gouda, du brie, et celui-là ressemble à un cheddar fort..., s'enthousiasme Vicky en prenant une bonne bouchée du premier.

Elle recrache aussitôt le tout dans sa serviette de table en tissu bourgogne en tentant d'être discrète malgré son écœurement bien senti. Du fromage plein les dents, elle vocifère :

— C'est dé-gueu-lasse...

— Ben oui, mais depuis quand l'Amérique du Sud est-elle réputée en matière de fromage ?

Entêtée, Vicky mange tout de même un autre petit morceau de chacun, puis elle commente :

— C'est pas un casse-tête, ils goûtent tous le vieux fromage de chèvre périmé.

— Moi, je trouve que les tomates sont un peu dures, mais bonnes. Je sais pas pourquoi elles sont vertes de même, par contre...

— Les concombres aussi sont pas pires !

— Les patates pilées, on oublie ça. C'est délavé, avec mottons en prime, ça me roule dans la bouche! Les fèves dans la sauce rouge non plus, c'est pas très bon... Y'a une épice très forte... je crois que c'est du romarin? En tout cas, on dirait qu'ils ont échappé un sapin dedans!

— Ça va super bien notre affaire. «Le manger» était bien meilleur au Mexique, me semble?

— Ouin. Aaaah! la viande est pas mangeable non plus...

— Je vais aller me chercher des concombres pis des tomates..., se motive Vicky en reculant sa chaise.

— Les frites sont super bonnes! s'écrie Caro comme si elle venait de gagner 250 000 pesos convertibles. Mais le ketchup... Ark, c'est pire que la marque maison du Super C!

— Concombres, tomates vertes... et des frites alors, sans ketchup, complète Vicky en s'éloignant avec l'air dépressif d'un caniche en manque de toilettage.

En attendant d'être servie au bar de la plage, Katia fait un brin de jasette avec le beau Mike.

— Je suis tombé dans mon lit comme une roche, mais je me sens encore fatigué, on dirait, confie celui-ci. Vive les vols de nuit!

— Nous aussi, on s'est couchées assez tôt. Ouf! Mais ce soir, on devrait être plus en forme pour faire la fête, envoie Katia avec un sourire ravageur.

— Ah oui? Je vais me taper une petite *siesta* d'après-midi, alors..., lui indique-t-il en lui décochant une œillade tout aussi éloquente. Tsé, je suis vieux, moi!

— Bah! Arrête! T'es pas vieux! Ben... un peu, mais pas tant que ça...

Elle lui assène un petit coup de coude se voulant plus *cute* que violent, et elle agrippe ses verres pour retourner auprès de ses amies.

Le sourire aux lèvres, Katia qui vole en avançant sur la plage, regrette d'emblée de ne pas avoir apporté un verre supplémentaire, puisque Sylvio se trouve près de leurs chaises longues. La petite puce juchée sur ses épaules, il tend un carton mauve à Caroline. Katia n'entend qu'une bribe de la fin de la conversation en arrivant près d'eux. Caroline, la main sur la poitrine en guise de reconnaissance, le remercie chaudement:

— Merci! Vraiment, c'est super gentil!

— C'est quoi? demande Katia.

— Il nous a refilé un coupon donnant droit à un rabais de 50 % sur chacune de nos croisières en catamaran!

— Ah wow! Merci beaucoup! On va aller réserver tantôt. Il fait vraiment plus chaud aujourd'hui! se réjouit Katia en tendant les cocktails à qui de droit.

— Kat, tu viens de parler de température…, se déçoit Vicky, comme si cela constituait un grave affront aux valeurs intrinsèques du groupe.

Visage déconfit à l'appui, Katia joue le jeu de la fille sérieusement désolée et elle se repent :

— Je m'excuse, les filles… vraiment…

— Et j'ai repensé à votre projet d'aller à La Havane, continue Sylvio. Puisque je dois y aller souvent pour affaires, je vous propose de vous y conduire cette semaine. Je fais mes emplettes, je vous montre quelques trucs intéressants là-bas et on revient. Le périple sera moins long qu'en bus avec trente autres touristes…

— Ben là, c'est trop ! Les filles ? On accepte ? s'étonne Katia, complètement ahurie par la générosité du type.

— Moi, je trouve ça parfait ! accepte Vicky.

— Super ! Je vous avertirai aussitôt que je saurai quel jour exactement je dois m'y rendre. Est-ce la première fois que vous venez à Cuba ?

— Non, moi, je suis déjà venue une fois, mais je ne suis pas allée à La Havane…

S'ensuit une discussion à propos d'elles, de leur vie, leur travail d'enseignante, leur famille, et patati et patata. Comme Camila s'impatiente de son immobilité forcée, ainsi juchée sur les épaules de son père, elle grogne ce qui semble être une plainte avant de battre des pattes à vive allure sur la poitrine de son pauvre papa.

— *Bien, bien, vamos, vamos, mi corazón*[16], lui répond Sylvio pour la calmer un peu.

Les filles sourient en guise de *No problemo!*

— De toute façon, le temps file et ma femme doit me chercher. Vous avez vu ce petit modèle réduit quand elle n'est pas contente ? Vous pouvez donc très bien imaginer sa mère ! *¡Ja! ¡ja! ¡ja!* ajoute Sylvio en se prenant le front d'une main, mi-découragé, mi-hilare.

Les filles rigolent en le saluant, puis il quitte en direction du bar de la plage où il s'arrête brièvement pour parler à un des employés en poste.

Le sachant loin, Caroline se confie à ses amies :

— Il est vraiment trop fin, lui !

— Oui ! Et sa petite fille est tellement *cute*, renchérit Vicky.

— Il tente pas de nous *cruiser* non plus ; il nous parle de sa femme, complète Katia.

— Heureuse de constater que ça existe, du monde juste gentil, de nos jours !

Au même moment, le serveur du bar de la plage arrive près d'elles. Il tient en équilibre, sur un plateau, trois flûtes et un sceau de glace, qu'il dépose au bout de la chaise longue de Katia.

---

16. «Bien, bien, allons-y, allons-y, mon cœur!»

Dans un anglais acceptable, le type explique :

— Une livraison de la part de Sylvio. *¡El vino especial*[17] !

— Eh ben coudonc ! Lui, son projet me rejoint vraiment ! Plus que l'autre avec son jeu débile d'œufs dans le maillot ! clame Vicky, en extase devant la bouteille de vin mousseux.

— *¡Gracias !*

Pendant que l'employé regagne son poste, Katia saute aux conclusions :

— Vous voyez, c'est le propriétaire de la place, c'est certain ! Et c'est notre ami ! Trop génial !

Les filles terminent leur cocktail avant d'entamer la bouteille de vin, bien au frais dans le sceau.

— Toi, le beau Mike ?

— Aaah ! on dirait que j'ai de la misère à le cerner. Hier, l'avez-vous vu ? Il est parti de la discothèque en me disant un simple « Bye », sans trop montrer qu'il voulait qu'il se passe quelque chose entre nous.

— Oui, mais on était tous brûlés, justifie Caroline.

— Peut-être… J'avoue que tantôt, au bar, il m'a fait des yeux doux. C'est ce soir que ça se passe ou rien ! se convainc Katia, bien décidée à mettre le grappin dessus.

---

17. Ai-je vraiment besoin de traduire cela ?! ☺

— Hé, regardez là-bas! C'est quoi? demande Vicky à voix haute en désignant la plage au loin.

— Un... panda, remarque Caroline, l'air neutre comme jamais.

Comme de fait, un type habillé avec un costume représentant l'animal déambule avec joie sur la plage.

— Un panda?

— Ce doit être organisé par l'hôtel. Une mascotte pour amuser les enfants, peut-être?

— C'est certain, sinon qui, dans la vie, voyagerait avec un costume de panda dans ses valises[18]?

Au moment où les filles se servent des bulles dans une allégresse manifeste, un élément extérieur vient faire ombrage:

— Yo! les «ron coco»! crie Dave de très loin.

— Ah non, pas le fatigant..., murmure Katia entre ses dents.

— Vous m'excuserez, les filles, mais je vous le laisse. Urgence toilette. Be-bye! se défile Vicky en s'enfuyant, telle une joggeuse s'entraînant pour le marathon de Montréal,

---

18. Moi, j'en connais un... Ça vous dit quelque chose, les consœurs?

trop heureuse d'avoir «quelque chose d'important à faire» au moment crucial où la mouffette débarque.

Discrètement, Katia déconne avec ironie :

— Aaah ! T'es vraiment chanceuse d'avoir le «flu» pour vrai...

JOUR 8

AÉROPORT MONTRÉAL-TRUDEAU
SALLE 315 – **9 H 27**

Caroline, qui espère récupérer son téléphone cellulaire de manière imminente, fixe la porte comme si elle prophétisait que quelqu'un allait entrer d'une minute à l'autre.

— Hum..., émet Katia comme seul commentaire.

— Ouin..., ajoute Vicky.

— Je me souviens que je ne me posais pas de questions du tout à son sujet, se souvient Caroline, peu fière que sa présumée naïveté ait vraiment été totale cette fois.

— *A priori*, ce gars-là semblait correct, se rappelle Katia, songeuse et déçue de n'avoir jamais remis en doute les motivations profondes de l'homme qu'elles connaissaient à peine.

Vicky gigote de gauche à droite sur sa chaise, puis elle se frotte un peu le côté de la fesse droite du revers de la main. Caroline, qui l'observe du coin de l'œil, lui reproche instantanément son manque de discrétion :

— Vicky ?! Lâche-toi le derrière un peu...

— Eille, laisse faire ! C'est pas à toi que c'est arrivé, pis ça paraît. Je capote tellement, les filles !

— Tu vas être correcte, Vic. Ce doit être juste une niaiserie. Tu en auras le cœur net demain.

— J'espère tellement. Sinon, je dirai quoi à Marc ? Hein ? Il va jamais me croire.

Caroline, l'avocate en chef du diable, ne peut s'empêcher de commenter :

— Il faut avouer que c'était pas très, très brillant votre affaire, non plus.

— En matière de gestion d'urgence toilettes, je pense que t'es tout simplement pas autorisée à te prononcer, ma chère, lui reproche Vicky en se frottant à présent l'arrière-train sans aucune retenue.

— C'est vrai. Le comité gérant le droit ou non de faire la morale aux autres t'a carrément retiré ton droit de donner ton opinion sur la question, et ce, pour l'éternité..., approuve Katia en laissant s'échapper un petit rire spontané.

— OK, d'abord..., se désiste-t-elle, sachant très bien à quelle anecdote ses deux amies font référence.

JOUR 2

CUBA, VARADERO
COSTA AZUL DEL MAR RESORT

Vicky, ayant eu le malheur de revenir aux chaises longues après une demi-heure d'absence, doit tout de même endurer la mouffette qui ennuie tout le monde à mourir depuis déjà un petit moment avec une savoureuse histoire concernant son père lors d'une visite à la ferme. Elle s'est à peine installée dans sa chaise longue que Katia, n'en pouvant probablement plus du monologue de Dave, se lève à son tour et, pour une raison inconnue, prend la clé des champs. Dave ne se rend pas compte que les filles ne l'écoutent plus du tout, mais qu'elles méditent plutôt, le nez au vent. Cerveaux en fuite pour survivre. En plein milieu d'une phrase, Vicky se lève elle aussi pour retourner une fois de plus à la salle de bains. Remplie de compassion, Caroline lui demande :

— Pauvre toi ! Ça va pas encore ?

— Bah, il faut que j'y retourne... C'est pas grave.

Dave semble comprendre entre les branches de quoi elles parlent, et commente avec entrain :

— Avez-vous la chiasse ? Moi, le soir que j'ai mangé le plateau de fruits de mer, j'en ai eu pour trois jours à m'en remettre. Ha ! ha ! ha !

Vicky, qui s'éloignait d'un pas décidé, s'arrête d'un coup. Elle pivote tranquillement sur elle-même en entendant sa déclaration. Sa tête tourne lentement, comme dans les scènes au ralenti du film *La Matrice*. Elle fusille Dave d'un regard funeste, avant de s'indigner :

— T'aurais pu nous le dire, innocent ! T'es ben niaiseux de nous avoir conseillé d'en manger !?

— Ben, je me suis dit que ça m'arrivait à moi, mais peut-être pas aux autres, yo !

Vicky le fixe en grinçant des dents. Caroline baisse la tête.

— Câlin ? demande la mouffette pour détendre l'atmosphère.

— Ne-non... Cibole... laisse faire le câlin, vitupère Vicky qui s'éloigne en secouant la tête de découragement.

Chemin faisant, Vicky passe tout près de Katia qui discute avec le beau Mike et son fils au bar. En apercevant le visage décomposé de son amie, Katia saisit d'emblée sa détresse et lui fait signe de venir les rejoindre. Mais comme Vicky semble un peu pressée, Katia décide de laisser son *prospect* et son fiston en plan afin d'accompagner son amie pour faire la lumière sur la situation.

— Qu'est-ce qui se passe ? Tu te sens encore mal ?

— Pas si pire, mais il faut que j'y retourne. Mais tu sais pas la meilleure ? L'autre mouffette de con-d'inutile-de-la-vie vient de nous confier avoir eu super mal au ventre après avoir mangé le plateau de fruits de mer !

— Voyons? Gros colon! Il aurait pu nous mettre en garde à la place de nous dire de prendre ça...

— Je te le fais pas dire! Je te jure, j'avais le goût de lui donner une toute petite tapette en arrière de la tête avec ma chaise de plage! Mais bon, pour le moment, j'ai d'autres priorités...

En aboutissant à proximité des deux toilettes situées les plus près du bar de la plage, les filles constatent à leur grand désarroi qu'environ une dizaine de personnes y font déjà le pied de grue.

— Ah non..., rouspète Vicky en se tortillant comme un serpent de mer.

Rapide sur la gâchette et empreinte d'une sincère empathie à son égard, Katia propose à sa copine:

— Allons à celles que j'ai vues proches des spas, c'est toujours tranquille par là... Viens!

Une vacancière qui attend en queue de peloton les aborde au passage:

— Il fait plus chaud qu'hier, hein?

— Ben oui, ben oui, fait chaud, fait chaud, marmonne Vicky en prenant le large vers le petit chemin.

Toujours très compatissante au besoin pressant de son amie, Katia lui emboîte le pas à étripe-cheval. L'air d'avoir une olive coincée entre les deux fesses, Vicky la suit en avançant à pas de souris sur le pavé, craignant à tout moment de ne pas se rendre à temps. Atteignant enfin la petite maisonnette abritant les toilettes, elles sont ravies de constater que les lieux s'avèrent effectivement déserts.

— Merci pour la bonne idée, mon amie! apprécie Vicky en s'engouffrant dans une des deux cabines à la vitesse de l'éclair.

— De rien, répond Katia en entrant dans l'autre.

— Pfft, souffle Vicky en guise de soulagement, tandis qu'une musique de fond de bruits éloquents l'accompagne.

Pour masquer le tout, Katia se met à chanter très fort: «*Bará, bará, bará, berê, berê, berê...*» Comme elle termine la première, Katia sort et attend sur le seuil de la porte que son amie la rejoigne. Elle entend finalement Vicky qui chigne d'une petite voix:

— Katiaaaa? Y a plus de papier de toilette...

— Ah non! je viens juste de terminer le rouleau dans la mienne! Attends, je vais voir s'il y a du papier à main au lavabo.

Elle s'y rend, mais constate, hélas, qu'il n'y en a plus. Elle communique la navrante nouvelle à Vicky, qui hurle à tue-tête:

— Ben là, je fais QUOI?

— Euh... je sais pas. Veux-tu que j'aille au bar te chercher des essuie-tout?

— Ben non, c'est à l'autre bout du monde, ça va te prendre deux ans!

— Je sais pas quoi te dire, Vic…

— Je veux juste quelque chose pour m'essuyer, n'importe quoi, calvaire…

— La seule solution que j'entrevois serait de se dépanner *camping style* avec des feuilles…

— Des feuilles d'arbres ?

— Ouais.

Désinhibée par les bulles et motivée par son urgence sanitaire, Vicky accepte :

— Aaaah, pas le choix, trouve-moi-s'en !

Katia part en exploration aux alentours. Elle repère une plante à grand feuillage plus loin et en arrache quelques feuilles avant de revenir vers son amie pour les lui glisser sous la porte du cabinet.

— Ç'a pas de maudit bon sens… Dis JAMAIS ça à personne, toi[19] ! rigole tout de même Vicky, honteuse de la vulgarité de la scène.

— Promis ! Ha ! ha ! ha !

En sortant, Vicky regarde son amie et elles pouffent à l'unisson.

---

19. Ça restera entre nous…

— Bon, il ne s'est rien passé du tout... *Refill* de champagne?

— Oh que oui! Et il faut aller secourir Caro, qui se trouve certainement encore sous l'emprise de la mouffette!

Lorsque les filles arrivent enfin à la rescousse de la pauvre Caro, celle-ci discute avec la mouffette et Mathieu. Pince-sans-rire, Caroline met illico ses deux amies au courant d'un détail non négligeable:

— Les filles, Mathieu me disait que ça ne marchera pas, finalement, le Frisbee-aux-œufs.

— Hoooon, fait Vicky, comme si l'entièreté de ses vacances devenait tout à coup futile et sans intérêt.

— Trop dommage, oui. C'était trop compliqué. On trouvait pas de Frisbee, ils voulaient juste nous donner deux ou trois œufs au buffet, donc on oublie le jeu. Mais pas grave, on se reprend!

— C'est malheureux... ça avait l'air, comment dire? Su-per le *fun*! se désole Katia, en arborant elle aussi la mine d'une fille qui désire quasiment retourner à la maison sur le premier vol disponible tellement elle est déçue.

— Je sais..., envoie Mathieu, la tête basse et le bec à l'eau, puis il repart vers son groupe d'amis.

Dave-le-pot-de-colle, toujours présent, sourit à belles dents aux trois profs tout en se balançant d'avant en arrière, les mains dans les poches de son bermuda en jeans vert lime. L'intrus parti, il poursuit son histoire :

— Donc, je vais recommencer mon anecdote, vu que vous n'étiez pas là. Je racontais que, une fois, mon père, quand j'avais huit ans…

— Ah non, là ! Dave, excuse-nous, mais il faut vraiment qu'on parle entre filles, c'est sérieux, envoie Vicky avec empressement comme si elle avait été mandatée par l'Amérique au grand complet pour trouver une solution immédiate au conflit entourant la crise du pétrole au Moyen-Orient.

— Encore ?

— Oui ! renchérit Katia avec aplomb, espérant ainsi le voir s'en aller sans faire l'enfant.

— Bon, pas grave, je me suis fait plein d'amis par là-bas de toute façon, yo…

— Super, bye-bye !

Tandis qu'il se dirige d'un pas hésitant vers un autre groupe de vacanciers, Caroline partage ses remords de conscience :

— Il fait un peu pitié pareil…

— Ben oui, mais là, on passera pas la semaine avec lui, à écouter les souvenirs poches de son père sous prétexte «qu'il fait pitié», rationalise Katia.

— C'est beau vouloir être fine et à l'écoute, mais il est vrai-ment gossant. J'en reviens pas ! À cause de lui, je me suis payé une diarrhée à cinquante pesos, faut le faire, se plaint Vicky, dans la même veine.

— Je sais ben, mais...

Silence cubain.

— Changement de propos : je trouve *cute* le gars avec la camisole rouge, juste là. Je pense qu'il voyage tout seul, avoue Vicky en montrant du menton un homme qui bouquine, assis en solitaire près de la mer.

Les filles l'analysent un instant.

— Ouin, il est assez beau bonhomme. Petite bedaine, par contre. Bon, je vais aller prendre une douche. On réserve le catamaran pour quel jour, au juste ?

— Demain, ça serait l'idéal, je pense. Si on va à La Havane plus tard dans la semaine, ce serait bien de faire cette activité-là maintenant, propose Caroline.

— Moi, par contre, il faudrait que je me sente un peu mieux pour envisager passer des heures sur un bateau.

— Tu iras mieux demain, *no problemo*. C'est pas une vraie de vraie *turista*, ton affaire...

— T'as sûrement raison. On t'accompagne pour aller s'inscrire, alors.

Les filles se lèvent et suivent Caroline, visiblement à la tête des opérations.

— C'est par là, je m'en souviens.

— Cibole qu'il fait pas encore assez chaud à mon goût ! fait remarquer Vicky, prise d'un frisson en s'enroulant dans sa serviette de plage.

— Chut... «Ce dont on ne parle pas n'existe pas...»

JOUR 8

AÉROPORT MONTRÉAL-TRUDEAU
SALLE 315 – **9 H 34**

Pendant que Katia pianote sur la table la quatrième symphonie de Beethoven, le menton reposant au creux de sa main libre, Caroline tournicote encore une couette de sa queue-de-cheval défraîchie. Elle déprime une fois de plus à ce sujet :

— Mes maususses de cheveux...

— C'est pas si pire, Caro, pour vrai, tente Vicky pour l'apaiser.

— Pas besoin d'être fine, je sais que c'est horrible.

— C'était quand même notre meilleur souper du voyage, ce soir-là. Je pense que c'est la seule fois où j'ai mangé un repas complet.

— Moi aussi, approuve à son tour Vicky.

— C'est vraiment long leur affaire, eux autres, hein ?

— Oui, en effet. J'ai hâte de pouvoir donner des nouvelles à Éric... et d'en recevoir aussi, avoue Caroline, dont le timbre de voix est teinté d'ironie.

— Pauvre toi, c'est plate, être dans le doute de même. Disons que je te comprends, ma chère! compatit Vicky sur un ton laissant croire qu'elle a, à l'évidence, de bonnes raisons de sympathiser.

— Mets-en, je me sens tout croche, approuve Caro.

Celle-ci se remet à triturer nerveusement une de ses mèches en fixant le revêtement industriel gris pâle recouvrant le plancher de la terne salle d'interrogatoire 315.

Dans la lune, elle soupire :

— Et il va me voir la tête de même, en plus...

JOUR 2

CUBA, VARADERO
COSTA AZUL DEL MAR RESORT

En route vers le buffet, les filles s'examinent – vestimentairement[20] parlant – avec désolation.

— Ça fait juste trois jours qu'on est habillées pareil. Mon linge long n'est pas sale du tout, non, non, non!

---

20. Très beau pour mon *Petit Dubois illustré, ça!*

ironise Vicky en descendant un peu les manches de son chandail bleu marin en fin lainage, l'air déshonoré.

— Sérieusement, s'il fait encore froid demain soir, je dois absolument trouver du savon à linge pour pouvoir au moins laver mon chandail, annonce Caroline.

— Tu vois, nous aurions besoin illico presto d'un Québécois prêt à discuter de météo! déconne Katia en pivotant comme si elle s'apprêtait sérieusement à faire du recrutement dans les parages.

Les filles consultent ensemble l'ardoise posée sur un chevalet de bois à l'entrée du restaurant: on y annonce une thématique italienne pour le buffet du soir. Les pâtes étant un mets bien difficile à bousiller, elles ont bon espoir d'enfin pouvoir se régaler. En fait, et pour tout dire, elles sont si heureuses que si elles ne se retenaient pas, elles se mettraient à applaudir.

Ayant choisi une table à proximité de la terrasse, le trio s'amuse de l'accoutrement d'une voyageuse qui écrit dans un carnet, un peu plus loin.

— Elle porte une tuque dans le Sud[21], ça donne une idée du temps qu'il fait. Pose-nous avec elle en arrière-plan, demande Caroline en sortant son téléphone portable.

---

21. Ah, la fille avec la tuque, c'était moi! J'espionnais les trois profs en vacances à Cuba... ☺

— Quand c'est rendu que tu envies une fille habillée en hiver… On s'entend qu'on va attendre de porter notre linge d'été avant de se vanter sur Facebook d'être en voyage dans le Sud, se désole Vicky.

— Non, je veux pas mettre cette photo-là sur Facebook. Elle est pour nous seulement, en souvenir!

— Ben oui, j'imagine déjà le statut: «Allo tout le monde, nous sommes heureuses d'être à Cuba, il fait si chaud! *Yeah!*» Et tu vois une fille avec une tuque en arrière-plan, déclare Katia.

— Tu finis pas avouer: «OK, il fait plus froid qu'au Québec en ce moment…» *Big fail!*

Katia prend tout de même la photo de Caro et Vicky avec la fille derrière, juste pour le plaisir.

Une fois le vin rouge commandé à la serveuse, le trio se dirige vers le buffet où deux chefs aux longs chapeaux blancs confectionnent des pâtes sur mesure pour les clients. Il y a aussi, dispersés çà et là sur le buffet, des plats de pâtes déjà mélangées.

Katia murmure entre ses dents, à l'intention de ses amies:

— Prends pas celles aux fruits de mer, Vicky…

— Merci du conseil! Sérieux, j'en mangerai plus jamais de ma vie, je pense!

Divers aliments reposent dans de petits culs-de-poule devant les cuisiniers en poste derrière deux plaques chauffantes rehaussées d'un grand wok. Caroline montre au premier cuistot des piments verts coupés grossièrement, des champignons – en boîte, qui semblent un peu visqueux – et une sauce tomate un peu orangée et séchée sur le dessus, comme si elle reposait à l'air libre depuis des heures. Il mélange alors le tout dans un poêlon, ajoute des linguines déjà cuites à la mixture, puis fait habilement sauter le tout en propulsant le contenu du poêlon bien haut dans les airs avant de rattraper l'entièreté de la nourriture.

Vicky, qui a remarqué un fait étrange, demande à ses amies :

— Le gars qui fait sauter les pâtes, c'est le *lifeguard* qu'on voit toujours près de la plage ou j'hallucine ?

— Ah ouin ? s'étonne Caroline, pas certaine.

— Ben oui, c'est lui ! Vive les doubles tâches ! Il faut être polyvalent pour travailler dans un *résore* !

Vicky et Katia décident de plagier intégralement le choix de plat de Caroline, question de ne pas risquer à nouveau d'être victimes d'inconfort intestinal. De retour à leur table, elles entament le repas en mastiquant longtemps leur première bouchée.

— C'est pas de la grande gastronomie, mais ça fait la *job* !

— C'est juste de la sauce tomate en boîte, mais bon. Au moins, on remarque moins le fameux goût de beurre ou d'huile rance, émet Caroline.

— On va juste boire plus de vin! conclut Katia en s'envoyant une bonne rasade de *vino tinto* derrière la cravate.

Elle pose son verre de rouge et avale sa gorgée de travers en déclarant:

-*My God*, que mon vin est pas bon! C'est épouvantable!

— Moi, il est pas si pire...

La serveuse ayant terminé la bouteille dans le verre de Katia, celui-ci ne goûte pas la même chose que celui de Vicky et de Caroline, qui provient d'une seconde bouteille.

— Leurs grands crus sont variables, on dirait. Un verre, il est passable, et l'autre, il est pas buvable.

— On appelle ça des cépages aléatoires. C'est d'autant plus louche que j'ai bien vu que les deux bouteilles étaient identiques.

— C'est vrai..., songe Caroline à voix haute. J'avais moi aussi remarqué que les bouteilles sont toutes débouchées à l'avance... Peut-être qu'ils font juste les remplir?

— Oui, et c'est le *lifeguard*-chef cuisiner qui est également chargé de fabriquer le vin de contrebande dans son sous-sol, pouffe Vicky.

— Ha! ha! ha! vous êtes ben drôles, mais en attendant, j'ai toujours pas de vin potable à boire, moi! se plaint Katia qui essaie d'attirer l'attention d'une serveuse fuyante.

Caroline sort son téléphone portable de son sac et regarde furtivement pour voir si elle a reçu des messages. Vicky remarque son stratagème et lui demande si elle a eu des nouvelles de sa petite famille.

— Non. Je vais tenter de parler à Éric demain. On dirait que ça va ordinaire un peu, lui et moi, depuis un temps.

— Ah ouin?

— Je le sens distant, comme absent. On s'obstinait plus que d'habitude, aussi, avant que je parte, explique Caroline.

— Bizarre... tu comprends pas pourquoi?

— Non...

— Bah, ça vous fera du bien de passer une semaine à vous ennuyer l'un de l'autre, tente Vicky pour apaiser son amie, qui semble fort préoccupée par la situation.

Katia fait de grands signes à la serveuse pour lui indiquer qu'elle désire commander d'autre vin. Elle annonce avec désolation:

— Simonaque, il est sept heures du soir pis je suis même pas chaudaille!

— Mets-toi surtout pas de pression, réagit Caroline en grimaçant.

— C'est beau de pas répéter les mêmes erreurs, mais franchement, on est ben trop à jeun depuis le début de notre voyage plate de matantes «ron coco»!

— Je suis d'accord ! Il faut se reprendre pour rentrer dans notre argent, affirme Vicky en levant à son tour son verre de vin, prête à le boire d'un trait au compte de trois. Ils feront pas d'argent avec nous autres ! Tchin-tchin !

La serveuse qui arrive – enfin ! – ressert une nouvelle coupe à Katia, celle-ci ayant discrètement remisé la précédente sous la table pour ne pas avoir à la boire[22].

L'homme qui lisait sur la plage et qui avait capté l'intérêt de Vicky en fin de journée passe près de leur table, toujours seul, une assiette vide en main. Comme elle le dévisage, il lui sourit.

— Lui…, avoue-t-elle à la troupe sans étoffer davantage son commentaire rempli de sous-entendus coquins.

— Ton candidat pour «*frencher*-rien-que», peut-être ?

— Hum… Je pense que oui ! Ça me dérange pas, moi, les petites bedaines. Je trouve ça *cute*, même.

Ayant finalement mis à exécution leur noble projet de consommer plus d'alcool, les filles rient très fort à table depuis que Katia a carrément fait la demande qu'on leur apporte une bouteille de vin rouge complète.

---

22. J'ai vu ça… Eh oui !

— Sans blague, je suis quand même encore fatiguée. Le bon vin m'endort. Il me faudrait un petit remontant, avoue Caroline en bâillant, tout en faisant tourner entre ses doigts le pied circulaire de son verre de vin.

— Le «bon» vin, je te trouve généreuse, avec ton qualificatif, envoie Katia.

Caro, songeuse, flatte la nappe bourgogne avec ses deux paumes pour y faire disparaître quelques plis disgracieux.

— Moi aussi, je suis encore claquée. C'est super pratique les vols de nuit. En arrivant à destination, t'es brûlée de ta nuit blanche pendant trois jours. Ensuite, t'as trois jours de *break* où t'es plus en forme et, après, tu reviens de nuit, donc t'es à terre pour un autre trois jours ! Vraiment ! Vive les vacances ! exagère Vicky, aussi cernée qu'un vampire anémique.

Un Cubain, qui semble préparer des cafés spéciaux sur commande pour les touristes, passe près d'elles en bringuebalant une desserte sur roulettes.

— Ah oui ! Un bon café !

Caroline lui envoie un signe de la main. L'employé pousse alors son chariot vers leur table, enchanté de trouver des preneuses pour son service. Dans un anglais très limité, il explique sommairement les choix disponibles en présentant les bouteilles d'alcool associées à chacune des recettes. Caroline choisit le café «*Cuba especial*» aromatisé de liqueur de noisette, de rhum et de crème irlandaise. Le serveur allume alors un petit brûleur de propane pour infuser le café dans un percolateur.

Une fois le café prêt, à peine quelques minutes plus tard, il le verse dans une petite carafe en inox, puis il y ajoute une sorte d'épice brune qu'il qualifie de «secrète». Avec l'agilité prodigieuse d'un barman comptant plusieurs années de service, l'homme mélange la liqueur de noisette et le rhum dans un autre contenant pour ensuite les transvider de récipient en récipient dans le simple but de se donner en spectacle. Il embrase ensuite la mixture d'alcool, puis il poursuit en incorporant avec délicatesse la crème irlandaise à la surface du café régulier qu'il a préalablement versé dans une tasse de verre transparente. La crème créant une barrière, il fait ensuite couler l'alcool qui brûle toujours sur le dessus.

— Wow! se réjouit Caro en recevant son café trois étages dont la flamme bleutée grimpe encore jusqu'à la hauteur de ses yeux.

Un peu hypnotisée, elle fixe un instant l'ondulation saccadée de la flamme avant de faire un grand saut.

— HIP! crie-t-elle.

La mouffette, qui, comme toute bonne mouffette, vient de surgir de nulle part, lui plante avec robustesse les doigts dans les flancs dans le but de la surprendre. Afin de voir qui vient de l'assaillir de la sorte, elle se tourne brusquement. Au passage, le bout de sa tresse balaie la flamme ardente de son café et s'embrase. En une fraction de seconde, le serveur attrape une serviette de table de ratine noire qui reposait sur sa desserte et il l'enroule autour des cheveux de Caroline sans trop de ménagement. Réalisant tout à coup que quelqu'un tente d'éteindre sa couette en feu, Caroline se met à crier comme un putois:

— AAAAAAAAAAH!

Un silence presque complet s'installe dans le vaste restaurant. Stupéfaite face à la scène tragique, Vicky porte la main à sa bouche, sous le choc. Katia se lève de sa chaise, prête à intervenir. Hélas, jugeant que les dommages collatéraux doivent avoir été maîtrisés, le serveur retire sa serviette avec lenteur. Prise de panique, Caroline crache en direction de Dave:

— Voyons, gros cave! Qu'est-ce que tu fais!?

— Oups, je pensais pas que... yo...

N'ayant pas ressenti de sensation de brûlure en tant que telle, Caroline pousse un peu la main du serveur – alias son sauveur – afin de constater par elle-même les dégâts capillaires. Une forte odeur de cheveux calcinés embaume l'endroit dans un spectre assez large pour que les gens des deux tables d'à côté esquissent des mimiques éloquentes. Caroline estime que seulement la pointe des cheveux a été brûlée, le reste n'ayant été atteint qu'en surface. Elle reprend donc ses esprits et elle se tourne vers la mouffette, debout de biais avec elle. Les yeux de Caro lui lançant des missiles gorgés de colère, l'accusé recule de deux pas. De petits pas préventifs que son instinct juge nécessaire d'exécuter pour assurer sa survie potentielle dans ce bas monde.

— Coudonc, toi!? Es-tu venu au monde pour me faire chier, criss? hurle Caroline, complètement hors d'elle.

Puis, touchant avec désolation le bout de ses cheveux rabougris, elle pleurniche :

— Voyons donc, mes cheveux...

Vicky lève des yeux sidérés vers son amie. Elle ne l'a jamais vue aussi en furie de toute sa sainte vie.

— T'es lourd, toi, hein ? Le savais-tu ? vocifère Katia en enlignant la mouffette qui recule à nouveau de quelques pas, craignant plus que jamais de ne pas s'en sortir vivante.

— C'est un a-cci-dent... Je m'ex-cu-seeee, dit-il platement.

Puis Dave s'éloigne en ne semblant pas éprouver plus de remords.

— Je vais le tuer, sérieux... Je vais le tuer !

— C'est pas si pire, pour de vrai, Caro, la console Vicky, triste de constater que deux pouces de la chevelure de son amie ont littéralement fondu.

Une Cubaine en uniforme, qui semble en charge de la salle à manger, arrive au trot, alertée par le brouhaha entourant la catastrophe. Elle demande si tout va bien en toisant avec mépris le serveur, car elle en déduit à tort qu'il est responsable de l'incident. Celui-ci lève les deux bras en clamant son innocence, puis il explique la scène à sa supérieure avec l'impétuosité d'un être luttant pour sa survie. Maintenant au courant des faits, celle-ci touche le bras de Caroline pour tenter de l'apaiser. Toujours en beau fusil, Caro se lève et déguerpit vers la chambre, pressée de trouver un miroir.

Cinq minutes plus tard, Vicky et Katia arrivent en trombe à l'*habitación*, munies de leur verre de vin, de celui de Caroline ainsi que d'une nouvelle bouteille. Un petit remontant ne sera pas de trop, compte tenu du possible état de détresse de leur compagne à la tête roussie.

— Je ca-po-te! les avertit Caroline en les voyant passer le seuil.

En effet, ses cheveux maintenant libres laissent voir que ce n'est pas seulement le bout de sa couette qui a été touché. Comme sa tresse était du côté gauche, des strates de cheveux du côté droit s'avèrent désormais un peu plus courts que tout le reste.

— Caro, c'est pas si pire, il faudrait juste que tu coupes, genre, deux pouces, propose Vicky, un ton de désolation charitable dans la voix.

— Il a failli me faire passer au feu, l'autre zouf! s'indigne Caroline en imaginant le pire.

Katia, qui souhaite alléger l'atmosphère, cite les propos vociférés par son amie un peu plus tôt, et ce, en accentuant le blasphème – pas du tout dans les habitudes langagières de cette dernière :

— As-tu réellement dit : «Es-tu venu au monde pour me faire chier, CRISS ?»

Katia se tait en attendant la réaction de sa pauvre copine en peine. Vicky et Katia ne peuvent finalement pas se retenir et elles pouffent de rire. Caroline finit par les imiter.

— Eille, j'ai vraiment dit ça à quelqu'un...

— Et mon autre Katia qui rajoute : «T'es lourd toi, hein? Le savais-tu?» En ce moment, le pauvre gars doit être en train de se faire hara-kiri avec un couteau à beurre à genoux devant le comptoir à pain du buffet, exagère Vicky.

— Non mais, tsé, il fait peut-être pitié un peu, mais m'as-tu vu l'énergumène fatiguant!? Rien à faire avec lui, conclut Katia, en reservant du *vino tinto* à Caroline.

La voyant toujours en état de dépression avancée devant la glace, à tenter de déterminer ce qu'elle doit faire de ses cheveux, Vicky prend en charge la résolution du problème.

— On va trouver une coiffeuse demain. Il y en a peut-être une directement dans l'hôtel?

— Ouin... Je suis donc ben pas chanceuse avec mes maususses de cheveux! se désole Caro, attristée par son karma capillaire désastreux.

Installées sur la terrasse de leur chambre, les filles terminent la bouteille de vin en placotant. Vicky agrippe son téléphone. Du balcon, elles ont la chance de capter sporadi-quement le WiFi – lorsque celui-ci fonctionne, bien entendu. Comme il lui reste du temps sur la carte d'une heure qu'elle a achetée le matin même, elle se connecte sur Facebook. Sur le fil de nouvelles qui déroule, elle aperçoit des photos de Marc en vacances à Vegas avec trois de ses amis.

— Bon, son ami vient de mettre des photos…

Les filles la laissent constater les faits en silence. Comme elle fait instantanément une moue offusquée, Katia demande :

— Qu'est-ce qu'il y a ? Montre…

Deux des trois photos présentent les gars, ensemble à l'hôtel : l'une dans la chambre et la deuxième, sur le balcon. Le dernier cliché les montre dans le bar d'un casino où des filles souriantes en robes de soirée se trouvent près d'eux, assises sur des tabourets.

— Vicky, c'est sûr qu'ils rencontrent du monde et qu'ils leur parlent !

— Pfft ! Ben oui, je sais, je m'en fous !

Comme Vicky observe intensément la photo en l'agrandissant dans son téléphone à écran tactile pour scruter de plus près les filles en question, Katia adresse une mimique amusée à Caroline, étonnée du fait que son amie soit si jalouse.

Quelque temps plus tard, Katia s'étire un peu tandis que Vicky bâille un bon coup.

— Bon, il faudrait qu'on bouge, sinon je vais cailler sur place, annonce Katia en secouant la tête rapidement, l'air de vouloir se réveiller.

— Moi aussi! On va à la discothèque du *résore*? Faut que je «*frenche*-rien-que», envoie Vicky, une pointe évidente de vengeance dans la voix.

— *Yes*, madame!

— Avant, on prend une photo..., ordonne Vicky en levant bien haut son téléphone intelligent.

— Ah, je suis comme pas dedans, s'oppose Caro en se touchant la tête.

— Non, non, et on fait des faces de filles qui vivent les vacances de leur vie. Allez! commande Vicky, un peu bête, tout en affichant un visage de bonheur extrême.

Comme elle a retourné l'écran pour que les filles puissent se voir, elles s'exécutent. Vicky vérifie le cliché et commente:

— Non! Caro, t'as l'air dépressive, pis moi j'ai comme un double menton... on recommence...

Elle positionne son téléphone pour faire un second *selfie* de groupe.

Dix minutes plus tard, les filles prennent leur énième photo.

— Non, on dirait qu'on n'a pas assez de *fun*, leur reproche Vicky en voulant alors en prendre une autre.

— *Fuck off*, là, je suis tannée, se plaint Katia en se levant. La dixième était pas pire, non?

Résignée, Vicky télécharge sur son profil Facebook celle qui semble à ses yeux la meilleure du lot.

— Tiens ! Il va bien voir que nous aussi on s'amuse, bon ! dit Vicky, toujours frustrée.

— On s'amuse, c'est ma-la-de…, réagit Katia en voyant le visage aigri de son amie tout en bâillant aux corneilles.

Caroline soupire bruyamment en jouant avec ses cheveux. Silence.

— Facebook, méchante arnaque pareil. Présentement, tout le monde est certain qu'on vit le *highlight* de notre vie, alors qu'en vérité on pense juste à aller se coucher, souligne Katia. Je pense que je suis pas encore assez chaude.

— Justement, on s'en va à la discothèque ! Envoyez, ordonne Vicky d'un ton plus brusque qu'enjoué.

— Wow. Dis de même, c'est super invitant…

— Pas moi, les filles. Ça me tente pas. Je vais essayer de parler à Éric et je vais me coucher. De toute façon, regardez-moi la tête…

À la suite de cette dernière remarque, les deux filles n'ont pas d'autre choix que d'approuver la sage décision de leur amie.

— Bon, demain à la première heure, on arrange tes cheveux, Caro, promet Vicky en se repoudrant un peu le nez devant le miroir de la salle de bain.

JOUR 8
AÉROPORT MONTRÉAL-TRUDEAU
SALLE 315 – **9 H 39**

En se remémorant la triste scène de ses cheveux bousillés de manière fortuite, Caroline secoue la tête avant de colérer[23] une fois de plus :

— S'il m'avait dit «Câlin?» à ce moment-là, je l'aurais assassiné avec le percolateur en *stainless* du Cubain.

— «Viens! Je vais te faire un beau câlin avec mon poing dans ta face…», renchérit Katia en menaçant le vide, comme si elle répondait à la demande de la mouffette, les yeux chargés d'une rage inspirée candidement du film *Massacre à la tronçonneuse*.

— Et c'est là que j'ai appris pour Éric... Une maususse de belle soirée de voyage, ça, poursuit Caroline, dans un tout autre ordre d'idées.

— Ça va s'arranger, Caro. Je suis certaine que c'est juste un gros malentendu, réagit Katia, fermement convaincue que Caro crie au loup pour rien avec cette histoire.

— J'espère..., soupire Caroline, le visage à nouveau décomposé au beau milieu de la petite salle 315.

---

23. Le verbe «colérer» devrait déjà exister depuis longtemps, il me semble, non?

Silence pesant. Les filles guettent le néon qui peine encore à rester allumé de façon continue. Contrairement au tube fluorescent, Caroline semble tout à coup prise d'une illumination face à ladite soirée.

— C'est bien ce soir-là que c'est arrivé, l'histoire du gars qui était tout seul?

— Cibole! Il n'est RIEN arrivé, c'est ça l'affaire!

— Mais pourquoi que ç'a fait une grosse histoire de même, d'abord? Je comprends pas trop ce drame-là, je dois avouer, insiste Caroline, qui désire enfin jeter la lumière sur le sujet.

— Tout le monde a capoté pour rien, à cause de l'autre folle. Cet hôtel-là était plein de monde *fucké* dans la tête, voilà tout! rage Vicky, maintenant rendue sous les projecteurs au banc des accusés.

La lumière vacille toujours.

JOUR 2
CUBA, VARADERO
COSTA AZUL DEL MAR RESORT

L'ambiance de la discothèque pleine à craquer atteignant un niveau latino-festif plus qu'endiablé, les vacanciers improvisent tous des mérengués plutôt maladroits au rythme de la musique suave rugie par les grands haut-parleurs. Dans la zone du bar, Vicky et Katia discutent avec les gens autour, dont Mike et son fils qui ont pris place près d'elles.

— La vie, c'est comme une boîte de chocolats: on sait jamais ce qu'on va déballer, philosophe le soufflé de Drummond venu se joindre à l'improviste au groupe de voyageurs.

— Excuse-moi, mais tu l'as prise dans *Forrest Gump*, celle-là! s'interloque Vicky, ravie de coincer le pseudo-théoricien-songé du dimanche.

— Bah... pfft... mais j'ai..., s'embourbe-t-il, incapable d'organiser adéquatement sa défense.

D'orgueil, il redresse ses larges épaules vers l'arrière et ose pousser la note encore plus loin:

— Je me suis peut-être un peu inspiré, mais j'ai changé pour «déballer» alors qu'il disait «sur quoi on va tomber»... Ah!

— Meuh..., maugrée Vicky en roulant des yeux.

Démuni, il se cambre un peu le dos et s'éloigne vers un autre groupe de voyageurs en zigzaguant comme un skieur de slalom dans la foule dense, faisant mine d'hésiter entre plusieurs groupes de gens, l'air de se croire en demande comme jamais auparavant dans sa vie. Sa balade impro-visée se termine finalement aux abords d'un groupe de filles qui ne semblent même pas remarquer sa présence.

Mike rigole en s'informant auprès de Katia:

— Euh... c'était quoi, ça?

— Un grand penseur des temps modernes du Centre-du-Québec! T'avais pas remarqué? Tu m'étonnes.

— Oui, oui... De toute façon, on s'aperçoit dès le premier coup d'œil qu'il a une *shape* d'intellectuel, ironise Mike en adoptant une pose réfléchie.

Cédric, tout aussi sarcastique que son père, en rajoute :

— Je pense que je l'ai déjà vu dans une capsule Web, ce gars-là. Son propos était vraiment philosophique, justement. C'était quoi donc ? Ah oui ! C'était : «*Chest*, bras, bras, *chest, chest,* bras[24]...»

Complice de son fils, Mike poursuit avec un air sérieux de curé pendant la messe de Pâques :

— C'était pas plutôt «... *chest,* bras, bras», à la fin ?

— Ha ! ha ! ha ! Peu importe, c'est certain que c'est lui ! approuve Katia.

Vicky, qui s'amuse follement des couillonnades des deux gars, semble tout à coup un peu déconcentrée. Elle vient de repérer sa proie au loin, c'est-à-dire le gars seul à la petite bedaine. Elle tape le bras de Katia pour lui signifier de façon officielle qu'elle part à la chasse. À pas de loup en talons hauts, elle s'approche du type qui retient son attention depuis le début des vacances.

Comme s'il attendait sa venue, il l'accueille aussitôt d'un grand sourire charmant.

— Salut !

---

24. *Chest*-bras-de-Drummond, voilà maintenant son nom !

— Salut!

Fin trentaine, Simon arbore un *look* décontracté rehaussé d'une casquette des Blue Jays. N'étant pas celui que l'on remarque d'emblée pour sa belle apparence, le gars ressemble au type classique «petit banlieusard» sans histoire buvant une bière-Clamato le samedi avant le dîner tout en nettoyant sa piscine. Une barbe de quelques jours un peu rouquine lui confère un petit je-ne-sais-quoi irlandais.

Après les présentations d'usage et les échanges de détails comprenant les classiques: «Tu viens d'où?» et «T'es ici depuis quand?», le duo bascule avec brio en plein cœur du sujet «température». Comment y échapper...

— C'est pas chaud pour le Sud, hein?

— Eille, non! On s'attendait pas à ça...

Tout en discutant, Simon ne peut s'empêcher de rigoler en apercevant au loin la mouffette qui se trémousse comme un déchaîné sur la piste de danse. N'effectuant pas du tout les mouvements communs aux danses latines, il semble plutôt improviser un cours de Zumba en solo.

— Méchant spécimen, ce gars-là, pareil, affirme-t-il comme s'il le connaissait déjà.

— Tu dis! Tu l'as rencontré, toi aussi? Il a mis le feu à ma *chum* de fille tantôt au buffet!

— Quoi?

Vicky lui raconte la scène avec moult détails. Simon rit aux éclats. En riant de la sorte, une petite fossette se dessine sur sa joue droite, mais pas sur celle de gauche. Craquant.

Vicky s'esclaffe aussi, malgré sa grande compassion pour Caroline.

— On rit, mais c'est quand même pas si drôle...

— Moi, il m'a abordé sur la plage avant-hier en pensant que j'étais gai. En fait, il a foncé droit sur moi, comme un vrai maniaque !

— T'es pas gai ? le taquine Vicky en lui envoyant un clin d'œil.

— Non, mademoiselle, affirme Simon en souriant à sa charmante compagne du moment.

JOUR 8
AÉROPORT MONTRÉAL-TRUDEAU
SALLE 315 – 9 H 40

— La façon dont tu nous décris la scène, tout serait de sa faute ! tempête Katia en cognant son poing sur la table.

— Les filles, c'est carrément sa faute. Aucun doute là-dessus ! approuve Vicky, en détournant la tête pour fixer le carrelage du plancher.

— Méchant moron, lui aussi!

— Et je lui avais demandé d'être discret en plus… Merci, tsé! se fâche Vicky.

— Pas fort…

Vicky poursuit son histoire afin de rafraîchir la mémoire des filles:

— En fait, quand on s'est éclipsés de la discothèque…

JOUR 2
CUBA, VARADERO
COSTA AZUL DEL MAR RESORT

Simon, qui discute avec Vicky depuis plus d'une heure, termine son verre de bière d'un trait et se lève. Constatant l'imminence de son départ, Vicky demande:

— Tu t'en vas?

— Ouais, je suis encore un peu fatigué du vol de nuit…

— Moi aussi. Je rentre avec toi, alors.

À la hâte, Vicky passe indiquer à Katia qu'elle rentre à sa chambre et elle rejoint illico Simon qui l'attend déjà près de la porte. Les photos douteuses de Marc l'ayant motivée plus que jamais à mener à terme son projet «je *frenche*-rien-que», elle le suit en marchant très près. Désinhibée par l'alcool ingurgité autant que par la réceptivité évidente du gars, Vicky se tourne vers lui aussitôt qu'ils se retrouvent à l'écart des regards.

— Je te trouve vraiment charmant, Simon…, amorce-t-elle en s'avançant vers lui pour l'embrasser sans mettre davantage la table.

Leurs lèvres ont à peine le temps de s'effleurer que Simon la prend par les épaules pour la repousser avec hésitation.

— Oooh, un instant…, balbutie-t-il en guise d'explication.

Un peu étonnée de se faire ainsi maintenir à distance, Vicky demande :

— Quoi ?

— Euh, c'est que… je ne suis pas disponible.

— Aaah ! si t'as une relation pas officielle comme moi au Québec, ben, c'est pas grave ! On est dans le Sud, on s'amuse, l'encourage Vicky en avançant vers lui pour une deuxième tentative.

Il s'esquive de plus belle et détourne la tête.

— Voyons ? se surprend Vicky, un peu dans le néant.

— Non, non, tu comprends pas. Je n'ai pas une relation pas claire, j'ai une relation tout court et… ma blonde est ici, en voyage avec moi.

— Quoi ? Où ça ?

— Dans la chambre, elle est malade. Le premier soir, on a payé un supplément pour aller dans un resto sans réservation et elle a mangé une assiette de fruits de mer. Depuis, elle se sent pas très bien, disons.

— Franchement! T'aurais pu me le dire plus tôt!

— Je pensais pas que tu pensais que nous deux...

— Me semble que c'était évident qu'on flirtait, non?!

— Non, justement. Tu parles jamais à des gars sans vouloir les *frencher*, toi?

— Pfft! Ouais, souvent!

— C'est ce que je pensais. C'est pas grave, Vicky. C'est même très flatteur, d'ailleurs, crois-moi.

— C'est surtout humiliant...

— Arrête ça! Je le prends comme un compliment, je te jure.

— Dis ça à personne, s'il te plaît, j'ai l'air trop conne.

— Inquiète-toi pas. Sens-toi pas mal à l'aise non plus! Ce sont des choses qui arrivent. Avoir été tout seul..., et il lui adresse une mimique sous-entendant une évidence n'ayant pas besoin d'être nommée.

— OK, bon ben... bonne soirée.

— Salut!

Désenchantée et tout de même un peu honteuse devant son échec, Vicky s'éloigne pour se diriger vers sa chambre. Elle rebrousse finalement chemin et décide de retourner au bar, question de noyer à fond sa déconfiture. En l'apercevant, Katia – en proie à un état d'ivresse fort avancé – présume, en parlant fort :

— Ayoye, c'est vraiment pas long quand tu «*frenches*-rien-que»!

— Pfft! Laisse faire... *Shooter*?

JOUR 3
CUBA, VARADERO
COSTA AZUL DEL MAR RESORT

Le soleil, qui perce vaillamment à travers la mince fente entre les deux rideaux de la porte-fenêtre, pourrait laisser croire qu'il fait extrêmement chaud à l'extérieur. Caroline, déjà réveillée depuis plus de trente minutes, fait un brin de lecture au lit en attendant que Vicky bouge un peu.

— Ouf..., marmonne enfin la dormeuse en relevant légèrement la tête pour finalement l'enfouir bien profond entre ses deux oreillers.

— Bon, j'avais hâte que tu te réveilles. J'essaie de lire depuis tantôt, mais je suis comme incapable de me concentrer. Vic, je capote! Mon *chum* me trompe, pleurniche Caroline.

— Quoi?

— Hier, quand vous êtes parties, je suis allée au café Internet pour lui parler sur Skype parce que le WiFi ne fonctionnait plus ici. Je lui ai envoyé un message Facebook quand j'ai vu qu'il était en ligne. Pendant ce temps-là, je regardais le fil de nouvelles. Et là, j'ai vu qu'il avait récemment ajouté à ses amis une certaine «Julie Massé». Je regarde c'est qui, et là, je réalise que je la connais pas pantoute cette fille-là. Genre pitoune, super belle, avec plein de photos pas pire *sexy* sur son profil. Mon *chum* était toujours en ligne, mais il me répondait pas. J'ai réécrit: «Allo???». Il a lu mon message presque tout de suite – je le sais parce que j'ai vu le petit crochet en bas – mais il m'a pas répondu. J'ai attendu, genre, dix minutes et il ne m'a jamais donné de nouvelles... Il parlait avec elle, c'est sûr!

— C'est qui, la fille?

— Aucune idée. Ils n'ont pas d'amis en commun. Je te le dis, je capote! Le balancier de la vie me remet dans la face mes niaiseries du passé, regrette-t-elle, en mille miettes au beau milieu de son lit.

— Eille! C'est rendu que tu parles comme le soufflé de Drummond. Attends donc avant de sauter aux conclusions. Il y a sûrement une explication logique.

Caroline dépose son roman sur la table de chevet et elle se met à observer le mur devant elle avec un intérêt presque maniaque. Vicky, qui semble se remettre difficilement des excès de la veille, détaille pour sa part le plafond, ne sachant pas trop quoi ajouter.

Les filles entendent alors des pas dans le corridor. Quelqu'un cogne à la porte.

— ¡*Holaaa*! ¿*Mini barrr*? clame le même employé avec son accent toujours trop sensuel compte tenu de la nature de sa tâche.

— Aaaah! Pas encore lui! s'offusque Caro.

— ¡*Holaaa*! ¿*Mini barrr*? réitère le type qui cogne également à la chambre de Katia.

— AAAAAH! Simonaque! crie Katia de son lit.

Malgré son anxiété, Caroline ne peut s'empêcher de pouffer de rire après quelques secondes. Vicky aussi. Comme il récidive une troisième fois, Caro se lève pour aller ouvrir afin de lui dire qu'elles n'ont besoin de rien et, du coup, éviter que Katia l'assomme raide avec sa lampe de chevet.

Après dix minutes passées à rebattre les oreilles de Vicky avec les pires scénarios d'infidélité de la terre, Caroline se lève afin d'entrouvrir les rideaux de la porte-fenêtre.

— Gros soleil... me semble, oui, c'est sûrement une simple illusion. Si j'ouvre la porte, je gage que je vais constater qu'il fait huit degrés en réalité.

D'un coup de poignet décidé, elle fait glisser les deux pans de tissu beige sur la tringle. Le soleil qui pénètre à grands coups de rayons dans la chambre martèle le fond des iris de Vicky, ce qui amplifie son effroyable mal de bloc. Elle se prononce tout de même sur le sujet :

— Sérieusement, à la lumière des deux cents conversations concernant la température que j'ai eues à la discothèque hier soir, il devrait faire plus chaud aujourd'hui. Il me semble que, cette nuit, quand je suis rentrée, il faisait déjà plus doux. Quoique, dans l'état où je me trouvais, ce n'était peut-être qu'une illusion, ça aussi.

Presque craintive face à la mauvaise surprise qui l'attend assurément, Caroline regarde un moment à travers les vitres sans bouger. Les feuilles des palmiers qui valsent, la mer au loin et le dôme bleu azur bien dégagé la laissent un peu de glace compte tenu de ses préoccupations actuelles. Elle fait finalement glisser la grande porte d'un seul coup, comme propulsée par son aigreur du moment. Une bouffée d'air frais se faufile insidieusement dans la chambre.

— Ah, oui, il fait encore frais, mais c'est vraiment plus chaud qu'hier... et il est encore tôt, affirme-t-elle en avançant sur le balcon d'un grand pas, cette constatation apaisant son ressentiment l'espace d'un instant.

Après avoir admiré la vue en silence pendant un court moment, elle remet un pied dans la chambre, puis déclare :

— Facque, c'est ça. Je sais pas quoi faire du tout, pour Éric. Difficile d'éclaircir ça à distance. Pfft...

— J'avoue...

— Vous autres, votre fin de soirée ? C'était le *fun* ?

— Bof ! Le gars que je croyais célibataire est ici avec sa blonde, finalement.

— Qui ? La bedaine ?

Vicky lui explique alors toute l'histoire en omettant de dire qu'elle a tenté de l'embrasser à deux reprises, en vain.

— La maususse d'assiette de fruits de mer... En passant, ça ne débloque pas pantoute, mon côlon. On dirait que je suis enceinte de six mois. Je prendrai plus jamais d'Imodium de ma vie.

— Dans mon cas, ça va mieux, mais...

Vicky se palpe alors l'arrière-train sous les couvertures. Prise de panique, mais sans rien expliquer à son amie, elle se lève d'un bond et court s'enfermer dans la salle de bain. Caroline rigole un peu de sa course folle, en se remémorant des souvenirs pénibles de leur voyage précédent. Elle se gausse :

— Tu ne vas pas si bien que ça, finalement !

Enfermée dans la toilette, Vicky ne répond pas, mais Caro l'entend soupirer. Tout de même ravie d'être en mesure de s'habiller en vêtements courts, Caroline analyse le contenu de sa valise afin de décider ce qu'elle portera. Lorsque son amie sort enfin de la salle d'eau, elle la questionne :

— Urgence ?

— Non, c'est pas ça...

— Quoi ?

Caroline s'approche de Vicky, qui semble sur le point de pleurer, lui touche l'épaule et répète :

— Quoi ?

— Je panique solide, Caro ! Mes fesses, ça ne fonctionne pas du tout...

— Hein ? Tes fesses ?

— J'ai plein de petits boutons bizarres, pis ça pique.

— Comment ça ? T'es irritée à cause de la diarrhée ?

— Non...

Elle lui raconte alors en bref l'incident de la veille où Katia a dû lui refiler des feuilles provenant d'une plante mystère pour s'essuyer. Caroline, qui ignorait tout de cette péripétie enlevante, s'écrie :

— Ah mon Dieu ! Il fallait pas faire ça ! Surtout pas dans un autre pays !

— Je sais, mais j'étais assez prise au dépourvu merci, tu comprends...

— T'es peut-être infestée de bibittes ou, pire encore, d'œufs de bibittes... oui, des larves...

— Voyons donc, dis-moi pas ça ! couine Vicky, au bord du désespoir face à l'effroyable hypothèse.

— Montre !

— Es-tu malade ? C'est dégueulasse..., refuse Vicky en répétant, avec des larmes dans la voix : «Des larves de bibittes...» Ah non, pas ça !

— Faudrait que tu consultes un médecin au plus vite.

— Je vais attendre une autre journée. Ça va sûrement passer. De toute façon, on doit s'occuper de tes cheveux ce matin.

— Ouin, c'est vrai. J'y pensais plus. Eille, encore une fois, ça va super bien, ma vie… Wow ! s'apitoie la pauvre Caro, un trémolo dans la voix.

Accoudées à table devant un café et une assiette garnie de morceaux de pain grillé et de tranches d'un ananas qui a l'air d'avoir été cultivé au pôle Nord tant il est blanc et dur, Caroline et Vicky discutent telles deux potineuses du village. Pour se divertir, elles ont fait une gageure à savoir combien de temps passera avant que quelqu'un leur parle de température. Dix pesos cubains convertibles sont en jeu.

— La madame aux toasts avait vraiment envie de nous en parler, hein ? Mais elle s'est comme retenue…

— Je sens que quelqu'un passant près de notre table va nous en parler en premier, prophétise Caroline en scrutant toujours les alentours.

On voit alors apparaître Katia, cachée sous d'immenses lunettes de soleil dont elle n'a nullement besoin puisque le toit du restaurant à aire semi-ouverte bloque tous les rayons possibles. Sur sa route, Katia croise Cédric avec qui elle discute quelques minutes. Il porte aussi des verres fumés, indice irréfutable d'un probable état de lendemain de veille. Sa brève tournée du buffet s'étant avérée peu fructueuse, Katia rejoint ses amies avec seulement deux tasses de café pleines à ras bord. L'une d'elles se renverse un peu sur la nappe au moment où elle la pose.

— Voyons, on dirait que t'as vu un fantôme, lui reproche Caro.

— Non, non, je *feel* un peu drôle ce matin, c'est tout... J'ai trop bu hier. Donc? Vous êtes venues «pas déjeuner» au buffet?

— Exact! Toi, c'est ça ton repas? demande Caroline en désignant, du menton, les deux remontants.

— Oui, madame! Le mijoté de fruits de mer me tentait pas trop en me levant, donc... Eille, il fait chaud aujourd'hui! Maudit qu'on est bien à Cuba!

— *Yeah!* Moins de cinq minutes! Tu me dois dix pesos! se réjouit Vicky en assaillant Caroline d'un petit coup de poing sur l'épaule.

— Non! Kat, ça compte pas!

— Ah merci! Je compte pas, moi, se désole Katia sans même savoir de quoi il est question.

— Ça prend quelqu'un du *résore,* spécifie Caroline.

Les cinéastes amateurs, qui viennent tout juste de terminer leur long métrage quotidien «du manger», – un *remake* certainement digne d'être présenté à Cannes – passent près de la table des filles. La femme a troqué son fameux t-shirt zéro *sexy* pour une simple camisole blanche. Elle commente avec entrain:

— Il fait beau ! On est contents !

— Ben oui, concède Caroline, désappointée de perdre – en bonne et due forme, cette fois – dix pesos.

Vicky lui assène une ultime tape sur l'épaule, officialisant ainsi sa victoire.

— Ta nuit ? demande Vicky à Katia pour entrer rapidement dans le vif d'un sujet plus intéressant.

— Bof, on a bu pas mal de *shooters*, hein ?! Mike était complètement soûl, pour tout dire. On s'est embrassés au bar, mais son fils a dû m'aider en fin de soirée à le traîner dans ma chambre, ça vous donne une idée. On a vraiment ri, par contre. On a dormi collés tous les deux. Ce matin, c'était doux, c'était *cool*, mais il avait mal à la tête – naturellement, comme moi, d'ailleurs. Il est parti se recoucher dans sa chambre. Je peux pas en dire beaucoup plus sur lui à ce stade-ci, mais il me plaît bien, cet homme-là... Vous autres ?

— Personne n'est venu mettre le feu à ma tête ce matin, donc ça va pas si pire, je suppose. Seul petit hic : mon *chum* me trompe, donc...

— Hein ?

Elle lui raconte alors l'épisode de la veille. Katia ne semble pas s'en faire une miette.

— Caro, tout le monde ajoute n'importe qui sur Facebook de nos jours. Si ça se trouve, c'est peut-être la cousine d'un ami, genre.

— Ils auraient des amis en commun alors.

— La sœur de sa secrétaire, d'abord! N'importe qui...

Jugeant sa supposition trop facile, Caroline laisse tomber le sujet et tâte un peu le bout de ses cheveux roussis avant de dire :

— Faut que je fasse quelque chose avec ma tête au plus vite...

— Oui, on va trouver une coiffeuse, c'est notre mission du jour! On a le temps, le catamaran part juste à 13 h...

Toutes parées à mettre en branle leur projet de sauvetage capillaire, les filles partent à la recherche d'une coiffeuse et s'informent auprès de la réceptionniste de l'hôtel. Elles aboutissent près de la boutique de souvenirs, au début d'un long couloir perpendiculaire au lobby, et repèrent tout de suite ce qui ressemble à un centre de soins de beauté. Au même moment, une femme dans la soixantaine, fière comme Artaban, sort du lieu en question en arborant une coiffure haute et frisée ressemblant presque à la tour longiforme de Marge Simpson. Caroline fige sur place comme une statue de cire et elle dévisage ses amies avec horreur. Vicky pousse quand même la porte pour jeter un œil à l'intérieur. Les filles entrent à la queue leu leu, d'un pas timide. Une coiffeuse cubaine bien en chair finalise la mise en plis d'une seconde cliente âgée à qui elle semble confectionner le même genre de chignon haut et rabougri. Prise de panique, la pauvre Caroline ne laisse même pas le temps à la coiffeuse de les saluer et elle sort en trombe de la pièce. Les filles la rejoignent dans le corridor et s'informent :

— Caro ?

— Non, je peux pas. Depuis le congrès à Québec, j'ai développé une phobie des coiffeuses que je connais pas. C'est impossible, je peux pas…

— C'est si intense que ça ? Qu'est-ce que tu comptes faire, d'abord ?

— Je sais pas. Je pense qu'il faudrait juste égaliser le bas pour le moment. Tu voudrais pas me le faire, Vicky ? T'es capable…

— Non, non, non, oublie ça. Pas question que je sois responsable de ta tête.

Caro se tourne vers Katia en l'implorant des yeux telle une gamine de six ans désirant de tout cœur un chaton angora à l'animalerie. Celle-ci refuse aussi de but en blanc :

— Regarde-moi pas de même, c'est non !

— C'est beau, c'est beau, je vais le faire toute seule, d'abord !

— T'as des ciseaux ?

— Non, je vais aller en emprunter à la réception.

Caro s'éloigne d'un pas résolu pour accomplir sa mission. Mission qu'elle juge d'ailleurs d'une importance capitale.

Dans un anglais acceptable, elle baragouine sa demande à la femme postée derrière le comptoir. Confuse, l'employée ne semble pas trop comprendre pour quelle raison une vacancière cherche des ciseaux. Son instinct professionnel lui dicte de refuser la demande particulière de sa cliente, juste au cas où. Caroline insiste :

— S'il vous plaît, je me suis fait brûler les cheveux au buffet hier... Regardez !

Les yeux bien arrondis, la Cubaine hausse les épaules. Caroline poursuit donc son explication sans toutefois se montrer plus claire :

— Brû-ler... le gars du café... les flammes... pouf !

Toujours dans le brouillard, la femme demande finalement à un homme pas très loin d'elle de lui venir en aide pour gérer la situation singulière. Lorsque le Cubain avance vers les trois vacancières, Katia prend une fois de plus en main le volet «communication», question de ne pas y passer la journée.

Trouvant lui aussi la requête de la cliente bien inhabituelle, il refuse de la tête, craignant d'être ensuite réprimandé.

— Ils sont pas vite vite sur leurs patins, eux autres ! peste Caroline, ne sachant plus du tout comment expliquer sa revendication de façon claire.

— Coudonc, on leur demande pas de nous prêter un bazooka pour faire exploser la piscine, quand même ! s'interloque aussi Vicky.

Par chance, Sylvio arrive à la réception au même moment. Katia se rue sur lui pour lui faire part de leur imbroglio. Il écoute un moment avant de déblatérer sans plus attendre quelque chose en espagnol aux deux employés récalcitrants. La femme opine du chef puis se rend dans un petit bureau adjacent à la réception. Elle revient et tend une paire de ciseaux à Caroline, navrée de s'être montrée si méfiante pour rien. Ne lui en tenant pas rigueur, Caroline lui balance un reconnaissant :

— ¡Gracias!

Sylvio leur indique :

— Vous n'aurez qu'à les rapporter à la réception après. En passant, je crois bien devoir aller à La Havane dans deux jours. Est-ce que ça va toujours pour vous ?

— Oui, oui, parfait !

— Bon, bien, amusez-vous cet après-midi. À plus tard !

— Au revoir et encore merci !

Debout devant le miroir de la salle de bain, les épaules légèrement cambrées de découragement, Caroline panique :

— Ça marche pas pantoute. Ils coupent pas assez, ces ciseaux-là. Regardez ça, tout est coupé croche, c'est presque pire que c'était !

— Sérieusement, Caro, arrête de couper. Si tu veux pas aller voir la coiffeuse, je pense que t'as pas d'autre option que de t'attacher les cheveux pour le restant du voyage, conclut Vicky, qui ne souhaite toujours pas manier les ciseaux pour aider son amie.

— Ouin, attachés, ça paraît moins, se résigne la pauvre échevelée en posant l'outil trop usé sur le comptoir de la vanité.

S'apercevant que Vicky se gratte une fesse de façon non subtile, Katia lui demande :

— Qu'est-ce que t'as ?

Caroline répond à sa place :

— Elle a des larves de bibittes dans les fesses !

— ARK ! Arrête de dire ça !

Vicky explique alors son malaise à Katia.

— Ah ouin ? J'avais pris soin de prendre des feuilles super loin du chemin en plus, au cas où des messieurs auraient fait pipi dedans...

— AH MON DIEU ! J'avais même pas pensé à ça... je vais vomir, s'affole Vicky en se prenant la tête à deux mains, l'air de vouloir se la frapper contre le mur.

— Montre, demande Katia en lui faisant signe de baisser son bermuda.

— NON ! T'es malade ? Jamais. Ça va passer, là...

— Bon, à défaut de manger, on s'enfile un petit verre en attendant de larguer les amarres ? propose Katia, jugeant que l'urgence «crinière» a été réglée au maximum de leur capacité.

— OK...

Après avoir rassemblé leurs effets personnels en prévision de leur après-midi sur le catamaran, Katia, déjà un peu pompette, gambade dans le chemin en direction de la plage. Vicky et Caroline, qui ont également ingurgité quelques cocktails, semblent à présent faire fi de leurs soucis de la veille et du matin. Elles rigolent en voyant Katia sautiller comme une fillette trop excitée d'aller à la foire. Celle-ci fredonne à tue-tête l'éternelle chanson espagnole qu'elles entendent en rafale depuis le début de leur séjour :

— «*Bará, bará, bará, berê, berê, berê...*»

Elles ont à peine le temps de mettre le bout d'une sandale dans le sable qu'une voix cubaine, maintenant familière, les aborde :

— *¡Hola! ¿Bolleyboll? ¿Sí?*

— Voyons ? Il nous suit ou quoi ?

— *No, gracias, catamaran...*, se défile Katia, heureuse d'avoir dans sa manche une vraie défaite pour refuser.

Les filles ralentissent en arrivant près de l'endroit désigné comme lieu de départ et elles observent du coin de l'œil les vacanciers qui prendront part à l'aventure. Elles distinguent un couple dans la quarantaine qu'elles n'avaient jamais vu encore, puis un autre couple dans la trentaine. Une petite famille, composée des deux parents et de deux ados, patiente devant une affiche publicitaire en carton plantée de biais dans le sable et servant à promouvoir ladite croisière.

— On va voir plein de poissons, c'est trop excitant ! s'enflamme Vicky en agrippant le poignet de Caroline pour lui transmettre sa joie de vivre du moment.

Deux Cubains arrivent près du groupe avec de grands bacs de plastique contenant l'équipement de base pour pratiquer la plongée en apnée. À tour de rôle, les gens essaient des palmes, des masques et des tubas afin de dénicher la bonne taille. Un autre homme arrive avec des combinaisons courtes en néoprène pour ceux craignant d'avoir froid sous l'eau. Vicky refuse d'en enfiler une sous prétexte que les photos seront vraiment plus jolies sans la tenue de caoutchouc. De toute façon, le soleil ayant repris du service et se trouvant à son apogée, elle estime qu'elle ne devrait pas avoir froid. Katia aussi passe outre, tandis que Caroline en prend une qu'elle inspecte.

— Mets pas ça, Caro ! L'eau est chaude, c'est certain. Il y a eu du temps froid maximum quatre jours, tente de la convaincre Vicky. De toute façon, c'est dégueu, il paraît que tout le monde fait pipi là-dedans.

Écœurée par ce dernier détail, Caro redonne la combinaison au Cubain, résolue comme jamais à pratiquer l'activité sans l'enveloppe de protection thermique.

Une fille blonde et un peu rondelette vient soudainement se stationner près de Vicky, dont le nez est bien enfoui dans le bac à palmes, à la recherche de sa taille. Vicky relève la tête pour constater qui arrive près d'elle de la sorte. Sans aucune délicatesse, la Québécoise lui demande :

— C'est toi, la fille qui embrasse les *chums* des autres ?

— Hein…? fait Vicky, toujours accroupie devant le bac, perplexe devant l'accusation qui tombe sur la plage comme un couperet.

— Simon, c'est MON *chum*, en passant, et on vient juste de se fiancer, pour ton information. Il m'a dit que t'as essayé de l'embrasser, à ce qu'il paraît, pis deux fois en plus de ça !

— Euh… non, ment Vicky, ne sachant pas trop comment se sortir d'embarras.

— Ben, en tout cas, laisse-le tranquille pis trouve-toi donc un *chum* si tu veux embrasser un gars ! crache-t-elle en tournant les talons en mode traction arrière.

Non satisfaite, la blonde se retourne vers les filles du groupe pour les mettre en garde :

— Je vous conseille de surveiller vos *chums*, les filles ! dit-elle en quittant les lieux, la moutarde lui débordant du nez.

Tel le Chat botté dans *Shrek*, Vicky lève des yeux bulbeux vers les futurs plaisanciers, témoins de la scène. Les trois femmes qui sont en couple la dévisagent, les lèvres bien pincées, tandis que leurs conjoints regardent partout ailleurs comme des perruches aux aguets. Katia se penche vers sa pauvre amie humiliée, toujours accroupie, puis lui murmure entre ses dents avec discrétion :

— Quessé qui est arrivé, estiiii ?

— Rien. Il n'est RIEN arrivé, rectifie Vicky à voix forte en se redressant pour que tout le monde autour entende bien sa déclaration.

— Tu m'avais pas dit ça que t'avais essayé de le *frencher*, lui chuchote à son tour Caroline en prenant soin de parler en direction opposée des spectateurs.

— Pfft ! Eille, moi, le niaisage de même, là ! Une vraie folle, elle ! Je le connais même pas, son *chum* ! Simon ? C'est qui ça, Simon ? déclare Vicky à tue-tête, question de se tirer d'affaire en attrapant au vol un semblant de dignité.

À voir leur attitude scandalisée, les vacancières présentes ne semblent pas croire un traître mot de ce qu'elle avance. Craignant de devoir porter pour le reste du voyage la triste réputation de la fille-qui-courtise-les-hommes-des-autres, Vicky poursuit son plaidoyer de non-culpabilité en changeant son fusil d'épaule, faisant mine de ne parler qu'à ses amies :

— Ah ouiiiii ! OK ! Là, je me souviens. Simon… Imaginez-vous donc que sa blonde était malade et pognée dans la chambre, donc il en a profité pour essayer de m'embrasser, l'écœurant ! Un vrai beau crosseur, je vous le dis !

La fille dans la trentaine, qui semble douter de ce nouveau détail, prend un peu rudement la main de son *chum* en signe de possession. Au moment où Vicky jette un regard vers la foule qui l'observe toujours discrètement, l'ado de quatorze ans, un peu en retrait du groupe, en profite pour lui envoyer une œillade enflammée croyant ainsi avoir des chances que la vacancière aux mœurs légères tente un jour de l'embrasser.

— Pis en plus, j'en ai un, *chum* ! Pfft !

Le capitaine arrive heureusement sur ces entrefaites pour annoncer l'imminence du départ, faisant ainsi diversion à la scène chargée de malaises.

— *¡Vamos*[25] !

JOUR 8

AÉROPORT MONTRÉAL-TRUDEAU
SALLE 315 – **9 H 46**

Katia, qui se souvient très bien de la spectaculaire déconfiture publique de son amie, pouffe tout de même de rire.

— C'était une scène digne d'un film d'amour italien quétaine. La fille jalouse qui pète sa coche solide devant tout le monde... Pis toi qui dis: «Je le connais pas» pour finalement changer d'idée: «Ah oui, lui! Un beau

---

25. Allons-y!

crosseur!». T'étais zéro crédible, Vic. Inscris-toi jamais en théâtre, la taquine Katia.

— Je voulais fondre dans le sable comme un cornet de crème glacée molle, avoue Vicky.

— T'as quand même essayé d'embrasser son *chum*. Ce que tu avais omis de nous dire sur le coup, d'ailleurs, lui reproche Caroline, tout à coup très chatouilleuse face au sujet «infidélité».

— Bon, regardez QUI parle! s'offusque l'accusée, sans mettre de gants blancs.

Caroline croise les bras pour toute réponse. La voyant ainsi prête à monter sur ses grands chevaux, Vicky nuance ses propos.

— Je veux dire que, avoir su AVANT qu'il était en couple, je n'aurais pas essayé de le *frencher*.

— Mais c'est vraiment lui, le cave. Pas besoin de raconter ça à ta blonde, innocent! C'est quoi l'idée? vocifère Katia, hors d'elle.

— Je le sais. Ç'aurait évité toute une histoire.

— *Anyway*, je vais me souvenir de cette balade de catamaran là pour le reste de ma vie. Pour des raisons différentes, disons…, envoie Katia.

Caro approuve en hochant la tête de découragement:

— Moi aussi, crois-moi. Moi aussi…

JOUR 3

CUBA
EN PLEINE MER

Tout le monde à bord papote joyeusement, le nez au vent. Après plus d'une heure de balade en mer, l'embarcation s'immobilise à proximité d'une bouée rouge flottante surplombant un petit récif de corail. Craignant toujours comme le feu d'être jugée par les femmes présentes, Vicky déploie beaucoup d'efforts pour paraître sympathique à outrance. À grands coups d'éclats de rire pour les blagues de tout un chacun, elle en donne bien plus que le client en demande. Katia, quant à elle, carbure à plein régime dans la réserve de bière qui repose à l'avant, près du conducteur, conservée bien précieusement dans une immense glacière verte à l'effigie de la populaire compagnie Cristal. Un peu « cocktail », elle chantonne :

— *« Bará, bará, bará, berê, berê, berê*[26]*... »*

— Eille, on est-tu tannées de l'entendre, cette toune-là, pareil ? Me semble que ça joue en boucle depuis qu'on est arrivées, se plaint Caroline en enfilant sa veste de sauvetage.

— C'est vrai, répète la fille dans la trentaine qui enfile ses palmes à quelques mètres de Caroline.

---

26. Je vais finir par vous la mettre dans la tête hein ?! ☺

— Ouin! T'AS TELLEMENT RAISON! l'appuie Vicky avec emphase en fixant la fille, question de montrer qu'elle s'avère en accord total avec elle.

Ladite fille sourit à Caroline sans relever le commentaire de Vicky. Ainsi ignorée, Vicky tourne les yeux vers la mer.

— Je vois des poissons! s'enthousiasme-t-elle en se penchant quasi acrobatiquement par-dessus bord pour observer le tout de plus près.

Le copain de la trentenaire en profite alors pour reluquer le postérieur de Vicky – bien relevé compte tenu de sa position cambrée. La fille lui assène un coup de palme sur l'épaule en guise de représailles. Caroline voit la scène de bisc-en-coin, mais n'en fait pas de cas. Pour exciter les futurs plongeurs, le type qui accompagne le capitaine lance alors quelques bouts de pain dans l'eau tout près de la coque. En moins de trois secondes et quart, un banc de petits poissons rayés noir et jaune se pointe à la surface en frétillant pour attraper des morceaux du généreux repas.

— Ah mon Dieu! Il y a vraiment plein de poissons! s'électrise encore plus Vicky.

— Allez-y toutes les deux, je vais prendre une autre bière, moi, annonce Katia en s'allongeant dans un filet à larges mailles recouvrant la moitié du centre de l'embarcation et faisant office de lieu de détente pour les vacanciers.

Sans plus attendre, tout le monde s'élance à la mer. Caroline, la seule à avoir demandé une ceinture de sécurité, flotte comme un canard de bain près de l'embarcation.

Pataugeant pas très loin d'elle, Vicky admire la faune et la flore sous-marines, le masque bien immergé sous la surface de l'eau qui ondule au gré des vagues. Malgré que le récif ne soit ni très garni ni très coloré, plusieurs poissons barbotent autour, sans inquiétude. Les filles en repèrent deux gros bleus, un gris au nez assez long et d'autres très plats de couleur jaune serin.

Vicky retire alors le tuba de sa bouche pour implorer Katia – toujours à bord – de prendre quelques photos. La requête perturbe un peu sa pause *cerveza*, mais Katia collabore de bon cœur. Ses deux amies flottantes prennent la pose pour elle en levant le pouce et en gonflant les joues pour être comiques. Toujours à fond dans sa démarche d'avoir l'air – du moins aux yeux de Marc – de passer des vacances délirantes, Vicky implore Caroline :

— Aie l'air d'avoir *full* de *fun*, là !

— J'en ai aussi... Pas besoin de gérer mon enthousiasme, je suis capable, réplique Caro, un peu agacée.

Presque éblouie par une inspiration soudaine, Katia se dirige vers le Cubain qui a nourri les poissons précédemment et lui demande des bouts de pain. Il lui tend un sac de plastique bien garni.

— Attendez, on va en prendre une avec des poissons autour de vous !

— Ah oui ! On s'approche, alors, approuve Vicky.

Sans plus attendre, Katia jette deux grosses poignées de miettes dans l'eau juste devant ses amies qui avancent toujours, puis elle s'empare de l'appareil photo. Désirant collaborer à la démarche artistique de Katia, le Cubain avance pour en lancer d'autres à son tour. Cette fois, la surabondance de nourriture flottante attire des poissons non par dizaines, mais bien par centaines. Baignant maintenant dans une mare de pain mou et de poissons grouillants, les filles trouvent l'expérience comique pendant, tout au plus, trois secondes et quart.

— Ben là!? Il y en a trop... Ils me touchent partout... AAAAH! C'est dégueulasse! AH! HIII! C'est pas le *fun* pantoute! gueule Vicky comme une perdue.

— AAAAAAH, mon Dieu, j'aime pas ça, ils vont me mordre! HIP! HIP! panique Caroline en tentant de s'éloigner de la masse frétillante tout en battant des mains devant elle pour nager en petit chien.

— Esti que vous êtes drôles! se tord de rire Katia en prenant des tonnes de photos de la scène savoureuse.

Caroline sent alors quelque chose d'anormal se produire.

— AAAHHH! HEIN?? NON... J'ai... j'ai un poisson dans mon maillot! AAAHHH! panique-t-elle, plus hystérique que jamais.

Manquant cruellement de compassion, Katia rit toujours comme une hyène en continuant de photographier ses amies au bord de l'agonie.

— Je vais filmer à la place! décide-t-elle en changeant le mode de fonctionnement de l'appareil.

Toujours aux prises avec le poisson trop aventureux coincé dans sa culotte de maillot de bain, Caroline tente de l'enlever tout en roulant de tous les côtés comme une bille à cause de son gilet de sauvetage. Elle s'accroche désespérément à l'épaule de Vicky, charitablement venue à sa rescousse. Ainsi prise au piège, la pauvre Vicky cale un peu à son tour et avale une généreuse gorgée d'eau saline. Lorsque sa tête émerge à la surface, elle crache et tousse avant de gueuler par la tête à Caroline :

— T'es folle ou quoi ? Lâche-moi, tu vas me noyer !

— HIIII ! Le poisson, maudite marde ! crie toujours Caroline, les deux mains sous l'eau.

— C'est super bon, les filles ! Lâchez pas ! s'enflamme Katia tout en continuant à filmer.

La scène est si cocasse que Katia craint presque de s'échapper dans sa petite culotte à force de rire étant donné toute la bière ingurgitée depuis le début de l'après-midi.

Caroline tente le tout pour le tout pour se défaire du poisson prisonnier de son slip et elle relève les jambes pour l'enlever, la tête renversée et à moitié plongée dans la mer. Affolée et manquant d'air, elle réussit et se redresse à la surface. Désorientée et un peu sous le choc, elle échappe malencontreusement le morceau de tissu qui disparaît dans les fonds marins…

— *Shit !* J'ai échappé mon maillot ! dit-elle, catastrophée, en replongeant sans plus attendre la tête dans l'eau pour tenter de le repérer avec son masque.

Sur le bateau, Katia rigole, pliée en deux comme un cartable.

— Quoi? T'es toute nue, là? s'indigne Vicky, ahurie, puis elle examine son amie sous l'eau pour s'en assurer.

Aussitôt, son voisin, alias le *chum* de la trentenaire frustrée, plonge aussi dans l'eau en ayant tout à coup l'air d'avoir très envie d'explorer les fonds marins antillais. Pas dupe de sa manigance de voyeur de niveau un, sa blonde l'extirpe de l'eau par les cheveux avec une force herculéenne. L'ado, qui a également disparu sous l'eau aussitôt l'information de potentielle nudité transmise, reste là un bon moment à fixer Caro, le tuba en bouche et la caméra GoPro résistante à l'eau bien en main... Caro tente de peine et de misère de cacher ses parties intimes avec ses mains. La cordelette blanche de son tampon ondule paisiblement au gré du mouvement des vagues. Elle songe pendant un instant qu'un poisson pourrait bien croire qu'il s'agit d'un appât à croquer... En étirant le cou au maximum, elle beugle en direction de Vicky:

— Criss, Vic! Aide-moi à le trouver! Je suis pas capable de plonger avec ma ceinture!

Comme celle-ci appréhende toujours de se faire noyer *in extremis* par son amie hystérique et désormais à moitié nue, elle regarde sous l'eau à travers son masque tout en conservant une bonne distance entre elles. Le capitaine et son matelot, qui n'ont rien compris de la scène de désordre aquatique en cours, se questionnent:

— ¿Que passa[27]?

— No lo se[28]...

Caroline, les fesses à l'air, barbotte à la surface entre Vicky qui fouine du mieux qu'elle peut, le *chum* de la fille qui tente toujours subtilement de se rincer l'œil, et le jeune ado en pleine séance de voyeurisme qui la mire carrément avec sa caméra à un mètre d'elle sous l'eau.

Caro crache à Katia :

— Arrête de rire, Kat, pis lance-moi quelque chose pour que je me cache !

Katia, que les éclats de rire ininterrompus empêchent de collaborer, lui lance finalement à l'arraché une serviette de plage. Caroline tente de l'enfouir sous l'eau pour s'en entourer la taille, enfin. Aussitôt son laborieux projet mené à terme, l'ado remonte à la surface, déçu qu'elle se soit ainsi couvert le derrière en plein milieu de sa séance photo fructueuse. Dans le brouhaha de la scène, du sable s'est soulevé du fond marin peu profond laissant l'eau, jadis limpide, plutôt trouble. Ceci expliquant pourquoi personne ne trouve ledit bas de maillot.

— Asti de marde... de marde... voyons..., pleurniche Caro en regardant partout.

---

27. Que se passe-t-il ?
28. Je ne sais pas...

— Monte me rejoindre, ils vont le retrouver, propose Katia qui réussit à arrêter de rire pour prêter main-forte à son amie en détresse aquatique.

Caroline se résigne et grimpe dans l'échelle en tentant de maintenir sa serviette en place d'une seule main. Sa veste de sauvetage pesante – parce que gonflée d'eau – ne facilite pas du tout sa manœuvre. Tout le groupe de plongeurs se mobilise alors pour retrouver l'objet perdu. Même les femmes contribuent à l'effort de guerre, ne souhaitant pour rien au monde qu'une des filles de l'expédition reste ainsi, «en fesses». Le capitaine saisit enfin la nature de la crise en voyant Caroline grimper à bord avec sa serviette autour de la taille. Il ne peut s'empêcher d'éclater de rire à son tour. Katia se joint à lui.

— *¡Ja! ¡ja! ¡ja!*

— Bon, OK, ça va faire! s'offusque Caroline, agacée.

Debout au beau milieu du bateau, Katia explique en anglais aux membres de l'équipage ce qui vient de se produire.

— Le poisson dans son maillot, et là, oups! enlève le maillot... Plouf! dans la mer! Parti! Perdu! Bye-bye! Ha! ha! ha!

— *¡Ja! ¡ja! ¡ja!* rient maintenant les deux Cubains à l'unisson.

— On a compris! Voulez-vous que je refasse un exemple avec mon top, tant qu'à y être?

— Non, non, c'est déjà arrivé au Mexique, *anyway*! Ha! ha! ha! Je m'en souvenais plus!

Puis Katia explique sans plus attendre aux Cubains ladite scène du Mexique, il y a deux ans. Les deux types rient maintenant à ventre déboutonné. L'adolescente qui n'a pas dit un mot depuis de début de l'expédition remonte alors à la surface en brandissant bien haut le maillot de Caroline.

— Ah mon Dieu! Merci! dit celle-ci tandis que Katia se déplace près de l'échelle pour aller le récupérer.

Elle le tend ensuite à son amie, qui réussit en moins de deux à l'enfiler sans que la foule entrevoie son entrejambe. L'ado en rut, toujours dans l'eau, la reluque avec le sourire baveux du gars qui en a bien trop vu pour son âge.

— Bon, donnez-moi une bière, quelqu'un! s'exclame Caro, à bout de nerfs, en se levant et en dénouant la serviette d'autour de sa taille.

Katia donne le coup d'envoi à la fête en dansant quelques pas de mérengué.

— «*Bará, bará, bará, berê, berê, berê…*»

Après une heure de détente en mer – et trois autres bières ingurgitées par Katia –, l'embarcation se dirige vers la côte de l'île. Le ciel encore bleu clair et le soleil chaud pourraient laisser présager une mer calme, mais hélas, ce n'est pas le cas. Le vent s'étant levé, les vagues s'avèrent beaucoup plus houleuses que lors du départ. Les oscillations du catamaran, sévèrement secoué, donnent aux gens à bord l'impression de se retrouver en plein cœur d'une chaîne de collines fluviales. L'instinct de survie des touristes les force à se cramponner avec les moyens du bord afin de rester stables dans l'embarcation.

— *God*, que je me sens mal, se plaint Katia en soufflant par la bouche, les deux mains bien accrochées au mât central du catamaran.

— T'as bien trop bu, aussi, lui reproche Caroline, assise dans le grand filet et se tenant solidement au cordage.

— Je pensais pas qu'il allait y avoir de la «houle-ma-poule» de même... OOOH, se lamente Katia alors que l'embarcation percute de plein fouet un rouleau impressionnant.

L'adolescente à bord, maintenant rendue vert lime, se dirige avec difficulté vers le bastingage, aidée de sa mère qui lui tient un biceps et l'épaule. Remarquant que le teint de Katia semble de plus en plus verdâtre, Vicky lui demande :

— Coudonc ? Vas-tu être malade ?

— Je pense pas, mais j'ai le cœur au bord... Aaaah... Pfft...

Au même moment, la jeune fille se met à vomir son repas du midi dans la mer. Le capitaine ralentit la vitesse de croisière pour éviter de perdre une plaisancière par-dessus bord. En moins de deux secondes, Katia se rue à son tour vers le garde-corps afin de dégobiller elle aussi. C'est maintenant au tour de Caroline de se payer la gueule de son amie. Quasiment ravie de la voir ainsi en peine, Caro agrippe l'appareil photo et elle immortalise la scène.

— Avec l'eau turquoise en arrière-plan, c'est super beau, Kat! apprécie-t-elle en continuant, toute joyeuse, de photographier son amie qui expulse tripes et boyaux au grand jour.

— Hé, Kat! «*Bará, bará, bará, berê, berê, berê...*»

— Ferme-la, sti, réussit à gémir Katia entre deux vomissements.

— Ah! Je pense que je vais filmer à la place!

JOUR 8

AÉROPORT MONTRÉAL-TRUDEAU
SALLE 315 – 9 H 51

Vicky et Caroline sont crampées de rire en se remémorant la scène burlesque. Katia les coupe:

— Ben oui, ben oui, c'était TRÈS drôle...

— Sérieux, je vais mettre une de ces excellentes photos-là sur Facebook, c'est certain! déconne Caroline.

— Oui, et moi je vais en mettre une de toi, paniquée, qui remonte dans le bateau les fesses à l'air...

Trouvant tout à coup l'idée beaucoup moins comique, Caroline se ravise :

— C'était une farce...

— Et c'est ainsi qu'elle fit honte à la célèbre compagnie Cristal en vomissant toutes ses bières par-dessus bord..., conclut Vicky en imitant la voix de Pierre Bruneau au bulletin de nouvelles de 18 h.

— Sérieux, j'ai vu plein de poissons rayés jaune et noir venir rôder près du bateau pour profiter du «festin»...

— ARK..., s'égosille Caro en battant des mains. Les maususses de poissons rayés...

— Ouin, ce fut toute une excursion de *snorkeling* sans *snorkeling*, mon affaire, réalise Katia qui n'a finalement même pas mis le bout d'un orteil dans l'eau.

— Vous souvenez-vous de l'autre clown qu'on a revu ce jour-là ?

— Lui, il était drôle pareil ! Un genre d'hyperactif...

JOUR 3
CUBA, VARADERO
COSTA AZUL DEL MAR RESORT

Tout en donnant un coup de main aux employés pour ranger l'équipement dans les bacs, les filles rigolent de l'épopée du mal de mer de Katia.

— Ça va mieux ?

— Ouais, je savais que si quelqu'un était malade, j'allais l'être moi aussi. Je supporte pas de voir ça...

— Oui, les bières que tu t'es descendues tout l'après-midi en plein soleil n'avaient sûrement RIEN à voir là-dedans..., ironise Caroline.

— Meuh... non. C'était la mer déchaînée...

En se rendant vers leurs chambres, les filles croisent le gars qui désirait organiser le jeu compliqué de Frisbee aux œufs la veille. En proie à une énergie foudroyante, Mathieu les aborde, les bras écartés et en mouvement de chaque côté du corps comme s'il tentait de s'envoler.

— Les filles, les filles ! C'est super que je vous croise ici, j'ai eu une méga idée ! On va essayer de louer un bateau à un pêcheur pour aller attraper des langoustes en mer. Ensuite, on va trouver des BBQ ou faire un feu sur la plage, c'est selon, et s'organiser un genre de repas collectif. Les gens paieront genre cinq ou dix pesos et on ira chercher des pommes de terre, des salades et d'autres accompagne-ments au buffet. De toute façon, c'est pas grave de payer un peu, c'est un « tout inclus ». L'avez-vous payé cher, votre voyage, vous autres ?

— Non, imagine-toi donc qu'on l'a gagné ! lui envoie Vicky, super fière.

— Ah ouin !? Dans un concours ?

— Euh..., fait Vicky, plus tout à fait certaine de devoir ou non livrer la vérité.

— Oui, dans un concours de coiffeuses !

— Vous êtes coiffeuses ? s'étonne le gars en posant son regard dubitatif sur la tignasse négligée de Caroline.

— Oui ! ment d'instinct Katia, toujours prête à jouer le jeu.

— Bah… c'est une longue histoire, disons, se ravise plutôt Vicky en faisant des yeux ronds à Katia, pas certaine de vouloir jouer à nouveau à ce petit jeu de mensonges[29].

— Alors, ça vous tente ?

Faisant preuve d'une logique implacable, Caroline se désiste :

— Oui, mais pas aujourd'hui. Il est trop tard, déjà dix-sept heures…

— Ouin, mais on y va tout de suite !

— Des langoustes, c'est sûrement pas si facile que ça à pêcher, ajoute Vicky.

— Ouin… en tout cas, on vous en reparle ! À plus !

Trouvant une fois de plus que ce pauvre hère se complique la vie pour rien, Vicky commente :

— Eille, lui, avec ses projets IKEA en cent cinquante-huit étapes faciles…

---

29. Comme lors d'un certain congrès à Québec…

Sortant de la douche, Vicky confie à sa colocataire de chambre :

— Sérieusement, l'eau salée de la mer ne semble pas avoir aidé du tout ma situation « foufounesque »...

Les filles ayant pris l'habitude de laisser leurs portes de chambre respectives ouvertes pour pouvoir communiquer, Katia demande à voix forte de sa chambre, pas certaine d'avoir bien entendu :

— Quoi ? Ton infection de fesses ne va pas mieux ?

— Franchement ! Crie-le donc sur le balcon, tant qu'à y être !

À voix basse, Vicky poursuit :

— Non, c'est pire. Il faudrait vraiment que je consulte un médecin demain. Il doit bien exister une crème ou quelque chose pour guérir ça...

Caroline approche de Vicky et lui regarde le visage attentivement.

— Vic, euh...

— Ah oui, je sais. J'ai vu ça en sortant de la douche, se rembrunit la prof d'arts plastiques.

Malgré qu'elle ait pris soin de s'appliquer de la crème solaire, Vicky a tout de même bronzé beaucoup, la puissance du FPS dans sa crème n'ayant pas résisté à la baignade. On distingue nettement le contour de ses lunettes de soleil sur son visage hâlé.

Fin prête, Katia aboutit dans la chambre de ses voisines et remarque aussitôt son bronzage imparfait.

— Hon! *Hello, racoon!*

— Eille, ça va super bien mes affaires, se désole Vicky en tentant de masquer un peu les inégalités avec un fond de teint plus foncé.

— T'as juste à pas porter de lunettes demain et ça sera correct. Au moins, t'as pas attrapé de coup de soleil, l'avise Katia.

Vêtues de tenues de soirée décontractées et légèrement maquillées, les trois amies partent à la conquête du buffet. Le soir est tombé et les étoiles scintillent dans le ciel limpide. Quelques croassements de lézards se font entendre de part et d'autre du sentier que les filles ont emprunté. À présent habituées aux nombreuses pistes tortueuses du complexe, Caro, Katia et Vicky s'orientent facilement malgré la pénombre. Chemin faisant, elles doivent céder le passage à une voiturette de golf qui conduit de nouveaux arrivants vers leur chambre. En entrant près du restaurant, les filles constatent d'emblée la thématique culinaire du soir: souper de fruits de mer.

— Ayoye, ça me rejoint pas pantoute, ce menu-là. Je mangerai pas de fruits de mer, certain, annonce Vicky, malgré que ses inconforts intestinaux du deuxième jour soient désormais chose du passé.

— Il y aura autre chose, c'est sûr.

Katia part en chasse pour trouver quelque chose à manger dans le généreux buffet. L'hôtel étant très populaire auprès des Italiens, un groupe de voyageurs provenant de ce pays fait son entrée dans la zone de restauration. Un homme d'environ soixante-cinq ans passe près d'elle en la reluquant sans gêne et lui adresse un large sourire éloquent. Étonnée qu'un homme de cet âge puisse espérer la séduire, elle lui renvoie un sourire coincé, par pure politesse. L'homme agrippe une assiette et se poste derrière elle dans la file défilant devant les mets du buffet. Constatant du coin de l'œil que l'homme la fixe sans arrêt, Katia décide de l'ignorer pour ne pas avoir à lui parler. Mine de rien, elle se sert un peu de lasagne bolognaise dans un grand plat carré puis repose la spatule. L'homme sur ses talons s'empare de l'outil à son tour et se sert également une portion de lasagne. Katia continue d'avancer et aperçoit un peu plus loin ce qu'elle croit être des gnocchis dans une sauce blanche non identifiée, probablement une béchamel. Elle décide de tenter le coup et d'y goûter. L'homme l'imite encore une fois en reproduisant les mêmes faits et gestes. Il semble même s'assurer de prendre la même quantité de nourriture qu'elle.

«Qu'est-ce qu'il fait là, lui?», se demande Katia en observant le bizarre stratagème de séduction de son nouvel admirateur.

Déterminée à l'ignorer coûte que coûte, elle se dirige vers le comptoir de pain où elle attrape une petite baguette longue et sèche. Il fait de même. Elle tourne finalement les yeux vers lui et, ravi, il lui décoche une œillade suggestive. Cette fois-ci, elle répond d'un sourire très amer et elle poursuit sa route vers la table des marinades où elle sélectionne à la hâte quelques petits oignons doux, un cornichon sucré, des olives noires, un piment dans l'huile et des champignons marinés. Ayant peine à la suivre, il se dépêche de reproduire ses choix, mais il oublie malheureusement les champignons, n'ayant pas eu le temps de bien voir l'assiette de sa soupirante qui vient de prendre la poudre d'escampette. Elle prend place à sa table sans même daigner lever les yeux vers lui tandis qu'il retourne rejoindre ses compagnons de voyage, bredouille.

À l'autre bout de la pièce, Vicky et Caroline se servent divers morceaux de pizza.

— Elle a pas l'air super bonne, mais bon, il faut bien se nourrir.

La pizza semble avoir été concoctée à l'aide d'une croûte de pain rassis et de champignons en boîte bien poreux. Sur le dessus, on distingue de petites boules de fromage un peu étrange à mi-chemin entre la feta et le bocconcini. Quelques morceaux de poivron vert discrets ainsi que des cubes de jambon grisâtres ornent l'ensemble. Vicky attrape à la volée quelques frites pour remplir davantage son assiette peu garnie.

En rejoignant Katia à la table, les deux filles remarquent que celle-ci affiche une mine amusée.

— Qu'est-ce que t'as?

— Je viens de vivre un beau moment.

— Quoi? T'as trouvé des coquerelles dans le buffet?

— Parle pas de coquerelles, Vic! J'y pensais pu! se plaint Caro.

— Je viens de vivre la pire technique de *cruise* de l'histoire du *cruising* du monde entier...

— Laquelle, donc? Pas la technique de faire semblant d'échapper quelque chose dans ton décolleté pour pouvoir te pogner une boule? demande Vicky en se mettant deux frites à la fois dans la bouche.

Ses deux amies se retournent vers elle, stoïques comme deux chevreuils figeant devant les phares allumés d'une voiture en plein milieu de l'autoroute.

— Euh... Dis-nous pas que quelqu'un t'a déjà fait ce coup-là, Vic?

— Ouin? ajoute Caroline.

— Bah... non... je disais ça de même.

Silence. Les filles ne la croient pas.

— *Anyway*, c'était plutôt la technique de la synchronicité des goûts alimentaires. Ou, si vous préférez, «Je prends les mêmes choses que toi dans le buffet pour que tu voies qu'on est faits pour être ensemble. On mange les mêmes affaires, c'est évident que le bonheur nous attend quelque part pas loin d'ici!» Wow!

— Enfin! Nous nous sommes trouvés, mon amour!

— Quelqu'un a fait ça pour vrai? Qui? demande Caroline.

— Lui, la chemise blanche là-bas au bout de la grande table, précise Katia.

— Ark, le vieux pet?

— Oui, madame!

— Dégueu...

— Là, tu vas pas coucher avec? s'interpose Vicky en frappant doucement son poing sur la table.

— J'y pense, peut-être. Je vais voir comment je *feel*.

— Je vais vomir, envoie Caroline.

— Mais si t'es malade maintenant, on ne saura pas si c'est à cause de cette pizza dégueulasse ou à cause de Katia qui se pogne un papi... Tu comprends, ce serait pas clair.

— Hi! hi! T'es drôle, Vic! Mais sérieusement, parlant de tactiques de *cruise* efficaces... Pensez-vous que j'aurais dû tenter de croiser Mike, tantôt...?

— Tu lui avais dit qu'on partait en catamaran?

— Oui, oui. Mais je veux quand même paraître intéressée un minimum, question qu'on tombe amoureux au plus vite.

— Ouin, il va sûrement venir souper ici.

Changeant de sujet, Vicky annonce :

— Des gens croisés à la plage m'ont dit qu'il fallait sortir en ville ce soir. Ils vont à un bar qui s'appelle le Havana Club. Il paraît que c'est super le *fun*.

— Ah, moi, ça me tente ! Ça va me changer les idées, tente de se convaincre Caro en mâchant avec difficulté un morceau de pizza durci.

Katia attrape machinalement un peu de lasagne froide dans son assiette, sans relever les propos de ses amies. Face à son mutisme, Caro lui demande :

— Allo ?

Katia sort des limbes puis relève la tête.

— Quoi ? Je pensais que je devrais trouver Mike pour lui proposer de venir avec nous.

Katia marque une pause. Puis, lançant sa fourchette dans son assiette :

— C'est dégueulasse, ces pâtes-là ! Tiens, je te vole des frites, Vic.

— Je vais aller en chercher une assiette pleine pour tout le monde, décide Caro.

— Bonne idée ! Merci !

Elle se lève et revient à peine quelques instants plus tard, son assiette chargée à bloc d'un énorme monticule de frites. Elle annonce à ses amies :

— Tantôt, je suis allée fouiller sur le profil Facebook de la fille que mon *chum* a ajoutée... Madame court des marathons et s'implique dans le bénévolat pour les paniers de Noël dans le temps des Fêtes. C'est un genre de mère Teresa, mais avec des fesses de béton. Elle me fait tellement suer, sérieux...

— Ah, Caro, arrête de te torturer avec ça. Je te le dis, c'est sûrement rien, insiste Katia.

— Ben oui, mais c'est QUI ? pleurniche Caroline.

— Personne...

— Demain, c'est le jour de l'An ! s'excite Vicky pour changer de sujet.

— Ouin, je me demande bien ce qu'ils vont organiser comme soirée spéciale !

— Ça sera sûrement le plus beau jour de l'An de notre vie !

Le nez en l'air pour observer les alentours, Vicky remarque que la blonde de Simon se trouve à une table avec plusieurs couples de vacanciers. Tout à coup, Simon se met à rire à gorge déployée et l'ensemble des occupants de la table se tourne vers elle. Se doutant bien du sujet dont il est question à cette tablée, Vicky baisse la tête de honte tout en s'enfouissant une énorme poignée de frites dans la bouche.

Près d'un palmier légèrement à l'abri des regards, Katia et Mike s'embrassent. Pour leur part, Vicky, Caro et Cédric attendent des taxis devant l'hôtel pour se rendre en ville. Caroline, observant discrètement Katia et Mike, donne un petit coup de coude à Cédric.

— Avoue qu'ils sont trop *cutes*! Et elle «paranoïe» encore qu'il ne soit pas intéressé…

— Ben oui, ben oui, marmonne le jeune homme, l'air blasé, tout en reportant les yeux sur son téléphone intelligent.

Ne comprenant pas trop sa réaction, les filles laissent tomber le sujet. Peut-être est-il déçu qu'elle s'accapare ainsi son père? Un premier taxi qui arrive dérange les amoureux.

— Bon, je saute dedans avec mon gars et on se rejoint à la *Calle* 62[30], annonce Mike en embrassant une ultime fois Katia comme s'il devait la quitter pour des mois.

— OK, sourit Katia en le regardant s'engouffrer dans le véhicule en étendant un peu la main comme une femme éplorée d'autrefois, saluant son mari qui part pour la guerre.

---

30. La 62e Rue, c'est vraiment un *must* à Varadero!

— Vous êtes vraiment *in love*, c'est fou, souligne Caroline, ravie pour sa copine.

— Les filles, je me sens étrange. On dirait que, lui, je voudrais le revoir pour de vrai à notre retour. Je sens pas que c'est un simple flirt de vacances.

— Tant mieux! Vas-y tranquillement, alors. Comme si c'était une vraie *date* au Québec, disons.

— Ouin, c'est un peu ce que je me dis.

Un deuxième véhicule se gare devant elles et coupe court à la conversation. Croyant qu'il s'agit d'une voiture personnelle, les filles s'éloignent un peu du chemin afin de libérer l'espace. La rutilante décapotable américaine rose bonbon semble directement sortie d'un film des années 1950. Voyant l'air ébahi des filles immobilisées sur le pavé, le chauffeur demande timidement:

— *¿Taxiii?*

— C'est vraiment un taxi?

— Malade! Une décapotable! Pensez-vous que c'est plus cher?

— Je sais pas. Je vais lui demander, dit Katia, avant de le questionner en anglais à propos du prix pour la course jusqu'au centre-ville.

— *Quince*[31].

---

31. Quinze.

— On nous avait dit que ça coûterait entre quinze et vingt pesos, donc il compte parmi les moins chers! *Let's go!* crie presque Vicky avant d'ouvrir la petite portière arrière, excitée comme une puce.

Caroline entre de l'autre côté tandis que Katia s'installe aux côtés du chauffeur, qui sourit de bonheur.

— ¡Vamos[32]!

Au moment où il démarre, quelqu'un qui arrive du lobby crie très fort: «Attendez-moi!» Le conducteur immobilise la voiture. Tout le monde se tourne pour observer la mouffette qui arrive au galop. Les genoux dans le front, il contourne la voiture et ouvre grand la portière du côté de Caroline pour ensuite la presser en douceur de se pousser au milieu afin qu'il puisse s'asseoir.

— Hé, yo! les salue-t-il, la fleur au fusil, en levant son verre de rhum sans glace qu'il n'a même pas daigné jeter avant d'entrer dans le véhicule.

Soudainement le mors aux dents, Caro reste muette et croise les bras.

— Qu'est-ce que tu fais là? glapit Katia.

Pas certain que l'intrus à la tignasse bicolore soit admis de façon légitime dans leur cohorte, le chauffeur ne redémarre pas.

---

32. Allons-y!

— Ah, je m'excuse, là, «ron coco»! Je voulais pas te brûler les cheveux par exprès, se repent le pauvre gars.

Silence. Malaise. Le chauffeur attend toujours, épiant la conversation dans son rétroviseur. Décidant alors que la rancœur ne devrait pas miner leur soirée, Caroline accepte ses excuses :

— OK, c'est beau, là.

— *Good!* envoie Dave, heureux, en ébouriffant les pauvres cheveux de Caroline de la main.

— Dépeigne-moi pas! Ç'a été assez difficile de faire quelque chose de potable avec ça, s'indigne celle-ci, trouvant le geste tout ce qu'il y a de plus déplacé compte tenu du contexte.

— Câlin, d'abord?

— Non plus, PAS de câlin. Bon, on s'en va.

Le perspicace chauffeur saisit, même sans rien comprendre, que la bonne entente règne maintenant au sein de son véhicule. Il démarre. Katia juge bon de remettre les pendules à l'heure avec le nouveau venu.

— Là, là, toi... Tu nous parles pas de ton père, OK? On le sait que ça te fait de la peine pis toute, mais là, on est en vacances et on veut que ça demeure léger.

— OK, promis, je vais être *light, light, light*! Yo!

Le soufflé de Drummond, qui sort du lobby avec des amis, les interpelle d'un «Hé!», le bras en l'air, juste avant que le tacot bifurque vers l'artère principale.

— Bon, l'autre moron, astheure... On partira jamais, je pense, se plaint Katia en se retournant.

Le gars arrive à son tour en courant près de la voiture.

— *Nice car*, les filles! Vous allez à la *Calle* 62?

— Oui, approuvent celles-ci, désabusées.

— Parfait, on vous suit! Que la vie nous guide où la vie nous mène...

— C'est ça, c'est ça, l'interrompt Katia en faisant signe au chauffeur de partir.

— Ayoye! Y en aura pas de facile, conclut Vicky en riant tout de même dans sa main.

— On part! Ouuuuuh! s'excitent les filles, enthousiastes face à la balade à venir.

Arrivés à destination, le chauffeur s'immobilise près du trottoir du côté de Vicky. Les filles sont dans tous leurs états.

— Décapotable de marde! Cibole, *checkez*-moi la tête! Dire que j'étais un peu *cute* avant de partir. Mais là? se plaint Vicky dont le beau chignon bien serré s'avère maintenant tout en broussailles.

— Seigneur, j'étais déjà désavantagée côté cheveux... Imaginez maintenant? beugle Caro en tentant de rapailler sa tresse démantibulée.

— Moi, il faut que je me peigne au plus vite, j'ai des nœuds partout, annonce Katia dont les cheveux étaient libres.

— On s'en fout, de vos cheveux! On va danser! *Woop! Woop!* s'excite la mouffette, qui ne semble pas plus dépeignée que d'habitude malgré la randonnée.

— Oui, on le sait que tu t'en fous des cheveux, toi, envoie Caroline.

— C'est où? interroge Vicky, qui voit seulement un hôtel de son côté de la route.

— De l'autre côté. Vous voyez la rue barrée? C'est là, explique Dave.

Les filles, déprimées par leurs efforts de mise en plis gaspillés en moins de dix minutes, sortent du véhicule l'air d'avoir passé la nuit sur la corde à linge.

— Ç'a valu la peine de se pomponner pendant une heure..., chiale Vicky en traversant la rue en compagnie du reste de la troupe.

Des hommes en uniforme et d'autres en civil s'entretiennent près d'une barrière de plastique jaune installée pour bloquer la fameuse soixante-deuxième rue, ayant inspiré le nom du bar Calle 62. L'établissement à aire ouverte est en fait un coin d'immeuble sans murs, offrant à la clientèle la joie de voir un spectacle à demi en plein air au cœur de la ville. Un bar longe le mur intérieur et un groupe sur la scène – devant laquelle sont disposées plusieurs tables – offre une prestation musicale latino. Les filles repèrent rapidement Mike et son fils, debout dans la rue, les sièges étant malheureusement tous occupés.

Au bar Calle 62, le touriste moyen côtoie de près la faune locale qui adore prendre d'assaut la rue afin d'y faire la fête toute la nuit. Des relents de fumée provenant de grillades qui crépitent sur la plaque d'un restaurant de rue juste en face confèrent une ambiance très typique de l'Amérique du Sud et centrale à l'endroit. La rue vibre littéralement à la cadence des piétinements et des corps qui s'entremêlent dans des mouvements rotatifs.

Katia fait un signe de la main à Mike avant de se diriger vers le bar avec les filles pour y cueillir une Cristal bien froide. À son retour, tout le monde apprécie la musique entraînante en observant tout autour les Cubains, pour qui l'heure de la fiesta a sonné. Les filles reconnaissent la chanson pour l'avoir entendue à quelques reprises sur le site du complexe hôtelier. Les gens dansent devant le groupe de musique, entre les tables, dans la rue, partout. On remarque des couples de toutes sortes : deux Cubains ou encore deux touristes, mais aussi beaucoup de couples métissés formés de touristes féminines et de Cubains. Les pieds de tous s'entremêlent au sol tantôt de façon habile, tantôt de façon maladroite. Les trois filles dansent plutôt sur place, la tête relevée vers la scène. Tout à coup, la chanson change et la foule s'anime comme jamais.

— Ah, tu vois, ce doit être une chanson super populaire ici, apprécie Caroline qui se laisse transporter par l'engouement ambiant en se dandinant avec allégresse.

Beau moment.

Au rythme du groupe latin *live* qui endiable la portion piétonnière de la *Calle* 62, Vicky se rend au bar pour commander un petit seau de bières pour tous. Katia en profite pour aller se soulager aux toilettes.

En arrivant à destination, elle bute sur une Cubaine installée derrière une petite table et qui lui tend la main, la paume vers le haut. Comprenant que la préposée exige de l'argent pour utiliser les cabinets de toilette, elle fouille dans sa poche à la recherche de quelques pesos.

En recevant son dû, la femme déroule alors un rouleau de papier hygiénique duquel elle déchire deux carreaux. Perplexe, Katia agrippe le chiche don et le brandit en l'air en demandant :

— *More, please...*

Sérieuse, voire un peu bête, l'employée fait non de la tête.

— Ben voyons ? se scandalise Katia en bon français.

La femme réitère son signe de tête avec aplomb en lui signalant de circuler.

— *Dos more, please...*, baragouine Katia dans les deux langues.

De plus en plus impatiente, la femme balaye de nouveau l'air devant elle pour signifier à la touriste harcelante qu'elle refuse ferme de lui en fournir davantage.

Katia s'éloigne finalement en la dévisageant sans révérence :

— Franchement! C'est assez *cheap*, merci! Quessé que tu veux que je fasse avec ça? en élevant bien haut les deux minuscules carrés de papier.

Pendant ce temps, Vicky, qui attend toujours au bar, remarque que la blonde de Simon se trouve tout près d'elle dans la file. Vicky baisse la tête afin de ne pas être repérée. Comme les clients entre les deux filles se retirent au fur et à mesure qu'ils ont été servis, le mouvement de la foule les force à se rapprocher pour ne pas perdre leur place. Malgré le fait que Vicky n'apprécie pas la manière dont la fiancée de Simon l'invective ouvertement devant tout le monde pour lui jeter au visage son échec, elle adopte le silence en espérant ainsi ne pas détériorer davantage leur «relation». Dans un état d'ivresse avancée, la mouffette pousse légèrement les gens du coude pour venir se stationner derrière les deux filles qui ne se regardent même pas, chacune faisant semblant de ne pas avoir vu l'autre. Reconnaissant la blonde de Simon avec qui il a jasé en début de journée, Dave déclare :

— Eille! Allo!

— Allo! s'illumine la fille en souriant de toutes ses dents, question de prouver à Vicky qu'elle est la personne la plus sympathique qui soit.

— Vous connaissez-vous ? On est tous au même hôtel ! précise la mouffette en prenant les deux filles par le cou.

— Oui, avoue sèchement la blonde de Simon, son sourire de dentiste se transformant du coup en un rictus d'arracheuse de dents.

Dave lui confie alors :

— Elle, c'est une «ron coco» qui «*frenche*-rien-que» ! Ha ! ha ! ha !

— Je le sais, ça ! rage la fille en grimaçant.

De nouveau honteuse et repentante, la pauvre Vicky se dégage de l'étreinte de la mouffette en secouant l'épaule puis elle regarde partout autour. La fille frustrée ayant été servie en premier, elle quitte le plateau sans mot dire.

Vicky se tourne vers Dave :

— Sérieux, toi, t'es jamais là au bon moment pis tu dis jamais la bonne affaire !

— Quoi ? Yo !

— Laisse faire...

Le groupe ayant terminé sa performance depuis un petit moment, la soirée s'essouffle au Calle 62. Le mouvement de foule semble diriger les fêtards vers le Havana Club, situé tout au fond de la rue, à environ deux minutes à pied. Tout le groupe se met d'accord pour s'y rendre.

Après avoir payé les frais pour entrer dans le club, ils aboutissent dans un espace pas très grand, mais déjà bien rempli de gens se dandinant. Le plancher de danse surplombé de deux boules disco est en contrebas et on y accède en descendant deux marches. Deux grands écrans géants un peu *vintage* projettent le vidéoclip de la chanson en cours. Le bar qui court le long du mur de gauche est entouré de blocs de verre dont certains sont éclairés, d'autres non. Le reste de l'établissement est noir – la peinture, le plancher ainsi que le comptoir du bar –, ce qui confère à l'endroit un air quelque peu lugubre.

La bande s'accoude au comptoir en faux marbre en attendant de recevoir un verre.

Vicky, qui danse avec un gars anglophone depuis déjà un bon moment, s'amuse comme une folle. Stuart, un homme d'environ quarante ans et résidant à Vancouver, est dégourdi et bien divertissant. Il l'invite à fumer un cigare dehors ; elle le suit. Au passage, elle aperçoit Mike, son fils et les deux filles qui s'enfilent des *shooters* au bar. Elle s'approche.

— T'as trouvé un autre *prospect* pour «*frencher*-rien-que»? demande discrètement Katia à son amie en zieutant Stuart qui se dirige vers la sortie.

— Je pense bien que oui… et il n'est pas en couple, lui, au moins ! Je lui ai déjà demandé, se réjouit Vicky en lui adressant un demi-sourire.

Tandis que Stuart discute avec un voyageur qu'il connaît, Vicky sort son téléphone, qu'elle a pris soin de connecter au réseau WiFi en arrivant au bar. Elle se rend sur le profil de Marc afin de voir s'il a affiché d'autres clichés de son voyage de gars. Deux nouvelles photos s'y trouvent, dont une de lui et ses amis avec quatre super belles filles. À première vue, Vicky semble reconnaître une des filles qui se trouvait aussi sur la photo précédente. «Encore elle?», rage intérieurement Vicky. Prise d'une illumination, elle demande à une fille à proximité de prendre une photo d'elle et de ses deux nouveaux «amis», et ce, malgré le fait qu'elle n'ait même pas adressé un traître mot à l'ami de Stuart.

Les deux gars collaborent en se plaçant côte à côte près de Vicky, qui sourit en levant les bras dans les airs comme si elle vivait la soirée la plus extraordinaire de toute sa vie. Satisfaite, elle regarde à peine la photo, puis elle la met en ligne.

Tentant de faire fi de la jalousie qui foisonne dans son cœur, elle rejoint ses amies à l'intérieur pour s'enfiler toujours des *shooters*, question de noyer ses tourments. Emplie d'une énergie tirant ses origines à la fois des effluves d'alcool et du déni, elle retourne danser auprès de Stuart. Tout en effectuant un ridicule mouvement de *moonwalk* raté, la mouffette se joint à eux. Le trouvant clairement moins fatigant lorsqu'il danse sans parler, Vicky lui sourit en se déhanchant.

Près d'une heure plus tard, la fête bat toujours son plein dans les entrailles de ce semblant de grotte cubaine. Vicky, en sueur, suit le rythme accompagnée d'un groupe de jeunes voyageurs dont fait partie Stuart. Tentant un rapprochement plus explicite, Vicky se colle contre l'homme en question en espérant que celui-ci comprenne bien évidemment son intention sous-jacente. Il répond de façon positive à sa manœuvre suggestive et la fait tournoyer sur elle-même comme on le fait en exécutant une danse latine. Comprenant que Stuart s'avère réceptif à son opération séduction, elle l'entraîne alors, en le tenant par la main, vers un coin sombre du bar pour prendre un *shooter*. Persuadée dur comme fer que Stuart craque raide dingue pour elle, Vicky boit cul sec son petit verre d'alcool et elle tente de nouveau un contact plus étroit. Les yeux un peu fuyants, elle triture les rebords du veston léger de son prétendant, l'air coquin. Il lui dit alors en anglais :

— T'es vraiment une femme très gracieuse, belle Vicky.

Saisissant la balle au bond, Vicky ferme les yeux et rapproche *prestissimo* son visage de celui de Stuart afin de l'embrasser. Tombé des nues, celui-ci plaque deux doigts sur ses lèvres au tout dernier moment avant d'avouer :

— Non, non, je suis pas…

— Hein ?

Confuse, elle ouvre les yeux et écarte les bras en le regardant.

— Je suis gai, Vicky. Me semble que c'est évident.

— Aaaah…

Vicky s'excuse, la mâchoire rendue au plancher, avant de lui sourire de façon étrange, honteuse de cette seconde tentative de séduction ratée.

Caroline, qui l'aperçoit surgir presque au pas de course, s'informe :

— Et puis ? Ça *frenche* pas mal ?

L'air cafardeux et sans dire un mot, Vicky lui désigne Stuart s'éclatant comme jamais auparavant avec la mouffette qui lui tient bien fermement les hanches par-derrière.

— Aaaaah, constate Caroline, qui comprend la situation sans avoir besoin d'un dessin.

Katia remarque aussi la scène au loin, avant d'avouer à son amie :

— Je voulais pas te le dire, Vic, mais c'était comme évident qu'il était aux hommes.

Mathieu, alias le gars qui tente toujours d'organiser plein d'activités, s'immisce dans le groupe comme un cheveu sur la soupe :

— Eille ! Vous êtes ici ! Super ! Je voulais vous dire, les filles, ç'a pas marché le souper de langoustes, finalement. On peut pas faire de feu sur la plage, pis on n'a pas trouvé de bateau à louer non plus… En tout cas…

— Hon, c'est plate, hein, se désole Katia en donnant un coup de pied discret à Caroline qui ricane sous cape.

— On se reprendra. Je suis sûre que tu vas avoir une autre bonne idée d'activité de même d'ici la fin du voyage ! en rajoute Vicky, ironique.

— Oui ! J'ai tout le temps plein d'idées !

JOUR 8

AÉROPORT MONTRÉAL-TRUDEAU
SALLE 315 – **9 H 58**

Alors qu'elles s'amusent à souhait en se remémorant le deuxième échec humiliant de leur amie, les filles se font déranger par un agent frontalier qui entre dans la pièce accompagné d'une collègue. Ils leur apportent leurs sacoches et leurs bagages à main.

— Enfin ! Dieu soit loué ! réagit Caro, heureuse, les deux bras vers le ciel.

— On nous a demandé de vous remettre vos effets personnels et de vous dire que la visite de l'inspecteur Biron devrait avoir lieu sous peu.

— Merci beaucoup, leur envoie Vicky en serrant son sac contre son cœur comme s'il était rempli de pièces d'or.

Les deux agents quittent les lieux aussitôt, pressés de retourner traiter un cas plus urgent.

À leur sortie, les filles lâchent simultanément un «Bon!» de soulagement puis sortent leur cellulaire en quatrième vitesse, comme si elles en avaient besoin pour respirer.

— Justement, Vicky, tu regarderas comme il faut la photo que t'a mise sur Facebook. Tu vas voir que c'était évident, pour ton gars de Vancouver.

— Je le sais. Je m'en suis bien rendu compte après...

Effectivement, Vicky se souvient qu'elle avait porté une attention plus particulière au cliché le lendemain matin. Les deux types se tenaient par la taille près d'elle, et l'ami de Stuart ne regardait pas du tout l'objectif, mais mirait plutôt le beau Canadien, avec une tendresse digne d'un jeune marié.

Vicky ajoute:

— Et moi, je la *poste* en me disant que je vais faire suer Marc à distance... Échec. Il a juste «aimé» la photo, mais il devait avoir le goût d'écrire: «Wow! Ils ont l'air le *fun* tes nouveaux amis gais!»

— Il n'y avait absolument rien pour rendre un gars jaloux là-dedans, crois-moi. *Epic fail*, ton affaire! s'amuse Katia.

— Ah! Mon *chum* s'inquiète..., commente Caroline, les yeux rivés sur son téléphone.

— Explique-lui pas la situation par texto, c'est trop compliqué. Il va capoter pour rien, conseille Vicky en constatant à sa grande déception qu'elle n'a pas reçu de message de Marc.

— Je sais. Je vais juste lui écrire que nous allons arriver bientôt sans trop lui expliquer où nous sommes. De toute façon, il me dit qu'il a couché au Best Western, hier, explique Caroline tout en écrivant.

Vicky fouille dans sa sacoche pour s'assurer qu'il n'y manque rien. Afin d'accéder à quelque chose tout au fond, elle sort une pile de papiers. En voyant les feuilles sur la table, Caroline lui demande :

— Comment ça fonctionne, pour les assurances ?

— La femme au téléphone m'a dit que je devais garder les originaux dans mes affaires, même si le cabinet de médecin leur en a télécopié une copie. Juste au cas où, je suppose.

Katia prend les documents de son amie et les inspecte.

— C'est écrit en espagnol. Je comprends absolument rien...

— Oui, je sais, mais les compagnies d'assurance doivent être habituées de recevoir de la paperasse dans plusieurs langues.

— Au moins, la bonne nouvelle, c'est qu'ils vont te rembourser. On nous déduit assez d'argent sur notre paie pour cette maudite assurance-là !

— Oui, oui, c'est certain. Une chance !

— Ça va mieux de ce côté-là ?

— Dur à dire. Ça pique encore, mais je pense que c'est parce que ça guérit.

— Voilà au moins une situation qui aura été simple à régler durant le voyage. Plate que ça arrive, mais pas trop complexe. J'imaginais que la démarche pour voir un médecin à l'étranger serait beaucoup plus laborieuse, dit Caroline.

— Oui, moi aussi. J'avoue que le tout s'est très bien passé...

JOUR 4

CUBA, VARADERO
COSTA AZUL DEL MAR RESORT

— Bon, c'est l'heure, fait Vicky en regardant sa montre.

— Oui, on va t'attendre ici, c'est correct? lui indique Katia en prenant place dans un fauteuil de rotin du lobby de l'hôtel.

— Oui.

Ayant demandé à la réception la marche à suivre pour rencontrer un médecin, Vicky a réussi à obtenir un rendez-vous dans l'heure suivante. Elle a cru comprendre que plusieurs docteurs se relaient dans les divers complexes hôteliers de Varadero afin que les voyageurs aient accès à des soins de santé particuliers au besoin. Elle a aussi contacté à frais virés sa compagnie d'assurance collective étant donné qu'elle avait déjà lu sur Internet que, lorsqu'on doit recevoir des soins à l'étranger, il faut contacter sa compagnie le plus tôt possible et de préférence avant de voir un médecin, sinon les frais pourraient ne pas être couverts[33]. L'employé de sa compagnie lui a aussi fourni un numéro de télécopieur où le détail de la consultation, dûment signé par le professionnel de la santé, devra être envoyé. Comme tout s'est orchestré très rapidement, Vicky a emprunté aux filles la somme nécessaire pour payer la consultation puisque seuls les paiements en espèces sont acceptés.

Un peu nerveuse, elle se dirige vers le corridor où se trouvent la coiffeuse, le centre de santé et la boutique de souvenirs.

En pénétrant dans la petite salle dont la porte est déjà ouverte, Vicky remarque que l'endroit ressemble plus à un salon de massage qu'à une clinique médicale. La grande pharmacie vitrée qui donne l'impression de contenir divers médicaments reste le seul indice permettant de deviner la vocation de la pièce.

À sa grande joie, sa requête intérieure secrète est exaucée ; une femme médecin se trouve en poste.

— *¡Hola[34] !* l'accueille la Cubaine d'une cinquantaine d'années.

— *¡Hola !*

---

33. Petit détail informatif ici. Ça peut être utile, sait-on jamais… ☺
34. Bonjour !

Dans un anglais à l'accent bien senti, la dame lui demande de s'asseoir sur la table et lui fait signe d'enlever ses sandales. Vicky ayant menti à la réceptionniste quant à la nature de la blessure à évaluer, elle doit maintenant rectifier le tir.

— Non, je n'ai pas vraiment mal au pied…, puis elle montre du doigt son postérieur à la femme.

— ¿Qué[35]?

Perplexe, la femme désigne le visage de Vicky, bronzé inégalement et de façon étrange.

— Non, non, j'ai juste bronzé avec mes lunettes de soleil…

Extrêmement gênée, Vicky lui baragouine une explication un peu bâclée lui relatant la cause de son malaise actuel. Une rainure large comme un labour du printemps se creuse dans le front de la pauvre docteure hispanophone. Elle ne saisit visiblement rien à son histoire rocambolesque de feuille d'arbre utilisée en ultime recours en guise de papier hygiénique.

— Un palmier? reprend la femme, confuse, toujours en anglais.

— Non, pas vraiment un palmier, mais une autre plante. Je ne sais pas trop laquelle en vérité, rectifie Vicky en évitant de croiser le regard du médecin.

---

35. Quoi?

Jugeant que de constater les faits par elle-même l'aidera sûrement davantage à faire la lumière sur ce cas singulier, la docteure lui demande d'enlever son short. Morte de honte, Vicky s'exécute en se disant : «Méchante connerie pareil...».

Les petits boutons et les rougeurs étant surtout situés au niveau de son interfessier, Vicky doit se coucher sur la table et relever le derrière afin que la dame aperçoive bien les symptômes visibles de son malaise. Ayant revêtu des gants de caoutchouc, la femme écarte un peu les fesses de sa patiente pour bien investiguer la situation.

— *Aaah, si. Comprendo*[36].

Heureuse que le médecin saisisse si rapidement la nature de sa désastreuse irritation cutanée, Vicky se réjouit. «Je dois pas être la seule de l'Univers à être entrée en contact avec cette plante toxique là...»

S'étant aussitôt fait une tête sur le cas, la femme retire ses gants et invite Vicky à se rhabiller.

Impatiente de connaître enfin le diagnostic, Vicky monte ses culottes sans se faire prier et elle s'approche de la femme qui rédige déjà le dossier. En silence, elle prend place sur la chaise devant elle, n'osant pas la déranger compte tenu de sa grande concentration. Elle espère en secret que la docteure aura un traitement concret et rapide à la portée de la main.

---

36. Ah oui. Je comprends.

Après avoir pris soin de relire ses notes deux fois plutôt qu'une en répétant quelques mots espagnols à voix basse, la femme sourit à Vicky avant de se lever. Elle ouvre la porte aux gonds un peu tremblotants de la pharmacie de métal et elle y fouille en étirant le cou pour bien voir tout au fond. Après un petit moment de recherche, elle en extirpe deux contenants. Faisant maintenant dos à Vicky, elle prépare la posologie adéquate.

À sa patiente, elle explique simplement en anglais, tout en lui remettant un contenant de pilules non identifié :

— Deux par jour, trois jours.

— D'accord.

— Et trois par jour, sept jours, en lui donnant un petit pot rempli d'une crème blanche.

— OK.

La femme rédige ensuite la facture qu'elle joint à la feuille de diagnostic. Comme tout semble nickel et en règle, Vicky jette un œil sur la facture : 130 pesos convertibles pour la consultation, 20 de plus pour les frais de déplacement, 80 pour les comprimés et la crème et 15 pour faire parvenir la télécopie aux assurances. Se foutant bien du prix total étant donné le remboursement imminent à son retour au Québec, Vicky remet 245 pesos à la femme qui inscrit ensuite *pagado*[37] sur sa facture. Puis, elle faxe les documents en question.

----

37. Payé.

Satisfaits de la simplicité de la démarche, Vicky et son fessier irrité quittent la salle en remerciant la femme.

À sa sortie, la voyageuse soulagée raconte tout à ses amies qui la suivent jusqu'à la chambre.

— Ce soir, c'est le jour de l'An, yahou ! s'excite Katia en se déhanchant dans le petit chemin pour faire rigoler ses amies.

— «*Bará, bará, bará, berê, berê, berê*», chantonne Vicky question de l'accompagner musicalement de façon adéquate.

— Je me demande vraiment si cette toune-là va jouer ce soir…

— Je le sais ben pas ! Tout un suspense, hein, les amies ?

— Vicky, je te conseille d'enlever tes lunettes pour ne pas empirer ta face de *racoon*.

— Ah oui, c'est vrai. Mais je déteste ça. J'ai le soleil dans les yeux, fait-elle malgré tout en les retirant.

— Il faut que tu sois belle, belle pour «*frencher*-rien-que» ce soir !

— Je dois avouer que c'est pas super bien parti, mon projet. Et n'allez pas croire que ce soit par manque de motivation de ma part…

— Dans ma tête, *frencher* dans le Sud, c'est aussi facile que de croiser un cowboy au festival western de Saint-Tite, évalue Katia, avec beaucoup de sérieux.

— C'est peut-être plutôt là-bas que je devrais aller *frencher*?

— On va sur le bord de la piscine en avant-midi et à la plage en *aprèm*? propose Katia.

— Bon plan! l'appuie Caroline.

En étendant leurs serviettes sur des chaises longues installées de biais avec le bar de la piscine, les filles entendent un chant partisan qui s'élève.

— *Go Habs, go! Go Habs, go! Go Habs, go!* crie à tue-tête un groupe de jeunes Québécois qui s'enfilent des *shooters* derrière la cravate malgré l'heure matinale.

— Calvince, c'est vraiment agressant, se plaint Vicky, les mains vers le ciel, en dévisageant avec beaucoup de mépris le groupe de jeunes gens.

Sans se soucier d'elles, les gars continuent de s'époumoner:

— *Go Habs, go! Go Habs, go!*

— C'est n'importe quoi, ce gueulage-là! On s'apprête pas à gagner la coupe Stanley, quand même! Les Canadiens sont pas en train de jouer la *game* de leur vie dans la piscine non plus! s'offusque Katia.

— Des jeunes..., mentionne Caro pour tempérer ses amies qui enlignent les gars, debout, les mains sur les hanches comme deux enseignantes en beau fusil.

— Jeunes... mais surtout fatigants, oui!

— On entend ça dans les corridors de l'école de la première semaine après la rentrée à l'avant-dernière semaine avant le congé d'été. En vacances, ça me tente juste pas! explique Vicky.

— Voulez-vous leur donner une copie? Les mettre en retenue dans la barboteuse? Ou appeler leurs parents, peut-être? raille Caroline, en s'allongeant avec grâce sur sa chaise longue.

— Non, mais leur conseiller avec rudesse de sacrer le camp dans un autre pays, peut-être, suggère Katia qui secoue la tête en guise de fierté face à sa superbe idée.

Les filles aperçoivent alors la mouffette qui arrive par le petit chemin suivi de sa valise à roulettes.

— Ah mon Dieu! C'est vrai! Il s'en va, lui! constate Vicky, comme si elle annonçait une nouvelle réjouissante à ses amies.

— Quelle belle journée! s'enflamme Katia en allongeant les bras pour ensuite les placer sous sa tête.

La main sur la poitrine, Caro exagère:

— C'est le plus beau jour de ma vie!

Vicky expire longuement, de façon quasi méditative, en guise d'approbation, puis elle ajoute :

— Enfin, la paix ! Là, nos vacances commencent pour de vrai ! Je suis quasiment émue, les filles…

La mouffette repère ses trois « amies » de loin et elle accourt dans leur direction, sa valise presque sur une roue. En arrivant à proximité, Dave feint un visage triste à souhait.

— Je m'en vais. Je vais pleurer…

— Nous autres aussi ! Regarde-nous la face ! déconne Katia, son sourire allant bien à l'encontre de son affirmation.

— Ça m'a fait plaisir de vous rencontrer. Je vous aime ! pleurniche Dave. Câlin ?

Conscientes qu'elles donneront la dernière accolade de leur vie à ce gars étrange, les filles acceptent en étendant les mains de façon nonchalante, sans même prendre la peine de se lever. Il les serre chacune leur tour et empoigne sa valise.

— Bon… Bye…

— Bye-bye, là ! lance Katia, encore extrêmement joyeuse.

Puis la mouffette disparaît de leur champ de vision – et de leur vie – à tout jamais[38].

––––––––––

38. Alléluia !

— Voulez-vous un petit mojito pour fêter ça, les filles ? demande Vicky en ne quittant pas des yeux le gars qui s'éloigne, comme si elle craignait qu'il revienne.

— Oh oui, un double ! Il faut célébrer en grand !

— Je vais en profiter pour aller dire leurs quatre vérités en pleine face aux jeunes débiles qui crient là-bas !

— Vicky…, soupire Caroline, prônant plutôt le «vivre et laisser vivre».

Tandis que Vicky se dirige vers le bar telle une furie, un couple accompagné de deux jeunes enfants passe devant Caro et Katia. Comme Caroline admire, avec des yeux de mère qui s'ennuie de sa progéniture, la gamine de tout au plus trois ans qui trottine avec un sceau de plastique rouge dans les mains, sa maman la salue :

— Bonjour ! Il fait beau !

— Ben oui !

La petite famille poursuit sa route. Katia attend un peu avant de s'avancer vers la chaise de Caro pour lui cracher :

— Sérieux, je suis plus capable des commentaires sur la température… OK, il faisait frais les deux premiers jours, mais depuis il fait super beau. Donc ça va, on peut en revenir, tout le monde ! On est dans le SUD les amis, donc on «trippe» pas tant que ça parce qu'il fait beau ! C'est pas la surprise de l'année du tout. Si on était en voyage en Sibérie en plein hiver et que là, on constatait : «Ayoye, il fait 35 degrés ?» on mentionnerait aux nouvelles que ce n'est JAMAIS arrivé dans toute l'histoire de la Sibérie. Là, ce serait impressionnant et pas normal, donc ça vaudrait la peine d'en parler souvent, tsé… MAIS LÀ, C'EST JUSTE NORMAL, SIMONAQUE!

— Calme-toi, Kat, tu me postillonnes dessus.

— Excuse-moi. Je me suis laissé emporter…

— C'est un comportement typiquement québécois, on n'y peut rien. Chaque fois que je mets de l'essence proche de chez nous, la fille à la caisse me décrit la température qu'il fait dehors, du genre: «Il pleut aujourd'hui?» ou «Y a des nuages, hein?» C'est juste pour faire la conversation, je pense.

— Tu vois? Pourquoi décrire à quelqu'un la température du moment? EILLE, CHOSE? ALLO? JE LE SAIS CRISS, J'ARRIVE DE DEHORS! Si tu veux me communiquer une information adéquate, dis-moi: «On annonce un méga tsunami, il faut vite aller aux abris!» ÇA, c'est pertinent! Mais me dire qu'il fait soleil dehors, pendant que je me mets de la FPS 30 dans la face en suant ma vie, c'est I-NU-TI-LE!

-Coudonc, vas-tu être menstruée toi aussi ou quoi? demande Caroline.

— Ben non… j'ai juste soif, c'est pour ça. Voyons, c'est vraiment long son affaire, fait remarquer Katia en levant le nez en direction du bar.

Curieusement, Vicky est toujours là, debout près du comptoir. En analysant la scène avec plus d'attention, les filles remarquent qu'elle est entourée du groupe de jeunes garçons avec qui elle discute, étant donné qu'ils ont cessé de scander des encouragements inutiles pour leur équipe sportive préférée. Les trois cocktails, qui semblent prêts, reposent devant elle.

— Elle est en train de les chicaner, tu crois ? se désole Caroline.

Contre toute attente, Vicky éclate alors de rire à en perdre haleine avant de taper son voisin immédiat sur le torse en réaction à son excellente blague.

— Bon… elle *cruise* ! Sacrée Vicky…, rectifie Caroline en secouant la tête de découragement.

— T'aimerais pas ça, te pogner un jeune, toi ? ose Katia en fixant la piscine pour ne pas affronter le regard de son amie.

— Ark, non ! Du genre plus un poil, parce qu'il se l'épile au Neet ? Non merci !

— Un jeune avec un peu de poil, mettons.

— Quel âge, s'il a du poil ?

— Je sais pas, mais plus jeune que toi de plusieurs années.

— Pis son poil est où exactement ?

— Aaaah, laisse faire, Caro… Il fait beau soleil, hein ?

Vicky, qui revient au bercail en trottinant avec candeur, arbore le sourire radieux d'une jeune mariée en pleine lune de miel. Elle claironne un «madame» poli en distribuant aux filles les cocktails.

— Coudonc?! Viens-tu juste de «*frencher*-rien-que» sans qu'on te voie?

— Euh... non, mais ils sont super fins, les jeunes, finalement!

— Tiens, Caro se demandait justement: Ont-ils du poil? Si oui, où? Et à quel âge le premier a-t-il poussé?

— Hein? De quoi vous parlez? J'ai pas remarqué leurs poils pantoute, mais je sais juste que je me suis fait complimenter solide! Oh que oui, mesdames!

— Ah oui?

— Je suis très *cute,* il paraît! déclare Vicky, le nez en l'air, fière comme une paonne.

— Ça fait toujours plaisir!

— Celui à la camisole rouge a un peu gâché le portrait avant que je parte en précisant que j'étais belle «pour une vieille», mais bon. Il était plus soûl que les autres et il ressemblait à un hobbit, alors je m'en fous!

— *Go Habs, go,* d'abord! envoie Katia en levant son verre de plastique.

Voyant qu'il contient autre chose que le mojito espéré, elle s'informe:

— Euh, c'est quoi, au juste?

— Ben oui, c'était long au bar parce qu'ils n'avaient plus de rhum, imaginez-vous donc !

— Hein ? s'étonne Caroline. On n'est pas à Cuba ? Me semble que c'est leur spécialité, ça, et que ça coûte juste deux dollars la bouteille, non ?

— Ben oui. Je sais pas c'est quoi l'affaire. En tout cas, un des barmans est parti depuis vingt minutes pour aller en chercher, ce qui explique pourquoi il y avait un *line-up* de deux cents personnes. Je nous ai rapporté des vodkas-limonade à la place, ça me tentait pas d'attendre !

Après avoir sapé une bonne gorgée de son verre, Katia crache avec dépit :

— Limonade ? C'est pas ça pantoute ! C'est du Seven-Up !

Caroline qui a aussi goûté au cocktail, ajoute :

— Je veux pas avoir l'air de te reprendre Kat, mais je dirais plutôt du Seven-Up « flat ».

— On va surveiller le retour du préposé au rhum...

Comme Katia revient auprès des filles après avoir passé quelque temps à barboter plus loin avec son soupirant, Caroline la taquine :

— Hé ! Tu t'amuses bien avec ton *chum* et ton beau-fils !?

— Ouais... On a du gros, gros *fun*..., fait Katia en souriant à demi tout en mirant les alentours.

— Parle-nous-en un peu, de lui ! T'es vraiment discrète, je trouve...

Katia fait alors diversion en désignant un objet non identifié reposant au bord de la piscine en face de leurs chaises.

— C'est à qui, ça ?

— C'est quoi ? fait Vicky en approchant. Ah mon Dieu ! crie-t-elle en réalisant de quoi il s'agit.

— Quoi ? demande Caro, restée un peu plus loin.

— Hon, hon, hon... Je suis prise au dépourvu, je sais pas quoi faire, avoue Vicky, les deux mains bien hautes en observant les alentours à la recherche de renfort immédiat.

Les filles approchent et pouffent de rire en identifiant à leur tour l'objet en question.

— Hein...

— Ayoye ! Il faut faire quelque chose. Il faut intervenir ! décide Caroline, en regardant aussi tout autour.

— Bon...

Les trois filles fixent de très près – comme si elles n'avaient jamais vu ça de leur sainte vie – un dentier reposant tranquillement sur le bord de la piscine.

— C'est quoi? Il faut faire le tour des gens étendus autour de la piscine en leur demandant s'ils ont perdu leurs dents?

— On fait un appel à tous au haut-parleur?

— Ou on demande à mes amis de crier : «DENTIER!!!» à la place de «*Go Habs, Go!*», propose Vicky qui désire secrètement se faire à nouveau complimenter par la jeunesse environnante.

— Ou encore, on va au buffet pour identifier quelqu'un qui se prend une assiette de manger mou? s'illumine Katia, fière de son idée géniale.

— Vous êtes tartes! On va juste le rapporter à la réception, décide Caroline.

— OK! Prends-le, toi, Caro!

— Ark, non...

— On va le mettre dans un de nos verres vides, propose Vicky.

Elle agrippe donc un verre vide dans la généreuse pile reposant sous la chaise de Vicky – le gars du rhum étant revenu depuis une heure. En moins de deux secondes, elle réalise avoir besoin d'un second outil pour soulever le dentier afin de le mettre dans le verre sans avoir à y toucher. Elle s'étire alors pour attraper deux autres verres vides dont elle se sert comme des pinces pour prendre l'objet afin de le déposer dans le premier verre. Le dentier tombe tout au fond entre des restants de limette et des feuilles de menthe encore trempées.

— Voilà! Je vais aller le porter.

— Eille, je veux absolument voir la face de la réceptionniste! J'y vais avec toi!

— Moi aussi! C'est une grosse mission! Il faut faire ça en groupe...

En arrivant au comptoir, Vicky y dépose le verre de plastique contenant le dentier au mojito et elle sourit en direction de l'employée qui avance vers elle, l'air perplexe à souhait.

— *¿Dientes*[39]*?*

— *¡Si! ¡La piscina!*

Démunie, la femme tourne la tête à gauche, puis à droite, comme si elle espérait voir surgir un collègue pour lui refiler illico l'étrange dossier. Personne ne vient. Elle tire donc un peu le verre vers elle avec dédain, puis remercie les trois filles en reculant le visage comme si elle craignait d'attraper le scorbut à distance.

Les filles, qui s'amusent de la situation, repartent.

— Qu'est-ce qu'ils vont faire avec, vous pensez?

— Aucune idée.

---

39. Des dents?

Après quelques verres supplémentaires sirotés bien confortablement dans la piscine, les filles mettent fin à leur petite saucette afin de prendre un bain de soleil. Une voix qu'elles reconnaissent bien les fait tressaillir :

— Eille, les «ron coco qui *frenchent*-rien-que»!

— QUOI ? Non… Non…, crie Vicky aux aguets, ne comprenant pas comment cela est possible.

— Hein ? Il est revenu ? C'est un vrai cauchemar…, se scandalise Katia, les yeux bien ronds.

En moins de deux, Dave atterrit près d'elles et se rue sur Caroline pour la serrer dans ses bras.

— Câlin !

— Non, non, non, s'oppose celle-ci, puis elle lève une main dans les airs lui signalant ainsi de reculer de son espace vital en effectuant au minimum trois pas.

Dave s'exécute docilement.

— Je voulais juste un petit mini câlin pour fêter une belle nouvelle…

— Qu'est-ce que tu fais encore ici ? lui crie par la tête Katia.

— Imaginez-vous donc que c'est la tempête du siècle à Toronto ! L'avion ne décollera pas ! Ils ont ramené tout le monde à leur hôtel. On partira demain, après-demain ou l'autre après-demain, on le sait pas encore. C'est génial!

— Hein? Il y avait pas d'autres options? fait de nouveau Katia, l'air abattu.

— Ouin... Aucun vol ce soir? enchaîne Vicky, comme si elle négociait la situation pour elle-même.

— Non! Câlin?

— Ne-non... Pis arrête de dire «câlin» tout le temps. On aime pas ça, les câlins, bon! répond sèchement Katia pour lui signifier de se calmer les ardeurs affectives un peu.

Déçu du refus de rapprochement, il observe les filles sans rien dire. Les trois vacancières fixent maintenant la piscine devant, en dépression totale. Affichant toujours la mine radieuse du gars trop heureux de revenir au complexe hôtelier, il respire un bon coup avant de demander:

— En passant, Caroline... si je tire, qu'est-ce que je gagne? Ha! ha! ha!

— Hein? De quoi tu parles, encore?

— Si je tire, est-ce que tu t'allumes comme une grosse luciole?

— Laisse faire «la grosse», s'il te plaît! Tirer sur quoi, au juste? Je comprends pas, s'impatiente Caroline, craignant qu'il s'apprête indirectement à mettre la table pour livrer un autre témoignage touchant concernant son père.

Katia expire bruyamment son désarroi au grand jour sans trop lui prêter attention pendant que Vicky envoie la main aux jeunes du bar qui la jaugent encore de loin.

— Tirer sur… ÇA! crie la mouffette en désignant du doigt l'entrejambe de Caroline.

— Hein? Ah mon Dieu! panique celle-ci en cachant du coup la cordelette fuyante de son tampon qui sortait tel un bébé couleuvre du bas de son maillot de bain.

Katia explose de rire.

— Quoi? Son tampon? réagit Vicky, un peu à retardement.

Katia étant trop crampée pour répondre, Caro pleurniche la réponse à sa place:

— Ouiiiii… Franchement, vous auriez pu me le dire, les filles! finit-elle par rugir en fusillant du regard ses amies qui rient toujours comme deux folles. C'est donc ben compliqué de gérer ça en voyage…

— Gère Caro! Gère! finit par scander Katia, le visage tordu.

— Bon, sur ce, je vous laisse. Je pars en balade annoncer à tout le monde que je suis revenu! indique Dave en effectuant un saut dans les airs pour ensuite joindre ses deux talons ensemble d'un petit coup sec.

Sans rien ajouter, la mouffette s'enfuit en gambadant comme un jeune écolier trop heureux le jour de la rentrée. Vicky, encore à son émoi, analyse:

— Avant, il m'énervait tout court. Maintenant, je le déteste. Il me tape tellement sur les nerfs d'être revenu !

— Il me tape sur les nerfs ! Toronto me tape sur les nerfs ! L'hiver me tape sur les nerfs ! exagère Katia.

Un tapage cacophonique dérange son allocution haineuse envers la mouffette.

— Oléé ! Olé ! Olé ! Olé ! Oléé ! Oléé !

— Ah ! voyez-vous, mes *chums* ont changé de toune pour encourager à distance les Canadiens qui jouent même pas !

JOUR 8

AÉROPORT MONTRÉAL-TRUDEAU
SALLE 315 – **10 H 04**

Katia se remémore avec joie la scène du cordon indésirable, puis éclate de rire à nouveau :

— Le fameux Tampax, quel classique savoureux ! C'est indémodable !

— Laisse faire...

— Parlant d'incontournable, encourager les Canadiens en gueulant n'importe où dans le monde, voilà un autre grand classique québécois, je pense, souligne pertinemment Vicky.

— Ouin, c'est un drôle de comportement, analyse Katia. Ça sert à quoi de crier de même dans un autre pays ? Non, mais si t'es au Centre Bell, je peux comprendre, mais sinon...

— Une fois, en vacances avec le petit et Éric dans un chalet au lac Memphrémagog, nos voisins immédiats avaient chanté ça pendant trois heures d'affilée au bord de leur feu de camp, se rappelle Caroline, pas certaine non plus de trouver la chose très brillante.

— C'était très, très bizarre...

— Comme l'intégralité de ce voyage, d'ailleurs.

— Et dire qu'on a commencé l'année de même...

— Quand ça ? À la soirée du jour de l'An la plus extra-ordinaire de notre vie ? suppose Vicky, ses yeux roulant d'ironie jusqu'au plafond.

JOUR 4

CUBA, VARADERO
COSTA AZUL DEL MAR RESORT

Après avoir mangé une soupe claire au goût étrangement laiteux – question de survivre –, les filles s'installent sur la plage, bien décidées à continuer de profiter au maximum de cette journée festive. Le ciel est entièrement dégagé et au loin, on entend la musique latino qui accompagne le concours de hula-hoop qui se déroule à la piscine. Un magnifique pélican effectue un plongeon vertigineux tout près de la plage, ce qui tire Vicky de sa rêverie.

— Ah wow!

— On dirait que je ne réalise comme pas qu'on change d'année ce soir, souligne Caro en admirant le splendide panorama, qui rend la perspective du changement d'année si abstraite.

— Me semble qu'aujourd'hui, j'aurais aimé ça faire partie d'une gang le *fun* comme durant notre voyage au Mexique, songe Vicky en observant les gens autour.

— Écoute, t'as du choix en masse! Nous avons le soufflé de Drummond pas trop loin à notre droite, propose Katia, toute main levée, l'air de lui présenter le tableau des cocos à l'émission *La Poule aux œufs d'or*.

— Ah non, pas de phrases sur «la vie» toute une journée de temps, pitié!

— Désolée, j'ai pas le temps de penser à notre vie sociale en ce moment, je suis bien trop occupée à m'assurer que ma corde de tampon ne sorte pas de mon maillot, dit Caro, sérieuse comme si sa mission s'avérait au premier plan d'une liste d'enjeux importants.

— Oui, gère ça! rigole Vicky.

Katia poursuit:

— Sinon, ma chère Vicky, il y a toujours le couple qui filme n'importe quoi tout le temps! Tu pourrais les suivre toute la journée et faire des vidéos avec eux! Le rêve, quoi!

— Non, merci. À moins que je me joigne plutôt à eux ? propose Vicky en désignant du menton la blonde de Simon et trois autres couples qui s'amusent en buvant un coup à quelques mètres d'elles.

Les filles les espionnent furtivement. La blonde de Simon parle fort. Mesquine, elle jette de temps à autre un regard méprisant vers Vicky, question de lui faire sentir à tout instant qu'elle l'a à l'œil. Curieusement, Simon n'est pas avec eux.

— Eille… elle va-tu en revenir à un moment donné, la grosse pas fine ?

Les trois profs observent les alentours afin de poursuivre la blague concernant Vicky qui se cherche des amis. Elles aperçoivent alors au loin des vacanciers qui les fixent de leurs chaises longues.

— Ah mon Dieu ! Ils sont encore là, eux autres ? On ne les avait jamais revus ! s'étonne Caroline en leur riant au nez.

Subtiles comme trois astronautes dans un rassemblement de moines tibétains, les filles détaillent les deux Russes rencontrés lors de leur première soirée. Les deux types, qui ont visiblement choisi leur chaise en fonction de leur voisinage immédiat, dévisagent en alternance les trois filles à leur droite ainsi que deux autres jeunes femmes devant eux qui lisent tranquillement sous leur *palapa*. Buvant avec une inextinguible soif de la bière dans un énorme thermos «*I love Cuba*», les deux gars secouent la tête tout comme lors de cette fameuse soirée à la discothèque de l'hôtel.

— *Bobbleheads... The Return!* envoie Katia avec une voix de présentatrice de gala.

— Sérieux, pourquoi ils font ça avec leur tête? se questionne à nouveau Caroline, désireuse d'en apprendre davantage sur les particularités synergologiques des pays nordiques.

— «Il est grand, le mystère de la foi...», proclame Vicky.

— Une simple façon de communiquer avec son prochain? Ils parlent pas un mot d'anglais, les pauvres...

Un gars motivé à souhait arrive alors au trot devant les filles qui lézardent toujours dans leur chaise en papotant à propos des autres[40].

— Les filles! Les filles! J'ai eu une super idée d'activité pour aujourd'hui!

— Aaaah, on t'écoute! feint de s'enthousiasmer Katia en reconnaissant bien Mathieu, l'hyperactif-super-motivé toujours enclin à proposer un nouveau projet saugrenu impossible à réaliser.

— Écoutez ça! C'est comme le jeu de limbo, mais plus sportif et modifié, mettons. On fait jouer la fameuse chanson de limbo que tout le monde connaît. Tsé là, tut, tut, tut, tututu, tut, tut, tutut...

---

40. Activité classique de «tout inclus». Vrai ou pas?

Mathieu fredonne l'air de la chanson jusqu'à ce que Vicky le coupe :

— Oui, oui, ZE chanson de limbo, là !

— Ouais, mais au lieu du jeu traditionnel avec le bâton et tout, c'est à vélo ! En fait, on remplace le bâton horizontal par une saucisse au bout d'une tige. Là, quelqu'un tient la saucisse bien haute. Environ cinq personnes participent en même temps, disons. Si on est plus, on fera deux équipes. Là, les gens doivent tourner en rond à bicyclette et, quand ils passent devant le gars qui tient la saucisse, ils doivent réussir à l'attraper en mordant dedans. Ce qui est drôle, c'est qu'on trempe la saucisse dans la moutarde avant... Ha ! ha ! ha ! Malade, hein ? Ça vous tente ?

Comme s'il leur racontait avoir aperçu une bonne douzaine d'extraterrestres verdâtres sur le bord de la piscine, les filles le contemplent, la bouche ouverte, interloquées.

Comme elles restent muettes, il répète :

— Ça vous tente ?

— Ben, euh...

— Pourquoi la moutarde, au juste ? s'informe Caroline pour avoir l'air de s'intéresser un minimum aux aspects techniques entourant son activité débile.

— Ah ben là, ça peut être du ketchup aussi. Pas de trouble ! Un condiment, n'importe lequel. Donc, on va essayer d'aller louer des vélos, de se procurer des saucisses... Euh, ça va nous prendre aussi une radio, c'est vrai...

Silence. Bruits de criquets cubains.

— Facque... vous autres vous aimez mieux du ketchup, c'est ça ?

— Euh, pas celui du buffet en tout cas...

— Bon, je vous tiens au courant ! Bye !

— Oui, oui, c'est ça... Bye ! le congédie cavalièrement Katia, considérant que l'activité qu'il vient de leur proposer se situe en tête de liste des moins intéressantes sur terre.

Comme il est reparti aussi vite qu'il était arrivé, les filles ont le champ libre pour commenter dans son dos :

— J'ai jamais vu un gars partir sur des bulles de fou de même !

— Il consomme du LSD de façon quotidienne, c'est certain !

— On dirait Louis-José Houde en *overdose* de *speed* !

— Un limbo-bicycle-saucisses ? On aura tout vu ! approuve Caro, presque étourdie par la complexité du projet.

— Juste à en entendre parler, je suis brûlée, exagère Vicky.

— Cette fois, je suis sans mot, les filles… *My god*, j'ai besoin d'un *drink* au plus vite pour m'en remettre ! conclut Katia en se levant.

Après avoir empilé beaucoup trop de verres vides sous leur *palapa*, les filles sont prises d'une idée de génie à leur tour. Un concept farfelu, mais tout de même plus classique que ceux de Mathieu.

— On enterre quelqu'un dans le sable et on prend une photo drôle pour mettre sur Facebook !

— OUIIIII !

— OK ! Mais pas moi…, répond Caroline en replaçant ses lunettes de soleil avant de revérifier que sa fameuse corde ne dépasse pas.

Vicky, qui voit là une superbe opportunité de montrer à Marc que ses vacances s'avèrent les plus démentiellement amusantes du monde entier, propose sans hésiter sa candidature.

— Moi ! Moi ! Et vous me ferez un habit en coquillages par-dessus le sable ! ajoute-t-elle, incapable de se défaire de son esthétisme d'enseignante d'arts plastiques.

— Tsé, ça c'est un projet amusant de voyage dans le Sud… Pas un limbo-saucisse-bicycle-machin, souligne Caroline, enjouée comme jamais par la proposition.

Sans plus attendre, les filles s'activent. Elles creusent d'abord un genre de fossé avec leurs mains pour que Vicky puisse être un peu en dessous du niveau de la mer et soit ainsi plus facile à recouvrir de sable. Sans surprise, les trois filles à genoux – donc les fesses relevées – attirent le regard de plusieurs voyageurs qui observent – l'air de rien – le panorama avantageux que le projet des belles touristes leur procure. Pendant le travail, qui s'avère tout de même ardu pour des vacances, Katia s'informe d'un détail non négligeable :

— Caro, tu gères ta corde, j'espère ?

— QUOI ? Dis-moi pas qu'elle est encore sortie ?

— Je l'ignore, mais je sais juste que je dénombre minimum deux cents pervers qui vous matent le cul en ce moment.

Vicky et Caroline, qui sont côte à côte face à la mer, se tournent alors vers le *résore* pour constater d'elles-mêmes les allégations de Katia. Les quelques hommes qui se rinçaient l'œil – Katia ayant largement exagéré leur nombre – détournent tous le regard au même moment, comme s'ils n'avaient jamais, mais au grand jamais, osé « échapper » les yeux sur le postérieur d'une femme n'étant pas la leur.

Davantage intéressées à poursuivre leur mission qu'à identifier les vicieux qui les épient, les deux filles se remettent à la tâche en creusant de plus en plus profondément, donc en relevant encore plus le derrière. Au moment où Katia a conscience qu'un jeune homme prend une photo de la scène avec son téléphone intelligent, elle met ses amies en garde à nouveau.

— Vos culs vont se retrouver sur Facebook, je vous le dis...

— Ben voyons? Gang d'obsédés!? s'indigne Vicky avec agacement en pivotant une fois de plus vers la berge.

Cette fois, elle aperçoit bien l'énergumène qui les a prises en photo sans leur consentement. Le jeune – ayant tout au plus vingt-cinq ans – et son ami sont assis, pénards, sous une ombrelle de feuilles de bambou. Un peu «cocktail», Vicky monte sur ses grands chevaux et fonce droit sur eux.

— Euh, les gars? Quand on prend la photo d'une fille sur la plage, on le fait dis-crè-te-ment au cas où vous le saviez pas!

— *Chill out*, là! On se calme! l'apaise l'un d'eux, une main vers le ciel.

— Capote pas, on te trouve belle, c'est tout.

Vicky, un peu prise de court de se faire ainsi flatter l'*ego* alors qu'elle est supposée être choquée noir, hésite à poursuivre ses invectives.

— Ah... ben... merci...

— *Anyway*, on a rencontré un gars qui s'appelle Simon, hier, et on a eu vent que t'étais du type «chaude lapine» pas mal! ajoute l'autre en lui envoyant une œillade complice comme s'il envisageait sérieusement d'amorcer une histoire olé olé avec elle.

— Pfft! souffle Vicky, de nouveau offusquée à souhait, en tournant les talons pour revenir près des filles sans avoir rien trouvé à répliquer à ce commentaire désobligeant.

— Lui, là! Lui, là!

— Quoi? Qui?

— Le Simon qui répand partout sur le *résore* que je suis une charrue, je vais lui... je vais lui... je vais me venger! Ah oui! Cibole que oui!

— Ah oui! Venge-toi! C'est drôle quand tu te venges! l'encourage Katia, avide de susciter des dénouements croustillants pour cette semaine de vacances beaucoup trop tranquille à son goût.

— Comment tu vas faire? s'informe Caroline, plus craintive qu'emballée.

— Regardez-moi bien aller! Je vais trouver quelque chose...

Katia continue de creuser en cherchant elle aussi comment son amie pourrait bien le faire payer pour sa langue sale. En fixant le sable qui s'accumule près de ses genoux, elle sourit mesquinement...

Une fois le trou assez large et profond pour que Vicky puisse s'y glisser, celle-ci s'y allonge comme dans un tombeau exotique. Elle change finalement d'idée à la dernière minute et elle se relève pour aller chercher ses verres fumés.

— Pour la photo, ça va être plus joli avec mes lunettes, dit-elle en reprenant position dans son terrier.

Elle en ressort une fois de plus en plaidant :

— Non, je veux vous aider à trouver les décorations avant !

Caroline agrippe un des deux sacs de plage dans lesquels elles glissent leurs effets personnels de valeur, et les trois vacancières se séparent pour partir en expédition dans les environs. Katia, qui longe la mer, trouve de beaux petits coquillages blancs tandis que Caroline déniche, le long d'un muret de briques délimitant la zone du complexe hôtelier, deux branches de bois poreux un peu grugées par l'érosion ainsi que des feuilles de palmier. Vicky découvre sur la plage une partie de noix de coco triangulaire qui pourrait très bien servir, selon elle, à faire le bas de son maillot de bain fictif. D'instinct, les trois filles convergent finalement vers le bar, succombant à l'appel aérien subliminal d'un bon mojito bien frais.

S'étant acquittées de leur mission principale dans un temps record, elles reviennent à leur point de départ investies d'une énergie festive foudroyante.

— Ça va être trop *hot* !

— Belle photo en perspective..., fantasme Vicky.

— Ark, c'est quoi ça? s'inquiète Katia en approchant de quelque chose d'étrange et de poilu gisant dans le sable.

— Hein? On dirait un animal mort!

Katia trouve un bâton et soulève le truc à la hauteur de ses hanches. Vicky, qui a hérité du verre de Katia tandis que celle-ci s'acquitte de sa mission, s'écrie:

— Une moumoute?

— Ouais, c'est vraiment un *top* de tête, juste le dessus, analyse Katia. Une demi-perruque.

— Ah ben, coudonc! Un dentier, et maintenant des cheveux? Il y a un monsieur Patate qui se démantibule quelque part sur le *résore*, certain!

— C'était quand même naïf de sa part de penser jouer dans les vagues sans la perdre...

— On s'entend que je ne vais pas porter ce truc-là à la réception, décide Katia en laissant choir le bâton ainsi que la perruque dans le sable, près de leur paillote.

— C'est peut-être au vieux qui te *cruisait* au buffet en prenant le même «manger» que toi? s'illumine Vicky.

— Il est justement là-bas, regardez...

L'homme au torse poivre et sel, qui paresse sur une chaise de plage, est entouré de deux splendides Latinos ayant sans l'ombre d'un doute l'âge d'être ses filles. Les Cubaines rigolent en buvant un verre, visiblement ravies de relaxer à ses côtés.

— Aaaark! Vieux dégueu...

— Il se paie de la compagnie... Pas juste une, mais bien DES putes. Y a rien de trop beau pour la classe ouvrière, hein, chuchote Katia, comme si la police écoutait leur conversation à l'aide de micros dissimulés dans le sable.

Retournant à leur occupation, les filles ensevelissent Vicky en débutant par les pieds et les jambes. Katia tapote avec vigueur la surface, debout sur le monticule recouvrant la moitié du corps de Vicky. Cette dernière s'inquiète :

— Pas trop compact, je vais rester prise là, après !

Progressant vers le haut du corps, les filles font des mouvements de pieds énergiques pour rabattre la terre humide sur leur amie.

— Hum... C'est frais, apprécie Vicky en prenant une dernière gorgée de son verre avant de le poser dans le sable.

Vicky allonge les bras le long de son corps telle une momie pour ainsi permettre à ses complices de terminer son ensevelissement. Après avoir pris soin de ne pas accumuler de sable trop près de son visage, les filles compactent la surface avec leurs mains avant de commencer à sculpter avec habileté la zone supérieure afin de lui donner un genre de forme humaine.

— On va te faire des belles rondeurs de femme bien en chair...

— D'énormes seins, surtout !

— Oui, oui!

— Eille, je vous le dis, les filles, même en forçant, j'arrive pas à sortir mes bras du sable...

Un vieil homme vêtu d'un ensemble à motifs hawaïens approche des filles sur la plage, puis leur offre des arachides emballées dans de petits sacs de plastique.

— *No, gracias*, le remercie Katia, bien trop occupée pour collationner.

Le type repart vers d'autres vacanciers.

Les deux apprenties artistes fignolent la décoration de leur corps de sable en apposant la coquille de noix de coco en guise de bas de bikini. Constatant qu'il manque des coquillages pour terminer le haut de bikini, elles partent à la chasse aux trésors en laissant Vicky en plan avec le sac de plage. Celle-ci patiente, tout sourire, le nez vers le ciel. Les vacanciers qui passent s'amusent de la voir dans cette drôle de posture. Les filles reviennent avec le nécessaire pour lui confectionner un haut de maillot de bain en coquillages digne d'une robe de soirée de la Petite Sirène.

— Ça va être vraiment beau!

— Bon! Donnez-moi une gorgée, quelqu'un!

Caroline approche le verre et place la paille dans la bouche de son amie comme on le ferait pour nourrir un individu ayant perdu l'usage de ses membres supérieurs.

— Tu vois, même dans l'adversité la plus pénible, on t'abreuve ! C'est ça, l'amitié ! souligne Katia, presque émotive face à la scène de solidarité touchante.

— Merci, j'apprécie !

— J'ai le goût de mettre des feuilles de palmier proche de ton derrière, en souvenir de ta mésaventure ! dit Katia.

— Laisse faire...

— Juste pour nous... personne ne va comprendre l'allusion, insiste Katia qui s'exécute en mettant une petite feuille de palmier près du bas de bikini de coco de la momie de sable.

Une fois le montage terminé, les filles admirent leur travail, debout devant Vicky.

— Wow !

— C'est super beau !

Au moment de prendre l'appareil photo pour immortaliser la scène, Caroline semble apercevoir quelque chose d'intéressant au loin.

— Ah mon Dieu ! Regarde ! s'exclame-t-elle en frappant l'épaule de Katia.

— Wow !! s'excite celle-ci à son tour.

— Quoi ? Je peux pas voir. C'est quoi ? veut savoir la pauvre Vicky, confinée à regarder les nuages dans le ciel.

— Attends !

Katia décampe telle une gazelle.

— Ça va être trop malade, Vic!

— C'est quoi? panique toujours celle-ci, craignant le pire.

— Tu vas voir!

Après quelques minutes, Vicky entend Katia qui revient auprès d'elle en compagnie d'un homme parlant espagnol.

— *¿Aquí*[41]?

— *¡Sí!*

Toujours sans que Vicky puisse apercevoir ce qui se passe, l'homme dépose quelque chose près d'elle. Avant même qu'elle puisse identifier de quoi il s'agit, des plumes balayent le côté de son visage tandis qu'un caquètement sonore parvient à ses oreilles. Elle tourne la tête.

— QUESSÉ ÇA, CALVAIRE! crie Vicky en voyant finalement apparaître, à cinq centimètres de son visage, un énorme ara bleu et or.

L'homme ignore sa panique du moment et dispose un second oiseau de l'autre côté de sa tête. Un ara rouge, cette fois.

— Les filles! HIIIIII!

_____

41. Ici?

— Ben non, capote pas, c'est juste des oiseaux domes-tiqués. Ils font juste ça, prendre des photos avec les touristes. Pour vrai, l'effet est malade, Vic! Bouge pas.

Vicky-la-momie tourne la tête vers la volaille à sa droite qui semble un peu stupéfaite de sa position inhabituelle dans le sable. La seconde bête à sa gauche lui envoie un : « ¡Hola! » aussi parfait que s'il avait été prononcé par une voix humaine.

— Ils parlent en plus! C'est incroyable!

— ¡Hola! caquette encore son voisin ailé au dos de feu.

Caroline, qui n'en revient tout simplement pas, ajoute :

— Hooooooon! Vicky! T'entends ça? Ils parlent!

— J'entends, certain. Il crie direct dans mon oreille.

— Ils disent autre chose que « hola », vous pensez ?

— Je m'en sacre comme de l'an quarante qu'ils disent « hola », « gracias » ou n'importe quoi d'autre, sérieux. Prenez votre maudite photo au plus vite, sinon ils vont me bouffer la face comme dans le film d'Hitchcock...

Impatient, le spécimen de droite bat des ailes dans le visage de Vicky.

— Il m'attaque! crie celle-ci, faisant ainsi sursauter le second volatile qui, soudainement inquiet, donne aussi quelques petits coups d'ailes avant de crier un autre « hola ».

— *¡Tranquilo! ¡Tranquilo*[42]*!* la prie l'homme en ajustant son appareil.

— *Tranquilo*, toi-même, chose! C'est pas toi qui t'es fait bouffer l'oreille par un lézard au Mexique.

— Bouge pas, Vicky…, la supplie Katia qui supervise la séance photo, debout derrière le photographe.

Le type prend deux photos consécutives de Vicky avec les oiseaux. Rebelle, Katia en prend deux supplémentaires par-dessus son épaule avec son cellulaire, malgré qu'elle n'en ait pas le droit, les photos de touristes constituant le gagne-pain du type. L'homme hispanophone revient vers Vicky qui grimace toujours de peur. Il reprend ses oiseaux, qu'il pose agilement sur ses épaules et il baragouine à moitié en anglais, à moitié en espagnol, qu'il reviendra dans dix minutes afin de leur remettre les clichés.

L'homme s'éloigne et Katia en profite pour jeter un œil à ses photos illégales.

— Hish, j'espère que les siennes seront belles parce que t'aimeras pas les miennes…

Le vieux Cubain des arachides ressurgit près des filles et leur demande:

— *Picture?*

— Hein?

---

42. Calmez-vous! Calmez-vous!

— *Picture ?*

Confuse, Katia en déduit :

— On dirait qu'il nous offre de prendre une photo avec toi...

— Pis ses *peanuts* ? C'est quoi le rapport ?

— Je sais pas mais bon, je veux sortir d'ici. Aidez-moi donc un peu...

— *No, thanks,* répond Katia à l'homme qui s'éloigne ensuite.

Au moment où Katia tente d'aider son amie, une volée d'oiseaux aquatiques passe au-dessus d'elles dans le ciel. Certains volatiles en profitent pour, comment dire, relâcher leur sphincter.

— ARK !! gueule Katia qui sent une matière visqueuse douteuse atterrir sur son bras ainsi que sur son épaule.

— Ah ! tu vois ! T'as voulu me faire suer, les oiseaux se vengent sur toi ! la nargue Vicky en se délivrant enfin de son sarcophage sablonneux.

— *¡Hola ! ¿Bolleyboll ? ¿Sí ?* s'informe l'éternel employé motivé qui passe en trottinant à petits pas.

— *Nooooo,* lui répond Katia pour une ultime fois avant de se diriger vers la mer pour nettoyer son cadeau d'oiseau.

Le type au ballon poursuit sa route, plus confiant que jamais de réussir à les convaincre un jour...

Le photographe revient avec la photo et leur demande les quinze pesos convenus avant même de leur présenter le cliché.

— Calvince, le prix a augmenté, hein! Méchante inflation! commente Vicky qui se souvient avoir déboursé dix dollars au Mexique pour une photo de ce genre.

Katia le paie sans broncher, trop curieuse de voir le résultat. À la réception de la photo, elle fait une drôle de tête.

— Ah! C'est trop drôle!

Vicky lui arrache le cliché des mains sans ménagement.

— Montre... Cibole, c'est épouvantable! M'as-tu vu la face?

Comme de fait, sa peur des oiseaux se traduit par une grimace éloquente, faisant en sorte qu'elle crispe la bouche en se tournant sur le côté. Elle a ainsi l'air d'avoir le double menton d'une femme pesant trois cents livres.

— Ouin..., se désole Caroline en toisant l'image par-dessus l'épaule de Vicky, incapable de lui mentir.

— Ark, pis en plus, t'avais mis la moumoute dégueu sous le bas de maillot... T'es conne! Brûlez-moi ça!

— Ben non, ben non...

Remises de leurs émotions, les trois filles poursuivent avec ardeur leur «tournoi» de mojitos au bar de la plage en compagnie de Mike, de son fils et de quelques autres voyageurs qui profitent de la fin d'après-midi pour étancher généreusement leur soif.

— «*Bará, bará, bará, berê, berê, berê*», chantonne Katia en même temps que la musique.

Son fils étant un peu plus loin, Mike en profite pour se confier à Katia.

— Tu comprends que je passe beaucoup de temps avec lui et moins avec toi, hein?

— Ben oui, tu m'en as parlé ce matin et c'est normal.

— C'est notre premier voyage père-fils et c'est important pour moi de passer du temps de qualité en sa compagnie.

— Je comprends tout à fait, crois-moi! fait Katia en lui volant un baiser sur les lèvres au passage.

Elle le regarde s'éloigner pour rejoindre son fils qui est assis au bar et qui fixe toujours et à jamais l'écran de son portable.

— Vous êtes *cutes* à mort! remarque Caroline en se déhanchant au son de la musique, malgré le fait que celle-ci soit toujours aussi redondante.

— Ouin, avec lui, c'est spécial. Je me sens différente, avoue Katia en l'épiant, l'air songeur.

— Comment? Parle-nous-en! Tu nous racontes presque jamais rien! lui reproche une fois de plus Vicky.

— Différente, c'est tout...

Les trois amies gardent le silence quelques minutes. Chacune étant plongée dans des réflexions profondes. Vicky sort son téléphone intelligent. Elle souhaite fureter un peu sur le fil de nouvelles Facebook étant donné que le WiFi est disponible au bar. Caroline fait de même.

— Ah, *god*, lâchez vos cellulaires, les filles! beugle Katia.

— KAT? T'as «posté» ça? crie Vicky en apercevant l'horrible cliché d'elle avec les oiseaux.

La photo prise par Katia est moins pire que le cliché officiel pris par le photographe, mais l'objectif a tout de même immortalisé sa peur des volatiles.

— C'est juste drôle, arrête!

— Je suis dégueu! C'est pas drôle pantoute! Enlève-la!

— Trop tard...

Se résignant, car il est en effet trop tard pour faire quoi que ce soit étant donné que soixante-sept personnes – dont Marc – ont déjà «aimé» ledit cliché, elle continue à dérouler le fil de nouvelles. Elle y aperçoit une nouvelle photo mettant en vedette Marc et ses amis dans la rue principale de Las Vegas, les bras bien hauts, l'air d'avoir intégré les rangs d'un groupe de conquérants urbains aguerris. Trois filles assez jolies se trouvent derrière un peu en retrait et elles rigolent de la photo comique que les gars prennent.

— Regardez. ENCORE une photo avec des filles ! se désole Vicky en présentant son téléphone à ses amies. On dirait que c'est encore les mêmes, en plus...

— Vic, tu capotes, pour de vrai. Premièrement, c'est certain qu'il rencontre du monde là-bas, dont «des filles». Deuxièmement, tu voulais profiter de tes derniers moments de célibat officiel pour «*frencher*-rien-que» à Cuba, donc...

Éteignant son téléphone d'un geste prompt, Vicky rouspète :

— Pfft ! Et, à part de ça, je veux même plus *frencher*... Ça me tente pu. Bon, je m'en vais à la chambre. Bye !

— Moi, je veux parler à mon *chum* ! décide Caroline malgré qu'elle soit un peu sous l'effet de l'alcool.

Vicky quitte la scène.

— Mauvaise idée pour toi aussi. Il faut pas que tu lui parles de tes inquiétudes maintenant, Caro. C'est pas le temps, lui signale Katia.

— Coudonc, toi ! T'es rendue conseillère matrimoniale ou quoi ? réagit Caroline. Moi, je pense que je serais mieux de mettre ça au clair main-te-nant ! Il faut battre le frère pendant qu'il est chaud !

— Le frère ?

— Le fer, je veux dire ! Le fer !

— T'as raison ! Je vais battre mon frère quand il aura bu trop de vin ! Ha ! ha ! ha !

En grimaçant, Caroline pose son verre sur le zinc pour se diriger un peu à l'écart afin de tenter de rejoindre son *chum* via Skype.

Elle enfile ses écouteurs et lance l'appel. À son grand bonheur, son destinataire répond.

— Alloooo ! fait Caroline, le ton à mi-chemin entre la joie et l'ambivalence.

— Tu vas bien ?

— Ouais, ça va bien. Toi ?

— Oui, je suis tranquille. J'ai loué *Les Bagnoles 2* avec le petit. On va regarder ça tantôt. Là, on se faisait des croquettes de poulet...

— Aaahh. C'est le *fun*...

— Ça va ? T'as l'air drôle...

— Bah, ça va, oui, mais je me demandais... Euh...

La mouffette, qui surgit par-derrière, se mêle impoliment de la conversation de Caroline.

— Alloooo ! À quiiii tu parles ? demande-t-il en étirant le cou pour voir l'écran de son téléphone.

— C'est qui? demande Éric, confus, en voyant surgir rapidement la tête d'un gars par-dessus l'épaule de sa blonde.

— Personne, il a pas rapport... Tasse-toi! le rabroue Caroline en le poussant du coude.

— C'est ton *chum*? Je pensais que vous étiez des matantes «ron coco qui *frenchaient*-rien-que», moi! Ha! ha! ha!

Éric, qui a mal entendu la phrase au complet, a par contre perçu nettement le mot *frenchaient*. Il fronce les sourcils.

— DÉGAGE! crie Caroline avant de revenir à la conversation.

— Pourquoi il dit ça? C'est qui, lui?

— Aucun rapport, il est tellement fatigant, t'as pas idée. Regarde, il m'a même brûlé les cheveux un soir au buffet, ajoute-t-elle en lui montrant sa tresse tristement amochée.

— Brûlé?

— Ouais...

Silence. Une petite voix appelle Éric dans la maison.

— Attends, mon grand, papa arrive, dit Éric en réponse à leur fils qui le réclame au loin.

— Je veux voir le petit...

— C'est pas vraiment un bon moment. Il m'appelle des toilettes, donc je vais y aller. On se reparle, OK?

— OK, oui, bonne soirée...

— Ouin... toi aussi, la salue Éric, suspicieux et pas très jovial.

Caroline raccroche et fonce sur la mouffette, qui s'est jointe à Katia et aux deux autres gars pour prendre un verre.

— T'es vraiment le roi des cons, toi?!

— Quoi? s'enquiert Katia, surprise par l'agressivité subite de son amie.

— Imagine-toi qu'il est allé dire devant Éric que j'embrassais des gars!

— Voyons?

— J'ai pas dit ça...

— Je vais te frapper, sérieux!

Alors que plusieurs personnes se retournent en entendant la menace – qui semble très sincère –, Katia prend doucement Caroline par le bras.

— Viens, on s'en va...

— C'était vraiment cave, ça! gueule encore Caroline en suivant tout de même son amie.

Les filles quittent l'aire du bar comme deux voleuses, puis se dirigent vers le petit chemin. Katia se tient très près de Caroline pour éviter que celle-ci ne retourne auprès de la mouffette pour lui crêper le chignon.

— Gros épais! pleurniche encore Caroline. Il va briser mon couple!

— Caro, arrête de t'en faire, là. Éric va comprendre quand tu vas lui expliquer.

— Non mais, toutes les filles rêvent d'avoir un ami gai... Eille, le voulez-vous quelqu'un? On le vend pas cher et avec grand plaisir en plus!

— Non, non, on va le donner...

— Le con est revenu ici juste pour me faire suer, je pense.

Arrivées près des chambres, les filles se taisent, n'ayant rien d'autre à ajouter sur le sujet. Caroline glisse sa carte magnétique dans la fente et elle entre. Katia insère la sienne à son tour lorsqu'elle entend:

— Vicky? Franchement!

Katia fait demi-tour et bondit vers la chambre des filles pour voir ce qui s'y passe. Elle a tout juste le temps de voir Vicky, à moitié nue sur le lit, qui replie avec empressement le couvre-lit sur elle.

— Qu'est-ce que tu faisais là? demande Caroline, une pointe d'écœurement marqué dans la voix.

— Aaaaaah…, grogne Vicky sans rien expliquer en soufflant ensuite avec sa bouche.

— Vicky? insiste Katia comme pour la forcer à s'expliquer.

— Vicky? Te masturbais-tu? Tu peux nous le dire, ajoute Caroline avec un air bienveillant de maman d'ado prête à encaisser la réponse pour ensuite se lancer dans un brin d'éducation concernant l'endroit et le moment où c'est possible de faire la chose, sans lui transmettre que c'est «mal».

— Ah! Franchement, Caro! Bon, bon, bon… Je prenais juste une photo cochonne pour Marc. Je me suis dit: «Il rencontre plein de filles, donc je vais lui montrer que c'est moi la plus belle.»

— Ah, OK, envoie Caroline, soulagée, mais seulement à moitié.

Katia retourne dans sa chambre sans rien ajouter, mais en pouffant de rire.

Les portes grandes ouvertes comme à leur habitude, les filles conversent d'une chambre à l'autre.

— S'il n'avait encore rien fait avec l'autre fille, là, il va passer à l'action, c'est certain! panique Caroline, hors d'elle.

— Caro, Éric est fou de toi, il ferait jamais ça. C'est quoi cette jalousie-là, tout d'un coup? crie Katia de sa chambre, plus que jamais convaincue que Caroline divague gravement.

— Je suis insécure, comme si... Eille, en plus, avec tout ça, je lui ai même pas souhaité «bonne année».

— Pas grave, tu lui enverras un message ce soir, ou tu le rappelleras demain.

— Pas trop le goût de lui parler maintenant, après l'intervention de l'autre tata...

— La mouffette...

— Ce gars-là est officiellement venu sur terre pour me faire chier. J'en suis maintenant certaine, exagère Caroline.

— Moi aussi, je suis sûre!

Katia effectue son entrée dans la chambre des filles, vêtue d'une superbe robe fuchsia à fines bretelles. Elle a remonté ses cheveux en chignon. Elle resplendit de beauté.

— Bon, les filles, c'est le jour de l'An! Vous mettez la plus belle robe de votre valise et on va s'amuser comme jamais, en mettant de côté la paranoïa à propos de vos *chums*, OK?

— Ouin..., essaie de se convaincre Vicky, la babine inférieure lui descendant presque jusqu'au plancher.

— T'as raison! approuve Caroline en tentant de remonter aussi ses cheveux de façon adéquate malgré sa coupe inégale et ses cheveux rêches.

JOUR 8

AÉROPORT MONTRÉAL-TRUDEAU
SALLE 315 – **10 H 13**

Toujours recluses dans la salle 315, les filles pianotent sur leur téléphone avec nonchalance. Caroline dépose finalement le sien sur la table et se prend la tête à deux mains.

— Reste que mon *chum* doit vraiment se faire des idées en ce moment. Le con qui dit ça devant lui et ensuite, le drame de la fin. Il ne doit rien comprendre. La seule chose que j'ai pu lui écrire est : «Chéri, on a manqué notre avion! Trop long à t'expliquer. Nous prendrons le prochain vol à 2 h 30. Je te texte en arrivant à Montréal!»

— Marc doit se poser beaucoup de questions lui aussi, souligne Vicky.

— En réalité, Mike aussi doit bien se demander pourquoi nous n'étions pas dans l'avion... Pouf! Disparue dans la nature, la belle Katia!

— C'est vrai, ils devaient être sur la même envolée que nous, eux! allume Vicky, qui n'avait pas songé à ce détail.

— La honte... Les filles, si la commission scolaire apprend la nouvelle, qu'est-ce qui va nous arriver?

— Caro, je te répète, ENCORE, que les douaniers qui nous ont interrogées ont affirmé que le dossier était confidentiel. C'est pas comme si on avait reçu des accusations, élabore Katia en levant les deux mains en guise de «calmons-nous».

— J'espère…

— Moi, ce dont je veux me souvenir, c'est pas de l'imbroglio à la fin du voyage, mais des bons moments qu'on a passés ensemble. Le *party* du jour de l'An était quand même le *fun*, il faut le dire, se rappelle Katia.

— Ouais… parle pour toi…

JOUR 4

CUBA, VARADERO
COSTA AZUL DEL MAR RESORT

Les filles font la queue un petit moment avant de parvenir à pénétrer dans l'aire du buffet, qui a été revampée pour l'occasion. Fébriles, elles regardent partout autour d'elles.

— Wow! Regardez toutes les sculptures de glace! C'est vraiment beau.

Un groupe de Cubains a érigé des sculptures de glace impressionnantes un peu partout dans le restaurant et dans le lobby. Certaines représentent des animaux ou des oiseaux et d'autres des personnages de bandes dessinées. Une grosse étoile trône au milieu de la place et des coupes ont été disposées en pyramide sur une table tout près pour éventuellement y accueillir le festif mousseux du Nouvel An.

— Comment ça se fait que ça fond pas ?

— J'imagine que ça va fondre à un moment donné...

Comme un homme se donne en spectacle devant l'un des blocs sculptés, les filles approchent un peu.

— Impressionnant, décrit Caroline.

L'artisan taille l'aile de ce qui semble être un grand aigle. Soucieuse du détail, Vicky émet une remarque :

— C'est pas le gars qui sert les *drinks* au bar de la plage tous les jours, lui ?

— Ah oui ! On dirait bien qu'il a une double tâche lui aussi...

Les filles observent les différentes sculptures qui se succèdent jusqu'à la réception. Elles commentent le tout, en admiration devant la minutie nécessaire pour accomplir son art. En arrivant près du comptoir de la réception, Caroline pousse un cri :

— Ah mon Dieu ! ÇA, c'est très drôle !

— Quoi ? fait Katia tandis que son amie, crampée en deux, lui montre quelque chose du doigt.

Sur le comptoir de marbre, un petit aquarium rempli d'eau jusqu'à la moitié met en valeur le fameux dentier perdu. Sur une feuille blanche collée en haut, on peut lire : « *Found near the pool*[43] ».

— Eille, je peux pas croire que, présentement, il y a une personne pas de dents qui déambule dans le *résore* sans chercher à les retrouver !

— C'est clairement épique !

En riant comme des gamines, elles rebroussent chemin pour revenir vers le buffet. Sylvio arrive près d'elles accompagné de sa fille et d'un autre bambin.

— Allo !

— Allo ! Je vous présente Alejandro, mon grand garçon.

Celui-ci fait un signe de tête gêné avant d'enfouir la phalange de son pouce dans sa bouche, tandis que sa petite sœur, timide aussi, s'accroche à la sécurisante jambe de son père.

— Ma femme est là-bas, dit-il en désignant du menton une splendide Latino aux cheveux noirs très longs, encore plus jolie que sur la photo qu'il leur avait montrée quelques jours plus tôt.

— Il y a beaucoup de Cubains à l'hôtel ce soir, on dirait, remarque Katia.

— Oui, ici, les complexes hôteliers sont aussi des clubs privés, donc les gens locaux peuvent payer un forfait

---

43. Trouvé près de la piscine.

annuel et venir avec leur famille les week-ends ou lors des fêtes comme ce soir.

— Ah ouin, je le savais pas, affirme Caroline. C'est bien...

— Voilà pourquoi, ce soir, il y a presque autant de touristes que de gens locaux.

Sylvio s'éloigne un peu, sa progéniture trottinant derrière lui. Galant à souhait, il revient illico muni de deux coupes de champagne qu'il tend à Caro et à Katia, puis il retourne de nouveau à la table et en agrippe une supplémentaire pour Vicky. Il attrape également au passage trois splendides couronnes cartonnées du Nouvel An ornées de faux brillants.

— Wow! Merci! s'exclament les filles, ravies, en revêtant avec fierté leur couvre-chef festif.

— Demain, ça va toujours pour La Havane?

— Oui, pas trop tôt, j'espère?

— Disons neuf heures?

— D'accord, c'est bien!

— Parfait! Bonne soirée les filles, à plus tard, les salue Sylvio en retournant auprès de sa famille et de ses amis.

— Santé! Ça va être le plus beau jour de l'An de notre vie, les filles! prophétise Katia.

JOUR 8

AÉROPORT MONTRÉAL-TRUDEAU
SALLE 315 – **10 H 16**

— Méchante soirée plate à mort ! rage Vicky.

— Pas si pire quand même ! envoie Katia.

— Toi, on le sait bien que t'as eu du *fun*…

— Je me suis chicanée avec Éric juste avant le décompte. Wow !

— Le pire jour de l'An de ma vie pour de vrai, déclare Vicky.

— N'exagère pas !

— Tu le sais pas, toi, crois-moi…

JOUR 4

CUBA, VARADERO
COSTA AZUL DEL MAR RESORT

Assise près de Caroline qui se dispute avec Éric par le biais de messages Facebook au sujet des propos tenus par la mouffette lors de leur conversation précédente, Vicky semble abattue, la tête reposant au creux de la paume, faisant ainsi remonter sa joue presque jusqu'à son nez. Elle observe à la dérobée la blonde de Simon qui parle dans son dos depuis le début du voyage. Tout le monde placote à la table voisine et, tout à coup, des gens éclatent de rire. Certains se retournent pour la regarder en tentant d'avoir l'air discret. «Je pense que je deviens dingue et que je paranoïe avec toute cette histoire», se convainc Vicky en remettant vraiment en question sa capacité à faire preuve de jugement.

— Franchement, mon *chum* est chez son oncle, il est un peu soûl et il remet en doute ma fidélité, panique Caroline, les yeux rivés sur la messagerie de son portable.

— Et lui? La fille?

— Je sais. Je lui demande et il fait l'innocent en me disant ne pas comprendre de quoi je parle. Il me ment carrément en pleine face.

Un peu plus loin, Katia ondule contre Mike au son de la musique exotique qui emplit la salle de restauration. Un spectacle de danse est en cours. Elle décide finalement de rejoindre ses amies qui semblent bien tranquilles assises à une table en retrait.

— À plusssss tard, minaude-t-elle en envoyant des yeux coquins remplis de suppositions à son charmant soupirant de Saint-Jérôme.

Heureuse, elle vole jusqu'à ses amies comme une princesse couronnée de matière recyclable.

— Aaaaaaah! Belle soirée, hein!?

— Bof!

— Je vous annonce une troisième double tâche pour un des membres du personnel. Le gars sensuel du «*mini barrrrr* » le matin est aussi un danseur ! Voilà ! Ce doit être pour ça qu'il a un ton de voix suave-latino-*sexy* de même, suppute Katia en pointant le Cubain au loin qui se dandine en costume à paillettes or et rouge.

— Voyons, il me répond plus. En-co-re. Il est parti où ? crie Caroline, hors d'elle, en fixant son cellulaire.

Katia envoie un regard interrogateur à Vicky qui lui articule en retour un « Éric » sans faire de son en agitant un peu sa main droite pour la mettre au courant que la situation ne va pas très bien.

— Moi, j'attends le décompte pour aller me coucher, déclare Vicky, en proie à une dépression majeure, sa couronne de princesse tenant un peu croche sur sa tête.

— Ben là..., réagit Katia, déçue que le niveau de bonheur à cette soirée s'avère aussi inégal. As-tu envoyé ta photo cochonne ?

— Oui, et il me répond pas... Il m'avait déjà souhaité « bonne année » avant que je l'envoie parce qu'il repartait vers Montréal aujourd'hui, je pense...

— Bon, tant pis, je range mon cell. Je suis assez en maudit de même ! décide Caro en insérant son téléphone dans sa bourse.

— Bon ! s'enthousiasme Katia.

Caroline, l'air en beau maudit, tourne la tête pour observer les gens tout autour sans sourire. Vicky remet son menton au creux de sa main en soupirant.

— Eille, wow! Vous êtes de bonne humeur, c'est effrayant!

La mouffette surgit subitement de nulle part, comme toujours, et elle aborde les filles en criant avec frénésie:

— C'est-tu à vous autres, ça?

— Ah lui! marmonne Caroline en respirant profondément pour éviter de lui sauter au visage.

Les filles pivotent en même temps pour le regarder. Les yeux ronds et la bouche ouverte, il étend les bras comme un clown surgissant dans une fête d'enfants. Sa tête est garnie d'un genre de perruque défraîchie qui ressemble étrangement à celle dégotée par les filles sur la plage.

— Ark...

— J'ai trouvé ça sur la plage, et là, je la porte pour que le propriétaire puisse l'identifier!

Vicky, toujours d'une humeur peu festive, répète simplement:

— Ark-eeee...

— Bon, je vais poursuivre ma tournée! annonce la mouffette en repartant au galop vers le groupe de voyageurs de la table voisine.

— Les filles, le mot «inutilité» est trop insignifiant pour décrire ce gars-là...

— Une plaie de lit...

JOUR 8

AÉROPORT MONTRÉAL-TRUDEAU
SALLE 315 - **10 H 25**

La conversation des filles est interrompue par quelqu'un qui entre dans la salle d'interrogatoire. Enfin! Un homme qu'elles n'avaient pas encore rencontré pénètre dans la pièce d'un pas décidé.

— Bonjour, je suis l'inspecteur Biron, des Services frontaliers du Canada.

Les filles le saluent en retour avec politesse en s'assoyant bien droites sur leur chaise, les mains sur les cuisses. Elles ont l'air de trois jeunes étudiantes qui s'apprêtent à se faire gronder pour avoir copié lors d'un important contrôle de fin d'année.

Un agent qui l'accompagne ressort aussitôt de la pièce sans même avoir pris la peine de saluer les filles. Il revient en moins de temps qu'il n'en faut pour crier «lapin» avec deux chaises supplémentaires, qu'il place près du grand bureau, afin de faire face aux trois témoins.

— Désolé pour le délai, mesdames. J'ai pris rapidement connaissance des dépositions de mes collègues, mais pour être certain de bien comprendre la situation et de rédiger des rapports adéquats, j'aurais quelques questions supplémentaires à vous poser.

— D'accord...

Les trois enseignantes observent avec attention l'homme chauve âgé d'une cinquantaine d'années qui prend place au centre. Ses yeux bleu clair presque dépourvus de cils parcourent les feuilles devant lui avec diligence. Il prend bien le temps de repérer certaines informations, question d'orienter adéquatement le début de son interrogatoire. La carrure de l'homme cloche avec le fait qu'il soit de petite taille – son large cou et ses épaules massives donnent l'impression d'avoir été posés sur un tronc trop frêle pour lui.

— Premièrement, revenons au premier janvier. Les rapports mentionnent que vous avez aperçu monsieur Sanchez sur le complexe hôtelier en début de journée. C'était où et à quelle heure exactement ? J'ai besoin de connaître tous les détails, même ceux qui paraissent anodins pour vous. Pour le moment, je n'ai presque rien à ce sujet. J'aimerais que vous me racontiez cette journée à partir du début.

— D'accord...

JOUR 5

CUBA, VARADERO
COSTA AZUL DEL MAR RESORT

Au moment où le réveille-matin du téléphone de Katia sonne, Mike retire sa tête de sous l'oreiller.

— Câline... c'est fort, ça...

— Oui, j'avais peur de passer tout droit.

Il s'étire comme un chat avant de soupirer. Katia lui précise :

— T'es pas obligé de te lever, Mike. Reste ici et rendors-toi. Juste à fermer la porte en sortant, je vais apporter ma carte.

— Non. C'est toi qui pars pas, murmure-t-il en l'enlaçant de côté et en enroulant ses jambes autour d'elle tel un boa constricteur désirant étouffer sa proie pour ensuite l'avaler tout rond.

— Eille ! Lâche-moi, il faut que je parte ! pleurniche un peu Katia, malgré qu'elle se sente heureuse comme jamais.

Se libérant finalement de son étreinte, elle se dirige vers la salle de bain pour y faire un brin de toilette.

Elle se prépare en quatrième vitesse, question de ne pas faire attendre les filles et, surtout, Sylvio. Chaque fois qu'elle passe près du lit, Mike grogne et la tire vers lui pour lui voler quelques baisers à l'arraché...

En arrivant à l'entrée du complexe quelque quinze minutes en retard, Katia s'excuse auprès du groupe :

— Désolée, j'ai été retenue, dit-elle en envoyant un regard coquin aux deux filles qui lèvent les yeux vers le ciel.

— T'as eu le temps d'aller chez le fleuriste, par contre ? questionne Vicky en remarquant que sa queue-de-cheval est ornée de deux hibiscus bien rouges.

— C'est un cadeau... Bon, je prendrais bien un café, moi. J'ai pas eu le temps de passer par le buffet.

— Nous non plus.

Sylvio s'interpose, bien fier :

— Non, attendez. En route, je vous ferai boire le meilleur café que vous aurez jamais bu de votre vie.

— Parfait ! Allons-y, alors ! Ça va être une super journée ! se réjouit Katia, beaucoup trop enthousiaste compte tenu de son manque de sommeil et de l'heure hâtive.

— Seigneur ! Qu'est-ce que t'as fumé ? demande Caroline, étonnée de la voir si enjouée à la perspective d'endurer deux heures de route.

— Je suis de bonne humeur, c'est tout !

— On tient à te faire un suivi sur un dossier très important : le dentier se trouve toujours dans son aquarium à la réception, mais là, la moumoute est rendue à côté...

— Pas vrai ? Ha ! ha ! ha ! Merci de me mettre au courant. Voilà donc deux dossiers importants à suivre...

Vicky se prononce avec désolation :

— Imaginez, commencer la nouvelle année sans dents ni cheveux. Me semble que ça laisse rien présager de bon pour l'avenir !

— Mais est-ce que les deux appartiennent à la même personne ? Là est la vraie question...

Sylvio emboîte le pas aux trois filles. Au même moment, celles-ci se font aborder par un type qui traverse le lobby en joggant :

— *¿Bolleyboll? ¿Sí?*

— C'est une blague..., grince Caroline en dévisageant l'animateur.

— *No*, La Havane..., lui annonce Katia, faussement désolée.

Ahurie, Vicky rigole :

— Voyons donc ? Il est partout, lui ? Rendu là, je pense qu'on peut statuer que c'est du harcèlement !

Le gars poursuit sa route, son ballon volant dans les airs au rythme de ses pas de course.

Clopin-clopant, le groupe se dirige donc vers le station-nement adjacent à l'hôtel où l'automobile de Sylvio est garée. En approchant, les filles prennent place à bord, l'esprit léger comme la brise...

JOUR 8
AÉROPORT MONTRÉAL-TRUDEAU
SALLE 315 – **10 H 37**

L'inspecteur Biron, qui prend en note les détails qu'il juge essentiels, demande sans lever la tête :

— De quelle marque de voiture s'agissait-il?

Trois paires de yeux le dévisagent comme s'il venait de poser sa question en mandarin.

— La couleur, au moins?

— Euh... grise, prétend Caroline, tandis que Vicky se tourne vers elle, les sourcils en accent circonflexe, prête à douter de son affirmation.

Biron lève des yeux globuleux vers Vicky et il hausse les épaules.

— Foncée, précise Vicky en croyant ainsi éclaircir le mystère de la foi, question de passer à autre chose.

Comme l'inspecteur jette un coup d'œil en direction de son collègue, l'air de dire: «On n'est pas sortis du bois avec ces trois-là!», Katia ajoute son grain de sel.

— Une quatre portes, gris *charcoal*. Comme un vieux Pontiac avec du bois dans le dedans des portes. Genre, gros char de vieux mononcle cochon.

— «De vieux mononcle cochon»? répète Biron.

— Un Pontiac? C'est quoi donc, un Pontiac? se demande Caroline comme si elle doutait incontestablement de l'information livrée par son amie.

Hésitant à noter des détails imprécis dans sa déposition, Biron écarquille les yeux avant de respirer bien profondément.

— Bon... Peu importe. Ensuite?

— Vous n'êtes pas curieux de savoir si on a joué ou non au «*bolleyboll*», finalement ? déconne Katia, question d'alléger l'atmosphère.

L'accompagnateur de l'inspecteur échappe un petit rictus.

— Continuez, je vous prie.

JOUR 5
CUBA, VARADERO
COSTA AZUL DEL MAR RESORT

Le propriétaire de la *tienda*[44] en bordure de la rue principale semble très heureux de voir Sylvio débarquer à l'improviste. Ce dernier lui explique que «*¡Las tres amigas necesitan un buon caffè*[45] !» Ravi, l'homme dans la soixantaine se lève de sa chaise de fortune, installée dans la rue devant son petit commerce, pour serrer la main des filles. Il part ensuite au galop à l'intérieur pour s'acquitter de son heureuse mission.

Quelques minutes plus tard, il ressort avec trois gobelets cartonnés coiffés d'un couvercle de plastique. Comme si l'élixir allait instantanément enjoliver sa journée, Vicky porte sans plus attendre le verre à ses lèvres. Les deux

___

44. Magasin.
45. Les trois amies ont besoin d'un bon café !

filles l'imitent sous le regard inquisiteur du vieil homme, en attente de leur réaction.

Katia s'écrie :

— *My god* ! C'est le meilleur café que j'ai bu de toute ma vie !

— Incroyable, hein ? approuve Caroline en se léchant la lèvre supérieure.

— C'est fou !

Communément ravis, les deux hommes échangent un regard complice et Sylvio paie le Cubain avant de lui serrer la pince, puis de retourner près de sa vieille Oldsmobile noire qu'il aime tant[46]. Les filles montent à bord, leur délicieux café en main.

Le soleil radieux rend la balade en voiture des plus agréables. Les trois filles se délectent du paysage en silence, bercées par la musique cubaine métissée que diffuse doucement la radio de Sylvio. Les Québécoises se pâment devant tant d'exotisme, Sylvio les aidant à repérer les champs d'ananas et les manguiers, ainsi que les arbres auxquels poussent des avocats en été. En bordure de la route, des animaux domestiques paissent librement, comme s'ils n'appartenaient à personne et à tout le monde en même temps. Un paysan dans sa charrue vétuste tirée

---

46. Un Pontiac, han ?

par une bourrique leur envoie la main, comme à de vieilles connaissances.

En arrivant à la frontière de la province de Matanzas, les filles commentent la signalisation en bordure de la route.

— C'est étrange, hein ? Quand on change de région, c'est inscrit sur les pancartes avec un trait dessus comme pour la rayer et ils inscrivent la nouvelle en dessous.

— Oui, on entre présentement dans la province Mayabeque.

Plusieurs personnes tenant des plateaux sont postées le long de la route longeant diverses plantations de bananes. Sylvio explique aux filles que ces gens vendent illégalement du fromage.

— Eh ben ! C'est quand même assez inoffensif comme marché noir.

Sylvio leur indique ensuite que le marché noir du bœuf s'avère plus complexe. On interdit aux Cubains de consommer cette viande rouge, car elle est réservée uniquement aux touristes.

— Hein ? C'est sacré comme en Inde ?

— Non, c'est juste prohibé. Les méthodes d'élevage étant ancestrales et complexes, on réserve ce privilège aux touristes, pour des raisons économiques.

— Les gens doivent quand même pas aller en prison pour avoir mangé de la viande ! s'exclame Katia.

— On écope de vingt-cinq ans de prison si on trouve du bœuf dans ton congélateur, jure Sylvio. Mais je ne connais personne qui se soit fait prendre...

— Seigneur! C'est vraiment radical!

Au su de cette information socio-politico-culturelle draconienne, les filles ressentent une certaine culpabilité d'avoir droit à un aliment si banal qu'elles voient passer à grands coups de steak au buffet, en plus. Elles constatent qu'il existe un gouffre culturel entre leurs deux univers. Un silence pesant, lourd de sous-entendus, enveloppe les occupants de la voiture...

JOUR 8
AÉROPORT MONTRÉAL-TRUDEAU
SALLE 315 – **10 H 44**

— Ç'a pas de maudit bon sens, hein? s'offusque Katia, furieuse devant cette injustice.

Comme elle semble chercher l'approbation des deux agents frontaliers devant elle, ceux-ci l'appuient vaguement.

— Non, en effet. C'est assez radical comme pratique...

— C'est juste de la viande! renchérit Katia, les baguettes en l'air. Imaginez, vivre là-bas, vous seriez peut-être pas des douaniers, mais bien des polices du bœuf!

— Franchement Kat, t'exagères avec ta police du bœuf, fait Caro.

Les deux agents se dévisagent une fois de plus. Biron les prie, en regardant sa montre :

— Allons, non pas que la situation sociopolitique cubaine nous laisse indifférents, mais il faudrait poursuivre, s'il vous plaît.

Bien qu'elle soit aussi touchée par cette inégalité que son amie, Vicky juge bon de poursuivre avec du concret :

— Donc, en arrivant à La Havane, on a admiré le gros Jésus qui surplombe la ville, mais de l'autre côté de la rivière. C'était beau. On a visité une vieille forteresse, mais on n'a pas payé pour entrer dedans. On a juste vu le plus gros cigare roulé à la main du monde entier qui se trouve dans une petite boutique à l'entrée. Ensuite, on est allées en ville. On n'a pas regretté du tout d'y être allées en tout cas. C'est tellement beau, cette ville-là !

Biron écoute attentivement sans prendre de notes. Puisque les vacancières ont suivi un itinéraire classique, rien de spécifique ne semble contribuer à l'enquête en cours.

— Est-il resté avec vous toute la journée ?

— Oui.

Caroline rectifie :

— Euh... non...

JOUR 5

CUBA, LA HAVANE

En quittant l'antique hôtel abritant en ses murs la fameuse chambre ayant servi pendant plusieurs années de repaire d'inspiration mystique à l'écrivain Ernest Hemingway, les filles foulent d'un pied nonchalant les dalles usées entourant la Plaza de Armas, littéralement transformée en librairie à ciel ouvert. Les bouquins d'âge mûr qui jaunissent tranquillement au soleil s'y comptent par milliers. Cette vieille partie de La Havane, à cause de son côté rustique et des carrioles servant à promener les touristes, rappelle aux filles le Vieux-Québec. Un joyeux désordre et une ambiance décontractée caractérisent par ailleurs cette portion de la ville, qui semble vibrer au rythme de la musique et des rires cubains voyageant entre les portes des bâtiments ouvertes au grand jour. L'odeur des *churros*[47] grésillant dans l'huile se mêle aux effluves des *tacos*, des cigares et des *empanadas*[48] qui se succèdent sans suivre d'ordre à chaque coin de rue. Deux chiens errants qui roupillent, flegmatiques, au pied d'une table où quatre vieux Cubains se disputent une partie de dominos comme si leur vie en dépendait, confèrent à l'ensemble du tableau une petite touche de nonchalance. Et partout, dans cette

---

47. Une sorte d'entre-deux entre le beignet et la pâte à choux ; ça comble une envie de sucré n'importe quand !
48. Pochette de pâte renfermant diverses mixtures de poulet, légumes et sauce.

métropole littéralement prise d'assaut par des touristes venant des quatre coins du monde, on peut apercevoir des bagnoles américaines des années 1950 aux couleurs de l'arc-en-ciel, toutes plus rutilantes les unes que les autres. Classique zénith cubain ici présent.

À la fois émerveillées et curieuses d'en apprendre davantage, les trois vacancières savourent chaque instant, les yeux grands comme des soucoupes. En guide attentif, Sylvio estime que leur estomac respectif doit crier famine. Il leur propose de trouver une terrasse agréable près du Capitolio, le temps qu'il effectue ses propres commissions pour l'hôtel. Les filles prennent donc place au Café de Paris en se laissant tomber lourdement sur le tressage de plastique des chaises colorées, heureuses de s'accorder une petite pause…

JOUR 8

AÉROPORT MONTRÉAL-TRUDEAU
SALLE 315 – **10 H 50**

Un silence pesant s'installe dans la salle d'interrogatoire 315. L'agent accompagnant Biron a levé la main pour prier les filles de s'interrompre un instant. Les trois comparses cessent donc de parler, en attente de son intervention.

— Alors, monsieur Sanchez vous a quittées ?

— Oui, je l'ai écrit dans ma déposition, moi, se défend Katia en se montrant du doigt.

— Ah, OK. Moi, j'ai surtout décrit la scène d'hier, mais j'ai pas parlé de ce jour-là, se repent Vicky, les idées un peu embrouillées, cognitivement éreintée par toute cette saga.

— Voilà pourquoi on refait le tour ensemble. Donc, où est-il parti à ce moment-là ?

Caroline commence :

— On le sait pas. Il a tourné à droite dans la rue du resto et...

— Non, il a continué tout droit, sur le même chemin par lequel on était arrivés.

— Droite ou gauche, ça dépend si tu parles quand t'es face au resto ou pas ?

— Face à la porte ou de dos, mettons ? Si c'est de dos, il s'est dirigé à droite.

Les deux agents, visiblement découragés, se dévisagent de nouveau pendant de longues secondes avant que Biron décide :

— Bon, bon, bon, peu importe. Vous ne savez pas ce qu'il a fait, aucun indice concernant son emploi du temps ? Aucun détail ? Pensez-y bien.

— Non, il est revenu une heure trente plus tard sans rien nous dire.

— D'accord...

— Ensuite, on est passées par une rue pour visiter une petite église et on est retournées au stationnement. On a pris une voiture et on est rentrées, complète Vicky.

— Pourquoi dites-vous «une» voiture? Vous n'avez pas repris le même véhicule?

— Le Pontiac? fait Caro, toujours pas convaincue de ce détail.

— Le même véhicule que pour l'allée, répète Biron.

— Non, on a changé d'auto. Elle était garée presque à la même place, mais deux ou trois espaces de stationnement plus loin.

— Il nous a dit: «Mon ami m'a demandé de retourner à Varadero avec son automobile pour faire changer les roues. Je reviendrai chercher la mienne cette semaine.»

Comme si les filles réalisaient tout à coup, en le racontant, que ce détail recelait sans l'ombre d'un doute un lien avec les événements de la veille, elles se regardent, un peu honteuses de ne pas avoir fait le lien avant. Caroline calme les ardeurs de regret du groupe:

— On ne pouvait pas savoir, pour de vrai.

— Est-ce que l'autre véhicule était toujours là?

— Le Pontiac? répète encore Caro.

— Eille! Reviens-en avec ton Pontiac, Caro! On sait même pas si c'était ça, lui reproche Vicky.

— Je veux dire, est-ce que le véhicule du départ était toujours à la même place dans le stationnement, précise l'agent.

Les trois filles contemplent l'agent, le visage en forme de point d'interrogation, l'air de dire : «Pensez-vous réellement qu'on se souvient de ce genre de détail insignifiant?»

— Bon... pouvez-vous décrire le nouveau véhicule, au moins?

— Bleu marin.

— Bleu marin.

— Oui, bleu et PAS un Pontiac.

— Caro? Tu sais même pas c'est quoi, un Pontiac, tu l'as dit tantôt! Comment peux-tu affirmer que c'en était pas un? la chicane Katia.

— Ben, si l'autre c'était un Pontiac, le deuxième était différent, c'est tout ce que je veux dire...

— Ouin, les deux chars étaient différents! conclut Vicky.

Les trois profs se réjouissent intérieurement d'être ainsi au diapason dans leur déclaration. Voilà au moins un élément unanime et valide qui pourra servir adéquatement à l'enquête. Quant à eux, les enquêteurs échangent encore un regard complice, s'amusant du manque de connaissances des trois témoins en matière d'automobile. L'inspecteur poursuit tout de même :

— Ensuite?

JOUR 5

CUBA, VARADERO
COSTA AZUL DEL MAR RESORT

De retour à l'hôtel, dans le corridor menant à leurs chambres, les filles discutent de leur périple.

— Je suis vraiment contente d'être allée, en tout cas! Wow! Quelle belle journée!

— Moi aussi!

— Avec un chauffeur privé en plus. Vous avez vu les gros bus de touristes pleins à craquer qui devaient attendre après tout le monde à chaque endroit à visiter? ARK!

— Et c'était super bon, au resto!

— Mais ce soir, ce sera encore «le manger» du maudit buffet…On oublie tout le temps d'aller réserver dans les restos à la carte, soupire Caroline.

— C'était TA *job*, ça, lui rappelle Katia.

— On pourrait toujours aller en ville, suggère Vicky.

Katia arrive devant sa porte et remarque une petite feuille insérée dans la craque, près de la poignée. Elle s'en saisit avec délicatesse et la déplie.

— Ah! C'est donc ben fin. Mike a justement réservé au resto Kahori pour nous tous! Un truc chinois, sûrement. Il fallait être en groupe.

— C'est vraiment gentil! apprécie Vicky. À quelle heure?

— Dans une heure.

— Parfait, on se prépare et on se rejoint au lobby?

— Oui, super!

Prête la première et vêtue d'une splendide robe crème à bretelles, Katia se dirige vers le lobby question d'y siroter un verre tranquille en attendant les filles. En y mettant les pieds, elle constate que Mike et Cédric s'y trouvent déjà.

— Allo, dit-elle en embrassant discrètement Mike sur une joue avant de tapoter un peu maladroitement l'épaule de son fils.

— Et puis? La Havane? demande Mike.

— C'est incroyablement beau, cette ville! Avec un chauffeur privé, c'était le *top*! Au fait, merci pour le resto, c'est une super idée. C'est chinois?

— Je sais pas trop, honnêtement. Peu importe c'est quoi, ça va faire changement du buffet!

— Qu'est-ce que vous avez fait, vous deux?

— On s'est baladés dans le ciel! Du parachute ascensionnel, le truc tiré par le bateau, là... Nous aussi c'était *top*, hein? répond Mike en regardant son fils qui se tient bien droit à ses côtés.

— Ouais ! approuve celui-ci sans même daigner tourner la tête.

Vicky et Caroline arrivent et bientôt, le petit groupe se met en route vers le resto en question. Katia, déçue, annonce, tout en marchant le cou bien allongé :

— Les filles, j'ai un suivi-client important pour vous : le dentier et la moumoute sont encore à la même place...

En pénétrant dans une petite pièce partiellement fermée par des paravents de papier de riz, le groupe est accueilli par un couple de vacanciers s'y trouvant déjà.

— Allo !!! lance le fameux duo de cinéastes amateurs tout en filmant l'arrivée des convives avec qui ils partageront ce souper asiatique.

— Aaaah ! Regarde donc la belle surprise, toi..., se réjouit Katia en regardant ses amies, ironique comme pas une.

— Présentez-vous à la caméra, les prie le type en les filmant à tour de rôle.

Les présentations, gênantes et trop officielles, ayant créé un beau malaise, tout le groupe reste planté devant les tables *hibachi*, ne sachant trop quoi faire pour se tirer d'embarras.

— Vous n'êtes pas obligés de tout filmer, non plus ! Nous souhaitons rester incognito, vous savez... Ce qui se passe à Cuba, reste à Cuba! déconne Katia pour faire sa comique et du coup, passer un message clair au couple quant à la portion «filmographique» de la soirée.

— C'est très bon ça, comme expression! Redis-le à la caméra! exige la femme en arrachant l'appareil des mains de son mari pour effectuer un gros plan sur le visage de Katia.

Malgré son agacement, celle-ci s'exécute tout de même avant de changer de sujet de façon intentionnelle:

— Aaaah, wow! Ils vont cuisiner devant nous!

Tout le monde prend donc place en faisant fi de la caméra qui capte leurs moindres faits et gestes.

Un Cubain coiffé d'un chapeau de chef blanc longiligne apparaît. Il est déguisé en japonais – une perruque raide et noire dépasse de son couvre-chef et ses vêtements ressemblent étrangement à un habit de judo – et il a bridé ses yeux d'un trait de crayon khôl sur le dessus et sur le dessous. En imitant de façon peu convaincante un accent anglais asiatique, il salue tout le monde en effectuant une minicourbette, les mains jointes à la hauteur de la poitrine.

À la table en forme de demi-lune pouvant accueillir dix personnes, les convives se rapprochent encore plus afin de se réunir autour d'une plaque de cuisson géante qui servira de plan de travail au cuistot. Caroline, qui se trouve tout au bout, est juste à côté du chef. Elle affirme avec excitation:

— Wow! J'ai jamais mangé dans ce genre de restaurant!

Fébrile, la femme place finalement la caméra, toujours en marche, sur un trépied afin de libérer ses mains pour le reste du repas. Une fois que tout le monde a fait son choix, le cuistot nomme en anglais les ingrédients qu'il dépose sur la plaque bien chaude : «Poulet, piment, oignon, brocoli…», puis il jette une huile aux effluves de safran et de gingembre sur les aliments avant d'embraser le tout en un clin d'œil.

En voyant la flamme s'élever, Caroline s'extirpe de sa chaise en virevoltant comme une toupie pour finalement atterrir en petit bonhomme et de dos contre le paravent de papier de riz qui tremblote derrière elle.

— HÉ ! crie-t-elle en se prenant la tête.

— Voyons donc…, fait la femme à la caméra en donnant un coup de coude à son mari pour que celui-ci tourne la caméra afin de capter la scène absurde.

Demeuré de marbre, le chef continue à brasser à l'aide de deux larges spatules en inox le repas qui grésille sur sa plaque. Son air stoïque sied bien à son rôle de chef cuisinier japonais. Mike dévisage Katia avec de grands yeux étonnés. Vicky fait peu de cas de la commotion, puis elle explique avec désinvolture :

— Elle aime pas le feu… Un genre de traumatisme.

Réalisant que sa réaction s'avère trop vive, Caroline se redresse un peu et ajoute avec honte :

— Je suis rendue avec une phobie des coiffeuses et du feu… Ça va super bien mon affaire !

Ne regagnant pas sa chaise initiale, elle se déplace plutôt vers Vicky, assise au milieu de la tablée et la pousse un peu du bras pour lui faire comprendre qu'elle désire changer de place avec elle. Compatissante à la détresse aussi évidente que démesurée de son amie, cette dernière collabore.

Sans plus d'explications, le repas se poursuit. Caroline recule sa chaise au maximum et se place ainsi en retrait du groupe. Faisant fi des événements perturbants précédents, le très habile Cubain exécute en rafale des tours d'adresse tantôt en faisant bondir les aliments dans les airs, tantôt en les déplaçant rapidement sur la plaque à l'aide de ses spatules. Il concocte même un grand cœur avec des œufs avant de les mélanger puis de les ajouter au sauté de poulet et de légumes. Impressionnés, les convives manifestent leur appréciation en applaudissant.

Après avoir laissé le temps aux clients de déguster la première partie du repas, le cuisinier se remet à l'œuvre. Il badigeonne un peu d'huile sur la plaque avant d'y jeter des petites crevettes et des pois mange-tout qu'il nappe d'une sauce claire parfumée aux agrumes. Afin de poursuivre son spectacle d'acrobaties culinaires enlevant, le chef cubain-japonais demande à Cédric, assis devant lui, d'ouvrir grand la bouche. Sans faire de chichis, celui-ci s'exécute. Le cuistot attrape alors une crevette qu'il lance habilement et directement dans la bouche du jeune homme. Tout le monde s'esclaffe. Le chef fait de même pour le caméraman et sa femme. Exalté comme jamais, le couple demande alors à Cédric de prendre la caméra afin que le cuisinier recommence la manœuvre, question de capter la scène intégrale sur pellicule. Lorsque vient son tour de recevoir son repas volant, Katia ouvre grand la bouche. À la dernière minute, cependant, elle perçoit que le projectile va manquer son objectif, donc elle bouge un peu vers le bas. Par malheur, la crevette – bien visée par le cuistot dès le départ – vient percuter le haut de son nez avant de retomber sur la table.

— Ben voyons…, se désole celle-ci en saisissant sa serviette de table pour s'essuyer le visage.

— Ne pas bouger…, ordonne le cuistot qui désire aussitôt répéter l'expérience.

Katia ouvre la bouche de plus belle. Son instinct la rendant incapable de ne pas bouger, elle tente de nouveau d'attraper par elle-même la crevette en se déplaçant, cette fois, vers la gauche. Ainsi déviée de sa trajectoire par le visage de Katia, la crevette vient s'échouer sur sa belle robe beige, la laissant donc maculée d'une tache de sauce brunâtre.

— Ah, calvaire…, s'impatiente Katia qui étend encore plus la tache disgracieuse en essayant tant bien que mal de la frotter à l'aide de la serviette de tissu.

— Faut pas que tu bouges, lui rappelle Mike, juste pour bien faire.

— Oui, mais…

Sous les encouragements de toute la tribu, elle se positionne pour une ultime tentative. La même chose se produit, son cerveau lui commandant à tort de se mouvoir pour réussir l'exploit. La crevette tombe à nouveau sur sa robe, maculant à présent son sein droit d'une splendide salissure bien fraîche.

— Il fait exprès ou quoi? rugit Katia, aussi souillée qu'en colère.

— Ne pas bouger, madame, réitère le type déguisé en japonais qui semble vouloir refaire un autre essai.

— Ne-non, *fuck off*, ça me tente pu pantoute, maugrée Katia, au désespoir, en élargissant encore plus la seconde tache sur son bustier à l'aide de la serviette.

— J'ai du Tide to Go à la chambre, la rassure Caroline, qui rit tout de même dans sa barbe en voyant la détresse vestimentaire de son amie.

Au tour de Mike de réceptionner le fruit de mer volant. Tout se passe à merveille. Curieusement, il en va de même pour le reste des convives.

Ne comprenant pas du tout pourquoi elle a été la seule à ne pas être épargnée, Katia rouspète:

— Il a fait exprès..., en toisant d'un regard quasi meurtrier le pauvre Cubain à toque qui sue à grosses gouttes derrière la plaque chaude.

JOUR 8

AÉROPORT MONTRÉAL-TRUDEAU
SALLE 815 – **10 H 59**

L'inspecteur au cou trop large regarde les filles avec les yeux suspicieux d'un homme trouvant leur histoire irréellement abracadabrante, quoiqu'inutile aux fins de l'enquête. Il semble même suspecter qu'elles tirent volontairement dans tous les sens pour brouiller les pistes. Caroline, qui décode très bien l'expression perplexe sur son visage, sent le besoin d'expliquer :

— Écoutez, chaque fois qu'on sort ensemble quelque part, il nous arrive toujours les catastrophes les plus pathétiques de la terre. Au quotidien, c'est pas de même. Moi, je suis une fille vraiment tranquille, voire quasiment plate, d'habitude.

— On a une problématique au niveau de notre karma de groupe. Individuellement, notre vie est très ennuyante, mais ensemble, on dirait que tout se complique…

Trouvant les explications ésotériques de Vicky à des années-lumière de ses croyances rationnelles personnelles, Biron fronce une fois de plus les sourcils et il répète simplement : «karma ?», l'air de se dire : «On ne montera pas un dossier criminel international étoffé avec des conclusions de ce genre.»

— Un instant ! Moi, je suis pas aussi plate qu'eux autres dans la vraie vie, précise Katia, qui ne souhaite pas du tout porter ce chapeau peu avantageux.

— Peu importe. À moins qu'il ne se soit produit quelque chose de significatif la veille du départ, passons outre, si ça ne vous dérange pas. Parlez-nous d'hier matin, s'il vous plaît.

— Aussi bien comme ça, parce que le sixième jour, il s'est rien passé de toute façon, soupire Caroline, laissant ainsi croire qu'elle s'était ennuyée à mort.

— Parle pour toi !

— Ah oui, c'est vrai, hormis le fait que Katia a *frenché* Mike toute la journée, rectifie celle-ci. Et que le couple qui faisait suer Vicky a rompu sur la plage, devant tout le monde. On n'a jamais compris cette scène-là, d'ailleurs, hein ?

— Non. Quelle crise tout de même..., ne peut s'empêcher de débuter Katia.

JOUR 6
CUBA, VARADERO
COSTA AZUL DEL MAR RESORT

Assises sur la plage depuis déjà un bon bout de temps, les trois vacancières profitent à fond de leur dernière journée complète à la plage. Caroline dévore un roman tandis que Vicky, Katia et Mike discutent, Cédric étant parti faire une balade. Sans aucune surprise et avec une prévisibilité à ennuyer un mort, un Cubain les aborde au passage :

— *¿Bolleyboll? ¿Sí?*

— ...

Le groupe l'observe, hébété. Caroline lève les yeux de son bouquin. Katia et Mike se consultent du regard. Vicky les observe un instant avant de reporter ses yeux sur le type avec le ballon.

— Pourquoi pas ! envoie Katia.

— Ouin, ça me tente, fait aussi Caro.

— *¡Bien! ¡Fantástico!* apprécie l'employé, pour qui c'est officiellement le plus beau jour de sa vie.

Les filles et Mike l'observent vivre ce qui semble être un moment de félicité indescriptible. Il poursuit :

— *¡Sí! ¡Bien! ¡Bien! ¡Bolleyboll, sí!*

— Ayoye ! Je pense qu'il est heureux, spécule Vicky.

— Imaginez sa joie : il a essayé si fort pendant six jours... Pour lui, ce doit être comme arriver en haut de l'Everest, s'imagine Katia en levant l'index vers le ciel.

— C'est touchant de voir ça, complète Mike, tout aussi ironique.

Des cris stridents viennent alors déranger leur moment cocasse.

— Voyons donc, calvaire!? Ici? Pendant que je suis malade à notre chambre! J'en reviens pas, criss...

— C'est même pas vrai! Je te le jure, Simon! C'est pas vrai...

— Non, il me l'a dit! Des gens vous ont vus dans la piscine... Si tu veux savoir, là, quin, *fuck* l'ostie de mariage, crie Simon avant de propulser ce qui semble être une bague sur la chaise longue de sa fiancée avant de déguerpir.

Du sable se soulève de terre à chacun de ses pas tellement il est en beau fusil. Tout le groupe de futurs sportifs reste muet. L'employé, qui n'a rien compris à la pièce de théâtre se déroulant en français, redemande tout de même à voix basse, juste pour être certain de son coup:

— *¿Bolleyboll? ¿Sí?*

JOUR 8

AÉROPORT MONTRÉAL-TRUDEAU
SALLE 315 – **11 H 07**

Katia, qui savoure ce genre de querelle comme une enfant de quatre ans se servant à deux mains dans un plat de Smarties rouges, sourit aux anges à l'évocation du doux souvenir:

— Quand tu dis solide «pétage de coche»... Hon! *Anyway*, on saura jamais ce qui s'est réellement passé, au fond...

— Ben…, hésite Vicky avec le visage repentant d'une bonne sœur ayant commis le péché de la chair à quarante-trois reprises.

— Hein?

— Vicky?

En ne disant rien, les douaniers l'avalisent secrètement à poursuivre, malgré que le topo des trois témoins s'avère complètement hors sujet pour le dossier, encore une fois.

— Aaaaah! C'était pas supposé se passer de même du tout, bon. Mon plan de génie a comme dérapé en cours de route…

— Quoi? Qu'est-ce que t'as fait? s'inquiète Caroline.

— On t'écoute…, salive encore plus Katia.

Vicky souffle avec la bouche avant de se lancer:

— Le soir du jour de l'An…

JOUR 4

CUBA, VARADERO
COSTA AZUL DEL MAR RESORT

La mouffette se tient devant les filles avec la perruque sur la tête.

— J'ai trouvé ça sur la plage, et là, je la porte pour que le propriétaire puisse l'identifier!

Vicky, toujours d'une humeur peu festive, répète simplement :

— Ark-eeee…

— Bon, je vais poursuivre ma tournée ! annonce la mouffette en repartant au galop vers le groupe de voyageurs de la table voisine.

— Les filles, le mot «inutilité» est trop insignifiant pour décrire ce gars-là…

— Une plaie de lit…

— *Anyway !* Vous êtes plates, toutes les deux, facque je retourne voir mon mec ! Bye !

Caroline l'écoute à peine et s'exclame :

— Bon, Éric est revenu !

La prof de français rive les yeux sur son cellulaire.

Vicky s'emmerde. Elle tend l'oreille vers la mouffette qui présente sa perruque à la table voisine. La blonde de Simon est là, mais pas lui. Celle-ci lance une blague à la tablée :

— C'est peut-être la perruque à mon *chum* et je le sais pas ! Mais bon, en ce moment, il fait des allers-retours aux toilettes dans la chambre, donc c'est pas un bon moment pour aller le lui demander !

Vicky se tourne alors vers l'extrémité de la salle où elle aperçoit le soufflé de Drummond qui sirote un verre tout seul. Une idée « de génie » la frappe alors de plein fouet. Le ciel s'illumine. Les archanges descendent du ciel.

Elle se lève d'un bond et part le rejoindre en tentant d'avoir l'air subtil.

— Salut !

— Allo ! Que la fraîcheur de cette nouvelle année nous apporte le frais nécessaire pour éventer nos vies...

— Ben oui, ben oui, le frais pis toute... Écoute, je sais pas trop comment te dire ça, mais tu vois la fille là-bas, celle à la robe noire avec un col en V ?

— Oui, elle est super fine !

— Tu peux garder un secret ?

— Oui, oui. Secret bien gardé arrive toujours à point...

— Elle capote sur toi ! Elle est en couple ici, mais elle le regrette tellement ! Elle « trippe » raide sur toi. Elle te trouve intelligent, beau comme un Dieu, tout ce que tu dis la touche...

— Ah ouin ?

— Je te jure, c'est fou. Et là, son *chum* est désagréable et malade, donc elle est toute seule. C'est triste pour commencer la nouvelle année, je trouve...

— Hon, oui..., s'émeut le soufflé de Drummond en bombant son torse démesuré en direction de la fille en question.

— En tout cas, je voulais te le dire. Ça fait toujours plaisir de savoir qu'on plaît à quelqu'un à ce point-là !

— C'est bon, mordicus et bouche cousue...

JOUR 8

AÉROPORT MONTRÉAL-TRUDEAU
SALLE 315 – **11 H 08**

— Non, non, non..., refuse de croire Caroline en se prenant la tête.

— C'est de l'abus envers un pauvre être humain intellectuellement incapable de se défendre, ça ! crie Katia, réjouie comme jamais par ce coup de théâtre prodigieux.

— Qu'est-ce que vous pensez qui est arrivé ? Il a sauté sur l'opportunité à pieds joints, le pauvre, explique Vicky. Je l'ai vu rôder autour d'elle toute la soirée et, croyez-le ou non, elle avait l'air d'avoir du gros *fun* avec !

— Hein ? J'ai jamais remarqué ça ! avoue Caro.

— Moi non plus. J'avais même pas remarqué que son *chum* était pas dans les parages.

Le visage de Vicky s'assombrit de nouveau :

— Disons que c'est le lendemain que j'ai poussé ma chance un peu. Quand on est allées prendre un verre au bar de l'hôtel, après le souper au Kahori...

JOUR 5

CUBA, VARADERO
COSTA AZUL DEL MAR RESORT

Katia ayant dû aller se changer après les attaques de crevettes en rafale, les filles arrivent les dernières à la discothèque. Vicky remarque d'emblée le soufflé de Drummond qui discute avec la blonde de Simon. Il semble la charmer, à demi avachi sur le bar, tout près d'elle. Ladite fille sourit. Vicky aussi.

Les trois vacancières approchent du bar pour commander un verre. Katia se colle sur Mike illico tandis que Caroline placote avec une autre voyageuse à sa droite. Pensant vite, Vicky accroche au passage la mouffette qui déambule, l'air de ne pas trop savoir où elle va.

— Hé! Allo!

Heureux qu'elle semble ravie de le voir pour une fois, il tente d'en abuser :

— Yo! Câlin?

Ayant mesquinement besoin de lui, elle s'exécute en gémissant un cri de bonheur extrême.

— Écoute, je suis tellement mal à l'aise, là… Tu connais la fille, là-bas?

— Oui.

— Je l'ai vue *frencher* avec le gars qui l'accompagne dans la piscine aujourd'hui... Ils se cachaient...

— Hein ? Elle ne va pas se marier avec Simon bientôt ?

— Ben oui... c'est pas *cool*, hein ?!

— Non... pauvre Simon !

— Tu parles. Il est malade dans sa chambre en plus, et là, je me dis : «Il faut que quelqu'un lui en parle...»

— Ah oui, c'est vrai...

— Mais en même temps, je trouve que c'est délicat. Me semble que d'homme à homme ce serait plus facile...

Elle ne termine pas sa phrase et observe, du coin de l'œil, Dave qui analyse à distance les ricanements du présumé couple adultère au bar.

— Je vais y dire, moi !

— Ah, t'es certain ? Mais là, je veux pas que tu dises que c'est moi qui ai dit ça...

Comme si elle venait d'hériter d'une mission digne de sa grandeur d'âme, la mouffette relève les épaules et proclame :

— Fais-moi confiance, je sais comment agir dans ce genre de situation là.

— Ah merci, c'est vraiment généreux de ta part.

— Je sais...

JOUR 8

AÉROPORT MONTRÉAL-TRUDEAU
SALLE 315 – **11 H 08**

Maintenant la tête couchée entre ses bras sur la table, Vicky répète :

— Je sais, je sais, je sais… c'est n'importe quoi !

— Franchement ! L'autre colon pas de savoir-vivre qui se vante : «Je sais comment agir…» Mon œil, oui !

— Moi, j'adore ça ! Je trouve ça parfait !

— L'instinct gossant de la mouffette à faire suer tout le monde a vu là une opportunité incroyable de foutre le trouble, donc vous connaissez la suite. Mais sans blague, j'espérais qu'ils se chicanent un peu, pas qu'ils divorcent avant de se marier !

— Elle t'a humiliée toute la semaine, et lui aussi, donc c'est bien fait pour eux !

— Bon, bon, bon. Non pas que votre histoire soit inintéressante, mais revenons à l'essentiel, s'il vous plaît, mesdames…

— Oui, oui, désolée.

— Je continue donc l'affaire «Sanchez», enchaîne Katia. Il nous a fait part de son «offre» à notre retour de

La Havane. On a tout de suite trouvé l'idée géniale, en se disant que ça nous donnerait un peu plus de temps pour profiter de la plage et du soleil...

JOUR 7
CUBA, VARADERO
COSTA AZUL DEL MAR RESORT

En bouclant leurs valises à la chambre, Caroline et Vicky discutent de leur itinéraire de retour.

— Cette fois-ci, les heures de vol sont super chouettes. On va pas revenir brûlées à la maison comme à notre arrivée ici, se réjouit Caroline.

— Oui, parce que le retour à l'école va arriver vite !

— Il nous reste au moins encore quelques jours pour retomber sur nos pattes.

— C'est vraiment gentil qu'il ait proposé de nous reconduire à l'aéroport. On n'aura pas besoin d'attendre une heure trente pour rien, ni de faire le tour des hôtels en autobus comme à notre arrivée.

— Oui, la fameuse «*run* de lait» pour aller chercher des voyageurs dans toute la ville.

— Bon, on se dépêche pour profiter de la plage une dernière fois ? Je veux prendre plus de photos aussi. Me semble que j'en ai pas beaucoup...

La porte de la chambre de Katia étant toujours ouverte, Vicky lui demande d'une voix forte :

— Es-tu prête, Kat ?

— Oui, donnez-moi dix minutes...

— OK, on passe par le buffet pour manger une croûte avant ?

— Ouais...

Au même moment, un bruit de chariot se fait entendre dans le corridor.

— *¡Holaaa ! ¿Mini barrr ?*

— Voilà encore l'autre zouf avec son ton de voix inadéquat..., se plaint Katia.

— Ben oui, et danseur en plus.

— Il fallait bien terminer ce voyage en beauté...

Installées à une table de la salle à manger devant une rôtie sèche, les filles discutent à propos des gens qui se trouvent tout autour. Plusieurs voyageurs attrapent des trucs à la hâte, question de respecter l'horaire serré qui leur est imposé pour leur transport vers l'aéroport.

— Tout le monde est pressé. Il doit y avoir une grande file d'attente au lobby et nous, on s'épargne tout ça !

Vraiment une superbe idée! Quand tu prends le transport organisé dans le forfait, tu perds presque trois heures au final, analyse Katia.

— C'est vrai, on va s'épargner d'aller chercher tout le monde en bus aussi.

— Ah zut, le WiFi ne marche pas encore. Marc a peut-être répondu à ma photo...

— Grosse cochonne!

— T'as raison. Pour moi non plus, rien ne fonctionne, confirme Caroline en regardant son téléphone.

Mike surgit dans l'aire de repas et repère avec facilité les trois vacancières. Il approche de quelques pas tandis que son garçon reste en plan, absorbé par un jeu sur son cellulaire. Katia, qui comprend qu'ils doivent quitter l'hôtel avec le transport de groupe, se lève en terminant à la hâte sa bouchée avant de s'essuyer la commissure des lèvres avec une serviette de table. Elle boit une gorgée d'eau et agrippe sa sacoche pour y dénicher une gomme. Les filles lui sourient avec tendresse sans rien dire.

Elle rejoint Mike près du mur de l'entrée du buffet, un peu à l'écart des regards.

— Donc, voilà, susurre-t-elle en enroulant ses bras autour de son cou.

— Même si on va se croiser à l'aéroport, j'avais envie de te dire au revoir, ici, à l'hôtel. Le lieu de notre rencontre..., commence-t-il, romantique.

— On en a déjà parlé souvent, mais... Mike, j'aimerais vraiment te revoir au Québec... Je sais qu'habituellement les amours de voyage durent pas, que la réalité rattrape souvent les gens et que, finalement, ça marche pas... Étrangement, avec toi, je ressens plutôt le contraire.

— Pareil pour moi, ma belle. Je te trouve dynamique, belle, le *fun*. En toute franchise, t'es exactement le genre de femme que je recherche.

— Tu le dis pas pour me *bullshitter*? Je vais pas arriver chez moi et tenter de te contacter pour finalement réaliser que tu m'as refilé un faux numéro de téléphone? demande Katia en s'inspirant bien évidemment d'une histoire vécue par une certaine amie dans le passé[49].

— Qu'est-ce qui me dit que c'est pas toi, la croqueuse d'hommes qui me fera faux bond?

Constatant que l'insécurité est partagée des deux côtés, Katia sourit et l'embrasse avec douceur. Entre deux baisers, elle murmure:

— Pas de chance que ça arrive, je t'assure...

— Mais je dois te dire, je suis un vrai gars de la construction macho qui se lave les cheveux avec du savon pour le corps et qui fait jamais la vaisselle.

— Hum... t'as un lave-vaisselle?

---

49. Mexique, Patrice... ah lui... Grrr!

— Ouais, mais je la rince jamais avant de la mettre dedans...

— Ah ouin... je sais plus trop, alors. Peut-être que ça ne fonctionnera pas nous deux, finalement.

Il l'attrape par la nuque pour la rapprocher de lui de nouveau. Elle résiste et fait mine de s'opposer à son geste autoritaire pour être taquine.

— Eille!

Mike rigole doucement.

Une dernière embrassade empreinte d'émotion clôture cet au revoir officiel.

— On se revoit à l'aéroport...

— Oui! Oui! Bye! À plus tard...

Katia revient vers ses amies et les valises en arborant un large sourire.

— Cibole! T'as pas l'air en amour pantoute, Kat!

— Mon Dieu! Vas-tu ENFIN avoir un *chum*? Je dois halluciner, lui lance Caroline, ravie par la perspective.

— Peut-être. Ç'a pas de bon sens... Qui rencontre un gars en voyage, dans la vie?

— Toi!

— Mais, attendez, on va voir comment se déroule la suite. Qui sait comment il est pour de vrai au quotidien?

— Tu vas voir…

— Oui, on s'est promis de se voir dès cette semaine étant donné que je suis encore en congé… et que son gars passe la semaine chez sa mère.

— Ouuuuuuh !

Katia sourit en saisissant un autre morceau de pain, une douce euphorie bien accrochée au cœur.

JOUR 8

AÉROPORT MONTRÉAL-TRUDEAU
SALLE 815 – 11 H 11

L'inspecteur, qui semble trouver le temps un peu long, prie les filles d'en arriver aux faits en roulant une main dans les airs.

— Non pas que votre idylle amoureuse soit ininté-ressante, mais je crois que cela ne sert à rien pour notre enquête.

— Oui, oui, mais vous avez dit «en détail». Je vous raconte les détails…

— Allez donc droit au but, s'il vous plaît, mesdames.

Presque insultée, Katia poursuit sans trop le montrer :

— D'accord. Donc, en terminant de manger…

JOUR 7
CUBA, VARADERO
COSTA AZUL DEL MAR RESORT

Les filles se lèvent de table et remarquent que Sylvio vient de faire son entrée dans la grande pièce à aire ouverte. Il semble pressé.

— Ah! Allo! Je vous cherchais! Donc, on va partir dans environ une heure trente, ça vous va?

— Oui, oui, parfait. On va aller flâner un peu sur la plage en prenant un dernier verre et on ira ensuite faire le *check-out*!

— Profitez-en, vous vous faites conduire, après tout. À plus tard!

— Merci encore!

Les filles se dirigent vers une petite pièce fermée à proximité de la réception afin d'y déposer leurs valises jusqu'au moment du grand départ. Comme elles ont gardé tout le nécessaire à la portée de la main, elles se rendent en moins de deux vers la mer en transportant un seul sac de plage commun.

Arrivées à bon port, elles s'allongent en balayant d'un regard nostalgique le panorama grandiose. Les flots sont d'un turquoise incomparable et la blancheur du sable fin est quasi éblouissante. Les plages sont vraiment magnifiques, à Cuba, et les filles ne se lassent pas de contempler le roulis apaisant des vagues qui semblent venir s'étendre comme de la gelée transparente sur des dunes de sucre très fin. Après un bref interlude admiratif, Katia juge que l'ambiance se prête bien à un bilan récapitulatif.

— On a fait un drôle de voyage, mais un beau voyage quand même.

— Ouin... Moi, il m'en est arrivé des vertes et des pas mûres, je trouve..., rappelle Vicky, plus ou moins d'accord avec son amie.

— Oui, mais rien de SI dramatique! Même votre coquerelle imaginaire est jamais revenue! C'est heureux ça, non!? tempère Katia.

— Elle était vraiment là! Je l'ai vue! se défend Caroline, indignée que ses amies la croient plus ou moins.

— Mes foufounes, c'est pas réglé, je vous signale. Même avec les médicaments, ça ne guérit pas vite.

— Tu pourras voir un médecin dès notre retour. T'en auras le cœur net, la rassure Caroline.

— Avouez que ce fut un voyage rempli de monde bizarre. Ma conclusion est: «Maudit que le monde est *fucké* dans la vie, pareil», affirme Katia avec candeur.

— Une autre chose que l'on doit retenir: Cuba, au mois de janvier, ça peut être légèrement frisquet. Et honnêtement, la formule «tout inclus» revient au même tout le temps. Regardez, hier, on a été à la piscine, à la plage, on a soupé au buffet et on a bu des verres à la discothèque.

Un peu redondant comme horaire. Je passerais pas deux semaines ici, en tout cas…, note Vicky.

— C'est comme une cassette qui tourne en boucle: «¡Hola! ¿Mini barrr?», «¿Bolleyboll?», «Bará, bará, bará, berê, berê, berê»…

— Oui, c'est vrai. T'oublies le sujet température, ça aussi c'était lassant. Mais une chance que ç'a bien fini de ce côté-là. Imaginez-vous un voyage au complet à quatorze degrés…

— Ouache! Et avec le buffet qu'on nous repasse de jour en jour, ça aide pas… Toujours les mêmes ananas durs, les sempiternelles saucisses style chorizo pleines d'huile et… les frites. Mais bon, dans mon cas, le voyage m'a fait réaliser comme une claque dans la face que Marc et moi, on niaise pour rien. Je l'aime vraiment, ce gars-là. Je voudrais qu'on forme un couple de façon officielle. C'est maintenant clair et net.

— Quand il verra ta photo, il va vouloir te marier! déconne Katia.

— Sans blague, Vic, je trouve que ça va de soi. La peur de l'engagement, faut en revenir à un moment donné. On n'a plus vingt ans, affirme Caro en se tournant vers ses amies.

— Ayoye, j'ai quand même hâte de voir la tête des autres profs quand ils apprendront la nouvelle[50].

---

50. Marc étant prof d'éducation physique à leur école, je vous le rappelle.

— La prof de mathématiques de secondaire III le sait déjà, je pense. La prof de chimie s'en doute aussi...

— Je pense que plusieurs personnes sont au courant. Ça ne créera pas une si grosse commotion, conclut Caroline. Regardez bien ça, vous allez toutes les deux vous retrouver en couple, et moi, je vais me séparer...

— Ah, Caro, arrête de dire des niaiseries. Tu divagues, on te l'a dit...

— Bien hâte de savoir c'est qui, cette fille-là, en tout cas, s'attriste-t-elle en fixant la mer diaphane qui s'étend à perte de vue devant elle.

— Dernier mojito, les femmes ? demande Katia en se levant.

— Ouais !

En se rendant au lobby, elles constatent avec joie l'absence de voyageurs dans les alentours. Seule une femme qu'elles ne connaissent pas discute avec un membre du personnel dans une chaise près de la réception. Le dentier se trouve toujours dans son aquarium et la perruque siège fièrement à ses côtés.

— La fameuse étape qui me fait peur, émet Vicky, presque nerveuse de devoir remettre les cartes des chambres.

— Ben non, calme-toi ! *¡ No problemo !*

— Jamais deux sans trois. Peut-être que je devrais sortir ma carte de crédit tout de suite, pour être prête...

Les filles avancent vers la réceptionniste qui s'empare des cartes de chambre avant d'ouvrir le fichier associé à chacune d'elles dans son ordinateur.

Pour faire la conversation et être polie, la Cubaine demande en anglais :

— Avez-vous passé un bon séjour dans notre hôtel ?

— Ouiiii, hésite Vicky en la regardant de côté, les yeux ronds, comme un cheval qui voit surgir son cavalier par surprise.

— Parfait... hum..., débute la femme en semblant analyser que tout est en règle.

Vicky, qui la toise avec suspicion, semble attendre la suite avec une appréhension douloureuse. Katia bâille un peu en mettant la main devant la bouche.

— Tout est correct ! Merci beaucoup et au plaisir de vous revoir, conclut la femme hispanophone en déposant les mains devant elle sur le comptoir.

— « Tout est correct » ? répète Vicky, incrédule.

— Oui..., approuve l'employée en fronçant les sourcils.

— En êtes-vous bien certaine ? réitère Vicky, la main posée sur sa sacoche, prête à dégainer sa carte de crédit.

— Oui..., envoie l'employé, l'air de ne rien comprendre.

— Tout est beau! crie Vicky en assénant une tape de joie sur l'épaule de Katia qui bâillait de nouveau.

— Ben là, tu t'attendais à quoi? demande Caroline, qui s'amuse de sa réaction d'extase face au *check-out* effectué sans aucune mauvaise surprise.

— Tout est beau! répète pour la deuxième fois Vicky, en souriant largement.

— Reviens-en, Vic..., s'impatiente Katia pour la ramener un peu sur terre.

Après avoir récupéré leurs bagages en deux temps trois mouvements, les filles attendent sagement Sylvio dans le *lobby*.

— Voyons? C'est ben long. Il est en retard ou quoi? demande Caroline en allumant son cellulaire pour y voir l'heure.

Katia sort aussi le sien et elle compte dans sa tête.

— Oui, il est en retard de dix minutes, disons.

— Ouin, il faudrait pas manquer notre avion, quand même.

— Mais non, il va arriver, la rassure Katia en tournant la tête vers les portes, intérieurement tout aussi inquiète que ses amies.

— Le WiFi ne fonctionne toujours pas, remarque Caroline.

— Hé! Yo! Vous êtes encore là, les «ron coco»?

— Oui, toi aussi, visiblement…

— Ouin, je sais pas encore quand je pars! En fait, je pourrais rester ici pour le reste de ma vie, ça me dérange pas! répond la mouffette, heureuse, un verre de rhum pur à la main.

Deux Québécoises viennent alors le rejoindre. Elles se présentent rapidement aux filles.

— On vient d'arriver! On «trippe» tellement, là!

— C'est le *fun*! répond Caroline, contente pour elles.

— Et on s'est fait un nouvel ami aussitôt arrivées! spécifie une des jeunes filles, l'air de vivre une véritable lune de miel avec Dave.

— Ça aussi, c'est le *fun*! répète Caroline, ambivalente.

— Bon, ben, bon retour à vous trois! Bye! saluent les filles qui s'éloignent, chacune accrochée à un bras de Dave.

— Ayoye! Elles ont tellement pas idée dans quoi elles s'embarquent…, se désole Katia en secouant la tête de pitié.

— Pauvres elles…

Les trois filles décident alors de sortir dehors pour voir Sylvio arriver.

— Qu'est-ce que ça fait quand tu manques ton avion? demande Caroline au moment où elles aboutissent sur le trottoir.

— Je sais pas[51]...

— Es-tu obligée de rester sept jours de plus ? s'informe à nouveau Caro en imaginant le pire.

— Non, regarde la mouffette. Il y a des vols presque tous les jours en saison touristique, je pense.

— Ça doit coûter cher, en tout cas..., ajoute Vicky.

— Arrêtez de « paranoïer » ! Il va arriver.

— On nous conseille toujours d'arriver au moins trois heures avant le vol, mais là, on va être tout juste deux heures avant. J'espère que ce sera correct...

— Oui, deux heures avant, ça va, dans les petits aéroports comme ici. On n'est pas à l'aéroport d'Atlanta quand même ! On va juste s'éviter la cohue en n'étant pas en même temps que le reste des touristes. On sauvera du temps puisqu'on évitera les longues files d'attente au comptoir d'enregistrement et à la guérite pour payer les taxes de départ. Donc, les filles, on se calme et, de toute façon...

Katia n'a même pas le temps de terminer sa phrase qu'une voiture apparaît dans la cour et fait le tour d'une enceinte de brique en forme d'arche, garnie de plantes grimpantes ornées de fleurs.

---

51. Votre auteure le sait, elle... Hon, hon, hon...

— Ah bon, voilà! se réjouit Katia, heureuse d'avoir raison.

Sylvio, au volant d'un nouveau véhicule, envoie la main aux filles...

JOUR 8

AÉROPORT MONTRÉAL-TRUDEAU
SALLE 315 – **11 H 23**

L'inspecteur et son collègue, qui écoutent attentivement le récit de Katia, la coupent en levant la main.

— On a remarqué une certaine discordance dans vos dépositions à ce niveau-ci, indique l'inspecteur Biron en replaçant les trois piles de papiers devant lui avant de poursuivre. Voyons voir, l'une a dit: «Une auto bleu foncé quatre portes du genre Toyota Camry. Ma tante en a une et ça ressemblait à sa voiture.»

L'inspecteur marque une pause et lève les yeux vers Vicky. Il poursuit avec la seconde déposition qu'il tient dans son autre main. C'est celle de Caroline.

— Vous, madame, vous décrivez: «Une Audi bleu foncé. Il me semble que j'ai vu des cercles à l'arrière»... Et vous, madame, vous dites: «Un char quatre portes, bleu, avec des roues "flashantes" en inox. Je ne sais pas quelle marque. Je ne connais rien aux chars et ça ne m'intéresse pas.»

Les trois filles, qui sont tout sauf des passionnées de voitures – nous le savons depuis longtemps – se dévisagent, un peu honteuses de leur performance douteuse quant à ce détail tout de même important.

— C'est vrai que ça ne m'intéresse pas, les chars…, avoue Katia, un peu perplexe en repensant à sa réponse un tantinet inadéquate.

— Ce n'était pas une Audi, Caro, mais bien un genre de Camry, comme celle de ma tante.

— Bleue ! Comme tantôt, on est toutes certaines qu'elle était bleue, insiste Katia, bien fière qu'elles soient du moins unanimes concernant cet aspect.

Voyant que la confusion règne toujours au sein du groupe de témoins, l'inspecteur récapitule :

— Donc, une berline, quatre portes, bleue ? De toute façon, on devrait être en mesure de faire le lien avec le rapport des autorités de Cuba.

— Sérieusement, on était en retard et un peu anxieuses. On se foutait bien de l'auto à ce moment-là. On voulait juste arriver à temps. Et, de toute façon, on est des filles… Si vous voulez, je peux vous dire ce que portait une fille au bar ce jour-là parce que je trouvais ça vraiment beau. Elle avait une robe à l'effigie de l'hôtel vert pomme avec un foulard brun et rose au cou, de petites paillettes vert plus foncé sur les bretelles et des escarpins qui…

L'inspecteur lève la main.

— Ça va, ça va, je comprends le principe.

— Une question d'intérêt, vous comprenez !

— Donc ? Vous placez vos bagages dans le coffre, vous montez avec lui et puis ?

— Non, on embarque dans l'auto et *il* place *lui-même* les bagages dans le coffre, c'est important. Je l'avais expliqué de cette manière, moi, pas vous ? précise Katia qui semble croire que l'inspecteur les accuse encore d'une dissemblance quant aux faits.

— Moi aussi.

Comme s'il ne se souvenait pas de ce détail, l'inspecteur jette un œil sur les trois dépositions avant de déclarer :

— Ah oui, pour ça, c'est bon. Ensuite ? Qu'est-ce que monsieur Sanchez vous a raconté ?

— Il nous a juste dit…

JOUR 7
CUBA, VARADERO
COSTA AZUL DEL MAR RESORT

— Désolé pour mon léger retard, s'excuse Sylvio qui sort du véhicule aussitôt celui-ci immobilisé près des filles.

Il inspecte à gauche, puis à droite, en remontant nerveusement la taille de son pantalon comme si celui-ci était trop grand pour lui. Il semble différent d'à son habitude, et particulièrement angoissé.

— On commençait à se demander ce qui se passait !

Comme Caroline se dirige vers l'arrière de l'automobile pour insérer sa valise dans le coffre, Sylvio l'arrête net en levant les deux mains :

— Non, non, je vais le faire. Allez plutôt vous asseoir dans l'auto.

— Ah, d'accord. C'est vraiment un service tout compris !

Il sourit succinctement et incline la tête pour avaliser son propos. Les filles prennent place à bord. Caroline, sur la banquette arrière aux côtés de Vicky, ouvre son cellulaire pour y voir l'heure.

— On va être juste correctes, je pense.

Sylvio finit de ranger les valises dans le coffre et reprend place derrière le volant. Les passagères ouvrent toutes grandes les vitres du véhicule pour dissiper la chaleur étouffante. De la racine de ses cheveux jusqu'à ses tempes, des gouttelettes perlent sur la peau basanée de leur conducteur privé.

— Ouf ! Il fait chaud ! Si jamais on vous demande pourquoi je vous conduis à l'aéroport, dites que vous étiez en retard et que vous avez manqué le bus...

Vicky dévisage Caroline pendant que Katia demande spontanément :

— Pourquoi ?

— Les autorités préfèrent que les touristes s'en tiennent au fonctionnement habituel durant leur séjour pour éviter que les gens manquent leur avion. N'oubliez pas qu'un visa de séjour temporaire vous a été remis à votre arrivée. Tout est très surveillé, à Cuba.

— Ah, OK. Pas de problème, alors, envoie Katia, tout de même perplexe à l'idée d'éventuellement devoir mentir à propos d'un détail qu'elle juge anodin.

Il démarre et s'engage sur la rue principale, c'est-à-dire l'artère centrale qui traverse Varadero et longe la côte sur plusieurs kilomètres. Mélancoliques et un peu songeuses, les filles observent la vie qui frétille dans les rues de la charmante station balnéaire. Comme Sylvio a dû ralentir à cause d'un feu rouge, deux jeunes enfants cubains à vélo dépassent le véhicule en imitant, à tue-tête, le cri d'un singe. Katia sursaute. Les deux taquins s'esclaffent de rire. Une femme enceinte de plusieurs mois, tenant la main d'un jeune môme de tout au plus trois ans, attend patiemment son tour pour traverser l'avenue. Le petit garçon qui l'accompagne fixe Katia, assise à l'avant de la voiture, et sa mère lui assène un petit coup sur le bras et le rabroue en espagnol. Le petit lève alors la main en direction de Katia. Touchée, celle-ci lui renvoie la main en esquissant un grand sourire. Vicky observe aussi, par la vitre, le ciel bleu à peine parsemé de quelques nuages floconneux. Elle réalise du coup que, dans quelques heures, elles devront affronter les rigueurs de l'hiver québécois. Cette triste réalité la force à expirer bruyamment sans raison. Caroline, qui comprend d'instinct son état d'esprit, l'observe avec compassion, victime elle aussi d'une légère nostalgie. Elle fait part de sa réflexion à ses amies :

— Moi, en tout cas, la prochaine fois que j'irai en voyage, je partirai avec Éric. Si on est encore ensemble, bien sûr...

Vicky lui flatte l'avant-bras, question de l'encourager à rester positive. Katia remarque qu'un bouchon de circulation évident semble se présenter devant. «Ah non, on n'a pas vraiment le temps...», songe-t-elle sans le dire à ses amies pour ne pas faire paniquer Caroline, qui s'avère perpétuellement inquiète.

JOUR 8
AÉROPORT MONTRÉAL-TRUDEAU
SALLE 315 – 11 H 28

L'inspecteur consulte la déclaration de Katia et lui demande :

— Dans votre témoignage, vous avez effectivement indiqué : «En arrivant près d'un bouchon de circulation...» Donc, vous pensiez que c'est ce dont il s'agissait ?

— Moi, je regardais pas vers l'avant. Je pensais à autre chose, avoue Caroline.

— Dans mon cas, je me désolais à l'idée qu'on gèlerait en cibole en arrivant ici. Je n'ai pas trop prêté attention au fait qu'on ralentissait.

— Et Sanchez, comment était-il? Décrivez-moi son attitude à ce moment-là.

— Il ne parlait pas. Rien. Il était comme froid depuis le début du trajet. Je me souviens m'être dit : «Coudonc, on dirait que ça le fait suer, finalement, de venir nous reconduire», se souvient Katia.

— Puisqu'on était sur la banquette arrière, on ne le voyait pas. Mais c'est vrai qu'il était moins de bonne humeur que d'habitude.

Activement replongée dans le récit de la scène, Caroline contemple le sol un instant avant d'éclater en sanglots. Pour marquer une pause en guise d'humanité envers son témoin éprouvé, l'inspecteur dépose les papiers sur la table. Vicky tapote d'une main le dos de son amie :

— C'est correct, Caro...

— Non mais, tsé..., pleurniche à nouveau celle-ci en levant les yeux vers le ciel.

Se levant, le deuxième agent demande aux filles :

— Voulez-vous un bon café?

— Ouais, c'est pas de refus, approuve Katia.

— Je reviens tout de suite.

Un silence pesant envahit la petite pièce. L'inspecteur observe à tour de rôle les filles tandis que Vicky frictionne le dos de Caroline, qui sanglote doucement. Katia se tourne vers Biron.

— On est fatiguées…, lui lance-t-elle, presque au bord de la crise de nerfs elle aussi.

— Je comprends tout à fait. On a presque terminé. Mais tout d'abord, vous devez me raconter la suite. Je dois absolument l'entendre pour éviter d'avoir à vous rappeler ici dans les prochaines semaines afin de rectifier les faits, vous comprenez ?

— Oui.

Reprenant le contrôle d'elle-même, Caroline se calme peu à peu. Dans sa bourse, elle déniche un mouchoir qu'elle porte à son nez. Le dos cambré comme une vieille femme de quatre-vingts ans, elle se dirige vers la poubelle près de la porte pour y jeter le bout de tissu souillé par-dessus ceux jetés précédemment. L'énergie flottant dans la pièce est maintenant si lourde qu'on a l'impression d'assister à des funérailles. Vicky soupire bruyamment. Bien que les trois filles aient rigolé en racontant certaines anecdotes du voyage, l'ambiance n'est désormais plus à la fête, la triste réalité de la fin de leur voyage ayant vite ressurgi à la surface.

Le deuxième homme revient avec les cafés. Dans un silence de plomb, tous ajoutent sucre et crème au breuvage fumant.

— Je peux aller aux toilettes ? demande Vicky.

— Ah oui, moi aussi !

— Prenons une petite pause.

L'agent ayant apporté les cafés escorte les filles aux toilettes les plus proches.

JOUR 8
AÉROPORT MONTRÉAL-TRUDEAU
SALLE 315 – **11 H 37**

Au retour de tout le monde, l'inspecteur qui fait tournoyer le café dans son verre, propose :

— Donc, on termine ?

Vicky se frotte les yeux de fatigue, Caroline sirote une gorgée de café et Katia écrase son visage au creux de ses mains, ce geste lui donnant l'air d'un chien sharpeï particulièrement plissé. Elle concède :

— Ouais.

— Quand est-ce que vous avez compris exactement ce qui se passait ?

— Moi, je regardais pas pantoute devant, comme je disais..., répète Vicky.

— Moi aussi, ç'a été long. Je suivais pas trop les événements, ajoute Caroline.

À cause de sa position à l'avant du véhicule, Katia s'est vite douté de quelque chose. Elle secoue la tête :

— Non, moi j'ai tout de suite trouvé ça très bizarre…

JOUR 7

CUBA, VARADERO
AVENIDA PRIMERA

Des hommes en uniforme se tiennent aux abords de la route et semblent *a priori* gérer la circulation. S'agit-il de la police ? Ou plutôt de simples contrôleurs routiers ? Katia ne sait pas, étant donné que leur habit bleu pâle – différent des uniformes des forces de l'ordre du Québec – pourrait appartenir autant à un groupe qu'à l'autre. Un homme au centre dirige vers la droite deux véhicules devant eux, puis deux autres vers la gauche, les faisant ainsi pénétrer dans deux rues adjacentes à la rue principale.

— N'oubliez pas. Je vous conduis, car vous avez manqué votre transport, répète Sylvio, qui semble tout à coup encore plus nerveux.

— Oui, oui…, approuve Katia, toujours perplexe face à ce détail qui semble si important à ses yeux.

Sylvio surveille tout autour, les deux mains bien agrippées au volant. À gauche. À droite. Katia remarque qu'il se concentre à analyser la scène. Comme les véhicules devant sont dirigés dans des directions opposées, l'automobile de Sylvio se retrouve seule devant le groupe de gens gérant le trafic. Katia reporte son attention vers un homme qui parle au *walkie-talkie* sur le trottoir à sa droite. Il semble sérieux. En tournant la tête, elle remarque que Sylvio, quant à lui, fixe un autre type parlant dans le même genre d'appareil, mais se tenant à gauche du véhicule, donc de son côté. Plongées dans leurs pensées, Vicky et Caroline fixent les alentours par leur fenêtre respective.

En moins de deux et sans rien dire à personne, Sylvio place l'embrayage au neutre et ouvre la portière. Tel un fugitif, il s'éloigne et se met à courir en diagonale pour passer entre deux hommes, avant de poursuivre sa course vers le trottoir. Un homme devant la voiture hurle quelque chose en espagnol et trois des hommes dégainent leur arme à feu. Puis, cinq policiers surgissent de derrière le véhicule et l'encerclent en gesticulant et en invectivant les passagères en espagnol.

— AH MON DIEU ! s'épouvante Caroline en sortant des limbes.

— BEN VOYONS ? clame à son tour Vicky, venant aussi de se faire brutalement sortir de sa rêverie du moment.

— TABARNAK ! fait Katia en levant les bras pour montrer à l'homme qui gesticule à côté de sa portière qu'elles ne sont pas menaçantes.

Sylvio, qui s'est rapidement fait intercepter par deux policiers, est projeté au sol avec rudesse et on lui passe les menottes sans ménagement.

— ¡Pasaporte! crie un Cubain aux trois touristes assises dans la voiture, en brandissant la main avec insistance.

— Quoi? s'affole Caroline.

— Passeport, passeport, lui indique Katia en effectuant des mouvements lents pour sortir le sien de son sac à main.

Elle récupère ceux des filles et les tend à l'homme debout près de la voiture, son arme toujours en main. Sans plus attendre, celui-ci les ouvre et il annonce fortement à ses confrères :

— Canadiense.

S'étant éloignés un peu, trois hommes discutent un moment en espagnol en regardant les papiers d'identification des filles, tandis que Sylvio est conduit vers une auto de police qui vient d'arriver sur les chapeaux de roues par une rue adjacente.

Caroline explose et se met à pleurer.

— On se calme, on n'a rien fait de mal, rationnalise Katia, blanche de peur.

— Hiiiiiii, se lamente Caroline, convaincue qu'elles seront tout bonnement abattues sur la place publique cubaine sans que personne ne sache pourquoi.

Voyant la pauvre femme en pleine décompensation névrotique sur la banquette arrière, le policier se radoucit un peu.

— *¡Sales[52]!* ordonne-t-il en ouvrant la portière de Caroline, pour la mettre en confiance.

Ne voulant pas se retrouver seule de son côté du véhicule, Vicky glisse sur le siège pour sortir par la même portière que Caroline. Elle s'accroche à sa main. Une fois dehors, les trois filles se regroupent en se collant les unes aux autres comme si cette proximité physique assurait ainsi leur survie dans ce bas monde. L'air d'avoir été kidnappées par une tribu de cannibales se terrant au fond de la brousse et s'apprêtant à concocter un mijoté de chair blanche fraîche, les trois touristes regardent leurs assaillants avec crainte tout en tentant de déchiffrer leurs intentions.

— *¿Conoce a este hombre[53]?*

En anglais, Katia murmure :

— Quoi? En anglais?

— *Ella está pidiendo Inglés[54].*

Tout le monde se met à crier «*Inglés*» dans la rue, à la recherche d'un traducteur maison. Un homme, vêtu

---

52. Sortez.
53. Connaissez-vous cet homme?
54. Elle demande à parler en anglais.

lui aussi d'un uniforme bleu, accourt vers la scène. En aboutissant près des filles, toujours regroupées épaule contre épaule comme si elles étaient ligotées en vue d'être incessamment déposées dans la marmite d'eau bouillante, il explique dans la langue de Shakespeare :

— Vous étiez avec un homme que la police tente de coincer depuis un bout de temps.

— Il ne faisait que nous conduire à l'aéroport ; nous avons manqué notre transport, ment d'instinct Katia, en le regrettant aussitôt...

JOUR 8

AÉROPORT MONTRÉAL-TRUDEAU
SALLE 315 - **11 H 44**

— Vous avez donc menti aux autorités cubaines..., constate l'inspecteur d'un ton de voix affirmatif plutôt qu'interrogatif.

— Ben... il nous avait tellement averties de dire ça. C'était rentré dans ma tête. De toute façon, je tentais seulement d'éviter la mort en plein milieu de la *Main* de Varadero, figurez-vous ! s'insurge Katia en croisant les bras sous sa poitrine, honteuse de se faire ainsi prendre comme une gamine la main dans le sac.

— Compte tenu de la conclusion de l'histoire, ça n'a pas vraiment d'importance…, avoue l'inspecteur sans pour autant cesser d'avoir l'air très déçu de son comportement.

— J'espère, franchement.

— Poursuivez, s'il vous plaît, les prie-t-il en prenant quelques notes sur une feuille.

JOUR 7
CUBA, VARADERO
AVENIDA PRIMERA

Le Cubain traducteur maison, à proximité des trois autres hommes, demande aux filles de reculer. Ceux-ci les encerclent. Comme si leurs pieds et leurs torses s'avéraient littéralement soudés ensemble, les filles se déplacent à petits pas vers l'arrière, tel un saucisson humain. Devant leurs yeux pétrifiés, un des hommes ouvre le coffre de la voiture. Malgré qu'elles se trouvent un peu loin, les filles peuvent tout de même y apercevoir leurs bagages.

— *¿Son estos sus maletas?*

— Est-ce que ce sont vos valises? répète le traducteur maison.

— Oui… *Sí*…, répond Katia, des sueurs froides et chaudes lui descendant le long de la colonne vertébrale.

Un homme enfile des gants en kevlar et extirpe chacune des valises avec précaution, comme si celles-ci pouvaient renfermer une bombe atomique prête à exploser. Apparaissent alors, tout au fond du coffre, trois boîtes de carton – de la grosseur de boîtes de chaussures – scellées avec du ruban adhésif rouge et parsemées d'étiquettes variées laissant croire que cette marchandise s'apprêtait à être expédiée à l'étranger. L'homme fait un signe de la tête affirmatif en direction du traducteur. Celui-ci approuve aussi la découverte en agitant la tête de haut en bas.

— Nous devons prendre notre avion... bientôt..., tente Katia avec une petite voix suppliante, en se plaquant encore plus le corps contre celui de ses amies.

Le traducteur répète cette affirmation à l'homme qui semble responsable de l'intervention policière. Celui-ci lui répond une phrase rapide en espagnol. Il traduit aux filles :

— Impossible. Vous devez être interrogées avant de quitter le pays...

— Mais non ! beugle Caroline, hors d'elle, en tournant la tête vers Katia comme si celle-ci détenait le pouvoir d'éviter cette fatalité.

Le supérieur tend leurs passeports à un homme à sa gauche et celui-ci s'empare des papiers en sortant son téléphone.

— Nous allons avertir la compagnie aérienne que vous ne serez pas sur le vol...

Caroline se remet à pleurer de plus belle tandis que les filles sont escortées vers un véhicule de police. De sa fenêtre, Sylvio regarde les voyageuses en grappe qui se déplacent à contrecœur vers leur transport.

JOUR 8

AÉROPORT MONTRÉAL-TRUDEAU
SALLE 315 – **11 H 51**

L'inspecteur, qui a rondement saisi la situation d'arrestation, acquiesce de la tête, compatissant face à la dure épreuve vécue par les trois innocentes aux traits tirés se tenant le dos rond devant lui. Caroline – dont le mascara a coulé et dont la tignasse paraît encore plus rêche maintenant qu'elle est ébouriffée – semble avoir passé une nuit épouvantable dans les entrailles de la prison d'Alcatraz. Elle enligne l'agent avec le regard qu'aurait un beagle désirant sortir de sa cage à la fourrière. Katia, cernée et un peu pâle, soupire en faisant tournoyer son reste de café froid dans le fond de son verre de carton. Vicky, chez qui on distingue encore un peu le bronzage inégal à la hauteur des yeux, a par mégarde décelé une entaille à l'ongle de son annulaire droit. Elle sort donc une lime à ongles en carton de son bagage à main et elle rectifie la situation en frottant quelques petits coups rapides dessus avant de glisser l'objet dans sa pochette pour le ranger. Impatiente d'en finir, elle pose une question sans contenu :

— Bon?

— Bon quoi? demande l'agent frontalier, croyant que celle-ci amènera une information inédite à l'enquête.

— Vous voulez la suite, je suppose?

— Naturellement.

— Je vais continuer, si tu permets, Kat, question de te donner une pause, pauvre toi!

— Nous vous écoutons, alors, approuve Biron, ravi de ne pas devoir pousser davantage dans le dos des témoins pour poursuivre.

— Là, ils nous ont emmenées dans une bâtisse proche de l'aéroport, un genre de quartier général des douaniers cubains. Et la femme est arrivée un peu plus tard.

— La femme de l'ambassade du Canada?

— Oui, exactement. Elle arrivait de La Havane et elle nous a expliqué toute la situation... la drogue, l'arrestation, le passé de Sylvio Sanchez et tout. Elle a bien vu dès le départ que nous n'avions absolument rien à voir là-dedans. Voyons! Trois petites profs tranquilles de Gatineau. Elle nous a posé des questions et elle a vérifié des choses, puis elle a assisté à notre interrogatoire avec les agents frontaliers cubains. Une chance qu'elle était là, pour de vrai.

— C'est là qu'elle nous a appris que...

JOUR 7
CUBA, AÉROPORT DE VARADERO
SALLE D'INTERROGATOIRE 2

La femme d'une cinquantaine d'années, assise à une table, les mains jointes ensemble comme si elle priait, tente de calmer les vacancières, et ce, en français.

— Non, mesdames, il n'était pas le propriétaire de l'hôtel du tout. Ce complexe appartient à une famille de Madrid qui possède quelques centaines d'hôtels un peu partout dans le monde, donc ils ne viennent jamais ici. Peu de complexes hôteliers appartiennent à des Cubains, en réalité. Ce sont plutôt des entrepreneurs européens qui les gèrent.

— Ben voyons, il nous a bien dit ça, les filles ? demande Caroline à ses amies.

— Pas exactement, Caro. Souviens-toi. Il a dit : « Je suis dans l'administration… » C'était assez flou, merci, comme réponse, mettons, rectifie Katia.

— Dans l'administration de quoi, misère ? Un réseau de trafiquants de mojitos illégaux ?

La femme les éclaire du mieux qu'elle le peut :

— Non, lui, c'était plutôt la drogue, mesdames. La cocaïne.

— Oui, les boîtes dans le coffre… on s'en doutait.

— Mais, dites-nous, il voulait faire quoi avec la drogue? C'était quoi son but en nous amenant à l'aéroport? s'inquiète Caroline, ne comprenant toujours pas le rôle qu'elles devaient jouer dans l'histoire.

— À ce stade-ci, c'est trop tôt pour sauter aux conclusions. Je ne fais pas trop dans les affaires criminelles de ce genre habituellement, donc je ne peux pas vous informer davantage à ce sujet.

— Il souhaitait que l'on soit accusées à sa place? demande Katia, tout aussi perdue que le reste du groupe.

— Il voulait mettre ça dans nos valises? panique à son tour Vicky.

JOUR 8

AÉROPORT MONTRÉAL-TRUDEAU
SALLE 815 – **11 H 59**

Katia, qui écoute son amie raconter les faits, s'interroge à nouveau à ce propos.

— Le savez-vous? Qu'est-ce qu'il nous voulait, au juste?

L'inspecteur Biron appuie ses larges épaules contre le dossier de la chaise en expirant comme un ballon qui se dégonfle sous la force de la pression. Il examine les filles à tour de rôle avant de commencer à rouler un peu la manche gauche de son chemisier. Tout en s'exécutant avec minutie, il explique :

— Pour le moment, les hypothèses sont : soit Monsieur Sanchez voulait seulement faire diversion pour le transport de la marchandise vers un lieu X, soit il projetait d'en glisser dans vos bagages pour que vous effectuiez le transport jusqu'à Montréal – ce qui, soit dit en passant, aurait été très fâcheux et lourd de conséquences pour vous.

— AH MON DIEU ! Je me sens pas bien..., s'alarme Caroline en se prenant la tête à deux mains, presque sur le bord de perdre connaissance.

— *God !* Imaginez la scène ! Trois profs arrêtées aux douanes pour trafic de drogue international... Eille... Comment aurait-on pu se défendre si la drogue avait été trouvée dans NOS bagages ? panique Katia en envisageant le pire.

— J'y pense, pis j'ai de la misère à respirer, souffle Caroline qui visualise très clairement son fils pleurant à fendre l'âme en la voyant, à travers le grillage de l'enceinte principale, pénétrer dans l'établissement de détention pour femmes afin d'y purger une sentence de vingt-cinq ans sans possibilité de libération conditionnelle.

— Très complexe, en effet. Mais l'hypothèse première du côté des services frontaliers cubains, autant que du nôtre, reste vraisemblablement la théorie de la facilitation du transport, tout simplement. Ou, tout au plus, un alibi pour circuler de façon justifiée sur le territoire de l'aéroport sans paraître trop suspect...

— Ah ouin, c'est bon. D'où la raison pour laquelle il voulait nous faire dire que nous avions raté notre autobus, approuve Katia, en espérant ainsi calmer un peu Caroline, au bord de la crise d'hyperventilation.

— Donc, vous avez parlé à la femme de l'ambassade, on vous a interrogées en sa compagnie et ensuite ?

— La femme nous a aidées pour organiser notre retour, étant donné que nous avions manqué notre vol de l'après-midi.

— Oui, et là, je ne sais pas si c'est pertinent pour l'enquête, mais j'ai pété une solide coche…, avoue Vicky, honteuse.

— Une coche ? C'est pas le mot ! envoie Katia, à mi-chemin entre l'amusement et le reproche.

— Oui, c'est inscrit noir sur blanc dans le rapport de déclaration de la représentante de l'ambassade canadienne, affirme l'inspecteur en arborant l'air neutre d'un homme simplement en train de rappeler des faits.

— J'étais tellement à boutte…, se justifie Vicky.

JOUR 7
CUBA, AÉROPORT DE VARADERO
SALLE D'INTERROGATOIRE 2

Les douaniers sortent de la petite pièce d'interrogatoire, où l'air climatisé ne fonctionnait malheureusement pas, créant ainsi, en ouvrant la porte, une vague de fraîcheur qui ragaillardit les trois filles. Il était temps, car les fesses bien collées sur leurs chaises de bois depuis plus de quatre heures dans ce cubicule, elles étaient carrément en train de suffoquer. La femme de l'ambassade les félicite :

— Ç'a très bien été, mesdames, vous avez bien fait ça. De retour au Canada, vous ne devriez pas avoir de problèmes avec cette malencontreuse histoire. Mais, à l'avenir, avant de faire confiance à des gens en voyage, vous devriez vraiment savoir à qui vous avez affaire.

— Oui, on a eu notre leçon! Moi je ne parlerai plus jamais à personne de ma vie en voyage! C'est réglé! décide Caroline, certaine de son coup.

— Il ne faut pas exagérer, tout de même, mais il faut faire attention, rester prudent. Bon, je vais vous donner un coup de main pour réserver des billets vers Montréal. Ça ne devrait pas être trop compliqué, nous sommes en haute saison.

— Comment ça fonctionne? demande Vicky.

— Je crois que le plus simple serait d'appeler directement à l'aéroport pour entrer en contact avec les compagnies aériennes qui ont des vols d'ici les prochaines vingt-quatre heures...

— Qui va payer? L'ambassade ou la police? ose Vicky, toujours aussi préoccupée face à tout ce qui concerne l'argent.

— Euh..., hésite la femme, tout à coup mal à l'aise.

Les trois filles la dévisagent curieusement en attente de sa réponse.

— Je suis désolée, mais le soutien fourni par l'ambassade canadienne ne peut couvrir le prix des billets d'avion. Je suis seulement venue vous prêter main-forte en raison de la barrière de la langue, et pour nous assurer que des citoyens canadiens ne soient pas accusés injustement d'un délit. Si votre situation avait découlé d'une catastrophe naturelle, d'un attentat terroriste ou autre chose du genre, nous aurions pu vous aider financièrement. Dans ce cas-ci, vous avez suivi cet homme de votre plein gré. Vous aviez mal interprété la situation au départ – et j'en suis navrée pour vous –, mais je ne peux rien faire en ce qui a trait au montant à débourser pour les billets d'avion...

— QUOI ? gronde Vicky, en beau fusil. Mais *c'était* pourtant un attentat, ça, non ? J'ai eu des *guns* pointés directement sur moi, j'ai vu l'intérieur d'un fusil jusqu'au mécanisme de la gâchette tellement il était proche de ma foutue tête, cibole ! C'est pas un attentat, ça, peut-être ? Ça prend quoi pour que ce soit classé comme un attentat ? Du sang qui revole jusqu'au ciel ? Il aurait fallu se faire tirer dessus une ou deux fois ? Est-ce que c'est le nombre de morts qui détermine si c'est un attentat ? La quantité de litres de sang retrouvés dans la rue, peut-être ? Dites-moi, parce que je ne comprends pas... VRAIMENT PAS !

— Non, madame, je vous certifie que ça ne peut être considéré comme un attentat terroriste. Nous sommes bien loin de là, même. De plus, je vous signale que je vous ai secondé du mieux que j'ai pu dans votre mésaventure, donc...

— Oui, Vic, arrête de crier de même, la supplie Caroline.

— Ben, moi, je vais leur en faire un criss d'attentat à l'ambassade du Canada! J'aurais dû prendre son *gun* pis tirer trois, quatre coups en l'air, comme ça. Avec des coups de feu, on aurait sûrement eu le droit de faire classer notre affaire comme un «attentat»!

La femme, qui avait établi un véritable lien de confiance avec les trois touristes, semble trouver la tournure des événements bien désolante. Elle secoue la tête, pince les lèvres et ouvre grand les yeux, à la fois agacée et étonnée par la perte de contrôle de Vicky.

Katia prend le bras de sa copine pour qu'elle se calme.

— Vic, on peut rien faire...

— On peut rien faire? On peut rien faire? Euh, je m'excuse, ça va nous coûter le prix du criss de voyage qu'on a gagné! Tu trouves pas que c'est de la marde, ça, toi? Pis toi? rage-t-elle en regardant tour à tour Katia et Caroline.

— C'est certain, mais bon... C'est pas comme si on avait le choix.

— Ben non, c'est comme mes fesses, ça! Hein? J'avais-tu le choix ou pas de me retrouver avec une maladie grimpante cubaine pour une niaiserie de même... Hein? Hein?

La femme, maintenant plutôt écœurée que surprise, dévisage Vicky un bon moment, pas certaine de comprendre de quoi elle souffre exactement.

Vicky sent le besoin de rectifier :

— Bah... Ça, c'est un autre dossier...

JOUR 8

AÉROPORT MONTRÉAL-TRUDEAU
SALLE 315 – 12 H 06

L'inspecteur vient de lire à haute voix la déclaration de la femme de l'ambassade concernant cette portion de l'histoire. Tout le monde baisse les yeux au sol. Malgré le côté dramatique de la situation, Katia ricane dans le creux de sa main en analysant d'un œil intéressé comment son amie se tirera d'embarras face aux deux agents frontaliers perplexes.

— Oui... euh... j'ai eu un petit problème de santé en voyage, mais ç'a pas rapport dans ce dossier-là, regrette Vicky, qui a littéralement perdu les pédales dans cette portion touchante de sa confession.

Les douaniers l'examinent, semblant se demander si cela doit ou non faire l'objet d'une investigation. Elle les prie de passer outre.

— Oublions ce passage, OK ? Aucun rapport, ça n'aurait même pas dû se retrouver là-dedans...

— D'accord...

Silence radio. Vicky enchaîne rapidement :

— Bon, donc là, on a trouvé des billets d'avion, aller simple en pleine nuit à 799 $, taxes incluses! Hourra! On était assez contentes! ironise-t-elle.

Le douanier qui leur a servi du café, silencieux depuis le début de l'interrogatoire, se prononce sur le sujet:

— Vous êtes chanceuses, croyez-moi. À la dernière minute comme ça, et pour un aller simple au Canada, j'ai déjà vu le double.

— Ah wow! On «trippe», d'abord! dit Vicky avec mesquinerie.

Caroline lui donne un coup de genou sous la table pour lui signifier de cesser son petit manège. Elle se cale dans son siège et soupire pour ainsi passer le micro à quelqu'un d'autre, capable de narrer calmement la fin du récit. Caroline l'attrape.

— Donc, nous avons trouvé un vol qui décollait sept heures plus tard. Nous avons imprimé nos billets électroniques, passé les douanes, puis nous sommes allées dormir sur des bancs dans la salle d'attente de l'aéroport. Ils nous avaient naturellement averties que nous serions interceptées en arrivant à Montréal.

— Ça, c'est le bout le *fun* de toute l'histoire. Nous avons réussi à dormir, genre, trois secondes sur les bancs... Hein, les filles? Environ trois secondes? déconne Katia.

— Quatre, je pense. Quatre secondes, oui...

Le terminal de l'aéroport étant fait sur le long, les filles marchent nonchalamment pour repérer la porte par laquelle elles entreront dans l'avion. En y arrivant, le vol inscrit n'est naturellement pas le leur, étant donné qu'elles ne partent qu'à 2 h 30 du matin.

Le vol suivant étant dans plus de deux heures, peu de personnes se trouvent dans les parages. Ravies de voir les lieux ainsi déserts, les trois filles passent à la vitesse de l'éclair devant les petites boutiques de cigares et de rhum local puis, épuisées à mort, elles se jettent à corps perdu sur des rangées de bancs afin d'essayer de dormir un peu. Ayant encore plusieurs heures d'attente devant elles, elles pourront ainsi récupérer de leur journée et soirée plus que mouvementées.

En moins de deux, les filles se mettent à somnoler tranquillement, la tête appuyée sur leur chandail à manches longues roulé en boule pour faire office d'oreiller de fortune. Des bruits sourds réveillent Katia en premier. Caroline, qui se trouve sur le banc devant ses deux amies, ouvre à son tour les yeux. Boum! Boum! Boum!

— C'était quoi? grogne Vicky en s'étirant un peu le cou.

Trois jeunes hommes qui viennent d'arriver dans l'aire d'attente font une cacophonie avec les tam-tams qu'ils ramènent au pays en guise de souvenirs. Tout le monde autour trouve ça amusant, à l'exception des filles, et surtout de Katia, qui rage extérieurement[55].

— Voyons, gang de TOURISTES!? Allez jouer du tam-tam ailleurs, on dort, nous autres! C'est quoi l'idée, calvaire!

En un clin d'œil, la salle se remplit de vacanciers canadiens bien bronzés, en attente du prochain vol, à destination de Toronto. Caroline, Vicky et Katia se voient même forcées de se rasseoir normalement à cause d'une famille qui s'installe près d'elles dans le but de servir une collation à leurs trois enfants. Résignées à être peu confortables, les filles – muettes, aigries et fatiguées – somnolent, semi-assises sur leur chaise, l'air d'avoir abusé des bonnes choses avant le grand départ. Des voyageurs leur parlent en anglais croyant qu'elles s'envolent elles aussi en direction de Toronto.

— Vous étiez à quel hôtel, nous ne vous avons jamais vues?

— Costa Azul del Mar Resort, répond avec peu d'enthousiasme Katia à la mère de famille qui essuie la morve au nez de son jeune fils qui a attrapé froid durant le voyage.

---

55. Habituellement, on rage «intérieurement» à propos de quelque chose, mais là, avec Katia...

— Ah, vous êtes de France ? Génial ! Paris ?

— Non, du Québec, poursuit Katia, expéditive, en espérant que la femme lise dans son attitude peu loquace qu'elle ne recherche pas nécessairement le contact avec son prochain.

Vicky, qui a presque réussi à se rendormir, se tient la tête au creux de la main, son coude étant accoté sur l'appuie-bras. Le banc voisin étant vide, elle a le loisir de s'avachir de côté à sa guise. Un couple bien en chair arrive tout près. La femme d'environ quatre cents livres avance péniblement en trottinant comme un éléphant faisant des pas lourds, mais discrets. Son mari, tout aussi bien enrobé, prend le banc devant elle. À voix haute, la femme s'excuse d'emblée de son arrivée, faisant ainsi ouvrir les yeux à une somnolente Vicky. D'instinct, et sans trop prêter attention, celle-ci se pousse pour laisser à l'inconnue qui vient de surgir la chance de s'asseoir. Elle se replace donc en position assise conventionnelle. La Canadienne rotationne[56] alors d'un demi-tour et elle baisse tranquillement son énorme fessier vers le siège. Réalisant ce qui se passe et se croyant presque en danger de mort par écrasement, Vicky se serre contre Katia qui sommeille, la tête renversée vers l'arrière et la bouche entrouverte. Réalisant que son amie vient d'entrer en collision avec elle, Katia s'en offusque en gémissant :

— Ahhh… voyons ?

---

56. Du verbe «rotationner» bien sûr ! À paraître dans *Le Petit… (vous connaissez la chanson)*.

— Ben là, chuchote Vicky, en espérant que son amie cesse de grogner pour ne pas mettre la femme obèse davantage mal à l'aise.

— Simonaque..., en rajoute Katia, sans filtre et vraiment de mauvais poil.

Caroline, qui a tout vu de sa place, fusille son amie d'un regard rempli de reproches.

En entendant la femme échanger en anglais avec son mari, Katia en profite :

— Ben non, elle comprend pas ce que je dis, c'est une Anglaise, la grosse...

— Franchement, Kat, t'es vraiment immature, la semonce Caroline, qui ne trouve pas ça drôle du tout.

Ayant envie de s'obstiner comme jamais compte tenu de son humeur de chien, Katia poursuit :

— Oh, excuse-moi ! Elle est pas grosse pantoute, la madame ! Comment ça d'abord que la madame super mince à côté de Vic fait en sorte que celle-ci doive s'asseoir avec moi sur mon banc parce qu'elle est tellement mini qu'elle prend un banc au complet plus les trois quarts du sien ? Hein ? C'est pas parce que la madame mange trop de Big Macs, ça hein ! Non ! Non ! Non !

Caroline souffle en roulant les yeux pour toute réponse, jugeant qu'il vaut mieux la boucler.

Vicky se tourne alors vers la femme obèse. Celle-ci regarde les filles attentivement. Pendant un instant, Vicky croit que ladite femme est bilingue et qu'elle a compris les propos insultants de Katia. Silence. Malaise. La vacancière dévisage Vicky, qui la fixe en retour.

— Il fait chaud, hein? exprime-t-elle enfin, dans la langue de Shakespeare teintée d'un accent texan, tout en secouant sa main bien potelée devant son visage.

Des gouttes de sueur miroitant sous les néons puissants du plafond perlent sur ses tempes. N'en pouvant plus, elle extirpe finalement son passeport de son étui pour s'en éventer le visage.

— Notre karma est déjà assez pourri de même, faudrait juste pas en rajouter, explique Vicky à Katia, presque rendue assise par terre et toujours grognonne.

— Je m'en sacre, de ton karma! rouspète celle-ci en tentant d'au moins remettre une fesse sur le siège. *Anyway*, on pourrait pas descendre plus bas. Rien ne pourrait être pire que cette aventure-là, je suppose…

— Hé! les «ron coco»! les interpelle une voix bien connue.

Dave les rejoint en gambadant, les genoux dans le front, trop heureux d'avoir repéré des amies pour passer le temps en attendant son vol de retour.

— Calvaire… Là, c'est ben le boutte du boutte…, soupire Katia, désormais trop épuisée pour être en colère.

— Qu'est-ce que vous faites là? Votre vol n'était pas hier?

Une voix aérienne demande aux passagers de se diriger vers la porte d'embarquement numéro 3. Tout le monde se meut dans un désordre plus ou moins contrôlé.

— Bon, allez-vous-en, gang de fatigants, qu'on dorme en paix ! soupire Katia.

— C'est pas fin pour moi, ça ! lui fait remarquer Dave.

Personne ne répond. Pour sa part, Katia ne l'entend carrément plus, son cerveau ayant déjà fui vers d'autres rives. Aussitôt que le couple grassouillet se lève, elle semble cependant reprendre parfaitement le contrôle d'elle-même et elle pousse Vicky sur l'épaule pour la projeter vers sa place initiale. Ainsi brusquée, Vicky se recule pour s'asseoir plus loin en attendant que les derniers voyageurs présents dans la zone ramassent leurs effets personnels et se dirigent vers la file d'attente. Quelques minutes plus tard, les filles reprennent pleine possession de l'espace et s'étendent de tout leur long, et sans aucune élégance, sur les sièges.

— Bon, ben, bye ! Câlin ? espère la mouffette qui se lève en étendant largement les bras.

Considérant avoir dit au revoir à ce gars au moins trois fois depuis le début du voyage, elles ne répondent pas. Aucune ne daigne même bouger le petit orteil.

— Bon…, se résigne Dave en s'éloignant bredouille et nostalgique à l'idée de quitter ces amies avec qui il a tissé des liens si solides.

Les filles ont à peine de temps de se reposer quelque vingt-cinq minutes que les premiers voyageurs du vol vers Montréal commencent à envahir les lieux. Le décollage étant dans moins de trois heures, les transports ont déjà commencé à déverser les vacanciers à l'aéroport.

Trois jeunes femmes animées s'assoient à quelques bancs en diagonale des filles. En chantant très fort : «*Bará, bará, bará, berê, berê, berê*… Ha! ha! ha!». Elles semblent se souvenir des moments inoubliables de leur voyage.

Au même moment, un groupe de gars québécois entre dans le terminal en scandant :

— *Go Habs, go! Go Habs, go!*

Une bière Cristal en main, les partisans-voyageurs profitent de leur voyage jusqu'à la dernière goutte, et ce, malgré que l'on soit en pleine nuit.

— Esti! Je capote! Pu capable! grince Katia entre ses dents, en direction de Caroline qui est couchée devant elle.

— On va survivre, l'encourage celle-ci.

Les voyageurs étant à nouveau de plus en plus nombreux, plusieurs semblent convoiter les places près des filles. Soucieuse de son karma comme jamais auparavant, Vicky se relève pour laisser l'opportunité à tout le monde de s'asseoir. Caroline fait de même. Katia reste couchée, attendant que quelqu'un lui demande de se lever. «Premier arrivé, premier servi! *Fuck off!*», se dit-elle en mettant les mains sur ses oreilles pour atténuer les bruits environnants.

Deux heures trente plus tard, l'agente de bord annonce l'embarcation imminente des passagers du vol 7821 en direction de YUL, Montréal. Les filles se lèvent d'un bond, bien décidées à être les premières à entrer dans cet avion, question d'accéder au plus vite à des sièges plus confortables que ceux du rudimentaire aéroport cubain. Le roupillon dans l'avion sera assurément plus réparateur que celui espéré dans ces lieux trop bruyants.

Leur plan ayant fonctionné à merveille, les filles se retrouvent presque les premières à embarquer dans l'appareil, tout juste après les parents voyageant avec de jeunes enfants. Compte tenu de l'achat tardif de leurs billets, elles ne sont pas assises ensemble, mais au moins leurs sièges se situent tous dans la même section. Katia se retrouve dans la rangée de sièges du milieu, juste après une des sorties de secours.

— Ah *nice*! Plein d'espace pour les jambes!

— Chanceuse, remarque Vicky en s'assoyant juste derrière elle, au milieu aussi.

Caroline, quant à elle, prend place dans un banc donnant sur l'allée dans la même rangée de sièges que celui de Vicky.

Sans plus attendre, les filles s'installent confortablement pour dormir tandis que les gens prennent place à bord de l'Airbus. Les yeux clos et dans un état de demi-sommeil, Katia perçoit quelqu'un qui s'immobilise tout près d'elle. Sans le faire exprès, il accroche ses jambes au passage. En fait, la silhouette généreuse de l'homme qui projette de s'asseoir à ses côtés laisse croire qu'il empiétera sur son banc par-dessus l'accoudoir. Comme ledit accoudoir le gêne, il le relève en se penchant de peine et de misère avant de se tourner pour prendre place. Katia ouvre les yeux à ce moment précis. Un homme presque aussi obèse que la Torontoise de l'aéroport s'échoue alors près d'elle dans un mouvement faisant onduler les matières adipeuses de son abdomen sous son chandail de coton. Une âcre et puissante odeur de transpiration monte au nez de Katia[57]. Le cœur au bord des lèvres, elle s'avance pour voir Caroline de biais afin de lui partager son désespoir du moment. Les deux autres filles, malgré qu'elles soient dans la rangée derrière, ont bien évidemment remarqué l'homme corpulent qui vient de prendre place à côté de leur amie. Vicky, qui voit là un signe supplémentaire pour appuyer sa théorie ésotérique orientale, articule sans aucun bruit le mot «karma» en direction de Caroline. Celle-ci acquiesce de la tête en souriant de malaise. Tentant d'attraper sa ceinture de sécurité

---

57. Fait vécu personnellement... sur un vol de douze heures en direction de Bangkok...

coincée entre son abdomen et l'accoudoir extérieur, l'homme se recule tout contre Katia. L'odeur nauséabonde qui se propage deux fois plus lorsqu'il bouge les bras lui fait presque hausser les épaules d'écœurement.

— Excusez-moi, dit le pauvre homme, terriblement gêné.

— Ça va, ça va, le rassure Katia, qui tente de récupérer quelques points karmiques positifs.

L'homme réussit tant bien que mal à attraper la ceinture et à la faire glisser entre ses doigts pour en atteindre l'extrémité. Il élargit le truc au maximum, mais il constate à son grand désespoir que le modèle n'est pas assez grand pour faire le tour de son abdomen géant. Comme si elle présageait que la situation allait se produire, une agente de bord se pointe à ses côtés pour constater les faits. Devant l'homme honteux et dépourvu de moyens, elle ouvre un compartiment à bagages tout près pour en ressortir une ceinture d'appoint servant à allonger le modèle original. Elle l'installe aisément. Cependant, même avec cette extension, c'est très juste. Visualisant les pénibles heures de vol à venir, Katia roule des yeux vers le téléviseur fixé au mur devant elle. Une femme âgée et son mari arrivent alors à leur tour dans l'allée. La femme octogénaire semble avoir de la difficulté à lire les chiffres sur sa carte d'embarquement, et elle s'obstine avec son mari, tout aussi âgé qu'elle.

— C'est un huit ça, pas un six. Je trouve pu mes lunettes, torvisse. Je pense que je les ai oubliées dans ma grosse valise. Mais bon, tu vois pas plus clair que moi de toute façon, donc laisse-moi tranquille, envoie-t-elle en direction de son mari. Au moins, moi, je n'ai pas oublié mon dentier su'l bord de la piscine pour le retrouver dans un aquarium à la réception trois jours plus tard ! Bon, voici nos sièges, je pense...

— Meuheuheu, marmonne son mari, la bouche molle comme s'il ne portait pas lesdites dents supposément retrouvées.

Katia, qui les observe se chicaner en plein milieu de l'allée, réprime l'envie de se retourner pour dévoiler aux filles ce qu'il est advenu du pauvre dentier abandonné[58].

— Ma petite madame, c'est quoi le chiffre ici, là ? s'informe la vieille dame en présentant son carton à Katia, toujours écrasée contre le côté de son siège telle une croûte de pain au fond d'un sac.

— 38D, c'est ici, juste à côté, lui indique Katia, heureuse à souhait que ses seconds voisins figurent dans les barèmes de leur poids santé.

— Je te l'avais dit, torvisse ! Bon, bon, bon, fait la femme en essayant de placer leurs bagages à main dans le compartiment se trouvant à proximité.

Pressentant les difficultés à venir, un bon samaritain se lève pour leur donner un coup de main.

---

58. Voilà au moins un gros dossier de réglé ! Je ne peux par contre pas vous donner de détails concernant la moumoute. Vous devrez donc vivre dans le doute pour le reste de votre vie... Je suis vraiment désolée.

— Merci bien, jeune homme. C'est plein de beaux jeunes dans cet avion-là, hein? observe la femme en prenant place près de Katia. Les jeunes, y «wéyagent» pas mal de nos jours...

Malgré que Katia trouve la femme bien rigolote, elle sourit par politesse en espérant avoir maintenant la paix pour dormir.

Une fois bien installée, la grand-maman se tourne vers Katia:

— Bon! On as-tu eu du beau temps, hein? Sauf le premier soir, il faisait frette en torvisse, hein, Raymond? Mais bon, ça arrive, des fois, dans le Sud. Imaginez-vous donc, ma petite madame, que nous autres, une fois, on était aux Bahamas avec un groupe organisé du Club de l'âge d'or de Saint-Rémi – c'est Mariette qui organise toujours des beaux «wéyages» de même; est assez fine, c'te Mariette-là, mais je connais plus sa sœur, Ginette; est plus de mon âge, mais est veuve depuis deux ans et demi... –, mais là, y avait fait environ moins trois degrés. Eille, j'avais même pas amené mon chapeau chaud en peau de mouton, du vrai de vrai mouton à part de ça, j'avais reçu ça le Noël d'avant et là...

La mamie est interrompue dans son histoire foison-nante de détails inutiles par l'hôtesse de l'air qui demande à Katia de ranger son bagage à main dans les compar-timents supérieurs, et non sous le banc, étant donné qu'elle se trouve dans la zone de la sortie de secours. Katia réprime une grimace de déception. Pensant que sa voisine est fâchée de devoir patienter pour connaître la suite de son histoire, la vieille dame la rassure :

— Allez-y, allez-y. De toute façon, j'ai trois grosses heures et demie pour vous raconter toute ça ! Je suis pas fatiguée «pintoute», moi ! À mon âge, on dort moins.

«Esti de marde, de marde…», songe Katia, en ayant subitement le goût de se rouler en boule dans la soute à bagages pour avoir enfin la paix…

JOUR 8

AÉROPORT MONTRÉAL-TRUDEAU
SALLE 315 – 12 H 15

Les inspecteurs, qui ont encore droit à des fragments d'histoire largement au-delà de leurs intérêts, agitent la tête en guise de compréhension.

— Le pire vol de toute ma vie, je vous jure. La madame m'a raconté son voyage dans les Bahamas au grand complet, ainsi que TOUS les autres périples qu'elle a faits dans sa vie. Que dire du récit mémorable et détaillé de son voyage de noces à Niagara Falls, en 1959…

Commençant bien malgré eux à trouver les trois touristes bien attachantes avec leurs histoires farfelues, le deuxième agent frontalier laisse échapper un petit soupir de compassion en arquant les sourcils.

— T'avais juste à pas rire de la première grosse madame, la nargue Vicky, fidèle à elle-même.

— Aaaah! Lâche-moi un peu avec ton maudit karma!

— Si t'as besoin de plus de preuves que ça pour y croire, c'est ton affaire, l'obstine Vicky, en croisant les bras.

— Sérieusement, ses histoires qui n'en finissaient plus de finir entremêlées avec mon voisin et son odeur de... son odeur de... de vidanges mortes! se révolte Katia, encore perturbée par son expérience olfactive traumatisante.

Les deux agents rient maintenant de bon cœur. Caroline, qui rigole aussi, commente à son tour:

— Des vidanges vivantes, ça pue déjà, donc imagine quand elles sont mortes! Hish...

— Et quand je pensais au fait que je payais le gros prix pour ce billet-là, en plus. Même les hôtesses de l'air me regardaient avec des faces de pitié pis des regards de compassion, l'air de dire: «Eh Seigneur, c'est pas le *fun* ta vie!».

— Bref, en arrivant ici, vous connaissez la suite. En se présentant aux douanes, ils nous ont escortées jusque dans vos bureaux...

— Une chance que la femme de l'ambassade nous avait averties. On s'y attendait, au moins.

L'inspecteur réfléchit en scrutant une ultime fois les papiers devant lui. Il prend la parole:

— Si vous permettez, j'aimerais juste revenir sur un détail qui me chicote...

Katia poursuit sa phrase pour faire sa comique :

— Les vidanges mortes ?

Il sourit :

— Non, j'ai bien visualisé ce passage, je vous assure.

— L'histoire du dentier aussi est close ! Vous ne vous attendiez pas à ça, hein ? en rajoute Katia.

L'agent ne répond pas, mais il enchaîne plutôt :

— Monsieur Sanchez ne vous a jamais, en aucun cas durant le voyage, offert de la drogue ou une quelconque substance illicite ?

— Non, clame Vicky, sans hésiter.

— Non, non, confirme Caroline.

Silence. Tout le monde se tourne vers Katia, qui, faisant celle qui n'a pas entendu la question, lève les yeux au ciel. Bruit de criquets. Tout le monde observe avec intérêt celle qui semble être subitement devenue muette.

— Ben là...

— QUOI ? gueule Caroline, qui devine bien évidemment la signification de son mutisme.

— Si je ne m'abuse, rien dans votre déclaration ne stipule qu'il vous avait offert quoi que ce soit, se souvient Biron en dévisageant Katia.

— Ben... Dans le contexte, vous allez comprendre pourquoi que... On dirait que je m'en souvenais pas[59], mais en racontant le voyage, ça me revient comme... un peu..., explique vaguement Katia, le regard fuyant.

— Bon! Une autre affaire! beugle Caroline, au bout du rouleau.

— On vous écoute, insiste l'inspecteur, tout à coup très intéressé par le sujet.

— Pourquoi je sens que je serai pas fière de toi, tout à coup? lance Caroline, prématurément en beau maudit envers son amie.

Katia inspire profondément, comme pour prendre son courage à deux mains, puis elle débute:

— Le deuxième soir, en revenant de la discothèque de l'hôtel...

JOUR 2
CUBA, VARADERO
COSTA AZUL DEL MAR RESORT

— Allez! Aide-moi! Tiens-lui l'autre bras, au moins! crie Katia en direction de Cédric, le fils de Mike, qui l'aide à ramener son père dans sa chambre.

---

59. Phénomène étrange nommé scientifiquement «Le syndrome de la commission Charbonneau».

Visiblement sous l'effet de l'alcool, les deux complices s'amusent à souhait de l'état d'ivresse pratiquement comateux de Mike.

— J'ai jamais vu mon vieux de même ! rigole Cédric en le soutenant sous le bras tel que demandé.

Mike se prononce sur le sujet avec peu de conviction :

— Chus correct, mon fils, chus correct... Chuste ben fatigué...

— Ben oui, c'est ça ! Ha ! ha ! ha !

— Chuste un peu fatssigué. Che vous le dis...

Une fois dans la chambre, Katia manque de trébucher par-dessus bord en laissant choir Mike sur le lit comme un cadavre. Cédric s'assoit au pied du lit et il gonfle les joues pour souligner leur effort. Katia, qui dépose sa bourse sur le bureau, expire bruyamment.

— Bon...

— Mon père boit pas souvent de *shooters* dans la vie, ça paraît-tu ! ?

— Oui, ça paraît !

Cédric détaille Katia un instant avant de lui déclarer :

— *Dater* une belle fille comme toi... méchant tata de se retrouver faite de même !

Mike, qui ronfle déjà, en étoile sur le couvre-lit, n'entend bien évidemment pas les taquineries de son fils.

— Viens avec moi! l'invite Cédric en lui faisant signe de sortir.

Passablement soûle elle aussi, elle ne comprend pas trop le but de sa démarche. Elle le suit tout de même, heureuse d'établir un contact plus étroit avec le fils de son soupirant quasi décédé. Une fois dehors, tout près du bloc de chambres, Cédric s'écrase sur une chaise longue à proximité de la piscine du complexe hôtelier. Il débute alors un récit un peu hors contexte lui racontant la rupture de ses parents, il y a de ça plusieurs années. Elle tente de l'écouter du mieux qu'elle peut, la vision trouble et l'esprit un peu embrouillé par les vapeurs d'alcool. Le fils de Mike étant un très beau garçon, elle focalise plutôt son attention sur son corps d'apollon, ses jeunes épaules robustes exerçant sur elle un attrait hypnotique inadéquat compte tenu de son statut de «presque beau-fils».

— Alors voilà, ma mère est partie avec l'autre connard plein de *cash*…

— Ouin, c'est pas évident, ça.

— Moi, je lui en ai pas voulu, en réalité. Tsé, dans la vie, on rencontre beaucoup de monde intéressant. Moi, je suis pour l'amour libre! Ouin… vive l'amour libre!

Katia rit à gorge déployée sans trop savoir pourquoi. Au même moment, et sans crier gare, Cédric s'approche d'elle pour l'embrasser.

Confuse, mais tout de même réceptive, elle l'embrasse durant quelques secondes…

JOUR 8

AÉROPORT MONTRÉAL-TRUDEAU
SALLE 315 – 12 H 21

— QUOI ? s'emporte Caroline, complètement sous le choc.

L'écho de son cri semble résonner pendant un siècle entre les murs ternes.

— Calvaire, elle s'est pognée le père ET le fils ! Ah ben là, c'est ben le boutte du boutte ! T'as pas d'allure, Kat ! beugle Vicky, les deux bras levés au ciel en signe de découragement.

— T'as AUCUNE morale ! C'est épouvantable, gueule Caro.

Un peu éberlués aussi, les deux inspecteurs la jaugent, car ils ne connaissent pas trop le contexte ni le passé amoureux de la voyageuse. Jugeant la situation entre les filles un peu trop explosive pour intervenir, ils adoptent tous deux une position de retraite démonstrative en s'appuyant le dos contre le dossier de leur chaise. Katia encaisse les insultes sans rien dire tel un boxeur en ronde finale du championnat du monde. Caroline s'insurge à nouveau :

— Katia ? Voyons donc ?

— Cédric… Hon ! hon ! hon ! J'en reviens juste pas, rajoute Vicky en secouant la tête.

— OK! Ça suffit, laissez-moi m'expliquer, s'il vous plaît!

Katia marque une pause pour laisser la chance à ses amies de prendre sur elles. Silence. Désirant rattraper au vol un minimum de dignité, Katia lève les paumes vers la table de façon distinguée, puis elle poursuit :

— Alors...

JOUR 2
CUBA, VARADERO
COSTA AZUL DEL MAR RESORT

Katia, qui réalise tout à coup l'inadéquacité[60] de la situation, reprend ses esprits et repousse le charmant jeune homme d'une main.

— Cédric, qu'est-ce que tu fais là, voyons?

— Bah... l'amour libre, tsé...

— Non, non, non, ça marche pas de même, quessé ça?! Je m'excuse, j'aurais jamais dû faire ça, franchement. C'est ton père qui m'intéresse, pas toi. T'es ben trop jeune pour moi, *anyway*!

— Non, je viens d'avoir dix-neuf ans!

---

60. Ah oui! Ça vaut la peine d'inventer un mot ici!

— *Oh my God*..., s'affole Katia, qui panique littéralement en apprenant cette horrible nouvelle.

Elle se redresse un peu, puis elle cligne des yeux comme si elle sortait tout droit d'un mauvais rêve. Elle sursaute lorsque Sylvio, approchant au détour du chemin, les aborde :

— Allo ! Excusez-moi... juste vous dire que si vous cherchez quelque chose cette semaine pour vous amuser, n'hésitez pas à me le demander.

— Ah ouin..., semble s'intéresser Cédric, qui a très bien saisi le sous-entendu évident du Cubain.

Confuse, Katia ne répond pas, encore trop sous le choc de ce qui vient tout juste de se produire. Emballé comme pas un, Cédric lui chuchote :

— On fait de l'*ecstasy* ! T'es *game* ?

Tel un homme derrière le comptoir d'un casse-croûte en bordure de l'autoroute, Sylvio reste là, pour voir si ses deux clients potentiels passeront une commande ou non. Désormais revenue à elle – du moins à une version d'elle-même tout de même suffisamment ivre –, Katia se lève d'un bond :

— Non, non, non ! On veut rien. Voyons donc ! Bonne nuit !

Puis elle s'éloigne vers le bâtiment des chambres...

Puisqu'elle semble ainsi apposer un point final à sa tranche de vie croustillante, tout le monde l'observe avec suspicion. Les agents froncent les sourcils. Les deux filles aussi.

— Faites pas ces faces-là !

— Quelle face veux-tu ? Dis-nous ! Parce que là, je trouve pas de face témoignant à quel point tu me décourages !

— T'es vraiment retournée à ta chambre ? demande Caroline, qui peine à cacher son doute titanesque.

— Vous avez refusé son offre ? enchaîne l'inspecteur Biron, plus intéressé par les détails légaux que par sa potentielle aventure tropicale coquine avec un juvénile.

— Ça me sert à quoi de dire la vérité si personne me croit ?

— C'est juste que la vérité arrive un peu tard, on trouve, ajoute Vicky.

— Je voulais vous en parler depuis qu'on est venues rejoindre Caro dans cette salle, mais vous aviez l'air de vous en contrefoutre comme de l'an quarante.

L'inspecteur ajoute des notes manuscrites au bas de la déclaration de Katia. Il change finalement d'idée et il lui tend une nouvelle feuille lignée de haut en bas sur laquelle il inscrit «annexe 1». Katia comprend sans avoir besoin d'un dessin qu'elle doit rédiger la nouvelle information révélée *in extremis*. Elle soupire :

— Je pensais pas que c'était si important...

— Les autorités cubaines voudront assurément savoir que monsieur Sanchez a fait ce genre «d'offre» à des clients en vacances dans un complexe hôtelier, donc oui, c'est très important, précise l'inspecteur, un peu agacé que Katia ait omis ce détail crucial.

Ses deux amies, qui semblent partager l'opinion de l'agent frontalier, la dévisagent d'un air pas très fier.

— Regardez-moi pas de même. C'est NOTRE spécialité de groupe, les révélations qui explosent à la toute fin, je vous rappelle, soutient Katia en toisant ses amies qui ont toutes deux jadis performé très habilement sous cet angle.

Estimant que Katia vient ici de marquer un point important, les filles se taisent. Katia entreprend sa rédaction sous le regard inquisiteur des agents.

— Est-ce que je dois vraiment écrire que j'ai *frenché* le fils de ma *date* ? C'est pas super valorisant...

— Non, non. Indiquez juste le lieu, la date et le contexte entourant l'offre de Sanchez, précise l'agent.

Ne pouvant s'empêcher d'émettre un commentaire, Caroline ajoute :

— Ça, c'est SI tu l'as juste *frenché*...

Dégageant malgré lui l'air du gars ayant très envie de le savoir également, le deuxième agent examine Katia avec attention, curieux de connaître sa réponse. Un peu poussée par les regards inquisiteurs de tout le monde, Katia cesse d'écrire pour répondre :

— Non, Caro, j'ai pas couché avec lui. Mais c'est vraiment un petit criss. Excusez-moi de sacrer, mais oui, c'est un vrai petit criss...

JOUR 3
CUBA, VARADERO
COSTA AZUL DEL MAR RESORT

On voit alors apparaître Katia, cachée sous d'immenses lunettes de soleil dont elle n'a nullement besoin puisque le toit du restaurant à aire semi-ouverte bloque tous les rayons possibles. Elle entreprend une rapide tournée des mets proposés, question de dénicher de quoi se mettre sous la dent. Cédric, qui porte aussi ses verres fumés, l'accoste alors qu'elle se penche pour inspecter de plus près le contenu d'un plat.

— Salut !

— Salut..., hésite Katia, honteuse, en tournant la tête vers un plat mijoté ressemblant à des fruits de mer dans une sauce blanche.

«Drôle de mets pour un petit-déjeuner», s'étonne-t-elle. En humant l'effluve de crustacés qui s'en dégage, elle s'éloigne de deux grands pas, prise d'un haut-le-cœur puissant.

— Sauve-toi pas! dit Cédric qui la regarde étrangement.

— Je me sauve pas...

Ne sachant ni quoi dire ni quoi faire, Katia brasse en alternance deux autres plats, sans par contre s'en servir. Les saucisses dans une sauce rouge et les œufs brouillés aux poivrons rouges ne lui disent rien qui vaille. Cédric, qui s'amuse un peu à ses dépens, explique:

— Aussitôt revenu de ta chambre, il y a dix minutes, mon père s'est recouché...

Faussement absorbée par l'offre culinaire peu alléchante du moment, Katia commente, et ce, sans aucun rapport:

— Du poisson le matin, c'est bizarre, hein, quand même? Les habitudes culturelles en termes d'alimentation... c'est tellement différent...

Semblant désormais animer une émission de variétés traitant des mœurs culinaires des pays du Sud, elle continue de remuer les différents plats du buffet en ignorant Cédric qui l'observe en catimini. Celui-ci se décide enfin à apaiser son anxiété du moment:

— Relaxe un peu. Je l'ai pas dit à mon père, pour hier, si c'est ça qui te tracasse... Du moins, pas encore...

— Comment ça, «pas encore»? panique la pauvre Katia en levant d'un coup la louche d'œufs brouillés dont le contenu se renverse à côté du réceptacle de métal, occasionnant ainsi un beau dégât inutile.

— Je te niaise, je dirai rien… à condition que tu…

— Que je quoi?

— Que tu sois fine, fine, fine…

— T'es un genre de maniaque sexuel ou quoi?

— Non, non, mais on devrait vraiment faire un *trip* à trois, toi, moi et mon père! Ce serait *hot,* un genre de moment père-fils. Il serait content, je pense.

— *Ah my God!* T'as vraiment un grave problème de santé mentale, se lamente Katia, au bord de la crise de panique devant le gâchis d'œufs brouillés qu'elle picosse toujours avec la louche.

— En tout cas, on n'est pas obligés de planifier le tout maintenant. On a toute la semaine! Bye!

Cédric s'éloigne avec son assiette, puis il se positionne près d'une table pour la regarder, heureux comme un pape à la fenêtre du Vatican. Katia, immobile, les yeux bien ronds et la bouche ouverte, se replonge dans l'observation des plats.

Après un long moment de réflexion ne lui donnant absolument aucune issue probable, elle passe par la machine à café où elle se verse deux cafés noirs avant de rejoindre ses amies, déjà assises à une table.

— Voyons? On dirait que t'as vu un fantôme, lui reproche Caro.

— Non, non, je *feel* un peu drôle ce matin, c'est tout... J'ai trop bu hier. Donc? Vous êtes venues «pas déjeuner» au buffet?

JOUR 8

AÉROPORT MONTRÉAL-TRUDEAU
SALLE 315 – **12 H 32**

Caroline, qui a pratiquement le goût de pleurer, dévisage son amie en gémissant:

— Eille, t'as pas, euh... t'as pas fait ça, Katia?

— Ben non! Franchement!

L'inspecteur se tourne à demi vers Caroline, semblant surpris qu'elle ait même envisagé la chose possible. Il le témoigne sans gêne en la regardant un peu de travers. Désirant justifier son soupçon légitime, Caroline explique au douanier:

— C'est parce qu'elle a déjà fait un *trip* à trois avec un couple de vieux au Mexique, facque...

— BEN VOYONS? Racontes-y pas ça! Veux-tu lui montrer des photos, tant qu'à y être?

— Ah? parce que t'as des photos, en plus? demande Vicky.

— Je disais juste que tu l'as déjà fait, alors logiquement t'aurais pu le refaire, c'est tout, rationalise Caroline, n'accordant que peu d'importance à son accusation précédente.

Katia, le visage allongé comme une courge spaghetti, se prend la tête à deux mains, hochant le nez de découragement. Honteuse de ses deux amies, de la situation et de l'ensemble de leur voyage, Vicky émet un :

— Ayoyeeee... Ç'a pas de maudit bon sens.

Le bec cloué par toute cette saga rocambolesque, les deux douaniers peinent à reprendre le contrôle de l'interrogatoire qui dérape dans tous les sens. Comme de fait, Katia enchaîne en dévisageant Caroline :

— Avant que mon amie ici présente délire en vous racontant une bifurcation PERSONNELLE et sans intérêt de ma vie TRÈS passée, j'expliquais simplement que le jeune s'est mis à me niaiser avec ça, tout le temps...

JOUR 3

CUBA, VARADERO
COSTA AZUL DEL MAR RESORT

S'amusant dans la discothèque en forme de grotte depuis déjà quelques heures, Vicky, qui suit Stuart pour aller fumer un cigarillo dehors, passe tout près des filles qui s'enfilent quelques *shooters* derrière la cravate avec Mike et son fils.

— T'as trouvé un *prospect* pour «*frencher*-rien-que»? demande discrètement Katia à son amie en zieutant Stuart qui se dirige vers la sortie.

— Je pense bien que oui… et il n'est pas en couple, lui, au moins! Je lui ai déjà demandé, se réjouit Vicky en lui adressant un demi-sourire.

Mike annonce:

— Je vais aux toilettes.

— Moi aussi, je te suis! déclare à son tour Caroline avant de lui emboîter le pas.

Katia, qui reste en plan avec Cédric, fait comme si de rien n'était en balayant des yeux la piste de danse grouillante. Celui-ci la fixe de biais avec amusement et sans bouger. Il approche finalement son visage d'elle, question de bien se faire entendre malgré la musique.

— Tsé Katia, un petit *trip* à trois tranquille, quelque chose de *relax*, là. Ne viens pas me dire que t'as jamais fait ça?

— Eille, t'es vraiment troublé, pauvre toi! Voyons donc! Hier, nos lèvres se sont frôlées parce que j'étais soûle raide, mais là, arrête de me parler comme ça. C'était une grosse erreur, OK?

— Capote pas. Ce serait *cool*, c'est tout. On est en vacances!

Katia s'éloigne de lui afin de commander des bières pour tout le monde au bar. Il l'épie toujours, le sourire fendu jusqu'aux oreilles. Ne sachant pas du tout comment interpréter son attitude, Katia garde la tête en direction opposée pour masquer son inconfort. Mike revient auprès d'eux et Cédric lui annonce :

— Ah! Pa! On parlait justement de toi!

Katia se tourne pour le dévisager d'une expression mi-figue, mi-raisin. Cédric pose sa main sur l'épaule de son père, l'air de vouloir lui faire une confession d'importance capitale.

— Ah oui? En bien, j'espère?

— Oui, oui, en bien. Mais c'est un secret entre Kat et moi...

JOUR 8

AÉROPORT MONTRÉAL-TRUDEAU
SALLE 315 - 12 H 39

L'ambiance ayant un peu tourné au vinaigre depuis les derniers détails de Katia à propos du jeune homme en question, Caroline fend le silence en deux et risque un commentaire :

— C'est assez délicat comme situation, j'avoue...

— Délicat? C'est pas le mot, je trouve. Je dirais plutôt *heavy* raide, commente Vicky, qui commence presque à trouver que son amie fait bien pitié dans toute cette histoire.

— Je comprends pourquoi il ne semblait pas si emballé par votre histoire quand on lui disait «vous trouver *cutes*» quand vous vous embrassiez en attendant les taxis pour aller à la discothèque, justement, analyse Caroline, en fine renarde.

— Voilà! confirme Katia.

— Il lui a dit ou pas finalement? questionne Vicky, très curieuse de connaître la conclusion de ce quiproquo.

— Attends la suite, tu vas voir. Le matin qu'on a trouvé le dentier sur le bord de la piscine...

Complètement absorbés par les confidences de Katia, les deux douaniers ne s'opposent pas à la poursuite de son récit. Ils jettent même un œil furtif aux déclarations en faisant semblant d'y faire un peu d'ordre, se languissant secrètement d'entendre la suite de la saga.

JOUR 4

CUBA, VARADERO
COSTA AZUL DEL MAR RESORT

Pendant que les filles sirotent tranquillement un cocktail en bordure de la piscine, Mike et Katia se lovent dans un coin du bassin d'eau, un peu à l'abri des regards. Mike lève les yeux vers son fils, qui écoute de la musique à l'ombre d'un palmier, pour éviter de cuire sous le soleil qui brille de mille feux dans le ciel cubain.

— Je me sens un peu mal. J'ai pas envie qu'il s'ennuie parce que j'ai rencontré une femme, tu comprends?

— Mike, je comprends tout à fait, le rassure Katia.

— Une femme magnifiquement belle, soit dit en passant, confie Mike en enlaçant Katia de côté avant d'embrasser son épaule humide avec une infinie tendresse. Je veux vraiment qu'on fasse des activités père-fils, mais ça me dérange pas du tout que tu sois avec nous..., poursuit-il en avançant avec douceur son index et son majeur sur l'avant-bras de Katia, comme on le fait pour imiter quelqu'un qui marche.

Paranoïaque, Katia, qui perçoit un sous-entendu non subtil, beugle:

— COMME FAIRE QUOI?

Mike cesse d'instinct de parler pour se tourner vers elle, ne comprenant pas du tout son ton de voix défensif. Katia, qui réalise soudain qu'elle a l'air complètement désaxée, tente de se reprendre en se radoucissant:

— Des trucs sportifs ou culturels, tu veux dire?

— Je sais pas trop. J'ai pas d'idées précises. Aimes-tu les sports? Mon fils capote sur le football. Pas trop de chance de jouer à ça ici, par contre...

— Aaaaah, des sports de même, OK, OK...

Soulagée d'avoir fabulé, Katia pivote un peu dans l'eau en balançant ses mains de gauche à droite pour faire des vagues. Mike observe toujours son fils de loin.

— Bon, il s'emmerde, je le sais. Je vais lui dire de venir se baigner avec nous, décide Mike en avançant vers le bord de la piscine pour crier : «Cédric ! Viens dans la piscine avec nous !»

Katia marmonne entre ses dents :

— Peut-être que ça lui tente juste pas de se baigner, aussi. Il écoute de la musique...

Cédric accepte gaiement l'invitation de son père, enlève son chandail et saute dans l'eau en moins de deux. Il approche rapidement du couple en arrosant Katia de la main.

— Ouuuuh ! Ha ! ha ! haaa, rit celle-ci sans conviction en ne répondant que peu à son attaque aquatique.

Cédric plonge dans l'eau pour lui attraper une jambe.

— Ben voyons ?! s'inquiète Katia, terriblement mal à l'aise de ce rapprochement amical qui prend pour elle une tout autre signification.

— Il t'attaque ! Venge-toi ! l'encourage Mike, heureux que son fils tisse des liens sociaux avec sa nouvelle flamme en la taquinant.

Katia saisit alors la tête de Cédric à deux mains puis elle la maintient sous la surface avec force. Il se débat un peu. Elle cède finalement dans l'unique but d'éviter de se retrouver à la cour criminelle accusée de meurtre au premier degré.

De retour à la surface, Cédric la regarde avec des yeux semblant davantage la déshabiller que la mettre au défi. Il a visiblement apprécié cette manœuvre de soumission. Il ose même hausser les sourcils quelques fois dans sa direction, tel un don Juan appréciant les possibilités érotiques qui pourraient en découler.

— Bon, je vous laisse vous battre entre père et fils, décide Katia en quittant illico les deux hommes pour nager vers les filles qui ont finalement sauté à l'eau pas trop loin d'eux.

— Elle a peur de toi! rigole Mike en prenant son fils par les épaules.

— Ouais, c'est ça! crie Katia en s'éloignant.

— Hé! On dirait que tu t'amuses bien avec ton *chum* et ton beau-fils! déconne Caroline en la voyant arriver près d'elles.

— Vraiment... On a du gros, gros *fun*, là..., fait Katia en souriant à demi tout en mirant les alentours.

JOUR 8
AÉROPORT MONTRÉAL-TRUDEAU
SALLE 315 - **12 H 44**

Ses auditeurs étant muets comme des carpes, Katia hausse les épaules en émettant un:

— Hum...

— Un vrai *freak,* lui! commente Vicky, ne sachant pas trop quoi penser de toute cette conjoncture.

— Je dois avouer que, à ce moment-là, j'ai réellement fantasmé de voir son corps de petit fendant inerte et bleuté sur le bord de la piscine...

Les douaniers lèvent des sourcils sévères.

— Je ni-ai-se. Un peu... Sans blague, des fois, je me disais: «Ah, il me nargue, c'est tout!» D'autres fois, je faisais plutôt: «Ne-non, il est très sérieux...» J'avais tellement de la misère à le lire, ce gars-là, explique Katia. Mais là, plus la semaine avançait, plus j'aimais vraiment beaucoup Mike. Le soir de l'incident, je m'en foutais un peu. Je venais tout juste de le ramener complètement soûl dans ma chambre pis je le connaissais à peine...

Trouvant tout de même les égarements de ce soir-là lourds de conséquences, Biron réplique d'un bref signe de tête affirmatif, semblant dissimuler un jugement évident. Comme Katia semble percevoir son attitude, elle se justifie à nouveau:

— Ben là... dans le Sud... un peu «chaudaille» et... célibataire... *Anyway!* Vous souvenez-vous, les filles, quand il est venu me voir au jour de l'An?

— Non. Je me disputais avec Éric, lui rappelle Caroline.

— Moi non plus. En ne sachant pas toute l'histoire, je prêtais pas attention à lui. De toute façon, j'étais occupée à faire mon mauvais coup merdique, avoue Vicky.

— Et moi qui croyais que vous formiez une belle famille reconstituée harmonieuse.

— Hish..., souffle Katia pour tout commentaire.

JOUR 4
CUBA, VARADERO
COSTA AZUL DEL MAR RESORT

Katia s'approche de Mike pour lui souhaiter «bonne année». Il tend les deux mains dans sa direction, mais elle se sent tout à coup terriblement gênée. Que dire? Mike possède un potentiel suffisant pour éventuellement développer quelque chose de plus sérieux, mais en même temps, elle le connaît si peu... Leur couple – qui n'en est même pas un officiellement – a déjà un passé et des secrets puisqu'elle a embrassé Cédric «par accident» avant même de coucher avec Mike. Confuse et un tantinet déroutée, elle se tord les mains en planifiant son discours dans sa tête pour du moins être un minimum adéquate. Elle décide d'y aller avec son cœur en exposant une partie de la vérité:

— C'est comme gênant, hein?

— Ouin, je sais pas trop quoi te dire moi non plus. Je veux pas avoir l'air trop intense, ni trop indifférent...

— Moi, ni trop dépendante folle amoureuse ni trop «je m'en fous royalement, on fait juste coucher ensemble durant un voyage»...

— Je sais même pas trop quoi te souhaiter non plus. On se connaît pas assez…

— Tes buts, tes rêves… je sais pas non plus. Imagine que je te dise : « Une bonne santé pour l'année qui vient » et que tu finis tout juste des traitements pour un cancer. Euh, malaise…

— Imagine que je te souhaite : « Du succès dans ta *job* », pis que t'es sur le chômage et dépressive depuis des mois… Héééé…

— Ou encore, imagine que je t'avoue : « Je souhaite te revoir cette année » et que tu me trouves trop entreprenante.

— Ou bien que je te dise : « De l'argent en masse ! » et que t'es accotée au crédit et que tu viens d'hypothéquer ta maison parce que t'es une joueuse compulsive…

— Bon ben, coudonc ! On est deux à pas savoir quoi se dire…

— On se dit-tu juste « bonne année », pour faire ça simple ?

— Ouais, ouais, ouais. On recommence.

Bon joueur, Mike lâche les mains de Katia pour s'éloigner d'environ cinq mètres. Elle tourne la tête en direction opposée pour se prêter au jeu. Il approche d'elle à nouveau comme s'il la voyait pour la première fois depuis dix ans.

— Hé, Katia ! Câline ! Bonne année !

— Ah ben, ah ben, ah ben! C'est-tu pas le beau Mike! Eille, bonne année, toi aussi!

Le couple rigole un peu de leur connivence naturelle avant de s'embrasser de façon aussi passionnée que s'ils venaient tout juste de prononcer leurs vœux maritaux devant le curé de la paroisse. Leurs baisers entrecoupés de rires complices sont interrompus par Cédric, qui crève leur bulle.

— Oh, excusez-moi de vous déranger, mais... bonne année, Katiaaaa!

— Ah, t'es donc ben fin..., improvise Katia, offusquée que celui-ci les dérange et vienne possiblement la narguer, et ce, juste en face de son père, encore une fois.

Mike se recule pour lui céder la place, ravi de voir son fils faire les premiers pas auprès de Katia.

— Alors, c'est ça, bonne année! répète Cédric.

— Toi aussi! Tout ce que tu souhaites...

— TOUT ce que je souhaite? demande Cédric en riant en coin.

— Tout ce que tu souhaites qui est possible, bien sûr..., envoie Katia avec un sourire factice.

Cédric approche pour lui faire une accolade. Tout près de son oreille, il murmure:

— Content de t'accueillir dans la famille, on va avoir BEN du *fun*!

Katia met fin à l'étreinte de façon précipitée, puis elle rejoint Mike qui s'était éloigné pour admirer, de loin, la scène touchante.

JOUR 8

AÉROPORT MONTRÉAL-TRUDEAU
SALLE 315 – 12 H 50

Katia marque une pause pour réfléchir. Personne ne parle. L'inspecteur Biron regarde sa montre. Le temps file. Désirant tout de même arriver à la conclusion de cette triangulation malsaine – malgré qu'elle soit hors sujet face à l'enquête –, Katia poursuit :

— À ce moment-là, j'ai compris : «Bon, c'est un débile profond pour de vrai!»

— Avec raison! Il s'immisce dans ton moment d'intimité avec son père pour t'aiguiller de la sorte, commente Caroline, complètement prise de pitié pour son amie victime d'intimidation.

— Vous n'avez pas entendu ses commentaires au restaurant Kahori?

— Non, j'étais trop occupée à me sauver du feu, explique Caroline en se tortillant une mèche de cheveux, preuve ultime d'un douloureux souvenir.

— Et moi, j'étais dans le jus à rire de toi quand tu te faisais lancer des crevettes par la tête! rigole Vicky.

— Écoutez ça, alors...

JOUR 5
CUBA, VARADERO
COSTA AZUL DEL MAR RESORT

Afin de poursuivre son spectacle d'acrobaties culinaires enlevant, le chef cubain-japonais demande à Cédric, assis devant lui, d'ouvrir grand la bouche. Sans faire de chichis, celui-ci s'exécute. Le cuistot attrape alors une crevette qu'il lance habilement et directement dans la bouche du jeune homme. Tout le monde s'esclaffe. Le chef fait de même pour le caméraman et sa femme. Exalté comme jamais, le couple demande alors à Cédric de prendre la caméra afin que le cuisinier recommence la manœuvre, question de capter la scène intégrale sur pellicule. Il collabore. Lorsque vient son tour de recevoir son repas volant, Katia ouvre grand la bouche.

Sans que personne à table entende, Cédric se dissimule avec la caméra et il murmure :

— Lui aussi il veut te mettre quelque chose dans la bouche...

Faisant mine de ne pas entendre son commentaire déplacé, Katia ne rétorque pas, mais la nervosité la fait broncher au moment où le chef envoie le missile. La crevette rate la cible et atterrit en plein sur le haut de son nez...

JOUR 8
AÉROPORT MONTRÉAL-TRUDEAU
SALLE 315 – 12 H 53

— Quand je vous disais : « Un p'tit criss… » Il en manquait pas une, je vous jure.

— C'est pour cette raison que tu bougeais tout le temps ?

— Oui, il me disait plein de conneries sans que personne entende.

Le douanier accompagnant l'inspecteur ne peut retenir un commentaire :

— C'est assez déplacé comme attitude, je dois avouer…

— Je ne vous le fais pas dire. Mais là, à la discothèque de l'hôtel ce soir-là, j'ai vidé mon sac et pas à peu près. J'en pouvais plus, sérieusement…

JOUR 5
CUBA, VARADERO
COSTA AZUL DEL MAR RESORT

Gentil avec tout le monde comme à son habitude, Mike discute depuis un bon moment avec un homme d'Ottawa et son épouse, accoudés au bar de la discothèque de l'hôtel. Cédric s'y trouve aussi, regardant en alternance les gens autour et l'écran de son téléphone. Craintive de recevoir en pleine poire un autre commentaire déplacé de sa part, Katia le reluque du coin de l'œil de temps à autre, mais sans plus. Posant sa bière Cristal sur le bar, Cédric s'éloigne vers les salles de bain. Sans trop réfléchir, Katia le prend en chasse. En arrivant dans une section plus isolée, tout près desdites toilettes, elle lui accroche le biceps avec vigueur afin qu'il se retourne.

Un peu surpris par l'assaut, il pivote sur lui-même, puis sourit aussi malicieusement qu'un vendeur d'assurance en voyant de qui il s'agit. Sans aucune hésitation, il lui demande :

— Tu viens à la toilette avec moi ou quoi ? Coquine…

La fumée lui sortant par les oreilles tel un geyser d'Islande en pleine éruption, elle approche impoliment son index très près de son jeune visage.

— Eille, toi, chose, c'est assez ! Je sais pas à quoi tu joues, ni c'est quoi ton criss de problème, mais là, tu vas arrêter de me faire chier, OK ! Je regrette mon geste, c'est-tu correct ? Ça te va ? On va en revenir, à un moment donné ! Je connaissais pas trop ton père ce soir-là, mais là, il se trouve qu'il me plaît vraiment, facque c'est pas vrai qu'un petit baveux la couche aux fesses pis pas de poils dans face de dix-neuf ans comme toi va me faire sentir comme de la marde ! CRISS-MOÉ LA PAIX ! C'TU ASSEZ CLAIR ?

Comme Katia a avancé son doigt à deux millimètres de lui en criant ses dernières insultes, le pauvre Cédric a d'instinct reculé d'un pas, les yeux ronds comme des boules de quilles. En fixant l'ongle au vernis rouge sang de Katia – bien assorti avec son visage enragé écarlate – Cédric s'appuie le dos contre le mur, n'osant rien dire. Katia replace alors chastement son chemisier vaporeux, lève le menton bien haut et s'engouffre dans la salle de bain des filles sans demander son reste.

JOUR 8

AÉROPORT MONTRÉAL-TRUDEAU
SALLE 315 – 12 H 57

Comme Katia a livré sa performance avec la même intensité que ce soir-là, les deux agents frontaliers se retrouvent avec le doigt du témoin en furie, maintenant debout, entre leurs deux têtes – son vernis s'avérant par contre moins impeccable que lors de l'événement. Presque apeurés, ils fixent Katia sans oser dire quoi que ce soit.

— Bon ! termine Katia en se rassoyant, un peu gênée de s'être ainsi laissé emporter par l'émotion.

— C'était assez clair, merci, comme « pétage de coche », réagit Vicky, pas vraiment étonnée quant à la réaction colérique de son intense copine.

— T'avais pas peur de le mettre en maudit plus qu'autre chose ? demande Caroline, de nature moins explosive.

— Non, non. Les petits cons de même, il faut les accoter au pied du mur pour leur faire comprendre le bon sens. Mais sachez que je ne fais pas ça avec mes élèves, croit bon de justifier Katia, tout de même soucieuse de son image professionnelle.

Les agents frontaliers éberlués observent avec stupéfaction Katia, qui enchaîne enfin pour conclure l'histoire.

— Donc ensuite, il s'est mis à m'ignorer. Il ne m'a pas regardée ni parlé du reste du voyage ou presque. Disons que mon niveau de stress a augmenté plus qu'autre chose parce que je savais pas quoi penser. Allait-il le dire ou pas à son père ? Je savais pas...

— Et puis, finalement ? s'informe Caroline.

— J'en suis là, j'en sais pas plus. Possiblement que je vais rappeler Mike en arrivant chez moi tantôt et qu'il va me dire : «Laisse faire, t'as *frenché* avec mon fils, grosse pouffiasse!», suppose Katia en devenant un peu tristounette.

— Peut-être qu'il va seulement garder l'égarement secret, commente l'agent frontalier, dérogeant de ses fonctions principales d'enquêteur pour jouer à brûle-pourpoint le rôle d'analyste en relations humaines.

Touchée par son conseil se voulant tout aussi spéculatif que réconfortant, Katia lui sourit gentiment.

— Bon, terminons l'entretien, si ça ne vous dérange pas. Nous devons vite retourner au brouhaha qui règne dans l'aéroport.

— Oui, oui. Il manque encore de l'information ?

— Hum... laissez-moi voir...

Biron, qui doit se remettre dedans, farfouille un peu dans les déclarations à la recherche de potentiels détails nécessitant des précisions. Les filles patientent. Le néon au plafond s'éteint finalement après avoir frémi pendant de longues secondes, semblant ainsi sonner la fin de l'interrogatoire. Tout le monde lève les yeux pour lui rendre un dernier hommage. R.I.P.

— Non, c'est complet, je crois, déclare l'agent en terminant de ranger la paperasse.

Comme Éric doit depuis longtemps se demander ce qui se passe, Caroline le texte aussitôt que tout le monde se lève, question de lui dire qu'il peut enfin s'en venir. Il doit attendre ce message depuis déjà de longues heures. Le fait que ses beaux-parents s'occupent de leur fils depuis hier rassure tout de même Caroline. «Mon *chum* doit être dingue d'inquiétude…», se dit-elle en ramassant ses effets personnels.

— Donc, juste à venir avec nous, mesdames.

Dans le long corridor adjacent à la salle d'interrogatoire, les deux douaniers escortent les filles comme si elles avaient quelque chose de très grave à se reprocher. Épuisées, elles avancent, dociles et la tête basse comme si c'était effectivement le cas. Elles arrivent enfin à la zone des douanes, qui regorge de monde. Les innombrables voyageurs rentrant au pays avancent à petits pas entre les cordons de sécurité. En apercevant la foule massive, Vicky, impatiente de rentrer à Gatineau pour enfin serrer Marc dans ses bras, émet un souffle puissant digne d'écorner un buffle à dix mètres de distance.

— Pfft!!! Pas vrai… J'en peux plus.

L'inspecteur, qui a rallumé son émetteur-récepteur radio à la sortie de la salle, demande aux filles de s'immobiliser en étendant la main vers le mur pour leur bloquer le passage. Biron s'éloigne un peu et il parle un instant dans l'appareil avant de revenir vers le groupe.

— On a l'autorisation de passer à la 1, annonce l'inspecteur à son collègue.

Le cortège – les filles étant prises en sandwich entre les deux agents frontaliers – amorce donc la descente du grand escalier faisant face aux différents postes de douane. L'air cerné des trois vacancières donne l'impression que celles-ci reviennent tout droit de la guerre, et plusieurs curieux à la fin de l'interminable file d'attente les dévisagent. Les touristes escortées attirent encore plus l'attention au moment où elles contournent littéralement la foule par la droite. Convaincues que les trois femmes se sont fait arrêter pour un truc illégal lourd de conséquences, certaines personnes lèvent le nez en l'air, semblant s'amuser mesquinement de leur triste sort. Caroline, qui épie les spectateurs qui l'observent, perçoit des regards froids et distants la jugeant incontestablement. Cependant, plus les filles avancent, plus les regards changent. Katia ne comprend pas trop ce qui se passe. Vicky lui chuchote :

— Tout le monde nous regarde croche. Où est-ce qu'on va, là ?

— Je sais pas...

En arrivant devant un bureau de douane dépourvu de file d'attente, Vicky lit l'enseigne : «Dignitaires étrangers». Biron s'avance pour discuter avec le douanier en poste. Tout à coup très fière de se retrouver là, Vicky se tourne vers les gens «normaux» pour lever à son tour le menton en guise de vengeance. Le cou presque en train de lui casser par en arrière elle aussi, Katia arbore un air distingué comme si elle n'était rien de moins que la reine d'Angleterre en personne. Pour sa part, Caroline jette des coups d'œil aléatoires à la foule qui semble en effet plus clémente à leur égard que tout à l'heure. Au moment où l'inspecteur revient vers elles, quelques minutes plus tard, les filles affichent désormais la mine ultrablasée de trois superstars internationales en tournée mondiale réclamant au plus vite une limousine, une suite luxueuse et du champagne.

— Vous pouvez y aller les trois ensemble. Juste à présenter votre passeport, comme d'habitude.

Les filles avancent en grande pompe vers l'homme.

— Avez-vous passé un bon voyage? demande le douanier, par réflexe.

— Bah…, répond Katia en se tournant une fois de plus vers la foule qui regarde toujours les filles en tentant de deviner la raison justifiant ce passe-droit avantageux.

En moins de deux, les filles sont admises au pays. Les douaniers les escortant toujours, elles se dirigent, le nez terriblement haut, vers les escaliers roulants pour descendre à la réclamation des bagages, située à l'étage inférieur. Sur place, les deux employés les dirigent vers une petite salle où leurs bagages ont été remisés après avoir été fouillés de fond en comble, bien entendu. Une fois leurs valises récupérées et de nouveau regroupés en peloton, les deux mêmes douaniers les accompagnent jusqu'aux grandes portes automatiques menant à la sortie. Ils passent tout droit au dernier contrôle servant à valider la carte que le douanier ne leur a pas remise.

— Bon bien…, fait Katia, ambivalente quant au protocole d'adieu à adopter dans ce genre de situation.

Étant donné que les douaniers en ont appris davantage à propos des filles qu'ils ne l'auraient pensé au départ, ils semblent aussi tous deux se demander comment conclure professionnellement une entrevue aussi loufoque. L'inspecteur prend la parole :

— Écoutez, mesdames, les services frontaliers du Canada vous sont très reconnaissants de votre collaboration et nous espérons ne pas vous avoir trop importunées avec nos démarches et les quelques retards encourus.

— Nous autres, on s'excuse de vous avoir importunés avec son *trip* à trois ! Ha ! ha ! ha ! déconne Vicky, étourdie par la fatigue.

— Ta gueule ! J'ai PAS fait de *trip* à trois ! s'offusque Katia en assenant une petite tape sur l'épaule de son amie.

— Mais au Mexique, oui ! complète Caroline sans trop savoir pourquoi.

— Eille, c'est quoi votre problème ? On se disait juste « bye », là !

Les agents sourient, amusés de voir les filles toujours et à jamais en train de s'obstiner. Biron remet, à chacune d'entre elles, sa carte professionnelle. Katia, encore très agacée, supplie alors les agents :

— Pouvez-vous garder ces deux-là ici ? Je vous dis, elles sont pas normales !

— Bye, bon retour à la maison, conclut Biron avant de tourner les talons.

— On entame notre retour à la vraie vie, maintenant, déclare Caroline en se dirigeant vers les portes vitrées, l'air de craindre pour la suite.

Au moment où les portes s'ouvrent, les filles se mettent illico à chercher Éric du regard. Une impression de déjà-vu de leur voyage au Mexique les enveloppe. Caroline fouille des yeux la vaste salle bondée de gens, mais n'y repère pas son conjoint. Les filles continuent d'avancer en zigzaguant entre les groupes de gens excités attendant familles et amis.

— Voyons ?! angoisse Caro en s'immobilisant, constatant bien évidemment qu'Éric n'est pas encore arrivé.

Elle agrippe son cellulaire. Éric lui a justement envoyé un texto il y a de ça dix minutes.

(Un peu en retard, on arrive !)

— Ah non, il est avec le petit…, constate Caroline.

— Je pensais qu'il devait le laisser avec ses parents, se souvient Vicky.

— Il a dû changer d'idée dans l'espoir de me faire une surprise. Pauvre petit minou, il doit être tanné d'attendre.

— C'est pas bien grave, Caro. Il devait plutôt être excité de dormir à l'hôtel avec son père.

— Oui, mais hier soir, ils ont dû attendre longtemps ici…

Les filles se positionnent pas très loin des portes rotatives menant vers l'extérieur pour attendre Éric, qui stationnera probablement la voiture juste devant afin d'accélérer le processus.

Vicky, qui a sorti un miroir de sa bourse, s'inspecte le visage sous tous les angles. Elle constate avec grand regret :

— Ouin, je suis pas la plus *cute* en ville, disons. Calvince, j'ai encore mon bronzage de raton...

— Je comprends, on vient de vivre les vingt-quatre heures les plus absurdes de notre vie.

— Les filles, c'est plate, mais je vous annonce officiellement que je ne repars plus jamais nulle part avec vous autres. Cette fois, c'est très sérieux.

— Bah, arrête donc, Caro...

— C'est très vrai. Voyons donc ! Voir si, MOI, je vis des affaires de même dans la vie ! Je vous jure, partir en voyage avec Éric, ce serait sûrement les vacances les plus monotones du monde, mais au moins, je m'en sortirais vivante et sans casier judiciaire !

— Caro, t'exagères encore...

— Non, non, je suis sérieuse. Réalisez-vous que, pour moi, un samedi qui sort de l'ordinaire dans ma petite vie, c'est d'aller au cinéma avec mon *chum* après avoir fait les courses au Costco ? C'est presque le comble de la folie pour nous. Un genre de grosse sortie. Avec vous deux, ben...

— Avoue que, pour ce voyage-là, c'est pas de notre faute du tout. RIEN n'était de notre faute en vérité, conclut Katia, fière de ne pas avoir été à la tête des conneries vécues par le trio.

— Oui, mais Caro a raison, Kat. Ça nous arrive pareil ! Pourquoi ? Pour-quoi ?

— Je sais pas, se désole Katia, qui approuve tout de même l'idée générale véhiculée par le groupe.

Les filles sont dérangées dans leur réflexion post-voyage par Caroline, qui voit arriver la voiture d'Éric.

— Il est là !

Elles sortent en moins de deux à l'extérieur. La froideur de janvier les enveloppe aussi confortablement qu'une couverture de clous.

Les deux portières avant s'ouvrent. Coup de théâtre. Ce n'est pas le fils du couple qui accompagne Éric, mais bien Marc. Il sort. Prise d'une joie intense de le voir, amalgamée au flot des émotions vécues durant la dernière semaine, Vicky court vers lui en criant très fort son nom avant de se jeter dans ses bras comme une épouse de militaire retrouvant son tendre mari après une mission de six ans au front. Celui-ci l'accueille avec joie en lui embrassant la tempe. Caroline se rue aussi avec force sur Éric pour se cramponner à son cou. Esseulée, mais sincèrement contente pour ses amies, Katia observe les retrouvailles touchantes en songeant à Mike…

Une fois la vague de tendresse passée, les gars s'emparent à la hâte des mallettes pour ne pas retarder la file de voitures attendant patiemment derrière. Étrangement, ils ne demandent aucun détail aux trois filles quant à la raison justifiant le fait qu'elles aient raté l'avion.

— On dirait que vous êtes comme nos sauveurs! s'amuse Vicky en s'agglutinant au bras de Marc, trop heureuse de cette surprise.

— Attendez qu'on vous raconte ce qui s'est passé! Vous ne croirez pas ça! débute Caroline en soufflant avec la bouche et en se demandant visiblement par où commencer.

L'air sérieux, Marc se tourne vers Éric:

— On leur dit?

Le visage d'Éric s'assombrit alors d'un seul coup et il chuchote dans sa direction:

— Non! En arrivant à Gatineau, comme on en avait parlé...

— De quoi? s'informe Caroline.

— Rien, rien, tente de la rassurer Éric en déplaçant une des valises pour être en mesure de bien fermer le coffre.

— Eille, c'est quoi l'affaire? demande à son tour Katia, qui sent visiblement que quelque chose cloche.

— Marc, esti..., grince Éric, en colère que celui-ci ait ouvert la porte sur un sujet délicat.

Dans une ambiance empreinte de lourdeur, les deux gars déplacent toujours les bagages dans le coffre, Marc ayant décidé d'apporter son aide à Éric pour ainsi éviter le regard de Vicky. Éric découvre un objet coincé sous la première valise:

— Hé, regarde, Caro ! C'est monsieur Tom ! Le petit le cherchait…, se réjouit-il en brandissant devant les yeux de sa conjointe une peluche en forme d'ourson.

— Laisse faire monsieur Tom, là ! Éric ? insiste Caroline sur un ton autoritaire, voire quasi menaçant.

Il approche et lui prend la tête à deux mains, avant de dire :

— On a une longue route à faire, vous devez être épuisées, on va reparler de tout ça en arrivant, OK ?

Un automobiliste impatient qui klaxonne derrière eux force Éric à refermer le coffre. Croyant que le malaise a un lien avec la fille inconnue qui s'est ajoutée sur son Facebook pendant son absence, Caroline redresse le cou comme un braque allemand ayant repéré une proie :

— Éric, j'embarque pas dans l'auto tant que tu me dis pas c'est quoi…

Fait comme un rat, celui-ci décoche un regard outré à Marc.

Convaincue que le secret s'avère plutôt en lien avec le voyage de Marc, Vicky se plante à son tour près de Caroline en croisant les bras, signifiant qu'elle exige également de savoir avant de bouger. Se retrouvant ainsi devant les trois filles qui font du piquetage avec des têtes de manifestantes contre le massacre des blanchons sur les glaciers, les gars n'ont d'autre choix que de s'ouvrir. Malgré le froid, les filles semblent fermes et solidaires. L'automobiliste derrière s'impatiente une fois de plus.

— OK, LÀ, TOI! Fais de l'air! rugit Caroline, en balayant l'air d'une main.

La voiture recule pour finalement passer près d'eux à vive allure en leur envoyant un sympathique doigt d'honneur.

— Dis-leur, toi, t'as commencé, décide Éric, qui anticipe visiblement une réaction négative de la part des trois protestataires congelées.

— Ben, euh…, débute Marc.

Celui-ci marque une pause, laissant ainsi croire que le sujet est en effet très grave. Katia s'impatiente :

— Accouchez, simonaque !

— En fait, euh… On le sait un peu ce qui vous est arrivé…

— Quoi? Comment ça? Caro te l'a écrit? s'étonne Vicky, pas trop au courant des messages échangés entre eux depuis leur arrivée en sol canadien.

— Non, je t'ai rien raconté, rectifie celle-ci, bien au courant.

— Capotez pas, tout est sous contrôle, mais… c'est passé à la télé, hier. Sur LCN… On vous a vues…

— QUOI??? s'étouffe Caroline en s'appuyant sur la carrosserie de la voiture, au bord de l'évanouissement.

— HEIN? beugle à son tour Vicky.

— *WHAT!* grogne Katia en se prenant le front.

— Calmez-vous, les filles, c'est pas si grave…

— Ma mère doit capoter…, fait Vicky, les deux mains sur la tête.

— Tout le monde capote un peu, à vrai dire, rectifie Marc.

— Esti de MARDE… DE MARDE ! gueule Katia.

CAGE AUX SPORTS DE GATINEAU. TROIS MOIS PLUS TARD…

— ET LE BUUUT ! crie Marc en se levant d'un bond de sa chaise, les deux bras dans les airs.

Au même moment, une sirène digne de celle des pompiers retentit derrière le bar central du populaire resto-bar de Gatineau. Dans la cacophonie des fans hystériques du tricolore venus voir le match tant attendu contre les Bruins de Boston, les filles tentent de poursuivre leur conversation, en vain.

— *Yes sir!* Un but, ma blonde ! s'exclame Marc en se rassoyant près de Vicky.

— Ben oui, je l'ai vu. Surtout «entendu», mettons, répond Vicky en roulant des yeux en direction de Katia qui se trouve devant elle.

— Gang de Boston à marde, esti que je les hais, commente Marc, soulevé par la partie en cours[61].

---

61. Bon, votre auteure en profiterait-elle pour afficher au grand jour ses couleurs sportives ? ☺

— Mais moi, si les Nordiques reviennent à Québec, je vous abandonne et je change de camp, annonce Mike d'un air tout à fait assumé.

— Bon... Il vient de rentrer dans gang depuis cinq minutes et il s'arrange déjà pour qu'on parte en guerre, se désole Marc en donnant un coup de coude à Éric.

Ils rigolent tous les deux un moment avant de lever leur bière en direction du nouveau *chum* de Katia, qu'ils connaissent depuis à peine quelques semaines. Bon joueur, Mike fait semblant d'être offusqué un instant avant d'éclater de rire et de choquer son verre contre celui de ses nouveaux amis.

Katia, quant à elle, sourit de toutes ses dents en direction de Vicky, heureuse de voir que l'intégration de son nouveau *chum* se passe bien. Caroline soupire en direction de la machine à *popcorn* tout près de la table, l'air de se dire : « Alléluia ! Mes amies sont ENFIN en couple ! »

— Moi, c'est Canadiens *forever*, à la vie à la mort. J'ai le CH de tatoué sur le cœur, statue Éric, un doigt en l'air avec son éternel air de chimiste un peu coincé.

Vicky se lève pour aller aux toilettes.

— Ah ! J'y vais avec toi, l'interpelle Katia, avant d'embrasser Mike passionnément – étant donné qu'elle va le quitter pendant au moins cinq minutes.

— Moi siiiii ! décide Caroline, juste dans le but de se joindre au groupe.

En s'engouffrant dans les toilettes du restaurant, les filles se sourient.

— C'est comme notre première soirée multicouple officielle! C'est *cool*, hein? se réjouit encore une fois Caroline.

— Oui, les gars s'entendent bien, je pense. C'est vraiment le *fun*! approuve Vicky.

— Les filles, je suis tellement *in love*, là! pleurniche Katia, presque au bord de la syncope amoureuse.

— Ah! c'est vraiment le *fun*! Je suis TELLEMENT contente que vous soyez ENFIN en couple!! *Yeah!* s'excite Caroline comme si elle ne le réalisait pas.

— Reviens-en, Caro, s'il te plaît. T'en parles souvent, lui envoie délicatement Vicky, un peu tannée de la redondance quasi journalière de ses propos.

Katia enchaîne en se vidant le cœur:

— Tout compte fait, disons que j'ai été sur les nerfs assez longtemps, avec son tannant de fils. Là, je suis soulagée...

— Ouin, il te testait, le p'tit maudit, comprend Caroline.

— Oui, peut-être, mais il est correct dans le fond. Quand on s'est vraiment expliqués, il m'a avoué qu'il n'avait jamais pris la relation naissante entre son père et moi au sérieux à Cuba. Il a changé d'idée quand il a vu qu'on se fréquentait au Québec.

— Il faut dire que c'est dur de prendre au sérieux une femme qui ramène ton père à coucher dans sa chambre en te *frenchant* en même temps, relance Vicky, du tac au tac.

— «En même temps», faudrait pas exagérer, quand même, rectifie Katia en s'inspectant dans la glace entre deux affiches faisant la promotion des nouveaux plats mexicains sur le menu.

— Euh... OK, d'abord, dans la minute suivante, affirme Vicky comme si elle y était.

— On s'en fout! Veux-tu le temps en millième de secondes, un coup partie? *Anyway*, on n'en parle plus, ça n'existe pas, bon! fulmine Katia, trouvant que son incartade ne pèse pas vraiment dans la balance.

— Mais tout est bien qui finit bien, affirme Caroline en se retenant à deux mains de proférer une autre déclaration de joie relative au fait que les filles sont désormais en couple.

— Il aime son père et il voit qu'on est heureux, conclut Katia. C'est l'homme de ma vie, les filles! LUI! Le vrai! LE président! J'ai enfin trouvé...

Ses amies rigolent en la voyant se dandiner comme une adolescente en pâmoison entre le comptoir et le sèche-mains.

— Je suis aussi très contente que Marc et moi, on ait officialisé notre relation. Je pense que ça m'insécurisait trop, notre formule «union libre», avoue Vicky.

— T'as jamais su s'il a eu une aventure avec une fille à Vegas? demande Caroline.

— Non. En fait, étant donné que j'ai tenté de «*frencher-rien-que*» la moitié du *résore* de mon bord, j'ai jugé bon de ne pas revenir sur nos vacances respectives. Dans le fond, ce qui compte, c'est à partir du moment où l'on s'est dit être vraiment un couple, admet Vicky.

— Pis ta photo ? Eille, tu nous as jamais reparlé de ça, cachottière ! se souvient tout à coup Katia.

Vicky lève vers ses amies des yeux de cocker honteux.

— Alors ? insiste Katia.

— Si je vous en ai pas reparlé, il y a sûrement une raison...

— Il a aimé ça, c'est certain, voyons ! C'est un gars !

— Il AURAIT probablement aimé ça, oui...

— Comment ça « aurait » ?

Vicky hésite un instant. Elle inspire.

— Les filles, ç'a pas de bon sens...

JOUR 8

GATINEAU
MAISON DE MARC

Enlacés dans le lit comme deux amoureux à leurs premiers jours, Vicky et Marc rigolent en s'embrassant.

— Je vais tellement dormir pendant des heures, se délecte Vicky, enfin heureuse d'être bel et bien arrivée à Gatineau après ce long périple à la finale peu reluisante.

— Je me suis ennuyé de tes fesses, commente-t-il en lui triturant le derrière à deux mains comme un pervers.

— Ha! ha! ha! rigole Vicky en tentant de se défaire de son étreinte, de peur qu'il ne remarque les petits boutons encore bien présents sur son postérieur.

Réussissant enfin à se dégager, elle réagit en se souvenant tout à coup:

— En tout cas, j'ai pas eu beaucoup de commentaires à propos de ma surprise...

— Quelle surprise?

— La photo...

— Quelle photo?

Elle soupire de découragement en croyant que celui-ci n'a simplement pas ouvert son message sur Facebook. Elle attrape son téléphone sur la table de chevet et appuie sur l'icône de son profil. Elle ouvre ensuite sa boîte de messages privés et elle repère leur conversation.

— Cette photo-là... Hein? Voyons? Elle est plus là...

— Quoi? Tu m'as envoyé une photo *sexy*? s'excite Marc en lui empoignant la taille.

— Attends. Comment ça, elle est pas là?

Elle fouille un instant sur son appareil avant de deviner:

— Ah non! Ah non! Ah non! Dis-moi pas que..., puis elle ouvre une autre boîte de messages.

Celle qui se trouvait tout en haut de la liste.

— AH NON ! Belle conne, je l'ai envoyée à ma mère !

— Pouah ! Pas vrai !?

— Franchement ! J'ai honte…

— Je peux-tu juste la voir au moins ? demande Marc avec un petit air piteux.

CAGE AUX SPORTS DE GATINEAU. TROIS MOIS PLUS TARD…

Katia se tord de rire, à demi couchée sur le sèche-mains automatique.

— HAAAAAA ! pleure de rire Caroline, quant à elle pliée en deux, la tête pendant vers le plancher.

— Bon, c'est correct, là, s'offusque Vicky. Vous comprenez maintenant pourquoi j'en reparlais pas…

— Ta mère… Ha ! ha ! ha !

— Et là, quand j'ai vu ça chez Marc, je me suis rendu compte qu'elle avait lu le message le lendemain matin et qu'elle n'avait rien répondu. Pauvre petite maman. Me semble de lui voir la face en prenant son café le matin : «Ah, ma belle fille chérie m'a écrit un message de bonne année… Voyons voir. Clic ! Ah mon Dieu !» Et elle me voit, écartée sur le lit, à moitié «chaudaille» et en bobettes, rien de moins que les seins à l'air. Épouvantable.

— C'est hilarant ! Elle t'a rien dit d'autre quand vous vous êtes vues ?

— Non, après la commotion due à notre arrestation et tout, j'ai voulu lui en parler. Elle m'a coupée sec en disant: «J'avais compris. N'en parlons plus! Bon, j'ai fait des pâtés au poulet, en veux-tu?» Je pense qu'elle est traumatisée. Elle fait du déni...

— Je comprends donc.

— Imaginez, sa fille lui envoie une photo dépravée et elle la voit aux nouvelles, impliquée dans une arrestation et une affaire de drogue à Cuba. Elle a dû dire à mon père: «Ouin, on a vraiment manqué notre coup avec elle...» Donc, pour répondre à ta question, Kat: oui, mon *chum* a aimé la photo, quand j'ai fini par la lui montrer...

— En tout cas, les filles, moi j'ai appris que, même en couple, rien n'est jamais gagné. Ce n'est pas nécessairement mauvais de craindre que l'autre puisse aller voir ailleurs un jour. L'histoire d'Éric, qui avait ajouté comme amie la super belle fiancée de son nouveau collègue au travail – qui n'a PAS de compte Facebook –, m'a donné une bonne frousse. Même si j'ai déjà fait des conneries dans le passé, j'ai refermé cette porte pour toujours. Éric, c'est le père de mon fils et l'homme avec qui je veux passer le reste de mes jours, dit sincèrement Caroline, la mine tristounette à cause des squelettes dans son placard.

— La fiancée de son nouveau collègue... Je savais tellement que c'était quelque chose du genre. Quand j'y repense, t'as fait toute une histoire avec rien, hein? se désole Katia.

— Eille, parlant de Facebook. L'autre mouffette de con... je l'ai accepté comme ami, mais je lui ai barré tous les accès; je ne vois rien de lui et il ne peut pas voir mon mur. En fait, il est dans mon réseau et c'est tout! Non mais, des plans pour qu'il ramène quelque chose de super compromettant sur la table de façon vraiment hors contexte. *No way!* s'amuse Vicky.

— Moi, je l'ai même pas accepté. Paquet de troubles, lui, confie Katia.

— Moi non plus! Des fois, je pense à lui et paf! il apparaît dans ma tête comme un parasite et je suis en beau maudit pour le reste de la journée, avoue Caroline.

— Pauvre toi, ce sont certainement des symptômes classiques de choc post-traumatique, diagnostique Katia en secouant la tête, portée par une compassion palpable.

Prise d'une illumination, Vicky interrompt leur discussion ironique :

— Ah les filles! Je vous avais pas dit ça! J'ai eu le verdict final de notre compagnie d'assurances pour le remboursement de mes frais médicaux à Cuba, hier...

— Puis?

— Cibole, ils payeront PAS! leur annonce Vicky, tout à coup hors d'elle.

— Comment ça? C'est vraiment niaiseux!

— C'est à cause de l'autre incompétente de médecin qui a écrit sur son rapport médical que j'avais pogné une maladie transmise sexuellement. Franchement! J'ai pris des médicaments pour l'herpès pendant trois jours...

— Ha! ha! ha! Excuse-moi, mais je trouve ça un peu beaucoup drôle..., se bidonne Caroline en riant de nouveau à ventre déboutonné.

— Bah... moi, pas tant que ça. Encore un maudit voyage qui m'a coûté les yeux de la tête au final. C'était une simple infection cutanée comme de l'herbe à puce... Franchement! C'est juste à moi que ça arrive, des affaires de même!

Les filles se taisent un instant sans raison apparente. Katia fend le silence en deux en éclatant de rire. Les deux autres l'imitent.

— C'est vrai que, toi, Vicky, tu coûtes cher à sortir en maudit! Ha! ha! ha!

— Ma facture est toujours plus élevée que celle des autres, oui. Parlez-en pas à Marc, il le sait pas encore. Des plans pour qu'il me quitte par peur de manquer de fonds dans son compte.

Les filles terminent ce qu'elles avaient à faire et retournent auprès de leurs *chums*. Marc les accueille en les mettant au courant des derniers faits saillants :

— Vous avez manqué une échappée de fou de Pacioretty, les filles! Mais on n'a pas compté.

— Ah bon, font celles-ci en reprenant leur place respective à table sans témoigner plus d'intérêt à la nouvelle.

Éric les taquine :

— Vous avez l'air bizarre? Avez-vous fait des niaiseries aux toilettes?

— Ben non..., nie Caroline en roulant des yeux vers son *chum*.

— De toute façon, Éric, si elles ont fait des niaiseries, pas de trouble, on va en entendre parler aux nouvelles tout de suite après le match! rigole Marc.

— Aaah! Ah! Très drôle, commente Vicky en lui tirant la langue.

— C'est correct pour cette histoire de LCN et tout, au fait? demande Mike. Vous avez réglé ça comment avec la commission scolaire?

Katia, qui ne se souvient pas lui avoir livré les derniers développements à ce sujet, lui explique brièvement :

— En réalité, la commission scolaire avait donné le mandat à la direction de notre école de nous rencontrer à ce sujet. On a raconté l'intégralité de notre mésaventure à notre directeur et tout s'est bien passé. Dans le fond, c'était pas notre faute du tout.

— On a tout raconté, encore une fois…, souffle Caroline, les yeux ronds.

— Et on s'est fait écœurer par les trois quarts de nos étudiants qui nous avaient vues aux nouvelles, complètement sous le choc au beau milieu de l'avenue principale de Varadero et entourées de policiers cubains… Eille… Franchement…

Éric rit de la situation loufoque et met Mike en garde :

— Toi, tu sais pas dans quoi tu t'embarques avec elle, dit-il en montrant Katia du doigt. Chaque fois qu'elles se retrouvent les trois ensemble, c'est l'enfer sur terre, il paraît!

— Ah ouin?

— Bah…, commente sans conviction Katia.

— Assez que moi, j'ai décidé que ma blonde ne partirait plus jamais sans moi, affirme Éric en volant à l'arraché un baiser rapide sur les lèvres de Caroline.

— Moi non plus, d'abord! affirme Marc en regardant tendrement Vicky, l'air de se demander s'il peut ou non exiger une telle chose.

— Ça veut dire qu'il faudrait partir en couples la prochaine fois? évalue Mike en embrassant la joue de Katia, qui est presque assise sur le rebord de sa chaise afin d'être le plus près possible de lui, et ce, en tout temps.

— Aaaaaah! Ce serait une excellente idée, ça! envoie Katia en regardant ses amies.

— Ouin…, dit Caroline avec peu d'entrain, pas certaine de l'excellence de ladite idée.

— On irait où, mettons? demande Vicky en tournant la tête vers Marc.

— Paris? propose Éric. J'ai toujours rêvé d'aller là, et toi aussi, mon amour…

— Je sais pas trop, se défile Caroline, en regardant à tour de rôle ses amies.

— Vegas, c'était *top* aussi, affirme Marc.

— Faudrait voir… Un des deux…

Autres titres d'Amélie Dubois

Dans la série « Chick Lit »

MARQUIS

Québec, Canada